13-64

THE GUINNESS
WHO'S WHO
OF

SECOND EDITION

Edited & Compiled by
Colin Larkin

GUINNESS PUBLISHING

Dedicated to Alan McGee

First Edition 1992
Second Edition published in 1995 by
GUINNESS PUBLISHING LTD
33 London Road, Enfield, Middlesex EN2 6DJ, England

All Editorial correspondence to
The Editor: Guinness Encyclopedia Of Popular Music
Square One Books Ltd
Iron Bridge House, 3 Bridge Approach, Chalk Farm, London NW1 8BD

GUINNESS is a registered trademark of Guinness Publishing Ltd

British Library Cataloguing-in-Publication data
A catalogue record for this book is available from the British Library

ISBN 0-85112-657-X

Conceived, designed, edited and produced by Colin Larkin for
SQUARE ONE BOOKS LTD
Iron Bridge House, 3 Bridge Approach, Chalk Farm, London NW1 8BD

Production Editor: Susan Pipe
Desk Editor: Miles Hutchinson
Senior Contributor: Alex Ogg
Special thanks to David Roberts of Guinness Publishing,
John Reiss, Steve Gillett, Mustafa Sidki and Jane Stobart

Printed and bound in Great Britain by the Bath Press

EDITOR'S NOTE

The Second Edition of *The Guinness Who's Who Of Indie And New Wave* forms a part of the multi-volume series taken from the *Guinness Encyclopedia Of Popular Music*. It has been considerably enlarged, updated, corrected and now has an Index of names. Fifteen specialist single volumes and four new editions have already been published and new titles are being planned for the near future.

Already available:
The Guinness Who's Who Of Heavy Metal.
The Guinness Who's Who Of Reggae.
The Guinness Who's Who Of Film Musicals.
The Guinness Who's Who Of Rap, Dance And Techno.
The Guinness Who's Who Of Fifties Music.
The Guinness Who's Who Of Sixties Music.
The Guinness Who's Who Of Seventies Music.
The Guinness Who's Who Of Jazz.
The Guinness Who's Who Of Country Music.
The Guinness Who's Who Of Blues.
The Guinness Who's Who Of Soul.
The Guinness Who's Who Of Folk Music.
The Guinness Who's Who Of Stage Musicals.
The Guinness All Time Top 1000 Albums.

In the three years since the first edition of this confusingly titled Who's Who appeared, the definition of the genre is at last being understood. I have been asked countless times on radio broadcasts and by letter: What do you mean by Indie? To counterbalance this however, the many thousands who bought the first edition obviously knew or were not bothered. Also, there is an important sub-title: New Wave Pop. My real title for this book was: *The Guinness Who's Who Of Music After the Sex Pistols Played By Creative On The Edge Musicians With Lots Of Nice Guitars That Sound A Bit Like The Byrds, Velvet Underground and the MC5.*

It is an attitude with a sound, it does not mean it has to be relased on Cream Pie Nosebag records with a limited pressing of 47. It does not mean you have to have been in the *NME* and not *Smash Hits*. Finally it does not mean that if you are enormously successful you lose the right to be included.

It is fair to say however, that the heart and soul of this book comes from record labels such as Creation, Sub Pop, 4AD, Beggars Banquet, Demon, Stiff, One Little Indian, Indolent and Cherry Red. The past two years (1994-95) have produced a 'silver age' for Indie, one look at the line-up for the past two Glastonbury Festivals or the Lollopallooza Fest in the USA will illustrate what musically fertile times we live in. Not since the great festivals of the late 60s (mostly in the USA) have we had such mouth-watering bills.

The current leader in the field must be Creation Records who in addition to watering great bands such as Teenage Fanclub, Swervedriver, 18 Wheeler and the Boo Radleys have found their Oasis in Oasis. Arguably the finest pop group since the

Beatles, it is hoped that they don't blow it, as another Stone Roses-type hiatus would surely not be tolerated. Oasis will in turn spawn dozens of bands signed by both major and independent companies over the next few months because they sound and write songs like Oasis. I would not object if the quality is good. Nobody objected to the Beatles being followed by the Small Faces, the Who, the Hollies and the Zombies in the UK. Nobody objected to the Beatles being followed by the Byrds, the Lovin' Spoonful or the Buffalo Springfield in the USA.

I am very grateful to all the musicians , bands and record companies who sent polite letters with suggestions, additions and corrections. I think you will see that I have listened. And to those reviewers who will point out who is missing in some smart alec way - please, why not think about those who are included instead.

One important plea to all bands and artists: Many of you are reluctant to give dates and places of birth. Please could we receive a flood of mail from you all to make this book truly comprehensive?

Some of the entries from the original edition have only been expanded and updated. This is not through laziness or dishonesty it was simply that some of our contributors wrote very well. For example both Simon Williams and John Eley's contributions stand up very well. I hope they have gone on to fame and fortune. Other contributors from the first edition were Jon Staines, Dave Wilson, Dave Laing, Mark Hodkinson, Ben Watson, Lionel Robinson, Chris Spencer, Tom Collier, Johnny Rogan, Jeff Tamarkin, Brian Hogg, Alan Rowett and Alex Ogg.

The last-named joined us two years ago as a full-time writer. Alex has since been responsible for updating many of the entries and for writing most of the new additions. Myself, Johnny Black and Brian Hogg added the others.

The outstanding photographs reproduced inside were nearly all taken by Steve Gillett. Steve is a compulsive gigger and can be seen at dozens of concerts happily flashing away with his partner Angela Lubrano! I am really glad he got in touch with us. The remaining photographs were supplied by the previously mentioned Angela (Nitzer Ebb and the Pastels) and Creation Records for 18 Wheeler (Roger Sargent), Alan McGee, Oasis (Steve Double); A Witness (Ian T. Tilton); Indolent Records for Sleeper (Kevin Westenberg); Rykodisk for Morphine and Reprise Records for Mudhoney (Charles Peterson).

Many thanks to the press offices of the record companies for supplying biogs and CDs. Apologies to those who I have ommitted but we acknowledge: Angela Gibbs at Warners, Andy Childs, Pat and Jody at Rykodisk, Colleen and Tony at 4AD, Sue and Lesley at Beggars Banquet, Vanessa Cotton, Andy and Cle at Creation, Sandra at RMP, Dave Shack at RCA, Alan Robinson at Demon, Miles at Topic, Stuart Bridgeman at Soundcakes, Steve Lowes at Indolent Records, Ian McNay at Cherry Red, K. Snowden at One Little Indian, Berni Kilmartin at Chrysalis, Judy at Phonogram, Sue and Dave Williams at Frontier Promotions, Alan King, the names on the compliment slips that I cannot read at Go! Discs, Food Records, Costermonger, Cooking Vinyl, Epic Records, East West, Matt at Fleming Molloy, Tish Ferry at Alan James PR, Ruth at Polydor, Alison at Columbia and Anglo Plugging.

Many thanks also to: Susan Pipe who quietly knows how to flow text, process entries, make an index and paginate in Quark XPress; Miles Hutchinson, who has already demonstrated that he was an excellent choice for the over-subscribed post of Desk Editor; Mike Kaye of ACI who wrote the new database and continues to suffer our pleas for it to work; John Reiss who looks after everything when I am delivering a new book; my mother who at 82 thought that Oasis doing 'Whatever' on television at Christmas was marvellous; Tom and Dan Larkin who are fast getting to the stage when they can take me to see their favourite band, and finally to my partner Diana Luke who insists on writing her name in big black felt tip on my Indie CDs.

Colin Larkin, July 1995

A Certain Ratio

No UK act has crystalized independent, punk-influenced funk more than Manchester's A Certain Ratio. The original line-up comprised Jeremy Kerr (bass), Simon Topping (vocals/trumpet), Peter Terel (guitar), Martin Moscrop (guitar/trumpet), Martha Tilson (ex-Occult Chemistry; vocals; although she had left by 1982) and Donald Johnson (drums, replacing a drum machine) - signed to Factory Records in 1979, for the cassette-only release, *The Graveyard And The Ballroom*. One side was recorded at Graveyard Studios, the other live, supporting Talking Heads at London's Electric Ballroom. After releasing 'All Night Party', in May 1979 there was a pause before 'Flight', a UK independent Top 10 chart hit over a year later. In the meantime, the band had teamed up with Factory's European sister, Benelux, for a cover of Banbarra's mid-70s funk classic, 'Shack Up', in July 1980. This edgy but rhythmic version offered an excellent snapshot of the band's innovative studio technique. *To Each...*, the band's official debut album, attracted BBC disc jockey John Peel in 1981, a year that also yielded 'Do The Du' (officially intended for release in the USA) and in December 'Waterline' also fared well. 1982 kicked off with a move from the independent to the national charts as *Sextet* further established ACR. Like *To Each...*, *Sextet* housed an intriguing, mostly instrumental collection hinged around funk rhythms. A 12-inch single for Benelux, 'Guess Who', surfaced in July, followed by the *Knife Slits Water* EP in October, coinciding with the release of *I'd Like To See You Again*. The band also issued an obscure 12-inch single on the Rock Steady label, 'Abracadabra', under the guise Sir Horatio, in September 1982. A year later, 'I Need Someone Tonight' was released, reaching the UK independent Top 10. Topping and Terel had departed, to be replaced by Andy Connell, and 'Brazilia' became the band's first project of 1985, preceding 'Wild Party' in July. Those in anticipation of a new ACR album had to wait until the end of 1986 for *Force*, although a compilation, *The Old And The New*, had provided some consolation earlier in the year. 'Mickey Way' promoted *Force* and continued ACR's run of independent hits. By 1987, the band had outgrown the confines of mere cult status and, looking to branch out, signed with A&M Records. To bridge the gap, the Dojo label issued *Live In America* in February, alongside 'Greetings Four', for the European label Materiali Sonari. It was not until the summer of 1989 that new ACR product arrived; and both 'The Big E' and 'Backs To The Wall' revealed a shift towards a more accessible sound. But neither these, nor 'Your Blue Eyes' in October, the *Four For The Floor* EP in February 1990 nor 'Won't Stop Loving You' in May could provide that elusive hit. As a result September 1989's *Good Together* made little impact and ACR left A&M soon afterwards. The group then switched to New Order manager Rob Gretton's Rob's Records, though Creation Records

reissued their back catalogue and also unveiled a sampler album of remixes from their vast discography (including contributions from Electronic and 808 State). Their experimental work and love of collage material has ensured their status as one of the most uncompromisingly original acts working in the post-punk era.
Albums: *The Graveyard And The Ballroom* (Factory 1980, cassette only), *To Each...* (Factory 1981), *Sextet* (Factory 1982), *I'd Like To See You Again* (Factory 1982), *Force* (Factory 1986), *Live In America* (Dojo 1987), *Good Together* (A&M 1989), *MCR* (A&M 1990), *Up In Downsville* (Rob's 1992), *Looking For A Certain Ratio* (Creation 1994). Compilations: *The Old And The New* (Factory 1986), *Sampler* (Creation 1994).

A House

A House are a witty, intelligent post-punk pop band from Dublin, Eire, led by lyricist Dave Couse (vocals), with Fergal Bunbury (guitar) and Martin Healy (bass). The band were originally signed by Geoff Travis for his Warner Brothers Records-backed Blanco Y Negro label in 1987, on the strength of debut single, 'Kick Me Again Jesus', and support slots with the Waterboys. However, their debut album failed commercially. Still tied to a two album deal, the band then made *I Want Too Much*. It was highly acclaimed for bright, defiant songs such as 'The Patron Saint Of Mediocrity'. However, many considered that to be the end of the band, but they regrouped. Keith Cullen had recently set up the Setanta Records label (also home to Frank 'n' Walters and Into Paradise) and invited them to join the roster. Their 'new' career started with an EP, *Doodle*, then the controversial 'Endless List' single. This attracted the wrath of feminists who noted that out of the dozens of names recounted by Couse in a spoken tribute to those who had furthered humanity's, none were female. The result was a second 'list', this time composed entirely of women. *I Am The Greatest* followed in October 1991, but its impact was lessened by distribution problems (BBC Radio 'play listed' it, but unable to the get the record into the shops, the band had to request that the BBC *not* play it). It was produced by Edwyn Collins on a shoestring budget ('He isn't really a producer as such, he just comes up with ideas and gets the drinks in'), and proved another superb showcase for Couse's lyrical aptitude and affecting vocals. Rereleased and repromoted, it eventually entered the UK Top 50. *Wide Eyed And Ignorant* was not as accomplished a collection of songs, with the production credits shared this time between Collins and Phil Thornalley.
Albums: *Big Fat Merry Go Round* (Blanco Y Negro 1988), *I Want Too Much* (Blanco Y Negro 1990), *I Am The Greatest* (Setanta 1991), *Wide Eyed And Ignorant* (Setanta/Parlophone 1994)

A Witness

Formed in Manchester, England, A Witness shared the distinctive sound adopted by the Ron Johnson label acts; fast, quirky songs with an obvious debt to both Captain Beefheart and Pere Ubu. The band comprised, Keith Curtis (vocals), Rick Aitken (b. 18 August 1956, d. October 1989; guitar), Vince Hunt (bass) and Alan Brown (drums). An EP,

A House

Loudhailer Songs, in 1985, attracted the *New Musical Express*, who included the band on their seminal *C86* sampler tape. An album, *I Am John Pancreas*, followed in 1986, full of manic, awkward guitar riffs and off-beat lyrics. After the release of another EP, *One Foot In The Groove* (1988), the Ron Johnson label folded, prompting a short-lived period at Fundamental Records who issued A Witness's second album, *Sacred Cow Heart*. The Membranes' Vinyl Drip label was responsible for the band's next and possibly finest single, 'I Love You Mr. Disposable Razors' (1990). Since then, Strange Fruit Records have combined A Witness's two 1988 sessions for BBC disc jockey John Peel on a mini-album. The band have also covered the Doors' 'Break On Through' on a tribute album to the music of 1967, *Through The Looking Glass*.

Albums: *I Am John Pancreas* (1985), *Sacred Cow Heart* (1988), *Double Peel Sessions* (1989).

A's

This minor new wave band from Philadelphia, USA recorded two albums for Arista Records in 1979 and 1981 but failed to make a significant impression. The group consisted of singer Richard Bush, his songwriting partner, Rocco Notte (keyboards), Rick DiFonzo (guitar), Terry Bortman (bass) and Mike Snyder (drums). The A's built a reputation on the east coast club scene with a strong power pop sound and an energetic, good-time stage show. Their self-titled debut album was praised by *Rolling Stone* but failed to catch on with the record-buying public. The follow-up, *A Woman's Got The Power*, produced by Nick Garvey of the Motors, found the band taking a more serious approach and reached the lower rungs of the US album chart. The band broke up in the early 80s.

Albums: *The A's* (1979), *A Woman's Got The Power* (1981).

Absolute Gray

Based in Rochester, New York, USA, and influenced by the 'psycho-pop' of Echo And The Bunnymen and Dream Syndicate, Absolute Gray's career spanned the mid 80s with a string of consistently pleasing recordings focused through the vocals and lyrics of Beth Brown (ex-new wave band Hit & Run). Formed in October 1983, the quartet played their first gig together in January of the following year. Their recording career began with an eight-track collection for the Earring label, including a live rendition of the Velvet Underground's 'Beginning To See The Light' and a lustful appreciation of the Bunnymen's Ian McCulloch, 'More Walnuts'. It was later reissued by Midnight Records, whom Absolute Gray joined for 1986's *What Remains*. Produced by Tim Lea of the Windbreakers, this was a low-key set of great depth and colour, accentuated by Brown's growing personality, which stamped the recording with a lovelorn desolation. 'Grey Farewell', in particular, was an almost peerless slice of 80s melancholy pop, and was written about the impending break-up of the band. Afterwards drummer Pat Thomas attempted a reflective but unremarkable solo album, and, with original guitarist/violinist Matt also leaving, Absolute Gray were reduced to Brown and Mitch Rasor (guitar/bass) for their final EP, *The Painted Post*. Thereafter Absolute Gray reformed briefly in 1987, a

meeting documented by *Sand Down The Moon*, but there was no permanent reunion.

Albums: *Green House* (Earring 1984, mini-album), *What Remains* (Midnight 1986), *A Journey Thru The Past* (Greek Di-Di Music 1988), *Sand Down The Moon* (Greek Di-Di Music 1989). Pat Thomas solo: *Pat Thomas* (Heyday 1988).

Accelerators

Hailing from North Carolina, USA, and unconnected to the New Jersey or Los Angeles bands of with the same name (and several others in different territories), these Accelerators were led by singer/guitarist and songwriter Gerald Duncan. It was he who largely orchestrated the band's competent but unenthralling mid-80s career. He had help, however, in the shape of renowned producer and musician Don Dixon, and local star Mitch Easter of Let's Active, who both appeared on the band's appealing debut, *Leave My Heart*. However, only Duncan and drummer Doug Welchel survived the transition to the Accelerators' second line-up, that also featured guitarist Brad Rice. *The Accelerators* featured two songs produced by Dixon, and it was significant that among the strongest tracks was a remake of the debut album's track 'Two Girls In Love'. Another was the cover of the Box Tops' 'The Letter'. Given the four-year interval between recordings, it did not bode well for their future, a suspicion confirmed when the band effectively disappeared from view again, only re-emerging once more in 1991 for the perfunctory *Dream Train*.

Albums: *Leave My Heart* (Dolphin 1983), *The Accelerators* (Profile 1987), *Dream Train* (Profile 1991).

Actifed

Actifed, formed in Hounslow, London, never made a great impact outside of the early 80s UK punk scene. The band, which consisted of David Rogers (vocals/lead guitar), John Bristow (bass), Clinton Grace (guitar) and Stuart Hemphill (drums), were acclaimed on the London club scene of 1981 and such was their following that they appeared on the front cover of *Sounds* magazine the following year before they had released any records. In retrospect it did them few favours. By the year's end the same magazine had crowned them with the 'Here Today, Gone Tomorrow' award, after no records had been released after protracted contractual problems with the promoter John Curd. Further complications arose from the concern shown by the pharmaceuticals company Actifed about the use of their name by four young men with anti-social haircuts. The upshot was a crucial delay in the beginning of the band's recording career. They finally plucked up courage to ask original singer Weazel to leave on 1 March 1983, prior to *Dawn Of Legion*, a sprightly four-track 12-inch released on Jungle Records which was produced by former Generation X member Tony James. They then set about a major UK tour and a second single, 'Crucifixion', followed in June 1984. However, the planned debut album was dropped from the schedules when the group collapsed later that year. This left Actifed to be remembered as a classic case of squandered talent.

Action Pact

This pop-punk band originating from Essex, England,

A Witness

helped to brighten the early 80s with infectious diatribes on the state of the nation. The line-up featured Kim Igoe (bass), Des 'Wild Planet' (guitar), Joe Fungus (drums) and George Cheex (b. 1966; vocals). John, later guitarist for Dead Man's Shadow, was the original singer when the band were known as Bad Samaritans. Joe was recruited from local punk band Savage Upsurge. When John left, female vocalist George was auditioned and recruited. Fresh Records, after releasing one DMS single, decided to release a joint single with both bands. Their debut release was titled 'Heathrow Touchdown', and was aired while two of the band members were still at school. Action Pact's two tracks, 'London Bouncers' and 'All Purpose Action Footwear' were given heavy airplay by BBC disc jockey John Peel. After completing their first session for his Radio 1 show, the anti-glue sniffing 'Suicide Bag' emerged on Fall Out. Fungus was then replaced on drums by Grimly Fiendish, who was not about to reveal his real name either. Kim 'Dr Phibes' left the band after the sessions for the debut album were completed, although he continued to write lyrics for them. His temporary replacement was Phil Langham (ex-the Dark). Another BBC radio session was completed, this time for disc jockey David 'Kid' Jensen. 'Thistles' took over on bass, and was in place in time for the band's performance at the Leeds *Futurama '83* festival. Two more enticing singles, 'A Question Of Choice' and 'Yet Another Dole Queue Song', prefaced the band's final album.
Albums: *Mercury Theatre On the Air Again* (Fall Out 1983) *Survival Of The Fattest* (Fall Out 1984).

AD

Formed in Brooklyn, New York, USA this rock/rap crossover group take their name from lead rapper Anthony DeMores' (b. 1969, Brooklyn, New York, USA) high school adventures, as MC AD. He met guitarist David Tarcia at Bard College, a liberal arts school in New York State. Despite the luxury of their education (DeMore was a theatre student with one play behind him), he was brought up in the Bronx and Brooklyn, the son of a lorry driver father. 'Bard made me more political. I saw people who didn't have the slightest understanding of my culture, and saw how they reacted to me and the other blacks and Latinos who were in that white middle-class world.' Joined by bassist Aaron Keane and drummer Mervin Clarke, DeMore took this specific indignation into the recording world with their debut album on Rage Records. Not to be confused with the group of the same name who recorded for Kerygama in the late 80s.
Album: *AD* (Rage 1993).

Adam And The Ants

Formed in April 1977, this initially punk outfit comprised Adam Ant (b. Stuart Leslie Goddard, 3 November 1954, London, England; vocals/guitar), backed by Lester Square (guitar), Andy Warren (vocals/bass) and Paul Flanagan (drums). Heavily influenced by the Sex Pistols, they incorporated bondage gear and sado-masochistic imagery into their live act and repertoire. The line-up was relatively *ad hoc* between 1977-79 with Mark Gaumont replacing Lester Square (who joined the Monochrome Set - as Andy

Warren would later do) and colourful manager Jordan occasionally taking vocals. Adam appeared with Toyah in Derek Jarman's movie *Jubilee* where he seemed more convincing than onstage. Although the first generation Ants released one album *Dirk Wears White Sox*, their critical reputation among new wave writers was poor. At the end of the decade, Ant sought the advice of Pistols manager Malcolm McLaren, who took on the role of image consultant for a £1,000 fee. His advice was a radical shift of musical policy and a daring new look combining Native American (Apache) imagery and piratical garb. In January 1980, however, the Ants fell victim to McLaren's charisma and abandoned their leader to form the newsworthy Bow Wow Wow. At this point, most observers assumed that Ant's career was over. In fact, it was just beginning.

With an entirely fresh set of Ants consisting of Marco Pirroni (b. 27 April 1959, London, England; vocals/guitar), Kevin Mooney (vocals/bass) and two drummers, Terry Lee Miall (8 November 1958, London, England) and Merrick (b. Chris Hughes, 3 March 1954, London, England), Ant effectively reinvented himself. Out went the punk riffs and bondage to be replaced by a sound heavily influenced by the Burundi Black drummers. With his Red Indian warpaint and colourful costume, the new Ant enjoyed three UK hits in 1980 culminating in the number 2 'Ant Music', in which he boldly dismissed his rivals and proclaimed his sound to be of the moment. His prognosis was correct. 1981 was the year of Adam And The Ants whose pop prescience was captured in a series of excellently produced videos. With his striking ex-anorexic looks and clever use of costume, Adam was a natural pin-up. His portrayal of a highwayman ('Stand And Deliver') and pantomime hero ('Prince Charming') brought two UK number 1 hits and ushered in an era of 'New Pop', where fancy dressing up and catchy melodic songs without a message became the norm. In 1981 Mooney was replaced by ex-Roxy Music member Gary Tibbs (b. 25 January 1958, London, England). Having dominated his group since 1977, it came as little surprise when Adam announced that he was dissolving the unit in early 1982 to pursue a solo career as Adam Ant.

Albums: *Dirk Wears White Sox* (Do It 1979), *Kings Of The Wild Frontier* (CBS 1980), *Prince Charming* (CBS 1981). Compilation: *Antmusic: The Very Best Of* (Arcade 1993). Videos: *Hits 1980-1986* (1986), *Prince Charming* (1988), *Antmusic: The Very Best Of* (1993).

Further reading: *Adam And The Ants*, Mike West, *Adam And The Ants*, Chris Welch, *Adam And The Ants*, Fred and Judy Vermorel, *Adam Ant Tribal Rock Special*, Martha Rodriguez (Design), *The Official Adam Ant Story*, James Maw, *Adam And The Ants Kings: The Official Adam And The Ants Song Book*, Stephen Lavers.

Videos: *Hits 1980-1986* (1986), *Prince Charming* (1988), *Antmusic: The Very Best Of* (1993).

Adicts

The Adicts can be singled out from the host of other UK punk hopefuls of the early 80s largely due to their image. The adoption of black bowler hats and face make-up shared more than a passing resemblance to those rather unruly characters in Stanley Kubrick's controversial film, *A Clockwork Orange*, and reflected the Adicts' brand of bootboy new wave music. The group were originally based in Ipswich, Suffolk, England, and comprised lead singer Monkey (b. Keith Warren), who had grotesquely perfected droog Alex's grin, plus Kid Dee (b. Michael Davison; drums), Pete Davidson (guitar) and Mel Ellis (bass). Their debut EP, *Lunch With The Adicts*, was the first release for the Dining Out label in 1981. This was followed by *Songs Of Praise* for DWED in October, which has subsequently become something of a cult classic in third wave punk collecting circles. The band then moved to the punk label Fall Out for 'Viva La Revolution', before they again changed labels, settling at the appropriately named Razor Records. There they achieved two UK Independent Top 10 singles, 'Chinese Takeaway' (1982) and 'Bad Boy' (1983). The ensuing album, *Sound Of Music*, even managed to scrape into the lower reaches of the UK chart for one week, which was only 380 weeks less than Julie Andrews' similarly titled collection. All was then quiet for two years, until the Adicts popped up in 1985, back at Fall Out, with a new EP, *Bar Room Bop*. The compilation, *This Is Your Life*, covered the band's earliest recordings from 1978-80. Since then there has been a trickle of albums to little interest outside of hardened punk audiences in Europe and the US.

Albums: *Songs Of Praise* (DWED 1981), *Sound Of Music* (Razor 1982), *Fifth Overture* (1987), *Live And Loud!* (Dojo 1987), *Rockers In Rags (Live In Alabama)* (1990). Compilation: *This Is Your Life (1978-80)* (Fall Out 1985). Videos: *Live At The Manhattan Club* (1983), *Let's Go* (1994).

Adolescents

The first line-up of the hardcore band the Adolescents, from Fullerton, Orange County, California, USA, comprised Frank Agnew (rhythm guitar), Rikk Agnew (lead guitar), Casey Royer (drums/vocals), Tony 'Montana' Brandenburg (vocals) and Steve 'Soto' Rodgers (bass/vocals). Montana formed the band with the other three, who were all formerly members of Social Distortion. Rikk Agnew, in addition, had formerly played with several Los Angeles bands including the Detours, while Rodgers had been part of Agent Orange. Following a flirtation with Posh Boy Records (the 'Amoeba' single, of which only 15 copies were pressed), the band's debut emerged on Frontier Records in 1981. Straight afterwards the band collapsed. Rikk Agnew went on to release a solo album for Frontier the following year, which largely consisted of songs written for the intended second Adolescents album. Afterwards he would go on to play with both Christian Death and T.S.O.L. The Adolescents reformed for reunion gigs in 1986 and effectively became an active unit once more. *Brats In Battalions*, released on the group's own label, included guitarist Alfie Agnew deputising for brother Frank on a powerful punk/metal hybrid. The line-up switched for *Balboa Fun *Zone*, but the songwriting of the remaining original members Rikk Agnew and Rodgers was seen to its best advantage. It was followed by a live album taken from concerts recorded five years apart. Agnew's second solo effort, credited to Rikk Agnew's Yard Sale, featured his returning two brothers, Alfie and Frank. The Adolescents finally called it a day in 1989.

Albums: *Adolescents* (Frontier 1981), *Brats In Battalions*

(SOS 1987), *Balboa Fun*Zone* (Triple X 1988), *Live 1981 and 1986* (Triple X 1989). Rikk Agnew solo: *All By Myself* (Frontier 1982). Rikk Agnew's Yard Sale: *Emotional Vomit* (Triple X 1990).

Adult Net

This 60s revivalist pop band from the UK was fronted by Laura Elise (aka 'Brix') Smith, b. California, USA. Her dual role after she relocated to England was as a member of husband Mark E. Smith's band, the Fall. The Adult Net was inaugurated in 1985 when Brix, who was brought up in Hollywood, took the phrase from a line in 'Stephen's Song', from the Fall's *Wonderful And Frightening World Of*. She had previously worked in Rage and Burden Of Proof. In contrast to the Fall, whom many noted she pushed in a more commercial direction, Adult Net chose vocal harmony and bubblegum pop which harked back to her Californian roots, and the Beach Boys in particular. Her accomplices at one time included three ex-members of the Smiths; Andy Rourke, Mike Joyce and Craig Gannon, the line-up that saw the band make their live debut. Hastily arranged in order to impress Geffen Records, the band nevertheless acquired a contract from Fontana Records. 'Incense And Peppermints' (Strawberry Alarm Clock) and 'Edie', a tribute to the Andy Warhol protégé, attracted plenty of press but few record sales. A cover of the Grass Roots' 'Where Were You' preceded *The Honey Tangle*, an album of seamless but occasionally sickly pop. The line-up had transformed to include Clem Burke (ex-Blondie) and James Eller (ex-The The), while Gannon was retained from the earlier formation. A previous album, recorded in 1987 for Beggars Banquet Records, titled *Spin This Web*, remained unreleased. As *Honey Tangle*, named after a racehorse, was released, the personal and professional split between Brix and Mark E. Smith became public. Subsequently a version of Donovan's 'Hurdy Gurdy Man', featuring new current boyfriend Nigel Kennedy on violin, was shelved when Fontana dropped the band in October 1990. Smith laid low for a while before tentatively rehearsing with Hole as replacement bass player. In 1995 she returned to the Fall to guest on that year's *Cerebral Caustic*, evidently having made up with ex-husband Mark E. Smith. Album: *The Honey Tangle* (Fontana 1989).

Adventures

Formed in early 1984, the Adventures' story can be traced back six years to the Belfast, Northern Ireland powerpop/punk group the Starjets, which featured vocalist Terry Sharpe and guitarist Pat Gribben. The duo eventually sought their fortune on the London pub circuit and put together the Adventures with Pat Gribben's wife Eileen on vocals, aided by Gerard 'Spud' Murphy (guitar), Tony Ayre (bass) and Paul Crowder (drums). A deal with Chrysalis Records brought minimal chart success during 1984 and 1985, prompting the group to take a sabbatical in order to rethink their approach. A new deal with Elektra Records saw them achieve modest acclaim for *The Sea Of Love*, while the single, 'Broken Land', entered the UK Top 20. Although they attempted to consolidate their position, 'Down In The Sea Of Love' failed to reach the Top 40 and their subsequent career proved less than eventful.

Albums: *Theodore And Friends* (Chrysalis 1985, issued in US as *The Adventures* (Chrysalis 1985), *The Sea Of Love* (Elektra 1988), *Trading Secrets With The Moon* (Elektra 1989), *Lions & Tigers & Bears* (Elektra 1993).

Adverts

The Adverts first came to prominence in 1976 at the celebrated London punk venue, the Roxy Club. Fronted by vocalist Tim 'TV' Smith and Gaye Advert (vocals/bass), the line-up was completed by Howard Pickup (guitar) and Laurie Driver (drums). Damned guitarist Brian James was so impressed by their performance that he offered them a support slot, as well as introducing them to the hip new wave label, Stiff Records. On tour they were initially promoted with the witty poster: 'The Adverts can play one chord, the Damned can play three. Come and see all four at . . .' Their debut single, the self-effacingly titled 'One Chord Wonders' was well received, but it was their second outing that attracted controversy and chart fame. 'Gary Gilmore's Eyes', a song based on the death-row criminal who had requested permission to donate his eyes to science, was a macabre but euphoric slice of punk/pop which catapulted the Adverts into the UK Top 20. One of the first punk groups to enjoy commercial success, the quartet also boasted the first female punk star in Gaye Advert. Despite some tabloid newspaper publicity, the next single, 'Safety In Numbers' failed to chart, though its successor 'No Time To Be 21' reached number 38. The group barely had time to record their debut album, *Crossing The Red Sea With The Adverts*, before Laurie Driver was ousted and replaced by former Chelsea/Generation X drummer John Towe, who himself left shortly afterwards, succeeded by Rod Latter. Changing record labels, personnel problems and unsuitable production dogged their progress while *Cast Of Thousands* was largely ignored. On 27 October 1979, with a line-up comprising Smith, Dave Sinclair (drums), Mel Weston (keyboards), Eric Russell (guitar) and former Doctors Of Madness bassist, Colin Stoner, the Adverts gave their last performance at Slough College of Art. Smith would go on to record with TV Smith's Explorers, then Cheap and finally solo through a contract with Cooking Vinyl Records.
Albums: *Crossing The Red Sea With The Adverts* (Bright 1978), *Cast Of Thousands* (RCA 1979), *Live At The Roxy Club* (Receiver 1990).

Afghan Whigs

From Cincinnati, and originally stalwarts of the Sub Pop Records empire, in the 90s Afghan Whigs were classified widely as favoured proponents of grunge, though there is much of a more traditional nature in their music. Their *Uptown Avondale* EP, for example, was a collection of classic soul covers, while as early as *Up In It* they were bastardising country rock on tracks like 'Son Of The South'. The band numbers Rick McCollum (guitar), Steve Earle (drums) and John Curley (bass) alongside the distinctive vocals ('I think Camel cigarettes are a big influence on my voice') of mainman Greg Dulli (vocals/guitar). With his origins in Hamilton, a steeltown 30 miles outside of Cincinnati, Dulli quit his film course to attempt to pick up acting parts (apparently making it into the last 50 at the auditions for the

Breakfast Club's 'weirdo'). He first met bassist John Curley in jail, where they were being held overnight for urinating in front of a police officer and drug-dealing respectively. When Afghan Whigs went major, Dulli insisted that he produce their records and direct their videos (in fact before signing Dulli had handled band management). Elektra Records agreed to his conditions, and to financing a movie project. Their major label debut, *Gentlemen*, concerned familiar Afghan Whigs subjects: alienation and the seedier side of life. One of the songs, 'My Curse', was so personal that Dulli couldn't sing it himself - employing Marcy Mays of Scrawl instead. Marketing the album also became the subject of a College Music Journal seminar. In 1994 Dulli was part of the supergroup who recorded a soundtrack for the Stuart Sutcliffe (Beatles) biopic, singing as John Lennon. Other band members were Mike Mills (R.E.M.), Don Fleming (Gumball) Dave Grohl (Nirvana) and Thurston Moore (Sonic Youth).

Albums: *Big Top Halloween* (Ultrasuede 1988), *Up In It* (Sub Pop 1990), *Congregation* (Sub Pop 1992), *Gentlemen* (Elektra 1993).

Afraid Of Mice

Previously known variously as Beano, the Press and the Jones, Liverpool's Afraid Of Mice were formed in early 1979 by ex-Next member Philip Franz Jones (guitar/vocals), who for six years struggled with continuously fluctuating personnel to find a suitable, permanent line-up. With the emergence of bands like Echo And The Bunnymen, Teardrop Explodes and Orchestral Manoeuvres In The Dark, there was a great deal of interest in the second 'Liverpool Scene'. Consequently their appearance on a local compilation, *A Trip To The Dentist*, initiated a deal with Charisma Records. Following two well-received singles, 'I'm On Fire' and 'Intercontinental', 1982 saw the release of *Afraid Of Mice*, with one-time David Bowie producer Tony Visconti at the controls. Described as 'power-pop with an edge', its mixture of punchy guitars, angry lyrics and simple classic pop achieved considerable critical acclaim. Even so, commercial success was to prove much more elusive. After one last single, 'At The Club', and a give-away flexi-disc, 'Transparents', they parted company with Charisma. Although they continued to play live under various names, including the Lumberjack Ballet, Afraid Of Mice's final vinyl appearances were the live *Official Bootleg* in 1983 and a solitary track, 'Don't Take Your Love Away', on the *Jobs For The Boys* compilation in 1985. The Mice were finally laid to rest in 1986 when Phil Jones teamed up with Alex McKechnie (ex-Passage and Modern Eon) in Two's A Crowd, who eventually became Up And Running.

Albums: *Afraid Of Mice* (Charisma 1982), *Afraid Of Mice - The Official Bootleg* (Own label 1983).

Age Of Chance

Hard, guitar fuelled dance raiders from Leeds, Yorkshire, England who at one point looked likely to translate Gang Of Four's vision to a mass audience: 'We're part experimental, part bop and we look pretty good as well.' With a line-up boasting Steve Elvidge (vocals), Neil Howbs (guitar), Geoff Taylor (bass) and Jan Penny (percussion, stand-up drums)

their first single was 'Motorcity', on their own label, which proved a big hit with BBC disc jockey John Peel. A follow-up, 'Bible Of The Beats', pushed them further in the direction of caustic dance. Although their early live sets rarely extended beyond 20 minutes, they proved attractive to a media which could make photogenic capital out of their lavish costumes (such as designer cyclist garb). Their metallic treatment of Prince's 'Kiss' was a mutant dance mini-classic, while a reading of the Trammps' 'Disco Inferno' brought them to within sniffing distance of the UK Top 40. Signing to Virgin Records, a succession of anonymous singles failed to get them any closer. Only the Public Enemy remixed 'Take It' (featuring embryonic rapping) was of much interest, before Steve E left among considerable acrimony. Despite drafting in a replacement, Charles Hutchinson, the band were soon dropped by Virgin. When he in turn deserted, Perry briefly handled vocals before the group finally gave up the ghost in 1991. Elvidge persevered with his love of samples and loops by working with Mad Love, who went nowhere. Elvidge is currently a DJ in Leeds and York, while Howson publishes a listings magazine, *View*. Perry works for Leeds Council, and Taylor for the Grand Theatre in the same city.

Albums: *1,000 Years Of Trouble* (Virgin 1987), *Mecca* (Charisma 1990).

Video: *Crush TV* (1988).

Agent Orange

Named after the chemical defoliant so chillingly used by the USA in the Vietnam war, Agent Orange were one of a number of bands formed in the highly active 'So-Cal' hardcore scene of Fullerton, Orange County, Los Angeles. The original line-up combined Mike Palm (vocals/guitar), Steve 'Soto' Rodgers (bass) and Scott Miller (drums). However, Rodgers left early in their development to put together another local punk attraction, the Adolescents. His replacement was James Levesque. The band's first important supporter was KROQ disc jockey Rodney Bingenheimer, who was fundamental to the promotion of many similar outfits. Their debut release, the *Bloodstains* EP, was the only one to feature Rodgers, and its title-track was the first song the fledgling group wrote. Afterwards they signed to prominent local label Posh Boy Records, run by Robbie Fields. A debut album followed, which showed the band rising above the usual three chord bluster of hardcore with a melodic approach which recalled 60s surf instrumental bands (the Ventures being the most obvious influence). However, the group stormed out of the studio near to the album's completion, complaining about being 'produced' and Fields' behaviour in general, leaving engineer David Hines and Jay Lansford (of Simpletones, Stepmothers and Channel 3 fame) to finish off the recordings. 1982's *Bitchin' Summer* EP subsequently became one of the first skate/surf punk crossover items, with three energised surf guitar instrumentals establishing the group's future direction. Various problems delayed the next release until the group signed with Enigma Records for 1984's *When You Least Expect It* EP, which saw a conscious and largely unsuccessful attempt to accommodate a more disciplined, polished sound, a mistake compounded by a pointless cover of Jefferson Airplane's 'Somebody To Love'. However, all the

elements came together for *This Is The Voice* - the overdriven guitar mesh now allied to first-rate song writing and delivery. This time the cover of 'Dangerman' was fine but subordinate to the Agent Orange originals. Levesque had been replaced by Brent Liles (ex-Social Disortion) a year later, although they have been largely quiet since, save for a 1991 live album and various reissues.
Albums: *Living In Darkness* (Posh Boy 1981), *This Is The Voice* (Enigma 1986), *Real Live Sound* (Restless 1991).

Aire, Jane, And The Belvederes

This group was one of several new wave acts discovered in Akron, Ohio, USA, by producer Liam Sternberg, and subsequently introduced to Stiff Records. Jane Aire (b. Jane Ashley, 2 December 1956, Akron, Ohio, USA) recorded initially for the *Akron Compilation LP* in 1978 and became the first of the featured artists to release a single - 'Yankee Wheels'. Sternberg used a band called the Edge as both session musicians and tour band but renamed them the Belvederes (after a type of turret-like building). The Edge consisted of former Damned guitarist Lu Edmunds (later in Athletico Spizz 80, the Mekons and PiL), respected session players Gavin Povey and Glyn Havard on keyboards and bass respectively, plus drummer Jon Moss (b. 11 September 1957), who played with numerous punk bands including London and the Damned before finding fame with Culture Club. As well as backing Jane Aire, the Edge also played on some of Kirsty MacColl's early recordings and released their own material. After the Stiff single, Aire was signed to Virgin Records to record an album that featured the above musicians plus Chris Payne (trombone), Ray Warleigh (saxophone) and backing singers Rachel Sweet and Kirsty MacColl. After marrying the Boomtown Rats' Pete Briquette in 1980 and assembling a new bunch of Belvederes in Paul Cutler (guitar), Ian Curnon (keyboards), Sam Hartley (bass), Dave Ashley (drums) and former Deaf School saxophonist Ian Ritchie, Aire returned to Stiff to make a further single - a version of Dusty Springfield's 'I Close My Eyes And Count To Ten' - in 1982.
Album: *Jane Aire And The Belvederes* (Virgin 1979).

Airhead, (Jefferson)

This engaging UK pop band consisted of lyricist Michael Wallis (vocals), Steve Marshall (keyboards), Ben Kesteven (bass), and Sam Kesteven (drums). Marshall and Wallis grew up in Snodland, Kent, England. They had played together in bands from 1987 onwards, but achieved little until they joined with the Kesteven brothers. Initial demos prompted interest from the major labels, and they were initially signed to WEA/Korova as the Apples in September 1990. Their opening single, 'Congratulations', was released in February 1991, produced by Leigh Gorman (Soho, ex-Bow Wow Wow) who also produced the band's second single, 'Scrap Happy', by which time they had become Jefferson Airhead, inspired by Jefferson Airplane. After objections from representatives of Jefferson Airplane's record label they became simply Airhead. Their debut *Boing* and its catchy single 'Funny How' surfaced soon after the name change.
Album: *Boing* (1991).

Alarm

Formed in Rhyl, Wales, during 1981, this energetic pop group comprised Mike Peters (b. 25 February 1959; vocals/guitar), David Sharp (b. 28 January 1959; vocals/guitar), Eddie MacDonald (b. 1 November 1959; bass) and Nigel Twist (b. 18 July 1958; drums). Originally known as Seventeen, they changed their name after recording a self-penned song titled 'Alarm Alarm'. Peters was anxious to steer the group in the direction of U2, whose commitment and dedication appealed to his sense of rock as an expression of passion. However, by the time of the Alarm's first UK hit, '68 Guns', their style and imagery most closely recalled punk rockers the Clash. The declamatory verve continued on 'Where Were You Hiding When The Storm Broke' and the traditional rock influence was emphasized in their long spiked hair, skin tight leather trousers and ostentatious belts. Behind the high energy, however, there was a lighter touch which was eloquently evinced on their reading of Pete Seeger's 'The Bells Of Rhymney', which they performed in aid of the coal miners' strike in 1984. The original U2 comparisons began to make more sense on the fourth album, *Electric Folklore Live*, which displayed the power of their in-concert performance. *Change* (produced by Tony Visconti) saw them investigating their Celtic origins with the assistance of members from the Welsh Symphony Orchestra. It was also issued in a Welsh language version. The much-maligned Mike Peters embarked on a solo career in the 90s following the dissolution of the band.
Albums: *Declaration* (IRS 1984), *Strength* (IRS 1985), *Eye Of The Hurricane* (IRS 1987), *Electric Folklore Live* (IRS 1988, mini-album), *Change* (IRS 1989), *Raw* (IRS 1991). Compilation: *Standards* (IRS 1990).
Videos: *Spirit Of '86* (1986), *Change* (1990).

Alberto Y Lost Trios Paranoias

This Manchester-based rock comedy troupe in the vein of the Bonzo Dog Doo-Dah Band and National Lampoon, was formed in 1973 by two former members of Greasy Bear; Chris 'C.P.' Lee (vocals/guitar) and Bruce Mitchell (drums), with Les Prior (vocals), Jimmy Hibbert (vocals/bass), Bob Harding (vocals/guitar/bass), Simon White (steel guitar/guitar), Tony Bowers (bass/guitar) and Ray 'Mighty Mongo' Hughes (second drummer). The group mercilessly parodied the major rock names of the 70s - 'Anadin' was a reworking of Lou Reed's 'Heroin'/'Sweet Jane'. As with many comedy ensembles, the Albertos belied their comic aspirations by their exemplary musicianship, but by the time it came to committing to record their finely-honed act, the artists they had pilloried had ceased to become valid targets and the album flopped. The follow-up in 1977, *Italians From Outer Space*, went some way to re-establishing the Albertos' reputation, but once more the majority of songs were more miss than hit. That same year, the easy targets of the early 70s were put aside with the ascent of punk rock and the Albertos' highly acclaimed stage performance of C.P. Lee's rock play, *Sleak* at London's Royal Court Theatre, presented the story of the manipulation of an innocent, Norman Sleak, into giving the ultimate in rock performance - onstage suicide. This concept gave birth to 'Snuff Rock'. The play's run was punctuated by the comic disc jockey role

of Les Prior, quite possibly his finest performance. The accompanying EP *Snuff Rock*, released on Stiff Records, poked fun at the punk rock phenomenon, targeting the Sex Pistols ('Gobbing On Life'), the Damned ('Kill') and the Clash ('Snuffin' Like That') as well as a myriad of reggae bands in 'Snuffin' In A Babylon'. For once the Albertos act was successfully transferred to vinyl. They hit the UK Top 50 with the Status Quo spoof, 'Heads Down No Nonsense Mindless Boogie' in 1978. Chas Jankel and Roger Ruskin Spear assisted the Albertos on their last album, *Skite*. The group soldiered on into the 80s taking *Sleak* to the Squat Theatre Off-Broadway as well as producing a less successful stage production, entitled *Never Mind The Bullocks*. The death of Les Prior on 31 January 1980 from leukaemia left a large gap in the group, and although his illness had limited him to rare performances in his final years, his comic inspirations were sorely missed. On folding, Hibbert made an unsuccessful attempt to launch a heavy metal career with *Heavy Duty* (1980), but later found success as the writer and voiced character on the children's television cartoon, *Count Duckula*. Lee made a successful stage appearance portraying the hip-beat poet Lord Buckley, as well as releasing, on cassette only, under the title C.P. Lee Mystery Guild, *Radio Sweat* (1981) - a spoof on commercial radio stations. Bowers joined Durutti Column, and later Simply Red. There was a brief, but unsuccessful reformation, as the Mothmen.
Albums: *Alberto Y Lost Trios Paranoias* (Transatlantic 1976), *Italians From Outer Space* (Transatlantic 1977), *Skite* (Logo 1978). Compilation: *The Best Of The Albertos* (Demon 1991).

Alien Sex Fiend

Essentially an alias for the eccentric Nick Wade, Alien Sex Fiend emerged as part of the early 80s gothic punk movement from the UK, centred around London's Batcave venue. Wade previously served time with obscure acts such as the Earwigs and Mr. And Mrs. Demeanour before releasing two singles as Demon Preacher. This was shortened to the Demons for a third single, but like its predecessors it vanished without trace. After various short-lived projects, Wade eventually stumbled upon his long-term guise, Alien Sex Fiend in 1982, aided by David James (guitar), partner Christine Wade (synthesizer) and Johnny 'Ha Ha' Freshwater (drums). On the strength of a nine-track demo tape, the band played the Batcave at the end of the year. Live tracks were added to the tape and released as the cassette-only release, *The Lewd, The Mad, The Ugly And Old Nik*, before signing with Cherry Red Records subsidiary, Anagram. Wade, whose stage image of ghoulish thick white pancake make-up revealed his strongest influence, Alice Cooper, further essayed that debt with 'Ignore The Machine' (1983). *Who's Been Sleeping In My Brain*, was followed by 'Lips Can't Go' and in 1984 by 'R.I.P.'/'New Christian Music', 'Dead And Buried' and 'E.S.T. (Trip To The Moon)', to coincide with *Acid Bath*. Such was the album's reception in Japan that the group embarked on a tour there. *Liquid Head In Tokyo* celebrated the event, but was the last output for Johnny Ha Ha. As a three-piece, the band came up with 'I'm Doin' Time In A Maximum Security Twilight Home' (1985), accompanied by *Maximum Security*. *IT - The*

Album, in time for a tour supporting Alice Cooper. A cover of Red Crayola's late 60s classic, 'Hurricane Fighter Plane', surfaced in early 1987, followed by 'The Impossible Mission'. A retrospective, *All Our Yesterdays*, coincided with Yaxi Highriser's departure. Under the guise of the Dynamic Duo, Wade then issued 'Where Are Batman And Robin?' (on the Riddler label!). 'Bun Ho' was the next Alien Sex Fiend single, continuing a more open-minded musical policy. *Another Planet* confirmed this, while 'Haunted House' saw the adoption of out-and-out dance techniques. After a tour (with Rat Fink Junior and Doc Milton) was captured on the double album, *Too Much Acid?*, the band returned with 'Now I'm Being Zombified' in September 1990. That same month, Alien Sex Fiend released the experimental *Curse* and bounced back three years later with *The Altered States Of America*.
Albums: *Who's Been Sleeping In My Brain* (Anagram 1983), *Acid Bath* (Anagram 1984), *Liquid Head In Tokyo - Live* (Anagram 1985), *Maximum Security* (Anagram 1985), *IT - The Album* (Anagram 1986), *Here Cum Germs* (Anagram 1987), *Too Much Acid?* (Anagram 1989), *Curse* (Anagram 1990), *The Altered States Of America* (Anagram 1993). Compilation: *All Our Yesterdays* (Anagram 1988).
Videos: *A Purple Glistener* (1984), *Edit* (1987), *Overdose* (1988), *Liquid Head In Tokyo* (1991).

All About Eve

Originally called the Swarm, All About Eve emerged on the late 80s UK 'Gothic' scene. The group's nucleus of erstwhile rock journalist and Gene Loves Jezebel bass player Julianne Regan (vocals), along with Tim Bricheno (guitar; ex-Aemotti Crii), provided much of the band's song material. After various early personnel changes, the rhythm section was stabilized with Andy Cousin (bass; also ex-Aemotti Crii) and Mark Price (drums). Given encouragement by rising stars the Mission (for whom Regan had in the past sung backing vocals), All About Eve developed a solid following and with a backdrop of hippy mysticism and imagery, along with Regan's predilection for white-witchcraft and Tarot cards, provided a taste of the exotic with a mixture of goth-rock and 70s folk. Early singles 'Our Summer' and 'Flowers In Our Hair' achieved great success in the UK independent charts and after signing to Mercury Records, their modest showings in the national charts finally gave them a Top 10 hit in July 1988 with 'Martha's Harbour'. Both albums reached the UK Top 10, confirmed their aspirations to be among the frontrunners in British rock in the late 80s. However, this ambition was dealt a blow in 1990 when a rift between the group and guitarist Bricheno resulted in his departure to join the Sisters Of Mercy. The recruitment of Church guitarist Marty Willson-Piper on a part-time basis revitalized the group's drive, although the subsequent album, *Touched By Jesus*, only managed a brief visit to the UK Top 20, and indications that the group had undergone a born-again transformation have yet to be vindicated. A stormy dispute with their distributor, Phonogram, over the company's alleged priority for chart single success saw All About Eve leave the label in late 1991 and shortly afterwards sign to MCA Records.
Albums: *All About Eve* (1987), *Scarlet And Other Stories*

(1989), *Touched By Jesus* (1991), *Ultraviolet* (1992). Compilation: *Winter Words, Hits And Rarities* (1992). Videos: *Martha's Harbour* (1988), *What Kind Of Fool* (1989), *Evergreen* (1989).

Allin, G.G.

b. Kevin Allin, New Hampshire, USA. Of all the degenerate acts carried out in the history of rock 'n' roll, there can be few who have touched (preferably with disinfected gloves) the life and times of G.G. Allin. As one critic thoughtfully pointed out, 'If Allin was an insect he would not only be a dung beetle, he would be the dung beetle the other dung beetles avoided.' Usually taking the stage clad only in a jockstrap, Allin's shows gradually became more excessive as the 80s progressed. His antics included live sexual acts, drug taking and self-immolation. If you caught G.G. Allin on a 'good' night, you could expect to have a variety of bodily effluent flung at you - including vomit, urine and faeces - while simultaneously enjoying songs such as 'You Scum, Eat My Diarrhoea' and 'I'm Gonna Rape You'. These antics eventually led to a nationwide ban and several brushes with the law. Long a cult icon in some circles in Europe and North America, there is little point in attempting rational artistic judgement of his long and often painful recording career. The facts are these: His debut introduced the two regular facets of his career - basic but clumsy Stooges-derived garage punk, and lyrical vulgarity on a massive scale. The rock world had become accustomed to foul language, but on *Always Was, Is, And Always Shall Be*, it was applied with such ferocity and regularity, to all manner of bodily functions, that it became almost became an art form. The moronic 'Pussy Summit Meeting' was a typical title but is quite possibly Allin's best record. However, it all got worse from there. Allin's first band, the Jabbers, defected after recording the *No Rules* EP for Orange Records in 1983, but their leader regrouped with the Scumfucs after briefly fronting the Cedar Street Sluts. Whatever musical merit the Jabbers boasted was entirely lost on the primitive playing and production which accompanied the Scumfucs' recordings. Some argue that it was at this point that Allin actually began to believe lyrics he had previously written merely for shock value. After the Scumfucs split Allin laid low for a period, but interest was reactivated by the ROIR Records compilation, *Hated In The Nation*, which included his 1981 single with members of MC5, 'Gimme Some Head' and a collaboration with J. Mascis of Dinosaur Jr. From there Allin moved to Homestead Records, recording solo and with that label's boss, Gerard Cosloy, as the Holy Men. In the early 90s Allin served a four-year jail sentence in Michigan's Jackson State Prison for aggravated assault with intent to mutilate. Throughout his imprisonment Allin claimed that he would commit suicide live on stage on his return, but he was denied the opportunity, when, following release in 1993, he died in a much more conventional rock 'n' roll way - a drugs overdose. He had left his last show in New York on 27 June, completely naked, attacking innocent passers by, before succumbing to a cocaine/heroin overdose among 'friends'. Suitably, his last recordings were attributed to the Murder Junkies. Albums: With G.G. Allin And The Jabbers: *Always Was, Is,*

And Always Shall Be (Orange 1980), *Banned In Boston* (Black And Blue 1989). With G.G. Allin And The Scumfucs: *Eat My Fuc* (Blood 1984). With G.G. Allin And The Scumfucs/Artless: *G.G. Allin And The Scumfucs/Artless* (Starving Missle/Holy War 1985). With G.G. Allin And The Holy Men: *You Give Love A Bad Name* (Homestead 1987). G.G. Allin And The Murder Junkies: *Bloodshed And Brutality For All* (1993). G.G. Allin solo: *Hated In The Nation* (ROIR 1987, cassette only), *Freaks, Faggots, Drunks & Junkies* (Homestead 1988), *Doctrine Of Mayhem* (Black And Blue 1990).

Altered Images

Formed in 1979, this Glasgow pop ensemble featured Clare Grogan (vocals), Johnny McElhone (guitar), Tony McDaid (bass) and Michael 'Tich' Anderson (drums). Even before their recorded debut, Grogan found herself cast in a film, *Gregory's Girl*, by director Bill Forsyth. In 1980 Altered Images toured with Siouxsie And The Banshees and subsequently employed the services of their bassist, Steve Severin, as producer. Another champion of their work was the influential UK disc jockey, John Peel. Their BBC radio sessions resulted in the offer of a major recording contract by Epic Records, and two unsuccessful singles followed; the early 80s indie classic 'Dead Pop Stars' and 'A Day's Wait'. With the addition of guitarist Jim McInven, the group completed their debut, *Happy Birthday*, in 1981. The infectious title-track, produced by Martin Rushent, soared to number 2 in the UK charts, establishing the elfin Grogan as a punkish Shirley Temple. 'I Could Be Happy' and 'See Those Eyes' were also hits, but the group's second album, *Pinky Blue*, was not well-received by the critics. With 1983's *Bite*, Grogan took on a more sophisticated, adult image, lost Tich and McInven, gained Stephen Lironi (guitar/drums) and found new producers, Tony Visconti and Mike Chapman. The experiment brought another Top 10 hit, 'Don't Talk To Me About Love'. Following a brief tour with the addition of David Wilde (drums) and Jim Prime (keyboards) the group disbanded. Grogan pursued an acting career (notably in television sitcome *Red Dwarf*), recorded a solo album, *Love Bomb*, and later reappeared fronting a new group, Universal Love School. Meanwhile, Altered Images' guitarist Johnny McElhone moved on to Hipsway and Texas. Albums: *Happy Birthday* (Epic 1981), *Pinky Blue* (Epic 1982), *Bite* (Epic 1983). Compilations: *Collected Images* (Epic 1984), *The Best Of Altered Images* (Receiver 1992).

Alternative TV

Formed in 1977, ATV was the brainchild of Mark Perry, the editor of Britain's seminal punk fanzine, *Sniffin' Glue*. The original line-up featured Perry (vocals), Alex Fergusson (b. 16 December 1952, Glasgow, Scotland; guitar), Micky Smith (bass) and John Towe (ex-Generation X, drums), but this unstable group later underwent several changes. Although ATV completed numerous albums during their career, they are best remembered for a series of uncompromising singles, including their self-effacing debut, 'Love Lies Limp' (free with *Sniffin' Glue*) and the declamatory 'How Much Longer?'. A disillusioned Perry abandoned the group in 1979 in favour of the Good

American Music Club

Missionaries and subsequent projects, namely the Door And The Window and the Reflections. He returned to recording under the ATV banner in 1981 and continued to do so sporadically throughout the 80s. Fergusson went on to join Psychic TV, up until 1986, subsequently turning his hand to producing for Gaye Bykers On Acid and the Popguns. With residual interest in Alternative TV still strong, Perry was stated to be working with Fergusson once more in 1995.

Albums: *The Image Has Cracked* (Deptford Fun City 1978), *Vibing Up The Senile Man Part One* (Deptford Fun City 1979), *Live At The Rat Club '77* (Crystal Red 1979), *Strange Kicks* (IRS 1981), *Peep Show* (Anagram 1987), *Dragon Love* (Chapter 22 1990), *Live 1978* (Overground/Feel Good All Over 1992), *My Life As A Child Star* (Overground 1994). With Here And Now: *What You See... Is What You Are* (Deptford Fun City 1978). Compilations: *Action Time Vision* (Deptford Fun City 1980), *Splitting In Two* (Anagram 1989).

American Music Club

One of their country's most undervalued groups, San Francisco's American Music Club have taken a similar path to Australia's Go-Betweens in reaping rich harvests of critical acclaim not yet reflected in their sales figures. The group's mastermind and musical springboard is Mark Eitzel (b. 1959, Walnut Creek, San Francisco, California, USA; vocals/guitar), a lyricist of rare scope. The name of his publishing company, 'I Failed In Life Music', is a good indicator as to Eitzel's world view: 'I see humanity, including myself, as basically a bunch of sheep or ants. We're machines that occasionally do something better than machines.' The rest of American Music Club is Danny Pearson (bass), Tim Mooney (drums), Vudi (guitar) and occasionally Bruce Kaphan (steel guitar). When he was seven Eitzel's family moved to Okinawa, Taiwan, before settling in Southampton, England. He wrote his first songs aged 14, and was 17 when he saw the new punk bands. Two years later he moved to Ohio with his family. There he put together Naked Skinnies, who emigrated to San Francisco in 1981. It was during their show at the San Francisco punk venue, the Mabuhay Gardens, that Vudi walked in and saw them. From his earliest appearances Eitzel's on-stage demeanour rivalled the extravagances of Iggy Pop's. In the early days he was also a fractious heavy drinker, until the day AMC signed to a major label after several acclaimed independent albums. Before this he had quit the band twice, once after the tour to support *Engine*, and once after *Everclear*. He also temporarily fronted Toiling Midgets. Following *Everclear*, in 1991, *Rolling Stone* magazine elected Eitzel their Songwriter Of The Year, but as he conceded: 'Yes, I'm songwriter of the year for 1991; a month later I'm still songwriter of the year, and still no-one comes to see us play!' *Mercury* was the band's debut for a major record label, although song titles such as 'What Godzilla Said To God When His Name Wasn't Found In The Book Of Life' illustrated that Eitzel's peculiar lyrical scenarios were still intact. The album was primarily written

while Eitzel was living in the decidedly down-at-heel Mission District of San Francisco. The critical acclaim customarily heaped on the group could be heard for 1994's *San Francisco*, and *Melody Maker* journalist Andrew Mueller grew exasperated when reviewing one of the singles drawn from it, 'Can You Help Me?' - 'We're obviously not explaining ourselves tremendously well . . . Every album they have ever made we have reviewed with prose in the most opulent hues of purple . . . We have, in short, shouted ourselves hoarse from the very rooftops in this band's name, and still nobody who doesn't work here owns any of their records'.
Albums: *The Restless Stranger* (Grifter 1986), *Engine* (Grifter/Frontier 1986), *California* (Grifter/Frontier 1988), *United Kingdom* (Demon 1990), *Everclear* (Alias 1991), *Mercury* (Virgin 1993), *San Francisco* (Virgin 1994).

An Emotional Fish

This four-piece power pop band in the mould of U2 or INXS, was formed in Dublin, Eire, with a line-up of Gerard Wheland (vocals), Enda Wyatt (bass), Dave Frew (guitar) and Martin Murphy (drums). They began with two Irish hits on U2's Mother label, the second of which, 'Celebrate', was given a UK release. BBC disc jockey Mark Goodier invited them to do a session, and Radio 1 was so impressed by the band that they sponsored their UK tour. However, this soon backfired as the press made them scapegoats for what they saw as 'odious and corrupt' practices on behalf of a public broadcasting service. This fuelled further invective when the band's debut album was unveiled, 'weighty, overblown and held back by windy rhetoric' being among the kinder reviews. 'Lace Virginia' and 'Blue', the follow-up singles, sank without trace as Radio 1 judiciously withdrew from the controversy, failing to give the band airplay in the process. The outfit released their second album in 1993 to a still hostile critical reception, while 1995's *Sloper* saw them retreat from stadium rock bombast to a more textured, acoustic songwriting base.
Albums: *An Emotional Fish* (Warners 1990), *Junkpuppets* (Warners 1993), *Sloper* (ZYX 1995).

Anastasia Screamed

Formed in 1987 by Christopher Burdett (b. 8 March 1968, Boston, Massachusetts, USA; drums), Christopher Cugini (b. 23 November 1966, Malden, Massachusetts, USA; guitar), Andy Jagolinzer (b. 11 June 1969, Framingham, Massachusetts, USA; vocals) and Scott Lerner (b. 3 March 1966, Boston, Massachusetts, USA), the last being the first of a litany of short-term bass players to pass through the band's ranks. Chick Graning (b. 28 October 1966, Vancouver, Canada) replaced Jagolinzer before the end of the year, and added an extra touch of hysteria to a flowing, sub-hardcore guitar sound which hardly needed to be destabilized any further. Following a brace of independent singles which garnered much appreciation from the US college radio circuit, in 1989 the band solved their bass playing problems by bringing in Charlie Bock (b. 26 January 1965, Nashville, Tennessee, USA) and also relocated from Boston to Nashville. A year later Anastasia Screamed signed to the UK's Fire Records and started to earn applause from Europe, broadening their horizons with a topsy-turvy brand

of rock 'n' roll, touring extensively with Throwing Muses. Graning, indeed, would become romantically linked with the latter's Tanya Donelly prior to her switch to Belly. However, soon afterwards his band collapsed, which at the time, and retrospectively, seemed an awful waste of talent.
Albums: *Laughing Down The Limehouse* (Fire 1990), *Moontime* (Fire 1991).

And All Because The Lady Loves

Formed in 1987, this Newcastle born female duo, Nicky Rushton (b. 1961; guitar/vocals) and Rachel Collins (b. 1965; bass/vocals) achieved critical acclaim on the UK club circuit with their sets of bitter-sweet love songs, combined with a twist of political consciousness. Accompanied by simple, but effective, guitar and bass, their songs were off-set with strong - almost a cappella - vocal harmonies and punchy melodies. They toured with Microdisney and Michelle Shocked while promoting their 1988 EP, *If You Risk Nothing*, and this led to an album on the small independent label, Paint It Red, which won widespread critical acclaim. In 1990 they released their second album on the duo's own Newcastle-based label, Roundabout. Their most recent work has seen them employing the use of backing musicians, live and in the studio, though they remain one of the north east's best kept secrets.
Albums: *Anything But A Soft Centre* (Paint It Red 1988), *Centred* (Roundabout 1991), *Sugar Baby Love* (Roundabout 1991), *Sister Bridget* (Roundabout 1993).

Angelic Upstarts

This politically motivated hard-line punk quartet formed in 1977, in South Shields, England. They were the brainchild of Mensi (vocals), and strongly influenced by the Clash, Damned and Sex Pistols. With Cowie, Warrington and Taylor completing the line-up, they signed to the independent Small Wonder label and released the underground classic 'Murder Of Liddle Towers' in 1979. The song condemned police brutality and identified strongly with the youth culture of the day. It led to a deal with Warner Brothers, which produced *Teenage Warning* and *We Gotta Get Out Of This Place* in 1979 and 1980 respectively. Both these albums are punk classics, featuring provocative lyrics which ridiculed the politics of the government of Margaret Thatcher. Characterized by Mensi's nasal snarl, the band suffered from regular outbreaks of violence at their live shows from National Front fascist supporters, who sought to counter the group's left-wing politics after initially misinterpreting their patriotic stance. As the 80s progressed, the band gradually saw their fan-base disappear. They had become entrenched in a musical style that was rapidly becoming outdated. The Angelic Upstarts continued to release material, but with declining success. The band ground to a halt in 1986, but reformed for a brief period in 1988 and then once again in 1992, releasing *Bombed Out* on the Roadrunner label. In the 90s, Mensi has become a leading member of the Anti Fascist Action group.
Albums: *Teenage Warning* (Warners 1979), *We Gotta Get Out Of This Place* (Warners 1980), *2 Million Voices* (EMI 1981), *Live* (EMI 1981), *Still From The Heart* (EMI 1982), *Reason Why?* (Anagram 1983), *Last Tango In Moscow* (Picasso 1984,

Animals That Swim

live album), *Live In Yugoslavia* (Picasso 1985), *Blood On The Terraces* (Link 1987), *Power Of The Press* (Gas 1986), *Bombed Out* (Roadrunner 1992). Compilations: *Angel Dust (The Collected Highs 1978-1983)* (Anagram 1983), *Bootlegs And Rarities* (Dojo 1986), *Blood On The Terraces* (Link 1987), *Live And Loud* (Link 1988), *Greatest Hits Live* (Streetlink 1992).

Angry Samoans

Formed in August 1978, in Van Nuys, California, USA, the Angry Samoans were one of the original Los Angeles punk bands, along with Fear, Black Flag, Circle Jerks and X. The fact that they never achieved quite what those other bands did can be put down to a disappointingly curt discography. After numerous personnel changes, the most solid line-up consisted of core duo Mike Saunders (guitar/vocals) and Gregg Turner (guitar/vocals), plus Todd Homer (bass/vocals), Steve Drojensky (guitar) and Bill Vockeroth (drums). Leaning toward the humorous side of punk, in the same way as the Ramones and Dickies, some of the Samoans' songs featured titles such as 'I'm A Pig', 'My Old Man's A Fatso', 'Attack Of The Mushroom People' and 'They Saved Hitler's Cock'. Following two EPs and one album for Bad Trip, they laid low for some time, before re-emerging in the late 80s via the auspices of Triple X Records.
Albums: *Back From Somoa* (Bad Trip 1982), *STP Not LSD* (PVC 1988), *Live At Rhino Records* (Triple X 1990). Compilation: *Return To Somoa* (Shakin' Street 1990).

Animals That Swim

A quintet from north London, Animals That Swim comprise Hank Starrs (vocals/drums), Hugh Barker (guitar), Al Barker (guitar/keyboards), Del Crabtree (trumpet) and Anthony Coote (bass). Much praised in the press by peer groups Elastica and Blur during 1994, a series of seven inch singles for Ché Records were well-received. Previously, they had recorded on their own Beachheads In Space label, including their debut single, 'Roy', and the *50 Dresses* EP. However, *Workshy*, the group's debut long player, failed to make the same impression, although its musical strengths were just as obvious. The band regrouped in early 1995 for the more promising 'Pink Carnations', where the story of a recovering patient offered the sort of poetic deep irony which recalled the Smiths' 'Girlfriend In A Coma'. This was released on their new label, Elemental Records, a relationship which had begun when that record label's head, Nick Evans, had asked to borrow 50 pence off the band to buy their single. However, it was not yet enough for the band to be able to renounce their current day jobs, which include working as a chef at a gay vegetarian restaurant, a bookshop assistant and a rehearsal studio assistant.
Album: *Workshy* (Ché 1994).

Anti-Nowhere League

Leading lights in the early 80s UK punk scene along with contempories GBH and Exploited, this quartet from Tunbridge Wells, Kent, betrayed their talent in biker leather, chains and hardcore obscenity. Led by Animal (b. Nick Karmer; vocals) and Magoo (guitar), their catalogue of sexual outrage veered from the satirical to the genuinely offensive,

with a string of four-letter words, rabid misogyny and the glorification of bestiality. Their most memorable moment was a thrashy re-run of Ralph McTell's 'Streets Of London' which replaced the song's folky sentimentality with the barbed, snarling rhetoric of the gutter. Thousands of copies of the single were seized and destroyed by the police as the b-side, 'So What', was deemed obscene. This incident however, did nothing to prevent the group reaching number 1 in the UK Independent single charts, a feat accomplished a further three times in 1982 with 'I Hate People', 'Woman' and 'For You'. As their punkish appeal receded, the group abbreviated their name to the League and turned to a punk/metal hybrid in keeping with their biker image. Surprisingly, the results were not as appalling as might have been imagined, with *The Perfect Crime* boasting several fine songs, not least the very nearly subtle '(I Don't Believe) This Is My England'. The group disbanded in 1988 but there have been several revivals, including the one-off 1989 reunion recorded for release as *Live And Loud*.
Albums: *We Are...The League* (WXYZ 1982), *Live In Yugoslavia* (ID 1983), *The Perfect Crime* (GWR 1987), *Live And Loud* (Link 1990). Compilation: *Long Live The League* (Dojo 1986).

Anti-Pasti

Hailing from Derbyshire, England, Anti-Pasti were part of the commercially successful but critically reviled third wave of punk. The group, comprising the typically surname-less Will (bass), Dugi (guitar), Kev (drums) and Martin Roper (lead vocals), signed to the punk/heavy metal label Rondelet Records in 1980, and debuted with the *Four Sore Points* EP, followed by a second epistle, *Let Them Free*, in January 1981. Later that year, Anti-Pasti offered their debut album, *The Last Call*, which reached the UK Top 40. Their growing profile was confirmed when a third single, 'Six Guns', appeared at end of the year and reached number 1 in the UK Independent chart, as did the successful joint venture with Oi! punk legends the Exploited on a 12-inch single EP, *Don't Let 'Em Grind You Down*. 'East To The West', released in 1982, preceded the last Anti-Pasti album and single, both named 'Caution To The Wind', although a self-titled singles retrospective surfaced a year later.
Albums: *The Last Call* (Rondolet 1981), *Caution To The Wind* (Rondolet 1982). Compilation: *Anti-Pasti* (Rondolet 1983).

Antietam

With roots in Louisville, Kentucky outfit Babylon Dance Band, Antietam took their name from an 1862 battle in the American Civil War and based themselves in New York. Led by Tara Key (guitar/vocals) and husband Tim Harris (bass/vocals), with Michael Weinert the first of a rota of drummers, the group's debut dabbled in sloppy art-rock posturing to limited effect. The follow-up saw violin added by Danna Pentes of Fetchin Bones, one of a number of collaborators in the Antietam line-up of subsequent years. A third album, *Burgoo*, featured a third drummer in Charles Schultz, with production by Yo La Tengo's Ira Kaplan and Georgia Hubley. Though sound quality was undoubtedly better the married couple's squalling vocals still verged on irritation, however intelligent the lyrics. Some of this dubious approach to song writing was explained by Key as an attempt to make music 'like the sounds I feel in the pit of my stomach'. *Rope-A-Dope* saw the introduction of yet another drummer, Josh Madell, who also toured with Codeine, while Key enjoyed the fruits of a partially successful solo album (*Bourbon County*).

Albums: *Antietam* (Homestead 1985), *Music From Elba* (Homestead 1986), *Burgoo* (Triple X 1990), *Everywhere Outside* (Triple X 1991), *Rope-A-Dope* (Homestead 1995).

Apples

This four-piece band from Edinburgh, Scotland, were accused of attempting to cash in on the 'indie dance movement' when they stuttered into life in the early 90s. Their act was built around lyricist and vocalist Callum McNair, with a soundscape built on a pop rock beat punctuated by a multitude of samples (similar to EMF, and Jesus Jones). The similarity to the aforementioned saw the critics overlook their competent but uninspired music. Signed to Epic Records, their debut album included the single, 'Stay People Child', but their career was short-lived. Ex-Win member Ian Stoddart would go on to join Captain Shifty.

Album: *Here Is Tomorrow* (Epic 1991).

AR Kane

This act proved popular in the independent UK charts of the late 80s, and with critics who saw in them a brave, unconventional approach to music. The group comprised Alex Ayuli and Rudi Tambala from the east end of London, who have consistently shunned the press which so venerates them. Despite this, Ayuli claims to be the advertising copywriter who dreamt up the idea of using This Mortal Coil's 'Song To The Siren' as the soundtrack to the Thompson travel group's Freestyle Holiday advertisement. The band's first recording was 'When You're Sad' on One Little Indian Records, followed by the impressive *Lolita* EP for 4AD Records, sympathetically produced by Robin Guthrie of the Cocteau Twins. Later they collaborated with Colourbox for the M.A.R.R.S. one-off single, 'Pump Up The Volume', which topped the UK charts. *69* became the first long player for Rough Trade Records in 1988, making it a hat trick of prestigious independent labels who have employed their services. More importantly, it and the subsequent *i* brought about a huge breakthrough, a new pop animal forged from material components including Miles Davis, the Cocteau Twins and Robert Wyatt. Veering between riff onslaughts and open, quasi-ambient spaces, both albums offered an aural experience totally unique at that time. A hiatus prefaced *Americana*, which compiled tracks from their first two albums along with new material. It was released on David Byrne's Luka Bop label. After a five year gap the duo re-emerged in 1995 with *New Clear Child*, which was again radically different to all that had preceded it. This time there was little of the previous abrasiveness to temper the spaced out sequences, with the lyrics built on an unconvincing brand of new age mysticism. Despite this, it maintained AR Kane's proud tradition of sounding unequivocally different to anything else on offer.

Albums: *69* (Rough Trade 1988), *i* (Rough Trade 1989), *Americana* (Luka Bop 1992), *New Clear Child* (3rd Stone 1994).

Armoury Show

Formed in 1984 by Richard Jobson (b. 6 October 1960, Dunfermline, Fife, Scotland; vocals/guitar) and Russell Webb (bass/vocals), longstanding members of the Skids. The group was initially completed by John McGeoch (b. 28 May 1955, Greenock, Strathclyde, Scotland; guitar), formerly of Magazine and Siouxsie And The Banshees, and John Doyle (drums). Although the quartet enjoyed two minor hit singles with 'Castles In Spain' (1984) and 'We Can Be Brave Again' (1985), the two latter musicians proved incompatible and left following the completion of the group's sole album. *Waiting For The Floods* was an uncomfortable mix of different styles, but a 1987 single, 'New York City', which featured Jobson, Webb and sundry session musicians, showed a greater sense of purpose. Although redolent of early Simple Minds, the release suggested a newfound confidence, but the group broke up in the wake of Jobson's burgeoning modelling and media-based career.

Album: *Waiting For The Floods* (1985).

Artery

Latter-day interest in Artery tends to stem from the presence of Simon Hinkler (later to join the Mission). However, the Sheffield band's sound was an interesting blend of post-punk and funk, and worthy of attention in its own right. Hinkler was accompanied by Mark Gouldthorpe (vocals/guitar), Michael Fidler (vocals/guitar), Neil Mackenzie (bass) and Gary Wilson (drums), the team first appearing on 'Mother Moon' via the Limited Edition label in 1979. A move to Aardvark Records spawned two singles, 'Unbalanced' (with a free live EP) and 'Afterwards', before Artery signed to Red Flame Records. August 1982's 'The Clown' hinted at the promise found on their debut mini-album, *Oceans* and a further single, 'The Slide'. It was then over a year before Artery offered their rendition of 'Alabama Song' (a co-release with Virgin Records), and they left Red Flame soon after, signing to Golden Dawn Records. After 'Big Machine' in May 1984 and 'Diamonds In The Mine Field' in October, the band issued their first full-length album, *Terminal - The Second Coming*, but there was little response. Only a live album followed in 1986. However, some three years later, 'Afterwards' was issued as a cassette on the Pleasantly Surprised label.

Albums: *Oceans* (Red Flame 1982, mini-album), *Terminal - The Second Coming* (Golden Dawn 1985), *Live In Amsterdam* (Golden Dawn 1986).

Ash

Ash are a highly touted young band who began to make an impression in 1994, having arrived, as some commentators noted, 'Undertones-like', from Ulster, Northern Ireland at the age of 17. Rick McMurray (drums), Tim Wheeler (vocals/guitar) and Mark Hamilton (bass) were still studying for their A-Levels when their debut single, 'Jack Named The Planets', arrived in a 1,000-copy edition, soon awakening both the UK radio and press to their snappy, commercial

punk-pop. They also appealed to an American alternative climate where every A&R executive was searching for a new Green Day, and tantalizing offers followed to sign with either Warner-Reprise or Interscope. The band chose to fly to Los Angeles (missing several homework assignments in the process) and let their hosts squabble over them and indulge them beyond the expectations a young UK indie band has a right to. Following a seven song mini-album in late 1994, their topical fourth single, 'Kung Fu', featured a picture cover of Manchester United's football star Eric Cantona assaulting, kung fu-style, a fan of the opposing team, Crystal Palace. Released on Homegrown Records, it was recorded in Wales with Oasis producer Owen Morris. 'We wanted to write a really crap Ramones song and it was meant to be the b-side but it turned out too good.'
Album: *Home Grown* (Infectious 1994, mini-album).

Ash, Daniel
A founder member of Bauhaus, Tones On Tail, and Love And Rockets, Ash emerged in 1991 with his first solo album, *Coming Down*, on Beggars Banquet. It made number 109 in the US charts, on the back of Love And Rocket's US popularity. However, a single from it, 'This Love', though highly commercial, failed to chart.
Albums: *Coming Down* (1991), *Foolish Thing Desire* (1993).

Asphalt Ribbons
Nottingham, England, group whose promise was finally sustained in a spin-off band, Tindersticks. However, Asphalt Ribbons in their own right left more than band members Stuart Staples (vocals), Dave Boulter (keyboards) and Dickon Hinchcliffe (violin) behind for posterity. During their four year existence they also recorded three EPs, one for Lily records in 1988 and two (*The Orchid* in 1989 and *Good Love* in 1990) for the influential In Tape label. An album finally emerged in 1991 following In Tape's collapse, with sympathetic production by Jon Langford of the Mekons, but by this time the publicity originally generated had dissipated.
Album: *Old Horse And Other Songs* (ETT 1991).

Ass Ponys
This alternative rock band from Cincinnati, Ohio, USA, comprise Chuck Cleaver (vocals), John Erhardt (guitar), Randy Cheek (bass) and Dave Morrison (drums), the latter replacing original percussionist Dan Kleingers. Music obsessives to a man, the band formed in October 1989 and were soon compared to bands such as Hot Tuna, Pavement and the Minutemen. Cleaver and Kleingers had previously played together in the Lunchbuddies and Gomez, while Cheek enjoyed some small-time success with the Libertines. Erhardt had not played in rock bands before, previously working as part of a bluegrass collective. The group's independent debut for Okra Records in June 1990 was scuppered, however, when distribution agency Rough Trade Records of New York collapsed. At this stage the band's songs were still shambolic and erratic, although the germ of their talent was evident. The band returned to Ultrasuede Studios to begin recording material for a second album in October 1990. The working period lasted through winter 1990 and the summer of 1991 during which Kleingers was replaced by

Morrison. He was in place for four of *Grim*'s 16 tracks. *Grim* was a more subdued effort, but once again spoiled by industry machinations. Like previous albums produced by John Curley (the Afghan Whigs' bass player and proprietor of Ultrasuede Studios), *Electric Rock Music* synthesized the strengths of the biting emotional edge of the earlier material. Lyrics explored both large emotional targets and the seemingly insignificant. Despite the transition to a major label, the recording budget was a mere $2,500, and the lyrics had hardly brightened - Cleaver remained obsessed with the hopeless and the doomed, wallowing in the outsider's point of view.
Albums: *Mr. Superlove* (Okra 1990), *Grim* (Normal (Germany) 1992, Safehouse (USA) 1993), *Electric Rock Music* (A&M 1994).

Associates
Vocalist Billy MacKenzie (b. 27 March 1957, Dundee, Scotland) and Alan Rankine had performed in a variety of local groups before finally forming the Associates in 1979. After a minor label recording of David Bowie's 'Boys Keep Swinging', they were signed to Fiction Records where they released the critically acclaimed *The Affectionate Punch*. After a spell on the Beggars Banquet Records subsidiary, Situation 2, they formed their own Associates label, distributed by Sire/WEA. The extra push provided a Top 10 chart breakthrough courtesy of 'Party Fears Two', which boasted an engaging and distinctive keyboard arrangement. Two further Top 30 hits followed with 'Club Country' and '18 Carat Love Affair'/'Love Hangover'. Meanwhile MacKenzie became involved in other projects, most notably a cameo appearance on B.E.F.'s extravagant *Songs Of Quality And Distinction*. It was not until 1984 that the Associates reconvened and this was followed by several very low chart entries and a relatively poor selling album, *Perhaps*. Not surprisingly, Rankine and MacKenzie reverted to solo work, leaving the Associates as something of an occasional group. It was not until 1990 that the group returned with a new album, *Wild And Lonely*, which was stylistically similar to their earlier work.
Albums: *The Affectionate Punch* (Fiction 1980), *Sulk* (Sire 1982), *Perhaps* (Associates/WEA 1985), *Wild And Lonely* (Circa/Charisma 1990). Compilation: *Fourth Drawer Down* (Situation 2 1981).

Astley, Virginia
Astley was a former member of the Ravishing Beauties along with Nicola Holland and Kate St. John. As classically trained musicians they attempted, with some degree of success, to cross over into the pop field, working with amongst others, Echo And The Bunnymen and the Teardrop Explodes. Astley broke away to pursue a solo career in 1982. Her first single, 'Love's A Lonely Place To Be' was a melancholy paeon to the feeling of isolation when a love affair breaks down and the song's choral, almost boy soprano feel, gave it an ephemeral quality. It reached number 7 in the UK Independent chart and fitted in well with the then-current fashion for 'quiet pop'. Her debut album in 1983 confirmed her love of all things English and pastoral. Largely an instrumental album, this dreamy atmospheric piece

incorporated the sounds of the countryside on a summer's day. Complete with authentic bird songs and farm sounds, it gave the feel of a modern day piece by Delius. It took three years for her second album to be released and the Ryuichi Sakamoto produced *Hope In Darkened Heart* concentrated on Astley's preoccupation with the loss of childhood's innocence and adulthood's uncertainty. This accomplished musician remains for the time being, on the periphery of the music scene and can occasionally be found guesting for other artists.

Albums: *From Gardens Where We Feel Secure* (1983), *Hope In Darkened Heart* (1986).

Attila The Stockbroker

After graduating from the University of Kent with a degree in French, this performance poet (b. John Baine, 21 October 1957, England) really was a stockbroker, or on the way to becoming one, before he set out on the live music circuit. Accompanied on occasion by his own mandolin backing, he regaled his audience with good-humoured invective on the state of the world. Viewed as one of the new 'Ranting Poets', a term he disliked, his influences were poets Roger McCoughlan and Brian Patton, alongside Monty Python and the energy of punk. After playing in forgotten punk bands English Disease and Brighton Riot Squad, he joined Brussels based new wave band, Contingent. His usual early environment, indeed, was supporting punk bands. He played frequently enough to earn himself a session for BBC disc jockey John Peel, which in turn led to a deal with Cherry Red Records and his debut, *Ranting At The Nation*, was a highly colourful selection of verse and spoken word highlighting the absurdity of British life. Nightmare visions of Soviets running the social security system and his affection for obscure European soccer clubs were among the targets: 'So go to your Job Centre - I'll bet you'll see, Albanian students get handouts for free, and drug-crazed punk rockers cavort and caress, in the interview booths of the D.H.S.S.'. Critics were not convinced, however, one citing the contents as 'an inarticulate mish-mash of bad humour and popular cliches'. The *Cocktails* E.P., from October 1982, boasted some of his finest pieces to date, from the serious ('Contributory Negligence') to the absurd ('The Night I Slept With Seething Wells'). 1984's *Sawdust And Empire* saw a greater emphasis on music. Increasingly Attila was seeing himself as a folk artist, and in between releases was becoming a near permanent fixture at various festivals, working alongside John Otway and TV Smith (ex-Adverts). He has also managed The Tender Trap. He was involved in the staging of *Cheryl The Rock Opera*, alongside Otway and Blyth Power, for whom he occasionally plucks a fiddle, and has contributed to the pages of the *Guardian* with his essays on social change in eastern Europe while on tour in the region.

Albums: *Ranting At The Nation* (Cherry Red 1983), *Sawdust And Empire* (Cherry Red 1984), *Libyan Students From Hell* (Cherry Red 1987), *Scornflakes* (Probe 1988), *Live At The Rivioli* (Musidisc 1990), *Donkey's Years* (Musidisc 1991).

Attractions

Formed in May 1977 to back Elvis Costello, the Attractions provided sympathetic support to the singer's contrasting, and often demanding, compositions. Steve Nieve (b. Steven Nason; keyboards), Bruce Thomas (b. Stockton-on-Tees, Cleveland, England; bass) and Pete Thomas (b. 9 August 1954, Sheffield, Yorkshire, England; drums) were already experienced musicians - Bruce Thomas with the Sutherland Brothers and Quiver, Pete Thomas with Chilli Willi And The Red Hot Peppers and John Stewart - while Nieve's dexterity on keyboards added colour to many of the unit's exemplary releases. In 1980 the Attractions completed a low-key album, *Mad About The Wrong Boy*, but their position as Costello's natural backing group became increasingly unsure as their leader embarked on a plethora of guises. Nieve recorded a solo collection, *Playboy* (1987) and later led the houseband, along with Pete Thomas as Steve Nieve And The Playboys, on television's *Jonathan Ross Show*, while Bruce Thomas began a literary career with *The Big Wheel* (1990), an impressionistic autobiography.

Album: *Mad About The Wrong Boy* (1980).

Au Pairs

Arguably the Midlands' key contribution to the early 80s post-punk scene, Birmingham band the Au Pairs consisted of Lesley Woods (lead vocals/guitar) Paul Foad (lead guitar), Jane Munro (bass) and Pete Hammond (drums). The began their career in 1980 with the *You* EP on their own Human label, which also housed their long playing debut. Critically acclaimed for their social insight and thoughtful, agit-prop music, they continued with singles like 'It's Obvious' and 'Inconvenience', which brought them closest to a hit. Covering a variety of subjects from the controversial ('Armagh') to the frankly personal ('Sex Without Stress'), they signed to Kamera Records and released a live album on a.k.a. Records in 1983 before vanishing when Woods failed to show for a concert in Belgium. The latter artefact, recorded at the Berlin Women's Festival, is probably the best introduction to the band - missing as it does some of the duff tracks which marred their previous studio efforts. Woods later blamed the split on 'lack of money, nervous breakdowns and drugs...the usual rock 'n' roll story'. She settled in Europe for a few years before returning to London to undertake a law degree and form all-female band the Darlings. Foad formed End Of Chat with Hammond and trumpeter Graham Hamilton (who deputised for Woods on that aborted Belgium date). Munro, who left six months prior to the band's eventual dissolution, spent the early 90s training as an aromatherapist.

Albums: *Playing With A Different Sex* (Human 1981), *Sense And Sensuality* (Kamera 1982), *Live In Berlin* (a.k.a. 1983).

Ausgang

Formed in Birmingham, England, in 1983 from the ashes of Kabuki, some of Ausgang's members had previously been in the Solicitors. The main thread between all three bands was the drummer, Max. Having been ejected from art college in 1981, Max had DJ'd at various Birmingham clubs, before taking Jowan (vocals) from the Solicitors with him to form a new band. Bassist, Cub, was recruited for Kabuki when Max booked a band called Across The Room for one of his club nights at Snoopys. (Cub was so named because of his fondness for tigers.) Max and Jowan then recruited guitarist

Matthew at a youth club audition (Matthew previously played with the Detectives - fronted by subsequently famous house DJ, Dave Haslam) and Wilz joined on keyboards. The six piece line-up was completed by drummer Trynitron for their only release - a 1,000-copy pressing 7-inch single, 'I Am A Horse', for Kabaret Noir Records in 1982. However, Trynitron soon disappeared, and the remaining members of the band jettisoned Jowan, who departed for Spain, and Wilz, who joined Pavlov's Dogs (not to be confused with the 70s USA rock group, Pavlov's Dog). Max (drums), Cub (bass), Ibo (vocals) and Matthew (guitar) thus became Ausgang, following a suggestion from Ibo's German speaking girlfriend (Ausgang translating as 'way out'). The band made their live debut on 28 September 1983 at the Powerhouse in Birmingham. 'We were rocky, threatening and difficult. We played around a lot with time changes in our music, which meant it was never easy to dance to,' said Ibo. A tour support with the Wonder Stuff followed, before they met their manager John-Bill Lizard, while playing with Death Cult. After launching their own fanzine, *Stab The Sun*, they signed a recording contract with Criminal Damage Records. A 12-inch EP headed by 'Weight' was followed by a 7-inch single, 'Solid Glass Spine'/'Strip Me Down'. Both revealed a brittle, awkward dynamic, that combined some of the gothic movement's drama with a broader lyrical palette. By the advent of the group's final Criminal Damage release, the *Head On* EP, Cub had departed to concentrate on his love of motorcycles. Stu eventually replaced him on bass. The reshuffled line-up then signed to FM Revolver Records for whom their debut, *Manipulate*, followed in January 1986. These dense, fraught pop songs again set them apart from the 'new punk' and Bat Cave movements prevalent at the time. It was followed by the tense 'Hunt Ya Down' 12-inch single, before further label problems intervened. After touring with Gene Loves Jezebel the group set up the Shakedown label, and released the 'King Hell' 12-inch. They lengthened their name to Ausgang-A-Go-Go in 1987, releasing a mini-album that year (one side playing at 45 rpm, the other at other 33 rpm). However, with no support from record buyers the band dissolved. Matthew and Stu are now involved in video production.
Albums: *Manipulate* (FM Revolver 1986). As Ausgang-A-Go-Go: *Los Descamisados* (Shakedown 1987, mini-album).

Auteurs

Truculent UK indie stars the Auteurs are spearheaded by the imposing figure of Luke Haines (b. 7 October 1967, Walton-On-Thames, Surrey, England; vocals, guitar), alongside Glenn Collins (b. 7 February 1968, Cheltenham, Gloucestershire, England; drums) and Haines' girlfriend, Alice Readman (b. 1967, Harrow, Middlesex, England; bass). Both Haines and Readman had previously performed in 'shambling' band the Servants between 1987 and 1991, while Collins had worked with Dog Unit and Vort Pylon (they would be joined by cellist James Banbury in 1993). Together they took their new name from the film term (which initially appeared in the *Cahiers Du Cinema* journal and generally denotes director, or more literally author). Their debut public appearance came at the Euston Rails Club in London in April 1992, and it was December of that

year before their first vinyl emerged ('Showgirl'). This instantly saw them transported to the head of the post-Smiths bedsit/student throne, with Haines' impressive use of language (instructed by film, music and theatre) the focal point. Irrespective of the fact that they were tempestuously dispensed with as support to The The in 1993, their live performances were erratic, and sometimes awful. At least their debut album (recorded on a budget of £10,000 as an unsigned band) saw Haines confirm their arrival with a strong body of songs. Although it failed to ignite commercially, the critical reception was lavish, and the band missed out on the 1993 Mercury Prize award by just one vote. *Now I'm A Cowboy* continued the pattern of press eulogy and public indecisiveness, on a set soaked with Haines' class obsessions ('The Upper Classes', etc.), though negotiations to enlist the services of Vanessa Paradis to duet on 'New French Girlfriend' broke down. The promotional touring arrangements for *New Wave* were also inconvenienced by Haines having to spend much of the end of 1994 recuperating from a fall in Spain which broke both his ankles. 1995 saw the band return to the studio for sessions for their third album.
Albums: *New Wave* (Hut 1993), *Now I'm A Cowboy* (Hut 1994).

Avant Gardeners

Headed by Russell Murch (vocals/guitar) with Martin Saunders (guitar), Nigel Rae (bass) and Mike Kelly (drums), the Avant Gardener released their debut EP in the summer of 1977 on Virgin Records. Their 60s influenced rock style was obviously affected by the climate of the time, with strong overtones of punk. Consequently the new year saw two tracks from the EP, 'Gotta Turn Back' and 'Strange Girl In Clothes', included on Virgin's new wave showcase, *Guillotine*. Whereas the album was a stepping stone with varying degrees of success for most of the other bands, the Avant Gardener were ignored in the UK, although minor interest was shown abroad. With the addition of an 's' to their name and a revised line-up of mainman Murch (vocals/guitar), Rob Hill (bass) and Mike Roberts (guitar), they released *Dig It* on Appaloosa Records in 1980. Three tracks from the EP were included, as well as a cover version of Roky Erikson's 'Two Headed Dog'. This was a good indication of the band's future direction away from their punk debut and throughout the early 80s they continued to play live, releasing a single, 'Deadwood Stage', in 1983, and the quasi psychedelic *The Church Of The Inner Cosmos* in 1984.
Albums: *Dig It* (Appalosa 1980), *The Church Of The Inner Cosmos* (Appalosa 1984).

Avengers

Formed in San Francisco, USA, in 1977, the Avengers joined the Dils and Crime as one of the city's prime punk/hardcore attractions. The original line-up featured Penelope Houston (vocals), Greg Westermark (guitar), Johnathan Postal (bass) and Danny Furious (drums), but only Houston and Furious survived the unit's interminable changes. The group's debut release, 'Car Crash'/'We Are The One'/'I Believe In Me' (1977), captured their powerful sound, but a subsequent EP,

Aztec Cameras

The American In Me (aka *White Nigger*) (1979), produced by former Sex Pistols' guitarist Steve Jones, was also of merit. Both sets formed the basis of the Avengers' sole, and posthumous, album. Houston would go on to a solo career, perversely in the singer/songwriter tradition.
Album: *The Avengers 1977-1979* (CD Presents 1983).

B

Aztec Camera

This acclaimed UK pop outfit was formed in 1980 by Roddy Frame (b. 29 January 1964, East Kilbride, Scotland), as a vehicle for his songwriting talent. The other members, Campbell Owens (bass), and Dave Mulholland (drums), soon passed through, and a regular turnover in band members ensued while Frame put together the songs that made up the exceptionally strong debut *High Land, Hard Rain*. Their three hits in the UK independent charts on the influential Postcard label had already made the band a critics' favourite, but this sparkling album of light acoustic songs with a mature influence of jazz and Latin rhythms was a memorable work. 'Oblivious' reached number 18 in the UK singles chart, while excellent songs like the uplifting 'Walk Out To Winter' and the expertly crafted 'We Could Send Letters' indicated a major talent in the ascendant. The Mark Knopfler-produced *Knife* broke no new ground, but now signed to the massive WEA Records, the band was pushed into a world tour to promote the album. Frame was happier writing songs on his acoustic guitar back home in Scotland and retreated there following the tour, until *Love* in 1987. This introverted yet over-produced album showed Frame's continuing development with Elvis Costello-influenced song structures. The comparative failure of this collection was rectified the following year with two further hit singles 'How Men Are' and the catchy 'Somewhere In My Heart'. This stimulated interest in *Love* and the album became a substantial success. After a further fallow period, allowing Frame to create more gems, the band returned in 1990 with the highly acclaimed *Stray*, leaving no doubt that their brand of intelligent, gentle pop has a considerable following. In the summer of 1993 Roddy Frame finally delivered the album that fans and critics had waited for. *Dreamland* was an excellent collection of emotionally direct, honest songs that rivalled Aztec Camera's sparkling debut a decade earlier.
Albums: *High Land, Hard Rain* (1983), *Knife* (1984), *Aztec Camera* (1985, 10-inch album), *Love* (1987), *Stray* (1990), *Dreamland* (1993).
Videos: *Aztec Camera* (1989)

B-52's

The quirky appearance, stage antics and lyrical content of the B-52's belie a formidable musical ability, as the band's rhythmically perfect pop songs show many influences, including 50s' rock 'n' roll, punk and commercial dance music. However, it was the late 70s' new-wave music fans that took them to their hearts. The group were formed in Athens, Georgia, USA, in 1976, and took their name from the bouffant hairstyle worn by Kate Pierson (b. 27 April 1948, Weehawken, New Jersey, USA; organ/vocals) and Cindy Wilson (b. 28 February 1957, Athens, Georgia, USA; guitar/vocals). The line-up was completed by Cindy's brother Ricky (b. 19 March 1953, Athens, Georgia, USA, d. 12 October 1986; guitar), Fred Schneider (b. 1 July 1951, Newark, Georgia, USA; keyboards/vocals) and Keith Strickland (b. 26 October 1953, Athens, Georgia, USA; drums). The lyrically bizarre but musically thunderous 'Rock Lobster' was originally a private pressing of 2,000 copies and came to the notice of the perceptive Chris Blackwell, who signed them to Island Records in the UK. Their debut, *B-52's*, became a strong seller and established the band as a highly regarded unit with a particularly strong following on the American campus circuit during the early 80s. Their anthem, 'Rock Lobster', became a belated US hit in 1980 and they received John Lennon's seal of approval that year as his favourite band. Subsequent albums continued to defy categorization, their love of melodrama and pop culture running side by side with outright experimentalism (witness 50s sci-fi parody 'Planet Claire'). Ricky Wilson died of AIDS in 1985 (although it was initially claimed that cancer was the cause, to save his family from intrusion). Nevertheless the band reached a commercial peak in 1989, winning a new generation of fans with the powerful hit single, 'Love Shack', and its enticing accompanying video. *Cosmic Thing* showed that the band had not lost their touch and blended several musical styles with aplomb. In 1992 the group parted company with Cindy Wilson and recorded *Good Stuff* under the eyes of previous producer Don Was (Was (Not Was)) and Nile Rodgers (Chic). During a Democratic party fund-raising concert in April of that year, actress Kim Basinger stood in for Wilson, as did Julie Cruise the following year. 1994 brought huge commercial success with the theme song to *The Flintstones*, yet despite the 'cheese' factor, it remained hard not to warm to the full-blooded performances from Schneider and Pierson.
Albums: *B-52's* (Warners 1979), *Wild Planet* (Warners 1980), *Party Mix!* (Warners 1981 - remix of the first two albums), *Mesopotamia* (Warners 1982, mini-album), *Whammy!* (Warners 1983), *Bouncing Off The Satellites* (Warners 1986), *Cosmic Thing* (Reprise 1989), *Good Stuff* (Warners 1992). Compilations: *Best Of The B-52's: Dance This Mess Around* (Island 1990), *Party Mix-Mesopotamia* (Warners 1991).

B-Movie

This post-punk keyboard and guitar combo originated from Mansfield, England. They were often falsely linked with the early 80s fad of New Romanticism. Graham Boffey (drums) and Paul Statham (guitar) were one-time members of punk band the Aborted, formed, like so many others, in the wake of the first Clash album. The duo invited Steve Hovington (vocals/bass) along to rehearsals, changing their name to Studio 10 before settling on B-Movie. Studio manager Andy Dransfield sent a demo tape of the band to Lincoln-based independent record label Dead Good. The result was two tracks on the compilation *East*. Soon after Rick Holliday joined as keyboard player. Their *Take Three* EP, was warmly received by critics, ensuring several local radio sessions and a six-track 12-inch single, headed by 'Nowhere Girl'. Eccentric entrepreneur Stevo noticed the band and became their manager. Moving to Deram Records, 'Remembrance Day' became the second single to attract strong support in the press. Unfortunately Stevo's connection saw the band categorized as part of the New Romantic movement, a perception which would act as a major constraint in their future. After 'Marilyn Dreams' only scraped the charts the band set out on a major European tour, during which they acquired the services of Luciano Codemo on bass, relieving Hovington to concentrate on his vocals. In turn he was replaced by Mike Pedham (ex-Everest The Hard Way, now the Chimes), and soon Boffey too departed, joining Soft As Ghosts. Martin Smedley and Andy Johnson were the new recruits, but they arrived just in time to see the departure of a frustrated Holliday. He joined Six Sed Red then MCX while the reduced B-Movie line-up signed with Sire. A highly commercial but disappointing single, 'A Letter From Afar', was remixed by Jellybean Benitez. An album eventually followed, but by this time the band had effectively fallen apart (Al Cash and Martin Winter were among the latter-day cast). Statham would go on to work with Pete Murphy and Then Jerico, Hovington formed One before returning to work with Holliday, and Boffey is currently a member of Slaughterhouse 5.
Albums: *Forever Running* (1985), *The Dead Good Tapes* (1988), *Remembrance Days* (1991), *Radio Days* (1991).

B.A.L.L.

Formed in New York, USA in 1987, B.A.L.L. comprised of Mark Kramer (bass/vocals/production) and David Licht (drums) - both formerly of Shockabilly - and two ex-members of the Velvet Monkeys: Don Fleming (guitar/vocals) and Jay Speigel (drums). The quartet's debut, *Period (Another American Lie)*, established their sound wherein grunge-styled pop songs were driven by loud, distorted guitar work and the two drummers solid, uncompromising beat. Humour was an equally integral part of the group's raison d'etre, a facet which came to fruition on *Bird*. Its sleeve parodied the infamous Beatles 'butcher cover' and the second side was devoted to a pastiche of the *Concert For Bangla Desh*. Several sacred cows of rock were mercilessly savaged in a suite which married Ringo Starr's 'It Don't Come Easy', George Harrison's 'Wah Wah' and Marc Bolan's 'Buick Mackane'. However the concept was arguably stronger than the aural results and the group's own material lacked sparkle. Billed on the reverse as 'the disappointing third album', *Trouble Doll* was indeed inferior, comprising of one studio side and another recorded live at CBGB's, some of which was reprised from *Bird*. *Four (Hardball)* captures the quartet at their best, despite the fact they fell apart during its recording. The first side is devoted to powerful pop songs, its counterpart comprises of ravaged instrumentals. Fleming left the group before completing vocals. The friction was latterly resolved - a similarly-charged album, *Special Kiss* appeared in 1991 under a new name, Gumball - but the four achieved a greater profile elsewhere. Speigal and Fleming reformed the Velvet Monkeys; the latter became a producer of note (Teenage Fanclub, Free Kitten) while Kramer continued to administer his Shimmy Disc label, which issued B.A.L.L.'s albums, and record with Bongwater and as a solo artist.
Albums: *Period (Another American Lie)* (Shimmy Disc 1987), *Bird* (Shimmy Disc 1988), *Trouble Doll* (Shimmy Disc 1989), *Four...Hardball* (Shimmy Disc 1990).

Babes In Toyland

This hardcore rock trio spearheaded a new wave of US female bands at the turn of the 90s. Their origins can be traced back to 1987, when Kat Bjelland (b. Woodburn, Oregon, USA - adopted, though she did not know it until she was much older; vocals/guitar) moved to Minneapolis. Previously she had played in a band, Sugar Baby Doll, with Courtney Love (Hole) and Jennifer Finch (L7) in San Francisco. The trio was completed by Michelle Leon (bass) and Lori Barbero (drums/vocals). They first came to prominence at the legendary singles club at Sub Pop Records, then made a deep impression on a European support tour with Sonic Youth. A debut album, prooduced by Jack Endino, was recorded live with the vocals overdubbed. Soon after, WEA A&R representative Tim Carr saw the band live in Minneapolis and was impressed. After signing to the label, they recorded the 1992 mini-album, *To Mother*. Bjelland, meanwhile, was busy defending the band from the suspicious minds of a media that wanted to llump the band together with other all-girl bands to create a movement. 'Men and women play their instruments to a completely different beat. Women are a lot more rhythmic - naturally - than men. It doesn't even have anything to do with music, it all has to do with timing.' In 1992 Leon left the group and was replaced by Maureen Herman (b. Chicago, Illinois, USA). *Fontanelle* received excellent reviews throughout the rock and indie press, and a support tour with Faith No More brought them further plaudits, as they signed with their first manager, Debbie Gordon. However, when the group took a break in 1993, press speculation suggested their imminent demise. Lori Barbero formed her own label, Spanish Fly, home of Milk, while Kat worked with her husband Stuart Grey, singer with Australian noise outfit Lubricated Goat, on two projects, Crunt and KatSu. Babes In Toyland reconvened in time for the the Lollapalooza tour and in 1995 *Nemesisters* was a powerful return to form, with memorable cover versions of Sister Sledge's 'We Are Family' and Eric Carmen's 'All By Myself' sitting well alongside strong original compositions such as 'Memory' and 'Scherezadian 22'.

Back To The Planet

Albums: *Spanking Machine* (Twin Tone 1990), *To Mother* (Reprise/WEA 1991, mini-album), *Fontanelle* (Reprise/WEA 1992), *Painkillers* (Reprise/WEA 1994), *Nemesisters* (Reprise/WEA 1995).

Back To The Planet

This dance collective mix rave, ska and punk traditions. Based in Camberwell, London, the band consists of Fil 'the Girl' Walters (b. 31 January 1970, Dartford, Kent, England; vocals), Carl Hendrickse (b. 28 January 1970, London, England; bass), Fraggle (b. David Fletcher, 5 August 1968, Kent, England; guitar), Henry Nicholas Cullen (b. 10 October 1969, Lewisham, London, England; drums) and Guy McAffer (b. 27 May 1969; keyboards). Together they create an enchanting cocktail of simple but effective good time music whose lyrics are often overtly political. Their recordings have so far chiefly been available only on cassette, notably the album length *Warning The Public* which sold 3,000 copies at gigs alone. Their first vinyl release was the 12-inch 'The Revolution Of Thought', though 1993 singles 'Teenage Turtles' (a *New Musical Express* Single Of The Week) and 'Please Don't Fight' looked likeliest to see them accepted by a hesistant media. Signed to London Records subsidiary Parallel, after a minor bidding war amongst the majors, they began the new year headlining the *New Musical Express*'s 'On Into 93' showcase gig and gracing the cover of that magazine. However, the liaison with a major record label did not work out, and after just a year the band were again recording independently. Predictably, by the arrival of *Messages After The Bleep*, the mainstream music media had moved on.
Album: *Mind And Soul Collaborations* (Parallel 1993), *Messages After The Bleep* (Arthur Mix 1995)

Bad Brains

This black USA hardcore punk and dub reggae outfit originated in 1978. The band were all playing together earlier in a fusion outfit 'doing Chick Corea and Stanley Clarke type stuff'. They moved from Washington, D.C. to New York where they established a reputation as prime exponents, alongside the Dead Kennedys and Black Flag, of the new 'hardcore' hybrid of punk, based on a barely credible speed of musicianship. The line-up consisted of H.R. (b. Paul Hudson; vocals) and brother Earl Hudson (drums), Dr. Know (guitar) and Darryl Jennifer (bass). They would break up their sets with dub and reggae outings and attracted a mixed audience, which was certainly one of their objectives: 'We're a gospel group, preaching the word of unity.' It is frustrating that so little studio material remains to document this early period, though the singles 'Pay To Cum' and 'Big Takeover' are regarded as punk classics. They were due to support the Damned in the UK in October 1979, having sold most of their equipment to buy aeroplane tickets. On arrival, however, they were denied work permits. They continued through the 80s, although H.R. went on to a solo career. In May 1988 he was temporarily replaced by ex-Faith No More vocalist Chuck Moseley, while Mackie (ex-Cro-Mags) took over on drums. The move, which allowed the remaining founding members to gig, was singularly unsuccessful. Famed for their exhilarating live shows,

especially H.R.'s athletics, noted US rock critic Jack Rabid rated them, on form, the best he had ever seen. More recently bands like Living Colour have sung their praises as one of the forerunners of articulate black rock music, while in 1994 even Madonna took notice, offering them a place on her Maverick label, with H.R. returning to the fold. *God Of Love*, produced by Ric Ocasek, concentrated more on dub and rasta messages than hardcore, but proved again there was still fire in the belly of this group.
Albums: *Bad Brains* (ROIR 1982, cassette only), *Rock For Light* (PVC 1983), *I Against I* (SST 1986), *Live* (SST 1988), *Attitude: The ROIR Session* (ROIR-Important 1989), *Quickness* (Caroline 1989), *The Youth Are Getting Restless* (Caroline 1990), *Rise* (1993), *God Of Love* (Maverick 1995).

Bad Religion

This USA hardcore band were formed in 1980 in the suburbs of north Los Angeles, California. Their first incarnation comprised Greg Graffin (vocals), Brett Gurewitz (guitar), Jay Lishrout (drums) and Jay Bentley (bass), with the name originating from their mutual distaste for organized religion. Their debut release was the poorly produced EP, *Bad Religion*, on Epitaph records, formed by founder member Gurewitz. Following several appearances on local compilation albums, Pete Finestone took over as drummer in 1982. The milestone *How Could Hell Be Any Worse* was recorded in Hollywood, creating a fair degree of local and national interest. By the following year Paul Dedona and Davy Goldman had joined as the new bass guitarist and drummer respectively. The subsequent *Into The Unknown* proved a minor disaster, disillusioning hardcore fans with the emphasis shifted to slick keyboard textures, though the record itself stands up well. 1984 saw further internal strife as Graffin became the only surviving member from the previous year, with Greg Hetson and Tim Gallegos taking over guitar and bass, and Pete Finestone returning on drums, while Gurewitz took time out to conquer his drink and drug problems. A comeback EP, *Back To The Known*, revealed a much more purposeful outfit. A long period of inactivity was ended in 1987 when Gurewitz rejoined for a show which Hetson (working with former band Circle Jerks once more) could not attend. New material was written, and *Suffer* was released in 1988 to wide critical acclaim. The band's albums since then have featured intelligent lyrics set against their compelling punk sound. Despite this, Gurevitz retired in 1994 to spend more time looking after the Epitaph label, which was enjoying success with Offspring and others.
Albums: *How Could Hell Be Any Worse?* (Epitaph 1982), *Into The Unknown* (Epitaph 1983), *Suffer* (Epitaph 1988) *No Control* (Epitaph 1989), *Against The Grain* (Epitaph 1990), *Recipe For Hate* (Epitaph 1993).

Bad Seeds

(see Cave, Nick, And The Bad Seeds)

Badowski, Henry

After serving his apprenticeship in UK bands Norman And The Baskervilles, Lick It Dry and the New Rockets, Badowski joined punk band Chelsea on bass, but in early 1978, after only a few months, he left to enlist as drummer

for Stiff Records artist Wreckless Eric. During the summer of that year, he sang and played keyboards with the short-lived King, a punk/psychedelic group that included Dave Berk (drums; also Johnny Moped), Kim Bradshaw (bass) and ex-Damned, Captain Sensible (guitar). Consequently when King folded, Badowski took-up the bass with the re-formed the Damned off-shoot, the Doomed. With the new year came the new position of drummer with the Good Missionaries, an experimental band created by Mark Perry from Alternative TV. This association led to the start of his solo career in the summer of 1979, with the release of 'Making Love With My Wife' on Perry's Deptford Fun City label. Recorded at Pathway Studios, the track was performed completely by Badowski and displayed a strong 60s influence, with echoes of Syd Barrett and Kevin Ayers. The b-side, 'Baby Sign Here With Me', was originally part of the King live set and utilized the talents of James Stevenson (bass/guitar) from Chelsea, and Alex Kolkowski (violin) and Dave Berk (drums), both from the Johnny Moped Band. The single drew favourable reviews and within a month he had signed a contract with A&M Records, releasing a further two singles 'My Face' and 'Henry's In Love', closely followed by the album, *Life Is A Grand*, a classic slice of psychedelia that was to signal the end of Badowski's solo career.
Album: *Life Is A Grand* (A&M 1981).

Balaam And The Angel

This UK rock band included both post-punk gothic and 60s elements in their output. They were originally made up of the three Morris brothers, Jim (b. 25 November 1960, Motherwell, Scotland; guitar; occasional recorder/keyboards), Mark (b. 15 January 1963, Motherwell, Scotland; lead vocals/bass) and Des (b. 27 June 1964, Motherwell, Scotland; drums). They began their career playing working mens clubs as a children's cabaret act in their native Motherwell, encouraged by their father who had insisted they all watch television's *Top Of The Pops* as children. They eventually moved down to Cannock in Staffordshire, where they are still based. An early gig at the ICA in London in 1985, saw a completely different approach to that with which Balaam would later become identified. Playing in bare feet and pyjamas, they played numerous covers of 60s love paeans, and also a recorder solo. Somewhat falsely categorized as a gothic group after supporting the Cult on three successive tours, they were, in fact, self-consciously colourful in both appearance and approach. Early in their career they founded Chapter 22 Records, along with manager Craig Jennings. Their debut on the label came when 'World Of Light' appeared in 1984, although 'Day And Night' was their most impressive release from this period. Their debut set, *The Greatest Story Ever Told*, was named after the headline under which their first interview in *Melody Maker* appeared, and saw them rehoused on Virgin Records. Apparently intended to be reminiscent of the Doors, while there were stylistic similarities, it fell some way short of the visionary qualities associated with the west coast phenomenon. In September 1988 the band's second album was released after they had returned from support slots with Kiss and Iggy Pop in the USA. A new guitarist, Ian McKean, entered because of the need for two guitar parts on

Live Free Or Die. They were dropped by Virgin however, and their first tour for over four years took place in 1990. Press speculation that Mark would join the Cult as replacement bass player for Jamie Stewart collapsed as Ian Astbury decided that he was too much of a 'front man'. In 1991, they truncated their name to Balaam, marking the switch with the release of a mini-album, *No More Innocence*. By the advent of *Prime Time* any residual press interest in their career had dried up completely.
Albums: *The Greatest Story Ever Told* (Virgin 1986), *Live Free Or Die* (Virgin 1988), *No More Innocence* (Intense 1991, mini-album), *Prime Time* (Bleeding Hearts 1993).

Bambi Slam

An ambitious UK rock dance outfit, the Bambi Slam were formed in the mid-80s around would-be eccentric Roy Feldon (b. Lancashire, England). After a fairly inconsequential upbringing in the rosy suburbs of Pickering, Toronto, Canada, the expatriate Feldon moved to California for a spell. Coming to Britain to seek fame and fortune, he recruited Nick Maynard (drums) and Linda Mellor (cello), through an advert in the Royal Academy. Under the name Bambi Slam they toured the country, sending demos to dozens of record companies. The music contained on these cassettes resembled a rockier Public Image Limited. Product Inc., a subsidiary of Mute Records, picked up on them and released three singles, 'Bamp Bamp' through to the stirring 'Happy Birthday'. A tour supporting the Cult and a debut album were well under way and things were seemingly going to plan. However, Feldon suddenly underwent a period of artistic introspection resulting in the band going way over budget. This led to a split with Product Inc. and an unfinished album on which they owed a considerable amount of money. However, Rough Trade supremo Geoff Travis thought they had promise and signed them to Blanco Y Negro. There they released a flawed debut, after which Feldon jettisoned the rest of the band.
Album: *The Bambi Slam* (Blanco Y Negro 1987).

Band Of Susans

The membership of this articulate US guitar-based assembly was fluid but evolved around the songwriting partnership of Robert Poss (b. 20 November 1956, Buffalo, New York, USA; guitar/vocals) and Susan Stenger (b. 11 May 1955, Buffalo, New York, USA; bass/guitar/vocals). Poss had once been offered the guitarist's role in PiL when Keith Levene left. Both he and Stenger formerly worked with guitar composers Rhys Chatham, and eventually formed their own group. Their title was lifted from the fact that the original line-up contained three Susans. Other members of the group have included Ron Spitzer (drums, replaced by Joey Kaye), Page Hamilton (guitar/vocals, who later formed Helmet in 1992) and Anne Husick, who took over from Karen Haglof as third guitarist. Bruce Gilbert from Wire also temporarily filled in for Haglof because of her aversion to touring. However, personnel changes have had little effect on the internal dynamics of the band because when they audition new people 'we're not looking for an influx of new ideas, we like the way the band is . . . ' Two independent albums won them supporters on both sides of the Atlantic, after which they moved to Restless Records for 1991's *The Word And The Flesh*. The massed barrage of guitars on-stage remains a unique visual and aural experience which the *New Musical Express* described as 'nothing less than pure, demonic euphoria'. 1995's *Here Comes Success*, an ironic title given that the band was apparently on the verge of dissolution, opened with the charming 'Elizabeth Stride (1843-1888)', the tale of a Jack The Ripper victim who had lived on the same street as Stenger.

Albums: *Hope Against Hope* (Further/Blast First 1988), *Love Agenda* (Restless/Blast First 1989), *The Word And The Flesh* (Restless/Blast First 1991), *Veil* (Restless/Blast First 1993), *Here Comes Success* (Blast First 1995).

Bandit Queen

Based in Manchester, England, this three-piece emerged in the early 90s with a repertoire of singles such as 'Give It To The Dog' and 'Miss Dandys', which blended the pop sensibilities of early Blondie with the modern feminist swagger of the Breeders. Unsurprisingly, they won fans and influence quickly, resulting in the release of *Hormone Hotel* for Playtime Records in February 1995. However, the road to critical respect had not been an easy one for former music journalist and singer/guitarist Tracy Golding, who had spent several years in the widely-ignored indie pop outfit Swirl. Bandit Queen were formed with Janet Wolstenholme (bass) and David Galley (drums) to vent her anger at what she saw as indifference to home-grown UK talent. The name Bandit Queen was taken from the nickname for Phoolan Devi, an Indian woman of low caste who deserted her bullying husband only to be kidnapped and raped by bandits. She then became the bandit leader's lover, eventually rising to gang leader herself on his death. 'I was just inspired by her endurance,' stated Golding, who herself had not been without determination in her own career, starting Bandit Queen when she was in her 30s. The *Bandit Queen* film, controversially banned in parts of the subcontinent and released at the same time as the group's emergence, probably hindered and confused rather than aided their career.

Album: *Hormone Hotel* (Playtime 1995).

Bangles

Formerly known as the Colours, the Bangs and finally the Bangles, this all-female Los Angeles quartet mastered the art of melodic west coast guitar-based pop and like the Go-Go's immediately before them, led the way for all-female groups in the latter half of the 80s. The band was formed in 1981 and originally comprised Susanna Hoffs (b. 17 January 1962, Newport Beach, California, USA; guitar/vocals), Debbi Peterson (b. 22 August 1961, Los Angeles, California, USA; drums/vocals), Vicki Peterson (b. 11 January 1958, Los Angeles, California, USA; guitar/vocals) and Annette Zilinkas (bass/vocals). They emerged from the 'paisley underground' scene which spawned bands like Rain Parade and Dream Syndicate. The Bangles' first recordings were made on their own Downkiddie label and then for Miles Copeland's Faulty Products set-up which resulted in a flawed self-titled mini-album. On signing to the major CBS label in 1983, the line-up had undergone a crucial change. Zilinkas departed (later to join Blood On The Saddle) and was replaced by former Runaways member Michael Steele (b. 2 June 1954; bass/vocals). Their superb debut 'Hero Takes A Fall' failed to chart, as did their interpretation of Kimberley Rew's Soft Boys/Katrina And The Waves song 'Going Down To Liverpool'. The idea of four glamourous middle-class American girls singing about trotting down to a labour exchange in Liverpool with their UB40 cards, was both bizarre and quaint. The Bangles' energetic and harmonious style showed both a grasp and great affection for 60s' pop with their Beatles and Byrds-like sound. Again they failed to chart, although their sparkling debut *All Over The Place* scraped into the US chart. Following regular live work they built up a strong following, although it was not until the US/UK number 2 hit single 'Manic Monday', written by Prince and the huge success of *Different Light* that won them a wider audience. The media, meanwhile, were picking out Hoffs as the leader of the group. This sowed the seeds of dissatisfaction within the line-up that would later come to a head. Both album and single narrowly missed the top of both US and UK charts, and throughout 1986 the Bangles could do no wrong. Their interpretation of Jules Shear's 'If She Knew What She Wants' showed touches of mid-60s' Mamas And The Papas, while 'Walk Like An Egyptian' (composed by former Rachel Sweet svengali Liam Sternberg) was pure 80s quirkiness and gave the group a US number 1/UK number 3 hit. The unusual choice of a cover of the Simon And Garfunkel song 'Hazy Shade Of Winter', which was featured in the film *Less Than Zero*, gave them a US number 2 hit/UK number 11 hit in 1988. The third album, *Everything* continued to offer a collection of classy pop which generated the hit singles 'In Your Room' (US number 5, 1988) and the controversial 'Eternal Flame' in the spring of 1989, which gave the group a UK/US number 1 hit. Both these songs featured lead vocals from Hoffs, but 'Eternal Flame', was viewed by the other group members as an unnecessary departure from the Bangles' *modus operandi* with its use of string backing and barely little instrumental contribution from the rest of the group. Rather than harking back to the 60s the song was reminiscent of the pop ballads of the early-mid-70s of Michael Jackson and Donny Osmond. It also once again compounded the illusion in the public's eye that the Bangles were Hoffs' group. The year that had started so well for the group was now disintegrating into internal conflict. 'Be With You' and 'I'll Set You Free' failed to emulate their predecessors success and by the end of the year the decision was made to dissolve the group. Susanna Hoffs embarked on a solo career while the remaining members have yet to make any impact with their respective plans.

Albums: *All Over The Place* (Columbia 1985), *Different Light* (Columbia 1986), *Everything* (Columbia 1988). Compilations: *The Bangles Greatest Hits* (Columbia 1991), *Twelve Inch Mixes* (1993). Videos: *Bangles Greatest Hits* (1990).

Barenaked Ladies

Taking their name from a childhood slang term for a naked woman, the Barenaked Ladies are, in fact, five strapping lads from Scarborough, near Toronto, Canada. They were formed in 1988 by songwriters Steven Page (b. 22 June

Barenaked Ladies

1970; guitar/vocals) and Ed Robertson (b. 25 October 1970; guitar/vocals) while they were students. Brothers Jim (b. 12 February 1970; bass/keyboards) and Andy Creegan (b. 4 July 1971; congas) and Tyler Stewart (b. 21 September 1967; drums) were soon added to the line-up. The group set off on an intensive series of club dates, word of their prowess soon spread and their first release, a five-song EP, proved a big hit. Their debut album, *Gordon*, subsequently sold more than half a million copies in their native Canada, outselling acts like U2 and Michael Jackson. Their melodic pop with its strong harmonies and string-driven acoustics has led to them being unfairly dubbed the Fat Canadian Housemartins. Despite their undeniable debt to the British band, the Barenaked Ladies - who cite the Beach Boys and the Proclaimers among their influences - have carved out a distinctive sound. Songs such as 'Be My Yoko Ono' and 'If I Had A Million Dollars' are particular crowd favourites. Live, their self-deprecating humour, catchy songs and high energy make for a thoroughly entertaining show. However, with their tubby looks, spectacles and fondness for unflattering baggy shorts, it remains to be seen whether their success at home can be translated into hard sales in the rest of the world.
Album: *Gordon* (1992), *Maybe You Should Drive* (Sire 1994).

Barely Works

This eclectic folk group was assembled in 1988 by former Boothill Foot-Tappers singer and banjoist Chris Thompson (b. 19 March 1957, Ashford, Middlesex, England), together with Richard Avison (b. 9 July 1958, Rothbury, Northumberland, England; trombone/vocals - ex-Happy End and Dead Can Dance), Sarah Allen (b. 22 July 1964, Tiverton, Devon, England; accordion/tin whistle/flute - ex-Happy End and Di's New Outfit), Alison Jones (b. 6 April 1965, Sketty, Swansea, West Glamorgan, Wales; violin/vocals - ex-Di's New Outfit), Keith Moore (tuba - also a member of poet John Hegley's Popticians), Mat Fox (b. 8 November 1956; hammer dulcimer/percussion/vocals) and former Redskins drummer Paul Hookham, later replaced in 1990 by Tim Walmsley (b. 29 March 1956, Paddington, London, England - also ex-Happy End). This strange mixture of personalities signed to the radical world-music label, Cooking Vinyl and emerged from the UK folk club circuit in the late 80s and early 90s. Their performances boasted an broad range of traditional ('Byker Hill') and original material, mostly from Thompson and Allen as well as tackling the works of such artists as Captain Beefheart ('Tropical Hot Dog Nite'). The Barely Works have managed to break away from the constrictive pigeon-hole of an 'English Folk Group' and crossed over to the rock-club circuit where their virtuosity has proven them more than capable of moving a rock audience. Mat Fox left the group in early 1992 and Keith Moore was replaced by Alice Kinloch. In 1993 the group disbanded.
Albums: *The Beat Beat* (1990), *Don't Mind Walking* (1991), *Shimmer* (1992), *Glow* (1992).

Barracudas

Formed in 1979 as a neo-surfing band - their lone UK Top 40 entry in 1980 was the derivative 'Summer Fun' - Jeremy Gluck (vocals), Robin Wills (guitar/vocals), David Buckley (bass/vocals) and Nicky Turner (drums/vocals) eschewed this direction during the recording of their debut album, *Drop Out With The Barracudas*. Newer tracks, including 'I Saw My Death In A Dream Last Night', bore a debt to US-styled psychedelia and garage bands, and the group became one of the genre's leading proponents during its revival in the early 80s. The original rhythm section was then replaced by Jim Dickson and Terry Smith. However, the group only asserted an individual style with the arrival of Chris Wilson, formerly of the Flamin' Groovies. His influence was felt on the Barracudas' next two studio albums, *Mean Time* and *Endeavour To Persevere*, but these excellent releases were only issued in France. Failure to generate a British deal inevitably hampered the group's progress and they broke up in December 1984. Wilson and Wills were later reunited in a new venture, the Fortunate Sons, while Gluck, a former columnist on the music paper, *Sounds*, resumed his journalistic career, principally with *Q* magazine (as Jeremy Clarke) and also released two solo albums. Bentley ran his own vegitarian catering company before forming High Noon and, later, East West. Nick Turner joined Lords Of The New Church before taking a job at IRS Records. Gluck and Wills reformed the Barracudas in the 90s to record *Wait For Everything*, but were hampered by lack of money.
Albums: *Drop Out With The Barracudas* (Voxx 1981), *Mean Time* (Closer 1983), *Live 1983* (Coyote 1983), *Endeavour To Persevere* (Closer 1984), *Live In Madrid* (Impossible 1986), *Wait For Everything* (1993). Compilations: *The Big Gap* (Coyote 1984), *I Wish It Could Be 1965 Again* (GMG 1987), *The Garbage Dump Tapes* (Shakin' Street 1989, remixes and re-recordings), *The Complete EMI Recordings* (EMI 1991).

Bates, Martyn

Former lead singer of UK group Eyeless In Gaza, Bates split to perform solo in the late 80s having previously released a solo set, *Letters Written*, in 1982. Bates' songs were performed with no less a sense of intense, anguished passion than they once were with his erstwhile partners, but although he maintained a minor cult following, more widespread success eluded him. In 1990, with former Primitives guitarist Steve Dullaghan, he moved back to a group format with the formation of the five-piece Hungry I, releasing an EP, *The Falling Orchard*, in the summer of 1991. A further EP, *Second Step*, was recorded in October of that year, before the group 'exploded in acrimony and frustration' in March 1992. Whereupon Bates reunited with former partner Peter Becker to reform Eyeless In Gaza, releasing an album, *Fabulous Library*, in 1993. March 1994 saw the release of an album by Martyn Bates and M.J. Harris entitled *Murder Ballads/Drift*, with the former Napalm Death guiding light providing a brooding and intense 'ambient electronics' backdrop to a set of melodic and introspective, traditional folk-song sagas.
Albums: *Letters Written* (Cherry Red 1982), *Return Of The Quiet* (Cherry Red 1987), *Love Smashed On A Rock* (Integrity/Antler 1988), *Letters To A Scattered Family* (Integrity/Antler 1990), *Stars Come Trembling* (Ingegrity/Antler 1990), with M.J. Harris *Murder Ballads/Drift* (1994).

Bators, Stiv

b. Stivin Bator, 22 October 1949, Cleveland, Ohio, USA, d. June 1990. Bators' first bands, Mother Goose and Frankenstein, were transmuted into a seminal US 'no wave' band the Dead Boys. They moved to New York in 1976, and although they officially split in 1978 there were frequent reunions. Bators moved to Los Angeles where he recorded demos with friend Jeff Jones (ex-Blue Ash). He also gigged with Akron band Rubber City Rebels. The first release from the demos was a version of the Choir's (later the Raspberries) 60s single, 'It's Cold Outside', which was released on Greg Shaw's Bomp label. A second guitarist and debut album (USA only) followed in 1980, on which the duo was augmented by guitarist Eddy Best and drummer David Quinton (formerly in Toronto's the Mods). After appearing in John Walter's cult movie *Polyester*, Bators formed a touring band with Rick Bremner replacing Quinton. By 1981, Bators had become a permanent member of the Wanderers. The Stiv Bators Band played a final American tour in February 1981 with Brian James of the Damned guesting on guitar, after which Bators concentrated on the Wanderers until September 1981. After the impressive *Only Lovers Left Alive* (1981), Bators took Dave Treganna (ex-Sham 69) with him to join James and Nicky Turner (ex-Barracudas) in Lords Of The New Church. Following the Lords' demise, Bators resurfaced in London in 1989 for a 'Return Of The Living Boys' gig. This time his cohorts were drawn from a variety of local personnel, and it was not until he returned to Paris that he entered a recording studio once more. A new line-up included Dee Dee Ramone (Ramones), who had to be replaced by Neil X (Sigue Sigue Sputnik) before the sessions began, Kris Dollimore (ex-Godfathers) and guest appearances from Johnny Thunders. With six songs completed, Bators was hit by car in June 1990, and died the day after. There are hopes that his sessions will receive a posthumous release.

Album: *Where The Action Is* (Bomp 1980). Compilation: *The Church And The New Creatures* (Lolita 1983).

Bauhaus

Originally known as Bauhaus 1919, this Northamptonshire quartet comprised Peter Murphy (vocals), Daniel Ash (vocals/guitar), David Jay aka David J. (vocals/bass) and Kevin Haskins (drums). Within months of their formation they made their recording debut in 1979 with the classic, brooding, nine-minute gothic anthem, 'Bela Lugosi's Dead'. Their career saw them move to various independent labels (Small Wonder, Axix, 4AD and Beggars Banquet) and along the way they cut some interesting singles, including 'Dark Entries', 'Terror Couple Kill Colonel' and a reworking of T. Rex's 'Telegram Sam'. Often insistent on spontaneity in the studio, they recorded four albums in as many years, of which *Mask* (1981) proved the most accessible. A cameo appearance in the movie *The Hunger*, starring David Bowie, showed them playing their memorable Bela Lugosi tribute. They later took advantage of the Bowie connection to record a carbon copy of 'Ziggy Stardust', which gave them their only UK Top 20 hit. Although there was further belated success with 'Lagartija Nick' and 'She's In Parties', the group disbanded in 1983. Vocalist Peter Murphy briefly joined Japan's Mick Karn in Dali's Car and the remaining three members soldiered on under the name Love And Rockets.

Albums: *In The Flat Field* (1980), *Mask* (1981), *The Sky's Gone Out* (1982), *Press The Eject And Give Me The Tape* (1982), *Burning From The Inside* (1983). Compilation: *1979-1983* (1985).

Videos: *Shadow Of Light* (1984), *Archive* (1988).

Beastie Boys

Former hardcore trio who would go on to find international fame as the first crossover white rap act of the 80s. After forming at New York University original members John Berry and Kate Shellenbach would depart after the release of 'Pollywog Stew', leaving Adam 'MCA' Yauch (b. 15 August 1967, Brooklyn, New York, USA), Mike 'D' Diamond (b. 20 November 1965, New York, USA) and the recently recruited guitarist Adam 'Ad Rock' Horovitz (b. 31 October 1966, Manhattan, New York, USA) to hold the banner. The group was originally convened to play at MCA's 15th birthday party, adding Horovitz to their ranks from The Young And The Useless (one single, 'Real Men Don't Use Floss'). Horovitz, it transpired, was the son of dramatist Israel Horwitz, indicating that far from being the spawn of inner-city dystopia, the Beasties all came from privileged middle class backgrounds. They continued in similar vein to their debut with the *Cookie Puss* EP, which offerred the first evidence of them picking up on the underground rap phenomenon. The record, later sampled for a British Airways commercial, would earn them $40,000 in royalties. Friend and sometime band member Rick Rubin quickly signed them to his fledgling Def Jam label. They would not prove hard to market. Their debut album revealed a collision of bad attitudes, spearheaded by the raucous single, 'Fight For Your Right To Party', and samples of everything from Led Zeppelin to the theme to *Mister Ed*. There was nothing self-conscious or sophisticated about the lyrics, Mike D and MCA reeling off complaints about their parents confiscating their pornography or telling them to turn the stereo down. Somehow, however, it became an anthem for pseudo rebellious youth everywhere, scoring a number 11 hit in the UK. In the wake of its success *Licensed To Ill* became the first rap album to top the US charts. By the time follow-up singles 'No Sleep Till Brooklyn' and 'She's On It' charted, the band had become a media *cause celebre*. Their stage shows regularly featured caged, half-naked females, while their Volkswagen pendants resulted in a crime wave with fans stealing said items from vehicles throughout the UK. A reflective Horovitz recalled how that never happened in the US, where they merely stole the car itself. More disturbing, it was alleged that the band derided terminally ill children on a foreign jaunt. This false accusation was roundly denied, but other stories of excess leaked out of the Beastie Boys camp with grim regularity. There was also friction between the group and Def Jam, the former accusing the latter of withholding royalties, the latter accusing the former of withholding a follow-up album. By the time the band re-assembled after a number of solo projects in 1989, the public, for the most part, had forgotten about them. Rap's ante had been significantly raised by the arrival of Public Enemy and NWA, yet *Paul's Boutique* remains one of the

genre's most overlooked pieces, a complex reflection of pop culture which is infinitely subtler than their debut. Leaving their adolescent fixations behind, the rhymes plundered cult fiction (*Clockwork Orange*) through to *The Old Testament*. It was co-produced by the Dust Brothers, who would subsequently become a hot production item. Moving to California, *Check Your Head* saw them returning, partially, to their thrash roots, reverting to a guitar, bass and drums format. In the meantime the Beasties had invested wisely, setting up their own magazine, studio and label, Grandy Royal. This has boasted releases by Luscious Jackson, plus The Young And The Useless (Adam Horwitz's first band) and DFL (his hardcore punk project). Other signings included DJ Hurricane (also of the Afros), Noise Addict and Moistboyz. There has been a downside too. Horovitz pleaded guility to a charge of battery on a television cameraman during a memorial service for River Phoenix in 1993. He was put on two years probation, ordered to undertake 200 hours community service and pay restitution costs. His connections with the Phoenix family came through his actress wife Ione Sky. He himself had undertaken film roles in *The Santa Anna Project*, *Roadside Prophets* and *Lost Angels*, also appearing in a television cameo for *The Equalizer*. By this time both he and Diamond had become Californian citizens, while Yauch had become a Buddhist, speaking out in the press against US trade links with China, because of that country's annexation of Tibet. *Ill Communication* was another succesful voyage into inspired Beastie thuggism, featuring A Tribe Called Quest's Q Tip, and a second appearance from Biz Markie, following his debut on *Check Your Head*.
Albums: *Licensed To Ill* (Def Jam 1986), *Paul's Boutique* (Capitol 1989), *Check Your Head* (Capitol 1992), *Ill Communication* (Capitol 1994). Compilation: *Some Old Bullshit* (Capitol 1994).
Albums: *Ill Communication (Grand Royal/Capitol)* (1994).
Videos: *Sabotage* (1994), *The Skills To Pay The Bills* (1994).

Beat (USA)

Formed in San Francisco in 1979 the new wave/pop band the Beat were led by Paul Collins, who had previously played in the power pop band, the Nerves, with Peter Case, who later joined the Plimsouls, and songwriter Jack Lee (whose 'Hanging On The Telephone' was a hit for Blondie). The Beat signed with Bill Graham's management company and secured a recording deal with Columbia Records. Their debut, *The Beat*, was popular on college radio but never broke nationally. Their second album and a 1983 EP for Passport Records, recorded with a new line-up, failed to garner much interest and the group broke up.
Albums: *The Beat* (1979), *The Kids Are The Same* (1982), *To Beat Or Not To Beat* (1983, mini-album).

Beat Rodeo

Beat Rodeo was initially the name given to an EP recorded by Steve Almaas (b. Minneapolis, Minnesota, USA), a guitarist/vocalist formerly with the Minneapolis punk bands the Suicide Commandos and the Crackers. Almaas recorded the country-rock-oriented *Beat Rodeo* in 1981 with Richard Barone, formerly of the New York-New Jersey pop band the

Bongos and record producer Mitch Easter, at the latter's North Carolina recording studio, the Drive-In. The EP was released on the independent Coyote Records, after which Almaas formed the group Beat Rodeo, in 1982, along with guitarist/vocalist Bill Schunk (b. Riverhead, New York, USA). An early line-up of the group worked in clubs in the US north east and mid-west for two years before signing with I.R.S. Records. Their first version of their debut, *Staying Out Late*, was produced by Don Dixon at Easter's studio and released in Germany only in July 1984. That year, Almaas and Schunk replaced the original members with bassist Dan Prater and drummer Louis King. In early 1985 Almaas and Dixon returned to the Drive-In to remix the album and it was reissued, along with two new tracks added that year. *Home In The Heart Of The Beat* was recorded, with producer Scott Litt, in 1986. It failed to make a dent commercially and the band continued performing on the club circuit, but did not record.
Albums: *Staying Out Late* (1984), *Home In The Heart Of The Beat* (1986).

Beautiful South

This highly literate adult pop group were built from the ashes of the Housemartins. The line-up features vocalists Paul Heaton (b. 9 May 1962, Birkenhead, Merseyside, England) and David Hemmingway (b. 20 September 1960, England) from Hull's self-proclaimed 'Fourth Best Band'. In reference to their previous dour Northern image, Heaton sarcastically named his new band Beautiful South, recruiting Sean Welch (bass), Briana Corrigan (ex-Anthill Runaways; vocals), former Housemartins roadie David Stead (drums) and Heaton's new co-writer, David Rotheray (guitar). Continuing an association with Go! Discs, their first single was the ballad 'Song For Whoever' which gave them instant UK chart success (number 2 in June 1989). After the rejection of the original sleeve concept for their debut album (a suicidal girl with gun in her mouth), *Welcome To The Beautiful South* emerged in October 1989 to a good critical reception. 'A Little Time' became their first number 1 the following year. A bitter duet between Corrigan and Hemmingway, it was supported by a memorable video which won The Best Music Video award at the 1991 BRIT Awards. Lyrically, Heaton had honed his songwriting to a style which allowed the twists and ironies to develop more fully: 'I find it difficult to write straightforward optimistic love songs... I throw in a row, a fight, get a few knives out...'. Though giving the band their least successful chart position to date (number 43), 'My Book' provided one of Heaton's most cutting lyrics (including a hilarious reference to the football player Peter Beardsley) and also saw Jazzie B. of Soul II Soul sue for the slight use of the 'Back To Reality' refrain. Always a writer able to deal with emotive subjects in an intelligent and forthright manner, Heaton's next topic was lonely alcoholism in 'Old Red Eyes Is Back', the first fruits of a protracted writing stint in Gran Canaria. However, Corrigan became a little unsettled at some of the subject matter now expressed in Heaton's lyrics (notably '36D', a song about *The Sun* newspaper's 'Page 3' topless models, which was open to a variety of interpretations) and left the band after *0898*, although press statements suggested she may return in the

Beck

future. Her replacement, Jacqui Abbot, was introduced on 'Everybody's Talkin'', and more fully on the band's fourth studio album, *Miaow*. However, its success was dwarfed by the singles collection, *Carry On Up The Charts*, which dominated the listings in late 1994 and early 1995.
Albums: *Welcome To The Beautiful South* (Go! Discs 1989), *Choke* (Go! Discs 1990), *0898* (Go! Discs 1992), *Miaow* (Go! Discs 1994). Compilation: *Carry On Up The Charts* (Go! Discs 1994).
Video: *The Pumpkin* (1992).

Beck
b. c.1974, Los Angeles, California, USA. Beck Hansen rose swiftly to prominence in 1994 with his marriage of folk (Leadbelly, Woody Guthrie) and guitar noise. As a child he loitered around his bluegrass street musician father, living with his office-worker mother and half-brother in some of Los Angeles' worst addresses, picking up on the nascent hip hop scene there as a breakdancer. He also spent time in Kansas with his grandmother and Presbyterian preacher grandfather, and with his other grandfather, the artist Al Hansen, in Europe. His guitar playing, however, was primarily inspired by the blues of Mississippi John Hurt, which he would deliver with improvised lyrics while busking. After dropping out of school at 16 he moved to New York, though he was unable to join in with the local punk scene there. On his return to Los Angeles he played his first gigs in-between sets at clubs such as Raji's and Jabberjaw. His music was now a potpourri of those diverse early influences - street hip hop, Delta blues, Presbyterian hymns, punk with scat lyrics, and the whole was now beginning to take shape as he released his first single, 'MTV Makes Me Want To Smoke Crack', the title of which would be made ironic by his future success in that very medium. This was followed by a 12-inch for Los Angeles independent Bong Load Custom Records, titled 'Loser', produced with hip hop technician Karl Stephenson. Those who would try to read something sardonic into this title in retrospect should be reminded that Beck was at the time living in a rat-infested shed: 'I was working in a video store doing things like alphabetizing the pornography section for minimum wage'. When 'Loser' was finally released after a year's delay in the summer of 1993, critics fell over themselves to call it an anthem to doomed youth. Vaulted into the pop charts, Beck was suddenly viewed as a baby-faced saviour for the 'slacker' generation, a platform he was most unwilling to mount: 'I never had any slack. I was working a $4-an-hour job trying to stay alive. I mean, that slacker kind of stuff is for people who have the time to be depressed about everything.' The major labels s swooped for his signature. Geffen Records won possibly the most competitive chase for an artist in a decade, though not before David Geffen had rung Beck up at home and the artist had already set in motion two more independent records - 'Steve Threw Up' for Bong Load and a 10-inch album, *A Western Harvest Field By Moonlight*, on Fingerpaint Records. Despite this, the contract with Geffen was highly unusual in that it allowed Beck to record and release material for other companies should he wish - an option he took delight in exercising. The *Mellow Gold* debut album for Geffen was only one of three albums scheduled for release in 1994. The second, *Stereo Pathetic Soul Manure*, appeared on LA's Flipside, and the third, a collaboration with Calvin Johnson of Beat Happening, emerged on K Records.
Albums: *A Western Harvest Field By Moonlight* (Fingerpaint 1993), *Mellow Gold* (Geffen 1994), *Stereo Pathetic Soul Manure* (Flipside 1994).

Beggars Banquet Records
This independent UK record label was formed during the punk explosion of 1977. The label's first release was 'Shadow' by the Lurkers, Britain's three-chord answer to the Ramones. Signing the Doll, Johnny G., Jeff 'Duffo' Duff and Tubeway Army (Gary Numan) the same year, it was the latter's 'Are Friends Electric' that ensured Beggars Banquet's long-term future. This reached the number 1 spot in May 1979, during a 16-week residency in the UK singles charts. Tubeway Army, and lead vocalist Numan in particular, provided the main source of income for the label during the late 70s and early 80s. This allowed Beggars Banquet to sign a variety of mainly 'indie' bands and encourage their development. The label's roster subsequently included Goat, Bauhaus, the Fall, Icicle Works, Adult Net, Go-Betweens, Gene Loves Jezebel, Fields Of The Nephilim and Freeez.

Bel Canto
A chamber-rock trio drawing its members from Norway, Bel Canto (Italian for 'beautiful song') play a blend of alternative pop-rock with medieval atmospherics recreated by synthesizers. It can be an effective combination, producing an aural assimilation of the past which is hallmarked by an evocative sense of loss and sadness (similar to the Cocteau Twins). The idea behind the songs was drawn from energy fields, be they female power or the earth's gravitational pull, with vocals delicately etched by the alto of Anneli Marian Drecker. The orchestration by Nils Johansen and Geir Jennsen on the debut combined electronics with traditional instruments, sometimes departing from the pious imagery for upbeat Arabic numbers ('Agassiz') or cultured ambient soundscapes ('Blank Sheets'). Guest musicians for *Birds Of Passage* added flugelhorn, bouzouki and dozens of other instruments to achieve a bold, decidedly unusual though not necessarily uncommercial, sound.
Albums: *White-Out Conditions* (Crammed Discs 1987), *Birds Of Passage* (Nettwerk 1989), *Shimmering, Warm And Bright* (Crammed Discs 1992).

Belle Stars
A splinter group from the 2-Tone influenced Bodysnatchers, this UK, all-female septet comprised Sarah-Jane Owen (guitar), Miranda Joyce (saxophone), Judy Parsons (drums) and Jennie McKeown (bass). Signed by Stiff Records in 1981, they charted the following year with remakes of the Dixie Cups' 'Iko Iko' and Shirley Ellis's 'The Clapping Song'. Unable to sustain a long term commercial appeal and subject to changing personnel, they nevertheless produced one memorable smash hit, 'Sign Of The Times', a catchy pop tune with a spoken word section reminiscent of the great, girl group sound of the mid-60s.
Album: *The Belle Stars* (1983).
Video: *Live Signs, Live Times* (1989).

Beloved

Belly

Based in Newport, Rhode Island, USA, Belly consist of Tanya Donelly (b. 14 August 1966, Newport, Rhode Island, USA; vocals/guitar), Thomas Gorman (b. 20 May 1966, USA; lead guitar), Chris Gorman (b. Christopher Toll Gorman, 29 August 1967, USA; drums) and recent recruit Gail Greenwood (b. 3 October 1960, USA; bass). Donelly, along with half-sister Kristin Hersh, was a founding member of Throwing Muses. She was happy playing second fiddle (not literally) and writing the occasional song until Hersh took time out to start a family. Donelly eventually left, amicably, after recording *The Real Ramona*. She had already worked with the Breeders, a female punk pop super group featuring Kim Deal (Pixies) and Jo Wiggs (Perfect Disaster). However, this too was primarily someone else's band and Donelly finally moved on to Belly. They originally formed in December 1991 with brothers Tom and Chris Gorman (ex-Verbal Assault), and former Throwing Muses' bass player Fred Abong. He was replaced by Leslie Langston (also ex-Throwing Muses) who in turn was replaced by Greenwood, who had had stints with the all girl band the Dames and hardcore outfit Boneyard. She also works freelance as an illustrator, and designed Aerosmith's fan club Christmas cards. Belly had debuted with the EPs *Slow Dust* and then *Gepetto*, which preceded the album, *Star*. Recorded in Nashville, *Star* saw Donelly welding perverse, abusive and uplifting lyrics to a smothering mesh of guitar and sweet vocals. In its wake the *Feed The Tree* EP gave them unlikely daytime airplay and a first chart hit, before the album soared to number 2 in the UK charts. Included on it was a version of 'Trust In Me' (from Disney's *The Jungle Book*), a song that sums up the band's appeal: a clash of the nice and the nasty. *King* was recording during the end of 1994 in Nassau, Bahamas, with producer Glyn Johns and had writing contributions from both Tom Gorman and Greenwood for the first time, with Chris Gorman continuing to provide distinctive cover imagery. For Donelly's part the lyrics switched to a first person focus, though when pressed for a summary she would describe the album as 'just pop rock like everything else'. It is hard to expand on that description.
Albums: *Star* (Sire/4AD 1993), *King* (Sire/4AD 1995).

Beloved

Initially known in 1983 as the Journey Through and comprising Jon Marsh (b. c.1964), Guy Gousden and Tim Havard, UK band the Beloved fell into place a year later when Cambridge University student and ex-postman Steve Waddington (b. c.1959) joined on guitar. It was no straightforward initiation ceremony either. Marsh had placed an advert in the music press which ran thus: 'I am Jon Marsh, founder member of the Beloved. should you too wish to do something gorgeous, meet me in exactly three year's time at exactly 11am in Diana's Diner, or site thereof, Covent Garden, London, WC2'. Tentative stabs at heavy psychedelia evolved into a more pop orientated formula by the mid-80s, with the Beloved's dark, danceable sounds often being compared to New Order and garnering attention throughout Europe. Marsh became a contestant on television quiz show *Countdown* in 1987, featuring on nine programmes before being knocked out in the semi-finals. It was not until 1988, however, that the Beloved started living up to their name: Waddington and Marsh, heavily influenced by the nascent 'rave' scene in London at that time, split from Gousden and Harvard and started forging their own path. Unshackled from the confines of a four-cornered set-up, the revitalised duo dived into the deep end of the exploding dance movement, subsequently breaking into commercial waters with the ambient textures of 'Sun Rising'. The *Happiness* album, backed by Marsh and Waddington's enthusiastic chatter concerning the virtues of floatation tanks and hallucinogenic substances, perfectly embodied the tripped-out vibe of the times and sealed the Beloved's fashionable success in worldwide territories. By 1993's *Conscience*, Marsh had left his former partner Waddington, using his wife Helena as his new creative foil. The resultant album was more whimsical and understated than previous affairs, with a pop rather than club feel.
Albums: *Happiness* (Atlantic 1990), *Blissed Out* (remix of *Happiness*) (East West 1990), *Conscience* (East West 1993).

Benny Profane

Formed in the late 80s in Liverpool, England, Benny Profane featured Dave Jackson (vocals), Joseph McKechnie (guitar/drums), Robin Surtees (guitar), and Becky Stringer (bass). The permanent drummer had been Frank Sparks (ex-Ex Post Facto) but when he left both Roger Sinek and Dave Brown helped out on the band's debut album. Jackson, Stringer and Peter Baker, who filled in as an additional member providing organ, had all previously played in the Room. In many ways they were effectively an update of that commercially overlooked group. The new member McKechnie was rescued from the lay-out desk of the Merseyside health magazine *Who Cares?* They took their name from a character in Thomas Pynchon's book, *V*, and their first single, 'Where Is Pig', came from his dialogue in the novel. A succession of low-key gigs at Monroes pub in Liverpool gave them a high local profile. However, they never repeated the success of the other local group who made the venue their home, the La's, despite two strong albums and three fondly remembered sessions for the BBC disc jockey John Peel.
Albums: *Trapdoor Swing* (Play Hard 1989), *Dunbluck Charm* (Play Hard 1990).

Berry, Heidi

An American singer and songwriter, and former painter, who has lived in London since childhood, Berry saw the first of her compositions released on Creation Records in 1987 on the mini-album, *Firefly*. Numerous members of the Creation fold were used as backing musicians, notably Martin Duffy (Felt) on keyboards. Two years later the line-up also included her brother Christopher on acoustic guitar, and Rocky Holman on piano and synthesizer. However, after appearing on This Mortal Coil's *Blood*, singing a version of Rodney Crowell's 'Til I Gain Control Again', she switched to 4AD Records. The nucleus of Christopher Berry and Holman were retained for the subsequent *Love*, which proved to be her most accomplished and satisfying set to date. The album contained contributions from Terry Bickers and Laurence O'Keefe (Levitation), Martin McCarrick (Siouxsie And The

Bettie Serveert

Banshees), Lol Coxhill and Ian Kearey (Blue Aeroplanes). The original compositions were augmented by a cover of Bob Mould's 'Up In The Air'. *Heidi Berry* included the artist's first ever single, 'The Moon And The Sun', and saw Bickers return to provide guitar assistance.

Albums: *Firefly* (Creation 1987, mini-album), *Below The Waves* (4AD 1989), *Love* (4AD 1991), *Heidi Berry* (4AD 1993).

Beserkley Records

Independent record label founded in 1973 in Berkeley, California, USA, by Matthew King Kaufman, formerly of Baltimore, Maryland. Kaufman's initial goal was to revive the 45 rpm single in an era when the album had taken over as the primary format for record sales. His first signing was Earthquake, a band from the East Bay area of the San Francisco region, whose first single was a cover of the Easybeats hit, 'Friday On My Mind'. The label continued to release only singles for three years. Kaufman signed a brief distribution deal with the short-lived Playboy Records in the US and Jonathan King's UK Records in England. Ultimately, Beserkley signed three other acts that comprised the bulk of its catalogue: the eccentric Jonathan Richman And The Modern Lovers, mainstream pop-rockers Greg Kihn and popsters the Rubinoos. Kihn became the label's largest seller, logging a number 2 US single with 'Jeopardy' in 1983, although the label and its artists were consistently more popular in Europe, where it featured a larger roster of talent, including the Smirks and the Tyla Gang (see Sean Tyla). By the mid-80s Earthquake had disbanded, the Rubinoos had sued Kaufman for mismanagement, and Kihn and Richman had signed to other labels, forcing Kaufman to fold the label. In 1990 he was considering reviving it but as yet no new releases have appeared.

Compilation: *Beserkeley Chartbusters Volume One* (1979).

Bettie Serveert

Formed in Amsterdam, Holland, Bettie Serveert consist of Carol Van Dijk (vocals), Peter Visser (guitar), Herman Bunskoeke (bass) and Berend Dubbe (drums). In 1991 Visser and Bunskoeke were playing together in a band entitled De Arsten (the Doctors), for whom Dubbe was a roadie and Van Dijk the mixer, and when they broke up the four members began jamming together on material Van Dijk had written in her bedroom. The original idea was for her to sell these compositions to avoid having to go on stage and sing them, but 'nobody wanted to buy them'. Her musical partners decided to gather round to give those songs a home, and named the band after a line in a tennis instruction book written by the Dutch tennis player Bettie Stove (the literal translation for their name is 'Bettie serves'). The only obstacle remaining was Van Dijk's reluctance to go on stage, and well into the group's success stories continued to circulate about her having to be physically dragged onto the stage by her fellow band members. (She says that her shyness stems from her removal from Canada at the age of seven so that her father could start a photography business in Amsterdam.) Nevertheless, Bettie Serveert's debut was a buoyant record celebrating her new-found friendships. With a sound reminiscent of Belly at their most jovial, it sold

particularly well in the US. The title of the band's second album, *Lamprey*, came from the deep-sea creature whose insides implode if it comes too near the surface, and indicated a more introspective, blues-based approach, drawing on the singer's childhood alienation. Many were unprepared for its austerity, but as Van Dijk said: 'When something is super catchy it starts to fade after a while. Maybe the new songs are more like paintings that you don't really get at first glance, but something about them makes you look again and again.' These songs were warmly received on dates with Jeff Buckley in 1995, while 'Crutches', released as a single, found even UK critics, notoriously resistant to the mainland Europe rock/pop tradition, falling for the group.

Albums: *Palomine* (Beggars Banquet 1993), *Lamprey* (Beggars Banquet 1995).

Bevis Frond

Often mistakenly believed to be a group, the Bevis Frond is actually just one person: Nick Saloman. Influenced by Jimi Hendrix and Cream, Saloman formed the Bevis Frond Museum while still at school. The group disbanded and after a period playing acoustic sets in the Walthamstow area of London he formed the Von Trap Family, later known as Room 13. In 1982 Saloman was seriously hurt in a motorcycle accident. He used the money he received in compensation to record *Miasma* in his bedroom and it quickly became a collectors' item. *Pulsebeat* magazine referred to the tracks as 'like fireworks for inside your head'. Saloman then released *Inner Marshland* and *Triptych* on his own Woronzow Records and his long psychedelic guitar workouts mapped out a style that was shamelessly archaic but nevertheless appealing. London's Reckless Records re-released his first three albums and in 1988 provided *Bevis Through The Looking Glass* and, a year later, *The Auntie Winnie Album*. Saloman's brand of raw, imaginative blues guitar drew many converts and *Any Gas Faster*, recorded in better-equipped studios, was widely lauded. *Rolling Stone* magazine said of it: 'With so much modern psychedelia cheapened by cliché or nostalgia, the Bevis Frond is the actual out-there item.' In 1991 Saloman released a double set, *New River Head*, on his own Woronzow Records, distributed in the USA by Reckless. He followed it up with 1992's *Just Is*, again a double, and *Beatroots*, recorded under the pseudonym Fred Bison Five. As a tireless believer in the need for communication, he set up an underground magazine, *Ptolemaic Terrascope*, in the late 80s, and like Saloman's music, it is a loyal correspondent of the UK psychedelic scene.

Albums: *Miasma* (Woronzow 1987), *Inner Marshland* (Woronzow 1987), *Bevis Through The Looking Glass* (Woronzow 1987, double album), *The Aunty Winnie Album* (Reckless 1989), *Triptych* (Reckless 1989), *Any Gas Faster* (Woronzow 1990), *New River Head* (Woronzow 1991, double album), *London Stone* (Woronzow 1992), *Just Is* (Woronzow 1993, double album). Compilation: *A Gathering Of Fronds* (Woronzow 1992).

Bible

The Bible were formed in Cambridge, UK, and their debut single 'Gracelands' (1986), was a classy pop song, as was its

follow-up, 'Mahalia' (a tribute to the gospel singer Mahalia Jackson). The band consisted of Boo Hewerdine (vocals/guitar), Tony Shepherd (keyboards/percussion), Dave Larcombe (drums) and Leroy Lendor (bass), and by the time Chrysalis Records had signed them, they already had an album's worth of well-crafted songs in *Walking The Ghost Back Home*. Chrysalis duly reissued 'Gracelands' in early 1987, but it eluded the charts, and the band spent the year recording a second album. Released in January 1988, *Eureka* shared the melodic quality of the Bible's debut, but neither of the singles, 'Crystal Palace' in April and 'Honey Be Good' in September, made much impression. Desperate for success, they tried revamping 'Gracelands' and when that failed, reissued 'Honey Be Good'. A compilation release in late 1989, *The Best Of The Bible*, signalled the end of the band's association with their label. Hewerdine, who had previously played in short-lived bands such as the Great Divide, subsequently embarked on a fruitful solo career.
Albums: *Walking The Ghost Back Home* (Backs 1986), *Eureka* (Ensign/Chrysalis 1988). Compilation: *The Best Of The Bible* (Ensign/Chrysalis 1989).

Biff Bang Pow!

Biff Bang Pow! - a name derived from a song by 60s cult group the Creation - is an outlet for the musical aspirations of Glaswegian Alan McGee, the motivating force behind Creation Records, one of the UK's most inventive independent outlets. The group also featured business partner Dick Green (guitar) and despite its part-time nature, has completed several excellent releases, including the neo-psychedelic singles, '50 Years Of Fun' (1984) and 'Love's Going Out Of Fashion' (1986). *Pass The Paintbrush Honey* and *The Girl Who Runs The Beat Hotel* offered idiosyncratic, and often contrasting, views of pop, while *Love Is Forever* showed the influence of Neil Young, notably on 'Ice Cream Machine'. In the 90s, however, with his record label achieving major success with Oasis and the Boo Radleys, McGee has found less time for his own band.
Albums: *Pass The Paintbrush Honey* (Creation 1985), *The Girl Who Lives At The Beat Hotel* (Creation 1987), *Oblivion* (Creation 1987), *Love Is Forever* (Creation 1988), *Songs For The Sad Eyed Girl* (Creation 1990). Compilation: *The Acid House Album* (Creation 1989), *L'amour, Demure, Stenhousemuir* (Creation 1992).

Big Audio Dynamite

After Clash guitarist Mick Jones (b. 26 June 1955, Brixton, London, England) was fired from that group in 1984 he formed an ill-fated outfit with former Clash drummer Topper Headon, before linking up with ex-Roxy DJ and film-maker Don Letts to form Big Audio Dynamite (or BAD, as they were commonly known). With Jones (guitar), Letts (keyboards and effects), they completed the line-up with Dan Donovan (keyboards), son of famed photographer Terence Donovan, Leo Williams (bass) and Greg Roberts (drums). *This Is Big Audio Dynamite* proved to be a natural progression from tracks like 'Inoculated City' on *Combat Rock*, the last Clash LP that featured Jones, with cut up funk spiced with sampled sounds (the first time this technique has been used). The follow-up album featured writing

contributions from Joe Strummer, who happened across the band while they were recording in Soho, London. BAD continued to record but hit their first crisis in 1988 when Jones came close to death from pneumonia, which caused a delay in the release of *Megatop Phoenix*. This in turn led to the break-up of the band and by 1990 and *Kool-Aid*, Jones had assembled a completely new line-up (BAD II) featuring Nick Hawkins (guitar), Gary Stonadge (bass) and Chris Kavanagh (ex-Sigue Sigue Sputnik; drums). DJ Zonka was also drafted in to provide live 'scratching' and mixing. Jones also contributed to the *Flashback* soundtrack and 'Good Morning Britain' single from Aztec Camera. He summoned disdain, not least from former colleagues, by insisting on putting a BAD track on the b-side to the posthumous Clash number 1 'Should I Stay Or Should I Go'. Donovan married and separated from Eighth Wonder singer and actor Patsy Kensit. He went on to join the reformed Sigue Sigue Sputnik, while his former employers were being hailed as a great influence on the new wave of 90s Brit-dance-pop (EMF, Jesus Jones).
Albums: *This Is Big Audio Dynamite* (Columbia 1985), *No. 10 Upping Street* (Columbia 1986), *Tighten Up, Vol 88* (Columbia 1988), *Megatop Phoenix* (Columbia 1989). As B.A.D.: *Kool-Aid* (MCA 1990). As B.A.D. II: *The Globe* (Columbia 1991).

Big Black

Initially based in Evanstown, Illinois, USA, Big Black made its recording debut in 1983 with the six-track EP *Lungs*. Fronted by guitarist/vocalist Steve Albini, the group underwent several changes before completing *Bulldozer* the following year. A more settled line-up was formed around Albini, Santiago Durango (guitar) and Dave Riley aka Dave Lovering (bass) as Big Black began fusing an arresting, distinctive sound and *Atomizer* (1986) established the trio as one of America's leading independent acts. This powerful, compulsive set included 'Kerosene', a lyrically nihilistic piece equating pyromania with teenage sex as a means of escaping small-town boredom. The combined guitar assault of Albini and Durango was underpinned by Riley's emphatic bass work, which propelled this metallic composition to its violent conclusion. Melvin Belli (guitar) replaced Durango, who left to study law, for *Songs About Fucking*, Big Black's best-known and most popular album. Once again their blend of post-hardcore and post-industrial styles proved exciting, but Albini had now tired of his creation: 'Big Black are dumb, ugly and persistent, just like a wart' - and announced the break-up of the group prior to the record's release. He later became a respected but idiosyncratic producer, working with the Pixies (*Surfer Rosa*), the Breeders (*Pod*) and Tad (*Salt Lick*), before forming a new venture, the controversially-named and short-lived Rapeman. When that group shuddered under the weight of criticism at its name (though Albini insisted this was merely a UK phenomenon), he returned to production duties. Undoubtedly the highest profile of these would be PJ Harvey's *Rid Of Me* and Nirvana's *In Utero*. Afterwards he returned to a group format with Shellac.
Albums: *Atomizer* (Homestead/Blast First 1986), *Sound Of Impact* (Walls Have Ears 1987, live album), *Songs About*

Big Audio Dynamite

Fucking (Touch And Go/Blast First 1987). Compilations: *The Hammer Party* (Homestead/Blast First 1986), *Rich Man's 8-Track* (Homestead/Blast First 1987), *Pigpile* (Blast First 1992).

Big Flame

This Manchester trio featuring Alan Brown (bass), David 'Dill' Brown (drums) and Gregory O'Keefe (guitar) were perhaps the finest offering on the independent Ron Johnson label. Big Flame's uncompromising aural assault stemmed from their jagged, staccato guitar attack, first heard on the EP *Sink* (on the Plaque label) in April 1984. Almost a year later, their first Ron Johnson label EP, *Rigour*, surfaced, followed in September by *Tough! Why Popstars Can't Dance*. The band were featured on the *New Musical Express C86* compilation of new talent, showcasing the brief 'New Way (Quick Wash And Brush Up With Liberation Theology)'. A retrospective 10-inch EP, *Two Can Guru* preceded a new EP, *Cubist Pop Manifesto*. The latter brought Big Flame critical, if not commercial support. But after a 12-inch maxi-EP, *XPQWRTZ* (a co-release with German label, Constrictor), the band broke up, with ex-members forming Great Leap Forwards.

Big Head Todd And The Monsters

Formed at high school in Boulder, Colorado, USA, in 1986, the band put together two albums and several single releases to little outside interest. Gradually, however, songwriter Todd Park Mohr (vocals/guitar), Rob Squires (bass) and Brian Nevin (drums) earned a groundswell of support after financing the band from their own pockets. *Midnight Radio*, with cover artwork by Chris Mars of the Replacements, one of their most vociferous fans, began to take that 'buzz' to a national level, though despite the breakthrough the band remained with their own label for its release. Finally signing to Giant Records through the auspices of Irving Azoff in 1993, they made their major label debut with *Sister Sweetly*, produced with David Z (Prince/Fine Young Cannibals/BoDeans) at Paisley Park studios, where strong musical frameworks emboldened songs such as 'Broken Hearted Saviour' and 'True Groove Thing'. Guitarist Leo Kottke contributed to 'Soul For Every Cowboy', while the band, on the back of an 18-month US tour, had three singles in the *Billboard* AOR Top 10, performed enthusiastically on the *David Letterman* and *Today* shows, and supported Robert Plant. *Strategem* (deliberately misspelled) unveiled further gritty displays of rural blues rock, particularly 'Neckbreaker' (inspired by 14th Century mystic St John Of The Cross) and 'Angel Leads Me On'.
Albums: *Another Mayberry* (Big Records 1989), *Midnight Radio* (Big Records 1990), *Sister Sweetly* (Giant 1993), *Strategem* (Giant 1995).

Big In Japan

For a band that issued very little vinyl, Big In Japan received strong critical acclaim. The main reason for this interest was their line-up: Jayne Casey (vocals; later with Pink Industry/Military), Bill Drummond (guitar; later formed Lori And The Chameleons, ran the Zoo Records label, released a solo album and comprised half of the KLF), Dave

Balfe (bass; worked with Drummond in Lori And The Chameleons, was later enrolled as keyboard player in the Teardrop Explodes and then founded the Food Records label), Budgie (drums; later briefly with the Slits then, more permanently, Siouxsie And The Banshees), Ian Broudie (guitar; who subsequently joined the Original Mirrors before carving out a successful career as producer, and later enjoyed success under the guise of the Lightning Seeds) and finally Holly on bass. After two country-styled singles, Holly joined Frankie Goes To Hollywood and is now the solo artist, Holly Johnson. On the b-side of their 1977 self-titled debut single was a track from the Chuddy Nuddies, who turned out to be the Yachts. After Big In Japan split, Drummond used four of their tracks for the first Zoo single, *From Y To Z And Never Again*, which stands as a delightfully quirky period piece. The remaining members of Big In Japan (vocalist Ken Ward and drummer Phil Allen) failed to emulate the success of their fellow travellers.

Bikini Kill

Pioneers of the 90s radical feminist musical movement named Riot Grrrl, USA's Bikini Kill were widely perceived to be the transatlantic cousins of UK band Huggy Bear - an impression confirmed when they joined that band for a 1993 shared album which was one of the movement's most celebrated documents. Hailing from Olympia, Washington, and led by the haranguing voice of Kathleen Hanna, Bikini Kill believe that indie rock is just as sexist as mainstream rock. Their tactics in attempting to create a new artistic platform include asking men to make way for women at the front of their concerts. Musically they resembled some of the late 70s punk pioneers, particularly the Slits. Also in the group are Billy Boredom (guitar) and Kathin (bass). *Yeah Yeah Yeah* was followed later in the same year by the band's first album, *Pussy Whipped*. This included direct takes on sexual politics which spared no blushes. 'Rebel Girl', the group's anthem which had previously been recorded twice, once in single form with Joan Jett as producer, made a third appearance. While the initial spark of Riot Grrrl has died down, Bikini Kill's remains its most vibrant legacy.
Albums: *Bikini Kill* (K Records 1992, cassette only), *Bikini Kill* (Kill Rock Stars 1993, mini-album), *Yeah Yeah Yeah* (Kill Rock Stars 1993, split album with Huggy Bear), *Pussy Whipped* (Kill Rock Stars 1993). Compilation: *Bikini Kill/Yeah Yeah Yeah* (Kill Rock Stars 1995).

Biohazard

The mean streets of Brooklyn, New York, saw the formation of Biohazard in 1988 by Evan Seinfeld (bass/vocals), Billy Graziedi (guitar/vocals), Bobby Hambel (guitar) and Danny Schuler (drums), and the harsh realities of urban life provide constant lyrical inspiration for this socially and politically aware hardcore band. Modest beginnings supporting the likes of the Cro-Mags and Carnivore at the famous L'Amour club led to an independent debut, *Biohazard*. Constant touring built such a cult following that the band were able to sign to Roadrunner for one album and a subsequent major deal with Warner Brothers at the same time in 1992. *Urban Discipline* was recorded in under two weeks on a tiny budget, but proved to be the band's breakthrough album. Blisteringly heavy with lyrics to match - 'Black And White And Red All Over' was an anti-racism tirade to dispel a mistakenly-applied fascist label stemming from the debut's 'Howard Beach', which concerned a racially-motivated Brooklyn murder - the album drew massive praise, as did wild live shows during heavy touring with Kreator in Europe and Sick Of It All in the US. The band also recorded a well-received track with rappers Onyx for the *Judgement Night* soundtrack. The Warners debut, *State Of The World Address*, was recorded in seven weeks, and demonstrated that major label status did not mean any compromise on Biohazard's part, with a furiously heavy Ed Stasium production and an aggressive performance which gathered a succession of rave reviews. The band embarked on a successful US tour with Pantera and Sepultura as album sales took off, but a second appearance at Donington came to a controversially premature end due to the stage management's safety worries over Biohazard's penchant for encouraging their audience to join them on stage *en masse*. However, further European touring, including several festival dates, was problem-free, with the band constantly enhancing a deserved reputation for their ferocious live shows, before returning to the US for dates with House Of Pain and Danzig.

Albums: *Biohazard* (Maze 1990), *Urban Discipline* (Roadrunner 1992), *State Of The World Address* (Warners 1994).

Birthday Party

One of the most creative and inspiring 'alternative' acts of the 80s, this Australian outfit had its roots in the new wave band Boys Next Door. After one album, the band relocated to London and switched names. In addition to featuring the embryonic genius of Nick Cave (vocals), their ranks were swelled by Roland S. Howard (ex-Obsessions, Young Charlatans; guitar), Mick Harvey (guitar, drums, organ, piano), Tracy Pew (d. 5 July 1986; bass) and Phil Calvert (drums). They chose the newly launched 4AD Records offshoot of Beggars Banquet Records as their new home, and made their debut with the impressive 'Fiend Catcher'. Music critics and BBC disc jockey John Peel became early and long-serving converts to the band's intense post-punk surges. Back in Australia, they recorded their first album, a transitional piece which nevertheless captured some enduring aggressive rock statements. Their finest recording, however, was the single 'Release The Bats'. It was John Peel's favourite record of 1981, though its subject matter unwittingly tied the band in with the emerging 'Gothic' subculture populated by Bauhaus and Sex Gang Children. As Pew was imprisoned for three months for drink-driving offences, Barry Adamson (ex-Magazine), Roland Howard's brother Harry and Chris Walsh helped out on the recording of the follow-up, and the band's increasingly torrid live shows. After collaborating with the Go-Betweens on the one-off single, 'After The Fireworks', as the Tuf Monks, they shifted to Berlin to escape the constant exposure and expectations of them in the UK. Calvert was dropped (moving on to Psychedelic Furs), while the four remaining members moved on to collaborative projects with Lydia Lunch and Einsturzende Neubaten amongst others. They had already recorded a joint 12-inch, 'Drunk On The Pope's Blood', with Lunch, and Howard featured on much of

her future output. When Harvey left in the summer of 1983, the band seemed set to fulfil their solo careers, even though he was temporarily replaced on drums by Des Heffner. However, after a final gig in Melbourne, Australia in June the band called it a day. Howard went on to join Crime And The City Solution alongside his brother and Harvey, who also continued on Cave's solo band the Bad Seeds.

Albums: *The Birthday Party* (Missing Link 1980, Australia), *Prayers On Fire* (Thermidor 1981), *Drunk On The Pope's Blood* (4AD 1982, mini-album), *Junkyard* (4AD 1982), *It's Still Living* (Missing Link 1985, Australia, live album). Compilations: *A Collection* (Missing Link 1985, Australia), *Hee Haw* (4AD 1989), *The Peel Sessions Album* (Strange Fruit 1991).

Video: *Pleasure Heads Must Burn* (1988).

Biting Tongues

An undereevaluated Manchester group, Biting Tongues were formed by Graham Massey and Howard Walmsley in 1980, ostensibly to provide soundtracks for the latter's live film screenings. With Massey on guitar and Walmsley on saxophone, they added local writer Ken Hollings as vocalist, Colin Seddon on bass and Eddie Sherwood on drums. Fusing jazz, punk and dance music influences, Biting Tongues would release four albums over the 80s, the last of which saw them move to influential Manchester independent Factory Records. By this time Hollings and Sherwood had both departed, the latter going on to join Simply Red. Their replacements were Basil Clarke (vocals) and Phil Kirby (drums). The Factory album, accompanied by singles 'Trouble Hand' and 'Compressor', acted as a soundtrack to another Walmsley film (in addition there would be a full-scale video album in 1987, *Wall Of Surf*). However, as the 80s progressed Clarke and Kirby drifted off into the ranks of the increasingly successful Yargo, leaving the group's founding duo to return to work on video/soundtracks. A fifth album was aborted when their fifth record company, Cut Deep, collapsed. A final single, 'Love Out', was offerred, after which Massey moved on to 808 State, while Walmsley retured to full-time film and video pursuits, among his other engagements constructing visuals for his old partner's new outfit.

Albums: *Biting Tongues* (Situation 2 1982), *Libreville* (Paragon 1984), *Live It* (New Hormones 1985, cassette only), *Feverhouse* (Factory 1985), *Recharge* (Cut Deep 1990, unreleased).

Video: *Wall Of Surf* (1987).

Bivouac

Formed in Derby, England, this band consist of Paul Yeadon (vocals/guitar), Granville Marsden (bass) and Anthony Hodkinson (drums), who were inundated with acclaim in 1993 following a record company trawl to find the UK's answer to Nirvana. Particularly impressive were the early singles 'Bivouac', 'Slack' (1992) and 'Good Day Song' (1993). Support slots with Fugazi, Therapy? and Sugar, then a co-headlining tour with Jacob's Mouse, preceded the group's appearance at the Phoenix and Reading Festivals of 1993. Bivouac then toured Europe with the Jesus Lizard, who described them as 'the best goddam band in Britain'. In

Björk

1994 they consolidated their position in the US market with tours alongside Sup Pop Records' act Seaweed, while Keith York (ex-Doctor Phibes And The House Of Wax Equations) became the group's new drummer. A second album finally arrived in 1995, by which time much of the buzz surrounding the band had dissipated.

Albums: *Tuber* (Elemental 1993), *Full Size Boy* (Elemental/Geffen 1995).

Björk

b. Björk Gudmundsdóttir, 21 October 1966, Reykjavic, Iceland. The former Sugarcubes vocalist, armed with a remarkable, keening vocal presence, has crossed over to huge success via her club-orientated material. The success of *Debut* culminated in awards for Best International Newcomer and Best International Artist at the 1994 BRIT Awards. However, she had made her 'debut' proper as far back as 1977, with an album recorded in her native territory as an 11-year old prodigy (including covers of pop standards by the Beatles and others). It was only the start of a prodigious musical legacy. Her next recording outfit were Tappi Takarrass (which apparently translates as 'Cork that bitch's arse'), who recorded two albums between 1981 and 1983. A more high profile role was afforded via work with KUKL, who introduced her to future Sugarcubes Einar Örn and Siggi. The group's two albums were issued in the UK on the Crass imprint. Björk returned to Iceland after the Sugarcubes six year career, partially to pay off debts, recording a first solo album in 1990 backed by a local be-bop group. She re-emerged in 1993 with *Debut* and a welter of more house-orientated material, including four hit singles. These chiefly came to prominence in the dance charts (Björk having placed a first toe in those waters with 808 State on *Ex:El*) via their big name remixers. The most important of these were Underworld and Bassheads ('Human Behaviour'), Black Dog ('Venus As A Boy'), Tim Simenon of Bomb The Bass ('Play Dead', which was also used on the soundtrack to *The Young Americans* cinema release and featured a distinctive Jah Wobble bass hook) and David Morales, Justin Robertson and Fluke ('Big Time Sensuality'). Björk would appear at the 1993 BRIT Awards duetting with PJ Harvey, while in 1994 she would co-write the title-track to Madonna's album, *Bedtime Stories*.

Albums: *Björk* (Fàlkinn 1977), with Trió Gudmundar *Gling-Gló* (Smekkylesa 1990), *Debut* (One Little Indian 1993).

Videos: *Björk* (1994), *Vessel* (1994).

Black

Originally a three-piece pop outfit from Roby, near Liverpool, England, the group featured Colin Vearncombe (vocals), Dave Dickie (keyboards) and Jimmy Sangster (bass). Vearncombe was previously in the Epileptic Tits at the age of 16, playing punk covers. He then moved on to producing his own tapes until Dickie (ex-Last Chant), then Sangster formed a unit together. A previous incarnation had released 'Human Features' on a local label. Black's next base was the Liverpool independent record label Eternal, sponsored by Pete Wylie and Wah. However, Vearncombe's distinctive voice soon attracted the attention of WEA Records. Unfortunately, after the failure of two singles, 'Hey Presto' (written about existential novel, *The Dice Man*) and 'More Than The Sun', they dropped the band. Despite this setback, Black soon found themselves with an unexpected hit on their hands. Vearncombe was approached by two brothers after a gig who wanted to put one of the band's singles out on their Ugly Man label. That single was the seductive, bittersweet ballad, 'Wonderful Life', and after using a record plugger it was played regularly on the radio and took off in the independent charts. Its success attracted the attention of A&M Records, and the second single for the label, 'Sweetest Smile', gave them a Top 10 UK hit. Their debut album followed, though 1988's *Comedy* was the more impressive long player, highlighting Vearncombe's natural romanticism. A hiatus followed which allowed Vearncombe time for marriage and new material, before a third album, titled simply *Black*. Produced by Robin Millar, guest vocalists included Robert Palmer and Sam Brown. A single featuring the latter, 'Fly To The Moon', also boasted an ironic cover of Janet Jackson's 'Control'. *Are We Having Fun Yet?* continued in a similar vein but received little commercial reward.

Albums: *Wonderful Life* (A&M 1987), *Comedy* (A&M 1988), *Black* (A&M 1991), *Are We Having Fun Yet?* (A&M 1993).

Black Flag

Formed in 1977 in Los Angeles, California, Black Flag rose to become one of America's leading hardcore groups. The initial line-up - Keith Morris (vocals), Greg Ginn (guitar), Chuck Dukowski (bass) and Brian Migdol (drums) - completed the *Nervous Breakdown* EP in 1978, but the following year Morris left to form the Circle Jerks. Several members would join and leave before Henry Rollins (vocals), Dez Cadenza (guitar) and Robo (drums) joined Ginn and Dukowski for *Damaged*, the group's first full-length album. Originally scheduled for release by MCA Records, the company withdrew support, citing outrageous content, and the set appeared on the quintet's own label, SST Records. This prolific outlet has not only issued every subsequent Black Flag recording, but also has a catalogue including Hüsker Dü, Sonic Youth, the Minutemen, the Meat Puppets and Dinosaur Jr. Administered by Ginn and Dukowski, the latter of whom left the group to concentrate his efforts more fully, the company has become one of America's leading, and most influential, independents. Ginn continued to lead Black Flag in tandem with Rollins, and although its rhythm section was still subject to change, the music's power remained undiminished. Pivotal albums included *My War* and *In My Head* while their diversity was showcased on *Family Man*, which contrasted a side of Rollins' spoken word performances with four excellent instrumentals. However, the group split up in 1986 following the release of a compulsive live set, *Who's Got The 10 1/2?*, following which Ginn switched his attentions to labelmates Gone. Rollins went on to a succesful solo career. The glory days of Black Flag are warmly recalled in one of Rollins' numerous books for his 2.13.61. publishing empire, *Get In The Van*.

Albums: *Damaged* (SST 1981), *My War* (SST 1984), *Family Man* (SST 1984), *Slip It In* (SST 1984), *Live '84* (SST 1984, cassette only), *Loose Nut* (SST 1985), *The Process Of Weeding*

Out (SST 1985, instrumental mini-album), *In My Head* (SST 1985), *Who's Got The 10 1/2?* (SST 1986). Compilations: *Everything Went Black* (SST 1982, double album), *The First Four Years* (SST 1984), *Wasted...Again* (SST 1988).

Video: *Black Flag Live* (1984).

Further reading: *Get In The Van*, Henry Rollins (1994).

Black, Frank

b. Charles Francis Kitteridge III. This US vocalist/guitarist led the Boston-based Pixies under the name Black Francis. When that group underwent an acrimonious split in 1993, Francis embarked on a solo career as Frank Black. His self-titled debut featured assistance from Nick Vincent (drums) and Eric Drew Feldman (guitar/saxophone). The latter, formerly of Captain Beefheart's Magic Band, also produced the set which featured cameos from fellow Beefheart acolyte Jeff Morris Tepper and ex-Pixies guitarist Joey Santiago. *Frank Black* showed its creator's quirky grasp of pop, from the abrasive 'Los Angeles' to the melodic 'I Hear Ramona Sing'. It also contained a version of Brian Wilson's 'Hang On To Your Ego', which the Beach Boys' leader recast as 'I Know There's An Answer' on *Pet Sounds*. The song gave Black a rare UK hit single. A sprawling double set, *Teenager Of The Year*, ensued, but critical reaction suggested the artist had lost his incisive skills and a year later it was announced he had been dropped by 4AD Records.

Albums: *Frank Black* (4AD 1993), *Teenager Of The Year* (4AD 1994, double album).

Blake Babies

This trio from Boston, Massachusetts, USA, comprised Julianna Hatfield, John Strohm (guitar/vocals) and Freda Love (drums). As part of a succession of groups that emerged from a healthy rock scene in the Boston area in the late 80s/early 90s, Blake Babies were able to mature slowly, showing signs of a major breakthrough in early 1992. Their debut, *Nicely Nicely*, was released on the group's own Chewbud label and the follow up, the mini-album *Slow Learner*, on Billy Bragg's re-activated Utility imprint. Signed to the North Carolina Mammoth label, *Earwig* and *Sunburn* consolidated the praise garnered from the music press, often drawing comparisons with fellow Bostonians, the Lemonheads. Hatfield would enjoy a celebrated romance with Evan Dando of the Lemonheads, while Strohm had also briefly been a member during their *Creator* sessions. The release of the EP *Rosy Jack World*, coupled with sell-out dates on a UK visit early in 1992 promised a bright future for the group. However Hatfield turned solo, just as *Sunburn* began to attract rave reviews. On her departure Hatfield concluded: 'When Blake Babies was happening it was really romantic to sleep on floors and not have any money. But when I look back on it, I can't believe some of the stuff we did.' Strohm and Love, meanwhile, went on to form Antenna.

Albums: *Nicely Nicely* (Chewbud 1988), *Slow Learner* (Utility 1989, mini-album), *Earwig* (Mammoth 1989), *Sunburn* (Mammoth 1990).

Blameless

Formed in Sheffield, England, the indie band Blameless do not cite run of the mill influences. The Pixies and Velvet Underground are ignored in interviews in favour of Hall And Oates and Don McLean. 'We haven't got a chirpy cockney accent or bouncy numbers, we have good songs and genuine music.' Consisting of Jared Daley (vocals), Jason (bass) and Jon (drums), they nevertheless maintain a musical intensity that distinguishes them from the recordings of heroes such as the Police. They first came to the attention of the UK press when they released 'Signs' for the Rough Trade Records singles club. China Records A&R man Paul Weighell remembered their first gig at the Falcon as 'like an A&R convention'. This was primarily caused by the circulation of strong demo-tapes. They made their debut for China with 'Town Clowns', before 'Don't Say You're Sorry' in February 1995. These and the debut album were produced in Boston by American Paul Q. Kolderie, who had previously worked with Dinosaur Jr, Hole and Radiohead. Daley later said, 'When China said we were going to Boston, we thought they meant Boston, Lincolnshire.' In the wake of its release came comparisons to everybody from Pearl Jam to the Wonder Stuff, the music covering a wide territory from fast indie rock to balladeering.

Album: *The Signs Were All There* (China 1995).

Blasters

Formed in Los Angeles, California, USA, in 1979, the Blasters were one of the leading proponents of the so-called US 'roots-rock' revival of the 80s. Originally comprising Phil Alvin (vocals), his songwriter brother Dave (guitar), John Bazz (bass) and Bill Bateman (drums), the group's first album in 1980 was *American Music* on the small Rollin' Rock label. Incorporating rockabilly, R&B, country and blues, the album was critically applauded for both Dave Alvin's songwriting and the band's ability to update the age-old styles without slavishly re-creating them. With a switch to the higher-profile Slash label in 1981, the group released a self-titled album which was also well-received. Pianist Gene Taylor was added to the line-up and 50s saxophonist Lee Allen guested (and later toured with the group). With Slash picking up distribution from Warner Brothers the album reached the Top 40, due largely to good reviews. (Three later albums would chart at lower positions.) A live EP recorded in London followed in 1982 but it was the following year's *Non Fiction*, a thematic study of the working class that critics likened to Bruce Springsteen and Tom T. Hall, which earned the band its greatest acclaim so far. By this time saxophonist Steve Berlin had also joined the fold. Berlin then joined Los Lobos when *Hard Line*, was issued in 1985. The album included a song by John Cougar Mellencamp and guest backing vocals by the Jordanaires. Dave Alvin departed the group upon its completion to join X and was replaced by Hollywood Fats, who died of a heart attack at the age of 32 while a member of the band. Phil Alvin and Steve Berlin kept a version of the group together until 1987 at which point it folded. Both Alvin brothers have recorded solo albums and worked on other projects.

Albums: *American Music* (Rollin' Rock 1980), *The Blasters* (Slash 1981), *Non Fiction* (Slash 1983), *Hard Line* (Slash 1985). Compilation: *The Blasters Collection* (Slash 1991).

Bleach

Bleach

Brothers Neil (b. 14 September 1965, Ipswich, Suffolk, England; guitar) and Nick Singleton (b. 2 February 1968, Ipswich, Suffolk, England; bass) acted as catalysts for Bleach when, in July 1989, they were joined by Steve Scott (b. 29 November 1963, Norwich, Norfolk, England; drums) and the initially reluctant vocalist, Salli Carson (b. 6 October 1966, Yorkshire, England). Within a year they had made their mark with the EP *Eclipse* - so called because it was actually recorded during an eclipse of the sun - on which their original twisted, spikey guitar sound was praised by the national music press. The follow-up EP, *Snag*, was also acclaimed, with the track 'Dipping' particularly singled out for praise. Tours of the Uk warranted a compilation of the singles to continue the momentum. However, Bleach soon found themselves swimming against the tide in the UK indie press. Critics turned their attention towards the nascent 'shoegazing' bands in preference to Bleach's more strident tones, and singer Carson shaved her head in an attempt to deflect accusations that she was a mere sex symbol.
Albums: *Killing Time* (Musidisc 1992), *Hard* (Musidisc 1993, mini-album), *Fast* (Musidisc 1993). Compilation: *Bleach* (Way Cool 1991).

Blegvad, Peter

b. 1951, New York City, New York, USA. Blegvad is a playful and witty songwriter and singer who has built up a cult following in the UK and the USA. Moving to England in the early 70s, he formed Slapp Happy with singer Dagmar Krause and keyboard player Anthony Moore. Described by one critic as a 'mutant cabaret group', they made two albums for Virgin Records and two more with *avant garde* band Henry Cow. When that group split in 1977, Blegvad worked briefly with the Art Bears before returning to New York. There he performed with John Zorn, the Ambitious Lovers and from 1985-87, Anton Fier's 'supergroup', the Golden Palaminos. Blegvad's solo recording career began in the mid-80s, when he made two albums for Virgin, with Andy Partridge of XTC producing *The Naked Shakespeare*. Previously he had recorded for the same label in 1977 in tandem with John Greaves. After making *Downtime* for *avant garde* label Recommended, Blegvad signed to Silvertone Records where Palaminos colleague Chris Blamey co-produced *King Strut*. Guest artists on the album included Syd Straw (vocals) and Danny Thompson (bass). Blegvad also began to contribute a weekly cartoon strip to the London newspaper *The Independent On Sunday*, entitled *Leviathan,* which displayed the same world-weary wit as his songwriting.
Albums: with John Greaves *Kew. Rhone* (Virgin 1977), *The Naked Shakespeare* (Virgin 1983), *Knights Like This* (Virgin 1985), *Downtime* (Recommended 1988), *King Strut & Other Stories* (Silvertone 1991).

Blind Melon

US pop-rock vehicle comprising Glen Graham (b. Columbus, Mississippi, USA; drums), Shannon Hoon (b. Lafayette, Indiana, USA; vocals), Rogers Stevens (b. West Point, Mississippi, USA; guitar), Christopher Thorn (b. Dover, Pennsylvania, USA; guitar) and Brad Smith (b. West Point, Mississippi, USA; bass) who broke big in 1993. One of their major claims to fame was introducing the phenomenon of the 'bee girl'. Back in their home base of Columbus, Mississippi, Graham was passing round a snap of his sister, Georgia, appearing in a school play. The band elected to use the shot, which presented young Georgia as an awkward, publicity shy youngster adorned in a bee-suit, on their debut album. The image would also re-appear on the video of their second single, 'No Rain', in June 1992. Directed by Sam Bayer (responsible for Nirvana's 'Smells Like Teen Spirit'), the Bee Girl was portrayed by 10 year old Heather DeLoach. MTV pushed the clip relentlessly, helping to boost the fortunes of their album. The young girl became a huge cult icon, beloved of sundry rock stars including Madonna, while Blind Melon profited greatly from their association with her. Their album had been shipped for several months and was languishing outside the US charts, but it soon re-entered and went on to strike number 3. However, success had not been as instantaneous as many assumed. Smith had long been a dedicated musician, playing drums, baritone saxophone and guitar, the last of which he taught to Stevens. The two left Columbus in 1989 for Los Angeles, where they met first Hoon, a small-town mischief maker who had left his sporting ambitions behind when he got into the drug scene, and Thorn, who had formerly played in a local heavy metal band, R.O.T. Together they scoured Hollywood for a drummer who did not reflect the LA metal scene's flashy overtones, and found fellow Mississippi refugee Graham. A demo tape was recorded, and, without their consent, circulated to the major record companies, who began queuing up for their services. This despite the fact that they had an armoury of just five songs. It was Atlantic Records who eventually grabbed their signatures. They were put to work in a LA studio, but were distracted by the presence of Hoon's old Indiana friend, Axl Rose, who was recording *Use Your Illusion* with Guns N'Roses. Hoon was invited to add backing vocals, and appeared in the video to 'Don't Cry'. After a support tour to Soundgarden the group relocated to Durham, North Carolina to find space and time to finish writing their debut set, before hooking up with producer Rick Parashar in Seattle. Afterwards events overtook them, and by November 1993 *Rolling Stone* magazine was parading them, naked, on their cover.
Album: *Blind Melon* (Capitol 1993).

Blondie

Blondie was formed in New York City in 1974 when Deborah Harry (b. 1 July 1945, Miami, Florida, USA; vocals), Chris Stein (b. 5 January 1950, Brooklyn, New York, USA; guitar), Fred Smith (bass) and Bill O'Connor (drums) abandoned the revivalist Stilettos for an independent musical direction. Backing vocalists Julie and Jackie, then Tish and Snookie, augmented the new group's early line-up, but progress was undermined by the departure of Smith for Television and the loss of O'Connor. Newcomers James Destri (b. 13 April 1954; keyboards), Gary Valentine (bass) and Clement Burke (b. 24 November 1955, New York, USA; drums) joined Harry and Stein in a reshaped unit which secured a recording deal through the aegis of producer

Blind Melon

Richard Gottehrer. Originally released on the Private Stock label, *Blondie* was indebted to both contemporary punk and 60s' girl groups, adeptly combining melody with purpose. Although not a runaway commercial success, the album did engender interest, particularly in the UK, where the group became highly popular. Internal disputes resulted in the departure of Gary Valentine, but the arrival of Frank Infante (guitar) and Nigel Harrison (b. Princes Risborough, Buckinghamshire, England; bass) triggered the group's most consistant period. Having freed themselves from the restrictions of Private Stock and signed to Chrysalis Records, *Plastic Letters* contained two UK Top 10 hits in 'Denis' and '(I'm Always Touched By Your) Presence Dear' while *Parallel Lines*, produced by pop svengali Mike Chapman, included the UK chart-topping 'Heart Of Glass' and 'Sunday Girl' (both 1979 yet the latter did not even chart in the USA). Although creatively uneven, *Eat To The Beat* confirmed Blondie's dalliance with disco following 'Heart Of Glass' and the set spawned two highly-successful singles in 'Union City Blue' and 'Atomic. A Further hit 'Call Me' was culled from the soundtrack of *American Gigolo* and produced by Giorgio Moroder, it reached number 1 in both the UK and USA. *Autoamerican* provided two further US chart toppers in 'The Tide Is High' and 'Rapture' while the former song, originally recorded by reggae group the Paragons, reached the same position in Britain. However, despite this commercial ascendancy, Blondie was beset by internal difficulties as the media increasingly focused on their photogenic lead singer.

The distinction between the group's name and Harry's persona became increasingly blurred, although a sense of distance between the two was created with the release of her solo album, *Koo Koo*. *The Hunter*, a generally disappointing set which Debbie completed under duress, became Blondie's final recording, their tenure ending when Stein's ill-health brought an attendant tour to a premature end. The guitarist was suffering from the genetic disease pemphigus and between 1983 and 1985, both he and Debbie Harry absented themselves from full-time performing. The latter then resumed her solo career, while former colleague Burke joined the Eurythmics.

Albums: *Blondie* (Private Stock 1976), *Plastic Letters* (Chrysalis 1978), *Parallel Lines* (Chrysalis 1978), *Eat To The Beat* (Chrysalis 1979), *Autoamerican* (Chrysalis 1980), *The Hunter* (Chrysalis 1982). Compilations: *The Best Of Blondie* (Chrysalis 1981), *Once More Into The Bleach* (Chrysalis 1988, contains remixes and rare cuts), *The Complete Picture - The Very Best Of Deborah Harry And Blondie* (Chrysalis 1991)

Videos: *Blondie-Live* (1986), *Eat To The Beat* (1988), *Best Of Blondie* (1988).

Blood On The Saddle

This Los Angeles group was a leading light of the city's 'cowpunk' movement of the mid-80s, which blended elements of country, rockabilly and US hardcore. Greg Davis (guitar/vocals), Ron Botelho (bass) and Hermann Senac (drums/vocals) founded the unit in April 1983, but within months the line-up had been augmented by Annette Zilinkas (vocals), formerly of the Bangles. The acclaimed *Blood On The Saddle* was released the following year, but critical approbation was not matched by commercial success. A second set, *Poison Love*, was undermined by low-key distribution, but *Fresh Blood*, issued by the influential SST label, achieved a much higher profile. The album confirmed the group's energetic style, but persistent public indifference has undermined early confidence.

Albums: *Blood On The Saddle* (New Alliance 1984), *Poison Love* (Chameleon 1986), *Fresh Blood* (SST 1987).

Blood Sausage

The excruciatingly titled UK band Blood Sausage consist of Dale Shaw (vocals/guitar), A.J.W. Bourton (guitar/bass/flute/keyboards), Owen Thomas (guitar/percussion), Jo Johnson (bass/drums) and Niki Elliot (drums). Signed to Wiiija Records, the group earned its reputation supporting Cornershop on dates throughout 1993. Each member, however has additional interests outside Blood Sausage. Shaw draws his own comic, *Dipper*, Bourton and Thomas play in surf instrumental band Cee Bee Beaumont (who have released records on Hangman, the record label run by Billy Childish); Johnson and Elliot are both members of Huggy Bear. The quintet recorded their debut 10-inch album at Toe Rag Studios in the East End of London using original 50s and 60s recording and mixing equipment, recording 15 tracks in just two days. It followed the group's debut EP, *Touching You In Ways That Don't Feel Comfortable*, which was Single Of The Week in the *New Musical Express*. The band continued its exploration of controversial issues on their album with songs such as 'Fucking A Junkie Without A Condom and 'Bill Joel', a jibe at Dale's former hero, plus a deranged and lyrically 'improved' version of 'Have Love Will Travel', with Elliot on vocals.

Album: *Happy Little Bullshit Boy* (Wiiija 1993).

Blue Aeroplanes

Since forming in Bristol, England, in the early 80s, the Blue Aeroplanes have had endless line-up changes, but maintained their original aim, a desire to mix rock and beat poetry and to involve a large number of musicians in an almost communal manner. The nucleus of the band has always revolved around deadpan vocalist Gerard Langley, his brother John (drums/percussion), Nick Jacobs (guitar), Dave Chapman (multi-instrumentalist) and dancer Wojtek Dmochowski. Along the way, individuals such as Angelo Bruschini (guitar/bass/organ), John Stapleton (tapes), Ruth Coltrane (bass/mandolin), Ian Kearey (guitar/banjimer/harmonium), Rodney Allen (guitar), Simon Heathfield (bass) and Caroline Halcrow (guitar - who later left to pursue a solo career as Caroline Trettine) have all contributed to the Aeroplanes' melting pot. After a debut album for the Abstract label, *Bop Art*, in April 1984, the band signed with the fledgling Fire Records. Several well-received EPs followed - *Action Painting And Other Original Works* (1985), *Lover And Confidante And Other Stories Of Travel* and *Religion And Heartbreak* (March, 1986) -

succeeded by their second album, *Tolerance* (October 1986). The Aeroplanes' third set, *Spitting Out Miracles*, surfaced in 1987. All were characterized by Langley's monotone verse and a deluge of instruments and sounds hinged around the guitar. 'Veils Of Colour' (1988) coincided with the release of *Night Tracks*, their February 1987 session for BBC Radio disc jockey, Janice Long. A double album, *Friendloverplane*, neatly concluded their time with Fire, compiling the Aeroplanes' progress to date. It was not until the start of the new decade that, following a stint supporting R.E.M. in the UK, the band re-emerged on the Ensign label with 'Jacket Hangs' in January 1990 and a new album, *Swagger*, the following month. Both suggested a more direct, straightforward approach, and this was confirmed on the EP *And Stones*. In 1991, an eight-strong line-up now comprising; Langley, Bruschini, Dmochowski, Allen, Paul Mulreany (drums - a former member of the Jazz Butcher), Andy McCreeth, Hazel Winter and Robin Key, released the roundly-acclaimed *Beatsongs*, co-produced by Elvis Costello and Larry Hirsch. Further activity in 1994 indicated a major push forward with that year's album for new home Beggars Banquet Records. *Life Model* sounded as fresh as the band ever has and engendered further press acclaim, and featured new recruits Marcus Williams (bass; ex-Mighty Lemon Drops), Susie Hugg (vocals; ex-Katydids).

Albums: *Bop Art* (Abstract 1984), *Tolerance* (Fire 1986), *Spitting Out Miracles* (Fire 1987), *Swagger* (Ensign 1990), *Beatsongs* (Ensign 1991), *Life Model* (Beggars Banquet 1994). Compilations: *Friendloverplane* (Fire 1988), *Friendloverplane 2* (Ensign 1992).

Blue Nile

The Blue Nile formed in Glasgow, Scotland in 1981 and consist of Paul Buchanan (b. Glasgow, Scotland; vocals/guitar/synthesizers), Robert Bell (b. Glasgow, Scotland; synthesizers) and Paul Joseph Moore (b. Glasgow, Scotland; piano/synthesizers). Their debut single, 'I Love This Life', was recorded independently and subsequently picked up on by RSO Records, which promptly folded. Eventually, their demo-tapes found their way to hi-fi specialists Linn Products, so the company could test various types of music at their new cutting plant. In spite of their lack of experience in the record retail market, Linn immediately signed the band to make 'A Walk Across The Rooftops', which came out in 1984 to considerable praise. Suddenly, thanks to some gently emotive synthetics and an overall mood which seemed to revel in nocturnal atmospherics, the unsuspecting trio were thrust into the limelight. Blue Nile pondered over the reasons for their success and, as a consequence, found themselves incapable of repeating the feats of the first album. Indeed, it was to be five years before the follow up, *Hats*, finally continued the shimmering legacy of its predecessor, whereupon the studio-bound collective took their first tentative steps into the live arena with enthusiastically-received shows in the USA and Britain before returning to the studio for another anticipated lengthy recording period. Another hold-up was caused by contractual difficulties with Linn and Virgin Records ('It's amazing how you can be generating fantastically small amounts of money and still have fantastically complicated

scenarios.'). In the 90s the band journeyed to California to record backing vocals for Julian Lennon, eventually working with Robbie Robertson and several others. They also signed a new contract with Warner Brothers Records in 1993, and by 1995 stated they had a large stockpile of songs written in the interim to draw upon.

Albums: *A Walk Across The Rooftops* (Linn/Virgin 1984), *Hats* (Linn/Virgin 1989).

Blue Orchids

This experimental pop group were a spin-off from the Manchester band the Fall. Una Baines (keyboards/vocals) and Martin Bramah (guitar/vocals) both found themselves outcasts from that band as the 80s dawned. They put together the Blue Orchids with Rick Goldstar (guitar), Steve Toyne (bass), and Joe Kin (drums), producing a sound that echoed the less esoteric moments of their former employer. Lyrics were usually spoken or half-sung, leaving a sinister and enticing set of songs which deserved a wider audience. These included their debut single 'The Flood', after which Ian Rogers became the first in a succession of drumming replacements. After the follow-up 'Work', the band embarked on a debut album. Toyne had left, leaving Bramah to fill in on bass, as their third drummer 'Toby' (ex-Ed Banger And The Nosebleeds) came into the line-up. *The Greatest Hit (Money Mountain)* was as ambitious and slightly flawed. Mark Hellyer filled the vacant bass position, while Goldstraw departed, leaving Bramah to handle guitar duties on his own. 'Agents Of Chance' was the final Blue Orchids release for some time, before they returned with one 12-inch single, 'Sleepy Town', in 1985. Nick Marshall (drums) was the back-up to Baines and Bramah this time, on an effort produced by another ex-Fall man, Tony Friel. Bramah moved on to Thirst, working, inevitably, with another Fall emigrate, Karl Burns. He would finally return to the Fall fold in 1989 to complete the cycle. However, the Blue Orchids reformed once more in 1991 with a single, 'Diamond Age', and the retrospective *A View From The City*. Contained among other forgotten period classics is 'Bad Education', better known for the cover treatment given it by Aztec Camera. The new line-up featured Bramah, Craig Gannon (ex-Bluebells and Smiths; guitar), Martin Hennin (bass), and Dick Harrison (drums). Baines, Bramah's now ex-wife, had departed. His new girlfriend was the Fall keyboard player Marcia Schofield who made a guest appearance on 'Diamond Age'. The Blue Orchids influence continues to be felt in the revival of the hammond organ sound, especially on the records of bands such as the Inspiral Carpets (who once asked Bramah to join as singer).

Albums: *The Greatest Hit (Money Mountain)* (Rough Trade 1982), *A View From The City* (Rough Trade 1991).

Bluebells

This Scottish quintet were formed in 1982, and originally comprised brothers David McCluskey (b. 13 January 1964; drums) and Ken McCluskey (b. 8 February 1962; vocals/harmonica), plus Robert 'Bobby Bluebell' Hodgens (b. 6 June 1959; vocals/guitar), Russell Irvine (guitar) and Lawrence Donegan (bass). The latter two were later replaced, respectively, by Craig Gannon (b. 30 July 1966) and Neal

Baldwin. The group were fine exponents of the 'jangly pop' being by Scottish bands such as Orange Juice and Aztec Camera. Despite strong airplay on British radio, the inexplicable failure of 'Cath' to rise any further than number 62 in the UK chart in 1983 perplexed critics and fans, as did the similar fate that befell 'Sugar Bridge' in the same year. The Bluebells did at last gain their deserved success in 1984 with the number 11 hit, 'I'm Falling', and 'Young At Heart' (co-written by Siobhan Fahey of Bananarama/Shakespears Sister) which breached the UK Top 10, while their solitary album for London Records achieved Top 30 status. Riding on the wave of this success, a re-issued 'Cath'/'She Will Always Be Waiting' belatedly hit the Top 40. After splitting, siblings Ken and David formed the McCluskey Brothers, releasing an album, *Aware Of All*, while Bobby formed Up and later worked with Paul Quinn (ex-Bourgie Bourgie). Craig Gannon stood-in, briefly, for the Smiths' bassist Andy Rourke, who was having drug problems, then on Rouke's return, Gannon continued with the Smiths as second guitarist, subsequently joining the Adult Net. In 1993 Volkswagen used 'Young At Heart' in one of their television advertisements. The song re-entered the UK charts in April, reaching number 1 and staying there for a month. However, the group promised 'not to outstay their welcome', with the McCluskey brothers returning to folk singing (releasing a new album, *Favourite Colours*). Bobby Bluebell was to be found in Bob's, his Glasgow house/hip hop club, while Russel Irvine had become a chef, but returned for their appearances on *Top Of The Pops*, replacing Donegan. The Bluebells' former bass player was ejected after a previous apearance on the programme, when he used the opportunity to write an exposé of the show for the *Guardian* newspaper.

Albums: *Sisters* (London 1984), *Bloomin' Live* (London 1993). Compilations: *Second* (London 1992, early, previously unreleased recordings), *The Singles Collection* (London 1993).

Video: *The Bluebells* (1989).

Blues Traveler

New York, USA blues-rock quartet, Blues Traveler are led by singer and harmonica player John Popper (b. 1967, Cleveland, Ohio, USA). Some of the interest in the band in the mid-90s arose from the fact that Popper was a close friend of Eric Shenkman and Chris Barron, putting the pair, who subsequently formed the Spin Doctors, in touch with each other. Just like that band and another set of friends, Phish, Blues Traveler share an appetite for extended jams, and at their best the spontaneous musicianship that flows through their live sets can be inspired. Popper first sought to play harmonica after being inspired by the film the *Blues Brothers*, while at school in Connecticut. He initially intended to become a comedian; his physical appearance has caused many reviewers compare him with the larger-than-life actor John Belushi. The band were befriended at an early stage by Blues Brother keyboard player Paul Shaffer, who since his five minutes of celluloid fame had become band leader and arranger for the David Letterman show. Letterman's sponsorship of the band stretched to over a dozen appearances in their first four years of existence, and was paramount in establishing their no-nonsense appeal.

Blur

When Popper moved to Princeton, New Jersey, to attend high school, he met drummer Brendan Hill, the duo calling themselves 'The Blues Band' by 1985. They were eventually joined by the younger, sports-orientated guitarist Chan Kinchla until a knee injury cut short that career. He moved instead to New York, with Hill and Popper. Bass player Bobby Sheehan joined in 1987. Playing low-key gigs at Nightingale's in the East Village, they eventually honed their organic rock into something a little more structured, changing their name to Blues Traveler at the end of the 80s. Recording and selling demo tapes at gigs eventually brought a high profile visitor to one of their gigs, Bill Graham. Through his influence they found themselves on bills with the Allman Brothers and Carlos Santana. Interest from A&M Records followed and the band recorded their debut at the end of 1989, for release early in the following year. The appearances on *Letterman* followed as part of a large promotional push which included over 800 gigs in three years. The only setback came in autumn 1992 when Popper was involved in a motorcycle accident which left him with major injuries. *Save His Soul*'s release was consequently delayed, but the incident necessitated a long hiatus from live touring, until he took the stage again in April 1993 in a wheelchair. He continued in this vein for a second H.O.R.D.E. tour (Horizons of Rock Developing Everywhere), an alternative to the Lollapalooza events, with Big Head Todd And The Monsters among others. A third stint was later undertaken with the Allman Brothers Band, Chuck Leavell of whom joined Paul Shaffer in contributing to *Four*. The group then appeared at Woodstock '94, but, true to form, they were unable to stay the whole weekend because of gig commitments elsewhere.

Albums: *Blues Traveler* (A&M 1990), *Travelers And Thieves* (A&M 1991), *On Tour Forever* (A&M 1992, bonus disc given away free with copies of *Travelers And Thieves*), *Save His Soul* (A&M 1993), *Four* (A&M 1994).

Blur

'When our third album comes out our position as the quintessential English band of the 90s will be assured.' A typical bullish statement which could have been made by any number of UK indie bands in 1990 - but from the mouth of Damon Albarn of Blur it amounts to prophecy. Blur were formed in London while Albarn (b. 23 March 1968, Whitechapel, London, England; vocals), Alex James (b. 21 November 1968, Bournemouth, Dorset, England; bass) and Graham Coxon (b. 12 March 1969, Rinteln, Hannover, West Germany; guitar) were studying at Goldsmith's College. Coxon had first seen Albarn when he played a debut solo gig at Colchester Arts Centre in 1988. Also in that audience was future Blur drummer Dave Rowntree (b. 8 May 1964, Colchester, Essex, England). Albarn's desire to make music was encouraged by his father, who moved in circles which exposed his son to artists such as Soft Machine and Cat Stevens, while his mother was a stage designer for Joan Littlewood's theatre company at Stratford. Rowntree's father was sound-engineer for the Beatles at the BBC, and had taken lessons on the bagpipes. When the four members convened in London (the first person James saw in halls of residence at Guildhall was Coxon) they formed a band -

initially entitled Seymour - and started out on the lower rungs of the gig circuit by playing bottom of the bill to New Fast Automatic Daffodils and Too Much Texas at Camden's Dingwalls venue. A year and a dozen gigs later, the quartet had signed to Food Records, run by ex-Teardrop Explodes keyboard player David Balfe and *Sounds* journalist Andy Ross, whose suggestion it was that they change their name to Blur. They earned a reputation with venue promoters for haphazardly implemented onstage stunts. Playing vibrant 90s-friendly pop with a sharp cutting edge, Blur's debut release, 'She's So High', which had initially got Seymour signed when included on their first demo tape, sneaked into the Top 50 of the UK chart. With the band displaying a justifiably breezy confidence in their abilities, there was little surprise when the infectious 'There's No Other Way' reached number 8 in the UK charts in the spring of 1991. This success continued when *Leisure* entered the UK charts at number 2 - a mere two years after formation. However, a relatively fallow period followed when 'Popscene' failed to rise above number 34 in the UK charts. As the 'baggy' and 'Madchester' movements died, the band were viewed with the same hostility which now greeted bands like Rain or the Mock Turtles as audiences looked away from the Byrds-fixated guitar pop of the period. Blur seemed set to disappear with the same alacrity with which they had conjured themselves, though their names were kept alive in press columns by their 'expert liggers' status. *Modern Life Is Rubbish* was presented to their record company at the end of 1992 but rejected, Balfe insisting that Albarn go away and write at least two more tracks. The resultant songs, 'For Tomorrow' and 'Chemical World', were the album's singles. When it finally emerged in 1993 its sales profile of 50,000 copies failed to match that of its predecessor or expectations, but touring and a strong headlining appearance at the Reading Festival rebuilt confidence. The 'new' model Blur was waiting in the wings, and saw fruition in March 1994 with the release of 'Girls & Boys', the first single from what was to prove the epoch-making *Park Life* album. This set wantonly upturned musical expectations, borrowing liberally from every great British institution from the Beatles, the Small Faces and the Kinks to the Jam and Madness topped off by Albarn's knowing, Cockney delivery. At last there seemed to be genuine substance to the band's more excessive claims. With the entire music media their friends again, Blur consolidated with a live spectacular in front of 8,000 fans at London's Alexandra Palace, while the album gained a Mercury Prize nomination and they went on to secure four trophies, including Best Band and Album, at the 1995 BRIT Awards.

Albums: *Leisure* (Food 1991), *Modern Life Is Rubbish* (Food 1993), *Park Life* (Food 1994).

Videos: *Star Shaped* (1993), *Showtime* (1995).

Further reading: *An Illustrated Biography*, Linda Holorney (1995).

Blurt

Poet Ted Milton formed this indie rock group in the early 80s, featuring his voice and alto saxophone, his brother Jake on drums and Pete Creese's guitar. England's 'No Wave' never got the attention it deserved, but Blurt's art-rock-plus-punk-rock had a certain charm. The band made their debut with the memorable 1980 single, 'My Mother Was A Friend Of The Enemy Of The People', going on to record a number of albums which mixed subversive lyrics with musical clatter and squeal. Milton has also recorded as a solo artist. Not since Lora Logic has the saxophone spoken so articulately in rock music.

Albums: *In Berlin* (Ruby 1981), B*lurt* (Red Flame 1982), *Bullets For You* (Devine 1984), *Friday The 12th* (Another Side 1985), *Poppycock* (Toeblock 1986), *Smoke Time* (Moving Target 1987), *Kenny Rogers' Greatest Hit (Take 2)* (Toeblock 1989), *The Body Live!* (Heute 1989). Videos: *Live At The Subs* (1990).

Blyth Power

The driving force behind this collection of post-punk train spotters (their name derives from the name of a steam engine) is drummer, lead singer and songwriter Josef Porta (b. 21 February 1962, Templecombe, Somerset, England). He had previously worked with a variety of bands; Valley Forge - while in Somerset in 1978, and on moving to London in 1979, Attitudes and the Entire Cosmos which was primarily made up from the road-crew of Here And Now. After brief stints joining and recording with Zounds, Null And Void and the Mob, Porta formed Blyth Power in 1983 with Curtis Youé. Porta's eloquent lyrics, coupled with a punk-influenced mixture of folk and rock drew analogies from England's history, such as Watt Tyler and Oliver Cromwell's army, to the state of present day politics, in particular a resistance to the Conservative government. His attacks on the ruination of the common man's right to English heritage have endeared them to an audience of kindred spirits, though this has been no exercise in austerity - Porta being just as likely to document the rise and fall of a cricket match as a government's fortunes.

Albums: *A Little Touch Of Harry In The Middle Of The Night* (96 Tapes 1984, cassette only), *Wicked Women, Wicked Men And Wicket Keepers* (Midnight 1986), *The Barman And Other Stories* (Midnight 1988), *Alnwick And Tyne* (Midnight 1990), *The Guns Of Castle Cary* (1991), *Pastor Skull* (1993). Compilation: *Pont Au-Dessus De La Brue* (1988).

BMX Bandits

Formed in Bellshill, Lanarkshire, Scotland in 1985, this idiosyncratic group revolves around Duglas Stewart, ex-Faith Healers and Pretty Flowers. Stewart chose the name 'BMX Bandits' because he assumed the band would last for one gig, but it quickly became one of the prime components of the 'anorak' or 'C86' movement. Yet despite an early, naive image - Stewart sometimes passed sweets out to his audience - the singer has proved himself a wry lyricist, akin to idol Jonathan Richman. The group's debut single, 'E102', was issued on 53rd & 3rd in 1986. Sean Dickson (keyboards), Jim McCulloch (guitar), Billy Wood (vocals) and Willie McArdle (drums) joined Stewart for this release, although within months, the first of a host of line-up changes was underway. Dickson formed the Soup Dragons, which McCulloch later joined and the Bandits were buoyed by the arrival of Joe McAlinden (vocals/guitar/saxophone) and Norman Blake (ex-Faith Healers, guitar/vocals). Both

musicians were involved in another band, the Boy Hairdressers, but were part of the reshaped line-up featured on *C-86*, mischievously dubbed so by Stewart when his group was denied a spot on the compilation tape of that name. Gordon Keen (guitar) and Francis MacDonald (drums) completed the 'new' Bandits which was aurally moving away from its early, jejune sound. Eugene Kelly (ex-Vaselines) joined the quintet for *Star Wars*, issued by a label based in Japan where the Bandits enjoyed a cult following. It showed the group's increased musical maturity although individual commitments to other projects defied convention. Blake found success with Teenage Fanclub, McAlinden had formed Superstar while Kelly and Keen forged Captain America, later known as Eugenius. The Bandits joined Creation Records in 1993, but attendant publicity announced that the last-named pair would no longer feature in the band. *Life Goes On* was another excellent set, buoyed by the inclusion of the memorable 'Serious Drugs'. The Bandits supported southern soul singer/songwriter Dan Penn on a rare live appearance prior to completing *Gettin' Dirty*. By this point a new line-up of Stewart, MacDonald, Finlay MacDonald John Hogarty and Sishil K. Dade (ex-Soup Dragons) had emerged. 'It's the first time the BMX Bandits have been a group, rather than friends backing me,' Duglas opined. The results were their finest album to date.

Albums: *C-86* (1990), *A Totally Groovy Live Experience* (Avalanche 1990) *Star Wars* (Vinyl Japan 1992), *Gordon Keen And His BMX Bandits* (Sunflower 1992, mini-album), *Life Goes On* (Creation 1994), *Gettin' Dirty* (Creation 1995). Compilation: *C-86 Plus* (Vinyl Japan 1992).

Bob

Formed in north London, UK, in 1986 by Richard Blackborow (b. 21 March 1966, Hackney, London, England), Simon Armstrong (b. 12 February 1966, Hull, Humberside, England), Jem Morris (b. Aberdare, South Wales; bass) and a drum machine, Bob were always destined to become an archetypal 'indie' pop band. Their first release was on flexi disc only, laying the ground rules for a series of small-scale single releases and British tours to build a passionate following in the provinces. Gary Connors (b. London, England) replaced the drum machine in 1988, only to soon make way for Dean Leggett (b. 30 August 1963), who had previously drummed for Jamie Wednesday (soon to become Carter USM). With solid support from influential BBC disc jockey John Peel and a healthy selection of earnest, old-fashioned guitar-based tunes such as 'Convenience', Bob ploughed an individualistic furrow around the outskirts of the music business, surviving another line-up alteration when Morris was replaced by the bassist from the Caretaker Race, Stephen Hersom (b. 28 April 1963, Plaistow, London, England). Perhaps fittingly after such a determined career, when Bob finally got round to making an album after five years the record's commercial potential was undermined by the collapse of the Rough Trade Records distribution system. Yet, far from being damaged by the experience, this disaster merely seemed to strengthen Bob's idiosyncratic resolve.

Album: *Leave The Straight Life Behind* (Rough Trade 1991). Compilation: *Swag Sack* (Rough Trade 1989).

Bobs

Not the San Francisco-based *a cappella* group of the same name, this version of the Bobs hailed from Fort Lauderdale and was led by vocalist/bass player Bob Rupe. Specialising in hard-edged pop with reggae, jazz and funk interludes, their style was first unveiled on a self-titled mini-album for Safety Net Records in 1983 (though it was recorded two years previously). Songs like 'Sounds Of People (Eating)' reminded some reviewers of Talking Heads, others suggesting British pop reference points like XTC. When the track-listing was expanded by one to seven for the follow-up collection, it was with a new three-piece line-up, with Rupe again the unifying factor. The group's satire on American society's underbelly was further refined with improved instrumentation, including pedal steel for the country pastiche, 'The Beer Belly'. Rupe subsequently joined New York country-rock conglomeration the Silos.
Albums: *The Bobs* (Safety Net 1983, mini-album), *White Gazebo* (Safety Net 1984, mini-album).

Bodines

This UK rock/pop combo achieved a degree of critical success in the mid to late 80s, principally, and unjustly, through their connections with the fashionable Creation Records label. The band's line-up featured: lyricist Mike Ryan (vocals), Paul Brotherton (guitar), Tim Burtonwood (bass) and John Rowland (drums). Ryan and Rowland were schoolfriends from Glossop, while Brotherton grew up in Salford. The band was put together while its members were unemployed. Their first demo tape included raw versions of songs which would surface later, and Alan McGee at Creation decided he was interested. They became the youngest band to play the Factory Funhouse (at the Hacienda, Manchester), and two singles on Creation, 'God Bless' and 'Therese', produced by Ian Broudie (Lightning Seeds), were impressive. However, they soon moved on when record sales failed to follow their good press. Subsequent singles 'Skankin' Queen' and 'Slip Slide' were undeservedly ignored, though their debut album was critically revered: 'Mick Ryan ... is not going suddenly to sing songs about being happy; he's still stuck with betrayal, guilt and worry, but these feelings aren't smothered in some wet blanket, they're distilled into a crystal glass.' By this time they employed a brass section (Graham Lambyekski and Nelson Pandela), but when new label Magnet disappeared, so did the Bodines.
Album: *Played* (Magnet 1987).

Bollock Brothers

The Bollock Brothers started off as an 'in joke', which rapidly became very unfunny indeed. Formed in the UK in 1982 and led by the 'legendary' Jock McDonald, they attempted to satirize the philosophy of punk by blatantly using songs, images and ideas that were the property of the Sex Pistols. However, their music was less than exciting and more akin to inept cabaret. They included funk, blues, soul, rock and even folk styles, but struggled to produce anything that was even vaguely memorable or original. The full-scale Pistols pastiche, *Never Mind The Bollocks*, is worthy of note, however, for including Michael Fagin on guest vocals. Fagin

was widely celebrated in the media previously for having broken into the Queen's bedroom in the middle of the night for a chat. Arguably stranger still, McDonald managed to enlist songwriters Vangelis and Alex Harvey for *Four Horsemen Of The Apocalypse*, but this set was still marred by his abominable vocals. Several albums/bootlegs credited to the Ex-Pistols have also had McDonald's dubious fingerprints all over them.
Albums: *Last Supper* (Charly 1983, double album), *Never Mind The Bollocks* (Charly 1983), *Live Performances* (Charly 1983, double album), *77, 78, 79* (Konnexion 1985), *Four Horsemen Of The Apocalypse* (Charly 1985), *Rock 'N' Roll Suicide* (Konnexion 1986), *Live - In Public In Private* (Charly 1985), *The Prophecies Of Nostradamus* (Blue Turtle 1987).

Bongwater

Bongwater evolved in New York, USA in 1987 when (Mark) Kramer (guitar), formerly of Shockabilly and the Butthole Surfers, joined forces with vocalist/performance artist Ann Magnuson. The pair were already acquainted from the latter's previous group, Pulsallama, and the new act was one of the first to record for Kramer's Shimmy-Disc label. The duo completed their debut EP, *Breaking No New Ground*, with the help of guitarist Fred Frith, and its content ranged from original material to a reconstructed interpretation of the Moody Blues' 'Ride My See-Saw'. The expansive *Double Bummer* introduced Dave Rick (guitar) and David Licht (drums) to a unit which would remain largely informal, although both contributed to subsequent releases. The new set included 'Dazed And Chinese', a version of Led Zeppelin's 'Dazed And Confused', sung in Chinese, as well as songs drawn from the Soft Machine, Monkees and Gary Glitter. Self-penned compositions embraced psychedelia, raped documentaries, pop culture and the *avant garde*, and if derided as self-indulgent by some, the album confirmed the group's sense of adventure. *Too Much Sleep* was more conventional and while 'Splash 1' (the Thirteenth Floor Elevators) and 'The Drum' (Slapp Happy) continued the duo's dalliance with the obscure, their original material, notably the title song and 'He Loved The Weather', showed an unerring grasp of melody. Magnuson's semi-narrative intonation flourished freely on *The Power Of Pussy*, which encompassed sexuality in many contrasting forms. Layers of guitar lines and samples enhanced a genuinely highly-crafted collection, which confirmed the promise of earlier recordings. Bongwater have also undertaken several entertaining live appearances and enter the 90s as one of the independent circuit's most imaginative acts.
Albums: *Breaking No New Ground* (EP)(1987), *Double Bummer* (1988), *Too Much Sleep* (1990), *The Power Of Pussy* (1991), *The Big Sell Out* (1992).

Boo Radleys

This UK outfit have taken an arduous route to the popular acclaim that they always anticipated and their talents demanded. Formed in 1988 in Liverpool by Sice (b. Simon Rowbottom, 18 June 1969, Wallasey, Merseyside, England; guitar/vocals), Martin Carr (b. 29 November 1968, Thurso, Highland Region, Scotland; guitar), Timothy Brown (b. 26 February 1969, Wallasey, Merseyside, England; bass) and

Boo Radleys

Steve Drewitt (b. Northwich, England; drums), they took their name from a character in the novel, *To Kill A Mockingbird*. Sice and Carr had played out childhood fantasies of pop stardom as children - waving to imagined fans and fielding self-composed interview questions - with the Beatles the cornerstone of their reference points. Carr's first venture into rock music was as a failed critic, writing two reviews for the *Liverpool Quiggins Market* paper. After several years of sporadic activity the Boo Radleys quietly released *Ichabod And I* on a small independent label which showcased the band's talent for guitar-blasted melodies, where timeless tunes were bolstered with up-to-date effects pedals; in truth a fairly accurate revision of Dinosaur Jr's caustic blueprint. The British music press were unusually late to arrive on the scene, only paying attention after disc jockey John Peel had championed the quartet on BBC Radio 1. In the summer of 1990 drummer Steve Drewitt left to join Breed and was replaced by Robert Cieka (b. 4 August 1968, Birmingham, West Midlands, England), just as the Boo Radleys signed to Rough Trade Records. Within six months the band had started to fulfil their commercial potential by entering the Top 100 of the UK charts with an EP, *Every Heaven*. However, when the Rough Trade ship went down, the Boo Radleys needed Creation Records intervention to continue. Their new record company's vision (hard critical commentary on the Boo Radleys at the time including corrupting their name to 'Do Baddleys') was rewarded with *Everything's Alright Forever*, which broke them firmly out of the indie ghetto. Songs like 'Lazy Days', which predicted their later optimistic direction, were actually inspired by Sice's reading of the Manson murders, while other moments simply gloried in guitar-led musical abandon. *Giant Steps* saw the band finally drop their previous standing as 'mediocre indie stalwarts' by producing a set which retraced the grandeur of Merseybeat, dripping with poise, attitude and melody, bringing them several Album Of The Year awards in the UK press. Surprisingly, the ante was further upped by *Wake Up*, now without any of the usual chaotic experimentalism, replaced instead by sweeping vistas of orchestrated pop. The buoyant, positive mood was only darkened by the occasional barbed lyric of '4am Conversation' or 'Wilder'. 'Joel' even attempted to preempt critics with the line 'All I want is harmony, Like some outmoded 60s throwback'. An evident attempt to wrest chart domination away from newcomers Oasis or the rejuvenated Blur, *Wake Up* sacrificed nothing apart from a previous inaccessibility. Despite an avowed intention to become chart fixtures, the album was recorded in Wales amid much catastrophe and artistic abandon, including a drunken but foiled attempt to 'polish sheep'. The spirit of the Boo Radleys obviously lives on despite the new commercial climate they find themselves in.

Albums: *Ichabod And I* (Action 1990), *Everything's Alright Forever* (Creation 1992), *Giant Steps* (Creation 1993), *Wake Up* (Creation 1995). Compilation: *Learning To Walk* (Rough Trade 1994).

Boomtown Rats

One of the first new wave groups to emerge during the musical shake-ups of 1977, Boomtown Rats were also significant for spearheading an interest in young Irish rock. Originally formed in 1975, the group comprised Bob Geldof (b. Robert Frederick Zenon Geldof, 5 October 1954, Dun Laoghaire, Eire; vocals), Gerry Roberts (vocals/guitar), Johnnie Fingers (keyboards), Pete Briquette (bass) and Simon Crowe (drums). Before moving to London, they signed to the recently established Ensign Records, which saw commercial possibilities in their high energy yet melodic work. Their self-titled debut album was a UK chart success and included two memorable singles, 'Looking After No. 1' and 'Mary Of The Fourth Form', which both reached the UK Top 20. The following summer, their *A Tonic For The Troops* was released to critical acclaim. Among its attendant hit singles were the biting 'She's So Modern' and quirky 'Like Clockwork'. By November 1978, a third hit from the album, the acerbic, urban protest 'Rat Trap', secured them their first UK number 1. In spite of their R&B leanings, the group were initially considered in some quarters as part of the punk upsurge and were banned in their home country. Unduly concerned about this they received considerable press thanks to the irrepressible loquaciousness of their lead singer, who made the press regard him as an individual, and certainly not a punk. A third album, *The Fine Art Of Surfacing* coincided with their finest moment, 'I Don't Like Mondays', the harrowing true-life story of an American teenage girl who wounded eight children and killed her school janitor and headmaster. The weirdest aspect of the tale was her explanation on being confronted with the deed: 'I don't like Mondays, this livens up the day'. Geldof adapted those words to produce one of pop's most dramatic moments in years, with some startlingly effective piano work from the appropriately named Johnny Fingers. A massive UK number 1, the single proved almost impossible to match, as the energetic but average follow-up, 'Someone's Looking At You', proved. Nevertheless, the Rats were still hitting the Top 5 in the UK and even released an understated but effective comment on Northern Ireland in 'Banana Republic'. By 1982, however, the group had fallen from critical and commercial grace and their subsequent recordings seemed passé. For Geldof, more important work lay ahead with the founding of Band Aid and much-needed world publicity on the devastating famine in Ethiopia. The Rats performed at the Live Aid concert on 13 July 1985 before bowing out the following year at Dublin's Self Aid benefit.

Albums: *The Boomtown Rats* (Ensign 1977), *A Tonic For The Troops* (Ensign 1978), *The Fine Art Of Surfacing* (Ensign 1979), *Mondo Bongo* (Ensign 1981), *V Deep* (Ensign 1982), *In The Long Grass* (Ensign 1984). Compilations: *Greatest Hits* (Ensign 1987), *Loudmouth - The Best Of The Boomtown Rats And Bob Geldof* (Vertigo 1994).
Videos: *A Tonic For The Troops* (1986), *On A Night Like This* (1989).

Boothill Foot-Tappers

Formed in 1982 by Chris Thompson (b. 19 March 1957, Ashford, Middlesex, England; banjo/vocals) and Kevin Walsh (guitar/vocals), the Boothill's full line-up was completed by Wendy May (b. Wendy May Billingsley; vocals), Slim (b. Clive Pain; accordion/piano), Marnie Stephenson (washboard/vocals), Merrill Heatley (vocals) and her brother Danny (drums). As part of an emerging 'country cow-punk' movement in the UK during the mid-80s (along with such acts as Helen And The Horns and Yip Yip Coyote), the Boothill Foot-Tappers proved to be the most adept at the genre and certainly one of the best live performers. They scored a minor UK hit on the Go! Discs/Chrysalis label with 'Get Your Feet Out Of My Shoes' in July 1984. Slim, who had been enjoying a parallel career as part of the Blubbery Hellbellies, left the group in 1983 before the recording of the Boothill's debut album and was replaced by Simon Edwards (melodeon) - although he occasionally re-joined the group for live performances. The group folded at the end of 1985 after touring to promote the album which failed to set the charts alight. After briefly working with B.J. Cole and Bob Loveday in the Rivals and later with the Devils In Disguise, Chris Thompson went on to form the Barely Works. Wendy May decided to concentrate on the running of the successful disco club 'Locomotion' at the Town And Country Club in Kentish Town, London.
Album: *Ain't That Far From Boothill* (1985).

Botany 5

UK band Botany 500 were formed by ex-Juggernauts (one single, 'Throw Yourself Under The Monstrous Wheels Of The Rock 'n' Roll Industry As It Approaches Destruction') vocalist Gordon Kerr (b. Sterling, Scotland) and David Galbraith. Their early use of ambient textures along with funk and jazz interludes was persuasive and pleasant. A debut single for Supreme, 'Bully Beef', even featured live string accompaniment. Kerr split from Galbraith in 1989, winning a Tennent's Live! talent competition run by Glasgow's Ca Va studio. He signed to Virgin, replacing his partner with Jason Robertson (guitar) and Stevie Christie (keyboards). The name was shortened to Botany 5 when a lawsuit was threatened from the American company Botany 500, responsible for wardrobe on television fare such as *Kojak*. A single, 'Love Bomb', preceded Botany 5's debut album, which was significantly ahead of its time; predicting the chill house tones of the Orb, Aphex Twin etc. It was created as a deliberate antidote to the excess of the Summer Of Love: 'Our album's for when kids come home from raves. No crazy, out of hand stuff. More artistic; slow, mellow, subdued...quiet'. The trio were joined for live extravaganzas by former Orange Juice drummer Zeke Manyika and Paul Weller associate, Carmel, in order to provide more organic backing.
Album: *Into The Night* (Virgin 1991).

Bow Wow Wow

Formed in London in 1980 by former Sex Pistols manager Malcolm McLaren, Bow Wow Wow consisted of three former members of Adam And The Ants: David Barbe (b. David Barbarossa, 1961, Mauritius; drums), Matthew Ashman (b. 1962, London, England) and Leigh Gorman (b. 1961; bass). This trio was called upon to back McLaren's latest protegee, a 14-year-old Burmese girl whom he had discovered singing in a dry cleaners in Kilburn, London. Annabella Lu Win (b. Myant Myant Aye, 1966, Rangoon, Burma) was McLaren's female equivalent of Frankie Lymon, a teenager with no previous musical experience who could be moulded to perfection. Bow Wow Wow debuted with 'C30, C60, C90, Go' a driving, Burundi Black-influenced paean to home taping composed by McLaren. Its follow-up the cassette-only *Your Cassette Pet* featured eight tracks in an EP format (including the bizarre 'Sexy Eiffel Towers'). In addition to the African Burundi-influence, the group combined a 50s sounding Gretsch guitar complete with echo and tremelo. Although innovative and exciting, the group received only limited chart rewards during their stay with EMI Records and like the Pistols before them soon sought a new record company. After signing with RCA, McLaren enlivened his promotion of the group with a series of publicity stunts, amid outrageous talk of paedophiliac pop. The jailbait Annabella had her head shaven into a Mohican style and began appearing in tribal clothes. Further controversy ensued when she was photographed semi-nude on an album sleeve pastiche of Manet's *Déjeuner sur l'Herbe*. A deserved UK Top 10 hit followed with 'Go Wild In The Country', a frenzied, almost animalistic display of sensuous exuberance. An average cover of the Strangeloves/Brian Poole And The Tremeloes' hit 'I Want Candy' also clipped the Top 10, but by then McLaren was losing control of his concept. A second lead singer was briefly recruited in the form of Lieutenant Lush, who threatened to steal the limelight from McLaren's *ingenue* and was subsequently ousted, only to reappear in Culture Club as Boy George. By 1983, amid uncertainty and disillusionment Bow Wow Wow folded. The backing group briefly soldiered on as the Chiefs Of Relief, while Annabella took a sabbatical, reappearing in 1985 for an unsuccessful solo career.

Albums: *See Jungle! See Jungle! Go Join Your Gang, Yeah, City All Over! Go Ape Crazy!* (1981), *I Want Candy* (1982), *When The Going Gets Tough, The Tough Get Going* (1983). Compilation: *The Best Of Bow Wow Wow* (1989).

Boys

Emerging alongside the first wave of UK punk bands, the Boys were always more than three chord wonders. They were formed by factory worker and guitarist John Plain (b. Leeds, Yorkshire, England) who recruited fellow workers Duncan Reid and Jack Black on bass and drums respectively. 'Honest' John Plain was also acquainted with Matt Dangerfield (b. Leeds, Yorkshire, England) and recruited him as second guitarist. Dangerfield had played two rehearsal gigs with the infamous punk ensemble, London SS, alongside Norwegian keyboards player Casino Steel. Steel, formerly of the Hollywood Brats, completed the line-up of the Boys in the summer of 1976. With Duncan 'Kid' Reid singing, and Steel/Dangerfield writing they made their name by touring with John Cale in April 1977. Signed to NEMS, 'I Don't Care' was their first single and although it did not fare well in the UK the Boys became successful on the continent particularly in Holland and Steel's native Norway. Further recordings followed for NEMS including the first of several Christmas singles recorded under the pseudonym the Yobs. In 1979 they signed with Safari where Dangerfield also acted

as a producer for Toyah early in her career. Popular with the press but unable to convert acclaim into sales the Boys eventually split. Plain teamed up with Pete Stride of the Lurkers as the New Guitars In Town for a short break in 1980, before the Boys final album was issued in 1981.

Albums: *The Boys* (NEMS 1977), *Alternative Chartbusters* (NEMS 1978), *To Hell With The Boys* (Safari 1979), *Boys Only* (Safari 1981). As the Yobs: *The Christmas Album* (Safari 1980).

Bragg, Billy

b. Steven William Bragg, 20 December 1957, Barking, Essex, England. Popularly known as 'The Bard Of Barking' (or variations of), Bragg is generally regarded as one of the most committed left-wing political performers working in popular music. After forming the ill-fated punk group Riff Raff, Bragg briefly joined the British Army (Tank Corp), before buying his way out with what he later described as the most wisely spent £175 of his life. Between time working in a record store and absorbing his new found love of the blues and protest genre, he launched himself on a solo musical career. Armed with guitar, amplifier and voice, Bragg undertook a maverick tour of the concert halls of Britain, ready at a moment's notice to fill in as support for almost any act. He confounded the local youth with what would usually be a stark contrast to the music billed for that evening. Seeing himself as a 'one man Clash', his lyrics, full of passion, anger and wit, made him a truly original character on the UK music scene. During this time, managed by ex-Pink Floyd supremo Peter Jenner, his album *Life's A Riot With Spy Vs Spy*, formerly on Charisma, but now with the emergent independent label, Go-Discs/Utility, had begun to take a very firm hold on the UK independent charts, eventually peaking in the UK national charts at number 30. His follow-up, *Brewing Up With Billy Bragg* reached number 16 in the UK charts. As always, at Billy's insistence, and helped by the low production costs, the albums were kept at a below-average selling price. His credentials as a songwriter were given a boost in 1985 when Kirsty MacColl reached number 7 in the UK charts with his song 'New England'. Bragg became a fixture at political rallies and benefits, particularly during the 1984 Miners Strike with his powerful pro-Union songs 'Which Side Are You On', 'There Is Power In The Union' and the EP title-track, 'Between The Wars'. He was instrumental in creating the socialist musicians collective 'Red Wedge', which included such pop luminaries as Paul Weller, Junior Giscombe and Jimmy Somerville. Despite the politicizing, Bragg was still able to pen classic love songs such as the much-acclaimed 'Levi Stubbs' Tears', which appeared on the UK Top 10 album *Talking To The Taxman About Poetry*. Bragg's political attentions soon spread to Russia and Central/South America. He often returned the host musician's hospitality by offering them places as support acts on his future UK tours.

In 1988 he reached the UK number 1 slot with a cover of the Beatles song, 'She's Leaving Home', on which he was accompanied by Cara Tivey on piano - this was part of a children's charity project of contemporary artists performing various Lennon And McCartney songs. Bragg shared this double a-side single release with Wet Wet Wet's version of

'With A Little Help From My Friends', which received the majority of radio play, effectively relegating Bragg's contribution to that of a b-side. In 1989 he re-activated the label Utility, for the purposes of encouraging young talent who had found difficulty in persuading the increasingly reticent major companies to take a gamble. These artists included Coming Up Roses, Weddings Parties Anything, Clea And McLeod, Caroline Trettine, Blake Babies, Jungr And Parker and Dead Famous People. In 1991, Bragg issued the critically acclaimed *Don't Try This At Home*, arguably his most commercial work to date. The album featured a shift towards personal politics, most noticeably on the liberating hit single, 'Sexuality'.

Albums: *Life's A Riot With Spy Vs Spy* (1983), *Brewing Up With Billy Bragg* (1984), *Talking With The Taxman About Poetry* (1986), *Workers Playtime* (1988), *Help Save The Youth Of America - Live And Dubious* (1988, a US/Canadian release), *The Internationale* (1990), *Don't Try This At Home* (1991), *The Peel Sessions Album* (1992, recordings from 1983-88). Compilation: *Back To Basics* (1987, a repackage of the first two albums).

Videos: *Billy Bragg Goes To Moscow And Norton, Virginia Too* (1990).

Further reading: *Midnight In Moscow*, Chris Salewicz.

Brainiac

Formed in Dayton, Ohio, USA, maverick art-rock band Brainiac played their first gig together at Rightstate University in March 1992. Straight away the band became a legend in their area by dabbling in the urban nether-worlds depicted in their songs. Following a splendidly adventurous debut album produced by Girls Against Boys keyboard player Eli Janney, Gary Gersch, managing director of Geffen Records, launched a £2 million offer for their services. Brainiac's response, allegedly, was to tell him to 'fuck off'. Instead they continued touring with Jesus Lizard and Shudder To Think as well as Girls Against Boys, and befriended R.E.M.'s Michael Stipe in Hollywood. Comprising Tim Taylor (vocals), Tyler Trent (drums), Michelle O'Dean (guitar) and Juan Monasterio (bass), the group have gone on to establish a reputation as one of American music's most forthright and entertaining live bands, while their ambition and irreverence was confirmed by the arrival of a second album in 1995: 'Too many American bands dress like lumberjacks and tell the kids 'we're with you'. Which means fuck. It's boring. The kids want something they can aspire to or make fun of.'

Albums: *Smack Bunny Baby* (Grass 1992), *Bonsai Superstar* (Grass 1995).

Branca, Glenn

Avant-garde composer/musician Branca emerged from New York's no-wave movement of the 70s. Although several contemporaries experimented with punk and deconstructed jazz, this artist advanced symphonies for guitar, wherein specially developed instruments ('mallet guitars') employed a radical tuning system to accentuate the intervals between 'true' notes on a scale. *Lesson No.1*, issued on the pivotal 99 label, featured repetitive motifs, redolent of Philip Glass, but played with both dissonance and volume. *The Ascension*

followed an equally challenging perspective, but furious bass and drum patterns tightened its rhythms. A collaborative album with poet John Giorno, *Who Are You Staring At?* ensued, on which Branca's contribution, 'Bad Smells', features music for a dance piece choreographed by Twyla Tharp. During the 80s Branca established the Neutral label which served as an early outlet for Sonic Youth. This innovative group was formed following the recording of *Symphony No. 1* on which two future members, Thurston Moore and Lee Ranaldo, participated. This association has continued on further recordings, helping attract other adventurous rock musicians to the Branca fold. Swans bassist Algis Kizys is one of 10 guitarists guesting on *Symphony No. 6*, on which booming riffs are punctuated by mesmerising keyboard fills. *The World Turned Upside Down - A Ballet For Orchestra In 7 Movements* featured the New York Chamber Sinfonia, exposing a poignant beauty in Branca's compositional technique. *Symphony No. 10 For Massed Guitars*, which received its world premier in Britain in February 1994, restated the composer's infatuation with loud music. Whether he will ever gain widespread recognition is a moot point, Branca was commissioned to compose the score for Peter Greenaway's film *The Belly Of An Architect* (1986). However, he and the director fell out, and only seven minutes remain in the final soundtrack. It is still recognisably 'Branca', the mark of an imaginative and gifted talent.

Albums: *Lesson No. 1* (1980), *The Ascension* (1981), with John Giorino *Who Are You Staring At* (1982), *Symphony No. 1 (Tonal Plexus)* (1983), *Symphony No. 3* (1983), *Symphony No. 6 (Devil Chairs At The Gates Of Heaven)* (1989), *The World Turned Upside Down (A Ballet For Orchestra In 7 Movements* (1992), *Symphony No. 2 (The Peaks Of The Sacred)* (1992).

Breeders

Restless with her subordinate role in Boston, USA guitar band the Pixies, bassist Kim Deal (b. 10 June 1961, Dayton, Ohio, USA; guitar/vocals/synthesisers) forged this spin-off project with Throwing Muses' guitarist Tayna Donelly (b. 14 August 1966, USA). The name Breeders, a derogatory term used by homosexuals to describe heterosexuals, had been the name of a group Deal fronted, prior to the Pixies, with her twin sister Kelly. Kim and Donelly initially undertook sessions with Muses' drummer David Narciso, but these sessions were abandoned. Now joined by bassist Josephine Wiggs (b. Josephine Miranda Cordelia Susan Wiggs, 26 February 1965, Letchworth, Hertfordshire, England) from British act the Perfect Disaster, the Breeders recorded *Pod* in Edinburgh, during a Pixies tour of Britain. Britt Walford from Kentucky hardcore group, Slint drummed on the record under the pseudonym Shannon Doughton. Distinctively 'engineered' by Big Black/Rapeman figurehead Steve Albini, the tenor of the album leant towards Deal's work with her parent group with plangent guitars, menacing melodies and uncompromised lyrics. The harrowing 'Hellhound' took the view of an aborted foetus, 'Iris' graphically detailed menstruation, while their reading of the Beatles 'Happiness Is A Warm Gun', expressed the tension only implicit in the original. A four-track EP, *Safari*, which

featured a thrilling version of the Who's 'So Sad About Us', followed. Here the group was augmented by Kelly Deal (guitar/vocals) and new drummer Mike Hunt. Yet despite critical and commercial acclaim, the Breeders remained a sideline. However, following the Pixies bitter split in the wake of *Trompe Le Monde*, Kim Deal rekindled the group in 1993. Tanya Donelly had already quit the Muses to form Belly and was thus unavailable. However Wiggs, who left Perfect Disaster during the Breeders' first inception, abandoned Honey Tongue, a group she formed with Jon Mattock from Spiritualized, to rejoin the Deal twins. Jim MacPherson (b. James Carl MacPherson, 23 June 1966, Dayton, Ohio, USA; drums), formerly of the Raging Mantras, completed the line-up featured on *Last Splash*. Less abrasive than its predecessor, this engaging set revealed Kim Deal's growing maturation as a songwriter, encompassing mock C&W ('Driving All Night'), grunge-styled instrumentals ('Roi') and moving ballads ('Do You Love Me Now?').
Albums: *Pod* (4AD 1990), *Last Splash* (4AD 1993).

Brickell, Edie, And The New Bohemians

The US group, the New Bohemians - Kenny Withrow (guitar), John Bush (percussion), Brad Houser (bass), and Brando Aly (drums) already existed as a unit in their own right before Edie Brickell (guitar/vocals) jumped up on stage to sing with them. Following their contribution to the Island compilation *Deep Ellum*, Aly left and was replaced by Matt Chamberlain, with Wes Martin joining as additional guitarist. The new line-up signed to Geffen Records and recorded their debut *Shooting Rubberbands At The Stars* from whence came the UK hit single 'What I Am'. The work immediately established Brickell as one of the most interesting new songwriters of her era with a distinctive vocal style. The group subsequently toured with Bob Dylan. Their follow-up single 'Circle' also charted but only reached number 74 in the UK. *Ghost Of A Dog* included guest vocals by John Lydon on 'Strings Of Love' and displayed Brickell's characteristically oblique lyrics. In June 1992, Edie married Paul Simon.
Albums: *Shooting Rubberbands At The Stars* (1988), *Ghost Of A Dog* (1991). Edie Brickell solo: *Picture Perfect Morning* (Geffen 1994).

Brigandage

This UK post punk (or 'positive punk') group were notable for creating an almost audible 'buzz' in the London area before fizzling out just as rapidly. The focus of the band was Michelle (b. c.1960). Based in Camden, London, both she and boyfriend Richard North had been 'faces' at the beginning of punk. The two also ran their own stall, The Art Of Stealing, in Camden Market. Michelle was able to boast of being both the first in the queue for the 100 Club 'Punk Festival', and of being escorted to hospital in an ambulance by Mick Jones of the Clash. The original line-up featured Michelle (vocals), Mick Fox (guitar) and brothers Ben (drums) and Scott Addisson (bass). However, their beliefs in 'positive punk' were savaged by critics, notably in the *New Musical Express*, and the band left Michelle with only the the name. Richard, the editor of *Kick* fanzine, (who also wrote

for *Zig Zag* as Richard Kick and the *New Musical Express* as Richard North), was the first to be drafted in on bass. His assertion that he could not play was dismissed by Michelle, who added David Eaves (guitar) and Tim Nuttal (drums), before he had time to argue about it. Brigandage Mark 1 had collapsed, ironically, following Richard's nearly infamous 'Positive Punk' piece in the *NME*. Unfortunately, they proved unable to capitalize on their live reputation and left little behind to testify to their talents.
Album: *Pretty Little Thing* (Gung-ho 1986).

Bright, Bette

b. Anne Martin, Whitstable, Kent, England. A founder member of Liverpool cult-favourites Deaf School, vocalist Bright embarked on a solo career following the group's demise. Her early singles, 'My Boyfriend's Back'- and 'Captain Of Your Ship', were remakes of well-known female-group classics by the Angels and Reparata And The Delrons respectively. The singer's sole UK Top 50 success was derived from a third release, 'Hello, I Am Your Heart'. Backed by the Illuminations which included Ian Broudie (guitar - later of Care and Lightning Seeds) and Clive Langer, Bette embarked on a tour of British clubs and colleges and completed a promising album which offered versions of Betty Wright's 'Shoorah Shoorah' and the Deaf School favourite, 'Thunder And Lightning'. Unable to make a significant commercial breakthrough, she guested on several live appearances by Clive Langer And The Boxes, before reverting to a domestic life following her marriage to Madness' singer Graham 'Suggs' McPherson.
Album: *Rhythm Breaks The Ice* (Korova 1981).

Bright, Len, Combo

Eric Goulden (guitar/vocal), Russ Wilkins (bass) and Bruce Brand (drums) presided over a mid-80s rock scene in England's Medway towns that was as self-contained in its quieter way as Merseybeat. Cultivating a comically seedy image and the artistic style of a backdated 60s beat group, the trio were popular on the college circuit with a set steered by Goulden's instinctive if indelicate audience control and monopolized by his compositions - some dating back to both his Captains Of Industry and an earlier incarnation as Wreckless Eric. By scorning a proper recording studio, the home-made passion of the Combo's debut album and its 'Someone Must've Nailed Us Together' single cost next to nothing to record on antiquated electronic paraphernalia assembled in Brand's Chatham attic. 1987's *Combo Time!* was a critical success but a commercial failure. Later that year, the trio was torn by dissent over future policy and Goulden's subsequent exit to resume his solo career.
Albums: *The Len Bright Combo Present...* (1986), *Combo Time!* (1987).

Brilliant

Brilliant, creatively fuelled by ex-Killing Joke bass player Youth (b. Martin Glover Youth, 27 December 1960, Africa), originally formed in England with Paul Ferguson (drums) and Paul Raven (bass). However, the latter pair soon defected back to Killing Joke. A second line-up featuring, among others, Tin Tin (b. France), Marcus (ex-Lemon Boys) and

Stephan was equally short-lived. Brilliant, meanwhile, persevered with Youth on bass, Jimmy Cauty on guitar and June Lawrence on vocals. Though neither of the new members were experienced musically, Lawrence had studied fashion at art school and Jimmy had been a prominent comic artist. Much adored by the music press, their sole breakthrough came with a sumptuous cover of James Brown's 'It's A Man's Man's Man's World'.
Album: *Kiss The Lips Of Life* (1986).

Brilliant Corners

Purveyors of intelligent and undervalued pop music, the Brilliant Corners originated from Bristol, England, and took their name from a Thelonious Monk jazz passage. Davey Woodward (b. c.1966, Avonmouth, Bristol, England; vocals/guitar), Chris (bass), Winston (percussion/backing vocals), Bob (drums) and Dan (occasional keyboards) comprised the line-up. Early material was absorbed into the *New Musical Express*' *C86* phenomenon, and comparisons to other 'shambling' bands became a near permanent albatross around the group's necks. Their own SS20 label would be home to their first three singles and mini-album *Growing Up Absurd*. However, their latter day career was characterized by an absence of press coverage, bearing no relation to the quality of the band's output. Thus far they had sustained only a single line-up change, losing a trumpeter, though a substitute guitarist called Phil was drafted in when Woodward broke his arm. In March 1988 the band set up their own label McQueen.
Albums: *Growing Up Absurd* (1985), *Somebody Up There Likes Me* (1988), *A History Of White Trash* (1993).
Video: *Creamy Stuff* (1991).

Buckley, Jeff

b. Jeffrey Scott Buckley, 1966, Orange County, California, USA. The son of respected singer/songwriter Tim Buckley, Jeff Buckley not-unnaturally takes exception to comparisons with his father, citing his mother as a greater influence. Having studied at the Los Angeles Musicians' Institute, Jeff moved to New York where he first garnered attention at a Tim Buckley tribute, organized by producer Hal Willner. The young singer performed 'One I Was' at this 1991 event. Jeff made numerous appearances at several of the city's clubs, including the Fez and Bang On, recording his debut mini-album at the Sin-e. This tentative four-song set included two original compositions alongside versions of Van Morrison's 'Young Lovers Do' and Edith Piaf's 'J n'en Connais Pas La Fin'. Having secured a major contract with Sony, Buckley completed the critically-acclaimed *Grace* with his regular group; Michael Tighe (guitar), Mick Grondhal (bass) and Matt (drums). An expressive singer with an astonishing range, Buckley soars and sweeps across this near-perfect collection which includes versions of Elkie Brooks' 'Lilac Wine' and Leonard Cohen's 'Hallelujah' alongside several breathtaking original songs. His live appearances have been acclaimed as revelatory, blending expressive readings of material from *Grace* with an array of interpretations ranging from Big Star ('Kanga Roo') to the MC5 ('Kick Out The Jams'). A gifted, melodic composer whose awareness of contemporary guitar band brings dynamism to the singer/songwriter form, Jeff Buckley has already proclaimed his unique talent.
Albums: *Live At The Sin-e* (Big Cat 1992), *Grace* (Sony 1994).

Buffalo Tom

This Boston, USA based melodic hardcore trio, feature Bill Janowitz (vocals/guitar), Tom Maginnis (drums) and Chris Colbourn (bass). They were formed in 1986 at Massachusetts University, and took their inspiration from bands such as Hüsker Dü and Soul Asylum. Their first album consisted largely of the catchy but hard pop format made famous by the above. The title, *Sunflower Suit*, was taken from the Hitchcock film, *The Birds*. It was released in America on underground label SST Records; in the UK it was simply called *Buffalo Tom*. The producer was Dinosaur Jr's J. Mascis, leading to similarities between the two bands being regularly overstated by critics (some nicknamed them Dinosaur Jr. Jr.) As was the follow-up, this time licensed to Beggars Banquet in the UK. When *Let Me Come Over* was released in 1992 the band had established a healthy reputation amongst both critics and live audiences, touring with the Wedding Present amongst others. Generally acknowledged as being of a superior hue to many members of the underground US rock movement, Buffalo Tom have yet to escape critical comparisons to inappropriate sources. Possibly the most accurate comparison mentioned thus far is a passing similarity to Neil Young.
Albums: *Sunflower Suit* (SST 1989), *Bird Brain* (Beggars Banquet 1990), *Let Me Come Over* (Beggars Banquet 1992), *Big Red Letter Day* (Beggars Banquet 1993).

Burnel, Jean Jacques

Out of the four original members of the Stranglers, bassist Jean Jacques Burnel (b. 1952, London, England) was probably the most forthright. Born of French parents he was staunchly pro-European. A keen biker, former skinhead, a black belt in karate and an Economics graduate from Bradford University. He was employed as a van driver in Guildford, Surrey when he first met Hugh Cornwell, through the American lead singer of the band Bobbysox whom Hugh was playing guitar with in the early 70s. Original plans to become a karate instructor were shelved (although he would return to this profession part-time), so he could play bass and sing in a band with Cornwell. As the Stranglers soared to success Burnel waged a personal battle with the press who dismissed the band as either being of higher intellect than their punk cohorts, or alternatively abject and brutal chauvinists. Several well-documented episodes led to violent resolution at Burnel's hands. Burnel was the first Strangler to work on a solo project, *Euroman Cometh*. As the title implied, this was a plea for the cause of European federalism, and somewhat ahead of its time. This was released early in 1979 with guests Brian James (guitar; ex-Damned), Lew Lewis (harmonica; ex-Eddie And The Hot Rods) with Carey Fortune (ex-Chelsea) and Pete Howells (ex-Drones) sharing drum duties. A short tour to promote the album was something of a disaster. The Euroband put together for the tour featured John Ellis (ex-Vibrators - who was also playing for the support band Rapid Eye Movement),

Jeff Buckley

Lewis, Howells, and Penny Tobin on keyboards. In 1980 'Girl From The Snow Country' was scheduled as a solo release but was withdrawn. Despite a later bootleg, the copies that slipped out are among the most collectable of new wave releases. The next musical project outside of the Stranglers was a collaboration with Dave Greenfield on a soundtrack for the Vincent Coudanne film *Ecoutez Vos Murs*. Ensuing years saw Burnel getting involved with a number of bands as either producer, guest musician or both. Typically the groups were largely non-English, including Taxi Girl (France), Ping Pong (Norway), the Revenge (Belgium) and ARB (Japan). The next major project was the formation in 1986 of a 60s cover outfit called the Purple Helmets. Consisting of Burnel, Ellis, Alex Gifford, and Laurent Sinclair the outfit was put together for a one-off gig at the *Trans Musicale Avant Festival* in France. So successful was the concert that the Helmets became an ongoing concern with Greenfield replacing Sinclair and Tears For Fears drummer Manny Elias joining. Burnel has since made one further solo album, *C'est Un Jour Parfait*, which was recorded almost entirely in French and released just about everywhere in Europe except Britain.
Albums: *Euroman Cometh* (1979), with Dave Greenfield *Fire And Water* (1983), *C'est Un Jour Parfait* (1989).

Bushwackers

Bush-rock is perhaps the only style of music which might be considered unique to Australia, unlike almost all other Australian music which is directly influenced by or even imitative of USA and UK trends. The style is a mixture of traditional Irish and Australian ballads, traditional folk dance music played on the usual rock musical instruments, with the addition of fiddle and accordion. The major proponents of this genre were the Bushwackers, themselves originally an all-acoustic band formed in 1971 playing folk dances and singing typical Australian 'bush' ballads and poems. The Bushwackers principal members comprised Dobe Newton (vocals/lagaphone), Jan Wozitsky (banjo/harmonica/vocals), Tommy Emmanuel (guitar) and Louis McManus (guitar/fiddle/mandolin). By the mid-70s the band had electrified and started playing the pubs, where they attracted the attention of the rock world, particularly with the album *Faces In The Street*, but the crossover took some years to complete. The Bushwackers toured the UK and continental Europe for several extended spells, and were popular with crowds at the summertime folk festivals. The band has at various times attracted regular rock players as members, such as Peter Farndon (bass; Pretenders) and Freddie Strauks (drums; Skyhooks) as well as some of Australia's finest folk musicians. The band also published three books of their songs and dance tunes, which sold in large quantities. By the mid-80s the band had eased back to a part-time concern, but still managed to retain a small, loyal following.
Albums: *Shearer's Dream* (1974), *And The Band Played Waltzing Matilda* (1976), *Murrumbidgee, Bushfire, The Dance Album* (1980), *Faces In The Street* (1981), *Down There For Dancing* (1982), *Warrigul Morning* (1988), *Beneath The Southern Cross* (1989), *Shoalhaven Man* (1989).

Butterfield 8

Butterfield 8 were the brainchild of former Higson's multi-instrumentalist Terry Edwards (b. Hornchurch, Essex, England) in collaboration with ex-Madness bassist Mark 'Bedders' Bedford (b. 24 August 1961, London, England). Edwards's long-time fascination with film and show scores fused with his other love of blues-tinged jazz in the Butterfield 8. The group provided a welcome outlet after the restriction of the funk-influenced Higsons. Named after the 1960 film starring Laurence Harvey and Elizabeth Taylor, the Butterfield 8's debut album included versions of Herbie Hancock's 'Watermelon Man' and the Viscounts 'Harlem Nocturne'. Among Edwards' other projects and collaborations, was the 70s glitter-glam parody, the Eight Track Cartridge Family. He has also performed with, and produced, Yeah Jazz, worked with the Simon Lewis Partnership and in 1991 he released two EPs celebrating the music of the Jesus And Mary Chain and the Fall.
Album: *Blow* (Go! Discs 1988).

Butthole Surfers

Formerly known as the Ashtray Baby Heads, this maverick quartet from Austin, Texas, USA, made its recording debut in 1983 with a self-titled mini-album (the name Butthole Surfers comes from an early song about beach transvestites). Gibson 'Gibby' Haynes (vocals) Paul Leary Walthall aka Paul Sneef (guitar) and King Koffey (drums) were initially indebted to the punk/hardcore scene, as shown by the startling 'The Shah Sleeps In Lee Harvey's Grave', but other selections were inspired by a variety of sources. Loping melodies, screaming guitar and heavy-metal riffs abound in a catalogue as zany as it is unclassifiable. Lyrically explicit, the group has polarized opinion between those who appreciate their boisterous humour and those deeming them prurient. Having endured a succession of bass players, including Kramer from Shockabilly and Bongwater, the Buttholes secured the permanent services of Jeff Pinker, alias Tooter, alias Pinkus, in 1985. The Surfers' strongest work appears on *Locust Abortion Technician* and *Hairway To Steven*, the former memorably including 'Sweet Loaf', a thinly disguised version of Black Sabbath's 'Sweet Leaf'. On the latter set, tracks are denoted by various simple drawings, including a defecating deer, rather than song titles. In 1991 the release of *Digital Dump*, a house-music project undertaken by Haynes and Tooter under the Jack Officers epithet, was followed closely by the Buttholes' ninth album, *Piough*, which showed that their ability to enrage, bewilder and excite remained as sure as ever. It was marked by a curiously reverential version of Donovan's 'Hurdy Gurdy Man'. This set was closely followed by Paul Leary's excellent solo debut, *The History Of Dogs*.
Albums: *Butthole Surfers* (Alternative Tentacles 1983), *PCP PEP* (Alternative Tentacles 1984), *Another Man's Sac* (Touch And Go 1985), *Rembrandt Pussyhorse* (Touch And Go 1986), *Locust Abortion Technician* (Touch And Go 1987), *Hairway To Steven* (Touch And Go 1988), *Pioughd* (Rough Trade 1991), *Independent Worm Saloon* (Capitol 1993). Compilations: *Double Live* (Latino Bugger 1989), *The Hole Truth ... And Nothing But* (Trance Syndicate 1995).

Buzzcocks

Originally formed in Manchester in January 1976, the group

consisted of Pete Shelley (b. Peter McNeish, 17 April 1955; vocals/guitar), Howard Devoto (b. Howard Trafford; vocals), Steve Diggle (bass) and John Maher (drums). A support spot on the Sex Pistols' infamous 'Anarchy' tour prefaced their debut recording, the EP *Spiral Scratch*, which included one of punk's most enduring anthems, 'Boredom'. The quartet's undeveloped promise was momentarily short-circuited when Devoto sensationally left in March 1977, only to resurface later that year with Magazine. A reshuffled Buzzcocks, with Shelley taking lead vocal and Garth Smith (later replaced by Steve Garvey) on bass, won a major deal with United Artists. During the next three years, they recorded some of the finest pop-punk singles of their era, including the Devoto/Shelley song 'Orgasm Addict' and, after the split, Shelley's 'What Do I Get?', 'Love You More', the classic 'Ever Fallen In Love (With Someone You Shouldn't've)', 'Promises' (with Diggle), 'Everybody's Happy Nowadays' and Diggle's 'Harmony In My Head'. After three albums and nearly five years on the road, the group fell victim to disillusionment and Shelley quit for a solo career. Steve Diggle re-emerged with Flag Of Convenience, but neither party could reproduce the best of the Buzzcocks. With hindsight, the Buzzcocks' influence upon British 'indie-pop' of the late 80s ranks alongside that of the Ramones or the Velvet Underground. The group reformed in the late 80s, then again in 1990 with former Smiths' drummer Mike Joyce added to their ranks. For their first major tour since the break-up, 1993's 35-date itinerary, Shelley and Diggle were joined by Tony Arber (bass) and Phil Barker (drums). Garvey was said to be a family man in New York, while Maher was unable to commit because of his devotion to motor racing. The Buzzcocks continue to be feted by the cognoscenti, and support tours with Nirvana and a genuinely riveting comback album (*Trade Test Transmissions*) simply add to their legacy.
Albums: *Another Music In A Different Kitchen* (United Artists 1978), *Love Bites* (United Artists 1978), *A Different Kind Of Tension* (United Artists 1979), *Trade Test Transmissions* (Castle 1993). Compilations: *Singles - Going Steady* (EMI 1981), *Lest We Forget* (ROIR 1988, cassette only), *The Peel Sessions Album* (Strange Fruit 1990), *Live At The Roxy, April '77* (Absolutely Free 1989), *Time's Up* (Document 1991, rec. 1976), *Product* (EMI 1989, 5 album/3 CD box set - contains previously unreleased recordings), *Operator's Manual - Buzzcocks Best* (EMI 1991), *Entertaining Friends* (EMI 1992).
Videos: *Auf Weidershehen* (1989), *Live Legends* (1990).

Byrne, David

b. 14 May 1952, Dumbarton, Scotland, but raised in Baltimore, Ohio, USA. A graduate of the Rhode Island School of Design, Byrne abandoned his training in visual and conceptual arts in favour of rock. He formed Talking Heads with two fellow students and this highly-respected unit evolved from its origins in the New York punk milieu into one of America's leading attractions. Much of its appeal was derived from Byrne's quirky, almost paranoid, diction and imaginative compositions, but the group rapidly proved too limiting for his widening artistic palate. *My Life In The Bush Of Ghosts*, a collaboration with Brian Eno, was widely praised by critics for its adventurous blend of sound collages,

ethnic influences and vibrant percussion, which contrasted with Byrne's ensuing solo debut, *The Catherine Wheel*. The soundtrack to Twyla Tharp's modern ballet, this fascinating set was the prelude to an intensive period in the parent group's career, following which the artist began composing and scripting a feature film. Released in 1985, *True Stories*, which Byrne also directed and starred in, was the subject of an attendant Talking Heads' album. *The Knee Plays*, on which David worked with playwright Robert Wilson, confirmed interests emphasized in 1987 by his collaboration with Ryuichi Sakamoto and Cong Su on the soundtrack for Bertolucci's *The Last Emperor*. This highly-acclaimed film won nine Oscars, including one for Best Original Score. Byrne meanwhile continued recording commitments to his group, but by the end of the 80s intimated a reluctance to appear live with them. He instead assembled a 14-strong Latin-American ensemble which toured the USA, Canada, Europe and Japan to promote *Rei Momo*, while a 1991 statement established that Talking Heads were on 'indefinite furlough'. *The Forest* confirmed the artist's prodigious talent by invoking European orchestral music while his Luaka Bop label served as an outlet for a series of world music albums, including several devoted to Brazilian recordings.
Albums: with Brian Eno *My Life In The Bush Of Ghosts* (1981), *The Catherine Wheel* (1981), *Music For The Knee Plays* (1985), with Ryuichi Sakamoto, Cong Su *The Last Emperor* (1987, film soundtrack), *Rei Momo* (1989), *The Forest* (1991), *Uh-Oh* (1992), *David Byrne* (Luaka Bop/Warner Brothers 1994).
Videos: *Catherine Wheel* (1989), *David Byrne: Between The Teeth* (1993).

C

Cabaret Voltaire

Formed in Sheffield, Yorkshire, England, in 1974, and named after the Dadaist collective, this experimental, innovative electronic-dance group consisted of Stephen Mallinder (bass/lead vocals), Richard H. Kirk (guitar/wind instruments) and Chris Watson (electronics and tapes). Influenced by Can and Brian Eno, the group strived to avoid the confines of traditional pop music and the trio's early appearances veered towards performance art. This attitude initially attracted the attention of Factory Records and the group contributed two tracks to the Manchester label's 1978 double EP, *A Factory Sample*. They eventually signed to Rough Trade Records that same year, producing the *Extended Play* EP which confirmed the band's experimental stance, although 'Nag, Nag, Nag' (1979) was a head-on rush of distorted guitar with a driving beat. The trio continued to break new ground, using sampled 'noise', cut-up techniques and tape loops. Often viewed as inaccessible, in the ensuing years Cabaret Voltaire released the UK Independent Top 10 singles 'Silent Command' (1979), 'Three Mantras' and 'Seconds Too Late' (both 1980). Their 1979 debut album, *Mix Up*, was followed by a more conventional offering, *The Voice Of America*. After *Live At The YMCA 27.10.79*, the group widened their horizons, with video and collaborative work, including outings on the Belgian label, Les Disques du Crépuscule and two Industrial label cassettes, *Cabaret Voltaire 1974-76* (their early recordings) and Kirk's solo *Disposable Half Truths*. In 1981, the group's prolific out-put was increased by the morbid but successful *Red Mecca* and by another cassette, *Live At The Lyceum*. Watson left in October 1981 to work in television and later resurfaced in the Hafler Trio. In 1982 Eric Random was recruited on guitar for a Solidarity benefit concert, performing under the name Pressure Company. The year also saw the release of *2 x 45*, 'Temperature Drop', plus the Japanese live album *Hai!* and a solo set from Mallinder, *Pow Wow*. Departing from Rough Trade in 1983, whilst also releasing 'Fools Game' on Les Disques du Crépuscule and 'Yashar' on Factory, the group signed a joint deal with Some Bizarre/Virgin Records. The first fruits of this move, 'Just Fascination' and 'The Crackdown' confirmed Cabaret Voltaire's new approach and signalled a drastic shift towards rhythmic dance sounds (assisted by Soft Cell, later Grid keyboard player, Dave Ball's presence). Yet another label entered the frame when Doublevision released the film soundtrack *Johnny Yesno*. Kirk's double set, *Time High Fiction*, came at the end of this productive year. Aside from a compilation video, *TV Wipeout*, 1984 was a quiet year, until 'Sensoria' (Some Bizarre) ripped the dance charts apart, setting the tone for much of Cabaret Voltaire's subsequent work, including 'James Brown', both featuring on *Micro-phonies*, and 'I Want You' (1985). In between, the pair concentrated on the video *Gasoline In Your Eye*, paralleled by the similarly-titled, double 12-inch 'Drinking Gasoline'. The critically acclaimed *The Covenant, The Sword And The Arm Of The Lord*, echoed the group's earlier phase. Kirk's solo work continued apace in 1986 with *Black Jesus Voice*, and a mini-album, *Ugly Spirit*, plus a project with the Box's Peter Hope resulting in *Hoodoo Talk* in 1987. By July 1987 the duo had transferred to EMI/Parlophone, debuting with 'Don't Argue'. As with the follow-up releases, 'Here To Go' and 'Code', its sound introduced a more commercial dance slant, lacking the pair's earlier, experimental approach. In 1988, Mallinder collaborated with Dave Ball and Mark Brydon, collectively known as Love Street, releasing 'Galaxy'. A new Cabaret Voltaire single, 'Hypnotised' (1989), reflected their visit to the house music capital, Chicago. Kirk's 'Test One' (1990), issued under the guise of Sweet Exorcist, was pure acid house. The group continued this style with 'Keep On' and *Groovy, Laid Back And Nasty*. In the meantime, Mute Records methodically reissued the band's early back catalogue on CD. Leaving EMI, Cabaret Voltaire returned to Les Disques du Crépuscule for 'What Is Real' (1991), followed by *Body And Soul*. This only consolidated Cabaret Voltaire's pivotal role in hi-tech dance music, which they have helped develop over a decade and a half.

Albums: *Mix Up* (Rough Trade 1979), *The Voice Of America* (Rough Trade 1980), *Live At The YMCA 27.10.79.* (Rough Trade 1980), *Red Mecca* (Rough Trade 1981), *Live At The Lyceum* (Rough Trade 1981), *2 x 45* (Rough Trade 1982), *Hai!* (Rough Trade 1982), *Johnny Yesno* (Doublevision 1983, film soundtrack), *Micro-phonies* (Some Bizarre 1984), *The Covenant, The Sword And The Arm Of The Lord* (Some Bizarre 1985), *The Crackdown* (Some Bizarre 1986), *Code* (Parlophone 1987), *Groovy Laid Back And Nasty* (Parlophone 1990), *Body And Soul* (Crepuscule 1991), *Percussion Force* (Crepuscule 1991), *International Language* (1993). As Pressure Company: *Live In Sheffield 19 January 1982* (Paradox Product 1982). Compilations: *Cabaret Voltaire 1974-76* (Industrial 1981), *The Golden Moments Of Cabaret Voltaire* (Rough Trade 1987), *8 Crépuscule Tracks* (Interior Music 1988), *Listen Up With Cabaret Voltaire* (Mute 1990), *The Living Legends* (Mute 1990), *Three Mantras* (Mute 1990), *Technology* (Virgin 1992). Solo albums: Richard H. Kirk: *Disposable Half Truths* (Rough Trade 1981), *Time High Fiction* (Rough Trade 1983), *Black Jesus Voice* (Rough Trade 1986), *Ugly Spirit* (Rough Trade 1986). Stephen Mallinder: *Pow Wow* (1982). With Peter Hope: *Hoodoo Talk* (Native 1987). As Sweet Exorcist: *Clonk's Coming* (Warp/Outer Rhythm 1991).
Videos: *TV Wipeout* (1984), *Gasoline In Your Eye* (1985), *Cabaret Voltaire* (1990).

Call

US band the Call's big, echoed rockers demanded comparisons with U2 from the very outset of their career. A Californian-based quartet, the songs written by vocalist Michael Been recalled the passion and melodrama of *Boy*-era U2, an impression compounded by the group's spiritual inclinations. Their 1986 debut was given over to rather self-satisfied Christian mysticism, but occasionally they struck the right note with more classy and less pretentious numbers - the best example being hit single 'Everywhere I Go'. *Let The Day Begin*, produced another memorable single in the title-track, as the Call moved over to Mercury Records. *Bad Moon* emerged as pressure mounted on Been to produce another 'Let The Day Begin'. Despite this, it was a rewarding set finding a more natural studio context to complement vocals that were always in danger of ill-advised grandeur. Again the title-cut was a standout, though this was ably backed up by a rash of bold song writing ventures including 'What's Happened To You' and the evocative 'This Is Your Life'. A subsequent compilation covering the band's Mercury years was compiled by Been and titled after the group's first breakthrough hit, 'Walls Come Tumbling Down'. However, the Call's long term fate was, as one reviewer offered, to be 'too politically tuff to be the Police, too strident to be the Cars, and too late to be the Clash'.
Albums: *Reconciled* (Elektra 1986), *Into The Woods* (Elektra 1987), *Let The Day Begin* (Mercury 1989), *Red Moon* (Mercury 1990). Compilation: *Walls Come Down - The Mercury Years* (Mercury 1991).

Camper Van Beethoven

A band for whom the term 'alternative' might first have been coined. In fact, principal songwriter David Lowery suggests

Call

that is exactly the case: '(We) were arguably the prototypical alternative band. I remember first seeing that word applied to us. The nearest I could figure is that we seemed like a punk band, but we were playing pop music, so they made up the word 'alternative' for those of us who do that'. Camper Van Beethoven were a witty, often sarcastic garage rock band formed in Redlands, California, USA, in 1983 by school friends, transferring to Santa Cruz when members attended college there. They were named by early member David McDaniels, though initial line-ups were frequently unstable. By 1987 the band solidified as Lowery (vocals/guitar), Greg Lisher (guitar), Chris Pederson (drums), Jonathan Segal (violin) and Victor Krummenacher (bass). Krummenacher was formerly a member of jazz ensemble Wrestling Worms. Their debut, *Telephone Free Landslide Victory*, contained the classic single cut 'Take The Skinheads Bowling', as well as the surreal ethnic instrumentation of 'Balalaika Gap' and 'Border Ska', and a strange Black Flag cover ('Wasted'). It was typical of an armoury of songs which included titles like 'The Day Lassie Went To The Moon', 'Joe Stalin's Cadillac', and 'ZZ Top Goes To Egypt'. They played their UK debut in March 1987, where 'Skinheads' had become something of a cult hit, but neither there nor in the US did their critical popularity transfer into sales. The anagramatical *Vampire Can Mating Oven* wrapped up the last of their Rough Trade distributed fare before a move to Virgin Records. *Our Beloved Revolutionary Sweetheart* found them in fine form with a bigger budget and a sympathetic producer, Dennis

Herring. However, the tone of *Key Lime Pie* proved infinitely more sombre than previous outings and prophesied their split. In retrospect it is hard to listen to a track like 'When I Win The Lottery' without reading it as allegory for the band's unsuccessful transition from indie to major label chart prospecting. A bizarre cover of Status Quo's 'Pictures Of Matchstick Men', released as a single, served as a reminder of their former discordant eclecticism. Four members of Camper Van Beethoven, Lisher Krummenacher, Pederson and former Ophelias guitarist David Immerglück (who joined the band over their final recordings) put together Monks Of Doom. Jonathon Segal released a solo album, and main songwriter David Lowery, after waiting fruitlessly for his former colleagues to return from their 'stupidity', finally made the deserved transition to that of major league player with Cracker.

Albums: *Telephone Free Landslide Victory* (Independent Project 1985), *Take The Skinheads Bowling* (Pitch-A-Tent 1986, mini-album), *Camper Van Beethoven II/III* (Pitch-A-Tent 1986), *Camper Van Beethoven* (Pitch-A-Tent 1986), *Vampire Can Mating Oven* (Pitch-A-Tent 1987, mini-album), *Our Beloved Revolutionary Sweetheart* (Virgin 1988), *Key Lime Pie* (Virgin 1989).

Candlebox

Formed in California Candlebox consist of Kevin Martin (vocals), Peter Klett (guitar), Bardi Martin (bass) and Scott Mercado (drums), and were widely celebrated as one of the

most exciting American rock bands to arrive in the mid-90s. They signed to Madonna's Maverick label and buoyed by the media interest that accompanies the singer's every move, Candlebox soon found themselves a major success. Both 'Far Behind' and 'You' were hits in the singles chart and in 1995 sales of *Candlebox* reached three million copies in the USA. *Candlebox* was co-produced by Kelly Gray and revealed a band happy to explore territory somewhere between traditional pop-metal and Seattle-styled grunge. This was an assured debut and one that places the band in the 'anticipated difficult second album' category.
Album: *Candlebox* (Maverick/Warner 1994).

Candyland

This multi-racial independent label dance band from south London, England, generated a modicum of critical attention in the early 90s. Their first demo was produced by Gil Norton (of Pixies fame) who 'discovered them'. Under the patronage of Jonathan King they played the Great British Music Weekend at Wembley before their first single, 'Fountain Of Youth', appeared. Felix Tod (vocals) and David Wesley Ayers Jnr (guitar) formed the band after a life of minor poverty. They met Kenediid Osman (b. Somalia; bass) on the steps of a local mosque. Later they added Derrick McKenzie (b. Jamaica; drums) and Colin Payne (b. Southend, Essex, England; keyboards/financial adviser), a former stockbroker who had lost millions for his company. Unfortunately, his investment in Candyland proved similarly unadvised, as the music press snubbed the band once they learned of its sponsors.
Album: *Suck It And See* (Non Fiction 1991).

Captain America

Formed in 1991, Captain America was one of several groups to emerge from the flourishing millieu centred on the Scottish town of Bellshill. Vocalist/guitarist Eugene Kelly and bassist James Seenan were former members of the Vaselines, while the original line-up also featured BMX Bandits' guitarist Gordon Keen and Teenage Fanclub drummer Brendan O'Hare. The last-named was replaced by Andy Bollen soon after the quartet's inception. Captain America completed two 12-inch EPs, *Captain America* and *Flame On*, both of which revealed a penchant for distorted guitarwork, but progress was halted when Marvel Comics, publishers of the *Captain America* title, threatened litigation. The C&A company also objected to the unit's use of their trading logo on *Flame On*, and having jetisoned Seenan and Bollen, Kelly and Keen re-emerged with a new rhythm section and a new name; Eugenius.

Captain Sensible

b. Raymond Burns, 24 April 1954, Balham, London, England. Having drifted from job to job after leaving school, Burns fell in with fellow reprobate Chris Miller, while working at the Croydon Fairfield Halls. Sharing common interests in drink, chaos and music, they eventually found themselves part of the burgeoning punk scene in west London in 1976. Together with Dave Vanian and Brian James, Miller (Rat Scabies) and Burns (Captain Sensible) formed what was to be one of the major punk bands of the

period; the Damned. Initially enrolled as their bass player, he moved on to guitar following James's departure from the group. A riotous character with an unnerving sense of charm, Sensible frequently performed at gigs dressed in various guises, often in a tu-tu, a nurse's uniform or even nothing at all. Behind the comic-strip facade lurked a keen fan of 60s and 70s psychedelia; he was often quoted in later interviews as being influenced by Jimi Hendrix and the Soft Machine. This went against the punk ethos of the time. He was able to indulge his esoteric taste in music by carving out a solo career by accident rather than design, owing to the frequent bouts of forced inactivity by the Damned. With ex-Chelsea bassist Henry Badowski, Sensible formed King, an outfit which lasted barely three months. That same year, he recorded 'Jet Boy Jet Girl', a lyrically improbable translation of Plastic Bertrand's 'Ca Plane Pour Moi' with the Softies and also performed on Johnny Moped's *Cycledelic*. A fervent campaigner for animal rights, and a CND supporter, he confirmed his anti-establishment credentials by recording an EP on the Crass label, *This Is Your Captain Speaking* in 1981. With fellow Damned member Paul Gray, he produced the Dolly Mixture singles, 'Been Teen' and 'Everything And More'. Signed by A&M as a solo act, he recorded a cover version of Richard Rodgers/Oscar Hammerstein II's 'Happy Talk' which included Dolly Mixture on backing vocals. The single shot to the UK number 1 position in the summer of 1982. With his distinctive red beret and round shades, he become an instant media and family favourite, revealing an endearing fondness for rabbits, cricket and trains. He subsequently released two albums in close collaboration with lyricist Robyn Hitchcock, and had further hit singles with 'Wot' and the glorious anti-Falklands war song 'Glad It's All Over'. Although he was keen not to let his solo success interfere with the Damned's activities, Sensible found himself gradually becoming isolated from the group due to internal politics and managerial disputes, resulting in his leaving the band in 1984, although he occasionally dropped in to guest on live performances.
One single in 1985 in partnership with girlfriend Rachel Bor of Dolly Mixture, billed as Captain Sensible & The Missus, 'Wot, No Meat?', emphasized his commitment to vegetarianism. He undertook one national tour in 1985, as well as studio work which culminated in the formation of his own Deltic label. His 1991 album *Revolution Now* received less favourable reviews. The double set did, however, show that his talent for catchy pop had not deserted him. He reunited with Paul Gray for some live performances in 1991, and in 1994 augmented by Gray, Malcolm Dixon (organ) and Garrie Dreadful (drums) he released *Live At The Milky Way*. This was the album the Captin should have made years ago as it captures both his humour and considerable songwriting talent. The band perform as if it is their last day on the planet, and rewarding versions of 'Neat Neat Neat', 'New Rose' and an energetic version of his number 1 hit 'Happy Talk' are but three gems from an excellent album. Sensible is enigmatic, hugely talented and highly underrated.
Albums: *Women And Captains First* (A&M 1982), *The Power Of Love* (1983), *Revolution Now* (1991), *Universe Of Geoffrey Brown* (1993), *Live At The Milky Way* (Humbug 1994). Compilation: *Sensible Singles* (1984).

Cardiacs

Formed in 1978 by Tim Smith (b. 3 July 1961, Carshalton, Surrey, England; guitar/vocals), brother Jim (b. 14 April 1958, Carshalton, Surrey, England), Peter Tagg (b. London, England; drums) and Mick Pugh (b. 21 September 1958, Kingston, Surrey, England; vocals), they started life known as Philip Pilf And The Filth which, although bizarre, was to be no less strange than the rest of a career riddled with personnel changes and eccentric activities. The name was soon switched to Cardiac Arrest, whereupon Colvin Myers (b. London, England; keyboards) joined for the first single, 'A Bus For A Bus On The Bus' in 1979. In the same year, Mark Cawthra replaced Tagg, who went on to form the Trudy. His departure was followed by Mick Pugh and Colvin Myers, who joined the Sound. The Cardiacs resolutely strived to avoid the traditional machinations of the record business by releasing a series of cassette-only albums. Saxophonist Sara Smith (b. 30 November 1960, Coleford, Gloucestershire, England) and drummer Dominic Luckman (b. 29 November 1961, Brighton, East Sussex, England) both merged with the ranks, as had William D. Drake (b. 7 February 1962, Essex, England; keyboards) and Tim Quy (b. 14 August 1961, Brixton, London, England; percussion) toward the end of 1983. Fortunately, this line-up was to remain stable for the next six years, allowing the Cardiacs to build a devoted live following with oddball performances involving flour, ill-fitting suits and several other crazy theatrical elements. Long over-due vinyl album releases followed, revealing how the band were perfecting a thoroughly unique musical sound which flummoxed the critics, although one offered the opinion that 'Genesis on a frantic amphetamine overdose' fitted the bill adequately. By 1988, the Cardiacs started to infringe upon the hitherto alien mainstream, reaching number 80 in the UK singles chart with the epic 'This Is The Life', but changes were on the way again as Sarah Smith, Tim Quy and William D. Drake all left and guitarist Christian Hayes (b. 10 June 1964, London, England) joined briefly before departing for the equally indefinable Levitation in 1991, paving the way for more chapters in the Cardiacs' fairy story. In 1995 the entire Cardiacs' back catalogue was reissued, together with a specially priced sampler CD. This comprised one track from each of their previous albums and one each from projected new releases from Tim Smith, WD Drake and Sarah Smith (*The Sea Nymphs*), Tim Smith's solo album (*Oceanland World*) and a new, as yet untitled Cardiacs studio album. The band then joined with Sidi Bou Said for a widespread UK tour and supported long-standing fans, Blur, at the Mile End Stadium in London.

Albums: *The Obvious Identity* (Alphabet 1980, cassette only), *Toy World* (Alphabet 1981, cassette only), *Archive Cardiacs* (Alphabet 1983, cassette only), *The Seaside* (Alphabet 1983, cassette only), *Mr & Mrs Smith And Mr Drake* (Alphabet 1984, cassette only), *Big Ship* (Alphabet 1985), *Rude Bootleg (Live At The Reading Festival, 1986)* (Alphabet 1986), *A Little Man And A House And The Whole World Window* (Alphabet 1988), *Cardiacs Live At The Paradiso, Amsterdam* (Alphabet 1988), *On Land And In The Sea* (Alphabet 1989), *Songs For Ships And Irons* (Alphabet 1990), *Heaven Born And Ever Bright* (Alphabet 1992), *All That Glitters Is A Mare's Nest* (Alphabet 1993). Compilation: *Cardiacs Sampler* (Aphabet 1995).

Video: *Cardiacs Live* (1990).

Cardinal

A collaboration between Richard Davies and Eric Matthews, Cardinal took shape when the unlikely duo met in Boston, Massachusetts, USA. Initially interested by each other's demo tapes, their partnership took shape despite native Australian songwriter Davies nearing the completion of a law degree. Having originally played in obscure garage band the Moles, Davies discovered his muse somewhat late in life, and was 30 by the time Cardinal's debut album was released. Conversely Matthews spent his childhood immersed in music, learning trumpet and classical composition. His conversion to indie pop came thus: 'I heard Richard's ideas and saw something special in them that I wanted to be part of'. Certainly Matthews intricate melodies contributed to his partner's song writing, with brass and harpsichord interludes a welcome visitor where a guitar riff might have been anticipated. Rather than the heavily orchestrated, pristine quality suggested by their name, songs like 'You've Lost Me There' and previous single 'Dream Figure' were powered by a surprisingly tough emotional dynamic.

Album: *Cardinal* (Flydaddy 1995).

Caretaker Race

Undervalued indie group formed by occasional rock journalist Andy Strickland (b. 16 August 1959, Newport, Isle Of Wight, England; guitar/lead vocals), Dave Mew (b. 11 May 1959, Epping, Essex, England), Henry Hersom (b. London, England; bass), Sally Ward (b. Preston, England; keyboards) and Andrew Deevey (b. 11 November 1964, Liverpool, England). The Caretaker Race came into existence in east London in 1986 after pivotal force Strickland left fellow London outfit the Loft, just as the independent circuit was held in the grip of the 'shambling' scene. While all around them feigned incompetence, however, the Caretaker Race chose a mature, melodic guitar path reminiscent of Australian group the Go-Betweens. This approach won them several friends and a stable sales figure. They started their own Roustabout Records in 1987 before switching to the Foundation label in 1989. Along the way they lost bassist Henry Hersom, who joined London outfit Bob, to be replaced by Jackie Carrera (b. 6 June 1964, London, England), and also Sally Ward, who left to take up teaching. They also lost momentum, and have been quiet in recent years.

Album: *Hangover Square* (Foundation 1990).

Carroll, Cath

b. 25 August 1960, Chipping Sodbury, Avon, England. Carroll had previously made a name for herself on the Manchester club and music scene, founding with friend Liz Naylor the magazine *City Fun*; forming the short-lived Gay Animals; and developing a penchant for cross-dressing. On moving south to London, she pursued a parallel career as a journalist and gossip columnist for the rock weekly, *New Musical Express* and listings magazine, *City Limits*. An often used pseudonym, Myrna Minkoff (influenced by the

character in John Kennedy Toole's novel, *A Confederacy Of Dunces*) was a direct contradiction of Carroll's true quiet nature. Leading the mid-80s 'indie' band, Miaow, which also comprised Chris Fenner (drums), Ron Caine (bass/guitar) and Steve MacGuire (guitar), she found herself linked with the *NME*'s seminal C86 project, contributing 'Sport Most Royal' for the album and appearing at London's ICA rock week celebration. Her smooth vocals coupled with the jangling rhythm section won critical acclaim, particularly with the anti-Thatcher song, 'Grocer's Devil Daughter', on the Venus label, and the triumphant 'yodelling' high point, 'When It All Comes Down', on Factory Records, which reached the UK independent Top 20. Their final single, 'Break The Code', gave some clue as to the musical direction Carroll was later to pursue. She subsequently became involved in low-key collaborations with Julian Henry in the Hit Parade, then married Big Black's guitarist Santiago Durango (who had left the group to study law), and continued her own solo career, spending recording time in San Paulo, Brazil, as well as London and Sheffield, England. Remaining with Factory as a solo artist (and becoming the label's first artist actually to sign a contract), Carroll recorded her debut album, assisted by Mark Brydon (guitar), Sim Lister (sax/drums/keyboards), Oswaldinho da Cuica (congas), Antenor Soares Gandra Neto (guitar), Dirceu Simoes de Medeiros (drums), Vincente da Paula Silva (piano), Valerie A. James (backing vocals), Steve Albini (guitar) and Santiago Durango (guitar). The result was the critically acclaimed *England Made Me*, released in the summer of 1991. The set confirmed the complete departure from Carroll's past English 'indie' workings, revealing a set of smooth, steamy latin-samba, mixed with electro-dance rhythms. She currently resides in Chicago, USA, but has been quiet following the collapse of Factory.
Album: *England Made Me* (Factory 1991).

Cars

In a recording career that started in 1977 the Cars' output has been a meagre 6 albums. Each one, however, has sold over a million copies and all have reached high chart positions in the USA. Formerly known as Cap'n Swing the stable line-up comprised; Ric Ocasek (b. Richard Otcasek, 23 March 1949, Baltimore, Maryland, USA; guitar/vocals), Benjamin Orr (b. Benjamin Orzechowski, Cleveland, Ohio, USA; bass/vocals), Greg Hawkes (keyboards), Elliot Easton (b. Elliot Shapiro, 18 December 1953, Brooklyn, New York City, New York, USA; guitar) and David Robinson (drums). Their catchy pop/rock songs have been hard to categorize and when they arrived with 'Just What I Needed' they were embraced by the new wave art-rock fraternity in the USA. They were an instant success in Britain, notching up a number of hits, debuting with a top 3 single, the irresistible 'My Best Friend's Girl'. The Cars have never deviated from writing catchy well-crafted songs, each containing at least one memorable and instantly hummable riff. Today they are accepted by the AOR market, which no doubt contributes to their massive record sales. In 1984 they enjoyed world-wide success with 'Drive,' and a year later the same song was opportunistically but tastefully used to pull at people's conscience during the Live Aid concert. A film

accompanying the song showing the appalling famine in Ethiopia will forever be in peoples' minds. As the lyric 'Who's gonna plug their ears when you scream' was played, it was replaced by a heart-rending scream from a small child. This memorable yet tragic segment left few dry eyes in the world. Predictably the song became a hit once more. The band broke up at the end of the 80s in favour of solo work, Ocasek became busy as a record producer, notably with Weezer in 1994.
Albums: *The Cars* (1978), *Candy-O* (1979), *Panorama* (1980), *Shake It Up* (1981), *Heartbeat City* (1984), *Door To Door* (1987). Rick Ocasek solo: *Beautitude* (1983), *Fireball Zone* (1991). Elliot Easton solo: *Change No Change* (1985). Compilation: *The Cars Greatest Hits* (1985).
Videos: *Heartbeat City* (1984), *Cars Live* (1988).

Carter USM

When the group Jamie Wednesday folded in the face of public apathy, they left two singles, 'Vote For Love' and 'We Three Kings Of Orient Aren't', on the Pink Records label, in their wake. Before that, there had been several bands, namely the Ballpoints, the End, Dead Clergy and Peter Pan's Playground. Then the south London pair of Jimbob (b. James Morrison, 22 November 1960) and Fruitbat (b. Leslie Carter, 12 February 1958) acquired a drum machine and took their name from a newspaper cutting, sometime in 1988, to create Carter The Unstoppable Sex Machine. The single, 'Sheltered Life', on the independent label Big Cat, revealed a dance formula that had more in common with other irreverent samplers such as the KLF than the Pet Shop Boys or Erasure. The single made little impression, unlike Carter's next single, 'Sheriff Fatman' (1989), an exciting amalgam of a great riff, strong rhythm and strident lyrics about a maverick landlord. *101 Damnations* was an innovative melting pot of samples, ideas and tunes, shot through with a punk-inspired ethos. Lyrically, the duo used a mix-and-match approach, swapping punned words and phrases in a manner that soon became a trademark. 'Rubbish' (1990) followed 'Fatman' into the UK indie charts, and attracted considerable attention, helped by a cover of the Pet Shop Boys' 'Rent' on the b-side. Carter had moved to Rough Trade Records by the end of the year, releasing their fourth single, 'Anytime, Anyplace, Anywhere'. After the export-only *Handbuilt For Perverts* and a special Christmas giveaway single, 'Christmas Shopper's Paradise', came the controversial 'Bloodsports For All' in 1991. This document of bullying in the military received little airplay as it coincided with the start of the Gulf conflict, but *30 Something* topped the UK Independent chart and reached the national Top 10. Financial upheaval at Rough Trade and Carter's growing success led to a deal with Chrysalis Records, commencing with a chart-bound reissue of 'Sheriff Fatman' in June. In the meantime, the band visited the USA and toured Japan later in the year. Carter's Top 20 hit later in 1991, 'After The Watershed', motivated lawyers representing the Rolling Stones to demand substantial payment (allegedly 100% of all royalties) for an infringement of copyright in using a snippet of the Stones' 1967 hit, 'Ruby Tuesday'. Meanwhile, Carter's lighting engineer and MC, Jon 'Fat' Beast, had ingratiated himself within the group's entourage (prompting the legendary cries of 'You Fat Bastard' at gigs), though he and the band would amicably part company in early 1992 when his fame became disproportionate to that of the group. Carter's albums from here on displayed a gradually more sophisticated approach, though the cornerstone of their appeal remained their incisive lyrics and propulsive live shows. For 1995's *Love Bomb*, their fourth consecutive Top 10 UK album, the group had recruited a full-time drummer, Wez, who had formerly played in the Byrds-inspired early 90s band, Resque. The extravagant hair cuts and stage gear had also been toned down, in keeping with songs that now demanded more from the listener than had previously been the case.

Albums: *101 Damnations* (Big Cat 1990), *30 Something* (Rough Trade 1991), *1992 - The Love Album* (1992), *Post Historic Monsters* (Chrysalis 1993), *Starry Eyed And Bollock Naked* (Chrysalis 1994), *Worry Bomb* (Chrysalis 1995).
Video: *Flicking The V's - Live In Croatia* (1995).

Cassandra Complex

This electronic and guitar band was formed in Leeds, England, in the mid-80s, with a line-up consisting of Rodney Orpheus (vocals), Paul Dillon (keyboards) and Andy Booth (guitar). Their first single, 'March', came out in April 1985, on their own Complex RAP label. Lyrically, it concerned the perception of liberty: 'Everyone's got a concept of freedom. Some people think that freedom is having the right to work; to another way of thinking, having the right not to work is freedom'. Before this they had also constructed their own basement studio, and organized several 'events' which would take the form of live shows with visuals, run on an autonomous basis. They were originally housed on Rouska Records, a small independent based in Leeds, for which they released the singles 'Datakill' and 'Moscow Idaho', and the album *Grenade* in 1986. The latter contained some potent, though some argued egocentric, observations: 'When I grow up I'm gonna buy myself a bomb big enough to blow up the future' ran one lyric. Significantly, they were not averse to covering Throbbing Gristle's 'Something Came Over Me' live and on record. However, their real audience seemed to be Europe, where they are now based. Signing to Play It Again Sam Records, they released *Theomania* in the summer of 1988, followed by *Finland* two years later. One of the tracks on this album, 'Let's Go To Europe', was obviously semi-autobiographical. Their 1991 album took its title from a quote by Russian mystic Gurdjieff, and was typically cluttered with pseudo-intellectual baggage throughout. It is little surprise that their guitar/synthesizer hard pop remains more popular on the Continent than in their homeland.

Albums: *Grenade* (Rouska 1986), *Theomania* (Play It Again Sam 1988), *Satan, Bugs Bunny And Me* (Play It Again Sam 1989), *Finland* (Play It Again Sam 1990), *Cyberpunx* (Play It Again Sam 1990), *The War Against Sleep* (Play It Again Sam 1991).

Cast

With a line-up of John Power (vocals/guitar), Peter Wilkinson (bass), Keith O'Neill (drums) and Skin (guitar), much of the attention initially surrounding Liverpool pop-rock band Cast arose from Power's previous position as bass player in the near-mythical La's. When it became apparent that the band's second album was never going to materialise, Powers 'left to get something new. I was just feeling uninspired. I left to do my own stuff...somewhere along the line you have to make a decision about what you want out of life'. Hence Cast, who began their career as support to the Lightning Seeds, before signing to Polydor Records (largely through their reputation for working with Jimi Hendrix and the Who - evidently the 60s were still a big factor in the evolution of Powers musical style). The choice of producer for the band's debut album would be John Leckie.

Catherine Wheel

After partaking of various local bands Rob Dickinson (b. 23 July 1965, Norwich, Norfolk, England; vocals) and Brian Futter (b. 7 December 1965, London, England; guitar) instigated the Catherine Wheel in the spring of 1990 by acquiring an eight track tape machine and embarking on bedroom recording sessions. Joined by the rhythm section of Neil Sims (b. 4 October 1965, Norwich, Norfolk, England; drums) and David Hawes (b. 10 November 1965, Great Yarmouth, Norfolk, England; bass) for live shows, the band had an immediate impact which took them by surprise. Armed with a guitar-propelled sound which was sufficiently fashionable to attract attention without sacrificing creative depth, they released a debut EP, *She's My Friend*, on the Wilde Club label at the start of 1991. This hinted at a potential which warranted certain members of the group to forsake lucrative jobs in the local oil industry in order to concentrate on playing full-time. British tours with such names as Blur and the Charlatans gave the Catherine Wheel an even higher profile, resulting in a major deal with Fontana Records during the summer of the same year. Admirably, they never sought to exploit the family ties between singer Rob Dickinson and cousin Bruce, former Iron Maiden vocalist. Their debut album included the seven minute 'Black Metallic', a US college radio hit. However, by the end of 1992 the press had turned on what it perceived to be the 'shoegazing' scene, and the Catherine Wheel were also targeted for volleys of abuse despite aural evidence to the contrary. *Chrome* was again produced by Gil Norton and featured cover artwork by Hipgnosis designer Storm Thorgesen (Pink Floyd's *Dark Side Of The Moon*, etc.) but failed to revive fortunes in the UK, though their international audience continued to grow. 1995's *Happy Days* included a duet with Tanya Donelly (Belly) on 'Judy Staring At The Sun', while the album's uncompromising, bitter aftertaste was summed up by one of its titles, 'Eat My Dust You Insensitive Fuck'.

Albums: *Ferment* (Fontana 1992), *Chrome* (Fontana 1993), *Happy Days* (Fontana 1995).

Cave, Nick, And The Bad Seeds

After the Birthday Party split, the enigmatic Australian vocalist Nick Cave retained his association with Berlin by teaming up with ex-Einsturzende Neubauten member Blixa Bargeld (guitar), together with ex-Magazine personnel Barry Adamson (bass and other instruments) and multi-instrumentalist Mick Harvey. The debut album, *From Here*

Nick Cave

To Eternity, was accompanied by a startling rendition of the Elvis Presley classic, 'In the Ghetto', showing Cave had lost none of his passion or the ability to inject dramatic tension in his music. *The First Born Is Dead* followed a year later, promoted by the excellent 'Tupelo', but the Bad Seeds made their mark with *Kicking Against The Pricks* in the summer of 1986, bolstered by the UK Independent number 1, 'The Singer'. Cave had always drawn from a variety of sources, from Captain Beefheart to delta blues, and the Bad Seeds' material betrayed a claustrophobic, swamp-like aura. Although purely cover versions, *Kicking Against The Pricks* (which included drummer Thomas Wylder) fully displayed his abilities as an original interpreter of other artist's material. The subsequent *Your Funeral, My Trial* emphasized the power of his self-penned compositions, with improved production giving his vocals added clarity. After a brief hiatus from recording, it was two years before Cave returned, but it was worth the wait. 'The Mercy Seat' was a taut, brooding example of Cave's ability to build a story, followed by the milder 'Oh Deanna', which still contained considerable menace in its lyric. Both elements were present on October 1988's *Tender Prey*, as well as a more melodious approach to both his song constructions and singing voice. 'The Ship Song', released in February 1990, continued Cave's exploration of the more traditional ballad, and was followed by another strong album, *The Good Son*, in April. This accentuated several themes previously explored; notably spirituality and mortality, aided by the introduction of strings. Cave's literary aspirations had already been given an outlet by Black Spring Press in 1989, who published his first novel, *And The Ass Saw The Angel*. His film appearances include Wim Wenders' *Wings Of Desire* (1987) and a powerful performance as a prison inmate in the Australian production, *Ghosts Of The Civil Dead* (1989).
Albums: *From Here To Eternity* (Mute 1984), *The First Born Is Dead* (Mute 1985), *Kicking Against The Pricks* (Mute 1986), *Your Funeral, My Trial* (Mute 1986), *Tender Prey* (Mute 1988), with Mick Harvey, Blixa Bargeld *Ghosts Of The Civil Dead* (Mute 1989, film soundtrack), *The Good Son* (Mute 1990), *Henry's Dream* (Mute 1992), *Live Seeds* (Mute 1993), *Let Love In* (Mute 1994).
Video: *Road To God Knows Where* (1990).
Further reading: a collection of song lyrics and verse, *King Ink*, Nick Cave.

CBGB's

CBGB's is practically as intrinsic to the development of American alternative rock music as the guitar. A downtown, 300-capacity New York nightclub/venue, its legendary status grew quickly among aficionados of the city's 'No Wave' scene, and the subsequent punk movement. Established in December 1963, the venue was founded by owner Hilly Kristal (b. c.1931), giving it the name Country, Bluegrass, Blues and Other Music for Uplifting Gourmandizers, though the last sections of these initials were soon dropped. Previously it had been a low-rent drinking establishment. The club came into its own in the mid-70s, when Television manager Terry Ork brought in new groups. A who's who of New York music quickly followed, including Patti Smith, Blondie, Richard Hell, Ramones, Dead Boys, Talking Heads

and the Cramps. A second generation also saw the light of day through CBGB's, including Sonic Youth and the Swans. In 1993 20th Anniversary Celebrations were held, with some of the venue's favourite artists taking part in the celebrations, including Joan Jett, the Damned, David Byrne and more recent graduates, Jesus Lizard and J. Mascis (Dinosaur Jr). The Dictators, Tuff Darts and the Shirts all reunited for the occasion. Other notable attractions over the years have included Guns N'Roses, AC/DC, Pearl Jam, and the Spin Doctors. Though many like Joey Ramone retain fond memories of its illustrious past as a 'birthplace', the venue remains popular to this day because of the booking policy, whereby bands receive 80% of the door minus expenses.
Selected album: *Live At CBGBs* (1976).
Further reading: *This Ain't No Disco*, Roman Kozak.

Chameleons

Formed in 1981 in Middleton, Manchester, this highly promising but ill-fated group comprised Mark Burgess (vocals/bass), Reg Smithies (guitar), Dave Fielding (guitar) and Brian Schofield (drums). After some successful BBC radio sessions, the unit were signed to the CBS subsidiary Epic and released 'In Shreds'. Its lack of success saw the group switch to the independent label Statik where they issued 'As High As You Can Go' and 'A Person Isn't Safe Anywhere These Days'. Their *Script Of The Bridge* and *What Does Anything Mean Basically?* revealed them as a promising guitar-based group with a strong melodic sense. Regular touring won them a contract with Geffen Records and their third album *Strange Times* was very well received by the critics. Just as a breakthrough beckoned, however, their manager Tony Fletcher died and amid the ensuing chaos the group folded. Two spin-off groups, the Sun And The Moon and the Reegs lacked the charm of their powerful but unrealized mother group.
Albums: *Script Of The Bridge* (1983), *What Does Anything Mean Basically?* (1985), *Fan And The Bellows* (1986), *Strange Times* (1987), *Tripping Dogs* (1990, early recordings), *Peel Sessions* (1990, early recordings), *The Free Trade Hall Rehearsal* (1992), *The Radio 1 Evening Show Sessions* (1993), *Strange Times* (1993).
Videos: *Live At Camden Palace* (1986).

Change Of Seasons

Dutch rock band founded in 1992, recording a demo tape a year later which received the 'demo of the month' award in one of Holland's metal magazines. Other European media were similarly impressed. Signing to Rock The Nation Records shortly thereafter, they re-recorded the songs before travelling to South River, New Jersey, to mix the finished album at Trax East Studios. *Cold Sweat* tapped the alternative sounds of Seattle and the Pearl Jam/Soundgarden axis as its main inspiration, also blending in progressive elements drawn from a wider musical vocabulary (press comparisons included Dream Theater).
Album: *Cold Sweat* (RTN 1994).

Channel 3

This US based hardcore band, comprised Mike McGrann (vocals/guitar), Kimm Gardner (guitar), Larry Kelley (bass) and Mike Burton (the most permanent of their first four drummers). Hailing from the suburban community of Cerritos in south Los Angeles, they originally formed in 1980. Their first release was an EP on Californian label Posh Boy in 1981. One track from this, 'Manzanar', was played heavily by UK disc jockey John Peel, which resulted in Posh Boy's Robbie Fields licensing a three track EP to No Future Records. This was headed by the title track 'I've Got A Gun'. 'Manzanar' was again present, and concerned McGrann's mother (he is partially of Japanese origin) being sent to a work camp in World War II. Considering it was early in the band's career, the lyrics showed surprising maturity: 'Adolf really caught your eye, ain't it fun to knock the Warsaw zone, but you turned the other way, when we screwed some of our very own'. 1982 saw Jack Debaun become their next drummer, and *Fear Of Life* was re-titled *I've Got A Gun* in the UK with some differences in the track-listing. *After The Lights Go Out* was a superior and more consistent effort, although it failed to recapture the spark of interest which came with their first UK single. 1985's collection for Enigma Records revealed that the band had navigated the transition to a more straightforward rock format comfortably, without losing that early spark. Despite which, it was to be their last recording. McGrann's summation of their brief existence ran thus: 'Channel 3 was a band formed around friendships, if we weren't playing guitars together we'd probably be bowling or robbing Laundramats together.'

Albums: *Fear Of Life/I've Got A Gun* (Posh Boy 1982), *After The Lights Go Out* (Posh Boy 1983), *The Last Time I Drank ...* (Enigma 1985).

Chapterhouse

Formed in Reading in 1987 by Andrew Sherriff (b. 5 May 1969, Wokingham, England; guitar/vocals), Stephen Patman (b. 8 November 1968, Windsor, Berkshire, England; guitar), Simon Rowe (b. 23 June 1969, Reading, Berkshire, England; guitar), Jon Curtis (bass) and Ashley Bates (b. 2 November 1971, Reading, Berkshire, England; drums), Chapterhouse took the unusual step of rehearsing and gigging for well over a year before recording even a demotape. They were initially lumped in with the British acid rock scene of the time, a mistake hardly rectified by the band's early performances supporting Spacemen 3. Chapterhouse eventually escaped from one genre only to find themselves thrust amongst the infamous 'shoegazer' groups of 1991 (with Lush, Moose and Slowdive), so called because of the bands' static live shows and insular, effects-pedal driven music. Bassist Jon Curtis left early on to study, being replaced by Russell Barrett (b. 7 November 1968, Vermont, USA) who also fronted his own garage band, the Bikinis. Chapterhouse eventually signed to the newly-formed Dedicated Records label, releasing a series of lavishly-acclaimed singles, including 'Pearl', which revelled in distorted melodies. The autumn of 1991 saw the band aiming their sights on the American market, but they were to make little headway. Back home in Britain, too, the press were now reluctant to embrace them, with the 'shoegazing' scene becoming the target of a traditional backlash. Reviews in the music papers for 1993's *Blood Music* were lukewarm at best.

Albums: *Whirlpool* (Dedicated 1991), *Blood Music* (Dedicated 1993).

Charlatans

Of all the 'Manchester' bands to emerge in 1989 and 1990, the Charlatans' rise was undoubtedly the swiftest. Hinging around Tim Burgess (b. 30 May 1968, Salford, Manchester, England; lead vocals, ex-Electric Crayons) and Martin Blunt (b. 1965; bass, ex-Makin' Time), supported by Jon Baker (b. 1969; guitar), Jon Brookes (b. 1969; drums) and Rob Collins (b. 1967; keyboards), the band fused 60s melodies, Hammond organ riffs and a generally loose feel that was instantly adopted by those taken with the Stone Roses and the Happy Mondays. The group's stage presentation was boosted by the recruitment of veteran Californian lightsman 'Captain Whizzo' who provided the psychedelic visuals. With all the optimism that accompanies a new decade, 1990's 'Indian Rope', a 12-inch only debut on their own Dead Dead Good label, sold well enough to secure a contract with Beggars Banquet Records/Situation 2. That was nothing compared to 'The Only One I Know', a swirling, grooved pop song that borrowed from the Byrds and Booker T. And The MGs to provide the perfect summer anthem. A UK Top 10 hit, the single catapulted the Charlatans into the big league, and was consolidated by the follow-up, 'Then', and the band's debut album later that year. With the delightful compositions that made up the UK chart-topping *Some Friendly*, the band ended the year on a high note. 1991 proved far quieter on the recording front, although a fourth single and a further hit, 'Over Rising', steered away from the band's organ-based approach. However, 1992 brought more than its fair share of problems. *Between 10th And 11th* disappointed, bass player Martin Blunt suffered a nervous breakdown, guitarist Baker flew the nest (replaced by Mark Collins) and, most bizarrely, keyboard player Rob Collins was jailed for being an accessory to an armed robbery on a Northwich off-licence. *Up To Our Hips* repaired some of the damage with confident songs such as 'Can't Get Out Of Bed' and 'Autograph', though despite a strong fan base the Charlatans were still widely perceived to be yesterday's men, press interest fading as quickly as it had sprung up.

Albums: *Some Friendly* (Situation 2 1990), *Between 10th And 11th* (Situation 2 1992), *Up To Our Hips* (Beggars Banquet 1994).

Chefs

The Chefs, from Brighton, East Sussex, England, only survived three singles before splitting, and one of those was a reissue. Along with other aspiring local talent in the late 70s, the Chefs - Helen McCookerybook (b. Helen McCallum; vocals/bass), James McCallum (guitar), Russell Greenwood (drums), Carl Evans (guitar) - were signed to the town's resident label, Attrix Records. The EP, *Sweetie*, issued in September 1980, was far from being sweet, dealing frankly with sex, personal hygiene and other matters. But '24 Hours' (1981) was nothing short of a great pop song and was strong enough to warrant a reissue on the Midlands label, Graduate Records. The band changed their name to Skat for a guitar-based cover of the Velvet Underground's 'Femme Fatale'. Helen McCookerybook then left to form Helen And The

Horns, a bold brass dominated group with influences taken from the American west. 'Pioneer Town' and a remake of Doris Day's 'Secret Love' were both interesting excursions, although the band eventually floundered due to Helen's increasing stage fright.

Chelsea

This London-based punk unit was formed in 1977 by vocalist Gene October, the only constant in a myriad of line-ups. Initially recruiting Brian James (guitar), Geoff Myles (bass) and Chris Bashford (drums), like many of their immediate peers Chelsea were a band with a strong social conscience. Specializing in sub-three minute vitriolic outbursts on unemployment, inner city decay and the deconstruction of society under British Prime Minister Margaret Thatcher's rule, their lyrics were always more interesting than their music. The songs generally formed a similar pattern of uptempo numbers, marred by basic studio techniques (October's delivery, occasionally gruesome, was nevertheless the glue in the formula). Taken as a body of work the songs become jarring, but individually their music is exciting and energetic. Their most noteworthy song is 'Right To Work', which became a working-class anthem during the late 70s (though it would later transpire that the basis of the song was, perversely, anti-union - and October was not exactly a veteran of any council estate). They have continued to record throughout the 80s, but with an ever-changing line-up and an image that is as anachronistic as their music.
Albums: *Chelsea* (Step Forward 1979), *Alternative Hits* (Step Forward 1980), *Evacuate* (IRS 1982), *Rocks Off* (Jungle 1986), *Under Wraps* (IRS 1989). Compilations: *Just For The Record* (Step Forward 1985), *Backtrax* (Illegal 1988), *Unreleased Stuff* (Clay 1989).
Video: *Live At The Bier Keller* (1984).
Films: *Jubilee* (1978).

Cherry Vanilla

This USA punk outfit was fronted by the sexually provocative Cherry Vanilla (b. New York, USA). With the addition of Stuart Elliot (drums), Howie Finkel (bass), Louis Lepere (guitar) and Zecca Esquibel (keyboards), they specialized in commercial pop-rock anthems, rather than hard-line punk. Signing to RCA, they supported Johnny Thunders And The Heartbreakers on their UK tour in 1978. Following the release of the follow-up *Venus De Vinyl*, the group left RCA for an uncertain future.
Albums: *Bad Girl* (1978), *Venus De Vinyl* (1979).

Chesterfields

For a while, the Chesterfields' charming, jolly guitar pop, was very much in vogue. They were formed in Yeovil, Somerset, England, in the summer of 1984, by David Goldsworthy (guitar/vocals), Simon Barber (bass/vocals) and Dominic Manns (drums). In 1985 they were joined by guitarist Brendan Holden. They contributed 'Nose Out Of Joint' alongside a track from Scotland's Shop Assistants, whom they joined at Bristol's Subway Organisation Records in time for the EP, *A Guitar In Your Bath* (1986), four slices of frothy guitar pop. 'Completely And Utterly' continued

the formula, but for the next single, 'Ask Johnny Dee' in 1987, the Chesterfields offered a less abrasive style. *Kettle* showcased the band's songwriting talents admirably. Back in April, Holden had left the band, and was temporarily replaced by Rodney Allen (later with the Blue Aeroplanes) and former Loft guitarist Andy Strickland (on loan from the Caretaker Race). A more permanent guitarist was later found in Simon's brother, Mark Barber. A compilation of the band's singles, *Westward Ho!*, coincided with the release of their session for BBC disc jockey, Janice Long. A month later, the band set up their own label, Household. In March 1988 they issued 'Goodbye Goodbye' a more melancholy offering than previous efforts. This was followed by 'Blame' and a new album, *Crocodile Tears*. The latter was not as warmly received as *Kettle* and both Goldsworthy and Manns left soon after. The Chesterfields continued with Simon and Mark Barber co-fronting the band, assisted by various drummers and guitarists, before splitting up in July 1989. Their last offering, 'Fool Is A Man', was perhaps their finest moment. Simon went on to front Yeovil-based Basinger, while Mark led the Bristol-based Grape.
Albums: *Kettle* (Subway 1987), *Crocodile Tears* (Household 1988). Compilation: *Westward Ho!* (Subway 1987).

Chilli Willi And The Red Hot Peppers

Although fondly recalled as a leading 'pub rock' attraction, Chilli Willi began life as a folksy-cum-country duo comprising of Martin Stone (b. 11 December 1946, Woking, Surrey, England; guitar/mandolin/vocals) and Phil 'Snakefinger' Lithman (b. 17 June 1949, Tooting, London, England; guitar/lap steel/fiddle/piano/vocals). Both were former members of Junior's Blues Band, an aspiring early 60s group, but while Lithman moved to San Francisco, Stone found a measure of notoriety with the Savoy Brown Blues Band and Mighty Baby. The friends were reunited on *Kings Of The Robot Rhythm*, an informal, enchanting collection which featured assistance from blues singer Jo-Ann Kelly and several members of Brinsley Schwarz. In December 1972 the duo added Paul 'Dice Man' Bailey (b. 6 July 1947, Weston-super-Mare, Somerset, England; guitar/saxophone/banjo), Paul Riley (b. 3 October 1951, Islington, London, England; bass) and Pete Thomas (b. 9 August 1954, Sheffield, Yorkshire, England; drums) and over the ensuing two years, the quintet became one of Britain's most compulsive live attractions. Despite its charm, incorporating many diverse American styles such as blues, country, western swing, rock and R&B, *Bongos Over Balham* failed to capture the group's in-concert passion and a disillusioned Chilli Willi split up in February 1975. Pete Thomas later joined the Attractions, Paul Riley played with Graham Parker's band, while Bailey helped form Bontemps Roulez. Martin Stone joined the Pink Fairies prior to leaving music altogether, while Lithman returned to San Francisco where, as Snakefinger, he resumed his earlier association with the Residents.
Albums: *Kings Of The Robot Rhythm* (1972), *Bongos Over Balham* (1974).

Chills

The ever-changing line-ups that have made up New Zealand guitar pop band the Chills are kept constant by founder member Martin Phillipps (b. 1963, Dunedin, New Zealand) whose musical apprenticeship began when he was asked to join punk band the Same as guitarist in 1978. Inspired by New Zealand's top punk acts the Enemy and the Clean, the Same churned out a standard set of 60s garage band covers without ever recording. When that band split Phillipps took his sister Rachel, and bassist Jane Todd (later of the Verlaines) into the first incarnation of the Chills in 1980. Signed to the influential New Zealand independent label, Flying Nun Records, the Chills began to release a number of seminal guitar-pop singles, mostly in New Zealand. Other members to pass through the band over the years included Fraser Batts (keyboards), Terry Moore (bass), Martin Kean (guitar), Peter Allison (keyboards), Alan Haig (drums), and Martyn Bull (drums) - the latter of whom died in 1983 of leukæmia. It was to him that Phillipps dedicated 'I Love My Leather Jacket', as the said apparel was Bull's parting gift. In 1985, already on their ninth line-up, Phillipps brought the Chills to London for some dates and Alan McGee released the *Kaleidoscope World* compilation on his Creation Records label. On returning to New Zealand the band dissolved again and Phillipps once more found new musicians including Justin Harwood (bass), Andrew Todd (keyboards), Caroline Easther (drums) and Jimmy Stephenson (drums). Despite the constant upheavals, and the relative lack of recorded material for a band with a 10-year career, the Chills have continued to produce honest, clean guitar driven pop.

Albums: *Kaleidoscope World* (Creation 1986), *Brave Words* (Flying Nun 1987), *Submarine Bells* (Slash/Warners 1990).

China Crisis

This UK, Liverpool-based group was formed in 1979 around the core of Gary Daly (b. 5 May 1962, Kirkby, Merseyside, England; vocals) and Eddie Lundon (b. 9 June 1962, Kirkby, Merseyside, England; guitar). In 1982, their first single, 'African And White', initially on the independent Inevitable label, was picked up for distribution by Virgin Records and made a critical impact, despite only just breaking into the UK Top 50. The single's b-side was 'Red Sails', a perfect early example of China Crisis' pastoral electro-pop. Having now signed to the Virgin label, the duo formed a more permanent line-up with the recruitment of Gazza Johnson (bass) and Kevin Wilkinson (drums). The following single, 'Christian', taken from the debut album *Difficult Shapes And Passive Rhythms* was a UK number 12 hit. With the follow-up to their second album, they scored two further Top 50 hits with 'Tragedy And Mystery' and 'Working With Fire And Steel', the former featuring the trade-mark on the forthcoming album - the ethereal oboe accompaniment. 'Wishful Thinking' in 1984 gave the group a Top 10 hit, while the following year gave them two further Top 20 hits with 'Black Man Ray' and 'King In A Catholic Style (Wake Up)'. While *Flaunt The Imperfection*, produced by Walter Becker, reached the UK Top 10, the follow-up, the uneven *What Price Paradise?* (produced by Clive Langer and Alan Winstanley), saw a drop in China Crisis' fortunes, when the album peaked at number 63. A two-year hiatus saw a reunion with Becker which resulted in the critically acclaimed *Diary Of A Hollow Horse*, although this success was not reflected in sales. Since their split with Virgin and the release of a deserved

reappraisal of the group's career with a compilation in 1990, activities within the China Crisis camp has been low-key.

Albums: *Difficult Shapes And Passive Rhythms* (1983), *Working With Fire And Steel - Possible Pop Songs Volume Two* (1983), *Flaunt The Imperfection* (1985), *What Price Paradise?* (1986), *Diary Of A Hollow Horse* (1989), *Warped By Success* (Stardumb 1994). Compilations: *The China Crisis Collection* (1990), *China Crisis Diary* (1992).

Video: *Showbiz Absurd*.

Chris And Cosey

Chris Carter and Cosey Fanni Tutti (b. Christine Newby) became partners while with late 70s 'industrial' sound pioneers, Throbbing Gristle. When the latter split in 1981, the couple decided to operate both as Chris And Cosey and as CTI (Creative Technology Institute). Their debut album, *Heartbeat*, credited to CTI, drew from Throbbing Gristle's rhythmic undercurrents, but the pair's next collection, *Trance*, was soured by a disagreement with Rough Trade Records over its selling price. 1983 yielded two singles, the Japanese-only 'Nikki' (a collaboration with John Duncan) and the relatively mainstream 'October (Love Song)'. These were followed in 1984 by *Songs Of Love And Lust*. That year the duo also issued *Elemental 7* in collaboration with John Lacey on Cabaret Voltaire's Doublevision label and further projects, as CTI, with Lustmord's Brian Williams and Glenn Wallis of Konstructivitis. These projects were also accompanied by *European Rendezvous*. CTI's *Mondo Beat*, released in 1985, was originally conceived by Chris as a 12-inch single, but expanded beyond that format. By this time, the pair's relationship with Rough Trade had become strained and they left after *Techno Primitiv* and 'Sweet Surprise', a project with the Eurythmics. They then joined Vancouver label Nettwerk Productions, while in Europe they were handled by renowned Brussels label, Play It Again Sam (who have also reissued much of their product). Since then, Chris And Cosey have gradually steered towards the 'New Beat' dance sound, with singles such as 'Obsession', 'Exotica' (both 1987) and 'Rise' (1989). Early 90s albums *Reflection* and *Pagan Tango*, confirmed their adoption of hi-tech dance music.

Albums: *Heartbeat* (Rough Trade 1981), *Trance* (Rough Trade 1982), *Songs Of Love And Lust* (Rough Trade 1984), *Elemental 7* (Rough Trade 1984), *European Rendezvous* (Doublevision 1984), *Techno Primitiv* (Rough Trade 1985), *Action* (Licensed 1987), *Exotica* (Nettwerk 1987), *Trust* (Play It Again Sam 1989), *Reflection* (Play It Again Sam 1990), *Pagan Tango* (Play It Again Sam 1991), *Muzik Fantastique* (Play It Again Sam 1992). Compilations: *Best Of Chris And Cosey* (Play It Again Sam 1989), *Collectiv 1, 2, 3, & 4* (Play It Again Sam 1990).

Christian Death

This incredibly prolific art-rock group were formed in Los Angeles, California, USA, in 1979 by singer Rozz Williams. The original line-up additionally comprised Rikk Agnew (ex-Adolescents; guitar), James McGearly (bass) and George Belanger (drums), but afterwards the group's composition would fluctuate rapidly. In finding success in their homeland elusive, the group relocated to Europe in 1983, where they fitted in perfectly with the gothic rock fashion. Shunning the easy route to success, the band have since remained on the periphery of rock, and Christian Death's independence from prevailing trends has secured themselves a strong cult following, if little commercial or critical recognition. In 1986 the group fell under the control of songwriter and singer Valor Kand (b. Australia), who made radical changes to the line-up. Principal members now included Gitane Demone (vocals/keyboards) and David Glass (drums). Their often provocative material made as its principal target grand passion and organised religion, particularly that of Catholicism, citing corruption in the church and links with politicians. Album cover artwork, such as that which bedecked *Sex, Drugs And Jesus Christ*, which depicted a Christ-like figure injecting heroin, caused a suitable furore of publicity and controversy. As did *All The Hate*'s 'poignant' use of swastika imagery. Despite the attention-seeking nature of some of their product, their vast discography has rarely risen above such crude devices. It is complicated, too, by the fact that during the 90s there have been at least two bands operating under the same banner, resulting in all manner of litigation and dubious album issues.

Albums: *Only Theatre Of Pain* (Frontier 1982), *Catastrophe Ballet* (L'Invitation Au Suicide 1984), *Ashes* (Nostradamus 1985), *The Decomposition Of Violets* (ROIR 1986, cassette only), *Anthology Of Live Bootlegs* (Nostradamus 1986), *Atrocities* (Normal 1986), *Scriptures* (Jungle 1987), *Sex, Drugs And Jesus Christ* (Jungle 1988), *The Heretics Alive* (Jungle 1989), *All The Love* (Jungle 1989), *All The Hate* (Jungle 1989), *Insanus, Ultio, Proditio Misericordiaque* (Supporti Fonografici 1990), *Love And Hate* (Jungle 1992), *Sexy Death God* (Bullet Proof 1993). Compilations: *The Wind Kissed Pictures (Past And Present)* (Supporti Fonografici 1987), *Past, Present And Future* (Supporti Fonografici 1991), *Jesus Points The Bone At You* (Jungle 1992, singles collection from 1986-90).

Chrome

Formed in San Francisco in 1976, Chrome were one of the earliest and most influential American new wave/punk/industrial bands. Their first recording line-up featured John L. Cyborg (b. John Lambdin; vocals/guitar/bass), Gary Spain (vocals/guitar/bass), Mike Low (guitar/synthesiser/bass) and Damon Edge (guitar/synthesiser/drums). Only Cyborg had any previous experience worth noting, having played with the Flower Travellin' Band. This line-up recorded 1977's *The Visitation* for Siren Records. Low then departed and was replaced by Helios Creed. The band proceeded to record *Alien Soundtracks* as background music for live sex shows. Much of their material at this stage dealt with the theme of machines taking over from man, an idea expressed in several of their album titles for Siren. These also saw a gradual progression from guitar-based rock to synthesizer and taped experimental pieces with a sinister undercurrent of menace and urban anxiety which stamped the band as an American equivalent to Throbbing Gristle. In the early 80s the band fractured. Edge and Creed recruited new players John and Hilary Stench from Remeo Void and Vital Parts respectively. They had also played together in Pearl Harbor And The

Explosions. After *Third From The Sun*, the band effectively ground to a halt in 1983. However, Damon Edge resurrected the name for another slew of less satisfying albums released alternately on France's Mosquito and Germany's Dossier Records. The archive release of the *Chrome Box* set included four of their old albums, plus new recordings, *Chronicles 1 + 2*, while *No Humans Allowed* compiled their Siren material including deleted singles and EPs. These days Helios Creed regularly turns out solo metal/grunge albums on Amphetamine Reptile Records, and other former members are still active in a variety of bands.

Albums: *The Visitation* (Siren 1977), *Alien Soundtracks* (Siren 1978), *Half Machine Lip Moves* (Siren 1979), *Red Exposure* (Siren 1980), *Inworlds* (Siren 1980), *Blood On The Moon* (Siren 1981), *Third From The Sun* (Siren 1982), *Raining Milk* (Mosquito 1983), *Chronicles* (Dossier 1984), *Into The Eyes Of The Zombie King* (Mosquito 1984), *The Lyon Concert* (Dossier 1985), *Another World* (Dossier 1986), *Dreaming In Sequence* (Dossier 1987), *Live In Germany* (Dossier 1989), *Alien Soundtracks II* (Dossier 1989). Compilations: *No Humans Allowed* (Siren 1982), *Chrome Box* (Subterranean 1982, 6 album boxed set).

Chumbawamba

The multi-member Chumbawamba were originally an anarchist group formed in Leeds, England. out of a household situated in the shadow of Armley jail. In a similar manner to Crass, who were an obvious early influence, the group dynamic was powered by their communal life. First playing live in 1983, the band, whose regional origins are in Burnley and Bradford, alternated between instruments/theatricals on stage and record. The current line-up is Harry Hamer, Alice Nutter, Boff, Mavis Dillon, Louise Mary Watts, Danbert Nobacon, Paul Greco and Dunstan Bruce, with ages ranging from teens to 30s at inception. Their first single, 'Revolution', was startling, opening with the sound of John Lennon's 'Imagine', before having it removed from the stereo and smashed. It was just as precise lyrically: 'The history books from every age, Have the same words written on every page, Always starting with revolution, Always ending with capitulation, Always silenced by the truncheon, or bought out with concessions, Always repetition...'. It was a powerful introduction, finishing at number 6 in disc jockey John Peel's 1985 Festive 50 radio poll. The follow-up, 'We Are The World', was banned from airplay due to its explicit support of direct action. *Pictures of Starving Children Sell Records* used polemic and agit-prop to subvert a common theme in the music industry at that time, denouncing the self-indulgence of Band Aid. Other targets included multi-nationals (the band had published a booklet on immoral activities titled *Dirty Fingers In Dirty Pies*), apartheid and imperialism. Their discourse was made all the more articulate by the surprising virtuosity of musics employed, from polka to ballad to thrash. Pouring red paint over the Clash on their comeback 'busking' tour in Leeds demonstrated their contempt for what they saw as false prophets, while the second album considered the role of government in oppression and the futility of the vote. *English Rebel Songs* acknowledged their place in the folk protest movement, and *Slap!* saw hope in the rebellious dance music

Chumbawamba

which characterized the end of the 80s. By this time the group had somewhat abandoned their previous austerity - now Danbert (seemingly addicted to flowery dresses) and Alice (who wrote widely on the positive aspects of pornography) were all-singing, all-dancing comperes to a live show which celebrated resistance and deviance rather than complained about 'the system'. Anarchy!, somewhat ironically titled in view of new perceptions of the band, dismissed the blind-alley myopia of the punk set ('Give The Anarchist A Cigarette'), while still railing against intolerance ('Homophobia' gave a musical backdrop to a true story of a gay slaying in Bradford). Chumbawamba may no longer share the same living space, or even the same ideas, but they are as powerful and attractive a force in the underbelly of the British music scene as ever.

Albums: *Pictures Of Starving Children Sell Records* (Agit Prop 1986), *Never Mind The Ballots, Here's The Rest Of Your Life* (Agit Prop 1987), *English Rebel Songs 1381-1914* (Agit Prop 1989, mini-album), *Slap!* (Agit Prop 1990), *Anarchy* (One Little Indian 1994), *Showbusiness! Chumbawamba Live* (One Little Indian 1995). Compilation: *First 2* (Agit Prop 1993, comprises *Pictures Of Starving Children Sell Records* and *Never Mind The Ballots*).

Church

Formed in Canberra, Australia, in 1980, the Church, led by Steve Kilbey (b. England; bass/vocals), who emigrated with his family at an early age, comprised Peter Koppes (b. Australia; guitar/vocals), Marty Willson-Piper (b. England; guitar/vocals) and Nick Ward (drums). Richard Ploog (b. Australia; drums) would replace the latter after the completion of the group's debut album. That release came in 1981, when *Of Skins And Heart* gained some radio and television exposure. The European release, *The Church*, which included stand-out cut 'The Unguarded Moment' (with its accompanying early pixelated image effect video) gave indications of great promise. The Church's 60s/Byrds revivalist stance, coupled with a distinctive 12-stringed 'jangly' guitar approach was exemplified on *The Blurred Crusade* by such songs as 'Almost With You', 'When You Were Mine' and 'Fields Of Mars'. *Starfish* saw the band gain college radio airplay in the USA, earning them a US Top 30 hit with 'Under The Milky Way', and strengthened their audiences in parts of Europe - although generally the group found themselves restricted to a loyal cult following. Much of the group's activities have been interrupted periodically due to internal problems and for solo projects and collaborations. Ploog's departure in 1991 saw the addition of former Patti Smith and Television drummer, Jay Dee Daugherty. Willson-Piper released two solo albums and took on a part-time role as guitarist for All About Eve in 1991. Kilbey has recorded several albums as well as publishing a book of poems. In 1991 he teamed up with Go-Betweens guitarist Grant McLennan to record under the name of Jack Frost. Peter Koppes completed an EP, *When Reason Forbids*, in 1987, before embarking on his own sequence of album releases.

Albums: *Of Skins & Heart* (Parlophone 1981), *The Church* (Carrere 1982), *Blurred Crusade* (Carrere 1982), *Seance* (Carrere 1983), *Remote Luxury* (Warners 1984), *Heyday*

(Warners 1986), *Starfish* (Arista 1988), *Gold Afternoon Fix* (Arista 1990), *Priest = Aura* (Arista 1992), *Sometime Anywhere* (Arista 1994). Compilations: *Conception* (Carrerre 1988), *Hindsight* (EMI 1988), *A Quick Smoke At Spots (Archives 1986-1990)* (Arista 1991). Solo albums: Marty Willson-Piper: *In Reflection* (Chase 1987), *Art Attack Survival* (Rykodisc 1988), *Rhyme* (Rykodisc 1989). Peter Koppes: *Manchild & Myth* (Rykodisc 1988), *From The Well* (TVT 1989). Steve Kilbey: *Unearthed* (Enigma 1987), *Earthed* (Rykodisc 1988), *The Slow Crack* (Red Eye 1988), *Remindlessness* (Red Eye 1990). With Grant McLennan (as Jack Frost): *Jack Frost* (Arista 1991).

Videos: *Goldfish (Jokes, Magic And Souvenirs)* (1990).

Ciccone Youth

A satirical offshoot from New York rock innovators Sonic Youth, Ciccone Youth comprise essentially the same personnel Thurston Moore (guitar/vocals), Kim Gordon (bass/vocals), Lee Renaldo (guitar) plus, various drummers and other collaborators. The band had long been fascinated by the impact Madonna was having on a generation. Moore had previously mounted a photo of the artist on the cover of his own fanzine *Killer*. The band's infatuation was also prefaced with the track 'Madonna, Sean And Me' on Sonic Youth's *E.V.O.L.* album. It was November 1986 when the name Ciccone Youth was first employed, however. The single 'Into The Groove(y)' was a direct parody of Madonna's original, with Moore's vocals overlaid in a manner which suggested a duet. Assistance on the recording came from Firehose and Mike Watt (ex-Minutemen). Further pastiche was served up with *The Whitey Album*. Despite rumours that it would be made up entirely of covers of the Beatles' similarly titled original, it proved to be the band's most eclectic release to date. 'We just wanted to steal blatantly from these records. We're not trying to hide anything. We took the bass drums of L.L. Cool J and Run DMC records. We took stuff off Jimi Hendrix records . . .' Notable was the deliberately lifeless rendering of Robert Palmer's 'Addicted To Love', and the cover of John Cage's 'Silence' pastiche. While not an unqualified success, the album served to rid the band of some of their excesses without committing them to the catalogue of Sonic Youth.

Albums: *The Whitey Album* (Blast First 1989).

Circle Jerks

Formed in Los Angeles, California, USA, in 1980, this powerful punk band was founded by vocalist Keith Morris (ex-Black Flag) and guitarist Greg Hetson (ex-Redd Kross). Roger (Dowding) Rogerson (bass) and Lucky Lehrer (drums) completed the line-up featured on the quartet's forceful debut album. Their second, *Wild In The Streets*, was initially issued on Police manager Miles Copeland's Step Forward/Faulty label. It featured the services of hardcore's number one drummer, Chuck Biscuits (ex-DOA), but he would leave in 1984 for a career in Danzig. Appearances on several influential 'new music' compilations, including *Decline Of Western Civilisation* (they also had a starring role in the film of the same name) and *Let Them Eat Jelly Beans* confirmed the Circle Jerks' position at the vanguard of California's virulent hardcore movement. Longstanding members Morris and Hetson remained at the helm of this compulsive group which, by 1985, was fleshed out with the addition of Zander 'Snake' Scloss (bass; later Weirdos and Joe Strummer) and Keith 'Adolph' Clark (drums). *Wönderful*, from the same year, was something of a disappointment, but the Circle Jerks rescued their reputation with their final album, the staunch, Dictators-influenced *VI*. Albums: *Group Sex* (Frontier 1980), *Wild In The Streets* (Faulty 1982), *Golden Shower Of Hits* (LAX 1983), *Wönderful* (Combat Core 1985), *VI* (Relativity 1987).

Circus Lupus

Circus Lupus consist of Arika Casebolt (drums), Chris Hamely (guitar), Seth Lorinczi (bass) and Chris Thomson (vocals). They emerged in the 90s as one of the new breed of US alternative rock bands. Founded in Washington D.C., the band chose not to play the relentlessly intense hardcore sound associated with Washington state, but opted for a looser feel. On *Solid Brass* the producer Don Zientara emphasized Thomson's highly personal lyrics. It also included (on CD and cassette versions) the band's Joan Jett-produced single, 'Pop Man', a favourite of US college radio. Albums: *Super Genius* (Dischord 1992), *Solid Brass* (Dischord 1993).

Clarke, John Cooper

b. 25 January 1949, Salford, Manchester, England. With a 1965-style Bob Dylan suit and sunglasses and quickfire delivery, Clarke enjoyed a brief vogue as a 'punk poet'. His usually comedic compositions showed the influence of the punning wordplay of Roger McGough, combined with the tougher 'hip' approach of the American beats. Clarke recited his poetry in local folk clubs and working with Rick Goldstraw's group, the Ferretts, he began to mix his poems with musical backing. Goldstraw's involvement with the independent label, Rabid Records led, in 1977, to Clarke recording the co-produced Martin Hannett single, 'Psycle Sluts' - '...those nubile nihilists of the north circular the lean leonine leatherette lovelies of the Leeds intersection luftwaffe angels locked in a pagan paradise - no cash a passion for trash...' With the onset of punk, Clarke found himself encountering livelier audiences when he shared a bill with the Buzzcocks. The popularity of his performances with such audiences led to an increase in the phenomenon of the 'punk poet', giving rise to the careers of such 'second generation' artists as Attila The Stockbroker, Seething Wells and Joolz. After touring with Be-Bop DeLuxe, he was signed to Epic Records where Bill Nelson produced his debut album. The single, 'Gimmix', became a UK Top 40 hit in 1979. Again produced by Martin Hannett and with backing music by the Invisible Girls, it also appeared on *Snap Crackle And Bop*, along with 'Beasley Street', described by one reviewer as 'an English "Desolation Row"'. Clarke went into semi-retirement later in the 80s, forming a domestic partnership with ex-Velvet Underground singer Nico. In the 90s Clarke became active again on the pub and club circuit and is engaged in various film and book projects (his 1982 documentary, *Ten Years In An Open Necked Shirt*, was shown on UK television's Channel Four). Albums: *Disguise In Love* (Epic 1978), *Snap Crackle And Bop*

(Epic 1979), *Zip Style Method* (Epic 1982). Compilations: *Qu'est Le Maison De Fromage* (Rabid 1980), *Me And My Big Mouth* (Epic 1981).
Further reading: *Ten Years In An Open Necked Shirt*, John Cooper Clarke.

Clash

The Clash at first tucked in snugly behind punk's loudest noise, the Sex Pistols (whom they supported on 'the Anarchy tour'), and later became a much more consistent and intriguing force. Guitarist Mick Jones (b. 26 June 1955, London, England) had formed London SS in 1975, whose members at one time included bassist Paul Simonon (b. 15 December 1956, London, England) and drummer Nicky 'Topper' Headon (b. 30 May 1955, Bromley, Kent, England). Joe Strummer (b. John Graham Mellor, 21 August 1952, Ankara, Turkey) had spent the mid-70s fronting a pub-rock group called the 101ers, playing early rock 'n' roll style numbers such as 'Keys To Your Heart'. The early line-up of the Clash was completed by guitarist Keith Levene but he left early in 1976 with another original member, drummer Terry Chimes, whose services were called upon intermittently during the following years. They signed to CBS Records and during three weekends they recorded *The Clash* in London with sound engineer, Mickey Foote, taking on the producer's role. In 1977 *Rolling Stone* magazine called it the 'definitive punk album' and elsewhere it was recognized that they had brilliantly distilled the anger, depression and energy of mid-70s England. More importantly, they had infused the message and sloganeering with strong tunes and pop hooks, as on 'I'm So Bored With The USA' and 'Career Opportunities'. The album reached number 12 in the UK charts and garnered almost universal praise. CBS were keen to infiltrate the American market and Blue Öyster Cult's founder/lyricist Sandy Pearlman was brought in to produce *Give 'Em Enough Rope*. The label's manipulative approach failed and it suffered very poor sales in the USA but in the UK it reached number 2, despite pertinent claims that its more rounded edges amounted to a sell out of the band's earlier, much flaunted punk ethics. They increasingly embraced reggae elements, seemingly a natural progression of their anti-racist stance, and had a minor UK hit with '(White Man) In Hammersmith Palais' in July 1978, following it up with the frothy punk-pop of 'Tommy Gun' - their first Top 20 hit. Their debut album was finally released in the USA as a double set including tracks from their singles and it sold healthily before *London Calling*, produced by the volatile Guy Stevens, marked a return to almost top form. They played to packed houses across the USA early in 1980 and were cover stars in many prestigious rock magazines. Typically, their next move was over-ambitious and the triple set, *Sandinista!*, was leaden and too sprawling after the acute concentration of earlier records. It scraped into the UK Top 20 and sales were disappointing despite CBS making it available at a special cut-price. The experienced rock producer, Glyn Johns, was brought in to instigate a tightening-up and *Combat Rock* was as snappy as anticipated. It was recorded with Terry Chimes on drums after Headon had abruptly left the group. Chimes was later replaced by Pete Howard. 'Rock The Casbah', a jaunty, humorous song written by Headon, became a Top 10 hit in the USA and reached number 30 in the UK, aided by a sardonic video. During 1982 they toured the USA supporting the Who at their stadium concerts. Many observers were critical of a band that had once ridiculed superstar status, for becoming part of the same machinery. A simmering tension between Jones and Strummer eventually led to bitterness and Jones left in 1983 after Strummer accused him of becoming lazy. He told the press: 'He wasn't with us any more'. Strummer later apologised for lambasting Jones and admitted he was mainly to blame for the break-up of a successful songwriting partnership: 'I stabbed him in the back' was his own honest account of proceedings. The Clash struggled without Jones' input, despite the toothless *Cut The Crap* reaching number 16 in the the the UK charts in 1985. Mick Jones formed Big Audio Dynamite with another product of the 70s London scene, Don Letts, and for several years became a relevant force merging dance with powerful, spikey pop choruses. Strummer finally disbanded the Clash in 1986 and after a brief tour with Latino Rockabilly War and a period playing rhythm guitar with the Pogues, he turned almost full time to acting and production. He supervised the soundtrack to the film, *Sid And Nancy*, about the former Sex Pistols' bassist Sid Vicious and his girlfriend Nancy Spungen. In 1988 the Clash's most furious but tuneful songs were gathered together on the excellent compilation, *The Story Of The Clash*. They made a dramatic and unexpected return to the charts in 1991 when 'Should I Stay Or Should I Go?', originally a UK number 17 hit in October 1982, was re-released by CBS after the song appeared in a Levi's jeans television advertisement. Incredibly, the song reached number 1, thereby prompting more reissues of Clash material and fuelling widespread rumours of a band reunion, which came to nought.

Albums: *The Clash* (CBS 1977), *Give 'Em Enough Rope* (CBS 1978), *London's Calling* (CBS 1979, double album), *Sandinista!* (CBS 1980, triple album), *Combat Rock* (CBS 1982), *Cut The Crap* (CBS 1985). Compilations: *The Story Of The Clash* (CBS 1988, double album), *The Singles Collection* (CBS 1991).
Videos: *Rude Boy* (1987), *This Is Video Clash* (1989).

Classix Nouveaux

This 80s UK experimental quartet was fronted by the shaven-headed Sal Solo (b. 5 September 1954, Hatfield, Hertfordshire, England), whose uncompromising vocal style gelled uneasily with his musicians' synthesizer dance beat. Originally appearing on Stevo's Some Bizzare Records sample album, the group signed to Liberty Records in 1981 and recorded a series of albums, ranging from the gargantuan to the quirkily unmelodic. Four of their singles reached the UK Top 75 during 1981 and the following year they scored their biggest success with 'Is It A Dream' which climbed to number 11. Perpetually on the periphery, the group's limited chart success and affiliation with a major label did little to offset their determinedly *avant garde* approach. By the mid-80s, the unit folded with Sal going solo.
Albums: *Night People* (1981), *La Verité* (1982), *Secret* (1983). Solo: Sal Solo *Heart And Soul* (1985).

Clock DVA

One of a batch of groups forming the so-called 'industrial' scene of Sheffield in the early 80s, Clock DVA's first release was, appropriately, on Throbbing Gristle's Industrial label. The cassette-only (until its re-release in 1990) *White Souls In Black Suits* featured Adi Newton (ex-the Studs, the Future, Veer; vocals), Steven James Taylor (ex-Block Opposite; bass/vocals/guitar), Paul Widger (ex-They Must Be Russians; guitar), Roger Quail (drums) and Charlie Collins (saxophone). However, there had already been three previous line-ups, including guitarist Dave Hammond, and synthesizer players Joseph Hurst and Simon Elliot-Kemp. 1981 saw the band offer *Thirst*, available through independent label Fetish. With the ground for such 'difficult music' having been prepared by Throbbing Gristle, the press reaction was remarkably favourable. Nevertheless, the band disintegrated at the end of the year. Newton kept the name while the other three joined the Box. By 1983 replacements were found in John Valentine Carruthers (guitar), Paul Browse (saxophone), Dean Dennis (bass) and Nick Sanderson (drums). A brace of singles prefaced *Advantage*, their first album for Polydor Records. The following year Carruthers and Sanderson departed as Clock DVA continued as a trio. Though it would be five years before a follow-up, Newton was kept busy with his visual project the Anti Group (TAGC), and several singles. *Buried Dreams* finally arrived in 1989. By the time of 1991's *Transitional Voices*, Browse had been replaced by Robert Baker, a veteran of TAGC. Newton has long since described the process of making music as his research: 'We feel music is something that should change and not remain too rigid, evolve with ourselves as we grow, change our perception' Although their recorded history is sparse, it represents a more thoughtful and reflective body of work than that which dominates their peer group. In particular, Newton's grasp of the philosophical connotations of technology have placed him apart from the majority of its practitioners.
Albums: *White Souls In Black Suits* (Industrial 1980, cassette only), *Thirst* (Fetish 1981), *Advantage* (Polydor 1983), *Buried Dreams* (Interfish 1989), *Transitional Voices* (Amphetamine Reptile 1991), *Man-Amplified* (Contempo 1992), *Digital Soundtrack* (Contempo 1993).
Video: *Kinetic Engineering* (1994).

Close Lobsters

This atypical example of the 'indie shambling band' were formed in 1985 by Andrew Burnett (b. 11 February 1965, Johnstone, Scotland; vocals), brother Robert Burnett (b. 11 September 1962, Johnstone, Scotland; bass), Stewart McFadeyn (b. 26 September 1965, Paisley, Scotland; drums), Graeme Wilmington (b. 22 August 1965, Johnstone, Scotland; guitar) and Thomas Donnelly (b. 29 August 1962, Johnstone, Scotland; guitar). The Close Lobsters first crept into the limelight by featuring 'Firestation Towers' on the *C86* cassette organized by the *New Musical Express*, designed to bring together the best of the new independent bands appearing in 1986. Thanks to an intense mixture of agitated guitars and Andrew Burnett's peculiar - frequently unfathomable - lyrics, Close Lobsters manufactured a partisan following in Britain and garnered an enthusiastic response from US college radio stations. An invitation to the prestigious New York Music Seminar in 1989 led to an extensive Stateside tour as the band virtually emigrated to America in a bid to crack that market. In spite of respectable sales the pressure was too much for Donnelly, who departed at the close of the year. His ex-colleagues followed this example by taking a two-year break from the public eye before returning to the live circuit at the start of 1991. Sadly, when a Close Lobsters song did crack the UK Top 20 the following year ('Let's Make Some Plans'), it was as the b-side version to the Wedding Present's 'California'.

Albums: *Foxheads Stalk This Land* (Fire 1987), *Headache Rhetoric* (Fire 1989).

Cockney Rejects

Discovered by Jimmy Pursey of Sham 69, this east London-based skinhead group came to the fore in 1980 with an irreverent brand of proletariat punk/rock. The group comprised Jefferson Turner (vocals), Vince Riordan (bass/vocals), Micky Geggus (guitar/vocals) and Keith Warrington (drums). Daring and anti-everything, they were virtually a parody of the 'kick over the traces' punk attitude, while also betraying a stubborn parochialism in keeping with their group title. The 'anarchic' contents of their albums were reflected in their garishly tasteless record sleeves. Yet they had a certain subversive humour, titling their first two albums *Greatest Hits* when the sum of their UK Top 40 achievements rested with 'The Greatest Cockney Ripoff' at number 21 and the West Ham United football anthem, 'I'm Forever Blowing Bubbles', at number 35. On their second album they included the 'Oi! Oi! Oi!' song/chant, thereby giving birth to a musical sub-genre which came to define the brash inarticulacy of skinhead politics. Their gigs during this time also became an interface for working class culture and the extreme right, though just like Sham 69 the Rejects were judged guilty by default. By the time of 1982's *The Wild Ones* the group were veering away from their original punk influences towards heavy metal. Significantly, their new producer was UFO bassist Pete Way. Equally significantly, their career was well on the decline by this point. The group disbanded in 1985 but reformed to public apathy at the turn of the decade, *Lethal* hardly living up to its title.

Albums: *Greatest Hits Volume 1* (Zonophone 1980), *Greatest Hits Volume 2* (Zonophone 1980), *The Power And The Glory* (Zonophone 1981), *The Wild Ones* (AKA 1982), *Rock The Wild Side* (Heavy Metal 1984), *Lethal* (Neat 1990). Compilations: *Unheard Rejects* (Wonderful World 1985, early/unreleased recordings), *We Are The Firm* (Dojo 1986), *Greatest Hits Volume 3 (Live And Loud)* (Link 1987).

Cocteau Twins

Hailing from Grangemouth, Scotland, the Cocteau Twins are responsible for some of the most unique and emotive contemporary pop music to emerge in the 80s. An enigmatic collection of musicians, centering on the duo of Elizabeth Fraser (b. 29 August 1958) and Robin Guthrie, inevitably the central focus has rested on the remarkable vocal presence of Fraser. Able to convey the most astonishing variety of moods and inflections, using words more for their sound than their meaning, her voice has become one of the most recognisable and imitated of the last two decades. The musical backdrop to all this has been controlled by Fraser's partner, Robin Guthrie. As composer (utilizing guitar, tape loops, echo boxes and drum machines) and studio producer, he has served as driving force and artistic controller. Guthrie formed the group in 1982 with his friend, bass player Will Heggie, and had recruited Fraser as a singer reputably after seeing her dancing in a Grangemouth discotheque. Subsequent demo tapes fell into the hands Ivo Watts-Russell, the owner of 4AD Records. His enthusiasm for the Cocteau's music prompted the band's move to London to record for the label. The first album generated enormous interest and airplay from BBC Radio 1 disc jockey, John Peel. The ensuing debut album, *Garlands*, released in 1982, initially encouraged lazy comparisons to Siouxsie And The Banshees, but this legacy was soon erased as the Cocteau Twins began to carve their own niche in modern music. By spring 1983, Heggie had departed (later to re-emerge in Lowlife), leaving Fraser and Guthrie to record the second, transitional album, *Head Over Heels*. Having smoothed over the rougher edges of its predecessor with Guthrie adding layers of echo and phased drum effects the album allowed Fraser's voice full rein. This resulted in a dreamlike quality (encouraging the famed but hated ethereal tag) that permeated songs which, despite an absence of structure, were no less emphatic. During this period the group were also involved in the 4AD label project, This Mortal Coil, for which Fraser and Guthrie's version of the Tim Buckley song, 'Song To the Siren', has since been acknowledged as one of the finest independent label recordings of the 80s. Simon Raymonde had by now been enrolled as bass player, eventually becoming a valuable asset in composing, arranging and production. The release of two superb EP collections, *Sunburst And Snowblind* and *Pearly-Dewdrops' Drops*, dominated the independent charts, with the latter broaching the national Top 30. The Cocteau's reluctance to reveal anything of their private lives or play the music business game won them respect from many quarters and annoyance from others. This did leave them, however, less able to counter the image imposed upon them by fans as fey, mystical creatures - in the interviews the band did acquiesce to the principals transpired to be earthy, cantankerous and most definitely of this world. One benefit of their refusal to place photos of the group on record sleeves was the superb cover art produced by the 23 Envelope art studio. The arrival of *Treasure* in 1984 saw the group scaling new heights, comfortably justifying its status as the band's most essential album. The next couple of years were marked by the release of several EPs; *Aikea-Guinea*, *Tiny Dynamine* and *Echoes In A Shallow Bay*, each displaying rich, complex textures without ever repeating themselves. *Victorialand* featured a lighter, neo-acoustic sound, marked by the absence of Raymonde. It included instead a guest role for Richard Thomas (saxophone/tablas) of 4AD stablemates Dif Juz, though for the first time some critics detected an absence of conviction in the project. Raymonde returned for the subsequent EP set, *Love's Easy Tears*, and a not altogether successful collaboration with Harold Budd in late 1986. A hiatus of almost two years ended with the release of *Blue Bell*

Knoll, though the contents hardly refuted accusations that the Cocteau Twins had lost their touch. The emotional impact of the birth of Fraser and Guthrie's child seemed to revive their career, however, an event that was keenly reflected in the songs on the stunning *Heaven And Las Vegas*. The single, 'Iceblink Luck', also saw a return to the UK Top 40 and combined with a renewed urgency to take the music onto the road, including the unlikely setting of Las Vegas. This burst of activity coincided with the Cocteau's desire to break away from the confines and protective enclaves of their long time 'spiritual home', 4AD Records, in March 1991. For much of that year Guthrie continued with studio production work, notably with the promising new 4AD group, Lush. The Cocteau Twins eventually signed a new deal with Fontana Records in March 1992. Following lengthy treatment with her speech therapist, Liz Frazer was coaxed back into the recording studio and completed *Four-Calender Café*, released in the autumn of 1993. There were some surprises in store for the band's long term supporters - for the first time Fraser's lyrics were audible, and the band then unveiled a festive single, 'Frosty The Snowman'. Scotland's cherubic aesthetes obviously had a sense of humour, too.

Albums: *Garlands* (4AD 1982), *Head Over Heels* (4AD 1983), *Treasure* (4AD 1984), *Victorialand* (4AD 1986), *Blue Bell Knoll* (4AD 1988), *Heaven Or Las Vegas* (4AD 1990), *Four-Calender Café* (Fontana 1993). Harold Budd, Elizabeth Fraser, Robin Guthrie and Simon Raymonde: *The Moon And The Melodies* (4AD 1986), Compilations: *The Pink Opaque* (4AD 1986), *The Singles Collection* (Capitol 1991).

Codeine

USA Band Codeine consist of Steve Immerwahr (bass/vocals), John Engle (guitar), with Douglas Scharin and then Matthews McGuigan (ex-Coral) replacing Come guitarist Chris Brokaw as drummer. Signed to the Sub Pop Records label, Codeine play at a deliberate, slovenly lo-fi pace: 'It's not a see how slow you can go thing, more a compositional tool. A lot of the songs are about having a very low amount of energy or being physically unable to move. So it's performing the songs in a way that's analogous to what they're about - moments of inertia.' *Barely Real* is on first hearing slightly soporific and listless, but it rewards repeated listening with its depth and emotional texture. Afterwards they moved to Louisville, Kentucky, to rehearse songs that would form *The White Birch*, which was eventually recorded in Chicago. Inspired by a painting from American artist Thomas Dewing, it prompted the German magazine Howl to describe Codeine as 'a group that uses tears instead of notes'.

Albums: *Barley Real* (Sub Pop 1993, mini-album), *The White Birch* (Sub Pop 1994).

Coil

UK sound manipulators and experimentalists Coil were formed in the aftermath of Throbbing Gristle's artistic fallout when Peter Christopherson (keyboards, programming) split from Genesis P. Orridge's Psychic TV to join John Balance (vocals, percussion) in 1982. Balance had already been recording under the name Coil. The band has

gone on to include numerous other personnel, notably Clint Ruin (Foetus). However, the core members remained Balance, Christopherson and Stephen Thrower (programming, keyboards) until the early 90s. They set their stall out with a 1985 long-playing debut, *Scatology*. This, regarded as a work of unequalled genius in some sectors of the industrial community, used elementary electronics and primitive samples as a basis for exploring lyrical themes which included religion, sexual freedom and alchemy: 'I'm obsessed with the idea of turning base matter into gold, transmuting base materials, i.e. raw sound, into something else'. Housed in a black and white sleeve which only reinforced the hostility of some of the enclosed music, *Scatology* was an innovative staging post in music's post-punk revolution. Ruin was in attendance to aid the keyboard runs, and also added horns to the follow-up, *Horse Rotorvator*. A less ostentatiously uncompromising audio experience, this collection saw the group supplant the more abrasive elements of its sound with classical and jazz textures, though the messages thus sweetened remained grim. Occasionally the more prominent placing of the poetry/vocals, aided by a musical background drawing from Arabic and Middle Eastern cultures, produced an uncharacteristically accessible, clean sound. *Unreleased Themes From Hellraiser* contained exactly that - a series of mood instrumentals written for the film but rejected. Clive Barker's loss proved boon to Coil fans on an often overlooked set which is among the most evocative in the band's consistently excellent discography. Although *Gold Is The Metal With The Broadest Shoulders* is a compilation, it is worth consideration in its own right as the versions of the songs contained (drawn from the previous albums and EPs plus compilation appearances) are often in radically different form. The same is true of *Unnatural History*, which culls material from debut EP *How To Destroy Angels* and the band's collaboration with Current 93, as well as including a 17 minute eulogy to 'male sexual energy'. By the advent of *Love's Secret Domain* five years had passed since a studio album proper (through lack of finances rather than lack of energy), and Coil had moved with the times. Incorporating acid house beats and some of the ephemera of dance music, *Love's Secret Domain* was nevertheless as deeply impersonal as previous outings: 'I hate people. I can only stand two or three at a time. If I see large numbers of people enjoying themselves, I automatically start having a bad time'. Despite Thrower's truculence, Balance admitted that he had been influenced by attendance at the Shoom and Confusion clubs which first imported Balearic Beat to the UK. The additional member photographed on the sleeve, meanwhile, turned out to be Otto Avery, a 'mad acid kid' who didn't do anything on the record but merely turned up and asked to be credited. More substantial input came from Annie Anxiety (backing vocals) and Marc Almond (guitar - having previously added vocals to earlier Coil recordings). By 1995 the band had signed to Nothing Records, the label run by Trent Reznor of Nine Inch Nails, releasing *Backwards* This, with Thrower replaced in the central trio by Dean McCowall, saw the band retreat to earlier lyrical concerns, though they also experimented with field recordings in homage to occultist Austin Osman Spare. In the meantime the group were being name checked by a new breed of sonic

experimentalists, leading to collaborations with Autechre, Atom Heart, Bill Laswell and Tetsu Inoue. They also worked with William Burroughs on a track included on *Backwards*, and provided a video to Ministry's 'Just One Fix'. This new sprouting of commercial activity resulted in two other new albums - *The Sound Of Music* compiled Coil music written for the Derek Jarman films *Blue* and *Journey To Avebury*, along with the earlier Clive Barker recordings, while *Worship The Glitch* was credited to ELpH: 'ELpH is when we no longer recognise our presence in the music. It's the idea of taking the dead spaces, the mistakes, and extending them'.
Albums: *Scatology* (K.422/Some Bizarre 1985), *Horse Rotorvator* (Some Bizarre/Relativity 1987), *Unreleased Themes From Hellraiser* (Solar Lodge 1988), *Love's Secret Domain* (Wax Trax 1991), *Backwards* (Nothing 1995). Compilations: *Gold Is The Metal With The Broadest Shoulders* (Threshold House 1990), *Unnatural History* (Threshold House 1990), *The Sound Of Music* (Eskaton 1995). As ELpH: *Worship The Glitch* (Eskaton 1995). With Current 93: *Nightmare Culture* (Laylah 1985).

Cole, Lloyd, (And The Commotions)

b. 31 January 1961, Buxton, Derbyshire, England. Despite his birthplace, this literate singer-songwriter emerged from Glasgow's post-punk renaissance. Neil Clark (b. 3 July 1955; guitar), Blair Cowan (keyboards), Lawrence Donegan (b. 13 July 1961; bass) and Stephen Irvine (b. 16 December 1959; drums) completed the line-up responsible for *Rattlesnakes*, a critically lauded set which merged Byrds-like guitar figures to Cole's languid, Lou Reed inspired intonation. A representative selection from the album, 'Perfect Skin', reached the UK Top 30 when issued as a single, while a follow-up album, *Easy Pieces*, spawned two Top 20 entries in 'Brand New Friend' and 'Lost Weekend'. However, the style which came so easily on these early outings seemed laboured on *Mainstream*, after which Cole disbanded his group. Retaining Cowan, he switched bases to New York, and emphasized the infatuation with Lou Reed's music by recruiting sidemen Robert Quine (guitar) and Fred Maher (drums), the latter of whom also acted as producer. *Lloyd Cole* showed signs of an artistic rejuvenation, but Cole was yet to stamp a wholly original personae and capitalize on his undoubted talent. Both *Don't Get Weird On Me, Babe* and *Bad Vibes* failed to lift the atmosphere of bookish lyrics rendered without the requisite soul, but neither were these collections without merit. Instead the listener was once again left to reminisce about the power of writing and performance which coalesced on tracks like 'Down On Mission Street' and 'Forest Fire' from the artist's debut.
Albums: *Rattlesnakes* (Polydor 1984), *Easy Pieces* (Polydor 1985), *Mainstream* (Polydor 1987). Solo: *Lloyd Cole* (Polydor 1989), *Don't Get Weird On Me, Babe* (Polydor 1991), *Bad Vibes* (Fontana 1993). Compilation: *1984-1989* (Polydor 1989).
Videos: *Lloyd Cole & The Commotions* (1986), *From The Hip* (1988), *1984 - 1989* (1989).

Colenso Parade

This interesting pop/rock act was formed in October 1984 in Belfast, Northern Ireland. They released two singles,

'Standing Up' and 'Down By The Border' on their own Goliath label before an early appearance at the Futurama Festival saw Stiff Records put them in touch with manager Dave Bedford. Soon after, they moved to London where Bedford had set up Fire Records. From the original line-up Oscar (vocals), Linda Clandinning (keyboards) and Neil Lawson (bass) remained the nucleus of the band. Terry Bickers (later of House Of Love and Levitation) replaced the original guitarist Jackie Forgie after the first single, and was in turn dropped in favour of John Watt (though Bickers was in place for the album sessions, by the time *Glentorran* appeared he had moved on). Owen Howell (ex-Big Self) would also replace Robert Wakeman as drummer. Following 'Hallelujah Chorus' they scored heavy airplay with 'Fontana Eyes' in 1986, a classic 12-bar blues workout founded on captivating lyrical epigrams, 'I'm holding my breath, cos there's no-one to hold'. A split came soon after their only album when a deal with a major label fell through. Further demos were recorded but nothing surfaced, although Oscar was asked to join Echo And The Bunnymen as singer following the departure of Ian McCulloch. He declined the invitation, and is now working in video. Lawson is currently an aircraft photographer, while Linda Clandinning has trained as a hairdresser. Only Robert Wakeman has continued in the music industry, with indie hopefuls Salad. Album: *Glentorran* (Fire 1986).

Collective Soul

Formed in Stockbridge, Georgia, USA, Collective Soul have earned their reputation with strong, hook-laden pop rock songs, the best example of which is 'Shine', which topped *Billboard*'s Rock Album Tracks poll in May 1994. The band's history up to then, though, had been a tortuous one of over a decade. Ed Roland (vocals/guitar) grew up in a strict family, with access to music and radio denied by his parents. Despite this, he left Stockbridge to study guitar at Boston's Berklee School Of Music. When he ran out of money he returned to Stockbridge to work in a 24-track recording studio, where he taught himself production technique and formed the band Collective Soul. (The only surviving member of that version of the group is the drummer Shane Evans.) After years of rejection from major labels, Ed Roland disbanded the group in 1992. 'I didn't know where to go, or what to do. I just knew I had to do something, so I put together a songwriter demo, figuring I'd write tunes for other people.' A year later he was contacted after radio stations expressed interest in 'Shine'. This led to a contract with Atlantic Records and together with his brother Dean Roland (guitars), Ross Childress (lead guitar), Will Turpin (bass) and Evans, Collective Soul were re-formed. Although the follow-up single, 'Breathe', failed to replicate the success of 'Shine', the group's debut album (now on Atlantic) was re-packaged to become a million-seller by the year's end. The quintet began 1995 with 'Gel', the first single from their second album. With strong rotation play from MTV, it was also featured on the soundtrack of the cult *Jerky Boys* film. In March 1995 they set out on a maror tour supporting Van Halen.
Albums: *Hints, Allegations & Things Left Unsaid* (Atlantic 1993), *Collective Soul* (Atlantic 1995).

Collins, Edwyn

Following the collapse of Orange Juice, a band acclaimed in the UK music press but who did not enjoy commercial success, Edwyn Collins launched a solo career that has had a similar pattern. Both the Orange Juice producer, Dennis Bovell, and their drummer, Zeke Manyika, are present on Collins' solo debut, *Hope And Despair*, which also featured Aztec Camera's Roddy Frame. The single 'Don't Shilly Shally' was produced by Robin Guthrie of the Cocteau Twins who handled the lighting at early Orange Juice gigs. *Hellbent On Compromise* is a more intimate and atmospheric recording, and Collins said in interviews that his intention was to present a 'cinematic' effect. Afterwards Collins produced A House, Vic Goddard and Frank And Walters, and worked with the Setanta Records roster. *Gorgeous George* was produced by Collins on an old EMI/Neve mixing console and is filled with cantankerous phrases such as 'the truly detestable summer festival'. Paul Cook (ex-Sex Pistols) drummed. Collins' writing is sharper than on the slightly morose *Hellbent On Compromise*, especially on tracks such as 'A Girl Like You' and 'Make Me Feel Again'. The former, released as a single, became the most successful instalment in his 15 year recording career when it entered the Top 10s of both Australia and France.

Albums: *Hope And Despair* (Demon 1989), *Hellbent On Compromise* (Demon 1990), *Gorgeous George* (Setanta 1994).

Colorblind James Experience

Hailing from Rochester, New York, USA, this quartet were led by the evidently talented but somewhat unhinged Colorblind James (vocals/vibraphone/guitar), with Phillip Marshall (lead guitar/vocals), Bernie Heveron (bass/vocals) and Jim McAvaney (drums). Together they utilized the myriad forms of North American musical expression open to them, from country, cocktail-lounge jazz, folk, rockabilly and blues to good-time rock 'n' roll, in order to express James' odd-ball view of the world. It was BBC disc jockey John Peel who first gave them the exposure necessary to make them realize they were achieving something that an audience might also appreciate. Their debut album was an eclectic work, notable for its engaging black humour. The high point of the collection, the sprawling 'I'm Considering A Move To Memphis', was reminiscent of David Byrne's less self-conscious efforts. By the time of the release of their second album, *Why Should I Stand Up?*, the line-up had increased to a sextet with the addition of John Ebert (trombone/tuba/vocals), Ken Frank (bass/violin/vocals - replacing Heveron) and Dave McIntire (sax/clarinet/vocals). On occasions the group have put aside their electric instruments, thereby standing revealed as Colorblind James And The Death Valley Boys, indulging in more basic country-blues, gospel and jug band music. The result of these sessions was *Strange Sounds From The Basement*, which carried on Colorblind's infatuation with the underside of contemporary American life.

Albums: *Colorblind James Experience* (Earring 1987), *Why Should I Stand Up?* (Death Valley/Cooking Vinyl 1989). As Colorblind James And The Death Valley Boys: *Strange Sounds From The Basement* (Death Valley/Cooking Vinyl 1990).

Colour Field

After appearing with the Specials and the Fun Boy Three, Terry Hall (b. 19 March 1959, Coventry, West Midlands, England; guitar/vocals) formed the Colour Field with Karl Sharle (bass) and Toby Lyons (guitar/keyboards) in 1983. Having been involved in a band that was responsible for the ska/mod revival, (then a vocal based trio), Hall's third band of the 80's was a basic group of three musicians. He was aided by friends, and produced strong pop songs featuring his rather flat vocals. After the instant success of his two previous bands, Colour Field found the going hard. Although they had positive reviews from the music press, it took nearly 18 months for the band to break into the UK Top 20 with 'Thinking Of You' in 1985. Their debut album reached number 12 in the UK, but the failure of subsequent singles soon reduced them down to a duo of Hall and Lyons. They reappeared in 1987 with a weak cover version of Sly And The Family Stone's 'Running Away' and a second album which gave a poor showing on the UK chart, which resulted in the group dissolving. Hall later released a solo album with assistance from Blair Booth (keyboards/vocals) and Anouchka Grooe (guitar).

Albums: *Virgins And Philistines* (1985), *Deception* (1987). Solo album: Terry Hall *Ultra Modern Nursery Rhymes* (1989).

Come

Formed in 1991, this highly-rated quartet centres on musicians already involved in New York's alternative music circuit. Singer/guitarist Thalia Zedek began her recording career with the Dangerous Birds and Uzi, before joining the influential Live Skull. Guitarist Chris Brokaw was formerly drummer in Codeine, while Sean O'Brien (bass) and Arthur Johnson (drums) were both ex-members of the Bar B Q Killers. Come made its debut in August 1991 with 'Car', a slow, menacing performance issued on the Sub Pop Records label. The equally atmospheric 'Fast Piss Blues' succeeded it, backed by a languid version of the Rolling Stones' 'I Got The Blues'. These served as the prefect introduction to *Eleven: Eleven*, rightly lauded as one of 1992's finest releases. The spirit of Patti Smith, Delta blues and the Stooges permeated this startling collection which highlighted Zedek's emotive voice and Brokow's dense guitar work. A period of seclusion ensued, but Come re-emerged with 1994's powerful second collection, which included further high calibre recordings in 'Finish Line' and 'Let's Get Lost', as Come went on to support Throwing Muses on their 1995 British tour.

Album: *Eleven: Eleven* (Beggars Banquet 1992), *Don't Ask, Don't Tell* (Beggars Banquet 1994).

Coming Up Roses

This unit was formed in 1986 by the songwriting partnership of ex-Dolly Mixture members, Debsey Wykes (b. 21 December 1960, Hammersmith, London, England; guitar/vocals) and Hester Smith (b. 28 October 1960, West Africa; drums) along with Nicky Brodie (vocals/percussion), Patricia O'Flynn (saxophone, ex-Shillelagh Sisters), Leigh Luscious (guitar) and ex-Amazulu bassist Claire Kenny, later replaced by Sophie Cherry (bass). Their melodic pop dance style, described by the group as 'ballroom soul', mixed witty

and caustic lyrics - in 'I Could Have Been Your Girlfriend (If You'd Asked Me To)' Wykes sang; 'She's so dumb, she's so sweet/I didn't think she'd last a week ... She's so pretty she's so fine, she is such a waste of time/Well so she's cute, well I don't care, she's got stinking underwear!'. They signed to Billy Bragg's Utility Records label releasing one album in 1989. The group had already toured the UK as part of the pop-socialist collective Red Wedge troupe in 1987. After various personnel changes, but still retaining the nucleus of Wykes and Smith along with Brodie, the group settled on a more stable line-up in 1990 with Tony Watts (lead guitar), Midus (bass) and Jane Keay (saxophone). However, disillusion with the music business's preoccupation with current trends prompted the group's demise in March 1991, leaving behind a legacy of timeless pop songs.
Album: *I Said Ballroom* (Utility 1989).

Comsat Angels

Three major record deals, no hit singles, legal complications - and yet the Comsat Angels survived to make thoughtful, expressive guitar music for more than 10 years. Formed in Sheffield, England, at the end of the 70s as Radio Earth, they initially merged the zest of punk with a mature songwriting approach, using keyboards quite strongly on their promising debut, *Waiting For A Miracle*. The line-up of Stephen Fellows (guitar/vocals), Mik Glaisher (drums), Kevin Bacon (bass) and Andy Peake (keyboards) was to remain constant throughout their early career. In the USA they were forced to shorten their name to CS Angels after the communications giant, Comsat, threatened legal action. *Sleep No More* was their highest UK chart placing at number 51 but after *Fiction* only skimmed the lower reaches of the Top 100, Polydor Records lost patience and the band moved to the CBS Records subsidiary, Jive. *Land* spawned a near hit with the catchy 'Independence Day' which had previously appeared on their first album. The single was released in various formats, including a double-single set, but did not provide the success the band required. Other groups with a similar driving guitar sound fared better and they were surpassed commercially by the likes of Simple Minds and U2. The band invested heavily in their own recording studio in Sheffield and it has become a focus for the city's musical creativity. Another attempt to regenerate their career was made by Island Records in the late 80s but early in 1990 the band announced they were changing their name to Headhunters in the hope that it would bring about a change of fortune. However, they reverted to the name Comsat Angels shortly afterwards, signing to RPM Records who released a new album, *My Mind's Eye*, in addition to two compilations of radio sessions.
Albums: *Waiting For A Miracle* (Polydor 1980), *Sleep No More* (Polydor 1981), *Fiction* (Polydor 1982), *Land* (Jive 1983), *Seven Day Weekend* (Jive 1985), *Chasing Shadows* (Island 1987), *My Mind's Eye* (RPM 1992). Compilations: *Enz* (Polydor 1984, Dutch release), *Time Considered* (RPM 1992), *Unravelled* (RPM 1994).

Concrete Blonde

After spending several years in the embryonic form of Dream 6 (under which name they released an EP for Happy Hermit in France), Hollywood, California, USA rock band Concrete Blonde formed in 1986. The founders of the group, former Sparks personnel Earle (production) and Jim Mankey (guitars) plus Johnette Napolitano (bass/vocals), were joined by Harry Rushakoff (drums) for their debut on IRS Records. Its alluring mix of energy, sensitivity and streetwise wit secured Concrete Blonde a positive response from both the music press and maturer rock audiences. For *Free* Napolitano handed over bass duties to new member Alan Bloch, allowing her to concentrate on singing. Irrespective of which she remained the focus of the band - her remarkable voice, which sounds both assertive and vulnerable, gives Concrete Blonde much of its poignancy and power. *Bloodletting* is perhaps the band's strongest album in terms of emotional intensity, with its painful dissection of an ailing relationship (all songwriting handled by Napolitano). It saw the introduction of new percussionist Paul Thompson (ex-Roxy Music), with the group now effectively a trio of Napolitano, Jim Mankey and Thompson. Their most recent release, *Mexican Moon*, includes Hispanic influences, and continues the vein of sincere, sassy and seductive rock which has made Concrete Blonde such a welcome presence over the last decade.
Albums: *Concrete Blonde* (IRS 1986), *Free* (IRS 1989), *Bloodletting* (IRS 1990), *Walking In London* (IRS 1992), *Mexican Moon* (IRS 1993).

Conflict

This anarchist punk band were formed in south east London in 1979, previously existing under a variety of names such as Splattered Rock Stars. Having followed Crass around the country they were essentially motivated by similar concerns; pacifism, animal welfare, anarchism. 'We call ourselves anarchists. That doesn't mean we believe in chaos - our ideal society would be one of small self-governing communities, with people being able to run their own lives. But above all we're trying to say that we don't want to be used by the political left or right.' They played their first gig in their native Eltham in April 1981. The basic line-up featured Colin Jerwood (b. 6 May, 1962, London, England; vocals) Graham (guitar) Ken (drums) and John Clifford (bass), although their early line-ups were very fluid, with newcomers Steve and Paco taking over on guitar and drums soon after. Paul Fryday, meanwhile, became technician, visuals supervisor and general motivator. Their debut EP, *The House That Man Built*, came out on the Crass label, with Pauline Beck adding vocals. 'To A Nation Of Animal Lovers', on which Crass' Steve Ignorant guested, saw the band faced with incitement charges over the cover. Their policy of direct action in protest to many causes, in particular the Orkney seal hunters, led to many live appearances being broken up by police action. After this there were numerous line-up changes, the most significant of which was the two-year tenure of Ignorant as joint vocalist between 1987 and 1989. Jerwood, meanwhile, had been assaulted at a pub in Eltham, nearly losing the use of his eye in the process. Conflict set up their own Mortarhate label, going on to release albums throughout the 80s for a loyal audience of social miscreants. The best of their efforts were the studio side of *Increase The Pressure* and *The Ungovernable Force*, in

1984 and 1985 respectively. The widescale rioting which occurred after the band's 1987 Brixton Academy gig was documented by *Turning Rebellion Into Money*. In 1993 the group recorded their first 7-inch single since 1985, followed in December with an album, *Conclusion*.

Albums: *It's Time To See Who's Who* (Corpus Christi 1983), *Increase The Pressure* (Mortarhate 1984), *The Ungovernable Force* (Mortarhate 1985), *Only Stupid Bastards Help EMI* (New Army 1986), *Turning Rebellion Into Money* (Mortarhate 1987), *The Final Conflict* (Mortarhate 1989), *Against All Odds* (Mortarhate 1989), *Conclusion* (Mortarhate 1993). Compilation: *Standard Issue* (Mortarhate 1989).

Contortions

Formed by James Siegfried in 1980, James Chance And The Contortions were a collision of punk and harmolodic jazz that, along with Bill Laswell's Material and James Blood Ulmer, constituted New York's No Wave scene. Siegfried went to school with Mark Johnson (Cassandra Wilson's drummer) and recruited guitarist Bern Nix from Ornette Coleman's Prime Time. This awareness of cutting-edge jazz - and a defiantly original saxophone style, an unholy combination of Captain Beefheart and Maceo Parker - injected punk with a brittle energy that was unmatched. A later version of the band, James White And The Blacks, fomented Defunkt as a separate entity, kick-starting the black rock movement that begat Living Color. Heroin problems prevented James Chance reaching a large audience, but his spiky, beautiful music remains to testify that jazz chops do not necessarily make for tedious rock music.

Albums: *Buy* (1979), *Live In New York* (1981), as James White And The Blacks *Off White* (1979), *Sax Maniac* (1982), *James White's Flaming Demonics* (1983), *Soul Exorcism* (1991, live 1980 recording in Amsterdam).

Cope, Julian

b. 21 October 1957, Deri, Mid Glamorgan, Wales. Cope first attracted attention as an integral part of Liverpool's post-punk renaissance, most notably as a member of the short-lived but seminal group, the Crucial Three, which also included Ian McCulloch and Pete Wylie. In 1978 Cope began writing songs with Ian McCulloch in A Shallow Madness, but the pair quickly fell out over the direction of the group. While McCulloch formed Echo And The Bunnymen, Cope founded the Teardrop Explodes whose early releases enjoyed critical acclaim. The band scored several hit singles but an introspective second album, *Wilder*, was heavily criticized before dissension within the ranks led to their inevitable demise. In 1984 Cope embarked on a solo career with *World Shut Your Mouth* but misfortune dogged his progress. The singer intentionally gashed his stomach with a broken microphone stand during an appearance at London's Hammersmith Palais and his pronouncements on the benefits of mind-expanding substances exacerbated an already wayward, unconventional image. The sleeve of his second album, *Fried*, featured a naked Cope cowering under a turtle shell and commentators drew parallels with rock casualties Roky Erickson and Syd Barrett, both of whom Cope admired. Another of his heroes, Scott Walker, enjoyed a upsurge in interest in his recordings when Cope constantly

gave the reclusive 60s singer name-checks in interviews. A third album, *Skellington*, was rejected by his label, which resulted in Cope switching to Island Records. Paradoxically he then enjoyed a UK Top 20 single with a newly-recorded version of 'World Shut Your Mouth'. *Saint Julian* became the artist's best-selling album to date, but a tour to promote Cope's next collection, *My Nation Underground*, was abandoned when he became too ill to continue. Over subsequent months Cope maintained a low profile, but re-emerged in 1990 at London's anti-Poll Tax demonstration dressed in the costume of a space alien, Mr Sqwubbsy. However, this unconventional behaviour was tempered by a new realism and in 1991 he scored another major hit with 'Beautiful Love'. Commentators also noted a newfound maturity on the attendant double album, *Peggy Suicide*, which garnered considerable praise. Two albums for his own mail order record companies followed. However, none of this was enough to discourage Island from dropping the artist following the release of *Jehovakill*, though the move caused considerable surprise within critical circles (in retrospect it may have had more to do with Cope's legendary contrariness and recessionary times than any comment on his ability). Soon afterwards he announced a new US deal with American Records in June 1993 and published a book on lay lines. *Autogeddon* provided no clear-cut evidence as to whether or not his powers were on the wane, but kept the faithful happy for another year.

Albums: *World Shut Your Mouth* (Mercury 1984), *Fried* (Mercury 1984), *Saint Julian* (Island 1987), *My Nation Underground* (Island 1988), *Skellington* and *Droolian* (Capeco-Zippo 1990 and Mofoco-Zippo 1990, both fan club only releases), *Peggy Suicide* (Island 1991, double album), *Jehovahkill* (Island 1993), *Autogeddon* (Echo 1994). Compilation: *Floored Genius - The Best Of Julian Cope And The Teardrop Explodes 1981 - 1991* (Island 1992). Video: *Copeulation* (1989).

Cornershop

Half-Asian, half white indie band who rose to prominence in the UK in 1993 by attacking some dubious statements made at that time by former idol Morrissey. The band; Ben Ayers (b. 30 April 1968, St John's, Newfoundland, Canada; guitar, vocals), Tjindar Singh (b. 8 February 1968, New Cross, Wolverhampton, England; guitar), Avtar Singh (b. 11 May 1965, Punjab, India; bass, vocals) and David Chambers (b. 1969, Lincoln, Lincolnshire, England; ex-Dandelion Adventure; drums) are based in Leicester, London and Preston. Signing to Wiiija Records they were invited to comment on Morrissey after his Finsbury Park glorification of skinhead culture and 'British' values. In the process, they became willing spokesmen for what seemed a significant debate, though it was just as well their own musical abilities were not under the microscope. They had evolved out of the ashes of General Havoc in 1991, whose whole ethos was enshrined in the motto: 'Don't rehearse; hardly play; get media attention'. The debut single, 'In The Days Of Ford Cortina', whilst in many ways charming, was proto-punk amateurism at best. It also came in 'curry-coloured' vinyl, while other song titles included 'Kawasaki, Hotter Than Chapati'. Evidence that while Morrissey may have slipped in

to dubious philosophical territory, Cornershop looked unlikely to rival him in his use of irony. By 1995's *Woman's Gotta Have It* the style had been refined but hardly remodelled - with tracks like 'Hong Kong Book Of Kung Fu' recalling the world of children's cartoons to good effect.
Albums: *Hold On It Hurts* (Wiiija 1994), *Woman's Gotta Have It* (Wiiija 1995).

Cornwell, Hugh

Cornwell (b. 28 August 1949, London, England) had long since launched his solo career before his defection in August 1990 from the Stranglers, with whom he was lead vocalist and guitarist. His extra-curricular activities began in 1979, when he recorded an album, *Nosferatu*, with Captain Beefheart drummer Robert Williams, which also featured contributions from members of Devo. It is of considerable interest to Stranglers' fans as it prefigures some of the lyrical and musical aspects of the band in the next decade. Cornwell returned to the Stranglers for much of the 80s, enduring several adventures, not least a jail term for heroin possession which he would later recall in a privately published indictment of the justice system - *Who Guards The Guards?*. He also appeared alongside Bob Hoskins in a London stage play. Cornwell's next album, *Wolf*, was a hugely disappointing affair, a limp attempt to craft himself a pop niche. Rightly considered a potent songwriter for his work with the Stranglers, this attempt to convert himself into a gruff Ray Davies fell flat, despite the presence of old pals Jools Holland and Manny Elias (Tears For Fears). The album had been prefaced by one notable single, 1987's 'Facts And Figures', which featured on the soundtrack of the animated film *When The Wind Blows*. Following his departure from the Stranglers after 16 years, Cornwell started to develop songs he had already half-written while still with the band. Before unveiling these he collaborated with Robert Cook and Andy West for the largely ignored *CCW* album. Afterwards he recruited former collaborator Williams (drums), Alex Gifford (bass), Ted Mason and Chris Goulstone (guitars) and Art Of Noise producer Gary Langan to shape *Wired*. Far superior to its predecessor, this collection of songs revealed a grasp of vibrant pop.
Albums: with Robert Williams *Nosferatu* (Liberty 1979), *Wolf* (Virgin 1988), with CCW *CCW* (UFO 1992), *Wired* (Transmission 1993).

Corrosion Of Conformity

This seminal hardcore crossover band, originally known as No Labels, was formed in Raleigh, North Carolina, by Reed Mullin (drums), Woody Weatherman (guitar) and Mike Dean (bass/vocals) in 1982, and rose to become one of the biggest draws in the US underground with their stunning live shows. *Eye For An Eye*, with vocals supplied by Eric Eyke, separated them from the pack by mixing hardcore speed with Black Sabbath and Deep Purple-influenced power riffing. A more metallic crossover style became evident with *Animosity*, although the group lost neither their aggression nor their hardcore ideals. The blistering *Technocracy*, with Simon Bob (ex-Ugly Americans) on vocals, saw the band's audience expand with the rise of thrash, but record company problems and the loss of Simon Bob and Dean led to Corrosion Of

Conformity's collapse. However, just as it seemed that *Six Songs With Mike Singing* was to be their epitaph, Corrosion Of Conformity returned, with Mullin and Weatherman joined by Karl Agell (vocals, ex-School Of Violence), Pepper Keenan (guitar/vocals) and Phil Swisher (bass). Impressive tours with DRI and Danzig helped gain a new deal, and the acclaimed *Blind* saw the band adopt a slower, more melodic, but still fiercely heavy style. It also continued the hardcore lyrical stance of an increasingly politically active band, challenging social, political and ecological issues. Success with 'Vote With A Bullet' and electrifying live shows, including a UK tour supporting Soundgarden, re-established Corrosion Of Conformity as a force, but the departure of Agell and Swisher slowed the momentum once more. *Deliverance*, with Keenan taking lead vocals and Dean back in place, saw the band incorporate ever more diverse influences into their weighty sound, adding southern rock grooves and, perhaps most surprisingly, Thin Lizzy-style guitar harmonies for a varied album which was a considerable departure from their hardcore musical roots.
Albums: *Eye For An Eye* (No Core 1984), *Animosity* (Death/Metal Blade 1985), *Technocracy* (Metal Blade 1987, mini-album), *Six Songs With Mike Singing* (Caroline 1988, rec. 1985, mini-album), *Blind* (Relativity 1991), *Deliverance* (Columbia 1994).

Cortinas

Originally an R&B band, the Cortinas were formed during July 1976 in Bristol, England by Jeremy Valentine (vocals), Nick Sheppard (guitar), Mike Fewins (guitar), Dexter Dalwood (bass) and Daniel Swan (drums). The advent of the late 70s 'new wave' brought a change to their usual live set of 60s cover versions, which were replaced with self-penned tracks like 'Television Families' and 'I Wanna Have It With You'. The remainder were given the 'punk treatment', which created an exciting live spectacle. In the beginning of June 1977, 'Fascist Dictator' was released on the Step Forward label, capturing perfectly the raw energy of the time, although it lacked any real originality. This new-found popularity brought with it problems, as many of their hometown gigs ended in trouble, prompting the band to cut their ties with punk. Consequently the live set saw a return to cover versions, where even 'Fascist Dictator' was excluded. *True Romances* was released on CBS in 1978 and contained a remake of Smokey Robinson's 'First I Look At The Purse', together with 12 originals. The album had lost the power and bite of previous offerings, the result being mediocre. One last single 'Heartache' was extracted before they split at the end of the year. Mike Fewins joined Essential Bop, whereas Nick Sheppard formed the Spics, two of the most prominent new wave bands to emerge from Bristol in 1979.
Album: *True Romances* (1978).

Costello, Elvis

b. Declan McManus, 25 August 1955, Paddington, London, England, but brought up in Liverpool. The son of singer and bandleader Ross McManus first came to prominence during the UK punk era of 1977. The former computer programmer toured A&R offices giving impromptu performances. While appealing to the new wave market, the sensitive issues he wrote about, combined with the structures he composed them in, indicated a major talent that would survive and outgrow this musical generation. Following a brief tenure in Flip City he was signed to Dave Robinson's pioneering Stiff Records. Costello failed to chart with his early releases, which included the anti-fascist 'Less Than Zero' and the sublime ballad 'Alison'. His Nick Lowe-produced debut, *My Aim Is True*, featured members of the west-coast cult band Clover, who in turn had Huey Lewis as their vocalist. The album introduced a new pinnacle in late 70s songwriting. Costello spat, shouted and crooned through a cornucopia of radical issues, producing a set that was instantly hailed by the critics. His debut hit single, 'Watching The Detectives', contained scathing verses about wife-beating over a beautifully simple reggae beat. His new band, the Attractions, gave Costello a solid base: the combination of Bruce Thomas (b. Stockton-on-Tees, Cleveland, England; bass), ex-Chilli Willi And The Red Hot Peppers' Pete Thomas (b. 9 August 1954, Sheffield, Yorkshire, England; drums) and Steve Nieve (b. Steven Nason; keyboards), became an integral part of the Costello sound. The Attractions provided the backing on the strong follow-up, *This Year's Model*, and further magnificent singles ensued prior to the release of another landmark album, *Armed Forces*. This vitriolic collection narrowly missed the coveted number 1 position in the UK and reached the Top 10 in the USA. Costello's standing across the Atlantic was seriously dented by his regrettably flippant dismissal of Ray Charles as 'an ignorant, blind nigger', an opinion which he later recanted. 'Oliver's Army', a major hit taken from the album, was a bitter attack on the mercenary soldier, sung over a contrastingly upbeat tune. By the end of the 70s Costello was firmly established as both performer and songwriter with Linda Ronstadt and Dave Edmunds having success with his compositions. During 1981 he spent time in Nashville recording a country album, *Almost Blue*, with legendary producer Billy Sherrill. George Jones's 'Good Year For The Roses' became the album's major hit, although a superb reading of Patsy Cline's 'Sweet Dreams' was a comparative failure. The following year, with seven albums already behind him, the prolific Costello released another outstanding collection, *Imperial Bedroom*. Many of the songs herein were romantic excursions into mistrust and deceit, including 'Man Out Of Time' and 'I'm Your Toy'. The fast paced 'Beyond Belief' was a perfect example of vintage Costello lyricism: 'History repeats the old conceits/the glib replies the same defeats/keep your finger on important issues with crocodile tears and a pocketful of tissues'. That year Robert Wyatt recorded arguably the best-ever interpretation of a Costello song. The superlative 'Shipbuilding' offered an imposingly subtle indictment of the Falklands War, with Wyatt's strained voice giving extra depth to Costello's seamless lyric. The next year Costello as the Imposter released 'Pills And Soap', a similar theme cleverly masking a bellicose attack on Thatcherism. Both *Punch The Clock* and *Goodbye Cruel World* maintained the high standards that Costello had already set and he also found the time to produce albums by the Specials, Squeeze, the Bluebells and the Pogues (where he met future wife, Cait O'Riordan). During 1984 he played a retarded brother on BBC television

in Alan Bleasdale's *Scully*, which would not be the last time he would attempt a low-key acting career. The following year he took to a different stage at Live Aid, and in front of millions poignantly sang John Lennon's 'All You Need Is Love' accompanied by his solo guitar (some critics pointed out that no, what people actually needed was food). His version of the Animals' 'Don't Let Me Be Misunderstood' was a minor hit in 1986 and during another punishing year he released two albums; the rock 'n' roll influenced *King Of America*, with notable production from T-Bone Burnett and guitar contributions from the legendary James Burton and, reunited with the Attractions and producer Nick Lowe, Costello stalled with the less successful *Blood And Chocolate*. Towards the end of the 80s he collaborated with Paul McCartney and co-wrote a number of songs for *Flowers In The Dirt*, and returned after a brief hiatus (by Costello standards) with the excellent *Spike* in 1989. During 1990 he wrote and sang with Roger McGuinn for his 1991 comeback album, *Back To Rio*. During that year a heavily bearded and hirsuite Costello also co-wrote the soundtrack to the controversial television series, *GBH*, (written by Alan Bleasdale) and delivered another artistic success, *Mighty Like A Rose*. With lyrics as sharp as any of his previous work, this introspective and reflective album had Costello denying he was ever cynical - merely realistic. His perplexing collaboration with the Brodsky Quartet in 1993 was a brave yet commercially ignored outing. *Brutal Truth* brought him back to critical approbation, before *Kojak Variety*, a second album of cover versions recorded in 1991 but released four years later, with selections from major artists such as Screaming Jay Hawkins, Supremes, Bob Dylan, Willie Dixon, Ray Davies and Bacharach And David.

Albums: *My Aim Is True* (Stiff 1977), *This Year's Model* (Radar 1978), *Armed Forces* (Radar 1979), *Get Happy* (F-Beat 1980), *Trust* (F-Beat 1981), *Almost Blue* (F-Beat 1981), *Imperial Bedroom* (F-Beat 1982), *Punch The Clock* (F-Beat 1983), *Goodbye Cruel World* (F-Beat 1984), *King Of America* (Demon 1986), *Blood And Chocolate* (Demon 1986), *Spike* (Warners 1989), *Mighty Like A Rose* (Warners 1991), with the Brodsky Quartet *The Juliet Letters* (Warners 1993), *Brutal Youth* (Warners 1994), *Kojak Variety* (Warners 1995). Compilations: *Ten Bloody Marys And Ten Hows Your Fathers* (Demon 1980), *The Best Of Elvis Costello - The Man* (Telstar 1985), *Girls Girls Girls* (Demon 1989), *Out Of Our Idiot* (Demon 1987).

Videos: *Best Of Elvis Costello* (1986), with the Brodsky Quartet *The Juliet Letters* (1993).

Films: *Americation* (1979).

Further reading: *Elvis Costello: Completely False Biography Based On Rumour, Innuendo And Lies*, Krista Reese. *Elvis Costello*, Mick St. Michael. *Elvis Costello: A Man Out Of Time*, David Gouldstone. *The Big Wheel*, Bruce Thomas.

Count Bishops

This high energy UK R&B act was similar in tone to peers such as Dr. Feelgood and Eddie And The Hot Rods. Their original line-up was led by vocalist Mike Spenser from Brooklyn, New York, USA. Spenser arrived from the US and worked as a road manager in London for Chrome. Initially he sang two or three numbers with the band before

eventually taking over that platform. After phoning his friend Johnny Guitar, who flew in from the States to join them, they changed their name to the Count Bishops. They signed to the pioneering independent Chiswick Records label in 1975, and their *Speedball* EP was one of the earliest 'new wave' releases. Although Spenser sang on the EP (released in December) he was quickly replaced by the gravel-throated Dave Tice. Spenser would later lead the Cannibals. The dual guitar attack of Zenon De Fleur and Johnny Guitar was underpinned by the rhythm section of Pat McMullan (bass), and Paul Balbi (drums). By the adventof 1978's 'I Want Candy', the band had dropped the prefix and become simply the Bishops. They recorded a live album at the Chalk Farm Roundhouse in February 1978, but tragedy struck a year later. Zenon De Fleur suffered a fatal heart attack after being involved in a car crash in London. He was just 28. His death pre-empted the release of *Cross Cuts* and the band split soon afterwards, though a handful of gigs were played without him. They returned in December 1979 to record live at the Hope And Anchor pub in Islington, for the compilation album, *The London R&B Sessions*. The line-up at that point was Dave Tice (vocals/harmonica), Johnny Guitar (guitar), Pat McMullan (bass) and Charles Morgan (drums). Johnny Guitar would go on to replace John Mayo in Dr. Feelgood, though the Bishops made one final recording in 1984.
Albums: *Count Bishops* (Chiswick 1977). As The Bishops: *The Bishops Live* (Chiswick 1978), *Cross Cuts* (Chiswick 1979), *Good Gear* (Chiswick 1984).

Counting Crows

Berkeley Hills, California based folk-rock band comprising Adam Duritz (b. c.1964; vocals), David Bryson (guitar), Mat Malley (bass), Steve Bowman (drums), Charlie Gillingham (Hammond organ, keyboards) and Dan Vickrey (lead guitar, mandolin). Early reports suggested the influence of the singer-songwriter tradition, notably Van Morrison. Other comparisons were made with the Band. While in interview Duritz was keen to point out that they were more than a retro outfit, he applauded the organic approach to musicianship which lay behind the Band and their ilk. This was reflected on their well-received debut, produced by T-Bone Burnett, which mixed traditional R&B elements with a raw, rocky delivery. The MTV rotation of 'Mr Jones' undoubtedly augmented sales, as did crticial reaction, David Cavanagh noting in *The Independent* that: 'Its musical warmth makes it sound like a bunch of understated anthems in which, conceivably, millions could find solace'. By mid-1995 their remarkable debut had sold over 5 million copies in their homeland.
Album: *August And Everything After* (Geffen 1993).

Cowboy Junkies

Toronto-based musicians, Michael Timmins (b. 21 April

Cowboy Junkies

1959, Montreal, Canada; guitar) and Alan Anton (b. Alan Alizojvodic, 22 June 1959, Montreal, Canada; bass), formed a group called Hunger Project in 1979. It was not successful and, basing themselves in the UK, they formed an experimental instrumental group, Germinal. Returning to Toronto, they joined forces with Timmins' sister Margo (b. 27 June 1961, Montreal, Canada; vocal) and brother Peter (b. 29 October 1965, Montreal, Canada; drums). As the Cowboy Junkies (which was simply an attention-grabbing name), they recorded their first album, *Whites Off Earth Now!!*, in a private house. Their second album, *The Trinity Session*, was made with one microphone in the Church of Holy Trinity, Toronto for $250. The band's spartan, less-is-more sound captivated listeners and, with little publicity, the second album sold 250,000 copies in North America. The tracks included a curious reinterpretation of 'Blue Moon' called 'Blue Moon Revisited (Song For Elvis)' and the country standards, 'I'm So Lonesome I Could Cry' and 'Walking After Midnight'. Lou Reed praised their version of his song, 'Sweet Jane', and, in 1991, they contributed 'To Lay Me Down' in a tribute to the Grateful Dead, *Deadicated*. Their 1990 album, *The Caution Horses*, included several vintage country songs which, true to form, were performed in their whispered, five miles-per-hour style. The extent of the Cowboy Junkies' fast growing reputation was sufficient for them to promote the 1992 album *Black-Eyed Man* at London's Royal Albert Hall.

Albums: *Whites Off Earth Now!!* (1986), *The Trinity Session* (1988), *The Caution Horses* (1990), *Black-Eyed Man* (1992), *Pale Sun, Crescent Moon* (RCA 1993).

Cracker

A rowdy update of the 70s Californian folk rock fraternity, Cracker are fronted by Redlands natives David Lowery (formerly the founder of skewed rock architects Camper Van Beethoven) and fellow guitarist Johnny Hickman (b. c.1959). Vocalist Lowery (b. c.1961) has been recording offbeat pop songs from the age of 16, issuing a number of tapes before joining covers bands. From there he graduated to original material with Box Of Laughs and Estonian Gauchos - who included Hickman. When Camper Van Beethoven imploded on tour in 1989, Lowery once again approached Hickman, who had been unable to join the latter band due to solo commitments and work with ill-fated country band the Unforgiven. Immediately the duo picked up the Lynyrd Skynyrd mantle also appropriated with less raucous abandon by the Counting Crows, with whom they would tour during 1994. Cracker had by this time already recorded its self-titled debut album for Virgin Records, who still had Lowery under contract following the dissolution of Camper Van Beethoven. The album, with guest help from Jim Keltner (drums; of Little Village) and Benmont Tench (bass; Tom Petty And The Heartbreakers) melded influences as diverse as psychedelia, country rock and Delta blues, forging a style that was at once ethnic yet universal - its wry centre piece, 'Teen Angst', being the first to alert commentators to something a little special about their activities. *Cracker* would sell over 200,000 copies, a figure soon doubled by follow-up collection, *Kerosene Hot*, which saw a more permanent rhythm aggregation in David

Lowering and Bruce Hughes. Much of the 'buzz' concerned opening single 'Low', and its black and white video featuring Lowery boxing Sandra Bernhardt - the perfect backdrop to the song's moody, overpowering grunge guitar and lyrical paranoia. Now based in Richmond, Virginia, where Lowery co-owns a studio, some of Camper Van Beethoven's more dizzy excesses spilled over on to the album. These included a final listed track, 'Hi-Desert Biker Meth Lab', which they never got round to finishing, inserting a 40 second sound collage instead. The CD release was then programmed with 99 tracks, most of which consisted of three seconds of silence. However, *Kerosene Hat* also worked on a more sober level. 'Nostalgia' offered salutations to the lonely Soviet cosmonaut who spent a year drifting (space being a recurring theme). Other fine moments included a cover version of the Grateful Dead's 'Loser', or the neo-Rolling Stones interlude, 'Take Me Down To The Infirmary'.

Albums: *Cracker* (Virgin 1992), *Kerosene Hat* (Virgin 1994).

Cramps

Formed in Ohio, USA, in 1976, the original Cramps, Lux Interior (b. Erick Lee Purkhiser; vocals), 'Poison' Ivy Rorschach (b. Kirsty Marlana Wallace; guitar), Bryan Gregory (guitar) and his sister, Pam Balam (drums), later moved to New York, where they were embroiled in the emergent punk scene centred on the CBGBs rock venue. Miriam Linna briefly replaced Balam, before Nick Knox (b. Nick Stephanoff) became the group's permanent drummer. The Cramps' early work was recorded at the famed Sun Records studio under the aegis of producer Alex Chilton. Their early singles and debut album blended the frantic rush of rockabilly with a dose of 60s garage-band panache and an obvious love of ghoulish b-movies. Bryan Gregory's sudden departure followed the release of the compulsive 'Drug Train' single. Former Gun Club acolyte, Kid Congo (Powers) (b. Brian Tristan), appeared on *Psychedelic Jungle*, but he later rejoined his erstwhile colleagues and the Cramps have since employed several, often female, replacements, including Fur and Candy Del Mar. Despite the group's momentum being rudely interrupted by a protracted legal wrangle with the IRS Records label during the early 80s, the Cramps' horror-cum-trash style, supplemented with a healthy dose of humour and sex, has nonetheless remained intact throughout their career. However, the best examples of their work can still be found on their early albums (and compilations), with songs such as 'You've Got Good Taste', 'Human Fly' and 'I'm Cramped' perfectly capturing a moment in time in the evolution of alternative rock music. Next best is probably 1986's *A Date With Elvis*, which appealed because the formula was still relatively fresh. Wary of outside manipulation, the Cramps continue to steer their own course to good effect by touring and recording, proving themselves the masters of their particular genre. Their live shows, especially, are rarely found wanting in terms of entertainment value. In 1991 Interior and Rorschach re-emerged fronting a rejuvenated line-up with Slim Chance (bass) and Jim Sclavunos (drums). Now signed to Creation Records a further album was issued in 1994 with a new amended line-up of Harry Drumdini not surprisingly on drums. *Flamejob* was as provocative and funny as their past efforts.

Cranberries

Albums: *Songs The Lord Taught Us* (Illegal/IRS 1980), *Psychedelic Jungle* (IRS 1981), *Smell Of Female* (Enigma 1983), *Bad Music For Bad People* (IRS 1984), *A Date With Elvis* (Big Beat 1986), *Stay Sick* (Enigma 1990), *Look Mom No Head!* (Big Beat 1991), *Flamejob* (Creation 1994). Compilation: *Off The Bone* (IRS 1983).

Further reading: *The Wild, Wild World Of The Cramps*, Ian Johnston.

Cranberries

This band hail from Limerick, Eire, and boast the honeyed voice of Delores O'Riordan (b. Delores Mary Eileen O'Riordan, 1971, Ballybricken, Limerick, Eire). From a conservative, rural Catholic background, she had sung since the age of four in schools and churches. Her guitarist and main co-songwriter is Noel Hogan, and the line-up is completed by his brother, Mike (bass) and Fergal Lawler (drums). The male members had been involved as a band for some time but it never amounted to much until they joined forces with O'Riordan. Their original singer had given them their original name - The Cranberry Saw Us. Their debut EP *Uncertain* was released in late 1991 on the Xeric label, whose owner, Pearse Gilmore, became their manager. With its circulation the buzz surrounding the band transferred to mainland UK, where Island Records underwent tough negotiations (not least due to Gilmore's self-interested protectionism) to tie-up a six album deal. However, *Uncertain* disappointed many journalists who had been given a preview of the far superior songs on the demo (which included 'Put Me Down', 'Dreams' and 'Linger'). Sessions for their debut album also produced rancour, with Gilmore attempting to act as producer, leading to the end of that relationship. The band contacted Rough Trade Records supremo Geoff Travis, who had been interested in signing them but who instead took over management (with Jeanette Lee, a former member of Public Image Limited). The album was started from scratch at Windmill Studios, Dublin, with Stephen Street. *Everybody Else Is Doing It, So Why Can't We?* was finally released n March 1993, following the issue of 'Dreams' and 'Linger' as singles. By now much of the original impetus had dissipated, though a 1993 tour with Belly at least seemed to offer some exposure. It helped the band renew their confidence, and was followed by dates with Hothouse Flowers. But it would be American audiences who would first truly appreciate the band. On 10 June they began a six week tour with The The and they were picked up by college radio. The US proved to have none of the preconceptions associated with the capricious British press, and the band soon became a hot radio and concert ticket. In July 1994 O'Riordan married their tour manager, Don Burton, in a ceremony distinguished by her see-through bridal attire. The Americans kept buying the album in their droves, and was successful in the UK too, reaching number 1 in the UK charts in June 1994. *No Need To Argue* followed in October - and with its release the Cranberries crowned as the new kings of AOR. Including the strong single 'Zombie' (despite its rather crude and untimely lyrics concerning the Northern Ireland struggle), the album meant the band were now welcomed anew by the UK media which had long since deserted them. The only doubt hanging over the band's future was the much repeated opinion that Delores was the star and that, ultimately, she didn't need her compatriots.

Albums: *Everybody Else Is Doing It, So Why Can't We?* (Island 1993), *No Need To Argue* (Island 1994).

Video: *Live* (1994).

Cranes

Portsmouth, England band the Cranes continued the musical metaphors of their obvious forebears the Cocteau Twins and My Bloody Valentine in the late 80s and early 90s. They were formed by sister/brother team Alison (b. c.1964; vocals/bass) and Jim Shaw (drums), who comprise the principal song writing unit. As children they would listen to New Order, Nick Cave and the Young Gods, which became an approximation of their later sound (though they ferociously objected to the 'Gothic' tag they earned in their early days). The line-up is completed by Mark Francombe (guitar) and Matt Cope (bass/guitar). After five years of introspection, writing and perfecting songs for themselves, and contributions to a plethora of various artist compilations, the band picked up support from disc jockey John Peel with 1990's mini-album, *Self-Non-Self*. They signed to BMG/RCA subsidiary Dedicated in July 1990, attracting further plaudits for *Wings Of Joy*, described variously as 'foetal, minimalist, metallic and funereal'. *Forever* saw the band pick up world tour support slots with an admiring Cure, while *Loved*, a more accessible offering with Shaw's vocals noticeably more prominent in the mix, suggested they may break through in the wake of the Cranberries' commercialisation of 'dream pop', an American term which still fits this UK band admirably.

Albums: *Fuel* (Bite Back 1987, cassette only), *Self-Non-Self* (Dedicated 1990, mini-album), *Wings Of Joy* (Dedicated 1991), *Forever* (Dedicated 1993), *Loved* (Dedicated 1994).

Crash Test Dummies

When songwriter Brad Roberts (vocals/guitar) graduated from the University of Winnipeg, Canada, with an honours degree in English Literature, he was still a dedicated student, planning to take a Ph.D. become a professor. His chronic asthma and penchant for the lyrics of XTC's Andy Partridge did little to dispel his 'college geek' image. However, when the band he had started with friends in the mid-80s took off, his academic interests had to be suspended. Building on impromptu get-togethers as a group formed at an after-hours club in Winnipeg, the name Crash Test Dummies was eventually decided upon. When record company executives heard some of Roberts' demo tapes (which he had been using to try to get the band festival gigs), the interest encouraged him to concentrate more fully on music. The band comprised Roberts, his younger brother Dan (bass), Benjamin Darvill (mandolin/harmonica) and Ellen Reid (piano/accordion/backing vocals). Their debut , *The Ghosts That Haunt Me*, rose to number 1 on the Canadian chart on the back of the hit single, 'Superman's Song'. A blend of blues-based rock 'n' roll and folk-pop, its best moments occurred when Roberts strange vocal amalgam of Scott Walker and Tom Waits combined with Darvill's harmonica. However, despite selling over a quarter of a million copies domestically, the rest of north America were uninterested.

Crash Test Dummies

This situation was radically amended with the release of *God Shuffled His Feet*, which introduced drummer Michel Dooge and was co-produced by Talking Heads' Jerry Harrison. Their breakthrough arrived with another distinctive single, 'Mmmm Mmmm Mmmm', with its stuttering title as the song's chorus. A catchy radio-friendly novelty song, it was only partly representative of the band's more astute and perky pop compositions. Nevertheless, it rose to number 12 on the *Billboard* chart in March 1994. *God Shuffled His Feet* was a fairly strong album, although occasionally its references to literature and schools of philosophy, such as Dada, Cubism and Sartre, overbalanced some of the songs. At other times Roberts' questioning intelligence worked to better effect: 'How does a duck know which direction south is?' being just one of many wide-eyed but entertaining observations.

Albums: *The Ghosts That Haunt Me* (Arista 1991), *God Shuffled His Feet* (RCA 1994).

Video: *Symptomology Of A Rock Band: The Case Of Crash Test Dummies* (1994).

Crass

Formed in 1978 by Steve Ignorant and Penny Rimbaud, Crass's music was a confrontational hybrid of buzzsaw, off-beat guitars, military drumming and shouted vocals, but this was always secondary to their message. They believed in anarchy (which they defined as 'respect for yourself and others as human beings') in the UK and took their multi-media performances to hundreds of unlikely venues. Formed by the members of a commune based in Epping, Essex, England, Crass had a fluid line-up and its members wore black and adopted pseudonyms to save their message becoming diluted by personalities. *Feeding The 5,000* was raw and frantic, peppered with swear words but clearly authentic and heartfelt. *Stations Of The Crass*, a double album, offered more of the same and challenged contemporary issues like the dissolution of the punk ethos ('White Punks On Hope') and British class divisions ('Time Out'). The group's most notorious offering was the post-Falklands war single, directed at the Prime Minister, Margaret Thatcher, 'How Does It Feel (To Be The Mother Of A 1,000 Dead)', which topped the UK Independent chart. The line-up at the time was listed as: Ignorant (vocals), Rimbaud (drums), Eve Libertine (vocals), Joy De Vivre (vocals), Phil Free (guitar), N.A. Palmer (guitar), Pete Wright (bass) and Mick 'G' Duffield (backing vocals). Crass maintained a high degree of autonomy through their own Crass Records label and supported other like-minded groups, notably Flux Of Pink Indians and Conflict. They issued three compilation albums of other people's music, *Bullshit Detectors 1, 2* and *3* (a title borrowed from the Clash song, a group that Crass often accused of 'selling out') and released records by the Poison Girls, Captain Sensible, Rudimentary Peni, the Mob (which included Josef Porta, later of Blyth Power), the aforementioned Conflict and Flux, and many others. On *Penis Envy* the female members took on lead vocals and the record was a sustained and tuneful attack on sexism in modern society. It marked the band's creative apex because by *Christ The Album* and *Yes Sir, I Will* - where poetry and experimental music were combined - the

initial energy and inspiration was missing. The group split in 1984, as they often said they would, and to this day remain one of the few groups to loyally adhere to their original ideals. Steve Ignorant joined Conflict in the latter part of 80s.

Albums: *The Feeding Of The 5,000* (Small Wonder 1978), *Stations Of The Crass* (Crass 1980), *Penis Envy* (Crass 1981), *Yes Sir, I Will* (Crass 1982), *Christ The Album* (Crass 1983, double album). Compilations: *Best Before 1984* (Crass 1987, a singles collection), *You'll Ruin It For Everyone* (Pomona/Crass 1993).

Video: *Christ The Movie*.

Cravats

From the UK midlands town of Redditch, Worcestershire, England, the Cravats' weird brand of rock was first heard on the classic 'Gordon', a co-release with Small Wonder Records and their own label in October 1978. After joining Small Wonder, the band, consisting of Shend (b. Chris Harz; vocals/bass), Robin Dallaway (guitar/vocals), Dave Bennett (drums) and Richard London (saxophone), put out a series of entertaining singles, starting with the EP *Burning Bridges* in 1979. It was over a year before 'Precinct' appeared in 1980, alongside what proved to be their only album, *Cravats In Toytown*. After releasing 'You're Driving Me' and 'Off The Beach' in 1981, the band moved to Glass Records for 'Terminus' in 1982, but it was to prove a one-off single. Only the superb 'Rub Me Out', on the Crass label, made any headway in the UK Independent chart. A retrospective EP, *The Cravats Sing Terminus And Other Hits*, surfaced before the band laid low. A solitary EP, *In The Land Of The Giants*, on the Reflex label some three years later, was all the band could offer before mutating into the Very Things. Pursuing an acting career, Shend later made various minor television appearances, in particular the BBC television soap opera, *EastEnders*.

Album: *The Cravats In Toytown* (Small Wonder 1980).

Crazyhead

This guitar band formed in Leicester, England in 1986, were signed to the fledgling Food label. Their first two releases saw quick independent chart success; '(What Gives You The Idea That) You're So Amazing Baby?' and 'Baby Turpentine' both reaching number 2. In common with Gaye Bikers On Acid, Bomb Party and Pop Will Eat Itself, the group were linked with the media-fuelled 'biker' or 'grebo' rock genre. By the time of their third single 'Time Has Taken Its Toll On You' and debut album in 1988 their career was in decline, despite later minor national chart success in 1989 with the *Have Love, Will Travel* EP and 'Like Princes Do' on the Food label's Christmas EP. Enjoying ludicrous names like Vom, Superfast Blind Dick, Ian 'Anderson Pork Beast' (vocals) and stranger still, Kevin, they were dropped from Food in 1989. Their second album, produced by Pat Collier, saw them housed on Black records.

Albums: *Desert Orchid* (1988), *Some Kind Of Fever* (1990), *Live In Memphis* (1993).

Creaming Jesus

This satirical UK hardcore/metal quintet were formed in

Crazyhead

1987 by vocalist Andy and guitarists Richard and Mario. With the addition of drummer Roy and bassist Tally, they signed to the independent Jungle label. Their amusingly titled debut saw chainsaw guitars collide with machine-gun drumming, whilst the lyrics dealt with contemporary issues such as television evangelists, sexual perverts, childhood anxieties and warmongerers. Never big on subtlety, Creaming Jesus, whose name in itself is enough to send the weak-hearted into apoplexy, have sustained a rudimentary talent over a succession of albums.

Albums: *Too Fat To Run, Too Stupid To Hide* (Jungle 1990), *Guilt By Association* (Jungle 1992), *Chaos For The Converted* (Jungle 1994).

Creation Records

This UK independent record label was formed by music business entrepreneur/reformed British Rail clerk Alan McGee (b. 29 September 1960, Glasgow, Scotland), whose first venture was the dubious Laughing Apple. Brought up in East Kilbride, Scotland, childhood friends included what would become Creation's first 'name' signing, the Jesus And Mary Chain. His first love was 60s music, particularly psychedelia, and he named his label after the UK cult band of the same name. With this he combined a fond regard for the energy and irreverence of punk, and after a tentative step into the world of fanzines with *Communication Blur*, he moved to London in 1982. There he established the Living Room, a venue of no fixed abode. The first release on Creation, however, did little to justify his already bold claims. ''77 In '83' was the work of The Legend!, a fanzine editor as eccentric by reputation as McGee. The next 20 singles cultivated a strong identity, if not fervent sales. They came in wraparound plastic sleeves, with 1,000 pressings for each. The best of these saw the debut of the Pastels, which had charm to compensate for the nostalgic arrangements and impoverished production values it shared with its brethren. Other featured bands included the Revolving Paint Dream, Jasmine Minks and McGee's own Biff Bang Pow!. There were, however, three milestone records which really signposted the arrival of the label. The first was the Loft's 'Why Does The Rain?', similar in feel to many Creation singles but with a much more focused and emotive delivery. The second was the Jesus And Mary Chain's 'Upside Down'. The Mary Chain crystalized the meeting of 60s songwriting with punk's brash shock value, inspiring massive interest in the band, the label, and the numerous imitators that sprung up around them. Finally, Primal Scream's 'Velocity Girl', although not their first record, was the one that brought them to the public's attention. Although the Loft would be short lived, and the Jesus And Mary Chain would switch to the Warner Brothers distributed Blanco Y Negro label, Creation had earned its spurs with the public. Primal Scream would prove pivotal, the lucrative jewel in the Creation crown. Although the glut of success dried up with the arrival of diverse acts such as Nikki Sudden, Clive Langer and Baby Amphetamine, the House Of Love revived fortunes in 1987. They were another band who later left for a larger record company, but new mainstays arrived with music press favourites My Bloody Valentine and then Ride. The high recording costs incurred by the former led to yet another

parting of the ways after 1991's *Loveless*. Although McGee sold part of the label to Sony to improve its financial position in the 90s, his inspired A&R track record continued. He was able to pick up the Boo Radleys following their split with Rough Trade Records, at a time when their career seemed doomed. This marriage found first critical success with *Giant Steps*, then enormous chart and commercial acceptance with 1995's garlanded *Wake Up*. Even more contagious than the Liverpool band's 60s revisionism was the astonishing overnight success of Oasis - typically signed by McGee on a whim after seeing them support his less headline-grabbing act, 18 Wheeler, at a Glasgow gig. Oasis' critical and chart domination throughout 1994 and 1995, despite looking as though they might implode at any moment, has surely established Creation's place in the music industry for decades to come.

In 1995 the UK charts were dominated by Oasis, Boo Radleys and Teenage Fanclub. McGee, meanwhile, continues to be as uniquely provocative as ever: 'No praise is high enough for Creation'. In truth, Creation can arguably lay claim to being the most genuinely innovative of the UK independents and are riding a crest in the mid-90s. As one critic of McGee noted: 'His willingness to give free reign to bands who seem impossible commercial ventures has resulted in occasionally great artistic, and ironically fiscal, success.'

Creatures

This on-off collaboration between Siouxsie And The Banshees members Siouxsie Sioux and drummer/percussionist Budgie won them a string of UK hits starting with 'Mad Eyed Screamer' (1981) and 'Miss The Girl' (1983) - both achieving Top 30 status. Their greatest success came that same year with Herbie Mann and Carl Sigman's swing composition, 'Right Now' which reached number 14. Away from the more rock constraints of the parent group, the Creatures allowed Budgie to experiment with more exotic percussive instruments and give the sound a freer, more expressive feel. Conceived primarily as a studio-only set-up, the Creatures did not make their live debut until 1990.

Albums: *Feast* (1983), *Boomerang* (1989). Compilation: *The Best Of* (1993).

Crenshaw, Marshall

b. 1954, Detroit, Michigan, USA. After portraying John Lennon in the stage show *Beatlemania*, Crenshaw forged a solo career as a solid and dependable performer of the classic urban American pop song. His rock 'n' roll songs were sprinkled with lyrics discoursing on the perennial problems of the love-lorn and that of being in love. With a echo-laden guitar sound that harked back to the 60s with a little Buddy Holly and Eddie Cochran thrown in for effect, Crenshaw's future looked bright with the release of his first album for Warner Brothers Records in 1982. Performing alongside his brother Robert (drums/vocals) and Chris Donato (bass/vocals), this debut album contained Crenshaw's only US single hit to date, 'Someday, Someway'. His album of modern pop also contained such classics as 'Cynical Girl' and 'Mary Ann', but only reached number 50 on the US chart.

His follow-up was dealt a similar fate. Although the album was packed with what seemed to be 'radio-friendly' hits, songs like 'Whenever You're On My Mind', 'What Time Is It?' and 'For Her Love' found only cult-status appreciation. The lean period of commercial success was relieved by the success of Owen Paul's cover of his 'My Favourite Waste Of Time', which reached the UK Top 3 in 1986. Crenshaw made film appearances in *Peggy Sue Got Married* and portrayed Buddy Holly in *La Bamba*. Further acclaimed album releases have seen the guitarist cover other artists' songs including sterling performances of Richard Thompson's 'Valerie' and John Haitt's 'Someplace Where Love Can't Find Me' on *Good Evening*. A split with Warners in 1990 saw Crenshaw sign to MCA and the release of *Life's Too Short*.

Albums: *Marshall Crenshaw* (1982), *Field Day* (1983), *Downtown* (1985), *Sings Mary Jean & Nine Others* (1987), *Good Evening* (1989), *Life's Too Short* (1991).

Crime

Formed in San Francisco, California, USA, in 1976, this talented punk act originally comprised Frankie Fix (guitar), Johnny Strike (guitar), Ron Greco (aka Ron the Ripper, bass; ex-Chosen Few) and Ricky James (drums). Greco had previously been dumped by the Chosen Few just as they were about to transmute into the Flamin' Groovies. His new group made their debut on their own Crime label with 'Hot Wire My Heart'/'Baby You're So Repulsive' in 1976, the a-side of which was later covered by Sonic Youth on *Sister* and is considered to be something of a classic of early US hardcore. Afterwards James quit the band to join Flipper, then Toiling Midgets. 'Murder By Guitar'/'Frustration' was issued the following year with new drummer Brittley Black In place, and taken together these singles confirmed the quartet as one of the Bay Area's leading new wave attractions. A projected album was, however, shelved and the quartet disbanded following the release of 'Maserati'/'Gangster Funk' (1980). Between these two singles Black played briefly in the Flamin' Groovies (late joining Death). He had been replaced by the group's third and most permanent drummer, Hank Rank. It was he who was in place for the various studio and live sessions which appeared in bootleg and ultimately official format following the band's demise. However, he too would depart in 1980, with Black returning to drum on the poorly received 'Maserati'. Rank would form Other Music, while Johnny Strike put together an 'experimental drum group', Rev.

Album: *San Francisco's Doomed* (Solar Lodge 1983, reissued on CD by Overground 1993).

Crime And The City Solution

Formed from the ashes of the Birthday Party, Crime And The City Solution have become a repository for a number of musicians and artists working under that verbose banner. Their inital mainstay was Rowland S. Howard (vocals/guitar), who, together with brother Harry Howard (bass), brought fellow Birthday Party journeyman Mick Harvey (drums) to the fold. Early line-ups fluctuated rapidly, and included stays for the likes of Epic Soundtracks (drums, ex-Swell Maps). The first pivotal change, however, came when Simon Bonney (b. Tasmania, Australasia; vocals/guitar) arrived. Bonney, whose own band shared a near parallel career to Boys Next Door (a precursor to the Birthday Party), had known the other members from their days together in Melbourne, Australia. The brothers Howard would later split with Bonney to form These Immortal Souls, effectively leaving the band's destination in his hands. In the meantime, Mick Harvey drummed with Nick Cave And The Bad Seeds, while new recruit Alexander Hacke (guitar) continued to play with Einsturzende Neubaten, for whom Bonney was also an occasional member. Hacke had joined in time for *Shine*, whereupon the band had re-located to Berlin from England. This allowed them to work with a variety of new media, notably appearing in Wim Wenders' film *Wings Of Desire*. Their liaison was so successful the director asked them to compose the soundtrack to his next film *To The Ends Of the World*. The line-up for later albums added multi-instrumentalist Chrislo Hass, Thomas Stern (bass) and Bronwyn Adams (violin), with whom Bonney was now co-writing. Despite the personnel shifts, the band's output has remained remarkably constant, though the textures have undoubtedly altered; emotive and intense vignettes on the dark side of life, the evocation of mood as much a keynote as is the case with former cohort Nick Cave.

Albums: *Room Of Lights* (1987), *Shine* (1988), *The Bride Ship* (1989), *The Paradise Discotheque* (1990), *The Adversary - Live* (1993).

Crispy Ambulance

Many bands tired to emulate the moody magnificence of Joy Division but few succeeded as well as fellow Mancunians Crispy Ambulance. So similar were they that vocalist Alan Hempsall stood in for Ian Curtis at a Joy Division gig when the singer was incapacitated by an epileptic attack. They were formed in Manchester in 1978 by Hempsall, Robert Davenport (guitar), Keith Darbyshire (bass) and Gary Madeley (drums) - a line-up which would remain constant throughout the band's existence. They began by playing Hawkwind and Magazine covers but by 1979 the influence of their famous peers had become evident. A debut single, 'From The Cradle To The Grave', was released on their own Aural Assault label, and was brought to the attention of Rob Gretton, manager of Joy Division and later New Order. He arranged for their next release - the 10-inch single 'Unsightly and Serene' - to come out on Factory Records, while future releases such as 1981's excellent 'Live On A Hot August Night' 12-inch single (produced by Martin Hannett) appeared on Factory Benelux. The band split in November 1981 but later reformed as Ram Ram Kino with some additional members. They would release one single on Genesis P. Orridge's Psychic Temple label late in 1985.

Album: *The Plateau Phase* (Factory 1982).

Cro-Mags

This US thrash/hardcore band was formed in 1984 by bassist (and sometime singer) Harley Flanegan, a follower of the Hare Krishna doctrine, who nevertheless represents an intimidating, multi-tattooed presence on stage. After a series of false starts, vocalist John 'Bloodclot' Joseph, drummer Mackie and guitarists Doug Holland (ex-Kraut; who joined in time for *Best Wishes*) and Parris Mitchell Mayhew were recruited to cement the band's line-up. When Joseph left Flanegan would take over vocal duties. They specialized in a fusion of thrash, hardcore and heavy metal and the influences of Motörhead, the Dead Kennedys and Metallica were quite apparent on their debut, *The Age Of Quarrel*. They built up a small but loyal cult of supporters, and regularly headlined major hardcore events at New York's CBGB's during the mid to late 80s. Primarily remarkable for their sheer sonic intensity, the group were at the forefront of a musical genre which became increasingly adopted by the metal fraternity as time wore on. Unlike most, however, Cro-Mags offered lyrical diversity and invention to back up their 'mosh' epics, notably on tracks like 'The Only One', which delivered a sermon on their leader's religious position. Line-up changes were numerous, the most pertinent of which was Mackie's decision to join Bad Brains.

Albums: *The Age Of Quarrel* (GWR 1987), *Best Wishes* (Profile 1990), *Alpha Omega* (Century Media 1992).

Cuban Heels

This UK group was headed by John Malarky (vocals), previously a member of Johnny And The Self Abusers, the Scottish punk band that metamorphosed into Simple Minds. Cuban Heels' formation in Glasgow 1978 was completed with the addition of Laurie Cuffe (guitar), Paul Armour (bass) and Davie Duncan (drums). Initially an R&B band with the odd punk track, they soon found growing popularity with the mod revival crowd. Consequently their live set was balanced between originals like 'Modern Girl', 'Too Much, Too Loud', 'Samantha's World' and 'Young Pretender', plus covers such as Cat Stevens' 'Matthew And Son' and Cliff Richard's 'On The Beach'. The debut single released on the Housewives Choice label in March 1978, was a pop-punk reworking of Petula Clark's hit, 'Downtown'. With the new year came a change in line-up, with Nick Clarke (bass) and Ali McKenzie (drums), replacing Armour and Duncan. Throughout 1979-80 they continued an exhausting live schedule and released two more independent singles, 'Little Girl' and 'Walk On Water'. Their lack of commercial success prompted the band to settle on a more comfortable pop sound, with an image to match. A deal with Virgin Records saw *Walk Our Way To Heaven* and a string of singles, 'Sweet Charity', 'My Colours Fly' and a remake of 'Walk On Water', suffer the same fate as previous offerings. The band split during 1982.

Album: *Walk Our Way To Heaven* (Virgin 1981).

Cud

Cud were formed in Leeds in 1987 by Carl Puttnam (b. 1967, Ilford, Essex, England; vocals), Mike Dunphy (b. 1967, Northumberland, England; guitar), William Potter (b. 1968, Derby, England; bass) and Steve 'The Drummer From Cud' Goodwin (b. 1967, Croydon, Surrey, England; drums). The quartet sprung into existence when they discovered the remains of a deserted drum kit in a rubbish skip. They

debuted on the Wedding Present's Reception label and spent two years building up a small but fanatical north England following with a comical hybrid of funk and the uglier elements of independent music. Threatened by a not entirely undeserved 'joker' tag - helped by Cud's desire to perform absurd versions of Hot Chocolate and Jethro Tull songs - 1990 brought 'a new sense of sanity and professionalism' to the band. Critical acclaim coincided with a more nationwide spread of supporters, and their newfound attitude reaped commercial dividends when the 'Robinson Crusoe' single reached number 86 in the UK charts, closely followed by 'Magic' peaking at number 80. With financial viability suddenly outweighing the band's odder idiosyncracies, major labels tussled for their signatures until Cud decided to go with A&M Records in 1991 for the simple reason that the label's logo 'had the trumpet'. This move saw the release in the summer of 1992 of *Aquarius*, which earned the group glowing reviews. However, the transition from indie chart to mainstream pop territory was not as easy as this early victory might have suggested. A&M launched the band with a seemingly endless collection of promotional gimmicks (balloons, mobiles, etc.) but failed to reap significant commercial reward. Despite this, the critics were still kind to *Showbiz*, wherein Cud provided a less insular pop sound and 'mature' lyrics (mature in comparison to previous efforts, but hardly by anyone else's standards).

Albums: *When In Rome, Kill Me* (Imaginary 1989), *Leggy Mambo* (Imaginary 1990), *Aquarius* (A&M 1992), *Showbiz* (A&M 1994). Compilation: *Elvis Belt* (Imaginary 1990). Video: *When At Home, Film Me* (1990).

Cuddly Toys

Emerging from the ashes of glam-punk outfit Raped, the Ireland-based Cuddly Toys consisted of Sean Purcell (vocals), Tony Baggett (bass), Faebhean Kwest (guitar), Billy Surgeoner (guitar) and Paddy Phield (drums). Both their 1980 offerings, *Guillotine Theatre* and a cover of Marc Bolan and David Bowie's 'Madmen', were co-releases for Raped's old label Parole and Fresh Records. 'Astral Joe' came later that year, followed by 'Someone's Crying' in 1981, but the band seemed derivative in comparison to more exciting members of their peer group and soon endured line-up changes. Terry Noakes joined on guitar and Robert Parker on drums. After 'It's A Shame' and a second album, *Trials And Crosses*, in 1982, the group disappeared from view.

Albums: *Guillotine Theatre* (Fresh 1981), *Trials And Crosses* (Fresh 1982).

Cult

Originally known as first Southern Death Cult then Death Cult, the band were formed by lead singer Ian Astbury (b. 14 May 1962, Heswell, Merseyside, England) in 1981. After a youth spent in Scotland and Canada (where he gained early exposure to the culture of native Indians on the Six Nations Reservation, informing the early stages of the band's career), Astbury moved into a Bradford, Yorkshire, house and discovered a group in rehearsal in the basement. The group's personnel included Haq Qureshi (drums), David 'Buzz' Burrows (guitar) and Barry Jepson (bass). As their vocalist, Astbury oversaw a rapid rise in fortunes, their fifth gig and

London debut at the Heaven club attracting a near 2,000-strong audience. Southern Death Cult made their recording debut in December 1982 with the double a-side, 'Moya'/'Fatman', and supported Bauhaus on tour in early 1983. However, by March the group had folded, Astbury reeling from his perceived image of 'positive punk' spokesman, and the fact that his native Indian concept was being diluted by the group's format. His new band, operating under the truncated name Death Cult, would, he vowed, not become a victim of hype in the same way again (Qureshi, Jepson and Burrows would go on to join Getting The Fear, subsequently becoming Into A Circle before Qureshi re-emerged as the centrepiece of Fun-Da-Mental's 'world dance' ethos under the name Propa-Ghandi). A combination of the single, demo and live tracks was posthumously issued as the sole SDC album. Death Cult comprised the rhythm section of recently deceased gothic band Ritual, namely Ray 'The Reverend' Mondo (drums) and Jamie Stewart (bass), plus ex-Ed Banger And The Nosebleeds and Theatre Of Hate guitarist Billy Duffy (b. 12 May 1959, Manchester, England). They made their debut in July 1983 with an eponymous four-track 12-inch, at which time Astbury also changed his own name (he had previously been using Ian Lindsay, which, it later transpired, was his mother's maiden name). After an appearance at the Futurama festival Mondo swapped drumming positions with Sex Gang Children's Nigel Preston (d. 7 May 1992), a former colleague of Duffy's in Theatre Of Hate. However, 1984 brought about a second and final name change - with the band feeling that the Death prefix typecast them as a 'Gothic' act, they became simply the Cult. They recorded their first album together, *Dreamtime*, for release in September 1984, its sales boosted by a number 1 single in the indepedent charts with the typcially anthemic 'Spiritwalker'. Another strong effort followed early the next year, 'She Sells Sanctuary', but this was to prove Preston's swansong. Mark Brzezicki of Big Country helped out on sessions for the forthcoming album until the permanent arrival of Les Warner (b. 13 February 1961), who had previously worked with Johnny Thunders, Julian Lennon and Randy California. The band's major commercial break came with *Love* in 1985, which comprised fully-fledged hard rock song structures and pushed Duffy's guitar lines to the fore. It spawned two UK Top 20 hit singles in the aforementioned 'She Sells Sanctuary' and 'Rain'. *Electric* saw the band's transition to heavy rock completed. There was no disguising the group's source of inspiration, with Led Zeppelin being mentioned in nearly every review. Part-produced by Rick Rubin, *Electric* was a bold and brash statement of intent, if not quite the finished item. It became a success on both sides of the Atlantic, peaking at number 4 and 38 in the UK and US charts respectively. The gigs to promote it saw the band add bass player Kid 'Haggis' Chaos (b. Mark Manning; ex-Zodiac Mindwarp And The Love Reaction), with Stewart switching to rhythm guitar. Both he and Warner were dispensed with in March 1988, the former joining 4 Horsemen. Reduced to a three-piece of Astbury, Stewart and Duffy, the sessions for *Sonic Temple* saw them temporarily recruit the services of drummer Mickey Curry. It was an album which combined the atmospheric passion of *Love* with the unbridled energy of *Electric*. A 1989 world tour saw the band augmented by Matt Sorum (drums) and Mark Taylor (keyboards; ex-Alarm, Armoury Show). Stewart quit in 1990, while Sorum would go on to a tenure with Guns N'Roses. *Ceremony* was released in 1991, with the help of Charley Drayton (bass) and the returning Mickey Curry. This was a retrogressive collection of songs, that had more in common with *Love* than their previous two albums. Nevertheless, having already established an enormous fan-base, success was virtually guaranteed. 1994's *The Cult* saw them reunited with producer Bob Rock once more, on a set which included the rather clumsy Kurt Cobain tribute, 'Sacred Life'.

Albums: As Southern Death Cult: *Southern Death Cult* (Beggars Banquet 1986). Compilation: *Complete Recordings* (Situation Two 1991). As the Cult: *Dreamtime* (Beggars Banquet 1984), *Love* (Beggars Banquet 1985), *Electric* (Beggars Banquet 1987), *Sonic Temple* (Beggars Banquet 1989), *Ceremony* (Beggars Banquet 1991), *The Cult* (Beggars Banquet 1994). Compilation: *Pure Cult* (Beggars Banquet 1993).

Videos: *Dreamtime Live At The Lyceum* (1984), *Electric Love* (1987), *Cult: Video Single* (1987), *Sonic Ceremony* (1992), *Pure Cult* (1993).

Cure

Formed in 1976 as the Easy Cure, this UK group was based around the musicianship of Robert Smith (b. 21 April 1959, Crawley, Sussex, England; guitar/vocals), Michael Dempsey (bass) and Laurence Lol Tolhurst (b. 3 February 1959; drums). After struggling to find a niche during the first flashes of punk, the group issued the Albert Camus-inspired 'Killing An Arab' on the independent Small Wonder Records in mid-1978. It proved sufficient to draw them to the attention of producer and Fiction Records label manager Chris Parry, who reissued the single the following year. By May 1979, the group were attracting glowing reviews, particularly in the wake of 'Boys Don't Cry', whose style recalled mid-60s British beat, with the added attraction of Smith's deadpan vocal. The attendant album, *Three Imaginary Boys*, was also well-received, and was followed by a support spot with Siouxsie And The Banshees, on which Smith joined the headliners onstage. Another strong single, 'Jumping Someone Else's Train' performed predictably well in the independent charts but, in common with previous releases, narrowly missed the national chart. A pseudonymous single, 'I'm A Cult Hero', under the name the Cult Heroes, passed unnoticed and, soon after its release, Dempsey was replaced on bass by Simon Gallup. Amid the shake-up keyboards player Mathieu Hartley was added to the line-up. By the spring of 1980, the Cure were developing less as a pop group than a guitar-laden rock group. The atmospheric 12-inch single, 'A Forest', gave them their first UK Top 40 hit, while a stronger second album, *17 Seconds*, reached the Top 20. Thereafter the Cure's cult following ensured that their work regularly appeared in the lower regions of the charts. After consolidating their position during 1981 with 'Primary', 'Charlotte Sometimes' and 'Faith', the group looked to the new year for a new direction. A major breakthrough with *Pornography* threatened to place them in the major league of new UK acts, but there were

internal problems to overcome. The keyboards player, Hartley, had lasted only a few months and, early in 1982, the other 'new boy', Gallup, was fired and replaced by Steve Goulding. Meanwhile, Smith briefly joined Siouxsie And The Banshees as a temporary replacement for John McGeogh. As well as contributing the excellent psychedelic-tinged guitar work to their hit, 'Dear Prudence', Smith subsequently teamed up with Banshee Steve Severin and Jeanette Landray in the Glove. The Cure, meanwhile, continued to record and during the summer enjoyed their first UK Top 20 single appearance with the electronics-based 'The Walk'. Four months later they were in the Top 10 with the radically contrasting pop single, 'The Love Cats' (Smith subsequently attempted to distance himself from this song, which was initially intended more as a parody). Further success followed with 'The Caterpillar', another unusual single, highlighted by Smith's eccentric violin playing. This chart success confirmed the Cure as not only one of the most eclectic and eccentric ensembles working in British pop - but one of the very few to make such innovations accessible to a wider audience. Smith's heavy eye make-up, smudged crimson lipstick and shock-spiked hair was equally as striking, while the group's videos, directed by Tim Pope, became increasingly wondrous. In 1985 the group released their most commercially successful album yet, *The Head On The Door*. The following year, they re-recorded their second single, 'Boys Don't Cry', which this time became a minor UK hit. By now, the group was effectively Smith and Tolhurst, with members such as Gallup and others flitting through the line-up from year to year. With the retrospective *Standing On A Beach* singles collection the Cure underlined their longevity during an otherwise quiet year. During 1987 they undertook a tour of South America and enjoyed several more minor UK hits with 'Why Can't I Be You?', 'Catch' and 'Just Like Heaven'. The latter also reached the US Top 40, as did their double album, *Kiss Me, Kiss Me, Kiss Me*. A two-year hiatus followed before the release of the follow-up, *Disintegration*. A fiendishly downbeat affair, with some of Smith's most moribund lyrics, it nevertheless climbed into the UK Top 3. During the same period the group continued to register regular hits with such singles as 'Lullaby', 'Lovesong', 'Pictures Of You' and the fiery 'Never Enough'. Along the way, they continued their run of line-up changes, which culminated in the departure of Tolhurst (to form Presence), leaving Smith as the sole original member. Although it was assumed that the Cure would attempt to consolidate their promising sales in the USA, Smith announced that he would not be undertaking any further tours of America. 1990 ended with the release of *Mixed Up*, a double album collecting re-recordings and remixes of their singles. By 1992 the Cure line-up comprised Smith, a reinstated Gallup, Perry Bamonte (keyboards/guitar), Porl Thompson (guitar) and Boris Williams (drums), and with the critically acclaimed *Wish*, the band consolidated their position as one of the world's most consistently successful groups. Thompson would leave the unit in June 1993, at which time former member Tolhurst would sue Smith, the band and its record label, for alleged unpaid royalties. The ensuing court transcripts made for colourful reading, and confirmed the Cure's reputation for drinking excess

(Tolhurst was summarily defeated in the action and left with a huge legal debt).

Albums: *Three Imaginary Boys* (Fiction 1979), *Boys Don't Cry* (Fiction 1979), *Seventeen Seconds* (Fiction 1980), *Faith* (Fiction 1981), *Pornography* (Fiction 1982), *The Top* (Fiction 1984), *Concert - The Cure Live* (Fiction 1984), *Concert And Curiosity - Cure Anomalies 1977-1984* (Fiction 1984), *Head On The Door* (Fiction 1985), *Kiss Me, Kiss Me, Kiss Me* (Fiction 1987), *Disintegration* (Fiction 1990), *Entreat* (Fiction 1991), *Wish* (Fiction 1992), *Show* (Fiction 1993), *Paris* (Fiction 1993). Compilations: *Japanese Whispers - The Cure Singles Nov 1982-Nov 1983* (Fiction 1983), *Standing On The Beach - The Singles* (Fiction 1986), *Mixed Up* (Fiction 1990).

Videos: *Staring At the Sea: The Images* (1986), *Close To Me* (1989), *The Cure In Orange* (1989), *The Cure Play Out* (1991), *Cure Picture Show* (1991), *The Cure Show* (1993).

Further reading: *Ten Imaginary Years*, Lydia Barbarian, Steve Sutherland and Robert Smith. *The Cure: A Visual Documentary*, Dave Thompson and Jo-Anne Greene. *The Cure Songwords 1978 - 1989*, Robert Smith (ed.). *The Cure: Success Corruption & Lies*, Ross Clarke. *The Cure On Record*, Darren Butler. *The Cure: Faith*, Dave Bowler and Bryan Dray.

Curve

Curve were a chart topping indie act who never quite made the transition to commercial success despite an armoury of impressive songs. Their most prominent feature was the distinctive and opinionated voice of Toni Halliday (b. c.1965), one of three children born to a liberal Roman Catholic mother and single parent. Her major collaborator and song writing partner was Dean Garcia (guitar). The original precocious child, Halliday secured her first record deal at the age of 14, moving to London where she floundered with pop duo the Uncles. She later met David A. Stewart in Sunderland and they stayed friends, making the acquaintance of another member of Stewart's inner sanctum, Garcia, who had played on the Eurythmics albums *Touch* and *Be Yourself Tonight*. They joined forces in the equally pallid State Of Play, who were signed to Virgin Records and released two singles and an album, *Balancing The Scales*. After their acrimonious split, Halliday released a ghastly solo album, *Hearts And Handshakes*, before reuniting with Garcia to sign to the Eurythmics' Anxious label as Curve. Halliday had taken a tape of the song 'Ten Little Girls' to Stewart, who was immediately impressed. The results were three EPs, *Blindfold*, *Frozen* and *Cherry*, which were well-received by the UK indie rock press, and purchased in hefty quantities despite cynics citing Halliday as a stubborn careerist. The groundwork laid for a potentially rich recording career continued with the creation of their own studio and an expanded line-up including Debbie Smith and Alex Mitchell (guitars) and Monti (drums). However, though the critics remained somewhat in awe of the band's distant resonance, two albums and a series of singles (later efforts like 'Blackerthreetracker' merging the Curve sound with industrial and techno elements) failed to build on the press profile. The band eventually sundered, amicably, in 1994. 'We finished the tour and Dean was really upset because he

had two kids and he didn't really know them. He said he didn't want to tour any more. . . I 'm still signed, but they (the band's label) dropped Dean . . . there's no animosity between us'. Halliday would collaborate with cult remix team Leftfield for 1995's 'Original', while Debbie Smith would go on to join Echobelly.

Albums: *Doppelganger* (Anxious 1992), *Cuckoo* (Anxious 1993). Compilation: *Radio Sessions* (Anxious 1993).

D

DAF

This German band specialized in minimalist electro-dance music. The initials stood for Deutsch Amerikanische Freundschaft and the line-up comprised Robert Gorl (drums/synthesizer), W. Spelmans (guitar), C. Hass (saxophone/synthesizer/bass) and Gabi Delgado-Lopez (vocals). Their first UK album was released on the Mute label in 1980, the title, *Die Kleinen Und Die Bosen*, is translated as The Small And The Evil. Recorded in London, the album was uneven and was generally considered as unrepresentative, dominated by 'songs' whose heritage combined *Pink Flag* era Wire and Can influences. Afterwards Gorl and Delgado-Lopez continued as a duo. They recorded three albums for Virgin in an 18-month period. These comprised a mixture of Teutonic fantasy, love songs, and social statements. Delgado-Lopez's refusal to sing in English, condemned them to a minority international market. Contrary to their dour image, there is much to admire in the exemplary pop of singles such as 'Verlieb Dich In Mich'.

Albums: *Die Kleinen Und Die Bosen* (1980), *Alles Ist Gut* (1981), *Gold Und Liebe* (1981), *Fur Immer* (1982), *DAF* (1988). Robert Gorl solo *Night Full Of Tension* (1984).

Daisy Chainsaw

Contrived but fun pop punk outfit whose sudden appearance brightened up the independent scene of the early 90s, though their subsequent disappearance was just as mercurial. Led by fragile singer Katie Jane Garside, the band also comprised Richard Adams (bass), Vince Johnson (drums) and Crispin Grey (guitar). They debuted with the *LoveSickPleasure* EP, which spiralled in to the UK Top 30, aided by the highly colourful video for lead track 'Love Your Money'. Radio 1 had picked up on the song's frenetic pace, and the indie media were similarly impressed by Garside's 'Victorian chimney sweep' image, barefooted with torn dresses and covered in dirt. Allegations of sexual and psychological abuse suggested by one interview were later vehemently denied, but there is little doubt that the band's presentation was disturbingly resonant of the child as victim. The success of the EP encouraged them to sign with larger independent One Little Indian Records, despite tantalizing offers from the majors. However, their record company must have soon learned to regret their enthusiasm. Shortly after a hit and miss debut album produced by Ken Thomas (although there were strong tracks in 'Lonely Ugly Brutal World' and 'Use Me Use Me'), Garside announced her departure. The band attempted to soldier on but to no interest whatsoever.

Album: *Eleventeen* (One Little Indian/Wayward 1992).

Dalek I Love You

From the ashes of Liverpool punk band Radio Blank, Alan Gill (guitar/vocals) and David Balfe (bass/vocals/synthesizer), formed Dalek I Love You in November 1977. Disagreement over the band's name - David wanted the Daleks, whereas Alan preferred Darling I Love You - resulted in the compromised title, and with the addition of Dave Hughes (keyboards), Chris 'Teepee' Shaw (synthesizer), plus a drum machine, the first of many loose line-ups was complete. In July 1978 Balfe left to join Big In Japan. After a string of critically acclaimed synthesizer-pop singles, 1980 saw the release of *Compass Kum'pass*, which came in the wake of groups like O.M.D. and Tubeway Army bringing electronics into the mainstream charts. A worldwide deal with Korova Records produced the singles, 'Holiday In Disneyland', 'Ambition' and the album, *Dalek I Love You*, which meshed layered synth and psychedelic fragments with starry-eyed vocals, augmented by excellent harmonies. Again, none achieved any real commercial success and Phil Jones decided to put the band 'on ice'. During this period he was busy writing and recording the soundtrack for the film, *Letter To Brezhnev* (1985), and formed the Bopadub label in Birkenhead, which put out a series of cassettes culminating in 1985 with *Naive*, recorded by the reformed Dalek I. In 1986, after eight years of tentative existence, Phil Jones was still optimistic about future releases and subsequently, *Compass Kum'pass* was re-released by Fontana in 1989, acknowledging the importance of this seminal electronic band.

Albums: *Compass Kum'pass* (1980), *Dalek I Love You* (Korova 1983). As Dalek I: *Naive* (Bopadub 1985, cassette only).

Dali's Car

This was a brief a partnership between Bauhaus frontman Peter Murphy and Japan's distinctive bassist Mick Karn. Dali's Car first surfaced on a compilation cassette, *Jobs Not Yobs*, in 1982, but it was over two years before they signed with Virgin Records subsidiary 10. 'The Judgment Is The Mirror', in 1984, accompanied an album, *Waking Hour*, released a month after, but the project was not warmly received and the pair soon went their separate ways.

Album: *Waking Hour* (Virgin 1984).

Damned

Formed in 1976, this UK punk group comprised Captain Sensible, Rat Scabies (b. Chris Miller, 30 July 1957, Surrey, England; drums), Brian James (b. Brian Robertson, England; guitar) and Dave Vanian (b. David Letts, England; vocals).

Scabies and James had previously played in the unwieldy punk ensemble London SS and, joined by Sensible, a veteran of early formations of Johnny Moped, they backed Nick Kent's Subterraneans. The Damned emerged in May 1976 and two months later they were supporting the Sex Pistols at the 100 Club. After appearing at the celebrated Mont de Marsan punk festival in August, they were signed to Stiff Records one month later. In October they released what is generally regarded as the first UK punk single, 'New Rose', which was backed by a frantic version of the Beatles' 'Help'. Apart from being dismissed as a support act during the Sex Pistols' ill-fated Anarchy tour, they then released UK punk's first album, *Damned Damned Damned*, produced by Nick Lowe. The work was typical of the period, full of short, sharp songs played at tremendous velocity, which served to mask a quite phenomenal level of musical ability (some critics, unable to believe the speed of the band, wrongly accused them of having speeded up the studio tapes). During April 1977 they became the first UK punk group to tour the USA. By the summer of that year, they recruited a second guitarist, Lu Edmunds; and soon after drummer Rat Scabies quit. A temporary replacement, Dave Berk (ex-Johnny Moped), deputized until the recruitment of London percussionist Jon Moss. In November their second album, *Music For Pleasure*, produced by Pink Floyd's Nick Mason, was mauled by the critics and worse followed when they were dropped from Stiff's roster. Increasingly dismissed for their lack of earnestness and love of pantomime, they lost heart and split in early 1978. The members went in various directions: Sensible joined the Softies, Moss and Edmunds formed the Edge, Vanian teamed-up with Doctors Of Madness and James founded Tanz Der Youth. The second part of the Damned story re-opened one year later when Sensible, Vanian and Scabies formed the Doomed. In November 1978 they became legally entitled to use the name Damned and, joined by ex-Saints bass player Algy Ward, they opened this new phase of their career with their first Top 20 single, the storming 'Love Song'. Minor hits followed, including the equally visceral 'Smash It Up' and the more sober but still affecting 'I Just Can't Be Happy Today'. Both were included on *Machine Gun Ettiquette*, one of the finest documents of any band of this generation, as the group again became a formidable concert attraction. When Ward left to join Tank he was replaced by Paul Gray, from Eddie And The Hot Rods. The group continued to reach the lower regions of the chart during the next year while Captain Sensible simultaneously signed a solo deal with A&M Records. To everyone's surprise, not least his own, he zoomed to number 1 with a novel revival of 'Happy Talk', which outsold every previous Damned release. Although he stuck with the group for two more years, he finally left in August 1984 due to the friction his parallel career was causing. However, during that time the Damned remained firmly on form. *The Black Album* was an ambitious progression, while singles such as 'White Rabbit' (a cover of Jefferson Airplane's pscyhedelic classic) and 'History Of The World' revealed a band whose abilities were still well above the vast majority of their peers. So too *Strawberries*, which announced a more pop-orientated direction, but one accomodated with aplomb. With Sensible gone a third phase in the group's career ushered in new members Roman Jugg (guitar/keyboards) and Bryn Gunn (bass), joining the core duo of Scabies and Vanian. Subsequent releases now pandered to a more determined assault on the charts. In 1986 they enjoyed their biggest ever hit with a cover of Barry Ryan's 'Eloise' (UK number 3). Another 60s pastiche, this time a rather pedestrian reading of Love's 'Alone Again Or', gave them a further minor UK hit. However, the authenticity of the Damned's discography from here on in is open to question, while their back-catalogue proved ripe for exploitation by all manner of compilations and poorly produced live albums, to further muddy the picture of a genuinely great band. *Phantasmagoria* and more particularly the lacklustre *Anything* failed to add anything of note to that legacy. The band continue to tour into the 90s, sometimes with Sensible, and there are numerous side projects to entertain afficionados, but it is unlikely that the Damned will ever match their peerless early 80s phase.

Albums: *Damned Damned Damned* (Stiff 1977), *Music For Pleasure* (Stiff 1977), *Machine Gun Etiquette* (Chiswick 1979), *The Black Album* (Chiswick 1980, double album), *Strawberries* (Bronze 1982), *Phantasmagoria* (MCA 1985), *Anything* (MCA 1986). Compilations/live albums: *The Best Of The Damned* (Chiswick 1981), *Live At Shepperton* (Big Beat 1982), *Not The Captain's Birthday Party* (Stiff 1986), *Damned But Not Forgotten* (Dojo 1986), *Light At The End Of The Tunnel* (MCA 1987), *Mindless, Directionless Energy* (ID 1987), *The Long Lost Weekend: Best Of Vol. 1 & 2* (Big Beat 1988), *Final Damnation* (Essential 1989, live 1988 recording), *Totally Damned (Live And Rare)* (Dojo 1991), *Skip Off School To See The Damned - The Stiff Singles* (Stiff 1992), *School Bullies* (Receiver 1993), *Sessions Of The Damned* (Strange Fruit 1993).

Video: *Light At The End Of The Tunnel* (1987).

Further reading: *The Book Of The Damned: The Light At The End Of The Tunnel*, Carol Clerk.

Dancing Did

Hailing from Evesham in Worcestershire, England, the Dancing Did's brand of rustic rock 'n' roll proved you could write songs about the English countryside without embracing the comic style of the Wurzels or the Yetties. Dancing Did took their name from 'didicoi' - otherwise known to town-dwellers as Gypsies. The band comprised Tim Harrison (vocals), Martyn Dormer (lead guitar/synthesizer/vocals), Roger Smith (bass) and Chris Houghton (drums). Formed in 1980, they released two singles on first their own Fruit And Veg label, then Stiff Records, before moving to the ill-starred Kamera Records. Musically they resembled a marriage of the Clash with Steeleye Span, but their true appeal lay in the imagery of Harrison's lyrics, as shown in such titles as 'A Fruit Picking Fantasy (The Day Bo Diddley Nearly Came To Evesham)', 'Badger Boys' - a celebration of country delinquents, 'Ballad Of The Dying Sigh' - a tale that would not be out of place in Fairport Convention's repertoire - and the rousing 'Wolves Of Worcestershire'. That the subject matter was of such a rural hue limited their attraction within the cities to a mere cult following, securing their eventual demise in 1983. Dormer became first a clothes shop owner then mobile

telephone salesman, while Houghton continued part-time in pub cover band, the Bassetts, while continuing to run a market stall. Smith went on to study farming and played intermittently with Rhythm Oil, while Harrison used his graphic design degree to obtain employment at *Punch*, then *Chat* and *Q* magazines.

Album: *And Did Those Feet* (Kamera 1982).

Daniels, Phil, And The Cross

Daniels, a graduate of London's Anna Scher Theatre School and a member of the Royal Shakespeare Company, had flirted with pop as part of Renoir. Following his involvement in the Mod blockbuster, *Quadraphenia*, the persona of Jimmy the Mod was launched into the rock world with the aid of Peter Hugo-Daly (keyboards), Barry Neil (bass) and John McWilliams (drums), Daniels himself handling both vocal and guitar duties. A solitary album on RCA was offered, but sales were minimal. This despite full-page advertisements in the music press, a charitable reaction from some critics and a concert itinerary centred on the metropolis. Daniels returned to stage, television and film work, notably satirising the music industry in Hazel O'Connor's *Breaking Glass*. In 1994 he was to be found singing in a new West End production of *Carousel*, whilst also being celebrated as a cult icon of the 70s and 80s (being featured on the cover of the hip dance compilation, *The Junior Boy's Own Collection*). His vocals on Blur's *Parklife* title track gave him further exposure.

Album: *Phil Daniels And The Cross* (RCA 1980).

Danse Society

These UK gothic rock innovators evolved from Sheffield bands Y? and Lips-X. The two groups merged as Danse Crazy, establishing the line-up as Steve Rawlings (vocals) Paul Gilmartin (drums) Lyndon Scarfe (keyboards) and Paul Nash (guitar), as additional guitar and keyboard players were jettisoned. These included Paul Hampshire (aka Bee and Paul Hertz). They came to prominence first at the Futurama Festival 2 in Leeds which was filmed by the BBC. After a slight change of name to Danse Society, and the filling of the bass position with Tim Wright, they performed their first gig at the Marples venue in Sheffield. The self-produced 'Clock' single provided the band with some acclaim, despite its short run of 1,000 copies. Management duties were taken over by Marcus Featherby, who released their EP, *No Shame In Death*, on his own Pax Records label. However, they soon returned to their own Society Records. The mini-album, *Seduction*, garnered strong support in the media and the band embarked on a series of interviews and live dates. Following one more independent single they signed to Arista Records: 'We'd done the Society Records thing and taken it as far as we could independently, we were totally out of money.' The dramatic 'Wake Up' was their debut, its sense of mystery and dark charm pre-dating the 'gothic' scene by at least a year. *Heaven Is Waiting* provided their first full album's worth of material, and further airplay from BBC disc jockeys John Peel and Janice Long kept them in the ascendent. However, internal rifts saw the replacement of Scarfe with former Music For Pleasure member David Whitaker. Relations with their record company also deteriorated when

Darling Buds

Arista failed to back a US tour. Litigation delayed further activities until a compromise was reached in March 1985. When they returned with 'Say It Again' (produced by Stock, Aitken And Waterman), it was to a bemused audience who had not anticipated such a sudden shift in style. The more commercial nature of their subsequent work failed to impress, and Arista rejected their proposed second album, *Heaven Again*. When they split in April 1986, Rawlings attempted to persevere with the funk-orientated Society, while the rest of the band continued briefly as Johnny In The Clouds

Albums: *Seduction* (Arista 1982), *Heaven Is Waiting* (Arista 1984).

Darling Buds

Formed in Wales in 1987 by Andrea Lewis (b. 25 March 1967, Newport, Wales; vocals), Harley Farr (b. 4 July 1964, Singapore; guitar), Bloss (drums) and Chris McDonagh (b. 6 March 1962, Newport, Wales; bass), the early part of the Darling Buds' career was as much a pure adrenalin rush as was their poppy/punk music. Following in the tradition of classic pop records by Blondie and the Waitresses, the Buds produced a series of sparkling sub-three minute singles on the independent Native Records label ('Shame On You' etc.), becoming embroiled in the superfluous 'Blond' scene of that time alongside the Primitives. With the added incentive of increasingly celebrational live performances, Epic Records swiftly signed the band in 1988 and earned moderate chart success for subsequent singles 'Burst' and 'Hit The Ground'. Unfortunately, in the true spirit of bubblegum pop, the Darling Buds' balloon soon began to deflate. Drummer Bloss was replaced by Jimmy Hughes (b. Liverpool, England) and the band's second album, *Crawdaddy*, witnessed a new sophisticated approach to recording which was at odds with their early material, creating few ripples in the musical pond. *Erotica* then emerged just one month before Madonna's opus of the same title, though doubtless it would have been ignored by a now disinterested music media no matter what flag it sailed under.

Albums: *Pop Said* (Epic 1989), *Crawdaddy* (Epic 1990), *Erotica* (Epic 1992).

Daryll Ann

Dutch indie guitar band who moved to Amsterdam from outlying villages in 1993, and cut a cheap cassette mini-album which led to them signing to Virgin Record subsidiary, Hut Records, in the UK. Comprising (male) guitarist Anne Soldaat, Jelle Paulusma (vocals/guitar), Jeroen Vos (bass) and Jeroen Kleign (drums), the group took its name from a character in the television series *Hill Street Blues*. Kleign had kicked out their previous drummer at the end of 1993, and Jelle was actually the replacement of original singer Coem Paulusma, his twin brother, who left to become a biologist. Their debut EP for Hut, *I Could Never Love You*, immediately revealed their classic, guitar rock construction, an impression further essayed by support slots in the UK to Verve and Smashing Pumpkins. A debut album followed, including a humorous high point in a cover version of Carly Simon's 'You're So Vain'.z

Album: *Seaborne West* (Hut 1995).

Dax, Danielle

b. Southend, Essex, England. Dax first came to prominence in 1980 with Karl Blake in the engaging Lemon Kittens. After *We Buy A Hammer For Daddy* and *The Big Dentist*, the group broke up in 1982. Dax next pursued a more straightforward pop route, mixed with forays into ethnic music and the *avant garde*. Her first solo album, *Pop-Eyes*, featured her playing 15 instruments, as well as composing and producing. She also displayed talents as a sleeve designer, contributing to Robert Fripp's *League Of Gentlemen* among others. After a brief detour into acting, during which she appeared in the film, *A Company Of Wolves*, she returned to the recording scene in 1984. *Jesus Egg That Wept* was a mini-album which preceded an extensive UK tour during which she was backed by Dave Knight, Steve Reeves, Ian Sturgess and Martin Watts. Former artistic partner Blake also made a comeback on that album's 'Ostrich'. Her 1985 single, 'Yummer Yummer Man', was well-received and revealed her love of 60s psychedelia. *Inky Bloaters* was an exceptionally eclectic work which maintained that reputation, and saw reviewers recall a myriad of influences in an attempt to get a handle on its contents. After appearing at the new music seminar in Boston, she was signed more permanently by Seymour Stein to Sire Records. He launched her on the US market with *Dark Adapted Eye*, which added five new picks to selections from *Inky Bloaters*. Her fourth album, *Blast The Human Flower*, produced by Stephen Street, included a revival of the Beatles' 'Tomorrow Never Knows', but was an unhappy mainstream compromise which sacrificed Dax's earlier esotericism for accessibility.

Albums: *Pop-Eyes* (Initially 1983), *Jesus Egg That Wept* (Awesome 1984, mini-album), *Inky Bloaters* (Awesome 1987), *Dark Adapted Eye* (Sire 1988), *Blast The Human Flower* (Sire 1990).

Video: *Danielle Dax* (1987).

dB's

Founder members of the US pop unit the dB's, Chris Stamey (guitars/vocals), Gene Holder (bass) and Will Rigby (drums) had made their name around North Carolina, USA, with the Sneakers, alongside Mitch Easter (guitar/vocals). After two EPs (in 1976 and 1978) on Alan Betrock's Car label, Easter departed (later surfacing with Let's Active), the remaining three teamed up with keyboardist Peter Holsapple (ex-H-Bombs), to create the dB's. Stamey and Holsapple had previously worked together in Rittenhouse Square as early as 1972, while Stamey had indulged in a solo effort, 'Summer Sun' on Ork, in 1977. The dB's' debut single, 'I Thought (You Wanted To Know)', on the Car label, was issued towards the end of 1978, by which time the band had relocated to New York City. Signing with Shake, they then came up with 'Black And White', attracting attention in the UK, and sealing a contract with Albion. The dB's delivered two albums in as many years for Albion, both capturing an evocative blend of melodic, occasionally Beatles-styled songs and new wave sensibilities. 'Dynamite', 'Big Brown Eyes' and 'Judy' were drawn from *Stands For Decibels* (1981) while the following year's *Repercussions* spawned 'Amplifier', 'Neverland' and 'Living A Lie'. However, the dB's failed to make any significant commercial impact. Stamey was the first to leave and release a solo work, *In The Winter Of Love*, in 1984. An apathetic British reception meant that his second album, *It's Alright* on A&M Records, failed to secure a UK release. In the meantime, the dB's replaced Stamey with Jeff Beninato and reunited for *The Sound Of Music* on IRS, joined by guests Van Dyke Parks and Syd Straw. Since then, Peter Holsapple has been busy working in the wings with R.E.M..

Albums: *Stands For Decibels* (1981), *Repercussions* (1982), *Like This* (1985), *The Sound Of Music* (1987). Compilation: *Amplifier* (1986).

Dead Boys

One of the first wave punk/no wave bands in the USA, the Dead Boys formed in Cleveland in 1976 but relocated to New York the following year. They won their spurs playing the infamous Bowery club, CBGB's, the starting place for other bands such as the Ramones, Television, Blondie and Talking Heads. The band consisted of Stiv Bators (vocals), Jimmy Zero (rhythm guitar), Cheetah Chrome (b. Gene Connor; lead guitar), Jeff Magnum (bass) and Johnny Blitz (drums). The group took its cue from Iggy Pop And The Stooges by being as menacing, snarling and aggressive as possible. Signed to Sire Records in 1977, they released their debut album, the appropriately titled *Young, Loud And Snotty*, one of the very earliest US punk records, which included the band's anthem, 'Sonic Reducer'. It was followed a year later by the less convincing *We Have Come For Your Children*, produced by Felix Pappalardi. The band sundered in 1980 (*Night Of The Living Dead Boys* is a posthumous live issue), with Bators recording a pair of solo albums before invoking Lords Of The New Church with former Damned and Sham 69 member, Brian James. He was killed in an automobile accident in France in June 1990.

Albums: *Young, Loud And Snotty* (Sire 1977), *We Have Come For Your Children* (Sire 1978), *Night Of The Living Dead Boys* (Bomp 1981). Compilation: *Younger, Louder And Snottier* (Necrophilia 1989).

Dead Famous People

Hailing from New Zealand and signed to the independent Flying Nun Records label, the group comprised Donna Savage (vocals), Biddy Leyland (keyboards), Wendy Kjestrup (guitar), Jenny Renals (bass) and Robin Tearle (drums). After achieving a modest degree of success on the New Zealand independent circuit the group transferred operations to the UK. Tearle, unable to travel, was replaced by Gill Moon, and later by Frances Gant. They were picked up by Utility Records, run by Billy Bragg, for whom Biddy Leyland had previously helped to organize a tour in New Zealand. The mini-album, *Arriving Late In Torn And Filthy Jeans*, included tracks originally recorded in New Zealand for Flying Nun and became Utility's biggest-selling release. The set featured highly lyrical and melodic songs such as 'Barlow's House' and 'Postcard From Paradise'. The sexual politics revealed in 'Traitor To The Cause' won critical acclaim from many quarters. After a string of successful live appearances on the London club/bar circuit, the group looked set for higher things. However, by the middle of 1990 a rift within the group caused a split, leaving the main songwriters, Savage

and Leyland, to work solo. An unexpected taste of success came later that year for Donna when she guested on Saint Etienne's version of the Field Mice song, 'Let's Kiss And Make Up'. The following year saw the release of an album on the La-Di-Da label, *All Hail The Daffodil*, which consisted of material recorded in early 1990 and vindicated much of the group's early promise.

Album: *Arriving Late In Torn And Filthy Jeans* (Utility 1989). Compilation: *All Hail The Daffodil* (La-Di-Da 1991).

Dead Kennedys

The undoubted kings of US punk, San Francisco's Dead Kennedys arrived on the 80s music scene with the most vitriolic and ultimately persuasive music ever to marshal the US underground (at least until the arrival of Nirvana). Even today the sight of their name can send the uninitiated into a fit of apoplexy. Originally a quintet with a second guitarist called 6025, he left before recordings for the debut album took place, leaving a core group of Jello Biafra (b. Eric Boucher, 17 June 1958, Denver, Colorado, USA; vocals), Klaus Flouride (bass), East Bay Ray Glasser (guitar) and Ted (b. Bruce Slesinger; drums). However, as soon as they hit a studio the results were extraordinary. Biafra, weaned partially on 70s Brit Punk as well as local San Francisco bands like Crime and the Nuns, was the consummate front man; his performances never far away from personal endangerment, including stage-diving and verbally lambasting his audience. He was certainly never destined to be an industry conformist - some of his more celebrated stunts included getting married in a graveyard, running for Mayor of San Francisco (he finished fourth), allowing the crowd to disrobe him on stage, etc. Lyrically, the Dead Kennedys always went for the jugular but twisted expectations; writing an anti-neutron bomb song called 'Kill The Poor' is a good example of their satire. The band's debut single, 'California Uber Alles' attacked the 'new age' fascism of Californian governor Jerry Brown, a theme developed over a full blown musical roller coaster ride. Just as enduring is its follow-up, 'Holiday In Cambodia', which mercilessly parodied college student chic and the indifference to the suffering caused to others by America's foreign policy: 'Playing ethnicky jazz to parade your snazz on your five grand stereo/Bragging that you know how the niggers feel cold and the slum's got so much soul'. 'Too Drunk To Fuck', naturally despite a complete absence of airplay, made the UK Top 40 (there were a number of prosecutions linked to those wearing the accompanying t-shirt). Biafra established his own Alternative Tentacles Records after a brief flirtation with Miles Copeland's IRS Records label (Cherry Red Records in the UK), and this has gone to on be a staple of the US alternative record scene, releasing music by both peers and progeny: Hüsker Dü, T.S.O.L., D.O.A., No Means No, Beatnigs, Alice Donut, etc. Slesinger broke away to form the Wolverines at this point, having never been quite in tune with the Kennedys' musical dynamic. His eventual replacement was Darren H. Peligro (ex-Nubs, Speedboys, Hellations, SSI etc., who had also played guitar with the Jungle Studs and was the drummer for an early incarnation of Red Hot Chilli Peppers). If the band's debut album, *Fresh Fruit For Rotting Vegetables*, had followed a broadly traditional musical format,

In God We Trust Inc. indulged in full blown thrash. Undoubtedly the long-term inspiration behind literally hundreds of US noise merchants, it certainly took many by surprise with its minimalist adrenaline ('Dog Bite/On My Leg/S'Not Right, S'posed to Beg' practically encompassed the entire lyrics to one song). *Plastic Surgery Disasters* saw the band branch out again. Though it did not share *Fresh Fruit's* immediacy, there were several stunning songs on offer once more ('Trust Your Mechanic' with Biafra's typically apocalyptic delivery, attacked the values of the service industry, and 'Well Paid Scientist', which mocked the career ladder). *Frankenchrist* was more considered, allowing songs like 'Soup Is Good Food' to bite hard. The cornerstone of the recording was 'Stars And Stripes Of Corruption', which predicted some of Biafra's later solo excursions by relentlessly pursuing a single theme. *Bedtime For Democracy* was the band's final studio recording, and a return to the aggressive speed of the previous mini-album, though without the shock value. Meanwhile Biafra was on trial for the artwork given away with *Frankenchrist*, a pastiche of American consumerism by H.R. Giger (*Landscape #20* - often referred to as 'Penis Landscape'), which made its point via a depiction of row upon row of male genitalia entering anuses (graphic shorthand for everybody fucking everybody else). Long an irritant to the US moral 'guardians', the PMRC now had Biafra in their sights. In truth the band had elected to call it a day anyhow, but there was a long hibernation while Biafra weathered the storm (he was eventually cleared on all counts and the case thrown out of court) before embarking on his next creative phase - an episodic solo career marked by collaborations with D.O.A., No Means No, etc. Flouride would release two albums for Alternative Tentacles, while East Bay Ray formed Scrapyard. The Dead Kennedys' contribution, meanwhile, is best measured not by the plethora of copy bands who sprung up around the world, but by the enduring quality of their best records and Biafra's admirable and unyielding stance on artistic censorship.
Albums: *Fresh Fruit For Rotting Vegetables* (IRS/Cherry Red 1980), *In God We Trust Inc.* (Alternative Tentacles/Faulty 1981, mini-album), *Plastic Surgery Disasters* (Alternative Tentacles 1982), *Frankenchrist* (Alternative Tentacles 1985), *Bedtime For Democracy* (Alternative Tentacles 1986). Compilation: *Give Me Convenience Or Give Me Death* (Alternative Tentacles 1987).
Video: *Live In San Francisco* (1987).

Dead Milkmen

US cypto punk band the Dead Milkmen hailed from the active Philadelphian underground scene of the mid-80s and drew members who rejoiced in the unlikely names Joe Jack Talcum (guitar/vocals), Rodney Anonymous Melloncamp (vocals), Dave Blood (bass) and Dean Clean (drums). With each of their album titles punning a more famous rock release and songs such as 'Takin' Retards To The Zoo', 'Beach Party Vietnam', and 'The Thing That Only Eats Hippies', the Dead Milkmen were always destined for college favouritism. Utilising an uncomplicated adolescent punk rock foundation, the group's debut album set out its stall by loading up on youthful satire and demanding to know the answer to the eternal questions - like why does anybody like the Doors. As basic but slightly more astute was *Eat Your Paisley!*, its b-movie song titles suggesting there was no immediate end in sight for the Milkmen's hyperactive juvenilia. *Bucky Fellini* saw a more fully fledged musical format, aided by guest musicians and improved song writing - though with lyrical targets including '(Theme From) Blood Orgy Of The Atomic Fern' and 'Nitro Burning Funny Cars' it was obvious that the band had not yet turned into a 'proper' rock group. *Beelzebubba* boasted the minor hit single 'Punk Rock Girl', but was undistinguished elsewhere. The best song title yet arrived in 'If You Love Somebody, Set Them On Fire', drawn from the improved *Metaphysical Graffiti*. Guests included Butthole Surfers' Gilby Clarke, on the near-hysterical prog rock bluff, 'Anderson, Walkman, Buttholes and How!'.
Albums: *Big Lizard In My Back Yard* (Fever/Enigma 1985), *Eat Your Paisley!* (Fever-Restless 1986), *Bucky Fellini* (Fever/Enigma 1987), *Instant Club Hit (You'll Dance To Anything)* (Fever/Enigma 1987, mini-album), *Beelzebubba* (Fever/Enigma 1988), *Metaphysical Graffiti* (Enigma 1990).

Deaf School

Art-rock band that practically started the Liverpool new wave scene single-handed. Deaf School were formed in January 1974 by a large group of students at Liverpool Art College. The original line-up could be as big as 15 but the basic 12 were singers Bette Bright (b. Ann Martin, Whitstable, Kent, England), Ann Bright, Hazel Bartram, and Eric Shark (b. Thomas Davis), Enrico Cadillac Jnr, (b. Steve Allen), guitarists Cliff Hanger (b. Clive Langer) and Roy Holder, bassist Mr Average (b. Steve Lindsay), keyboards player the Rev. Max Ripple (b. John Wood), drummer Tim Whittaker and saxophonists Ian Ritchie and Mike Evans. Sandy Bright soon left to get married and she was quickly followed by Bartram, Evans and Holder, the last of whom was fired. The remaining eight-piece line-up developed an entertaining blend of rock music and almost vaudevillian stage theatrics. This combination helped them win a *Melody Maker* Rock Contest in which the prize was a recording contract with WEA Records. The debut - *Second Honeymoon* - came out in August 1976 (by which time former Stealers Wheel guitarist Paul Pilnick had been added to the line-up). Hugely popular, particularly in Liverpool, their audience contained a host of names soon to make it in their own right. Two more albums and three singles emerged before the band finally dissolved after Bette Bright appeared in the *Great Rock 'N' Roll Swindle*, recorded two singles for Radar and a third for Korova with her backing band The Illuminations (variously Glen Matlock, Rusty Egan, Henry Priestman, Clive Langer, and Paul Pilnick). In 1981 she married Suggs from Madness. Eric Shark quit music to run a shop in Liverpool, Enrico Cadillac reverted to his real name and formed the Original Mirrors. Clive Langer formed the Boxes but had more success as a producer. Steve Lindsay replaced Holly Johnson in Big In Japan, went on to the Secrets and then found limited success with the Planets. The Rev. Max Ripple became the head of the Fine Art department at Goldsmiths College in London. Tim Whittaker concentrated on session work with such Liverpool luminaries as Pink Military. Ian Ritchie finished up with

Jane Aire. Steve Lindsay released a solo single ('Mr Average') while still in Deaf School, and another as Steve Temple in 1981, before forming the Planets. Steve Allen later joined with Steve Nieve in Perils Of Plastic. Various ex-Deaf School kids have also turned up in the deliberately dreadful Portsmouth Sinfonia. In 1988 Cadillac, Bright, Shark, Langer, Lindsay and Ripple reformed for five sell-out shows to celebrate the 10th anniversary of their demise, a concert commemorated with the 1988 release of *2nd Coming*.

Albums: *Second Honeymoon* (Warners 1976), *Don't Stop The World* (Warners 1977), *English Boys Working Girls* (Warners 1978), *2nd Coming: Liverpool '88* (Demon 1988).

Deep Freeze Mice

Deep Freeze Mice is effectively a front operation for Alan Jenkins (b. 16 March 1959, Dudley, West Midlands, England; guitar/clarinet/vocals). Jenkins' one-man battle against the heads (and underlings) of the corporate music industry has seen him lead various bands since the late 70s. Along with the Chrysanthemums, Jody And The Creams and Ruth's Refrigerator, the majority of his output has been released under the Deep Freeze Mice moniker. Formed in 1979, the group's line-up has included Sherree Lawrence (b. 24 May 1959, Rushden, Northamptonshire, England; keyboards), Michael Bunnage (b. 21 December 1958, Romford, Essex, England; bass) and Graham Summers (b. 30 July 1958, Wellingborough, Northamptonshire, England; drums). Peter Gregory replaced Summers in 1983. The group's brand of English psychedelia, which drew upon such influences as Syd Barrett, Captain Beefheart, the Mothers Of Invention, Soft Machine, plus a soupçon of the Velvet Underground, often made for uncomfortable listening, but conversely also displayed a talent for commercial pop songs. Jenkins has privately published a booklet entitled *How To Be In A Pop Group* (1990), an accurate, but highly amusing account of the pitfalls to be endured along the road to possible fame and failure, naming names in the process. He continues to record on the periphery of the music business which he studiously despises for its lack of adventure.

Albums: *My Geraniums Are Bulletproof* (Cordella 1979), *Teenage Head In My Refrigerator* (Cordella 1981), *The Gates Of Lunch* (Cordella 1982), *Saw A Ranch House Burning Last Night* (Mole Enbalming 1983), *I Love You Little Bobo With Your Delicate Golden Lions* (1984), *Hang On Constance Let Me Hear The News* (1985), *War, Famine, Death, Pestilence And Miss Timberlake* (1986), *Rain Is When The Earth Is Television* (1987), *Live In Switzerland* (1988), *The Tender Yellow Ponies Of Insomnia* (1989). As the Chrysanthemums: *Is That A Fish On Your Shoulder, Or Are You Just Pleased To See Me?* (1987), *Little Flecks Of Foam Around Barking* (1988), *Odyssey And Oracle* (1989). As Jody And The Creams: *A Big Dog* (1990).

Deep Freeze Productions

DFP are a London music collective consisting of Richard Belben (musician), Chris Jones (engineer), Paul Sims (disc jockey) and Mal (vocals). All four members were in their early 30s when they first began to make music together and had therefore experienced the passing of several musical styles, from punk to reggae and acid house, and they decided to compress these influences into a highly rhythmic package which spanned acid jazz, deep house, reggae and funk. *Slowbone* collects some of their earlier releases, including the powerful 'The Lost Soul Of Arch Stanton'. The group's members had grown with the emergent club culture - from February 1992's debut single, 'Get Yo Body', through DJing stints at clubs such as Submission, High On Hope and Paul Oakenfold's Confusion, and remixes for vocalists such as Glen Goldsmith, Shay Jones and Marvelle. A recording contract with Go! Discs subsidiary Go! Beat fell through, although DFP went on to produce artists for Big Life Records, including James Taylor Quartet. Afterwards they set up their own Sureshot Records for EPs such as *Space Button* and *Feeling Good*. With the release of their debut album the group also became in-house production gurus for new label Wired Records, working with artists such as Shola (punk poetry), Shio (reggae) and Stephanie (guitarist).

Album: *Slowbone* (Sureshot 1995, double album).

Del Amitri

A Glaswegian semi-acoustic rock band who emerged in the wake of the Postcard Records scene when they were formed by 16 year old singer, pianist and bassist Justin Currie (b. 11 December 1964, Scotland) and his guitarist friend Iain Harvie (b. 19 May 1962, Scotland). They were joined for their debut on the No Strings independent label, 'Sense Sickness', by Bryan Tolland (guitar) and Paul Tyagi (drums). Numerous sessions for disc jockey John Peel and tours with everyone from the Fall to the Smiths ensured a cult following and a growing reputation for Currie's wry lyrics. Having taken second guitarist David Cummings and drummer Brian McDermott aboard, they came to the attention of Chrysalis Records who signed them to their own 'indie' label, Big Star. Del Amitri, meaning 'from the womb' in Greek, released their debut album in 1985 but fell foul of the label shortly afterwards. The band's career entered a restorative period during which they toured via a network of fans who organized and promoted events in individual regions. A tour of the US led to Del Amitri being signed to A&M Records in 1987 and resuming their recording career. They hit the UK singles chart with 'Kiss This Thing Goodbye', 'Nothing Ever Happens', and 'Spit In The Rain'. The re-issue of 'Kiss This Thing Goodbye' helped to break them in the US, while domestically the plaintive protest ballad, 'Nothing Ever Happens', won many supporters: 'And computer terminals report some gains, On the values of copper and tin, While American businessmen snap up Van Goghs, For the price of a hospital wing'. Though their singles success abated somewhat, this was tempered by the platinum success of 1992's *Change Everything*. Touring continued throughout that year while most of 1993 was spent at Haremere House in East Sussex, working on their fourth album. *Twisted* was produced by Al Clay (Frank Black, Pere Ubu) and further refined the band's familiar AOR formula, with the lyrics almost exclusively dealing in loneliness and the establishment and breakdown of relationships. Of their transition from indie word smiths to stadium rockers, Currie, philosophically, preferred to think that 'Del Amitri fans only hold ironic lighters aloft'.

Albums: *Del Amitri* (Chrysalis 1985), *Waking Hours* (A&M 1989), *Change Everything* (A&M 1992), *Twisted* (A&M 1995).

Del Lords

Bronx, New York, USA rock band founded by ex-Dictators guitarist/vocalist Scott Kempner (then known as Top Ten), whose straightforward enthusiasm for uncomplicated rock has brought a new lustre to a tried and tested formula. Backed by the equally strident guitar (and occasional lead vocals) of Eric 'Roscoe' Ambel, the group's 1984 debut featured basic but impressive rock 'n' roll in 'Burning In The Flame Of Love', 'Feel Like Going Home' and 'How Can A Poor Man Stand Such Times And Live' (a cover of Alfred Reed's classic revitalized by the unlikely urban blues of the Del Lords). Drafting in Pat Benatar's producer husband Neil Geraldo, *Johnny Comes Marching Home*, from its title onwards, was a set which utilised folk tradition, but squeezed it through a taut electric guitar mesh, producing peerless rock songs which defied both its roots and its participants' ages. A third album pushed the strident choruses and strong melody lines to the forefront, in an obvious effort on Geraldo's part to convert critical reverence into commercial accessibility. Though *Based On A True Story* was consequently weakened, the natural strengths of songs like 'Judas Kiss' and 'The Cool And The Crazy', an anthemic party rocker, won through. Guests included Mojo Nixon ('Rivers Of Justice') and Syd Straw. Adept covers of the Flamin' Groovies on *Howlin' At The Halloween Moon* could not disguise the mediocrity of a disappointing live set, but this proved an uncharacteristic qualitative hitch. *Lovers Who Wander* saw Kempner and Ambel produce the best work of their respective careers. Abandoning the commercial ambition of their previous studio set, this collection focused instead on the innate strengths of previous Del Lords releases - spirited, emotive rock songs delivered with unreconstructed passion. Of no small consequence was the band's most sympathetic production yet - courtesy of Thom Panunzio and bass player Manny Caiati. Shortly after release Ambel would depart for a solo career (having already recorded one album in 1988).
Albums: *Frontier Days* (Enigma/EMI 1984), *Johnny Comes Marching Home* (Enigma/EMI 1986), *Based On A True Story* (Enigma 1988), *Howlin' At The Halloween Moon* (Restless 1989), *Lovers Who Wander* (Enigma 1990). Eric Ambel solo: *Roscoe's Gang* (Enigma 1988).

Delta 5

Leeds, England-originated post-punk band who had much in common with the Au Pairs - though the inspired amateurism that fuelled their early releases proved more reminiscent of the Slits. They released several singles on Rough Trade Records which highlighted insipid but endearing hook lines, the John Peel favourite 'Mind Your Own Business' being a good example (they also recorded two 1980 radio sessions for the programme). The line-up featured Julz Sale (vocals), Alan Riggs (guitar), Ros Allen (bass), Bethan Peters (bass/vocals) and Kelvin Knight (drums). Sale and Peters were the only two remaining following a major transformation in personnel as they moved

to Pre Records. They split up shortly after, though history would prove them to be a great influence on mid-80s indie pop bands like the Shop Assistants and Tallulah Gosh.
Album: *See The Whirl* (Pre 1981).

Denison/Kimball Trio

Misnomered US duo featuring the talents of Duana Denison (Jesus Lizard) and James Kimball (Mule), this project existed in splendid isolation to the guitar barrage more familiar to long term camp followers. Instead the band's 1994 debut album offered an exercise in ambient escapism as part of a soundtrack for an independent film starring Jesus Lizard vocalist David Yow. Repetitive jazz licks dominated the instrumentation, for an effect not dissimilar to that of Barry Adamson's experimental soundscapes.
Album: *Walls In The City* (Skin Graft 1994).

Dentists

Formed in Chatham, Kent, England, this group comprised Michael Murphy (b. 8 October 1963, Bexley, Kent, England; guitar/vocals), Robert Collins (b. 12 June 1965, Gillingham, Kent, England; lead guitar), Mark Matthew (b. 15 May 1965, Farnborough, Hampshire, England; bass) and drummer Ian Smith, subsequently replaced by Alun Gwynne Jones (b. 3 February 1966, Chatham, Kent, England) in 1986, and later by Robert Grigg (b. 28 July 1968, Canterbury, Kent, England) in 1991. The initial line-up was forged from the ashes of local bands Split Decision and The Ancient Gallery in December 1983. The contemporaries of other Medway town bands such as the Milkshakes and the Prisoners, the hard-working Dentists have been plying their brand of melodic, driving pop (reminiscent in parts of the Smiths) on the London club circuit into the 90s and have built up a sizeable, loyal following. The group made their debut with the whimsical 'Strawberries Are Growing In My Garden' in January 1985. Their early EP, *Down And Out In Parts And Chatham* (1986), garnered critical acclaim as did *Writhing On The Shagpile*, which made an appearance in the UK independent chart in 1987. Since then press attention has been minimal leaving the band to quietly go about their business, issuing several EPs and albums on various labels. Their 1990 debut long player, *Heads And How To Read Them*, their strongest collection to date, secured favourable press reviews, but not strong enough to push the group out of the lower divisions in the UK they have inhabited since their inception. However, during 1991-92 the Dentists would appear to have gained an appreciable audience on the US college circuit, indicating that, in common with the Jazz Butcher and Robyn Hitchcock, a potentially profitable future may lay ahead for them there.
Albums: *You And Your Bloody Oranges* (Spruck 1985), *Beer Bottle And Bannister Symphonie* (Antler 1988), *Heads And How To Read Them* (1990), *Dressed* (1992), *Powdered Lobster Fiasco* (1993).

Denzil

Denzil have been compared to XTC and Squeeze. They earned more praise initially in the USA than in the UK, and signed to Giant Records who released the band's debut album there in 1994. The group went on to play over 100

gigs in the USA, supporting the Posies, Grant Lee Buffalo and American Music Club. The album was eventually released in the UK through BMG Records, where an audience quickly formed for Denzil Thomas's storytelling and unusual song construction. In 1995 he added a rhythm section of Jeremy Stacy (ex-Tori Amos, World Party; drums) and Martin Burden (bass) in an attempt to bolster the band's live sound. They joined core members Thomas (vocals/guitar) and Craig Boyd (guitar).
Album: *Pub* (Giant 1994).

Department S

Taking their name from the 60s television series, Department S evolved from the punk/ska combo Guns For Hire. Although it featured several members during its lifetime, Guns For Hire was essentially occasional *Face* writer Vaughan Toulouse (b. Vaughan Cotillard, 30 July 1959, St Helier, Jersey, Channel Islands, d. August 1991; vocals), Mike Herbage (guitar), Tony Lordan (bass), Eddie Roxy (b. Edward Lloyd Barnes; keyboards - replaced by Mark Taylor in 1981), and Stuart Mizan (drums; replaced by Mike Hasler). Hasler, who drummed for Madness in their Invaders days and also managed the Nips, wrote Guns For Hire's only single - 'I'm Gonna Rough My Girlfriend's Boyfriend Up Tonight' - which emerged on Korova Records. The group became Department S with the addition of Mark Taylor and Stuart Mizan. They made their live debut at the Rock Garden, London, in July 1980. Demon Records released their debut single, 'Is Vic There?', in 1981. It was produced by former Mott The Hoople members, Buffin and Overend Watts, but its success led to the better equipped RCA Records picking it up. The b-side, 'Solid Gold Easy Action', featured Bananarama on backing vocals. Two further singles followed on Stiff Records but a planned album was aborted when neither single charted. Vaughan returned to work as a disc jockey, before re-emerging with Main T on Paul Weller's Respond label. When two further singles flopped it proved to be the end of his performing career, with the exception of contributions to Weller's Council Collective off-shoot on 'Soul Deep', a miners' strike benefit. He was also linked with the Style Council as one of the personalities behind the 'Cappacino Kid', whose writing graced the band's sleeves. Vaughan died in August 1991 after a long illness brought on by AIDS. Of the remainder of the band, Lordan and Taylor were most recently accounted for as being a postman and cab driver respectively.
Compilation: *Is Vic There?* (1993).

Depeche Mode

During the UK post-punk backlash at the turn of the 80s, when bands dispensed with guitars and drums in favour of synthesizers and drum machines, Depeche Mode were formed, taking their name from a phrase in a French style magazine. More than a decade later they are recognized as the most successful 'electro-synth' group ever. Ironically enough, given their reputation as the kings of synth-pop, they had made their debut as a trio playing only guitars at Scamps in Southend. The band originally came together in the nieghbouring borough of Basildon, Essex, England, in 1980, and comprised: Vince Clarke (b. 3 July 1960,

Basildon, Essex; synthesizer, ex-No Romance In China), Andy Fletcher (b. 8 July 1960, Basildon, Essex; synthesizer) and Martin Gore (b. 23 July 1961, Basildon, Essex; synthesizer, ex-The French Look, Norman & The Worms). Following a series of concerts which attracted packed houses at the Bridge House Tavern in London's Canning Town, they were spotted by Daniel Miller. Shortly afterwards they were signed to his independent Mute label, where they remain. They had already tasted vinyl exposure by issuing one track on Stevo's *Some Bizzare* compilation in 1981. This had been recorded by the original trio, with Clarke on vocals, before they elected to recruit Dave Gahan (b. 9 May 1962, Epping, Essex) as their permanent lead vocalist.
'Dreaming Of Me' in 1981 started a remarkable run of hit singles which by the turn of the decade had totalled 23 chart entries. Principal songwriter Vince Clarke left shortly after *Speak And Spell* to form Yazoo with Alison Moyet, and the writing reins were taken over by Martin Gore, as Alan Wilder (b. 1 June 1959, England; synthesizer, vocals, ex-Dragons, Hitmen) settled into Clarke's place. The gentle, hypnotic ambience of 'See You' was an early demonstration of Gore's sense of melody.
Only briefly have Depeche Mode found their craft compatible with the tastes of the music press, yet their success reamins a testament to the power of their music, which is arresting yet generally easy on the ear, and often compulsively danceable. Lyrically Gore has tended to tackle subjects a shade darker than the musical content might suggest, including sado-masochism ('Master And Servant'), capitalism ('Everything Counts') and religious fetishism ('Personal Jesus'). As the 90s dawned their albums continued to make the UK Top 10, and they also began to make inroads on the European and American markets, which were late in discovering them. The *Violator* tour would make them huge concert stars in the USA, selling several million copies worldwide. The album presented a harder sound, informed by Gahan's patronage of the American rock scene, which was continued on *Songs Of Faith & Devotion*. As their standing throughout the world continued to be enhanced by ambitious stage shows, the latter album debuted in both the US and UK chart at number 1 on its week of release. This despite the fact that thinly-veiled acrimony seemed to surround the Depeche Mode camp as it entered the 90s.
Albums: *Speak And Spell* (Mute 1981), *A Broken Frame* (Mute 1982), *Construction Time Again* (Mute 1983), *Some Great Reward* (Mute 1984), *Black Celebration* (Mute 1986), *Music For The Masses* (Mute 1987), *101* (Mute 1989, double album), *Violator* (Mute 1991), *Songs Of Faith & Devotion* (Mute 1993). Compilation: *The Singles 81-85* (Mute 1985). Videos: *Some Great Videos* (1986), *Strange* (1988), *101* (1989), *Strange Too - Another Violation* (1990), *Devotional* (1993), *Live In Hamburg* (1993).
Further reading: *Depeche Mode: The Photographs*, Anton Corbijn. *Depeche Mode: Some Great Reward*, Dave Thompson.

Descendents

Los Angeles, California, USA punk band, whose first stage of development was as a three-piece; Frank Navetta (vocals/guitar), Tony Lombardo (vocals/bass) and Bill

Stevenson (drums), playing power pop along the lines of the Buzzcocks. It was this formation who were intact for the debut 'Ride The Wild' single. They hooked up with singer Cecilia for some six months before the near legendary Milo Auckerman became the first regular vocalist. The resulting period was characterised by songs about fishing and food. Titles like 'Weinerschnitzel' and the self-parodying 'Fat' hail from these merry times. There was also a predilection for loading up on caffeine and measuring the results in song velocity on tour. Shortly after things got more serious, as they recorded their debut album for posterity. Again the title was self explanatory, with Milo indeed being college-bound. There was something of a hiatus in the band's fortunes following this traumatic experience, with Ray Cooper replacing Navetta on guitar in 1985 (he originally tried out as vocalist). Doug Carrion (bass; ex-Anti, Incest Cattle) came in around 1986. He would later serve in Dag Nasty. Stevenson joined up with Black Flag. Milo remembers his choice of career as being a question of priorities: 'I went to El Camino College for my first year, then I went to UC San Diego. I have a problem. I like to immerse myself in things. I'm obsessed with music and I'm obsesssed with biology - so what can I do?'. When the band got back together three years later, *I Don't Want To Grow Up* followed swiftly on the heels of the reunion. This time the production values were more polished: 'On 'Grow Up' I was more melancholy. We're singing about the same things, just approaching it in a different way. To bring out the feeling behind it rather than just punking it out'. The Descendents were hugely popular in the US because they addressed the burning issues facing their audience; relationships and the hassles of being young. Milo's eventual replacement in the band was Dave Smalley (ex-DYS, Dag Nasty). Stevenson also played guitar in the unspeakable Nig Heist. After the Descendents finished the members formed All, who continued in much the same vein, but without Lombardo or Carrion. Their influence on UK pop punk outfits like Mega City Four and particularly the Senseless Things (who covered 'Marriage') should not be underestimated.
Albums: *Milo Goes To College* (New Alliance 1982), *I Don't Want To Grow Up* (New Alliance 1985), *Enjoy* (New Alliance 1986), *All* (SST 1987), *Liveage* (SST 1987, live album), *Hellraker* (SST 1989, live album). Compilations: *Bonus Fat* (New Alliance 1985), *Two Things At Once* (SST 1988, combines *Milo Goes To College* and *Bonus Fat*).

Desperate Bicycles

One of the first independent, do-it-yourself pop bands of the new wave era, the Desperate Bicycles hinged around vocalist Danny Wigley, the only member to survive an ever-fluctuating line-up. At one stage he was aided and abetted by Roger Stephens (bass), Dan Electro (guitar), Dave Papworth (drums) and Nick Stephens (keyboards), although Jeff Titley also served time behind the drum kit. In 1977 'Smokescreen'/'Handlebars' was released, featuring the two tracks on both sides, in mono on the band's own label, Refill. This set the pattern for all subsequent Desperate Bicycles product. After several singles - 'The Medium Was Tedium', the *New Cross New Cross* EP, 'Occupied Territory' (all 1978) and 'Grief Is Very Private' (1979) - the group released a well-regarded album, *Remorse Code*, and subsequently disbanded.
Album: *Remorse Code* (Refill 1979).

Destroy All Monsters

This Detroit-based group revolved around ex-Stooges guitarist Ron Asheton and former MC5 bassist Michael Davis. Such experience ensured attention in the new group's fortunes, particularly in the light of the concurrent punk rock explosion. With the group also comprising Niagara (vocals), Larry Miller (guitar), Ben Miller (saxophone) and Rob King (drums) Destroy All Monsters made its recording debut in 1978 with 'Bored'/'You're Gonna Die', issued in the UK by the independent Cherry Red label. The same outlet released a further two singles, while in the US the band completed two privately pressed EPs, *Live* (1979) and *Black Out In The City* (1980). The group was then disbanded, following which Asheton formed New Race with another former MC5 member, drummer Dennis Thompson.
Albums: *November 22nd 1963 - Singles And Rarities* (1989), *Live* (1989). Compilation: *Bored* (1991).

Destructors

Peterborough, England based punk band who produced a welter of recorded material in line with the vogueish third generation concerns of pacifism, anarchism and human rights. Animal rights, another favoured topic of the time, was notable for its absence; it was later revealed that one member, Allen Adams, actually worked at an animal research foundation. The band were formed in 1977 from two defunct Peterborough outfits. Phil Atterson (guitar) and Allen Adams (vocals), then added Dip (bass; ex-Now) for their first half-dozen gigs, without the aid of a permanent drummer. Andy Jackson joined on rhythm guitar but soon left taking Atterson with him to form the Blanks. He did at least introduce the remaining Destructors to Andy Butler who became their permanent drummer. By 1979 Adams had quit and he and Butler also moved on to the Blanks. This band achieved minor notoriety when they released an inflammatory single 'The Northern Ripper'. Released during the days of the Yorkshire Ripper it earned Adams an interview with the special task force set up by the Police to detect the criminal. However, the Blanks dissolved after a disastrous Discharge support, and the nucleus of the band decided to resurrect the Destructors moniker (Allen Adams; vocals, Andy McDonald; drums, Dave Ithermee; rhythm guitar, Dave; lead guitar). Together they made their second debut in August 1981. They went on to release a plethora of unremarkable, sloganeering punk which did at least have the occasional above average lyric to distinguish it.
Album: *Bomb Hanoi, Bomb Saigon, Bomb Disneyland* (Carnage 1984).

Devine And Statton

After laying low for several years after the demise of Weekend, and working with various local Cardiff bands while pursuing college studies, singer Alison Statton (b. March 1958, Cardiff, South Glamorgan, Wales) quietly re-emerged in 1989 with the album *The Prince Of Wales*, a set of songs written by former Ludus member Ian Devine (b. Ian Pincombe; guitar/vocals), which was released on the Belgian independent label, Les Disques Du Crepuscule. The album echoed the strong Celtic background of both members, blending folk styles with a polished, almost-MOR feel while the duo were backed admirably by Blaine I. Reininger (violin/mandolin/keyboards), Nicolas Fizman (bass) and Frank Michiels (percussion). Lyrically, the album professed a staunch sense of Welsh patriotism, most evident in the song, 'Turn The Aerials Away From England'. However, Statton's quiet English-sounding voice and light melodies belied this instinct. Their cover version of New Order's 'Bizarre Love Triangle' received favourable reviews and attracted the attention of New Order's Peter Hook, who expressed a desire to record with the duo on their next album. The duo also recruited guest guitarist, Marc Ribot, who in the past had recorded with Tom Waits. The defiantly-titled *Cardiffians* continued where the debut left off and included a version of the Crystal Gayle hit, 'Don't It Make My Brown Eyes Blue'. The duo have yet to prove themselves on the live circuit, and Statton has publicly expressed a desire to contain her renewed musical career as a part-time venture.

Albums: *The Prince Of Wales* (Les Disques Du Crepescule 1989), *Cardiffians* (Les Disques Du Crepescule 1990).

Devo

Formed during 1972 in Akron, Ohio, this US new wave band, who fitted the term better than most, comprised Gerald Casale (bass/vocals), Alan Myers (drums), Mark Mothersbaugh (vocals/keyboards/guitar), Bob Mothersbaugh (guitar/vocals), and Bob Casale (guitar/vocals). The philosophical principle on which Devo operated, and from which they took a shortened name, was devolution: the theory that mankind, rather than progressing, has actually embarked on a negative curve. The medium they pioneered to present this was basic, electronic music, with strong robotic and mechanical overtones. The visual representation and marketing exaggerated modern life, with industrial uniforms and neo-military formations alongside potato masks and flower-pot headgear. Their debut album was among their finest achievements; a synthesis of pop and sarcastic social commentary. Produced by Brian Eno, it caught the prevailing wind of America's new wave movement perfectly. It also offered them their biggest UK hit in a savage take on the Rolling Stones' '(I Can't Get No) Satisfaction'. It wasn't until their third studio album, however, that Devo confirmed they were no novelty act. *Freedom Of Choice* contained Devo standards 'Girl You Want' and 'Whip It', the latter giving them a million selling single. At the peak of their powers, Devo inspired and informed many, not least one of Neil Young's great albums, *Rust Never Sleeps*. However, as the 80s unfolded the band seemed to lose its bite, and *New Traditionalists* signalled a creative descent. Successive albums were released to diminishing critical and commercial returns, and after *Shout* songwriters Gerald Casale and Mark Mothersbaugh moved into soundtrack work. Devo had previously performed the theme to Dan Ayckroyd's movie *Doctor Detroit*, and they added to this with TV work on *Pee-Wee's Playhouse* and *Davis Rules*. Mothersbaugh had also cut a pair of studio LPs solo, largely consisting of keyboard doodlings and 'atmosphere' pieces. These arrived at the same time as Devo's first original

work together in four years, *Total Devo*, which saw Myers replaced by David Kendrick (ex-Gleaming Spires, Sparks). Devo's absence had not, however, made critics' hearts grow fonder. As was unerringly pointed out, the band had long since lost its status as innovators, and been surpassed by a generation of electronic outfits it had helped to inspire. Despite falling out of fashion as the 80s wore on, Devo nevertheless saw themselves venerated in the new decade by bands who hailed their early work as a significant influence. Nirvana would cover an obscure Devo cut, 'Turnaround', and both Soundgarden and Superchunk offered re-makes of 'Girl You Want'. A new wave tribute album, *Freedom Of Choice*, adopting the band's own 1980 title, included the latter. Gerald Casale was bemused by the sudden attention: 'I think we were the most misunderstood band that ever came down the pike because behind the satire, our message was a humanistic one, not an inhumane one. If there's any interest in Devo now, it's only because it turned out that what was called an art-school smartass joke - this de-evolution rap, about man devolving - now seems very true as you look around.'

Albums: *Q: Are We Not Men? A: We Are Devo!* (Warners 1978), *Duty Now For The Future* (Warners 1979), *Freedom Of Choice* (Warners 1980), *Dev-o Live* (Warners 1981, mini-album), *New Traditionalists* (Warners 1981), *Oh No, It's Devo* (Warners 1982), *Shout* (Warners 1984), *Total Devo* (Enigma 1988), *Smooth Noodle Maps* (Enigma 1990). Compilations: *E-Z Listening Disc* (Rykodisc 1987), *Now It Can Be Told* (Enigma 1989), *Greatest Hits* (Warners 1990), *Greatest Misses* (Warners 1990), *Hard Core Devo* (Rykodisc 1990), *Hardcore Devo 1974-77, Volumes 1 & 2* (Fan Club 1991), *Live: The Mongoloid Years* (Rykodisc 1992). Mark Mothersbaugh solo: *Muzik For Insomniaks Volume 1* (Enigma 1988), *Muzik For Insomniaks Volume 2* (Enigma 1988).

Devoto, Howard

b. Howard Trotter. One writer perceptively dubbed the bespectacled new wave intellectual as 'the Orson Welles of punk'. After leaving the Buzzcocks just as they seemed destined for greatness (which they actually managed to achieve without him), Manchester student Howard Devoto formed the altogether more sober Magazine. After widespread critical acclaim, the band split in the early 80s, and Devoto briefly embarked on a straightforward solo career with 1983's *Jerky Visions Of The Dream*. Despite two singles ('Rainy Season' and 'Cold Imagination'), the album failed to achieve the impact that Magazine had attained. Devoto approached later work using various disguises, such as Luxuria. Highly-influential during the punk era, Devoto's role as a much-quoted spokesperson and innovator declined in the 80s.

Album: *Jerky Visions Of The Dream* (Virgin 1983).

Dharma Bums

A garage band in the best traditions of the MC5 and early 80s college-rock bands like Rain Parade and R.E.M., Dharma Bums comprised Jeremy Wilson (b. c.1969; vocals), John Moen (drums, vocals), Eric Lovre (guitar, vocals) and Jim Talstra (bass). They originated from Portland, Oregon, USA and began their career in 1987. A first album, *Haywire*,

was recorded quickly for the PopLlama label in 1989, which had been advised of the band by Young Fresh Fellows' Scott McCaughey. He repeated the favour by playing their debut album to Frontier Records boss Lisa Fancher. 1990 saw the more polished *Bliss* emerge. Featuring greatly improved songwriting, it covered subjects from rape and adolescence to suicide, in a mature fashion built on ragged rock textures.
Albums: *Haywire* (1989), *Bliss* (1990).

Dickies

Formed in 1977 in Los Angeles, California, USA, the Dickies were a punk rock band which specialized in speedy renditions of humorous songs, many of which were cover versions of earlier rock hits. The group consisted of Chuck Wagon (keyboards), guitarist Stan Lee (guitar), Billy Club (bass), Leonard Graves Phillips (vocals) and Karlos Kaballero (drums). Wearing fashionably ludicrous, often grotesque clothing, the Dickies quickly became one of the most popular of the original LA punk bands, and were signed to A&M Records in 1978. In addition to their self-penned songs, the Dickies' early recordings included such previously-bombastic numbers as the Moody Blues' 'Nights In White Satin' and Black Sabbath's 'Paranoid', played at a furious pace and often clocking in at under two minutes. During their career they would also cover the Monkees, Led Zeppelin and others. Their original material often took its cue from cult b-movies, similar in style and attitude to New York's Ramones. After a prolific recording schedule in the early 80s, the Dickies kept a low profile for the rest of the decade and were still recording new material in 1988, although they were no longer in the spotlight.
Albums: *The Incredible Shrinking Dickies* (1979), *Dawn Of The Dickies* (1979), *Stukas Over Disneyland* (1983), *We Aren't The World!* (1986), *Second Coming* (1988).

Dictators

Formed in 1974 in New York City, the Dictators pre-dated the punk rock of bands such as the Ramones and Sex Pistols by two years, yet they exhibited many of that genre's hallmarks from their inception. Purveying loud, three-chord rock without long solos and drawing their lyrical inspiration and visual image from such disparate facets of popular culture as fast food, professional wrestling, cult movies and late-night television, the Dictators built a devoted fan-base in their hometown and selected hip pockets in the USA and Europe, but were unable to succeed commercially and are rarely acknowledged for their pioneering efforts in helping to establish the new rock 'n' roll of the 70s and 80s. The group originally consisted of guitarists Scott 'Top Ten' Kempner and Ross 'The Boss' Funicello, bassist Andy Shernoff and drummer Stu Boy King. Vocalist 'Handsome Dick Manitoba' (b. Richard Blum) guested on the group's debut album and subsequently joined. King left after the release of that album and was replaced by Richie Teeter, and bassist Mark 'The Animal' Mendoza also joined at that time (1975), allowing Shernoff to switch to keyboards. That first album, *The Dictators Go Girl Crazy*, featured original songs by Shernoff with titles such as 'Teengenerate', '(I Live For) Cars And Girls' and a cover of Sonny And Cher's 'I Got You Babe'. It was released on Epic Records, which then dropped

the group when the album failed to catch on. After the personnel shuffle of 1975, the Dictators signed to Asylum/Elektra Records in late 1976 and released *Manifest Destiny*, their only album to chart. Before they recorded their third and last album, *Bloodbrothers*, in 1978, Mendoza left to join heavy metal outfit Twisted Sister. When the third album failed, they were dropped by Elektra and disbanded. The Dictators have reunited several times for single concert dates, one of which was recorded and released as a cassette-only in 1981, *Fuck 'Em If They Can't Take A Joke*. During the 80s Kempner went on to form the Del-Lords, another straight-ahead rock group popular in New York. Manitoba and Shernoff formed the quasi-metal band Manitoba's Wild Kingdom. Funicello joined the short-lived Shakin' Street. The Dictators reunited once more in December 1993 to play at the 20th Anniversary celebrations for CBGB's.
Albums: *The Dictators Go Girl Crazy* (Epic 1975), *Manifest Destiny* (Asylum 1977), *Bloodbrothers* (Asylum 1978), *Fuck 'Em If They Can't Take A Joke* (ROIR 1981).

Die Cheerleader

British four-piece consisting of Rita Blazyca (guitar), Sam Ireland (vocals), Debbie Quargnolo (bass) and lone male member Andy Semple (drums). Die Cheerleader play chunky, punk-edged, hard rock, featuring feisty, semi-surreal songs about relationships and life's many downturns. In the process they have managed to straddle both the heavy metal and indie genres, capturing the attention of journalists from both camps and securing a publishing deal with poet and punk legend Henry Rollins. Tours with well-regarded punk and rock bands Terrorvision, Bad Religion and Iggy Pop helped to establish their reputation as a hard working, talented live act. *Filth By Association* collected their well-received first three EPs (*D.C.E.P.*, *Saturation* and *69 Hayloft Action*) in updated form, along with two new tracks to complete the package. Later Rollins sought to launch them in the US by tying up a deal with London Records, who released the US-only *Son Of Filth*, an album split between old material remixed by Rollins and new songs produced in London with Steve Mack (ex-That Petrol Emotion).
Albums: *Filth By Association* (Abstract 1993), *Son Of Filth* (London 1995, US only).

Die Kreuzen

This punk/thrash band was formed in Milwaukee, USA, in 1981, their name derived from the German for 'the crosses'. The band, featuring Dan Kubinski (vocals), Brian Egeness (guitar), Keith Brammer (bass) and Eric Tunison (drums), started life with a highly regarded album of embryonic thrash (incorporating all six tunes from their 1982 debut EP, *Cows And Beer*). Since that debut their material has revealed a much stronger inclination towards traditional rock structures, though they were widely congratulated for bringing intelligence and lyrical diversity to the heavy metal sphere. *Century Days*, for example, includes both piano and horns on several tracks, whilst maintaining an allegiance to the band's traditionally hard sound. Brammer would transfer to Wreck in 1989. Signed to Chicago independent Touch And Go Records, their 1991 album was produced by Butch Vig (Killdozer, Tad, Nirvana).

Albums: *Die Kreuzen* (Touch & Go 1984), *October File* (Touch & Go 1986), *Century Days* (Touch & Go 1988), *Gone Away* (Touch & Go 1989, mini-album), *Cement* (Touch & Go 1991).

Die Krupps

Tracing their origins to the turn of the 80s, German outfit Die Krupps have been a pioneering force in experimental music ever since. The band was formed in 1981 by Jurgen Engler (vocals, keyboards, guitars and group spokesman; ex-famed German punk band Male) and Ralf Dorper (previously part of Propaganda). Together with Front 242 they helped to formulate the Body Music sub-genre of Euro rock, a sound lush in electronics but harsh in execution. Several albums of synthesized material emerged, and were duly snapped up by Die Krupps' loyal fan base. However, Engler spent the mid-80s, which were largely quiet for the band, ingesting the new sounds pioneered by Metallica and others who were pushing back the frontiers of metal. When Die Krupps eventually returned in 1992 they took all by surprise by adding layers of metal guitar, consequently picking up a new audience which spanned several genres. The most famous of two excellent sets in that year was a tribute album to the band who had revolutionized Engler's thinking: 'Metallica were coming to Germany for some dates and I wanted to present something to them because I really admired what they did. So we put together this tape, and that's all it was intended for, but our label heard of it and wanted to put it out...'. Lars Ulrich was reportedly highly impressed with the results, though he proved unable to meet an engagement to help out on the recording of *The Final Option*. This set saw the recruitment of Lee Altus (guitar; ex-Heathen) and Darren Minter (drums), and a continuation of Die Krupps' bleak lyrical thematic (notably on 'Crossfire', a reaction to the Yugoslavian conflict). A remix album, with contributions from Gunshot, Jim Martin (ex-Faith No More), Andrew Eldritch (Sisters of Mercy) and Julian Beeston (Nitzer Ebb, who in 1989 had remodelled the group's classic 'Wahre Arbeit, Wahrer Lohn') was also unveiled.
Albums: *Stahlwerksinfonie* (Zick Zack 1981), *Volle Kraft Voraus* (WEA 1982), *Entering The Arena* (Statik 1984), *Metalle Maschinen Musik 91-81 Past Forward* (Rough Trade 1991, double album), *One* (Rough Trade 1992), *Metal For The Masses Part II - A Tribute To Metallica* (Rough Trade 1992), *The Final Option* (Rough Trade 1993), *The Final Mixes* (Rough Trade 1994). Compilation: *Die Krupps Box* (Rough Trade 1993, 3-CD box set)

Dif Juz

Formed in west London in 1980, Dif Juz were one of the first signings to the fledgling 4AD Records roster, and comprised brothers Dave (guitar) and Alan Curtis (guitar), plus Gary Bromley (bass) and Richie Thomas (drums/saxophone). Rising to prominence via support slots with the Birthday Party and Jah Wobble, the group's highly atmospheric music was in keeping with the 'ethereal' tag which 4AD soon earned, but a million miles away from their beginnings in punk band London Pride. They made their debut in 1981 with two EPs, *Huremics* and *Vibrating Air*,

with a third collection of sharp, minimalist pieces following for Red Flame Records in 1983 as the *Who Says So?* EP. After a break of two years they released their first, cassette-only long player, this time totally improvised in the studio. Afterwards the quartet reunited with 4AD Records, supporting the Cocteau Twins at UK venues such as the Royal Albert Hall and Sadler's Wells Theatre. A new album for the label, *Extractions*, featured guest appearances from Cocteau Twins' nucleus Liz Fraser, their first ever vocalist, and Robin Guthrie (Richard Thomas would return the compliment by guesting on the Cocteau's *Victorialand* on tablas and saxophone). Dif Juz's final recording was a mini-album in 1986. Comprising re-recordings and remixes of earlier material (the *Huremics* and *Vibrating Air* EPs), it passed by to minimal critical interest. The arrival of ex-Dead Can Dance bass player Scott Roger for European touring did little to avert their impending collapse. Thomas would subsequently become drummer for Butterfly Child (having previously played with Jesus And Mary Chain), while Dave Curtis now plays guitar for Wolfgang Press. His brother Alan has relocated to New York, while Bromley currently works as an electrician.
Albums: *Time Clock Turn Back* (Pleasantly Surprised 1985, cassette only), *Extractions* (4AD 1985), *Out Of The Trees* (4AD 1986, mini-album).

Dils

Formed in San Diego, California, USA, in 1977, the Dils' most stable line-up comprised Chip Kinman (guitar/vocals), Tony 'Nineteen' Kinman (guitar/vocals) and Endre Alquover (drums), who had replaced Pat Garrett. The trio was an integral part of the Los Angeles punk movement, completing two powerful singles in 'I Hate The Rich' and 'Class War' (both 1977). Drummers Rand McNally and John Silvers later passed through the line-up, but the group's only other release was their *Made In Canada* EP (1980). The Dils then evolved into Rank And File, in which the Kinman brothers were joined by ex-Nuns' guitarist Alejandro Escovado. The new act revived 'Sound Of The Rain' on their *Long Gone Dead* album. Despite an existence spanning four years, when the Dils broke up in 1980 there remained only the aforementioned three singles to document their existence, until the advent of a pair of posthumous live albums.
Albums: *Live: Dils* (Iloki/Triple X 1987), *The Dils* (Lost 1990).

Dim Stars

Formed in New York in 1991, Dim Stars is an occasional project featuring Richard Hell (ex-Television, Heartbreakers; vocals/bass), Don Fleming (ex-Velvet Monkeys, B.A.L.L.; guitar, vocals) and two members of Sonic Youth; Thurston Moore (guitar/vocals) and Steve Shelly (drums). A live 3-single pack, *Dim Stars* was issued that year on Sonic Youth's Ecstatic Peace! label. It included a lengthy version of 'You've Got To Lose', first featured on Hell's *Blank Generation* album. *Three Songs*, an EP credited to 'Richard Hell' ensued, although this featured the Dim Stars' line-up. The quartet's eponymous album is an informal, but exciting, set, combining Hell's visionary lyrics with the debauched ease of the Rolling Stones' classic *Exile On Main Street*. Guitarist

Robert Quine, formerly of Richard's group, the Voidoids and Jad Fair assist the proceedings, the highlight of which is a memorable take of Howlin' Wolf's 'Natchez Burning'. Prior commitments to Sonic Youth preclude Dim Stars from becoming a permanent fixture, but the album is an excellent restatement of Richard Hell's talent.
Album: *Dim Stars* (1993).

Dinosaur Jr

This rock band from the university town of Amherst, Massachusetts, USA, were originally called simply Dinosaur. Their musical onslaught eventually dragged them, alongside the Pixies, into the rock mainstream of the late 80s. Both J. Mascis (vocals/guitar) and Lou Barlow (bass) were formerly in the hardcore band Deep Wound, along with a singer called Charlie. He recruited his best friend Murphy (b. Patrick Murphy; ex-All White Jury) from Connecticut, and was rewarded by the first line-up of Dinosaur ejecting him and thus becoming a trio. Mascis had by this time switched from drums to guitar, to accommodate the new arrival. Mascis, apparently a huge fan of Sham 69 and the UK Oi! movement, had actually known Murphy at high school but they had never got on. He formed Deep Wound as a response to seeing 999 play live when he was 14 years old. During Dinosaur Jr's career internal rifts never seemed far from the surface, while their leader's monosyllabic press interviews and general disinterest in rock 'n' roll machinations gave the impression of 'genius anchored by lethargy'. Two albums for Homestead were issued then SST Records saw them establish their name as a credible underground rock act. The best of the pair was *You're Living All Over Me*, which featured backing vocals from Sonic Youth's Lee Renaldo. However, their debut album had brought them to the attention of ageing hippie group Dinosaur, who insisted the band change their name. Mascis elected to add the suffix Junior. Real recognition came with the release of the huge underground anthem 'Freak Scene', which more than one journalist called the perfect pop single. Its sound was constructed on swathes of guitar and Mascis's laconic vocals, which were reminiscent of Neil Young. However, the parent album (*Bug*) and tour saw Barlow depart (to Sebadoh) and Donna became a temporary replacement. This line-up recorded the version of the Cure's 'Just Like Heaven' which so impressed Robert Smith and led to joint touring engagements. Soon after they signed to Warner Brothers subsidiary Blanco Y Negro, remixing their Sub Pop Records cut, 'The Wagon', as their debut major label release. Subsequent members included Don Fleming (Gumball etc.) Jay Spiegel and Van Connor (Screaming Trees), while Mascis himself flirted with other bands, principally as a drummer, such as Gobblehoof, Velvet Monkeys and satanic metal band, Upside Down Cross. By the advent of *Green Mind* Dinosaur Jr. had effectively become the J. Mascis show, with him playing almost all the instruments. Murphy departed because of misgivings about the band's finances. However, although critically acclaimed *Where You Been* did not manage to build on the commercial inroads originally made by *Green Mind*. *Without A Sound* included several strong compositions such as 'Feel The Pain' and 'On The Brink', with the bass now played by Mike

Johnson. Mascis has also produced other artists including the Breeders, and wrote the soundtrack for and appeared in Allison Anders' film, *Gas, Food, Lodging*. Mascis appeared solo in 1995 and it would now appear that the future of the band is in the balance.
Albums: As Dinosaur: *Dinosaur* (Homestead 1985). As Dinosaur Jr: *You're Living All Over Me* (SST 1987), *Bug* (SST 1988), *Green Mind* (Blanco Y Negro 1991), *Where You Been* (Blanco Y Negro 1993), *Without A Sound* (Blanco Y Negro 1994)

Discharge

There are some who would argue that Discharge are the most influential punk band after the Sex Pistols. Certainly their caustic wall of sound (a million miles away from anything Phil Spector could ever have envisaged when he invented the term) has inspired both punk and metal bands throughout the UK and USA. Discharge were formed in 1978 in Birmingham, England. Like many of the early 80s punk bands, Discharge's line-up was fluid and consisted of people who refused to offer anything other than nicknames to the press - but the nucleus of the band has always been demonic singer Cal (b. Kevin Morris) and long-serving bass player Rainy. Other early members of the band included Bones (guitar) and Rainy's brother, Tezz (drums), who was subsequently replaced by Bambi and then Gary. Their debut EP, released in 1980 as the first record on Stoke-On-Trent label Clay Records, preceded their participation on the renowned Apocalypse Now tour, on which they joined such punk luminaries as the Exploited, Chron Gen and Anti-Pasti. Like each of these bands Cal's lyrics decried the horror of war, but they eschewed the melody pursued, to varying degrees, by the others. They were also closest of these bands to Crass's ideals about cheaply priced records, vegetarianism, and suspicion of the press. Later *Sun* newspaper critic Gary Bushell, whose *Sounds* music paper was the only one interested in documenting this emerging scene, railed at their methodology: 'Umpteen versions of the same pneumatic drill solo . . . awful . . . no tunes, no talent, no fun . . . dull, boring and monotonous . . . the musical equivalent of glue-sniffing.' However, others did not agree, and the band soon built up a considerable following through EPs such as *Realities Of War*, *Why?* and *Fight Back*. Over a full album Discharge could be a uniquely intimidating experience, and their impact dwindled as the 80s progressed. However, the impact of their sonic assaults can still be heard in a thousand or more bands, including practically everything on Earache Records through to mainstream metal bands Guns N'Roses and Metallica.
Albums: *Hear Nothing, See Nothing, Say Nothing* (Clay 1982), *Never Again* (Clay 1984), *Brave New World* (Clay 1986), *The Nightmare Continues* (Clay 1988), *Live At City Garden* (Clay 1990), *Shootin' Up The World* (Clay 1994). Compilation: *Discharge 1980-1986* (Clay 1987).

Dislocation Dance

Quirky jazz-pop was the speciality of Manchester outfit Dislocation Dance. Signed to the Buzzcocks' New Hormones label after forming in late 1978, the band consisted of Ian Runacres (vocals/guitar), Dick Harrison

(drums), Paul Emmerson (bass) and Andy Diagram (trumpet/vocals). An EP, *It's So Difficult* (1980), was a co-release with the band's Delicate Issues label. The EP, *Slip That Disc* (1981) included an offbeat version of the Beatles' 'We Can Work It Out', and was followed by, what was for the group, a transistional album, *Music Music Music*. Having now been joined by Kath Way (vocals/saxophone), Dislocation Dance then issued the comparatively poppy 'Rosemary' (1982), but left New Hormones after the fashionably bossa-nova tinged 'You'll Never Never Know' (both 1982). In 1983 a one-off single, 'Violette' for the Music Label, passed the time, before the band signed to Rough Trade later that year, releasing 'Show Me'. A second album, *Midnight Shift*, also appeared, but they left the label soon after. A final 12-inch single 'What's Going On' on the Slipped Discs label, signalled the end of Dislocation Dance in late 1985. Andy Diagram, also fronted the Diagram Brothers and later appeared with the Pale Fountains.
Albums: *Music Music Music* (New Hormones 1981), *Midnight Shift* (Rough Trade 1984).

Disorder

This punk band from Bristol, England, blended breakneck thrash with tales of gargantuan cider consumption. The first incarnation dated from 1980 with Mick (bass), Steve (guitar), Virus (drums) and Dean (vocals). They produced a demonstration tape which was sent to Riot City Records. Turned down, they formed their own Disorder Records instead. After the release of 'Complete Disorder', Mick left and was replaced by Steve Robinson. The *Distortion Till Deafness* EP was subsequently released, before bizarre developments followed. Robinson split with girlfriend Beki Bondage (of Vice Squad, the band who had vetoed Disorder joining Riot City) and took up glue sniffing as a hobby. Then the CID caught up with Virus concerning the ownership of his new drumkit. Dean left too, going on to salubrious employment as toilet cleaner in Taunton. He was replaced by Taff (ex-X-Certs Review). With Taff on bass, they persuaded Boobs, their roadie, to take over vocals. Luckily he was almost through his current sentence for fraudulently sabotaging his electricity meter. After the recording of 'Perdition', they set about a short touring stint with the Varukers. Their first foreign tour was sabotaged by a typical series of farcical miscalculations concerning European geography and train timetables. Virus felt enough was enough and was replaced by Glenn (ex-Dead Popstars), while the band moved into a shared squat with friends Amebix. Later releases were somewhat more restrained, daring to flirt with melody on occasion.
Albums: *Perdition* (Disorder 1982), *Under The Scalpel Blade* (Disorder 1984), *Live In Oslo* (Disorder 1985), *One Day Son, All This Will Be Yours* (Disorder 1986), *Violent World* (Disorder 1989). Compilation: *The Singles Collection* (Riot City 1984).

Distractions

This Manchester, England new wave band was first formed in 1975 by college friends Mike Finney (vocals) and Steve Perrin-Brown (guitar), together with Lawrence Tickle (bass) and Tony Trap (drums). Restructured under the influence of the Buzzcocks towards the end of 1977, Finney and Brown stabilized the line-up with the addition of Pip Nicholls (bass), Adrian Wright (guitar) and Alec Sidebottom (drums), who had previously played with the Purple Gang in the 60s. Their live set composed of 'Waiting For The Rain', 'Doesn't Bother Me', 'Pillow Talk', 'Do The', 'Valerie' and 'Paracetomol', mixing the spirit of punk with a taste of the 60s. After supporting most of the main bands in the Manchester area, they made their debut in January 1979 with 'You're Not Going Out Dressed Like That'. This resulted in a contract with Tony Wilson's Factory label, and the release of 'Time Goes By So Slow'. Originally the b-side 'Pillow Fight' was to be the main track, but was flipped over at the last minute. Both good pop songs, they had the potential to climb the national charts, but failed through lack of radio play and promotion. At the end of September they signed to Island Records and released a re-recorded version of 'It Doesn't Bother Me'. In 1980 *Nobody's Perfect* was issued, a mixture of new and old songs from their early live set, followed by the singles 'Boys Cry' - a remake of the old Eden Kane hit - 'Something For The Weekend', the EP *And Then There's*. All received favourable reviews, but commercial success remained elusive, causing the inevitable split in 1981.
Album: *Nobody's Perfect* (1980).

Divine Comedy

These days the Divine Comedy is just one man, Neil Hannon (b. 7 November 1970, Londonderry, Northern Ireland), the son of the Bishop of Clogher. Influenced as much by classical as popular music, his opening salvo on Setanta Records (a spiritual home for wayward pop stars such as Frank 'n' Walters and A House) was *Fanfare For The Comic Muse*. Filled with elegant, resourceful observations on the perversities of Irish and British life, this proved the most pop-orientated of his 90s work. Of his ensuing albums he would confess: 'I was very interested in the purity of three chords and all that but I was lured away by polyphonic harmony.' *Fanfare* also saw the departure of a 'band' concept, with Hannon candidly pointing out that the decision was partially down to '...them realising Neil's an arrogant, egocentric bastard'. The prevailing influences on *Liberation* and *Promenade* included Michael Nyman, European art and Scott Walker. Critics were full of praise for both albums, partly because of Hannon's ability to provide self-conscious but highly amusing interview copy. *Promenade* included 'The Booklovers', in which Hannon recounted the names of some 60 authors, leaving a gap for them to answer (many of the replying voices were provided by the Irish comedian, Sean Hughes).
Albums: *Fanfare For The Comic Muse* (Setanta 1991), *Liberation* (Setanta 1993), *Promenade* (Setanta 1994).

Divinyls

Led by the provocative Chrissie Amphlett, whose songwriting with guitarist Mark McEntee is the basis of the band, the Divinyls have recorded some excellent work. Amphlett's sexy image complemented the mesmerizing urgency of the music, and the band was guaranteed the audience's undivided attention. They formed in Sydney in

Divine Comedy

1981, and their first mini-LP was written for the 1982 film *Monkey Grip*, and produced the Australian Top 10 single 'Boys In Town' as well as the excellent ballad, 'Only The Lonely'. Signing with the UK label Chrysalis, their first album *Desperate* was a hit in Australia. Several hit singles and extensive touring bridged the gap to *What A Life* (1985), which was greeted enthusiastically; but the sales did not match the reviews. Later material, with the exception of the next single 'Pleasure And Pain' did not compare well with their earliest work. The band now is basically a duo, with musicians added whenever a tour is undertaken. It has undergone a revival with its controversial single 'I Touch Myself', a deliberately blatant reference to masturbation, released in 1991 and reaching the UK Top 10.

Albums: *Desperate* (1983), *What A Life* (1985), *Tempermental* (1988), *Divinyls* (1991).

Dixon, Don

Better known as producer to a generation of influential US pop-rock bands (R.E.M., Smithereens, Let's Active), Dixon toiled for 14 years as part of North Carolina's Arrogance before releasing his solo album in 1985. This wonderfully titled debut consisted partly of leftover Arrogance tracks, as well as several other cast-offs and demos from Dixon's recent history. Clearly evident, as with all his recordings, was his abiding affection for clean-cut 60s pop. Guests included Mitch Easter on a version of Nick Lowe's 'Skin Deep'. Indeed, if Dixon has a UK equivalent, then it is probably Lowe whose wry sense of humour is possibly an influence on the ironic nostalgia of the title-track. Spongetones' guitarist Jamie Hoover, Dixon's wife Marti Jones and Easter all played on *Romeo At Juilliard*, an album which fulfilled the promise of the debut with a more fully realised and better produced collection of pop songs. Picking from a vast canon of songs Dixon used this set to reassert his credentials as a fine singer-songwriter, rather than merely the highly-regarded right-hand-man of better known artists. The strength of these and previous compositions allowed them to work well live, and this was confirmed by the release of *Chi-Town Budget Show* in 1988. Both this and the subsequent studio album were illuminated by powerful duets with Marti Jones, with *EEE* featuring more forceful instrumentation (notably brass) as Dixon pursued a commercially appetizing pop-soul direction. That he did so without sacrificing the quality, added further to his growing reputation.

Albums: *Most Of The Girls Like To Dance But Only Some Of The Boys Like To* (Enigma 1985), *Romeo At Juilliard* (Enigma 1987), *Chi-Town Budget Show* (Restless 1989), *EEE* (Enigma 1989).

Do Ré Mi

One of the more respected post-punk bands, Do Ré Mi has achieved limited success both in Australia and overseas since its formation in Sydney in 1981. It had success with its second single 'Man Overboard' from its debut album in 1985, although previously releasing a rather obscure mini-album in 1982. Subsequent releases did not catch the mainstream listeners and thus its excellent album *Domestic Harmony*, while critically acclaimed did not sell well. Lead vocalist, Deborah Conway, is currently pursuing a solo career

and her talent has attracted the attention of Pete Townshend. Albums: *Domestic Harmony* (1985), *Happiest Place In Town* (1988).

DOA

Explosive band based in Vancouver, Canada, who formed in 1978, and rose to become their country's most popular and influential hardcore act. The line-up featured Joey 'Shithead' Keithley (lead vocals/guitar), Randy Rampage (bass/vocals), Chuck Biscuits (drums), and also Brad Kent (guitar; ex-Avengers). Early releases included the *Disco Sucks* EP on their own Sudden Death Records, an impossibly rare artefact. Apart from their long playing debut, 1980 also saw Dave Gregg added as second guitarist to fill out the band's sound (Kent was only a temporary member). In the early 80s they toured incessantly, and not only defined their own sound but much of the subsequent 'hardcore' genre. The *Positively DOA* EP and *Hardcore 81* proved hugely important to the development of north American punk. The latter actually gave the movement an identity, not only in name, but a political agenda too. The band's most successful line-up collapsed in 1982. Biscuits left to join the Circle Jerks (and subsequently Black Flag and Danzig), while Randy Rampage went on to a solo career. In came Gregg 'Dimwit' James (drums; ex-Subhumans, Pointed Sticks, actually Chuck Biscuits' elder brother) and Brian 'Wimpy Boy' Goble (bass/vocals; ex-Subhumans). DOA's product in this incarnation is almost as invigorating. However, the third album 'proper' would realise fully the potential of the two which preceded it. *Let's Wreck The Party* was a definitive, hard-rocking, intelligent punk record. After its release, James departed and was replaced on drums by Jon Card (ex-Personality Crisis and SNFU). Chris Prohourn aka 'Humper The Dumper' (guitar/vocals; ex-Red Tide) joined as well, when Dave Gregg started his own band, Groovaholics. Keithley, meanwhile, appeared alongside old friend Jello Biafra in the film *Terminal City Ricochet*, as a biker cop. DOA would subsequently record a ferocious album in tandem with the former Dead Kennedys' vocalist. Asked in 1994 if he saw himself as a punk Tom Jones (DOA having covered one of the Welshman's songs), Keithley offered this career summation: 'Well, DOA can't keep going on forever, though some people say it already has, but I gotta think of my career later on in life, y'know, down in Vegas and Reno.'

Albums: *Something Better Change* (Friend's 1980), *Hardcore '81* (Friend's 1981), *Let's Wreck The Party* (Alternative Tentacles 1985), *True (North) Strong And Free* (Rock Hotel/Profile 1987), *Murder* (Restless 1990), with Jello Biafra *Last Scream Of The Missing Neighbours* (Alternative Tentacles 1990, mini-album), *Talk Minus Action Equals Zero* (Roadrunner 1991), *13 Flavours Of Doom* (Alternative Tentacles 1992). Compilation: *Bloodied But Unbowed* (CD Presents 1984).

Video: *Assassination Club* (1984).

Doctor And The Medics

This psychedelic UK pop-rock outfit came to prominence in 1986 with a cover of Norman Greenbaum's 'Spirit In The Sky'. The single hit number 1 in the UK, but they found it difficult to consolidate their success, with the subsequent

'Burn' and 'Waterloo' only achieving UK chart placings of 29 and 46 respectively. *Laughing At The Pieces* peaked at number 25 in the charts, primarily on the back of major single success. Since then, every release has sunk without trace and the band were dropped by their label.

Albums: *Laughing At The Pieces* (1986), *Keep Thinking It's Thursday* (1987), *The Adventures Of Boadicea And The Beetle* (1993).

Doctors Of Madness

When punk exploded on an unsuspecting UK music scene in 1976, several relatively established bands waiting in the wings were somehow dragged along with it. The Doctors Of Madness were one such group. Comprising weirdo Richard 'Kid' Strange (vocals, guitar, keyboards, percussion), Stoner (bass, vocals, percussion), Peter (drums, percussion, vocals) and Urban (guitar, violin), the Doctors were already signed to Polydor Records and had issued two rock albums verging on the theatrical by late 1976: *Late Night Movies, All Night Brainstorms* and *Figments Of Emancipation*. Much of their momentum was lost, however, when they issued only one single in 1977, 'Bulletin', and it was not until 1978 that *Sons Of Survival* appeared. By that time, the post-punk era had arrived, awash with new ideas, and the Doctors Of Madness seemed acutely anachronistic. They broke up soon after, their career later summarized on a compilation, *Revisionism*. Richard Strange, meanwhile, set about an erratic but fascinating solo career, which included such singles as 'International Language' (1980) on Cherry Red Records and the narcissistically-entitled album, *The Phenomenal Rise Of Richard Strange* (1981), on Virgin Records.

Albums: *Late Night Movies, All Night Brainstorms* (Polydor 1976), *Figments Of Emancipation* (Polydor 1976), *Sons Of Survival* (Polydor 1978). Compilation: *Revisionism (1975-78)* (Polydor 1981).

Dodgy

A pop trio based in north London, the roots of Dodgy can be traced to mid-80s Birmingham, where Nigel Clarke (vocals/bass) joined local goth band Three Cheers For Tokyo, finding a musical ally in drummer Matthew Priest. Their shared tastes included The The's *Infected* album and a revulsion for their guitarist's Flying V exhibitionism. The pair relocated to London instead and placed an advert in *Loot* which read simply: 'Wanted: Jimi Hendrix'. Andy Miller (guitar) rallied to the call, and the trio moved to Hounslow. They spent a year there practising the three part harmonies which would become their trademark, and fighting over whose turn it was to empty the dustbin/ashtray. Taking the name Dodgy, the band played their first gig at the John Bull pub in Chiswick. Afterwards the 'Dodgy Club' was introduced. By taking over a Kingston wine bar, the group created their own weekly hangout with DJ's mixing up indie and dance cuts, with the band playing as the finalé. Guests included Oasis, Shed Seven and even Ralph McTell. The group's first demo, featuring an early take on 'Lovebird', won BBC disc jockey Gary Crowley's 'Demo Clash' for several consecutive weeks, before A&M Records requested their signatures. *The Dodgy Album*, filled with buoyant 60s-styled pop tunes, nevertheless failed to sell, though The

Dodgy Club was now being exported as far afield as Amsterdam and Scandinavia. 1994 was the group's breakthrough year, with *Homegrown* producing two memorable singles in 'Staying Out For The Summer' (a hit when reissued in 1995) and 'So Let Me Go Far'. Despite lacking any discernible image aside from that of three wide-eyed and unspoilt souls with a fondness for dressing down (matching red trousers apart) and big, eminently hummable songs, Dodgy were now welcome guests in both the charts and the pop press.

Albums: *The Dodgy Album* (A&M 1993), *Homegrown* (A&M 1994).

Doll

Formed in late 1977, this UK new wave group originally comprised Marion Valentine (b. 1952, Brighton, Sussex, England; vocals/guitar), Christos Yianni (b. 6 September 1954, London, England; bass), Adonis Yianni (b. 10 October 1957, London, England; keyboards) and Mario Watts (b. 1958, London, England; drums). After signing to Beggar's Banquet, the group issued 'Don't Tango My Heart', but it was their second single, infectious 'Desire Me' that propelled them into the UK charts in 1978. Inter-group politics, exacerbated by the inevitable promotion of their female singer and lyricist, caused several line-up changes. By the time they came to record their sole album, *Listen To The Silence*, Dennis Hayes (keyboard), Jamie West-Oram (guitar) and Paul Turner (drums) had joined. The group split soon after, and although it was expected that the feline Valentine (complete with leopard-skin guitar and jump-suit) would be launched as a solo, she concentrated instead on songwriting, eventually retiring from the music business.

Album: *Listen To The Silence* (1979).

Doll By Doll

Essentially a vehicle for singer Jackie Leven, this UK rock group was formed in 1977 and first came to the fore in 1979, riding on the coat-tails of the punk explosion, with *Remember*. An interesting debut, the work featured Leven's wide-ranging vocal work to startling effect. Despite constant line-up changes, which included Joe Shaw (guitar), David McIntosh (drums) and Robin Spreafico (bass, later replaced by Tony Waite), Leven's group produced some well-arranged albums during the early 80s but never quite crossed over into the mainstream. Their adoption of an unfashionable rock style, coupled with an uneasy relationship with the music press hampered the groups progress. Signed with Magnet Records, they released the accomplished *Doll By Doll* which provided them with a minor hit in 'Carita' (1981). With *Grand Passion*, Leven teamed up with vocalist Helen Turner for his most ambitious and experimental piece, but the critical reception proved lukewarm. On the break-up of the group, Leven continued under his own name.

Albums: *Remember* (1979), *Gypsy Blood* (1979), *Doll By Doll* (1981), *Grand Passion* (1982).

Dolly Mixture

This female UK pop trio comprised Debsey Wykes (b. 21 December 1960, Hammersmith, London, England; bass/piano/vocals), Rachel Bor (b. 16 May 1963, Wales;

Dodgy

guitar/cello/vocals) and Hester Smith (b. 28 October 1960, West Africa; drums). The group was formed by the three school-friends in Cambridge, with a musical style that echoed the Shangri-Las and the 70s Undertones. Championed by influential UK disc jockey, John Peel, the group released a cover of the Shirelles hit, 'Baby It's You' on the Chrysalis label in 1980 - which at the time of issue the group disowned, protesting at the label's attempted manipulation of their image. They were one of the first bands to record for Paul Weller's Respond label, releasing, 'Been Teen' (1981) and 'Everything And More' (1982), both of which were produced by Captain Sensible and Paul Gray of the Damned. The UK record-buying public found difficulty coming to terms with the trio's idiosyncratic mode of dress and independent attitude; something that some of the music press also had problems with. They proved their worth, however, in their exhilarating live performances. In 1982 they released a double album, on their own Dead Good Dolly Platters label, featuring demo tapes collected over the previous four years. The album has since achieved cult status among later 80s independent groups. Dolly Mixture eventually found national fame by acting as Sensible's backing vocalists on his UK number 1 single, 'Happy Talk', in 1982. They also guested on his subsequent singles and albums, while Rachel and the Captain formed a romantic partnership. Meanwhile, their own career floundered, despite the critical plaudits. The trio dissolved as a working band in 1984, leaving as their swan song *The Fireside EP*, released on Cordelia Records, a set consisting mainly of 'pop/chamber' music, featuring their often ignored talents on piano and cello. In 1986 Debsey and Hester resurfaced with Coming Up Roses.

Album: *The Demonstration Tapes* (Dead Good Dolly 1982, double album).

Done Lying Down

Led by Boston born Jeremy Parker (vocals/guitar), Done Lying Down are nevertheless a UK-based outfit who were widely venerated by a number of sources throughout 1994. The line-up filled out by English personnel Ali Mac (bass), Glen Young (guitar) and James Sherry (drums), their list of achievements in that year included a series of EPs (*Heart Of Dirt*, *Family Values*, *Negative One Friends* and *Just A Misdemeanour*) which brought gradually increasing indie chart returns, radio sessions for John Peel, and video appearances on UK television's *Chart Show*, alongside feverish touring with Girls Against Boys, Compulsion, Ned's Atomic Dustbin and many others. The first of their EPs, released in 1993, was produced by Membranes/Sensurround leader and journalist John Robb. The three tracks were headed by 'Dissent', a forceful cut accentuated by a stop-start construction reminiscent of Nirvana (a comparison which stuck to the band throughout the course of their early career). An album, *John Austin Rutledge*, was named after a friend of Parker who co-wrote some of the songs therein: 'All he wanted was a credit, but we decided to name it after him and put his photo on the cover!', advised a slightly contrary Parker.

Album: *John Austin Rutledge* (Black And White Indians/Abstract 1994).

Dr Phibes And The House Of Wax Equations

Formed in the late 80s at South Cheshire College of Further Education, where they all studied music, Dr Phibes quickly became one of the north west's most important dance bands. The name is taken from two separate Hammer Horror films. The band comprise Howard King Jnr. (vocals/guitars), Lee Belsham (bass), and Keith York (drums). Their vinyl debut came with the 1990 12-inch 'Sugarblast', which preceded their long playing debut in April 1991. Topping the independent charts for two weeks, it generated significant media coverage and critical acclaim. Their music is an eclectic, but primarily rhythmic mix, of blues, funk and psychedelia. Recording sessions for their second album were disturbed when Belsham injured a shoulder. His colleague York drove off in their van, unbeknownst to Belsham who was still lying on top of it. At the time of writing the band desperately needs a successful second album to launch them out of the ghetto of cult popularity they currently inhabit. Albums: *Whirlpool* (1991), *Hypnotwister* (1993).

Dream Syndicate

The early 80s were an exciting time for those with a taste for American west coast rock. Several aspiring new acts appeared in the space of a few months that were obviously indebted to the late 60s, but managed to offer something refreshingly vital in the process. The Dream Syndicate's debut, *The Days Of Wine And Roses* (recorded in September 1982), more than justified the attention that the 'paisley underground' bands were attracting. Consisting of songwriter Steve Wynn (guitar/vocals), Karl Precoda (guitar), Kendra Smith (bass) and Dennis Duck (drums), the band chose their finest song, 'Tell Me When It's Over', for their first UK single, issued on Rough Trade Records in late 1983. A deal with A&M Records followed, and *Medicine Show* appeared in 1984. Like their debut, there was a definite acknowledgement to the influence of both Lou Reed and Neil Young. By this time, though, Kendra Smith had joined partner David Roback in Opal. *This Is Not The New Dream Syndicate Album*, released the following year, recycled their early recordings live, but it was to be their last engagement with A&M. Another move, this time to Chrysalis Records' offshoot Big Time, resulted in *Out Of The Grey* a year later, but the band's approach was gradually shifting to the mainstream. After a 12-inch single, '50 In A 25 Zone', the Dream Syndicate moved to the Enigma Records label, distributed in the UK by Virgin Records. 1988's *Ghost Stories* was followed by 'I Have Faith', and then came a live swansong offering, *Live At Raji's*, in 1989. However, the band never surpassed the dizzy heights of their first album, leaving Wynn to go on to a similarly acclaimed but commercially unsuccessful solo career.

Albums: *The Days Of Wine And Roses* (Ruby 1982), *Medicine Show* (A&M 1984), *This Is Not The New Dream Syndicate Album* (A&M 1984, live mini-album), *Out Of The Grey* (Big Time 1986), *Ghost Stories* (Enigma 1988), *Live At Raji's* (Restless 1989). Compilation: *It's Too Late To Stop Now* (Fan Club 1989).

DRI

This thrash metal band were formed in Houston, Texas,

USA, in 1982. The band's original line-up consisted of Kurt Brecht (vocals), Spike Cassidy (guitar), Dennis Johnson (bass) and Kurt's brother, Eric Brecht (drums). Originally calling themselves Dirty Rotten Imbeciles, they shortened it to DRI and signed to Roadrunner Records in the UK. In the US they would first use their own indpendent label, subsequently signing with Metal Blade/Enigma. Their debut album, *Dirty Rotten LP,* was released in 1984, and preceded the band's relocation to San Francisco. It quickly established DRI at the forefront of their genre with its vicious mixture of punk, hardcore and thrash metal (Slayer's Dave Lombardo would cite them as a major influence). Before the next album, *Dealing With It,* founder member Eric Brecht left the band to be replaced by Felix Griffin, though this was only one of numerous personnel changes over the band"s lifetime. DRI continued to bridge punk and metal audiences, even going as far as to call their third album *Crossover.* They would eventually move into a more traditional speed metal style for the release of *Four Of A Kind* in 1988. Perhaps to remind their fans of their 'roots', the band re-mixed and re-released the *Dirty Rotten LP* in the same year, also including four extra tracks which had originally been released as an EP, *Violent Pacification,* back in 1984. Soon after this the band hit problems on a short tour of Mexico as new bass player John Menor was viciously attacked and robbed. However, this did not deter the band from producing their most accomplished album to date, *Thrash Zone,* though it would prove to be their swansong.
Albums: *Dirty Rotten LP* (Rotten 1984), *Dealing With It* (Metal Blade/Enigma 1985), *Crossover* (Metal Blade/Enigma 1987), *Four Of A Kind* (Metal Blade/Enigma 1988), *Dirty Rotten LP* (Rotten/Roadrunner 1988, remixed version of debut with 4 extra tracks), *Thrash Zone* (Metal Blade/Enigma 1989).
Video: *Live At The Ritz* (1989).

Drones

Very few punk bands actually stuck to their principles and shunned the lurid advances of the major record companies. Whether the Drones from Manchester, England, were such a band, or whether they were never given the opportunity, is debatable. Either way, the band issued three singles and an ephemeral album that now seems to personify the new wave. Second division punk they may have been, but they were exciting and vital nonetheless. The Drones' humble recording career began with an EP on the Ohm label, *Temptations Of A White Collar Worker,* in the spring of 1977. The release of 'Bone Idol' on their own Valer label later in the year was swiftly followed by a rough but enthusiastic album, entitled *Further Temptations.* The group ended the year with the inclusion on the Beggars Banquet Records sampler, *Streets.* After that, M.J. Drone (lead vocals/rhythm guitar), Gus Callender (Gangrene to his friends; lead guitar/vocals), Pete Perfect (drums) and Steve 'Whisper' Cundall (bass) kept a low profile, turning up on the essential live punk document, *Short Circuit - Live At The Electric Circus,* in mid-1978. After a final single, 'Can't See' on the Fabulous label in 1980, the band struggled on, breaking-up finally in 1981.
Album: *Further Temptations* (Valer 1977).

Droogs

Formed in 1972, this Los Angeles-based group initially included Rich Albin (vocals), Roger Clay (guitar/vocals), Paul Motter (bass) and Kyle Raven (drums). Unashamedly inspired by 60s garage bands, the quartet founded their own label, Plug & Socket, on which they recorded cover versions of favourite songs and originals inspired by their heroes. Having completed a mere six singles in the space of 10 years, during which time the group's rhythm section underwent several changes, the Droogs found themselves avatars of the then in-vogue 'Paisley Underground' scene. *Stone Cold World* was sadly obscured in the flurry to praise Green On Red, the Long Ryders and Bangles, but Albin and Clay doggedly pursued their chosen direction when the fashion faded. *Want Something,* issued following a protracted absence, featured material by John Hiatt, the Kinks and Peter Holsapple (of the dB's), and continued the unit's dalliance with psychedelic guitar pop.
Albums: *Stone Cold World* (1984), *Kingdom Day* (1987), *Want Something* (1991).

Drugstore

Led by Isabel Monterio (b. Sao Paulo, Brazil; vocals/bass), who relocated to England in 1990, Drugstore are a London three-piece specialising in dreamy but occasionally spiteful punk pop. They additionally comprise Daron Robinson (guitar) and Mike Chylinski (drums), Monterio meeting the latter, previously in a series of Los Angeles rock bands, after she had played bass in minor London groups. Drugstore came to nation-wide prominence at the 1994 Phoenix Festival, at which Monterio took the stage in the national football strip of Brazil (this being only one of several unusual stage costumes adopted). This was enough to gain the attention of Go! Discs, who signed the band following the release of just one single ('Alive') on their own Honey label (just before Robinson had joined the band). Tours with Gene, Tindersticks and Echobelly followed as did second single 'Modern Pleasures', before the advent of a debut album in 1995. With their vocalist proffering highly unusual lyrical matter with a delivery akin to Mazzy Star, there was delicious menace behind the seductive sound (sample lyric from *Drugstore* - 'I've still got the knife that I used to get rid of that guy' - from 'Nectarine'). A complementary single, 'Solitary Party Groover', earned numerous Single Of The Week awards as Drugstore's rise continued.
Album: *Drugstore* (Honey/Go! Discs 1995).

Drum Theatre

This cosmopolitan UK-based group comprised Kent B. (drums/keyboards), Gari Tarn (drums/vocals), Paul Snook (drums/bass guitar). Originally a very exciting visual act, they boasted six members, all of whom played the drums at some point. By the time the band were signed to a recording contract they had been slimmed down to a trio. They received attention when their first single of 1986, 'Living In The Past' made a small impact on the UK charts, while they were supporting the Human League on a European tour. The reissue of their 1985 single 'Eldorado', in 1987 received plenty of radio airplay and just missed the Top 40, and their debut album was released to mixed reaction and poor sales.

The same fate met their subsequent singles.
Album: *Everyman* (1987).

Drummond, Bill

b. 29 April 1953, Butterworth, South Africa. After relocating to Scotland as a child, Drummond rose to fame in the music business during the late 70s rock renaissance in Liverpool. Drummond formed the Merseyside trio, Big In Japan, which lasted from 1977-78. Drummond subsequently founded the influential Zoo Record label and backed Lori Larty in Lori And The Chameleons. He then enjoyed considerable success as a manager overseeing the affairs of Echo And The Bunnymen and the Teardrop Explodes. When the Liverpool group scene saw artists moving south, Drummond left the city, and during the next decade was involved in a number of bizarre projects, which testified to his imagination and love of novelty. The controversial JAMMS (Justified Ancients Of Mu Mu), whose irreverent sampling was extremely innovative for the period, was a typical example of Drummond's pseudonymous mischief. The chart-topping Timelords was another spoof and, by the 90s, Drummond found himself at the heart of the creative sampling technology with the critically acclaimed and best-selling KLF. Along the way, the eccentric entrepreneur even managed to record a minor solo album, most notable for the track 'Julian Cope Is Dead', an answer song to the former Teardrop Explodes singer's witty 'Bill Drummond Said'.
Album: *The Man* (1987).

Dub War

A collision of ragga and punk, shot through with steely metallic guitar, Dub War emerged in 1994 as a high octane, highly political extension of hard rock's new found ability to merge new styles with old. Formed in Newport, Wales, in 1993, the four-piece, who comprise Jeff Rose (guitar), Richie Glover (bass), Martin Ford (drums) and Benji (vocals), all came from diverse musical backgrounds. Glover had played in several minor punk bands, while Benji's apprenticeship came in reggae dancehalls, and he had previously worked with Mad Professor. The group made its debut at the end of 1993 with a self-titled 12-inch EP, which simultaneously managed to appear in three different *New Musical Express* charts - the 'Vibes', 'Turn Ons' and 'Hardcore' listings. Following a debut mini-album in 1994, they switched to Earache Records for the *Mental* EP, joining Pop Will Eat Itself and Manic Street Preachers on touring engagements. *Mental* featured remixes from Senser, Brand New Heavies and Jamiroquai, and was followed by a further EP, *Gorrit*. Their first full album came in February 1995 with *Pain*, by which time the band had established a strong live following to augment their press profile.
Albums: *Dub Warning* (1994, mini-album), *Pain* (Earache 1995).

Dugites

The Dugites emerged from Perth, Australia in 1978, at the tail-end of punk, and in the middle of a period heralding the arrival of several other other Australian bands which featured female lead singers, such as the Eurogliders, Divinyls and Do Ré Mi. While their early material was naive pop, their later work glistened with good production values and good playing, and deserved better recognition. Their first single, the plaintive 'In My Car' charted, but by the time the band gelled and matured for their last excellent album, their audience had lost interest.
Albums: *The Dugites* (1980), *West Of The World* (1981), *Cut The Talking* (1984).

Dukes Of Stratosphear

An alter ego of XTC, this group was a vehicle for Andy Partridge's psychedelic frustrations of being born a decade or two out of time. Both albums released so far contain brilliant pastiches of virtually every pop band during the mid-to late 60s. In many cases the Dukes' tongue-in-cheek parables are far superior to the songs to which they are gently alluding. It was suggested that their albums actually outsold the XTC product available at the same time.
Albums: *25 O'Clock* (1985), *Psonic Psunspot* (1987). Compilation: *Chips From The Chocolate Fireball* (Virgin 1987).

Durutti Column

One of the more eclectic bands to emerge from Manchester's punk scene, Vini Reilly (b. Vincent Gerard Reilly, August 1953, Manchester, England) and his Durutti Column combined elements of jazz, electronic and even folk in their multitude of releases. However Vini's musical beginnings were as guitarist in more standard 1977 hopefuls Ed Banger And The Nosebleeds. Two other groups from 1977 - Fastbreeder and Flashback - had since merged into a new group, who were being managed by Manchester television presenter and Factory Records founder, Anthony Wilson. Wilson invited Reilly to join guitarist Dave Rowbotham and drummer Chris Joyce in January 1978, and together they became the Durutti Column (after a political cartoon strip used by the SI in Strasbourg during the 60s). They were joined by vocalist Phil Rainford and bass player Tony Bowers and recorded for the famous 'A Factory Sampler EP' with the late Martin Hannett producing. These were the only recordings made by this line-up and the band broke up. Reilly carried on with the Durutti Column alone, while the others (except Rainford) formed the Moth Men. The debut *The Return Of The Durutti Column* appeared on Factory in 1980 and was largely recorded by Reilly, although Hannett, Pete Crooks (bass), and Toby (drums) also contributed. Durutti Column soon established a solid cult following, particularly abroad, where Reilly's moving instrumental work was widely appreciated. Live appearances had been sporadic, however, as Reilly suffered from an eating disorder and was frequently too ill to play. The album was notable for its sandpaper sleeve, inspired by the anarchist movement Situationist Internatiside. Reilly and producer Hannett helped out on Pauline Murray's first solo album later in 1980. The Durutti Column's own recordings over the next few years were a mixed batch recorded by Reilly with assistance from drummers Donald Johnson, then Bruce Mitchell (ex-Alberto Y Lost Trios Paranoias), Maunagh Flemin and Simon Topping on horns, and much later further brass players Richard Henry, Tim Kellett, and Mervyn Fletcher plus violinist Blaine Reininger and celloist

Caroline Lavelle. Dozens of other musicians have joined the nucleus of Reilly and Mitchell over the years and the band are still active today. A striking example of late period Durutti Column was captured on *Vini Reilly*, released in 1989. The guitarist cleverly incorporated the sampled voices of Joan Sutherland, Tracy Chapman, Otis Redding and Annie Lennox into a moving world of acoustic/electric ballads. Reilly has also lent some mesmerizing guitar to a host of recordings by artists such as Anne Clarke and Richard Jobson, and fellow Mancunian and friend Morrissey. On 8 November 1991, former Durutti guitarist Dave Rowbotham was discovered axed to death at his Manchester home. A murder hunt followed.

Albums: *The Return Of The Durutti Column* (Factory 1980), *Another Setting* (Factory 1983), *Live At The Venue London* (VU 1983), *Amigos En Portugal* (Fundacio Atlantica 1984, live album), *Without Mercy* (Factory 1984), *Domo Arigato* (Factory 1985), *Circuses And Bread* (Factory 1986), *The Guitar And Other Machines* (Factory 1987), *Live At The Bottom Line New York* (ROIR 1987, cassette only), *Vini Reilly* (Factory 1989), *Obey The Time* (Factory 1990), *Lips That Would Kiss Form Prayers To Broken Stone* (Factory 1991), *Dry* (Materiali Sonori 1991). Compilations: *Valuable Passages* (Factory 1986), *The Durutti Column - The First Four Albums* (Factory 1988). As Vini Reilly: *The Sporadic Recordings* (Sporadic 1989).

Dury, Ian

b. 12 May 1942, Upminster, Essex, England. The zenith of Dury's musical career, *New Boots And Panties*, came in 1977, when youth was being celebrated amid power chords and bondage trousers - he was 35 at the time. Stricken by polio at the age of seven, he initially decided on a career in art, and until his 28th birthday taught the subject at Canterbury School of Art. He began playing pubs and clubs in London with Kilburn And The High Roads, reinterpreting R&B numbers and later adding his own wry lyrics in a semi-spoken cockney slang. The group dissolved and the remainder became a new line-up called the Blockheads. In 1975 Stiff Records signed the group and considered Dury's aggressive but honest stance the perfect summary of the contemporary mood. The Blockheads' debut and finest moment, *New Boots And Panties*, received superlative reviews and spent more than a year in the UK albums chart. His dry wit, sensitivity and brilliant lyrical caricatures were evident in songs like 'Clever Trevor', 'Wake Up And Make Love To Me' and his tribute to Gene Vincent, 'Sweet Gene Vincent'. He lampooned the excesses of the music business on 'Sex And Drugs And Rock And Roll' and briefly crossed over from critical acclaim to commercial acceptance with the UK number 1 'Hit Me With Your Rhythm Stick' in December 1979. *Do It Yourself* and *Laughter* were similarly inspired although lacking the impact of his debut, and by his third album he had teamed up with Wilko Johnson (ex-Dr. Feelgood) and lost the co-writing services of pianist Chaz Jankel. He continued to work towards a stronger dance context and employed the masterful rhythm section of Sly Dunbar and Robbie Shakespeare on *Lord Upminster* which also featured the celebrated jazz trumpeter Don Cherry. He continued to make thoughtful, polemic records in the 80s

and audaciously suggested that his excellent song, 'Spasticus Autisticus', should be adopted as the musical emblem of the Year Of The Disabled. Like many before him, he turned to acting and appeared in several television plays and films in the late 80s. In 1989 he wrote the musical *Apples* with another former member of the Blockheads, Mickey Gallagher. In the 90s Dury was seen hosting a late night UK television show *Metro* and continued to tour, being able to dictate his own pace.

Albums: *New Boots And Panties* (1977), *Do It Yourself* (1979), *Laughter* (1980), *Lord Upminster* (1981), *Juke Box Dury* (1981), *4,000 Weeks Holiday* (1984), *The Bus Driver's Prayer And Other Stories* (1992). Compilation: *Greatest Hits* (1981).

Easterhouse

Formed in Manchester, England, by the Perry brothers, singer Andy and guitarist Ivor, during the mid-80s, Easterhouse first came to prominence after being championed by Morrissey of the Smiths. Taking their name from a working-class area of Glasgow, they signed to Rough Trade Records and were widely praised for early singles 'Inspiration' and 'Whistling In The Dark', which merged Andy's left wing political rhetoric with Ivor's echo-laden guitar patterns. *Contenders*, a confident debut, also featured Peter Vanden (bass), Gary Rostock (drums) and Mike Murray (rhythm guitar). Contained within were entirely convincing accomodations between music and politics - the hard line of Andy Perry's lyrics exemplified by the bitter assault on the betrayal of the working class by Britain's labour party in the compelling 'Nineteen Sixty Nine'. Arguments broke out soon after its release and Ivor Perry went on to form the short-lived Cradle. Andy Perry kept the name Easterhouse, but by the time of *Waiting For The Red Bird* he was the only remaining original band member. He was joined on theis disappointing, over-ambitious record by David Verner (drums), Neil Taylor (lead guitar), Lance Sabin (rhythm guitar) and Steve Lovell (lead guitar). 'Come Out Fighting', with its anthemic rock pretensions failed to make the singles chart and the new Easterhouse, with all songs written solely by Perry, was heavily criticized: the political content was still high with tracks like 'Stay With Me (Death On The Dole)' but the soul and subtle melodies were no longer present. Easterhouse's impact was, aside from one great album, probably minimal, but along with other Manchester guitar groups like the Chameleons, they laid the foundations for the later explosion of interest in the city in the late 80s.

Albums: *Contenders* (Rough Trade 1986), *Waiting For The Red Bird* (Rough Trade 1989).

Easy

If Abba had stereotyped Sweden with a boy/girl pop tag since the early 70s, Easy seemed the most likely fellow countrymen to make the international scene look at the Scandinavian nation in a new light. Formerly known as TV Pop Crisis, Easy was formed in 1990 with Johan Holmlund (b. 13 July 1965, Jonkoping, Sweden; vocals), Tommy Ericson (b. 23 March 1966, Umea, Sweden), Anders Peterson (b. 12 November 1965, Jonkoping, Sweden), Rikard Jormin (b. 2 August 1965, Jonkoping, Sweden) and Tommy Jonsson (b. 15 June 1966, Vastervik, Sweden). Because the band was heavily influenced by the noisier British acts such as the Jesus And Mary Chain, it was a logical move for the quintet to sign to the UK arm of Blast First records. Similarly, Easy relished the opportunity to tour the British mainland and, thanks to support slots with Lush, the Charlatans and House Of Love, the group gouged a small but significant niche in the independent pop market by virtue of their moody guitar growls. It proved to be a temporary assignation however, and the group retreated to Sweden shortly thereafter.

Album: *Magic Seed* (Blast First 1990).

Eat

Based in King's Cross, London, Eat first formed in 1986, though their roots were in the picturesque location of Bath, Avon, rather than the squats of the capital. With music described as 'Louisiana swamp mindfuck blues', they signed to Fiction Records, initially on a one-off contract for the *Autogift* EP. The band, comprising brothers Paul and Max Nobel (guitar), Ange Dolittle (vocals), Tim Sewell (bass) and Pete Howard (drums), soon ingratiated themselves with their north London following by playing frequently at the underground Mutoid Waste events, while both Paul Nobel and Sewell could be found DJing at warehouse parties during the rise of acid house. There was always an endearing quality to the band; at a gig at London's Borderline club in its opening week they handed cash out to the audience after deciding the entrance fee was 'a rip off'. Disc jockey John Peel regularly played one track from the debut, 'Skin', leading to a full five album contract with Fiction Records and a second EP, *The Plastic Bag Tour*. This time pinned around the anti-yuppie anthem, 'Babyboom', it further revealed the depth of the band, with Dolittle' vocals distinctively cast through a Bullit harmonica microphone. Always a somewhat fractious band, after their debut album there was a split between the Nobel brothers and the rest of Eat in November 1990 (the second album was consequently delayed). As Dolittle pointed out: 'It got to the point where we just couldn't bear to be in the same room as each other'. Paul and Max Nobel would form TV Eye. In 1991 the band were reformed with Dolittle joined by former members Sewell and Howard, plus guitarists Jem Moorshead and Maz Lavilla. The cover of 1992's *Gold Egg* EP showed Dolittle naked with his privates airbrushed out, causing complaints from various councils who vowed not to put up the posters. The singer also exposed himself on stage with the Wonder

Stuff, a band rarely outdone in on-stage excess. However, despite generally positive reviews for 1993's *Epicure*, much of the momentum earned on tours with the aforementioned band and James had evidently elapsed. In 1995 Doolittle would join with former members of the Wonder Stuff to become Weknowhereyoulive.

Albums: *Sell Me A God* (Fiction 1989), *Epicure* (Fiction 1993).

Eater

This UK punk rock band formed in 1976 while the band members were still at school. Comprising Andy Blade (vocals), Dee Generate (drums), Brian Chevette (guitar) and Ian Woodcock (bass), they made their vinyl debut with '15' (a bastardized version of Alice Cooper's 'Eighteen'), on *The Roxy, London W.C.2.* compilation, recorded during the spring of 1977. With equipment purchased from Woolworths, they were picked up by The Label, which released five singles including 'Outside View' and 'Lock It Up', with the latter featuring a dire version of T. Rex's 'Jeepster' on the b-side. An album followed later the same year, but it only served to further highlight the band's obvious musical limitations. For all that Eater are fondly remembered by many for being the epitome of punk's orignal 'get up and go' ethos.

Albums: *The Album* (The Label 1977), *The History Of Eater Vol.1* (DeLorean 1985).

Echo And The Bunnymen

The origins of this renowned 80s Liverpool, England group can be traced back to the spring of 1977 when vocalist Ian McCulloch (b. 5 May 1959, Liverpool, England) was a member of the Crucial Three with Julian Cope and Pete Wylie. While the last two later emerged in the Teardrop Explodes and Wah!, respectively, McCulloch put together his major group at the end of 1978. Initially a trio the group featured McCulloch, Will Sergeant (b. 12 April 1958, Liverpool, England; guitar); Les Patterson (b. 18 April 1958, Ormskirk, Merseyside, England; bass) and a drum machine which they christened 'Echo'. After making their first appearance at the famous Liverpool club, Eric's, they made their vinyl debut in March 1979 with 'Read It In Books', produced by whizz kid entrepreneurs Bill Drummond and Dave Balfe. The production was sparse but intriguing and helped the group to establish a sizeable cult following. McCulloch's brooding live performance and vocal inflections were already drawing comparisons with the Doors' Jim Morrison. After signing to Korova Records (distributed by Warner Brothers) they replaced 'Echo' with a human being: Pete De Freitas (b. 2 August 1961, Port Of Spain, Trinidad, West Indies, d. 14 June 1989). The second single, 'Rescue', was a considerable improvement on its predecessor, with a confident, driving sound that augured well for their forthcoming album. *Crocodiles* proved impressive with a wealth of strong arrangements and compulsive guitar work. After the less melodic single, 'The Puppet', the group toured extensively and issued an EP, *Shine So Hard*, which crept into the UK Top 40. The next album, *Heaven Up Here*, saw them regaled by the music press. Although a less accessible and melodic work than its predecessor, it sold well and topped numerous polls. *Porcupine* reinforced the group's appeal, while 'The Cutter' gave them their biggest hit so far. In 1984 they charted again with 'The Killing Moon', an excellent example of McCulloch's ability to summon lazy melodrama out of primary lyrical colours. The epic quality of his writing remained perfectly in keeping with the group's grandiloquent musical character. The accompanying 1984 album, *Ocean Rain*, broadened their appeal further and brought them into the US Top 100 album charts. In February 1986 De Freitas left the group to be replaced by former Haircut 100 drummer, Mark Fox, but he returned the following September. However, it now seemed the band's best days were behind them. The uninspiringly titled *Echo And The Bunnymen* drew matching lacklustre performances, while a version of the Doors' 'People Are Strange' left both fans and critics perplexed. This new recording was produced by Ray Manzarek, who also played on the track, and it was used as the haunting theme for the cult film, *The Lost Boys* (1989). Yet, as many noted, there were simply dozens of better Bunnymen compositions which could have benefitted from that type of exposure. In 1988 McCulloch made the announcement that he was henceforth pursuing a solo career. While he completed the well-received *Candleland*, the Bunnymen made the unexpected decision to carry on. Large numbers of audition tapes were listened to before they chose McCulloch's successor, Noel Burke, a Belfast boy who had previously recorded with St Vitus Dance. Just as they were beginning rehearsals, De Frietas was tragically killed in a road accident. The group struggled on, recruiting new drummer Damon Reece and adding road manager Jake Brockman on guitar/synthesizer. In 1992 they introduced the next phase of Bunnymen history with *Reverberation*, but public expectations were not high and the critics unkind, and it was to be a final instalment. The Bunnymen Mark II broke up in the summer of the same year, with Pattinson going on to work with Terry Hall while Sergeant conducted work on his ambient side project, B*O*M, and formed Glide for one single. McCulloch, whose solo career had stalled after a bright start, and Sergeant would eventually work together again from 1993 as Electrafixion, also pulling in Reece from the second Bunnymen incarnation.

Albums: *Crocodiles* (Korova 1980), *Heaven Up Here* (Korova 1981), *Porcupine* (Korova 1983), *Ocean Rain* (Korova 1984), *Echo And The Bunnymen* (WEA 1987), *Reverberation* (Korova 1990). Compilation: *Songs To Learn And Sing* (Korova 1985), *Live In Concert* (Windsong 1991), *The Cutter* (WEA 1993). Solo: Will Sergeant: *Themes For Grind* (92 Happy Customers 1983); Ian McCulloch: *Candleland* (WEA 1988), *Mysterio* (WEA 1992).

Echobelly

This stylish UK indie pop band consist of Anglo-Asian singer Sonya Aurora Madan, guitarists Glenn Johansson (b. Sweden) and Debbie Smith (ex-Curve), Andy Henderson (drums) and Alex Keyser (bass). After breaking the UK Top 40 with 'I Can't Imagine The World Without Me', the group

Echobelly

was quickly adopted by the British music media, who saw in Madan a new and articulate role model. The group also began to make friends in the USA by appearing at New York's New Music Seminar, leading to a deal with Sony Records. On the album's release *Vox* magazine said they had made 'a storming debut album by a major new British pop group'.
Album: *Everyone's Got One* (Rhythm King 1994).

Eddie And The Hot Rods

Formed in 1975, this quintet from Southend, Essex, England, originally comprised Barrie Masters (vocals), Lew Lewis (harmonica), Paul Gray (bass), Dave Higgs (guitar), Steve Nicol (drums) plus 'Eddie', a short-lived dummy that Masters pummelled on stage. After one classic single, 'Writing On The Wall', Lewis left, though he appeared on the high energy 'Horseplay', the flip-side of their cover of Sam The Sham And The Pharoahs' 'Wooly Bully'. Generally regarded as a younger, more energetic version of Dr. Feelgood, the Rods pursued a tricky route between the conservatism of pub rock and the radicalism of punk. During the summer of 1976, the group broke house records at the Marquee Club with a scorching series of raucous, sweat-drenched performances. Their power was well captured on a live EP which included a cover of ? And The Mysterians' '96 Tears' and a clever amalgamation of the Rolling Stones' 'Satisfaction' and Them's 'Gloria'. The arrival of guitarist Graeme Douglas from the Kursaal Flyers gave the group a more commercial edge and a distinctive jingle-jangle sound. A guest appearance on former MC5 singer Robin Tyner's 'Till The Night Is Gone' was followed by the strident 'Do Anything You Want To Do', which provided a Top 10 hit in the UK. A fine second album, *Life On The Line*, was striking enough to suggest a long term future, but the group fell victim to diminishing returns. Douglas left, followed by Gray, who joined the Damned. Masters disbanded the group for a spell but reformed the unit for pub gigs and small label appearances.
Albums: *Teenage Depression* (Island 1976), *Life On The Line* (Island 1977), *Thriller* (Island 1979), *Fish 'N' Chips* (EMI America 1980). Compilations: *The Curse Of The Rods* (Hound Dog 1990), *Live And Rare* (Receiver 1993).

Edge

This UK group was formed in 1978 by former Damned members Jon Moss (b. 11 September 1957, London, England; drums) and guitarist Lu Edmunds. They were joined by bassist Glyn Havard and pianist Gavin Povey. Although they gigged extensively and undertook studio work, backing Kirsty MacColl on the single 'They Don't Know' and touring as Jane Aire And The Belvederes, their own work was largely ignored. They issued three singles ('Macho Man', 'Downhill' and 'Watching You') during the late 70s, and issued the album *Square 1* in 1980 before disbanding. Moss went on to join Culture Club, while Edmunds teamed-up with Athletico Spizz 80 and later the Mekons. The remaining members returned to session work.
Album: *Square 1* (1980). Compilation: *The Moonlight Tapes* (1980).

808 State

Manchester's finest dance combo of the late 80s/early 90s, comprising Martin Price (b. 26 March 1955), owner of the influential Eastern Bloc record shop, Graham Massey (b. 4 August 1960, Manchester, Lancashire, England; ex-Beach Surgeon, Danny & The Dressmakers, Biting Tongues), Darren Partington (b. 1 November 1969, Manchester, Lancashire, England) and Andy Barker (b. 2 November 1969, Manchester, Lancashire, England). The final two had already worked together as DJ double act the Spin Masters. Massey had previously worked in a cafe opposite the Eastern Bloc shop, while Partington and Barker had been regular visitors to the premises, proffering a variety of tapes in the hope of getting a deal with Price's Creed label. Together with Gerald Simpson, they began recording together as a loose electro house collective, and rose to prominence at the end of 1989 when their single, 'Pacific State', became a massive underground hit. It proved to be a mixed blessing for the band, however, as they were lumped in with the pervading Manchester indie dance boom (a term they despised). *Newbuild* and *Quadrastate* helped to establish them as premier exponents of UK techno dance, leading to a lucrative deal with ZTT Records. However, Simpson had left to form his own A Guy Called Gerald vehicle, and launched a series of attacks on the band concerning unpaid royalties in the press. *Ex:El* featured the vocals of New Order's Bernard Sumner on 'Spanish Heart', and then-Sugarcube Björk Gudmundsdottir on 'Oops' (also a single) and 'Qmart'. They also worked with Mancunian rapper MC Tunes on the LP *North At Its Heights* and several singles. In October 1991 Price declined to tour the US with the band electing to work on solo projects instead, including managing Rochdale rappers the Kaliphz, and his own musical project, Switzerland. 808 State persevered with another fine album in 1993, which again saw a new rash of collaborations. Featured this time were Ian McCulloch (ex-Echo And The Bunnymen) adding vocals to 'Moses', and samples from the Jam's 'Start', UB40's 'One In Ten' and even *Star Wars*' Darth Vader. 1995 saw the announcement of plans for a new 808 State album in the autumn, while Massey occupied himself with co-writing Björk's 'Army Of Me' single.
Albums: *Newbuild* (Creed 1988), *Quadrastate* (Creed 1989), *808:90* (Creed 1989), *Ex:El* (ZTT 1991), *Gorgeous* (WEA 1993). With MC Tunes: *North At Its Heights* (ZTT 1990).

18 Wheeler

Formed in Scotland, 18 Wheeler consist of Sean Jackson (guitar/vocals), Neil Halliday (drums), Alan Hake (bass) and Steven Haddow (guitar). They released two singles, 'Nature Girl' and 'Suncrush', which bore the obvious influence of Glasgow's early 80s Postcard Records' scene. They were followed in 1994 by 'Kum Back' and 'The Revealer'. On the debut album their familiar bubblegum pop was allied to rhythms drawn from folk, country and dub. Described in the *Guardian* newspaper as '1994's lost pop classic', this was not widespread opinion as others saw the band as insubstantial and retrogressive. A more accomplished collection, *Formanka*, followed a year later, by which time the band's fortunes had been significantly outstripped by another Creation act, Oasis, who had once been third

18 Wheeler

support to 18 Wheeler at a gig in Glasgow.
Album: *Twin Action* (Creation 1994), *Formanka* (Creation 1995).

Einsturzende Neubaten

Formed out of the Berlin Arts Conglomerate Geniale Dilletanten, Einsturzende Neubaten made their live debut in April 1980. The line-up comprised Blixa Bargeld, N.U. Unruh, Beate Bartel and Gudrun Gut. Alexander Van Borsig, an occasional contributor, joined in time for the band's first single, 'Fur Den Untergang'. When Bartel and Gut departed to form Mania D and Matador they were replaced by F.M. (Mufti) and Einheit (ex-Abwarts). Einheit and Unruh formed the band's rhythmic backbone, experimenting with a variety of percussive effects, while Bargeld provided vocals and guitar. Their first official album (there were previously many tapes available) was *Kollaps*, a collage of sounds created by unusual rhythmic instruments ranging from steel girders to pipes and canisters. Their 1982 12-inch single, 'Durstiges Tier', involved contributions from the Birthday Party's Rowland S. Howard and Lydia Lunch, at which point Van Borsig had joined the band permanently as sound technician alongside new bass player Marc Chung (also ex-Abwarts). A British tour with the Birthday Party introduced them to Some Bizzare Records which released *Die Zeichnungen Das Patienten O.T.* 1984's *Strategien Gegen Architekturen* was compiled with Jim Thirlwell (Foetus), while the band performed live at the ICA in London. Joined by Genesis P. Orridge (Psychic TV), Frank Tovey (Fad Gadget) and Stevo (Some Bizzare), the gig ended violently and attracted heated debate in the press. Bargeld spent the rest of the year touring as bass player for Nick Cave, going on to record several studio albums as a Bad Seed. In 1987 Einsturzende Neubaten performed the soundtrack for *Andi*, a play at the Hamburg Schauspielhaus, and also released *Funf Auf Der Nach Oben Offenen Richterskala*. This was intended as a farewell album, but they, nevertheless, continued after its release. Bargeld's part-time career with the Bad Seeds continued, and in 1988 he featured alongside them in Wim Wenders' film *Angels Über Berlin*. Von Borsig, ironically, was now contributing to the work of Crime And The City Solution, featuring Cave's old Birthday Party colleagues. The band reunited, however, in time for 1989's *Haus Der Luge*.
Albums: *Kollaps* (Zick Zack 1981), *Die Zeichnungen Des Patienten O.T.* (Some Bizzare 1983), *Strategien Gegen Architekturen* (Mute 1984), *Half Mensch* (Some Bizzrre/Rough Trade 1985), *Funf Auf Nach Oben Offenen Richterskala* (Some Bizzare 1987), *Haus Der Luge* (Some Bizzare 1989), *Tabula Rasa* (Mute 1992), *Malediction* (Mute 1993).
Video: *Liebeslieder* (1993).

Elastica

One of the most prominent members of the 90s UK independent scene, Elastica are Justine Frischmann (b.

c.1970, Twickenham, London, England; vocals/guitar), Donna Matthews (bass), Justin Welch (drums) and Annie Holland (guitar). Frischmann is the daughter of a Hungarian refugee, while her mother's family ran a corner shop in Glasgow, before she attended a single sex private school in London. Some of Elastica's original notoriety sprang from the fact that Frischmann was in an early incarnation of Suede and was romantically linked with that group's singer, Brett Anderson, then Blur's Damon Albarn. Indeed, one of Elastica's songs, 'See That Animal' - the b-side to 'Connection' - was co-written with Anderson when both parties attended University College London. They lived together in a dilapidated north London house filled with 20 year old students, throwing mouldy plates into the garden rather than wash them, while Suede looked for a deal. She left in October 1991 just before they were signed: 'Bernard and Brett would refuse to have anything to do with what I'd written. In the end I thought they'd be a lot better off without me. And they were, unfortunately'. There was more to Elastica, however, than nepotism, as they demonstrated with a series of stunning singles after they formed as a result of Frischmann placing adverts in the British music press. Wearing punk and new wave influences as diverse as Adam And The Ants, Blondie and Bow Wow Wow on their sleeves, they nevertheless chose to avoid the New Wave Of The New Wave bandwagon, consolidating their appeal with a place on the bill of 1994's Reading Festival. 'Waking Up', practically a musical re-write of the Stranglers' 'No More Heroes', was nevertheless as exciting a single as any to hit the charts in early 1995. This, together with three earlier singles, was included on the group's debut album. While the chord sequences could too often be linked directly to particular antecedents - 'Line Up' and 'Connection's similarities to *Chairs Missing*-era Wire being the best of several examples (and one which resulted in a royalty settlement, as did 'Waking Up' with the Stranglers' publishers), Frischmann's lyrics fitted the post-feminist 90s perfectly, as 'Car Song' proved: 'You could call me a car lover, Cause I love it in a motor, Every shining bonnet, Makes me think of my back on it'. Critics also leaped on 'veiled' references to her past and present paramours: 'We were sitting there waiting and I told you my plan, You were far too busy writing lines that didn't scan'.

Album: *Elastica* (Deceptive 1995).

Electro Hippies

This eccentric 'grindcore' outfit formed in Liverpool, England, in 1988. Specializing in low-technology studio techniques, they went on to issue a sequence of albums for Peaceville, and, later, Necrosis. In each case, a distorted, bass-laden barrage was over-ridden by stomach-churning vocals that lacked both finesse and cohesion (though that was hardly the intention anyway). The group's initial line-up included the surname-less Simon (drums), Dom (bass/vocals) and Andy (guitar/vocals). Chaotic and extreme, Electro Hippies used their platform to chastise the whole

Elastica

recording industry. Their mantle was upheld in the first case by Radio 1 disc jockey John Peel, for whom the group recorded a July 1987 session consisting of some nine tracks. Titles such as 'Starve The City (To Feed The Poor)' and 'Mega-Armageddon Death Part 3' summed up both their appeal and limitations.

Albums: *Peel Sessions* (Strange Fruit 1987), *The Only Good Punk Is A Dead One* (Peaceville 1988), *Electro Hippies Live* (Peaceville 1989), *Play Loud Or Die* (Necrosis 1989). Compilation: *The Peaceville Recordings* (Peaceville 1989).

Electronic

This powerful UK duo comprised Johnny Marr (b. John Maher, 31 October 1963, Manchester-, England) and Bernard Sumner (b. 4 January 1956, Manchester, England), both formerly key members of very successful Manchester-based bands, the Smiths and New Order respectively. Although they first worked together in 1983, Electronic was not formed until 1989. A somewhat unlikely pairing, *Q* magazine commented, 'It was a marriage made not in heaven,' because of their previous mutual mistrust. After a brief period as guitarist for Matt Johnson's The The and work with various well-known artists, such as David Byrne and the Pretenders, Electronic marked Marr's move into more commercial territory. His instinct for infectious, melodic pop guitar and Sumner's songwriting and programming ability proved to be an effective combination. Their first single, 'Getting Away With It' was released in 1989 on Manchester's highly respected Factory Records and featured the Pet Shop Boys' Neil Tennant as guest vocalist. This inspired move helped the record to number 12 in the UK chart. The individual track records of the three musicians immediately gave the band a high profile, arousing the interest of both the press and the public. This attention was intensified by the excitement surrounding the 'baggy' dance scene emerging from Manchester and the city's explosion of new musical talent, sparked by bands such as Happy Mondays and the Stone Roses. Electronic capitalized on the new credibility that dance music had acquired and were influenced by the fusions that were taking place, using 'electronic' dance rhythms and indie guitar pop. In July 1991, a self-titled debut album followed two more UK Top 20 singles, 'Get The Message' and 'Feel Every Beat'. The singles were witty and distinctive and were praised by the critics. Not surprisingly, the album was also very well-received, reaching number 2 in the UK chart (number 1 the indie chart). After a short gap 'Disappointed' consolidated their early promise by reaching number 6 in the UK in June 1992. Intelligent, original and fashionably marrying the sounds of the guitar and the computer much was expected but did not arrive.

Album: *Electronic* (1991).

Eleventh Dream Day

This US group was formed in Chicago in the mid-80s and comprised Rick Rizzo (guitar/vocals), Janet Beveridge Bean (drums), Douglas McCombs (bass) and Baird Figi (guitar/vocals). Its brand of college-rock, in the mould of the Pixies and Dream Syndicate, drew on music from the 60s and 70s, with the guitar histrionics of Television, Neil Young

and Crazy Horse combined with a whiff of psychedelia. Signed to the Atlantic label, Eleventh Dream Day seemed set to break away from their cult-status in the 90s. This impetus was struck a blow early in 1991 when Figi quit and was replaced by Wink O'Bannon. *Lived To Tell* was recorded in a studio-converted Kentucky barn in an attempt to obtain the feeling of a live recording.

Albums: *Eleventh Dream Day* (1987), *Prairie School Freakout* (1989), *Beet* (1990), *Lived To Tell* (1991), *El Moodio* (1993).

EMF

Formed in the Forest of Dean, Gloucestershire, England, in 1989 EMF consist of James Atkin (b. 28 March 1969; vocals), Ian Dench (guitar/keyboards), Derry Brownson (keyboards/samples), Zak Foley (bass) and Mark Decloedt (drums), and Milf (DJ). All of them had previously been in local indie bands; Dench in Apple Mosaic, and Foley in the IUC's. The band claimed EMF stands for Epsom Mad Funkers or more controversially, and more attractive to the gutter press, Ecstasy Mother Fuckers. Parlophone Records countered that it stood for Every Mothers' Favourites, which is hard to believe given the band's notorious touring antics. Their record company signed them after just four gigs and without the advance warning of a demo. However, their opportunism was rewarded when debut single, 'Unbelievable', became a Top 5 UK hit. The follow-up, 'I Believe' was criticised in many quarters for being a straight rewrite, while many were also suggesting that the band had stolen Jesus Jones' pop/sample thunder. However, their ability to win over the teen-pop market was proven by debut album sales of over two million. Together with the aforementioned Jesus Jones, the band proved particularly successful in cracking the US, where they were bracketed as part of a new 'British Invasion'. The band ran into some trouble with Yoko Ono over 'Lies', where a sample of the voice of John Lennon's killer Mark Chapman reciting Lennon lyric 'Watching The Wheels' from his prison cell resulted in an out of court settlement of $15,000 and a retraction of the offending voice from subsequent pressings. Other samples proved less controversial, and included Radio 3 announcers and Kermit The Frog. 1992's *Stigma* disappointed with sales less than one fifth of its debut, a fact blamed by chief song writer Dench on an over-demanding schedule and tabloid controversy: 'It was a self-conscious record and deliberately anti-commercial. At least we got everything out of our system.' Their label encouraged the band to spend their time getting new material right, leaving to a near three year gap between 1992's *Unexplained* EP and 1995's *Cha Cha Cha*. Band suggestions for producer included Jim Foetus and Butch Vig, but these were eventually rejected in favour of Johnny Dollar, who had previously worked with Youssou N'Dour and Neneh Cherry.

Albums: *Schubert Dip* (Parlophone 1991), *Stigma* (Parlophone 1992), *Cha Cha Cha* (Parlophone 1995).

Emotionals

This charming but derivative pop group much in the mould of the Primitives and Darling Buds emerged from London, England, in the late 80s. Featuring Emma Vine (vocals), Pete Maher (guitar/vocals), Roz Laney (bass) and Kieron James (drums/percussion), the Emotionals was originally formed in Brixton in 1988. Vine and Maher had met at school, but were more interested in following Richard Hell And The Voidoids than attending lessons. They moved to London and, from the summer of that year, they began an exhaustive promotional campaign which has barely ceased since its inception. Winning early support from US disc jockey Rodney Bingenheimer and Blondie's Nigel Harrison, they signed to Native Records from whence their two rather average albums emerged. When Native went down the pan the Emotionals followed quickly thereafter.

Albums: *Personal Pleasure* (Native 1990), *In Response* (Native 1991).

Epic Soundtracks

Better known for starting art punk renegades Swell Maps with his brother, Nikki Sudden, in the mid-70s, then collaborations with Crime & The City Solution and These Immortal Souls, Epic's late-starting solo career has revealed more to his artistic muse than that normally associated with a jobbing drummer. However, in interviews he admitted to seeing his resumé as something of a drag, and wishing that his solo career had started about two decades previously (there had previously been two singles, 'Jelly Babies' and 'Rain Rain Rain', released on Rough Trade Records under his name in 1981 and 1982). Just as he largely disowned his past, so he confessed to having little affection for the style of music pioneered by the punk years. His solo career instead concentrated on a more soulful, singer-songwriter approach. This despite the appearance of indie and punk luminaries like Kim Gordon of Sonic Youth, J. Mascis of Dinosaur Jr. and Will Pepper of Thee Hypnotics on his second album, *Sleeping Star* (Mascis and Gordon had also worked on the debut). He would also tour with Evan Dando of the Lemonheads, both artists sharing an abiding affection for Gram Parsons evident in their own work.

Albums: *Rise Above* (Rough Trade 1993), *Sleeping Star* (Rough Trade 1995).

Eric's Trip

Drawing its personnel from the Canadian fishing village of Moncton, New Brunswick, Eric's Trip formed because, as they were keen to point out, 'nothing much else happens there'. The band comprise Julie Doiron (bass/vocals), Chris Thompson (guitar), Rick White (guitar/vocals) and Mark Gaudet (drums). Their sound, self-described as 'punk rock that isn't afraid to dream', first came to light on a series of cassette-only releases at the turn of the 90s. These transmuted into profligate 7-inch singles and compilation appearances, before landing on Sub Pop Records in 1993 for their long-playing debut (the first Canadian artists on the roster). Though their descriptions of their sound may have invoked notions of gentility, by their second album they were still averaging one minute per song - just enough time to crystallise a single idea around a simple riff. Lyrics concerned themselves primarily with small-town issues. Unsurprisingly, perhaps, as band members still held down day jobs in Moncton, be they photo lab, record store or fast food outlet.

Albums: *Love Tara* (Sub Pop 1993), *Forever Again* (Sub Pop 1994).

Essential Logic

Formed in London, England, in 1978 by Lora Logic, X-Ray Spex's erstwhile original saxophonist, Essential Logic's first single was 'Aerosol Burns', a punk masterpiece of brash guitar and hiccoughing rhythms. The group delighted in odd, jangling harmonies and eccentric song shapes: Lora Logic's loopy punk vocals (a strong influence on more successful female-led groups of the 80s such as Throwing Muses and Fuzzbox) and gorgeously primitive saxophone made *Beat Rhythm News* special. Her solo album, *Pedigree Charm*, had a smoother sound, but her sideline work with Red Crayola retained the harshness and power. Logic later joined the Hare Krishna cult, just like X-Ray Spex's Poly Styrene before her, and has now left music altogether.

Albums: *Beat Rhythm News* (Rough Trade 1979). As Lora Logic: *Pedigree Charm* (Rough Trade 1982).

Eugenius

Formed in Glasgow, Scotland, Eugenius were led by Eugene Kelly, who had previously been part of the Vaselines, who were hailed as influential after their demise. On the other hand Kelly described them as 'a bunch of drunken, useless, awful idiots'. That did not stop Kurt Cobain of Nirvana praising the Vaselines and Kelly's subsequent bands. Two years after their break up, a promoter invited Kelly to support the Lemonheads, even though he didn't have a band at that time. He borrowed Gordon Keen (guitar) from BMX Bandits, James from the Vaselines and Brendan O'Hare from Teenage Fanclub to make the gig. The quartet wrote a couple of songs together and called themselves Captain America. Despite being only a half-hearted exercise, word quickly spread. Just four months after that debut performance Captain America were invited to support Nirvana, just as 'Smells Like Teen Spirit' was taking off (Cobain was frequently spotted wearing a Captain America T-shirt). However, as soon as they made their debut with the *Wow* EP on Dangerhouse Records, *Marvel Comics* in America took legal action to prevent them using the name again. Captain America became Eugenius as the group replaced Keen and O'Hare with Roy Lawrence and Ray Boyle, and signed to Creation Records. The press were still interested, but as the band admitted, 'The Nirvana connection could be a bit of a bastard at times. Through some bizarre logic, people automatically assumed that we would sound like them - just because Kurt wore our T-shirt on the cover of the NME.' *Oomalama* took three weeks in total to complete, though the band found themselves somewhat over-extended as it was originally intended to be a mini-album. Some of the fanfare surrounding the band had died down by the time they began recording *Mary Queen Of Scots*, a mature, reflective album, still dependent on the group's buzzsaw guitars and insistent melodies. One of the best examples of their new sound was 'Caesar's Vein', a track about the band's first US tour in 1992, and the first single to be lifted from these sessions.

Albums: *Oomalama* (Creation 1992), *Mary Queen Of Scots* (August Records 1994).

Everything But The Girl

The duo of Tracey Thorn (b. 26 September 1962, Hertfordshire, England) and Ben Watt (b. 6 December

1962, England), first came together when they were students at Hull University, their name coming from a local furniture shop. Thorn was also a member of the Marine Girls who issued two albums. They performed together in 1982 and released a gentle and simply produced version of Cole Porter's 'Night And Day'. Thorn made a solo acoustic mini-album in 1982, *A Distant Shore*, which was a strong seller in the UK independent charts, and Watt released the critically acclaimed *North Marine Drive* the following year. They subsequently left Cherry Red Records and signed to the major-distributed Blanco y Negro label. In 1984 they made the national chart with 'Each And Everyone', which preceded their superb *Eden*. This jazz-flavoured pop collection hallmarked the duo's understated but beautific compositional skills, displaying a great leap from the comparative naivete of their previous offerings. Their biggest single breakthrough, meanwhile, came with a version of Danny Whitten's 'I Don't Want To Talk About It', which reached the UK Top 3 in 1988. Their subsequent albums have revealed a much more gradual growth in songwriting, though many contend they have never surpassed that debut. *The Language Of Life*, a collection more firmly fixated with jazz stylings, found further critical acclaim, and stands as their best effort post-*Eden*. One track, 'The Road', featured Stan Getz on saxophone. However, a more pop-orientated follow-up, *World-wide*, was released to mediocre reviews in 1991. *Amplified Heart* repaired the damage somewhat, with contributions from Danny Thompson, Dave Mattacks, Richard Thompson and arranger Harry Robinson.
Albums: *Eden* (Blanco y Negro 1984), *Love Not Money* (Blanco y Negro 1985), *Baby The Stars Shine Bright* (Blanco y Negro 1986), *Idlewild* (Blanco y Negro 1988), *The Language Of Life* (Blanco y Negro 1990), *World-wide* (Blanco y Negro 1991), *Amplified Heart* (Banco y Negro 1994). Compilation: *Home Movies: The Best Of* (Blanco y Negro 1993). Tracey Thorn solo *A Distant Shore* (Cherry Red 1993). Ben Watt solo *North Marine Drive* (Cherry Red 1993).

Ex

Unconventional Dutch conglomerate formed in 1977 when punk first hit Holland and a variety of like minds came together as a politically active musical and social unit. The Ex were formed from the ashes of two small local bands, with the membership at various times including G.W. Sok (vocals), Terrie Hessels (guitar), Katrin Bornfeld (drums), Jos Kley (vocals), Sabien Witteman (drums), Joke Laarman (bass), Luc Klaassen (bass), Wineke T. Hart (violin), Kees vanden Haak (saxophone), Dolf Planteydt (guitar) and Tom Greene (guitar). They were strongly linked to a variety of left field concerns in general and the Amsterdam squatting movement in particular. Although the sound started life as strictly agit-prop punk, they later incorporated elements such as Eastern folk music, funk and various other styles. *Scrabbling At The Lock*, for instance, was a collaboration with experimental violin player Tom Cora. Guests on other works include Thurston Moore and Lee Renaldo (Sonic Youth), Jon Langford (Mekons), the Dog Faced Hermans, etc. Their attitude to the place of rebel music in the scheme of things can best be summised by a statement on the rear of 1985's

Pokkeherrie: 'Where have all the musicians gone? The ones who made sound disturb, who pulled down the stage, who forged music into a weapon. Where have all the musicians gone? They perform in supermarkets and have their instruments tuned. 'Our ears are deaf and our strings are wrapped up in silk. We hurt nobody." A lowlands equivalent to Fugazi then, but with arguably more stylistic variation.
Albums: *Disturbing Domestic Peace* (Verrerecords), *History Is What's Happening* (More DPM 1982), *History Of Labour* (VGZ 1983), *Tumult* (FAI 1983), *Blueprints For A Blackout* (Pig Brother Productions 1983), *Pokkeherrie* (Pockabilly 1985), *Too Many Cowboys* (Mordam 1987), *Live In Wroclaw* (Red 1987, cassette only), *Hands Up You're Free* (Ex 1988), *Aural Guerilla* (Ex 1988), *Joggers And Smoggers* (Ex 1989), *Scrabbling At The Lock* (Ex 1991).

Exploding White Mice

This hard-hitting guitar band was formed in Adelaide, Australia in early 1985 featuring Jeff Stephens (lead guitar), Paul Gilchrist (vocals) and Giles Barrow (rhythm guitar). Their style drew influences from the tough Detroit sound of the early Stooges with just a hint of Ramones-style 'dumb fun'. In fact they took their name from the laboratory rodents that featured in the Ramones' movie *Rock 'N' Roll High School*. Their debut recording featured three originals and three covers including 'Pipeline' and a burning version of Bo Diddley's 'Let The Kids Dance', and indicated a young band with considerable talent. Exploding White Mice quickly developed a huge live reputation and their 1987 double a-sided single, John Kongos' 'He's Gonna Step On You Again', should have broken them to a wider audience. However, another version by the seasoned cover band Party Boys, received more attention. Their first full-length album proved them to be one of the finest trash pop bands in the country. On their most recent album, the band have developed their pop sensibilities to the point where commercial acceptance is becoming a distinct possibility.
Albums: *Brute Force & Ignorance* (1988), *Exploding White Mice* (1990).

Exploited

This abrasive and unruly Scottish punk quartet was formed in East Kilbride in 1980 by vocalist Wattie Buchan and guitarist 'Big John' Duncan. Recruiting drummer Dru Stix (b. Drew Campbell) and bassist Gary McCormick, they signed to the Secret Records label the following year. Specializing in two-minute blasts of high-speed blue vitriol, they released their first album, *Punk's Not Dead*, in 1981. Lyrically they sketched out themes such as war, corruption, unemployment and police brutality, amid a chaotic blur of crashing drums and flailing guitar chords. The band quickly become entrenched in their own limited musical and philosophical ideology, and earned themselves a certain low-life notoriety. Songs such as 'Fuck A Mod', for example, set youth tribe again youth tribe without any true rationale. 'Sid Vicious Was Innocent', meanwhile, deserves no comment whatsoever. Yet they were the only member of the third generation punk set to make it on to *Top Of The Pops*, with 1981's 'Dead Cities'. Continuing to release material on a regular basis, they have retained a small, but ever-declining, cult following. The line-ups have fluctuated wildly, with Duncan going on to join Goodbye Mr Mackenzie and, very nearly, Nirvana, while Buchan has stayed in place to marshal the troops. The diminutive but thoroughly obnoxious lead singer, with a multi-coloured mohican haircut, strikes an oddly anachronistic figure today as he presides over his talentless musical curio.

Albums: *Punk's Not Dead* (Secret 1981), *On Stage* (Superville 1981), *Troops Of Tomorrow* (Secret 1982), *Let's Start A War* (Pax 1983), *Horror Epics* (Konnexion 1985), *Death Before Dishonour* (Rough Justice 1989), *The Massacre* (Rough Justice 1991). Compilations: *Totally Exploited* (Dojo 1984), *Live On The Apocalypse Now Tour '81* (Chaos 1985), *Live And Loud* (Link 1987), *Inner City Decay* (Snow 1987), *On Stage 91/Live At The Whitehouse 1985* (Dojo 1991).

Extreme Noise Terror

A band whose name truly encapsulates their sound, Extreme Noise Terror formed in January 1985 and were signed by Manic Ears Records after their first ever gig. Their debut release was a split album with Chaos UK, and although there were musical similarities, ENT, along with Napalm Death, were already in the process of twisting traditional punk influences into altogether different shapes. Along with the latter, they became the subject of disc jockey John Peel's interest in 1987, recording a session (one of three) which would eventually see release on the Strange Fruit imprint. Afterwards drummer Mick Harris, who had left Napalm Death to replace the group's original drummer, in turn departed, joining Scorn. His replacement was Stick (Tony Dickens), who joined existing members Dean Jones (vocals), Phil Vane (vocals) and Pete Hurley (guitar). Mark Bailey had by now replaced Mark Gardiner, who himself had replaced Jerry Clay, on bass. Touring in Japan preceded the release of *Phonophobia*, while continued Peel sessions brought the group to the attention of the KLF's Bill Drummond. He asked them to record a version of the KLF's '3am Eternal', with the intention of the band appearing on *Top Of The Pops* live at Christmas to perform the tune (The BBC decided this was not in the best interests of their audience). Eventually released as a limited edition single, the two band's paths crossed again in 1992 when the KLF were invited to perform live at the 1992 Brit Awards. This crazed event, which included the firing of blanks into the audience, has already passed into music industry legend. Back on their own, 1993 saw Extreme Noise Terror touring widely, and the group signed to premier noise stable Earache the following year. By this time the line-up had swelled to include Lee Barrett (bass; also Disgust) replacing Bailey, and Ali Firouzbakht (lead guitar), with a returning Pig Killer on drums. Together they released *Retro-bution*, ostensibly a compilation, but nevertheless featuring the new line-up on re-recorded versions of familiar material.

Albums: *Radioactive* (Manic Ears 1985, split with Chaos UK), *A Holocaust In Your Head* (Hurt 1987), *The Peel Sessions* (Strange Fruit 1990), *Phonophobia* (Vinyl Japan 1992), *Retro-bution* (Earache 1995). Video: *From One Extreme To The Other* (1989).

Eyeless In Gaza

Taking their name from Aldous Huxley's famous novel, this UK group was the brainchild of vocalists/musicians Martyn Bates and Peter Becker. Known for their tortured vocals and impressive arranging skills, the group established a reasonable following on the independent circuit with their 1981 debut, *Photographs As Memories*. Several more albums for the Cherry Red label saw them alternate between a melodramatic and meandering style that increasingly veered towards improvisation. Bates subsequently teamed up with former Primitives bassist Steve Gullaghan in Hungry I, also working solo. Eyeless In Gaza reformed in 1992, releasing an album titled *Fabulous Library* the following year as a trio comprising Bates, Becker and chanteuse Elizabeth S. Reverting to the original two-pice line-up later in 1993, the two recorded and toured Europe and the US extensively with self-styled 'performance poet' Anne Clark, also collaborating with Derek Jarman film soundtrack composer Simon Turner. 1994 saw Eyeless In Gaza signing to the Belgian based dance/experimental label Antler Subway.

Albums: *Photographs As Memories* (Cherry Red 1981), *Caught In Flux* (Cherry Red 1981), *Pale Hands I Loved So Well* (Uniton 1982), *Drumming The Beating Heart* (Cherry Red 1983), *Rust Red September* (Cherry Red 1983), *Back From The Rains* (Cherry Red 1986), *Kodak Ghosts Run Amok* (Cherry Red 1987), *Transience Blues* (Integrity/Antler 1989), *Fabulous Library* (Orchid 1993). Compilation: *Orange Ice And Wax Crayons* (Cherry Red 1992).

Fabulous

This UK post-punk band was formed in the wake of the media success of the Manic Street Preachers. Fabulous comprised Simon Dudfield (vocals), plus Martin Goodacre (guitar), 'Hodge' (drums), Russel Underwood (second guitar) and Ronnie Fabulous (bass). They were managed by former *NME* assistant editor James Brown. Dudfield was a contributor and both Goodacre and Underwood were photographers on the same paper. Live they were characterized by Dudfield's studied Iggy Pop impersonations, while musically and ideologically they borrowed from the situationist tack of the Sex Pistols. Their first single 'Destined To Be Free' was just a small part of their stated agenda to reinvent 1977 and rid the UK music scene of the 'Ecstasy' mentality. They also made a point of exhibiting a stolen carpet from EMI's offices. As more than one journalist has noted, the Sex Pistols had taken that record company for £50,000, which puts Fabulous' achievements in some sort of perspective.

Factory Records

Cambridge graduate Tony Wilson (b. 1950, Salford, Lancashire, England) was a regional television reporter working in Manchester when he started the Factory label in 1978. He was also responsible for the *So It Goes* and *What's On* television programmes, which in themselves had acted as an invaluable platform for the emerging new wave scene. Previously he had edited his university's *Shilling Paper*. From there he joined television news company ITN as a trainee reporter, writing bulletins for current events programmes. It was on regional news programmes based in Manchester that he first encountered his future collaborators in the Factory operation; Alan Erasmus, Peter Saville, Rob Gretton (manager of Joy Division) and producer Martin Hannett. Erasmus and Wilson began their operation by jointly managing the fledgling Durutti Column, opening the Factory Club venue soon after. The label's first catalogue number, FAC 1, was allocated to the poster promoting its opening event. This typified Wilson's approach to the whole Factory operation, the most famous assignation of which was FAC 51, the Hacienda nightclub. However, it was their records, and the impersonal, nondescriptive packaging that accompanied them, which saw the label make its mark. Among the first releases were OMD's 'Electricity' (later a hit on Dindisc), and A Certain Ratio's 'All Night Party'. But it was Joy Division, harnessing the anxieties of Manchester youth to a discordant, sombre musical landscape, that established the label in terms of public perception and financial security. With Curtis gone, New Order continued as the backbone of the Factory operation throughout the 80s, establishing themselves in the mainstream with the biggest selling 12-inch up until that time, 'Blue Monday'. Other mainstays included Section 25 and Stockholm Monsters, who steered a path too close to that of New Order, and the resourceful Durutti Column. It took the brief arrival of James to restore a pop sensibility (their subsequent departure would be a huge body blow), while New Order, somewhat astonishingly, took the England Football Squad to number 1 in the UK Charts with 'World In Motion'. The latter-day success of Electronic, the most successful of various New Order offshoots, and the Happy Mondays, a shambolic post-punk dance conglomerate, has diffused accusations of Factory being too reliant on a single band. Reported cashflow problems in 1991, although vehemently denied by Wilson, will most likely be eased by a bumper crop of albums on the horizon, including new material by New Order and the Happy Mondays. Additionally the four-album compilation, *Palatine*, showcased the label's achievements, of which Wilson has never been reticent: 'In my opinion (popular art) is as valid as any other art form . . . a lot of the tracks on *Palatine* are phenomenal art. We're 35 years into pop now, and great records do not lose their power. The deference with which we treat this stuff is deserved.'
Album: *Palatine* (1991).

Fad Gadget

Effectively a moniker for UK-born vocalist and synthesizer player Frank Tovey, Fad Gadget enjoyed cult success with a series of bizarre releases on the Mute Records label during the early 80s. Tovey's background lay in his study of performance art at Leeds Art College. After moving to London, he transferred this interest into an unpredictable, often self-mutilating stage show. The first artist to sign with Daniel Miller's Mute label, Fad Gadget's 'Back To Nature' was released in 1979. 'Ricky's Hand' further combined Tovey's lyrical skill (observing the darker aspects of life) with an innovative use of electronics. Both these traits were evident on 'Fireside Favourites', a single and also the title of Fad Gadget's debut album. For the latter, Tovey was joined by Eric Radcliffe (guitar/bass), Nick Cash (drums), John Fryer (noises), Daniel Miller (drum machine/synthesizer) and Phil Wauquaire (bass synthesizer/guitar). After 'Make Room' in 1981 came *Incontinent*, which was more violent, unnerving and disturbing than before. Tovey had also recruited new staff, working with Peter Balmer (bass/rhythm guitar), David Simmons (piano/synthesizer), singers B.J. Frost and Anne Clift, John Fryer (percussion), plus drummer Robert Gotobed of Wire. In 1982 'Saturday Night Special' and 'King Of Flies' preceded a third album, *Under The Flag*. Dealing with the twin themes of the Falklands conflict and Tovey's new-born child, the album featured Alison Moyet on saxophone and backing vocals. The following year saw new extremes as Tovey returned from a European tour with his legs in plaster, having broken them during a show. On the recording front, the year was fairly quiet, apart from 'For Whom The Bell Tolls' and 'I Discover Love'. 'Collapsing New People' continued an impressive run of singles at the start of 1984, and was followed by Fad Gadget's final album, *Gag*. By this time, the band had swelled and supported Siouxsie And The Banshees at London's Royal Albert Hall. But Tovey opted to use his real identity from this point on. In November, he teamed up with American Boyd Rice for *Easy Listening For The Hard Of Hearing*. Since then, Tovey has issued four solo works, each of them as highly distinct and uncompromising as Fad Gadget's material.
Albums: *Fireside Favourites* (Mute 1980), *Incontinent* (Mute 1981), *Under The Flag* (Mute 1982), *Gag* (Mute 1984). Compilation: *The Fad Gadget Singles* (Mute 1986). As Frank Tovey: with Boyd Rice *Easy Listening For The Hard Of Hearing* (Mute 1984), *Snakes And Ladders* (Mute 1985), *Civilian* (Mute 1988), *Tyranny And The Hired Hand* (Mute 1989). Frank Tovey with the Pyros: *Grand Union* (Mute 1991).

Fairground Attraction

This jazz-tinged Anglo/Scottish pop band comprised Eddi Reader (b. 28 August 1959, Glasgow, Scotland; vocals), Mark Nevin (guitar), Simon Edwards (guitaron, a Mexican acoustic guitar shaped bass) and Roy Dodds (drums). After art school Reader made her first musical forays as backing singer for the Gang Of Four. She moved to London in 1983 where session and live work with the Eurythmics and Alison Moyet kept her gainfully employed. She first hooked up with Nevin for the Compact Organisation sampler album *The Compact Composers*, singing on two of his songs. Nevin and Reader began their first collaborations in 1985, after Nevin had graduated by playing in one of the numerous line-ups of Jane Aire And The Belvederes. He was also closely involved with Sandie Shaw's mid-80s comeback. Around his songs

Fairground Attraction

they built Fairground Attraction, adding Edwards and Dodds, a jazz drummer of over 20 years' standing who had spent time with Working Week and Terence Trent D'Arby. They signed to RCA and quickly set about recording a debut album, as the gentle skiffle of 'Perfect' topped the UK singles charts in May 1988. They subsequently won both Best Single and Best Album categories at the Brit awards. A slight hiatus in their career followed when Reader became pregnant. They followed their natural inclinations by filming the video for their 1989 single 'Clare' in Nashville, and were supplemented on tour by Graham Henderson (accordion) and Roger Beaujolais (vibes). The group's promise was then cut short when the band split, and Reader went on to acting (appearing in a BBC drama *Your Cheatin' Heart*, about the Scottish country and western scene) and a solo career releasing her debut, *Mir Mama*, in 1992.
Albums: *First Of A Million Kisses* (1988), *Ay Fond Kiss* (1990).

Faith Brothers

A passionate brand of rock, spiced with an old soul feel allowed the Faith Brothers to address important political and moral issues, without needing to preach. Their debut single, 'Country Of The Blind', in 1985, set the tone, an attack on a nation in the clutches of consumer fever and a decaying welfare state. 'Stranger On Home Ground', (1985), was closer to their hearts, dealing with the band's attitude towards the loss of community, not least where they grew up

around west London's Fulham area. The year ended with the more optimistic 'Eventide (A Hymn For Change)', a title shared by the Faith Brothers' debut album released on the Virgin Records' subsidiary 10. Alongside the main songwriter Billy Franks (guitar/vocals) were Lee Hirons (bass), his brother Mark (guitar), Henry Trezise (keyboards), Mark Waterman (saxophone), Will Tipper (trumpet) and Steve Howlett (drums). The immediacy of the singles seemed to be lost on *Eventide*, which sounded strained and tame in comparison. 'Whistling In The Dark' was taken as a further single in 1986, but failed to chart. The Faith Brothers returned in 1987 with *A Human Sound*, but like its two singles, 'That's Just The Way It Is To Me' and 'Consider Me', it lacked the bite of the band's early singles and made little impression. They disbanded shortly thereafter.
Albums: *Eventide* (10 1985), *A Human Sound* (Siren 1987).

Faith No More

Formed in San Francisco in 1980, Faith No More, titled after a greyhound the members had bet on, were among the first outfits to experiment with the fusion of funk, thrash and hardcore styles which effectively became a new musical sub-genre. The band initially comprised Jim Martin (b. 21 July 1961, Oakland, California, USA; guitar; ex-Vicious Hatred), Roddy Bottum (b. 1 July 1963, Los Angeles, California, USA; keyboards), Bill Gould (b. 24 April 1963, Los Angeles, California, USA; bass), Mike Bordin (b. 27 November 1962, San Francisco, California, USA; drums) and Chuck Moseley

Faith Brothers

(vocals). Bottum had attended the same school as Bould, while Bordin was recruited from his course at Berkeley University in tribal rhythm. Gould had met Moseley on the Los Angeles club circuit in 1980, while Martin had been recommended by Metallica's Cliff Burton. This line-up recorded a low-budget, self-titled debut on the independent Mordam label, followed by the ground breaking *Introduce Yourself* on Slash, a subsidiary of Warner Brothers. It encompassed a variety of styles but exuded a rare warmth and energy, mainly through Moseley's melodramatic vocals, and was well received by the critics (not least for signature tune, 'We Care A Lot'). However, internal disputes led to the firing of Moseley on the eve of widespread press coverage and favourable live reviews, though it had been reported that the band underwent a period when every single member walked out at some point. Moseley would go on to gig, temporarily, with Bad Brains, before putting his own band together, Cement. Against the odds his replacement, Mike Patton (b. 27 January 1968, Eureka, California, USA), was even more flamboyant and actually more accomplished as a singer (it was also rumoured that Courtney Love of Hole auditioned/rehearsed with the group). *The Real Thing*, the album which followed Patton's recruitment, was a runaway success, with the single, 'Epic', denting the UK Top 20 singles chart. Their style was now both offbeat and unpredictable, yet retained enough melody to remain a commercial proposition. Despite the universal adulation, however, it transpired that the band still pretty much hated each other off stage. *Live At The Brixton Academy* was released as a stop-gap affair, while the band toured on for nearly three years on the back of the worldwide success of their last studio album. After Patton temporarily defected back to his original, pre-Faith No More outfit, Mr Bungle, the group finally returned with *Angel Dust*. A tougher, less accessible record in keeping with the group's origins (despite a cover of the Commodores' 'I'm Easy'), it made the US Top 10 as their commercial ascent continued. However, in 1994 following a good deal of press speculation, the ever volatile line-up of Faith No More switched again as Jim Martin was ousted in favour of Trey Spruance, who had formerly worked in Patton's earlier and sometimes concurrent band, Mr Bungle.

Albums: *Faith No More* (Mordam 1984), *Introduce Yourself* (London 1987), *The Real Thing* (London 1989), *Live At The Brixton Academy* (London 1991), *Angel Dust* (London 1992), *King For A Day...Fool For A Lifetime* (London 1995). Video: *Live At Brixton* (1990).

Further reading: *Faith No More: The Real Story*, Steffan Chirazi.

Faith Over Reason

This English group emerged on the independent scene in the early 90s. Their version of Nick Drake's 'Northern Sky' pigeon-holed the group as one firmly planted within the pastoral sound of the British folk/rock era of the 70s, although conversely, the group's sound has often been compared with that of the Sundays and Smiths. Formed in Croydon, south London, the group consists of Moira Lambert (b. 13 October 1970, Chicester, West Sussex, England; lead vocals/acoustic guitar), William Lloyd (b. 17

March 1971, London, England; bass/keyboards), Simon Roots (b. 1 September 1970; guitar) and Mark Wilsher (b. 1 May 1970, Croydon, Surrey, England; drums). The release of two EPs in 1990, *Believing In Me* ('Evangeline'/'Believing In Me'/'Northern Sky') and *Billy Blue* ('High In The Sun'/'Ice Queen'/'Billy Blue'/'Move Closer') on the Big Cat label, drew well-earned praise from the music press. Lambert in the meantime contributed vocals to Saint Etienne's 'Only Love Can Break Your Heart', an indie-dance hit in 1990. The group's momentum was disrupted in late 1991 by the departure of Roots.

Album: *Eyes Wide Smile* (Big Cat 1992).

Fall

Formed in Manchester, England, in 1977, the Fall was the brainchild of the mercurial Mark E. Smith (b. Mark Edward Smith, 5 March 1957, Salford, Manchester, England). Over the years, Smith ruthlessly went through a battalion of musicians while taking the group through a personal odyssey of his wayward musical and lyrical excursions. His truculent press proclamations, by turns hysterically funny or sinister, also illuminated their career. Just as importantly, BBC disc jockey John Peel became their most consistent and fervent advocate, with the group recording a record number of sessions for his Radio 1 programme. The first Fall line-up, featuring Una Baines (electric piano), Martin Bramah (guitar), Karl Burns (drums) and Tony Friel (bass), made their debut on 'Bingo Master's Breakout', a good example of Smith's surreal vision, coloured by his relentlessly northern working class vigil. Initially signed to the small independent label Step Forward the group recorded three singles, including the savage 'Fiery Jack', plus *Live At The Witch Trials*. In 1980 the unit signed to Rough Trade Records and went on to release the critically acclaimed but still wilful singles 'How I Wrote Elastic Man' and 'Totally Wired'. Meanwhile, a whole series of line-up changes saw the arrival and subsequent departures of Marc Riley, Mike Leigh, Martin Bramah, Yvonne Pawlett and Craig Scanlon. The Fall's convoluted career continued to produce a series of discordant, yet frequently fascinating albums from the early menace of *Dragnet* to the chaotic *Hex Enduction Hour*. At every turn Smith worked hard to stand aloof from any prevailing trend, his suspicious mind refusing to make concessions to the mainstream. An apparent change in the group's image and philosophy occurred during 1983 with the arrival of future wife Brix (Laura Elise Smith). As well as appearing with the Fall as singer/guitarist, Brix later recorded with her own group, the pop-orientated Adult Net. She first appeared on the Fall's *Perverted By Language*, and her presence was felt more keenly when the group unexpectedly emerged as a potential chart act, successfully covering R. Dean Taylor's 'There's A Ghost In My House' and later the Kinks' 'Victoria'. Despite this, Mark E. Smith's deadpan vocals and distinctive, accentuated vocals still dominated the band's sound. That and his backing band's ceaseless exploration of the basic rock riff. On later albums such as the almost flawless *This Nation's Saving Grace* and *The Frenz Experiment*, they lost none of their baffling wordplay or nagging, insistent rhythms, but the work seemed more focused and accessible. The line-up changes had slowed,

although more changes were afoot with the arrival of drummer Simon Wolstenscroft and Marcia Schofield. Proof of Smith's growing stature among the popular art cognescenti was the staging of his papal play *Hey! Luciani* and the involvement of dancer Michael Clark in the production of *I Am Kurious Oranj*. Any suggestions that the Fall might be slowly heading for a degree of commercial acceptance underestimated Smith's restless spirit. By the turn of the decade Brix had left the singer and the group (he maintains he 'kicked her out'), and Schofield followed soon after. A succession of labels did little to impare the band's 90s output, with the Fall's leader unable to do wrong in the eyes of the band's hugely commited following, which now had outposts throughout America. Brix returned in time to guest on 1995's *Cerebral Caustic*, although Smith had persevered in her absence, recording four consistently strong albums. Unpredictable and unique, the Fall under Smith's guidance remain one of the most uncompromising yet finest groups in British rock history.

Albums: *Live At The Witch Trials* (Step Forward 1979), *Dragnet* (Step Forward 1979), *Totale's Turns (It's Now Or Never) (Live)* (Rough Trade 1980), *Grotesque (After The Gramme)* (Rough Trade 1980), *Slates* (Rough Trade 1981, mini-album), *Hex Enduction Hour* (Kamera 1982), *Room To Live* (Kamera 1982), *Perverted By Language* (Rough Trade 1983), *The Wonderful And Frightening World Of ...* (Beggars Banquet 1984), *This Nation's Saving Grace* (Beggars Banquet 1985), *Bend Sinister* (Beggars Banquet 1986), *The Frenz Experiment* (Beggars Banquet 1988), *I Am Kurious Oranj* (Beggars Banquet 1988), *Seminal Live* (Beggars Banquet 1989), *Extricate* (Cog Sinister/Fontana 1990), *Shiftwork* (Cog Sinister/Fontana 1991), *Code Selfish* (Cog Sinister/Fontana 1992), *The Infotainment Scan* (Cog Sinister/Permanent 1993), *Middle Class Revolt* (Permanent 1994), *Cerebral Caustic* (Permanent 1995). Compilations: *77 - Early Years - 79* (Step Forward 1981), *Live At Acklam Hall, London, 1980* (Chaos 1982, cassette only), *Hip Priests And Kamerads* (Situaton 2 1985), *In Palace Of Swords Reversed (80-83)* (Cog Sinister 1987), *458489* (Beggars Banquet 1990), *458489-B Sides* (Beggars Banquet 1990), *The Collection* (Castle 1993), *BBC Live In Concert* (Windsong 1993, rec. 1987).

Further reading: *Paintwork: A Portrait Of The Fall*, Brian Edge.

False Prophets

'Our aim is to disarm the mechanics of oppression through persistent 'making and doing' of words and music in an invocation of the ancient magic which empowers humankind through the massing of voices in sacred speech/song.' With this impressive philosophy in mind, the False Prophets, comprising Stephan Ielpi (vocals), Debra De Salvo (guitar/vocals), Steven Taylor (guitar/vocals), Nick Marden (bass/vocals) and Billy Atwell III (drums/vocals) - burst into life in the early 80s as part of the famed US hardcore scene which also spawned Black Flag and Hüsker Dü. Their hypothesis was intelligence, intellect and knowledge as opposed to the horror show shock tactics used by so many US punk acts. This approach led to a contract with Jello Biafra's Alternative Tentacles Records in 1986, from which sprang *False Prophets* and *Implosion*. These albums showed a willingness to experiment and break away from pure punk thrash-outs. *Invisible People*, on Konkurrel, saw them start the new decade in style, an innovative fusion of hardcore punk, Latin rhythms, hard rock and polemic sculpted into a uniquely compelling record. They continued their quest for equality and freedom through the 80s with this theory as their cornerstone: 'All music, particularly rock, is ecstatic activity, and ecstasy itself is revolutionary.'

Albums: *False Prophets* (Alternative Tentacles 1986), *Implosion* (Alternative Tentacles 1987), *Invisible People* (Konkurrel 1990).

Family Cat

Originally from Yeovil, Somerset, the Family Cat were formed in 1988 and comprise Paul 'Fred' Frederick (lead vocals/guitar), Stephen Jelbert (guitar), Tim McVey (guitar), John (bass) and Kevin (drums). Based in south London, the group drew their influences from a variety of styles, in particular Sonic Youth and the Pixies, and found critical praise for their frenetic live appearances. A mini-album, *Tell 'Em We're Surfin'*, followed on from the unexpected success of their debut single, 1989's 'Tom Verlaine', on the Bad Girl label. Despite the accolades from the British music press the group found it difficult to break out of the 'independent' mould. The Family Cat's persistence eventually paid off with well-received singles in 'Remember What It Is That You Love' and 'A Place With No Name' (both 1990), and 'Colour Me Grey' (1991, with backing vocals from the then future indie star, PJ Harvey). A new album in 1992 on the Dedicated label, *Furthest From The Sun*, surprised many with a effective display of power and confidence, generating some of their best reviews yet. However, by the advent of *Magic Happens* the band had seemingly been forgotten by the majority of the British music press.

Albums: *Tell 'Em We're Surfin'* (Bad Girl 1989, mini-album), *Furthest From The Sun* (Dedicated 1992), *Magic Happens* (Dedicated 1994).

Family Fodder

This independent band comprised Dominique Pearce (vocals), Alig Levillian (guitars/keyboards/saxophone, vocals), Felix Friedorowicz (keyboards/bassoon/violin), Mick Hobbs (bass/organ), Martin Frederick (bass/vocals), Rick Wilson (drums/vocals), Charles Bullen (drums, guitar/viola/vocals), Buzz Smith (drums) Mark Doffman (drums), Ian Hill (vocals/percussion), Judy Carter and Jan Beetlestone (backing vocals). Their best remembered contribution to modern music was the tribute single, 'Debbie Harry', though other efforts such as 'Playing Golf', 'Warm', 'Savoire Faire' and 'Film Music' were entertaining for their idiosyncratic experimentalism. However, despite a reasonable line in songwriting craft from Pearce, it would have required greater commercial aptitude to sustain the legions of personnel. A greatest hits album was an ironic artefact in retrospect.

Album: *Monkey Banana Kitchen* (Fresh 1981). Compilation: *Greatest Hits* (Crammed Discs 1984).

Farm

If perseverance warrants its own unique award, the Farm could expect the equivalent of the Nobel prize for their incessant efforts. Formed in 1983 by former youth worker Peter Hooton (b. 28 September 1962, Liverpool, England; vocals), Steve Grimes (b. 4 June 1962, Liverpool, England; guitar), Phillip Strongman (bass) and Andy McVann (drums), the Farm were to become synonymous with so many cultural 'scenes' over the ensuing years that their music was rendered almost irrelevant. For much of the 80s the band flirted with politics, tagged 'The Soul Of Socialism', the 'Scally' fashions of their Liverpool hometown, and maintained strong soccer interests - primarily through singer Peter Hooton's fanzine, *The End*, a precursor to the explosion of football fanzines at the end of the decade. By 1984 John Melvin, George Maher, Steve Levy and Anthony Evans had joined, bringing with them a brass section and adding a northern soul influence to the Farm's unfashionable pop sound. Two years on, the line-up changed again as McVann was killed in a police car chase. He was replaced by Roy Boulter (b. 2 July 1964, Liverpool, England) and the line-up was bolstered by Keith Mullen (b. Bootle, England; guitar) and new bassist Carl Hunter (b. 14 April 1965, Bootle, England). The horn section departed and Ben Leach (b. 2 May 1969, Liverpool, England; keyboards) completed a new six-piece collective which was destined to change the Farm's fortunes. After the synthpop flop of their fourth independent release, 'Body And Soul', the Farm started their own Produce label and had a fortuitous meeting with in vogue dance producer, Terry Farley. Consequently, a cover version of the Monkees' 'Stepping Stone' was augmented with fashionable club beats and samples and, come 1990, the Farm suddenly found themselves being caught up in the Happy Mondays' 'Baggy' boom. The anthemic 'Groovy Train' and 'All Together Now', (the latter incorporating the sampling of the 17th century composer Johann Pachelbel's 'Canon And Gigue'), swept the band into the Top 10 of the UK charts, to be followed in 1991 by their debut album, *Spartacus*, going straight into the UK charts at number 1. If these placings were not proof enough of the Farm's new-found fame, the next achievement certainly was: the band's football connection was sealed when toy manufacturers Subbuteo designed a unique teamkit, just for the band. Later they also had the great honour of playing, alongside frequent collaborator Pete Wylie, Ian McCulloch and Gerry Marsden, to 15,000 Liverpool soccer fans for the 'Last Night Of The Kop', before Liverpool FC's legendary terrace was demolished. However, as the UK media tired of the 'baggy' sound, so a decline in the Farm's fortunes set in. *Love See No Colour* was bland and, indeed, colourless. Few bands can have gone from an album which entered the UK charts at number 1 to one which failed to break the Top 75 with such velocity. The blame lied in some outrageous squandering of the money earned through their debut album, and a total lack of direction in the songwriting. The group's new deal with Sony (which fostered their own End Product label) was over as quickly as it had started. Help, surprisingly, came from the US, where Seymour Stein of Sire Records saw some remaining commercial potential in the band. 1994 saw them retreat to a more orthodox guitar/bass/drums approach for

Hullabaloo. Thus the Farm's strange story of superhuman endurance continues apace.

Albums: *Spartacus* (Produce 1991), *Love See No Colour* (End Product 1992), *Hullabaloo* (Sire 1994).

Farmers Boys

Along with the Higsons, the Farmers Boys emerged from Norwich, Norfolk, England, in the early 80s with an amusing brand of wacky guitar pop. The excellent 'I Think I Need Help', issued in April 1982, was Baz, Frog, Mark and Stan's first offering (they never used surnames), followed by the equally impressive 'Whatever Is He Like' in the summer. For December's 'More Than A Dream', the band veered towards country and western, a formula successful enough to warrant its reissue as the Farmers Boys' first single for EMI. 'Muck It Out', issued in April 1983, played on the band's rural name in the search for a novelty hit, but chart success was something that would always elude them. After the catchy 'For You' in July, the group's only album appeared in the autumn, but despite charm and melodic strength, *Get Out And Walk* could not sustain the impact of their singles over two sides. 'Apparently', issued in the late spring of 1984, benefited from the band's horn section of Andrew Hamilton (saxophone), Noel Harris (trumpet) and John Beecham (trombone), while a cover of Cliff Richard's 'In The Country' became the closest thing to a Farmers Boys hit in August. But after two further singles, 'Phew Wow' in October and the excellent 'I Built The World' early in 1985, the writing was on the wall and the band split up soon after.

Album: *Get Out And Walk* (EMI 1983).

Fashion

This band from Birmingham, England blended offbeat funk with an independent spirit that seemed destined to ensure them commercial success. Originally a trio, comprising John Mulligan (bass), Dix (drums) and Luke (guitar), Fashion issued three diverse singles on their own label, spurred on by the D.I.Y. attitudes in the wake of punk. After November 1978's 'Steady Eddie Steady' came 'Citinite' in June and then *Perfect Product*, an impressive debut album. 'Silver Blades' followed in March 1980, ensuring a deal with Arista. Now swelled to a six-piece with Martin Stoker (ex-Dance; Bureau) on drums, vocalist Tony (ex-Neon Hearts) and main songwriter De Harriss, many predicted that their resultant singles would break the band on the back of the futurist scene of the early 80s. 'Street Player - Mechanik', in March 1982, 'Love Shadow' in August and later, 'Eye Talk' in January 1984, all scraped the lower reaches of the chart, but failed to establish the band in the public eye. Despite this, Fashion enjoyed a strong undercurrent of support, reflected in a UK Top 10 album *Fabrique*, in June 1982. But interest gradually waned, the band moved to Epic, and *Twilight Of The Idols*, issued exactly two years on, was not as warmly received, despite two singles, 'Dreaming' in April 1984 and 'You In The Night' in June.

Albums: *Perfect Product* (1979), *Fabrique* (1982), *Twilight Of The Idols* (1984), *The Height Of Fashion* (1990).

Fatima Mansions

A category defying group formed in August 1989 by Cork

singer Cathal Coughlan, fresh from his stint with the more restrained Microdisney, with the inspiration for the new name coming from a decrepit Dublin housing estate. They were almost immediately ensconced in a London studio by Kitchenware Records to record their debut album. *Against Nature* was released in September 1989 to almost universal critical acclaim and a large degree of astonishment; 'staggering in its weight of ideas ... never loses its capacity to suddenly stun you' stated the *New Musical Express*. Its abrasive lyrics might have been anticipated given Coughlan's pedigree, but the directness of the musical attack certainly was not. Andreas O'Gruama's guitar contributed richly to the final results, though otherwise the Fatima Mansions served primarily as a vehicle for its singer and songwriter. It was followed by 'Blues For Ceausescu', a fire and brimstone political tirade which held prophetic warnings of East European tragedy. Its operatic tilt enabled it to be at once hysterical, comic and sinister. Coughlan was now established in the press as a delicious anti-hero and mischief maker. *Bugs Fucking Bunny* was sadly dropped as the title of the second album, in favour of the comparatively non-descript *Viva Dead Ponies*. This time Coughlan's lyrics were totally submerged in vitriolic observations on the absurdities of living in the UK. The title-track, for instance, considered the case of Jesus being reincarnated as a Jewish shopkeeper. A particular vehemence, as ever, was reserved for British imperialism. It prompted the *Guardian* newspaper to number Coughlan as 'the most under-rated lyricist in pop today', while John Peel confirmed he could 'listen to Cathal Coughlan sing the phone book'. Further paranoia, bile and doses of his full-bodied vocal were poured in to the mini-album, *Bertie's Brochures*, in 1991. Notable amongst its eight tracks was a full-scale assassination of REM's 'Shiny Happy People'. The title-track this time referred to an Irish artist wrongly imprisoned for terrorism, coinciding with highly topical, real-life events. In 1992 Coughlan managed to alienate a Milan audience ostensibly there to see headliners U2 by attempting to insert a Virgin Mary shampoo holder into his anus whilst singing 'fuck the Pope, I want to fuck your traitor Pope'. After a sojourn in Newcastle Coughlan returned in 1994 with the release of *Lost In The Former West*, which again identified him as the sort of left field maverick genius who makes the broad church of pop music infinitely more entertaining than it might otherwise be. The only thing holding him back are the minuscule sales figures which have been his curse since Microdisney days.
Albums: *Against Nature* (Kitchenware 1989), *Viva Dead Ponies* (Kitchenware 1990), *Bertie's Brochures* (Kitchenware 1991, mini-album), *Valhalla Avenue* (Kitchenware 1992), *Lost In The Former West* (Radioactive 1994).
Video: *Y'Knaa* (1994).

Fear

One of the most entertaining and influential of the punk bands which grew up in the late 70s in Los Angeles, California, Fear consisted of Lee Ving (vocals, guitar, harmonica), Philo Cramer (guitar), Derf Scratch (bass) and Johnny Backbeat (drums). Formed in 1978, the band's sarcastic, almost nihilistic stance, captured on Penelope Spheeris' *The Decline Of Western Civilization* film, formed the basis of a recorded career which never quite captured the band's stroppy, chaotic live shows. The debut album *The Record* was, nevertheless, a searing document of the band's potent rock 'n' roll, despite some primitive attitudes to women and homosexuals. Animated by a musical ability far beyond many of their peers, and fortified by Ving's bar blues vocal presence, it is one of only two essential Fear recordings within a limited discography. The other was the band's debut single, 'I Love Living In The City', a sneering put-down of Hollywood. Their most famous live appearance, meanwhile, came as Halloween guests on the syndicated *Saturday Night Live* television show. In true punk style, the event ended in chaos and controversy, with the station quite appalled at the 'slam dancing' generated by Fear fans which accompanied the filming. Later in 1982 Scratch was replaced by future Red Hot Chili Peppers' bass player Flea in time for the release of 'Fuck Christmas'. Shortly afterwards Lorenzo (ex-Dickies) became the permanent bass player. 1985's *More Beer* repeated the debut album's formula, with occasional stylistic variation but little else to recommend it. It featured drummer Spit Stix, who was formerly in the Nina Hagen band.
Albums: *The Record* (Slash/Warners 1982), *More Beer* (Restless 1985), *Live...For The Record* (Restless 1991).

Feelies

Formed in New Jersey, USA in 1977, the Feelies originally consisted of Glenn Mercer (b. Haledon, New Jersey, USA; lead guitar/vocals), Bill Million (b. William Clayton, Haledon, New Jersey, USA; rhythm guitar/vocals), Keith DeNunzio aka Keith Clayton (b. 27 April 1958, Reading, Pennsylvania, USA; bass) and Dave Weckerman (drums). Weckerman departed from the line-up and was replaced by Vinny DeNuzio (b. 15 August 1956) prior to the group's debut album, *Crazy Rhythms* which featured Anton 'Andy' Fier. This exceptional release brought to mind the jerky paranoia of an early Talking Heads and the compulsion of the Velvet Underground, while at the same time established the Feelies' polyrhythmic pulsebeats and Mercer's scratchy, but effective guitarwork. Despite critical acclaim, *Crazy Rhythms* was a commercial failure and the group broke up. Fier subsequently formed the Golden Palaminos, an *ad hoc* unit featuring contributions from various, often contrasting, musicians including Jack Bruce and Syd Straw. Mercer and Million then embarked on several diverse projects which included work with three different groups; the Trypes, the Willies and Yung Wu. The latter unit also featured Weckerman and their lone album, *Sore Leave*, led directly to a Feelies' reformation. Stanley Demeski (drums) and Brenda Sauter (bass) joined the group and with Weckerman switching to percussion, the reformation was complete. The Feelies' second album, *The Good Earth*, was produced by R.E.M. guitarist Peter Buck, a long-time fan of *Crazy Rhythms*. Despite the gap between the releases, the new quintet showed much of the same fire and purpose, a factor confirmed by a third collection, *Only Life*. The group remains one of America's most inventive post-punk ensembles.
Albums: *Crazy Rhythms* (1980), *The Good Earth* (1986), *Only Life* (1989).

Felt

Cultivated, experimental English pop outfit formed in 1980 whose guru is the enigmatic Lawrence Hayward (vocals/guitar). Early collaborators included Maurice Deebank (guitar) and Nick Gilbert (bass), who practiced together in a small village called Water Orton just outside Birmingham. By the time of their first album released on Cherry Red Records, drummer Tony Race was replaced by Gary Ainge, and Gilbert departed to be replaced on bass by Mick Lloyd. Martin Duffy joined on organ for *Ignite The Seven Cannons*. Cult status had already arrived with the archtypal Felt cut, 'Penelope Tree'. The critical respect they were afforded continued, though they enjoyed little in the way of commerical recognition. The nearest they came was the 1985 single 'Primitive Painters', where they were joined by Elizabeth Fraser of the Cocteau Twins in a stirring, pristine pop song produced by fellow Cocteau Robin Guthrie. They signed to Creation Records in 1985. However, as Felt's contract with Cherry Red expired, so did the tenure of Lawrence's fellow guitarist and co-writer, Deebank. The latter, classically trained, had been an important component of the Felt sound, and was chiefly responsible for the delicate but intoxicating drama of early releases. Their stay at Creation saw high points in *Forever Breathes The Lonely Word* (1986) and *Poem Of The River* (1987). On the latter they were joined by Marco Thomas, Tony Willé and Neil Scott to add to the melodic guitar broadside. Felt bowed out with *Me And A Monkey On The Moon*, after a final move to Él Records, at which time guitar duties had switched to John Mohan. By the end of the 80s the band were no more, having achieved their stated task of surviving 10 years, 10 singles, and 10 albums (*Bubblegum Perfume* is an archive release of their Creation material, *The Felt Box Set* compiles their Cherry Red recordings). Lawrence had chosen to concentrate on his new project; 70s revivalists Denim.

Albums: *Crumbling The Antiseptic Beauty* (Cherry Red 1982, mini-album), *The Splendour Of Fear* (Cherry Red 1983, mini-album), *The Strange Idols Pattern And Other Short Stories* (Cherry Red 1984), *Ignite The Sevon Cannons* (Cherry Red 1985), *Let The Snakes Crinkle Their Heads To Death* (Creation 1986), *Forever Breathes The Lonely Word* (Creation 1986), *The Pictorial Jackson Review* (Creation 1988), *Train Above The City* (Creation 1988), *Me And A Monkey On The Moon* (Él 1989). Compilations: *Gold Mine Trash* (Cherry Red 1987), *Bubblegum Perfume* (Creation 1990), *The Felt Box Set* (Cherry Red 1993, 4-CD).

Fiat Lux

This three-piece synthesizer outfit took their name from the Latin for 'Let There Be Light'. Fiat Lux came together in Wakefield, Yorkshire, England in 1982. Vocalist Steve Wright and keyboard player David P. Crickmore had been at drama college together and Wright went on to join the well known Yorkshire Actors group. One of that company's patrons was the local guitarist and synthesizer wizard Bill Nelson (ex-Be Bop Deluxe and Red Noise) who on occasion provided music for their productions. Wright and Crickmore were writing material together and Wright decided to use his contact with Bill Nelson and send him a demo tape. Bill was impressed and decided to release the song 'Feels Like Winter Again' on his own Cocteau label. The first recordings were made using local session musicians but in April 1982 Bill's brother Ian, a saxophonist and keyboards player, was enrolled into Fiat Lux. Polydor picked up on the band and they recorded their first album in Liverpool. Tours with Blancmange and Howard Jones followed and their second and third Polydor singles - 'Secrets' and 'Blue Emotion' - both made the charts. 1985's 'Solitary Lovers' was not a success, however, and as synthesizer pop fell out of favour the band fell by the wayside, although Ian Nelson would go on to work occasionally with his brother.

Album: *Hired History* (1984).

Field Mice

Formed in Surrey, England in 1987 by principal songwriter Robert Wratten (b. 5 August 1966, Carshalton, Surrey, England; guitar/vocals) and Mark Dobson (b. 27 April 1965, Hartlepool, England; drums), the Field Mice linked up with Bristol-based Sarah Records for a series of records which unwittingly pigeon-holed both band and label as exponents of whimsical, sensitive pop songs. With the label's initial independent idealism - which manifested itself in seven inch-only releases in the era of 12-inch singles and compact disc singles - merely adding fire to cynics' vitriol. The Field Mice helped found a small yet fanatical following which spread as far as Japan by virtue of gently struck acoustic guitars and lyrics of the decidedly lovelorn variety. The line-up was expanded by the arrival of label-mate Harvey Williams (b. 31 December 1965, Cornwall, England; guitar), who had previously worked under the name Another Sunny Day. It was unfortunate that the prejudice of the music business ensured that the Field Mice remained condemned to the periphery even though the band were furthering their eclectic tastes by developing a penchant for danceable electronics ('Triangle') and experimental noise ('Humblebee'). And this was in spite of contemporary dance outfit Saint Etienne taking the Field Mice into the nation's clubs by covering the band's 'Let's Kiss And Make Up' single. In 1990 the trio became a quintet with the arrival of Michael Hiscock (b. 24 February 1966, Carshalton, Surrey, England; bass) and Annemari Davies (b. 9 February 1971, Oxfordshire, England; guitar/keyboards). Having previously only issued material on 7-inch and mini-albums (including the 10-inch *Snowball*), it was not until 1991 that the group released their first full albums. The first, *Coastal*, was a retrospective and *For Keeps*, a mature collection that promised much in the future. However, after the release of the acclaimed 'Missing The Moon', the Field Mice's frustrating reluctance to pursue a potentially rewarding higher profile, and a growing estrangement with their label, eventually led to the group dissolving in November 1991.

Albums: *Snowball* (Sarah 1989, mini-album), *Skywriting* (Sarah 1990), *For Keeps* (Sarah 1991). Compilation: *Coastal* (Sarah 1991).

Fields Of The Nephilim

This British rock group were formed in Stevenage, Hertfordshire, in 1983. The line-up comprised Carl McCoy

(vocals), Tony Pettitt (bass), Peter Yates (guitar) and the Wright brothers, Nod (b. Alexander; drums) and Paul (guitar). Their image, that of neo-western desperados, was borrowed from films such as *Once Upon A Time In America* and *The Long Ryders*. They also had the bizarre habit of smothering their predominantly black clothes in flour and/or talcum powder for some of the most hysterically inept videos ever recorded. Their version of Goth-rock, tempered with transatlantic overtones, found favour with those already immersed in the sounds of the Sisters Of Mercy and the Mission. Signed to the Situation Two label, Fields Of The Nephilim scored two major UK Independent hit singles with 'Preacher Man' and 'Blue Water', while their first album, *Dawn Razor*, made a modest showing on the UK album chart. The second set, *The Nephilim*, reached number 14, announcing the group's arrival as one of the principal rock acts of the day. Their devoted following also ensured a showing on the national singles chart, giving them minor hits with 'Moonchild' (1988 - also an independent chart number 1), 'Psychonaut' (1989) and 'Summerland (Dreamed)' (1990). In October 1991 McCoy left the group taking the 'Fields Of The Nephilim' name with him. The remaining members have since vowed to carry on. With the recruitment a new vocalist, Alan Delaney, they began gigging under the name Rubicon in the summer of 1992, leaving McCoy yet to unveil his version of the Nephilim.
Albums: *Dawn Razor* (Situation 2 1987), *The Nephilim* (Situation 2 1988), *Elyzium* (Beggars Banquet 1990), *Earth Inferno* (Beggars Banquet 1991), *BBC Radio 1 In Concert* (Windsong 1992), *Revelations* (Beggars Banquet 1993).
Videos: *Forever Remain* (1988), *Morphic Fields* (1989), *Earth Inferno* (1991), *Revelations* (1993).

Fingerprintz
This quirky Scottish new wave band was led by Jimmy O'Neil. They also included drummer Dogdan Wiczling, and acted as Lene Lovich's backing band for a time (O'Neil wrote her hit single 'Say When'). Their own releases included the 1981 single 'Shadowed', and their second album was produced by Nick Garvey of the Motors. O'Neil and Wiczling went on to play on Jaquie Brooke's album *Sob Stories*. Wiczling also toured and recorded with Adam Ant.
Albums: *The Very Dab* (1979), *Distinguishing Marks* (1980), *Beat Noire* (1981).

Finitribe
Scottish dance unit, who shared the same One Little Indian label as their fellow countrymen the Shamen, but failed to replicate their success. It was not through want of effort, or, for that matter, talent. The band took their name from 'Finny Tribe', a name given to the fish species by Irish religious sect the Rosicrucians, as well as the common people of that country. Originally a six-piece formed in Edinburgh in 1984, they founded their own label, striking out with a debut EP, *Curling And Stretching* in October. One month later they played their first gig together supporting Danielle Dax at London ULU. By 1986 they had acquired their first sampler, and released 'DeTestimony', an influential cut in both the balearic and, later, house movements. The following year they begun an ill-fated liaison with Chicago's

Wax Trax Records, releasing a version of Can's 'I Want More'. Following problems with the label vocalist Chris Connelly eventually elected to remain, ostensibly as part of Ministry and Revolting Cocks, also recording solo. Finitribe re-emerged in 1989 with the curtailed line-up of Mr Samples (b. John William Vick, 6 November 1965, Edinburgh, Scotland), Philip Pinsky (b. Philip David Pinsky, 23 March 1965, Appleton, Wisconsin, USA) and David Miller (b. David Francis Ashbride Miller, 20 July 1962, Moffat, Dunfrewshire, Scotland). Vick and Pinsky had previously been colleagues in Rigor Mortis, Miller having served in Explode Your Heart. Their influences remained both traditional rock and indie giants (Dog Faced Hermans, Magazine) and a myriad of new and old dance innovators (Jah Wobble, Tackhead, Sparks, Sub Sub, Orbital). A succession of well-regarded releases on One Little Indian failed to deliver them much in the way of commercial reward. The first and most notable of these was the acidic 'Animal Farm', which sampled the 'Old McDonald' nursery rhyme and laid torrents of abuse at the door of the McDonald's hamburger chain. The ensuing fuss, hardly deflated by a 'Fuck Off McDonald's' poster campaign, brought the band significant media exposure for the first time. Entering the 90s they looked as though they might expand beyond cult tastes with a new, kitsch image (white boiler suits peppered with stars) and more pop-dance-orientated material. As critics pointed out, they resembled an underground version of the Pet Shop Boys. By 1992 they had resurrected the Finiflex label and opened their own studio complex in Leith.
Albums: *Noise Lust And Fun* (Finiflex 1988), *Grossing 10K* (One Little Indian 1990), *An Unexpected Groovy Treat* (One Little Indian 1992).

Fire Engines
Alongside fellow Postcard Records bands such as Orange Juice and Josef K, the Fire Engines were part of a burgeoning Scottish music scene in the early 80s. Formed in 1979 by David Henderson (vocals/guitar), Murray Slade (guitar), Russell Burn (drums/percussion) and Graham Main (bass), the band's debut surfaced on the independent label, Codex Communications, in late 1980. 'Get Up And Use Me' was a manic burst of estranged, frenetically delivered guitar broken by sharp vocal outbursts. It also cut through the surrounding tendency for dense, synthesized sounds or second rate punk. The group received considerable promotion in the music press and were strongly tipped for success by the *New Musical Express*. *Lubricate Your Living Room (Background Music For Action People!)*, a mini-album's worth of near-instrumentals on the Accessory label, contained a similar barrage of awkward, angular funk guitar riffs. By spring 1981 the band had signed with aspiring Scottish label Pop: Aural, releasing the excellent 'Candy Skin'. More overtly pop (Henderson's nasal tones were to the forefront for the first time), the single was backed by 'Meat Whiplash', a superb slab of nasty, breakneck guitar work conflicting with an aggressive drum rhythm. By comparison, 'Big Gold Dream' (1981) was relatively melodic, perhaps in an attempt to reach a wider audience. It failed, although all the Fire Engines' product fared well in independent terms, and it was to be the

band's last release. Ideologically, the Fire Engines tapped a similar aesthetic to Josef K, fuelled by a vehement hatred of 'rock' in the general sense and the realization that punk's spirit of innovation had to be continued. Both bands remained true to that ethic, imploding rather than growing stale. Henderson went on to form Win, managed by Postcard founder Alan Horne, then Nectarine No. 9.
Album: *Lubricate Your Living Room (Background Music For Action People!)* (Pop: Aural 1981). Compilation: *Fond* (Creation 1992).

Firehose

This propulsive USA hardcore trio (usually titled fIREHOSE) was formed by two ex-members of the Minutemen, Mike Watt (vocalss/bass) and George Hurley (drums), following the death of the latter group's founding guitarist, David Boon, in 1985. Ed Crawford, aka eD fROMOHIO, completed the new venture's line-up, which made its debut in 1987 with the impressive *Ragin', Full-On*. Although undeniably powerful, the material Firehose offered was less explicit than that of its predecessor, and showed a greater emphasis on melody rather than bluster. Successive releases, *If'n* and *fROMOHIO*, revealed a group which, although bedevilled by inconsistency, was nonetheless capable of inventive, exciting music. At their best these songs merged knowing sarcasm (see 'For The Singer Of REM') with an unreconstructed approach to music making (as on drum solo, 'Let The Drummer Have Some'). This variety argued against commercial fortune, but the band were still picked up by a major, Columbia Records, in 1991, who released the slightly more disciplined *Flyin' The Flannel* that year. Later Mike Watt would also unveil a solo album for the same record company, completed with an all-star cast of US hardcore and punk legends.
Albums: *Ragin', Full-On* (SST 1987), *If'n* (SST 1988), *fROMOHIO* (SST 1989), *Flyin' The Flannel* (Columbia 1991).

Fischer Z

Basically a vehicle for the talents of musician/songwriter John Watts, Fischer Z was a bridge between new wave pop and the synthesizer wave of the early 80s. Watts and three other musicians performed on their first two albums, but by the time of the third Watts had taken over the keyboards and was co-producing as well. The first two singles, 'Wax Dolls' and 'Remember Russia', were both well received. The latter even boasted a Ralph Steadman cartoon illustration on the sleeve. However, it was 'The Worker' in 1979 that gave them their sole single success. In 1982 Watt started recording under his own name. However, singles like 'I Smelt Roses In The Underground' and 'Mayday Mayday' attracted little interest.
Albums: *Word Salad* (United Artists 1979), *Going Deaf For A Living* (1980), *Red Skies Over Paradise* (1981), *Destination Paradise* (1992), *Kamikaze Shirt* (Welfare 1994). John Watts solo *One More Twist* (1982), *The Iceberg Model* (1983).

Fishbone

Funk metal hybrid from Los Angeles, USA, who have now been active for over a decade. Five of the seven band members met through the Los Angeles School Bussing Program; a scheme designed to encourage black and white kids to visit each other's schools. Although their recorded output is sparse given their longevity, their hard political edge and high octane rythmic onslaught is every bit as deserving of mass attention as the Red Hot Chili Peppers or Living Colour. Their line-up boasts Chris 'Maverick Meat' Dowd (b. Christopher Gordon Dowd, 20 September 1965, Las Vegas, Nevada, USA; trombone, keyboards), 'Dirty' Walter Kibby (b. Walter Adam Kibby II, 13 November 1964, Columbus, Ohio, USA; trumpet, horn, vocals), 'Big' John Bigham (b. 3 March 1969, Lidsville, USA), Kendall Jones (b. Kendall Rey Jones, USA; guitar), Philip 'Fish' Fisher (b. 16 July 1967, El Camino, Los Angeles, California, USA; drums - has guested for Little Richard, Bob Dylan and others), John Fisher (b. John Norwood Fisher, 9 December 1965, El Camino, Los Angeles, California, USA; bass) and Angelo Moore (b. Angelo Christopher Moore, 5 November 1965, USA; lead vocals). Norwood was stabbed on stage early in their career when Fishbone played alongside hardcore bands such as the Dead Kennedys (the influence of Bad Brains is obvious in their output). After a debut mini-album the production expertise of David Kahne saw them touch on a more conventional metal direction, before exposing their true talents for the first time on *Truth And Soul*. This was helped in no small part by the airplay success of a cover of Curtis Mayfield's 'Freddie's Dead'. Subsequent recordings saw Fishbone branching out and working with rap artists like the Jungle Brothers, though *The Reality Of My Own Surroundings* had more in common with the hard-spined funk of Sly Stone. 'Fight The Youth' and 'Sunless Saturday' demonstrated a serious angle with socio-political, anti-racist and anti-drug lyrics in contrast to their lighter side on the humorous 'Naz-tee May'en'. Fishbone live shows continued to sell out without a hit to be seen, and Moore caused a minor sensation by ending a London show naked but for his saxophone. However, just as transatlantic commercial breakthrough offered itself with the *Monkey* set, bizarre press stories began to circulate concerning the activities of Jones, who, at the instigation of his father, had left the flock to join a religious cult. The group, whom he had renounced, were accused of attempted kidnap in their attempts to retrieve him.
Albums: *Fishbone* (Columbia 1985, mini-album), *In Your Face* (Columbia 1986), *Truth And Soul* (Columbia 1988), *The Reality Of My Surroundings* (Columbia 1991), *Give A Monkey A Brain & He'll Swear He's The Centre Of The Universe* (Columbia 1993).

Five Thirty

This north London based trio consisted of Tara Milton (vocals/bass), Paul Bassett (vocals/guitar) and Phil Hooper (drums). The name was taken as a reaction against the grind of 9 to 5 employment: 'It's the time when everyone goes home and gets ready to go out'. A previous incarnation featuring Milton and Bassett had recorded the single 'Catcher In The Rye' shortly after they had left school. After three further singles with the new line-up, and a series of well received, energetic live outings, they recorded their album debut, *Bed*, on East West Records. Motivated by the Jam, in spirit if not style, they were one of a number of similar sounding bands to break through in 1991, and achieve approval from the rock press for their energetic live performances. Afterwards, however, things went ominously silent.

Album: *Bed* (East West 1991).

Flaming Lips

Taking their name from a movie marquee in their home town of Oklahoma City, the Flaming Lips have won a deserved reputation in the late 80s and early 90s for their discordant, psychedelia-tinged garage rock. They are led by lyricist, vocalist and guitarist Wayne Coyne (b. Wayne Ruby Coyne, 17 March 1965, Pittsburgh, Pennsylvania, USA), who started playing music during his high school days to avert boredom. His inspiration came from his brother, who would invite musicians to hang out at the family home: 'I didn't know they were guitar lessons at the time, but there was always someone showing me a cool way to play 'Stairway To Heaven''. Following a debut bow at a transvestite bar in the mid-80s the Flaming Lips have gone on to record a fine body of work which escapes the worst excesses of the generic, drug-addled material which befalls many of their peers - whilst still being wonderfully off-kilter and unpredictable. 'I think a lot of things that we do are pretty normal rock-band kind of things. I mean, we do quiet songs, we do loud songs - but somewhere in there, people are drawn to the element of childlike images. It borderlines on being retarded in some ways'. Coyne was originally joined in the group by his brother, Mark Coyne, who is best remembered for his vocals on the debut album's 'My Own Planet'. Taking up the microphone following his brother's departure, Wayne Coyne now fronts a line-up which is filled out by Steven Drozd (b. Steven Gregory Drozd, 6 December 1969, Houston, Texas, USA; drums/vocals), Ron Jones (b. Ronald Lee Jones, 26 November 1970, Angeles, Philippines; guitars/vocals) and Michael Ivins (b. Michael Lee Ivins, 17 March 1965, Omaha, Nebraska, USA; bass/vocals). John 'Dingus' Donahue, of Mercury Rev fame, was also a member during the sessions for *In A Priest Driven Ambulance*. 1993 brought an acclaimed appearance at the Reading Festival, and tours with Porno For Pyros, Butthole Surfers and Stone Temple Pilots. They returned to Reading in 1994 to support the release of 'She Don't Use Jelly' which finally took off on MTV over the following year. This, combined with a storming appearance on the second stage at Lollapalooza, at last helped to build a substantial popular as well as critical following.

Albums: *The Flaming Lips* (Restless 1985), *Hear It Is* (Pink Dust 1986), *Oh My Gawd!!!* (Restless 1987), *Telepathic Surgery* (Restless 1989), *In A Priest Driven Ambulance* (Restless 1990), *Hit To Death In The Future Head* (Warners 1992), *Transmissions From The Satellite Heart* (Warners 1993).

Flamingoes

Mod-inspired UK indie trio featuring identical twin brothers Jude (vocals/guitar) and James (bass/vocals; both b. c.1970) Cook, plus lunatic drummer and ex-dustman Kevin. The Flamingoes formed in Hitchin, Hertfordshire, in April 1993,

before relocating to Camden, London, with the express intention of becoming 'pop stars'. They took their name from a Roxy Music lyric, though central influences such as the Jam and Clash were the ones acknowledged in early singles 'Chosen Few' and 'Scenester'. Previously they had won disc jockey Gary Crowley's *Demo Clash* competition on BBC GLR radio with 'Teenage Emergency'. Caught up in the *New Musical Express*-christened New Wave Of The New Wave, they played the famed New Art Riot gig in December with S*M*A*S*H and These Animal Men, attracting positive press in both the *Evening Standard* and *News Of The World* as well as more traditional music journals. Meanwhile Kevin was earning himself a reputation as a second generation Keith Moon, attacking audiences with sanitary towel bins and regularly throwing equipment about on stage. But their intention remained rigidly one of world domination: 'We ain't competing with Blur. I want to move right over Blur's heads and go straight for East 17'. To this end they recorded a debut album with the assistance of Dick Meany, after celebrated support gigs around the UK with label mates (at the time) Echobelly.

Album: *Plastic Jewels* (Pandemonium 1995).

Flatmates

The Flatmates were formed in Bristol, England, by Subway Organization label boss and guitarist Martin Whitehead in the summer of 1985, while he was promoting gigs. Whitehead recruited Rocker (drums), and was soon joined by Deb Haynes (vocals) and Kath Beach (bass), spurred on by the sounds of the Velvet Underground, Blondie, the Stooges and the Ramones. After Beach was replaced by Sarah Fletcher in 1986, the Flatmates issued the frothy 'I Could Be In Heaven' on Subway. 'Happy All The Time' continued the power pop vein the following year, which also saw Joel O'Bierne drafted in as the new drummer. The Flatmates' third single, 'You're Gonna Cry' (1987), was followed by 'Shimmer' (1988), the latter featuring guitarist Tim Rippington's debut. Like its predecessors, this fared well in the independent charts and justified the release of the band's BBC radio session for disc jockey Janice Long. Fletcher's departure was followed by the release of 'Heaven Knows', although this proved to be the band's last single. Rippington left in October 1988 after an on-stage fight with Whitehead, and the Flatmates eventually split the following April. A retrospective singles compilation, *Love And Death*, rounded it all off, by which time ex-members were busy with other projects. Martin and Joel formed the Sweet Young Things, later member Jackie Carrera (bass) had joined the Caretaker Race and Rocker teamed up with the Rosehips. After Subway folded in the spring of 1990, Whitehead started up a new label and fanzine, *Blaster!* As a final aside, the Flatmates' road manager Paul Roberts has since enjoyed a higher commercial profile than the band ever did with his outfit K-Class.

Compilation: *Love And Death* (Subway 1989).

Flesh For Lulu

This UK rock band were the creation of singer/guitarist Nick Marsh and drummer James Mitchell and took their name from an American cult movie. They were joined by Rocco

Barker (ex-Wasted Youth) on guitar and Glen Bishop, replaced by Kevin Mills (ex-Specimen) on bass after the single 'Restless'. Derek Greening (keyboards/guitar) became the fifth member shortly afterwards. Previously their debut single had been 'Roman Candle' prefacing a first album which they would 'rather forget about'. *Blue Sisters Swing*, on the tiny Hybrid label, followed as a stop gap. The sleeve illustration of two nuns kissing resulted in bans in the USA and Europe. The release of *Big Fun City* was the first to do the band justice, even though it was hampered by artwork problems at Polydor Records, and featured everything from country ballads to basic rock 'n' roll. Their succession of labels grew longer as they moved on to Beggars Banquet Records in 1986. *Long Live The New Flesh* followed a year later, recorded at Abbey Road Studios and produced by Mike Hedges. Their approach to the sophistication of their new surroundings was typical: 'Forget the cerebral approach - just turn up them guitars!' Their most pop orientated album to date, *Plastic Fantastic*, was recorded in Australia by Mark Opitz, several titles from which were later employed for film soundtracks (*Uncle Buck* and *Flashback*). By this time, original members Marsh, Barking and Greening had been joined by Hans Perrson (drums) and Mike Steed (bass). Despite stronger songwriting than had been evident on previous recordings, the album failed and Beggars did not renew their option.
Albums: *Flesh For Lulu* (Polydor 1984), *Blue Sisters Swing* (Hybrid 1985, mini-album), *Big Fun City* (Caroline 1985), *Long Live The New Flesh* (Beggars Banquet 1987), *Plastic Fantastic* (Beggars Banquet 1990).

Flesheaters

Innovative rock outfit built around cult hero Chris 'D' Desjardins (vocals), who had been active on the Los Angeles, California scene from the 70s, making films and acting as well as co-ordinating the Flesheaters. Their first established line-up added Robyn Jameson (bass), Don Kirk (guitar), and Chris Wahl (drums). However, something of the nature of the band can be summised by the frequency of its personnel shifts. Those passing through the ranks include; Bill Bateman (drums), Steve Berlin (saxophone), Gene Taylor (keyboards), John Bazz (bass), Dave Alvin (guitar) all ex-Blasters; Pat Garrett (guitar/bass), Joe Ramirez (bass), Joe Nanini (drums) all ex-Black Randy; John Doe (bass), Don Bonebrake (drums), Excene Doe (vocals) all ex-X. Stan Ridgway (Wall Of Voodoo; guitar) and Tito Larriva (Plugz; guitar) were also present in an early incarnation. These represent only a fraction of former members in a band which effectively operated in a 'pick up and play' mode. This did not diminish their appeal however; 'The one thing that we do that mystifies our audience is we don't play in one category. The music that we play is real loud. Its real metallic. It could be described as heavy metal, or what was in 1977 punk.' Chris D split the band at the end of the 80s after the years of cut and paste line-ups finally took their toll. By the 90s, however, they were back on the circuit once more. *Dragstrip Riot*, with which Desjardins reinstated the band after years of inactivity, was a sprawling double album set that saw the band crashing out riotous swamp rock of a virulent, Cramps type character. The intervening years had

seen him operate with his own band, Chris D And The Divine Horsemen, whilst Jameson also played with Alex Gibson and Passionel.
Albums: *No Questions Asked* (Upsetter 1979), *A Minute To Pray, A Second To Die* (Ruby 1981), *Forever Came Today* (Ruby 1982), *A Hard Road To Follow* (Upsetter 1983), *Dragstrip Riot* (SST 1991, double album), *Sex Diary Of Mr Vampire* (SST 1991). Compilations: *Greatest Hits - Destroyed By Fire* (SST 1986), *Prehistoric Fits* (SST 1990).

Fleshtones

Formed in 1976 in the Queens district of New York City, the Fleshtones were first heard on British shores as part of a 'package' tour in 1980 with the dB's, the Raybeats and the Bush Tetras. Each band was different, drawing energy from punk but ideas from a myriad of other musical forms. In the Fleshtones' case, Keith Strong (guitar), Peter Zaremba (vocals/keyboards), Jan Marek Pukulski (bass) and Bill Milhizer (drums, ex-Harry Toledo Band and Action Combo), this involved the fusion of the new wave with R&B and rockabilly. The group caught the attention of Miles Copeland's IRS Records label via 'American Beat', their debut single from 1979 on the Red Star label. The 12-inch EP *Up-Front* duly surfaced in 1980 in America, although it was not until 1981 that its strongest track, 'The Girl From Baltimore', secured a British release. It was followed by 'The World Has Changed' (though only in the US), and 'Shadow-Line' in early 1982. This coincided not only with the band's first official long player, *Roman Gods* but also *Blast Off!*, a cassette of their unreleased 1978 studio album on Reach Out International (ROIR) Records. All was comparatively quiet for over a year until the Fleshtones' unleashed their best record, *Hexbreaker*, promoted by two singles, 'Right Side Of A Good Thing' and the evocative 'Screaming Skull' (both 1983). The material shared the hard rock 'n' roll sound of *Roman Gods*, but the band soon curtailed their activities, apart from the strange *Fleshtones Vs Reality* set in 1987 and three live albums. However, they were back on the case come the 90s.
Albums: *Roman Gods* (IRS 1981), *Blast Off!* (ROIR 1982, cassette only), *Hexbreaker* (IRS 1983), *Speed Connection* (IRS 1985), *Speed Connection* (IRS 1985), *Fleshtones Vs Reality* (1987), *Soul Madrid* (Impossible 1989), *Beautiful Light* (Naked Language 1994). Compilation: *Living Legends Series* (IRS 1989).

Flipper

San Francisco punk band Flipper formed in 1979 with original members Will Shatter (bass/vocals), Steve DePace (drums), both former members of Negative Trend, Bruce Lose (bass/vocals) and Ted Falconi (guitar), also of Negative Trend, on drums. Following the single, 'Love Canal'/'Ha Ha', on Subterranean Records, the group released its debut, and best-known album, *Generic*, in 1982. Sporting topical lyrics and both hardcore punk and noise dirges, the collection was instantly recognised as a classic of west coast punk. However, these were no stereotypical three chord thrashes, the band experimenting instead with the wildly overblown 'Sex Bomb Baby' and the super-minimalist 'Life'. Other albums followed on Subterranean in 1984 and 1986 but failed to match their debut's impact, and the following year Shatter died of an accidental heroin overdose. Three out of four of the original members of Flipper reformed in 1990, resulting in the release of *American Grafishy*.

Albums: *Generic* (Subterranean 1982), *Gone Fishin'* (Subterranean 1984), *Public Flipper Ltd.* (Subterranean 1986), *American Grafishy* (1993). Compilation: *Sex Bob Baby!* (Subterranean 1988).

Flowered Up

As cultural phenomenons go, rarely has a band mirrored their social surroundings more graphically than Flowered Up from the UK. Formed on a north London housing estate in 1989, they were immediately championed by so many disparate causes (the working classes, the drug dealer, proud Southerners) that their rise to fame was virtually inevitable. Born out of the ecstasy boom which swept the musical underground at the turn of the 90s, Flowered Up's first gig at the close of 1989 was a shambolic affair which outraged as many onlookers as it excited. Within six months the line-up had settled down with Liam Maher (vocals), brother Joe (guitar), Andy Jackson (bass), Tim Dorney (keyboards), John Tovey (drums), and a man called Barry Mooncult who had taken to dancing with the band onstage, wearing a giant flower. The release of their debut single, 'It's On', encouraged the UK weekly music papers to take the unusual step of putting a brand new band on its front pages, but all the accusations of hype were drowned out by Flowered Up revellers convinced that the band were London's answer to Manchester's Happy Mondays. They weren't, nor were they another Clash, or another Madness, mainly because Flowered Up's flowing rock/funk grooves graced the Top 40 of all the UK charts, yet failed to upset the commercial applecart, in spite of all the attention. By 1991, much of the fuss had fizzled out and *A Life With Brian* appeared to show that the band, for all their Cockney quirkiness, could make an album that stood on its own two feet without fear of falling over. It would also provide the band with their tombstone, however, with Tim Dorney going on to work with Clive Langer, while Liam Maher returned to his bootleg stall in Camden Market.

Album: *A Life With Brian* (Heavenly 1991).

Flux Of Pink Indians

This UK Punk band was formed from the ashes of the Epileptics (who later changed their name to Epi-X due to letters of complaint from The British Epilepsy Association). Two surviving members were Colin (vocals) and Derek Birkett (b. 18 February 1961, London, England; bass), who would go on to form Flux Of Pink Indians, with guitarist Andy and drummer Sid. Their debut EP *Neu Smell*, emerged on Crass Records. Alongside standard rejections of society, war, and the eating of flesh lay the joyful 'Tube Disasters', the sort of humour which was in short order in the grim world of anarcho punk. Sid (later Rubella Ballet) was soon replaced by Bambi, formerly of Discharge, while Andy was replaced by Simon. However, both departed quickly for their original band, the Insane, and were replaced by old Epileptics guitarist Kevin Hunter and drummer Martin Wilson. Their debut album, *Strive To Survive Causing Least Suffering*

Possible, confirmed the promise of the single, and premiered the band's own Spiderleg label. Alongside standard thrash numbers were highly perceptive attacks on consumer society. The anti-religious 'Is Anybody There' was a particularly effective example, using simple but jarring lyrics to emphasize its point. The follow-up, *The Fucking Cunts Treat Us Like Pricks*, was unsurprisingly banned by retailers HMV, and copies were seized by Greater Manchester police from Eastern Bloc record shop, which was charged with displaying 'Obscene Articles For Publication For Gain'. The album, ironically, concerned violence between men and women, based on the experiences of a band member who had been sexually assaulted. The music contained within, was little short of a directionless cacophony, however. *Uncarved Block* was the most unexpected of the band's three studio albums, delivering more polemic allied to dance and funk rhythms which left their previous audience totally non-plussed. It was a brave effort, and one which, alongside their debut, stands up to repeated listening. Birkett, making use of his experiences with Spiderleg, has gone on to set up the highly successful One Little Indian Records, and still uses the Flux title for occasional projects: 'Flux is just me and whoever I happen to be recording with'.

Albums: *Strive To Survive Causing Least Suffering Possible* (Spiderleg 1982), *The Fucking Cunts Treat Us Like Pricks* (Spiderleg 1984), *Uncarved Block* (One Little Indian 1986).

Flys

This Coventry, England-based group enjoyed a minor league role in the new wave, but owed more to power pop and astute songwriting than punk. Singer and guitarist Neil O'Connor (brother of Hazel O'Connor) met school kids David Freeman (guitar/vocals) and Joe Hughes (bass/vocals) in the mid-70s, and formed Midnight Circus, eventually recruiting Pete King on drums. A name change to the Flys coincided with the discovery of punk's first tremors, but a demo in April 1977 brought an apathetic response from the usual channels. The band issued *Bunch Of Five*, an energetic EP, on their own Zama Records label in time for Christmas. Quick as a flash, EMI Records snapped them up, rushing out one of the EP tracks (and perhaps their finest ever moment), 'Love And A Molotov Cocktail', as a single. After a tour with the Buzzcocks and John Otway And Wild Willy Barrett came 'Fun City', recorded at Pathway Studios. *Waikiki Beach Refugees* (also the title of their next single) emerged in October 1978 to an enthusiastic response, while the band toured Europe. 1979 saw a flurry of singles - 'Beverley' in February, 'Name Dropping' in April and 'We Are The Lucky Ones' - but internal quarrels led to the recruitment of a riotous new drummer Graham Deakin (ex-Frankie Miller and John Entwistle's Ox). *Flys Own*, rawer than their debut, coincided with a tour with the Ruts in autumn 1979. The EP, *Four From The Square*, was released in February as the band transferred to Parlophone Records. This was followed by 'What Will Mother Say' in May 1980. Internal pressures began to erupt and the Flys broke up soon after. O'Connor joined Hazel for two years and two albums before becoming a musical arranger, and then producer and engineer. Freeman issued a cover of the Supremes' 'Stop! In The Name Of Love', took a degree, published his poetry, sung on Alison

Moyet's *Raindancing* and later formed The Lover Speaks with Hughes (after his spell with ex-Specials Roddy Radiation And His Tearjerkers). Pete King, meanwhile, joined After The Fire, but sadly died aged 26. See For Miles Records recently compiled an excellent self-titled retrospective of the band.

Albums: *Waikiki Beach Refugees* (EMI 1978), *Flys Own* (EMI 1979). Compilation: *The Flys* (See For Miles 1991).

Foetus

You've Got Foetus On Your Breath, Scraping Foetus Off The Wheel, Foetus Uber Alles, Foetus Inc ... all these titles are actually the pseudonym of one person: Australian emigre, Jim Thirlwell, alias Jim Foetus and Clint Ruin. After founding his own record company, Self Immolation in 1980, he set about 'recording works of aggression, insight and inspiration'. Backed with evocatively descriptive musical slogans such as 'positive negativism' and 'bleed now pay later', Foetus released a series of albums, several of which appeared through Stevo's Some Bizzare label. With stark one-word titles such as *Deaf*, *Ache*, *Hole* and *Nail*, Thirlwell presented a harrowing aural netherworld of death, lust, disease and spiritual decay. In November 1983, Foetus undertook a rare tour, performing with Marc Almond, Nick Cave and Lydia Lunch in the short-lived Immaculate Consumptive. Apart from these soul-mates, Foetus has also played live with the Swans' Rolli Mossiman in Wiseblood, Lydia Lunch in Stinkfist, and appeared on albums by several artist including The The, Einsturzende Neubauten, Nurse With Wound and Anne Hogan. In 1995 Thirlwell announced plans to release his first studio album in seven years.

Albums: *Deaf* (Self Immolation 1981), *Ache* (Self Immolation 1982), *Hole* (Self Immolation 1984), *Nail* (Self Immolation 1985), *Bedrock* (Self Immolation/Some Bizzare 1987, mini-album), *Thaw* (Self Immolation/Some Bizzare 1988), *Gash* (Big Cat 1995).

Food Records

This record label was formed by David Balfe (ex-Big In Japan, Teardrop Explodes manager) in 1984, and its first release was Brilliant's single, 'Soul Murder'. However, it was with the arrival of economics graduate and *Sounds* journalist Andy Ross (b. 31 January 1956) that the label was given a figurehead. Ross would conduct the day-to-day running of the label, which would focus on those bands linked with the 'indie' sector which had the greatest commercial potential. (Both Balfe and Ross would become co-managers of Voice Of The Beehive, a group they discovered playing above the Enterprise pub in Chalk Farm, London.) The earliest signees to Food also included Diesel Park West and Crazyhead, on the strength of which EMI Records first took a stake in the label in 1988. The arrival of Jesus Jones the following year was instrumental in the longterm success of the label. By this time Food's second strongest outfit were Blur. Their number 8-peaking single, 'There's No Other Way', gave the label its first significant success. By 1991 Jesus Jones' debut album had entered the chart at number 1 and the future looked bright. However, as Jesus Jones success tailed off, Blur too found themselves unable to live up to expectations. When

Balfe rejected their second album *Modern Life Is Rubbish* (correctly, in hindsight), it spoiled the label's relationship with the band. But for Ross's intervention the group were about to leave the label, but Balfe instead jumped ship, electing to return to management with Voice Of The Beehive and selling his shares to EMI. Ross's belief in Blur was vindicated by the enormous subsequent success of *Park Life*, though Shampoo too offered huge commercial reward, going double platinum in Japan. Other bands such as Sensitize and Whirlpool have not proved as successful, but that has not stopped the label investing in new talent, including Planet Claire and Dubstar.

Selected albums: Jesus Jones: *Doubt* (Food 1991). Blur: *Modern Life Is Rubbish* (Food 1993), *Park Life* (Food 1994). Shampoo: *We Are Shampoo* (Food 1994).

4AD Records

Few independent record labels can boast as distinctive a roster as 4AD, both aesthetically and musically. The label was formed in early 1980 by Ivo Watts-Russell and Peter Kent (who were both then working at Beggars Banquet Records) reputedly after hearing a demo from new act Modern English. At first, the label was called Axis for the initial clutch of singles by the Fast Set, the Bearz, Shox and most importantly, Bauhaus, but this was changed to avoid confusion with a similarly-named company and 4AD was born. A loan of £2,000 from Beggars Banquet ensured that 4AD got off the ground, signing Modern English, In Camera, Mass, Dance Chapter and Rema Rema, among others. Kent soon left to set up Situation 2, working heavily with Bauhaus who shortly graduated to Beggars Banquet. 4AD, however, steered away from their parent company, witnessing a one-off single for the then-unknown The The (and later, Matt Johnson's solo album), plus several uncompromising recordings from Australian outfit the Birthday Party, and providing a home for ex-Wire personnel Bruce Gilbert, Graham Lewis/Cupol and Colin Newman. 1981-82 brought new acts as eclectic as Sort Col, the Past Seven Days, My Captains, Dif Juz and the Happy Family, alongside solo works from ex-Bauhaus individuals David Jay and Daniel Ash/Tones On Tail and a collaboration between Lydia Lunch and the Birthday Party's Rowland S. Howard. More significantly, Ivo stumbled upon the Cocteau Twins, who were to prove the act that aside from emerging as the label's major artists, crystalized the ethereal nature often associated with 4AD product, aided later by the oblique yet attractive sleeve designs from Vaughn Oliver's 23 Envelope art studio. There was also Colourbox, another 4AD mainstay who embodied the label's experimental approach to recording and the studio, as well as the more sinister X-Mal Deutschland. Ivo soon teamed with the Cocteaus among others, for his own project in 1983, This Mortal Coil, which enjoyed both critical and commercial support. Apart from Dead Can Dance, Xymox, Richenel and the Wolfgang Press, the mid-80s saw few signings as 4AD concentrated on their existing roster. The late 80s, on the other hand, signalled a slight reappraisal, with the departure of Colourbox and the signing of new American acts Throwing Muses, Boston exports the Pixies and New York's Ultra Vivid Scene. The influential but often-ignored AR Kane also arrived for a brief

time, which spawned a one-off project with members of Colourbox, M.A.R.R.S's 'Pump Up The Volume'. A UK number 1 hit, this pivotal single was perhaps the first successful mesh of white rock and rhythm, paving the way for a commercial and artistic revolution in both British dance and independent music. Then came the two-pronged attack of guitar bands Lush and the Pale Saints to see in the new decade, as the Pixies made serious commercial headway. In their wake came the Breeders, a project involving the Pixies, Throwing Muses and others. When the Pixies dissolved it was to much wringing of hands in the music press, but 4AD soon picked up Frank Black as a solo artist (though he would eventually be dropped after two albums). Greater consolation came with the commercial approbation of Throwing Muses' spin-off, Belly. Which was just as well, as the quintessential 4AD group, the Cocteau Twins, had now moved on to a major. Treading a tightrope between financial well-being and artistic purity, 4AD has spotlighted an impressive yet diverse roster since its inception, and continues to excel in bringing idiosyncratic music into the commercial mainstream.
Compilation: *Lonely Is An Eyesore* (4AD 1987).

400 Blows

Coming together in 1981 in Croydon, London, this versatile ensemble combined funk, reggae, African music and disco. Their obvious influences, in addition to various ethnic styles, included 23 Skidoo and Throbbing Gristle. The debut release was 'Beat The Devil', much in the vein of Cabaret Voltaire, which attracted the attention of Illuminated Records. The band is basically the creation of Edward Beer, who dismissed original collaborator Scott Fraser after the single. The two Anthonys, Thorpe and Lea, were roped in though Beer continued to maintain artistic control. Early controversy surrounded the title of their debut album, *If I Kissed Her, I'd Have To Kill Her First*, which prompted the question of whether they liked women. 'Oh, maybe sexually I like them, but I don't like having them around that much. They just get on my nerves,' was Beer's reply. A minor hit came with 'Movin'', an update of the old Brass Construction number, at which point he had been joined by female vocalist Lee. By the late 80s and early 90s they were turning to the beat of acid house, releasing singles like 'Champion Sound' on Warrior records. Thorpe would go on to significant solo success as the Moody Boyz, also remixing for the KLF.
Albums: *If I Kissed Her, I'd Have To Kill Her First* (Illuminated 1985), *The Good Clean English Fist* (Dojo 1986), *Look* (Illuminated 1986), *Yesterday, Today, Tomorrow, Forever* (Concrete 1989), *New Lords On The Block* (Concrete 1989).

4 Non Blondes

San Francisco quartet who formed in 1989, making a slow rise through the traditional round of bar shows and club dates, going on to win a Best Unsigned Band award and then a prestigious support date to Primus. In 1993 their commercial arrival corresponded to that of fellow San Franciscans the Spin Doctors, scoring a UK number 2 single ('What's Up') and a Top 10 debut album, *Bigger, Better,*

Faster, More!, produced by Prince associate David Tickle. Selling half a million copies in the US where it was originally released in 1992, it also topped charts in Germany and Sweden. The group comprise the strong visual and almost hectoring vocal presence of Linda Perry (b. c.1965; guitar/vocals) alongside Christa Hillhouse (b. 1962, Oklahoma, USA; bass), Roger Rocha (guitar) and Dawn Richardson (drums). Rocha stepped in to replace original incumbent Shanna Hall during sessions for the debut album, with Richardson having replaced Wanda Day shortly before pre-production was embarked on. 'Token bloke' Rocha is the grandson of abstract expressionist Clyfford Still and an art school veteran, while Richardson is a trained percussionist with a degree from California State University and several years experience in jazz and salsa bands. Hillhouse and Perry began the band together, having to cancel their first ever rehearsal on 7 October 1989 when an earthquake hit the Bay Area. Hillhouse had first spotted Parry playing an acoustic set, and Perry's songs quickly became the dominant force within 4 Non Blondes. Some of her youth had been mis-spent as a self-confessed acid head, a predilection which she decided to end after falling from a third floor balcony. Prior to her musical career she had also worked, more soberly, as an accountant. Many of the band's songs were lifted directly from her solo repertoire, including 'Spaceman', the follow-up to 'What's Up'. However, suspicions were raised in the press that 4 Non Blondes represented a corporate chart raid, providing designer grunge for the post-Nirvana and Lemonheads (to whose label, Interscope/Atlantic Records they signed) generation. Support slots to Prince and Neil Young did little to dispel these assumptions, but there was an undeniable infectious simplicity to 'What's Up' which indelibly marked it as one of the records of 1993.
Album: *Bigger, Better, Faster, More!* (Interscope 1992).

4 Skins

As their name suggests, this London, England band comprised four skinheads, who specialized in vitriolic three-chord 'yob-rock'. Their membership was fluid, including no less than four lead singers, with only Hoxton Tom (bass) still resident between their first and second albums. Taking their musical brief from outfits such as Sham 69, the Angelic Upstarts and the Cockney Rejects, they were a third generation punk band heavily associated with the Oi! movement alongside fellow travellers the Business. With a blatantly patriotic image, the band attracted National Front supporters to their live shows, which occasionally erupted into full-scale riots. Lyrically they expounded on racism, police brutality and corrupt governments. However, musically they were not so adventurous, being rigidly formularized and unable to develop from their simplistic origins (basic punk spiced by the odd foray into skinhead's 'other' music, ska). From a creative standpoint, the band had ground to a halt by 1983. Their fan-base continued to contract and they soon faded into oblivion, though re-releases and compilations have reminded many of their enduring street popularity.
Albums: *The Good, The Bad And The 4 Skins* (Secret 1982), *A Fistful Of 4 Skins* (Syndicate 1983), *From Chaos To 1984* (Syndicate 1984). Compilations: *Wonderful World Of The 4*

Skins (Link 1987), *A Few 4 Skins More Vol. 1* (Link 1987), *A Few 4 Skins More Vol. 2* (Link 1987), *Live And Loud* (Link 1989).

14 Iced Bears

Few bands epitomized the mid-80s 'shambling' pop music scene in Britain more succinctly than Brighton's 14 Iced Bears. Formed in 1985 by Rob Sekula (b. 12 December 1963, Camberwell, Surrey, England), Alan White and Nick Emery, the band quickly became embroiled in an alternative network peppered with anoraks, cheap fanzines and guitar-based songs for which the word 'amateur' could have been invented. With more line-up changes than record releases, 14 Iced Bears' history is almost as shambolic as their music. Alan White soon departed to form Pleasure Splinters, to be replaced by Dominic Minques and guitarist Kevin Canham (b. 10 October 1964, Aldershot, Hampshire, England). Nick Roughley (b. West Riding, Yorkshire, England) joined for the band's second single in 1987 before leaving to form Blow Up. Steve Ormsby and Bill Cox briefly replaced Minques and Emery before 1988 when 14 Iced Bears - then consisting of Sekula, Kevin Canham, Will Taylor (b. 23 August 1968, Brighton, Sussex, England; bass) and Graham Durrant (b. 10 October 1963, Camberwell, Surrey, England; drums) - finally got around to making an album. After suffering from the curse of 'shambling', *14 Iced Bears* demonstrated an admirable progression towards heavier, more psychedelic territories and benefitted from a scattering of warmly surprised responses from the UK music press. Fittingly, this line-up remained stable until 1991 when Tim White (b. 30 March 1967, Essex, England) replaced Taylor, who had moved over to Blow Up, and 14 Iced Bears recorded their second 60s-tinged album, *Wonder*. Soon after, an extra chapter was added to the Bears' story when White made way for Rob Colley (b. 27 June 1963, Brighton, Sussex, England) formerly in Whirl.
Albums: *14 Iced Bears* (1988), *Wonder* (1991). Compilation: *Precision* (1990).

Foxton, Bruce

b. 1 September 1955, Woking, Surrey, England. Following the break-up of the Jam, guitarist Foxton set out on a predictably difficult solo career. During the summer of 1983, he enjoyed UK Top 30 success with 'Freak'. His strong, straightforward pop, with often distinct Jam overtones, was generally well-produced, with Steve Littlewhite's 'This Is The Way', proving particularly effective. In 1984, Foxton released *Touch Sensitive*, which featured all-original compositions and another solid production. While deserving chart success, Foxton's work has, not surprisingly, been compared unfavourably with that of the Jam and, consequently, his solo career has suffered.
Album: *Touch Sensitive* (1984).
Further reading: *Our Story*, Bruce Foxton and Rick Buckler with Alex Ogg.

Foxx, John

b. Dennis Leigh Chorley, Lancashire, England. Foxx moved to London in 1974 and was a key instigator of 70s electro-pop. He was the founder member of Ultravox with whom he wrote, sang and dabbled in synthetic noises, before handing over to Midge Ure. Gary Numan cited him as his main influence, which was some consolation for the fact that Numan was having hits when Ultravox were dropped by Island Records. Foxx went solo in 1979 and formed his own label MetalBeat, distributed by Virgin. The infectious 'Underpass' began a short string of minor Top 40 UK hits which included 'No-One Driving', 'Burning Car' and 'Europe After The Rain'. Foxx's appearances on the singles and album charts ended in the mid-80s.
Albums: *Metamatic* (1980), *The Garden* (1981), *The Golden Section* (1983), *In Mysterious Ways* (1985).

Frank And Walters

Highly promising three piece band from Cork, Ireland, named after two tramps who inhabit a nearby village. Made up of Paul Linehan (vocals/bass), Niall Linehan (guitar) and Ashley Keating (drums), the group attracted immediate press attention through a debut EP on the homely Setanta label (also responsible for Into Paradise), the song writing on which was highly unassuming in its parochial good humour. 'Michael', for instance, concerned the band's best friend who was the star of the town via his expensive car, until he crashed it and reverted to the use of a bicycle. Paul's tender lyrics emphasized the cathartic nature of this body blow in a manner heavily reminiscent of the slow passage of time and wisdom in rural Ireland. Two Single of The Week awards later, 'Fashion Crisis Hits New York' proved another instant favourite: 'Fashion Crisis hits New York, I saw a blind man who was eating his fork, He said that's what you've got to do to be cool, you eat your cutlery instead of your food'. This was enough to ensure Go Discs! would step in to shepherd future releases, as the band took up residence at a YMCA in Wimbledon. A third EP, led off by a typically infectious 'Happy Busman', was piloted by Edwyn Collins. However, the resulting debut album failed to fulfil critical expectations for journalists primed on the band's superior early material (which was largely rehashed to less immediate effect). 'This Is Not A Song' and a reissued 'Fashion Crisis Hits New York' offered chart hits via bigger promotion and production. Afterwards the band retreated to Cork in an attempt to recover from the 'too much too early' syndrome which, as some critics were already suggesting, had robbed them of their native charm.
Album: *Trains, Boats And Planes* (Go! Discs 1992).

Frank Chickens

Japan's ebullient Frank Chickens were formed by Kazuko Hohki (b. 1952, Tokyo, Japan; vocals) and Kazumi Taguchi (later replaced by Atsuko Kamura). The duo met in London in 1978 while working with the Japanese-American Toy Theatre. The JATT would perform extracts from classic fiction using toy figurines, mechanical robots and 'Godzilla' models as the central characters to the play. This bizarre concept was given publicity by BBC Radio 1 producer John Walters' *Walters' Week*. The Frank Chickens achieved something of a cult hit with 'Blue Canary' in 1985, which received strong airplay from disc jockey John Peel (whose producer was Walters). As well as depicting a socio-comic view of the modern Japanese woman in western society, the

Frank Chickens also tackled the subject of the western male's perception of Japanese women in general, as in 'Yellow Toast'. Their best known number, however, remained the proto-feminist 'We Are Ninja' ('We Are Ninja/Not Geisha'). Kazuko was, to some degree, also instrumental in popularizing the phenomenon of Karaoke to English culture by way of the Channel Four television programme, *The Karaoke Klub*. The Frank Chickens have continued to perform on the London fringe theatre and cabaret club circuit into the 90s.

Albums: *We Are Frank Chickens* (Kaz 1984), *Get Chickenised* (Flying Lecords 1987), *Club Monkey* (Flying Lecords 1988), *Do The Karaoke* (Flying Lecords 1989). Compilation: *The Best Of Frank Chickens* (Kaz 1987).

Frazier Chorus

Originally a four-piece band from Brighton, England, who - under the name Plop! - set out to be the antithesis of Wham!. However, singer and keyboardist Tim Freeman's songs were circulated on a demo and he and the rest of the band Michéle Allardyce (percussion), Kate Holmes (flute) and Chris Taplin (clarinet) were signed to 4AD under the name Frazier Chorus, a title taken from the back of a 50s US baseball jacket. With their unusual instrumental line-up which lent an almost synth-pop/pastoral feel, the 4AD debut, 'Sloppy Heart' (1987), did not fit easily with the harder edge the label were moving towards in the mid-80s. The band soon switched to Virgin. In 1989 they released their debut long player, *Sue* which featured orchestral arrangements from David Bedford and contributions from Tim Sanders (tenor saxophone), Roddy Lorimer (trumpet/flugelhorn) and Simon Clarke (piccolo/saxophones). Freeman's lyrics, delivered in an almost whispered singing style, eloquently chronicled a mundane existence with keen, ironic observations of 'everyday' life and sexual relations. Minor UK hits with 'Dream Kitchen' and 'Typical' promised much, but their single releases all failed to break any higher than 51. A reissue of 'Sloppy Heart' featured a laid-back version of the Sex Pistols' 'Anarchy In The UK' on its b-side. Allardyce left acrimoniously during the recording of the second album (with the Lightning Seeds' Ian Broudie on production) leaving the band as a trio. Allardyce, whose orientation was geared more to dance music, would continue to work as a journalist for disc jockey magazine *Jocks*. Further minor hits with the Paul Oakenfold re-mix of 'Cloud 8' and 'Nothing', and 1991's 'Walking On Air' confirmed that Frazier Chorus's cult appeal had peaked. Freeman also collaborated on the 4AD house project This Mortal Coil, while Taplin would go on to join Vanessa Quinnones in the duo, Espiritu.

Albums: *Sue* (1989), *Ray* (1991).

Free Kitten

Founded in New York by Sonic Youth bassist Kim Gordon and former Pussy Galore guitarist Julie Cafritz, Free Kitten announced their arrival with a series of singles, including a version of X-Ray Spex's 'Oh Bondage, Up Yours'. These were later collected on *Free Kitten*. The duo's brand of angry, 'post-punk' music was more forcibly unveiled on *Call Now*, a six-track set issued on Sonic Youth's Ecstatic Peace label. Elements of both musicians' antecedents were present,

notably on the extended 'Falling Backwards'. Bouyed by the addition of Mark Ibald (bass) and Yoshimi (drums, trumpet, harmonica), Free Kitten undertook a UK tour to promote *Nice Ass* on which the experimental nature of the group's music was placed within a more disciplined, rock-based structure.

Albums: *Call Now* (Ecstatic Peace 1992), *Unboxed* (Wiiija 1994), *Nice Ass* (Wiiija 1995). Compilation: *Free Kitten* (Wiiija 1994).

Freshies

The seeds of this UK pop group were sown in 1971 when Chris Sievey and his brother hitched a lift to London and staged a sit-in at the Beatles' Apple Records headquarters - eventually going on to do a session. Subsequently Sievey recorded numerous demos which were sent to record companies, resulting in an avalanche of rejection slips he later published as a small book. Another book was dedicated to Virgin Records rejections alone. His own label Razz was formed in 1974, releasing a variety of singles, videos and over 60 cassettes. In the meantime, Sievey attempted to form his own band under the title the Freshies. Among a stream of musicians who collaborated were Martin Jackson (later Magazine and Swing Out Sister) and Billy Duffy (later the Cult). The most consistent line-up however, was Barry Spencer (guitar), Rick Sarko (bass, ex-Ed Banger And The Nosebleeds) and Mike Doherty (drums, ex-Smirks), the line-up operating between 1980 and 1982. After several small pressings on Razz, Sievey finally hit the charts with 'I'm In Love With The Girl On The Manchester Virgin Megastore Checkout Desk', when it was re-released by MCA in 1981. Two other curious but enduring singles were also released on the major, the ambiguous anti-war ode 'Wrap Up The Rockers', and the paean to record collecting, 'I Can't Get (Boing Boing) Bouncing Babies By The Teardrop Explodes'. However, after a solitary single on Stiff the band split. Sievey, ever the optimist, went on to a similarly bizarre solo career alongside appearances with his alter-ego Frank Sidebottom. Incredibly, for a band with literally hundreds of songs behind them, the Freshies never released an album.

Freur

Trio who comprised Karl Hyde, Rick Smith and Alfie Thomas, formed at college in Cardiff, Wales in 1981. Their name was actually written as a hieroglyphic squiggle, to the amusement and bemusement of writers and chart compilers everywhere. 'Freur' was the phonetic pronunciation. They employed drummer Bryn Burrows (ex-Fabulous Poodles, his party trick of banging his head on his cymbals once led to him being carried offstage totally unconscious) and video guru John Warwicker. The group signed to CBS in 1983 and scored a minor chart success with 'Doot Doot'. Its popularity was made all the more unlikely by the fact that their record company had issued the original demo version rather than the recording the band had made with Conny Plank and Holger Czukay in Cologne. The record was also a big hit throughout Europe and topped the Italian charts. A second album was withheld from release by CBS, after which Smith and Hyde quit to form Underworld with Baz Allen.

Album: *Doot Doot* (CBS 1983).

Friends Again

This Glasgow, Scotland pop band featured Chris Thomson (vocals/rhythm guitar/song writing), Neil Cunningham (bass), Stuart Kerr (drums/vocals), Paul McGeechan (keyboards) and James Grant (lead guitar/vocals/song writing), who emerged in 1982. They released their independently financed debut single, 'Honey At The Core', the same year. It was followed by two further singles on Moon Records, 'Sunkissed' and 'State Of The Art'. However, when the band signed to Mercury Records, they not only re-released 'Honey At The Core', but also issued the lavish *Friends Again* EP. This elaborate package included new versions of the previous two singles plus the affecting, delicately orchestrated lead track, 'Lullaby No. 2', which nevertheless hid typically sombre lyrical matter from Thomson ('Everyone's the same, they've got deep dark hearts'). However, debut album *Trapped And Unwrapped* failed to showcase the band adequately, given too frail a production by Bob Sargent. With its lack of sales Grant departed in 1984, conscious that he wanted his own song writing platform, though at first he linked with Hipsway. Friends Again imploded in his absence, with Thomson going on to work under the title the Bathers. Grant would eventually forge Love And Money from the ashes of Friends Again, using the services of McGeechan, Kerr and, temporarily, Cunningham. Kerr would later also join Texas.
Album: *Trapped And Unwrapped* (Mercury 1984).

Front 242

A duo of Patrick Codenys (b. 16 November 1958, Brussels, Belgium; composition, computers, synthesizers, guitars, vocals) and Daniel Bressanutti (b. 27 August 1954, Brussels, Belgium; programming/samples), Front 242 have earned their long-standing reputation within the industrial/*avant garde* community via a largely compelling series of experimental exercises in sound. Originally Front 242 was just Codenys, for the 1982 single 'Principles', then a trio with Jean-Luc De Meyer and Bressanutti. These early releases were more in tune with the elementary synth-pop of artists such as Depeche Mode, and it was not until after the release of *Geography* that they would appear live. A fourth member, Geoff Bellingham, was added for this purpose, though he would be replaced by ex-roadie Richard 23. Front 242's journey through the 80s gradually saw them becoming a more distinctive unit, however, with politically-motivated samples filtering through the repetition. On the back of an awesome reputation for live events and visuals, they were launched out of cult status by the success of *Official Version*. This introduced the intemperate, militaristic rhythms which would become a signature, as well as a diversity enshrined by nods to disco and pop in other tracks. It was not until the advent of *Tyranny For You* that the ingredients were significantly re-arranged once more, this time to instil a darker, chaotic overtone to proceedings (the album emerged at the same time as the Gulf War and proclamations of a New World Order). Influenced by the German anti-rock movement (Can, Neu, Faust) cinema and architecture, the duo (following De Meyer's departure in the 90s) continue to run the Art & Strategy design company and record label.
Albums: *Geography* (Mask 1982), *No Comment* (RRE 1985),

Official Version (RRE 1987), *Front By Front* (RRE 1988), *Tyranny For You* (RRE 1991), *Live Target* (Guzzi 1993), *06:21:03:11 Up Evil* (RRE 1993), *05:22:09:12 Off* (RRE 1993). Compilations: *Back Catalogue* (RRE 1987), *Geography 1981-1983* (RRECD 1992), *No Comment 1984-1985* (RRECD 1992), *Back Catalogue 1981-1985* (RRECD 1992), *Official Version 1986-1987* (RRECD 1992), *Front By Front 1988-1989* (RRECD 1992).

Fudge Tunnel

UK noise operatives Fudge Tunnel were formed in 1989 by 18 year old vocalist, guitarist and songwriter Alex Newport when he moved to Nottingham. He quickly sought out like-minds in the shape of Dave Ryley (bass) and Adrian Parkin (drums). Their first ever release, 1990's *Sex Mammoth* EP, was immediately made Single Of The Week in the *New Musical Express*. Six months later came *The Sweet Sound Of Excess* EP, then touring commitments with Silverfish and Godflesh. 1991 saw them gain a permanent home at Earache Records, which culminated in the release of their debut album, which arrived with the self-explanatory title of *Hate Songs In E Minor*. This immensely caustic epistle was released in May 1991 after initial copies, featuring a drawing of a decapitation taken from the John Minnery book, *How To Kill*, were confiscated by Nottingham vice police. The acclaim the Colin Richardson-produced disc eventually accrued in metal and indie magazines was huge however, with barely a word of dissent and plenty more which earmarked Fudge Tunnel as the ultimate in brutal music. A commercially successful EP, *Teeth* (UK indie chart number 4 - a major landmark for such extreme music) preceded the release of a second album, *Creep Diets*. Despite continued progress, the band were unhappily bracketed with the emerging Seattle 'grunge' sound (which they had actually anticipated) and some of the momentum waned. As well as touring 1993 saw Newport working with Max Cavalera (Sepultura) on the Nailbomb project. Fudge Tunnel then reconvened at Sawmill Studios in Cornwall for their third album. *The Complicated Futility Of Ignorance* saw the grunge comparisons dropped as the group processed a further increase in their already massively violent sound.
Albums: *Hate Songs In E Minor* (Earache 1991), *Fudge Cake* (Pigboy/Vinyl Solution 1992; comprises *Sex Mammoth* and *Sweet Sound Of Excess* EPs), *Creep Diets* (Earache 1993), *The Complicated Futility Of Ignorance* (Earache 1994).

Fugazi

The thinking person's modern hardcore band, and vocalist/guitarist Ian MacKaye's most permanent institution since his Minor Threat days. More so than Henry Rollins, and arguably Jello Biafra, Fugazi have continued and expanded on the arguments of their antecedents. Door prices are kept down, mainstream press interviews are shunned, and they maintain a commitment to all-age shows which shames many bands. They have also been among the first to object publically to the ridiculous macho ritual of slam-dancing: 'We're about challenging crowds, confronting ourselves and them with new ideas and if I was a teenager now, I would not be doing a dance that's been going on for ten years'. It is a shame that Fugazi's press seems to focus unerringly on MacKaye's Minor Threat connections, as the contribution from his co-lyricist Guy Picciotto (ex-Rites Of Spring; vocals/guitar) deserves to be ranked above that of supporting cast. His more abstract, less direct communiques blend well with his partner's realism. The other members of the band are Brendan Canty (drums) and Joe Lally (bass), and together they have forged one of the most consistent and challenging discographies within the US underground. Although they have concentrated primarily on touring rather than studio efforts, each of their albums has gone on to sell more than 100,000 copies, produced entirely independently within their own Dischord Records framework. In a rare mainstream music press interview in 1995 MacKaye continued to decry those who would use the guise of punk rock to record for major corporations, commenting on the success of Green Day and Offspring by stating: 'They'll be forgotten, 'cos they're the fucking Ugly Kid Joe's of the 90s'. Fugazi's own record of the time, *Red Medicine*, proved just as abrasive and disciplined an exercise as usual.

Albums: *Repeater* (Dischord 1990), *Steady Diet Of Nothing* (Dischord 1991), *In On The Killtaker* (Dischord 1993), *Red Medicine* (Dischord 1995). Compilation: *13 Songs* (Dischord 1988, comprises previous 12-inches 'Fugazi' and 'Margin Walker').

Furniture

Bright indie pop band formed by life-long friends James Irvin (b. 20 July 1959, London, England; lead vocals) and Timothy Whelan (b. 15 September 1958, London, England) with Hamilton Lee (b. 7 September 1958, London, England) in 1981. Having released a single on their own The Guy From Paraguay label, the trio were joined by Sally Still (b. 5 February 1964, London, England; bass) and Maya Gilder (b. 25 April 1964, Poonah, India; keyboards) in 1982, as the band forged a sound peppered with jazzy touches and fuelled by a cinematically-orientated 'bedsit angst'. Basically, Furniture created moody music. Unfortunately, a series of legal disasters undermined any commercial potential: having finally broken through into the mainstream in 1986 with the 'Brilliant Mind' single, Furniture saw the record reach number 21 in the UK chart before their new label, Stiff Records, collapsed, thus halting the rise. The album, *The Wrong People* - a delight for critics and fans alike by virtue of its stark emotional textures, sweeping pop sensibilities and gentle eccentricities - found itself part of a rescue package from ZTT Records, who eventually fulfilled the 30,000 advance orders and promptly deleted the album. Two years of legal wrangles later, Furniture were able to sign to Arista Records, but a radical restructuring of company personnel saw the band's new album, *Food Sex And Paranoia*, overlooked in all the upheaval. Mutual distrust saw the group depart for pastures new, but when another promised deal fell through Furniture went their separate ways, playing a farewell performance at the Reading Festival in 1990. James Irvin and Sally Still both became journalists on *Melody Maker*, Maya Gilder gained employment at the BBC, while Timothy Whelan worked on a new musical venture named the Transmittors.

Albums: *When The Boom Was On* (Survival 1983), *The Wrong People* (Stiff 1986), *Food Sex And Paranoia* (Arista

1990). Compilations: *The Lovemongers* (Stiff 1986), *She Gets Out The Scrapbook* (1991).

Fuzztones

Obsessed with the psychedelic punk sound of the late 60s, the Fuzztones emerged from New York in the mid-80s. The group consisted of Rudi Protrudi (vocals/guitar, ex-Tina Peel and Devil Dogs), Deb O'Nair (organ, also ex-Tina Peel), Elan Portnoy (guitar), Michael Jay (bass) and Michael Phillips (drums, ex-Polyrock). They had formed during 1980 after the break-up of Tina Peel, and spent their formative years gigging around the east coast of the USA. The Fuzztones' first UK release was a live album, *Leave Your Mind At Home*, on the Midnight Music label in 1984, which combined brash garage guitar riffs with a definite nod to the Cramps. 1985's *Lysergic Emanations* on the independent ABC label was less forthright and delved further into acid rock, although the singles, 'She's Wicked' (1985) and 'Bad News Travels Fast' (1986), were all-out slabs of loud, raunchy guitar rock. All was quiet in their wake as the Fuzztones returned to the States for a while, finally resurfacing in 1988 with 'Nine Months Later' on Music Maniac. However, the label folded after *Creatures That Time Forgot* early in 1989 and the band transferred to Situation 2. 'Hurt On Hold' accompanied the band's second album of that year, *In Heat*. 'Action Speaks Louder Than Words' continued the staple diet of garage trash in 1990 but, by then the Fuzztones' formula seemed to be wearing thin and they have since kept a low profile.

Albums: *Leave Your Mind At Home - Live* (Midnight 1984), *Lysergic Emanations* (ABC 1984), *Live In Music* (Music Maniac 1987), *Creatures That Time Forgot* (Music Maniac 1989), *In Heat* (Beggars Banquet/RCA 1989).

Fuzzy

This pop quartet from Boston, USA, consist of Hilken Mancini (vocals), Chris Tappin (vocals/guitar), Winston Braman (bass) and David Ryan (also Lemonheads; drums). The band was formed by Mancini and Tappin when they worked in a record shop and discovered they had similar tastes in music and shared a lack of success with bands and boyfriends. Braman introduced himself to Mancini at a party, and the trio set about booking themselves into the Lemonheads' rehearsal studios, whereupon Ryan decided he would like to join the band. However, he disappeared before their first show, which was performed with a stand-in drummer known as Tom The Monk. Despite a catastrophic performance, Soul Asylum's Dave Pirner was impressed by their potential and encouraged the band, and Ryan returned after finishing touring commitments with the Lemonheads. Fuzzy's debut album was spearheaded by a well-regarded single, 'Flashlight', though touring was complicated by Ryan's availability.

Album: *Fuzzy* (1994).

G

G.B.H.

Formerly known as Charged G.B.H. (truncating the name by the release of 1986's *Oh No It's G.B.H. Again!* EP), the band originated as the initial impetus of the punk movement was petering out in 1980, counting the Exploited and Discharge among their peer group. Comprising Cal (b. Colin Abrahall; vocals), Jock Blyth (guitar), Ross (bass) and Wilf (drums), they brokered a violent and aggressive image (G.B.H., of course, standing for grievous bodily harm), sporting multi-coloured mohican haircuts and *de rigeur* studded and chained leathers. Musically, they combined influences such as the Ramones and Venom into a hardcore metallic barrage of testosterone-led frustration. With 'smash-the-system' sloganeering in place of lyrics, they were an uncompromising and extreme musical outfit during the early 80s, and exerted some influence on the thrash and hardcore movements which followed. While musically they could always be exciting, any enjoyment was downgraded by the poverty of intellect behind the lyrics (notable examples being the anti-feminist tract, 'Womb With A View', from *City Baby's Revenge*, or 'Limpwristed', from *Midnight Madness*). Their success was also always going to be limited by an inability to progress musically. Kai replaced Wilf on drums in 1989, as the band veered away from regimented hardcore towards speed metal. This trend has continued with the arrival of new bassist Anthony Morgan. Even the mohicans had disappeared on their 1993 tour to promote *From Here To Reality*, which the *New Musical Express* kindly reviewed as having 'no redeeming features whatsoever'.
Albums: *Leather, Bristles, Studs And Acne* (Clay 1981, mini-album), *City Baby Attacked By Rats* (Clay 1982), *Live At City Garden* (Clay 1982), *City Babies Revenge* (Clay 1983), *Midnight Madness And Beyond* (Rough Justice 1986), *A Fridge Too Far* (Rough Justice 1989), *No Need To Panic* (Rough Justice 1989), *Diplomatic Immunity* (Clay 1990), *From Here To Reality* (Music For Nations (1990), *Chruch Of The Truly Warped* (Rough Justice 1993). Compilations: *Leather, Bristles, No Survivors And Sick Boys* (Clay 1982), *The Clay Years 81-84* (Clay 1986).
Videos: *Live At Brixton* (1983), *A Video Too Far* (1989).

Galactic Cowboys

This US metallic art-rock quartet was formed in 1990 by vocalist Ben Huggins and guitarist Dane Sonnier. With the addition of bassist Monty Colvin and drummer Alan Doss, they specialized in complex and densely melodic song structures that typically exceeded the six-minute mark. Combining elements of Kings X, Metallica and Neil Young with state-of-the-art technology, they produced one of 1991's most impressive debut albums. Defying simple categorization, they surprised the listener with what initially seemed the *ad hoc* juxtaposition of incompatible styles. Somehow, the strange fusion worked; manic thrashing giving way to harmonica solos, which in turn are followed by four-part vocal harmonies. The Galactic Cowboys' flair for innovation was further confirmed by 1993's *Space In Your Face*, a second chapter in what promises to be an intriguing career.
Albums: *Galactic Cowboys* (MCA 1991), *Space In Your Face* (MCA 1993).

Galas, Diamanda

A confrontational writer whose glass shattering, pristine vocals are derived from the Schrei (shriek) opera of German expressionism where 'sounds become corporal and movements aural'. On stage this is achieved with the aid of four microphones and a system of delays and echoes. Galas is a classically trained Greek American who signed to Y Records in 1982, for which she recorded her debut, before moving on to Mute Records. Her self-titled 1984 album is typical, comprising; two 'endless plays of pain'. 'Panoptikon' deals with Jeremy Bentham's harrowing prison regime, while 'Song From The Blood Of Those Murdered' is dedicated to the Greek women killed by the Junta between 1967 and 1974. Galas continues to produce a series of albums dominated by her remarkable banshee-like delivery, rooted more in performance art than any notions of popular music.
Albums: *Litanies Of Satan* (1982), *Diamanda Galas* (1984), *The Divine Punishment* (1986), *Saint Of The Pit* (1987), *You Must Be Certain Of The Devil* (1987), *Plague Mass* (1991), *Vena Cava* (1993), with John Paul Jones *The Sporting Life* (Mute 1994).

Galaxie 500

Ex-Harvard College alumni Dean Wareham (b. New Zealand; guitar/vocals), Naomi Yang (bass/vocals) and Damon Krukowski (drums) formed this group in Boston, Massachusetts, USA. Having released one track, 'Obvious', on a flexi-disc given away with the magazine *Chemical Imbalance*, they moved to New York. Maverick producer Kramer allowed the trio's brittle amateurism to flourish on *Today*, wherein Wareham's plaintive voice and scratchy guitarwork inspired comparisons with the Velvet Underground and Jonathan Richman. A version of the latter's 'Don't Let Our Youth Go To Waste' was featured on this engaging set which inspired Rough Trade Records to sign the group. *On Fire* continued their established métier and a growing self-confidence imbued the songs with resonance and atmosphere. *This Is Our Music* provided a greater emphasis on light and shade, sacrificing some of Yang's silky bass lines for traditional dynamism. A cover version of Yoko Ono's 'Listen, The Snow Is Falling' proved captivating, but the set lacked the warmth of its predecessors. Rumours of internal disaffection proved true when Wareham left the group in 1991. He subsequently formed the enthralling Luna 2, later known simply as Luna, while his former Galaxie 500 partners continued as Pierre Etoile, then simply Damon And Naomi. After releasing a 1992 album (*More Sad Hits*) as such, the duo joined Magic Hour.
Albums: *Today* (Aurora 1987), *On Fire* (Rough Trade 1989), *This Is Our Music* (Rough Trade 1990).

Galactic Cowboys

Gallon Drunk

Gallon Drunk

High energy rock 'n' roll band who emerged as contenders for the vacant Birthday Party throne in the early 90s. The band's line-up was James Johnston (vocals/guitar/organ), Mike Delanian (bass) - both of whom were at school together, Max Decharne (drums, also keyboard player with The Earls Of Suave) and Joe Byfield (maracas), the latter having spent a brief spell with My Bloody Valentine. Formed early in 1990 and based in north London, original drummer Nick Combe was soon jettisoned. They quickly garnered plaudits from the music press, the *New Musical Express* describing them thus: '...a synthesis of quite disparate elements, from Memphis soul slew to primal rockabilly'. Others noted a similarity to the more raucous Birthday Party/Nick Cave recordings. After releasing singles on their manager's own Massive label, they moved on to Clawfist where 1992 saw the release of their debut album. Given their high press profile, this proved to be a little lacklustre, with strong songs smothered by a flat production. *From The Heart Of Town* was much closer to the mark, with Johnson's lyrics given a strong empathy by the band's voodoo rhythms and dry musicianship (including the contribution of new Gallon Drunk horn player Terry Edwards). Johnson's vignettes included some startling depictions of the grubbier elements of life in the capital populated by characters of the grim majesty of 'Jake On The Make' and the tramp in 'Arlington Road'.
Albums: *Gallon Drunk* (Clawfist 1992), *From The Heart Of Town* (Clawfist 1993).

Game Theory

Based in Sacramento, California, USA, rock band Game Theory comprised: Scott Miller (guitar/vocals/synthesizer), Nancy Becker (keyboards), Fred Juhos (bass/vocals) and Michael Irwin (drums), making its recording debut in 1982. Although loosely associated with the Los Angeles' Paisley Underground movement (Miller was previously a member of Alternative Learning, with Joe Becker of True West and Thin White Rope), the quartet's progress was determined by their guitarist's infatuation with classic US pop and melody, rather then musical fashion. The best example of their early muse, following a scene-setting, competent debut, is *Dead Center*, which compiles the EPs *Pointed Accounts Of People You Know* and *Distortion*. The latter tracks were co-produced by Michael Quercio (Three O'Clock), which cemented their ties to the Paisley scene. Matters improved further with *Real Night Time*, wherein covers of Big Star's 'You Can't Have Me' stand shoulder to shoulder with Miller's increasingly adventurous lyrical scenarios. Though his occasional co-writer Juhos had departed before its release, *The Big Shot Chronicles* continued to demonstrate Game Theory's excellence in power pop construction. Miller's fusion of 60s and 80s styles is expertly captured on *Lolita Nations*, another fruitful partnership with R.E.M./dBs producer Mitch Easter (their relationship having begun with *Real Night Time*), and *Two Steps From The Middle Ages*, which placed his group on a pop/rock pantheon with the equally accomplished, and under-rated, Shoes. Both titles saw a new five-piece line-up, with the addition of Donnette Thayer (guitar; ex-Veil (US)) and Gil Ray (drums). After their failure to break through with *Two Steps...*, the line-up fluctuated once more, with Quercio joining full-time on bass, Jozef Becker (ex-Thin White Rope) on percussion and Ray swtiching to guitar/keyboards. Thayer, meanwhile, moved on to Hex. Miller's creation thus survived several personnel changes, including the leader's own temporary defection, without losing its sense of direction. Persistent though they were, Game Theory finally called it a day in the 90s. Miller would go on to form a new vehicle for his under-valued talents, Loud Family.
Albums: *Blaze Of Glory* (Rational 1982), *Dead Center* (Lolita 1984), *Real Night Time* (Rational 1985), *The Big Shot Chronicles* (Rational 1986), *Lolita Nations* (Rational 1988), *Two Steps From The Middle Ages* (Enigma 1988). Compilation: *Tinker To Evers To Chance* (Rational 1990).

Gang Green

This quartet from Boston, Massachusetts, USA, specializing in a fusion of hardcore and thrash, was put together by guitarist/vocalist Chris Doherty. Although formed originally in 1982, it was the 1985 re-incarnation that inked a deal with Taang! Records (Doherty had spent some of the intervening period with Jerry's Kids). After numerous line-up changes, a degree of stability was achieved for *You Got It* with Doherty, plus Brian Betzger (drums), Fritz Erickson (guitar; replacing Chuck Stilphen), and Joe Gittleman (bass), the latter eventually replaced by ex-DRI member Josh Papp. Extolling the virtues of alcohol and skateboarding, and ridiculing the PMRC at every opportunity, their music was fast, aggressive and occasionally abusive. One career highlight was the mini-album, *I81B4U*, where the group's irreverent sense of fun puts 'two fingers up' at Van Halen's *OU812*. They also released one record as a skateboard-shaped picture disc. Unable to progress on the songwriting front, their sound neverthless grew louder and more impressive as time wore on, particularly on *Older, Budweiser*, which also took their obsession with the eponymous beer to new excesses.
Albums: *Another Wasted Night* (Taang! 1986), *You Got It* (Roadracer 1987), *I81B4U* (Roadracer 1988, mini-album), *Older, Budweiser* (Emergo 1989), *Can't Live Without It* (Emergo 1990), *King Of Bands* (Roadrunner 1991).

Gang Of Four

Formed in Leeds, Yorkshire, England in 1977, Gang Of Four - Jon King (vocals/melodica), Andy Gill (guitar), Dave Allen (drums) and Hugo Burnham (drums) - made their debut the following year with *Damaged Goods*. This uncompromising three-track EP introduced the group's strident approach, wherein Burham's pounding, compulsive drumming and Gill's staccato, stuttering guitarwork, reminiscent of Wilko Johnson from Dr. Feelgood, framed their overtly political lyrics. The quartet maintained this direction on *Entertainment*, while introducing the interest in dance music which marked future recordings. Its most impressive track, 'At Home He's A Tourist', was issued as a single, but encountered censorship problems over its pre-AIDS reference to prophylactics ('rubbers'). Internal strife resulted in Allen's departure, later to join Shriekback, in July 1981. He was replaced by Sara Lee, formerly of Jane Aire And The

Belvederes, as the group pursued a fuller, more expansive sound. *Songs Of The Free* featured the tongue-in-cheek single, 'I Love A Man In Uniform', which seemed destined for chart success until disappearing from radio playlists in the wake of the Falklands 'conflict'. Burnham was fired in 1983 and a three-piece line-up completed *Hard* with sundry session musicians. This disappointing release made little difference to a group unable to satisfy now divergent audiences and they split up the following year. However, following several rather inconclusive projects, King and Gill exhumed the Gang Of Four name in 1990. The reunion was marked by *Mall* for Polydor Records, which justified the decision to resume their career with a set of typically bracing, still politically-motivated songs.

Albums: *Entertainment* (Warners 1978), *Solid Gold* (Warners 1981), *Songs Of The Free* (Warners 1982), *Hard* (Warners 1983), *At The Palace* (Phonogram 1984), *Mall* (Polydor 1991). Compilation: *A Brief History Of The Twentieth Century* (Warners 1990).

Garon, Jesse, And The Desperadoes

This Edinburgh-based act emerged in 1986. Initially viewed as an informal venture - its founding line-up was largely drawn from members of another group, Rote Kopelle - the Desperadoes nonetheless established themselves as a leading exponent of the city's 'shambling' scene alongside the more feted Shop Assistants. Fran Schoppler (vocals) Andrew Tully (guitar/vocals), Angus McPake (bass) and Marquerita Vazquez Ponte (drums) provided the core of a unit which made its debut with the melodic 'Splashing Along', a single sympathetically produced by ex-Jesus And Mary Chain bassist Douglas Hart. The Desperadoes' deft blend of charm and melancholia was captured on a series of excellent singles, including 'The Rain Fell Down' and 'And If The Sky Should Fall', although their lone album, *Nixon*, revealed a more forthright perspective. The Desperadoes split up at the end of the decade, unable to fully exploit their substantial early promise.

Album: *Nixon* (Avalanche 1989). Compilation: *A Cabinet Of Curiosities* (Velocity 1988).

Gaye Bykers On Acid

This UK rock group employed an image which combined traditional biker attire with elements of psychedelia and hippie camp. They were led by the colourful figure of Mary Millington, aka Mary Mary (b. Ian Garfield Hoxley; vocals), alongside Kevin Hyde (drums), Robber (b. Ian Michael Reynolds; bass) and Tony (b. Richard Anthony Horsfall; guitar). They were later complemented by disc jockey William Samuel Ronald Monroe ('Rocket Ronnie'). Mary Mary, who had once come second in Leicester's Alternative Miss Universe competition, was often to be seen in platform shoes and dresses, which fuelled the critics' confusion with regard to the band's name and gender orientation. Their debut album, *Drill Your Own Hole*, required purchasers to do just that, as the record was initially issued without a hole in its centre. After leaving Virgin Records they set up their own label, Naked Brain, quite conceivably because nobody else would have them. Subsequent to the band's demise, which may or may not prove permanent, Kevin instigated a

new band, G.R.O.W.T.H., with Jeff (ex-Janitors). Tony teamed up with Brad Bradbury in Camp Collision, while Mary Mary joined ex-members of Killing Joke, Ministry and PiL in the multi-member outfit, Pigface. The 90s would bring a more permanent home for his talents in the shape of Hyperhead, formed with Karl Leiker (ex-Luxuria, Bugblot).

Albums: *Drill Your Own Hole* (Virgin 1987), *Stewed To The Gills* (Virgin 1989), *GrooveDiveSoapDish* (Bleed 1989), *Cancer Planet Mission* (Naked Brain 1990), *From The Tomb Of The Near Legendary* (1993).

Video: *Drill Your Own Brain* (1987).

Gene

Foppish aesthetes Gene formed in the summer of 1993, quickly melding a waspish chemistry from the base components of Steve Mason (guitar), Martin Rossiter (vocals), Kevin Miles (bass) and Matt James (drums). Writing songs together and honing their live profile, their influences were culled from Paul Weller, the Small Faces and, most obviously, the Smiths. Their debut release, the double a-side 'For The Dead'/'Child's Body', released on the fledgling Costermonger label in May 1994, set out a distinct musical agenda. Single Of The Week and Month awards followed from *New Musical Express* and *Select* magazines, with the limited 1,994 pressing selling out within two days after it was playlisted by BBC Radio 1. A strong reaction was also gained as support to Pulp at London's Forum, where Rossiter's stage presence illuminated Gene's performance. August brought a second single, this time promoted as a 'triple a-side', featuring 'Be My Light, Be My Guide', 'This Is Not My Crime' and 'I Can't Help Myself'. Gaining pole position in the UK independent poll, and reaching number 54 in the UK charts proper, the band set out on their first headlining UK tour. Following further positive press the band signed with Polydor Records, though they retained the Costermonger imprint for UK releases. A third single, 'Sleep Well Tonight', followed an appearance at the Reading Festival, also playing mainland Europe for the first time with Elastica and Oasis. *Select*'s description of the single, 'ace crooning and rock and roll iridescence', came closest to cornering Gene's appeal. It saw them break the Top 40, as they featured highly in various end of year polls for brightest UK newcomers. The release of 'Haunted By You' in February 1995 prefigured a debut album proper, produced by Phil Vinall. With less direct, even nebulous material sandwiching the energy of the singles, there was much for critics to reflect on. Eschewing the self-consciously fey approach of Suede, the uncouth voyeurism of Pulp or the 'new lad' abrasiveness of Oasis, Rossiter's dramas were dominated instead by a wholly unromantic cast of characters inhabiting a down at heel, broken world with little hope of redemption.

Album: *Olympian* (Costermonger 1995).

Gene Loves Jezebel

Identical twins Jay (John) and Mike Aston, ostensibly Gene Loves Jezebel, enjoyed cult appeal, largely within the UK gothic rock community, but achieved greater success in America. The pair grew up in the South Wales town of Porthcawl, together with guitarist Ian Hudson. After moving

Gene

to London, they made their debut in late 1981 supporting the Higsons. A recording deal with Situation 2 resulted in 'Shavin' My Neck' (a collection of demos) the following May. The dense, experimental sound was matched by live performances, featuring bassist Julianne Regan and drummer Dick Hawkins, where they mixed almost tribal rhythms with furious guitar work. Hawkins was replaced by a succession of drummers, including John Murphy (ex-Associates and SPK) and Steve Goulding, while Regan left to front All About Eve. Her space was filled by Hudson, allowing Albio De Luca (later of Furyo) to operate as guitarist in time for 'Screaming (For Emmalene)' in 1983. Following Luca and Goulding's departure, Hudson reverted to guitar and Hawkins/Murphy offered a two-pronged drum attack. Murphy then left before a third single, the strong, commercial sound of 'Bruises' (1983). Hot on its heels came the Jezebels' powerful debut album, *Promise*, promoted by a John Peel BBC radio session. A trip to the USA in 1984 to work with John Cale ensued, before returning for two quick-fire singles 'Influenza (Relapse)' and 'Shame (Whole Heart Howl)'. Marshall then left, Mike Aston briefly switching from rhythm guitar to play bass, before Peter Rizzo was recruited. Ex-Spear Of Destiny drummer Chris Bell arrived in place of Hawkins, but it was a year before 'The Cow' hit the UK independent charts, preceding *Immigrant* in June 1985. After 'Desire' in November, the band left for a further north American tour, a traumatic time that led to Hudson's departure, ex-Generation X guitarist James Stevenson taking his place. The group skirted the Top 75 with 'Sweetest Thing' and *Discover* (which included a free live album) while 'Heartache' hinted at a passing interest in dance music. They subsequently concentrated their efforts on the US market. However, all was not well in the Jezebels camp, and Mike Aston left the group in mid-1989. In 1993 Gene Loves Jezebel, now comprising Jay Aston, Rizzo, Stevenson and Robert Adam, released *Heavenly Bodies*.

Albums: *Promise* (Situation 2 1983), *Immigrant* (Beggars Banquet 1985), *Discover* (Beggars Banquet 1986), *House Of Dolls* (Beggars Banquet 1987), *Kiss Of Life* (Beggars Banquet 1990), *Heavenly Bodies* (Savage/Arista 1993).

Generation X

UK punk group Generation X emerged during the punk explosion of 1976. Billy Idol (b. William Broad, 30 November 1955, Stanmore, Middlesex, England; vocals) had previously worked with Tony James (bass/vocals) in the short-lived Chelsea. With Bob Andrews (guitar/vocals) and John Towe (drums), Generation X made their performing debut in London during December 1976. By the following May, Towe was replaced on drums by Mark Laff, while record companies sought their hand. Eventually they signed with Chrysalis Records. The group soon arrived in the lower regions of the UK chart with 'Your Generation' and 'Ready Steady Go'. The latter, strange for a punk group, was an affectionate tribute to the 60s, full of references to Bob Dylan, the Beatles, the Rolling Stones and Cathy McGowan (the legendary presenter of the UK music programme, *Ready Steady Go!*). Following 'Friday's Angels' in June 1979, former Clash drummer Terry Chimes stepped in for Laff. The group lasted until 1981, but were soon regarded as a rock band in

punk garb. Their biggest commercial success was with the 1979 single 'King Rocker', which reached number 11 in the UK. Idol later went on to solo stardom, departed drummer John Towe reappeared in the Adverts, Terry Chimes rejoined the Clash, while Tony James reinvented himself in Sigue Sigue Sputnik.

Albums: *Generation X* (Chrysalis 1978), *Valley Of The Dolls* (Chrysalis 1979). As Gen X: *Kiss Me Deadly* (Chrysalis 1981). Compilation: *Best Of Generation X* (Chrysalis 1985), *Perfect Hits (1975-81)* (Chrysalis 1991), *The Original Generation X* (MBC 1987), *Generation X Live* (MBC 1987).

Germs

Los Angeles, California, USA punk band the Germs were formed in April 1977 and quickly became the most influential band of their generation. The original members were Darby Crash (b. Paul Beahm; vocals), Pat Smear (guitar), Lorna Doom (bass) and Belinda Carlisle (drums), later of the Go-Gos. She soon left and was replaced by a succession of percussionists, including future X drummer D.J. Bonebrake and Don Bolles of 45 Grave. The group's first single, 'Forming', was issued on What? Records in 1977 and is considered by some to be the first example of the post-punk 'hardcore' genre, later popularized by bands such as Black Flag and the Dead Kennedys. Their next single was issued on Slash Records, which in 1979 released the group's only album, *GI*. The group disbanded in early 1980 but reformed later that year. A week after their first reunion concert, however, singer Crash died of a heroin overdose. The catalyst to a thousand US punk bands, though few modelled themselves on Crash's legendary self-destructive nature, the Germs were only ever going to provide a musical flashpoint rather than a career blueprint.

Albums: *GI* (Slash 1979), *What We Do Is Secret* (Slash 1981), *Germicide* (ROIR 1982). Compilation: *MIA* (Slash 1994).

Ghost Dance

If ever a supergroup were created to fulfil the demands of the enormous 'goth' fraternity in Britain during the mid-80s then, on paper at least, Ghost Dance fitted the bill. Formed in 1985 by Gary Marx (guitar) from Sisters Of Mercy and Anne Marie (vocals), previously with Skeletal Family, the duo recruited Etch (bass) from the Citron Girls and added 'Pandora' the drum machine. Throughout 1986, Ghost Dance attracted a ready-made audience with their brand of brooding rock, utilizing extra guitarists Steve Smith and Paul Southern from Red Lorry Yellow Lorry and swiftly releasing three independent singles that became highly collectable items. At the close of the year Richard Steel joined on guitar and John Grant replaced the drum machine. Their commercial position fortified by 'A Word To The Wise' entering the Top 100 of the UK chart and a sell out nationwide tour, Ghost Dance signed to Chrysalis Records and struggled to lose the 'gothic' tag. Unfortunately, while recording their debut album, various band members started to drift apart, and the 'Celebrate' single, a further attempt to broaden the band's musical horizons, merely served to alienate Ghost Dance's diehard fans. Perplexed by their protegés' evolution, the label dropped the band halfway through an ironically successful European tour with the

Ghost Dance

Ramones, encouraging the personal ructions to come to the fore and subsequently causing Ghost Dance to split at the beginning of 1990. Anne Marie embarked upon an unsuccessful solo career, Etch played guitar with the Mission and Loud, while Gary Marx concentrated on collaborating with local musicians.

Album: *Stop The World* (Chrysalis 1989). Compilation: *Gathering Dust* (Chrysalis 1988).

Giant Sand

Formed by singer/songwriter Howe Gelb (vocals/guitar/bass/keyboards) in his hometown of Tucson, Arizona, USA, in 1980 with Rainer Ptacek (guitar) and Billy Sed (drums). The line-up recorded a four track EP as Giant Sandworms on a local label before departing for New York, where Sed's drug escapades forced a return to Arizona. They were joined by Dave Seger (bass) for a further EP, before he left to join Naked Prey. His replacement was Scott Gerber. Shortly afterwards the band's name was switched to Giant Sand (the original name had unintentional connotations with the wildlife in the science fiction novel *Dune*), with Gelb firing all personnel except Gerber in the process. Ptacek, though, reappeared in Gelb's countrified *alter ego* group, the Band Of Blacky Ranchette. Tom Larkins, who played concurrently with Naked Prey, joined as drummer, and together they recorded *Valley Of Rain* with guest pianist Chris Cavacas from Green On Red. Gelb's girlfriend Paula Brown joined on bass and guitar, and together they had their

first child. After recording *Ballad Of A Thin Line Man* Gerber left to join the Sidewinders, eventually moving on to Los Cruzos with former Sandworm drummer Sed. A variety of personnel have populated more recent recordings, including Neil Harry (pedal steel guitar), John Convertino (drums) and Mark Walton (ex-Dream Syndicate; bass). It is this line-up which was most recently seen on tour. The band's early stark sound (often described as 'desert rock') has evolved into a crisp mix of swing, country, rock, and beatnik lyricism. It remains tempered, as ever, by Gelb's evocative, arid imagery.

Albums: *Valley Of Rain* (1985), as the Band Of Blacky Ranchette *The Band Of Blacky Ranchette* (1985), *Ballad Of A Thin Line Man* (1986), as the Band Of Blacky Ranchette *Heartland* (1986), *Storm* (1988), *The Love Songs LP* (1988), *Giant Songs* (1989), *Long Stem Rant* (1990), as the Band Of Blacky Ranchette *Sage Advice* (1990), *Ramp* (1991), *Center Of The Universe* (1992), *Purge And Slouch* (Restless 1994), *Glum* (Imago 1994). Compilation: *Giant Sandwich* (1989).

Gilbert, Bruce

Bruce Gilbert forged a reputation as a purveyor of challenging music as guitarist/vocalist and composer with Wire. When this acclaimed art/punk quartet broke up in 1980, he joined group bassist Graham Lewis in Dome, a unit which continued its predecessor's *avant garde* inclinations. The duo also worked as P'o and Duet Emmo, the latter of which marked a collaboration with Mute label boss, Daniel

Miller. Although Wire were reunited in 1984, Gilbert embarked on a concurrent solo career with *This Way*, the enthralling nature of which was maintained on the artist's second set, *The Shivering Man*. Both albums confirm his position as one of Britain's most innovative musicians.
Albums: *This Way* (1984), *The Shivering Man* (1989).

Glove

The Glove was essentially a one-off project for UK guitarist/vocalist Robert Smith of the Cure and bassist/multi-instrumentalist Steve Severin of Siouxsie And The Banshees, with singer/dancer Jeanette Landray. Heavily influenced by 60s cult imagery and psychedelia, the Glove (the name taken from the film *Yellow Submarine*) recorded two singles, 'Like An Animal' (a minor hit) and 'Punish Me With Kisses', and a distinctive album, *Blue Sunshine*, issued on the Banshees' Wonderland label in August 1983. Although the material's multi-layered sound was endearing, the Glove was plainly a self-indulgent exercise for Severin and Smith (who was also a Banshee at that time) and rubbed off on both parties. The Banshees, especially, later injected a strong late 60s feel into their music, not least with a cover of the Beatles' 'Dear Prudence'. The Glove, meanwhile, were destined to become a historical curio, although demand was strong enough to warrant a reissue of *Blue Sunshine* in 1990.
Album: *Blue Sunshine* (Wonderland 1983).

Go! Discs

Small but perfectly formed record label founded by managing director Andy McDonald in 1983 with a loan of £1,500. By the following year the label had found additional finance with a world-wide licensing deal through Chrysalis Records. The highest profile early name attached to the label would be Billy Bragg, but it was the Housemartins who made the commercial breakthrough. Their 'Happy Hour' made the number 3 slot in 1986 and was followed by the Christmas number 1, 'Caravan Of Love'. Polygram took out a minority stake in the company in the following year, by which point their most successful act were on the verge of transmuting into the Beautiful South. *Welcome To The Beautiful South* duly emerged in 1989 as the label's first million-selling release. By the turn of the decade the same band's 'A Little Time' had gone to number 1, as had Beats International with 'Dub Be Good To Me' - a strong Housemartins connection maintained as that group were headed by former drummer Norman Cook. A rare talent was unearthed with the discovery of the La's, while Go! Discs envisioned future trends by launching a dance subsidiary, Go! Beat (headed by Ferdy Hamilton). However, 1991 brought the first major setbacks. With bands like Father Father, Southernaires and Sound Systemme failing to recoup the label's promotion of them, and the recession biting, by the following year McDonald had been forced to lay off five staff. This was merely a temporary blip, and one straightened by the arrival of a revitalized Paul Weller. The Frank And Walters failed to sell in nearly the quantities envisaged, but this was compensated for by a number 1 single from Gabrielle. Weller's second album for the label, *Wild Wood*, was nominated for the Mercury Music Prize in 1994, before the multi-platinum Beautiful South compilation *Carry On*

Up The Charts became Go! Discs' first number 1 album. Arguably just as significant was the arrival of the critically-drooled over Portishead. New arrivals for 1995 include Drugstore, Brit hip bop act the Muddie Funksters, while Go! Beat's roster boasts Gabrielle and Gloworm.
Selected albums: Housemartins: *London 0 Hull 4* (Go! Discs 1986). Beautiful South: *Welcome To The Beautiful South* (Go! Discs 1989), *Carry On Up The Charts* (Go! Discs 1994). La's: *The La's* (Go! Discs 1990). Paul Weller: *Wild Wood* (Go! Discs 1994). Portishead: *Dummy* (Go! Discs 1994).

Go-Betweens

Critics' favourites the Go-Betweens were formed in Brisbane, Australia, by Robert Forster (b. 29 June 1957, Brisbane, Queensland, Australia; guitar/vocals) and Grant McLennan (b. 12 February 1958, Rockhampton, Queensland, Australia; bass/guitar/vocals). These two songwriters were influenced by Bob Dylan, the Velvet Underground, the Monkees and the then-burgeoning New York no wave scene involving Television, Talking Heads and Patti Smith. Although sharing the same subject matter in trouble torn love songs, melancholy and desolation, Forster and McLennan's very different compositional styles fully complemented each other. The Go-Betweens first recorded as a trio on the Able label with drummer Dennis Cantwell. McLennan took on bass playing duties for 'Lee Remick'/'Karen' (1978) and 'People Say'/'Don't Let Him Come Back' (1979). By the time of the latter release the line-up had expanded to include Tim Mustafa (drums), Malcolm Kelly (organ), and Candice and Jacqueline on tambourine and vocals. The duo later reverted to the trio format on recruiting ex-Zero drummer, Lindy Morrison (b. 2 November 1951, Australia). At the invitation of Postcard Records boss Alan Horne, the band came to Britain to record a single, 'I Need Two Heads'. After this brief visit the group returned to Australia and recorded *Send Me A Lullaby* for the independent label, Missing Link. This roughly-hewn but still charming set was heard by Geoff Travis at Rough Trade Records in London, who picked it up for distribution in the UK. Travis proposed that the Go-Betweens return to the UK, sign a recording deal and settle in London, which the group accepted. *Before Hollywood* garnered favourable reviews prompting many to predict a rosy future for the group. The highlight of this set was McLennan's evocative, 'Cattle And Cane', one of the Go-Betweens' most enduring tracks (later covered by the Wedding Present). The problem of finding a permanent bass player was solved with the enrolment of Brisbane associate Robert Vickers (b. 25 November 1959; Australia) to the post, thus enabling McLennan to concentrate on guitar and giving the group a fuller sound. The move to a major label, Sire Records, brought expectations of a 'big breakthrough' in terms of sales, but for all the critical acclaim heaped upon *Springhill Fair*, success still eluded them. The break with Sire left the group almost on the brink of returning to Australia. The intervention of Beggars Banquet Records led them to a relationship which allowed the group to develop at their own pace. *Liberty Belle And The Black Diamond Express* presented what was by far their best album to date. The successful use of violins and oboes led to the introduction of a fifth member, Amanda Brown (b. 17 November 1965, Australia; violin/oboe/guitar/keyboards), adding an extra dimension and smoother texture to the band's sound. With *Tallulah* in 1987, the Go-Betweens made their best showing so far in the UK album chart, peaking at number 91. That same year, Robert Vickers left the group to reside in New York and was replaced by John Willsteed (b. 13 February 1957, Australia). Prior to the release of *16 Lovers Lane* in 1988 the single, 'Streets Of Your Town', an upbeat pop song with a dark lyric tackling the subject of wife-battering, was given generous airplay. However, once again, the single failed to make any impact on the charts despite being lavished with praise from the UK music press. The album only managed to peak at number 81, a hugely disappointing finale. After touring with the set, Forster and McLennan dissolved the group in December 1989. Remaining with Beggars Banquet, they both released solo albums. Forster's collection, *Danger In The Past*, was recorded with substantial assistance from Bad Seeds member, Mick Harvey. McLennan released an album with fellow Antipodean, Steve Kilbey from the Church, under the title Jack Frost (for Arista Records), before crediting himself as G.W. McLennan. His full solo set, *Watershed*, proved that neither artist was lost without the other. Lindy Morrison and Amanda Brown meanwhile, had formed a group, Cleopatra Wong. Since McLennan joined Forster on-stage in 1991, rumours of a Go-Betweens reformation were strengthened by a Forster/McLennan support slot with Lloyd Cole in Toronto that same year.

Albums: *Send Me A Lullaby* (Missing Link/Rough Trade 1981), *Before Hollywood* (Rough Trade 1983), *Springhill Fair* (Sire 1984), *Liberty Belle And The Black Diamond Express* (Beggars Banquet 1986), *Tullulah* (Beggars Banquet 1987), *16 Lover's Lane* (Beggars Banquet 1988). Compilations: *Very Quick On The Eye* (Man Made 1982), *Metals And Shells* (PVC 1985), *Go-Betweens 1978-1990* (Beggars Banquet 1990). Solo: Robert Forster: *Danger In The Past* (Beggars Banquet 1990), *Calling From A Country Phone* (Beggars Banquet 1993). As Jack Frost: *Jack Frost* (Arista 1990). Grant McLennan: *Watershed* (Beggars Banquet 1991), *Fireboy* (Beggars Banquet 1993).

Video: *That Way* (1993).

Go-Go's

This all-female group, originally called the Misfits, were formed in California, USA, in 1978 by Belinda Carlisle (b. 17 August 1958, Hollywood, California, USA; lead vocals) and Jane Wiedlin (b. 20 May 1958, Oconomowoc, Wisconsin, USA; rhythm guitar/vocals). They were joined by Charlotte Caffey (b. 21 October 1953, Santa Monica, California, USA; lead guitar/keyboards), Elissa Bello (drums) and Margot Olaverra (bass). Inspired by the new wave scene, the Go-Go's performed bright, infectious harmony pop songs and were initially signed to the UK independent label Stiff Records and to Miles Copeland's IRS Records in the US, where they would enjoy practically all their success. By the time of the release of debut album *Beauty And The Beat*, Olaverra was replaced by ex-Textone Kathy Valentine and Bello by Gina Schock. Produced by Richard Gottehrer, who had earlier worked with a long line of female singers in the 60s, the sprightly pop qualities of *Beauty And The Beat* drew comparisons with Blondie, with whom Gottehrer had also worked. The album, which stayed at the US number 1 spot for 6 weeks in 1981, included 'Our Lips Are Sealed' (US Top 20), which was co-written by Wiedlin with Terry Hall of the Fun Boy Three, and 'We Got The Beat', which gave the group a US number 2 hit the following year. The second album provided a further US Top 10 hit with the title-track, but the group were by now showing signs of burn-out. Despite their 'safe' image, it later transpired that the Go-Go's were more than able to give the average all-male group a run for their money when it came to on-road excesses, which eventually took their toll. *Talk Show* reached the US Top 20, as did the most successful single culled from the set, 'Head Over Heels' (1984). With the break-up of the group in 1984, Belinda Carlisle subsequently pursued a successful solo career with assistance from Charlotte Caffey, who, for a time, appeared in her backing group. Caffey later formed the Graces with Meredith Brooks and Gia Campbell and recorded for A&M Records, releasing *Perfect View* in 1990. As well as recording as a solo artist, Wiedlin attempted to break into acting with a few minor film roles. Galvanized by her, the Go-Go's reformed briefly in 1990 for a benefit for the anti-fur trade organization, PETA (People for the Ethical Treatment of Animals). A fuller reunion took place in 1994 for well-paid shows in Las Vegas. Prompted by which, IRS issued *Return To The Valley Of The Go-Go's*, a compilation of the band's best known moments with the addition of two new tracks.

Album: *Beauty And The Beat* (IRS 1981), *Vacation* (IRS 1982), *Talk Show* (IRS 1984). Compilation: *Go-Go's Greatest* (IRS 1990), *Return To The Valley Of The Go-Go's* (IRS 1995).

Goddard, Vic, And The Subway Sect

Goddard, a native of the London suburb of Mortlake, put the band together during 1976, centring it on the friends with whom he used to attend Sex Pistols' gigs. Subway Sect made their live debut on 20 September 1976 at the 100 Club, featuring Goddard (vocals), Paul Myers (bass), Robert Miller (guitar), and Paul Smith (drums). They rehearsed in the Clash's studio. Their name came from brief flirtations with busking upon their inauguration. A series of short sets followed around the capital, featuring embryonic songwriting prowess to add to the abrasiveness they learnt at the hands of the Pistols. They opened for the Clash at Harlesdon and subsequently joined them for their *White Riot* tour. Mark Laff had replaced Smith, but he too was lured away (to Generation X) before they set out on their first European trek. Bob Ward was their new drummer when they released their April 1978 debut 'Nobody's Scared'. However, a major split followed leaving Ward and Goddard to recruit John Britain (guitar), Colin Scott (bass) and Steve Atkinson (keyboards) in the summer of 1978. 'Ambition' was a trailblazing single, but afterwards the band fell into inactivity before reviving in 1980 with another new line-up with definite New Romantic leanings. This time the group featured Rob March (b. 13 October 1962, Bristol, England; guitar), Dave Collard (b. 17 January 1961, Bristol, England; keyboards), Chris Bostock (b. 23 November 1962, Bristol, England; bass) and Sean McLusky (b. 5 May 1961, Bristol, England; drums). *Songs For Sale* presented a collection of slick, swing-style songs with Goddard adopting a cocktail-lounge, crooner image. Supports with the Clash and Buzzcocks had transformed into guest spots on the Altered Images tour, and Goddard's new backing band would depart to find commercial success with JoBoxers. Disillusioned, Goddard has since retired from the music scene.

Albums: *What's The Matter Boy* (1980), *Songs For Sale* (1982), *Trouble* (1986). Compilation: *A Retrospective (1977-81)* (1985). Vic Goddard *The End Of The Surrey People* (1993).

Godfathers

A tough R&B fired rock band, the Godfathers centred on brothers Peter and Chris Coyne (b. London, England). The group's beginnings were in the south London punk quartet, Sid Presley Experience (the Coynes on vocals and bass, plus Del Bartle - guitar, and Kevin Murphy - drums) who released two singles in 1984 and toured with Billy Bragg on the 'Jobs For Youth' tour. They split in 1985 and Bartle and Murphy toured as the New Sid Presley Experience before recruiting Mad Dog Lucas and forming the Unholy Trinity. The Coyne brothers also retained the Sid Presley moniker for a while but having recruited Mike Gibson (b. London, England; guitar), Kris Dollimore (b. Isle Of Sheppey, Kent, England; guitar) and George Mazur (b. Bradford, Yorkshire, England; drums), they became the Godfathers. 'Lonely Man' was released on their own Corporate Image label in 1985 and *Hit By Hit* came out the following year, collecting together their first three singles with other tracks. In 1986 came the first of their regular St Valentine's Day gigs in London which would take place at such venues as the London Dungeon as well as more conventional halls. With their reputation growing they were signed to the American arm of the Epic Records organization who released their best known work - *Birth, School, Work, Death*. Kris Dollimore left in 1989 (he would later work with Stiv Bators) and was replaced in January 1990 by Chris Burrows. Burrows had previously worked with many bands including the Presidents Of Explosion which had also included former Sid Presley drummer Kevin Murphy. Constant touring, particularly in Europe, followed, and *Unreal World* followed in 1991. However, by this time much of the band's impetus had been lost, and despite a staunchly resilient fan base, the group had effectively petered out by the early 90s.

Albums: *Hit By Hit* (Corporate Image 1986), *Birth, School, Work, Death* (Epic 1988), *More Songs About Love And Hate* (Epic 1989), *Unreal World* (Epic 1991). Compilation: *Dope, Rock 'n' Roll, And Fu**ing In The Streets* (Corporate Image 1992).

Godflesh

The Godflesh partnership was inaugurated by Justin Broadrick (guitar, vocals) and G. Christian Green (bass) in 1988, when the former left the venerated (by John Peel at least) hardcore industrial trio, Head Of David. Green had formerly served time in industrialists Fall Of Because, and

Godfathers

Godflesh were completed by the addition of a drum machine. An eponymous EP was released on the Swordfish label before moving to the more permanent home of Earache Records. By the advent of their debut album, the group had expanded to temporarily include guitarist Paul Neville (also ex-Fall Of Because). With strong critical reaction, they toured with Loop, and as part of the Earache Grindcrusher USA package, alongside Napalm Death. Broadrick had actually appeared with the latter as guitarist on side one of the legendary *Scum* album. 1991 produced three limited edition 12-inches (including one for the Sub Pop empire), which were eventually collected together as the *Slavestate* mini-album. With Neville opting to concentrate on his own project, Cabel Regime, Robert Hampson of Loop stepped in for additional guitar duties on the group's excellently-reviewed *Pure*. He would choose to stay at home, however, as the duo embarked on a promotional European tour. 1993 would see Broadrick branching out by providing guitar tracks for label mates Scorn (on their *Vae Solis* debut), and he also produced a 'biomechanical' remix of Pantera's 'Walk'. This 'biomechanical' method is described by Green as involving: 'stripping them (the tracks) down and reconstructing them from scratch with different drum patterns, different vocal lines etc.'. Meanwhile Godflesh's first own-name project in nearly two years, the *Merciless* EP, resurrected an eight-year old Fall Of Because song. October 1994 saw the introduction of a major new work, *Selfless*, a stunningly direct and brutal album from a band whose quality threshold has hardly wavered since their inception.
Albums: *Streetcleaner* (Earache 1989), *Slavestate* (Earache 1990; mini-album), *Pure* (Earache 1992), *Selfless* (Earache 1994).

Golden Palominos

This unorthodox rock group's profile has been much enhanced by the glittering array of celebrities who have contributed to their work. They are led by drummer Anton Fier, who gave birth to the group in 1981. Prior to this he had spent time in the ranks of experimental bands Lounge Lizards and Pere Ubu. The band's albums have seen guest appearances by John Lydon (Sex Pistols, PiL), Michael Stipe (R.E.M.), Daniel Ponce, T-Bone Burnett, Jack Bruce and Syd Straw amongst others. The other core members of the band have been Bill Laswell (bass), Nicky Skopelitis (guitar) and Amanda Kramer (vocals). *Drunk With Passion* featured Stipe on 'Alive And Living Now', while Bob Mould provided the vocal on the excellent 'Dying From The Inside Out'. Richard Thompson also put in an appearance. Both Thompson and Stipe had already made their bow with the Palominos on *Visions Of Excess*, along with Henry Kaiser and Lydon. The maverick talents employed on *Blast Of Silence* included Peter Blegvad and Don Dixon, though it failed to match the impact of the debut - an obvious example of the sum not being as great as the parts. For *This Is How It Feels* in 1993, Frier avoided the super-session framework, recruiting instead singer Lori Carson who added both warmth and sexuality to that and the subsequent *Pure*. Mainstays Skopelitis and Laswell were additionally joined by the guitar of Bootsy Collins. His more recent work has also seen Frier adopted by the techno cognoscenti of Britain,

where he believes the most innovative modern music is being made. This has led to remixes of Golden Palominos' work from Bandulu and Psychick Warriors Of Gaia appearing in UK clubs.
Albums: *The Golden Palominos* (OAO/Celluloid 1983), *Visions Of Excess* (Celluloid 1985), *Blast Of Silence* (Celluloid 1986), *A Dead Horse* (Celluloid 1989), *Drunk With Passion* (Restless 1991), *This Is How It Feels* (Restless 1993), *Pure* (Restless 1995).

Goodbye Mr. Mackenzie

One of Scotland's highly tipped 80s pop exports, Goodbye Mr Mackenzie combined the emotive songwriting style of fellow Scots Deacon Blue or Del Amitri, with inspiring guitar work by 'Big' John Duncan. They formed in Edinburgh in 1986 and additionally featured Martin Metcalfe (vocals/guitar), Rona Scobie (keyboards/vocals) and Shirley Manson (keyboards/vocals), Chuck Parker (bass) and Derek Kelly (drums). A debut single, 'The Rattler', appeared on the Precious Organisation label (also home to Wet Wet Wet's first releases) in September 1986 and attracted a degree of attention, earning them supportive press and several radio sessions. Jimmy Anderson was brought in on guitar allowing Metcalfe to concentrate on singing, and Neil Baldwin replaced Parker in time for a second single - this time on the Claude label. In February 1988 they signed to EMI/Capitol and shortly afterwards Fin Wilson took over bass duties while Big John Duncan (from the Blood Uncles and, before that, the Exploited) replaced Anderson, thus forming the best known and most successful line-up. Their often anthemic sound, embellished with a touch of melodrama, drew upon such influences as David Bowie, the Doors' Jim Morrison and Bruce Springsteen. Their first UK national chart appearance came with 'Goodbye Mr Mackenzie' in the summer of 1988, and a year later 'The Rattler' (re-recorded) finally made an impact on the charts, reaching the Top 40. This followed the release of their debut, *Good Deeds And Dirty Rags*, and later, *Fish Heads And Tails*, both housed on Capitol Records. However, a second studio album for Capitol, *Hammer And Tongs*, went unissued, until it was unearthed by new home Radioactive (a subsidiary of MCA Records) in 1991. It did little to revive fortunes. Duncan would later go on to guest with Nirvana on various touring engagements, where he acted as their guitar roadie (he was rumoured to be joining the band at one point).
Albums: *Good Deeds And Dirty Rags* (Capitol 1989), *Hammer And Tongs* (Radioactive/MCA 1991), *Live - On The Day Of Storms* (Radioactive 1993), *Five* (Radioactive 1993). Compilation: *Fish Heads And Tails* (Capitol 1989, mini-album).

Gorillas

Originally known as the Hammersmith Gorillas this English trio played their own brand of punk meets rhythm and blues meets heavy rock. Initially riding on the back of the punk movement they built up a loyal fan base and released a string of excellent singles during the mid to late 70s including 'You Really Got Me' (a cover of the Kinks classic), 'Gatecrasher', 'It's My Life' and 'She's My Gal'. Bandleader Jesse Hector (vocals/guitar), ably supported by Alan Butler (bass) and

Grant Lee Buffalo

Gary Anderson (drums), was influenced by several dead 'stars'. The extravagantly side-burned singer was a noted self-publicist, whose passionate belief in the importance of the Gorillas' as the 'future of rock music' was taken all in, surprisingly, good humour by the UK music press. These included Elvis Presley, Eddie Cochran, Buddy Holly, Brian Jones, Marc Bolan and Jimi Hendrix. Indeed, several of the tracks on the Gorillas album were delivered in the musical style of his heroes, most notably a superb cover of Hendrix's 'Foxy Lady' and the Marc Bolan-influenced 'Going Fishing'. After a lengthy absence, Hector was to be found working the London live circuit in 1992 with his group, the Sound. Album: *Message To The World* (1978).

Grant Lee Buffalo

Los Angeles, USA band comprising Grant Lee Phillips (b. Stockton, California; vocals/12 string guitar), Paul Kimble (bass/keyboards) and Joey Peters (drums). Phillips grew up in California the son of a minister, and the grandson of a Southern gospel singer grandmother, before enrolling in film school. Grant Lee Buffalo began to evolve in 1989 when Phillips joined Peters and Kimble in Shiva Burlesque, but despite existing critical acclaim they soon realised that the band's impetus was stalling. The trio became the only ones turning up for rehearsals, and sacked the other two members to concentrate on a new band. Mouth Of Rasputin, Rex Mundi, Soft Wolf Tread and The Machine Elves were all

rejected as names, choosing Grant Lee Buffalo after their singer's Christian names and the image of a buffalo to symbolise all 'that had gone wrong in this country'. It had previously been employed by Phillips for a set of solo country standards he would sing before his then band King Of The World came on-stage. Their influences were 'the music of America from the 30s to the 60s that's based on story-telling and improvisation, blues, jazz or country'. By the autumn of 1991 the band had recorded 11 songs in Kimble's home studio, a tape of which was passed to Bob Mould, who released 'Fuzzy' as a 7-inch on his Singles Only Label (SOL). A month later they had earned a deal with Slash Records, primarily because the band felt an affinity with several other acts on the label (X, Los Lobos, Violent Femmes). A debut album was recorded in two weeks in San Francisco, with Kimble again producing. The songs attacked modern America's complacency and pursuit of material wealth, harking back to a golden age of American optimism. Phillips' acute observation and lyrical poignancy, which earned comparisons to Neil Young and Mike Scott (Waterboys), was steeped in a grainy, cinematic sweep which saw the set lauded by Michael Stipe of REM as '1993's finest album, hands down'. 'America Snoring', released as a single in both the US and UK, symbolised the faithless, faceless climate of the US so despised by the author, and was written as a response to the Los Angeles riots. A companion piece, 'Stars N' Stripes', was Phillips' evocative homage to Elvis

Presley's Vegas period, and offered another passionate chapter in his thematic dissection of modern Americana. *Mighty Joe Moon* proved more restrained, with its anger at the vulgarity of characters and situations tempered by greater texture and guile. The keynote spirituality implicit in earlier recordings was maintained by 'Rock Of Ages', one of the few dramatic gestures on offer.

Albums: *Fuzzy* (Slash 1993), *Mighty Joe Moon* (Slash 1994).

Greedies

This UK-based trio featured Thin Lizzys' Phil Lynott (b. 20 August 1951, Dublin, Eire, d. 4 January 1986; vocals/bass) and the Sex Pistols' Steve Jones (b. 3 September 1955, London, England; guitar) and Paul Cook (b. 20 July 1956, London, England; drums). They amalgamated in December 1979 as the Greedies for the one-off UK hit, a frantic version of 'We Wish You A Merry Christmas' titled 'A Merry Jingle', which peaked at number 28 in the first week of January 1980. Later on in the year Jones and Cook, recording as the Professionals, narrowly missed the UK Top 40 with '1-2-3'. Lynott died aged 34, from liver, kidney and heart failure and pneumonia following a drug overdose.

Green Day

With alternative rock music going overground in the early 90s, few acts were better positioned to exploit the commercial possibilities than Green Day - Billy Joe Armstrong (vocals/guitar), Mike Dirnt (bass/vocals) and Tre Cool (drums). Armstrong and Dirnt had been playing together since the age of 11 in the refinery town of Rodeo, California, originally titled Sweet Children. Two indie albums followed for Lookout, the first of which, *39/Smooth*, was recorded in a single day. Like the subsequent *Kerplunk*, however, it sold 30,000 copies. That figure was dwarfed following their decision to move to Warner Brothers. Their major label debut, *Dookie*, gradually stalked the charts, going on to double platinum status in the band's native territory. Their arduous touring schedule was paramount in this rise, and was topped off by appearances on the 1994 Lollapalooza package and the revived Woodstock event. The other factor was the estimable quality of their song writing, and a terrific simplicity of execution on numbers such as 'Basket Case'. As Dirnt would concede: 'We just figured out a formula and Billie Joe writes real good songs, that's all'. With sales of *Dookie* topping four million copies, it came as no surprise when the band were nominated in no less than four Grammy categories.

Albums: *39/Smooth* (Lookout 1990), *Kerplunk* (Lookout 1992), *Dookie* (Warners 1994).

Green On Red

Formed as the Serfers in Tucson, Arizona, USA in 1981, the group featured Dan Stuart (guitar/vocals), Jack Waterson (bass) and Van Christian (drums). Christian was replaced by Alex MacNicol, and Chris Cacavas added on keyboards for the first EP *Two Bibles*, released under their new group name. The band attracted attention as part of the 60s-influenced 'paisley underground' alongside the Rain Parade and the Dream Syndicate. However, Green On Red's sound owed more to Neil Young and country/blues traditions, an influence that became more apparent when Chuck Prophet IV joined on lead guitar in 1984. Sophisticated arrangements on 1987's *The Killer Inside Me* saw the group pushing for mainstream recognition, but shortly afterwards Waterson and Cacavas left to pursue solo careers. The remaining duo, Prophet and Stuart, forged ahead, using session musicians for the excellent *Here Come The Snakes*. Both members have operated outside the confines of the group, most notably Stuart's involvement on *Danny And Dusty* featuring Steve Wynn and members of the Long Ryders. In 1991 Green On Red re-emerged with *Scapegoats* recorded in Nashville with the help of Al Kooper on keyboards. Prophet's solo career took off in 1993 with the well received *Balinese Dancer*.

Albums: *Green On Red* (1982), *Gravity Talks* (1984), *Gas Food Lodging* (1985), *No Free Lunch* (1985), *The Killer Inside Me* (1987), *Here Come The Snakes* (1989), *Live At The Town And Country Club* (1989, limited edition mini-album), *This Time Around* (1990), *Scapegoats* (1991), *Too Much Fun* (1992). Solo albums: Chuck Prophet *Brother Aldo* (1990), *Balinese Dancer* (1993); Dan Stuart *Danny And Dusty - The Lost Weekend* (1985); Chris Cacavas *Junkyard Love* (1989); Jack Waterson *Whose Dog* (1988).

Green River

Seattle band Green River may go down in history as the first 'grunge' band, and were certainly the first to release a record on the Sub Pop label. They first came together in 1984 with Jeff Ament (ex-Deranged Diction) on bass, drummer Alex Shumway, guitarist/vocalist Mark Arm and former Mr Epp guitarist Steve Turner. Soon the line-up was expanded with the addition of ex-Ducky Boys/March Of Crimes guitarist Stone Gossard and they began to air their wares on the local north west scene. By 1985 they had appeared alongside the Melvins on the *Deep Six* compilation album on the C/Z label, released a six song EP, *Come On Down*, for Homestead, and were playing the same clubs as another local band, Soundgarden. Both bands came to the attention of Sub Pop owner Bruce Pavitt, who decided to expand his cassette-based fanzine into a full record label and worked with them in producing the 12-inch EP, *Dry As A Bone*, which was released in June 1987. Turner left soon after and was replaced by another Deranged Diction member, Bruce Fairweather. In May 1988 they released the mini-album, *Rehab Doll* (cassette and CD vesions adended *Dry As A Bone*) but the band were already falling apart with musical differences between Arm and Ament which led to them splitting in June. Arm joined Turner with ex-Melvins' bassist Matt Lukin and drummer Dan Peters to form Mudhoney. Ament, Gossard and Fairweather regrouped with ex-Malfunkshun vocalist Andrew Wood and drummer Regan Hagar and formed Lords Of The Wasteland, who quickly evolved into Mother Love Bone. After the death of Wood in March 1990 that band fractured with Gossard and Ament forming the hugely successful Pearl Jam. Green River thus became an important footnote in the development of the 90s strongest rock movement, though their light was re-ignited temporarily on 30 November 1993 at the Aladdin Hotel in Las Vegas when Pearl Jam ended their live set early to make way for a one-off reformation of Green River with Gossard,

Arm, Turner and Ament joined by Chuck Treece (bassist from Urge Overkill) playing drums.

Album: *Rehab Doll* (Sub Pop 1988, mini-album).

Guadalcanal Diary

This quartet were formed in Marietta, Georgia, USA, in 1981 by vocalist/guitarist Murray Attaway and guitar player Jeff Walls, initially as a vehicle to perform renditions of Civil War songs. However, with a line-up of Robert Crowe (bass) and John Poe (drums), they went on to specialise in guitar-led songs with impassioned and wilful lyrics, in a manner which prefigured the 90s rise of Grant Lee Buffalo. Mainly written by Attaway, who once led a Yes covers band, these songs looked at Americana, personal disasters and spirituality - notably a fascination with southern Baptist culture summed up by one critic as 'gospels, damnations and hallelujahs'. Named after a soldier's history of the World War II Guadalcanal campaign, the group made its debut in 1983 with the EP, *Watusi Rodeo*. Two of the songs also appeared on their first long player, as did 'Watusi Rodeo', which had given the EP its title but which had not actually featured. Afforded the production expertise of Don Dixon but little else in the way of financial indulgence, the album married the group's strong songwriting to emotive lyrical themes like the loss of innocence ('Trail Of Tears') and the group's suspicion of religious fervour ('Why Do The Heathen Rage?'). The latter contrasted with a seemingly heartfelt rendition of 'Kumbayah'. The producer for *Jamboree* was Rodney Mills, with help from Steve Nye. With an improved budget the musical values were brought to the fore, but the more inspired lyrics lay on *2 x 4*, which saw Dixon return to the producer's chair. The bold arrangements introduced on the last album were also present here, but this time they did not overshadow compositions such as 'Let The Big Wheel Roll', a lovely example of southern country rock. The group's final album arrived two years later, and saw the emergence of Poe as a strong songwriting force (Jeff Walls was now more withdrawn in this respect). Attaway went on to work solo following the band's demise while Poe joined Love Tractor.

Albums: *Walking In The Shadow Of The Big Man* (DB 1984), *Jamboree* (Elektra 1986), *2 x 4* (Elektra 1987), *Flip-Flop* (Elektra 1989).

Guana Batz

The late 70s UK rockabilly revival inspired the subsequent appearance of several new wave rockabilly - or psychobilly - acts such as the Guana Batz. Formed in Feltham, Middlesex, England, the Guana Batz began gigging in 1983. The original line-up boasted Pip Hancox (vocals), Stuart Osbourne (guitar), Dave Turner (drums) and Mark White, though his electric bass was soon swapped for the stand-up double bass of Sam Sardi. With musical peers the Meteors and King Kurt spearheading the new high energy format ('We prefer to describe it as modern rockabilly'), the Guana Batz were soon signed to Big Beat records. An EP and single were released, but the breakthrough came when the band featured on the *Stompin' At The Klubfoot* compilation, the latter proving the premiere venue for psychobilly bands. ABC/ID records released their debut *Held Down To Vinyl ... At Last* in 1985, gaining a high placing in the UK

independent charts. Unfortunately on the tour Hancox broke a leg while attempting to hurdle two double basses on a BMX bike, and was forced to complete the tour in plaster. After a spirited assassination of Bruce Springsteen's 'I'm On Fire' their second album, *Loan Sharks*, entered the UK independent charts at number 2. The following year, *Live Over London* was only completed when Meteors' drummer Ginger stepped in to temporarily replace the injured Turner. After the fourth album he left permanently, leaving the position vacant for Johnny Bowler (ex-Get Smart). After 1990's *Electra Glide In Blue*, Sardi was replaced on bass by Mark Pennington (ex-Caravans). The group continue to tour heavily, especially in Europe where they retain great popularity.

Albums: *Held Down To Vinyl ... At Last* (ABC/ID 1985), *Loan Sharks* (ID 1986), *Live Over London* (ID 1987), *Rough Edges* (ID 1988), *Electra Glide In Blue* (World Service 1990). Compilations: *Best Of The Batz* (Wrongco 1988), *Guana Batz 1985-1990* (Streetlink 1991).

Videos: *Still Sweatin'* (1986), *Live Over London* (1988).

Gun Club

Briefly known as Creeping Ritual, the Gun Club were formed in Los Angeles, California, USA, in 1980. Led by vocalist Jeffrey Lee Pierce, the group was initially completed by Kid Congo Powers (b. Brian Tristan; guitar), Rob Ritter (bass) and Terry Graham (drums). *Fire Of Love* established the unit's uncompromising style which drew from delta blues and the psychobilly tradition of the Cramps. The set included anarchic versions of Robert Johnson's 'Preaching The Blues' and Tommy Johnson's 'Cool Drink Of Water', but progress was undermined by Congo's defection to the Cramps. *Miami* was the first of several Gun Club recordings for Animal Records, owned by ex-Blondie guitarist Chris Stein. Although lacking the passion of its predecessor, it established the group as one of America's leading 'alternative' acts, but further changes in personnel, including the return of the prodigal Congo, ultimately blunted Pierce's confidence (which itself was hardly aided by a self-destructive alcohol problem). He disbanded the group for a solo career in 1985; *Two Sides Of The Beast* was then issued in commemoration, but the singer later reconstituted the Gun Club with Kid Congo, Nick Sanderson (drums) and Romi Mori (bass), thereby continuing to provide a benchmark for impulsive, powerful music.

Albums: *Fire Of Love* (Ruby 1981), *Miami* (Animal 1982), *Las Vegas Story* (Animal 1984), *Sex Beat 81* (Lolita 1984), *Danse Kalinda Boom* (Dojo 1985), *Mother Juno* (Fundamental 1987), *Pastoral Hide And Seek* (Fire 1990), *Divinity* (New Rose 1991), *Ahmed's Wild Dream* (Solid 1993). Compilations: *The Birth, The Death, The Ghost* (ABC 1984), *Two Sides Of The Beast* (Dojo 1985).

Video: *Live At The Hacienda, 1983* (1994).

Gymslips

This east London post-punk all-female trio was formed in 1982 by Paula Richards (b. 1 August 1963, Kent, England; guitar/vocals), Suzanne Scott (bass/vocals) and Karen Yarnell (b. 2 April 1961; drums/vocals) and, on some live performances, Kathy Barnes (keyboards). The effervescent group recorded the classic tribute to alcoholic revelry, 'The Drinking Song', among other less notable misdemeanours. They also provided a series of singles for the Abstract label, including a cover of Suzi Quatro's hit, '48 Crash'. Their sole album, *Rockin' With The Renees*, was also issued on Abstract, which was subjected to many reissues over the years. After the group split in 1986 Yarnell briefly joined Norwich band, Serious Drinking before re-joining Paula who, in the meantime, had been working with the Deltones and Potato 5, in the Renees in the following year.

Album: *Rockin' With The Renees* (Abstract 1983).

H

Haig, Paul

b. 1960, Scotland. Haig was the former lead singer of the late 70s, Edinburgh post-punk 'art' band, Josef K. His work with the band led many to expect great things when he launched his solo career. Working with the group project, Rhythm Of Life, his releases confirmed that Haig was still a man with promise, with the singles 'Big Blue World', 'Heaven Sent' and 'The Only Truth' displaying such. However, throughout the 80s the critical acclaim never moved Haig any further than a cult following, although his talents were appreciated in France and Belgium. The atmospheric *Cinematique...* displayed a maturity in style and adventurousness far removed from his humble beginnings in the 70s and yet it appears it will be in that latter capacity he will be remembered for.

Albums: *Rhythm Of Life* (1983), *Sense Of Fun* (1985), *European Sun* (1988), *R.O.L.* (1990), *Cinematique - Themes For Unknown Films, Volume One* (1991).

Half Japanese

Formed by brothers David (drums) and Jad Fair (vocals/guitar) in 1975, this cult US group has undergone numerous changes since its inception. Despite an erratic history, the unit remains an important outlet for the disparate talents of Jad Fair, who has also pursued a musically indistinguishable solo career. Always remarked upon by the US press as looking rather like nerds from a prep chemistry class, Half Japanese performances were nevertheless events in the truest sense, often featuring two sets of drums, brass bands, magicians and up to four guitars. The most regular outside contributor was David Stansky, though all sorts of guest appearances punctuate the band's extensive recording career, Kramer (Shockabilly, Bongwater), Don Fleming (B.A.L.L., Gumball), Fred Frith (ex-Henry Cow) and John Zorn among them. However, all releases are hallmarked by Jad Fair's idiosyncratic talent, which latterly combined the

naivety of Jonathan Richman with a love of classic 60s pop. Half Japanese's body of work taken as a whole represents an almost inconceivable run of diversity and experimentation. As Jello Biafra, an early advocate, once noted: 'They just attack people with what they're doing'. Early songs like 'I Want Something New' could easily be classified unlistenable. Later titles like 'Thing With A Hook', 'Rosemary's Baby' and 'Vampire' (all from the *Horrible* EP), illustrate Fair's ability to take any genre (in this case gothic punk-pop) and sound absolutely convincing. Their best-known releases, including the more mainstream-targeted *The Band That Would Be King*, were issued on the 50 Skidillion Watts label, for which Maureen Tucker also recorded. In 1991 the former Velvet Underground drummer produced 'Everybody Knows' for Half Japanese in gratitude. However, it should not be a roll-call of distinguished colleagues which provide Jad Fair and Half Japanese with their notoriety, but the stature of their music and lyrics which have played a large part in the development of the US underground. In 1993 a feature-length movie tribute, *Half Japanese: The Band That Would Be King*, started touring small cinema venues, and the band were approached to open for Nirvana.

Albums: *Half Gentlemen, Not Beasts* (Armageddon 1980), *Loud* (Armageddon 1981), *Our Solar System* (Iridescence 1984), *Sing No Evil* (Iridescence 1984), *Music To Strip By* (50 Skidillion Watts 1987), *Charmed Life* (50 Skidillion Watts 1988), *The Band That Would Be King* (50 Skidillion Watts 1989), *We Are They Who Ache With Amorous Love* (Ralph 1990).

Half Man Half Biscuit

Five piece 'scally' outfit whose penchant for seeing the funny side of British society's underbelly won them many friends in the mid-80s. From Birkenhead, Merseyside, England, their line-up comprised Nigel Crossley (vocals/bass), S. Blackwell (guitar), N. Blackwell (vocals/guitar), D. Lloyd (keyboards) and P. Wright (drums). Their original demo tape for Skeleton Records was heard by Probe Plus boss Geoff Davies; who signed the band to his label in 1985. Test pressings of their first release were dispatched to BBC Radio 1 disc jockey John Peel who immediately arranged a session. *The Trumpton Riots* 12-inch EP, released in February 1986, became a resident in the indie charts for weeks, propelled by the Biscuits endearing view of the idiosyncracies of British life. Their songwriting vernacular included cult television programmes and celebrities (Snooker referee Len Ganley; sports presenter Dickie Davies) in unforgettable song titles; '99% Of Gargoyles Look Like Bob Todd', 'I Love You Because (You Like Jim Reeves)', 'Rod Hull Is Alive - Why?'. Throughout their work they displayed an admirable lack of careerism; turning down key television appearances owing to favoured football club Tranmere playing at home that evening. They also decided to split up at the peak of their success, though they did reform in mid-1990 to release a remarkable version of 'No Regrets'; featuring another cult television personality, Margi Clarke, on vocals. The subsequent *McIntyre, Treadmore And Davitt* and *This Leaden Pall* continued to mine the band's parochial good humour and downbeat view of life, including songs of the calibre of 'Outbreak Of Vitas Geralitis', Everything's AOR' and '13

Eurogoths Floating In The Dead Sea'.
Albums: *Back In The DHSS* (Probe Plus 1986), *McIntyre, Treadmore & Dewitt* (Probe Plus 1991), *This Leaden Pall* (Probe Plus 1993), *Some Call It Godcore* (Probe Plus 1995). Compilations: *Back Again In The DHSS* (Probe Plus 1987), *ACD* (Proble Plus 1989, same album as *Back Again* on CD with extra tracks).

Hannett, Martin

b. May 1948, Northside, Manchester, England, d. 9 April 1991. In his role as producer Hannett worked with practically all the bands from the Manchester area that came to prominence in the late 70s. He also intermittently produced the groups of the 80s that established Manchester's international reputation as a hot-bed of young musical talent. After completing further education, where he had spent all his time playing bass guitar in bands and promoting local concerts, he toured with Paul Young (ex-Sad Cafe, later Mike And The Mechanics). He also managed a musicians' co-operative and worked as a soundman before being approached by the Buzzcocks to produce their *Spiral Scratch* EP in 1977. Following this he helped Joy Division fashion their sound in the studio, producing them, and encouraging their use of synthesizers. This resulted in the brutal and isolating feel of *Unknown Pleasures* on the one hand, and the mesmerizing beauty of *Closer* on the other, both now considered classic albums. The band worked with Hannett on 1981's *Movement*, their debut as New Order, but were disappointed with the results; this was to be their last collaboration. An integral part of the band's subsequent success, Hannett was made co-director of their label, Factory Records. This, however, did not interfere with his production schedule, working with U2, the Only Ones, OMD, Psychedelic Furs, Magazine and numerous other bands in the early 80s. As Manchester flourished for a second time in the late 80s, again it was Hannett who helped shape the sound that had a profound influence on the UK music scene. He produced the Stone Roses' debut single, 'So Young', and Happy Mondays' *Bummed* album, which provided the blueprint for a host of young hopefuls as the 90s began. He was held in high regard throughout the UK music business, described by those who worked with him as a genius whose instincts behind the mixing desk almost always paid off. But away from the studio he had a reputation for irresponsible behaviour and his drink-and-drugs lifestyle accelerated his declining health. He died from a heart attack on 9 April 1991.
Compilation album: *Martin* (Factory 1991, contains selection of artists produced by Hannett).

Happy Mondays

Few debut records could lay claim to have had the impact (or length of title) of *Happy Mondays' Squirrel And G-Man Twenty Four Hour Party People Plastic Face Carnt Smile (White Out)*. The sextet's raw brand of urban folk with Shaun Ryder's accented, drawled vocals was almost universally acclaimed. John Cale, formerly of the Velvet Underground, produced and gave the record a fresh, live feel. The original line-up remained unchanged (apart from the addition of backing singer, Rowetta) since the group formed in Manchester, England, early in the 80s. Joining singer Ryder (b. 23 August 1962) was his brother, Paul Ryder (b. 24 April 1964; bass), Mark Day (b. 29 December 1961; guitar), Gary Whelan (b. 12 February 1966; drums), Paul Davis (b. 7 March 1966; keyboards) and Mark Berry (percussion). Nicknamed 'Bez', the latter was widely noted for his manic onstage antics, especially his gaunt, skeleton dance appearance. Martin Hannett, famous for his work with a number of Manchester bands including Joy Division, produced *Bummed*, and layered their music with diverse but strong dance rhythms. In 1990 they covered John Kongos' 'He's Gonna Step On You Again' (retitled 'Step On') and reached the Top 10 in the UK. *Pills 'N' Thrills And Bellyaches* went to number 1 in the UK and established the band as a major pop force. The album also coincided with support and re-promotion of 60s singer Donovan, who appeared alongside them on the front covers of the music press. They even recorded a tribute song, 'Donovan', which paraphrased the lyrics of the singer's 60s hit, 'Sunshine Superman'. Strong support from Factory Records and an unusually consistent output meant Happy Mondays quickly rose to the status of favourite sons, alongside the Stone Roses, of the readership of the *New Musical Express* and *Melody Maker*, and they were achieving sales to match. However, the band's successes were tempered with a fair share of unpleasant publicity which came to a head when Sean Ryder announced he was a heroin addict and was undergoing detoxification treatment. A highly publized strife-torn recording session in the Caribbean, with producers Tina Weymouth and Chris Frantz (of Talking Heads), resulted in ... *Yes Please!*. However, its impact was dulled by a fall off in press interest, at least outside of Ryder's drug habits. Fittingly, the Happy Mondays eventual collapse could not be tied to a specific date, with various members breaking off at various points throughout 1993. The band's focal points, Ryder and Bez, would eventually re-emerge in 1995 as part of a new coalition, Black Grape, after Ryder had contributed vocals to 'Can You Fly Like You Mean It' by fellow Mancunians Intastella.
Albums: *Squirrel And G-Man Twenty Four Hour Party People Plastic Face Carnt Smile (White Out)* (Factory 1986), *Bummed* (Factory 1988), *Pills 'N' Thrills And Bellyaches* (Factory 1990), ... *Yes Please!* (Factory 1992).

Harper, Charlie

b. David Charles Perez, 25 April 1944, London, England. Forming his first band at the age of 20, Charlie Harper's Free Press gave way to the Charlie Harper Band, although he made several appearances in another band called Bandana. By the advent of punk in 1976, Harper was playing with the Marauders, subsidized in part by his employment as a hairdresser. The Marauders would eventually transmute in to the Subs, and finally the UK Subs. With the UK Subs established, Harper was able to indulge himself a little in his favourite hobby, playing R&B and classic rock cover versions. Two singles, 'Barmy London Army' and 'Freaked' emerged in 1980 and 1981. The first was a tribute to Jimmy Pursey, the second notable for the oddly poignant b-side, 'Jo'. These were followed a year later by *Stolen Property* on Flickknife Records. Notable covers included 'Pills', 'Louie Louie', 'Hey Joe', 'Light My Fire', 'Waiting For the Man',

'Femme Fatale' and 'Hoochie Coochie Man'. His other major project outside of the Subs has been the Urban Dogs, who released two albums in 1982 and 1985. They included various old members of the UK Subs, in addition to Knox (ex-Vibrators) and Simon Smith (ex-Merton Parkas). In 1986 Harper teamed up with old friends from Hanoi Rocks and Cherry Bombz in the Suicide Twins. Throughout the 80s and early 90s, he has continued to perform with the UK Subs, milking former glories as sustenance.
Album: *Stolen Property* (Flicknife 1981).

Harrison, Jerry

b. Jeremiah Harrison, 21 February 1949, Milwaukee, Wisconsin, USA. He built his reputation as guitarist and keyboard player for Talking Heads. Previously he had played in a similar capacity for Jonathon Richman And The Modern Lovers, between 1970 and 1974, before going on to study at Harvard and work with computers in Boston. Like other core members of the Talking Heads, he has enjoyed several fruitful extra-curricular pursuits. These began with a debut solo album in 1981, titled *The Red And The Black*. Recorded while the parent group were enjoying a sabbatical, many of those who had contributed to recent Talking Heads fare such as *Remain In Light* - including Adrian Belew, Bernie Worrell and Nona Hendryx - were on hand to aid Harrison. However, apart from scant critical interest there was little public support for this exploration of international rhythms and ethnic music. Harrison then returned to his role in Talking Heads before 1984 brought a solitary 12-inch release for rap label, Sleeping Bag Records. Titled '5 Minutes' and credited to Bonzo Goes To Washington, this combined a Bootsy Collins bass riff with a sample of President Reagan declaring 'We begin bombing . . . .'. Although a footnote to Harrison's own career, this document pre-empted much of the politically motivated sampling which spread through the remainder of the 80s. The artist retained a political agenda for his second album, released in 1987. Joined by a core of accomplished musicians (the 13-piece Casual Gods), the music was once again primarily a rhythmic experience, moving from funk to urban hip hop. Three years later, and with the Talking Heads' career seemingly on permanent hold, Harrison returned to the Casual Gods. The resultant album, *Walk On Water*, credited to Jerry Harrison's Casual Gods, revealed a more pop/rock-orientated sound. The additional personnel this time included former Modern Lover colleague Ernie Brooks, Dan Hartman, Bernie Worrell and the Thompson Twins. Although the musicianship remained exemplary, critics were still dissuaded against the overall merits of the project by Harrison's somewhat untutored vocal delivery. Perhaps this has given impetus to his position in the 90s as overseer of a steady influx of production work (notably Crash Test Dummies). He also worked with some of his previous musical collaborators, notably on Bernie Worrell's *Funk Of Ages* album.
Albums: *The Red And The Black* (Sire 1981), *Casual Gods* (Sire 1987), as Jerry Harrison's Casual Gods: *Walk On Water* (Fly/Sire 1990).

Harry Crews

Taking their name from a cult US novelist and professor,

Harry Crews was a sideline project featuring Lydia Lunch and Sonic Youth bassist/vocalist Kim Gordon. Drummer Sadie Mae completed the line-up featured on *Naked In The Garden Hills*, recorded live in London and Vienna during a 1988 European tour. Initially set for release on Blast First, this confrontational set was issued on Lunch's Widowspeak outlet in the US and on Big Cat in the UK. Interspersed by angry polemics, the content is more akin to Gordon's previous work although the noise quotient is noticeably more informal. The trio was disbanded following the tour; Gordon later formed another part-time venture, Free Kitten.
Album: *Naked In The Garden Hills* (Widowspeak 1989).

Hart, Grant

While his erstwhile song writing partner Bob Mould has gone on to critical and commercial approbation with Sugar, former Hüsker Dü drummer and vocalist Hart has worked largely outside of the media glare following that band's collapse in December 1987. Hart, who quit or was fired (depending on which of the two conflicting accounts you choose to believe), took little time to regroup, and was the first of the two to release vinyl under his own name. 1988's *2541* EP was released on SST Records, home to Hüsker Dü before their major label days with Warner Brothers, and observers looking for insights into the sundering of one of alternative rock's most productive partnerships were not disappointed. The number used as its title was in fact the same as the address of their former office and studio. His anger at the ending of Hüsker Dü (an interpretation widely divined from the record by critics, despite Hart's own silence on the matter), was eloquently mounted on the back of a downbeat, acoustic number. He had warmed to the subject by the arrival of his solo debut, *Intolerance*, with Mould less cryptically the target of 'You're The Victim'. But this was just one episode in Grant's evidently troubled life which he used the record to address, with other subjects including his well-publicised travails with hard drugs ('The Main') and the suicide of Hüsker Dü manager Dave Savoy in 1987 ('She Can See The Angels Coming'). Self-produced and played, the artist resurrected a group format at the end of 1989 with the unveiling of Nova Mob (nothing to do with the 70s Liverpool band who included Julian Cope and Pete Wylie). After making their debut with 'All Of My Senses', a re-working of a track from Grant's solo album, in 1991 they released the *Admiral Of The Sea* EP, before Nova Mob went on to complete an astonishing concept album for Rough Trade Records later that year. Envisaged as a 'rock opera', *The Last Days Of Pompeii* explored grandiose historical themes, with the project balanced by Hart's enduring sense of pop melody. He confined himself to guitar and vocal duties within the trio, who additionally included Michael Crego, drums, and Tom Merkl, bass. However, that line-up soon splintered, with Crego replaced by Steve Sutherland, and Chris Hesler added as lead guitarist. In 1994 *Nova Mob* offered a quasi-rock anthem in the six-minute 'Shoot Your Way To Freedom': Interpreted as a rock anthem in press circles, it apparently concerned toilet sex instead. Thankfully, it seems Hart will never quite be able to play the straight mainstream rock star role.
Album: *Intolerance* (SST 1989).

Harvey, Polly (PJ)

(see PJ Harvey)

Hatfield, Juliana

b. c.1967, Duxbury, Massachusetts, USA. Formerly with the Blake Babies, Hatfield is a singer/songwriter/guitarist who became a favourite of the early 90s indie media through her on-off liaisons with the Lemonheads' Evan Dando, her self-professed virginity, and her excessively vulnerable songs. Her first musical experience came when singing Police covers in a school band, fronting the mildy diverting Blake Babies before her solo bow. She has been heard to denounce her debut, finding its revelations overtly embarassing once handed over to probing journalists. By the time of her second collection, Hatfield had become more strident and self-assured, adding the services of Dean Fisher (bass) and Todd Philips (ex-Bullet LaVolta; drums), to become the Juliana Hatfield Three. There was even a tribute track, 'President Garfield', to tough guy Henry Rollins. Hatfield's breathless vocals were still very much in place for 1995's *Only Everything*, which saw her retreat to solo billing, but this time the familiar charm bedecked a set of songs which were just as long on resignation as expectation ('Dumb Fun' being the compulsory allusion to Kurt Cobain's suicide).
Albums: *Hey Babe* (Mammoth 1992), *Become What You Are* (Mammoth 1993), *Only Everything* (Mammoth 1995).

Havana 3 A.M.

This rock band were formed by ex-Clash bass player, Paul Simonon (b. 15 December 1955, Brixton, London, England), and also consist of Nigel Dixon (guitar/vocals; ex-Whirlwind), Gary Myrick (guitar/vocals) and Travis Williams (drums). However, despite Simonon's pedigree, the group initially found it difficult to acquire a contract in their native territory, recording and releasing their debut album in Japan before a contract with IRS Records was forthcoming. However, much of the album had been inspired by Simonon's adventures in the USA. Following the dissolution of the Clash, he had concentrated on oil painting in Notting Hill, London, and New York,. Eventually he persuaded his friend, Dixon, to buy Harley Davidson motorbikes for a tour of North America. From El Paso, Texas they journeyed through Mexico to California. By the time these travels had finished, both Simonon and Dixon were ready for a new musical outlet, and their journey provided much of the ammunition. Simonon recounted his vision for the band thus: 'The parts of the cake are the singing style of Gene Vincent and Billy Fury - which is why Nigel is in, because he can sing like that. Then I wanted the guitars to sound as close to motorcycles as possible, like the Ventures. I wanted an electronic drum kit where you could hit a button and have a reggae beat, a Latin rhythm or an Ennio Morricone mood. You could say that I looked through my own record collection and decided to go for a particular atmosphere rather than something specific.' On the evidence of the band's debut album this largely worked, notably on 'Surf In The City', which recalled the Clash's version of 'Brand New Cadillac'. However, the group broke up in 1993.
Album: *Havana 3 A.M.* (IRS 1991).

Heart Throbs

Formed by Rose Carlotti (b. Rosemarie DeFreitas, 16 December 1963, Barbados; guitar/vocals) and Stephen Ward (b. 19 April 1963, Chelmsford, Essex, England; guitar/vocals) from an idea conceived at college in Birmingham and developed in Reading in 1986, when Rose's sister, Rachael (b. 25 May 1966, Oxfordshire, England; bass/vocals) and Mark Side (b. 24 June 1969, Oxfordshire, England; drums) completed the line-up. Within a year the Heart Throbs had made inroads towards infamy, supporting the Jesus And Mary Chain on tour and releasing 'Bang' in a controversial 'car crash' record sleeve. Further publicity followed at the close of the decade when the band started up their own Profumo label, named after the political sex scandal which shocked Britain in the early 60s, and which prompted tastefully 'saucy' pictures of singer Rose posing as the notorious Christine Keeler had done 20 years earlier, (added to which one of the main scandal protagonists shared the same name as guitarist Ward). In spite of these tactics and several waves of acclaim for their harshly bittersweet pop songs, commercial success remained out of reach. A deal with the One Little Indian Records label in the UK coincided with the band signing to Elektra Records in the USA. Now joined by guitarist Alan Barclay (b. 4 April 1968, Singapore), they achieved moderate success on both sides of the Atlantic with the long-awaited debut album, *Cleopatra Grip*, which included the superb 'Dreamtime', and embarked on a tense tour towards the end of 1990 which resulted in the departure of both bassist Rachael Carlotti and drummer Mark Side. They were dropped by Elektra and a subsequent deal with A&M Records for the US also collapsed, while the line-up struggles were compounded by a change of management, leaving Rose Carlotti to say of this period 'I just wanted to go out and kill a lot of people, really.' Colleen Brown took over on bass for the disjointed but largely ignored *Jubilee Twist*. By *Vertical Smile* Rose Carlotti was once again speaking out: 'Vertical Smile basically means cunt. So it's a rather nice allusion to the smile I have between my legs, and there are quite a few songs that are personal to my own experience. I wanted to concentrate on writing songs that confront sexuality in a way that is a departure from the banalities that this industry normally provides.' It was another strong album, but the Heart Throbs struggled to regain the ground they had lost in the intervening period, and the band ground to a halt the following year.
Albums: *Cleopatra Grip* (One Little Indian 1990), *Jubilee Twist* (One Little Indian 1992), *Vertical Smile* (One Little Indian 1993).

Heartbreakers

The Heartbreakers were formed in New York in 1975 when Richard Hell, former bassist with Television, joined forces with Johnny Thunders (guitar/vocals) and Jerry Nolan (drums), disaffected members of the New York Dolls. The new act made one live appearance as a trio before adding Walter Lure (guitar/vocals) to the line-up. The original Heartbreakers enjoyed cult popularity, but by the following year the mercurial Hell left to found the Voidoids. Drafting Billy Rath as his replacement, the quartet later moved to London, eager to embrace its nascent punk movement. They supported the Sex Pistols on the aborted *Anarchy* tour (December 1976) and were then signed to the ailing Track Records. 'Chinese Rocks', a paean to heroin co-written by Dee Dee Ramone of the Ramones, and the subsequent *L.A.M.F.*, gave an indication of the group's 'wrong side of the tracks' rock 'n' roll strengths, but was marred by Speedy Keen's unfocused production. Nolan left the band in disgust, but returned to fulfil outstanding commitments. The Heartbreakers then severed connections with Track, but having broken up in November 1977, reformed the following year with new drummer Ty Styx. The name was subsequently dropped and resurrected on several occasions, notably in 1984, but such interludes vied with Thunders' other, equally temporary, outlets, until he was found dead in mysterious circumstances in April 1991.

Albums: *L.A.M.F.* (Track 1977), *Live At Max's Kansas City* (Max's Kansas City 1979), *D.T.K. Live At The Speakeasy* (Jungle 1982), *Live At The Lyceum Ballroom 1984* (ABC 1984), *L.A.M.F. Revisited* (Jungle 1984, remixed version of debut album). Compilation: *D.T.K. - L.A.M.F.* (Jungle 1984).

Heavenly

After the break-up of Oxford, England's Talulah Gosh in 1988, Amelia Fletcher, Mathew Fletcher and Peter Momtchiloff re-formed in the summer of 1989, this time adapting the name Heavenly. The line-up was completed with the addition of the original 'Gosh bassist Robert Pursey (b. 27 May 1964, Chipping Sodbury, Avon, England). Whilst retaining the upbeat musical outlook and, at times, some of the tweeness of the previous outfit, Heavenly displayed a tighter, more mature sound, particularly in Amelia Fletcher's love-lorn lyrics and Momtchiloff's guitar playing. Recording for Sarah Records, Heavenly's debut single in 1990, 'I Fell In Love Last Night', was followed by 'Our Love Is Heavenly'. The debut mini-album, *Heavenly Vs Satan*, was a perfect statement from the group, highlighted by 'Shallow' and 'Stop Before You Say It'. A good example of Amelia Fletcher's self-depreciating sense of humour was to found in the b-side, 'Escort Crash On Marston Street (a re-working of the debut album's 'Wish Me Gone'). The group's line-up was enlarged in the summer of 1991 by the arrival of Cathy Rogers (b. 29 May 1968, Tatsfield, Surrey, England; keyboards/vocals) for the recording of *Le Jardin de Heavenly*. With the break-up of the Field Mice in 1991, Heavenly can now claim to be the Sarah label's greatest assest. Amelia also recorded a one-off solo EP, *Can You Keep A Secret*, for the Fierce label in 1988.

Albums: *Heavenly Vs Satan* (Sarah 1991, mini-album), *Le Jardin De Heavenly* (Sarah 1992).

Heavenly Records

Record label set up in 1990 by Jeff Barrett in a riposte to a previous decade he cited as 'horrible', when old friend and music journalist Bob Stanley rang him up about a new dance track, 'Only Love Can Break Your Heart', he had written for his band, Saint Etienne. The Heavenly label was promptly set up in response, though the first release would be Sly & Lovechild's 'The World According To', in May 1990. Barrett had already garnered a deal of experience in the UK

independent scene, as a former Creation Records' employee, gig promoter and a public relations representative for Happy Mondays, Primal Scream and several other Factory/Creation acts. After Saint Etienne earned their own niche, Flowered Up became a hugely hyped but, perversely, undervalued musical force, who Barrett met when 'buying drugs off them'. The Manic Street Preachers' 'Motown Junk' and 'You Love Us' then premiered one of the UK's most important bands. The Manic Street Preachers made an amicable switch to Columbia/Sony Records shortly thereafter, amid a barrage of press speculation - Heavenly's artists have rarely struggled to fill column inches. The Manic Street Preachers rewarded Barrett's faith in them with a royalty on their debut album, and partially as a consequence of this Heavenly linked themselves with the Japanese corporation, Sony. Despite considerable record company support, country rock act the Rockingbirds failed to take off, while the label again demonstrated its eclecticism by unveiling Latin dance group, Espiritu. 1992 brought a special Right Said Fred cover version EP featuring the Rockingbirds, Saint Etienne and Flowered Up, which pushed both the bands' and label's profile. The company also branched out into other media by publishing a book, Kevin Pearce's *Something Beginning With O*.

Selected album: St. Etienne: *Fox Base Alpha* (Heavenly 1991).

Further reading: *Something Beginning With O*, Kevin Pearce.

Helen And The Horns

(see Chefs)

Hell, Richard

b. Richard Myers, 2 October 1949, Lexington, Kentucky, USA. A seminal figure on New York's emergent punk scene, Hell embodied the fierce nihilism of the genre. In 1971 he was a founder member of the Neon Boys with guitarist Tom Verlaine. Hell first performed several of his best-known songs, including 'Love Comes In Spurts', while in this group. He also published a handful of poems, under his own name, during this period. The Neon Boys subsequently mutated into Television where Hell's torn clothing, the result of impoverishment, inspired Malcolm McLaren's ideas for the Sex Pistols. Personality clashes resulted in Hell's departure in 1975. He then formed the Heartbreakers with former New York Dolls' guitarist Johnny Thunders and drummer Jerry Nolan, but once again left prematurely. Hell reappeared in 1976 fronting his own unit, Richard Hell and the Voidoids, with twin-lead guitarists, Bob Quine and Ivan Julian, alongside drummer Marc Bell. The quartet's debut EP appeared later that year - Stiff Records secured the rights in Britain - and the set quickly achieved underground popularity. One particular track, 'Blank Generation', achieved anthem-like proportions as an apposite description of punk, but Hell intended the 'blank' to be filled by the listener's personal interpretation. A re-recorded version of the same song became the title-track of the Voidoids dazzling debut album, which also featured the terse, but extended epic, 'Another World', and a fiery interpretation of John Fogerty's 'Walk Upon The Water'. Raw, tense and edgy, with Richard intoning 'cut-up'-styled lyrics delivered in a style

ranging from moan to scream, *Blank Generation* is one of punk's definitive statements. Bell's departure for the Ramones in 1978 undermined the group's potential and Quine subsequently left to pursue a successful career as a session musician and sometime Lou Reed sideman. A three-year gap ensued, during which Hell only issued one single, the Nick Lowe-produced 'The Kid With The Replaceable Head'. An EP combining two new songs with a brace of Neon Boys' masters served as a prelude to *Destiny Street*, another compulsive selection on which the artist's lyricism flourished. Quine returned to add highly expressive guitar work while Material drummer Fred Maher supplied a suitably crisp frame. Despite the power of this release, Hell once again withdrew from recording. Indeed on his liner notes to *R.I.P.*, a compilation drawn from all stages in his career, Richard declared it a swansong. Instead he opted for film work, the most notable example of which was his starring role in Susan Seidelman's *Smithereens*. Sporadic live appearances did continue, some of which were reflected on *Funhunt*, a composite of three Voioid line-ups (1977, 1979 and 1985) which, despite its poor quality, is enthralling. In 1991 Hell resumed recording as part of the Dim Stars, a group completed by Thurston Moore and Steve Shelley (from Sonic Youth) and Don Fleming (Gumball etc). A live three-single set, issued on Sonic Youth's Ecstatic Peace label, was succeeded by *3 New Songs*, an EP credited to Hell, but comprising Dim Stars' recordings. A 1993 album, *Dim Stars*, showed Hell's powers undiminished. In 1995 he was said to be working on a novel with guitarist Quine, excerpts from which were released in spoken word format as *Go Now*.
Albums: *Blank Generation* (Sire 1977), *Destiny Street* (Red Star 1982), *Go Now* (Codex 1995, double spoken word album). Compilations: *R.I.P.* (ROIR 1984, cassette only), *Funhunt* (ROIR 1990, cassette only).

Helmet

Moving to New York, USA to pursue a Masters degree in jazz guitar, Page Hamilton 'discovered distortion' and new influences such as Big Black, Killing Joke and Sonic Youth during his tenure with Band Of Susans, leading him to form Helmet with fellow Oregon native Henry Bogdan (bass), Australian guitarist Peter Mengede and classically-schooled drummer John Stanier, a veteran of the Florida hardcore scene. The band's close-cropped, clean-cut anti-image contrasts with their brutally heavy music. Hamilton's lyrics draw from his life in New York, and are delivered with an angry roar in economical song structures, overlaid with an intense barrage of staccato riffing; the band play with rigid discipline, avoiding the high speed delivery of many thrash and hardcore bands and generating enormous power as a result. While selling modestly, *Strap It On* created considerable interest in Helmet, and the major label debut, *Meantime*, showed progression as the band established smoother rhythmic flows without compromising their sound. The band toured widely, with Faith No More in the USA and Ministry in Europe, before undertaking headline dates of their own. Helmet subsequently parted company with Mengede, replacing him in mid-1993 with ex-postal worker Rob Echeverria. Before the release of a third album for new label Atlantic Records/East West, the group recorded

'Just Another Victim' with House Of Pain for the *Judgement Night* soundtrack. *Betty* featured co-production from Todd Ray, plus one track concocted with Butch Vig, 'Milquetoast', which also featured on a soundtrack, this time *The Crow*.
Albums: *Strap It On* (Amphetamine Reptile 1991), *Meantime* (Interscope 1992), *Betty* (East West 1994). Compilation: *Born Annoying* (Amphetamine Reptile 1995).

Hersh, Kristin

b. c.1966, Atlanta, Georgia, USA. Also the lead singer of Throwing Muses, one of alternative US rock music's most influential and enduring groups, Hersh elected to pursue a simultaneous solo career after the parent band nearly dissolved in 1992. With her half-sister and band-mate Tanya Donelly setting out to form the commercially successful Belly, Hersh kept the name Throwing Muses but also began to write songs destined for self-accompaniment. She had already explored some disconcerting mental and psychological imagery in previous Muses' albums, not least the loss of custody of her son, Dylan (she now has a younger son, Ryder, five years' Dylan's junior). It had resulted in Hersh relocating to her son's home town of Newport, Rhode Island, where she herself grew up, sheltered from a stormy adolescence by her X and Violent Femmes records. Though her own parents were free-thinking types, she was equally influenced by her Baptist grandparents. She moved to Newport from Atlanta when she was six years old, and her father taught courses in Zen Buddhism and American Indian mythology. Her parents divorced at the age of 11, but this offered an unexpected boon, the father of her best friend, Tanya Donelly, marrying her mother. It was Hersh who was primarily behind the formation of Throwing Muses with Donelly, allowing her an outlet for the songs she had been writing from childhood. Some of these made extremely uncomfortable listening, and with the Muses' rise she found the new-found celebrity difficult to cope with. By the advent of her solo career Hersh had partially conquered her psychological battle with the aid of lithium, and by the mid-90s she felt able to continue without recourse to pharmaceuticals at all. Some of this turbulence was captured in the fibre of *Hips And Makers*, but so was a great deal more, the artist herself describing it as 'a real life record. It's personal, literally so; full of skin and coffee, shoes and sweat and babies and sex and food and stores - just stupid stuff that's a really big deal.' Michael Stipe of R.E.M. guested on backing vocals for promotional single 'Your Ghost', though elsewhere just Hersh's voice, guitar and intermittent cello carried the songs, produced by Lenny Kaye (Patti Smith). By now she had become wary of being characterized as the mad woman with a guitar, and the collection reflected her resentment with female creativity being so unobjectively linked with mental instability. After returning to the Throwing Muses format with palpable enthusiasm for *University* in 1995, she also revealed news of a first film project, *Guess What's Coming To Dinner*, written with husband and manager Billy O'Connell.
Album: *Hips And Makers* (Warners/4AD 1993)

Hewerdine, Boo

b. 1961, London, England. Singer-songwriter Hewerdine is

a proud resident of Cambridge, England, where he moved with his parents aged 12 and which he likes because 'nothing every happens here. You can get on with things.' However, at age 18 he returned to London to live in his late grandmother's house in Edgware, London, which set about a downward personal spiral. He suffered from agoraphobia and was (unjustly) accused of theft and fired from his job at a record shop. However, he found a friend with similar experiences and together they began to explore music as an outlet for their traumas. He returned to Cambridge to form Placebo Thing, then the marginally more successful The Great Divide. The latter released two singles for Enigma Records after being recommended to the label by Mike Scott of the Waterboys. These attracted a fair degree of attention within the UK's small press, but more mainstream media support was not forthcoming. In January 1985 Hewerdine once again returned to Cambridge to work in a record shop, and set up a third band, the Bible. Working with jazz drummer Tony Shepherd he wrote an album of songs, *Walking The Ghost Back Home*, released through Norwich independent Backs Records in 1987. Two singles drawn from the set, 'Graceland' and 'Mahalia', achieved had a slight success, with the album also earning a lot of critical support. With the band having expanded to a quartet the Bible signed with Chrysalis Records and just missed the UK Top 40 with a re-recorded 'Graceland' and 'Honey Be Good'. After the disappointing commercial performance of 1988's *Eureka*, Hewerdine grew unhappy about the band's direction, 'I thought we were turning into an ordinary group.' He began playing his first solo gigs as a result, while the rest of the Bible became Liberty Horses. Hewerdine then made the acquaintance of American 'new country' artist Darden Smith. Together they spent four days writing songs which became the collaborative *Evidence* album (they would also work together on Darden's solo album). Hewerdine's own solo debut came as a result of sessions spent recording nearly 30 songs at Church Studio in north London in 1990. These songs were whittled down and augmented with the help of co-producer Rob Peters (formerly of Birmingham's Dangerous Girls) to produce *Ignorance*. The lyrics addressed the period during the late 70s when the artist was slowly falling apart in north London, but escaped the morbidity that might have been triggered by those events with some bright, uplifting instrumentation. With support slots to Tori Amos and another widely-applauded single, 'History', the album did just enough commercially to sustain Hewerdine's status. He also wrote songs for Eddi Reader (notably 'Patience of Angels') and Clive Gregson and production work with Laurie Freelove.
Albums: with Darden Smith *Evidence* (Ensign 1989), *Ignorance* (Ensign 1992).

High

The High were instigated in Manchester, England, in October 1987 by Andy Couzens (b. 15 July 1965, Macclesfield, Cheshire, England; guitar), who had previously plied his trade in the yet-to-blossom Stone Roses. Joined by John Matthews (b. 23 September 1967, Torquay, Devon, England; vocals), Simon Davies (b. 24 January 1967, Manchester, England; bass) and Chris Goodwin (b. 10

August 1965, Oldham, Lancashire, England; drums), the High immediately eschewed the traditional paths open to small bands by avoiding the pitfalls of incessant touring. Instead, the quartet fabricated a set of unashamedly classic guitar/pop songs and signed to London Records after just one high profile hometown show. Armed with such a simple musical formula, the High were able to work at an unusually brisk pace, releasing three singles in 1990, each of which gradually pushed the band further towards the brink of the public's consciousness. Eventually, at the turn of the year, a remixed version of their debut, 'Box Set Go', worked its way up to number 28 in the UK charts, allowing them to concentrate on creating new material throughout 1991 However, along with the less worthy Northside, the High soon topped critical assassination lists in the backlash against all things 'baggy'. The result was an almost total absence of publicity to accompany the aptly titled *Hype*.
Albums: *Somewhere Soon* (London 1990), *Hype* (London 1993).

Higsons

Formed at Norwich University, England in 1980 by Charlie 'Switch' Higson (lead vocals), Terry Edwards (guitar, saxophone, trumpet), Stuart McGeachin (guitar), Simon Charterton (drums), Colin Williams (bass) and Dave Cummings (guitar), who left the line-up early on. They originally appeared under a plethora of guises such as the Higson 5, the Higson Brothers, the Higson Experience and had settled for the Higsons by the time their first single 'I Don't Want To Live With Monkeys' (1981) on the independent label Romans In Britain was released. The song typified the Higsons' brand of quirky, tongue-in-cheek funk/pop and was treated to extensive airplay by the influential BBC radio disc jockey John Peel, achieving a number 2 position in the UK independent chart. A new label, Waap, brought with it a second single, 'The Lost And The Lonely' (1981), followed by 'Conspiracy' (1982). A contract with Chrysalis/2-Tone ensued for two singles, 'Tear The Whole Thing Down' (1982) and 'Run Me Down' (1983). They returned to Waap for 'Push Out The Boat' (1983) and yet another change of labels (Uptight) for a cover of Andy Williams' 'Music To Watch Girls By' (1984). The single failed to provide that elusive hit and was followed by the album, *The Curse Of The Higsons*, combining several single sides with new material. Another move, to EMI's R4 label, yielded 'Take It' in 1985, but although Cummings had rejoined for the single, the Higsons played their final gig in March 1986. A posthumous release by Waap, *Attack Of The Cannibal Zombie Businessmen*, married both sides of the first three 45s with six unreleased cuts, including a cover of the Buddy Miles track 'Them Changes'. By that time, Charlie Higson had turned his hand to writing for the UK television comedy series *Saturday Night Live* and most notably for comedian Harry Enfield. Charterton formed the short-lived Eat My Bed, and then Brazilian Nightmare with ex-Serious Drinking pair Pete Saunders (ex-Dexy's Midnight Runners) and Jem Moore. Terry Edwards later performed with, and produced Yeah Jazz, released a single as New York, New York ('Roger Wilson Said') and teamed up with Madness's Mark 'Bedders' Bedford as the Butterfield 8. Dave Cummings,

180

meanwhile, joined Lloyd Cole's Commotions in 1986 and later joined Del Amitri.
Albums: *Live At The Jacquard Club, Norwich* (1982), *The Curse Of The Higsons* (1984), *Attack Of The Cannibal Zombie Businessmen* (1987).

Hindu Love Gods
The Hindu Love Gods are of most interest to R.E.M. fans, for three quarters of that band, Pete Buck (b. 6 December 1956, Athens, Georgia, USA; guitar), Mike Mills (b. 17 December 1956, Athens, Georgia, USA; bass) and Bill Berry (b. 31 July 1958, Hibbing, Minneapolis, USA; drums), were in attendance at the 1987 sessions at which the band was formed. The group's singer/guitarist is Warren Zevon. In fact, the R.E.M. axis had contributed to two previous solo albums for Zevon, before forming the Hindu Love Gods as an *ad hoc* offshoot in 1986. Following the release of singles 'Narrator' and 'Good Time Tonight', the full recording of their meeting was finally released in 1990. This, a collection of blues standards and an unlikely Prince cover, was little more than an adequate bar room blues session, and has not subsequently been repeated.
Album: *Hindu Love Gods* (Giant/Reprise 1990).

Hipsway
Hipsway emerged in the mid-80s onto a Scottish pop scene that had enjoyed a high profile, both commercially and critically, with acts like Orange Juice, the Associates, Simple Minds and Altered Images. It was ex-Altered Images' bassist Jon McElhone who teamed up with guitarist Pim Jones, drummer Harry Travers and vocalist Graham Skinner (previously in the White Savages) around 1984. As Hipsway, the band secured a deal with Mercury Records who were impressed enough to strongly promote both 'Broken Years' in June and the catchy 'Ask The Lord' later in 1985, though neither made much impact. However, the momentum led to a chart hit with their third single, 'Honey Thief', early in 1986, and in its wake came both Hipsway's self-titled album and a reissue of 'Ask The Lord' in April. Unfortunately, Graham Skinner's dramatic vocal style was the only distinctive feature aside from the previous promising singles. Drawn from the album came 'Long White Car' in August, but both fell quickly by the wayside after a modest chart run. It was three years before Hipsway would return but unfortunately they failed to manage what their second album, *Scratch The Surface*, suggested. 'Young Love' disappeared without trace, the album followed suit, and Hipsway broke up soon afterwards. Skinner and Jones moved on to Witness.
Albums: *Hipsway* (Mercury 1986), *Scratch The Surface* (Mercury 1989).

His Name Is Alive
Formed in 1987 and hailing from Livonia, Michigan, USA, His Name Is Alive (an obscure reference to Abraham Lincoln) was formed by Warren Defever (b. 1969; guitar, bass, vocals, samples) with high school friends Angela Carozzo (vocals) and Karin Oliver (guitar/vocals). Their first single was the independently released cassette, 'Riotousness And Postrophe' (1987), and was followed by the

idiosyncratic 'His Name Is Alive' (1987), 'I Had Sex With God' (1988) and 'Eutectic' (1988 - a commissioned piece for the Harbinger Dance Company in Detroit). The group slotted in perfectly in the set-up at 4AD Records, a label which provided a natural home for their brand of elegant, dream-like songs. After the release of *Livonia*, titled after their home town, the group expanded to a sextet, despite the departure of Carozzo, to comprise Defever, Oliver, Denise James (vocals), Melissa Elliott (guitar), Jymn Auge (guitar) and Damian Lang (drums). Often compared to the Cocteau Twins and This Mortal Coil, Defever's eclecticism took a pervese turn when a cover of Ritchie Blackmore's 'Man On The Silver Mountain', was included on the 1992 EP, *Dirt Eaters*.
Albums: *Livonia* (4AD 1990), *Home Is In Your Head* (4AD 1991), *Mouth By Mouth* (4AD 1993).

Hitchcock, Robyn
The possessor of a lyrical vision of a latter-day Syd Barrett, UK born Hitchcock made his early reputation with the post-punk psychedelic group, the Soft Boys, having previously appeared in various groups including the Beetles and Maureen And The Meat Packers. After the Soft Boys split in 1981 he spent some time writing for Captain Sensible, then formed his own group, the Egyptians, around erstwhile colleagues Andy Metcalfe (bass), Morris Windsor (drums) and Roger Jackson (keyboards). Hitchcock's live performances were punctuated by epic, surreal monologues of comic invention capable of baffling the uninitiated and delighting the converted. His sharp mind and predilection for the bizarre has revealed itself in many titles, such as 'Man With The Light Bulb Head' ('. . . I turn myself on in the dark'), 'My Wife And My Dead Wife' a tragi-comedy of a man coming to accept the intrusion into his life of a deceased spouse, 'Trash' a well aimed diatribe against hopeless rock star hangers-on, 'Trams Of Old London' a love and remembrance saga of an era long gone, and a guide to bringing up children in the a cappella 'Uncorrected Personality Traits'. A move to A&M Records saw the release of *Globe Of Frogs*, which included the 'Ballroom Man', a favourite on US college radio which went some way to breaking new ground and earning Hitchcock a fresh audience. As a result, and despite his devoted cult following in the UK, the artist has in the early 90s concentrated more on recording and performing in the United States (occasionally guesting with R.E.M.). He has also reformed the Soft Boys and seen his back-catalogue re-packaged with loving commitment by Sequel Records. It remains to be seen whether the odd-ball workings of this endearing eccentric's mind will find a way into anything other than the US collegiate consciousness.
Albums: *Black Snake Diamond Role* (Armageddon 1981, includes material recorded with the Soft Boys), *Groovy Decay* (Albion 1982), *I Often Dream Of Trains* (Midnight Music 1984), *Element Of Light* (Glass Fish 1986), *Eye* (Twin/Tone 1990), *Perspex Island* (1991), *Respect* (1993). With the Egyptians: *Fegmania!* (Slash 1985), *Gotta Let This Hen Out!* (Relativity 1985), *Exploding In Silence* (Relativity 1986), *Invisible Hitchcock* (Glass Fish 1986), *Globe Of Frogs* (A&M 1988), *Queen Elvis* (A&M 1989).

Hole

Hole

US hardcore guitar band fronted by the effervescent Courtney Love (b. 1965, though this is a date some dispute; vocals/guitar). An ex-stripper and actress, who had small roles in Alex Cox's *Sid And Nancy* and *Straight To Hell*, she was born to hippy parents (including Grateful Dead associate Hank Harrison and Oregon therapist Linda Carroll) and even attended Woodstock as a baby. She spent the rest of her childhood years at boarding schools in England and New Zealand, where her parents had bought a sheep farm, before travelling around the world in her teens. She spent some time in San Francisco, joining ill-fated line-ups of Sugar Baby Doll (with L7's Jenifer Finch and Kat Bjelland, also participating in a formative line-up of the latter's Babes In Toyland). Returning to Los Angeles, Love appeared for a while as vocalist with Faith No More in an incarnation which only reached the rehearsal stage. Still in LA, she formed Hole with Caroline Rue (drums), Jill Emery (bass) and Eric Erlandson (guitar), following the urging of Sonic Youth's Kim Gordon. The band quickly produced a trio of fine singles; 'Retard Girl', 'Dicknail', and 'Teenage Whore', which were pointed and unsettling dirges, set in a grimly sexual lyrical environment. Favourable UK press coverage, in particular from the *Melody Maker*'s resident sycophant Everett True, helped make Hole one of the most promising new groups of 1991. Equally impressive was a debut album, produced by Don Fleming (Gumball, B.A.L.L. etc.) and Kim Gordon (Sonic Youth), followed by massive exposure supporting Mudhoney throughout Europe. It was on this jaunt that Courtney achieved further notoriety by being the first woman musician to 'trash' her guitar on stage in the UK. In March 1992 Love married Nirvana singer/guitarist Kurt Cobain. That same month bassist Emery departed from the group line-up, with Rue following in short order. Love's domestic travails would continue to dominate coverage of her musical project, with Cobain's death on the eve of the release of *Live Through This* practically obliterating that album's impact. Which served to do the much-maligned Love a genuine disservice: this was another startling collection of songs written with intellect as well as invective. It included 'I Think That I Would Die', co-written with old friend and sparring partner Kat Bjelland, as well as a cover of the Young Marble Giants' 'Credit In The Straight World'. Replacements for Emery and Rue had been found in Kristen Pfaff (bass) and Patty Schemel (drums), though tragedy again followed Love when Pfaff was found dead from a heroin overdose in her bathtub, shortly after the album's release, and just two months after Cobain's death. She would be replaced by Melissa Auf Der Maur for Hole's 1994 tour, which extended into the following year with stays in Australasia and Europe. These dates again saw Love dominate headlines with violent and/or inflammatory stage behaviour.

Albums: *Pretty On The Inside* (City Slang 1991), *Live Through This* (Geffen 1994).

Holly And The Italians

Holly Beth Vincent (b. Chicago, Illinois, USA) formed the band in Los Angeles in 1978 with herself on vocals and guitar, Mark Henry on bass, and New York born Steve Young on drums. Feeling more affinity with the UK music scene they flew to London shortly after their inauguration. There they met disc jockey Charlie Gillett and signed to his Oval label, putting out 'Tell That Girl To Shut Up', which was later covered by Transvision Vamp. They played around the pub and club circuit before coming to prominence as support to Blondie. Signed to Virgin, they cut two fine new wave pop singles in 'Miles Away' and 'Youth Coup', with a debut album produced by Richard Gottehrer. However, soon after its release the group split, leaving behind just two further singles. Vincent moved on to pursue a solo career, with the confusingly titled album *Holly And The Italians*, which was credited solely to Holly Beth Vincent. She duetted with Joey Ramone on 'I Got You Babe', alongside further solo singles for Virgin. After a brief spell replacing Patty Donahue in the Waitresses, she appeared in an *ad hoc* combo called the Wild Things with Anthony Thistlethwaite of the Waterboys. They provided a track, 'Siberian Miles', for a fanzine *What A Nice Way To Turn 17*, with Vincent doing her best to sound like Peter Perrett (Only Ones).

Albums: *The Right To Be Italian* (1981), *Holly And The Italians* (1982).

Hollywood Brats

In 1973 the Hollywood Brats came together in London and recorded an album that would later be cited as one of the most influential of the punk era, even though it was not released in the UK until 1980. The group was led by Canadian vocalist Andrew Matheson, but arguably their strength was Norwegian keyboard player, Casino Steel. The rest of the band was Eunan Brady (guitar), Wayne Manor (bass) and Louis Sparks (drums). *Hollywood Brats* featured elements of the Flamin' Groovies and the New York Dolls welded to the ethos of the new wave, which endeared it to European fans and consequently some copies crept into the UK. However, by the time Cherry Red Records finally put out their 1979 single, the memorable 'Then He Kissed Me', and the album the following year, the band had gone their separate ways. Matheson was still recording with Brady helping out in between spells with the Tools and Wreckless Eric's Last Orders. Steel joined the infamous London SS and did a couple of rehearsals before Mat Dangerfield dragged him off to help form the Boys in June 1976.

Album: *Hollywood Brats* (Cherry Red 1980).

Honey Bane

b. Donna Tracy, England. Honey Bane was previously the young singer of the Fatal Microbes who released an EP *Violence Grows* and shared a 12-inch single release with the Poison Girls. She started her solo career in 1979 after escaping from a reform centre where she was admitted for alcohol abuse. 'You Can Be You' on the Crass label was recorded in a single day. Her backing band were the Kebabs, actually a pseudonym for Crass, although the three 'anarcho-punk' songs still retained the spirit of Fatal Microbes. It was almost a year before the follow-up, 'Guilty' was released, on Honey's own label, and stirred up enough interest to secure a deal with EMI subsidiary, Zonophone. With the help of Peter Godwin from Metro and Jimmy Pursey from Sham 69, they tried to manufacture a pop star. In January 1981 'Turn

Me On, Turn Me Off' peaked at number 37. Her provocative 'naughty girl' image had short-lived appeal and after one further glimpse at the charts with a cover version of the Supremes' 'Baby Love', her popularity made a rapid decline. Successive singles 'Jimmy . . . (Listen To Me)', 'Wish I Could Be Me' and 'Dizzy Dreamers', passed unnoticed, prompting Honey to concentrate on her acting career.

Honeysmugglers

Formed in London at the end of the 80s by Chris Spence, Steve Dinsdale, Ged Murphy and Steve C., the Honeysmugglers struggled to loosen the retrogressive tag awarded to them by virtue of their bold, Hammond organ-infested sound. In reality, the quartet were far more contemporary than most people gave them credit for, fusing 60s melodic instincts with the fluent rhythms of the 90s to create a boisterously tuneful panorama. After singles on Non-Fiction and Ultimate Records however, the Honeysmugglers split up acrimoniously in 1991, without ever releasing an album.

Hoodoo Gurus

An Australian rock band whose belief in the power of the bar chord has never diminished, Sydney's Hoodoo Gurus share links with that city's other major alternative rock attraction of the 80s, the Scientists (after both relocated from Perth) That connection was instigated by singer/songwriter Dave

Faulkner, who had previously played in a band titled the Gurus, before joining Scientists guitarist Rod Radalj (guitar) in an untitled band. Bolstered by the arrival of another ex-Scientist member, drummer Jim Baker, the trio named their new band Le Hoodoo Gurus. That group would eventually evolve into the tight, hypnotic garage rock machine which, under a slightly abbreviated title, became widely venerated in underground circles through their releases for a variety of American labels. Indeed, much of their popularity stemmed from the US, where tours of the west coast made them as popular as the musically aligned Fleshtones. Led by the power pop playing of Brad Sheperd (guitar/harmonica), with the rhythm section of Baker (drums) and Clyde Bramley (bass), their ceaseless exploration of the riff has seen them compared to everyone from the Cramps to the Fall, beginning with their influential *Stoneage Romeos* debut of 1983. Dedicated to US television sitcom legends Arnold Ziffel and Larry Storch, it included the stage favourite '(Let's All) Turn On' and the nonsensical 'I Was A Kamikaze Pilot'. *Mars Needs Guitars!*, with Mark Kingsmill taking over on drums, was slightly hampered by inferior production, but the tunes were still memorable and even adventurous given their limited musical range, which veered from country punk to booming, bass-driven sleaze rock. A rarer outbreak of melodicism was introduced on *Blow Your Cool!*, with the band joined by the Bangles on several selections, although elsewhere they retreated to pounding rhythms and tough

Hothouse Flowers

rock 'n' roll. The gap between albums in 1988 saw Bramley replaced by Rick Grossman on bass. More feedback and heightened songwriting tension, together with improved production, produced the band's finest album to date in 1989s *Magnum Cum Louder*. *Kinky* mined a similar furrow, drawing lyrical targets from US and Australian pop culture, though there was little stylistic variation to the band's themes. It seems unlikely that the Hoodoo Gurus will now rise above their current cult status.

Albums: *Stoneage Romeos* (Big Time/A&M 1983), *Mars Need Guitars!* (Big Time/Elektra 1985), *Blow Your Cool!* (Big Time/Elektra 1987), *Magnum Cum Louder* (RCA 1989), *Kinky* (RCA 1991).

Hootie And The Blowfish

This South Carolina quartet were formed at the turn of the 90s and are led by Darious Rucker, whose soulful vocals add sparkle to an otherwise fairly formulaic rock sound. Their debut was a slow burner on the US charts, climbing into the Top 10 after over seven months on the chart. Rucker was a strong live performer on their vast 1994 tour (of more than 300 dates), presiding over a clutch of songs about emotional isolation and yearning. Part of the 'buzz' surrounding the band followed US television talk show host David Letterman's pronouncement that Hootie were 'my favourite new band'. *Cracked Rear View* took its title from a John Hiatt lyric and was produced by R.E.M./John Cougar Mellencamp associate Don Gehman. It documented the band's career to date, and included the single 'Hold My Hand', one of several numbers to address ecological concerns and human frailty, which featured guest vocals from David Crosby.

Album: *Cracked Rear View* (East West 1994).

Hothouse Flowers

This folk-inspired Irish rock group, who took their name from the title of a Wynton Marsalis album, are based around the nucleus of Liam O'Maonlai and Fiachna O'Broainain. O'Maonlai was formerly in a punk band called Congress which would later evolve into My Bloody Valentine. They started performing together as the Incomparable Benzini Brothers and busked in their native Dublin. In 1985 they won the Street Entertainers Of The Year Award. Recruiting Maria Doyle they became the Hothouse Flowers and landed a regular gig at the Magic Carpet Club just outside Dublin. Their notoriety spreading, they were highly praised in *Rolling Stone* magazine before they had even concluded a record deal. An appearance on RTE's Saturday night chat programme - *The Late Show* - led to the issue of a single on U2's Mother label. 'Love Don't Work That Way' came out in 1987 and though it wasn't a great success it brought them to the attention of PolyGram who signed them up. Their debut single for the major - 'Don't Go' - was a number 11 UK hit. Further hits followed, including a cover of Johnny Nash's 'I Can See Clearly Now', 'Give It Up', and 'Movies'. Their debut, *People*, reached number 2 in the UK charts. The band exist as part of a larger, looser 'Raggle Taggle' musical community, and members can be heard on material by the Indigo Girls, Adventures, Michelle Shocked and Maria McKee. In the early 90s they made their 'acting' debut in an episode of the UK television series *Lovejoy*.

Albums: *People* (1988), *Home* (1990), *Songs From The Rain* (1993).

House Of Love

After a short spell with the ill-fated glam-rock inspired Kingdoms, UK-born vocalist/guitarist Guy Chadwick teamed up with drummer Pete Evans, guitarist Terry Bickers, bassist Chris Groothuizen and vocalist/guitarist Andrea Heukamp to form UK group, the House Of Love. Throughout 1986, the quintet played at small pubs and despatched a demo tape to Creation Records which, after constant play in the office, attracted the attention of label head, Alan McGee. He financed the recording of their debut single, the sparkling 'Shine On', which was released in May 1987. A follow-up, 'Real Animal', was also issued, but sold relatively poorly. After touring extensively under tough conditions, Andrea Heukamp decided to leave the group. Continuing as a quartet, the House Of Love spent the spring of 1988 recording their debut album, which cost an astonishingly meagre £8,000 to complete. A pilot single, 'Christine', was rightly acclaimed as one of the best UK independent singles of the year. Its shimmering guitar work was exemplary and indicated the enormous potential of the ensemble. The debut album did not disappoint and was included in many critics nominations for the best record of 1988. Already, the House Of Love were being tipped as the group most likely to succeed in 1989 and the release of the excellent 'Destroy The Heart' reinforced that view. Speculation was rife that they would sign to a major label and eventually PhonoGram secured their signatures. In keeping with their 60s/guitar-based imag,e the group's releases were subsequently issued on the newly-revived Fontana Records label. A torturous period followed. The first two singles for the label, 'Never' and 'I Don't Know Why I Love You' both stalled at number 41, while the album suffered interminable delays. By Christmas 1989, guitarist Terry Bickers had quit over what was euphemistically termed a personality clash. He was immediately replaced by Simon Walker, and early the following year the group's long-awaited £400,000 second album, *Fontana*, appeared to mixed reviews. As Chadwick later acknowledged: 'We'd stated everything on the first album'. Extensive touring followed, ending with the departure of Walker, tentatively replaced by original member Andrea Heukamp, who returned from Germany. Thereafter, Chadwick suffered a long period of writer's block while the departing Bickers enjoyed acclaim in Levitation. Although the House Of Love lost ground to newly-revered guitar groups such as the Stone Roses, they re-emeged in October 1991 with an acclaimed EP featuring the excellent 'The Girl With The Loneliest Eyes'. In 1992, the group's long-awaited new album, *Babe Rainbow*, was released to a degree of critical acclaim, but the impression of under-achievement was hard to avoid. Following 1993's *Audience Of The Mind* the band collapsed, Chadwick re-emerging a year later with the Madonnas.

Albums: *House Of Love* (Creation 1988), *Fontana* (Fontana 1989), *Babe Rainbow* (Fontana 1992), *Audience Of The Mind* (Fontana 1993). Compilation: *A Spy In The House Of Love* (Fontana 1990).

Housemartins

Formed in 1984, this UK pop group comprised Paul Heaton (b. 9 May 1962, Hull, Humberside, England; vocals/guitar), Stan Collimore (b. 6 April 1962, Hull, Humberside, England; bass), Ted Key (guitar) and Hugh Whitaker (drums). After signing to Go! Discs the group humorously promoted themselves as 'the fourth best band from Hull'. Their modesty and distinctly plain image disguised a genuine songwriting talent, which soon emerged. During late 1985, Key departed and was replaced by Norman Cook (b. 31 July 1963, Brighton, Sussex, England). By 1986, the group achieved their first UK hit with their third release, the infectious 'Happy Hour', which climbed to number 3. Their UK Top 10 debut album *Hull 4, London 0* displayed a wit, freshness and verve that rapidly established them as one of Britain's most promising groups. In December 1986, their excellent a cappella version of 'Caravan Of Love' gave them a deserved UK number 1 hit. Early in 1987 the Housemartins received a coveted BPI award as the Best Newcomers of the year. In the summer, they underwent a line-up change, with Dave Hemmingway replacing drummer Hugh Whitaker. Another acclaimed album *Five Get Over Excited* followed, after which the group displayed their left-wing political preferences by performing at the 'Red Wedge' concerts. After securing another Top 20 hit with the catchy 'Me And The Farmer', the group issued their final studio album, the self-mocking *The People Who Grinned Themselves To Death*. Although still at the peak of their powers, the group split in June 1988, annoucing that they had only intended the Housemartins to last for three years. The power of the original line-up was indicated by the subsequent successes of offshoot groups such as the Beautiful South and Beats International. In 1993 Hugh Whitaker was charged and sentenced to six years imprisonment for wounding with intent and three arson attacks on a business acquaintance.

Albums: *London 0, Hull 4* (1986), *The People Who Grinned Themselves To Death* (1987). Compilation: *Now That's What I Call Quite Good!* (1988).

Huggy Bear

Brighton, England based three female/two male band at the forefront of the 'Riot Grrrl' collective philosophy on female emancipation in the music industry. Riot Grrrl has origins in America, a subversive counter-culture dedicated to 'cutting the tripwires of alienation that separate girls from boys'. In the UK Huggy Bear are at the leading edge of this movement, their activities incorporating fanzine production (*Huggy Nation*) as well as the band. Their musical arm comprises Jo (vocals/bass), Nicky (vocals), Chris (vocals), Karen (drums), John (guitar), though their ethos has more to do with musical access than practice. Despite this, their stirring proto-punk anthems, particularly the rallying 'Her Jazz', helped stir considerable media interest in 1993. This despite the fact that they still resist attempts to be interviewed by the mainstream music press. Their antagonistic stance has thus far led to two significant incidents; after performing 'Her Jazz' on the television programme *The Word*, they were among a number of men and women to vocally object to an item on 'Bimbos' being

screened after their performance. The band were ejected from the building among allegation and counter-allegation of physical violence. Shortly afterwards a gig at the Derby Warehouse on 15 March 1993 ended in chaos' when, according to several press reports, the band were accosted by a male member of the audience and his girlfriend. The man in question had proved resistant to the band's 'girls only at the front' performance dictates. Though their career is still in its infancy (releases include debut EP *Rubbing The Impossible To Burst* and a shared album with similarly confrontational US band Bikini Kill), they have done much to bring the divisive nature of sexism in the music industry back in to focus.

Album: with Bikini Kill *Our Troubled Youth/Yeah! Yeah! Yeah! Yeah!* (Wiiija 1993).

Hula

Based in Sheffield, England, Hula were one of the city's most prominent exponents of the independent music scene, churning out numerous albums and 12-inch singles of funky, synthesized pop for Yorkshire's Red Rhino label. Hula hinged around Mark Albrow (keyboards/tapes), Alan Fish (drums/percussion; later replaced by Nort) and Ron Wright (vocals/guitar/tapes/clarinet), helped at first by Chakk's Mark Brydon (bass/percussion). Their debut EP, 1982's *Back Pop Workout*, was well-received, but it was a year before their debut album, *Cut From Inside*, was released. 1984 brought perhaps their best-known single, 'The Fever Car', in September, alongside a second album, *Murmur In November*. 'Get The Habit' and 'Walk On Stalks Of Shattered Glass' (for which Hula was joined by John Arery) were followed early in the new year by *One Thousand Years* and then *Freeze Out*, taken from sessions for BBC Radio 1 disc jockey John Peel. For *Shadowland*, Hula were aided by Adam Barnes and sleeve designer Simon Crump. This preceded 'Black Wall Blue' in November and 'Poison' in March 1987, produced by Daniel Miller. In May, Hula unleashed *Voice*, again enlisting outside help from Alan Fisch, Justin Bennett and Darrell D'Silva, to add a wider instrumental range. 'Cut Me Loose' in August and *Threshold* in November meant that 1987 was Hula's busiest year; but strangely, it turned out to be their last. Red Rhino went bankrupt soon after and without the freedom the label had given them, Hula as a band disappeared, although members continued to work within Sheffield's active music scene.

Albums: *Cut From Inside* (Red Rhino 1983), *Murmur* (Red Rhino 1984), *One Thousand Hours* (Red Rhino 1986), *Shadowland* (Red Rhino 1986), *Voice* (Red Rhino 1987), *Threshold* (Red Rhino 1987).

Hurrah!

Originally known as the Green-Eyed Children, Hurrah! consisted of Paul Handyside (b. 28 September 1960, Newcastle-upon-Tyne, Tyne And Wear, England; guitar/vocals), David 'Taffy' Hughes (b. 16 March 1961, Southmoor, Northumberland, England; guitar/vocals), David Porterhouse (b. 17 August 1961, Gateshead, Tyne And Wear, England; bass) and Mark Sim (drums). Switching to the moniker of Hurrah!, the quartet signed to the new Kitchenware Records label in 1982. Mark Sim soon departed

to be replaced by Damien Mahoney, whereupon a series of acclaimed singles such as 'The Sun Shines Here' and 'Hip Hip' earned the band great respect from the British Independent sector. Based upon the pivotal force of the singing/guitar-playing/songwriting partnership of Paul Handyside and David Hughes, Hurrah! mastered a jittery, urgent style rich in melodic content. By 1986, however, the band had pushed their sound towards a rockier terrain, replacing the initial charm with power and passion. Damien Mahoney left to join the police force in the spring of that year, allowing Steve Price to fill the vacant drum stool. Their debut, *Tell God I'm Here*, saw the light of day in 1987, swiftly followed by a support date with U2 at London's Wembley stadium and, on a more bizarre note, live shows in Iraq, Egypt and Jordan after accepting an invitation from the British Council. In spite of the band's determination, commercial success remained elusive. When *The Beautiful* failed to have a significant impact on the marketplace Hurrah! parted company with the 'misunderstanding' Arista Records label and returned to the independent sector. Adrian Evans (b. 6 March 1963, County Durham, England) became the band's fourth drummer when Steve Price emigrated to America, but by then the band were in their death throes.
Albums: *Tell God I'm Here* (Kitchenware 1987), *The Beautiful* (Arista 1989). Compilation: *Boxed* (Kitchenware 1985).

Hüsker Dü

Formed in Minneapolis, Minnesota, USA, in 1979, Hüsker Dü were a punk trio consisting of guitarist/vocalist Bob Mould, bassist Greg Norton and drummer Grant Hart, whose melding of pop and punk influences inspired thousands of UK, US and European bands. Indeed, it is hard to think of a single other band who have had such a profound impact on modern alternative music than this trio. Taking their name, which means 'Do you remember?', from a Norwegian board game, they started out as an aggressive hardcore thrash band before challenging that genre's restrictions and expanding to other musical formats. Their primary strength, like so many other truly great groups, was in having two songwriting partners (Mould and Hart) that for the entirety of their career fully complemented each other. Their first single, 'Statues', was released on the small Reflex label in 1981. The following year, a debut album, *Land Speed Record*, arrived on New Alliance Records, followed by an EP, *In A Free Land*. *Everything Falls Apart* in 1983 saw them back on Reflex. By the advent of their second EP, *Metal Circus* (now on SST Records), Hüsker Dü had become a critics' favourite in the USA - a rapport which was soon to be exported to their UK brethren. *Zen Arcade* in 1984 brought about a stylistic turning point - a two-record set, it followed a single storyline about a young boy leaving home and finding life even more difficult on his own. A 14-minute closing song, 'Reoccurring Dreams', in which it was revealed the boy's entire ordeal was a dream, broke all the rules of punk. A non-album cover of the Byrds' 'Eight Miles High' followed, and a 1985 album, *New Day Rising*, maintained the trio's reputation as a favourite of critics and college radio stations, with its irresistible quicksilver pop songs. After *Flip Your Wig* the band signed with Warner

Brothers Records (there were several other interested parties), with whom they issued *Candy Apple Grey* in 1986 and *Warehouse: Songs And Stories*, another double set, the following year. In 1988 Hart was dismissed from the group (though there are many conflicting versions of events leading up to this juncture), who summarily disbanded. Mould and Hart continued as solo artists, before Mould formed Sugar in 1991.
Albums: *Land Speed Record* (New Alliance 1982), *Everything Falls Apart* (Reflex 1982), *Zen Arcade* (SST 1984), *New Day Rising* (SST 1985), *Flip Your Wig* (SST 1985), *Candy Apple Grey* (WEA 1986), *Warehouse: Songs And Stories* (WEA 1987), *The Living End* (WEA 1994, rec 1987). Compilation: *Everything Falls Apart And More* (WEA 1993).

Hypnotics, (Thee)

Formed in High Wycombe, Buckinghamshire, England, this MC5 and Stooges-influenced group was the product of James Jones (vocals), Ray Hanson (guitar), Will Pepper (bass) and Mark Thompson (drums). On the strength of 'Love In A Different Vein' (1988), their debut single on the Hipsville label, the band signed to Beggars Banquet Records offshoot, Situation 2, and enjoyed independent chart success early the following year with the eight-minute 'Justice In Freedom'. Awash with loud, distorted, wah-wah guitars and blues riffs, the single had to be re-pressed due to popular demand. The powerful 'Soul Trader' followed later that year, and after supports to Spacemen 3 and Gaye Bykers On Acid the band commemorated their first national tour with a live mini-album, *Live'r Than God!*. A tour of the USA with the Cult won them praise across the Atlantic, before the band's first studio album surfaced early in 1990. *Come Down Heavy* was more refined and showed a definite nod towards early Santana, with guest appearances from Pretty Things' Dick Taylor and Phil May. Two singles followed, 'Half Man Half Boy' and 'Floatin' In My Hoodoo Dream', before the band appeared at the 1990 Reading Festival. However, in 1992 Craig Pike died of a heroin overdose. 1994's *The Very Crystal Speed Machine* (only released in the UK a year later) saw production from Chris Robinson and friends from the Black Crowes, and reflected on his passing with the mournful 'Goodbye'.
Albums: *Live'r Than God!* (Sub Pop 1989), *Come Down Heavy* (Beggars Banquet 1990), *Soul, Glitter And Sin* (Beggars Banquet 1991), *The Very Crystal Speed Machine* (SPV/American 1994).

Icicle Works

Emerging from the profligate network of Liverpudlian bands that existed during the punk rock and new wave era, the Icicle Works were formed by Ian McNabb (b. 3 November 1962; vocals/guitar), Chris Layhe (bass) and Chris Sharrock (drums). McNabb was formerly in City Limits with the near legendary Edie Shit (Howie Mimms), and Sharrock played with the Cherry Boys (who also included Mimms at one point). Taking their name from a science fiction novel - *The Day The Icicle Works Closed Down* - they made their recording debut with a six-track cassette entitled *Ascending*, released on the local Probe Plus emporium in 1981. The band then founded their own Troll Kitchen label on which they prepared 'Nirvana', their premier single. Gaining a lot of support from BBC disc jockey John Peel they came to the attention of Beggars Banquet Records, initially through their Situation 2 offshoot. Their second single, 'Birds Fly (Whisper To A Scream)', was an 'indie' hit but they had to wait for the next effort, 'Love Is A Wonderful Colour', to breach the UK Top 20. The subject matter was typically subverted by McNabb's irony and cynicism ('When love calls me, I shall be running swiftly, To find out, just what all the fuss is all about'). Teaming up with producer Ian Broudie (ex-Big In Japan, Care, and later Lightning Seeds) he helped them to a string of single successes over the ensuing years including 'Hollow Horse' and 'Understanding Jane', with their sound gradually shifting from subtle pop to harder rock territory. In 1986 they recruited Dave Green on keyboards, but the following year the group was turned upside down when both Sharrock and Layhe left within a short space of time. Sharrock joined the La's and later drummed for World Party. Layhe's role was taken by former Black bassist Roy Corkhill, whilst the drummer's stool was claimed by Zak Starkey whose father Ringo Starr formerly drummed for another Liverpool band. This line-up prospered for a short while but in 1989 McNabb assembled a new band. Retaining only Corkhill he added Mark Revell on guitar, Dave Baldwin on keyboards, and Paul Burgess on drums. The band signed a new deal with Epic Records and released an album before McNabb left to go solo. 1993 brought his debut album, *Truth And Beauty*. One of England's most under-rated, natural lyricists, his cult status looks set to continue, while his time with the Icicle Works has left behind a rich legacy of songwriting.

Albums: *The Icicle Works* (Beggars Banquet 1984), *The Small Price Of A Bicycle* (Beggars Banquet 1985), *If You Want To Defeat Your Enemy Sing His Song* (Beggars Banquet 1987), *Blind* (Beggars Banquet 1988), *Permanent Damage* (Epic 1990). Compilations: *7 Singles Deep* (Beggars Banquet 1986), *The Best Of* (Beggars Banquet 1992).

Iggy Pop

b. James Jewel Osterburg, 21 April 1947, Ypsilanti, Michigan, USA. The emaciated 'Godfather Of Punk', Iggy Pop was born just west of Detroit to an English father and raised in nearby Ann Arbor. He first joined bands while at high school, initially as a drummer, most notably with the Iguanas in 1964 where he picked up the nickname Iggy. The following year he joined the Denver blues-styled Prime Movers, but a year after that dropped out of the University Of Michigan to travel to Chicago and learn about the blues from former Howlin' Wolf and Paul Butterfield Blues Band drummer, Sam Lay. On returning to Detroit as Iggy Stooge, and further inspired after seeing the Doors, he formed the Psychedelic Stooges with Ron Asheton of the Chosen Few. Iggy was vocalist and guitarist, Asheton initially played bass, and they later added Asheton's brother Scott on drums. Before the Chosen Few, Ron Asheton had also been in the Prime Movers with Iggy. The Psychedelic Stooges made their debut on Halloween night, 1967, in Ann Arbor. The same year Iggy also made his acting debut in a long forgotten Françoise De Monierre film that also featured Nico. Meanwhile Dave Alexander joined on bass and the word 'Psychedelic' was dropped from their name. Ron switched to guitar leaving Iggy free to concentrate on singing and showmanship. The Stooges were signed to Elektra Records in 1968 by A&R man Danny Fields (later manager of the Ramones). They recorded two albums (the first produced by John Cale) for the label which sold moderately at the time but later became regarded as classics, featuring such quintessential Iggy numbers as 'No Fun' and 'I Wanna Be Your Dog'. Steven MacKay joined on saxophone in 1970 in-between the first and second albums as did Bill Cheatham on second guitar. Cheatham and Alexander left in August 1970 with Zeke Zettner replacing Alexander and James Williamson replacing Cheatham - but the Stooges broke up not long afterwards as Iggy fought a heroin problem. Stooge fan David Bowie tried to resurrect Iggy's career and helped him record *Raw Power* in London in the summer of 1972 (as Iggy and the Stooges, with Williamson on guitar, Scott Thurston on bass, and the Ashetons, who were flown in when suitable British musicians could not be found). The resultant album included the nihilistic anthem 'Search And Destroy'. Bowie's involvement continued (although his management company Mainman withdrew support because of constant drug allegations) as Iggy sailed through stormy seas (including self-admission to a mental hospital). The popular, but poor quality, live *Metallic KO* was released in France only at the time. Iggy Pop live events had long been a legend in the music industry, and it is doubtful whether any other artist has sustained such a high level of abject self destruction on stage. It was his performance on British television slot *So It Goes*, for example, that ensured the programme would never air again. After *Raw Power* there were sessions for *Kill City*, although it was not released until 1978, credited then to Iggy Pop and James Williamson. It also featured Thurston, Hunt and Tony Sales, Brian Glascock (ex-Toe Fat and later in the Motels), and others. The Stooges had folded again in 1974 with Ron Asheton forming New Order (not the same as the UK band) and then Destroy All Monsters. Steve MacKay later died from a drugs overdose and Dave Alexander from alcohol abuse. Thurston also joined the Motels. Interest was stirred in Iggy with the

Immaculate Fools

arrival of punk, on which his influence was self evident (Television recorded the tribute 'Little Johnny Jewel'), and in 1977 Bowie produced two studio albums - *The Idiot* and *Lust For Life* - using Hunt and Tony Sales, with Bowie himself, unheralded, playing keyboards. Key tracks from these two seminal albums include 'Night Clubbin'', 'The Passenger', and 'China Girl' (co-written with and later recorded by Bowie). Iggy also returned one of the several favours he owed Bowie by guesting on backing vocals for *Low*. In the late 70s Iggy signed to Arista Records and released some rather average albums with occasional assistance from Glen Matlock (ex-Sex Pistols) and Ivan Kral. He went into (vinyl) exile after 1982's autobiography and the Chris Stein produced *Zombie Birdhouse*. During his time out of the studio he cleaned up his drug problems and married. He started recording again in 1985 with Steve Jones (again ex-Sex Pistols) featuring on the next series of albums. He also developed his acting career (even taking lessons) appearing in *Sid And Nancy*, *The Color Of Money*, *Hardware*, and on television in *Miami Vice*. His big return came in 1986 with the Bowie-produced *Blah Blah Blah* and his first ever UK hit single, 'Real Wild Child', a cover of Australian Johnny O'Keefe's 50s rocker. His rejuventated *Brick By Brick* album featured Guns N'Roses guitarist Slash, who co-wrote four of the tracks, while his contribution to the *Red Hot And Blue* AIDS benefit was an endearing duet with Debbie Harry on 'Well Did You Evah?'. This was followed in 1991 by a duet with the B-52's Kate Pierson, who had also featured on *Brick By Brick*. 1993's *American Caesar*, from its jokily self-aggrandising title onwards, revealed continued creative growth, with longer spaces between albums now producing more worthwhile end results than was the case with his 80s career. Throughout he has remained the consumate live performer, setting a benchmark for at least one generation of rock musicians.

Albums: With the Stooges: *The Stooges* (Elektra 1969), *Fun House* (Elektra 1970). As Iggy And The Stooges: *Raw Power* (Columbia 1973), *Metallic KO* (Import 1974). As Iggy Pop: *The Idiot* (RCA 1977), *Lust For Life* (RCA 1977), with James Williamson *Kill City* (Bomp 1978), *TV Eye Live* (RCA 1978), *New Values* (Arista 1979), *Soldier* (Arista 1980), *Party* (Arista 1981), *Zombie Birdhouse* (Animal 1982), *Blah Blah Blah* (A&M 1986), *Instinct* (A&M 1988), *Brick By Brick* (Virgin 1990), *American Caesar* (Virgin 1993). Compilations: *Choice Cuts* (RCA 1984), *Compact Hits* (A&M 1988), *Suck On This!* (Revenge 1993), *Live NYC Ritz '86* (Revenge 1993).
Further reading: *I Need More*, Iggy Pop.

Immaculate Fools

UK pop band consisting of two sets of brothers from Kent, Kevin Weatherall (vocals), Paul Weatherall, Andy Ross and Peter Ross. They made their debut with 'Nothing Means Nothing' in September 1984, before hitting with 'Immaculate Fools' in January 1985. Afterwards they spent a lot of time touring the continent where they enjoyed more popularity, especially in Spain. Further singles included 'Hearts Of Fortune' and 'Save It' in 1985. Their second album, *Dumb Poet*, was well-received by critics (including a five star review in *Sounds* magazine), though it did not replicate earlier chart success. It spawned the singles 'Tragic Comedy' and 'Never Give Less Than Anything'. Barry Wickens (fiddle) joined in time for *Another Man's World*, but by then impetus had been lost, and the media proved less sympathetic to the group's summery, fey pop songs.
Albums: *Hearts Of Fortune* (A&M 1985), *Dumb Poet* (A&M 1987), *Another Man's World* (A&M 1990).
Video: *Searching For Sparks* (1987).

Inspiral Carpets

During the late 80s UK music scene, the city of Manchester and its surrounds spawned a host of exciting new groups and the Inspiral Carpets were at the head of the pack alongside Happy Mondays, James, the Stone Roses and 808 State. The group was formed in Oldham by schoolfriends Graham Lambert (guitar) and Stephen Holt (vocals). They were joined by drummer Craig Gill and performed in their hometown of Oldham with various other members until they were joined by organist Clint Boon and bassist David Swift. Boon met the group when they began rehearsing at his studio in Ashton-under-Lyne. His Doors-influenced playing later became the group's trademark. Their debut EP, *Planecrash*, was released by the independent label, Playtime, and the group were consequently asked to record a John Peel session for BBC Radio 1. In 1988 there was an acrimonious split between the band and label and also between the group members. Holt and Swift were replaced by Tom Hingley and Martin Walsh, formerly with local bands Too Much Texas and the Next Step respectively. The band formed their own label, Cow Records, and after a string of well-received singles they signed a worldwide deal with Mute Records. 'This Is How It Feels' was a hit and *Life* was critically acclaimed for its mixture of sparkling pop and occasional experimental flashes. Further singles had less impact and *The Beast Inside* received a mixed response, some critics claiming the band were becoming better known for their merchandise, like t-shirts and promotional milk bottles. The t-shirts, bearing the immortal words, 'Cool as Fuck!' inevitably aroused considerable controversy, particularly when a fan was arrested for causing offence by wearing such a garment. Afterwards the group journeyed onwards without ever arousing the same level of interest, though both *Revenge Of The Goldfish* and *Devil Hopping* had their moments. 'Bitch's Brew', from the former, stronger album, was a classy stab at Rolling Stones-styled sweeping pop revival, though elsewhere too many songs continued to be dominated by Boon's organ, which, once a powerful novelty, now tended to limit the band's songwriting range.
Albums: *Life* (Mute 1990), *The Beast Inside* (Mute 1991), *Revenge Of The Goldfish* (Mute 1992), *Devil Hopping* (Mute 1994).

Into Paradise

This rock-pop outfit formed in Dublin, Eire, in 1986, as Backwards Into Paradise. By 1988 their line-up had stabilized as Dave Long (vocals/guitar), James Eadie (lead guitar/keyboards), Rachael Tighe (bass), and Ronan Clarke (drums). They gathered few second glances until the release of *Under The Water*, early in 1990. A capricious and deceptive album, it secured many plaudits and a predictably

enthusiastic response from the media. Being from Dublin, they were automatically and inaccurately compared to both U2 and the Hothouse Flowers. Other critics noted the proliferation of drink orientated songs, which placed them in a more definite Irish tradition. The follow-up, *Churchtown*, on their new Ensign Records home, was given an altogether more terse reception. Ultimately, however, the accomodation with a major label went awry, and Into Paradise returned to original home Setanta Records, who in the meantime had enjoyed success with A House and Frank And Walters. This more sympathetic environment has seen Long continue to mine a strong creative furrow, though his lyrics may be a little too barbed for major success to come courting again.
Albums: *Under The Water* (Setanta 1990), *Churchtown* (Ensign 1991), *Down All The Days* (Setanta 1992), *For No One* (Setanta 1993).

Its Immaterial

This pop duo based in Liverpool, England scored a UK chart hit with 1986's 'Driving Away From Home (Jim's Tune)'. Following 'Eds Funky Diner' and the impeccable 'Space (He Called From The Kitchen)' they disappeared from view for a while, before J. Campbell and J. Whitehead re-emerged with an album on Siren Records. As before, the music was of a subdued, understated nature, with wry wit in the manner of the Pet Shop Boys.
Album: *Song* (1990).

J

Jacob's Mouse

At the age of 11 identical twins Hugo (guitar) and Jebb (bass) Boothby met Sam Marsh (vocals/drums) at a swimming competition, when all three boys were wearing heavy metal printed T-shirts. The band was formed and they soon graduated from Status Quo covers to writing their own material, drawing primary influence from the noisier acts appearing on UK disc jockey John Peel's radio show. (Peel later sponsored the band's career, and is a close neighbour of theirs in Bury St Edmunds, Suffolk, England.) Their name, hardly descriptive of their ferocious sound, was inspired by their cousin's pet, and was first used on a 7-inch EP, *The Dot*, released on the Liverish label in January 1991. It was Single Of The Week in the soon-to-be-defunct *Sounds* magazine, and heralded support slots with Nirvana, Carter USM, Senseless Things and others. Still without a record deal, they released *No Fish Shop Parking* (a name taken from a road sign in Bury St Edmunds) on their own Blithering Idiot label, which was run by the father of their manager, Sam Marsh. This brought them acclaim from UK disc jockeys John Peel

and Mark Goodier, and the band subsequently signed with Wiiija Records, whose Gary Walker had at first turned them down. After touring with Babes In Toyland they released the *Ton Up* EP in September 1992, and they also signed a US deal with Frontier Records to give them wider distribution. *I'm Scared* deserved the healthy amount of press it received with its low-fi hardcore sound draped in feedback and metal riffs. The band were also highly playful, pushing their sound in varied and quite unexpected directions in a manner reminiscent of Captain Beefheart. Live, they were equally distinctive, with Marsh's guttural, non-linear vocals used primarily as an instrument (the band humbly stating that, as they were so young, they would feel daft trying to impart wisdom to others) and the identical twins standing either side of the drum kit, flailing in unison. In the autumn of 1993 they released two further EPs, *Good* and *Group Of Seven*, after which the band took a break in preparation for a third album, which came out in March 1995.
Albums: *No Fish Shop Parking* (Blithering Idiot 1992), *I'm Scared* (Wiiija 1992), *Rubber Room* (Wiiija 1994). Compilation: *Wryly Smiling* (Wiiija 1994).

Jah Wobble

b. John Wardle, London, England. An innovative bass player, Wobble began his career with Public Image Limited. Previously he had been known as one of the 'four Johns' who hung around Malcolm McLaren's 'Sex' boutique. Heavily influenced by the experimental rhythms of bands like Can, his input to PiL's *Metal Box* collection inspired in turn many novice post-punk bass players. By August 1980 he had become one of the many instrumentalists to fall foul of Lydon in PiL's turbulent career, and set about going solo. 1983 saw him joining with his hero Holger Czukay and U2's The Edge for *Snake Charmer*, before he put together the Human Condition, a combo specializing in free-form jazz and dub improvisation. However, when they disbanded, the mid-80s quickly became wilderness years for Wobble: 'The biggest kickback I have had was from sweeping the platform at Tower Hill station. It was a scream. You felt like getting on the intercom and saying "The next train is the Upminster train, calling at all stations to Upminster and by the way, I USED TO BE SOMEONE!".' However, when he began listening to North African, Arabic and Romany music, he was inspired to pick up his bass once more. It was 1987 when he met guitarist Justin Adams, who had spent much of his early life in Arab countries. Their bonding resulted in Wobble putting together Invaders Of The Heart, with producer Mark Ferda on keyboards. After tentative live shows they released *Without Judgement* in the Netherlands, where Wobble had maintained cult popularity. As the late 80s saw a surge in the fortunes of dance and rhythmic expression, Invaders Of The Heart and Wobble suddenly achieved a surprise return to the mainstream. This was spearheaded by 1990's 'Bomba', remixed by Andy Weatherall on the fashionable Boy's Own label. Wobble was in demand again, notably as collaborator on Sinead O'Connor's *I Do Not Want What I Haven't Got* and Primal Scream's 'Higher Than The Sun'. This was quickly followed by Invaders Of The Heart's *Rising Above Bedlam*, in turn featuring contributions from O'Connor (the dance hit, 'Visions Of

You') and Natacha Atlas. Wobble's creative renaissance has continued into the 90s, with Invaders Of The Heart slowly building a formidable live repuation and releasing a series of infectious, upbeat albums for Island Records.

Albums: *The Legend Lives On...Jah Wobble In 'Betrayal'* (Virgin 1980), *Jah Wobble's Bedroom Album* (Lago 1983), *Psalms* (Wob 1987). With Holger Czukay and The Edge: *Snake Charmer* (Island 1983). With Ollie Morland: *Neon Moon* (Island 1985). With Invaders Of The Heart: *Without Judgement* (Island 1990), *Rising Above Bedlam* (Island 1991), *Take Me To God* (Island 1994).

Jam

This highly successful late 70s group comprised Paul Weller (b. 25 May 1958, Woking, Surrey, England; vocals/guitar), Bruce Foxton (b. 1 September 1955, England; bass/vocals) and Rick Buckler (b. Paul Richard Buckler, 6 December 1955, Woking, Surrey, England; drums). After gigging consistently throughout 1976, the group were signed to Polydor Records early the following year. Although emerging at the peak of punk, the Jam seemed oddly divorced from the movement. Their leader, Paul Weller, professed to voting Conservative (although he would later switch dramatically to support the Labour Party), and the group's musical influences were firmly entrenched in the early Who-influenced mod style. Their debut, 'In The City', was a high energy outing, with Weller displaying his Rickenbacker guitar to the fore. With their next record, 'All Around The World' they infiltrated the UK Top 20 for the first time. For the next year, they registered only minor hits, including 'News Of The World' (their only single written by Foxton) and a cover of the Kinks' 'David Watts'. A turning point in the group's critical fortunes occurred towards the end of 1978 with the release of 'Down In The Tube Station At Midnight'. This taut, dramatic anti-racist song saw them emerge as social commentators par excellence. *All Mod Cons* was widely acclaimed and thereafter the group rose to extraordinary heights. With *Setting Sons*, a quasi-concept album, Weller fused visions of British colonialism with urban decay and a satirical thrust at suburban life. The tone and execution of the work recalled the style of the Kinks' Ray Davies, whose class-conscious vignettes of the 60s had clearly influenced Weller. The superbly constructed 'Eton Rifles', lifted from the album, gave the Jam their first UK Top 10 single in late 1979. Early the following year, they secured their first UK number 1 with 'Going Underground', indicating the enormous strength of the group's fan base. By now they were on their way to topping music paper polls with increasing regularity. Throughout 1982, the Jam were streets ahead of their nearest rivals but their parochial charm could not be translated into international success. While they continued to log number 1 hits with 'Start' and 'Town Called Malice', the USA market remained untapped. In late 1982, the group's recent run of UK chart-toppers was interrupted by 'The Bitterest Pill (I Ever Had To Swallow)' which peaked at number 2. Weller then announced that the group were to break up, and that he intended to form a new outfit, the Style Council. It was a shock decision, as the group were still releasing some of the best music to come out of Britain and were most certainly at their peak. Their final single, the exuberant, anthemic 'Beat Surrender' entered the UK chart at number 1, an extraordinary conclusion to a remarkable but brief career. After the mixed fortunes of the Style Council Weller would embark on a solo career, a move Foxton made immediately after the Jam's dissolution. Buckler and Foxton would work briefly together in Time U.K., with Foxton then joining Stiff Little Fingers and Buckler retiring from the music industry as a furniture restorer.

Albums: *In The City* (Polydor 1977), *This Is The Modern World* (Polydor 1977), *All Mod Cons* (Polydor 1978), *Setting Sons* (Polydor 1979), *Sound Affects* (Polydor 1980), *The Gift* (Polydor 1982), *Dig The New Breed* (Polydor 1982), *Live Jam* (Polydor 1993). Compilations: *Snap!* (Polydor 1983, double album), *Greatest Hits* (Polydor 1991), *Extras* (Polydor 1992).

Videos: *Video Snap* (1986), *Transglobal Unity Express* (1988), *Greatest Hits* (1991), *Little Angels: Jam On Film* (1994).

Jane's Addiction

This innovative, art-rock quartet was formed in Los Angeles, USA, in 1986, by vocalist Perry Farrell. He had formerly starred in the Cure-influenced Psi Com, from whose ranks would also emerge Dino Paredes (Red Temple Spirits), while it is rumoured that two former members joined the Hare Krishna sect. With the addition of guitarist David Navarro, bassist Eric A. and drummer Stephen Perkins, Jane's Addiction incorporated elements of punk, rock, folk and funk into a unique and unpredictable soundscape. They debuted with a live album on the independent Triple X label, recorded at Hollywood's Roxy venue, which received widespread critical acclaim, despite a throwaway cover of Lou Reed's 'Rock 'n Roll' and Farrell's limited stage patter, largely consisting of profanities. Drawing inspiration from the Doors, PiL, Velvet Underground and Faith No More, they set about delivering a hypnotic and thought-provoking blend of intoxicating rhythms, jagged and off-beat guitar lines and high-pitched vocals of mesmeric intensity. *Ritual De Lo Habitual* is a work of depth and complexity, which requires repeated listening to reveal its hidden melodies, subtle nuances and enigmatic qualities. It included the video-friendly shoplifting narrative, 'Been Caught Stealing'. In the US, because of censorship of the album's provocative front cover (as with earlier work, featuring a Farrell sculpture), it was released in a plain envelope with the text of the First Amendment written on it. Farrell, meanwhile, helmed the 'Lollapalooza' concert series which for the first time filled large arenas with star-studded indie-rock/rap/alternative artists and events. Despite widespread media coverage, Jane's Addiction never made the commercial breakthrough that their talents deserved, and Farrell split the band in 1992. On his decision to defect to Porno For Pyros, taking drummer Perkins and bass player Martyn Le Noble with him, Farrell concluded: 'What it really boiled down to was, I wasn't getting along with them. I'm not saying whose fault it was. Even though I *know* whose fault it was'. The subject of such slurs, Navarro would go on to join the Red Hot Chili Peppers in 1994.

Albums: *Jane's Addiction* (Triple X 1987), *Nothing's Shocking* (Warners 1988), *Ritual De Lo Habitual* (Warners 1991).

Japan

Formed in London in early 1974, this group comprised David Sylvian (b. David Batt, 23 February 1958, Lewisham, London, England; vocals), his brother Steve Jansen (b. Steven Batt, 1 December 1959, Lewisham, London, England; drums), Richard Barbieri (b. 30 November 1958; keyboards) and Mick Karn (b. Anthony Michaelides, 24 July 1958, London, England; saxophone). A second guitarist, Rob Dean, joined later and the group won a recording contract with the German record company Ariola-Hansa. During the same period, they signed to manager Simon Napier-Bell. The group's derivative pop style hampered their prospects during 1978, and they suffered a number of hostile reviews. Eminently unfashionable in the UK punk era, they first found success in Japan. After three albums with Ariola-Hansa, they switched to Virgin Records in 1980 and their fortunes improved a year later thanks to the surge of popularity in the new romantic movement. Japan's androgynous image made them suddenly fashionable and they registered UK Top 20 hits with 'Quiet Life', 'Ghosts' and a cover of Smokey Robinson And The Miracles' 'I Second That Emotion'. Tin Drum, was also well received. Disagreements between Karn and Sylvian undermined the group's progress, just as they were achieving some long-overdue success and they split in late 1982. Sylvian and Karn went on to record solo with varying degrees of success.
Albums: Adolescent Sex (1978), Obscure (1978), Quiet Life (1980), Gentlemen Take Polaroids (1980), Tin Drum (1981), Oil On Canvas (1983). Compilations: Assemblage (1981), Exorcising Ghosts (1984), The Other Side Of Japan (1993).

Jayhawks

Def American Records producer George Drakoulias discovered the country/rock/R&B influenced Jayhawks after they had made two low-key records. Legend has it that he phoned Dave Ayers of Twin/Tone Records and overheard a collection of the band's demos, and signed them up. The band, who come from Minneapolis, Minnesota, USA, boasted a core line-up of Marc Olson (vocals/guitar) and Gary Louris (vocals/guitar), joined by Ken Callahan (bass), and subsequently Karen Grotberg (keyboards) and Marc Perlman, who replaced Callahan. Together since 1985, until their induction to Rick Rubin's eclectic label they had only sold approximately 10,000 records. Songs such as 'Waiting For The Sun' saw them compared to the Black Crowes (another Drakoulias discovery), combining rugged country imagery with harsh, rough hewn bar blues. Their second album, Blue Earth, threw up another name; that of Neil Young. For their own part they cited the Flying Burrito Brothers and Charles & Ira Louvin as their greatest influences. They also record widely as session musicians, including work for acts such as Soul Asylum, Counting Crows and Maria McKee. The group's rapid turnover of drummers continued on Tomorrow The Green Grass, with Don Heffington on hand in the studio and Tim O'Regan available for touring duties. Songs on this set included 'Miss Williams' Guitar', a tribute to Marc Olson's wife, Victoria Williams, and the exquisite single, 'Blue'. It saw them still playing simple, direct music, a traditional but never stultifyingly sound.

Albums: The Jayhawks (Bunkhouse 1986), The Blue Earth (Twin/Tone 1989), Hollywood Town Hall (Def American 1992), Tomorrow The Green Grass (American 1995).

Jazz Butcher

The Jazz Butcher are a prime example of British rock eccentricity. Formed in 1982 and hailing from Northampton, the group served as a vehicle for the idiosyncratic, melodic songwriting talents of Pat Fish (b. Patrick Huntrods; guitar/vocals), otherwise known as the Jazz Butcher. Although early group line-ups were erratic - including Rolo McGinty and Alice Thompson, (both later to emerge in the Woodentops) and ex-Bauhaus bassist David J. - the one constant member during much of the early years was lead guitarist Max Eider, whose light jazz/blues feel gave an eloquence to even the most heavy-handed of tunes. In terms of style, there was a large nod in the direction of Lou Reed and Jonathan Richman, while the songs' subject matter dealt with the diverse traumas of everyday life, taking in the joys and woes of small town living ('Living In A Village'), drink ('Soul Happy Hour'), fear and paranoia ('Death Dentist'), love ('Only A Rumour'/'Angels'), the virtues of public transport ('Groovin' In The Bus Lane'), film noir and Vladimir Ilyich Lenin. The classic Jazz Butcher line-up, including Max Eider, Felix Ray (bass) and 'Mr' O.P. Jones (drums), underwent a major upheaval in 1987 with the departure of Eider, resulting in the unit disintegrating. By the time of Fishcotheque, Fish was working virtually alone, but for a new partner in guitarist Kizzy O'Callaghan. The Jazz Butcher (Conspiracy) model of the band was rebuilt to comprise Fish, O'Callaghan, Laurence O'Keefe (bass), Paul Mulreany (drums) and Alex Green (saxophone), and saw group undergoing a change of label, moving from Glass to Creation Records. Subsequent albums saw an increasing use of cut-up film/television dialogue, and continued to garner encouraging reviews. While the Jazz Butcher has found a large audience in Europe, and more recently in the USA, substantial success in his homeland continues to elude him. 1995's Illuminated included the anti-Conservative government tract, 'Sixteen Years'. It saw some critics scoff at the way in which Creation's perseverance with the Jazz Butcher mirrored the British public's unwillingness to change administration.
Albums: The Jazz Butcher In Bath Of Bacon (Glass 1983), A Scandal In Bohemia (Glass 1984), Sex And Travel (Glass 1985), The Jazz Butcher And The Sikkorskis From Hell - Hamburg - A Live Album (Rebel 1985). As Jazz Butcher Conspiracy: Distressed Gentlefolk (Glass 1986). Fishcotheque (Creation 1988), Big Planet, Scary Planet (Genius 1989), Cult Of The Basement (Rough Trade 1990), Condition Blue (Creation 1991), Western Family (Live)(Creation 1993), Waiting For The Love Bus (Creation 1993), Illuminated (Creation 1995). Compilations: The Gift Of Music (Glass 1985), Bloody Nonsense (Big Time 1986), Big Questions - The Gift Of Music Vol 2 (Glass 1987), Edward's Closet (Creation 1991). Max Eider solo The Best Kisser In The World (Big Time 1987).

Jellyfish

This US band from San Francisco broke into the 90s by

brilliantly re-packaging the most gaudy elements of the 60s and 70s pop with irresistible kitsch appeal. The band's dress sense was particularly colourful, one critic observing that it could have been drawn from the wardrobes of colour blind charity shop consumers. The group is composed of Andy Sturmer (b. Pleasanton, San Fransisco, California, USA; drums/vocals), Jason Flakner (guitar), along with brothers Chris Manning (b. Pleasanton, San Fransisco, California, USA; bass) and Roger Manning (b. Pleasanton, San Fransisco, California, USA; keyboards). This hometown they describe as '*Twin Peaks* without the Tree'. Members of the band were previously in Beatnik Beach, a short-lived funk pop outfit on Atlantic. Their debut single, 'The King Is Half Undressed', was a classy slice of retro-pop. Allied to their childlike dress sense, the formula guaranteed immediate television exposure. An album followed shortly after, which was assured and close to outright Beatles pastiche with strange overtones of Earth Opera. It was produced by Albhy Galuten, his first job since *Saturday Night Fever*. However, subsequent highly commercial singles; 'Baby's Coming Back', 'I Wanna Stay Home', and 'Now She Knows She's Wrong', failed to build on a strong chart platform. Jellyfish were more than happy to be able to play with at least two of their heroes, Ringo Starr and Brian Wilson, following introductions from Don Was from Was (Not Was). Their debut album remains one of the more exciting debuts of the 90s and was followed in 1993 by a similarly crafted *Spilt Milk*. More complex arrangements and sometimes breathtaking harmonies showed definite influences of 10cc, Queen and Badfinger. The line up in 1993 included Eric Dover (guitar) who replaced Flakner and Tim Smith (bass), who took over from Chris Manning.

Albums: *Bellyhutton* (Virgin 1991), *Spilt Milk* (Virgin 1993).

Jesus And Mary Chain

Formed in East Kilbride, Scotland, this quartet comprised William Reid (vocals/guitar), Jim Reid (vocals/guitar), Douglas Hart (bass) and Murray Dalglish (drums). In the summer of 1984 they moved to London and signed to Alan McGee's label, Creation Records. Their debut, 'Upside Down', complete with trademark feedback, fared well in the independent charts and was backed with a version of Syd Barrett's 'Vegetable Man'. In November 1984, Dalglish was replaced on drums by Primal Scream vocalist Bobby Gillespie. By the end of the year, the group were attracting considerable media attention due to the violence at their gigs and a series of bans followed. Early the following year, the group signed to the WEA/Rough Trade label, Blanco Y Negro. The Reid brothers publically delighted in the charms of amphetamime sulphate, which gave their music a manic edge. Live performances usually lasted 20 minutes, which brought more controversy and truculence from traditional gig habitues, who felt short-changed. 'Never Understand' further underlined comparisons with the anarchic school of 1977 in general and the Sex Pistols in particular. For their next release, however, the group surprised many by issuing the more pop-orientated 'Just Like Honey'. By October 1985, Gillespie had grown tired of the Jesus And Mary Chain and returned to his former group, Primal Scream. One month later, the Reid Brothers issued their highly-

acclaimed debut, *Psychocandy*. Full of multi-tracked guitar distortion, underscored with dark melodies, many critics proclaimed it one of rock's great debuts. The following August the group reached the UK Top 20 with the melodic 'Some Candy Talking', which received curtailed radio play when it was alleged that the subject matter concerned heroin. During the same period, the group found a new drummer, John Moore, and parted from their manager, Alan McGee. Further hits with 'April Skies' and 'Happy When It Rains' preceded their second album, *Darklands*. Again fawned over by the press, though not to quite the same extent as their debut, it was followed by a tempestuous tour of Canada and America, during which one brother was briefly arrested then acquitted on a charge of assaulting a fan. In the spring of 1988 a compilation of the group's various out-takes was issued. This assuaged demand before the arrival of *Automatic* at the turn of the decade. The band was effectively just a duo for this, with programmed synth drums as backing to the usual barrage of distortion and twisted lyrics (the best example of which was the single, 'Blues From A Gun'). *Honey's Dead* also housed a powerful lead single in 'Reverence', which brought the band back to the charts. After which the Reid brothers changed tack for *Stoned & Dethroned*, with the feedback all but gone in favour of an acoustic, singer/songwriter approach. Self-produced and recorded at home, its more reflective texture was embossed by the appearance of guest vocalists Shane McGowan and Hope Sandoval (Mazzy Star).

Albums: *Psychocandy* (Blanco y Negro 1985), *Darklands* (Blanco y Negro 1987), *Automatic* (Blanco y Negro 1990), *Honey's Dead* (Blanco y Negro 1992), *Stoned & Dethroned* (Blanco y Negro 1994). Compilations: *Barbed Wire Kisses* (Blanco y Negro 1988), *Sound Of Speed* (Blanco y Negro 1993).

Jesus Jones

Blending the driving force of punk guitar with liberal use of samples and dance rhythms, Jesus Jones made an audacious debut with the single 'Info Freako'. The song was voted into the Top 10 year-end charts of all the UK music papers. Singer/songwriter Mike Edwards (b. 22 June 1964, City of London, England) is supported by Gen (b. Simon Matthews, 23 April 1964, Devizes, Wiltshire, England; drums), Al Jaworski (b. 31 January 1966, Plymouth, Devon, England; bass), Jerry De Borg (b. 30 October 1963, Kentish Town, London, England; guitar) and Barry D (b. Iain Richard Foxwell Baker, 29 September 1965, Carshalton, Surrey, England; keyboards). The group was formed in London, England, early in 1988, and was signed soon afterwards by Food Records. *Liquidizer* was an energetic debut which provided further UK hits with 'Never Enough' and 'Bring It On Down'. *Doubt*, produced mainly by Edwards, saw the band inject a stronger commercial element. After six weeks at the top of the US alternative chart it entered the *Billboard* chart and in the UK it reached number 1. In the summer of 1991 the band, who had always kept up a busy live schedule, became part of a nucleus of young UK bands scoring hits in the US. 'Right Here, Right Now' was a major success and along with EMF, whom many claim were stylistically indebted to Jesus Jones, they found their abrasive pop suddenly popular within the USA's generally conservative market. However, there was a consequent fall-off in their domestic popularity, highlighted by the poor chart returns afforded *Perverse*.

Albums: *Liquidizer* (Food 1989), *Doubt* (Food 1991), *Perverse* (Food 1993).

Jesus Lizard

Formed in 1989, the Jesus Lizard originally comprised David Yow (vocals), David Sims (bass) - both formerly of the Austin, Texas, act Scratch Acid - and Duane Denison (guitar), with the help of a drum machine. *Pure*, their abbreviated debut, maintained the uncompromising style of their former incarnation with its ponderous bass lines, growled vocals and crashing guitar. The set was produced by Steve Albini (ex-Big Black), with whom Sims had worked in the controversially-named Rapeman. Albini engineered and co-produced *Head*, on which the Jesus Lizard were joined by drummer Mac McNeilly. The group's sound remained as powerful and compulsive as ever, although some critics detected an artistic impasse. Jesus Lizard would join Nirvana on a joint single which broke the UK charts, but *Down* saw the band maintain a ferocity which deemed them very much a secular concern.

Albums: *Pure* (Touch & Go 1989, mini-album), *Head* (Touch & Go 1990), *Goat* (Touch & Go 1991), *Down* (Touch & Go 1994).

Jilted John

Rabid Records, a new wave label based in Manchester, England, received a recording of 'Jilted John', composed and performed by a thespian named Graham Fellowes. Rabid released this semi-monologue concerning the woes of a young lover, and were soon so overwhelmed by demand that EMI had to take over its marketing in 1978. Fellowes slipped into his Jilted John character in media interviews - a few similarly gormless appearances on BBC television's *Top Of The Pops* pushed the record to number 4 in the UK chart - and necessitated the issue of an album and an 'answer' single by John's rival, Gordon The Moron. After this episode, however, Fellowes returned to his acting career which has since included roles in the UK soap opera *Coronation Street* and a northern stage production of a play concerning John Lennon.

Album: *True Love Stories* (1978).

Jimmy The Hoover

Simon Barker (b. 22 July 1956, Malta; keyboards), Derek Dunbar (b. 31 August 1958, Aberdeen, Scotland; vocals), Carla Duplantier (b. Hollywood, Los Angeles California, USA; drums), Flinto (b. 11 March 1955, Zambia; bass) and Mark Rutherford (b. 14 April 1961, Hackney, London, England; guitar) formed the band in 1982. Malcolm McLaren gave them the name and a support tour with Bow Wow Wow. Cris Cole stepped in on bass guitar, and in 1983 they signed to CBS subsidiary Innervision. That year brought them their one hit 'Tantalise (Wo Wo Ee Yeh Yeh)' a good pop song with an African influence. Along with Innervision stablemates Wham! and Animal Nightlife, the group had 'legal' problems that interfered with the

promotion of the second single 'Kill Me Quick', and tied them up for many months.

Jobson, Richard

b. October 6 1960, Dunfermline, Scotland. Jobson was born the brother of John, a striker for Meadowbank Thistle Football Club, for whom Richard was also on the books. After the Skids four year tenure (1977-81) Jobson moved on to join the Armoury Show, which failed to repeat the success of any of its illustrious personnel's former bands. With their demise Jobson toured the UK with Scottish acting company Poines Plough. Turning to poetry, he hit the road once more, falling between two stools in terms of critical reception. On one side rock critics viewed the move suspiciously, castigating him as pretentious, while the poetry critics reacted with venom to the vulgar intrusion of a rock singer. Placed in its proper context, Jobson was capable of writing good poetry, but was too much at the whim of his own indulgence. The worst example of this was his infamous live rendition of Sylvia Plath's 'Daddy'. He continued to release albums throughout the 80s, the best of which was *16 Years Of Alcohol*, also the title of a book he wrote, which related his alcohol problems. He also suffers from epilepsy. Meanwhile Jobson had chanced upon further careers in television and fashion. He appeared variously as the pop correspondent on BBC television's *The Garden Party*, as presenter for *01 For London*, and most recently in regional arts programmes and the opinion show, *Biteback*. On top of this came his highly paid, and some might say unlikely, stint as a fashion model. Most notable were a series of car adverts, for which he also composed the music. His most recent recording, *Badman*, was released on Parlophone Records in 1988, produced by Ian Broudie (Lightning Seeds, etc). Though the imagery was typically grandiose, it did include a sprightly cover of Everything But The Girl's 'Angel'.

Albums: *The Ballad Of Etiquette* (Cocteau 1981), *An Afternoon In Company* (Crepuscule 1982), *Ten Thirty On A Summer Night* (Crepuscule 1983), *The Right Man* (Crepuscule 1986), *16 Years Of Alcohol* (Crepuscule 1987), *Badman* (Parlophone 1988).

Johansen, David

b. 9 January 1950, Staten Island, New York, USA. Johansen gained recognition in the early 70s as lead singer of the New York Dolls. A R&B/rock group taking inspiration from the likes of the Rolling Stones, the Dolls' street attitude and outrageous sense of dress, thrust them into the glitter/glam scene, although their music had little in common with others of that nature. Prior to joining the Dolls, Johansen joined his first band, the Vagabond Missionaries, in high school. At the age of 17 he moved to Manhattan, New York, and briefly worked with a band called Fast Eddie And The Electric Japs. The Dolls came together in late 1971 and quickly built a devoted audience at New York clubs such as the Mercer Arts Center and Max's Kansas City. They recorded two albums for Mercury Records and held on until late 1976. After their demise they became an inspiration to numerous artists, from the newly forming punk bands such as the Sex Pistols to Kiss to the Smiths. Johansen launched a solo career in 1978, recording for Blue Sky Records. Less flamboyant than the

Dolls' records, this was a solid rock effort that stressed Johansen's lyrical acumen. He released three other rock/R&B-oriented solo albums for Blue Sky and one for Passport Records before shifting career directions once again. In 1983 Johansen began booking small cabaret concert dates under the name Buster Poindexter, performing a slick, tightly-arranged set of vintage R&B numbers, show tunes, and jump blues. Dressing in a formal tuxedo and playing the lounge lizard, Poindexter built a following of his own, until Johansen the rocker literally ceased to exist; he completely gave up his rock act to pursue the new image full-time. He recorded two albums as Buster Poindexter, in 1987 and 1989, the first yielding a chart and club hit, a cover of Arrow's 1984 soca dance tune, 'Hot, Hot, Hot'. He was still popular as Poindexter in the early 90s, touring with a 10-piece band and packing clubs, his repertoire now including Caribbean-flavoured music, torch songs, blues, as well as the early R&B. He also launched an acting career in the late 80s, appearing in films including *Scrooged* and *Married To The Mob*.
Albums: *David Johansen* (1978), *In Style* (1979), *Here Comes The Night* (1981), *Live It Up* (1982), *Sweet Revenge* (1984); as Buster Poindexter *Buster Poindexter* (1987), *Buster Goes Berserk* (1989).

Johnny Moped

b. Paul Halford, London, England. The bizarre Moped Bands, in their various incarnations, have produced a stream of influential musicians and personalities. The outfit gradually emerged in Croydon, starting off with the Black Witch Climax Blues Band, before switching names to Genetic Breakdown from 1971-75. Some of the key personnel included Ray Burns (later Captain Sensible), his brother Phil, the Berk brothers, and the mysterious Xerxes. It was not until 1974 that Moped joined, as the band became known first as Johnny Moped And The 5 Arrogant Superstars, then Johnny Moped's Assault And Buggery. However, it was the birth of punk which saw Moped finding an audience for his 'moronic rock 'n' roll'. Getting support slots with the Damned introduced new wave audiences to the strange phenomenon of J. Moped, the performer. After the Berk brothers' stint in the Unusuals (with Chrissie Hynde, soon to be of the Moors Murderers then the Pretenders on vocals), they rejoined the re-christened Captain Sensible in the third Johnny Moped line-up. Having found success with the Damned, the Captain only stayed for three months, his place taken by the hideously titled Slimey Toad. With several singles behind them, notably the charming 'No One'/'Incendiary Device', they recorded the legendary *Cycledelic*, an album still acclaimed by both R.E.M. and the Ramones. The band disappeared after its release, although Dave Berk did replace Rat Scabies in the Damned when the latter stormed off during their European tour. Scabies had previously performed one gig with the Moped band. Against all odds, the Johnny Moped Big Band reformed in 1991, playing live for the first time in 12 years and recording *The Search For Xerxes*. Live, they were joined on stage by old colleagues Kirsty MacColl and the Captain. As Xerxes once stated: 'It is odd, that such an untalented bunch of people are still held in such affection'.

Albums: *Cycledelic* (1978), *The Search For Xerxes* (1991).

Johnson, Matt

b. 1961, Essex, England. From an early age Johnson turned to music. After beginnings with the school band, Road Star, he went on to the electronic trio, the Gadgets, who recorded three albums, the last of which was never released. His collaborators were Tom Johnson and Michael O'Shea, both of whom were ex-Plain Characters. While the band were still in progress, Johnson formed The The with Keith Laws (keyboards), Tom Johnston (bass) and Peter Ashworth (drums). Following two singles, one each for 4AD Records and Some Bizzare, the original formation disintegrated. Some backing tracks were salvaged, however, and these formed the basis of Johnson's solo effort, *Burning Blue Soul*, released in 1981. In cover design it parodied the Beatles' *Rubber Soul* period psychedelia, but in execution it was a very personal affair: 'It is pretty close to the bone. It was one of the most innocent albums made, probably. And very pure, almost virginal in a way. But when I listen to it, its very honest'. Back under The The's moniker, Johnson recorded tracks for a proposed debut album, *Pornography Of Despair*, which never appeared. Essentially a solo album, all of the tracks would eventually surface on subsequent The The albums or related releases.
Album: *Burning Blue Soul* (4AD 1981).

Josef K

This Edinburgh, Scotland-based band formed in the ashes of punk as TV Art and were influenced by New York bands such as Television, Talking Heads and the Velvet Underground. The original trio of Paul Haig (vocals), Malcolm Ross (guitar) and Ron Torrance (drums) were joined briefly by Gary McCormack (later with the Exploited), before a more permanent bassist was found in David Weddell. After a name change inspired by Franz Kafka's 1925 novel, *The Trial*, Josef K recorded a 10-track demo before committing 'Chance Meeting' to release on Steven Daly's Absolute label, in late 1979. Daly, who was also the drummer for Orange Juice, was the co-founder of Postcard Records, and thus signed Josef K to the newly-formed label. 'Radio Drill Time' was more frantic than their debut, dominated by hectic, awkward chords and Haig's thin, nasal voice. After numerous support slots, 1980 ended with the more low-key, melodic sound of 'It's Kinda Funny'. The single fared well and Josef K were all set to release their debut *Sorry For Laughing*, during the early months of 1981. Unhappy with its production, the band scrapped it at the test pressing stage and moved to a Belgian studio, in conjunction with the Les Disques du Crépuscule label. The session yielded the re-recorded title track and their strongest single, 'Sorry For Laughing' (1981), which joined tracks from the unreleased album as a session for BBC radio disc jockey John Peel, while the band returned to Belgium to work on their album. Back at Postcard, they drafted Malcolm's brother Alistair to play trumpet on a new version of 'Chance Meeting', issued just two months later, coinciding with a full session for Peel. *The Only Fun In Town* emerged in July to a mixed reception. Its frantic, trebly live sound appeared hurried, and betrayed the fact that it had been recorded in just six days. Josef K announced their demise soon after, prompted by Malcolm Ross' invitation to join Orange Juice. Crépescule issued Josef K's farewell single, 'The Missionary', in 1982, while other tracks surfaced on various compilations. After Ross had joined Orange Juice, Haig worked with Rhythm Of Life before embarking on a solo career. In 1987, Scottish label Supreme International Editions followed the excellent 'Heaven Sent' with *Young And Stupid*, a collection of Peel session material and tracks from the unreleased *Sorry For Laughing*. Then, in 1990, the entire recorded history of Josef K (plus tracks from their original demo) were compiled onto two definitive CDs by Les Temps Moderne.

Album: *The Only Fun In Town* (Postcard 1981). Compilations: *Young And Stupid* (Supreme International 1989), *The Only Fun In Town/Sorry For Laughing* (Les Temps Moderne 1990).

Joy Division

Originally known as Warsaw, this Manchester post-punk outfit comprised Ian Curtis (b. July 1956, Macclesfield, Cheshire, England, d. 18 May 1980; vocals), Bernard Dicken/Albrecht (b. 4 January 1956, Salford, Manchester, England; guitar/vocals), Peter Hook (b. 13 February 1956, Manchester, England; bass) and Steven Morris (b. 28 October 1957, Macclesfield, Cheshire, England; drums). Borrowing their name from the prostitution wing of a concentration camp, Joy Division emerged in 1978 as one of the most important groups of their era. After recording a regionally available EP, *An Ideal For Living*, they were signed to Manchester's recently formed Factory Records and placed in the hands of producer Martin Hannett. Their debut, *Unknown Pleasures*, was a raw, intense affair, with Curtis at his most manically arresting in the insistent 'She's Lost Control'. With its stark, black cover, the album captured the group still coming to terms with the recording process, but displaying a vision that was piercing in its clinical evocation of an unsettling disorder. With Morris's drums employed as a lead instrument, backed by the leaden but compulsive bass lines of Hook, the sound of Joy Division was distinctive and disturbing. By the time of their single, 'Transmission', the quartet had already established a strong cult following, which increased after each gig. Much of the attention centred on the charismatic Curtis, who was renowned for his neurotic choreography, resembling a demented marionette on wires. By the autumn of 1979, however, Curtis's performances were drawing attention for a more serious reason. On more than one occasion he suffered an epileptic seizure and blackouts onstage, the illness seemed to worsen with the group's increasingly demanding live schedule. On 18 May 1980, the eve of Joy Division's proposed visit to America, Ian Curtis was found hanged. The verdict was suicide. A note was allegedly found bearing the words: 'At this moment I wish I were dead. I just can't cope anymore'. The full impact of the tragedy was underlined shortly afterwards, for it quickly became evident that Curtis had taken his life at the peak of his creativity. While it seemed inevitable that the group's posthumously released work would receive a sympathetic reaction, few could have anticipated the quality of the material that emerged in 1980. The single, 'Love Will Tear Us Apart', was probably the finest of the year, a haunting account of a fragmented relationship, sung by Curtis in a voice that few realized he possessed. The attendant album, *Closer*, was faultless, displaying the group at the zenith of their powers. With spine-tingling cameos such as 'Isolation' and the extraordinary 'Twenty-Four Hours', the album eloquently articulated a sense of despair, yet simultaneously offered a therapeutic release. Instrumentally, the work showed maturity in every area and is deservedly regarded by many critics as the most brilliant rock album of the 80s. The following year, a double album, *Still*, collected the remainder of the group's material, most of it in primitive form. Within months of the Curtis tragedy, the remaining members sought a fresh start as New Order. In 1995 Curtis' widow, Deborah, published a book on her former husband and the band, while a compilation album and a re-released version of 'Love Will Tear Us Apart' were back on the shelves on the 15th anniversary of his death.

Albums: *Unknown Pleasures* (Factory 1979), *Closer* (Factory 1980), *Still* (Factory 1981). Compilations: *The Peel Sessions* (Strange Fruit 1986), *Permanent: The Best Of Joy Division* (London 1995). Further reading: *An Ideal For Living: An History Of Joy Division*, Mark Johnson. *Touching From A Distance*, Deborah Curtis.

June Brides

This mid-80s UK pop band were built around lyricist, guitarist and singer Phil Wilson. Operating in the independent sector, their sound was characterized by the unusual inclusion of a brass section; Jon Hunter (trumpet), Reg Fish (trumpet) and Frank Sweeney (viola), alongside Simon Beesley (guitar/vocals), Ade Carter (bass) and Dave Bickley (drums; replacing Brian Alexis). Their first release was 'In The Rain', followed by 'Every Conversation', on which That Petrol Emotion's John O'Neill was brought in to help with production. Their only album, however, was disappointing in relation to singles such as 'No Place Called Home'. Frank guested on a number of Creation Records artefacts (Peter Astor, Meat Whiplash), and had another claim to fame in being beaten-up badly by skinheads while trying to protect a pregnant woman. Hunter also played with Marc Riley for one EP. Press darlings for a couple of months, the June Brides nevertheless quickly departed from the scene because of 'frustration, lack of money, and some of us no longer enjoying being in the band'. Sweeney joined Brick Circus Hour and Wilson moved on to a solo career. A lavishly packaged compilation arrived in 1995, at which point a small-scale but relaxed reunion gig took place.

Album: *There Are Eight Million Stories* (Pink 1985). Compilation: *For Better Or Worse (1983-86)* (Overground 1995).

Justified Ancients Of Mu Mu

Also known as the JAMS, this coalition saw Bill Drummond and Jimmy Cauty engage in some startlingly imaginative methods of undermining the prevailing pop ethos. Drummond had cut his teeth in the Liverpool scene of the early 80s and played a large part in setting up Zoo Records. By 1987 he was working with Cauty and exploiting the techniques of sampling and computers. Their liberal use of other artists' material within the framework of their own songs resulted in a court case with Abba, following which all remaining copies of the JAMS' album, *1987 (What The Fuck Is Going On?)*, were legally bound to be destroyed. However, a handful of copies escaped annihilation and ended up on sale for £1,000 each. The following year the duo switched guises to become the Timelords, enjoying a worldwide hit with 'Doctorin' The Tardis', with Gary Glitter. A manual on how to have a number 1 single was written, to be succeeded by work on their own movie. By this time Drummond and Cauty were calling themselves the KLF and enjoying yet more global success with the 'Stadium House' trilogy of singles. In 1991 the JAMMS moniker was reactivated for 'It's Grim Up North', a dance single which owed several musical moments to composer William Blake. Whereupon Drummond and Cauty promptly slipped back into KLF mode to record with country singer Tammy Wynette.

Albums: *1987 (What The Fuck Is Going On?)* (KLF Communications 1987), *Who Killed The JAMS?* (KLF Communications 1987).

Katrina And The Waves

This pop group enjoyed their major hit with 'Walking On Sunshine' in 1985, but were also well-known for their original version of 'Going Down To Liverpool', which was successfully covered by the Bangles. The band consisted of Katrina Leskanich (b. 1960, Topeka, Kansas, USA; vocals), Kimberley Rew (guitar), Vince De La Cruz (b. Texas, USA; bass) and Alex Cooper (drums). Leskanich and De La Cruz are Americans, but came to Britain during 1976 when their military fathers served in the UK. Based at Feltwell, Norfolk, where the airforce base was, Rew and Cooper were both graduates of Cambridge University. Rew was formerly in the Soft Boys and after leaving them released the solo *The Bible Of Pop*, in 1982. Many of the songs he wrote for his solo career were carried over into Katrina And The Waves, where he became the chief songwriter. The band was formed in 1982 but their first two albums were only released in Canada. They followed up 'Walking On Sunshine' with 'Sun Street', which was their last hit, although they remained a popular act on the college circuit for some time thereafter. 1993 brought a series of reunion gigs, at first in their 'adopted city' of Cambridge.

Albums: *Walking On Sunshine* (Canada 1983), *Katrina And The Waves 2* (Canada 1984), *Katrina And The Waves* (Capitol 1985), *Waves* (Capitol 1985), *Break Of Hearts* (SBK 1989).

Kilbey, Steve

b. England, though his parents emigrated to Australia when he was a child. As leader and main writer of the Church, Kilbey led the resurgence of interest in Australia for 60s music. His performances on the 12-string guitar evoked the sound of the Byrds and their ilk of the psychedelic era. The band enjoyed considerable success on the college radio network in the USA and on the European live circuit. This enabled Kilbey to enjoy a prolific output outside the confines of the band with the publication of a book of poetry and the release of several solo albums on the small independent Red Eye label. This solo work often proved a little more adventurous than that of the Church. A 1991 collaboration with Grant McLennan of the Go-Betweens resulted in the album *Jack Frost*, though otherwise his most important partnership was that with Donnette Thayer (ex-Game Theory) under the title Hex (his only other project to see release outside of Australia).

Albums: *Unearthed* (Enigma 1987), *Earthed* (Rykodisc 1988), *The Slow Crack* (Red Eye 1988), *Remindlessness* (Red Eye 1990). As Hex: *Hex* (1989), *Vast Halos* (1990). As Jack Frost: *Jack Frost* (1991).

Kilburn And The High Roads

An important link between 'pub rock' and punk, Kilburn And The High Roads were formed in November 1970 by art lecturer Ian Dury (b. 12 May 1942, Upminster, Essex, England; vocals) and Russell Hardy (b. 9 September 1941, Huntingdon, Cambridgeshire, England; piano). As a frontman, Dury cut an almost Dickensian figure, with his growling, half-spoken vocals, squat figure, polio stricken leg and a withered hand, encased in a black leather glove. In fact, throughout the band's entire history their visual image was the antithesis of the prevalent glitter and glam-pop fashion. The initial line-up included Ted Speight (guitar), Terry Day (drums) and two former members of the Battered Ornaments, George Khan (saxophone) and Charlie Hart (bass). By 1973, despite a series of fluctuating line-ups, Dury and Russell had eventually settled down with a collection of musicians comprising: Keith Lucas (b. 6 May 1950, Gosport, Hampshire, England; guitar - a former art-school pupil of Dury's), Davey Payne (b. 11 August 1944, Willesden, London, England; saxophone), David Newton-Rohoman (b. 21 April, 1948, Guyana, South America; drums) and Humphrey Ocean (bass). The last would subsequently leave the Kilburns to concentrate on a successful career as an artist and be replaced by Charlie Sinclair in January 1974. The group's early repertoire consisted of rock 'n' roll favourites mixed with early 50s Tin Pan Alley pop, but this was later supplemented and supplanted by original material utilizing Dury's poetry, mostly depicting the loves and lives of every day east London folk. The Kilburns were, by this point, enshrined in London's 'pub rock' circuit. Managed by Charlie Gillett, they completed an album for the Raft label. This good fortune suffered a setback when the album's release was cancelled after the label went bankrupt. Warner Brothers, the parent company, chose to drop the group from its roster (but later released the sessions as *Wotabunch* in the wake of Dury's solo success). By late spring 1974, Gillett had left the scene, as

Katrina And The Waves

had Hardy, who was replaced by Rod Melvin. Later that year they signed to the Dawn label, and released two superb singles, 'Rough Kids'/'Billy Bentley (Promenades Himself In London)' and 'Crippled With Nerves'/'Huffety Puff'. The subsequent album, *Handsome*, released the following year, was a huge disappointment, largely due to the bland production which captured little of the excitement and irreverence of a Kilburn's gig. The album marked the end of this particular era as the group then disintegrated. Keith Lucas embraced punk with the formation of 999, performing under the name of Nick Cash, while Dury, Melvin and Payne became founder members of a revitalized unit, Ian Dury And The Kilburns. Ted Speight was also involved in this transitional band, during which time the singer introduced 'What A Waste' and 'England's Glory', two songs better associated with Ian Dury And The Blockheads, the group with which he found greater, long-deserved success.

Albums: *Handsome* (Dawn 1975), *Wotabunch* (Warners 1978). Compilation: *The Best Of Kilburn And The High Roads* (Warners 1977).

Killdozer

This US rock group imbue their slow, menacing soundscapes with only the loosest imitations of song structure. Killdozer trace their origins back to Madison, Wisconsin, and their origins in hicksville USA are regularly celebrated in their primal country blues. Featuring Michael Gerald (bass/vocals), plus the brothers Dan and Bill Hobson (guitar and drums, respectively), the trio have released a steady stream of albums which often highlighted their distaste at what they saw as the social and political malaise of their native country. They were just as likely to turn the spotlight on smalltown weirdness, however, or their singer's rampant confusion about the state of the world. In a respite from this angst, *For Ladies Only* was a project dedicated to covers of classic songs of the 70s, including 'One Tin Soldier' and 'Good Lovin' Gone Bad'. Guitarist Paul Zagoras came on board during the 90s, during which time Killdozer's formidable output was restrained somewhat due to Gerald taking accountancy exams (he is a former mathematics teacher). However, the band bounced straight back to form with albums in 1994 and 1995, both featuring further bizarre anecdotes and spiky, unreconstructed punk songs.

Albums: *Intellectuals Are The Shoeshine Boys Of The Ruling Elite* (Bone Air 1984), *Snakeboy* (Touch & Go 1985), *Burl* (Touch & Go 1986, mini-album), *Little Baby Buntin'* (Touch & Go 1987), *Twelve Point Buck* (Touch & Go 1988), *For Ladies Only* (Touch & Go 1989), *Uncompromising War On Art Under The Dictatorship Of The Proletariat* (Touch & Go 1994), *God Hears Pleas Of The Innocent* (Touch & Go 1995). Video: *Little Baby Buntin' Live* (1990).

Killing Joke

Immensely powerful post-punk band who combined a furious rhythm section with near psychotic performances from Jaz Coleman (b. Jeremy Coleman, Cheltenham, England; vocals/keyboards). The band came about when Coleman, of Egyptian descent, was introduced to Paul Ferguson, then drumming for the Matt Stagger Band. Coleman joined as a keyboard player, before they both quit to form their own group. This first incarnation added 'Geordie' (b. K. Walker, Newcastle, England; guitar) and Youth (b. Martin Glover Youth, 27 December 1960, Africa; bass), who had made his first public appearance at the Vortex in 1977 with forgotten punk band the Rage. After re-locating to Notting Hill Gate they paid for a rehearsal studio and borrowed money from Coleman's girlfriend to release the *Turn To Red* EP. Picked up by disc jockey John Peel, the band provided a session which would become the most frequently requested of the thousands he has commissioned. Via Island Records the band were able to set up their own Malicious Damage label, on which they released 'Wardance' in February 1980, notable for its remarkably savage b-side, 'Psyche'. A succession of fine, aggressive singles followed, alongside live appearances with Joy Division. They were in a strong enough position to negotiate a three album deal with EG, which allowed them to keep the name Malicious Damage for their records. After the release of a typically harsh debut album, the band were banned from a Glasgow gig when council officials took exception to posters depicting Pope Pius giving his blessing to two columns of Hitler's Brown Shirts (a genuine photograph). It was typical of the black humour which pervaded the band, especially on their record sleeves and graphics. After the recording of the third album was completed the band would disintegrate when Coleman's fascination with the occult led him to the conclusion that apocalypse was imminent, and he fled to Iceland. He was followed later by Youth. When Youth returned it was to begin work with Ferguson on a new project, Brilliant. However, having second thoughts Ferguson became the third Joker to flee to Iceland taking bass player Paul Raven (ex-Neon Hearts) with him. Brilliant continued with Youth as the only original member. The Killing Joke output from then on lacks something of the menace which had made them so vital. However, *Night Time* combined commercial elements better than most, proffering the hit single 'Love Like Blood'. While *Outside The Gate* was basically a Coleman solo album wrongly credited to the band, they returned with their best album for years with 1990's *Extremities, Dirt And Various Repressed Emotions*, which saw the drumming debut of Martin Atkins (ex-PiL). Regardless, the band broke up once more with bitter acrimony flying across the pages of the press the same year. While his former co-conspirators pronounced Killing Joke dead, Coleman pledged to continue under the name. He did just that after a brief sojourn into classical/ethnic music via a collaborative project with Anne Dudley. *Pandemonium* saw Youth return to join Geordie and Coleman, with the addition of new drummer Geoff Dugmore. This saw a revitalized Killing Joke, notably on 'Exorcism', recorded in the King's Chamber of the Great Pyramid in Cairo. They were welcomed back by a wide cross-section of critics (at least those who Coleman hadn't physically assaulted at some point) and friends. Indeed, bands claiming Killing Joke as a direct influence ranged from the Cult, Ministry and Skinny Puppy to Metallica and Soundgarden, while many noticed an uncanny similarity between the band's 'Eighties' and Nirvana's 'Come As You Are'.

Albums: *Killing Joke* (EG 1980), *What's THIS For...!* (EG 1981), *Revelations* (Malicious Damage/EG 1982), *Ha! Killing Joke Live* (Malicious Damage/EG 1982), *Fire Dances* (EG 1983), *Night Time* (EG 1985), *Brighter Than A Thousand Suns* (EG/Virgin 1986), *Outside The Gate* (EG/Virgin 1988), *Extremities, Dirt And Various Repressed Emotions* (RCA 1990), *Pandemonium* (Butterfly/Big Life 1994). Jaz Coleman with Anne Dudley: *Songs From The Victorious City* (China 1990). Compilations: *An Incomplete Collection* (EG 1990), *Laugh? I Nearly Bought One* (EG 1992), *Wilful Days* (Virgin 1995).

King

This Coventry-based group was formed in 1983 after the break-up of the Reluctant Stereotypes of which Paul King (vocals) was a member. The remainder of King comprised Tony Wall (bass), Mick Roberts (keyboards), James Jackel Lantsbery (guitar) and Adrian Lillywhite (drums; ex-Members). They made their debut supporting the Mighty Wah! and signed to CBS. Despite extensive touring and a sizeable following, their first three singles and *Steps In Time* sold poorly. The break came late in 1984 when they supported Culture Club and reached a whole new teen audience. 'Love And Pride' was released early next year, and made number 2 in the UK chart, while the album went to number 6. The hits continued throughout the year, most notably with 'Alone Without You', and King abruptly disbanded in 1986. Paul King pursued a solo career, which at best gave him a minor hit with 'I Know' which reached number 59. The group will probably be remembered as much for their trademark spray-painted Dr. Martens boots and Paul King's affable personality than for their engaging pop songs. Paul King later became a video jockey for MTV.

Albums: *Steps In Time* (1984), *Bitter Sweet* (1985).

King Missile

One of the more arresting crop of underground bands drawn from New York, USA, in recent years, King Missile are led by vocalist and spoken word/poetry maverick John S. Hall. His early albums (credited to King Missile (Dog Fly Religion)) for Kramer's Shimmy Disc label were expanded in sound by the latter's auxiliary musicianship and production, as well as the efforts of guitarist, Dogbowl. When the latter left, he took the parenthesized portion of the name with him, though Hall's instinct for black humour and caustic commentary remained. Dogbowl would go on to his own erratic solo career, while *Mystical Shit* saw Hall joined by Bongwater guitarist Dave Rick and multi-instrumentalist Chris Xefos (from When People Were Shorter). This included notable, gilt-edged cuts like 'Jesus Is Way Cool', which no doubt helped to entice Atlantic Records in the group's direction. King Missile began to break into the US college charts with *Happy Hour*, notably via the single, 'Detachable Penis', which was released a year before the John Wayne Bobbit case came to light. 1994's eponymous missive, meanwhile, saw production expertise from Daniel Rey (Ramones, White Zombie etc).

Albums: *Fluting On The Hump* (Shimmy Disc 1987), *Mystical Shit* (Shimmy Disc 1990), with Kramer *Real Men* (Shimmy Disc 1991), *The Way To Salvation* (Atlantic 1991), *Happy Hour* (Atlantic 1992), *King Missile* (Atlantic 1994). Compilation: *They* (Shimmy Disc 1988).

King Of The Slums

Formed near Manchester, England by vocalist Charley Keigher (vocals) and Sarah Curtis (electric violin), Salford's King Of The Slums first surfaced on the amateurish 'Spider Psychiatry' on SLR Records in 1986. The single went unnoticed and the band spent nearly two years refining their sound, before issuing the impressive EP, *England's Finest Hopes*, on the local Play Hard label in February 1988. Curtis's scratchy, John Cale-like violin playing and Keigher's vehement polemic were augmented by Jon Chandler (bass) although over the next few years the band used a succession of drummers - Trevor Rising, Ross Cain and Ged O'Brian, before eventually settling with Stuart Owen. 'Bombs Away! On Harpurhey' and the controversial 'Vicious British Boyfriend' (with its Enoch Powell/Union Jack sleeve), followed in quick succession early in 1989. A live appearance on BBC 2's *Snub TV* helped both singles into the independent charts, capturing one of the band's most electrifying moments, 'Fanciable Headcase'. *Barbarous English Fayre* compiled the group's Play Hard recordings, as the band moved to Midnight Music, acquiring a new bassist, James Cashan, along the way. Another independent hit, 'Once A Prefect', preceded King Of The Slums' first proper album, *Dandelions*. Titles like 'Up The Empire/Balls To The Bulldog Breed' and 'Barbarous Superiors' continued Keigher's fork-tongued lyrical attacks on racism and the establishment. By the time 'It's Dead Smart' arrived in 1990, Pete Mason had replaced previous guitarist Gary Sparkes, but the sound was just as razor-sharp, and the rhetoric no less poignant. *Blowzy Weirdos* followed a move to Cherry Red Records in 1991, and also saw the group catch a little of the spotlight that had fallen on Manchester in the wake of the Happy Mondays arrival. Sadly, it was not enough to ensure the survival of this talented act.

Album: *Dandelions* (Midnight 1990), *Blowzy Weirdos* (Cherry Red 1991). Compilation: *Barbarous English Fayre* (Play Hard 1989).

Kingmaker

Indie rock band founded in Hull, North Humberside, England, by Loz Hardy (b. Lawrence Paul Hardy, 14 September 1970, Manchester, Lancashire, England; vocals/guitar) with Myles Howell (b. 23 January 1971, Rugby, Warwickshire, England; bass) and John Andrew (b. John Ricardo Andrew, 27 May 1963, Hull, North Humberside, England; drums). The group was formed by Hardy and Howell during their year off after school, eventually recruiting the significantly elder Andrew, an ex-travelling puppeteer, to complete the unit. The band made their debut with *The Celebrated Working Man* EP, after which they signed to Chrysalis Records for a second EP, *Idiots At The Wheel*. They were immediately courted by the press, who invented a niche category for the group; New Cool Rock. At one time tipped by many as a potential next big

thing, Kingmaker rapidly fell out of favour with the fashionable climate of their genre. Paul Heaton of local stars the Beautiful South went so far as to accuse them of being middle class pretenders, living in castles on the outskirts of Hull. Nevertheless, Hardy's song writing prowess seems to have grown in inverse proportion to their stature. The songs on 1992's *Sleepwalking*, primarily located in Hardy's bitter world view, far surpassed anything on the debut album and early singles that won them most of the attention. Tucked away on the b-side to the BRIT Awards' baiting 'Armchair Anarchist', 'Everything's Changed Since You've Been To London' and 'Kissing Under Anaesthetic' stood head and shoulders above many of their peers. Their lyrical austerity, much ridiculed by some critics, was matched by strong musical craft (particularly Andrew's forceful, accomplished drumming) and an emotive resonance not confined to the young audience the band seem to attract. 1995's *In The Best Possible Taste* emerged within one month of the death of disc jockey, Kenny Everett, who had popularised the phrase, adding an unconscious irony to its use, with tracks such as 'One False Move' revealing a shift towards urban rockabilly.

Albums: *Eat Yourself Whole* (Chrysalis 1991), *Sleepwalking* (Chrysalis 1992), *To Hell With Humdrum* (Chrysalis 1993, mini-album), *In The Best Possible Taste* (Chrysalis 1995).

Kitchens Of Distinction

Formed in Tooting, London, England in 1986 by Patrick Fitzgerald (b. 7 April 1964, Basel, Switzerland), Julian Swales (b. 23 March 1964, Gwent, Wales) and Daniel Goodwin (b. 22 July 1964, Salamanca, Spain), Kitchens Of Distinction took their name from a Hygena advertisement and pursued a precarious path through the UK independent record industry. A debut single on their own Gold Rush Records in 1987, 'Last Gasp Death Shuffle', brought them a *New Musical Express* Single Of The Week award, and after signing to One Little Indian Records there were hints at an upturn in fortunes. Marrying a melodic sensibility with a stunning array of guitar effects, slight problems only appeared when the critical success of their first album, *Love Is Hell*, was not matched in commercial terms. The most popular theories for the band's slow rise centred upon their peculiar moniker and singer Patrick Fitzgerald's unwillingness to disguise or avoid the subject of his homosexuality, but whatever the reasons, the threesome struggled to break away from the threat of cult status. The battle seemed to pay dividends when the second album, *Strange Free World*, entered the UK charts at number 36, although the full-blown crossover their powerful, emotive songs so richly deserved was still not forthcoming. A nationwide tour with the Popinjays led to a friendship between the two groups, with the Kitchens often appearing under the pseudonym, the Toilets Of Destruction. Meanwhile the band found a more willing audience through college radio in the US. They returned in 1994 with *Cowboys And Aliens*, and a full blown UK headlining tour to re-establish their credentials.

Albums: *Love Is Hell* (One Little Indian 1989), *Strange Free World* (One Little Indian 1991), *The Death Of Cool* (One Little Indian 1992), *Cowboys And Aliens* (One Little Indian 1994).

Klark Kent

Whether this Klark Kent is the same man who works as a reporter for the *Daily Planet* is unclear. His close friend Stewart Copeland (b. 16 July 1952, Alexandria, Egypt), drummer with the Police tells us that Kent 'dabbles in politics, religion and anthropology'. He owns a huge multi-national company called the Kent Foundation, whose sinister influence is behind many world events. Kent is unable to tour because an unpleasant odour emitted from his body makes him intolerable to other musicians. . . The truth is, of course, that Kent and Copeland are one and the same. In 1978 when the Police were still waiting for their major breakthrough, Copeland was looking for some extra curricular activities, having previously been cited as a member of the unrealized group the Moors Murderers. Creating the *alter ego* of Kent, his first single 'Don't Care' was released on Kryptone in 1978 and later re-issued on A&M when it was a minor hit. The follow-up 'Too Kool To Kalypso' (back on the Krypton label) was pressed in lurid Kryptonite green, two more singles and a solitary mini-album followed, before Kent disappeared allowing Copeland to write film music and continue drumming with the Police. Album: *Klark Kent* (1980).

Kleenex

Widely regarded (especially by Greil Marcus) Swiss punk band, whose two releases on the fledgeling Rough Trade Records label, 'Ain't You' and 'You', attracted many admirers. Unfortunately they also attracted the attention of the tissue company of the same name, who took objection to the use of their patent. From 1980 onwards they consequently became Lilliput, going to to release two further singles and an album. The band included Marlene Marder (guitar), Klaudi Schiff (bass), Crigele Freund (vocals) and Lislot Ha (drums).
Compilation: *Lilliput* (Off Course 1993, also comprises Kleenex material).

KLF

Since 1987 the KLF have operated under a series of guises, only gradually revealing their true nature to the public at large. The band's principal spokesman is Bill Drummond (b. William Butterworth, 29 April 1953, South Africa), who had already enjoyed a chequered music industry career. As co-founder of the influential Zoo label in the late 70s, he introduced and later managed Echo & The Bunnymen and Teardrop Explodes. Later he joined forces with Jimmy Cauty (b. 1954), an artist of various persuasions and a member of Brilliant in the mid-80s. Their first project was undertaken under the title JAMS (Justified Ancients Of Mu Mu - a title lifted from Robert Shea and Robert Anton Wilson's conspiracy novels dealing with the *Illuminati*). An early version of 'All You Need Is Love' caused little reaction compared to the provocatively-titled LP which followed - *1987 - What The Fuck Is Going On?* Released under the KLF moniker (standing for Kopyright Liberation Front), it liberally disposed of the works of the Beatles, Led Zeppelin *et al* with the careless abandon the duo had picked up from the heyday of punk. One of the disfigured super groups, Abba, promptly took action to ensure the offending article was withdrawn. In the wake of the emerging house scene the next move was to compromise the theme tune to well-loved British television show *Dr Who*, adding a strong disco beat and Gary Glitter yelps to secure an instant number 1 with 'Doctorin' The Tardis'. Working under the title Timelords, this one-off coup was achieved with such simplicity that its originators took the step of writing a book; *How To Have A Number One The Easy Way*. Returning as the KLF, they scored a big hit with the more legitimate cult dance hit 'What Time Is Love'. After the throwaway send-up of Australian pop, 'Kylie Said To Jason', they hit big again with the soulful techno of '3 A.M. Eternal'. There would be further releases from the myriad of names employed by the duo (JAMS; 'Down Town', 'Its Grim Up North', Space, Space, Disco 2000; 'Uptight') while Cauty, alongside Alex Peterson, played a significant part in creating the Orb. Of the band's more recent work, perhaps the most startling was their luxurious video for the KLF's 'Justified And Ancient', featuring the unmistakable voice of Tammy Wynette. The song revealed the KLF at the top of their creative powers, selling millions of records worldwide while effectively taking the michael. They were voted the Top British Group by the BPI. Instead of lapping up the acclaim, the KLF, typically, rejected the comfort of a music biz career, and deliberately imploded at the BRITS award ceremony. There they performed an 'upbeat' version of '3AM Eternal', backed by breakneck speed punk band Extreme Noise Terror, amid press speculation that they would be bathing the ceremony's assembled masses with pig's blood. They contented themselves instead with (allegedly) dumping the carcass of a dead sheep in the foyer of the hotel staging the post-ceremony party, and Drummond mock machine-gunning the assembled dignitaries. They then announced that the proud tradition of musical anarchy they had brought to a nation was at a close: the KLF were no more. Their only 'release' in 1992 came with a version of 'Que Sera Sera' (naturally rechristened 'K Sera Sera', and recorded with the Soviet Army Chorale), which, they insisted, would only see the light of day on the advent of world peace. The KLF returned to their rightful throne, that of England's foremost musical pranksters, with a stinging art terrorist racket staged under the K Foundation banner. In late 1993, a series of advertisements began to appear in the quality press concerning the Turner Prize art awards. While that body was responsible for granting £20,000 to a piece of non-mainstream art, the K Foundation (a new vehicle for messrs Drummond and Cauty) promised double that for the worst piece of art displayed. The Turner shortlist was identical to that of the KLF's. More bizarre still, exactly £1,000,000 was withdrawn from the National Westminster bank (the biggest cash withdrawal in the institution's history), nailed to a board, and paraded in front of a select gathering of press and art luminaries. The money was eventually returned to their bank accounts (although members of the press pocketed a substantial portion), while the £40,000 was awarded to one Rachel Whiteread, who also won the 'proper' prize. Urban guerrillas specialising in highly original shock tactics, the KLF offer the prospect of a brighter decade should their various disguises continue to prosper.
Albums: *Towards The Trance* (KLF 1988), *The What Time Is*

Love Story (KLF 1989), *The White Room* (KLF 1989), *Chill Out* (KLF 1989). As JAMS: *1987 - What The Fuck Is Going On?* (KLF 1987), *Who Killed The JAMS?* (KLF 1988), *Shag Times* (KLF 1989).
Video: *Stadium House* (1991).

L

Knack

Formed in Los Angeles in 1978, the Knack comprised Doug Fieger (vocals/guitar), Prescott Niles (bass), Berton Averre (guitar) and Bruce Gary (drums). Taking their name from a cult British movie of the 60s, they attempted to revive the spirit of the beat-boom with matching suits, and short songs boasting solid, easily memorable riffs. After garnering considerable media attention for their club appearances on the Californian coastline in early 1979, they became the fortuitous recipients of a record company bidding war, which ended in their signing to Capitol Records. The fact that this was the Beatles' US label was no coincidence, for the Knack consistently employed imagery borrowed from the 'Fab Four', both in their visual appearance and record sleeves. Their prospects were improved by the recruitment of renowned pop producer Mike Chapman, who had previously worked with Blondie. During the summer of 1979, the Knack's well-publicized debut single 'My Sharona' promptly topped the US charts for six weeks, as well as reaching the UK Top 10 and selling a million copies. The first album, *The Knack*, was a scintillating pop portfolio, full of clever hooks and driving rhythms and proved an instant hit, selling five million copies in its year of release. Implicit in the Knack's abrupt rise were the seeds of their imminent destruction. In adapting 60s pop to snappy 70s production, they had also spiced up the standard boy/girl love songs with slightly more risque lyrics for their modern audience. Critics, already suspicious of the powerful record company push and presumptuous Beatles comparisons, pilloried the group for their overt sexism in such songs as 'Good Girls Don't' as well as reacting harshly to Fieger's arrogance during interviews. At the height of the critical backlash, the Knack issued the apologetically-titled *But The Little Girls Understand*, a sentiment which was to prove over-optimistic. Both the sales and the songs were less impressive and by the time of their third album, *Round Trip*, their powerpop style seemed decidedly outmoded. By the end of 1981, they voluntarily disbanded with Fieger attempting unsuccessfully to rekindle recent fame with Taking Chances, while the others fared little better with the ill-fated Gama.
Albums: *The Knack* (1979), *But The Little Girls Understand* (1980), *Round Trip* (1981). Compilation: *The Best Of ...* (1993).

L7

Guitarist/vocalists Donita Sparks (b. Chicago, Illinois, USA) and Suzi Gardner (b. Sacramento, California, USA) formed L7 in the mid-80s, linking with Jennifer Finch (b. Los Angeles, California, USA; bass/vocals) and trying several drummers, finally finding Dee Plakas (b. Chicago, Illinois, USA) after domestic touring to promote *L7*, supporting Bad Religion (drummer on their debut album was Roy Kolltsky). The band's raw punk-metal caught the interest of Sup Pop Records, who released *Smell The Magic*, a raucous grunge-flavoured blast which further enhanced the band's growing underground reputation. *Bricks Are Heavy* brought major success, with the surprisingly poppy 'Pretend We're Dead' becoming a major hit on both sides of the Atlantic. Subsequently the band became darlings of the music press with their multi-coloured hair and shock-tactic humour - at 1992's Reading Festival, Sparks retaliated against missile throwers by removing her tampon on stage and throwing it into the crowd, and later dropped her shorts during a live television performance on *The Word* - but the band's serious side led them to form Rock For Choice, a pro-abortion women's rights organisation which has gathered supporters from Pearl Jam to Corrosion Of Conformity for fund-raising concerts. L7 went on to appear as a band entitled Camel Lips in a John Waters' film, *Serial Mom*, before *Hungry For Stink* picked up where *Bricks Are Heavy* left off, blending serious and humorous lyrics against a still-thunderous musical backdrop.
Albums: *L7* (Epitaph 1988), *Smell The Magic* (Sup Pop 1990), *Bricks Are Heavy* (Slash/London 1992), *Hungry For Stink* (Slash/London 1994).

La's

Formed in 1986 in Liverpool, the La's featured Lee Mavers (b. 2 August 1962, Huyton, Liverpool, England; guitar/vocals), John Power (b. 14 September 1967; bass), Paul Hemmings (guitar) and John Timson (drums). Early demo tapes resulted in their signing with Go! Discs in 1987. After a well-received debut single, 'Way Out', which hallmarked the group's effortless, 60s-inspired pop mandate, they took a year out before issuing the wonderfully melodic 'There She Goes'. When this too eluded the charts, the La's, far from disillusioned, returned to the studio for two years to perfect tracks for their debut album. The line-up changed, too, with Lee's brother Neil (b. 8 July 1971, Huyton, Liverpool, England) taking up drums and ex-Marshmellow Overcoats' guitarist Cammy (b. Peter James Camell, 30 June 1967, Huyton, Liverpool, England) joining the line-up. In the meantime, 'There She Goes' became a massive underground favourite, prompting a reissue two years on (after the tuneful 'Timeless Melody'). In October 1990, it reached its rightful place in the UK Top 20. *The La's* followed that same month, an invigorating and highly

musical collection of tunes which matched, and some would argue outstripped, the Stones Roses' more garlanded debut. Its comparative lack of impact could be put down to Mavers truculence in the press, verbally abusing Go! Discs for insisting on releasing the record and disowning its contents. Any comparisons with the best of yesteryear stemmed from the band's obsession with real instruments, creating a rootsy, authentic air. After 'Feelin'' was drawn from the album, the La's set about recording tracks for a new work and spent much of 1991's summer touring America and Japan. Little was then heard of the band for the next four years, which took few acquainted with Mavers' studio perfectionism by surprise. The delays proved too much for Power, however, who departed to set up Cast. Back in the notoriously insular La's camp rumours continued to circulate of madness and drug addiction. A collaboration with Edgar Summertyme of the Stairs was vaunted, but no public assignments were forthcoming. 1994 finally brought a Mavers solo acoustic set in support of Paul Weller, which went so badly awry that he had the plug pulled on him. Finally, in April 1995, he spoke to the *New Musical Express* about a 'second' La's album.
Album: *The La's* (Go! Discs 1990).

Laibach

With origins in Tibovlje, Slovenia, Northern Yugoslavia, Laibach's powerful imagery has long been confused with the fascist icons they have tried to deconstruct. They were formed in 1980 by members of the Yugoslavian army, including Tomaz Hostnik (b. 1961, d. 1982; vocals) and Miran Mohar. They acted as the musical arm of the political art movement NSK (Neue Slowenische Kunst - New Slovian Art), conceived in 1980 and formulated in 1984. Laibach form one of three sections of the movement, the others being Irwin (painters) and Scipion Nasice (theatre). Laibach themselves have a constantly fluctuating line-up. However, the nucleus can be identified as Milan Frez, Dejan Knez, Ervin Markosek and Ivan Novak, the latter acting as spokesman. In 1982 they toured outside of their native country for the first time, releasing their first UK single 'Boji' in 1984. In the mid-80s they recorded Teutonic reworkings of rock classics such as 'Sympathy For The Devil', and appeared on *The South Bank Show*. The 1987 release 'Life Is Life', later covered by Opus, had the unfortunate effect of becoming an anthem for neo-Nazi's. Other notable pursuits included the commissioning of a soundtrack to *Macbeth* performed by the German theatre company Deutsches Schauspielhaus. It was played live during performances. In 1988 the band also covered the Beatles' *Let It Be*, bar the title track, in its entirety, in Wagnerian military style. They also released the German-only single, '3 Oktober', to celebrate reunification in 1990. Although they have achieved some degree of prominence, any realistic study of Laibach should focus on them as merely one component in a larger and more important artistic movement.
Albums: *Nova Arkopola* (1985), *Rekapitulacija* (1985), *The Occupied Europe Tour* (1986), *Opus Dei* (1987), *Krst Pod Triglavom-Baptism* (1987), *Let It Be* (1988), *Macbeth* (1990), *Sympathy For The Devil* (1990), *Kapital* (1992), *Ljubjana Zagreb Beograd* (1993).

Lambrettas

This English, Brighton-based band comprised Jez Bird (vocals/guitar), Doug Saunders (guitar/vocals), Mark Ellis (bass/vocals) and Paul Wincer (drums). Together with Secret Affair, the Merton Parkas and the Chords, they were part of the UK's short-lived mod revival of 1979-80. After securing a deal with Elton John's Rocket Records, they had 'Go Steady' included on the label's compilation *499 2139*, alongside fellow mod hopefuls the Act, the Escalators, Les Elite and the Vye. A month later, in November 1979, the same version of 'Go Steady' was released as a single, with little success, but drew much attention from the growing mod audiences. Success arrived with 'Poison Ivy', a catchy remake of the Leiber And Stoller-penned classic, reaching number 7 in the UK charts during 1980, eight places higher than the Coasters' original version of 1959. Their popularity continued with follow-up singles entering the charts, 'D-a-a-ance' climbed to number 12, and 'Another Day (Another Girl)' just managed to scrape into the UK Top 50, reaching number 49. The latter was originally called 'Page Three', but threatened legal action by *The Sun* newspaper, persuaded the band to rethink the title. Their debut *Beat Boys In The Jet Age* peaked at number 28 and was also their last glimpse of the charts. Successive releases: 'Steppin' Out', 'Good Times', 'Anything You Want', 'Decent Town' and 'Somebody To Love', had little impact on either critics or record-buying public, and by the time they issued *Ambience* in 1981, the mod revival was dead and buried and the band quickly folded. In 1985, Razor Records unearthed the Lambrettas' back catalogue, releasing a compilation of their singles, entitled *Kick Start*.
Albums: *Beat Boys In The Jet Age* (1980), *Ambience* (1981).
Compilation: *Kick Start* (1985).

Laugh

This UK, Manchester-based group first appeared via a flexidisc given free with the city's *Debris* magazine in 1986, with the punchy, guitar-dominated 'Take Your Time, Yeah!'. In November that same year the track fronted their first vinyl single on the Remorse label, but although it was well-received, Laugh had to wait until August the following year before their second offering, a decidedly-poppy effort entitled 'Paul McCartney'. This had been previewed on a 1986 session for disc jockey John Peel, which also featured the assistance of Smiths guitarist Craig Gannon. After 'Time To Lose' in 1988, which made the UK independent chart Top 30, the band moved to the short-lived Sub Aqua label for *Sensation No. 1*, the title of both the album and a single. Neither made any significant impact and Martin Mittler (bass), Spencer Birtwhistle (drums), Ian Bendelow (guitar) and Martin Wright (guitar/vocals) re-thought their strategy, later emerging as a dance outfit.
Album: *Sensation No.1* (Sub Aqua 1988).

Laughing Clowns

Based in Sydney, Australia, the Laughing Clowns were led by Ed Kuepper, who formed the band in 1979 after leaving the Saints. The group rehearsed for six months before gigging, and the music that emerged was complex. As the members: Louise Elliot (saxophone), Peter Doyle (trumpet), the

Wallace-Crabbe brothers Ben and Dan (bass and keyboards respectively), Peter Walsh (bass) and Jeffrey Wegener (drums), come from different disciplines such as jazz many of Kuepper's fans had difficulty appreciating what the band was attempting. The media found difficulties in pigeon-holing the Laughing Clowns as easily as their contemporaries. Representative of their style, and an in-concert favourite was 'Eternally Yours' (1984). Despite this lack of acceptance the band recorded often on independent labels (mainly their own called Prince Melon). The band toured the UK and Europe from 1982 onwards, releasing several records there as well, but to no great success. Undaunted, Kuepper continued solo, and formed a new outfit called the Yard Goes On Forever.

Albums: *Reign Of Terror* (1981), *Mr Uddich Schmuddich Goes To Town* (1981), *Law Of Nature* (1984), *Ghost Of Ideal Wife* (1985), *History Of Rock 'N' Roll, Volume 1* (1986, early 80s recordings).

Leather Nun

This post-punk group was founded in Goreburg, Sweden. In the mid-70s disc jockey, fanzine editor, and Iggy Pop/Ramones enthusiast Jonas Almqvist made frequent trips to London to see bands and while there he formed a friendship with Genesis P. Orridge of Throbbing Gristle. Almqvist played him a demo of a song - 'Death Threat' - that he had written and Orridge agreed to issue it on his own Industrial Records. Returning to Sweden, Almqvist recruited Bengt Aronsson (guitar), Freddie (bass) and Gert Claesson (drums) from what was regarded as Sweden's finest punk band, Strait Jacket. This was the first line-up of Leather Nun and later in 1979 they released the EP *Slow Death* on Industrial Records. Their use of hardcore gay-pornographic films to illustrate their material provoked allegations of obscenity. This led to Freddie eventually leaving the band, though not before recording the seminal 'Prime Mover' in 1983. His replacement was Haken, a singer-songwriter rapidly trained to play the bass. The band also added Nils Wohlrabe as second guitarist. They recorded for five different labels by 1985 and enjoyed cult attention in the UK with their cover of Abba's 'Gimme Gimme Gimme (A Man After Midnight)'. Anders Olsen replaced Haken on bass soon after.

Albums: *Slow Death* (1984), *Alive* (1985), *Lust Games* (1986), *Steel Construction* (1987).

Legendary Pink Dots

This east London experimental group was formed in 1981, based around lyricist and singer Edward Ka-spel, and keyboard player Phillip Knight, who emerged as part of the burgeoning do-it-yourself scene of the late 70s. Performing what they described as 'psychedelic' music - in an 'exploratory sense, rather than nostalgia' - they released their first album, *Brighter Now*, on the small, Birmingham, independent label, Phaze Records, eventually running through two other homes before settling with Play It Again Sam. The band emigrated to the Netherlands in 1985, after Ka-spel had become disenchanted with his native country's reaction to *The Tower* ('a really important album to me'). A series of recordings continued to fare better on the continent

than in the UK, while Ka-spel recorded the latest of several solo albums with Steve Stapleton of Nurse With Wound. He has also branched out with a side project, the Maria Dimension, and worked with Skinny Puppy (as Teargarden) The latest inauguration of Legendary Pink Dots, meanwhile, has added Nils Van Hoorne (saxophones/flute/bass/clarinet) and Bob Pisteer (guitars/bass/sitar). Ka-Spel's prolific recording schedule continues apace, despite the market for his marginalised electronic pop songs having barely enlarged since the early 80s.

Albums: *Brighter Now* (Phaze 1982), *Curse* (Terminal Kaleidoscope 1983), *Faces In The Fire* (Terminal Kaleidoscope 1984), *The Tower* (Terminal Kaleidoscope 1984), *The Lovers* (Ding Dong 1985), *Asylum* (Play It Again Sam 1985), *Island Of Jewels* (Play It Again Sam 1986), *Any Day Now* (Play It Again Sam 1988), *The Golden Age* (Play It Again Sam 1989), *Crushed Velvet Apocalypse* (Play It Again Sam 1990), *The Maria Dimension* (Play It Again Sam 1991), *Shadow Weaver* (Play It Again Sam 1992). Compilations: *Stone Circles* (Play It Again Sam 1988), *Legendary Pink Box* (Play It Again Sam 1989, 3-album box set). Solo albums: Edward Ka-spel *Laugh China Doll* (Torso 1984), *Eyes China Doll* (Scarface 1985), *Chyekk China Doll* (Torso 1986), *Perhaps We'll Only See A Thin Blue Line* (Play It Again Sam 1989).

Lemonheads

From their origins in the Boston, USA hardcore scene, the Lemonheads and their photogenic singer/guitarist Evan Dando (b. Evan Griffith Dando, 4 March 1967, Boston, Massachusetts, USA) have come full circle; from sweaty back-street punk clubs to teen-pop magazines such as *Smash Hits*. The group first formed as the Whelps in 1985, with Jesse Peretz on bass and Dando and Ben Deily sharing guitar and drum duties. Enthused by DJ Curtis W. Casella's radio show, they pestered him into releasing their debut EP, *Laughing All The Way To The Cleaners*, in a pressing of 1,000 copies, on his newly activated Taang! label. It featured a cover of Proud Scum's 'I Am A Rabbit', an obscure New Zealand punk disc often aired by the DJ. By January 1987 Dando had recruited the group's first regular drummer Doug Trachten, but he stayed permanent only for their debut album, *Hate Your Friends*, allegedly pressed in over seventy different versions by Taang! with an eye on the collectors' market. This was a more balanced effort than the follow-up, which this time boasted the services of Blake Babies drummer John Strohm. *Creator* revealed Dando's frustration at marrying commercial punk-pop with a darker lyrical perspective, evident in the cover version of Charles Manson's 'Your Home Is Where You're Happy' (the first of several references to the 60s figurehead). The band split shortly afterwards, following a disastrous Cambridge, Massachusetts gig were Dando insisted on playing sections of Guns N'Roses' 'Sweet Child O Mine' during every guitar solo. However, the offer of a European tour encouraged him to reunite the band, this time with himself as drummer, adding second guitarist Coorey Loog Brennan (ex-Italian band Superfetazione, and also a member of Bullet Lavolta). After *Lick* was issued in 1989, Deily, Dando's longtime associate and co-writer, decided to leave to continue his studies. He

Lemonheads

would subseqeuntly put together his own combo, Pods. However, for the second time Dando would split the Lemonheads, immediately following their acclaimed major label debut, *Lovey*. Peretz moved to New York to pursue his interests in photography and film, while new recruit David Ryan (b. 20 October 1964, Fort Wayne, Indiana, USA) vacated the drum stool. The new line-up featured Ben Daughtry (bass) and Byron Hoagland (drums; ex-Squirrel Bait). However, the new rhythm section was deemed untenable because Daughtry 'had a beard', so Jesse and David (both Harvard graduates) returned to the fold. The band, for some time hovering on the verge of a commercial breakthrough, finally achieved it by embarking on a series of cover versions; 'Luka' (Suzanne Vega) and 'Different Drum' (Michael Nesmith) were both *Melody Maker* singles of the week. There were also two covers on their *Patience And Prudence* EP; the old 50s chestnut 'Gonna Get Along Without You Now' plus a humorous reading of New Kids On The Block's 'Step By Step' - wherein Evan immitates each of the five vocal parts. Other choices have included Gram Parsons, hardcore legends the Misfits, and even a track from the musical *Hair*. However, the cover to make them cover stars proper was an affectionate reading of Simon And Garfunkel's 'Mrs Robinson'. By 1992 Nic Dalton (b. 6 June 1966, Canberra, Australia; ex-Hummingbirds and several other less famous Antipodeon bands) had stepped in on bass to help out with touring commitments, his place eventually becoming permanent. Dando had met him while he was in Australia, where he discovered Tom Morgan (ex-Sneeze, who had also included Dalton in their ranks), who would co-write several songs for the upcoming *It's A Shame About Ray* set. Dando's 'girlfriend' Juliana Hatfield (bass; ex-Blake Babies) also helped out at various points, notably on 'Bit Part'. She was the subject of 'It's About Time' on the follow-up, *Come On Feel The Lemonheads,* on which she also sang back-up vocals. Other guests included Belinda Carlisle. The success of *It's A Shame About Ray* offered a double-edged sword: the more pressure increased on Dando to write another hit album, the more he turned to hard drugs. Sessions were delayed as he took time out to repair a badly damaged voice, allegedly caused through smoking crack cocaine. That *Come On Feel The Lemonheads* emerged at the tail-end of 1993 was surprise enough, but to hear Dando's songwriting continue in its purple patch was even more gratifying.

Albums: *Hate Your Friends* (Taang! 1987), *Creator* (Taang! 1988), *Lick* (Taang! 1989), *Lovey* (Atlantic 1990), *It's A Shame About Ray* (Atlantic 1992), *Come On Feel The Lemonheads* (Atlantic 1993).
Video: *Two Weeks In Australia* (1993).

Let's Active

Ostensibly the vehicle for veteran US all-rounder Mitch Easter, Let's Active issued three melodic albums during the mid-80s. Easter previously played alongside various members of the dB's in the Sneakers in the late 70s, and also worked with the H-Bombs and the Cosmopolitans. His first solo outing graced *Shake To Date*, a UK compilation of material from the US Shake label, in 1981. In between 'discovering' R.E.M. and then producing their early work,

Easter eventually set up Let's Active. *Cypress* did not emerge until 1984, and featured Easter joined by Faye Hunter (bass) and Sam Romweber (drums). The songwriting skills were evident (and the debt to John Lennon and Paul McCartney was clear), but the album lacked bite. Almost two years later, Let's Active found that bite with *Big Plans For Everybody*, aided by drummers Eric Marshall and Rob Ladd and Angie Carlson (guitar/keyboards/vocals). Promoted by 'In Little Ways', the album seemed the perfect encapsulation of Easter's aims: superb production, an ingenious blend of instrumentation and, above all, strong songs. Easter's commitments elsewhere delayed the third Let's Active album for nearly three years, and as such *Every Dog Has His Day* (with John Heames now in the ranks) was slightly disappointing.

Albums: *Cypress* (1984), *Big Plans For Everybody* (1986), *Every Dog Has His Day* (1989).

Levellers

This five-piece unit from Brighton, Sussex, England combined folk instrumentation with rock and punk ethics: 'We draw on some Celtic influences because it's a powerful source, but we're a very English band - this country does have roots worth using'. They took their name, and much of their ideology, from the Puritans active at the time of the English Civil War between 1647 and 1649, whose agenda advocated republicanism, a written constitution and abolition of the monarchy. Their original line-up featured songwriter Mark Chadwick (lead vocals/guitar/banjo), Jonathan Sevink (fiddle), Alan Miles (vocals/guitars/mandolin/harmonica), Jeremy Cunningham (bass/bouzouki) and Charlie Heather (drums). Sevink's violin, like many of their instruments, was typically unconventional and ecologically pure, 'recycled' from three different broken violin bodies. Chadwick, meanwhile, used a guitar which had an old record player arm acting as pick-ups, as well as an amplifier acquired from the Revillos. The *Carry Me* EP was released on Brighton's Hag Records in May 1989, after label boss Phil Nelson had taken over their management. They signed to French label Musidisc in 1989, and Waterboys' producer Phil Tennant recorded their debut album. When their guitarist left during a tour of Belgium in April 1990, they recruited Simon Friend, a singer-songwriter and guitarist from the north of England, and set off on a typically extensive UK tour. After signing to China Records, they made a breakthrough into the national charts with minor 1991 UK hits, 'One Way' and 'Far From Home'. Their second album, *Levelling The Land*, reached the UK Top 20. A mixture of English and Celtic folk with powerful guitar driven rock, it was acclaimed throughout Europe where the band toured before performing sell-out UK concerts. In May 1992, the *Fifteen Years* EP entered the UK chart at number 11. Signed to Elektra Records in the USA, the Levellers made their initial impact touring small venues there before returning to the UK to stage three Christmas Freakshows, which combined music and circus acts at the Brighton Centre and Birmingham NEC. They also continued to play benefits for the environmental and social causes that are the subject of many of their songs. In 1993 they again toured Europe, released a compilation of singles and live tracks, *See Nothing,*

Levellers

Hear Nothing, Do Something, and recorded songs for a new album at Peter Gabriel's Real World studios. In the summer of that year 'Belaruse' registered high in the UK Top 20. The accompanying, self-titled album, also rose to number 2 in the UK charts, and followed a familiar formula in rousing, agit-prop folk rock. Their popularity, particularly in live appearances, made them regulars in the underground music press, wherein they took to criticizing The Men They Couldn't Hang and New Model Army who, paradoxically, appeared to be their biggest influences. The Levellers' affinity with the neo-hippie/new age travellers initially seemed likely to prevent them from achieving mass appeal, but the success of their records and their huge following continues to surprise many of the cynics.
Albums: *A Weapon Called The Word* (Musidisc 1990), *Levelling The Land* (China 1991), *Levellers* (China 1993). Compilation: *See Nothing, Hear Nothing, Do Something* (China 1993).
Video: *The Great Video Swindle (Live At Glasgow Barrowlands)* (1992).

Levitation

This rock-pop combo featured several experienced UK musicians, and was formed by Terry Bickers (vocals/guitar; ex-Colenso Parade) and Dave Francollini (drums; ex-Something Pretty Beautiful) after an altercation between the former's ex-group leader, Guy Chadwick of the House Of Love, in 1989. Levitation's line-up was completed by Christian 'Bic' Hayes (guitar; ex-Cardiacs), Robert White (keyboards) and Laurence O'Keefe (bass; ex-Jazz Butcher). Their pedigree was enough to see them shoot to prominence in the UK press, but two EPs, *Coppelia* and *After Ever*, revealed a band with no lack of enthusiasm or ideas. They were ousted from an early Transvision Vamp support officially because there was not enough room on stage for their equipment. Another story suggests that singer Wendy James was concerned that Levitation's growing live reputation might overshadow her own group. Bickers certainly enjoyed a reputation for being something of an eccentric, but initially seemed to have found a happier home for his obvious talents. Levitation's debut album featured John McGeoch, from PiL, guesting on guitar, and the critical response was strong. However, Bickers found himself moving on once more in 1993, making the following announcement live on stage at the Tufnell Park Dome in London: 'Oh dear. We've completely lost it, haven't we?'. While Levitation attempted to soldier on in his absence, Bickers disappeared to write songs, using the name Cradle to cover these exploits, though this was no band as such. An album was eventually recorded in 1995 with the help of various friends in a 'collective' set up, while Bickers also contributed guitar to the debut album by Oedipussy (who include Phil Parfitt, ex-Perfect Disaster).
Album: *Need For Not* (Rough Trade 1992).

Lewis, Lew

This R&B harmonica player extraordinaire was originally an asphalter by trade. He grew up amidst the Southend/Canvey

Island, Essex, UK musical scene, and made his first ventures with the Southside Jug Band in 1969, which featured Lee Brilleaux and Sparko of Dr. Feelgood, before transferring to the Fix which also included Dave Higgs. After they broke up, Lewis became a busker but later reunited with Higgs in 1973 when he formed Eddie And The Hot Rods. Lewis stayed with them until 1976, when a solo single emerged on Stiff Records. Although credited to Lewis, it featured the backing of Dr. Feelgood under pseudonyms. The a-side was 'Boogie On The Street', recorded in one take. April 1977 saw 'Out For A Lark' on United Artists, once more with the aid of Brilleaux and Sparko. Soon after he formed the Lew Lewis Reformer, consisting of Lewis (vocals/harp), Rick Taylor (guitar), Johnny Squirell (bass) and Buzz Barwell (drums). They recorded the unreleased Status Quo song, 'Win Or Lose', before setting out on a tour supporting Dave Edmunds' Rockpile in 1979. *Save The Wail* was recorded with the basic Reformer band and Gavin Povey from the Edge on keyboards. Lewis went on to guest on several albums of the time including Kirsty MacColl's *Desperate Character* in 1981. A year later he formed a short-lived band with Wilko Johnson. However, his musical career hit a low and in 1987 he held up a post office with a fake pistol (erroneously reported as a shotgun) and was sentenced to seven years' imprisonment for armed robbery. He has since been released. Coincidentally, Epic Records released his single, 'Shame Shame Shame', in August 1987.

Album: *Save The Wail* (Stiff 1980).

Leyton Buzzards

This new wave/pop outfit was formed by Geoffrey Deanne (b. 10 December 1954, London, England; vocals) and David Jaymes (b. 28 December 1954, Woodford, Essex, England; bass). They recruited Kevin Steptoe (drums) and Dave Monk (guitar). From playing R&B covers on the pub circuit, they changed direction in 1976 after witnessing the new punk movement at the Roxy Club in London. By the following year they had secured a record deal with Small Wonder Records, releasing the single '19 & Mad', and changing surnames to the likes of Nick Nayme (Deanne) to reinforce their new image. After the single, Monk was replaced by Vernon Austin. After entering The Band Of Hope And Glory contest, jointly sponsored by the *Sun* newspaper and BBC Radio 1, they won the final at the London Palladium. Their prize was a recording contract with Chrysalis. The result was the band's best-remembered moment, as 'Saturday Night (Beneath The Plastic Palm Trees)' saw them appearing on *Top Of The Pops*, celebrating band members' former weekend drinking and fighting antics. Shortening their name to the Buzzards, they were unable to capitalize on their early success, though their last Chrysalis single 'We Make A Noise' featured a cover designed by Monty Python's Terry Gilliam. The contract-fulfilling *Jellied Eels To Record Deals* compiled early singles, demos, and radio session tracks. Their final recording was a one-off single for WEA titled 'Can't Get Used To Losing You', before Deane and Jaymes set up the more successful, salsa-flavoured Modern Romance.

Album: *Jellied Eels to Record Deals* (1979).

Lightning Seeds

Contrary to the multiples suggested by the moniker, Lightning Seeds was the brainchild of one man, Ian Broudie (b. 4 August 1958, Liverpool, England), who had gouged a significant niche in the Merseyside music scene throughout the 80s. Originally a member of Big In Japan - a forerunner of the likes of Echo And The Bunnymen and Teardrop Explodes, not to mention a breeding ground for future Frankie Goes To Hollywood singer Holly Johnson and drummer Budgie, who was later to join Siouxsie And The Banshees. Broudie eventually ended up playing in the Original Mirrors and worked up an appetite for production work. His efforts on the first two Bunnymen albums acted as a springboard from whence Broudie was catapulted into the studio with numerous acts, including the Fall, Wah!, the Icicle Works and Frazier Chorus. On the creative front, Broudie collaborated with Wild Swans singer Paul Simpson under the name Care, releasing three immaculate singles and preparing the blueprint for his own pop-obsessed project come the end of the decade. Thus Lightning Seeds was born as an opportunity for Broudie to expand his own songwriting ideas. The project had an immediate impact when his first single, 'Pure', fuelled everyone's interest by virtue of being a deliberately low-key release, and went on to reach number 16 in the UK chart. *Cloudcuckooland* followed, encapsulating Broudie's notion of the perfect, sweet pop song, whereupon he put his producer's hat back on to work with contemporary bands such as Northside, the Primitives, Frank And Walters, Alison Moyet and Sleeper, among many others. He continued his work under the Lightning Seeds moniker in 1992 with *Sense*, another collection of perfect pop, but he would have to wait until 1994's *Jollification* for a further commercial breakthrough. This time he put together a full touring band, playing live for the first time since the Original Mirrors folded. The assembled line-up; Martin Campbell (bass; ex-Rain), Chris Sharrock (drums; ex-Icicle Works, La's) and Paul Hemmings (guitar; ex-La's) drew on his Liverpool connections, but Broudie remained very much the nucleus.

Albums: *Cloudcuckooland* (Epic 1990), *Sense* (Epic 1992), *Jollification* (Epic 1994).

Lilac Time

Turning his back on pop stardom as a solo performer, Stephen 'Tin Tin' Duffy dropped the 'Tin Tin' part of his name (after legal action by lawyers representing Hergé), and formed the Lilac Time with his brother, Nick (guitar), in 1987. Purposely low profile, the group's debut, *The Lilac Time*, was released by the tiny Birmingham label, Swordfish. The other group members were Michael Giri (bass) and Micky Harris (drums). The subtle blend of pop harmonies and folk instrumentation was well-received and Phonogram signed the band and re-released the debut. *Paradise Circus* was more commercial with pop gems like 'The Girl Who Waves At Trains'. *And Love For All*, produced jointly by Duffy, Andy Partridge of XTC and John Leckie, was more introspective and despite strong efforts by Phonogram the group failed to record a hit in the singles chart, mainly because of a general unwillingness to forget Duffy's rather twee past as a pop idol (he was also in the early line-up of

Lightning Seeds

Duran Duran). In 1991, the group signed with the leading independent label Creation and released *Astronauts*. In the week of its release it was announced that the group had split and that Duffy would revert once again to solo status.
Albums: *The Lilac Time* (1987), *Paradise Circus* (1989), *And Love For All* (1990), *Astronauts* (1991).

Lilliput

Formed from Rough Trade Records aspirants Kleenex, when the company was presented with legal pressure from the tissue manufacturer of the same name, Lilliput took their new moniker in 1980 and included the same line-up; Marlene Marder (guitar), Klaudi Schiff (bass), Crigele Freund (vocals) and Lislot Ha (drums). Their first release as Lilliput was 'Die Matrosen', followed by 'Eisgerwind' and a debut album, all housed on Rough Trade. However, by the time the album was released Lilliput were no more. Marder went on to form Danger Mice (two singles, 'I Have Got You' and 'Broken New Heart') during the mid-80s. She now runs a record shop in her native Zurich. Schiff, contrastingly, has become one of Switzerland's most celebrated painters.
Albums: *Lilliput* (Rough Trade 1983), *Some Songs* (Rough Trade 1983, Germany only). Compilation: *Lilliput* (Off Course 1993; comprises Kleenex/Lilliput material, different to debut of same title).

Liquid Jesus

This experimental, Los Angeles-based quintet were formed in 1990 by bassist Johnny Lonely and guitarist Scott Tracey. Adding Todd Rigione (guitar), Buck Murphy (vocals) and John Molo (drums), they gigged incessantly on the LA bar and club circuit. Fusing psychedelic, blues, jazz and metal influences to bizarre extremes, they debuted with an independently released live album. Tipped by some as the next Jane's Addiction, they were signed by Geffen Records in 1991 and delivered *Pour In The Sky*. This pooled their influences of Jimi Hendrix, Led Zeppelin, the Red Hot Chili Peppers and Queen, but accusations of plagiarism were sidestepped by virtue of their totally deranged and unpredictable delivery.
Albums: *Liquid Jesus Live* (Liquid Jesus 1990), *Pour In The Sky* (Geffen 1991).

Live

US rock band from York, Pennsylvania, Live comprise Ed Kowalcyzk (vocals), with Patrick Dahlheimer, Chad Taylor and Chad Gracey. The group was formed out of blue-collar friends attending high school because 'we share the same ignorance'. The group's dynamic is one of fraught pop which occasionally expands into full blown rock mode - with lyrics striking an idealistic tone. This was particularly true of the group's 1991 debut, the largely ignored *Mental Jewelery*, where spiritual overtones were also present. No less intense was the subsequent *Throwing Copper*, which would go on to sell over 2 million copies in the USA by 1995. However, by now Kowalcyzk's lyrics had developed a less literal level: 'I'm more into letting my subconscious write, I want to let go completely, without becoming addicted to anything - which is a danger'. Another danger was a track like 'Shit Towne', which addressed the populace of hometown York, and did

little to ingratiate the band to their old community.
Albums: *Mental Jewelry* (Radioactive 1991), *Throwing Copper* (Radioactive 1994).

Lloyd, Richard

Having established himself as a rhythm guitarist of standing in Television, Lloyd embarked on a solo career in 1979, releasing an album whose quality rivalled the efforts of his more illustrious ex-partners, Tom Verlaine and Richard Hell. *Alchemy* should have projected Lloyd towards a bigger audience but its reviews were not matched by its sales and Richard failed to exploit the work due to an alarming slump into drug addiction. It was five years before a chemical-free Lloyd returned with a new album, *Field Of Fire*, but since the mid-80s his output remained decidedly low. By 1991, he had joined Verlaine, Ficca and Smith in a reformed Television, spending much of early 1992 rehearsing and recording.
Albums: *Alchemy* (Elektra 1979), *Field Of Fire* (Mistlur/Moving Target 1985), *Real Time* (Celluloid 1987, live album).

Lloyd, Robert

Inspired by T. Rex and the fact that girls tended to pin posters of pop stars on their walls and not the professional footballers that Robert Lloyd (b. 1959, Cannock, Staffordshire, England) aspired to emulate, the teenager switched his allegiance from the football field to concert hall. Between 1974 and 1976 he played in several bands that never escaped the rehearsal room. He left school at the age of 16 and in 1976 attended a concert by the Sex Pistols. He started to follow the Pistols around on the Anarchy Tour and at one of the gigs, he persuaded a promoter to offer him some gigs. The result was the hurriedly assembled Prefects in February 1977, consisting of Lloyd, Alan and Paul Appelby, and Joe Crow. After one performance at a private party and one at the famous Barbarella's club in Birmingham, the Prefects were offered the chance of standing in for the Slits at a Clash concert. When the Buzzcocks dropped out of the subsequent tour, the Prefects were offered a permanent place. Although the band recorded two John Peel BBC radio sessions, no records were released until after the band's split in 1979. Lloyd's next move was to form the Nightingales and his own Vindaloo label. When the Nightingales fell apart in the mid-80s he concentrated on the label and songwriting, the results of which surfaced in further Peel sessions (he holds the record for the most sessions for Peel in his various forms) under the name Robert Lloyd And The New Four Seasons. This led to a single with the In-Tape label and in 1989 he signed to Virgin Records. After a few false starts, the album emerged in 1990 and featured Steve Nieve and Pete Thomas (the Attractions), Andy Scott (the Sweet) and Craig Gannon (ex-Bluebells, Aztec Camera, the Colourfield and the Smiths) amongst others. However, when it came to promoting the album, Lloyd had to assemble a new band centred around former Nightingale guitarist, The Tank.
Album: *Me And My Mouth* (Virgin 1990).

Loft

The Loft were formed in 1980 when Bill Prince (b. 19 July 1962, Devon, England) and Andy Strickland (b. 16 July

1959, Isle Of Wight, England; guitar/vocals) met with Peter Astor (b. 1959, Colchester, Essex, England), then singing in the group News Of Birds. Later joined by drummer Dave Morgan (drums), the band's first gig was under the name the Living Room which, by sheer coincidence, was also the banner of a small but significant London venue set up by Scottish entrepreneur, Alan McGee. Fortunately, the freshly-named Loft linked up with McGee's nascent Creation Records label to release the single, 'Why Does The Rain?', which encapsulated their stylishly downbeat driving guitar sound. A year later, the follow-up, 'Up The Hill And Down The Slope', furthered the Loft's cause and strengthened their cult-status, bolstered by championing from BBC disc jockey, Janice Long. As their reputation grew, so did tensions within the band, causing them to split just as their career appeared to be in full flow. As Astor recalled: 'We split for the same reason all bands do - people's feet smell.' Both Strickland and Prince pursued journalistic vocations and started up the Caretaker Race and the Wishing Stones respectively. Peter Astor and Dave Morgan formed the marginally successful Weather Prophets until they disbanded at the end of the 80s, allowing Astor to embark upon a solo career whilst Morgan went on to join the country-flavoured Rockingbirds. He would leave that band in 1994 to concentrate on a B.Sc in psychology, managing Bingo Salad, and playing sessions with several artists. After the demise of the Wishing Stones Prince would record a 1992 solo album for Heavenly Records. He became production editor for *Q* magazine in 1993.
Compilation: *Once Around The Fair* (Creation 1989).

London

As punk sent an electric shock through a complacent late 70s UK music scene, major labels were to be found signing acts, regardless of ability. London, like many other second division new wavers, were scooped up only to disappear after all the fuss had died down. Two releases in 1977, 'Everyone's A Winner' and 'No Time', were both of their time; punchy and urgent but ultimately lacking in substance. *Animal Games*, London's one and only album (and accompanying single) in 1978 followed suit, its power-pop feel lacking the true bite of punk's pioneers. Lead singer Riff Regan later had a stab at a solo career, while drummer Jon Moss joined the Edge before making his name in the early 80s with Culture Club.
Album: *Animal Games* (1978).

London SS

Historically London SS were one of the most important British bands of the punk era despite never playing in front of a paying audience, nor releasing any recordings. Musically they were either 'raw rock 'n' roll' or 'pretty crap' depending on which of their many members you care to ask. An *ad hoc* combo of London youth (or migrants drifting in from elsewhere), they were started around March 1975 by Tony James and Mick Jones. They spent the entire 10 months or so of the group's life auditioning musicians and rehearsing 60s beat and R&B classics. The only other semi-permanent member they found was guitarist Bryan James but amongst the others who traded licks and rimshots were: Terry Chimes (drums), who was rejected; Paul Simenon (vocals) rejected as

well; Nicky Headon (drums) turned the gig down; Tony James tried out for bass; Rat Scabies (b. Chris Miller) had a bash at the drum stool despite being in his own proto-punk group - Rot; Matt Dangerfield and Casino Steel of the Hollywood Brats popped in for two rehearsals on their way to forming the Boys; Roland Hot warmed the drum seat briefly as did Andy (whose surname has been lost to the mists of time; and another long-forgotten soul called George had a spell on the guitar). The only recording they ever made was a demo featuring the James/Jones/James/Hot line-up which was the penultimate assembly. In January 1976 they kicked Hot out, Bryan James went off with Rat Scabies to join the Subterraneans and then form the Damned. That left the two originators on their own again so James eventually went off and got a job before running into Billy Idol and joining Chelsea with him. They soon split Chelsea to form Generation X. Messrs Jones, Simenon and Chimes teamed up with 101ers vocalist Joe Strummer to form the Clash, and when Chimes left to form Jem, another London SSer, Nicky 'Topper' Headon, replaced him.

Lone Justice

This group of US country-rockers were fronted by Maria McKee (b. 17 August 1964, Los Angeles, California, USA) who is the half-sister of Love's Bryan MacLean. When she was just three-years-old her brother would take her to the various clubs along Los Angeles' Sunset Strip and she was befriended by the likes of Frank Zappa and the Doors. When she grew up, she and MacLean formed a duo initially called the Maria McKee Band, but later changed to the Bryan MacLean Band to cash in on *his* slightly higher profile. Heavily immersed in country music, McKee formed the first incarnation of Lone Justice with Ryan Hedgecock (guitar), Don Heffington (drums), Marvin Etzioni (bass) and Benmont Tench (keyboards, ex-Tom Petty And The Heartbreakers). The group were signed to the Geffen label at the recommendation of Linda Ronstadt. McKee's talents were also admired by artists such as Bob Dylan, U2's Bono, who offered them a support slot on tour, and Tom Petty, who donated songs to the first album. One of these, 'Ways To Be Wicked', while not achieving any notable chart status, was responsible for bringing the group to the attention of the UK audience via an imaginative black-and-white, cut-up-and-scratched video. The band's more established line-up transmuted to that of ex-patriot Brit Shayne Fontayne (guitar), Bruce Brody (keyboards, ex-Patti Smith and John Cale), Greg Sutton (bass) and Rudy Richardson (drums). They were managed by the respected producer, Jimmy Iovine. In 1985, former Undertones singer Feargal Sharkey scored a UK number 1 hit with McKee's 'A Good Heart'. Lone Justice split suddenly in 1987 with McKee going on to a solo career, taking only Brody with her from the remnants of Lone Justice.
Albums: *Lone Justice* (1985), *Shelter* (1987). Maria McKee solo *You Gotta Sin To Get Saved* (1993).

Long Ryders

Formed in November 1981, the Long Riders (as they were then known), initially included three ex-members of the Unclaimed - Sid Griffin (guitar/vocals), Barry Shank (bass/vocals) and Matt Roberts (drums). Steve Wynn completed this early line-up, but the guitarist was replaced by Stephen McCarthy on leaving to form the Dream Syndicate. Griffin and McCarthy remained at the helm throughout the group's turbulent history. As part of Los Angeles' 'paisley underground' movement, the Long Ryders' history is linked with, not only that of the Dream Syndicate, but also that of other guitar-oriented bands such as Rain Parade, (early) Bangles, Green On Red and Blood On The Saddle. A mini-album, *The Long Ryders*, was completed with Des Brewer (bass) and Greg Sowders (drums), although by the time the quartet secured a permanent deal, Tom Stevens had joined in place of Brewer. *Native Sons*, an excellent set influenced by Buffalo Springfield and Gram Parsons, suggested a promising future, but the Long Ryders were unable to repeat its balance of melody and purpose. They withered on record company indecision and, unable to secure a release from their contract, the group broke up in 1987.

Albums: *The Long Ryders* (1983), *Native Sons* (1984), *State Of Our Union* (1985), *Two-Fisted Tales* (1987), *10-5-60* (1987), *Metallic B.O.* (1989, early recordings).

Loop

Along with Spacemen 3, Loop, hailing from Croydon, London, England, proved to be the UK's answer to the onslaught of harsh, guitar-wielding acts that dominated the late 80s independent scene. Like the Spacemen, Loop refined fuzz-laden, pulsing guitar riffs, monotonous vocals and distinctive drum patterns to build bruised and intimidating soundscapes. An uncompromising blend of late 60s Detroit rock (Stooges and MC5) and Germany's early 70s *avant garde* (Can and Faust), the result was a dense, brooding mantra-like noise, not unlike early Hawkwind. Loop have always revolved around singer and guitarist Robert Wills (b. Robert Hampson), who formed the band with his wife, drummer Bex, and bassist Glen Ray in 1986. After the garage-like feedback on '16 Dreams' began their recording legacy in 1987, Bex was replaced by John Wills, who introduced a harder, rhythmic sound. This was further strengthened when James Endicott joined as second guitarist, after the reverberating psychedelia of 'Spinning' set the scene for Loop's impressive debut, *Heavens End*, in November. Alongside a cover of Suicide's 'Rocket USA' came a barrage of layered guitar noise awash with distortion and wah-wah. With a new bassist, John McKay, Loop moved to Midlands label Chapter 22 for April 1988's dynamic 'Collision', backed by a cover of the Pop Group's 'Thief Of Fire'. After the departure of James Endicott, and the Head label's compilation of their singles on *The World In Your Eyes* in August, Loop were ready to skirt the national charts with *Fade Out* in November. Its sparser, more discordant sound pushed the Can influence to the fore. Indeed, a cover of Can's hypnotic magnum opus, 'Mother Sky', turned up on the b-side of 'Black Sun' the following month. After a quiet year, Loop ended 1989 with the powerful 'Arc-Lite', their first single for Situation Two and with new guitarist Scott. Chapter 22 signalled their departure with another collection of two 12-inch singles, but this time, Loop publicly denounced the set. *A Gilded Eternity*, in 1990, again fared well commercially, and moved further towards ethereal soundscapes and away from the aggression of *Fade Out*. Since then, Loop have coveted a decidedly low profile with rumours of a split, with only 1991's *Wolf Flow*, a double set of sessions for BBC disc jockey John Peel, to indicate otherwise.

Albums: *Heavens End* (Head 1987), *Fade Out* (Chapter 22 1988), *A Gilded Eternity* (Beggars Banquet 1990). Compilations: *The World In Your Eyes* (Head 1988), *Eternal* (Chapter 22 1989), *Wolf Flow* (Reactor 1991, rec. 1987-90).

Lora Logic

London art student Susan Whitby originally adopted the pseudonym Lora Logic during her stint as saxophonist in X-Ray Spex. After leaving that group following their debut single, she soon re-emerged in 1978 with her own outfit, Essential Logic, who quickly recorded a couple of hard-edged EPs, *Aerosol Burns* and *Wake Up*. One album was recorded, *Beat Rhythm News* (1979), before Lora commenced on a series of solo recordings in 1981. Her quirky, occasionally arresting, vocals were in evidence on her sole album, *Pedigree Charm*, and she can also be heard on a number of recordings by other artists including the Raincoats, Stranglers, Swell Maps and Red Crayola.

Album: *Pedigree Charm* (Rough Trade 1982).

Lords Of The New Church

This rock band was made up of several well-known personalities, and often described as a punk 'supergroup'. The personnel was; Brian James (b. 18 February 1961; guitar, ex-Damned), Stiv Bators (b. 22 October 1956; Cleveland, Ohio, USA; vocals, ex-Dead Boys, Wanderers), Dave Treganna (b. 1954, Derby, England; bass, ex-Sham 69, Wanderers) and drummer Nicky Turner (b. 4 May 1959, ex-Barracudas). When Jimmy Pursey left Sham 69, the rest of the band had continued in the Wanderers, drafting in Stiv Bators. It was at this point that James contacted Bators with the view to setting up a group. Miles Copeland took on their management, their name coming from his original suggestion, Lords Of Discipline. They made their live debut in Paris in 1981. Their debut vinyl, 'New Church', helped to increase criticisms about the band's apparent blasphemy, hardly dispelled when the album appeared with lines like: 'Greed and murder is forgiven when in the name of the Church'. The self-titled debut premiered an authentic rock band with dark shades, flirting with apocalyptic and religious imagery. The single, 'Dance With Me', from *Is Nothing Sacred*, gained several MTV plays with a video directed by Derek Jarman. Unfortunately its success was scuppered after mistaken allegations about paedophilia saw it taken off air. Their final studio album, *Method To Our Madness*, revealed a band treading water with stifled heavy rock routines. They did not split officially until 1989, but before that Treganna had departed for Cherry Bombz, while Alistair Ward contributed some second guitar.

Albums: *Lords Of The New Church* (IRS 1982), *Is Nothing Sacred* (IRS 1983), *Method To Our Madness* (IRS 1984), *Live At The Spit* (Illegal 1988, rec. 1982). Compilation: *Killer Lords* (IRS 1985).

Love And Money

Lori And The Chameleons

Formed in 1979 in Liverpool, England, the group was a vehicle for the evocative teenage singer Lori Larty. With backing, production and songwriting provided by former Big In Japan alumni David Balfe and Bill Drummond, Lori emerged with an appealing, almost spoken-word tribute to Japan (the country), entitled 'Touch'. A sparkling arrangement, the disc entered the bottom of the UK charts and appeared to signal the emergence of a new talent. The concept of the group appeared to revolve vaguely around exotic, travelogue pop with each song title set in a specific geographical location: Japan, Peru, Russia and the Ganges River in India. The second single, 'The Lonely Spy', boasted another impressive, atmospheric vocal from Lori and an astonishing backing which emulated the bombastic scores associated with *James Bond* films. After four superb tracks, which represented some of the best UK pop of the period, the group ceased operating. The journeyman Troy Tate reappeared in the Teardrop Explodes, while Drummond turned to management and was later the brains behind a series of pseudonymous groups including the Justified Ancients Of Mu Mu (JAMS) and the Timelords who later emerged as the very successful KLF. Lori, meanwhile, spurned imminent pop success by returning to art college and effectively retiring from the music business. Her fleeting career provided as much mystery and instant appeal as the extraordinary discs on which she appeared.

Lotus Eaters

Rising from the ashes of the Wild Swans, Liverpool's Lotus Eaters enjoyed instant commercial success with a fragrant pop song, 'The First Picture Of You', their debut single from June 1983. Revolving around Peter Coyle (vocals) and Jeremy Kelly (guitar), plus Alan Wills (drums), Gerard Quinn (keyboards) and Phil (bass), the rhythm section was later replaced by Michael Dempsey (bass) and Steve Creese (drums). However, the band never managed to repeat their Top 20 status, despite four catchy follow-ups; 'You Don't Need Someone New' later in 1983, 'Set Me Apart' and 'Out On Your Own' (both 1984) and a final stab, 'It Hurts' (1985). Those who appreciate well-crafted, quality melodic pop should look no further than their only album, *No Sense Of Sin*, from 1984. Coyle and Kelly later reactivated the Wild Swans but were again unable to sustain significant interest.
Album: *No Sense Of Sin* (Sylvan 1984).

Love And Money

After the break-up of the Glasgow band, Friends Again in the mid-80s, guitarist James Grant formed the pop/funk influenced Love And Money, taking with him erstwhile 'Friends', Paul McGeechan (keyboards) and Stuart Kerr (drums), plus Bobby Patterson (bass). The group were named after Grant's personal pledge as to what he wanted to achieve in the coming year. Since then, the group have achieved a string of minor hit singles in the UK starting with 'Candybar Express' (1986) released on the Mercury label, followed by the Fontana issued 'Love And Money' (1987), 'Hallelujah Man' (1988), 'Strange Kind Of Love', 'Jocelyn Square' (both 1989) and 'Winter' (1991). Stuart Kerr left the group in 1987 and subsequently joined the Glasgow-based, Texas. Love And Money recorded their second album as a trio. By the time of *Dogs In The Traffic* the line-up was bolstered by the addition of Douglas McIntyre (guitar/vocals) and Gordon Wilson (drums). Seemingly, forever on the fringes of success, Love And Money have yet to achieve that major breakthrough
Albums: *All You Need Is Love And Money* (1986), *A Strange Kind Of Love* (1988), *Dogs In The Traffic* (1991), *Little Death* (Iona 1994).

Love And Rockets

This *avant garde* UK rock band formed in Christmas 1985 from the ashes of Bauhaus. When David Jay (aka David J) had finished working with the Jazz Butcher on the *Sex And Travel* and *A Scandal In Bohemia* albums, he linked up once more with old colleague Daniel Ash, who had been working with Tones On Tail. Kevin Haskins also came with Ash, forming the band's nucleus of David Jay (vocals, bass, keyboards), Daniel Ash (vocals, guitar, keyboards) and Haskins (drums, keyboards). Early singles included 'Kundiluni Express', concerning Tuntric meditation, and a cover of the Temptations 'Ball Of Confusion'. The band's debut *Seventh Dream Of Teenage Heaven*, was a celebration of the rituals of youth, based loosely on their own experiences of going to rock concerts to see bands like Roxy Music. Like all of the post-Bauhaus projects, the band have failed to cultivate a UK audience to rival their previous standing. However, they scored a big hit single in the US with 'So Alive', where their work still sells moderately well.
Albums: *Seventh Dream Of Teenage Heaven* (1986), *Express* (1986), *Earth Sun Moon* (1987), *Love And Rockets* (1989).

Lovich, Lene

Vocalist Lovich was one of several acts launched by the Stiff label in 1978. The former horror-film soundtrack screamer joined new signings Mickey Jupp, Rachel Sweet and Jona Lewie on the *Be Stiff* national tour, of which this charismatic performer emerged as the undoubted star. Her arresting, gypsy-like appearance, and warbled intonation was matched by a sense of pop's dynamics, as evinced by her UK Top 3 hit, 'Lucky Number'. Shaven-head guitarist Les Chappell provided a visual and compositional foil to a singer who enjoyed further, albeit minor, hits with 'Say When', 'Bird Song' (both 1979) and 'New Toy' (1981). Lovich also entered the album charts with *Stateless*, which derived its title from the air of mystery the artist cultivated about her origins. Subsequent releases fared less well and her 1982 single, 'It's You Only You (Mein Schmerz)', provided Lovich with her final chart entry. Problems within Stiff undermined the progress of a singer who sadly failed to maintain early promise.
Albums: *Stateless* (1978), *Flex* (1979), *No Man's Land* (1982).

Lowe, Nick

b. 25 March 1949, Woodbridge, Suffolk, England. Lowe has for many years been held in high esteem by a loyal band of admirers aware of his dexterity as producer, musician, vocalist and songwriter. His early apprenticeship as bass player/vocalist with Kippington Lodge, which evolved into

Brinsley Schwarz, made him a seasoned professional by the mid-70s. He then started a career as record producer, making his debut with the Kursaal Flyers' *Chocs Away*, followed by Dr. Feelgood's *Malpractice*. He also owns up to being responsible for an appalling novelty record, 'We Love You', a parody of the Bay City Rollers, recorded under the name the Tartan Horde. He formed Stiff Records with Jake Riviera and Dave Robinson in 1976 and was an early pioneer of punk music. His own singles were unsuccessful, but he was critically applauded for the catchy 'So It Goes', backed with the prototype punk song, 'Heart Of The City'. He was an important catalyst in the career of Elvis Costello, producing his first five albums and composing a modern classic with 'What's So Funny 'Bout (Peace Love And Understanding)'. Lowe became a significant figure in the UK, producing albums for the Damned, Clover and Dave Edmunds. In 1977, Lowe co-founded Rockpile and also managed to join the legendary 'Live Stiffs' tour. His own debut, *Jesus Of Cool* (US title: *Pure Pop For Now People*) was a critics' favourite and remains a strong collection of unpretentious rock 'n' pop. The hit single, 'I Love The Sound Of Breaking Glass', is still a disc-jockey favourite, although the equally impressive 'Little Hitler' failed miserably. In 1979 he produced another important single, 'Stop Your Sobbing', by the Pretenders, and released another excellent collection, *Labour Of Lust*, which contained the sparkling 'Cruel To Be Kind' and 'Cracking Up'. Lowe was indeed cracking up, from a surfeit of alcohol, as his brother-in-arms Dave Edmunds intimated in the UK television documentary, *Born Fighters*. Towards the end of a hectic year he married Carlene Carter. In the early 80s, as well as continuing his work with Costello, he additionally produced albums with John Hiatt, Paul Carrack, Carlene Carter and the Fabulous Thunderbirds. His own recordings suffered and were rushed efforts. In 1986 he reunited with Costello for *Blood And Chocolate*, although his own albums were virtually ignored by the public. He returned in 1988 with *Pinker And Prouder Than Previous*, with contributions from Edmunds, but once again it was dismissed, making his catalogue of flop albums embarrassingly large, a fact that Lowe observes with his customary good grace and humour. In 1992 Lowe formed a loose band with Ry Cooder, Jim Keltner and John Hiatt, known as Little Village, whose debut album received a lukewarm response. Much better was
Albums: *Jesus Of Cool* aka *Pure Pop For Now People* (Radar 1978), *Labour Of Lust* (Radar 1978), *Nick The Knife* (F-Beat 1982), *The Abominable Showman* (F-Beat 1983), *Nick Lowe And His Cowboy Outfit* (RCA 1984), *Rose Of England* (RCA 1985), *Pinker And Prouder Than Previous* (Demon 1988), *Party Of One* (Reprise 1990). Compilations: *16 All Time Lowes* (Demon 1984), *Nick's Knacks* (Demon 1986), *Basher: The Best Of Nick Lowe* (Demon 1989), *The Wilderness Years* (Demon 1991).
Films: *Americaion* (1979).

Lucas, Dick

Rarely gaining the recognition as an innovative, intelligent singer/songwriter with a strong social conscience that his work deserves, Lucas started his career as a teenager in anarcho-punks the Subhumans in the early 80s. During this initial period, it became clear that his lyrics and musical ambitions stretched beyond the usual punk rut. The 1983 mini-album, *Time Flies But Aeroplanes Crash*, included the melancholy 'Susan', a moving tale of a young girl resorting to suicide in order to escape from the restrictions of conventional life. It was something most of the Subhumans' contemporaries would never have dreamed of attempting. With his own record label - Bluurg - now established within the alternative scene, Lucas moved onto the upbeat tempo of ska, mixed with reggae references and punk politics. The vehicle for this was Culture Shock, arguably the most interesting and entertaining underground group of the late 80s, providing welcome relief from the usual uniformity and drabness of so-called 'political punk'. With Culture Shock, Lucas produced three fine albums, the best of which was undoubtedly *Onwards And Upwards*. On this excellent collection listeners were treated to lyrics on personal, emotional and socio-political subjects without ever devolving into empty rhetoric or personal deification. The stand-out tracks, 'You Are Not Alone' and 'Don't Worry About It', showed an extraordinary gift for tapping into the minds of isolated young listeners, marking Lucas as a Morrissey for the 'crusty' generation. Lucas decided to start the 90s with a new project, named Citizen Fish, embracing his philosophy that anarchists and libertarians are free-flowing souls trapped by the rules of civilisation. *Free Souls In A Trapped Environment* confirmed this stance, as Lucas struggled with the dilemma of expressing strong political views in an exciting way without losing the fun by being too rhetorical or burying the meaning with flippancy. A heavy dose of thrashing guitars/drums, offset by rootsy ska/dance tones proved to be the perfect solution. The lyrics, of course, were as astute as ever: 'Just to know that every up and down must balance out somehow/And there's a smile to end a conversation that was full of frowns/And here's a major chord to lift the minors up and dance around/And if the song seems far too long then tune in to another sound.' 1992's *Wider Than A Postcard* continued the social theory and skanky music, while the music press, whenever they deigned to actually write about them, compared Citizen Fish with the much-vaunted Manic Street Preachers - 'these are the REAL Generation Terrorists!'
Albums: Subhumans: *The Day The Country Died* (Spiderleg 1981), *Time Flies But Aeroplanes Crash* (Bluurg 1983), *From The Cradle To The Grave* (Bluurg 1984), *Worlds Apart* (Bluurg 1985), *EP-LP* (Bluurg 1986), *29:29 Split Vision* (Bluurg 1987). Culture Shock: *Go Wild!* (Bluurg 1987), *Onwards And Upwards* (Bluurg 1988), *All The Time* (Bluurg 1989). Citizen Fish: *Free Souls In A Trapped Environment* (Bluurg 1990), *Wider Than A Postcard* (Bluurg 1992).

Ludus

Founded in 1978, this Manchester, England-based quartet was consistently fronted by the enigmatic lyricist/vocalist Linder (b. Linda Mulvey, 1954, Liverpool, England). The backing was provided by Arthur Cadmon (b. Peter Sadler, Stockport, England), formerly of Manicured Noise and originally the musical genius behind the group. The line-up was completed by bassist Willie Trotter (b. 1959, Manchester, England) and drummer Phil 'Toby' Tolman (ex-

216

Ed Banger And The Nosebleeds). With their jazz-influenced forays and Linder's strong, sloganeering, elliptical feminist lyrics, the group were one of the most interesting of the Manchester new wave of the late 70s. The departure of Cadmon and later Trotter, replaced by Ian Devine (Ian Pincombe), saw the group change direction, though the jazz influence remained. Linder, a former girlfriend of the Buzzcocks' Howard Devoto, later became a well-publicized confidante of Morrissey. In spite of some inspired moments with Ludus, the group almost wilfully avoided the mainstream. As manager Richard Boon concluded: 'Ludus were totally improvisational and their set list would read: bass, drums, voice, next number. There was something self-limiting about Linder. Any time she seemed on the brink of a breakthrough, even if that meant selling 50 extra records, she would retreat, just like the poet Stevie Smith'. Ian Devine teamed-up in 1989 with ex-Weekend singer, Alison Statton, to form Devine And Statton.
Album: *Pickpocket* (New Hormones 1981).

Lunachicks

Legend has it that New York's Lunachicks were rescued from a life of streetgangs, drinking, idolatry and terrorism against humanity by being discovered by Sonic Youth, who recommended the all-female band to Blast First Records so vociferously that the Lunachicks' debut, *Babysitters On Acid*, was barely recorded before it was let loose upon an unsuspecting public. The 'not-at-all-nice-girls' turned their rebellious behaviour into a stage act. Becky (drums), Squid Sid (bass), Gina (lead guitar) and Sindi (guitar) were the musicians with a taste for excessive volume. Theo was the singer with a predilection for blood-splattered wedding gowns. The Lunachicks can only be described as 'different'.
Album: *Babysitters On Acid* (Blast First 1990), *Binge Purge* (Blast First 1993), *Jerk Of All Trades* (Go Kart 1995).

Lunch, Lydia

b. Lydia Koch, 1959, Rochester, New York, USA. The provocative Lydia Lunch was a pivotal figure in New York's 'no wave' scene of the late 70s and has worked with an array of talent since then. After spells with Teenage Jesus And The Jerks and Beirut Slump (the latter were restricted to one US single, 'Try Me'), Lydia Lunch opted for the freedom of solo work with 1980's acclaimed *Queen Of Siam* on the Ze label. Her next project, Eight-Eyed Spy, toyed with funk and R&B while retaining her uncompromising vocal style and violent, experimental musical approach. Then came *13:13* on the Ruby label, which benefited from a harder, more co-ordinated feel. In 1982 she shared a 12-inch EP with the Birthday Party on 4AD Records, *The Agony Is The Ecstacy*, revealing her increasing fascination with the baser instincts of human nature. Members of the Birthday Party also backed Lydia on 'Some Velvet Morning', while Einsturzende Neubauten joined her for 'Thirsty'. This marriage of the New York and Berlin undergrounds was further demonstrated on 'Der Karibische Western', on Zensor with Die Haut. Lunch continued this collaborative stance in 1983, working with Danish band Sort Sol. 1984's *In Limbo*, a mini-album for Cabaret Voltaire's Doublevision label, re-introduced her to solo work, and she soon founded

Widowspeak Productions in 1985 as an outlet to document her work, starting appropriately with the *Uncensored Lydia Lunch* cassette. After a project with Michael Gira, entitled *Hard Rock* (a cassette on Ecstatic Peace), Lydia homed in on New York pranksters Sonic Youth for 'Death Valley '69', a menacing start for Blast First Records in the UK. A sinister solo offering, *The Drowning Of Lady Hamilton*, was followed by a 10-inch EP recorded with No Trend, entitled *Heart Of Darkness* (1985). The next release for Widowspeak was a limited edition box, *The Intimate Diaries Of The Sexually Insane*, containing a cassette of chronic case histories, a booklet and a book, *Adulterers Anonymous*, co-written by Lydia. 1987's remixed and remastered double album retrospective, *Hysterie*, summarized her work from 1976-86, before she paired with the man behind Foetus and Clint Ruin, Jim Thirlwell, for the awesome Stinkfist project in 1989. That year also witnessed Harry Crews, an all-female wall of guitar sound for which Lunch was joined by Sonic Youth bassist, Kim Gordon. 1993 was spent working on a film script, *Psychomenstruum*. Lunch, in conjunction with her soul-mate Thirlwell, has also become known as an avid opponent of censorship. Her own work is uncompromisingly confrontational and lurid, including videos featuring highly explicit sexual activity. The politics of outrage remain her gospel.
Albums: *Queen Of Siam* (Ze 1980), *13:13* (Ruby 1982), *In Limbo* (Doublevision 1984), *Uncensored Lydia Lunch* (Widowspeak 1985), *The Drowning Of Lady Hamilton* (Widowspeak 1985), *Honeymoon In Red* (Widowspeak 1988), *Oral Fixation* (Widowspeak 1989), with Rowland S. Howard *Shotgun Wedding* (UFO 1991). Compilations: *Hysterie (1976-1986)* (Widowspeak 1989), *Crimes Against Nature* (Triple X, 3-CD set).
Video: *Lydia Lunch: The Gun Is Loaded* (1993).
Further reading: *Incriminating Evidence (Last Gasp)*, Lydia Lunch.

Lurkers

This first-generation UK punk quartet formed during 1977 in Uxbridge, London. Comprising Arturo Bassick (b. Arthur Billingsley; bass), Howard Wall (lead vocals), Pete Stride (guitar) and Manic Esso (b. Pete Haynes; drums), they were heralded as the British answer to the Ramones. They scored four minor UK hit singles between 1978-79, with 'Ain't Got A Clue' and 'I Don't Need To Tell Her' proving the most successful. Bassick had departed quickly, and was replaced first by Kim Bradshaw (ex-Saints) then, more permanently, Nigel Moore. The Lurkers specialized in two-minute blasts of punky rock 'n' roll, delivered with almost naive charm. Their simple, yet effective style was instantly accessible and exuded warmth as well as energy. They never received the recognition their talents deserved, however, because of a lack of image and media support. Pete Stride teamed-up with John Plain (the Boys) in 1980 to record *New Guitar In Town*. The material on this album was very much in a Lurkers vein, but again it met with limited success. The Lurkers were inactive for a short time at this juncture, with Stride and Moore then bringing in new singer Mark Fincham. The group reformed in 1988 (with the Stride/Bassick/Esso/Moore line-up) appearing on punk nostalgia bills and touring widely in Europe as well as recording new material.

Albums: *Fulham Fallout* (Beggars Banquet 1978), *God's Lonely Men* (Beggars Banquet 1979), *This Dirty Town* (Clay 1982), *King Of The Mountain* (Link 1989), *Wild Times Again* (Wesserlabel 1989, live album), *Powerjive* (Released Emotions 1990). Compilations: *Greatest Hit, Last Will And Testament* (Beggars Banquet 1980), *Totally Lurkered* (Dojo 1992).

Lush

Though they made their live debut at the Camden Falcon on 6 March 1988, little was heard of London-based Lush's serene pop qualities and full-bodied guitar sound until their mini-album, *Scar*, was issued in October 1989 on 4AD Records. It was a critically acclaimed debut, and red-haired Miki Berenyi (b. 18 March 1967, St Stephen's, London, England; vocals/guitar), Emma Anderson (b. 10 June 1964, Raynes Park, London, England; guitar/backing vocals), Steve Rippon (bass guitar) and Christopher Acland (b. 7 September 1966, Lancaster, Lancashire, England; drums) found themselves topping the independent charts. Previously Anderson, a former DHSS clerical assistant, had been bass player for the Rover Girls, Berenyi had played with I-Goat, Fuhrer Five and the Lillies, while Acland had been a member of Infection, Panik, A Touch Of Hysteria, Poison In The Machine and others. Tours with the Darling Buds and Loop followed Lush's initial breakthrough, plus an appearance on BBC2's *Snub TV* and a John Peel radio session. The EP, *Mad Love*, issued in February 1990, was less raw but soared to new heights with the help of producer Robin Guthrie from the Cocteau Twins. Lush's consistent coverage in the music press, not least for their perpetual appearances at pre/post-gig parties, made them one of the leading UK independent groups of the year; one that was taken up with tours in the UK and Europe and an appearance at the Glastonbury Festival. Another EP, *Sweetness And Light*, offered a further move towards a commercial pop sound and only narrowly missed the national charts. The three EPs were compiled, originally for the US market, on *Gala*. Much of 1991 was spent recording the long-awaited full debut album, during which time they also issued an EP, *Black Spring* (which included a cover of Dennis Wilson's 'Fallin' In Love'). When *Spooky* was finally released, many were disappointed, some insisting that Guthrie's production had swamped the group sound. Nevertheless, the album reached the national Top 20 and number 1 in the UK independent chart. During the winter of 1991/2 the group line-up changed when bassist Steve Rippon left amicably, to be replaced by *New Musical Express* picture researcher, Phil King (b. 29 April 1960, Chiswick, London, England). His musical apprenticeship had already included stints in the Servants, Felt, Biff Bang Pow! and See See Rider. The critical reception which awaited 1994's second album, *Split*, was fervent, with its cool guitar textures winning over many who had doubted their staying power. Berenyi and Anderson, dismissed in some quarters as 'two pissheads from London', had dispelled not only that notion, but also that of them being a 'typically glacial post-punk 4AD band' with a stunningly evocative collection of pop songs.

Albums: *Scar* (4AD 1989, mini-album), *Spooky* (4AD 1992), *Split* (4AD 1994). Compilation: *Gala* (4AD 1990).

M

Macc Lads

This trio from Macclesfield, Cheshire, England, comprised pseudonymous chancers The Beater (guitar/vocals), Muttley McLad (bass/vocals) and Chorley The Hord (drums). With a musical brief that incorporated elements of three-chord boogie, metallic riffs and punk, they insulted and entertained their audiences with a barrage of foul-mouthed one-liners and rock 'n' roll rugby songs. Lyrically, they extolled and exaggerated the virtues of the northern, macho, male-dominated pub scene: drinking real ale, 'pulling' women, Chinese takeaways and homophobia. Sample song titles include: 'Now He's A Poof', 'Eh Up Let's Sup', 'Dan's Big Log' and 'No Sheep 'Til Buxton'. Releasing a series of albums full of schoolboy humour, they gradually ran out of ideas. Shunned by nearly every record company and live venue in the land, the Macc Lads' grim philosophy, if such a polysyllabic word is appropriate, endures.

Albums: *Beer & Sex & Chips 'N' Gravy* (FM Revolver 1985), *Bitter, Fit, Crack* (FM Revolver 1987), *Live At Leeds - The Who?* (FM Revolver 1988), *From Beer To Eternity* (Hectic House 1989), *The Beer Necessities* (Hectic House 1990), *Turtle's Heads* (Hectic House 1991), *Alehouse Rock* (Up Not Down 1994). Compilation: *20 Golden Crates* (1991). Videos: *Come To Brum* (1989), *Quality Of Mersey* (1990), *Three Bears* (1990), *Sex Pies And Videotape* (1992).

MacColl, Kirsty

b. 10 October 1959, England. The daughter of the celebrated folk singer Ewan MacColl, Kirsty has enjoyed success in her own right as an accomplished songwriter and pop vocalist. Originally signed to Stiff Records as a 16-year-old, she was most unfortunate not to secure a massive hit with the earnest 'They Don't Know'. Many years later, the television comedienne Tracey Ullman took an inferior rendition of the song to number 2 in the UK charts. MacColl had to wait until 1981 for her first chart hit. A change of label to Polydor brought her deserved UK Top 20 success with the witty 'There's A Guy Works Down The Chip Shop Swears He's Elvis'. Her interest in country and pop influences was discernible on her strong debut *Desperate Characters*. In 1984, MacColl married producer Steve Lillywhite, and during the same year she returned to the charts with a stirring version of Billy Bragg's 'A New England'. During the next couple of years, she gave birth to two children but still found herself in-demand as a backing singer. She guested on recordings by a number of prominent artists, including Simple Minds, the Smiths, the Rolling Stones, Talking Heads, Robert Plant, Van Morrison and Morrissey. In December 1987, she enjoyed her highest ever chart placing at number 2 when duetting with Shane MacGowan on the Pogues' evocative vignette of Irish emigration, 'Fairytale Of New York'. In 1989, she returned to recording solo with the highly-accomplished *Kite*. The album included the powerful 'Free World' and an exceptionally alluring version of the Kinks' 'Days', which brought her back to the UK Top 20. Smiths guitarist Johnny Marr guested on several of the album's tracks and appeared on the excellent follow-up released in 1991. *Electric Landlady*, an amusing pun on the Jimi Hendrix Experience's *Electric Ladyland*, was another strong album which demonstrated MacColl's diversity and songwriting talent. The haunting, dance-influenced 'Walking Down Madison' gave her another Top 40 UK hit. Her career to date was sympathetically compiled on *Galore*, which demonstrated a highly accomplished artist even though four albums in fifteen years is hardly prolific.

Albums: *Desperate Characters* (1981), *Kite* (1989), *Electric Landlady* (1991), *Titanic Days* (ZTT 1994). Compilation: *Galore* (Virgin 1995).

Mackenzies

One of the more refreshing aspects of the *New Musical Express*/ICA Rock Week and accompanying *C86* cassette compilation was the Ron Johnson camp. This Manchester label threw up a handful of manic guitar acts whose shared sources appeared to be the Fall and Captain Beefheart. The Mackenzies were no exception. 'Big Jim (There's No Pubs In Heaven)' on *C86* started as a quirky thrash similar to the Fire Engines, then switched to militant jazz funk groove and back again. Similar ingredients were also found on 'New Breed' in April 1986 and the excellent 'Mealy Mouths' the following February. But the Mackenzies failed to capitalize on these, and nothing was heard from them, apart from a remix of 'Mealy Mouths' exactly a year later, in February 1988.

Madder Rose

Spuriously lauded on their arrival in 1993 as the 'new Velvet Underground', Manhattan-based New Yorkers Madder Rose comprised Billy Coté (b. New Jersey, USA; guitar), Mary Lorson (vocals), Matt Verta-Ray (bass) and Johnny Kick (b. Chicago, ex-Speedball; drums). The initial ripples were caused by singles such as 'Swim', a yearning, slow burning torch song reminiscent of Lou Reed's craft. However, they could hardly be described as anyone's 'new young thing', with all of the members aged over 30 at this early stage in their career. Each boasted an interesting, non-musical background. Lorson was an ex-busker and film student, while both Matt and Johnny worked at the Andy Warhol silk-screen factory and met the great man several times (a fact which helped to encourage the Velvet Underground comparisons). Coté had additionally spent much of the 80s working in No/New Wave bands Hammerdoll and Coté Coté, whilst struggling to overcome his heroin addiction. Covers of PiL's 'Rise' and the Cars' 'My Best Friends Girl' on stage further revealed Madder Rose's diversity, while their debut album was trumpeted by *Melody Maker* magazine as '*the* debut album of 1993'. Released on Atlantic Records' independently distributed subsidiary Seed, production was overseen by Kevin Salem of Dumptruck. Matt Verta-Ray left in February 1994, the departure agreed before the band recorded their second album, to concentrate on his own project, Speedball Baby. He was replaced for *Panic On* by Chris Giammalvo (ex-Eve's Plum), on a set co-produced with Clash/Breeders/Th' Faith Healers veteran, Mark Freegard. This saw Lorson emerge as a song writing force to rival Coté on some of the album's best numbers, including the appealing 'Foolish Ways'.

Albums: *Bring It Down* (Seed 1993), *Panic On* (Atlantic 1994).

Madness

This highly-regarded UK ska/pop group evolved from the London-based Invaders in the summer of 1979. Their line-up comprised Suggs McPherson (b. Graham McPherson, 13 January 1961, Hastings, Sussex, England; vocals), Mark Bedford (b. 24 August 1961, London, England; bass), Mike Barson (b. 21 April 1958, London, England; keyboards), Chris Foreman (b. 8 August 1958, London, England; guitar), Lee Thompson (b. 5 October 1957, London, England; saxophone), Chas Smash (b. Cathal Smythe, 14 January 1959; vocals/trumpet) and Dan Woodgate (b. 19 October 1960, London, England; drums). After signing a one-off deal with 2-Tone they issued 'The Prince', a tribute to blue beat maestro Prince Buster (whose song, 'Madness', had inspired the group's name). The single reached the UK Top 20 and the follow-up, 'One Step Beyond' (a Buster composition) did even better, peaking at number 7, the first result of their new deal with Stiff Records. An album of the same title revealed Madness' charm with its engaging mix of ska and exuberant pop, a fusion they humorously dubbed 'the nutty sound'. Over the next two years the group enjoyed an uninterrupted run of Top 10 UK hits, comprising 'My Girl', *Work Rest And Play* (EP), 'Baggy Trousers', 'Embarrassment', 'The Return Of The Los Palmas Seven', 'Grey Day', 'Shut Up' and 'It Must Be Love' (originally a hit for its composer, Labi Siffre). Although Madness appealed mainly to a younger audience and were known as a zany, fun-loving group, their work occasionally took on a more serious note. Both 'Grey Day' and 'Our House' showed their ability to write about working-class family life in a fashion that was piercingly accurate, yet never patronizing. At their best, Madness were the most able commentators on London life since the Kinks in the late 60s. An ability to tease out a sense of melancholy beneath the fun permeated their more mature work, particularly on the 1982 album, *The Rise And Fall*. That same year Suggs married singer Bette Bright and the group finally topped the charts with their 12th chart entry, 'House Of Fun' (which concerned the purchase of prophylactics and teenage sexuality). More UK hits followed, including 'Wings Of A Dove' and 'The Sun And The Rain', but in late 1983 the group suffered a serious setback when founding member Barson quit. The group continued to release some exceptional work in 1984 including 'Michael Caine' and 'One Better Day'. At the end of that year, they formed their own label, Zarjazz. It's first release was Feargal

Madness

Sharkey's 'Listen To Your Father' (written by the group), which reached the UK Top 30. Madness continued to enjoy relatively minor hits by previous standards with the contemplative 'Yesterday's Men', the exuberant 'Uncle Sam' and a cover of the former Scritti Politti success, 'The Sweetest Girl'. In the autumn of 1986, the group announced that they were splitting. Seventeen months later, they reunited as a four-piece under the name The Madness, but failed to emulate previous successes. One of Mark Bedford's projects was a collaboration with ex-Higson member Terry Edwards in Butterfield 8. Lee Thompson and Chris Foreman later worked under the appellation the Nutty Boys, releasing one album, *Crunch* (1990), and played to capacity crowds in London clubs and pubs. In June 1992 the original Madness reformed for two open air gigs in Finsbury Park, London, which resulted in *Madstock*, a 'live' document of the event. The group's renewed public image was rewarded with four chart entries during the year; three re-issues, 'It Must Be Love', 'House Of Fun', and 'My Girl'; along with 'The Harder They Come'. In 1993, a 'musical about homelessness', *One Step Beyond*, by Alan Gilbey, incorporated 15 Madness songs when it opened on the London Fringe. Further evidence, as if any was needed, of the enduring brilliance of Madness' irresistable songcraft.

Albums: *One Step Beyond* (Stiff 1979), *Absolutely* (Stiff 1980), *Madness 7* (Stiff 1981), *The Rise And Fall* (Stiff 1982), *Keep Moving* (Stiff 1984), *Mad Not Mad* (Zarjazz 1985). As The Madness: *The Madness* (Virgin 1988). As Madness: *Madstock* (Go! Discs 1992). Compilations: *Complete Madness* (Stiff 1982), *Utter Madness* (Zarjazz 1986), *Divine Madness* (Virgin 1992), *The Business - The Definitive Singles Collection* (Virgin 1993).

Videos: *Complete Madness* (1984), *Utter Madness* (1988), *Complete And Utter Madness* (1988), *Divine Madness* (1992).

Magazine

The Buzzcocks vocalist Howard Devoto left that group in January 1977, although he continued to be involved on the fringe of their activities for some time. In April he met guitarist John McGeogh and together they started writing songs. They formed Magazine with Devoto on vocals, McGeogh on guitar, Barry Adamson on bass, Bob Dickinson on keyboards and Martin Jackson on drums. The group played their debut live gig at the closing night of the Electric Circus, Manchester, in the autumn of 1977 as a last-minute addition to the bill. Their moody, cold keyboards and harsh rhythms were in sharp contrast to the mood of the day: 'Everybody was playing everything ultra fast, as fast as they could. I thought we could begin to play slow music again.' They were signed to Virgin Records but Dickinson left in November and, as a result, their debut, 'Shot By Both Sides', was recorded by the four remaining members. Dave Formula was recruited in time to play on *Real Life*. Next to leave was Jackson who departed after their first tour. Paul Spencer came in temporarily before John Doyle was recruited in October 1978. This line-up remained for the next couple of years, although McGeogh was also playing with Siouxsie And The Banshees, and, along with Adamson and Formula, in Steve Strange's Visage. Their albums received universal acclaim but only their first single and 1980's 'Sweetheart

Contract' dented the charts. As the latter was released McGeogh left to join Siouxsie full-time and Robin Simon (ex-Neo and Ultravox) was brought in on guitar. A tour of the USA and Australia - where a live album was recorded - led to Simon's departure and Ben Mandelson (ex-Amazorblades) came in for the band's last few months. The departure of Devoto in May 1981 signalled the unit's death knell. The work they left behind, however, is surprisingly enduring given its angular and experimental slant. Devoto would go on to a solo career before forming Luxuria.

Albums: *Real Life* (Virgin 1978), *Secondhand Daylight* (Virgin 1979), *The Correct Use Of Soap* (Virgin 1980), *Play* (Virgin 1980), *Magic, Murder And The Weather* (Virgin 1981). Compilations: *After The Fact* (Virgin 1982), *Rays & Hail 1978-81* (Virgin 1987), *Scree: Rarities 1978-1981* (Virgin 1990), *BBC Radio 1 Live In Concert* (Windsong 1993).

Magnapop

Based in Watkinsville, Athens, Georgia, USA, Magnapop's personnel is composed of Ruthie Morris (b. Florida, USA; guitar), Shannon Mulvaney (bass), David McNair (drums) and Linda Hopper (vocals). Linda had originally met Michael Stipe (R.E.M.) at art college in the early 80s, where he persuaded her to form a band with his sister (also called Linda), who were titled Oh OK. They lasted three years and briefly included McNair on drums. Mutual friends introduced her to Morris in Atlanta, and they started to write songs together in 1988, with their first demos produced by Stipe. Their debut single, 'Merry', was followed by the *Kiss My Mouth* EP, which found instant success in Holland and Belgium, their popularity demanding the release of a premature mini-album, essentially of demo tracks, in that area. This celebrity was based in part on an appearance at a Rotterdam festival, where Bob Mould, Nirvana and Frank Black were all playing. Magnapop created such a buzz that the promotor shifted them from a smaller platform to the main stage the following night, and Mould took an interest in the group, agreeing to produce their debut album proper. Mould proved not to be Magnapop's only star fan. Juliana Hatfield spoke highly of them whenever the opportunity arose, and even wrote a song, 'Ruthless', about their guitarist Ruthie Morris ('We're all suckers for a girl who really plays guitar/We're all pining for Ruthie/We all wish we were Ruthie/We're all dying for Ruthie').

Albums: *Magnapop* (1992), *Hot Boxing* (Play It Again Sam 1994).

Manic Street Preachers

These UK punk revivalists enjoyed a love-hate relationship with the music press which opened with a bizarre encounter in 1991. The catalyst was Richey Edwards, who cut the words '4 Real' into his forearm to the amazement of *New Musical Express* critic Steve Lamacq, when he dared to call into question the band's authenticity. The group hails from Blackwood, Gwent, Wales, and is comprised of James Dean Bradfield (b. 21 February 1969; vocals/guitar), Richey Edwards (b. 27 December 1969; rhythm guitar), Nicky Wire (b. Nick Jones; bass) and Sean Moore (b. 30 July 1970; drums). Their calculated insults at a wide variety of targets, particularly their peers, had already won them infamy following the release of their debut *New Art Riot* EP, and the Public Enemy-sampling 'Motown Junk' (a previous single, 'Suicide Alley', had been a limited pressing distributed to journalists only). Their personal manifesto was equally explicit: rock bands should cut down the previous generation, release one explosive album then disappear. Although the music press pointed out the obvious contradictions and naivete of this credo, the band polarized opinion to a degree which far outweighed their early musical proficiency. The singles, 'Stay Beautiful' and 'Love's Sweet Exile' (backed by the superior 'Repeat' - 'Repeat after me, fuck Queen and Country') were inconclusive, but the reissued version of 'You Love Us', with its taut, vicious refrain, revealed a band beginning to approach in power what they had always had in vision. Their debut album, too, was an injection of bile which proved perversely refreshing in a year of industry contraction and self-congratulation. Unfortunately, it never quite achieved its intention to outsell Guns N'Roses' *Appetite For Destruction*, nor did the band split immediately afterwards as stated. The polished, less caustic approach of *Gold Against The Soul* saw the Manics hitting a brick wall in expectation and execution, though as always there were moments of sublime lyricism (notably the singles 'Roses In The Hospital' and 'Life Becoming A Landslide'). *The Holy Bible* returned the group to the bleak worldview of yesteryear, notably on the haunting '4st 7lb', written by a near-anorexic Richey James before a nervous breakdown which saw him temporarily admitted to a mental facility. Other subject matter was drawn from prostitution, the holocaust and the penal system. Never easy listening at the best of times (despite the ability to write genuinely affecting songs like 'Motorcycle Emptiness'), the Manics have already produced enough inspired moments to justify their protracted early claims. However, all that seemed somehow irrelevant following Edwards' disappearance on 1 February 1995, with several parties expressing concern as to his well-being.

Albums: *Generation Terrorists* (Columbia 1992, double album), *Gold Against The Soul* (Columbia 1993), *The Holy Bible* (Columbia 1994).

Mann, Aimee

Having begun performing with the punk-inspired Young Snakes, Aimee Mann achieved recognition as the lead vocalist of the critically-acclaimed 'Til Tuesday. Frustrated with the industry trying to push a more mainstream approach - and suggestion that writers outside the group should contribute material - Mann left for a solo career in 1990. *Whatever* was a remarkable set, drawing rave reviews and the generous plaudits of Elvis Costello. A literate and skilled composer, Mann attacked the corporate music business on 'I've Had It' and detailed estrangement and heartbreak on 'I Should've Known' and 'I Know There's A Word' (allegedly concerning her former relationship with Jules Shear). Former Byrds' guitarist Roger McGuinn was

Aimee Mann

persuaded to contribute distinctive 12-string backing on a set reviving pop's traditions of melody and chorus, while placing them in an unquestionably contemporary context. Album: *Whatever* (Imago 1993).

March Violets

This rock band with definite 'gothic' leanings was formed in England during 1982. Hugh (bass) met Simon (vocals) in Leeds, and the latter recruited an old friend, Tom (guitar). Together with a hastily recruited female singer they entered the studios to record an EP which brought them subsequent exposure on BBC disc jockey John Peel's show. After further releases on the fashionable Merciful Release label, they acquired the services of Travis when he replaced the original drum machine in late 1984. Simon left owing to a 'mutual decision', while vocalist Cleo joined for their 'Snakedance' single in 1983. By this time the band behind her only retained Tom from the original line-up, with Loz the latest recruit on bass. In 1986, they signed to London Records, releasing 'Turn To The Sky', which just failed to scrape the charts. By this time they were trying to shake off the 'goth' tag, emphasizing that their influences were bands like Z.Z. Top, Led Zeppelin and the Pretenders. Critics used Cleo's blonde hair as justification for comparisons to Blondie, while musically they were somewhere between the two.
Album: *Natural History* (1984).

Marine Girls

This UK quartet was formed by four Hertfordshire school friends: Jane Fox (b. c.1963; bass/vocals), her sister Alice (b. c.1966; vocals/percussion), Tracey Thorn (b. 26 September 1962; guitar/vocals) and the soon-to-depart, Gina (percussion/vocals). The Marine Girls recorded their homemade *Beach Party* in a garden shed. Musically competent, within limitations, their lyrics showed remarkable strength and eloquence in dealing with the age-old problems of difficult boyfriends, new love and loneliness, often using the symbolic context of the sea and all its mysteries. With initial encouragement from the Television Personalities, the album was released by the Whaam! label and was later picked up Cherry Red Records, who signed the group for a second album. By this time, Tracey had left school to go to Hull University, where she struck up a romantic and artistic relationship with Cherry Red stable-mate Ben Watt. They recorded the Cole Porter song, 'Night And Day' under the name of Everything But The Girl. Thorn had also released a solo album in 1982, *A Distant Shore*, which was well-received by the critics and public. Pursuing a parallel career as a Marine Girl and as a duettist with Watt at first proved comfortable, but with the increasing popularity and media attention of Everything But The Girl, an amicable split with the Fox sisters came in late 1983, after the release of the successful *Lazy Ways*. Continuing their seaside/oceanic fixation, the sisters formed Grab Grab The Haddock, which produced two fine EPs on Cherry Red before folding in 1986. The line-up of Grab Grab The Haddock was notable for the inclusion of Lester Noel, who later joined former Housemartin Norman Cook in Beats International.
Albums: *Beach Party* (1981), *Lazy Ways* (1983).

Marion

Macclesfield, England quintet comprising Jamie Harding (b. c.1975; vocals), Anthony Grantham (guitar), Phil Cunningham (guitar), Julian Phillips (bass) and Murad Mousa (drums), who created an immediate stir in 1994 with the release of two independent singles ('Violent Men' and 'The Only Way'). This brace of fierce, anthemic songs, together with the fact that they were represented by ex-Smiths manager Joe Moss, helped ensure a frenzied A&R chase in the summer of that year, which was eventually concluded at the In The City seminar in September when they were signed by London Records. However, there was a degree of longevity to Marion's pursuits which might not have been suggested by their average age of 20 - Harding, Cunningham and Grantham had been in youthful bands together for nine years before this current incarnation. Their new label sent them to work with Stephen Street, provoking further Smiths' comparisons, which were hardly deflated by the news that Morrissey had attended two of their early gigs (he subsequently invited them to support him on UK dates). The first result of the new deal was the single, 'Toys For Boys'.

MARRS

A collaboration between two 4AD bands, Colourbox and AR Kane which, though a one off, was enough to set both the independent, dance and national charts alight during Autumn 1987. 'Pump Up The Volume' was augmented on the a-side by UK champion scratch mixer Chris 'C.J.' Mackintosh and London disc jockey/journalist Dave Dorrell. Primarily aimed at the dance market, the record was originally mailed to the 500 most influential regional club and dance DJs on an anonymous white label, in order that it received exposure six weeks prior to its stock version. On official release it entered the charts at number 35, a figure attained on 12-inch sales only. Daytime radio play ensured the single was the next weeks' highest climber, rising 24 places to number 11. The following two weeks it stayed at number 2 before reaching the number 1 spot on 28th September 1987. Originally the idea of 4AD supremo Ivo, the single featured samples of James Brown, a practice already common in hip hop which would soon come into vogue for an avalanche of dance tracks: 'We've used a lot of rhythms and time signatures from old records, classic soul records, but mixed that with modern electronic instruments and AR Kane's guitar sound', was how the single was described. The single was never followed-up, apparently due to acrimony between the involved personnel over finance, which was a great shame. As such the MARRS discography is a brief but blemishless one. Dorrell would go on to manage Bush while Mackintosh returned to the club circuit.

Martha And The Muffins

The roots of this Canadian new wave band stem back to the mid-70s, when Martha Johnson was the organist with Oh Those Pants, a 10-piece 60s covers/send-up band which also included future members of the Cads. This was followed by a spell in another Toronto band the Doncasters, who specialized in revamping 60s garage band material. In 1977, Johnson joined up with Mark Gane (guitar), Carl Finkle

(bass), Andy Haas (saxophone), and Tim Gane (drums) to form Martha and the Muffins. They were later joined by Martha Ladly, who initially played guitar but later moved to keyboards and trombone. They sent a tape to New York journalist Glenn O'Brien, who referred them to the fledgling DinDisc label. This led to the release of their debut single 'Insect Love'. Success came in 1980 with 'Echo Beach" which was a big hit in the UK. Follow-ups, including 'Saigon' (with its double groove b-side - playable backwards and forwards) fared less well. In 1981, Ladly left to work with the Associates and formed the Scenery Club who released a single on DinDisc. The Muffins signed to RCA and session player Clara Hurst played keyboards temporarily but joined the Belle Stars in 1982, when Martha And The Muffins split up. Johnson and Mark Gane formed M+M, who had a hit with 'Black Stations White Stations'.
Albums: *Metro Music* (1980), *Trance And Dance* (1980), *This Is The Ice Age* (1981), *Danseparc* (1983). Compilation: *Far Away In Time* (1993).

Matthews, Dave, Band
b. c.1967, South Africa. Dave Matthews moved to New York from his native country when he was just two years old. When his father died he moved back to Johannesburg with his mother, where he finished high school. He finally settled back in Charlottesville, and assembled his self-titled multi-racial band in the late 80s. These musicians forged a vibrant, individual sound from elements which included violin, saxophone and piano as well as the more traditional guitar, bass and drums. This eclectic mix significantly complemented Matthews own expanded world view. Together they built a formidable reputation on the back of a punishing touring schedule, which helped their self-produced and financed debut, *Remember Two Things*, sell over 100,000 copies. In its wake the group were afforded the luxury of picking from the majors. Eventually choosing RCA Records (who offered the most malleable contract), their major label debut, *Under The Table And Dreaming*, produced by Steve Lillywhite, entered the *Billboard* charts at number 34.
Albums: *Remember Two Things* (Bama Rags 1993), *Under The Table And Dreaming* (RCA 1994).

Maximum Joy
Like other Y label acts Shriekback and Pigbag, Bristol-based Maximum Joy explored a refreshing brand of independent funk that was in vogue in the UK during the early 80s. Formed by ex-Pop Group members John Waddington (guitar/vocals) and Dan Katsis (bass), the band was swelled by Janine Rainforth (vocals/clarinet/violin), Tony Wrafter (saxophone/flute/trumpet) and Charles Llewellyn (drums/percussion). The group's first two singles 'Stretch' (1981), 'White And Green Place' (1982) featured in the UK Independent Top 20. Later in the year, 'In The Air' preceded what was to be Maximum Joy's sole album, by which time Katsis had been replaced by Kevin Evans. Produced by Adrian Sherwood, this encapsulated Maximum Joy's at times quirky blend of percussion and funky instrumental flair, characterized by distinctive horns. With the departure of Wrafter later in the year, Dan Katsis rejoined for saxophone

duties. After a healthy rendition of Timmy Thomas' 70s soul classic, 'Why Can't We Live Together', Maximum Joy disbanded.
Album: *Station M.X.J.Y ...* (1982).

Mazzy Star
Highly regarded duo featuring the soothing timbre of singer Hope Sandoval's textured voice and guitarist David Roback. The partners had begun working together on a projected album as Opal (under which name Roback had formerly operated). Previous to which he had been a member of Paisley Underground legends the Rain Parade, and recorded the *Rainy Day* album with vocalists Susanna Hoffs (Bangles) and Kendra Smith. He met Sandoval while she was part of female duo Going Home. Enjoying a profitable working relationship, Roback and Sandoval adopted the name Mazzy Star for their sessions together, which eventually resulted in a critically lauded debut album. They released a comeback album on Capitol Records in 1993 after an absence that was mourned by many rock critics. Various musicians were employed, but the core of the project remained Roback and Sandoval (who would also contribute to the Jesus And Mary Chain's 'Sometimes Always' single). Contrary to expectations established by its forerunner, the resultant album included a cover of the Stooges' 'We Will Fall'. Elsewhere, however, Roback's stinging lyrical poignancy and effortless song construction continued to hold sway.
Albums: *She Hangs Brightly* (Rough Trade 1990), *So Tonight That I Might See* (Capitol 1993).

McAlmont
David McAlmont's first exposure to the music industry came as half of the highly-praised but under-achieving London duo Thieves, who split up in 1994. McAlmont has said about the Thieves split, 'It was just a case of who jumped first. I was very cowardly because I did it on the phone.' He subsequently teamed up with ex-Suede guitarist Bernard Butler. The relationship was never intended to be permanent, as both parties were unhappy about the dissolution of their former band. The two singles, 'Yes' and 'You Do', they co-wrote featured on McAlmont's typically lush solo debut.
Album: *McAlmont* (Hut 1995).

McCarthy
Barking Abbey Comprehensive school, in Essex, England, acted as a meeting point for McCarthy in the early part of the 80s. Eventually, in 1984, Malcolm Eden (b. 1 September 1963, Ilford, Essex, England; vocals), Tim Gane (b. 12 July 1964, Barking, Essex, England; guitar), John Williamson (b. 28 December 1963, Ilford, Essex, England; bass) and Gary Baker (b. 8 September 1963, Barking, Essex, England; drums) formed McCarthy and released a self-financed single, limited to 485 copies. The quartet's profile was further raised with the inclusion of 'Celestial City' on the *New Musical Express*' influential *C86* cassette, but while McCarthy certainly shared many contemporary bands' tastes for rough-edged guitars, they forced themselves away from the crowd by anointing their music with an extreme left wing political stance. Perhaps it was pure coincidence that the similarly-

McGee, Alan

minded songwriter Billy Bragg attended the very same school, yet the 'Red Sleeping Beauty' single - a poetically-veiled commentary on the Thatcher government of the time - was just one of a series of sharply toned releases where the message never suffocated McCarthy's melodic instinct. After a series of label changes and a highly successful last gasp evolution towards the more fashionable, upbeat sounds of 1990, McCarthy finally tired of battling against their apathetic surroundings and dissolved, playing their final gig at the London School of Economics at the start of the new decade. Gary Baker turned to radiography, Malcolm Eden concentrated on literary writing, while Tim Gane remained in music and started receiving numerous critical recommendations for his new band, Stereolab. He would also use his Duophonic imprint to release Malcolm Eden's first post-McCarthy venture, Herzfield.

Albums: *I'm A Wallet* (Pink 1987), *The Enraged Will Inherit The Earth* (September Records 1989), *Banking, Violence And The Inner Life Today* (Midnight 1990). Compilations: *That's All Very Well But* (Midnight 1989), *We'll Get You Soon You Creeps* (Midnight 1991).

McGee, Alan

b. 29 September 1960, Glasgow, Scotland. After leaving school at the age of 17, McGee became an electrician, then relocated to London where he worked as a clerk for British Rail. In his spare time, he promoted gigs for his nomadic club, the Living Room, booking acts such as the Nightingales and the Television Personalities. To his surprise, he found that he was making a profit, so elected to release records and formed the label Creation. During the early phase of the label's history, McGee issued singles by artists such as the Loft, the Pastels, Primal Scream, the Jasmine Minks and his own venture, Biff Bang Pow. After signing the Jesus And Mary Chain in 1984, McGee's credibility as a manager and label owner escalated dramatically. He stayed with the group for two, often stormy, years and along the way issued some fascinating product by Felt, the Bodines and the Weather Prophets. The ill-fated tie-up with Warner Brothers, Elevation Records, encouraged McGee to pursue the independent route with more vigour. During the latter half of the 80s, the Creation roster extended to include Nikki Sudden, Momus, Clive Langer and, most crucially, the House Of Love. After one album and two excellent singles, the latter signed to Phonogram. After 1988, McGee turned increasingly to the dance floor for inspiration. Initial releases by Love Corporation, Hynotone, JBC and DJ Danny Rampling were not commercial successes, but the new direction was sound. Ironically, it was former psychedelic outfit Primal Scream who embraced the dance culture most effectively, providing the label with hits such as 'Loaded'. Further success followed with the critically acclaimed and best-selling My Bloody Valentine, Ride, Oasis, Teenage Fanclub, and the Boo Radley's as Creation entered its most productive phase yet during the mid-90s. McGee's genuine love of music and thrust for innovation has made him one of the most influential music business entrepreneurs to emerge in the UK over the past decade.

McKee, Maria

Before her solo career Maria McKee was the singer with Lone Justice, a band formed by her brother, Brian McLean, the former Love guitarist and vocalist. Both Lone Justice albums, *Lone Justice* and *Shelter*, were critically acclaimed. After the break up of the band McKee took time to compose herself, and her debut solo album gave a good platform for her powerful voice and distinctive register (similar to a more cultured Janis Joplin) with more pop-orientated hooks. Predominantly concerned with romance and heartbreak, it included an unrepresentative UK number 1 single, 'Show Me Heaven', taken from the soundtrack to the Tom Cruise motor racing film, *Days Of Thunder*. Touring extensively in support of the album, McKee eventually decided to move to Ireland. This period also saw McKee collaborate with a variety of Irish musicians, including Gavin Friday at a series of gigs for the Dublin A.I.D.S. Alliance. She also recorded the UK club hit, 'Sweetest Child', with the help of noted producer Youth (Killing Joke, Brilliant). She eventually returned to Los Angeles in 1992 to begin work on a follow-up set. This time she recruited producer George Drakoulias, veteran of successful albums by Black Crowes and the Jayhawks both of whom sounded similar to Lone Justice. *You Gotta Sin To Get Saved* reunited three-quarters of the original line-up of that band: Marvin Etzioni (bass), Don Heffington (drums) and Bruce Brody (keyboards), alongside Gary Louris and Mark Olsen (guitar/vocals) of the Jayhawks. As McKee noted, 'We had everything in common musically so it just happened.' Bob Fisher provided guitar on live dates, with McKee seemingly much more comfortable with the return to rootsy material.

Albums: *Maria McKee* (Geffen 1989), *You Gotta Sin To Get Saved* (Geffen 1993).

McLaren, Malcolm

b. 22 January 1946, London, England. After a tempestuous childhood, during which he was reared by his eccentric grandmother, McLaren spent the mid-late 60s at various art colleges. In 1969 he became romantically involved with fashion designer Vivienne Westwood and they subsequently had a son together, Joseph. Malcolm was fascinated by the work of the Internationale Situationist, a Marxist/Dadaist group which espoused its doctrines through sharp political slogans such as 'be reasonable - demand the impossible'. Their use of staged 'situations', designed to gain the attention of and ultimately enlighten the proletariat, impressed McLaren, and would significantly influence his entrepreneurial career. In 1971 he opened the shop Let It Rock in Chelsea's Kings Road, which catered for Teddy Boy fashions. Among the shop's many visitors were several members of the New York Dolls, whose management McLaren took over in late 1974. It was to prove an ill-fated venture, but McLaren did spend some time with them in New York and organized their 'Better Dead Than Red' tour. After returning to the UK, he decided to find a new, young group whose power, presence and rebelliousness equalled that of the Dolls. The result was the Sex Pistols, whose brief spell of public notoriety ushered in the era of punk. McLaren was at the peak of his powers during this period, riding the wave of self-inflicted chaos that the Pistols spewed forth. The highlights included McLaren taking sizeable cheques from both EMI and A&M Records, who signed then fired the group in quick succession. The creation of the tragic caricature Sid Vicious, the conflict with Johnny Rotten, the involvement with Great Train Robber Ronnie Biggs and, finally, a self-glorifying film *The Great Rock 'n' Roll Swindle*, were all part of the saga. Following the Sex Pistols' demise, McLaren launched Bow Wow Wow, heavily promoting the 14-year-old singer Annabella Lu Win. Although their recordings were highly original for the period, the dividends proved unimpressive and the group split. In the meantime, McLaren had served as 'advisor' to and let slip through his hands 80s stars such as Adam Ant and Boy George (Culture Club). Eventually, he decided to transform himself into a recording star, despite the fact that he could not sing (ample evidence of which had appeared on his *Great Rock 'n' Roll Swindle* out-take, 'You Need Hands'). His singular ability to predict trends saw him assimilating various styles of music, from the Zulu tribes in Africa to the ethnic sounds of the Appalachian Mountains. The arduous sessions finally came to fruition with *Duck Rock*, which featured two UK Top 10 singles, 'Buffalo Girls' and 'Double Dutch'. The work pre-empted rock's interest in world music, as exemplified on *Graceland* by Paul Simon. McLaren next persisted with the music of urban New York and was particularly interested in the 'scratching' sounds of street hip hop disc jockeys. *Would Ya Like More Scratchin'* again anticipated the strong dance culture that would envelop the UK pop scene in the late 80s. Ever restless, McLaren moved on to a strange fusion of pop and opera with *Fans*, which featured a startling version of 'Madam Butterfly' that became a UK Top 20 hit. Following his experimental forays in the music business, McLaren relocated to Hollywood for a relatively unsuccessful period in the film industry. Nothing substantial emerged from that sojourn, but McLaren remains as unpredictable and innovative as ever.

Albums: *Duck Rock* (Island 1983), *Would Ya Like More Scratchin'* (Island 1984), *Fans* (Island 1984), *Waltz Darling* (Epic 1989), *Paris* (Disques Vogue 1994). Malcolm McLaren Presents The World Famous Supreme Team Show: *Round The Outside! Round The Outside!* (Virgin 1990).

Further reading: *Starmakers & Svengalis: The History Of British Pop Management*, Johnny Rogan, *The Wicked Ways Of Malcolm McLaren*, Craig Bromberg.

Meat Puppets

Formed in Tempe, Arizona, USA, Curt Kirkwood (guitar/vocals), Cris Kirkwood (bass/vocals) and Derrick Bostrom (drums) made their debut in 1981 with a five-track EP, *In A Car*. *Meat Puppets*, released the following year on the influential hardcore label, SST Records, offered a mix of thrash punk with hints of country, captured to perfection on the alternative cowboy classic, 'Tumblin' Tumbleweeds'. Their affection for roots music was fully realised on *Meat Puppets II*, a captivating set marked by dramatic shifts in mood and Curt Kirkwood's uncertain, but expressive, vocals. *Meat Puppets II* hauled country back to the campfire. *Up On The Sun* showed the trio moving further from their punk roots, embracing instead neo-psychedelic melodies. This evolution was enhanced further on *Mirage*, yet another

critically-acclaimed set. Having proclaimed an affection for Z.Z. Top, Curt Kirkwood introduced a more direct, fuzz-toned sound on *Huevos*, which was recorded in one marathon 72-hour session. Viewed by many longtime fans as a sell-out, the set's commercial appeal continued on *Monster*, the trio's heaviest, most 'traditional' set to date. Memorable hooklines were combined with hard-rock riffs and despite the qualms of those preferring the group's early work, the set was lauded as one of 1989's leading independent releases. Surprisingly the Meat Puppets then disbanded, reforming in 1991, buoyed by continued interest in their work and a proposed deal with London Records. Subsequent releases have kept interest in the group alive and in 1993 the Kirkwood brothers joined Nirvana on their now-legendary *Unplugged* appearance. Three songs from *Meat Puppets II*; 'Lake Of Fire', 'Plateau' and 'Oh Me', were immortalised during this affectionate collaboration.

Albums: *Meat Puppets* (SST 1982), *Meat Puppets II* (SST 1983), *Up On The Sun* (SST 1985). *Mirage* (SST 1987), *Huevos* (SST 1987), *Monsters* (SST 1989), *Forbidden Places* (London 1991), *Too High To Die* (London 1994). Compilation: *No Strings Attached* (SST 1990).

Medicine

US indie rock crew featuring Beth Thompson (b. 12 June 1967, St. Louis, Missouri, USA; vocals), Brad Laner (b. 6 November 1966, Los Angeles, California, USA; vocals, guitar), Jim Putnam (b. 30 September 1967, Hollywood, California, USA; guitar), Jim Goodall (b. 9 May 1952, Burbank, California, USA; drums) and Ed Ruscha (b. Edward Joseph Ruscha, 14 December 1968, Inglewood, California, USA; bass). Each of this membership had performed as part of other bands. Thompson had worked with Four Way Cross, Laner with Savage Republic and Steaming Coils, Putnam with SDF, Magic Beard and Bus Engines, Ruscha with SDF, Maids Of Gravity, Pita Hawks, Magic Beard and Dumb Speedway Children. The eldest member of the sect, Goodall has seen service with such established bands as the Flying Burrito Brothers and Canadian Sweetheart. Taking their name from an old Throbbing Gristle song, the group made their bow in Long Beach, California, in September 1991 (they had already been picked up for radio broadcast by west coast alternative radio guru Rodney Bingenheimer). Signed to English label Creation Records, they made their recorded debut in August 1992 with 'Aruca', which prefaced a well-received debut album. However, they left the UK independent's roster shortly afterwards, and sightings were fewer thenceforth until the release of *Sounds Of Medicine*, a mini-album with remixes by Billy Corgan (Smashing Pumpkins) and Robin Guthrie (Cocteau Twins). Again, this could hardly be described as light-hearted fare, but as Thompson declared to the press: 'I'm happy to make dark music. Fortunately you can't really make out our words so nobody's going to come to us and say we caused so and so's suicide'.

Albums: *Short Forth Self Living* (Creation 1992), *Sounds Of Medicine* (1994, mini-album).

Mega City Four

Thrash pop outfit influenced by early punks such as Stiff

Little Fingers and the Buzzcocks, stabilizing their output with a sustained melodicism and growing lyrical awareness. They started out in 1982 as Capricorn, who played a few gigs and recorded demos (including one 15 track affair entitled *The Good News Tape*). However, in 1986 original drummer Martin left, leaving the remaining members to undergo a re-think. A replacement, Chris Jones, was recruited from local bands Exit East and Moose Kaboose, joining Wiz (b. Darren Brown; vocals/guitar), Danny (b. Daniel Brown; rhythm guitar/backing vocals, brother of Wiz), and Gerry (b. Gerald Bryant; bass). Wiz had previously played one gig fronting a progressive rock band, Quilp, before joining Bryant in Capricorn, formed at Guildford technical college. On 1 January 1987, Mega City Four had their first practice. They took their name from the home base of *Judge Dredd*, the popular comic book enforcer. A demo appeared in March, and after nation-wide gigs a self-financed single, 'Miles Apart', was recorded in the autumn. Although it took six months to surface, reviews were impressive and disc jockey John Peel added his patronage. In the wake of its success it was reissued by Vinyl Solution subsidiary, Decoy Records, who became the band's permanent home. 'Distant Relatives' followed in November 1988, announcing Wiz's lyrical preoccupation with relationships, and was awarded Single Of The Week status by Steve Lamacq in *New Musical Express*. Another single, 'Less Than Senseless', arrived during a relentless 300-gig touring schedule throughout 1989. These experiences would result in the title of their debut album, *Tranzophobia* - a term invoked to convey the horror of touring for extended periods out of the back of a transit van. Though at the time it perfectly described the earnest, hard-working nature of the band, later it became an albatross around their necks when they found themselves unable to escape the lack of sophistication it implied. Despite this, Mega City Four, alongside peers and friends the Senseless Things, helped revitalize a flagging UK live scene with wholly committed performances. Sadly *Who Cares Wins* saw many of the band's newly acquired critical following renounce their previous advocacy, on a set neutered by flat production. Frustrated by budget restrictions, the band elected to move to Big Life Records for future recordings. 'Words That Say' and 'Stop', the latter a Top 40 success in January 1992, prefaced the band's long playing debut for their new home. *Sebastapol Road* was titled after the group's Farnborough rehearsal studio and comprised a succinct, energized collection of three minute pop songs with more highly-evolved lyrical themes than had previously been the case. A live album, less perfunctory than efforts by bands without Mega City Four's on-stage fluency, preceded 1993's *Magic Bullets*. With increasingly introverted song writing from Wiz - though his words were as direct and anti-glamour as ever - this was another fine, considered set, its quality emphasized by the promotional single, 'Iron Sky'. However, the group's fans had also moved on, to new favourites like Carter USM (one of many bands who started out as support act to MC4), and sales proved disappointing.
Albums: *Tranzophobia* (Decoy 1989), *Who Cares Wins* (Decoy 1990), *Sebastapol Road* (Big Life 1991), *Inspiringly Titled (The Live Album)* (Big Life 1992), *Magic Bullets* (Big Life 1993). Compilation: *Terribly Sorry Bob* (Decoy 1991).

Mekons

Although initially based in Leeds, England, the Mekons made their recording debut for the Edinburgh based Fast Product label in 1978. 'Never Been In A Riot', the outlet's first release, was the subject of effusive music press praise, and its joyous amateurism set the standard for much of the group's subsequent work. Having completed a second single, 'Where Were You', the Mekons were signed to Virgin Records where a line-up of Andy Carrigan (vocals), Mark White (vocals), Kevin Lycett (guitar), Tom Greenhalgh (guitar), Ross Allen (bass) and Jon Langford (drums, later guitar/vocals) completed *The Quality Of Mercy Is Not Strnen*. This unusual title was drawn from the axiom that, if you give a monkey a typewriter and an infinite amount of time, it would eventually produce the complete works of Shakespeare, a wry comment on the group's own musical ability. Nonetheless, the Mekons' enthusiasm, particularly in a live setting, was undoubtedly infectious and has contributed greatly to their long career. Despite numerous personnel changes (over 30 different members to 1995), they have retained a sense of naive adventurism, embracing world music, folk and roots material in their customarily ebullient manner. In the 90s three of the core members of the band (Greenhaigh, Langford and Sara Corina, Greenhaigh's violinist partner who joined in 1991) had relocated to Chicago, Illinois, USA, where the group enjoyed a loose recording contract with Quarterstick Records. This followed an unfortunate major label coalition with A&M Records. Other important contributors to the Mekons legacy include Sally Timms, vocalist and full-time member since the late 80s, who has released a brace of solo albums and is based in New York, and drummer Steve Goulding (ex-Graham Parker And The Rumour), a part-time journalist who has worked with Pig Dog Pondering. Langford would also work with Goulding on his part-time country band, Jon Langford & The Pine Valley Cosmonauts, who issued an album in Germany in 1994. He has also had numerous exhibitions of his paintings.
Albums: *The Quality Of Mercy Is Not Strnen* (Virgin 1979), *Mekons* (Red Rhino 1980), *Fear And Whiskey* (Sin 1985), *The Edge Of The World* (Sin 1986), *Honky Tonkin'* (Sin 1987), *New York Mekons* (ROIR 1987, cassette only), *So Good It Hurts* (Twin/Tone 1988), *Mekons Rock 'N' Roll* (A&M 1989), *The Curse Of The Mekons* (Blast First 1991), *I Love Mekons* (Quarterstick 1993), *Retreat From Memphis* (Quarterstick 1994). Compilations: *Mekons Story* (CNT 1982), *Original Sin* (RTD 1989).

Melvins

The late Kurt Cobain of Nirvana rated the Melvins as his favourite group. Unsurprising, perhaps, as they are the only other band of note to originate from his hometown Aberdeen (though they have since relocated to San Francisco), and he did once roadie for them. Drummer Dale Crover also played with Nirvana for a spell, while Cobain would guest and co-produce *Houdini* for the band. The other members of the Melvins, formed in 1984, numbered Buzz Osbourne (vocals/guitar) and Lori Beck (bass). Matt

Lukin (Mudhoney) was also a floating member. Reputed to be more influenced by the heavy rock angle than many who have fallen under the generic title 'grunge', the Melvins are big fans of Black Sabbath and even released three solo albums in a tribute to the Kiss strategy of similar pretensions. A cover of Flipper's 'Way Of The World' and 'Sacrifice' sat alongside Alice Cooper's 'Ballad Of Dwight Fry' on cover album, *Lysol*. *Stoner Witch*, their second album for Atlantic/East West, saw Crover and Osbourne joined by bass player Mark Deutrom, who had previously produced the band's first two albums. This time they were working with Garth Richardson of Red Hot Chili Peppers and L7 fame.
Albums: *Gluey Porch Treatments* (Alchemy 1986), *Ozma* (Boner 1987), *Bullhead* (Boner 1991), *Lysol* (Boner/Tupelo 1992), *Houdini* (Atlantic 1993), *Prick* (Amphetamine Reptile 1994), *Stoner Witch* (Atlantic 1994).

Members

One of the many UK bands inspired by punk, the Members came together in the summer of 1977, when former university student Nicky Tesco and French expatriate Jean-Marie Carroll, now a bank clerk in the UK, started working together. With Tesco on vocals and Carroll as guitarist and chief songwriter, they recruited Gary Baker on guitar, Adrian Lillywhite (brother of producer Steve Lillywhite) on drums, and a bass player. The bassist left after only a couple of months and was replaced by British Airways technician Chris Payne. They were based in Camberley, Surrey, England, where all the members (except Carroll) originated. The band's first recording - 'Fear On The Streets' - was for the Beggars Banquet punk compilation *Streets*. Despite this, it was Stiff Records that took the plunge and signed them. Their debut single, 'Solitary Confinement', was produced by Larry Wallis and earned them a contract with Virgin Records in November 1978, though by now Baker had departed and been replaced by Nigel Bennett. Their Virgin debut, 'Sound Of The Suburbs', was a hit in 1979, and was followed by the bloated but humorous reggae of 'Offshore Banking Business'. The b-side revisited 'Solitary Confinement', a song which the Newtown Neurotics would later update in the form of 'Living With Unemployment'. Their second album featured a guest appearance from Joe Jackson but it would be their last for Virgin, which they left in 1980. They were signed to Island Records briefly, but their third album came out on Albion Records, after which they disappeared. One other release of note is the Children Of 7's 'Solidarity' on Stiff, which featured both Carroll and Payne among the writing credits. More recently, 'Sound Of The Suburbs' featured as the title track to a nostalgic punk compilation which was advertised widely on UK television.
Albums: *At The Chelsea Nightclub* (Virgin 1979), *1980 The Choice Is Yours* (Virgin 1980), *Going West* (Albion 1983).

Membranes

Formed in Preston, Lancashire in 1977, this UK punk group was based in the seaside town of Blackpool, later immortalized as 'Tatty Seaside Town'. Founder member John Robb (b. 4 May, 1961; bass) was initially joined by Mark Tilton (guitar), Martin Kelly (drums) and Martin Critchley (vocals), the latter soon departing as Critchley

sidestepped from drums to keyboards, with 'Goofy Sid' Coulthart taking over behind the drumstool. Robb was to prove himself nothing if not a trier, organizing compilation appearances and inaugurating the near legendary, near indecipherable *Blackpool Rox* fanzine. Their first vinyl single was the 3-track 'Muscles' in 1981, gaining single of the week awards for its defiant, brash optimism and gaining ascendancy on the turntable of Radio 1's John Peel. It remains one of the most memorable DIY efforts of the early 80s. Steve Farmery joined on guitar after its release, with Martin Kelly leaving the keyboard position vacant. They joined Rondolet Records for 'Pin Stripe Hype', watching the label close down shortly after. This also saw off Farmery, leaving the band as a trio for much of the rest of their productive career. Missing out on the opportunity to be Creation Records first featured artists because of finance sent them down-market to Criminal Damage. It, too, proved a less than satisfactory home, and ultimately saw the group relocate to Manchester in 1983 in typically eternal optimism. The single which should have broken them was the acclaimed 'Spike Milligan's Tape Recorder', which somewhat pre-dated the guitar barrage of Big Black and Sonic Youth. However, distribution problems killed off the enthusiasm reciprocated by the media. The same problems applied to the 'Death To Trad Rock', 12-inch, after which Tilton left to be replaced by bass player, Stan. Although they finally made their postponed mark on Creation with the disappointing *Gift Of Life*, the band's fortunes were now in decline. Stan was replaced by Wallas as the band concentrated on the European circuit. Nick Brown was added on second guitar in 1987, followed in short order by Keith Curtis. Meanwhile, Robb was becoming more active as a freelance journalist for *Sounds*, and eventually *Melody Maker* and a host of other magazines. Despite the production services of Steve Albini (Big Black) on 1988's *Kiss Ass Godhead*, Wallas was the next departure, to be replaced by Paul Morley (ex-Slum Turkeys). However, total disintegration was imminent as Robb concentrated on his writing career, and launched his new dance project Sensurround.
Albums: *Gift Of Life* (Creation 1985), *Songs Of Love And Fury* (In Tape 1986), *Kiss Ass Godhead* (Homestead 1988), *To Slay The Rock Pig* (Vinyl Drip 1989). Compilations: *The Virgin Mary Versus Peter Sellers* (Vinyl Drip 1988), *Wrong Place At The Wrong Time* (Vinyl Drip 1993).
Video: *The Death To Trad Rock Special* (1988).

Men They Couldn't Hang, The

In their seven-year span, The Men They Couldn't Hang combined folk, punk and roots music to create an essential live act alongside a wealth of recorded talent. The band emerged as the Pogues' sparring partners but, despite a blaze of early publicity and praise, they failed to follow them upwards, dogged as they were by numerous label changes. Busking in Shepherds Bush, Welsh singer Cush met up with bassist Shanne (who had been in the Nips with the Pogues' Shane MacGowan), songwriter/guitarist Paul Simmonds, Scottish guitarist/singer Phil ('Swill') and his brother John on drums, in time for a ramshackle folk performance at London's alternative country music festival in Easter 1984.

Labelled as part of some 'cowpunk' scene, the band were quickly signed by Elvis Costello to his Demon label, Imp. A cover of Eric Bogle's 'Green Fields Of France' in October 1984 became a runaway indie success, and a favourite on BBC disc jockey John Peel's show. While playing live, the Men matched their own incisive compositions with entertaining covers. June 1985's 'Iron Masters' was just as strong, if more manic, and was accompanied by an impressive and assured debut, *The Night Of A Thousand Candles*.

Produced by Nick Lowe, 'Greenback' was less immediate, but its success swayed MCA to sign the group, resulting in 'Gold Rush' in June 1986. The group's second album, *How Green Is The Valley* continued their marriage of musical styles and a political sensibility drawn from an historical perspective. 'The Ghosts Of Cable Street' exemplified these ingredients. A move to Magnet Records catalyzed perhaps their finest work, with the commercial 'Island In The Rain' and the listenable *Waiting For Bonaparte*. 'The Colours' received airplay, but only skirted the charts. Fledgling label Silvertone's Andrew Lauder (who had worked with the group at Demon) signed the group in time for 'Rain, Steam And Speed' in February 1989. Hot on its heels came *Silvertown*. Two further singles followed: 'A Place In The Sun' and 'A Map Of Morocco'.

In 1990 they recorded their final studio album, for which the personnel was increased to six, with the addition of Nick Muir. On the strength of it, they supported David Bowie at Milton Keynes. Shortly afterwards they disbanded, following a long farewell tour, and a live album, *Alive, Alive - O*.

Albums: *Night Of A Thousand Candles* (1985), *How Green Is The Valley* (1986), *Waiting For Bonaparte* (1987, reissued 1988), *Silvertown* (1989), *The Domino Club* (1990), *Well Hung* (1991), *Alive, Alive - O* (1991).

Men Without Hats

Formed in Montreal, Canada, in 1980, this act was the brainchild of siblings Ivan (vocals) and Jeremy (drums) Arrobas, who manufactured remaining accompaniment on their records with synthesizers. An independent EP, *Folk Of The 80s*, created overseas cult interest to the extent that it was re-issued on Britain's Stiff label, along with an edit of its 'Antarctica' track as a single. However, just after the release of 1981's 'Nationale Seven', Jeremy left to allow composer Ivan to front a Men Without Hats with the brothers Stefan (guitar/violin) and Colin Doroschuk (keyboards) plus Allan McCarthy (drums). Produced by manager Marc Durand, *Rhythm Of Youth* reached number 14 in the USA in the wake of 'Safety Dance', a global smash born of a truce between electro-pop and medieval jollity that carried an anti-nuclear message over into an arresting video. A sure sign of its impact was a parody by Weird Al Yanovic. No more hits came the group's way, but their recordings still received a fair critical consideration.

Albums: *Rhythm Of Youth* (1982), *Folk Of the 80s Part III* (1984), *Pop Goes The Word* (1987).

Mental As Anything

Utilizing elements of rockabilly, rock and R&B combined with an energetic live act, Mental As Anything has proved a lasting, popular live and recording outfit. The group's debut album introduced Reg Mombasa (b. Chris O'Doherty, New Zealand; guitar/vocals), Wayne Delisle (b. Australia; drums) and the three songwriters: Martin Plaza (b. Martin Murphy, Australia; vocals/guitar), Greedy Smith (b. Andrew Smith, Australia; keyboards/harmonica/vocals) and Peter O'Doherty (b. New Zealand; bass). Despite their different writing styles, *Get Wet* achieved success, particularly with the enigmatically titled single 'The Nips Are Getting Better'. Their most fortuitous album, *Cats And Dogs*, saw the production smooth out the rough edges, and subsequent albums have maintained a high standard, with single releases constantly charting in Australia (two dozen to the end of 1990). Their single, 'Live It Up' gained considerable chart success in the UK in 1987, when it spent 13 weeks at number 3. Plaza has also released solo recordings which have enjoyed high sales in Australia.

Albums: *Get Wet* (1979), *Expresso Bongo* (1980), *Cats And Dogs* (1981), *Creatures Of Leisure* (1983), *Fundamental* (1985), *Mouth To Mouth* (1987), *Cyclone Raymond* (1989).

Mercury Rev

A six piece band from Buffalo, New York State, Mercury Rev burst onto the music scene in 1991 to unanimous critical acclaim for their enterprising mix of Pink Floyd and Dinosaur Jr dynamics. However, the sounds produced by Jonathan Donahue (vocals/guitar; ex-Flaming Lips), David Fridmann (bass), Jimmy Chambers (drums), Sean 'Grasshopper' Mackowiak (guitar), Suzanne Thorpe (flute) and David Baker (vocals/guitar) remain difficult to classify. Their album, *Yerself Is Steam*, although practically ignored in their native country, created the sort of snowballing press acclaim in the UK which has rarely been accorded a debut. The *Melody Maker*'s comment 'Universally acclaimed by UK critics as the draughtsmen behind the first, and so far only, great rock long player of 1991' was among the more conservative of the plaudits, and with only a handful of gigs under their belt they were to be seen filling support slots for the likes of My Bloody Valentine and, incredibly, Bob Dylan. Disc jockey John Peel summed up their appeal by stating that: 'Unlike many bands, you can't tell what's in their record collection'. The press undoubtedly saw them as the next step forward from the previous wave of influential US guitar bands like the Pixies, Sonic Youth and Dinosaur Jr. However, the ability to capitalize on this flying start rested, rather precariously, on their ability to remain together as a collective unit. A variety of stories filtered through concerning their self-destructive, almost psychotic behaviour. Already banned from one airline due to Donahue trying to remove Mackowiak's eye with a spoon, another minor crisis concerned Fridmann's disposal of the band's entire advance for their 'Carwash Hair' single on a holiday for his mother in Bermuda, without telling anyone. The band's writing and recording takes place in a similar, reckless manner: 'Basically, its whoever shouts loudest, or who has the biggest punch'. However, even by Mercury Rev's standards David Baker offered an unsettled musical visage, often simply stepping off the stage during performances to fetch a drink, and enriching the surreal nature of their songs with lines like 'Tonight I'll dig tunnels to your nightmare room' in 'Downs

Mercury Rev

Are Feminine Balloons'. This was drawn from *Boces*, another complex journey through multitudinous musical motifs and styles, producing a sonic anomaly drawing on the traditions of left field art rockers like Wire, Pere Ubu and Suicide. Baker was eventually deselected when his behaviour became intolerable in February 1994, with the miscreant electing to set out on a solo career instead. Reduced to a quintet, *See You On The Other Side* provided no other evidence of a reduction in the band's talents, revealing instead a more focused though no less exciting or adventurous sound.

Albums: *Yerself Is Steam* (Mint/Jungle 1991), *Boces* (Beggars Banquet 1993), *See You On The Other Side* (Beggars Banquet 1995). Compilation: *Yerself Is Steam/Lego My Ego* (Beggars Banquet 1992).

Merton Parkas

One of several late 70s mod revivalists to make the UK charts, the Merton Parkas began life as the Sneakers around 1975, playing old Motown classics. The line-up comprised brothers Mick (b. 11 September 1958; keyboards) and Danny Talbot (vocals), Neil Wurrell (bass) and Simon Smith (drums), and they chose their new name from Merton (the area of south London, they hailed from) and Parka (the ubiquitous item of mod attire). The Merton Parkas were great live favourites at the Bridgehouse in Canning Town, London but were unable to appear on the *Mods Mayday '79* live compilation because they were negotiating contracts with Beggars Banquet, after the label's first signing, the

Lurkers, had recommended them. They were one of the first neo-mod bands to record, and their debut single, 'You Need Wheels' was a hit in August 1979. Unfortunately, the rather trite lyrics had the Mertons branded as a novelty act, and they were often unfairly dismissed as bandwagon jumpers. Subsequent singles such as 'Plastic Smile', 'Give It To Me Now' (produced by Dennis Bovell of Matumbi), and 'Put Me In The Picture' failed to match the success of their debut. Mick Talbot was meanwhile making his name as an in-demand keyboard player on the Jam's *Setting Sons* and an album by the Chords. The Mertons soon disbanded and Talbot went on to join Dexys Midnight Runners and the Bureau and appeared in the Style Council. Smith, meanwhile, joined the psychedelic revivalists Mood Six, and spent a while with the Times, before returning to the reformed Mood Six.

Album: *Face In The Crowd* (1979).

Meteors

The Meteors were the first UK group to combine punk's energy with raw 50s rockabilly and invent a new musical form — psychobilly. In the USA, the Cramps had discovered a similar formula, but theirs was less violent and more dramatic. Together, they influenced a whole movement and an accompanying youth culture during the 80s, which enabled the Meteors to record some 15 albums over 10 years. In the late 70s, P. Paul Fenech (singer/guitarist) and Nigel Lewis (double bass/vocals) were churning out rockabilly and rock 'n' roll standards in acts such as the Southern Boys and, as a duo, Rock Therapy. Around 1980, drummer Mark Robertson was recruited, coinciding with a name change to Raw Deal, and they appeared on Alligator Records' *Home Crown Rockabilly* compilation. After a name change to the Meteors, the band issued a debut EP, *Meteor Madness*, jammed with compulsive, raw rockabilly, with lyrics drawing inspiration from graveyards and vampiric legend, all performed in a crazed, headlong amphetamine rush to the end of the song. 'Radioactive Kid' followed suit, and *In Heaven* was issued on their own Lost Souls label. Around the same time, the Meteors recorded an EP featuring a cover of the Electric Prunes' 'Get Me To The World On Time' under the guise of the Clapham South Escalators. Robertson left soon afterwards and was replaced by Woody, but after releasing demos, Lewis also departed to form the Tall Boys. Fenech was left to soldier on, bringing in electric bassist Mick White and Russell Jones for August 1982's 'Mutant Rock'. Another personnel change (Steve 'Ginger' Meadham joining on drums) preceded the Meteors second album, *Wreckin' Crew*, early in 1983, featuring the previous single, a wild cover of John Leyton's 'Johnny Remember Me'. That same year saw another departure, with White forming his own psychobilly act, the Guana Batz. His position was filled by Rick Ross for a national tour, captured on *Live*. Unfortunately, Ross left for the USA and in his place came Ian 'Spider' Cubitt, to record *Stampede*, 'I'm Just A Dog' and 'Fire, Fire'. *Monkey's Breath*, featuring new bassist Neville Hunt, surfaced in September 1985, alongside a cover of Creedence Clearwater Revival's 'Bad Moon Rising'. After two more unofficial offerings (*Live II* and the *Live And Loud*), the Meteors covered Jan And Dean's 'Surf City' and completed *Sewertime Blues. Don't Touch The Bang Bang Fruit* featured a version of the Stranglers' 'Go Buddy Go'. By this time, Spider's place had been filled by Toby 'Jug' Griffin and Austin H. Stones briefly deputized on bass. Lee Brown (ex-Pharaohs) took on a more permanent role on bass, in time for another punk cover in the Ramones' 'Somebody Put Something In My Drink'. Hot on its heels came *Only The Meteors Are Pure Psychobilly*, featuring new recordings of old 'classics'. Newer material was included on *Mutant Monkey And The Surfers From Zorch* later that year, although 'Rawhide' proved to be another popular cover. Even more powerful was *Undead, Unfriendly And Unstoppable*, which benefitted from new drummer Mark Howe. The release of 'Please Don't Touch' proved that, despite waves of imitators, the Meteors were still the most vibrant psychobilly band around. However, by the 90s the trail had finally run cold on the seemingly ever resilient Meteors.

Albums: *In Heaven* (Lost Soul 1981), *Wreckin' Crew* (ID 1983), *Live* (Wreckin' 1983), *Stampede* (Mad Pig 1984), *The Curse Of The Mutants* (Dojo 1984), *Monkey's Breath* (Mad Pig 1985), *Live II* (Dojo 1986), *Live And Loud* (Link 1986), *Sewertime Blues* (Anagram 1987), *Night Of The Werewolf* (Dojo 1987), *Don't Touch The Bang Bang Fruit* (Anagram 1987), *Only The Meteors Are Pure Psychobilly* (Anagram 1988), *Mutant Monkey And The Surfers From Zorch* (Anagram 1988), *Undead, Unfriendly And Unstoppable* (Anagram 1989). Compilation: *Teenagers From Outer Space* (Big Beat 1986).

Microdisney

This incendiary pop/folk group were formed in Cork, Eire, in 1980. There was little cohesion in their early formations; 'We used to be much more frenzied in those days, a Fall-type mess, and our line up was always changing. Originally Ocan (O'Hagan) was going to play guitar and I (Cathal Coughlan) was going to recite poetry, then one week it was guitar, bass, drums, then guitar keyboard and violin, then we had a drum machine. . .' After settling on the more traditional formation of drums, guitars, bass and keyboards, the band began releasing singles which eventually were collected together on *We Hate You White South African Bastards*. The title was typically inflammatory, and in direct opposition to that of their long-playing debut, *Everybody Is Fantastic*. An early clue to their subversive nature, on the surface Microdisney were purveyors of accessible and restrained pop music. This attracted Virgin Records, but the band had a dark edge in Coughlan's bitter lyricism. Their Virgin debut, 'Town To Town', dented the lower regions of the charts and was quickly followed by *Crooked Mile*. However, Microdisney elected to bite the hand that fed them with the near hit 'Singer's Hampstead Home', which thinly masked an attack on Virgin's fallen idol, Boy George. They bowed out with *39 Minutes*, by which time the vitriol was really flowing, counter-balanced as ever by O'Hagan's delicate country guitar. Despite critical acclaim, Microdisney's sales had remained disappointingly in the cult bracket. O'Hagan went on to release a solo album in 1990 (*High Llamas*), while Coughlan's Fatima Mansions has done much to spice up the late 80s and early 90s.

Albums: *Everybody Is Fantastic* (1984), *We Hate You White South African Bastards* (1984), *The Clock Comes Down The Stairs* (1985), *Crooked Mile* (1987), *39 Minutes* (1988), *Gale Force Wind* (1988).

Midnight Oil

Formed in Sydney, New South Wales, in 1975, and known as Farm, this strident band has pioneered its own course in Australian rock without relying on the established network of agencies and record companies. The original nucleus of the band comprised Martin Rotsey (guitar), Rob Hirst (drums) and Jim Moginie (guitar). They were later joined by law student Peter Garrett (lead vocals). The outfit became notorious for always insisting on total control over its recorded product and media releases, including photos, and when booking agencies denied the band gigs, the members organized their own venues and tours, taking advantage of the group's large following on the alternative rock scene. Joined by Dwayne 'Bones' Hillman (bass) in 1977 and changing their name to Midnight Oil, the group took a couple of album releases to refine its songwriting style, principally by Moginie and Hirst. As *Head Injuries* went gold in Australia, the imposing shaven-headed Garrett, who had by now received his law degree, began to make known his firm views on politics. Having signed a world-wide deal with CBS/Columbia, it was *10,9,8,7,6,5,4,3,2,1*, which saw the band gain mainstream radio airplay. Featuring songs about the environment, anti-nuclear sentiments, anti-war songs and powerful anthems of anti-establishment; it also propelled the band into the international market place. The

Microdisney

band performed at many charity concerts, promoting Koori (Australian aborigines) causes in Australia and the loquacious Garrett almost gained a seat in the Australian Parliament in 1984 while standing for the Nuclear Disarmament Party. The following album saw the band tour the USA and Europe, and *Rolling Stone* writers voted the album one of the best of 1989, despite a low profile there. While many regard *Red Sails In The Sunset* as their best work, the subsequent albums have been equally highly regarded. The group's peak album chart positions in the UK and USA were achieved with *Diesel And Dust* reaching the UK Top 20 and US number 21, while in the US the follow-up, *Blue Sky Mining* emulated that position. The group continued its antagonistic attitude towards major industrial companies in 1990, by organizing a protest concert outside the Manhattan offices of the Exxon oil company which was responsible for the Valdez oil slick in Alaska.

Albums: *Midnight Oil* (1978), *Head Injuries* (1979), *Place Without A Postcard* (1981), *10,9,8,7,6,5,4,3,2,1* (1982), *Red Sails In The Sunset* (1985), *Diesel And Dust* (1987), *Blue Sky Mining* (1990), *Scream In Blue-Live* (1992), *Earth And Sun And Moon* (1993).

Further reading: *Strict Rules*, Andrew McMillan.

Midway Still

UK indie rock band whose profile initially rose through supports to the likes of Cud and the more musically similar Mega City Four. Boasting a sound which also earned comparisons to Teenage Fanclub or Dinosaur Jr, the band comprised Paul Thomson (guitar/vocals), Declan Kelly (drums) and Jan aka John Kanopka (bass). Both of the latter were formerly members of USMF. Their first single, 'I Won't Try', emerged on Roughneck records (a subsidiary of Fire Records) in July 1991. Thematically it was dedicated to their pet python and attempts to feed it with mice who bred exponentially. Thomson was an interesting character, having met Keith Moon (Who) on holiday as a child, and sharing baths with a young Michela Strachan. Also in childhood, alas. The band were easily distinguished by their taste in Hawaiian shirts, though their efforts at running a competition in the *New Musical Express* to get a reader to design a logo for them ended in disaster. So too did their short but entertaining career with diminishing press returns for their second long player in 1993. As its title suggested, life may indeed by too long, but musical careers can also be disastrously short.

Album: *Dial Square* (Roughneck 1992), *Life's Too Long* (Roughneck 1993).

Mighty Lemon Drops

This UK independent label pop band broke through in 1985 with the highly-touted 'Like An Angel'. The band featured Paul Marsh (vocals/guitar), David Newton (guitar), Tony Linehan (bass) and Keith Rowley (drums), who had all enjoyed chequered careers in numerous Wolverhampton outfits. Newton had previously played with Active Restraint in 1982, which also included Marsh and Linehan. They in turn played regularly alongside Another Dream, and both bands featured on single releases by local label Watchdog Video And Records. Newton and Neal Cook of Another

Dream put together the Wild Flowers, alongside Dave Atherton (also ex-Another Dream; guitar/keyboards), Pete Waldron (bass) and Dave Fisher (drums). After a further single and a support to Simple Minds, Newton moved on once more, forming the Mighty Lemon Drops with Marsh and Linehan. The temporary drummer was Martin Gilks (later with the Wonder Stuff), before Keith Rowley stepped in full-time. As part of the *New Musical Express*' 'C-86' generation, they were snapped up by Chrysalis Records. Despite the charm of several singles in an Echo And The Bunnymen vein, they failed to translate independent chart success into hits. Although they were dropped by Chrysalis after three albums, they remained favourites on the US college circuit. Sadly this was not enough to sustain them, and they broke up in the early 90s leaving a compilation of live tracks and demos for release on Overground Records.

Albums: *Happy Head* (Chrysalis 1986), *World Without End* (Chrysalis 1988), *Sound* (Chyrsalis 1991), *All The Way - Live In Cincinnati* (Overground 1993).

Mighty Mighty

Like many of the UK indie guitar pop favourites of the mid-80s, Birmingham, UK's Mighty Mighty owed more than a passing debt to Orange Juice and the Postcard Records label. Hugh Harkin (vocals/occasional harp), Mick Geoghegan (guitar/lyric writer), brother Peter (organ/guitar), David Hennessy (drums) and Russell Burton (bass/vocals) first appeared as part of the *New Musical Express*/ICA Rock Week gigs and accompanying *C86* cassette compilation. This coincided nicely with Mighty Mighty's debut single, the catchy 'Everybody Knows The Monkey', in May 1986; like July's 'Is There Anyone Out There?' 12-inch, it was issued on the band's own Girlie label. However, aspiring local label Chapter 22 soon snapped them up, for a string of classy pop tunes that fared well on the independent sector. After December's 'Throwaway' (originally half of a fanzine flexidisc) came the raunchy 'Built Like A Car' in May 1987, 'One Way' in October and the attractive 'Born In A Maisonette' in the New Year. Unfortunately, Mighty Mighty failed to develop, and by the time *Sharks* was released in February 1988, their formula had worn thin. Apart from the excellent 'Blue And Green', *Sharks* had little to offer in the way of new ideas at a time when the independent scene was rapidly hardening. The ensuing collapse of the band was inevitable.

Album: *Sharks* (Chapter 22 1988).

Milkshakes

This UK, Chatham, Kent-based group were originally conceived in the late 70s by Pop Rivit roadies Mickey Hampshire and Banana Bertie as Mickey And The Milkshakes. Often appearing on the same circuit as fellow Medway town bands, the Dentists and the Prisoners, the group performed as a 'psychobilly' outfit, supporting the Pop Rivits from time to time with Wreckless Eric covers. Pop Rivit leader Billy Childish then began writing with Hampshire and in 1980 formed a new version of Mickey And The Milkshakes. Eventually settling on a line-up of Childish and Hampshire (guitars/vocals), Russ Wilkins (bass) and Bruce Brand (drums), they started recording a

string of albums featuring various R&B classics plus original material. After the first album they truncated their name. Later on, when John Agnew replaced Wilkins, they began to refer to themselves as Thee Milkshakes. In addition to their normal activities of gigging and recording, they also acted as the backing band to an all-girl vocal trio called the Del Monas. As prolific releasers of album material, The(e) Milkshakes were only modestly successful with singles, achieving two UK independent Top 20 hits with 'Brand New Cadillac' (1984) and 'Ambassadors Of Love' (1985). The group split in 1984 (although Milkshake material continued to be released long after), with Childish going on to form the equally productive Thee Mighty Caesars.
Albums: *Talkin' 'Bout Milkshakes* (1981), *Fourteen Rhythm And Blues Greats* (1982), *After School Session* (1983), *Milkshakes IV (The Men With The Golden Guitars)* (1983), *20 Rock And Roll Hits Of The 50s & 60s* (1984), *Nothing Can Stop These Men* (1984), *The Milkshakes In Germany* (1984), *Thee Knights Of Trash* (1984), *They Came, They Saw, They Conquered* (1985), *The Last Night Down At The Mic Club* (1986), *The 107 Tapes* (1986), *The Milkshakes Vs The Prisoners Live* (1987), *The Milkshakes Revenge* (1987), *Live From Chatham* (1987), *Still Talking 'Bout* (1992).

Ministry

'The difference between Ministry and other bands is that we sold out before we even started.' Alain Jourgensen (b. Havana, Cuba) began producing music under the Ministry name in the early 80s in Chicago, but was most unhappy with the Euro-pop direction in which his record company pushed him for *With Sympathy*, later describing it as 'that first abortion of an album'. Ministry took on a more acceptable shape for Jourgensen after *Twitch*, with the addition of Paul Barker (b. Palo Alto, California, USA) on bass/keyboards and drummer Bill Rieflin to Jourgensen's guitar/vocals/keyboards. The band evolved their own brand of guitar-based industrial metal, considering *The Land Of Rape And Honey* to be their true debut, and employed a variety of guest musicians for both live and studio work, with regular contributions from ex-Rigor Mortis guitarist Mike Scaccia and ex-Finitribe vocalist Chris Connelly. Despite Jourgensen's dislike of touring, Ministry developed a stunning live show, with a backdrop of disturbing visual images to accompany the intense musical barrage, and the sinister figure of Jourgensen taking centre stage behind a bone-encrusted mike stand. *In Case You Didn't Feel Like Showing Up (Live)* displays the metamorphosis of the songs as the band extend themselves in concert. At this stage, Jourgensen and Barker were working on numerous other studio projects in a variety of styles, including Lard with Jello Biafra, but Ministry remained one of two main acts. The other, the outrageous Revolting Cocks, served as a more blatantly humorous outlet for the pair's creative talents, in contrast to the dark anger and socio-political themes of Ministry. As alternative culture became more acceptable to the mainstream, Ministry achieved major success with *Psalm 69* (subtitled *The Way To Succeed And The Way To Suck Eggs*), helped by the popularity on MTV of 'Jesus Built My Hotrod', featuring a guest vocal and lyric from Butthole Surfer Gibby Haynes. The band were a huge draw on the 1992 Lollapalooza tour, playing second on the bill, and their debut European tour later that year was also a resounding success. In 1994 Rieflin was replaced on the drumstool by former Didjits' drummer Ray Washam.
Albums: *With Sympathy* (Arista 1983), *Twelve Inch Singles 1981-1984* (Wax Trax 1984), *Twitch* (Sire 1986), *The Land Of Rape And Honey* (Sire 1988), *The Mind Is A Terrible Thing To Taste* (Sire 1989), *In Case You Didn't Feel Like Showing Up (Live)* (Sire 1990), *Psalm 69* (Sire/Warners 1992).

Mink DeVille

The foundation of this unit was guitarist and songwriter Willy DeVille (b. 27 August 1953, New York City, New York, USA). He arrived in London in 1971 to form a band but, unable to find the right musicians, performed as a solo artist before heading to San Francisco and assembling the embryonic Mink DeVille. The basic trio became Willy (vocals/guitar/harmonica), Ruben Siguenza (bass) and Thomas R. Allen (drums). Allen had previously played with various blues musicians. They relocated to New York and recruited Louie X Erlanger on guitar. The band, by this time a wonderful live unit, recorded three tracks for the *Live At CBGB's* compilation and then in 1977 released their debut, which included the hit single 'Spanish Stroll'. The album, produced by Jack Nitzsche, also included a version of the Patti And The Emblems' classic, 'Mixed Up Shook Up'. The second album *Return To Magenta* was publicised by releasing 'Soul Twist' on purple vinyl, but overall the album was an unhappy compromise between the group's original new wave sound and Willy DeVille's more soulful ambitions. Like the debut, it included a Moon Martin cover, 'Rolene'. For the third album, *Le Chat Blue*, in 1980, the band comprised Willy and Erlanger, plus Kenny Margolis (keyboards), Jerry Scheff (bass), Ron Tutt (drums) and Steve Douglas (saxophone). Although it featured co-writing credits by songwriter Doc Pomus (Joe Turner, Dion, Drifters), the album failed to spark. *Savoir Faire* collected the best of the three Capitol albums, after which the band moved to Atlantic Records. Unfortunately, *Coup De Grâce* also failed to signal a revival. Despite Nitzsche returning to produce, only the occasional song had Mink DeVille's previous edge. Things improved, though, with the release of *Where Angels Fear To Tread* which removed some of the over-produced clutter from their sound. Willy DeVille's new songs paid tribute to his soul heroes without affecting the band's new-found strength. *Sportin' Life* continued the improvement, although afterwards De Ville left to renew his solo career.
Albums: *Mike DeVille* (Capitol 1977), *Return To Magenta* (Capitol 1978), *Le Chat Bleu* (Capitol 1980), *Coup De Grâce* (Atlantic 1981), *Where Angels Fear To Tread* (Atlantic 1983), *Sportin' Life* (Atlantic 1985), *Cabretta* (Razor 1987). Compilation: *Savoir Faire* (Capitol 1981).

Minutemen

Formed in 1980 in San Pedro, California, USA, and originally known as the Reactionaries. This influential hardcore trio initially comprised D. Boon (guitar/vocals), Mike Watt (bass) and Frank Tonche (drums), but the last named was replaced by George Hurley prior to recording. Although the trio donated tracks to several independent compilations, notably for the pivotal Radio Tokyo Tapes and the Posh Boy and New Alliance labels, their association with SST Records resulted in some of the genre's most impressive recordings. The unfettered rage of their early work was less apparent on *Buzz Or Howl Under The Influence Of Heat* and *Project: Mersh*, ('Mersh' is San Pedro slang for 'commercial'), but *Double Nickels On The Dime* and *3-Way Tie (For Last)* showed an undeterred passion and commitment. The Minutemen came to a premature end in 1986 following the death of D. Boon. Watt and Hurley decided to drop the group's name, and in its place formed Firehose with guitarist Ed Crawford.

Albums: *The Punchline* (1980), *Bean Spill* (1982), *What Makes A Man Start Fires* (1983), *Buzz Or Howl Under The Influence Of Heat* (1983), *Politics Of Time* (1984), *Double Nickels On The Dime* (1984), *Project: Mersh* (1985), *3-Way Tie (For Last)* (1986), *Ballot Result* (1987). Compilations: *My First Bells* (1985), *Post-Mersh Volume 1* (1985), *Post-Mersh Volume 2* (1987), *Post-Mersh Volume 3* (1989), *What Makes A Man Start Fires* (1991).

Miranda Sex Garden

Widely tagged with the terms 'classical' and 'pretentious' by UK critics, Miranda Sex Garden have faced sterner tests than that, including facing 20,000 unimpressed Depeche Mode fans on tour. The group comprise singer/songwriter Katharine Blake, and her cohorts, Ben Golomstock (keyboards), Donna McKevitt (violin) and Trevor Sharpe (percussion), having dropped original member Kelly McClusker, who formed the band with Blake after graduating from music college (Purcell School Of Music). All are accomplished musicians, and the three women each have strong falsetto voices. They spent their early days busking sixteenth century madrigals on London's underground, with an impressed Barry Adamson catching one performance on Portobello Road. Later they would contribute to his *Delusion* soundtrack. Their debut release comprised two versions of the madrigal 'Gush Forth My Tears', an *a cappela* treatment on one side, and a dance version on the other. Their talents won them a reception which was roughly equal in incredulity and wonder, and their voices soon appeared on Derek Jarman's soundtrack to *Blue* (on an unlikely song entitled 'Muff Diving Size Queen'). *Fairytales*, meanwhile, concerned sado-masochism, and they have actually played gigs under the title of Waltzing Maggots at fetish clubs, which included Blake performing half naked in Nazi regalia (finally destroying utterly their early press reputation for Victorian-esque primness).

Albums: *Madra* (Mute 1991), *Iris* (Mute 1992, mini-album), *Suspiria* (Mute 1993), *Fairytales Of Slavery* (Mute 1994).

Misfits

Like the Thirteenth Floor Elevators in the 60s and the New York Dolls in the early 70s, this US punk band was swiftly surrounded in a cloak of mythology and cult appeal. Long after their demise (they played their last live gig in 1983), their obscure US-only records were fetching large sums of money in collecting circles, by those fascinated by the band's spine-chilling mix of horror-movie imagery and hardcore. The Misfits were formed in New Jersey, New York, in 1977 by Gerry Only (bass) and Glenn Danzig (vocals) and, like many aspiring new wave acts, played in venues like CBGB's, adding guitarist Bobby Steele and drummer Joey Image. Later that year, 'Cough Cool' became their first single on their own Plan 9 label. A four-track EP, *Bullet* (in a sleeve showing J.F. Kennedy's assassination), was recorded before their debut album, and was followed by 'Horror Business'. A third single, 'Night Of The Living Dead', surfaced in 1979, the reference to the classic George A. Romero film revealing the Misfits' continued fascination with blood-and-guts horror. Then came an EP, *Three Hits From Hell*, recorded in 1980, but not issued until the following April, and a seasonal October single, 'Halloween'. Having now lost Steele to the Undead, replaced by Jerry's brother Doyle, Googy (aka Eerie Von) stepped in on drums during a European tour with the Damned as Joey's narcotic problems worsened. The Misfits rounded off 1981 by recording the seven-track mini-album *Evilive*, originally sold through the band's Fiend fan club, which also secured a German 12-inch release. The band's only original UK release was a 12-inch EP, *Beware*. Other Misfits releases included several patchy albums which failed to capture their live impact: 1982's *Walk Among Us*, *Earth A.D.* (aka *Wolfblood*) and the posthumous brace, *Legacy Of Brutality* and *Misfits*. Danzig issued his first solo single in 1981, 'Who Killed Marilyn?', later forming Samhain with Misfits' drummer Eerie Von. He was subsequently venerated in heavy metal magazines in the late 80s as his eponymous Danzig vehicle gained ground. The other Misfits mainstays, brothers Jerry and Doyle, formed the hapless Kryst The Conqueror, who released one five song EP with the help of Skid Row guitarist David Sabo.

Albums: *Beware* (Cherry Red 1979, mini-album), *Evilive* (Fiend 1981, mini-album), *Walk Among Us* (Ruby 1982), *Earth A.D.* (Plan 9 1983). Compilations: *Legacy Of Brutality* (Plan 9 1985), *The Misfits* (Plan 9 1986), *Evilive* (Plan 9 1987, expanded version of 1981 mini-album).

Mission

UK rock band who evolved from the Sisters Of Mercy, when Wayne Hussey (b. 26 May 1959, Bristol, England; ex-Walkie Talkies, Dead Or Alive) and Craig Adams split from Andrew Eldritch. They quickly recruited drummer Mick Brown (ex-Red Lorry, Yellow Lorry) and guitarist Simon Hinkler (ex-Artery). The original choice of title was the Sisterhood, which led to an undignified series of exchanges in the press between the band and Eldritch. In order to negate their use of the name, Eldritch put out a single under the name Sisterhood on his own Merciful Release label. Thus the title the Mission was selected instead. After two successful independent singles on the Chapter 22 label, they signed to Mercury in the autumn of 1986. Their major label debut, 'Stay With Me', entered the UK singles charts while the band worked on their debut album. *God's Own Medicine* was the outcome, revealing a tendency towards straightforward rock, and attracting criticism for its bombast. A heavy touring schedule ensued, with the band's on-stage antics attracting at least as much attention as their performances. A particularly indulgent tour of America saw Adams shipped home suffering from exhaustion. His temporary replacement on bass was Pete Turner. After headlining the Reading Festival, they began work on a new album under the auspices of Led Zeppelin bass player John Paul Jones as producer. *Children* was even more successful than its predecessor, reaching number 2 in the UK album charts, despite the customary critical disdain. 1990 brought 'Butterfly On A Wheel' as a single, providing further ammunition for accusations that the band were simply dredging up rock history. In February, the long-delayed third album, *Carved In Sand,* was released, revealing a more sophisticated approach to songwriting. During the world tour to promote the album, both Hinkler and Hussey became ill because of the excessive regime. Hinkler departed suddenly when they reached Toronto, leaving Dave Wolfenden to provide guitar for the rest of the tour. On their return, Paul Etchells took over the position on a more permanent basis. Hussey had meanwhile joined with the Wonder Stuff in proposing a fund-raising concert in London under the banner The Day Of Conscience, but the event self-destructed with a barrage of allegations about commercial intrusion. In a similar vein over the Christmas period, members of the band joined with Slade's Noddy Holder and Jim Lea to re-record 'Merry Xmas Everybody' for charity. However, 1992 would bring numerous further personnel difficulties. Craig Adams returned to Brighton, while Hussey brought in Andy Hobson (bass), Rik Carter (keyboards) and Mark Gemini Thwaite (guitar). A reflective Hussey, promoting the *Sum And Substance* compilation, would concede: 'We had an overblown sense of melodrama. It was great - pompous songs, big grand statements. We've never attempted to do anything that's innovative'. A nation of rock critics found something to agree with Hussey on at last.

Albums: *God's Own Medicine* (Mercury 1986), *Children* (Mercury 1988), *Carved In Sand* (Mercury 1990), *Masque* (Mercury 1992). Compilations: *The First Chapter* (Mercury 1987), *Grains Of Sand* (Mercury 1990), *Sum And Substance* (Vertigo 1994).

Videos: *South America* (1989), *Crusade* (1991), *From Dusk To Dawn* (1991), *Waves Upon The Sand* (1991), *Sum And Substance* (1994).

Further reading: *The Mission - Names Are Tombstones Baby*, Martin Roach with Neil Perry.

Mission Of Burma

Once cited as 'the ultimate collision of punk and pop', Boston, Massachusetts band Mission Of Burma were compared by others to the UK's art terrorists Wire. Certainly, they invoked a similar level of rapture among US critics and, much like Wire, self-consciously avoided the glare of the mainstream. The original line-up of Clint Conley (bass), Peter Prescott (drums), and Roger Miller (guitar) were greatly influential to a number of more commercially viable outfits. They formed in 1979, when Miller and Conley moved to Boston from Ann Arbor and New York respectively. They briefly put together Moving Parts before joining with resident Bostonian Prescott. Burma kicked off with supports for the UK's Gang Of Four. These went well and the Leeds funksters continued to sponsor them early in their development. They would split in 1985 after a career which embraced well defined but chaotic live and recorded work. Through a series of reissues on the venerated underground label, Taang! Recordrs, critics have now reassessed their historical importance. Among their staunchest admirers are R.E.M., who regularly covered 'Academy Flight Song' in their live sets. Prescott would go on to SST recording artists Volcano Suns.

Albums: *Vs* (Ace Of Hearts 1982), *The Horrible Truth About Burma Live* (Ace Of Hearts 1985), *Forget* (Taang! 1988), *Let There Be Burma* (Taang! 1990). Compilation: *Mission Of Burma* (Rykodisc 1988).

Mo-Dettes

Despite the name, the timing of their appearance on the music scene, and the fact that they covered the Rolling Stones' 'Paint It Black', the Mo-Dettes were not modettes and disliked anyone who said they were. They were originally formed for a one-off gig at the Acklam Hall, supporting the Vincent Units. Their line-up was built around Kate Korus (b. Katherine Corris, New York, USA; guitar), who played with the Castrators before lasting just three gigs with the earliest line-up of the Slits. She left (to be replaced by Viv Albertine) and attempted to form several bands. Korus took a long time finding musicians with whom she was happy, but gradually she came across (on the set of *The Great Rock 'N' Roll Swindle* where both had non-acting jobs) drummer June Miles-Kingston (the sister of Bob Kingston of Tenpole Tudor) and bassist Jane Crockford. Crockford had previously played in the Banks Of Dresden with Richard Dudanski. Through a mutual friend they met Ramona Carlier, a singer from Switzerland whose experience to date had been backing vocals at a few sessions plus a one-off party gig with a band called the Bomberettes, and had been in England about a year. The first product of their labours was 'White Mice' - on their own Mode label through Rough Trade. Ramona left late in 1981 to start a solo career, and was replaced by Sue Slack. Soon after, Korus split to be replaced by Melissa Ritter. The final split came shortly after in 1982, owing to further internal friction. Miles-Kingston moved on to Fun Boy Three's backing band, before she produced a solo single for Go! Discs, joined the Communards and sang on various sessions. Kate Korus also released a single with Jenny of the Belle Stars.

Album: *The Story So Far* (1980).

Mock Turtles

With their promising UK hit single, 'Can You Dig It?', the Mock Turtles followed a line of success stories that had emanated from Manchester, England, between 1989 and 1991. Like many of their contemporaries, the band had been playing the independent circuit for several years before realizing their potential. The band's lynch-pin was singer/guitarist/songwriter Martin Coogan, who had previously fronted Judge Happiness, won a Salford University talent contest and subsequently issued a single, 'Hey Judge', on the Mynah label in 1985. As the Mock Turtles, Coogan was joined by Steve Green (bass), Krzysztof Korab (keyboards) and Steve Cowen (drums), and their recordings surfaced on several of the Imaginary label's popular tribute compilations (covering Syd Barrett's 'No Good Trying', Captain Beefheart's 'Big-Eyed Beans From Venus', the Kinks' 'Big Sky', the Byrds' 'Why' and the Velvet

Underground's 'Pale Blue Eyes'), illustrating their eclectic tastez. Meanwhile, the band's first 12-inch EP, *Pomona*, was issued in 1987, and although it owed an obvious debt to early David Bowie and veered towards the overblown the confidence of musicians, string arrangements and songwriting was obvious. Guitarist Martin Glyn Murray joined the band in time for 'The Wicker Man' (inspired by the film of the same name), followed by 'And Then She Smiles'. From pure folk to powerful songs verging on the pompous, the Mock Turtles conveyed a distinctive feel within their music. But it was their next single, 1990's 'Lay Me Down', which hinted at bigger things, sporting a sparse yet infectious shuffling backbeat. Hot on its heels came a well-received debut album, *Turtle Soup*, in June, which fared well on the independent chart, as did the band's collaboration with one of Coogan's long-time influences, Bill Nelson, 'Take Your Time' (the b-side of their next single, 'Magic Boomerang'). This was enough to lure Siren Records, and for their first major label single, the band chose to rework the b-side of 'Lay Me Down', 'Can You Dig It?'. The single was an instant hit with BBC television's *Top Of The Pops* appearances to match, and in its wake came another reissue of sorts, 'And Then She Smiles'. This failed to consolidate the success of 'Can You Dig It', and the Mock Turtles' highly commercial *Two Sides* suffered from a low profile, despite its abundance of musical muscle and carefully-crafted songs. In the meantime, Imaginary compiled most of their early single tracks on *1987-90*, for those newcomers who had missed them first time around. However, the Mock Turtle's rapid progress soon transmuted into an equally swift decline. The band dissolved when Coogan formed a new band with Korab and Green after Murray left to pursue an acting career.
Albums: *Turtle Soup* (Imaginary 1990) *Two Sides* (Two Sides 1991). Compilation: *1987-90* (Imaginary 1991).

Models

The Models were Australia's premier 'new wave' band to emerge from the punk period in the second half of 1978. Original member Sean Kelly (guitar/vocals) and James Freud (bass; who joined in 1982), provided much of the Models' song material. Both had played together previously in Melbourne punk band, the Teenage Radio Stars. The fluctuating line-up of the Models has in the past included notables Andrew Duffield (keyboards; replaced in 1983 by Roger Mason), drummers Janis 'Johnny Crash' Friedenfields and Barton Price, Mark Ferrie (bass/vocals) and James Valentine (keyboards). The band recorded often, and despite having substantial success on the Australian alternative charts, toured frequently and extensively to repay debts that would eventually lead to acrimony between the principal songwriters. Commercial success finally came in 1985 with the 'Out Of Sight Out Of Mind' single and album, and the 'Barbados' single. The band's material was either dense rock music or melodic pop, which alienated its long-standing fans. Since the band broke up in 1987, Freud has recorded a solo album, but despite its high production costs, it did not perform very well. Kelly, eased himself back into the limelight by co-forming a band called the Absent Friends with various other well-known Australian musicians, including INXS bassist, Garry Beers. Initially conceived as a part-time affair, the band developed into a more fully-fledged outfit which earned high respect around Sydney. Albums: *Alphabetacharliedeltaechofoxtrot* (1980), *Local And/Or General* (1981), *Pleasure Of Your Company* (1983), *Out Of Sight Out Of Mind* (1985), *Media* (1986). Absent Friends *Here's Looking Up Your Address* (1990).

Modern English

Formed in Colchester, Essex, England, in 1979, Modern English's debut, *Mesh And Lace* was released in suitably arty packaging by 4AD Records two years later. It drew heavily on the gloom rock sound already patented by bands like Joy Division, and had little originality or focus. *After The Snow*, recorded by the same line-up of Robbie Gray (vocals), Gary McDowell (guitar/vocals), Richard Brown (drums), Mick Conroy (bass /vocals) and Stephen Walker (keyboards), was a minor revelation, as they introduced warmth and strong guitar harmonies, rejecting the tinny bleakness of the debut. It was well-received in the USA, and the band re-located to New York to consolidate a popularity encouraged by college radio. *Richochet Days* had a crisper production but less creative experimentation. By *Stop Start*, released by Sire Records in 1986, Stephen Walker and Richard Brown had left, and Aaron Davidson (keyboards/guitar) had joined. The band had tried too hard for commercial approval and was left with an unspecific rock/pop sound which caused them to split soon afterwards. Robbie Gray returned to England to form a new group. They reconvened in 1990 for *Pillow-Lips*, but to little interest
Albums: *Mesh And Lace* (4AD 1981), *After The Snow* (Sire 1982), *Richochet Days* (Sire 1984), *Stop Start* (Sire 1986), *Pillow Lips* (TVT 1990).

Modern Lovers

Formed in Boston, Massachusetts, USA, the Modern Lovers revolved around the talents of uncompromising singer/songwriter Jonathan Richman (b. May 1951, Boston, Massachusetts, USA). The group, which included Jerry Harrison (b. 21 February 1949, Milwaukee, Wisconsin, USA; guitar - later of Talking Heads), Ernie Brooks (bass) and future Cars drummer David Robinson, offered an inspired amalgam of 50s pop, garage bands, girl groups and the Velvet Underground, a style which both engendered a cult following and attracted the interest of ex-Velvet member John Cale, then a staff producer at Warner Brothers. However, having completed a series of demos, a disillusioned Richman disbanded the line-up and retreated to Boston, although Cale marked their association by recording his protégé's composition, 'Pablo Picasso', on *Helen Of Troy* (1975). In 1976, the unfinished tracks were purchased by the newly-founded Beserkley Records label, which remixed the masters, added two new performances and released the package as *The Modern Lovers*. The company also signed Richman, whose new album, *Jonathan Richman And The Modern Lovers*, was confusingly issued within months of the first selection. The second set revealed a less intensive talent, and his regression into almost child-like simplicity was confirmed on *Rock 'N' Roll With The Modern Lovers*. Richman's new group - Leroy Radcliffe (guitar), Greg 'Curly'

Kerenen (bass) and D. Smart (drums) - was purely acoustic and featured a repertoire which, by including 'The Ice-Cream Man', 'Hey There Little Insect', 'The Wheels On The Bus' and 'I'm A Little Aeroplane', was deemed enchanting or irritating, according to taste. The Modern Lovers nonetheless enjoyed two surprise UK hits with 'Roadrunner' and 'Egyptian Reggae', which reached numbers 11 and 5, respectively, in 1977. However, as the unit was undeniably a vehicle for Richman's quirky vision, the Modern Lovers' name was dropped the following year when the singer embarked on a solo tour. He has nonetheless revived the title on occasions, notably on *It's Time For Jonathan Richman And The Modern Lovers* and *Modern Lovers 88*.

Albums: *The Modern Lovers* (Beserkley 1976), *Jonathan Richman And The Modern Lovers* (Beserkley 1976), *Rock 'N' Roll With The Modern Lovers* (Beserkley 1977), *The Modern Lovers Live* (Beserkley 1977), *It's Time For Jonathan Richman And The Modern Lovers* (Upside 1986), *Modern Lovers 88* (Rounder 1988). Compilations: *The Original Modern Lovers* (Bomp 1981, early recordings), *Jonathan Richman And The Modern Lovers - 23 Great Recordings* (Beserkley 1990).

Momus

b. Nicholas Currie, 1960, Paisley, Scotland. After living in Canada for a spell as a teenager, Currie returned to the UK and, during the mid-80s, began recording on the independent circuit. His primary influence was Jacques Brel, whose earthy sexuality soon infiltrated Momus' work. An EP, *Beast With No Backs*, on El Records, garnered minor critical attention, as did the album *Circus Maximus*. Momus promised a follow-up, *The Poison Boyfriend*, but that title was abandoned after he signed with Creation Records. Finally, in 1988, Momus returned with *Tender Pervert*, a lacerating document of sexual and emotional psychoanalysis. His strength was his strong narrative line, particularly on songs such as 'Love On Ice' and 'Bishonen'. The following year, he issued *Don't Stop The Night*, which featured a more electronic, dance-orientated approach. One song, 'Righthand Heart', was a reworking of an essentially acoustic song on the previous album. Momus's lack of live experience has so far prevented any major excursion into performing. His 1991 album, *Hippopotamomus*, was less well received and was greeted with a zero out of 10 rating in the *New Musical Express* as a result of its moral perversity. The artist no doubt appreciated the irony. The early 90s saw Currie build on his audience within the gay community (parts of which admired his openess), contributing one track, 'Cocksucking Lesbian Man', to Derek Jarman's *Blue* movie. *Philosophy Of Momus* continued Curry's forays into the netherworld of twisted sexuality, utilising a third person mechanism as a defence against accusations of amorality.

Albums: *Circus Maximus* (El 1986), *The Poison Boyfriend* (Creation 1987), *Tender Pervert* (Creation 1988), *Don't Stop The Night* (Creation 1989), *Hippopotamomus* (Creation 1991), *Voyager* (Creation 1992), *The Ultracomformist* (Creation 1992), *Timelord* (Creation 1993), *The Philosophy Of Momus* (Cherry Red 1995). Compilation: *Monsters Of Love - Singles 1985-90* (Creation 1990).

Further reading: *Lust Of A Moron: The Lyrics Of Momus*, Momus.

Monochrome Set

Any all-encompassing classification of the Monochrome Set's music would be difficult. During a sporadic career that has spanned as many musical styles as it has record labels, they have been on the verge of breaking to a wider audience on a number of occasions. Formed in the UK during late 1976, Andy Warren (bass), Lester Square (guitar) and Bid (guitar/vocals) were playing in the B-Sides with Adam Ant. When the B-Sides became Adam And The Ants, Bid and Lester Square left. They formed the Monochrome Set in January 1978, later joined by Warren in 1979 after his role on the debut Ants album. With Jeremy Harrington (bass; ex-Gloria Mundi and Mean Street) and J.D. Haney (drums; ex-Art Attacks), the band issued singles during 1979-80 for Rough Trade Records including 'He's Frank', 'Eine Symphonie Des Graeuns', 'The Monochrome Set' and 'He's Frank (Slight Return)', each completely different in style and content. Their debut, *The Strange Boutique*, skirted the UK charts. After the title track came further singles '405 Lines' and 'Apocalypso', and a second album, *Love Zombies*. Lex Crane briefly sat in on drums before ex-Soft Boys member Morris Windsor joined for the release of the brilliant sex satire, 'The Mating Game', in July 1982, followed by 'Cast A Long Shadow' and the memorable *Eligible Bachelors*. By this time Carrie Booth had joined on keyboards while Nick Wesolowski took up the drums and Foz the guitar soon after. *Volume, Brilliance, Contrast*, compiled their Rough Trade recordings and selected BBC Radio 1 sessions, and coincided with another indie hit, 'Jet Set Junta' (like many Monochrome Set compositions deflating class/monetary division). 'Jacob's Ladder' seemed a sure-fire hit for 1985, but like 'Wallflower' later that year and the charming *The Lost Weekend*, eluded the charts. Disheartened, the band split and it was left to Cherry Red's El subsidiary to issue a sympathetic retrospective, *Fin! Live*, a year later. Various collections filtered out over the next three years (*Colour Transmission* featured much of the DinDisc material, while *Westminster Affair* highlighted their earliest recordings). In December 1989 the band reformed, with Bid, Lester and Warren joined by Orson Presence on guitar and keyboards, marking their return with *Dante's Casino*. From there on they have concentrated primarily on their cult following in the Far East, with frequent tours there.

Albums: *The Strange Boutique* (DinDisc 1980), *Love Zombies* (DinDisc 1980), *Eligible Bachelors* (Cherry Red 1982), *The Lost Weekend* (Blanco y Negro 1985), *Dante's Casino* (Vinyl Japan 1990), *Charade* (Cherry Red 1993), *Misere* (Cherry Red 1994). Compilations: *Volume, Brilliance, Contrast* (Cherry Red 1983), *Fin! Live* (El 1985), *Colour Transmission* (Virgin 1987), *Westminster Affair* (Cherry Red 1988). Video: *Destiny Calling* (1994).

Mood Six

Mood Six were central to the short-lived UK psychedelic revival that swept London's West End in the early 80s, and had evolved from various units with mod leanings. Drummer Simon Smith (b. 3 December 1958, Merton Park, London, England; ex-Merton Parkas), songwriter Tony Conway (b. 28 February 1958, Newbury, Berkshire, England) and Andy Godfrey (b. 28 December 1957, Ilford,

Essex, England) were both drawn from Security Risk, Paul Shurey and Guy Morley came from VIP's leaving only Phil Ward without high profile previous experience. The group debuted on WEA's 1982's new psychedelia compilation, *A Splash Of Colour*. The band contributed two tracks, the catchy 'Plastic Flowers' and the atmospheric 'Just Like A Dream', although both owed as much to late 60s pop as psychedelia. The resulting publicity surrounding that scene led to an interview on BBC television's *Nationwide* and a deal with EMI. 'Hanging Around' (later covered by Toni Basil) became the band's first single but was commercially disappointing and the follow-up, 'She's Too Far (Out)', was scrapped as the band were dropped from the label. Mood Six re-emerged early in 1985 on the psychedelic reissue label Psycho, with *The Difference Is…*, which saw the introduction of Chris O'Connor. This was followed in May by a re-recording of 'Plastic Flowers'. The band then moved to the Cherry Red label for 1986's classy, 'What Have You Ever Done?', drawn from *A Matter Of!*. Unfortunately, although Mood Six were writing endearing pop music, the final sound was occasionally bland, lacking that spark of originality. Keyboard player Simon Taylor (b. 28 December 1960, Redhill, Surrey, England) was inducted before the release of 'I Saw The Light' in May 1987, after which the band's relationship with Cherry Red fizzled out, and Phil Ward was ousted from the group. Simon Smith recently turned up in Small Town Parade, another band with strong mod connections, as did Taylor, though Mood Six continued in a low-key manner. Phil Ward's replacement on vocals would be Gerry O'Sullivan (b. 25 March 1963, Paddington, London, England). A new album was released in 1993 on the band's own label.
Albums: *The Difference Is…* (Psycho 1985), *A Matter Of!* (Cherry Red 1986), *And This Is It* (Lost Recording Company 1993).

Moose

This UK group comprised Russell Yates (vocals), Kevin McKillop (guitar), Damien Warburton (drums) and Lincoln Fong (bass). They inadvertently began the so-called 'shoegazing' movement, so dubbed because of the static nature of bands who focused on the floorboards instead of their audience, when Yates read lyrics taped to the floor. They rose to notoriety with supports to Lush, from whom they borrowed Chris Acland when Warburton failed to appear at gigs. Another temporary change arose when McKillop attended his child's birth, and Tim Gane from Sterolab stepped in. Conversely Yates moonlights as a Stereolab guitarist and McKillop has played with See See Rider. It is this sort of activity which fuelled 'The Scene That Celebrates Itself' tag, summoned by the *Melody Maker*'s Steve Sutherland to describe the incestuous nature of a clutch of upcoming bands who were not indulging in traditional rivalries. Three EPs comprised the original batch of recordings, the last of which was the first to confirm that the band could offer more than the voguish My Bloody Valentine influences. The C&W-tinged 'This River Will Never Run Dry' was applauded from almost all corners. Yates also achieved prominence through the Lillies, the brainchild of Stuart Mutler, editor of Tottenham Hotspurs'

soccer magazine, *The Spur*. This included Miki Berenyi and Chris Acland from Lush, Yates and Kevin McKillop from Moose, and was masterminded by Simon Raymonde of the Cocteau Twins. Together they recorded a flexi-disc entitled: 'And David Seaman Will Be Very Disappointed About That'. Despite strong critical reaction in their favour, Moose were dropped by Virgin Records subsidiary Circa when they failed to garner significant commercial reward for *XYZ*. The band relocated to Play It Again Sam, for whom *Honey Bee* further moved them away from indie rock territory, dabbling in soul, folk and country nuances. The critical response was still strong, but again did not provide an upsurge in sales.
Album: *XYZ* (Circa 1992), *Honey Bee* (Play It Again Sam 1993).

Morells

Formed in Springfield, Missouri, USA in 1982, the Morells recorded only one album, *Shake And Push*, on Borrowed Records. Although it never charted, this roots-rock group built a devoted following on the USA alternative circuit. Consisting of bassist Lou Whitney (who had once performed with soul singer Arthur Conley), his wife, Maralie (keyboards), D. Clinton Thompson (guitar) and Ron Gremp (drums), the group started in the late 70s as the Skeletons and then the Original Symptoms before settling in as the Morells, combining within their sound rockabilly, soul, blues and jazz. The group disbanded in the mid-80s. Lou Whitney went on to produce the debut album by New York rockers the Del-Lords before re-forming the Skeletons in 1988, with Thompson.
Album: *Shake And Push* (1982).

Morphine

Purveyors of quite startling, low-end alternative rock, Morphine are one of the few in the field who do not use guitars. Even vocalist Mark Sandman's bass is a rudimentary affair, composed of only two strings. Together with Dana Colley (saxophone) and Jerome Deupree (drums), the group was inaugurated by Sandman and Colley after the break-up the former's previous outfit, Treat Her Right. After playing a few tentative gigs they released their debut album, which, probably because no one had heard anything quite like it before, won many admirers. Their local community honoured them when they picked up Indie Debut Album Of The Year at the Boston Music Awards. Following its release Deupree departed, to be replaced by former Treat Her Right drummer Billy Conway. On the back of the attention they were receiving they picked up a deal with Rykodisc, while the band's music continued to be more influenced by literature, notably Jim Thompson, than musical peers.
Albums: *Good* (Accurate/Distortion 1992), *Cure For Pain* (Rykodisc 1993).

Morrissey

b. Steven Patrick Morrissey, 22 May 1959, Davyhulme, Manchester, England. Morrissey began his career with the vague intention of succeeding as a music journalist. Unemployed in Manchester during the late 70s, he frequently wrote letters to the music press and was eventually taken on by *Record Mirror* as a freelance local reviewer.

Morphine

During this period, he also ran a New York Dolls' fan club and even wrote a booklet about them. Another small illustrated volume, *James Dean Is Not Dead*, briefly catalogued the career of another Morrissey obsession. Two other projects, on girl groups and minor film stars, failed to reach the printed page. In the meantime, Morrissey was attempting unsuccessfully to progress as a performer. He had played a couple of gigs with local group the Nosebleeds and failed a record company audition with a relaunched version of Slaughter And The Dogs. By the early 80s his chance of fame had apparently expired. In 1982, however, he was approached by Wythenshawe guitarist Johnny Maher (later Marr) with the idea of forming a songwriting team. They soon developed into the Smiths, the most important and critically-acclaimed UK group of the 80s. Morrissey's arch lyrics, powerful persona and general newsworthiness made him a pop figure whose articulacy was unmatched by any of his contemporaries. By the late summer of 1987, the Smiths disbanded, leaving Morrissey to pursue a solo career. Early the following year he issued his first post-Smiths single, 'Suedehead', with Vini Reilly filling the guitarist's spot. The track was irresistibly commercial and reached the UK Top 5. The subsequent *Viva Hate* hit the top soon after, indicating that the singer could look forward to a long and successful future with EMI Records. A further UK Top 10 single with the John Betjemen-influenced 'Everyday Is Like Sunday' reiterated that point. In spite of his successes, Morrissey was initially keen on promoting a Smiths reunion but the closest

this reached was the equivalent of a farewell concert in the unlikely setting of Wolverhampton Civic Hall. On 22 December 1988, Morrissey performed alongside former Smiths, Andy Rourke, Mike Joyce and Craig Gannon for a 1,700 capacity audience, many of whom had queued for days in order to gain admittance to the venue. The following year brought several problems for Morrissey. Although he continued to release strong singles such as 'The Last Of The Famous International Playboys' and 'Interesting Drug', both reviews and chart placings were slighter less successful than expected. By the time of 'Ouija Board, Ouija Board', Morrissey suffered the most disappointing reviews of his career and, despite its charm, the single only reached number 18. Financial wrangles and management changes, which had characterized the Smiths' career, were repeated by Morrissey the soloist. A projected album, *Bona Drag*, was delayed and eventually cancelled, although the title served for a formidable hits and b-side compilation. In the meantime, Morrissey concentrated on the singles market, issuing some fascinating product, most notably the macabre 'November Spawned A Monster' and controversial 'Piccadilly Palare'. In March 1991, Morrissey issued the long-awaited *Kill Uncle*, a light yet not unappealing work, produced by Clive Langer and Alan Winstanley. By this time, the artist had not toured since the heyday of the Smiths, and there were some critics who wondered whether he would ever perform again. That question was answered in the summer and winter of 1991 when the singer embarked on a world tour, backed by a rockabilly group, whose raw energy and enthusiasm brought a new dimension to his recently understated studio work. The fruits of this collaboration were revealed on *Your Arsenal*, a neat fusion of 50s rockabilly influences and 70s glam rock. The presence of former David Bowie acolyte Mick Ronson as producer added to the effect. During 1992 Morrissey also hit the headlines when he issued a bitter attack on author Johnny Rogan. Prior to the publication of a book on the Smiths, which he had yet to read, Morrissey decreed: 'Personally, I hope Johnny Rogan ends his days very soon in an M3 pile-up'. The much publicised and long-running dispute merely served to focus attention on the book and heighten appreciation of his Smiths' work. Indications that interest may have peaked came as a result of the dismal failure of *Beethoven Was Deaf*, a live album which disappeared after only 2 weeks in the charts. However, Morrissey was now beginning to cultivate a following in the US way above the cult devotees who had followed the Smiths there. This offered welcome succour at a time when UK critics were predicting his imminent downfall and his domestic audience was undergoing a period of reduction. Then came the Madstock disaster - a live appearance in support of a reformed Madness that saw Morrissey bedecked in a Union Jack - which, when combined with song titles such as 'Bengali In Platforms' and 'The National Front Disco', saw a huge debate rage in the media over the artist's interpretation of 'Englishness'. *Vauxhall And I* ended the downward spiral, receiving 'born again' reviews throughout the UK music media. With the more sedate production from Steve Lillywhite, this was the closest the artist had come to matching his lyricism with the right material components since the Smiths. Indeed, as *Select* magazine decreed: 'If he keeps making albums like this, you won't want the Smiths back'.

Albums: *Viva Hate* (HMV 1988), *Kill Uncle* (HMV 1991), *Your Arsenal* (HMV 1992), *Beethoven Was Deaf* (HMV 1993), *Vauxhall And I* (HMV 1994). Compilation: *Bona Drag* (HMV 1990).
Video: *Live In Dallas* (1993).
Further reading: *Morrissey & Marr: The Severed Alliance*, Johnny Rogan, *Peepholism: Into The Art Of Morrissey*, Jo Slee. *Landsacapes Of The Mind*, David Bret.

Motello, Elton
Alan Ward had originally been the singer with punk hopefuls Bastard, which also included in its ranks future Damned guitarist Brian James. After the band split Ward assumed the pseudonym of Elton Motello, alternating between England and Belgium, where he had built up associations touring with Bastard. He made his debut appearance at the end of 1977 with 'Jet Boy, Jet Girl', first in Belgium on Pinball, followed a month later by a UK release on Lightning. The track achieved international success with the re-titled French version, 'Ca Plane Pour Moi', by pop-punk exponents Plastic Bertrand. Success for Motello's original was much more limited, even though it was released in many different countries. A few months later, 'Jet Boy, Jet Girl' was re-recorded to greater notoriety by Captain Sensible And The Softies. Towards the end of 1978 Motello recorded his debut album, *Victim Of Time*, which was released in March 1979

by Attic Records, but only in Canada. He was backed by various players including Peter (guitar), Nobby (drums) and Willie Change (bass), with the help of Jet Staxx (guitar), Tony Boast (guitar) and former Pink Fairies and Pretty Things drummer John 'Twink' Alder. In addition to the single, the album included a remake of the Small Faces' 'Sha La La La Lee' and another 11 compositions that fluctuated between pop and punk. With the new decade came two further releases: '20th Century Fox' and a second album, *Pop Art*.
Albums: *Victim Of Time* (Attic 1979), *Pop Art* (Attic 1980).

Motels
Formed in Berkeley, California, in the early 70s, the Motels comprised Martha Davis (vocals), Jeff Jourard (guitar), his brother Martin (keyboards/saxophone), former jazzer Michael Goodroe (bass) and UK session drummer Brian Glascock (ex-Toe Fat). Transferring to Los Angeles, the group assembled for appearances at Hollywood's Whiskey club throughout July 1978, attracting a modicum of music industry interest in the process. In 1979 their stunning debut album was issued by Capitol Records. Like its remaining tracks, the hit ballad, 'Total Control', was produced by John Carter and composed by central figure Davis, whose eclectic tastes included blues, Broadway musicals and Stravinsky. Her onstage presence was 'exceptionally charismatic', wrote *The Los Angeles Times*, wrongly predicting that she 'could become one of the most influential female performers in rock'. Her boyfriend, Tim McGovern (ex-Captain Kopter And The Fabulous Twirlybirds), replaced Jeff Jourard during sessions for *Careful*, with a sleeve adorned with a print of a Dougie Fields' painting. Though its singles, 'Whose Problem' and 'Days Are OK', flitted into the US and UK charts, they fared well in regional charts in Australasia, a territory where the group made its strongest impact. Their albums and tie-in singles tended to hover around the lower half of the UK Top 40 after *All Four One*, at number 16, marked the Motels' commercial zenith. In their homeland they scored two US Top 10 hits with 'Only The Lonely' (1982) and 'Suddenly Last Summer' (1983), but folded in 1987.
Albums: *The Motels* (Capitol 1979), *Careful* (Capitol 1980), *All Four One* (Capitol 1982), *Little Robbers* (Capitol 1983), *Shock* (Capitol 1985).

Mother Love Bone
This short-lived, Seattle-based quintet comprised Andrew Wood (vocals), Greg Gilmore (drums), Bruce Fairweather (guitar), Stone Gossard (guitar; ex-Green River) and Jeff Ament (bass; ex-Green River). Drawing influences from the Stooges, MC5 and the Velvet Underground they specialized in heavy-duty garage rock laced with drug-fuelled psychotic overtones. Signing to Polydor, they debuted with *Apple* in 1990 to widespread critical acclaim. Their promising career was curtailed abruptly by the untimely death of vocalist Andrew Wood in March, shortly after the album was released. Gossard and Ament would go on to enjoy further success with Temple Of The Dog and, to a much greater extent, Pearl Jam.
Album: *Apple* (Polydor 1990). Compilation: *Stardog Champion* (Polydor 1992).

Motorcycle Boy

This UK 'indie' pop group were formed in 1987 by former Shop Assistants singer Alex Taylor (vocals) with ex-Meat Whiplash personnel Michael Kerr (guitar), Paul McDermott (drums), Eddie Connelly (bass) and outsider, 'Scottie' (b. David Scott; guitar). Their debut single for Rough Trade Records, 'Big Rock Candy Mountain' (formerly a title for Burl Ives), reached number 3 in the UK independent chart. Despite this promising start, and much music press attention, they failed, largely from disorganisation, to set the live circuit alight and subsequently broke up soon after the release of their lone album which was recorded for major label Chrysalis Records. Alex Taylor was reportedly last spotted working as a shop assistant for a record store chain.
Album: *Scarlet* (Chrysalis 1989).

Motors

The Motors were based around the partnership of Nick Garvey (b. 26 April 1951, Stoke-on-Trent, Staffordshire, England) and Andy McMaster (b. 27 July 1947, Glasgow, Scotland) who first met in the pub rock band Ducks Deluxe. McMaster had a long career in pop music, having played in several bands in the 60s including the Sabres, which also featured Frankie Miller. McMaster released a solo single, 'Can't Get Drunk Without You', on President, and joined Ducks Deluxe in November 1974. Garvey was educated at Kings College in Cambridge and was an accomplished pianist, oboeist and trumpeter. Before he joined Ducks Deluxe in December 1972 he had acted as a road manager for the Flamin' Groovies. The pair left the Ducks early in 1975, just a few months before the unit disbanded. Garvey joined a group called the Snakes (along with future Wire vocalist Rob Gotobed) and they released one single. McMaster, meanwhile, went to work for a music publisher. Garvey's friend and manager Richard Ogden suggested that Garvey form his own band in order to record the songs he had written. This led to him contacting McMaster and in January 1977 they recorded demos together. The following month they recruited Ricky Wernham (aka Ricky Slaughter) from the Snakes on drums - he is the cousin of Knox from the Vibrators. Guitarist Rob Hendry was quickly replaced by Bram Tchaikovsky and the Motors were up and running. They made their live debut at the Marquee Club, London in March 1977 and signed to Virgin in May.
A tour with the Kursaal Flyers and the Heavy Metal Kids led to the release of their debut single, 'Dancing The Night Away', and first album, produced by Mutt Lange. However, it was their second single, 'Airport', which became a huge hit in the UK. It is widely used to this day as a stock soundtrack when television programmes show film clips of aeroplanes taking off or landing. Despite this success, the group were already burning out. After performing at Reading in August the Motors decided to concentrate on writing new material. Wernham took the opportunity to leave, while Tchaikovsky formed his own band with the intention of returning to the Motors, though he never did. Garvey and McMaster eventually re-emerged with some new material for *Tenement Steps*. It was recorded with the assistance of former Man bassist Martin Ace, and drummer Terry Williams (ex-Man and Rockpile, future Dire Straits). After *Tenement Steps* the Motors seized up, but both Garvey and McMaster have since released solo singles.
Albums: *The Motors I* (1977), *Approved By The Motors* (1978), *Tenement Steps* (1980). Compilation: *Greatest Hits* (1981).

Mould, Bob

The former guitarist, vocalist and co-composer of Hüsker Dü, Mould surprised many of that leading hardcore act's aficionados with his reflective solo debut, *Workbook*. Only one track, 'Whichever Way The Wind Blows', offered the maelstrom of guitars customary in the artist's work and instead the set was marked by a predominantly acoustic atmosphere. Cellist Jane Scarpantoni contributed to its air of melancholy, while two members of Pere Ubu, Tony Maimone (bass) and Anton Fier (drums; also Golden Palominos), added sympathetic support, helping to emphasize the gift for melody always apparent in Mould's work. Maimone and Fier also provided notable support on *Black Sheets Of Rain*, which marked a return to the uncompromising power of the guitarist's erstwhile unit. The set included the harrowing 'Hanging Tree' and apocalyptical 'Sacrifice Sacrifice/Let There Be Peace', but contrasted such doom-laden material with a brace of sprightly pop songs in 'It's Too Late' and 'Hear Me Calling', both of which echoed R.E.M.. Mould also formed his own record company, SOL (Singles Only Label), which has issued material by, among others, William Burroughs. The artist abandoned his solo career in 1993, reverting to the melodic hardcore trio format with Sugar.
Albums: *Workbook* (Virgin 1989), *Black Sheets Of Rain* (Virgin 1990).

Mudhoney

Mudhoney, forged from a host of hobbyist bands, can lay claim to the accolade 'godfathers' of grunge' more legitimately than most - whether or not they desire that title. The band comprises brothers Mark Arm (vocals) and Steve Turner (guitar), plus Matt Lukin (bass) and Dan Peters (drums). Arm and Turner were both ex-Green River, the band which also gave birth to Pearl Jam, and the less serious Thrown Ups. Lukin was ex-Melvins, Peters ex-Bundles Of Piss. Mudhoney were the band that first imported the sound of Sub Pop Records to wider shores. In August 1988 they released the fabulous 'Touch Me I'm Sick' single, one of the defining moments in the evolution of 'grunge', followed shortly by their debut mini-album. Contrary to popular belief, Turner chose the name *Superfuzz Bigmuff* after his favourite effects pedals rather than any sexual connotation. Early support included the admiration of Sonic Youth who covered their first a-side while Mudhoney thrashed through Sonic Youth staple 'Halloween' on the flip side of a split single. The first album proper was greeted as a comparative disappointment by many, though there were obvious standout tracks ('When Tomorrow Hits'). The EP, *Boiled Beef And Rotting Teeth*, contained a cover of the Dicks' 'Hate The Police', demonstrating a good grasp of their 'hardcore' heritage. They had previously demonstrated an ability to nominate a sprightly cover tune when Spacemen 3's 'Revolution' had appeared on the b-side to 'This Gift'. The

Mudhoney

band also hold the likes of Celibate Rifles and Billy Childish is high esteem. Members of the former have helped in production of the band, while on trips to England they have invited the latter to join as support. It was their patronage which led to Childish's Thee Headcoats releasing material through Sub Pop. Meanwhile, Mudhoney's shows were becoming less eye-catching, and progressively close to eye-gouging. Early gigs in London saw Arm invite the audience, every single one of them, on to the stage, with the resultant near destruction of several venues. *Every Good Boy Deserves Fudge* was a departure, with Hammond organ intruding into the band's accomplished rock formula. It demonstrated their increasing awareness of the possibilities of their own song writing. They are certainly not the wooden-headed noise dolts they are sometimes portrayed as: each comes from a comfortable middle class background, and while Arm is an English graduate, Turner has qualifications in anthropology. After much speculation Mudhoney became the final major players in the Sub Pop empire to go major when they moved to Warner Brothers Records, though many would argue that none of their efforts thus far has managed to reproduce the glory of 'Touch Me I'm Sick' or other highlights of their independent days. *My Brother The Cow*, however, revealed a band nearly back at its best. Released after extensive world-wide touring with Pearl Jam, songs such as 'Into Your Schtick' reflected on the passing of one-time friend Kurt Cobain. Jack Endino's production, meanwhile, added lustre and managed to capture the band's always compelling live sound better than had previously been the case.

Albums: *Superfuzz Bigmuff* (Sub Pop 1988), *Mudhoney* (Sub Pop 1989), *Every Good Boy Deserves Fudge* (Sub Pop 1991), *Piece Of Cake* (WEA 1992), *Five Dollar Bob's Mock Cooter Stew* (WEA 1993), *My Brother The Cow* (WEA 1995). Compilation: *Superfuzz Bigmuff Plus Early Singles* (Sub Pop 1993).
Video: *Absolutely Live* (1994).

Murphy, Peter

The former Bauhaus vocalist set out on his solo career after a brief stint as half of Dali's Car, with former Japan member Mick Karn (one album: *The Waking Hour*). Murphy was already famous in his own right for appearing as the enigmatic figure in a Maxell Tapes television advertisement. His first solo output was a cover version of Magazine's 'The Light Pours Out Of Me', for the Beggars Banquet sampler *The State Of Things*. This was included on his debut album, which boasted a massive credit list including Daniel Ash, his old songwriting partner in Bauhaus, John McGeogh (who played on the original of 'The Light Pours Out Of Me') and Howard Hughes. The debut set a precedent for critical apathy (in the UK at least) which has accompanied all subsequent recordings. 1987's *Love Hysteria* included a cover of Iggy Pop's 'Fun Time', amongst other typically dramatic gestures. By the third album a regular band had been formed, consisting of Peter Bonas (guitar), Terl Bryant (drums), Eddie Branch (bass) and Paul Statham (keyboards/guitar). All four had played on the previous album, Branch and Bonas on the first as well. One of the better songs from *Deep*,

'Cuts You Deep', won the Top Modern Rock Track in the 1990 *Billboard* Year In Music Awards.

Albums: *Should The World Fail To Fall Apart* (1986), *Love Hysteria* (1987), *Deep* (1989), *Holy Smoke* (1992).

Murray, Pauline, And The Invisible Girls

Following the demise of Penetration, Murray (b. 8 March 1958, Durham, England) departed, with bass guitarist Robert Blamire, to form a new group. Producers Martin Hannett and Steve Hopkins were claimed to be the 'Invisible' members, while the actual line-up consisted of John Maher (ex-Buzzcocks), Dave Rowbotham and Dave Hassell. The Invisible Girls would also act as studio and road band for John Cooper Clarke, and include among its ranks Pete Shelley, Karl Burns (the Fall), Bill Nelson, Vini Reilly (Durutti Column) and numerous others. A self-titled album and single, 'Dream Sequence', announced the arrival of Pauline Murray And The Invisible Girls, gaining strong critical support. The album featured guest appearances from Wayne Hussey (ex-Dead Or Alive, Sisters Of Mercy, the Mission) in addition to the previously mentioned Invisible luminaries. Despite this fine collection, the band split after two subsequent single releases from it: 'Searching For Heaven' and 'Mr. X'. Blamire went into production work while Murray took two years away from the music industry. 'I just . . . retreated from music really, just backed right out and decided what I wanted to do. Which took about a year to two years . . . I think Penetration to the Invisible Girls was such a vast leap that it lost everyone. It lost us as well'. Blamire and Murray reunited in the similarly short-lived Pauline Murray And The Storm.

Album: *Pauline Murray And The Invisible Girls* (1981).

Mute Records

Daniel Miller's brainchild was originally set up for a single under the guise of the Normal. 'T.V.O.D.'/'Warm Leatherette' became the first Mute single in early 1978, a pioneering utilization of electronics that paved the way for Mute's alignment with synthesized and hi-tech sounds. Several hundred albums later, Mute's singular artistic identity and experimental approach still cuts a distinctive chord through an apathetic music industry. Along with Factory and Rough Trade Records, Mute has demonstrated an ability to combine aesthetic autonomy with survival. Among the label's early group roster were Fad Gadget, D.A.F. and Depeche Mode. It was the success of the latter that convinced many that a post-punk independent label could succeed in producing a consistent chart act. Despite the offers made to the group from major labels, Depeche Mode resisted any temptation to move - a tribute to Miller's business acumen and his faith in Depeche Mode's artistic growth. The label has also been greatly assisted by ex-Depeche Mode member Vince Clark's series of projects from Yazoo through to Erasure. Owing to Depeche Mode and Erasure's continuing international success, Mute has been able to finance less commercial acts such as Laibach, Crime And The City Solution, Diamanda Galas and Nitzer Ebb. The label's acquisition of the back catalogues of Cabaret Voltaire, Can and Throbbing Gristle also ensured the continued availability of these seminal artists' output. In the 90s a subsidiary operation dealing with dance and techno, Novamute, was established, dealing with forerunning experimental artists such as Moby. On a more conventional front the parent label also signed the Inspiral Carpets, but the long-standing artist to best combine critical and commercial approbation has undoubtedly been Nick Cave.

Compilation: *International* (Mute 1991).

MX-80 Sound

Bruce Anderson (guitar), Rich Stim (guitar/keyboards/vocals/saxophone), Dave Sophiea (bass), Dave Mahoney (drums) and Jeff Armour, later replaced by Kevin Teare (drums). Hailing from Bloomington, Indiana, USA, MX-80 began as a trio of Anderson, Sophiea and Armour. In late 1975 they were joined by Stim and Mahoney. A single and EP on a local label were followed by their debut *Hard Attack* for Island Records. By this time they were based in San Francisco. *Hard Attack* achieved considerable attention; the avowed experimentation of the group (Captain Beefheart and Frank Zappa were often cited by critics) matched by a lyrical subject matter that fitted into the 'new wave' ethos of the period. The sound quality was also suitably murky. Signed to *Ralph*, the label run by the Residents, they produced two more albums and appeared on several compilations but their career tailed off in the early 80s. Stim entered law school and nothing further was heard except for Anderson's appearance in the Henry Kaiser Band. However, a clutch of tapes under a variety of names (Gizzards, Half-Life, O-Type) have appeared since 1987, apparently the work of Sophiea and Anderson, on the former's Quadruped label. These two, plus Stim and drummer Marc Weinstein, appear to constitute an MX for the 90s.

Albums: *Hard Attack* (1977), *Out Of The Tunnel* (1980), *Crowd Control* (1981).

My Bloody Valentine

It took several years for My Bloody Valentine to capture their ground-breaking hybrid of ethereal melodies and studio-orientated, discordant sounds which proved so influential on the independent scene of the late 80s. Their roots lay in Dublin, where singer/guitarist Kevin Shields joined drummer Colm O'Ciosoig in the short-lived Complex. Forming My Bloody Valentine in 1984, the pair moved to Berlin, joined by vocalist Dave Conway (vocals) and Tina (keyboards). A mini-album, *This Is Your Bloody Valentine*, on the obscure German Tycoon label in 1984, made little impression (although it was later reissued in the UK), so the band returned to London and recruited bassist Debbie Googe. The 12-inch EP, *Geek!* (and the accompanying, 'No Place To Go') emerged on Fever in mid-1986 which, like their debut, was strongly influenced by the Cramps and the Birthday Party. Later that year, the band signed with Joe Foster's fledgling Kaleidoscope Sound label for *The New Record By My Bloody Valentine* EP, which revealed a new influence, the Jesus And Mary Chain. A switch to the Primitives' label Lazy, produced 'Sunny Sundae Smile' (1987), which meshed bubblegum pop with buzzsaw guitars, a formula that dominated both the mini-album, *Ecstasy*, and 'Strawberry Wine', released later that year. The departure of

Conway signalled a change in musical direction, reinforced by the arrival of vocalist Belinda Butcher. A further move to Creation Records allowed for a drastic reappraisal in recording techniques, first apparent on the formidable *You Made Me Realise* EP in 1988. Enticing melodic structures contrasted with the snarling, almost unworldly collage of noise, developed more fully that year on My Bloody Valentine's pivotal *Isn't Anything*, from which was drawn the barrage of guitars, 'Feed Me With Your Kiss'. At last, the group had unearthed a completely new sound. Since then, their status has mushroomed. The release of an EP, *Glider* (1990), alongside a remix from the in-demand DJ Andy Weatherall, flirted with both dance music and the charts while 'Tremelo' (1991) must rank as arguably the most extreme piece of music to reach the Top 30. To quote the band, it 'sounded like it was being played through a transistor radio'. My Bloody Valentine's increasing maturity saw the meticulously-produced *Loveless* album reinforce their reputation as one of the prime influences on the late 80s' UK independent scene - one that groups such as Slowdive, Lush and Chapterhouse owe a great deal. However, the massive studio bills run up during that time saw My Bloody Valentine leave Creation, moving instead to Island Records. At which point another agonising gestation period was embarked upon, allegedly due to difficulty installing equipment in their own purpose built studio in south London.

Albums: *This Is Your Bloody Valentine* (Tycoon 1984), *Ecstasy* (Lazy 1987, mini-album), *Isn't Anything* (Creation 1988), *Loveless* (Creation 1991).

N

Naked Prey

This US group was founded in 1981 in Tucson, Arizona by Van Christian (guitar/vocals), formerly of the Serfers. David Seger (guitar/vocals), Richard Badenious (bass) and Sam Blake (drums) completed the line-up featured on the unit's mini-album debut. The set was produced by ex-Serfer Dan Stuart, guitarist in Green On Red, but although comparisons were naturally drawn between the two, Naked Prey offered a louder, heavier sound. This was more clearly heard on *Under The Blue Marlin*, on which Blake had been replaced by Tom Larkins. *40 Miles From Nowhere*, which featured the Rolling Stones 'Silver Train' and Glen Campbell's 'Wichita Lineman', was regarded as a disappointment, and the group's musical momentum noticeably faltered. Van Christian nonetheless continues to front his creation, although it now seems doomed to cult status.

Albums: *Naked Prey* (1984), *Under The Blue Marlin* (1986),

40 Miles From Nowhere (1987), *Kill The Messenger* (1989).

Napalm Death

This quintet from Birmingham, England, was formed in 1981. Dispensing with their original style by the mid-80s, they then absorbed punk and thrash metal influences to create the new sub-genre of grindcore, arguably the most extreme of all musical forms. Side one of their debut album featured Justin Broadrick (guitar), Mick Harris (drums) and Nick Bullen (bass/vocals), but by side two this had switched to Bill Steer (guitar), Jim Whitely (bass) and Lee Dorrian (vocals), with Harris the only survivor from that first inception (though that too had been subject to numerous changes). Broadrick would go on to Head Of David and Godflesh. *Scum* largely comprised sub-two minute blasts of metallic white noise, over-ridden by Dorrian's unintelligible vocal tirade. The lyrics dealt with social and political injustices, but actually sounded like somebody coughing up blood. Their main advocate was Radio 1 disc jockey John Peel, who had first picked up on *Scum*, playing the 0.75 second-long track 'You Suffer' three times before inviting them to record a session for the programme in September 1987. This would come to be acknowledged as one of the 'Classic Sessions' in Ken Garner's 1993 book on the subject, and introduced new bass player Shane Embury (also Unseen Terror, who split after one album in 1988). Elsewhere Napalm Death were the subject of derision and total miscomprehension. They were, however, the true pioneers of the 'blast-snare' technique - whereby the tempo of a given beat is sustained at the maximum physical human tolerance level. They went on to attract a small but loyal cult following on the underground heavy metal scene. From *Enslavement To Obliteration*, consisting of no less than 54 tracks on the CD, was a state of the artless offering which easily bypassed pervious extremes in music. However, following a Japanese tour in 1989 both Dorrian and Steer elected to leave the band, the former putting together Cathedral, the latter Carcass. Despite the gravity of the split replacements were found in vocalist Mark 'Barney' Greenway (ex-Bendiction) and US guitarist Jesse Pintado (ex-Terrorizer). To maintain their profile the band embarked on the European *Grindcrusher* tour (in their wake grindcore had developed considerably and found mass acceptance among the rank and file of the metal world) with Bolt Thrower, Carcass and Morbid Angel, before playing their first US dates in New York. A second guitarist, Mitch Harris (ex-Righteous Pigs) was added in time for *Harmony Corruption*, which, along with the 12 inch 'Suffer The Children', saw Napalm Death retreat to a purer death metal sound. During worldwide touring in 1992 sole surviving original member Mick Harris became disillusioned with the band and vacated the drum stool for Danny Herrara, a friend of Pintado's from Los Angeles. A fourth album, *Utopia Banished*, celebrated the band's remarkable survival instincts, while the heady touring schedule continued unabated. By 1993 the band had played in Russia, Israel, Canada and South Africa in addition to the more familiar European and US treks. A cover of the Dead Kennedys' 'Nazi Punks Fuck Off', issued as a single, reinstated their political motives. As *Fear, Emptiness, Despair* confirmed, however, they remain the antithesis of style, melody and taste - the punk concept taken to its ultimate extreme, and a great band for all the difficulty of listening to them.

Albums: *Scum* (Earache 1987), *From Enslavement To Obliteration* (Earache 1988), *The Peel Sessions* (Strange Fruit 1989), *Harmony Corruption* (Earache 1990), *Utopia Banished* (Earache 1992), *Fear, Emptiness, Despair* (Earache 1994). Compilation: *Death By Manipulation* (Earache 1992).

Video: *Live Corruption* (1990).

Native Hipsters

This London-based duo comprised William Wilding (b. 18 May 1953, Romford, Essex, England) and Blatt (b. Nanette Greenblatt, 9 March 1952, Cape Town, South Africa). Prior to 1980 they had worked under names such as the Wildings, then later as the Patterns with Robert Cubitt and Tom Fawcett. In that guise, they released the challenging but largely incoherent 'The B'Shop Is In The Fridge'. They next emerged as (And The) Native Hipsters, again with Cubitt and Fawcett. It was as the latter that Wilding and Blatt achieved national recognition with their 1980 release 'There Goes Concorde Again'. Blatt's repetitive child-like enthusiasm at the sighting of the famed 'silverbird' captured the attention of UK Radio One disc jockey, John Peel, resulting in the single peaking at number 5 in the UK independent charts. Wilding turned down an offer from producer Tony Visconti to re-cut the single for national consumption, preferring total artistic control. Their next release in 1982, a four track EP, *Tenderly Hurt Me*, won them a respect from the music press who had previously condemned them as quirky odd-balls. The Hipsters' inventive and bizarre mixture of surreal poetry, diverse musical styles, original and sampled sounds, plus a vast array of musical instruments of whatever came to hand, managed to establish a cult following. Variously assisted by friends such as Lester Square (guitar, from the Monochrome Set), Annie Whitehead (trombone), Chris Cornetto (cornet), Liduina Van Der Sman (saxophone) and Simon Davison (piano), Wilding and Blatt have over the years recorded countless sessions, live and in the studio, which were later compiled to form *Blatt On The Landscape*. During the early 90s Wilding performed on the London cabaret circuit as the iconoclastic Woody Bop Muddy, an act consisting of his passing a savage judgement on whatever and whoever's records passed through his hands, by way of smashing them with a hammer.

Albums: as the Wildings *Why Did I Buy Those Blue Pyjamas* (1979), *Blatt On The Landscape* (1988, cassette only).

Nectarine No.9

Formed in Edinburgh, Scotland, in 1993, Nectarine No.9 revolves around guitarist/vocalist Davey Henderson, an ex-member of both the Fire Engines and Win. Alan Horne, founder of Postcard Records took great interest in both groups and Henderson's newest venture was one of his first signings on reactivating the label. *The Nectarine No.9* reinstated Henderson's love of abrasive pop and quirky rhythms, inhabiting a musical world part T. Rex and part Fall. However, it lacked the focus of Henderson's previous

work and critical reaction was muted. *Guitar Thieves*, which collected various BBC Radio 1 sessions, included versions of Captain Beefheart's 'Frownland' and the Velvet Underground's 'Inside Of Your Heart', as well as an original song, 'Pull My Daisy', the title of which was drawn from a film featuring Allen Ginsberg and Jack Kerouac.

Albums: *The Nectarine No.9* (Postcard 1993), *Guitar Thieves* (Nightracks/Postcard 1994).

Ned's Atomic Dustbin

Formed in the West Midlands in 1988 by local characters Jonn Penney (b. 17 September 1968; lead vocals), Rat (b. 8 November 1970; guitar), Matt Cheslin (b. 28 November 1970; bass), Alex Griffin (b. 29 August 1971; bass) and Dan Warton (b. 28 July 1972; drums). After dubious Gothic beginnings, Ned's Atomic Dustbin began to find their feet in 1989 when a series of tour supports, notably with regional contemporaries the Wonderstuff, attracted a strong following. Notable for having two bassists, uniformly crimped hair and an unequivocally daft name (taken from the BBC radio's *The Goon Show*), the Ned's urgent, aggressive sub-hardcore sound still managed to offset any gimmicky connotations, turning a potential freak show into a challenging pop act. Armed with a plethora of original merchandising ideas - within three years the band produced 86 different t-shirt designs - their 'Kill Your Television' single entered the Top 50 of the UK chart and resulted in a major contract with Sony Music (formerly CBS). With the financial wherewithal to back their imagination, Ned's Atomic Dustbin soon translated their ideas into a phenomenal commercial success, peaking when *God Fodder* entered the UK charts at number four in 1991. The rest of the year was filled by hectic touring commitments, with America followed by Japan, a prestigious spot at the British Reading Festival, a UK number 21 hit with 'Trust', back to America (with Jesus Jones) and then a British tour which resulted in singer Jonn Penney collapsing from exhaustion on the last night.

Album: *God Fodder* (1991), *Are You Normal?* (1992).

Videos: *Nothing Is Cool* (1991), *Lunatic Magnets* (1993).

Nelson, Bill

b. William Nelson, 18 December 1948, Wakefield, West Yorkshire, England. Although noted chiefly for his innovative guitar work with Be-Bop Deluxe, his solo releases actually form more than four-fifths of his total output. *Smile* was a dreamy, acoustic debut after he had played throughout his home county with pre-progressive rock outfits like the Teenagers, Global Village and Gentle Revolution. He fronted Be-Bop Deluxe for most of the 70s before responding to punk and techno-rock forces by assembling Bill Nelson's Red Noise. *Sound-On-Sound*, released in 1979, was an agitated but confused debut from Red Noise and afterwards Nelson returned to solo work. The single 'Do You Dream In Colour?' provided his highest UK solo chart placing at number 52. It was released on his own label, Cocteau Records. Following a short-lived deal with Mercury Records he continued to release introspective, chiefly home-recorded albums. He was in demand as a producer and worked on sessions with many new-wave bands including the Skids and A Flock Of Seagulls. Surprisingly, after the demise of Be-Bop Deluxe he showed little inclination to use the guitar and preferred to experiment with keyboards and sampled sounds, composing thematic pieces which have been used in films and plays. He recorded backing music for the Yorkshire Actors Company's version of both *Das Kabinett* and *La Belle Et La Bette*, issued later as albums. Many of his releases throughout the 80s were of a whimsical, self-indulgent nature and missed the input of other musicians. Numerous albums were issued via his fan club and the quality was rarely matched by the prolificacy, which twice ran to four-album boxed sets, *Trial By Intimacy* and *Demonstrations Of Affection*. In 1991 he moved markedly towards a stronger and more defined melodic style with *Luminous* on Manchester's independent label, Imaginary, and also spoke of returning to his first love, the guitar.

Albums: *Smile* (1971), *Sound On Sound* (1979), *Quit Dreaming And Get On The Beam* (1981), *Sounding The Ritual Echo* (1981), *Das Kabinett* (1981), *La Belle Et La Bette* (1982), *The Love That Whirls* (1982), *Chimera* (1983), *The Two Fold Aspect Of Everything* (1984), *Trial By Intimacy* (1984), *Map Of Dreams* (1984), *Aconography* (1986), *Chamber Of Dreams* (1986), *Summer Of God's Piano* (1986), *Chance Encounters In The Garden Of Light* (1988), *Optimism* (1988), *Pavillions Of The Heart And Soul* (1989), *Demonstrations Of Affection* (1989), *Duplex* (1989), *Luminous* (1991), *Blue Moons And Laughing Guitars* (1992). Compilation: *Duplex: The Best Of Bill Nelson* (1990).

New Bomb Turks

Pleasantly appointed but noisy Ohio, USA-based band, the New Bomb Turks' manifesto was to rid their genre of its more dour concerns, re-establishing the sheer adrenaline rush and hedonism implicit in the musical format. Contrary to expectations, however, the band were no supporters of idiocy or ignorance, having met while studying at Ohio State University. Each member - Eric Davidson (vocals), Jim Weber (guitar), Matt Reber (bass) and Bill Brandt (drums) - obtained English degrees. They first worked together as DJ's on student radio station WSOR, gradually pulling together as a band via a series of small pressing 7-inch singles. It was with their debut album, however, that their arrival was signalled, *Maximum Rock 'n' Roll* magazine announcing it to be 'album of the year, maybe of the last five years'. In its wake New Bomb Turks gagged under the pressure somewhat, taking their time before a follow-up set, then blasting through the recording sessions to produce *Information Highway Revisited* in just sixty hours.

Albums: *!!Destroy-Oh-Boy!!* (Crypt 1992), *Information Highway Revisited* (Crypt 1994).

New Fast Automatic Daffodils

Manchester, UK based indie band whose arrival in 1989 coincided with their city's descent in to 'rave' culture and an upswing in the fortunes of 'baggy' bands Stone Roses and Happy Mondays. From their debut at the Manchester Polytechnic Poetry Society in 1988, they were described in one quarter as resembling 'a team of sex psychologists at a mass orgy'. The band, Andy Spearpoint (vocals), Justin Crawford (bass), Dolan Hewison (guitar), Perry Saunders

(drums) and Icarus Wilson-Wright (percussion) signed to Belgian label Play It Again Sam in 1989. Among their early singles, the caustic but wry 'Music Is Shit' gained most prominence. 'Get Better' was remixed by Joy Division producer, Martin Hannett, before second album, *Body Exit Mind*, was recorded with Craig Leon (Blondie, Ramones, Fall) at the helm. Their literate exposition of post-punk pop won them many friends in the media, though record sales failed to transpose to chart placings outside the 'independent' sector.

Albums: *Pigeon Hole* (Play It Again Sam 1990), *Body Exit Mind* (Play It Again Sam 1992).

Video: *Wake Up And Make Love Before 8:30 In The Morning* (1993).

New Model Army

With their roots embedded in the punk era, New Model Army were formed in Bradford, Yorkshire, in 1980, and immediately outlined their manifesto by naming themselves after the Sir Thomas Fairfax/Oliver Cromwell revolutionary army. The group was and is led by Justin 'Slade The Leveller' Sullivan (b. 1956, Buckinghamshire, England; guitar/vocals), a former platform sweeper and Mars Bar production line worker, with the help of Jason 'Moose' Harris (b. 1968; bass/guitar) and Robb Heaton (b. 1962, Cheshire, England; drums/guitar). Their brand of punk folk/rock attracted a loyal cult following, much of whom shared the band's grievances towards the Tory government policies of the 80s. This was best executed on their debut album, which combined militant themes such as 'Spirit Of The Falklands' and 'Vengeance' (a vitriolic anthem about getting even with one's trespassers) with the haunting lament for childhood, 'A Liberal Education'. The group's championing of traditional working class ethics saw an unexpected boost for a dying art and trade; that of the clog. New Model Army made their first public appearance at Scamps Disco in Bradford in October 1980. After releasing singles on Abstract Records, scoring a number 2 UK independent chart hit with 'The Price' in 1984, they formed an unlikely alliance with the multi-national EMI Records, which saw the band acquire a higher profile and a significantly increased recording budget. They eventually broke through to a wider audience with 'No Rest' which peaked at number 28 on the UK singles chart in 1985 - a position they were never to beat in an impressive run of 12 UK chart singles between 1985 and 1991. With often inflammatory lyrics, the band have never compromised their beliefs for commercial gain. They ran into trouble with the BBC's *Top Of The Pops* chart show for donning t-shirts with the (albeit laudable) slogan, 'Only Stupid Bastards Use Heroin'. This attracted some derision from the 'anarcho-punk' traditionalists Conflict, who replied with their own motif: 'Only Stupid Bastards Help EMI'. They subsequently continued to release quality albums, with considerable crossover potential, always maintaining credibility with their original fan base. In December 1991 the group left EMI, eventually finding a new home on Epic Records. Their first single for the label revealed few concessions to the mainstream: 'Here Comes The War' featured a picture of a charred body, and a pull-out poster instructing the user in how to prepare a nuclear bomb.

Albums: *Vengeance* (Abstract 1984), *No Rest For The Wicked* (EMI 1985), *Ghost Of Cain* (EMI 1986), *Radio Sessions* (Abstract 1988), *Thunder And Consolation* (EMI 1989), *Impurity* (EMI 1990), *Raw Melody Men* (EMI 1990), *The Love Of Hopeless Causes* (Epic 1993). Compilations: *The Independent Story* (Abstract 1987), *History* (EMI 1992).

New Musik

This UK pop group comprised Tony Mansfield (guitar/keyboards/vocals), Tony Hibbert (bass), Phil Towner (drums) and Clive Gates (keyboards). They came to prominence after a minor hit in 1979 with 'Straight Lines', during 1980 with three pop/synthesizer hits on the GTO label, 'Living By Numbers', 'The World Of Water' and 'Sanctuary'. Mansfield regarded their debut *From A To B* as rudimentary, but the succeeding *Anywhere* fared less well, despite its evident maturity. The change in style also took its toll on the band with the departure of Hibbert and Towner soon after its release. They were replaced by electronic percussionist Cliff Venner for the band's final and rather uninspired *Warp*. Full of empty electronic dance tracks it was notable for an daring attempt at the Beatles' *All You Need Is Love*. However, sales were very poor and they soon disbanded. Mansfield went on to produce hits for Captain Sensible, Mari Wilson, Naked Eyes and worked on A-Ha's debut album *Hunting High And Low*.

Albums: *From A To B* (1980), *Anywhere* (1981), *Warp* (1982).

New Order

When Joy Division's Ian Curtis committed suicide in May 1980 the three remaining members, Bernard Sumner (b. Bernard Dicken, 4 January 1956, Salford, Manchester, England; guitar/vocals), Peter Hook (b. 13 February 1956, Manchester, England; bass) and Stephen Morris (b. 28 October 1957, Macclesfield, Cheshire, England; drums) continued under the name New Order. Sumner took over vocal duties and the trio embarked upon a low-key tour of the USA, intent on continuing as an entity independent of the massive reputation Joy Division had achieved shortly before their demise. Later that same year they recruited Morris's girlfriend, Gillian Gilbert (b. 27 January 1961, Manchester, England; keyboards/guitar) and wrote and rehearsed their debut, *Movement*, which was released the following year. Their first single, 'Ceremony', penned by Joy Division, was a UK Top 40 hit in the spring of 1981, and extended the legacy of their previous band. Hook's deep, resonant bass line and Morris's crisp, incessant drumming were both Joy Division trademarks. The vocals, however, were weak, Sumner clearly at this stage feeling uncomfortable as frontman. Much was made, in 1983, of the band 'rising from the ashes' of Joy Division in the music press, when *Power, Corruption And Lies* was released. Their experimentation with electronic gadgetry was fully realised and the album contained many surprises and memorable songs. The catchy bass riff and quirky lyrics of 'Age Of Consent' made it an instant classic, while the sign-off line, on the otherwise elegiac 'Your Silent Face', 'You've caught me at a bad time/So why don't you piss off', showed that

Sumner no longer felt under any pressure to match the poetic, introspective lyricism of Ian Curtis. As well as redefining their sound they clearly now relished the role of 'most miserable sods in pop'. 'Blue Monday', released at this time in 12-inch format only, went on to become the biggest selling 12-inch single of all-time in the UK. In 1983 'disco' was a dirty word amongst the independent fraternity and 'Blue Monday', which combined an infectious dance beat with a calm, aloof vocal, was a brave step into uncharted territory. As well as influencing a legion of UK bands, it would be looked back upon as a crucial link between the disco of the 70s and the dance/house music wave at the end of the 80s. New Order had now clearly established themselves, and throughout the 80s and into the 90s they remained the top independent band in the UK, staying loyal to Manchester's Factory Records. Their subsequent collaboration with 'hot' New York hip-hop producer Arthur Baker spawned the anti-climactic 'Confusion' (1983) and 'Thieves Like Us' (1984). Both singles continued their preference for the 12-inch format, stretching in excess of six minutes, and stressing their lack of concern for the exposure gained by recording with mainstream radio in mind. *Low Life* appeared in 1985 and is perhaps their most consistently appealing album to date. While the 12-inch version of *Low Life*'s 'Perfect Kiss' was a magnificent single, showing the band at their most inspired and innovative, the collaboration with producer John Robie on the single version of 'Subculture' indicated that their tendency to experiment and 'play around' could also spell disaster. Their next album, 1986's *Brotherhood*, although containing strong tracks such as 'Bizarre Love Triangle', offered nothing unexpected. It wasn't until the UK Top 5 single 'True Faith' in 1987, produced and co-written by Stephen Hague hot on the heels of his success with the Pet Shop Boys and accompanied by an award-winning Phillipe Decouffle video, that New Order found themselves satisfying long term fans and general public alike. The following year Quincy Jones' remix of 'Blue Monday' provided the group with another Top 5 hit. If the recycling of old songs and proposed 'personal' projects fuelled rumours of a split then 1989's *Technique* promptly dispelled them. The album, recorded in Ibiza, contained upbeat bass-and-drums-dominated tracks that characterized the best of their early output. Its most striking feature, however, was their flirtation with the popular Balearic style, as in the hit single, 'Fine Time', which contained lines like 'I've met a lot of cool chicks, But I've never met a girl with all her own teeth', delivered in a voice that parodied Barry White's notoriously sexist, gravelly vocals of the 70s. Meanwhile the band had changed significantly as a live act. Their reputation for inconsistency and apathy, as well as their staunch refusal to play encores, was by now replaced with confident, crowd-pleasing hour-long sets. In the summer of 1990 they reached the UK number 1 position with 'World In Motion', accompanied by the England World Cup Squad, with a song that earned the questionable accolade of best football record of all time, and caused a band member to observe that 'this is probably the last straw for Joy Division fans'. Rather than exploiting their recent successes with endless tours, the group unexpectedly branched out into various spin-off ventures. Hook formed the hard-rocking Revenge, Sumner joined former Smiths' guitarist Johnny Marr in Electronic and Morris/Gilbert recorded an album under the self-effacing title, The Other Two. The extra-curricular work prompted persistent rumours that New Order had irrevocably split, but no official announcement or press admission was forthcoming. In the summer of 1991 the group announced that they had reconvened for a new album which was eventually released in 1993. *Republic* consequently met with mixed reviews reflecting critical confusion about their status and direction. While retaining the mix of rock and dance music successfully honed on *Technique*, the tone was decidedly more downbeat, even sombre. Sadly it arrived too late to help the doomed Factory label, and afterwards the band's membership would return to varied solo projects.

Albums: *Movement* (Factory 1981), *Power, Corruption And Lies* (Factory 1983), *Low Life* (Factory 1985), *Brotherhood* (Factory 1986), *Technique* (Factory 1989), *Republic* (London 1993). Compilations: *Substance* (Factory 1987), *The Peel Sessions* (Strange Fruit 1990), *Live In Concert* (Windsong 1992).
Videos: *Taras Schevenko* (1984), *Pumped Full Of Drugs* (1988), *Substance 1989* (1989), *Brixton Academy April 1987* (1989), *neworderstory* (1993), *(The Best Of) New Order* (1995).

New York Dolls

One of the most influential rock bands of the last 20 years, the New York Dolls pre-dated the punk and sleaze metal movements which followed and offered both a crash course in rebellion with style. Formed in 1972, the line-up stabilized with David Johansen (b. 9 January 1950, Staten Island, New York, USA; vocals), Johnny Thunders (b. John Anthony Genzale Jnr, 15 July 1952, New York City, New York, USA, d. 23 April 1991, New Orleans, Louisiana, USA; guitar), Arthur Harold Kane (bass), Sylvain Sylvain (guitar/piano) and Jerry Nolan (d. 14 January 1992; drums), the last two having replaced Rick Rivets and Billy Murcia (d. 6 November 1972). The band revelled in an outrageous glam-rock image: lipstick, high-heels and tacky leather outfits providing their visual currency. Underneath they were a first rate rock 'n' roll band, dragged up on the music of the Stooges, Rolling Stones and MC5. Their self-titled debut, released in 1973, was a major landmark in rock history, oozing attitude, vitality and controversy from every note. It met with widespread critical acclaim, but this never transferred to commercial success. The follow-up, *Too Much Too Soon*, was an appropriate title - and indicated that alcohol and drugs were beginning to take their toll. The album remains a charismatic collection of punk/glam-rock anthems, typically delivered with 'wasted' cool. Given a unanimous thumbs down from the music press the band began to implode shortly afterwards. Johansen embarked on a solo career and Thunders formed the Heartbreakers. The Dolls continued for a short time before eventually grinding to a halt in 1975, despite the auspices of new manager Malcolm McLaren. The link to the Sex Pistols and the UK punk movement is stronger than that fact alone, with the Dolls remaining a constant reference point for teen rebels the world over. Sadly for the band, their rewards were fleeting.

Jerry Nolan died as a result of a stroke on 14 January 1992 whilst undergoing treatment for pneumonia and meningitis. Thunders had departed from an overdose, in mysterious circumstances, less than a year previously. *Red Patent Leather* is a poor quality and posthumously-released live recording from May 1975 - *Rock 'N' Roll* offers a much more representative collection.

Albums: *New York Dolls* (Mercury 1973), *Too Much Too Soon* (Mercury 1974), *Red Patent Leather* (New Rose 1984). Compilations: *Lipstick Killers* (ROIR 1983), *Rock 'N' Roll* (Mercury 1994).

Newman, Colin

A founder member of Wire, guitarist/vocalist Newman began a solo career upon the group's demise in 1980. The engaging *A-Z* unsurprisingly furthered the tenor of his former act's work - much of it was intended for a provisional fourth Wire album - and ex-colleagues Mike Thorne (keyboards/production) and Robert Gotobed (drums) were on hand to further the sense of continuity. The set ably showcased Newman's grasp of dissonant pop and an ability to subvert the form while engaging with its rules. *Provisionally Entitled The Singing Fish* was a purely instrumental set which the artist produced and contributed an array of different instruments to. Newman's discipline and dark humour was nonetheless still evident. Within months he issued *Not To*, which echoed the style of his debut. Significantly Thorne had dropped from the picture, and the absence of his sometimes overstated keyboards allowed space for guitarist Desmond Simmons to develop. Simon Gillham (bass) and the ever-faithful Gotobed added punch to a collection blending new material with Wire and *A-Z* leftovers. Challenging, minimalist and sometimes splintered rhythmically, *Not To* captures Newman at his best. Paradoxically, he then withdrew from music for a period but, having obtained a grant, journeyed to India to undertake a series of recordings. His return in 1984 sparked the seeds of Wire's reunion two years later. Newman remained committed to the group, later dubbed Wir on Gotobed's departure, but continued his solo career with *Commercial Suicide*. Aided by Malka Spigel and Sean Bonnar/Samy Birnach of Minimal Impact - whose 1985 album, *Raging Souls*, Newman produced - the singer herein offered a quieter, more introspective style than on previous recordings. *It Seems* featured the same core trio, while the additional use of horn and reed players added depth, but in 1994 he formed Oracle with Birnbach and Speigel (now Newman's wife). The sumptious *Tree* followed, issued on the collective's Swim label. The album, recorded over a five-year period, contained a haunting version of the Lovin' Spoonful's 'Coconut Grove' and confirmed Newman's valued position on the periphary of modern music.

Albums: *A-Z* (Beggars Banquet 1980), *Provisionally Entitled The Singing Fish* (4AD 1981), *Not To* (4AD 1982), *Commercial Suicide* (Crammed Discs 1986), *It Seems* (Crammed Discs 1988).

Newtown Neurotics

Formed in the English post-war 'new town' of Harlow, Essex, the Newtown Neurotics produced a fine blend of pop and

punk rock with a strong left-wing political slant. Coming together in the spring of 1978, the group comprised Steve Drewett (vocals/guitars), Colin Dredd (bass/vocals) and Tiggy Barber (drums). 'Hypocrite' (1979) and 'When The Oil Runs Out' (1980) appeared on their own No Wonder label, after which Barber was replaced by Simon Lomond. The Neurotics became increasingly involved in the agit-pop and ranting poetry scenes throughout the 80s, regularly playing at benefit concerts and festivals with the likes of Attila The Stockbroker. The strong socialist rhetoric was apparent on their third single on the short-lived but impressive CNT label, 'Kick Out The Tories', in May 1982, followed in December by an attack on Britain's 'Licensing Hours'. When CNT folded, the Newtown Neurotics moved to Razor Records for their debut album. *Beggars Can Be Choosers* was an entertaining yet pertinent mix of scathing observation and new wave power and was promoted on single by a cover of the Ramones' 'Blitzkrieg Bop'. November 1984 saw the band move back to their No Wonder label for 'Suzie Is A Heartbreaker' (again hinting at a Ramones' connection), before the Neurotics dropped the 'Newtown' from their name, signing to Jungle Records in the process. The first fruits of this deal emerged as *Repercussions* in 1985, showcasing a group who'd lost none of their musical vigour or political evangelism. 'Living With Unemployment' followed in 1986 (with the help of ranting comedian Porky The Poet and the rumbustious Attila), preceding *Kickstarting A Backfiring Nation*. The Neurotics turned up occasionally during the late 80s (with *Is Your Washroom Breeding Bolshovics?*, for example) while the new decade was celebrated with *45 Revolutions Per Minute*, a singles compilation of the band's 'twelve blazing rock anthems' from 1979-84. The band had actually broken up in October 1988 when then bassist Colin Dredd contracted pleurisy, going on to play a series of astonishing farewell shows in Harlow with a stand-in bass player. Drewett and Mac would go on to form the Unstoppable Beat.
Albums: *Beggars Can Be Choosers* (Razor 1983), *Repercussions* (Jungle 1985), *Kickstarting A Backfiring Nation* (Jungle 1986), *Is Your Washroom Breeding Bolshovics?* (Jungle 1988). Compilation: *45 Revolutions Per Minute* (Jungle 1990).

Nightingales

After a series of low-key UK school bands, Robert Lloyd (b. 1959, Cannock, Staffordshire, England) formed the Prefects - one of the earliest punk bands - who toured with the Clash. They split up in 1979 and Lloyd assembled the Nightingales using the best of the musicians who had passed through the ranks of the Prefects. The first of many subsequent Nightingales line-ups were Alan and Paul Apperley, Joe Crow, Eamonn Duffy and Lloyd himself. They were ably championed by BBC disc jockey John Peel, for whom Lloyd has recorded more sessions under various guises than any other artist. Peel himself said of them: '(their performances) will serve to confirm their excellence when we are far enough distanced from the 1980s to look at the period rationally, and other, infinitely better known bands stand revealed as charlatans'. The Nightingales' debut single, 'Idiot Strength', was released in 1981 on the band's own Vindaloo label in association with Rough Trade Records. Joe Crow then

departed and his replacements, Nick Beales and Andy Lloyd, two of 15 personnel who would pass through the ranks, brought a totally different sound to the band. The Cherry Red label picked them up and the band's career began in earnest. Lloyd soon established himself as one of the more interesting lyricists of the independent chart. Most of his tirades were draped in humour: 'I'm too tired to do anything today, but tomorrow I'll start my diet, and answer some of my fan mail ('Elvis: The Last Ten Days'). Alternatively: 'I worked in a bakery ... the jokes were handed down like diseases, I only worked there for the bread.' The lack of success of subsequent releases led Lloyd and friends to the new Red Flame label started by Dave Kitson, the promoter of the Moonlight Club in London's Hampstead. Still unhappy with the way record companies were handling his band's career, Lloyd decided to reactivate the Vindaloo label. Ironically, this led to the demise of the Nightingales as Lloyd needed to spend more time as songwriter, producer and label boss for his relatively successful roster of artists such as We've Got A Fuzzbox And We're Gonna Use It and comedien Ted Chippington. When Fuzzbox toured America, taking the Nightingales' keyboard player with them, Lloyd dissolved the group and concentrated on a solo career. The Nightingales' legacy was wrapped up in 1991 with a compilation album for Mau Mau Records with sleevenotes written by a still devoted John Peel.
Albums: *Pigs On Purpose* (Cherry Red 1982), *Hysterics* (Red Flame 1983), *Just The Job* (Vindaloo 1983), *In The Good Old Country Ways* (Vindaloo 1986). Compilation: *What A Scream* (Mau Mau 1991).

Nine Inch Nails

Trent Reznor, the multi-instrumentalist, vocalist, and creative force behind Nine Inch Nails, trained as a classical pianist during his small-town Pennsylvania childhood, but his discovery of rock and early industrial groups, despite his dislike of the 'industrial' tag, changed his musical direction completely. Following a period working in a Cleveland recording studio and playing in local bands, Reznor began recording as Nine Inch Nails in 1988. The dark, atmospheric *Pretty Hate Machine*, written, played and co-produced by Reznor, was largely synthesizer-based, but the material was transformed on stage by a ferocious wall of guitars, and show-stealing Lollapalooza performances in 1991. Coupled with a major US hit with 'Head Like A Hole', it brought platinum status. Inspired by the live band, Reznor added an abrasive guitar barrage to the Nine Inch Nails sound for *Broken* (a subsequent remix set was titled *Fixed*), which hit the US Top 10, winning a Grammy for 'Wish'. 'Happiness In Slavery', however, courted controversy with an almost-universally banned video, where performance artist Bob Flanagan gave himself up to be torn apart as slave to a machine, acting out the theme of control common to Reznor's lyrics. Reznor also filmed an unreleased full-length *Broken* video which he felt 'makes 'Happiness In Slavery' look like a Disney movie'. By this time, Reznor had relocated to Los Angeles, building a studio in a rented house at 10050 Cielo Drive, which he later discovered was the scene of the Tate murders by the Manson Family (much to his disgust due to eternal interview questions thereafter about the

contribution of the house's atmosphere to *The Downward Spiral*). Occupying the middle ground between the styles of previous releases, *The Downward Spiral*'s multilayered blend of synthesizer textures and guitar fury provides a fascinating soundscape for Reznor's exploration of human degradation through sex, drugs, violence, depression and suicide, closing with personal emotional pain on 'Hurt': 'I hurt myself today, To see if I still feel, I focus on the pain, The only thing that's real'. *The Downward Spiral* made its US debut at number 2, and a return to live work with Robin Finck (guitar), Danny Lohneer (bass/guitar), James Woolley (keyboards) and Reznor's long-time friend and drummer Chris Vrenna drew floods of praise, with Nine Inch Nails being one of the most talked-about acts at the Woodstock anniversary show. 1994 saw the first non-Nine Inch Nails releases on Reznor's Nothing label, and the band also found time to construct an acclaimed soundtrack for Oliver Stone's film, *Natural Born Killers*. In the following year Reznor announced plans to record an album with circus 'freak show' specialist, Jim Rose, stating with typical bombast: 'the record will confront just about ever issue that upsets people. It will be non-PC in every way imaginable'.
Albums: *Pretty Hate Machine* (TVT 1989), *Broken* (Nothing 1992, mini-album), *Fixed* (Nothing 1992, mini-album), *The Downward Spiral* (Nothing 1994).

999

This London-based, UK punk band was formed in May 1977. Dispensing with earlier names such as the Dials, 48 Hours and the Fanatics, Nick Cash (b. Keith Lucas, 6 May 1950, Gosport, Hampshire, England; guitar/vocals) was a former Kilburn And The High Roads guitarist and studied at Canterbury College Of Art under Ian Dury. Cash teamed up with Guy Days (guitar), Jon Watson (bass) and Pablo LaBrittain (drums) who set out to establish themselves on the thriving live scene in the capital. After releasing the fiery 'I'm Alive' on their own LaBrittain Records, United Artists signed them and quickly re-issued it. Two further singles, 'Nasty Nasty' and 'Emergency' were equally memorable for their energetic melodies, though 1978's debut album featured several weaker tracks. *Separates* was stronger, with compelling numbers like the single 'Homicide' resorting to muscular choruses instead of simple speed. However, LaBrittain was the subject of a motoring accident on the band's return from Scandinavia, and was replaced by friend Ed Case. With high sales of all their product in the USA, the band undertook a series of lucrative tours across the Atlantic, which earned them a degree of resentment from domestic supporters. Following the return of LaBrittain to the fold, the group signed a new contract with Radarscope Records, eventually transferring to Polydor Records. *The Biggest Prize In Sport* and *Concrete* represented their most accomplished work, although two follow-up cover version singles were evidence that inspiration was in short supply. This observation is certainly true of 1983's *13th Floor Madness*, though their last studio album *Face To Face* was more convincing. By the end of 1985 Watson had left and was replaced by Danny Palmer, with the band once more concentrating on touring in Europe and America. In the 90s they have been the subject of a welter of compilations and

live albums in the wake of renewed interest in punk nostalgia, but the better elements of their back-catalogue argue strongly against the 'dregs of punk' tag which has hung around their necks in recent times.
Albums: *999* (United Artists 1978), *Separates* (United Artists 1978), *High Energy Plan* (PVC 1979, US version of *Separates* with different track-listing), *The Biggest Prize In Sport* (Polydor 1980), *Concrete* (Polydor 1981), *13th Floor Madness* (Albion 1983), *Face To Face* (Labritain 1985), *You Us It* (1994). Compilations: *The Singles Album* (United Artists 1980), *Greatest Hits* (Albion 1984), *In Case Of Emergency* (Dojo 1986), *Lust Power And Money* (ABC 1987, live album), *Live And Loud* (Link 1989), *The Cellblock Tapes* (Link 1990), *The Early Stuff - The UA Years* (EMI 1992).
Video: *Feelin' Alright With The Crew* (1987).

Nirvana

Formed in Aberdeen, Washington, USA, in 1988, the Nirvana which the MTV generation came to love comprised Kurt Cobain (b. Kurt Donald Cobain, 20 February 1967, Hoquiam, Seattle, USA, d. 5 April 1994, Seattle; guitar/vocals), Krist Novoselic (b. 16 May 1965, Croatia, Yugoslavia; bass) and Dave Grohl (b. 14 January 1969; drums). Grohl was 'something like our sixth drummer', explained Cobain, and had been recruited from east coast band Dave Brammage, having previously played with Scream, who recorded for Minor Threat's influential Dischord Records label. Their original drummer was Chad Channing; at one point Dinosaur Jr's J. Mascis had been touted as a permanent fixture, along with Dan Peters from Mudhoney. Having been signed by the Seattle-based Sub Pop Records, the trio completed their debut single, 'Love Buzz'/'Big Cheese', the former a song written and first recorded by 60s Dutch group, Shocking Blue. Second guitarist Jason Everman was then added prior to *Bleach*, which cost a meagre $600 to record. Though he was pictured on the cover, he played no part in the actual recording (going on to join Mindfunk, via Soundgarden and Skunk). The set confirmed Nirvana's ability to match heavy riffs with melody and it quickly attracted a cult following. However, Channing left the group following a European tour, and as a likely replacement proved hard to find, Dan Peters from labelmates Mudhoney stepped in on a temporary basis. He was featured on the single, 'Sliver', Nirvana's sole 1990 release. New drummer David Grohl reaffirmed a sense of stability. The revamped trio secured a prestigious deal with Geffen Records whose faith was rewarded with *Nevermind*, which broke the band worldwide. This was a startling collection of songs which transcended structural boundaries, notably the distinctive slow verse/fast chorus format, and almost single-handedly brought the 'grunge' subculture overground. It topped the US charts early in 1992, eclipsing much-vaunted competition from Michael Jackson and Dire Straits and topped many Album Of The Year polls. The opening track, 'Smells Like Teen Spirit', reached the UK Top 10; further confirmation that Nirvana now combined critical and popular acclaim. In early 1992 the romance of Cobain and Courtney Love of Hole was sealed when the couple married (Love giving birth to a daughter, Frances Bean). It was already obvious, however, that Cobain was struggling with his new role as 'spokesman for a generation'. The first big story to break concerned an article in *Vanity Fayre* which alleged Love had taken heroin while pregnant, which saw the state intercede on the child's behalf by not allowing the Cobains alone with the child during its first month. Press interviews ruminated on the difficulties experienced in recording a follow-up album, and also Cobain's use of a variety of drugs in order to stem the pain arising from a stomach complaint. The recording of *In Utero*, produced by Big Black/Rapeman alumni Steve Albini, was not without difficulties either. Rumours circulated concerning confrontations with both Albini and record company Geffen over the 'low-fi' production. When the record was finally released the effect was not as immediate as *Nevermind*, though Cobain's songwriting remained inspired on 'Penny Royal Tea', 'All Apologies' and the evocative 'Rape Me'. His descent into self-destruction accelerated in 1994, however, as he went into a coma during dates in Italy (it was later confirmed that this had all the markings of a failed suicide attempt), before returning to Seattle to shoot himself on 5 April 1994. The man who had long protested that Nirvana were 'merely' a punk band had finally been destroyed by the success that overtook him and them. The wake conducted in the press was matched by public demonstrations of affection and loss, which included suspected copycat suicides. The release of *Unplugged In New York* offered some small comfort for Cobain's fans, with the singer's understated, aching

delivery on a variety of covers and Nirvana standards one of the most emotive sights and sounds of the 90s. Grohl and Novoselic would play together again in the Foo Fighters, alongside ex-Germs guitarist Pat Smear (who had added second guitar to previous touring engagements and the band's *MTV Unplugged* appearance) following press rumours that Grohl would be working with Pearl Jam (much to Courtney Love's chagrin) or Tom Petty. In reality both former members would continue to work together under the Foo Fighters' moniker, with small club engagements in the US and the recording of a demo album.

Albums: *Bleach* (Sub Pop 1989), *Nevermind* (Geffen 1991), *In Utero* (Geffen 1993), *Unplugged In New York* (Geffen 1994). Compilation: *Incesticide* (Geffen 1992).

Video: *Live! Tonight! Sold Out!* (1994).

Further reading: *Come As You Are*, Michael Azerrad. *Nirvana And The Sound Of Seattle*, Brad Morrell. *Route 66: On The Road To Nirvana*, Gina Arnold. *Never Fade Away*, Dave Thompson. *Cobain - By The Editors Of Rolling Stone*.

Nitzer Ebb

The driving force behind this electronic based band are Douglas McCarthy (b. 1 September 1966, Chelmsford, England; vocals) and Bon Harris (b. 12 August 1965, Chelmsford, England; percussion/vocals). Frustrated by their environment at school in Chelmsford, and inspired by bands like D.A.F., Bauhaus and the Birthday Party, they began their

first experiments with synthesizers and drum machines in 1983. They were joined in their strictly amateur pursuits by school-mate David Gooday. They had summoned enough experience and confidence to release their first single the next year, 'Isn't It Funny How Your Body Works', on Power Of Voice Communications. They were nothing if not prolific, releasing a further five singles over the next twelve months, which led to a deal with the premier UK independent stable, Mute Records, and Geffen Records in the US. 1987 saw their first album on the shelves, *That Total Age*, home to surging minimalist aggression, and the beginning of a long-term relationship with producer Flood, who would remix the single 'Join In The Chant'. On Gooday's departure Julian Beeston was enrolled. After a lengthy European trek with Depeche Mode, the band recorded *Belief*, and in 1989 followed up their own world tour with *Showtime*. Their third album revealed a swing in attitude, with music that was less confrontational and more consumer friendly. This was particularly true in the US, where the single 'Fun To Be Had' peaked at Number 2 in the US dance charts. Their most recent album has confirmed their popularity with fans and a previously reluctant press. As McCarthy puts it: 'With the advent of *Ebbhead*, I think we've managed to twist listenability around to our way of thinking'.
Albums: *That Total Age* (Mute 1987), *Belief* (Mute 1988), *Showtime* (Mute 1989), *Ebbhead* (Mute 1991), *Big Hit* (Mute 1995).

Nordenstam, Stina

b. 1969, Stockholm, Sweden. Nordenstam came to music early through the jazz records and amateur playing of her father. She took to the fiddle and piano, and precociously began writing her own classically inspired compositions. At 15 she was singing modern classical music, but her next move, backed by the Flippermen learned towards jazz. Signed up by Swedish indie label Telegraph, she debuted with *Memories Of A Colour*, an ethereally evocative and occasionally disturbing journey through her psyche, setting her short story songs or vignettes to impeccably skewed jazzy arrangements. This soared to such Scandinavian success that the next opening of the Swedish parliament was accompanied by a rare Nordenstam gig. The oft-heard comparisons with Kate Bush and Joni Mitchell, whom she admires, are misleading. Nordenstam had taken her early passions (Cannonball Adderley, Erik Satie, John Coltane and Bartok), fused them with post-feminist angst and sang the results in a spooky *Village Of The Damned* little girl whisper. 1994's *And She Closed Her Eyes* was more of the same but better, tending towards ambient jazz with contributions from Jon Hassell and more guitar from Nordenstam.
Albums: *Memories Of A Colour* (Telegram 1992), *And She Closed Her Eyes* (Telegram 1994).

Northside

This UK independent label dance music band was formed in mid-1989 in Manchester by Warren 'Dermo' Dermody (vocals), Cliff Ogier (bass), Timmy Walsh (guitar) and Paul Walsh (drums). After signing to the premier Manchester independent, Factory Records, they released two singles in 1990, 'Shall We Take A Trip' and 'Rising Star', which

benefited from the 'Madchester' explosion brought about by the success of label mates Happy Mondays. Pilloried in the press as being an opportunistic 'baggy' band, these releases and an attendant album did little to persuade critics of any real significance to their shambolic dance shuffles.
Album: *Chicken Rhythms* (Factory 1991).

Nova Mob

(see Hart, Grant)

Nuns

Formed in San Francisco, California, USA, in 1977, the Nuns were one of the city's leading punk/new wave attractions, forerunning the rock and outrage antics of the Dead Kennedys. Their insubstantial progress was further limited by continual line-up problems, but such frustrations coalesced to astonishing effect in their 'Savage'/'Suicide Child' single. Their work appeared on several compilations, including *Rodney On The Roq* and *Experiments In Destiny*, but having split up in 1979, they reformed the following year to complete *The Nuns*, only to disband again. Ritchie Detrick (vocals), Jeff Olener (vocals), Alejandro Escovado (guitar), Jennifer Miro (keyboards), Mike Varney (bass) and Jeff Raphael (drums) were among those passing through the Nuns' ranks, of whom Escavado subsequently joined Rank And File. The Nuns reformed again in 1986 to record a completely different record, the icy, dance-fixated *Rumania*.
Albums: *The Nuns* (Posh Boy 1980), *Rumania* (PVC 1986).

O

O'Connor, Hazel

b. 16 May 1955, Coventry, England. O'Connor's introduction to showbusiness involved working as an dancer and starred with a minor movie role in *Girls Come First*. At the close of the 70s, she signed to the Albion label and issued the single 'Ee-I-Adio', which failed to sell. Her profile increased when she appeared in the film *Breaking Glass*, a melodramatic portrayal of a fictional rock star. O'Connor's aggressive singing style and confrontational appearance was used to good effect on the Tony Visconti produced 'Eighth Day' (complete with 'robotic' intonation) which reached the UK Top 5. The following year, she registered two further Top 10 singles, 'D-Days' and the uncharacteristic ballad 'Will You'. Various disputes with her record company and management slowed down her career. In 1984, she recorded *Smile* for RCA but the record sold poorly and the label declined to renew her option. O'Connor subsequently appeared in the musical *Girlfriends* in 1987.
Albums: *Breaking Glass* (1980), *Sons And Lovers* (1980),

Oasis

Glass Houses (1980), *Cover Plus* (1981), *Smile* (1984). Films: *Breaking Glass* (1980).

Oasis

From Manchester, England, Oasis became overnight sensations in 1994 on the back of sublime singles and exponentially increasing press interest, culminating in the fastest selling debut album of the 90s. Widely regarded in the press as natural successors to the Happy Mondays, Oasis proffered a similar working class roughneck chic. The group's creative axis is the Gallagher brothers, Noel (guitar/song writing) and Liam (vocals). They were brought up by Irish Roman Catholic parents in south Manchester suburb Burnage. While his younger brother was still in school, Noel, whose country and western DJ father has purchased a guitar for him at age 11, discovered punk, and like most of his peers happily engaged in truancy, burglary and glue-sniffing. After six month's probation for robbing a corner shop he began to take the instrument seriously at age 13, later finding his role model in Johnny Marr of the Smiths. Liam was not weaned on music until 1989 when his elder brother took him to see the Stone Roses. Afterwards Noel befriended Clint Boon of the Inspiral Carpets, subsequently becoming a guitar technician and travelling the world with them. When he rang home in 1991 he was informed by his mother that Liam had joined a band. Paul 'Bonehead' Arthurs (guitar), Tony McCarroll (drums) and Paul 'Guigs' McGuigan had been playing together as Rain (not the Liverpool group of similar moniker) before meeting with Liam, who became their singer, as they changed name to Oasis. When Noel returned to watch them play at Manchester's Boardwalk in 1992 he saw their promise, but insisted that they install him as lead guitarist and only perform his songs if he were to help them. Noel continued as roadie to the Inspiral Carpets to help purchase equipment, as the band set about establishing a local reputation. The incident which led to them being signed to Creation Records quickly passed into rock mythology. In May 1993 they drove to Glasgow with fellow denizens of the Boardwalk rehearsal studios, Sister Lovers, to support 18 Wheeler at King Tut's Wah Wah Club. Strong-arming their way on to the bill, they played five songs early in the evening, but these were enough to hypnotise Creation boss Alan McGee who offered them a contract there and then. However, they would not sign until several months later, during which time a copy of the band's demo had been passed to Johnny Marr, who became an early convert to the cause and put the band in touch with Electronic's management company, Ignition. With news spreading of the group's rise it seemed likely that the band would join any number of labels apart from Creation, with U2's Mother imprint rumoured to guarantee double any other offer. However, loyalty to the kindred spirits at Creation won through by October 1993, and two months later the label issued the group's 'debut', a one-sided 12-inch promo of 'Columbia' taken straight from the original demo. BBC Radio 1 immediately playlisted it (an almost unheralded event for such a 'non-release'). 1994 began with a torrent of press, much of it focusing on the group's errant behaviour. Punch-ups and the ingestion of large quantities of drink and drugs leading to gig cancellations, while frequent, often

violent bickering between the Gallagher brothers lent the group a sense of danger and mischief. 'Supersonic' reached the UK Top 40 in May 1995. 'Shakermaker', owing an obvious debt to the New Seekers' 'I'd Like To Teach The World To Sing', duly made number 11 two months later. High profile dates at the Glastonbury Festival and New York's New Music Seminar ensued, along with more stories of on the road indulgence. The Beatles-redolent 'Live Forever', with a sleeve featuring a photo of the house where John Lennon grew up, made the Top 10 in October. All of which ensured that the expectation for a debut album was now phenomenal. After scrapping the original tapes recorded at Monmouth's Monnow Studios, the songs had been completed with Mark Coyle and Anjali Dutt, with subsequent mixing by Electronic producer Owen Morris, at a total cost of £75,000. In August 1994 *Definitely Maybe* entered the UK charts at number 1, and, backed by a live version of the Beatles' 'I Am The Walrus', 'Cigarettes And Alcohol', a stage favourite, became the group's biggest UK singles success to date, when it reached number 7 in October 1994. In December they released 'Whatever' (not quite the Christmas number 1), a lush pop song with full orchestration that sounded astonishingly accomplished for a band whose recording career stretched over only eight months. Their assault on America began January 1995, and with a few gigs and word of mouth reports they were soon hovering around the US top 50. In mid-1995 it was announced that drummer McCarroll had amicably left the band. Few pop bands in recent years have created such a body of quality work in such a short time, and all done without resorting to media hype.
Albums: *Definitely Maybe* (Creation 1994), *Morning Glory* (Creation 1995).
Further reading: *Oasis. The Illustrated Story*, Paul Lester.

One Little Indian Records

The roots of the UK One Little Indian record label lie in the anarcho-punk scene of the early 80s particularly in one of its pioneering bands, Flux Of Pink Indians. The precursor to One Little Indian was Spiderleg, which released records by the System, Subhumans, and Amebix in addition to Flux's own material. Both labels were run by Derek Birkett (b. 18 February 1961, London, England), Flux's bass player, alongside friends and colleagues from the independent punk scene. Early releases included ones by Annie Anxiety, D&V and the Very Things. Reflecting on the mistakes made earlier, the label used expensive and tasteful cover art by Paul White's Me Company. When the Sugarcubes, a band Birkett previously knew when they were Kukl, broke through, financial security was assured. While One Little Indian retains its identity as the 'ethical indie', the operation is constructed on level-headed business practices: 'Our motives are artistic and business is reality'. Unlike many labels, the roster of bands does not have a uniform image or sounds. Music on the label includes the bright and breezy pop of the Popinjays, Heart Throbs and the Sugarcubes, the dance sound of the Shamen and Finitribe, the delicate, crafted pop of Kitchens of Distinction and the shattering volume of What? Noise. The label was also the temporary home for They Might Be Giants, who released *Lincoln* and two singles.

The recent mainstream success of the Shamen has consolidated their position in the independent charts. The massive success of Björk was long overdue and was financially very welcome, although other outfits, like Daisy Chainsaw, failed to fulfil expectations. Recent signings include Compulsion, Credit To The Nation and the revitalized Chumbawamba. The label has released several 'Best Of' compilations which act as a good introductions. Selected albums: Sugarcubes: *Life's Too Good* (One Little Indian 1988). Heart Throbs: *Cleopatra Grip* (One Little Indian 1990). Shamen: *Boss Drum* (One Little Indian 1992). Björk: *Debut* (One Little Indian 1993). Credit To The Nation: *Take Dis* (One Little Indian 1993). Chumbawamba: *Anarchy* (One Little Indian 1994).

101ers

Formed in London, England, in May 1974, the 101ers made their performing debut four months later at the Telegraph pub in Brixton. Led by guitarist/vocalist Joe Strummer, the group established itself on a fading pub-rock circuit about to be undermined by the advent of punk. Support slots by the Sex Pistols confirmed Strummer's growing agitation and he left to join the Clash in June 1976. The 101ers then broke up with Clive Timperley (guitar) later joining the Passions. Dan Kelleher (bass) moved on to the Derelicts and Richard Dudanski (drums) went on to work with the Raincoats and PiL. The group was commemorated by 'Keys To Your Heart', a 7-inch single issued on the independent Chiswick Records label the following month. In 1981 Strummer sanctioned the release of *Elgin Avenue Breakdown*, a collection of live recordings, BBC sessions and studio out-takes. The material ranged from traditional R&B - 'Too Much Monkey Business' and 'Route 66' - to ebullient originals which showed the singer's abrasive delivery already in place.
Album: *Elgin Avenue Breakdown* (Andulucia 1981).

1,000 Violins

This late 80s UK independent group were formed in Sheffield, Yorkshire, England, and comprised Darren Swindells (bass), Colin Gregory (guitar), Vincent Keenan (vocals), David Warmsley (keyboards/guitar) and Ian Addie (drums, replacing Sean O'Neil and Peter Day). Their routine but well executed brand of 60s influenced pop gave them three UK independent chart hits, the biggest being 'Locked Out Of The Love-In' (1987), which reached number 16. Their lone album was released on the US-based Immaculate Records. Despite critical plaudits that was the closest they came to establishing themselves, with one song recorded for a Janice Long BBC Radio 1 session, 'The Only Time I Got To Rock Was In My Granny's Chair', serving as something of an epitaph.
Album: *Hey Man, That's Beautiful* (Immaculate 1988).

Only Ones

The Only Ones were formed in 1976 with a line-up comprising: Peter Perrett (vocals/guitar), John Perry (guitar), Alan Mair (bass) and Mike Kellie (drums). Although touted as a new wave group, the unit included several old lags; Mair had previously worked with the Beatstalkers, while Kellie

had drummed with Spooky Tooth, Peter Frampton and Balls. Perrett's former band, England's Glory, would have their demos released retrospectively after the Only Ones' demise. After a promising independent single, 'Lovers Of Today', the group were signed by CBS Records and made their debut with the searing opus, 'Another Girl, Another Planet' - on eof the new wave's most enduring songs. Front man Perrett, with his leopard-skin jacket and Lou Reed drawl, won considerable music press attention and the group's self-titled debut album was very well-received. A second self-produced collection, *Even Serpents Shine,* was also distinctive, but internal group friction and disagreements with their record company hampered their progress. Producer Colin Thurston took control of *Baby's Got A Gun*, which included a guest appearance by Pauline Murray, but lacked the punch of their earlier work. With sales dwindling, CBS dropped the group from their roster and the Only Ones finally broke up in 1981, with Perrett by now in the throes of desperate drug addiction. Since that time the group, and in particular, Perrett, have frequently been hailed as influential figures. After over-coming his chemical dependencies, Perrett made known his intentions for a come-back in 1991. This eventually materialised when his new band, The One, took the stage at London's Underworld in January 1994. This coincided with reports that Perrett had now written over 40 new songs.
Albums: *The Only Ones* (CBS 1978), *Even Serpents Shine* (CBS 1979), *Baby's Got A Gun* (CBS 1980). Compilations: *Special View* (CBS 1979), *Remains* (Closer 1984), *Alone In The Night* (Dojo 1986), *The Only Ones Live In London* (Skyclad 1989; also released as *Only Ones Live*, Demon 1989), *The Peel Sessions* (Strange Fruit 1989), *The Immortal Story* (Columbia 1992), *The Big Sleep* (Jungle 1993).

Orange Juice

Formed in Scotland at the end of the 70s, this engaging and, in some quarters, revered, pop group comprised Edwyn Collins (b. 23 August 1959, Edinburgh, Scotland; vocals/lead guitar), James Kirk (vocals/rhythm guitar), David McClymont (bass) and Steven Daly (drums). They began their career on the cult independent label Postcard Records where they issued some of the best pop records of the early 80s, including 'Blue Boy' and 'Falling And Laughing'. Collins' coy vocal and innocent romanticism gave them a charm which was matched by strong musicianship. After signing to Polydor Records they issued *You Can't Hide Your Love Forever*, a highly accomplished effort that augured well for the future. At that point, the group suffered an internal shake-up with Kirk and Daly replaced by Malcolm Ross and Zeke Manyika. *Rip It Up* was another strong work, and the insistent title-track reached the UK Top 10. Further musical differences saw the group reduced to Collins and Manyika as they completed an energetic mini-album, *Texas Fever*, and an eponymous third album, which included the wistful 'What Presence?' Collins subsequently recorded a couple of singles with Paul Quinn, after which he embarked on a solo career that has only begun to fulfil its early promise in the mid-90s. Ross joined the line-up of Roddy Frame's Aztec Camera. Manyika also spawned solo projects on Polydor and Parlophone Records.

Albums: *You Can't Hide Your Love Forever* (Polydor 1982), *Rip It Up* (Polydor 1982), *Texas Fever* (Polydor 1984, mini-album), *Ostrich Churchyard* (Postcard 1992, live album). Compilations: *In A Nutshell* (Polydor 1985), *The Very Best Of* (Polydor 1992), *The Heather's On Fire* (Postcard 1993).

Orb

Basically the Orb is one man, Dr Alex Paterson (b. Duncan Robert Alex Paterson, hence the appropriation of the Dr title), whose specialist field is the creation of ambient house music. A former Killing Joke roadie, member of Bloodsport, and A&R man at EG Records, he formed the original Orb in 1988 with Jimmy Cauty of Brilliant fame (for whom he had also roadied). The name was taken from a line in Woody Allen's *Sleeper*. The band first appeared on WAU! Mr Modo's showcase set *Eternity Project One* (released via Gee Street), with the unrepresentative 'Tripping On Sunshine'. However, their first release proper came with 1989's *Kiss* EP, again on WAU! Mr Modo (which had been set up by Paterson with Orb manager Adam Morris). It was completely overshadowed by the success of the band's subsequent release, 'A Huge Ever-Growing Pulsating Brain Which Rules From The Centre Of The Ultraworld'. It was an extraordinary marriage of progressive rock trippiness and ambience, founded on a centrepoint sample of Minnie Riperton's 'Loving You' (at least on initial copies, being voiced by a soundalike due to cle`arance worries later). The group signed with Big Life, but Cauty departed in April 1990. He had wished to take Paterson and the Orb on board in his new KLF Communications set-up. There was no little acrimony at the time and Cauty re-recorded an album, which was to have been the Orb's debut, deleting Paterson's contributions, and naming it *Space* (also the artist title). In the event the ethereal 'Little Fluffy Clouds', with co writer Youth, was the next Orb release, though that too ran into difficulties when the sample of Rickie Lee Jones' attracted the artist's displeasure. Paterson did at least meet future co-conspirator Thrash (b. Kristian Weston) during these sessions, who joined in late 1991 from a punk/metal background, hence his name (though he had also been a member of Fortran 5). Their debut album (and the remix set of similar title) was based on a journey to dimensions beyond known levels of consciousness, according to the participants. It soared, or perhaps sleepwalked, to the top of the UK album charts, and led to a plunge of remixes for other artists (including Front 242 and Primal Scream). The album was fully in tune with, and in many ways anticipating of, the blissed out rave subculture of the early 90s, mingled with dashes of early 70s progressive rock (Pink Floyd were an obvious reference point). There was also an LP's worth of the band's recordings for John Peel's Radio 1 show. This included a 20 minute version of 'Huge Ever-Growing...' which prompted fellow disc jockey Andy Kershaw to ring the BBC to complain, mockingly, about the return of hippy indulgence on a gross scale polluting the nation's airwaves. The Orb signed to Island in 1993 following a departure from Big Life that took seven months and eventually the high court to settle. The deal with Island allowed Paterson to continue to work on collaborative projects, through their own label Inter-Modo, outside of the Orb name. Other projects included a remix album for Yellow Magic Orchestra, though a previous request by Jean Michel Jarre for them to do the same for his *Oxygene* opus was declined. They also took the opportunity to play live at unlikely venues like the Danish Island of Trekroner, and generally appeared to be having a hugely enjoyable time of their unlikely celebrity, Paterson even being awarded honorary president of Strathclyde University's Student Union. However, their first studio set for Island, *Pomme Fritz*, saw them witness the first signs of a critical backlash.

Albums: *The Orbs Adventures Beyond The Ultraworld* (WAU! Mr Modo/Big Life 1991), *Peel Sessions* (Strange Fruit 1991), *Aubrey Mixes, The Ultraworld Excursion* (WAU! Mr Modo/Big Life 1992), UFOrb (WAU! Mr Modo/Big Life 1992, double album, available as a triple in limited edition), *Live 93* (Island 1993), *Pomme Fritz* (Island 1994, mini album), *Orbvs Terrarvm* (Island 1995).

Other Two

The most pure dance-orientated of the three major New Order spin-offs, the Other Two features arguably the least attention-seeking of the Manchester quartet: Stephen Morris (b. 28 October 1957, Macclesfield, Cheshire, England) and Gillian Gilbert (b. 27 January 1961, Manchester, England). Recording at their own studio in rural Macclesfield, they debuted on the charts with the number 41-peaking 'Tasty Fish' in 1991. The follow-up, 'Selfish', came two years later, but featured fashionable remixes by both Moby and Farley And Heller. The Other Two would also tamper with the work of other artists, as well as earning several credits for television and soundtrack motifs.

Album: *The Other Two & You* (London 1993).

Otway, John

b. 2 October, 1952, Aylesbury, Buckinghamshire, England. The enigmatic madcap John Otway first came to prominence in the early 70s with his guitar/fiddle-playing partner Wild Willie Barrett. Otway's animated performances and unusual vocal style caught the attention of Pete Townshend, who produced the duo's first two Track label singles, 'Murder Man' and 'Louisa On A Horse'. Extensive gigging, highlighted by crazed and highly entertaining stage antics, won Otway and Barrett a loyal collegiate following and finally a minor hit with 'Really Free' in 1977. Its b-side, 'Beware Of The Flowers ('Cause I'm Sure They're Going To Get You Yeh)' was equally appealing and eccentric and augured well for further hits. Although Otway (with and without Barrett) soldiered on with syllable-stretching versions of Tom Jones's 'Green Green Grass Of Home' and quirky novelty workouts such as 'Headbutts', he remains a 70s curio, still locked into the UK college/club circuit.

Albums: *John Otway And Wild Willie Barrett* (1977), *Deep And Meaningless* (1978), *Where Did I Go Right* (1979), *Way And Bar* (1980), *All Balls And No Willy* (1982), *The Wimp And The Wild* (1989), *Under The Covers And Over The Top* (1992), *Live!* (Amazing Feet 1994). Compilations: *Gone With The Bin Or The Best Of Otway And Barre* (1981), *Greatest Hits* (1986).

Further reading: *Cor Baby That's Really Me*, John Otway.

Our Daughters Wedding

This New York, USA electronic trio comprised Keith Silva (vocal), Layne Rico (synthesizers/vocal) and Scott (keyboards). After extensive gigging, they relocated to the UK and signed to EMI. In the summer of 1981, they broached the UK Top 40 with the catchy 'Lawnchairs'. The follow-up EP *The Digital Cowboy* gained considerable press but proved less commercial. Despite a strong record company investment, the trio lost ground and their sole album was followed by their demise.
Album: *Moving Windows* (1982).

Out Of My Hair

Effectively a vehicle for lead singer and guitarist 'Comfort' (b. Simon Eugene, c.1970), so much so that he sacked the rest of the original line-up when they objected to his controlling influence, Out Of My Hair additionally comprise Sean Elliot (guitar), Kenny Rumbles (drums) and Jon George (bass). Formed in London, England, and signed to RCA Records, the sound was one of glamorous indie guitar pop, with Comfort offering a Rolling Stones/Jimi Hendrix-styled vocal performance at its heart. However, he and the band remained suspicious of the 'retro' tag that had dogged more mainstream artists like Lenny Kravitz: 'I'm not into all that hippie shit. I was watching Woodstock the other day and it just made me think, Fuck Off!'. Despite this, the group's debut single, 'In The Groove Again', had an obvious 60s, neo-acid rock feel. The follow-up, 'Heart's Desire', was less restrained and more sprawling, but still in the classic pop tradition. Or, as Comfort prefers to call it, 'psychedelic bubblegum folk'.

Outcasts

At one time the premier punk band stationed in Northern Ireland, the Outcasts line-up revolved around the three Cowan brothers; Greg (b. c.1961; bass/vocals), Martin (b. c.1955; guitar) and Colin (b. c.1957; drums). This was the nucleus, though Gordon Blair had temporarily replaced Greg when he was injured in a car crash. The line-up was completed by 'Getty' (b. Colin Getgood, c.1960; guitar) and Raymond Falls (b. c.1965; additional drums). An impressive early single, 'Magnum Force', earned them the support of BBC disc jockey John Peel. They went on to release a solid debut album, characterized by the heavy rhythms produced by the twin drummers. However, before the release of *Seven Deadly Sins*, Colin became the second of the brothers to be injured in a car crash, this time fatally.
Albums: *Blood And Thunder* (Abstract 1983), *Seven Deadly Sins* (New Rose 1984).

Ozric Tentacles

Predominantly an 80s UK festival band, Ozric Tentacles was originally a name conjured up by the band for a psychedelic breakfast cereal. Their original line-up featured Ed Wynne

Out Of My Hair

(guitar), his brother Roly (bass), Nick 'Tig' Van Gelder (drums), Gavin Griffiths (guitar) and Joie 'Ozrooniculator' Hinton (keyboards). They met at an open camp fire at Stonehenge in 1982. By the following year a second synthesizer player, Tom Brookes had joined. They started gigging in clubs such as the 'Crypt' in Deptford, south-east London. There they met their second percussionist, Paul Hankin. They soon became regulars at another psychedelic 'head' venue, the Club Dog, at the George Robey pub in Finsbury Park, north London. The band's long existence has seen a number of shifts in personnel. In 1984 Griffiths left to form the Ullulators, and Brookes left a year later. Hinton remained but also played for the aforementioned Ullulators and also the Oroonies. The next major change arrived in 1987 when Merv Peopler replaced Van Gelder. More recently Steve Everett has replaced Brookes on synthesizers, while Marcus Carcus and John Egan have added extra percussion and flute. Considering their lengthy career it might appear that the band have had a relatively sporadic, and recent, recording output. However, much of their work from the mid-80s onwards was made available on six cassette-only albums. Into the early 90s, with the British neo-hippy, new age travellers receiving a higher media profile and their role in organizing music festivals becoming increasingly important, bands such as the Ozric Tentacles and the Levellers benefited greatly and began to widen their audience.
Albums: *Pungent Effulgent* (Dovetail 1989), *Erp Land* (Dovetail 1990), *Strangeitude* (Dovetail 1991), *Jurassic Shift* (Dovetail 1993), *Aborescence* (Dovetail 1994).

P

Pale Fountains
Formed in Liverpool in the early 80s by songwriter Michael Head (guitar/vocals) and Chris McCaffrey (bass) with Thomas Whelan (drums) and Andy Diagram, formerly of Dislocation Dance and the Diagram Brothers. Having been assimilated into the early 80s 'quiet pop'/'Bossa Nova' movement, Pale Fountains also drew upon such influences as the Beatles, the Mamas And The Papas and Love, but were probably better known for wearing short baggy trousers. Previously on the Operation Twilight label, the group attempted to break into the big-time when they signed to the Virgin label. Despite this lucrative move, this highly-touted group never broke out of their cult status. Their highest national chart position was the UK Top 50 'Thank You' in 1982.
Albums: *Pacific Street* (1984), *From Across The Kitchen Table* (1985).

Pale Saints
Indie band formed in Leeds, Yorkshire, England, in 1989 by Ian Masters (b. 4 January 1964, Potters Bar, Hertfordshire, England; bass), Chris Cooper (b. 17 November 1966, Portsmouth, England; drums) and Graeme Naysmith (b. 9 February 1967, Edinburgh, Scotland; guitar), following an advertisement in a music paper. Aided by occasional guitarist Ashley Horner, who eventually concentrated on his other band, Edsel Auctioneer, on a full time basis, the Pale Saints spent a year playing local venues and perfecting an idiosyncratic array of material which relied heavily on textures and effects rather than traditional arrangements or blatantly commercial choruses. That was not to say that they were unattractive: their first ever London gig in the spring of 1989 brought them a record deal with 4AD Records, and their debut album of six months later, *The Comforts Of Madness*, earned the band much critical appreciation and the number 40 spot in the UK charts. Canadian emigrate Meriel Barham (b. 15 October 1964, Yorkshire, England) joined as a permanent guitarist/vocalist soon after, as Pale Saints continued their decidedly obtuse - if not downright perverse - path into the new decade with tours of Europe and Japan and an elegant cover version of Nancy Sinatra's 'Kinky Love', which reached number 72 in the UK charts. The subsequent *In Ribbons* housed a non-charting single in 'Throwing Back The Apple', before the band re-emerged in 1994 with *Slow Buildings*. By this time Masters had departed, leaving Barham in charge of lyric writing, while Hugh Jones' crisp production gave new impetus to the band's familiar grandeur.
Albums: *The Comforts Of Madness* (4AD 1990), *In Ribbons* (4AD 1992), *Slow Buildings* (4AD 1994).

Parachute Men
Formed in Leeds, Yorkshire, England, in 1985 by Fiona Gregg (b. 26 July 1963, Norwich, Norfolk, England; vocals), Stephen H. Gregg (b. 29 November 1960, Bishop Auckland, Co. Durham, England; guitar), Andrew Howes (bass) and Mark Boyce (drums), the Parachute Men proved to have a bat's ear for a tune, yet were persistently undersold by circumstance. Signing to Fire Records in 1987 was a promising move, particularly when 'The Innocents' was released to warm approval, but soon after Andrew Howes and Mark Boyce departed acrimoniously, leaving Fiona and Stephen H. Gregg to tour as an acoustic set-up until Matthew Parkin (bass) and Paul Walker (b. 7 July 1966, West Yorkshire, England; drums) filled the vacancies. The second album was released well over a year after it was recorded, costing the band valuable momentum and causing Matthew Parker to be replaced by Colleen Browne (b. 25 August 1966, Kelowna, Canada), but the Parachute Men continued to create lovingly-textured guitar sounds. However, the lack of media focus, undoubtedly exacerbated by their northern location, ensured that their talents remained the knowledge of a privileged few, and they disbanded soon after the release of *Earth, Dogs And Eggshells*.
Albums: *The Innocents* (Fire 1988), *Earth, Dogs And Eggshells* (Fire 1990).

Pale Saints

Paris Angels

This UK pop band was formed in November 1989 and were subsequently signed to Virgin Records. The embryonic line-up of Scott Carey (bass, harmonica), Rikki Turner (vocals/wind instruments), Simon Worrall (drums) and Paul Wagstaff (guitar) were joined by Jayne Gill (vocals, percussion) and Mark Adge (rhythm guitar, percussion), formerly the group's sound engineer. They blossomed with the addition of the computer-literate Steven Tajti to help with programming and effects. After releasing a version of David Bowie's 'Stay' they signed to Sheer Joy for 'Perfume' in June 1990. The group's blend of rock/dance pigeon-holed them as late arrivals to the Manchester scene and the award of a Single Of The Week in the *New Musical Express* and 10 weeks in the UK independent chart justified Virgin's decision to move in after two more singles on the independent label. The last of these, 'Oh Yes', in early 1991, became *Sounds* magazine's last ever single of the week, before the paper folded. However, their debut album and a re-recorded 'Perfume' failed to embrace the spirit of adventure that the single promised and the group floundered.
Album: *Sundew* (Virgin 1991).

Passions

This English post-punk group, with definite pop leanings, was formed in June 1978 and comprised Barbara Gogan (b. Dublin, Eire; vocals/guitar), Mitch Barker (vocals), Clive Timperley (guitar/vocals), Claire Bidwell (bass/vocals) and Richard Williams (drums). All save Timperley had featured in Rivers Of Passion, while all except Bidwell had spent time in the various incarnations of the Derelicts between 1974-76. During this time Timperley also played with Joe Strummer's 101er's. Gogan left her Dublin home at the age of 18 and settled in France within a Marxist commune. She came to London in 1972 and moved into a 'squat' near Ladbroke Grove, where she became involved with the Derelicts, a loose collection of like-minded left wingers. Evolving into the Passions they released their first single, 'Needles And Pins', on the tiny Soho label, also home of the Nips and the Inmates. They lost Barker in 1979 when a broken leg put paid to his musical activities. Continuing as a four-piece they signed to Fiction Records for their debut album, and one single, 'Hunted'. Bidwell left in July 1980 to form Schwarze Kapelle and then joined the Wall. David Agar, once a member of the fledgling Spandau Ballet, replaced her. Three days later they were dropped by Fiction but fell immediately on their feet with a contract for Polydor Records. They finally found success in 1981 with their second single for the label, 'I'm In Love With A German Film Star'. It would be their only hit, despite the eloquence and strength of later material. Timperley left to run a health shop in December 1981, while the recruitment of Kevin Armstrong (ex-Local Heroes SW9) on guitar and Jeff Smith (ex-Lene Lovich band) on keyboards failed to put the brakes on their commercial slide. Armstrong himself left in August 1982 to be replaced by Steve Wright, but by this time the band was in its death throes.
Albums: *Michael And Miranda* (Fiction 1980), *Thirty Thousand Feet Over China* (Polydor 1981), *Sanctuary* (Polydor 1982).

Pastels

Formed in Glasgow, Scotland, in 1982, the Pastels were one of the prime movers in the 80s 'shambling'/'anorak' independent scene that influenced later luminaries such as the Flatmates and Talulah Gosh. Group leader Stephen Pastel (b. Stephen McRobbie, Scotland; guitar/vocals) has since gone to great lengths to distance the Pastels from their past idolaters. Today they serve as a major influence on emerging Scottish bands like Teenage Fanclub (whose Norman Blake is a fan club member and would later play in the Pastels) and Captain America/Eugenius. However, their history has been characterized by the kind of lethargy which has doomed them to mere cultism: 'I just find careerism and naked ambition really ugly'. The Pastels themselves were motivated by a conglomeration of the Monkees and the Ramones. The early line-up also comprised Brian Superstar (b. Brian Taylor; guitar) and Chris Gordon (drums), but the latter's early departure signalled a recurring instability in the group's rhythm section. Their first release on the Television Personalities' Whaam! label, the *Songs For Children* EP, was the beginning of an unsettled relationship with a variety of labels including Rough Trade, Creation and Glass Records. Appearances on various compilations, not least a prestigious slot on the seminal *C86* collection ('Breaking Lines') from the *New Musical Express* increased their standing in the independent market, while their music combined ambitious vision with naive ability. A settled line-up; Pastel, Superstar, Aggi Wright (vocals), Martin Hayward (bass) and Bernice Swanson (drums) - completed two albums, *Up For A Bit With The Pastels* and *Sittin' Pretty*, wherein the group matured from the charming innocence of early releases to embrace a myriad of contrasting styles held together by McRobbie's commited vision. Material ranged from the bouyant 'Nothing To Be Done' to the lengthy 'Baby Honey' and 'Ditch The Fool', as the Pastels expanded their musical horizons with the temporary aid of Eugene Kelly (ex-Vaselines), Norman Blake and David Keegan, formerly of the Shop Assistants and Stephen's partner in the pivotal 53rd & 3rd Records label. By the early 90s Keegan had become a full-time member of the Pastels which, following a series of alterations, re-emerged centred around McRobbie, Wright (now on bass) and Katriona Mitchell (drums), the latter pursuing a concurrent path as a member of Melody Dog. Against the odds this trio was still in place for 1995's *Mobile Safari*, an enjoyable collection of raggamuffin odes to life in and outside of an under-achieving indie band, punctuated by songs such as 'Yoga' and 'Classic Lineup'.
Albums: *Up For A Bit With The Pastels* (Glass 1987), *Sittin' Pretty* (Chapter 22 1989), *Mobile Safari* (Domino 1995). Compilation: *Suck On The Pastels* (Creation 1988).

Pavement

Darlings of the US independent scene, formed in Stockton, California, in 1989. college dropouts Pavement were originally a duo with Steve Malkmus (vocals/guitar) and Scott 'Spiral Stairs' Kannberg (guitar). Later they extended to a five-piece by adding Gary Young (b. c.1954; percussion), a venerable live attraction who was as likely to perform handstands on stage as any musical duties, plus John Nastanovich (drums) and Mark Ibald (bass). However, as

Pastels

three of the band were located on the east coast (New York), rehearsals were initially limited to perhaps once a year, and recording sessions and tours proved equally sporadic, resulting in songs that were 'meant to sound like Chrome or the Clean, but ended up sounding like the Fall and Swell Maps.' Their debut release was 1989's *Slay Tracks (1933-1969)*, the first in a series of EP's to charm the critics. The attraction, undoubtedly, was Malkmus' dry, free-ranging lyrics, with their acute observational scope. Young left the band in 1993 (replaced by Steve West) when his stage behaviour became unbearable, but neither this, nor the insistence of UK critics that the band were a pale imitation of the Fall, hindered their rise to the top of the US alternative scene. *Wowee Zowee!* offered a more angular, less instantly accessible formula, with many of the tracks opting for outright experimentalism. Malkmus defended it thus: 'Its still a warm and open record if people are willing to join us'. Albums: *Perfect Sound Forever* (Drag City 191, mini-album), *Slanted And Enchanted* (Big Cat 1992), *Crooked Rain, Crooked Rain* (Big Cat 1994), *Wowee Zowee!* (Big Cat 1995). Compilation: *Westing (By Musket And Sextant)* (Big Cat 1993). Gary Young solo: *Hospital* (Big Cat 1995).

Paw

This Lawrence, Kansas, USA quartet formed in 1990 with brothers Grant (guitar) and Peter Fitch (drums) and bassist Charles Bryan, recruiting vocalist Mark Hennessy (b. Mark Thomas Joseph Brendan Hennessy, 6 May 1969, Kansas, USA) from local art-noise band King Rat, which Hennessy described as a period when 'I thought I was Nick Cave'. Paw were the leading local band, and picked up support gigs with Nirvana and the Fluid before recording their first seven-song demo at Butch Vig's Smart Studios in Wisconsin, which led to an enormous major label bidding war, won by A&M Records. *Newsweek* described Paw as 'the next Nirvana', but Hüsker Dü, Dinosaur Jr and the Replacements were perhaps better reference points for *Dragline*'s marriage of melody and raw guitar power, with a distinctive small-town storytelling aspect to the songs. 'Sleeping Bag' was perhaps the most poignant, telling the childhood story of a car crash which hospitalised the seriously injured Peter Fitch, and when older brother Grant feared the worst, he slept in Peter's sleeping bag, 'as corny as it sounds, just to be a little closer to him'. *Dragline* deservedly received universal acclaim, and the band toured exhaustively, earning an excellent live reputation, touring Europe with Therapy? and Hammerbox, the UK with Tool, and both the UK and USA with Monster Magnet, as singles 'Sleeping Bag', and 'Couldn't Know' brought them a wider audience. The band returned to the studio in late 1994, but without Bryan, who had tired of the endless touring.
Album: *Dragline* (A&M 1993).

Pearl Harbor And The Explosions

Formed in San Francisco, California in 1979, this much-touted attraction was centred on vocalist Pearl Harbor (b. 1958, Germany, of a Filipino mother), who, as Pearl E. Gates, had previously been a dancer in the Tubes live show. She subsequently joined Jane Dornacker in Leila And The Snakes, before taking the group's rhythm section - Hilary Stench (bass) and John Stench (drums) - in this new act. Their act continued the theatricality of the Tubes, but Gates was more interested in conventional rock 'n' roll. To this end she recruited Peter Bilt (guitar) and formed Pearl Harbor And The Explosions in October 1978. They specialized in old fashioned rock 'n' roll/rockabilly spiced with 'new wave' energy. Their debut single 'Drivin'' (which was later covered by Jane Aire And The Belvederes) came out on the independent 415 Records label and became an cult hit. Its success encouraged Warner Brothers to sign the group. Their self-titled debut was a strong, promising work, but the group failed to complete a follow-up. They split in June 1980 leaving Pearl to continue with a solo album *Don't Follow Me I'm Lost* under her new name Pearl Harbor. The album was produced by Nicky Gallagher (former member of Ian Dury's Blockheads). The Stench brothers joined ex-Jefferson Airplane guitarist Jorma Kaukonen in Vital Parts, before embarking on an association with cult *avant garde* act Chrome.
Albums: *Pearl Harbor And The Explosions* (1979), as Pearl Harbor *Don't Follow Me, I'm Lost* (1981).

Pearl Jam

This revisionist (or, depending on your viewpoint, visionary) rock quintet were formed in Seattle, USA, in the early 90s, by Jeff Ament (bass) and Stone Gossard (rhythm guitar). Gossard had played with Steve Turner in the Ducky Boys, the latter moving on to perform with Ament in Green River. Gossard would also become a member of this band when Mark Arm (like Turner, later to join Mudhoney) switched from guitar to vocals. Gossard and Ament, however, elected to continue working together when Green River washed up, and moved on to Mother Love Bone, fronted by local 'celebrity' Andrew Wood. However, that ill-fated group collapsed when, four weeks after the release of its debut album, *Apple*, Wood was found dead from a heroin overdose. Both Gossard and Ament would subsequently participate in Seattle's tribute to Wood, Temple Of The Dog, alongside Chris Cornell of Soundgarden who instigated the project, Soundgarden drummer Matt Cameron, plus Gossard's schoolfriend Mike McCready (guitar) and vocalist Eddie Vedder (ex-Bad Radio), from San Diego. He had been passed a tape of demos recorded by Ament, Gossard and McCready by Red Hot Chili Peppers' drummer Jack Irons. Both Vedder and McCready would eventually hook up permanently with Ament and Gossard to become Pearl Jam, with the addition of drummer Dave Krusen (having originally dabbled with the name Mookie Blaylock). The band signed to Epic Records in 1991, debuting the following year with the powerful, yet melodic *Ten*. A bold diarama, it saw the band successfully incorporate elements of their native traditions (Soundgarden, Mother Love Bone, Nirvana) with older influences such as the Doors, Velvet Underground, the Stooges and the MC5. The self-produced recording (together with Rick Parashar) showed great maturity for a debut, particularly in the full-blooded songwriting, best better demonstrated than on hit single 'Alive'. Dynamic live performances and a subtle commercial edge to their material catapulted them from obscurity to virtual superstars overnight, as the Seattle scene debate raged and Kurt Cobain

Pearl Jam

accused them of 'jumping the alternative bandwagon'. In the USA *Ten* was still in the Top 20 a year and a half after its release, having sold over 4 million copies in that country alone. The touring commitments which followed, however, brought Vedder to the verge of nervous collapse. He struggled back to health in time for the Lollapalooza II tour, an appearance on *MTV Unplugged*, and Pearl Jam's cameo as Matt Dillon's 'band', Citizen Dick, in the Cameron Crowe film, *Singles*. Vedder would also front a re-united Doors on their induction into the Rock 'n' Roll Hall Of Fame in Los Angeles at the Century Plaza hotel, performing versions of 'Roadhouse Blues', 'Break On Through' and 'Light My Fire'. The eagerly awaited 'difficult' follow-up was announced in October 1993, close on the heals of Nirvana's latest offering. Whilst reviews were mixed the advance orders placed the album on top of charts on both sides of the Atlantic. *Vitalogy* seemed overtly concerned with re-establishing the group's grass roots credibility, a strong clue to which arrived in the fact that the album was available for a week on vinyl before a CD or cassette release (a theme revisited on 'Spin The Black Circle'). There were also numerous references, some oblique, others not, to the death of Nirvana's Kurt Cobain. Ironically 1994 also saw drummer Dave Abbruzzese dispensed with, amid unfounded rumours that former Nirvana sticksman Dave Grohl would be invited in to the ranks.

Albums: *Ten* (Epic 1991), *Vs.* (Epic 1993), *Vitalogy* (Epic 1994).

Further reading: *Pearl Jam: The Illustrated Biography*, Brad Morrell. *Pearl Jam Live!*, Joey Lorenzo (compiler).

Peel, John

b. John Robert Parker Ravenscroft, 30 August 1939, Heswall, Cheshire, England. Having moved to the USA during the early 60s to work in his father's cotton business, Peel's musical knowledge engendered several guest appearances on Dallas radio stations. By cultivating his near-Liverpool birthright, he became something of a local celebrity in the wake of Beatlemania which in turn led to a full-time job as a disc jockey on Oklahoma's KOMA station. By 1966 he was working at KMEN in San Bernadino, California, but the following year John returned to Britain where his knowledge of emergent US underground rock led to his joining the pirate radio ship Radio London. Now stripped of his 'Ravenscroft' surname in favour of a snappier appellation, Peel achieved almost instant fame for his late-night *Perfumed Garden* programme which introduced the then-mysterious delights of Country Joe And The Fish, the Velvet Underground and Captain Beefheart And His Magic Band to unsuspecting UK audiences. When the Marine Offences Bill effectively outlawed pirate radio, Peel moved to the BBC's new Radio 1 where he latterly took control of Sunday afternoon's *Top Gear*. Here, he continued to promote 'new' music, airing progressive acts from Britain and America and giving a plethora of groups, including Pink Floyd, Soft Machine, Jethro Tull, Moby Grape, Grateful Dead, Jefferson Airplane, Buffalo Springfield and Fleetwood Mac, their first substantive airings. Peel also established the ambitious Dandelion label, the roster of which included Medicine Head and Kevin Coyne, but his closest ties lay with Marc

Bolan and Tyrannosaurus Rex, whose later success was due, in part, to Peel's unswerving support during their early career. Rod Stewart and the Faces were also strong favourites although the Peel's influence lessened during the early 70s as their music became increasingly predictable. Peel nonetheless promoted such experimental acts as Matching Mole and Can, as well as reggae and soul, before finding renewed enthusiasm with the advent of punk. Saturation airplay of the first Ramones album alienated many entrenched listeners, but it excited a new, and generally younger, audience. Once again Peel, with the guidance of ever-present producer John Walters, was in the vanguard of an exciting musical upheaval as he broadcast material by Siouxsie And The Banshees, Joy Division, the Undertones and the Fall, the latter two of which were particular favourites. John Peel remains an important and influential figure. The sole survivor of Radio 1's initial intake, his weekend shows still gnaw at the barriers of popular music, be it rap, hardcore, reggae or ethnic music. The highly-successful *Peel Sessions* EP series on the Strange Fruit label, drawn from the extensive library of live performances recorded for his programmes, are a tribute to his intuition.

Compilations: various artist sessions recorded especially for Peel's programmes *Before The Fall - The Peel Sessions* (1991), *Winters Of Discontent - The Peel Sessions* (1991), *The New Breed - The Peel Sessions* (1991), *Too Pure - The Peel Sessions* (1992).

Penetration

Durham, England band Penetration may have had a suitably outrageous name for a punk band, but their music took them far from conventional 'no future' concerns. Vocalist Pauline Murray and bass player Robert Blamire wrote songs which did not need to be hidden behind three-chord bluster, and, along with the Adverts, theirs remains one of the great undiscovered legacies of the era. After only four gigs the band gained a lucky break by being invited to support Generation X at the Roxy Club, London, on 29 January 1977. Formed like so many others after witnessing the Sex Pistols play Manchester Free Trade Hall, the line-up was crystallised with the addition of Gary Chaplin (guitar) and Gary Smallman (drums). After cutting a demo in the summer, their name was passed to Virgin Records by the manager of the same company's shop in Newcastle, resulting in their November debut, 'Don't Dictate'. A sterling, defiant punk statement, it quickly became a genre classic. Neale Floyd replaced Chaplin in time for the following year's 'Firing Squad'. The first of two John Peel sessions was completed in July, with Fred Purser now adding a second guitar, before a third single, 'Life's A Gamble', and debut album in October. *Moving Targets*, produced by Mick Glossop and Mike Howlett, was a deeply challenging album, adding covers of the Buzzcocks' 'Nostalgia' and Patti Smith's 'Free Money' to highly invigorating original songs like 'Future Daze' and 'Too Many Friends'. A second album, *Coming Up For Air*, followed in September 1979. Despite Steve Lillywhite's production, this all-original collection was a rather uninspired affair, without the clarity or purpose of the consistently exciting debut. The band announced their intention to split on stage in Newcastle on 14 October, just a month after its release. As Murray confirmed to the *New Musical Express*: 'I never wanted to be in Penetration and to be worrying all the time. I wanted it to be fun, not to be always thinking of hit singles and cracking America and writing for the next LP'. Posthumous releases included an official bootleg, while Murray went solo (originally with the Invisible Girls).

Albums: *Moving Targets* (Virgin 1978), *Coming Up For Air* (Virgin 1979), *Race Against Time* (Clifdayn 1979), *BBC Radio 1 Live In Concert* (Windsong 1993, split album with Ruts).

Perfect Disaster

Having tested the water as Orange Disaster, then the Architects Of Disaster, these calamitously-inclined types finally settled on the Perfect Disaster in 1984 as the original rhythm section departed to form Fields Of The Nephilim. The initial UK-based line-up consisted of Phil Parfitt, Allison Pates, John Saltwell and Malcolm Catto, although personnel changes were to plague the band's career. Ignored by the British music scene, the Perfect Disaster took their twisted, broody guitar sound to France for their self-titled debut album in 1985. There followed a couple of years of blank struggle on both sides of the English Channel before the band signed to Fire Records at home and released the critically-acclaimed *Asylum Road*. Prior to this, Saltwell and Pates both left, disillusioned, to be replaced by bassist Josephine Wiggs (b. Josephine Miranda Cordelia Susan Wiggs, 26 February 1965, Letchworth, Hertfordshire, England) and long-term guitarist Dan Cross. 1989 suggested that better prospects lurked over the horizon: the *Up* album, which stretched splendidly from fiery two-chord blasts to near-suicidal ramblings, coincided with prestigious live shows with the likes of the Jesus And Mary Chain. And the band's initial inspiration, based upon singer Parfitt's spell working at a Victorian mental institution, looked set to reap rewards. The public, alas, didn't share the critics' enthusiasm for the band. Wiggs left in 1990 to spend more time on the Breeders, a side project which also involved Tanya Donelly from Throwing Muses and Kim Deal of the Pixies, allowing John Saltwell to return on bass. The *Heaven Scent* album continued the Perfect Disaster's foray into the darker side of alternative music, but rumours of the band's demise, which persisted throughout 1991, were finally confirmed. Parfitt would go on to write alongside Jason Pierce (Spiritualized) before forming Oedipussy.

Albums: *The Perfect Disaster* (Kampa 1985), *Asylum Road* (Fire 1988), *Up* (Fire 1989), *Heaven Scent* (Fire 1990).

Perry, Mark

One of the first to spot the oncoming onslaught of UK punk, Mark Perry (b. c.1957, London, England) was a bank clerk who, inspired by the Ramones, started the *Sniffin' Glue (And Other Rock 'N' Roll Habits)* fanzine in mid-1976. After leaving his job and shortening his name to Mark P., he and south London pals like Danny Baker became the unofficial media messiahs of punk rock. *Sniffin' Glue* only lasted until August 1977 but by that time Perry was working on several labels and his new band, with Alex Ferguson; Alternative TV (signifying Alternative *to* TV). He had previously played in a trio called the New Beatles with Steve Walsh and Tyrone Thomas. Perry soon adapted the new band's name to ATV as everyone was either mispronouncing or misspelling it anyway. Their first release was a flexi on the Sniffin' Glue label. This was later reissued on Deptford Fun City, a label set up by Perry (in conjunction with Miles Copeland). ATV released several albums on DFC before becoming the Good Missionaries in 1979. After one album, *Fire From Heaven*, Perry left and recorded as the Reflection, the Door And The Window, and as a solo artist. There were just two 1980 singles credited to him but he also cropped up on various compilations. ATV reformed in 1981 for *Strange Kicks* only to break up again. Perry's album, *Snappy Turns*, also appeared in that year. ATV reformed for a second time in 1984, initially for a gig at the Euston Tavern in Kings Cross and this reformation lasted about a year. They split up just long enough to give themselves time to reform again and stayed together until 1987. More recently Perry has been involved in a band called Baby Ice Dog.

Album: *Snappy Turns* (Deptford Fun City 1981).

Peter And The Test Tube Babies

Punk rock can hardly stand as Brighton's major claim to fame, but the southern coastal town had its moments. In between the Piranhas' flirtations with the UK charts, Peter And The Test Tube Babies gained notoriety during the early 80s, with their brand of good-time Oi!-inspired punk. The group comprised Chris Marchant (bass), Nicholas Loizides (drums), Peter Bywaters (vocals) and Derek Greening (guitar). Locals may have remembered them from their contribution to resident label Attrix's *Vaultage 1978* compilation, which featured the provocative 'Elvis Is Dead'. But it wasn't until 1982 that the Test Tube Babies' first single emerged on the No Future label. 'Banned From The Pubs' was followed by 'Run Like Hell' that same year, before the band set up their own label, Trapper. After the gruesome 'Zombie Creeping Flesh' and 'The Jinx' (both 1983), they at last emerged with an album's worth of indecent exposure, *The Mating Sounds Of South American Frogs*. The inelegantly titled *Pissed And Proud* followed one month later. The next two years saw the group release albums and singles with various labels, including their own, Hairy Pie. The idiosyncratically entitled cassette-only release, *Journey To The Centre Of Johnny Clarke's Head*, was followed by the *Rotting In The Fart Sack* EP (1985) and *Another Noisy, Loud, Blaring Punk Rock LP*. The album *Soberphobia* saw the Test Tube Babies through to the end of 1986, but since then, all has been quiet, leaving it safe to assume that the band have returned to the pub.

Albums: *The Mating Sounds Of South American Frogs* (Trapper 1983), *Pissed And Proud* (No Future 1983), *Journey To The Centre Of Johnny Clarke's Head* (Hairy Pie 1984, cassette only), *Another Noisy, Loud, Blaring Punk Rock LP* (Hairy Pie 1985), *3 X 45* (Trapper 1985), *Soberphobia* (Dojo 1986). Compilation: *The Best Of Peter And The Test Tube Babies* (Dojo 1988).

Photos

Three-quarters of the Photos had previously been three quarters of DJM Records' token punk band Satans Rats, who

released three singles in the late 70s. Hailing from Evesham, Worcestershire, this trio comprised Steve Eagles (b. 1958; guitar) and Ollie Harrison (drums), who were at college together, and Dave Sparrow (bass) who had been in the Ipswich-band Quorum. The boys were in a club when they came across the photogenic Wendy Wu (b. 29 November 1959, Winson Green, West Midlands, England) who had previously managed a small band and been a hotel receptionist. Recruiting Wendy as their vocalist they became the Photos and signed with CBS in 1979. Their debut single was the stunningly accurate, if perhaps a little conceited, 'I'm So Attractive'. The four track EP released in 1980 included their own tribute to the Birmingham night-club Barbarellas. None of their singles on CBS/Epic dented the charts despite Tony Visconti being called in as producer. Wendy left in 1981 and was briefly replaced by Che from the Orchids. By 1983 they had moved on to the Rialto label but soon split up. Wendy would later work with Steve Strange in the band Strange Cruise. Steve Eagles went on to join Blurt and more recently re-emerged in one the most promising new bands of 1992, Bang Bang Machine.
Album: *The Photos* (Epic 1980).

Phranc

b. 1958, Los Angeles, California, USA. Before her career as the self-styled 'Jewish-American lesbian folksinger' Phranc had served an apprenticeship, of sorts, by appearing in LA 'hardcore' groups (Gender, Catholic Discipline and Castration Squad). On her return to acoustic playing in 1980, Phranc's sets consisted of autobiographical, part-comic songs, at times performed to similar hardcore audiences from her recent past. These appearances led to the gay coffee-house/folk circuit. Her warmly received *Folksinger* set a standard with titles such as 'Female Mudwrestling', 'Amazons' and 'One Of The Girls'. Her willingness to tackle such subjects as her sexuality, left-wing politics and her own family problems have so far prevented her from achieving anything beyond cult status. Phranc's third album was highlighted by her role as support act on Morrissey's first full British tour of 1991.
Albums: *Folksinger* (1986), *I Enjoy Being A Girl* (1989), *Positively Phranc* (1991).

Pigbag

Pigbag will be for ever linked with their debut single, and only hit, 'Papa's Got A Brand New Pigbag' (a play on words on the mid-60s James Brown classic, 'Papa's Got A Brand New Bag'). A quirky but nevertheless catchy funk/soul instrumental, the single was first released in May 1981, but took almost a year to reach the charts, peaking at number 3. Word had it that their label, Y, had deleted the single and then reactivated it when the demand was sufficient. The band had formed around the Gloucestershire and Avon region from the ashes of hardline militant funk act the Pop Group; Simon Underwood (bass) joined up with James Johnstone (guitar/keyboards), Ollie Moore (saxophone), Chip Carpenter (drums) and Roger Freeman (percussion). By the time of their hit, Pigbag already issued two further singles, 'Sunny Day' and 'Getting Up'. The debut album, *Dr Heckle And Mr Jive*, subsequently reached the UK Top 20.

Despite shrewd promotion, Pigbag's heyday was short-lived. 'Big Bean' (1982) peaked at number 40 and 'Hit The "O" Deck' (1983), failed to make any impact. After a live album, the band broke up, although 'Papa's Got A Brand New Pigbag' was later re-recorded in 1987, to coincide with *The Best Of Pigbag*.
Albums: *Dr Heckle And Mr Jive* (1982), *Pigbag - Live* (1983). Compilation: *The Best Of Pigbag* (1987).

Pil

(see Public Image Limited)

Pink Military/Pink Industry

This late 70s UK act were a central part of Liverpool's thriving post-punk scene. Distinctive vocalist Jayne Casey had fronted a now impressive-looking line-up in Big In Japan. But after their demise in the summer of 1978, she teamed up with John Highway (guitar), Wayne Wadden (bass), Paul Hornby (drums) and a certain Nicky (keyboards), to form Pink Military. An experimental 12-inch EP, *Blood And Lipstick*, appeared on local label Eric's (also the name of Liverpool's premier venue of the era), in 1979, and caused quite a stir. A deal with Virgin Records ensued, resulting in the more overtly commercial single, 'Did You See Her', in 1980. However, this belied the wealth and diversity of sounds to be found on the accompanying album, *Do Animals Believe In God?* By this time, Chris Joyce had been recruited on drums, while Wadden had been replaced by Martin on bass. But the Virgin/Eric's collaboration soon fell apart, and their next EP, *Buddha Waking/Disney Sleeping*, came out on Last Trumpet Records. Pink Military soon split and gave way to Pink Industry, Casey collaborating with Ambrose Reynolds, later a member of an early Frankie Goes To Hollywood line-up. The first fruits were extremely promising and 'Is This The End?' (1982) stands as one of the year's most outstanding singles. *Low Technology* emerged just over a year later, exemplifying the band's off-beat, haunting qualities. *Who Told You You Were Naked* hinted at eastern influences, while further embracing new instrument and studio techniques. There was a two-year gap before *New Beginnings*, accompanied by a single, 'What I Wouldn't Give' (with a sleeve adorned by a photograph of Morrissey) in mid-1985. An increasingly reclusive existence since then has been broken only by a retrospective self-titled album on Cathexis, promoted by 'Don't Let Go' in 1987.
Albums: As Pink Military *Do Animals Believe In God?* (Eric's 1980). As Pink Industry *Low Technology* (Zulu 1983), *Who Told You You Were Naked* (Zulu 1983), *New Beginnings* (Zulu 1985). Compilation: *Pink Industry* (Cathexis 1988).

Pixies

This US group was formed in Boston, Massachusetts, by room-mates Charles Michael Kittridge Thompson IV aka Black Francis (b. Long Beach, California, USA; vocals, guitar) and Joey Santiago (guitar). A newspaper advertisement, requiring applicants for a 'Hüsker Dü/Peter, Paul And Mary band', solicited bassist Kim Deal who in turn introduced drummer David Lovering. Originally known as Pixies In Panoply, the quartet secured a recording deal on the UK independent label 4AD Records on the strength of a

Pixies

series of superior demo tapes. Their debut release, *Come On Pilgrim*, introduced the band's abrasive, powerful sound and Francis' oblique lyrics. *Surfer Rosa*, produced by Big Black's Steve Albini, exaggerated the savage fury of its predecessor and the set was acclaimed Album Of The Year in much of the UK rock press. The superlative *Doolittle* emphasized the quartet's grasp of melody, yet retained their drive, and this thrilling collection scaled the national Top 10, aided and abetted by the band's most enduring single, 'Monkey Gone To Heaven'. The Pixies were now a highly popular attraction and their exciting live performances enhanced a growing reputation, establishing clear stage favourites in 'Debaser', 'Cactus', 'Wave Of Mutilation' and 'Bone Machine'. 1990's *Bossanova* showed an undiminished fire with a blend of pure pop with 'Allison' and sheer ferocity in 'Rock Music'. The band found themselves the darlings of the rock press and were once again widely regarded for recording one of the top albums of the year. Kim Deal, meanwhile, attracted glowing reviews for her offshoot project, the Breeders. *Trompe Le Monde* was, if anything, an even harsher collections than those which had preceded it, prompting some critics to describe it as the 'Pixies' heavy metal album'. Following the rechristened Frank Black's departure for a solo career in early 1993 the band effectively folded, but the group's reputation continues to outshine any of the membership's concurrent or subsequent projects.
Albums: *Come On Pilgrim* (4AD 1987), *Surfer Rosa* (4AD 1988), *Dolittle* (4AD 1989), *Bossanova* (4AD 1990), *Trampe Le Monde* (4AD 1991).

PJ Harvey

b. 9 October 1970, Corscombe, Dorset, England, Polly Jean Harvey, from whom her band's title is taken, was the daughter of hippie parents who exposed her to art rock bands like Captain Beefheart and folk singer-songwriters like Bob Dylan at an early age. After growing up on their farm and playing saxophone with eight-piece instrumental group Boulogne, she wrote her first songs as part of the Polekats, a folk trio who toured local pubs she was only just old enough to drink in. Afterwards she attended an art foundation course before joining Somerset based band Automatic Dlamini for two and a half years (from whence would come several future collaborators). Over this period she contributed saxophone, guitar and vocals, and toured Europe twice, also appearing on the chorus of local band Grape's 'Baby In A Plastic Bag' single, and singing backing vocals on Bristol-based Family Cat's 'Colour Me Grey'. Bored with playing other people's material, she moved to London, ostensibly to attend a course in sculpture (her other love), and elected to work with bass player Ian Olliver and drummer and backing vocalist Rob Ellis, both fellow Automatic Dlamini travellers. Together they played live for the first time in April 1991, using the name PJ Harvey. Independent label Too Pure Records, home of Th' Faith Healers and Stereolab, were so convinced by these nebulous performances that they mortgaged their home to finance the debut single, 'Dress' (Olliver left to be replaced by Stephen Vaughan on 'five-string fretless bass' after its release). Together with the most impressive 'Sheila-Na-Gig' and

debut album *Dry*, it was enough to bring her to the attention not only of Island Records but also the mainstream press. Subverting the traditions of the female singer-songwriter with outbreaks of fire and brimstone guitar, Harvey possessed the sort of voice which, whilst not cultured in the traditional sense, offered a highly emotive cudgel. Allied to lyrics which laid her own relationships and feelings naked, her revisionary attitude to feminism was demonstrated by the *New Musical Express* cover on which she appeared topless, with her back to the photographer. An evocative and disturbing songwriter, most considered that she would leave too bitter an aftertaste for a mass audience. A truism which was partially dispelled by support slots to U2 but hardly the choice of producer for *Rid Of Me*, Big Black/Rapeman controversialist Steve Albini. A vicious stew of rural blues, with Harvey's voice and guitar sounding almost animalised by the production, its title-track centre piece offered one of the most fearsome declarations ('You're not rid of me') ever articulated by rock music. Obsessive, haranguing imagery accompanied by stunning, committed musical performances (especially the distinctive drumming of Ellis), this was an album of such vehemence that its follow-up, by necessity, was forced to lower the extremity threshold. In the interim PJ Harvey (now officially a solo artist) made a memorable appearance at the 1994 BRIT Awards, duetting with Björk on a version of the Rolling Stones' 'Satisfaction'. For *To Bring You My Love* Harvey abandoned some of the psychosis, replacing it with a haunting, sinister ambience. With U2 producer Flood working in tandem with namesake Mick Harvey (of Nick Cave And The Bad Seeds), Polly left behind some of the less pleasant subject matter of yore (bodily dysfunction, revenge). The new approach was typified by the video to promotional single 'Down By The Water', evocative of Ophelia-like madness and sacrifice. Her band now consisted of guitarist John Parrish (another former colleague from Automatic Dlamini), Jean-Marc Butty (b. France; drums), Nick Bagnall (keyboards/bass), Joe Gore (b. San Francisco; ex-Tom Waits' band; guitar) and Eric Feldman (b. San Francisco; keyboards) - all musicians Harvey had met on previous travels. It was obvious, however, that she was still having problems with her public perception: 'If I hadn't been tarred with the angst-ridden old bitch cow image, it'd be something else. Now it's, oh, she's gone back to the farm'.
Album: *Dry* (Too Pure 1992), *Demonstration* (Too Pure 1992, 'demo' album given away with initial copies of *Dry*), *Rid Of Me* (Island 1993), *4-Track Demos* (Island 1993), *To Bring You My Love* (Island 1995).
Video: *Reeling* (1994).

Plasmatics

Formed in 1979 in New York City, USA, the Plasmatics were a theatrical hardcore band which incorporated such violent acts as blowing up Cadillacs and chainsawing guitars in half into its performances. Assembled by and masterminded by former pornography entrepreneur Rod Swenson, the original personnel of the group included vocalist Wendy O. Williams, a former star of sex shows, who wore see-through lingerie, but for the most part, appeared topless with strategically-placed masking tape. The remainder of the band comprised Richie Stotts (guitar), who wore a blue mohawk

haircut and a pink tutu on stage, Wes Beech (guitar), Stu Deutsch (drums) and Chosei Funahara (bass, later replaced by Jean Beauvoir). After releasing two EPs on the independent Vice Squad label in 1979, the Plasmatics signed with Stiff Records in the USA and the UK, releasing *New Hope For The Wretched* in 1980. It was largely panned by the critics but sold as a cult item due to the group's extensive press coverage, as did such singles as 'Butcher Baby' and 'Monkey Suit'. A second album, *Beyond The Valley Of 1984*, was issued on Stiff in 1981, as was an EP, *Metal Princess*. In 1982 the Plasmatics signed to Capitol Records and released *Coup D'Etat*, but by then they had evolved into an outright heavy metal outfit and had lost most of their novelty appeal. Williams and Beauvoir recorded solo albums following the Plasmatics' mid-80s break-up.
Albums: *New Hope For The Wretched* (1980), *Beyond The Valley Of 1984* (1981), *Coup D'Etat* (1982). Solo albums: Wendy O. Williams *Deffest! And Baddest!* (1988); Jean Beauvoir *Drums Along The Mohawk* (1986), *Jacknifed* (1988).

Pogues

The London punk scene of the late 70s inspired some unusual intermingling of styles and the Pogues (then known as Pogue Mahone) performed punky versions of traditional Irish folk songs in pubs throughout the capital. They were fronted by singer Shane MacGowan (b. 25 December 1957, Kent, England) and also included Peter 'Spider' Stacy (tin whistle), Jem Finer (banjo/mandolin), James Fearnley (guitar/piano accordion), Cait O'Riordan (bass) and Andrew Ranken (drums). MacGowan had spent his late teen years singing in a punk group called the Nipple Erectors (aka the Nips) which also contained Fearney. After several complaints the band changed their name (Pogue Mahone is 'kiss my arse' in Gaelic) and soon attracted the attention of the Clash who asked them to be their opening act. Record companies were perturbed by the band's occasionally chaotic live act where they would often fight onstage and Stacy kept time by banging his head with a beer tray. In 1984 Stiff Records signed them and recorded *Red Roses For Me*, containing several traditional tunes as well as excellent originals like 'Streams Of Whiskey' and 'Dark Streets Of London'. It announced a major songwriting talent in McGowan's evocative descriptions of times and places he had often visited first-hand. Elvis Costello produced *Rum, Sodomy And The Lash* on which Philip Chevron, formerly a guitarist with the Radiators From Space, replaced Finer who was on 'paternity leave'. The group soon established themselves as a formidable and unique live act and the record entered the UK Top 20. There were further changes when the multi-instrumentalist Terry Woods (a co-founder of Steeleye Span) joined and Cait O'Riordan was replaced by Darryl Hunt. She later married Elvis Costello. The group's intrinsicly political stance resulted in their video to accompany the single, 'A Pair Of Brown Eyes', having to be re-edited because the group were filmed spitting on a poster of Prime Minister, Margaret Thatcher. 'We represent the people who don't get the breaks. People can look at us and say, "My God, if that bunch of tumbledown wrecks can do it, so can I"', explained Chevron in a press interview. The band would later have

PJ Harvey

their protest ballad, 'Birmingham Six', banned from airplay. The album this was to be found on, *If I Should Fall From Grace With God*, was produced by Steve Lillywhite and embraced Middle Eastern and Spanish sounds. It sold more than 200,000 copies in the USA and 'Fairytale Of New York', a rumbustuous but poignant duet by MacGowan and Lillywhite's wife, Kirsty MacColl, was a Christmas number 2 hit in the UK in 1987. In the autumn of 1989 there were fears for the future of the group when MacGowan's heavy drinking led to him pulling out of several shows. He was due to join the band in the USA for a prestigious tour with Bob Dylan when he collapsed at London's Heathrow Airport. He missed all the support spots with Dylan and the band played without him. 'Other groups in a situation like that would've either said, "Let's get rid of the guy" or "Let's split up", but we're not the sort to do that. We're all part of each other's problems whether we like it or not', said Chevron. *Peace And Love* featured songs written by nearly every member of the group and its eclectic nature saw them picking up the hurdy-gurdy, the cittern and the mandola. Its erratic nature drew criticism from some quarters, mainly from original fans who had preferred the early folk-punk rants. While the rest of the group were clearly strong players it was widely accepted that MacGowan was the most talented songwriter. His output had always been highly sporadic but there were now fears that the drinking that fuelled his earlier creativity may have slowed him to a standstill. In an interview in 1989 he said he had not been 'dead-straight sober' since he was 14 and that he drank in quantity because 'it opened his mind to paradise'. It was announced in September 1991 that MacGowan had left the band and had been replaced by the former Clash singer, Joe Strummer. This relationship lasted until June the following year when Strummer stepped down and the lead vocalist job went to Spider Stacy. McGowan later re-emerged with his new band, the Popes, while his erstwhile colleagues continued to tour heavily, recording competent new material that lacked the flair of old.

Albums: *Red Roses For Me* (Stiff 1984), *Rum, Sodomy And The Lash* (Stiff 1985), *If I Should Fall From Grace With God* (Stiff 1988), *Peace And Love* (WEA 1989), *Hell's Ditch* (Pogue Mahone 1990), *Waiting For Herb* (PM 1993). Compilations: *The Best Of The Pogues* (PM 1991), *The Rest Of The Best* (PM 1992).

Poison Girls

The Poison Girls' firebrand political pop was first heard on a shared 12-inch EP, *Fatal Microbes Meet The Poison Girls*, a co-release for Small Wonder Records and the band's own label, Xntrix, in 1979. Poison Girls shared much of Crass' ideology (anarchism and communal living), though often through a more accessible musical medium. Aided by the strangely named Bernhardt Rebours (bass), Lance D'Boyle (drums) and Richard Famous (guitar), middle-aged Vi Subversa (vocals) also injected a strong feminist stance into their music. For their second EP, *Hex* (1979), the band co-opted with Crass' label, but it was almost a year before they released 'Persons Unknown', another shared single, this time with Crass themselves. The Poison Girls' long-playing debut proper, *Chappaquidick Bridge*, originally contained a free flexi-disc, 'Statement'. After 'All Systems Go' (1981), the

group parted with Crass and a live album, *Total Exposure*, appeared later that year. *Where's The Pleasure* followed in 1982, before the band moved to a new label, Illuminated Records. This relationship proved short-lived, and after 'One Good Reason' and 'Are You Happy Now?' (both 1983), the Poison Girls returned to Xntrix for *Seven Year Scratch* in 1984. That same year, '(I'm Not A) Real Woman' continued the band's lyrical tack, but their next album was to be their last. After *Songs Of Praise*, and a one-off 12-inch single for the Upright label (a memorable effort too in 'The Price Of Grain'), the Poison Girls broke up. In 1995 *Statement*, a 4-CD box set, was released to anthologise the group's output, and the group played a one-off reformation gig in London in June.

Albums: *Chappaquidick Bridge* (Crass 1980), *Total Exposure* (Xntrix 1982), *Where's The Pleasure* (Xntrix 1982), *Seven Year Scratch* (Xntrix 1984), *Songs Of Praise* (Xntrix 1985). Compilation: *Statement - The Complete Recordings* (Cooking Vinyl 1995).

Poison Idea

These hardcore heavyweights' broad appearance (nearly all members of the band could look on the term obese as a description of kindness) gave little credence to the harsh, speedy rock path they pursued. Formed in Portland, Oregon, USA, in late 1980, their first incarnation featured Jerry A. (vocals), Pig Champion (guitar), Chris Tense (bass) and Dean Johnson (drums). They debuted with the unwieldy EP *Pick Your King* which contained no less than 13 tracks, packaged in a sleeve featuring Elvis Presley on one side and Jesus Christ on the other. By the time of *Kings Of Punk* they were slightly more tuneful, but no less belligerent. However, Johnson and Tense were both fired and replaced by Steve 'Thee Slayer Hippy' Hanford (drums) and Tim Paul (ex-Final Warning, now Gruntruck; bass). The sound was also filled out with additional guitarist Vegetable (ex-Mayhem). However, Tim Paul only lasted one abortive gig (just one song, in fact) before being replaced by the returning Tense. His tenure, though slightly longer, lasted only until the release of *War All The Time*, after which Mondo (also ex-Mayhem) joined. The line-up wars continued after 'Getting The Fear' was released, with Vegetable sacked on New Year's Eve, replaced by Kid Cocksman (ex-Gargoyle; guitar), and Mondo quit after the appropriately titled 'Discontent'. Myrtle Tickner (ex-Oily Bloodmen) then became the band's fourth bass player. Aldine Striknine (guitar; ex-Maimed For Life) stepped in for the next casualty Kid Cocksman (apparently kicked out for being too thin) to record *Feel The Darkness*, after which Mondo returned once more, this time on second guitar. Despite the line-up confusions and obvious gimmickry, they produced a body of work of some substance, characterized by a lyrical preference for matters alcoholic and sexual, with some of the world's great song titles ('Record Collectors Are Pretentious Assholes', etc.). Live they were both enormously impressive, and impressively enormous. After *We Must Burn* Poison Idea disbanded with Tense and Johnson going on to form Apartment 3G.

Albums: *Kings Of Punk* (Pusmort 1986), *War All The Time* (Alchemy 1987), *Record Collectors Are Pretentious Assholes* (Bitzcore 1989), *Poison Idea* (In Your Face 1989), *Feel The*

Darkness (Vinyl Solution 1990), *Pajama Party* (Vinyl Solution 1992), *Blank, Blackout, Vacant* (Vinyl Solution 1992), *We Must Burn* (Vinyl Solution 1993).

Police

The reggae-influenced minimalist pop sound of this highly talented UK trio was one of the musical high-points of the late 70s and early 80s. Their individual talent and egos ultimately got the better of them and they fragmented, although each of the strong-willed former members has never ruled out the possibility of a re-match. The group comprised Stewart Copeland (b. 16 July 1952, Alexandria, Egypt; drums/percussion/vocals), Andy Summers (b. Andrew Somers, 31 December 1942, Poulton Le Fylde, Lancashire, England; guitar) and Sting (b. Gordon Sumner, 2 October 1951, Wallsend, Tyne And Wear, England; bass/vocals). Masterminded by Miles Copeland, ex-Curved Air member Stewart and ex-Last Exit bassist Sting came together with the vastly experienced Summers, leaving the original member Henry Padovani no alternative but to leave. He had previously played on their independent chart hit 'Fall Out', released on Miles' Illegal label. Summers, a former session musician and ex-Zoot Money, Dantalians Chariot, Eric Burdon And The New Animals, Soft Machine and Kevin Ayers, blended instantly with Copeland's back-to-front reggae drum technique and Sting's unusual and remarkable voice. Summers added a sparse clean guitar utilizing a flanger with echo, a sound he arguably invented and most certainly popularized; he found many imitators during his career with the Police. The mixture of such unusual styles gave them a totally fresh sound which they honed and developed over five outstanding albums; each record was a step forward both in musical content and sales. Astonishingly, their A&M debut 'Roxanne' failed to chart when first released, but this now-classic tale of a prostitute was a later success on the back of 'Can't Stand Losing You'. Their heavily reggae-influenced *Outlandos D'Amour* and *Regatta De Blanc* dominated the UK charts for most of 1979 and contained such chart-toppers as 'Message In A Bottle' and 'Walking On The Moon'. Sting's simple but intelligently written lyrics were complete tales. By the time *Zenyatta Mondatta* was released their punk-styled bleached hair had black roots; they were never to be touched up, as the Police were on their way to becoming one of the world's leading bands. This album was their big breakthrough in America, Europe, Japan and indeed the rest of the world. The group's third number 1 'Don't Stand So Close To Me', a tale of the temptations of being a schoolteacher (which Sting had been previously), was closely followed by the lyrically rich yet simply titled 'De Do Do Do De Da Da Da'. The following year, having now conquered the world, they released the outstanding *Ghost In The Machine*, which contained Sting's most profound lyrics to date and was enriched by Hugh Padgham's fuller production. The major hit singles from this album were the thought-provoking 'Spirits In The Material World', 'Invisible Sun', a brooding atmospheric comment on Northern Ireland and the joyous Caribbean carnival sound of 'Every Little Thing She Does Is Magic' which provided their fourth UK number 1.

Following yet another multi-million seller, the band relaxed in 1982 to concentrate on solo projects. Stewart resurrected his Klark Kent *alter ego*, releasing *Klark Kent*, and wrote the music for the film *Rumblefish*. Andy had a book of photographs published to coincide with an exhibition of his camera work and also made an album with Robert Fripp. Sting appeared in the film adaptation of Dennis Potter's *Brimstone And Treacle* and had the UK gutter press speculate on his sexual preferences. The Police re-convened in 1983 and released the carefully crafted *Synchronicity*; almost as if they knew this would be their last album. The package was stunning, a superb album containing numerous potential hit singles and a series of expertly made accompanying videos. The magnificent 'Every Breath You Take', arguably their greatest song, stayed at number 1 in the UK for four weeks, and for twice as many weeks in the USA, while the album stayed at the top for an astonishing 17 weeks. The collection varies from gentle songs like 'Tea In The Sahara' and 'Wrapped Around Your Finger' to the mercurial energy of 'Synchronicity II'. To finish on such a high and to depart as undefeated champions must have satisfied the band. In retrospect, it is better to have produced five classic albums than a massive catalogue of indifferent collections.

Albums: *Outlandos D'Amour* (1978), *Regatta De Blanc* (1979), *Zenyatta Mondatta* (1980), *Ghost In The Machine* (1981), *Synchronicity* (1983). Compilations: *Every Breath You Take - The Singles* (1986), *Greatest Hits* (1992).

Poly Styrene

b. Marion Elliot. Hailing from Brixton, London, England, the singer and main writer of X-Ray Spex, Poly Styrene, was writing songs by the age of nine. In 1976, a release on GTO Records, 'Silly Billy' by Mari Elliot, is believed to be her debut. Her subsequent work experiences on the sweet stall of Woolworths, and as a trainee clothes buyer, provided her with just as much songwriting stimulus. When punk reared its head Marion saw it as 'anti-racism, anti-nazism, and anti-sexism', and she quickly affirmed her identity with it. She assembled X-Ray Spex, wrote most of their material, and picked her new name from an advert. She was recognized as one of the leading lights of the punk movement in January 1978 when the BBC arts programme, *Omnibus*, broadcast the documentary *Who Is Poly Styrene?*. X-Ray Spex burnt out quickly and in 1980 Poly released her first solo single, 'Talk In Toytown', and the disappointing *Translucence* - especially moderate compared with the outstanding *Germ Free Adolescence* two years before. She then announced she was giving up pop music to devote herself to the Spiritual Life and Krishna Consciousness Movement, using the spiritual name Maharani Devi. She did, however, continue to play devotional music and to record at the temple's own studio (donated by George Harrison). At the bequest of her spiritual master she returned to pop music in 1986 with the Eastern-flavoured EP, *Gods And Goddesses*. In 1991 she reformed X-Ray Spex and announced that she was working on a 'counter culture street musical explosion' to be staged in 1992. She also appeared on Dream Academy's 1991 album, *A Different Kind Of Weather*, as vocalist on a version of John Lennon's 'Love'.

Album: *Translucence* (United Artists 1980).

Pooh Sticks

Mix a slapstick parody of the archetypal UK independent guitar band, a wicked sense of humour and an uncanny knack of turning out catchy, astute pop tunes and that ably defines the Pooh Sticks. They were formed in October 1987 in Wales when Hue Williams (b. 4 March 1968; son of ex-Man and Dire Straits drummer, Terry Williams) and friend Paul teamed-up with three schoolgirls Trudi, Alison and Stephanie. The band released a single almost immediately on local label, Fierce Records. 'On Tape' (1988) was a send-up of the independent scene at its most clichéd and attracted a great deal of interest, particularly as the band flew to New York for their first live appearance. A five-disc one-track single boxed set which included the legendary 'I Know Someone Who Knows Someone Who Knows Alan McGee Quite Well' (referring to the Creation Records head) followed in the summer, although these were transferred onto a one-sided self-titled mini-album by the end of the year. 1989 saw two live albums, *Orgasm* on the Scottish 53rd & 3rd label and *Trademark Of Quality*, while the Poohs covered the Vaselines' 'Dying For It' in 1990. The lampoonery continued with *The Great White Wonder* in 1991 when they tackled weightier icons from the 60s and 70s. In February of 1992 the Pooh Sticks signed a $1.2 million deal with the major BMG (formerly RCA Records) company in the USA.

Albums: *Pooh Sticks* (Fierce 1988, mini-album), *Orgasm* (53 & 3rd 1989), *Trademark Of Quality* (Fierce 1989), *Formula One Generation* (Sympathy For The Record Industry 1990), *Peel Sessions* (Overground 1991), *The Great White Wonder* (Sympathy For The Record Industry 1991), *Million Seller* (Zoo 1993), *Optimistic Fool* (Seed 1995).

Pop Group

This seminal UK punk group operated from Bristol, Avon, in the late 70s, combining abstracted funk with chaos and expressionist vocals courtesy of Mark Stewart. The topics under consideration - starvation, war, exploitation - were similar to those expounded by anarcho-punks Crass, but the Pop Group's music was much more sophisticated. Their records are by turns inspirational and intolerable, some of the most extreme music to have been pressed onto vinyl. The masterpiece was *For How Much Longer Do We Tolerate Mass Murder*. No one is able to maintain such a pitch of intensity: bassist Simon Underwood left to form Pigbag, a welcome relief from the drabness punk conformity had created, a riot of bright shirts, ethnic rhythms and James Brown references. Guitarist and saxophonist Gareth Sagar formed the irrepressible Rip Rig And Panic. Only singer Mark Stewart kept to his bleak viewpoint, forming the Maffia with the rhythm team from Sugarhill Records and working with producer Adrian Sherwood.

Albums: *Y* (Radar 1979), *For How Much Longer Must We Tolerate Mass Murder* (Rough Trade 1980), *We Are Time* (Rough Trade 1980).

Pop Will Eat Itself

This UK group took its name from the headine of an article on Jamie Wednesday (later Carter USM) by David Quantick in the *New Musical Express*. Having previously rehearsed and gigged under the names From Eden and Wild And Wondering, the group emerged as Pop Will Eat Itself in 1986 with a line-up comprising Clint Mansell (b. 7 November 1963, Coventry, England; vocals/guitar), Adam Mole (b. 1962, Stourbridge, England; keyboards), Graham Crabb (b. 10 October 1964, Streetly, West Midlands, England; drums, later vocals) and Richard Marsh (b. 4 March 1965, York, Yorkshire, England; bass). Making their live debut at the Mere, Stourbridge Art College, their first recording was the privately issued EP, *The Poppies Say Grr*, which was nominated as Single Of The Week in the *New Musical Express*. BBC Radio sessions followed and the group appeared in the independent charts with the follow-up EPs *Poppiecock* and *The Covers*. Already known for their hard pop and vulgarisms, they ran into trouble with the release of 'Beaver Patrol', which was criticized for its puerile sexism. Their debut album, *Box Frenzy*, followed in late 1987 and displayed their odd mix of guitar pop with sampling. The insistent 'There Is No Love Between Us Anymore' was their most impressive single to date and augured well for the future, as did 'Def Con One' in 1988. During that year they were invited to play in the USSR, and soon afterwards signed to the major, RCA Records. 'Can U Dig It' and 'Wise Up Sucker' were minor successes, as was their second album. A world tour sharpened their approach and during 1990 they achieved mainstream acclaim with 'Touched By The Hand Of Cicciolina', a paean addressed to the Italian porn star turned politician. Two further hit singles, 'X,Y & Zee' and '92 Degrees', followed in 1991. The group recruited a full-time (human) drummer in 1992 when Fuzz (b. Robert Townshend, 31 July 1964, Birmingham, England; ex-Pig Bros, General Public, Ranking Roger) joined, but following *Weird's Bar & Grill* a year later RCA dropped the band. Now effectively despised by the media, Pop Will Eat Itself continued despite expectations that this might signify the end of the band, forging a new contract with Infectious Records. The results of which have hardly endeared them to critics, though the title of the 1995 collection, *Two Fingers My Friends*, did at least underline their tenacity and self-sufficiency.

Albums: *Box Frenzy* (Chapter 22 1987), *Now For A Feast!* (Rough Trade 1989, early recordings), *This Is The Day, This Is The Hour, This Is This* (RCA 1989), *The Pop Will Eat Itself Cure For Sanity* (RCA 1990), *The Looks Or The Lifestyle* (RCA 1992), *Weird's Bar & Grill* (RCA 1993), *Dos Dedos Mes Amigos* (Infectious 1994), *Two Fingers My Friends!* (Infectious 1995).

Popguns

This Brighton, England-based group comprise Wendy Morgan (vocals), Simon Pickles (guitar), Greg Dixon (guitar), Pat Walkington (bass) and Shaun Charman (drums, ex-Wedding Present). The Popguns breezy power-pop and well-crafted songs, accompanied by Morgan's lyrics of boyfriend trouble 'n' bliss and post-teen alienation, found a ready audience. Despite a thin voice, she more than adequately made up for any shortcomings with an energetic, impassioned delivery. The two EPs released in 1989, *Landslide* and *Waiting For The Winter*, promised much, and were later compiled along with 1990's *Someone You Love* on

Eugenie for the Midnight Music label. The Popguns' first full album release in 1991 boasted a production credit for fellow Brighton resident, Psychic TV's Genesis P. Orridge. It achieved a healthy independent Top 10 chart position and promised further success, but gradually they were swept under by a music press ever watchful for the new, leaving them to stew in relative obscurity - though 1995's *Love Junky* still offered ambitious, bold songwriting.

Albums: *Snog* (Midnight Music 1991), *Love Junky* (3rd Stone 1995). Compilation: *Eugenie* (Midnight Music 1990).

Popinjays

Formed in London in 1988 by songwriters Wendy Robinson (b. 6 April 1964, Huddersfield, Yorkshire, England; vocals), Polly Hancock (b. 16 July 1964, Berkshire, England; guitar/vocals) and a drum machine, the Popinjays evolved out of the influential Timebox Club at the Bull & Gate pub in Kentish Town, north London (the duo later ran their own Pop Club at the same venue), by striving to perfect the ultimate pop formula. Dana Baldinger (b. 26 December 1963, California, USA; bass) joined in 1989 as the offer of a combination of sweets, comics and biscuits won the band a record deal with One Little Indian Records. Dana departed after one single, to be replaced by fellow countrywoman Anne Rogers (b. 17 October 1962, New York, USA) a move which was followed by a plethora of critical recommendations for the debut album, *Bang Up To Date With The Popinjays*. Ever conscious of the importance of fun in music, their promo video for the 'Vote Elvis' single featured much Monkees-style running around with special guest Cathal Coughlan from Fatima Mansions. Drummer Seamus Feeney (b. 19 November 1964, Middlesex, England), caused the drum machine to be sacked at the close of 1990, just as the Popinjays were beginning to garner appreciative attention from America. *Flying Down To Mono Valley* did little to embellish their reputation, and it was left to their 1994 album to produce a significant stylistic departure. *Tales From The Urban Prairie* saw forays into country rock and singer/songwriter melancholia, an affecting performance but one which left their traditional fan base in some degree of confusion.

Albums: *Bang Up To Date With The Popinjays* (One Little Indian 1990), *Flying Down To Mono Valley* (One Little Indian 1992), *Tales From The Urban Prairie* (One Little Indian 1994).

Popsicle

This Swedish indie pop outfit began to make an international breakthrough in 1993. The line-up initially comprised Andreas Mattson (vocals/guitar), Fredrik Norberg (vocals/guitar), Kenny Vikstrom (bass) and Per-Arne Wikander (drums), who met on a school trip to Stockholm. They formed in the mid-80s and experimented with a number of musical styles before shaping up as Popsicle in 1991. Their boisterous, Anglophile songs earned them a Scandinavian Grammy two years later. Freddy's inebriated acceptance speech at the ceremony included a death wish fatwa on Sweden's Eurovision Song Contest entrants. Vikstrom was replaced by Arvid Lind for *Abstinence*.

Albums: *Lacquer* (MNW 1993), *Abstinence* (Warners 1995).

Posies

Formed in Seattle, Washington, USA, the Posies play powerfully melodic music which pays tribute to Merseybeat and the harmonies of the Hollies. Growing up in Bellingham, 90 miles north of Seattle, Jonathon Auer (vocals/guitar) and Ken Stringfellow (vocals/guitar) were both in bands in their early teens, and even joined their high school choir. Stringfellow is married to Kim Warnick of the Fastbacks, and has mixed and produced for various Seattle/Sub Pop Records bands. He has also guested for Mudhoney. However, the Posies are equally influenced by Hüsker Dü as by the songwriting prowess of XTC, Elvis Costello and Squeeze. The duo's debut was recorded (originally on their own label as a cassette, later on PopLlama Products) in 1988 and introduced their penchant for sanguine, everyday lyrical topics. Entitled *Failure*, its title marked them out as singularly lacking in ambition, a trait which later became enshrined in the 'slacker' ethos. However, they signed to Geffen Records, and enlisted a rhythm section (Dave Fox and Mike Musburger) and brought in John Leckie to produce their major label debut. A varied, multi-textured album, it was reminiscent of the Stone Roses, whom Leckie also produced. The Posies' third album, *Frosting On The Beater*, a reference to masturbation, was produced by Don Fleming, and attracted wide acclaim, finishing in the higher reaches of many end of year critical polls. The group supported Teenage Fanclub and Big Star on European tours, and Auer and Stringfellow both took part in the reformation of the latter band.

Albums: *Failure* (23 1988, cassette only), *Dear 23* (Geffen 1990), *Frosting On The Beater* (Geffen 1993).

Possum Dixon

Possum Dixon are from the 'coffee house scene' of Los Angeles, California, USA. Named after a fugitive spotted on the US television programme *America's Most Wanted*, the group have earned a good deal of international support based on their rangy, expressive musicianship and lyrics, and have been compared to the Talking Heads, XTC and the Violent Femmes. Robert Zabrecky (vocals/bass) helped set up the Jabber Jaw club in the late 80s, which showcased local bands, as well as an unannounced Nirvana gig. Recruiting band members from this scene, Zabrecky started to put the band together and they released three independent singles. They eventually signed a contract with Interscope Records. Zabrecky described their music thus, 'There's a side that's experimental music, a stream of consciousness, trying to mix poetry, bullshit, abusive relationships, drugs, sex and coffee, things like that.' Songs such as 'We're All Happy' tackled the problem of a woman who came to vibrators late in life and overdosed on the resultant happiness they brought her. Better still was the single, 'Watch That Girl Destroy Me', produced by Earle Mankey, which followed acclaimed support slots to Compulsion in London.

Album: *Possum Dixon* (Interscope/East West 1993).

Postcard Records

After the impetus of punk's initial onslaught, like-minded individuals in every corner of Britain set about creating their own musical identity. If they could not play music, they went one better and founded their own label. Alan Horne set about realizing his ambition in late 70s Glasgow when he discovered local favourites Orange Juice. Here was a band that could be harnessed, and Horne set about creating Postcard Records with lead singer Edwyn Collins as the 'Sound Of Young Scotland'. Orange Juice's 'Falling And Laughing' was issued early in 1980, housed in distinctive foldaround, hand-coloured sleeves with a free flexi-disc. Much of the Postcard label's appeal would stem from the precious nature of its roster and the presentation of its releases as vital and desirable artefacts. To do this, Horne needed more than one band and after losing the Fire Engines, opted for manic Edinburgh act Josef K. Postcard's second release was also arguably their finest; Orange Juice's 'Blue Boy'. Their debut had caused a stir, certainly, but this formidable single, awash with frenetic guitar work and an unforgettably passionate melody, sent the critics reeling. Josef K's 'Radio Drill Time' was less accessible and more frenzied, but an aura had already surrounded the label.

Next came the Go-Betweens, an obscure Australian outfit whom Horne met while they were touring the UK. They promptly recorded 'I Need Two Heads', which became the fourth Postcard single, but this was to prove their only single for the label. Josef K's more relaxed 'It's Kinda Funny' and another Orange Juice classic, 'Simply Thrilled Honey' saw out 1980, and Horne took the end of year opportunity to redesign the label's image. The spartan brown labels (with a drum-beating pussycat) were replaced by a checked design to reflect the new sleeves, portraying a collage of Scottish national dress. In the meantime, Josef K hit a stumbling block. They were unhappy with the sound on their debut *Sorry For Laughing*, and eventually scrapped it before it reached the shops. Postcard instead relied on Orange Juice for 'Poor Old Soul', before introducing a new signing early in 1981, Aztec Camera. Fronted by the 16-year-old Roddy Frame, their debut, 'Just Like Gold', was more traditional than other Postcard material, but nonetheless endearing. Josef K teamed up with Belgian label Les Disques du Crépuscule for 'Sorry For Laughing' (the title track to the abandoned album), and followed this with 'Chance Meeting', a re-recording of their first single. By this time, mid-1981, Postcard was basking in the critical sunshine and Orange Juice succumbed to a seductive offer from Polydor Records. Their next single, 'Wan Light', was abandoned and from this point on, Postcard fell apart. Josef K finally took the plunge with a re-recorded album, *The Only Fun In Town*, and Aztec Camera continued to ply their acoustic sensibilities with 'Mattress Of Wire', but Horne soon moved on to pastures new, leaving numerous projects on the shelf. In addition to the first long player from Aztec Camera (*Green Jacket Grey*), Horne had allocated numbers to singles from the Bluebells (later to enjoy commercial success at London), the Jazzateers (who joined Rough Trade) and Secret Goldfish (reputedly an Orange Juice pseudonym). Aztec Camera and the Go-Betweens also moved to Rough Trade, and Josef K split up, while Horne eventually re-surfaced managing the labels Win and Swamplands.

Prefab Sprout

The intricate tales and thoughts in the lyrics of songwriter Paddy McAloon indicate a major songwriter. His Bob Dylan imagery and Elvis Costello bluntness have made Prefab Sprout one of the most refreshing pop bands of the late 80s and beyond. The band was formed in 1982 and comprised: Paddy McAloon (b. 7 June 1957, Durham, England; guitar/vocals), Martin McAloon (b. 4 January 1962, Durham, England; bass), Wendy Smith (b. 31 May 1963, Durham, England; vocals/guitar) and Neil Conti (b. 12 February 1959, London, England). Following a self-pressed single 'Lions In My Own Garden', Paddy attracted the attention of the independent label Kitchenware. They had further hits in the UK independent charts and their debut *Swoon* made the national chart. *Swoon* was a wordy album featuring songs with many chord changes that ultimately concentrated on lyrics rather than melody. Later that year the excellent 'When Love Breaks Down' failed to excite the single-buying public. A remixed version by Thomas Dolby was released the following year, but once again it failed. When *Steve McQueen* was issued in 1985 the band became media darlings, with Paddy McAloon coming near to over-exposure. The album was a critics' favourite and displayed hummable songs with fascinating lyrics, and it made a respectable showing in the charts. At the end of the year 'When Love Breaks Down' was issued for a third time and finally became a hit.

In the USA, *Steve McQueen* was forcibly retitled *Two Wheels Good*. A striking work, the album included a tribute to Faron Young and the arresting 'Goodbye Lucille # 1' (aka 'Johnny Johnny'). *From Langley Park To Memphis* in 1988 was a major success world-wide; Paddy had now refined his art to produce totally accessible yet inventive pop music. The album represented a courageous change of direction with McAloon employing strings and composing melodies which recalled the great show musical writers of the pre rock 'n' roll era. 'Nightingales' was very much in this vein, and the work ended with the strikingly melodramatic 'Nancy (Let Your Hair Down For Me)' and 'The Venus Of The Soup Kitchen'. Already the band had reached the stage of having superstar guests 'turning up on the album'. Both Stevie Wonder (harmonica solo on 'Nightingales') and Pete Townshend put in appearances. 'The King Of Rock 'N' Roll' became their biggest hit to date. *Protest Songs* was a collection scheduled to appear before their previous album and its success was muted by the continuing sales of both *Steve McQueen* and *From Langley Park To Memphis*. McAloon unleashed *Jordan: The Comeback* in 1990, and for many critics it was the album of the year. All McAloon's talents had combined to produce a concept album of magnificence. Over 64 minutes in length, the album boasted 19 tracks, full of striking melodies and fascinatingly oblique lyrics. The ghost of Elvis Presley haunted several of the songs, most notably the elegiac 'Moon Dog'. They are now established as one of Britain's major bands, and the media await their next move with interest.

Albums: *Swoon* (1984), *Steve McQueen* (1985), *From Langley Park To Memphis* (1988), *Protest Songs* (1989), *Jordan: The Comeback* (1990). Compilation: *A Life Of Surprises: The Best Of* (1992).

Pretenders

Chrissie Hynde (b. 17 September 1951, Akron, Ohio, USA),

came to England to seek her fortune during the early 70s. After meeting with *New Musical Express* writer and future boyfriend Nick Kent she joined the paper and gained entrance into the world of rock. During her pre-Pretenders days she worked at Malcolm McLaren's shop, SEX, played with Chris Spedding, joined Jack Rabbit, formed the Berk Brothers and made a tasteless, unreleased single as the Moors Murderers. By the time she assembled the band in 1978, Hynde had gained a great deal of experience. The classic Pretenders' line-up comprised: Pete Farndon (b. 2 June 1952, Hereford, England, d. 14 April 1983; bass), James Honeyman-Scott (b. 4 November 1956, Hereford, England d. 16 June 1982; guitar) and Martin Chambers (b. 4 September 1951, Hereford, England; drums). Their debut was a Nick Lowe produced version of the Kinks 'Stop Your Sobbing' in 1978. It scraped into the UK Top 40 the following year, having received critical praise and much interest. 'Kid' and the superb 'Brass In Pocket' followed. The latter was accompanied by a superb black and white video with Hynde portrayed as a waitress, and reached the number 1 position in the UK. It was their debut album that eventually put them on the road to becoming one of the decade's most important groups. *Pretenders* was a *tour-de-force* and remains their finest work. In addition to their previous singles the album contained the reggae-styled 'Private Life' (later recorded by Grace Jones), the frenetic 'Precious', the Byrds-like 'Talk Of The Town' and the beautiful ballad 'Lovers Of Today'.

Throughout 1980 they became a major stadium attraction in the USA; it was in America that Chrissie met and fell in love with her musical idol, the Kinks' Ray Davies. Davies had already expressed an interest in Hynde during an interview in the rock magazine *Dark Star*. Their tempestuous relationship lasted four years, almost resulting in marriage. Davies stated that they had gone to a registry office by bus but spent so much time arguing that they changed their minds and came home. During their romance they brought each other onstage to play with their respective bands, much to the chagrin of the band members. *Pretenders II* came in 1982; it was another collection of melodious rock played with new-wave enthusiasm. Stand-out tracks were 'Message Of Love', the brilliantly confessional, 'The Adulteress' and another Davies' chestnut, 'I Go To Sleep', first recorded by the Applejacks in 1964. During the turbulent month of June, Pete Farndon, whose drug abuse had been a problem for some time, was fired. Two days later Honeyman-Scott was found dead from a deadly concoction of heroin and cocaine. Nine months later Hynde gave birth to a daughter; the father was Ray Davies. Two months after this happy event, tragedy struck again. Pete Farndon was found dead in his bath from a drug overdose.

The new full-time Pretenders were Robbie McIntosh (ex-Average White Band) on lead guitar, and bassist Malcolm Foster. They set about recording a third album and the band ended the year with another hit single, the Christmassy '2000 Miles'. *Learning To Crawl* was released at the beginning of another successful year. The album was erratic, but it did contain some gems, notably the epic 'Thin Line Between Love And Hate', the powerful 'Middle Of The Road' and the melodic, yet poignant tribute to Honeyman-

Scott, 'Back On The Chain Gang'. The band embarked on another US tour, but Chrissie refused to be parted from her baby daughter who accompanied her, while Davies and his band were touring elsewhere. In May 1984, following a whirlwind affair, Hynde married Jim Kerr of Simple Minds. Back with the Pretenders she appeared at Live Aid at the JFK stadium in Philadelphia, and would enjoy success under her own name duetting with UB40 on the chart-topping reggae re-make of Sonny And Cher's 'I Got You Babe'. Following the birth of another daughter (Jim Kerr is the father), Chrissie effectively dismantled the band. *Get Close* was released at the end of 1987 and was well received. Both 'Don't Get Me Wrong' and 'Hymn To Her' were substantial hits. In 1988 a solo Hynde performed with UB40 at the Nelson Mandela Concert and the subsequent duet 'Breakfast In Bed' was a Top 10 UK hit. Hynde has since spent much of her time campaigning for Animal Rights. Her marriage to Kerr collapsed and in 1990 she returned with a new album *Packed*, still as the Pretenders. It was another critical and commercial success, demonstrating Hynde's natural gift for writing tight, melodic rock songs. 1994 brought *Last Of The Independents*, which saw her reunited with drummer Martin Chambers, alongside Adam Seymour (guitar) and Andy Hobson (bass).

Albums: *Pretenders* (1980), *Pretenders II* (1981), *Learning To Crawl* (1984), *Get Close* (1986), *Packed* (1990), *Last Of The Independents* (Sire/Warner Brothers 1994). Compilation: *The Singles* (1987).

Price

This UK pop punk combo began in the mid-80s. Leigh was playing with the Others, whilst Mick partnered In The Dark. Both were locals from the Uxbridge area, and when the groups folded Mick volunteered his drumming skills for the proposed band Leigh was inaugurating. They found vocalist Malcolm through an advertisement in the weekly *Sounds* music paper and bass player Gary, a multi-instrumentalist, who was one of the Others' original drummers. However, when he emigrated they drafted in another Gary, but he was as short-lived as his namesake. Huggy then stepped in as the permanent bass player. The final shift came in 1991 when Pete (also ex-Others) replaced Mick. Their first release came with a single jointly sponsored by *So What!* fanzine, 'The Price You Pay'. 1989 saw them joining the Released Emotions roster where they found Paul Fox (ex-Ruts) to produce their best recording, 'Between The Lies'. Their first album followed several months later.

Album: *Table Of Uncles* (Released Emotions 1990).

Primal Scream

The line-up which achieved so much success in 1991 consisted of Bobby Gillespie (b. 22 June 1964), Andrew Innes, Robert Young, Henry Olsen, Philip 'Toby' Tomanov, Martin Duffy and Denise Johnson, but Primal Scream had been a fluctuating affair since the middle of the 80s. Bobby Gillespie was the centrifugal force throughout, forming the band after a stint as stand-up drummer in the nascent Jesus And Mary Chain. Primal Scream achieved immediate popularity via the *New Musical Express's* alternative *C86* cassette compilation with 'Velocity Girl', an 80-second romp

Primitives

through the richer pastures of 60s guitar pop. After an album's worth of similarly melodic material in a brief liaison with the short-lived Elevation label, they veered towards rock territory near the end of the decade, revealing a penchant for leather trousers, wild guitars and idol-worshipping. The latter characteristic, at least, was to be a significant feature in their subsequent form, as Gillespie, encouraged by guitarist Andrew Innes, developed an interest in the burgeoning dance and drug scene. Come the start of the 90s, Primal Scream had been reinvented, with the aid of name remixers such as Andy Weatherall, into a groove machine. The 'Loaded' single was the first proof of the band's transformation, stealing from rock's heritage and cult biker movies yet invading Britain's dancefloors to become a Top 10 hit in the UK charts. Their iconoclastic ideals persisted, no more so than on the road, where Primal Scream's hedonistic indulgences were well-publicized. 1991's *Screamadelica* emphasized the band's cultural diversities and reaped rich critical acclaim and massive sales, just before the band relocated to Tennessee to work on the follow up. This finally emerged in 1994, produced by veteran Atlantic Records soul man Tom Dowd, revealing a stylistic debt to the Rolling Stones rather than the dance scene. Dowd was assisted by contributions from George Clinton and Black Crowes' producer George Drakoulias. Though the critical reception was frosty, Gillespie had once again reinvented himself and his band.

Albums: *Sonic Flower Groove* (Creation 1987), *Primal Scream* (Creation 1989), *Screamadelica* (Creation 1991), *Give Out But Don't Give Up* (Creation 1994).

Primitives

This highly-melodic group, from Coventry, England, formed in the summer of 1985, with a line-up featuring Kieron (vocals), Paul Court (b. 27 July 1965; vocals/guitar), Steve Dullaghan (b. 18 December 1966; bass) and Pete Tweedie (drums). Kieron was soon replaced by Tracy Tracy (b. Tracy Cattell, 18 August 1967, Australia). The group set up their own label, Lazy Records, and achieved a modicum of success on the UK independent circuit with 'Thru The Flowers', 'Really Stupid' and 'Stop Killing Me'. Despite the label now having status as a subsidiary of the major RCA Records set-up, the Primitives maintained their roots in the 'indie' scene and were, for a time, the pop press darlings. With echoes of Blondie and the Ramones, the Primitives' jangling guitar work brought them national fame in early 1988, when 'Crash', a classic piece of 'indie' pop, reached the UK Top 5. The accompanying album, *Lovely*, reached the UK Top 10, but any chance of consolidating this position was halted by personnel changes. The acrimonious ousting of Pete Tweedie saw the inclusion of Tig Williams, with further line-up changes when Andy Hobson replaced Dullaghan. Subsequent singles failed to emulate the success of 'Crash' and *Pure*, was only a partial success. The Primitives ended the 80s touring the USA and returned to UK to undergo extensive touring around Britain, hoping to regenerate those brief glory days. Both Dullahan and Tweedie would join Hate, while Hobson's tenure playing bass was a short one, being replaced in 1989 by Paul Samspon. When *Galore* failed to sell, the Primitives split-up.

Albums: *Lovely* (Lazy 1988), *Pure* (Lazy/RCA 1989), *Galore* (Lazy/RCA 1992). Compilation: *Lazy 86-88* (Lazy 1989).

Primus

The vast majority of reviewers can generally agree on one word to describe Primus - weird. Formed in San Francisco in 1984 by former Blind Illusion bassist Les Claypool, seven drummers passed through before Tim 'Herb' Alexander settled in, with Claypool's Blind Illusion colleague, ex-Possessed man Larry Lalonde replacing original guitarist Todd Huth shortly before the band recorded their debut. Musically, the band are highly talented and original, mixing funk, punk, thrash, metal and rock in their own intense manner, once described by Claypool as 'psychedelic polka'. Claypool and Alexander produce quirky, sometimes hypnotic rhythms, accentuating each other's playing, while former Joe Satriani pupil Lalonde creates and colours within the framework, although his playing owes more to Frank Zappa than to that of his old teacher. Claypool's vocals lean towards cartoonish narrative, with lyrics of a suitably abstract and humorous nature, drawing from both life and his film and literary influences. A common theme to all their albums is marine life, reflecting the band's passion for sea-fishing (they have played with fish-shaped covers on their vocal microphones). Their debut, *Such On This*, was a self-financed live set successfully released on their own Prawn Song label, and much of the material was to feature on *Fizzle Fry*, an independent studio release which won a Bay Area Music Award and, helped by touring with Faith No More, Jane's Addiction, 24-7 Spyz and Living Colour, a major record deal. *Sailing The Seas Of Cheese* further raised their profile, with their reworking of 'Tommy The Cat' from the debut (with a Tom Waits guest vocal) featuring in hit movie *Bill & Ted's Bogus Journey*. A lengthy world tour in support of Rush was then followed by stadium dates with U2. Any doubts as to the band being a sufficient draw for the closing (effectively headlining) slot on the 1993 Lollapalooza tour were dispelled when *Pork Soda* debuted in the US charts at number 7, producing a hit in 'My Name Is Mud'. Claypool would also hook up with Huth and former Primus drummer Jay Lane to form side-project Sausage, recording *Riddles Are Abound Tonight* for Interscope in 1994.

Albums: *Suck On This* (Prawn Song 1990), *Frizzle Fry* (Caroline 1990), *Sailing The Seas Of Cheese* (Interscope 1991), *Pork Soda* (Interscope 1993).

Prisoners

This mod-influenced group hailed from the UK's Medway Valley in Kent. Chief songwriter Graham Day (guitar/vocals), Allan Crockford (bass), James 'Jamie' Taylor (Hammond organ) and Johnny Symons (drums) emerged in 1982 with a rough and raucous debut, *A Taste Of Pink*, on their Own Up label. A deal with the Ace Records subsidiary, Big Beat, yielded *The Wisermiserdemelza* in 1983, a far more laid back, considered effort that ranged from powerful, 60s-influenced rock (the single, 'Hurricane') to tranquil ballads. The EP, *Electric Fit*, followed in 1984 and was notable for the excellent 'Melanie'. The band were featured on television's *The Tube* with other Big Beat acts, celebrated on the EP, *Four On Four: Trash On The Tube*, the Prisoners contributing the

awesome 'Reaching My Head'. The group were unhappy with the sound on their second album and returned to Own Up for *The Last Fourfathers*, a less slick production, but a more mature offering. It was enough to secure a deal with Stiff Records/Countdown, but from the start relations between band and label were poor. Although *In From The Cold* was an impressive album, it was far poppier and cleaner than the Prisoners had wished. Preceded by 'Whenever I'm Gone' (a re-recording from *The Last Fourfathers*), the album was badly promoted and the band, disillusioned with proceedings, split soon after. Aside from two live albums shared with the Milkshakes, there has since been an album's worth of rarities, *Rare And Unissued*. As to the Prisoners themselves, Taylor has since carved out a niche with his originally Booker T. Jones-influenced, and now rare groove-inspired, James Taylor Quartet. Crockford joined him for a while before reuniting with Graham Day (after his spell with Milkshakes offshoot, Thee Mighty Caesars) in the Prime Movers. The Prisoners lasting influence can be detected in many of the later Manchester bands, notably the Charlatans and the Inspiral Carpets, who also utilised the Hammond organ to propel their quasi-psychedelic pop songs.
Albums: *A Taste Of Pink* (Own Up 1982), *The Wisermiserdemelza* (Big Beat 1983), *The Last Fourfathers* (Own Up 1985), with the Milkshakes *The Last Night At The MIC Club* (Empire 1986), *In From The Cold* (54321 Countdown 1986), *Milkshakes V Prisoners Live* (Media Burn 1987). Compilations: *Revenge Of The Prisoners* (Pink Dust 1984), *Rare And Unissued* (Hangman 1988).

Professionals

This UK group was an offshoot from the notorious Sex Pistols and featured Paul Cook (drums/vocals) and Steve Jones (guitar/vocals) plus Ray McVeigh (guitar/vocals) and Paul Myers (bass, ex-Vic Goddard And The Subway Sect). The band received plenty of press attention thanks to the involvement of Cook and Jones but their debut album proved disappointing. A second album followed, plus a handful of singles, which still could not convince either the critics or the record-buying public that they had anything to offer.
Albums: *The Professionals* (1980), *I Didn't See It Coming* (1981).

Prong

This US thrash-hardcore rock trio was formed in the mid-80s. Hailing from New York's Manhattan lower east side, the band comprised Tommy Victor (vocals/guitar), Mike Kirkland (vocals/bass) and Ted Parsons (drums), and caused an immediate stir with their first release on the independent Spigot label. Emotionally angry, lyrically brutal, Prong partnered a relentless assault with some fierce guitar-riffing. Their second album for Epic Records, *Prove You Wrong*, in 1991, was their most significant work to date. By the advent of *Cleansed* the group had expanded to a four-piece. First they had added ex-Flotsam & Jetson bass player Tony Gregory, before recruiting Killing Joke musician Raven, who had previously worked with the band on their *Whose Fist Is It Anyway* remix EP. John Bechdel of Murder Inc. additionally expanded the band's sound with his

programming and sampling skills.
Albums: *Primitive Origins* (Spigot 1987), *Force Fed* (Spigot 1988), *Beg To Differ* (Epic 1990), *Prove You Wrong* (Epic 1991), *Cleansed* (Epic 1994).

Propaganda

This Euro pop/synthesizer band left their native Germany to arrive in England in 1983. Comprising Claudia Brücken (ex-Eggolinos; vocals), Michael Mertens (ex-Dusseldorf Symphony Orchestra; percussion), Susanne Freytag and Ralf Dorper (keyboards), they found an early advocate in Paul Morley of ZTT Records. Their first release, 'Dr. Mabuse', rallied well in the UK charts, reaching number 27. However, due to the label, and Trevor Horn's commitment to Frankie Goes To Hollywood, the follow-up would not be released until over a year later. 'Duel'/'Jewel' was more successful still as Brücken moved permanently to England to wed Morley. The group's first live performance in June 1985 saw their line-up bolstered by Derek Forbes (ex-Simple Minds) on bass and Steve Jansen (ex-Japan, brother of David Sylvian) on drums. *A Secret Wish* and the single from it, 'P-Machinery', emerged a month later. Their European tour saw another line-up shuffle with Brian McGee (also ex-Simple Minds) taking over drums, and Kevin Armstrong on guitar, alongside Brücken, Mertens, Freytag and Forbes. Dorper had departed on the advent of the tour, and eventually only Mertens remained from the original line-up. They became involved in a huge legal battle with ZTT, and Brücken decided to stay with her husband's label. She formed Act with Thomas Leer in 1987. When the litigation had finished in 1988 the new Propaganda line-up featured Besti Miller, an American expatriate based in Germany on vocals. They released *1-2-3-4* in 1990, with contributions from old hands Freytag and Dorper, as well as Howard Jones and David Gilmour. Meanwhile, Brücken had embarked on a solo career.
Albums: *A Secret Wish* (1985), *1-2-3-4* (1990). Solo album: Claudia Brücken *Love; And A Million Other Things* (1991).

Psychedelic Furs

Until the recruitment of a drummer (Vince Ely) in 1979, Richard Butler (b. 5 June 1956, Kingston-upon-Thames, Surrey, England; vocals), Roger Morris (guitar), ex-Photon John Ashton (b. 30 November 1957; guitar), Duncan Kilburn (woodwinds) and Tim Butler (b. 7 December 1958; bass) had difficulties finding work. The group were also dogged by an unprepossessing sullenness in interview, an equally anachronistic group name - inspired by the 1966 Velvet Underground track, 'Venus In Furs' - and Richard Butler's grating one-note style. It was not until a session on John Peel's BBC Radio 1 programme that they were invested with hip credibility - and a CBS Rcords recording contract. Under Steve Lillywhite's direction, their bleak debut album was followed by minor singles chart entries with 'Dumb Waiter' and 'Pretty In Pink', both selections from 1981's more tuneful and enduring *Talk Talk Talk*. Creeping even closer to the UK Top 40, 'Love My Way' was the chief single from *Forever Now*, produced in the USA by Todd Rundgren. On replacing Ely with Philip Calvert (ex-Birthday Party) in 1982, the outfit traded briefly as just 'the Furs' before *Mirror*

Moves emitted a UK Top 30 hit with 'Heaven' (which was underpinned with a fashionable disco rhythm). Lucrative too were 'Ghost In You' and a re-recording of 'Pretty In Pink' for inclusion on 1986's film of the same title. That same year, they appeared at the mammoth Glastonbury Fayre festival - which, to many of their fans, remains the most abiding memory of the Psychedelic Furs as performers. By 1990, Ashton, the Butler brothers and hired hands were all that remained of a band that had become mostly a studio concern. Three years later the band were just a very fond memory, with Richard Butler moving on to recapture 'the spark of surprise' with new outfit, Love Spit Love.

Albums: *Psychedelic Furs* (Columbia 1980), *Talk Talk Talk* (Columbia 1981), *Forever Now* (Columbia 1982), *Mirror Moves* (Columbia 1984), *Midnight To Midnight* (Columbia 1987), *Book Of Days* (Columbia 1989), *World Outside* (Columbia 1991). Compilations: *All Of This And Nothing* (Columbia 1988), *The Collection* (CBS 1991).

Psychic TV

This somewhat misrepresented UK *avant garde* collective have seen their aural experimentalism overshadowed by their connections with the literary underworld, or simply the underworld itself. They were formed by Genesis P. Orridge (b. c.1950; ex-Pork Dukes and Throbbing Gristle) and Peter Christopherson (ex-Throbbing Gristle). The line-up also included P. Orridge's long-term lover, Cosey Fanni Tutti and Geoff Rushton (former editor of *Stabmental* fanzine). However, Christopherson and Rushton soon left to form Coil. P. Orridge has been portrayed in much of the media as a deranged and dangerous madman. He had first come to the attention of the media and authorities as the organizer of the 'Prostitution' exhibition at London's ICA gallery in the late 70s. His shock tactics continued with his work in Throbbing Gristle and Psychic TV, and much use was made of fascinating/disturbing slide and film back projection at gigs. Alternatively, Genesis has repeatedly been revealed as a most personable and charming a character as the music industry has thrown up, albeit a little mischievous. P. Orridge takes his inspiration from the works of the Maquis De Sade, Charles Manson and particularly William Burroughs. Burroughs reciprocated the respect, and has stated of Psychic TV that they provide: 'the most important work with communication that I know of in the popular medium'. This is central to the band, and the philosophical congregation which backs them, the Temple Ov Psychick Youth. Their use of guerrilla tactics in the information war follows on from Throbbing Gristle's work, and makes use of broad readings of situationist and deconstructionist thought. P. Orridge's respect for 60s stars Brian Wilson and Brian Jones were revealed with two minor UK chart singles in 1986. The surprisingly poppy 'Godstar' celebrated the former Rolling Stones' guitarist, while the tribute to Wilson was a cover of 'Good Vibrations'. In an ambitious project, from 1986, the group aimed to issue 23 live albums on the 23rd of each month (23 being a statistically, symbolic number), each from a different country from their world tour. After walking out of their deal with Some Bizarre (who released their debut single 'Just Driftin') the band no longer involve themselves with the business concerns of music, like promotion. The

ranks of the band have been swelled by a variety of members, including John Gosling (ex-Zos Kia), Alex Ferguson (ex-Alternative TV), Daniel Black, Matthew Best, Dave Martin and many others. They have also branched out in to other media such as film and literature. (They made available recordings of Burroughs speeches for the first time.) Although the mainstream music press have continually painted a black picture of Psychic TV's music (and activities), it can at times be surprisingly bright and accessible. Conventional *society's* inability to come to terms with Psychic TV's message was demonstrated early in 1992 when police seized videos, books and magazines from Genesis P. Orridge's Brighton home after a performance art video was, it was claimed, shown out of context on a television programme about child abuse. The Orridges reportedly since fled the USA.

Albums: *Force The Hand Of Chance* (1982), *Dreams Less Sweet* (1983), *New York Scum Haters* (1984), *Themes* (1985), *Mouth Of The Night* (1985), *Live In Tokyo* (1986), *Pagan Day* (1987), *Live En Suisse* (1987), *Berlin Atonal, Vol. 1* (1987), *Live In Heaven* (1987), *Live In Reyjavik* (1987), *Live At Gottingen* (1987), *Temporary Temple* (1988), *Live At Mardi Gras* (1988), *Allegory And Self* (1988), *Live At Thee Circus* (1988), *Live In Glasgow* (1989), *Themes 3* (1989), *Live In Paris* (1989), *Live In Toronto* (1989), *Live At The Ritz* (1989), *Live At The Pyramid* (1989), *Kondole/Copycat* (1989), *Towards Thee Infinite Beat* (1990).

Public Image Limited

Public Image Ltd (PiL) was the 'company' formed by John Lydon (b. 31 January 1956, Finsbury Park, London, England) when he left behind both the Sex Pistols and previous moniker, Johnny Rotten, in January 1978. With Lydon on vocals, classically trained pianist and early Clash guitarist Keith Levene on guitar, reggae influenced bass player Jah Wobble (b. John Wordle), and Canadian drummer Jim Walker (ex-Furies), the band were put together with the working title of the Carnivorous Buttock Flies. By the time the debut single - the epic 'Public Image' - was released in its newspaper sleeve in September, they had adopted the less ridiculous name. Their live debut followed in Paris on 14 December, and they played the UK for the first time on Christmas Day. In January 1979 ex-101ers and Raincoats' drummer Richard Dudanski replaced Walker, who went on to punk band the Straps. The *Metal Box* set came out later that year as a set of 12-inch records housed in tin 'film' cans (it was later re-issued as a normal album). One of the most radical and difficult albums of its era, its conception and execution was a remarkable blend of Lydon's antagonism and Levene's climatic guitar. The single, 'Death Disco', also reached the UK charts. With Dudanski leaving, Fall drummer Karl Burns was enlisted until Martin Atkins (b. 3 August 1959, Coventry, England) from Mynd, joined in time to tour the USA in the spring of 1980. A live album, *Paris Au Printemps*, was recorded after which both Wobble and Atkins left. Wobble went on to record solo material and work for London Transport as a train guard while Atkins joined Brian Brain. In May 1981 Lydon and Levene, augmented by hired musicians, played from behind an onstage screen at the New York Ritz. The crowd failed to

Pulp

grasp the concept and 'bottled' the band. After *Flowers Of Romance* Pete Jones (b. 22 September 1957) became bass player, and Atkins returned on drums. Around this time subsidiary members Dave Crowe and Jeanette Lee, who had been with the band since the beginning in business roles, both departed and the group started a new era as Lydon decided to settle in Los Angeles. In 1983 Jones left as the hypnotic 'This Is Not A Love Song' became PiL's Top 5 hit, and Levene also departed as it was climbing the chart. In a relatively quiet period when Lydon collaborated with Afrika Bambaataa on the Time Zone single, 'World Destruction', PiL released only the 1984 album *This Is What You Want, This Is What You Get*, and another set of live recordings from foreign fields. Lydon also made his first feature film appearance in *Order Of Death*. They returned to the forefront with 1986's *Album*, from which came 'Single' aka 'Rise', featuring the drumming talents of Ginger Baker. The album included numerous guest/session musicians such as Steve Vai, Ryûichi Sakamoto and Tony Williams. The next year, Lydon assembled a permanent band once again, this time drawing on guitarists John McGeogh (ex-Magazine, Siouxsie And The Banshees, Armoury Show) and Lu Edmunds (ex-Damned, Mekons, 3 Mustaphas 3), bass player Allan Dias from America (formerly in nightclub backing bands and working with stars such as Tyrone Ashley and the *avant garde* Sun Ra), and drummer Bruce Smith (ex-Pop Group and various sessions). Lu Edmunds was forced to leave because he was suffering from tinnitus (Ted Chau was a temporary replacement) and Smith left as the band fell into inactivity again after 1988. The three remaining members came back to life in 1990 when Virgin Records put out a *Greatest Hits ... So Far* compilation, confidently including the new single 'Don't Ask Me' - Lydon's nod to the environmental problems of the world. After several years and countless line-ups, Lydon has remained the *enfant terrible* of the music industry, a constant irritant and occasional source of brilliance: 'I've learnt to manipulate the music business. I have to deal with all kinds of stupid, sycophantic people. I've just learnt to understand my power. Everyone should learn that, otherwise they lose control'. PiL then recruited new drummer Mike Joyce (ex-Smiths, Buzzcocks), but Lydon concentrated more on his autobiography and other musical projects (such as the Leftfield collaboration, 'Open Up') than PiL in the 90s.

Albums: *Public Image* (Virgin 1978), *Metal Box* (Virgin 1979), *Paris Au Printemps* (Virgin 1980), *Flowers Of Romance* (Virgin 1981), *Live In Tokyo* (Virgin 1983), *This Is What You Want, This Is What You Get* (Virgin 1984), *Album* (Virgin 1986), *Happy?* (Virgin 1987), *9* (Virgin 1989), *That What Is Not* (Virgin 1992). Compilation: *Greatest Hits ... So Far* (Virgin 1990).

Pulp

Camp pop troupe headed up by the inimitable Jarvis Cocker. Based in Sheffield, England, Cocker actually put the first version of Pulp together whilst still at school, recording a sole John Peel radio session in November 1981. That line-up boasted Cocker (vocals, guitar), Peter Dalton (keyboards), Jamie Pinchbeck (bass) and Wayne Furniss (drums). Bullied as a child for his angular, national health-bespectacled looks,

Cocker went on to work in a nursery for deaf children. Certainly his Pulp project could hardly be described as an overnight success. After the mini-album *It*, the first real evidence of Cocker's abilities as a lyricist arrived with 'Little Girl (With Blue Eyes)' ('There's a hole in your heart and one between your legs, you'll never have to wonder which one he's going to fill despite what he says'). Though singles like this and the subsequent 'Dogs Are Everywhere' and 'They Suffocate At Night' should have broken the band, it took a third chapter in their history, and a new line-up, to provide the impetus. Cocker's desire for success was always explicit: 'Until I've been on *Top Of The Pops* I will always consider myself a failure' (in fact by 1994 he was to be seen presenting an edition). By 1992 the group had coalesced to its current line-up, featuring Russell Senior (guitar, violin), Candida Doyle (keyboards), Stephen Mackay (bass) and Nicholas Banks (drums). The group's early 1994 single, 'Do You Remember The First Time?', was accompanied by a short film in which famous celebrities were quizzed on this very subject (the loss of their virginity). The *Sunday Times* described such songs as being like 'Mike Leigh set to music'. Which was ironic, given that the mother of Pulp member Doyle, who starred in the movie, had previously appeared in two Leigh films. She had also, more famously, played posh employer to Hilda Ogden's cleaner lady in *Coronation Street*. As well as this *His 'N' Hers*, nominated for the 1994 Mercury Prize, also contained minor hits in 'Lipgloss' and 'Babies'. It was their debut album for major label Island, with production supervised by Ed Buller, and offered a supreme evocation of the 'behind the net curtains' sexual morés of working class Britons.

Albums: *It* (Red Rhino 1983, mini-album), *Freaks* (Fire 1987), *Separations* (Fire 1992), *His 'N' Hers* (Island 1994). Compilations: *Intro - The Gift Recordings* (Island 1993), *Masters Of The Universe - Pulp On Fire 1985-86* (Fire 1994).

Purple Hearts

This UK group was one of a wave of late 70s UK mod revivalists, hailing from Romford, Essex. Previously they had been Jack Plug And The Sockets, who were closer to punk than mod. By May 1978 however, they had changed their name to the Purple Hearts (after a drug much favoured by mods in the 60s). The line-up featured Robert Manton (vocals), Simon Stebbing (guitar), Jeff Shadbolt (bass) and Gary Sparks (drums). They signed to Fiction, the new label formed by Chris Parry. The group came to prominence on the *March Of The Mods* tour with Secret Affair and Back To Zero. Their debut single came in September 1979 with 'Millions Like Us', with 'Frustration' and 'Jimmy' following shortly afterwards. The first and last of the trio brushed the lower regions of the charts. By 1980 they had moved on to the Safari label and released 'My Life's A Jigsaw' and 'Plane Crash', after which they split up. They reformed in 1982 for a one-off single, 'Scooby Doo', on Roadrunner Records. They returned once more in 1986 to record their second album for Razor.

Albums: *Beat That* (1980), *Pop-Ish Frenzy* (1986).

Q

Quick

This UK studio-based duo featured Col Campsie (vocals/guitar), George McFarlane (synthesizers/bass/guitar). They not only worked on their own material but also wrote for Chaka Khan and produced Haywoode, Blue Zoo and Second Image. The Quick debuted in 1980 and instantly became club favourites with a string of singles aimed at the dancefloor. Only one single 'Rhythm Of The Jungle' managed to cross over to the singles chart, just missing the UK Top 40 position by one place. On the strength of the hit an album containing all the singles to date plus some of the b-sides was released to little success. By 1983 they had found club success in the USA, but the limited following in the UK had dwindled so much that all future releases sank without trace. In 1988 the duo re-emerged as Giant Steps along with Gardner Cole (keyboards), Edic Lehmann (backgrounds), Bruce Gaitsch (guitar) and David Boruff (saxophone). The debut album and a single 'Another Lover' were both Top 20 hits in the USA.

Albums: *Fascinating Rhythm* (1982), *International Thing* (1984), *Wah Wah* (1986), as Giant Steps *The Book Of Pride* (1988).

R

R.E.M.

R.E.M. played their first concert in Athens, Georgia, USA on 19 April 1980. Their line-up, then as now, consisted of four drop-outs from the University of Georgia; Michael Stipe (vocals), Peter Buck (guitar), Mike Mills (bass) and Bill Berry (drums). Without the charisma of Stipe and his eccentric onstage behaviour, hurling himself about with abandon in between mumbling into the microphone, they could easily have been overlooked as just another bar band, relying on the harmonious guitar sound of the Byrds for their inspiration. Acquiring a healthy following among the college fraternity in their hometown, it wasn't long before they entered the studio to record their debut single 'Radio Free Europe', to be released independently on Hibtone Records. This was greeted with considerable praise by critics who conceded that the band amounted to more than the sum of their influences. Their country/folk sound was contradicted by a driving bassline and an urgency that put the listener more in mind of the Who in their early mod phase. Add to this the distinctive voice of Stipe and his, on the whole, inaudible, perhaps even non-existent, lyrics, and R.E.M. sounded quite unlike any other band in the USA, in the post-punk era of the early 80s. Gaining further favourable notices for the *Chronic Town* mini-LP, their debut full-length album was now eagerly anticipated; when it arrived in 1983 it surpassed all expectations, and was eventually made Album Of The Year by *Rolling Stone* magazine. As in the USA, the band earned a devoted cult following in Europe, largely comprised of college students, as a result of *Murmur*.

Reckoning appeared the following year and was permeated by a reckless spontaneity that had been missing from their earlier work. Recorded in only 12 days, the tracks varied in mood from frustration, as on 'So. Central Rain', to the tongue-in-cheek singalong '(Don't Go Back To) Rockville'. The songs were accessible enough but, as would be the case for most of the 80s, the singles culled from R.E.M.'s albums were generally deemed uncommercial by mainstream radio programmers. However, their cult reputation benefited from a series of flop singles on both sides of the Atlantic. Although received enthusiastically by critics, *Fables Of The Reconstruction* was a stark, morose album that mirrored a period of despondency within the band. Peter Buck summed it up in the 90s - 'If we were to record those songs again, they would be very different'. *Life's Rich Pageant*, in 1986, showed the first signs of a politicization within the band that would come to a head, and coincide with their commercial breakthrough, in the late 80s. Stipe's lyrics began to dwell increasingly on the prevailing amorality in the USA and question its inherited ethics, whilst still retaining their much vaunted obliqueness. Tracks like 'These Days' and 'Cuyahoga' were rallying cries to the young and disaffected; although the lyrics were reflective and almost bitter, the music was the most joyous and uplifting the band had recorded to date. This ironic approach to songwriting was typified by 'It's The End Of The World As We Know It (And I Feel Fine)', from the equally impressive *Document*. Released also as a single, it intentionally trivialized its subject matter with a witty and up-tempo infectiousness, more characteristic of the Housemartins.

Green arrived in 1988 and sold slowly but steadily in the USA, the attendant single 'Stand' reaching number 6 there, while 'Orange Crush' entered the UK Top 30. Apart from demonstrating their environmental awareness, particularly in 'You Are The Everything', the album laid more emphasis than previously on Stipe's vocals and lyrics. This, to the singer's dismay, led to his elevation as 'spokesman for a generation'. Already hero-worshiped by adoring long-term fans, Stipe insists 'Rock 'n' roll is a joke, people who take it seriously are the butt of the joke'. The world tour that coincided with the album's release saw R.E.M. making a smooth transition from medium-size venues to the stadium circuit, due as much to Stipe's individual choreography as to the elaborate, projected backdrops. After a break of two years the band re-emerged in 1991 with *Out Of Time*. Their previous use of horns and mandolins to embroider songs did not prepare their audience for the deployment of an entire string section, nor were the contributions from B-52s singer

Kate Pierson and Boogie Down Productions' KRS-1 expected. Ostensibly all love songs, the album was unanimously hailed as a masterpiece and entered the UK Top 5 on its release, topping both US and UK album charts shortly afterwards. The accompanying singles from that album 'Losing My Religion', 'Shiny Happy People', and 'Near Wild Heaven' gave them further hits. After picking up countless awards during the early 90s the band has maintained the high standard set by *Out Of Time*. *Automatic For The People* was released in October 1992, to universal favour. It reached the top of the charts in the UK and USA. Michael Stipe was seen both as pin-up and creative genius. The album produced a number of memorable singles including the moody 'Drive' and the joyous 'Man In The Moon', with its classic Elvis Presley vocal inflections from Stipe and an accompanying award-winning monochrome video. *Monster* showed the band in grungelike mode, not letting any accusations of selling out bother them, and certainly letting fans and critics alike know that they had not gone soft. 'What's The Frequency Kenneth?' started a run of further hit singles taken from the album and further awards were heaped upon them. Following the collapse of Bill Berry in Switzerland while on a major tour in 1995 the band were forced to rest. Berry was operated on for a ruptured aneurysm and he made a full recovery. The critical praise heaped upon the band has been monumental, through all the attention the band appear united, reasonably unaffected and painfully modest. They are one of the most important and popular groups to appear over the past three decades, and still retain massive credibility together with fresh ideas.
Albums: *Chronic Town* (IRS 1982, mini-LP), *Murmur* (IRS 1983), *Reckoning* (IRS 1984), *Fables Of The Reconstruction* (IRS 1985), *Life's Rich Pageant* (IRS 1986), *Document* (IRS 1987), *Dead Letter Office* (IRS 1987, out-takes and b-sides), *Green* (Warner 1988), *Out Of Time* (Warner 1991), *Automatic For The People* (Warner 1992), *Monster* (Warner 1994). Compilation: *Eponymous* (IRS 1988).
Videos: *Succumbs* (1987), *Pop Screen* (1990), *This Film Is On* (1991), *Tourfilm* (1991).
Further reading: *It Crawled From The South; An R.E.M. Companion*, Marcus Gray. *Remarks: Story Of R.E.M.*, Tony Fletcher. *R.E.M.: File Under Water, The Definitive Guide To 12 Years Of Recordings And Con*, Jon Storey. *R.E.M.: Behind The Mask*, Jim Greer. *R.E.M. Documental*, Dave Bowler and Bryan Dray.

Radical Dance Faction

Formed from the ashes of UK anarcho reggae outfit Military Surplus, RDF, as they are commonly abbreviated, set out in 1987. Their line-ups have been erratic but are based around the one constant, lyricist and vocalist Chris Bowsher. Using beat poetry, with its imagery of modern decay and capitalism gone wrong, their chosen musical outlet is reggae and ska. Bowsher was a veteran of the early punk explosion, and was particularly enamoured of bands like the Clash and Ruts who attempted to bridge the gap between rock and black music. Alongside the Levellers, they became prime movers in the media-christened 'crusty' movement (ie their following comprises largely the dispossessed and homeless, bonded by a political consciousness which has its roots in hippiedom,

beatnik romanticism and early 80s anarcho-punk).
Albums: *Borderland Cases* (1989), *Wasteland* (1991).

Radio Birdman

This highly-rated Australian group was formed in Sydney, New South Wales in 1974. Its Detroit/MC5 guitar-based sound was propelled by two American medical students Deniz Tek (b. Detroit, Michigan, USA; guitar) and Phillip 'Pip' Hoyle (guitar/keyboards), plus Rob Younger (vocals), Gilbert Warwick (guitar), Ron Keely (drums), Carl Rourke (bass) and, joining later, Chris Masuak (guitar). Because of study commitments the band was very much a part-time affair. This heightened the mystique which surrounded the band as they forged their own niche on the outer fringe of the Sydney music circuit from the mid-70s. A trip to the UK in 1978 saw a short tour and an album, but the band dissolved shortly afterwards. Radio Birdman have inspired many bands since, to the extent that Sydney is regarded as a nurturing ground for guitar-based bands. Lead singer Rob Younger has become one of the most important producers of underground and alternative bands in the past few years. One of the direct descendants of Radio Birdman was the hard rock band, the Hitmen of which comprised of Warwick, Masuak and former Saints' drummer Ivor Hay. Rob Younger, has lead his own group the New Christs since 1983. Another interesting chapter of the Birdman legend was the one-off band New Race in 1981, which comprised: Tek, Younger, and Gilbert with Ron Asheton (ex-Stooges) and Dennis Thompson of MC5 for a short tour and a live album.
Albums: *Radios Appear* (1978), *Living Eyes* (1981).

Radio Stars

This UK group was formed in 1977 by Andy Ellison (vocals), Ian McLeod (guitar) and Martin Gordon (bass), all of whom were previously members of Jet. Drummer Steve Parry completed the line-up of a group engendering considerable interest through its association with John's Children (Ellison) and Sparks (Gordon). A series of tongue-in-cheek singles, including 'Dirty Pictures' and 'Nervous Wreck', captured the quartet's brand of quirky pop/punk, but although the latter reached the fringes of the Top 40, the group was unable to achieve consistent success. Trevor White, also ex-Sparks, was later added to the line-up but Gordon's departure in December 1978 undermined any lingering potential and Radio Stars disbanded the following year. Ellison and White subsequently undertook several low-key projects and the singer later revived the group's name, but to little success.
Albums: *Songs For Swinging Lovers* (1977), *Radio Stars' Holiday Album* (1978).

Radiohead

The five members of Radiohead, widely tipped to steal U2's crown as the 90s progressed, first met at a private boys school in Abingdon, a small, picturesque town on the outskirts of Oxford. Thom Yorke (b. 7 October 1968, Wellingborough, Northamptonshire, England; vocals/guitar) had been given his first instrument, a Spanish guitar, at age eight by his mother. He formed his first band two years later, then joined

Radiohead

an existing school punk band, TNT. Singing for the first time, he realised he would require more sympathetic band members and formed what would become Radiohead with school friends Ed O'Brien (b. Edward John O'Brien, 15 April 1968, Oxford, Oxfordshire, England; guitar) 'who looked cool' and Colin Greenwood (b. Colin Charles Greenwood, 26 June 1969, Oxford, Oxfordshire, England; bass) 'because he was in my year and we always ended up at the same parties'. They shared an interest in Joy Division and the Smiths and Greenwood earned Yorke's sympathy for joining TNT after him. Mild-mannered drummer Phil Selway (b. Philip James Selway, 23 May 1967, Hemmingford Grey, England; drums) bound the group, titled On A Friday, together. The addition of Colin's brother and jazz fanatic, Jonny Greenwood (b. 5 November 1971, Oxford, Oxfordshire, England; guitar/keyboards) completed the line-up, originally on harmonica, after he pestered his elder brother and friends continually to let him join. A week after his first rehearsal with the band, On A Friday played their debut gig at the now defunct Jericho Tavern in Oxford. With a musical canon resembling a youthful Talking Heads, they added two saxophone-playing sisters to fill out the band. However, the band were then put on hold while the members pursued their academic careers, in an effort to appease already frantic parents (Jonny finished his schooling). Colin became entertainment's officer at Peterhouse College, Cambridge University, and helped get his friends together for occasional gigs there. At Exeter University Yorke played guitar in a techno band, Flickernoise, while Selway drummed for various theatrical productions (*Blood Brothers*, *Return To The Forbidden Planet*) while studying at Liverpool Polytechnic. The band finally regrouped in Oxford in the summer of 1991, deciding to dispense with the brass section and concentrate squarely on the band, now entitled Radiohead (after a Talking Heads song). Playing their first gig at the Hollybush Inn in July 1991, it was not long before they made a lasting impression. Their first commercial broadcast followed when 'Prove Yourself' was voted Gary Davies' 'Happening Track Of The Week' on BBC Radio 1. 'Creep' then became *the* alternative rock song in the UK during 1993, its self-loathing lyric stretched over driven guitars that at one point simply explode. Ignored when it was first released in September 1992, its re-release sparked enormous interest as the group toured with Kingmaker and James. Taking the band in to the UK Top 10, it also announced a Top 30 debut album, *Pablo Honey*. Unlike other celebrated UK indie hopefuls such as Suede, Radiohead also translated well to international tastes, from the US to Egypt. Two years of promotional activity followed, before the release of *The Bends*. With the pressure on following the plaudits, the recording process was not easy. With hardly a note recorded over two months, producer John Leckie ordered all bar Yorke out of the studio and told the singer to 'just fucking play it'. The songs came, and he and the rest of the band relocated to Abbey Road Studios to finish off the album in just three weeks. *The Bends* did not disappoint, with a vibrant mood range encouraging Yorke's prosaic yet affecting lyrics.

Albums: *Pablo Honey* (Parlophone 1993), *The Bends* (Parlophone 1995).

Video: *27/5/94 The Astoria London Live* (1995).

Railway Children

Formed in 1985 by Gary Newby (b. 5 June 1966, Australia), Brian Bateman (b. 3 August 1966, Wigan, Lancashire, England), Stephen Hull (b. 7 July 1966, Wigan, Lancashire, England) and Guy Keegan (b. 16 June 1966, Wigan, Lancashire, England), the Railway Children started playing small gigs around the north west of England. After a batch of demo tapes the four 19-year-olds found themselves being feted by numerous record companies, eventually settling on a contract-free deal with Factory Records. A brace of graceful singles which fused 60s harmonies with the early 80s pop sensibility of Liverpool paved the way for the fine *Reunion Wilderness* in 1987, and the Railway Children appeared set to follow guitar-based contemporaries the Smiths onto greater things. The band signed to Virgin Records that same year, and suddenly sounded a lot neater for it. The expensive production polish eradicated the quartet's rougher edges, and with pivotal creative force Gary Newby content to have his instinct smoothed by studio techniques, *Recurrence* appeared in 1988 to an uncertain audience confused by the band's independent beginnings and the new, mellower sound. Although singles regularly entered the Top 75 of the UK charts and the group flirted with fashionable dance beats with particularly encouraging results in USA, it was not until the start of 1991 that a re-released version of 'Every Beat Of The Heart' took the band into the upper echelons of the UK chart and thus validated their efforts of five years. However, when follow-ups 'Something So Good' and 'Music Stop' failed to emboss their new chart status, the band repaired to Lancashire. Rumours of a final split were hardly dispelled by a complete absence of new material until Virgin's compilation of their finer moments confirmed their demise.

Albums: *Reunion Wilderness* (Factory 1987), *Recurrence* (Virgin 1988), *Native Place* (Virgin 1990), *The Radio 1 Evening Show Sessions* (Nighttracks 1993). Compilation: *Listen On - The Best Of* (Virgin 1995).

Rain

This group originated in Liverpool, England in the late 80s and adopted the heritage of harmony pop in the vein of the Byrds. Rain were initially notable by dint of having three good harmony singers to back up their Rickenbacker guitar sound. They formed at the Merseyside Trade Union Community And Unemployed Resource Centre in Liverpool, set up with a £100,000 grant. The band's original locale was the severely depressed Huyton area, but eight months later they were signed to CBS and worked on album sessions with Nick Lowe. After a debut single, 'Lemonstone Desired', they courted controversy with the provocative nudity featured on the cover of *Taste Of Rain*. Their debut album was honed by months of rehearsal with guest appearances by Green On Red and blues musician Joe Louis Walker. The band comprise Ned Clark, Colin Murphy (singers, guitarists, songwriters), Martin Campbell and Tony McGuigan (bass, drums).

Album: *A Taste Of Rain* (1991).
Films: *Birth Of The Beatles* (1979).

Railway Children

Rain Parade

Part of Los Angeles' rock renaissance of the early 80s, the Rain Parade drew from late 60s influences to forge a new brand of psychedelia-tinged rock. After a promising debut single, 'What She's Done To Your Mind', on their own Llama label, the band - David Roback (vocals/guitar/percussion), brother Steve (vocals/bass), Matthew Piucci (vocals/guitar/sitar), Will Glenn (keyboards/violin) and Eddie Kalwa (drums) - issued *Emergency Third Rail Power Trip* to critical acclaim in 1983, followed by the excellent 'You Are My Friend' in 1985. Such was their impetus that the Rain Parade signed with Island Records, despite the loss of key figure David Roback (who then formed Opal with partner and original Rain Parade bassist Kendra Smith, eventually re-emerging in Mazzy Star). His replacement, John Thoman, arrived alongside new drummer Mark Marcum in time for *Beyond The Sunset*, drawn from live performances in Japan. A second studio set, *Crashing Dream*, emerged later in the year, but some of the original Rain Parade's other-worldly, evocative nature had been lost. Piucci would go on to form Gone Fishin'. He would also record an album with Neil Young's Crazy Horse.
Albums: *Emergency Third Rail Power Trip* (Enigma 1983), *Beyond The Sunset* (Restless 1985), *Crashing Dream* (Island 1985).

Raincoats

This female outfit epitomized the experimental approach that characterized much of punk's aftermath. The group were formed at Hornsea Art College, London, in 1976 by Gina Birch and Ana Da Silva. Augmented by Vicky Aspinall and manager Shirley O'Loughlin, they were originally joined by Palmolive before she left to concentrate on the Slits. This line-up was merely a nucleus for a flexible structure that involved numerous other musicians. As Birch recalls: 'We didn't exactly ignore the audience, but for us, playing was an emotional thing. We would struggle, we would cry, we didn't really know what we were doing half the time'. The Raincoats' debut, 'Fairytale In The Supermarket', appeared on Rough Trade Records (a label that shared their ground-breaking stance) in 1979. It would sell a healthy 25,000 copies. A self-titled album that same year boasted a similarly distinctive sound and both were revered by critics and a hardcore of admirers alike. *Odyshape* followed in 1981, but was less direct than their debut. Two further singles, a cover of Sly Stone's 'Running Away' (1982) and 'Animal Rhapsody' (1983) both hinted at unfulfilled potential. The Raincoats eventually delivered their swansong in 1984 with *Moving*. However, as fitting an epitaph as any can be found on *The Kitchen Tapes*, on the ROIR label, originally released in 1983. The group may have remained of historical interest only had not one of their biggest US fans, Kurt Cobain of Nirvana, tracked down Ana Da Silva to an antique shop in Notting Hill, London. In exchange for a customized original of the band's debut album, Cobain offered the Raincoats the chance to reform and support Nirvana on upcoming UK dates (he would also write sleevenotes for the CD reissues of their albums). Thus the 1994 model Raincoats, who featured Da Silva with Birch, joined by violinist Anne Wood and drummer Steve Shelley (a stand-in on loan from Sonic Youth). Palmolive was said to have departed for a life of religious evangelicism in Texas, while Aspinall was busy running a dance label.
Albums: *The Raincoats* (Rough Trade 1979), *Odyshape* (Rough Trade 1981), *The Kitchen Tapes* (ROIR 1983), *Moving* (Rough Trade 1984).

Ramones

The Ramones, comprising Johnny Ramone (b. John Cummings, 8 October 1951, Long Island, New York, USA; guitar), Dee Dee Ramone (b. Douglas Colvin, 18 September 1952, Vancouver, British Columbia, Canada; bass) and Joey Ramone (b. Jeffrey Hyman, 19 May 1952; drums) made their debut at New York's Performance Studio on 30 March 1974. Two months later manager Tommy Ramone (b. Tommy Erdelyi, 29 January 1952, Budapest, Hungary) replaced Joey on drums, who then switched to vocals. The quartet later secured a residency at the renowned CBGB's club where they became one of the city's leading proponents of punk rock. The fever-paced *Ramones* was a startling first album. Its high-octane assault drew from 50s kitsch and 60s garage-bands, while leather jackets, ripped jeans and an affected dumbness enhanced their music's cartoon-like quality. The group's debut appearance in London in July 1976 influenced a generation of British punk musicians, while *The Ramones Leave Home*, which included 'Suzie Is A Headbanger' and 'Gimme Gimme Shock Treatment', confirmed the sonic attack of its predecessor. *Rocket To Russia* was marginally less frenetic as the group's novelty appeal waned, although 'Sheena Is A Punk Rocker' gave the group their first UK Top 30 hit in 1977. In May 1978 Tommy Ramone left to pursue a career in production and former Richard Hell drummer Marc Bell, remodelled as Marky Ramone, replaced him for *Road To Ruin*, as the band sought to expand their appealing, but limited, style. They took a starring role in the trivial *Rock 'N' Roll High School* film, a participation which led to their collaboration with producer Phil Spector. The resultant release, *End Of The Century*, was a curious hybrid, and while Johnny baulked at Spector's laborious recording technique, Joey, whose penchant for girl-group material gave the Ramones their sense of melody, was less noticeably critical. The album contained a sympathetic version of the Ronettes' 'Baby I Love You', which became the group's biggest UK hit single when it reached the Top 10. The Ramones entered the 80s looking increasingly anachronistic, unable or unwilling to change. *Pleasant Dreams*, produced by Graham Gouldman, revealed a group now outshone by the emergent hardcore acts they had inspired. However, *Subterranean Jungle* showed a renewed purpose which was maintained sporadically on *Animal Boy* and *Halfway To Sanity*, the former containing 'Bonzo Goes To Bitburg', a hilarious riposte to Ronald Reagan's ill-advised visit to a cemetery containing graves of Nazi SS personnel. Although increasingly confined to pop's fringes, a revitalized line-up - Joey, Johnny, Marky and newcomer C.J. - undertook a successful 1990 US tour alongside fellow CBGB's graduate Deborah Harry and Talking Heads' offshoot Tom Tom Club. 1992 brought *Mondo Bizarro*, from which 'Censorshit', an attack on Tipper Gore, head of the PMRC, was the most notable moment. By 1995 and

Adios Amigos, rumours inferred that the two-minute buzzsaw guitar trail may have finally run cold, with the impression of a epitaph exacerbated by the album's title. As Johnny conceded: 'I know that you have to deal with a life without applause, and I'm looking forward to trying it. A lot of musicians are addicted to it and won't get out.'
Albums: *Ramones* (Sire 1976), *The Ramones Leave Home* (Sire 1977), *Rocket To Russia* (Sire 1977), *Road To Ruin* (Sire 1978), *It's Alive* (Sire 1979, UK only, double album), *End Of The Century* (Sire 1980), *Pleasant Dreams* (Sire 1981), *Subterranean Jungle* (Sire 1983), *Too Tough To Die* (Sire 1984), *Animal Boy* (Sire 1986), *Halfway To Sanity* (Sire 1987), *Brain Drain* (Sire 1989), *Loco Live* (Chrysalis 1991), *Mondo Bizarro* (Chrysalis 1992), *Acid Eaters* (Chrysalis 1993), *Adios Amigos* (Chrysalis 1995). Compilations: *Ramones Mania* (Sire 1988), *All The Stuff And More (Volume One)* (Sire 1990), *End Of The Decade* (Beggars Banquet 1990).

Rank And File
Formed in Los Angeles in 1981, Rank And File comprised of former members of the Dils, Chip Kinman (guitar/vocals) and Tony Kinman (bass/vocals), and ex-Nuns' guitarist/vocalist Alejandro Escovedo. Drummer Slim Evans completed the line-up featured on *Sundown*, an exemplary blend of new wave and country. The album included 'Amanda Ruth', later recorded by the Everly Brothers. The Kinman brothers then took control of the group and, having moved to Austin, Texas, completed *Long Gone Dead* with session musicians, including Richard Greene (fiddle) and Stan Lynch, drummer with Tom Petty And The Heartbreakers. The new set emphasized the duo's love of pop melody, but the contents were still infused with C&W. A long hiatus ensued, but their third album proved a major disappointment, lacking the verve and charm of its predecessors. Rank And File was then disbanded with the Kinmans later founding Blackbird. Escovedo reappeared leading the acclaimed True Believers before embarking on a solo career.
Albums: *Sundown* (1982), *Long Gone Dead* (1984), *Rank And File* (1987).

Rapeman
This controversially-named US act was created when Steve Albini (ex-Big Black; guitar/vocals) joined forces with two former members of Scratch Acid, David Wm. Sims (bass) and Rey Washam (drums). The trio was short-lived and their output comprised of a single, 'Inkis' Butt Crack', released on the cult Sub Pop label, *Budd*, a 4-track set, and *Two Nuns And A Pack Mule*. The album maintained the loud, uncompromising sound the two previous groups had offered - tight, crashing drums, pounding bass and sheets of metallic guitarwork - and included a startling interpretation of Z.Z. Top's 'Just Got Paid'. However, the group was unable to shake off criticism of its repellent name which Albini took from a character in contemporary Japanese comics. Several distributors objected to handling the album and many venues were forced under pressure, particularly at colleges and universities, to cancel appearances, which in part explained the trio's demise. Sims subsequently resurfaced in the Jesus Lizard, which Albini produced.
Album: *Two Nuns And A Pack Mule* (1988).

Razorcuts
Revolving around the songwriting talents of vocalist/guitarist Gregory Webster and bassist Tim Vass, the Razorcuts emerged at the tail end of the independent scene's melodic mid-80s phase. It was a time when bands wore their influences on their sleeves, from the Byrds to the Buzzcocks, and the Razorcuts were no exception. 'Big Pink Cake', issued on the Subway Organisation label in 1986, had all the familiar trademarks of the period; a simple melody, a childlike theme sung in a childlike, out-of-tune voice, a hand-drawn sleeve and jangly guitars. The songs possessed a certain charm, particularly evident on November's *Sorry To Embarrass You* EP. The presence of New Zealand drummer and music journalist David Smith led the band to antipodean label Flying Nun Records for their third single, 'I Heard You The First Time', released in June 1987. When the label ceased operations in the UK, the Razorcuts relocated, ending up at Creation Records, a label which sympathized with the band's 60s influences. And it was the Byrds' early sound which dominated *The Storyteller*. Issued in February 1988, it benefited from its musical intricacies, but did little to avoid accusations of plagiarism. A year later, *The World Keeps Turning* found a band struggling to develop their folk rock sound, despite the added clout of a second guitarist, Pete Momtchiloff, to beef up Webster's 12-string, a new drummer, Struan Robertson, backing vocals from Richard Mason and some attractive Hammond organ from producer John Rivers. When the Razorcuts split shortly afterwards, Vass formed Red Chair Fadeaway and combined folk elements with a laid-back psychedelic feel.
Albums: *The Storyteller* (Creation 1988), *The World Keeps Turning* (Creation 1989).

Real Kids
This American quartet, originally from Boston, gained recognition amid the punk-rock explosion in New York during the late 70s. Formed by vocalist/guitarist and part-time Modern Lover John Felice in 1975, they pre-dated the punk movement, but jumped on the bandwagon as soon as it started to roll. With bassist Allen 'Alpo' Paulino, Billy Borgioli (guitar) and Howard Ferguson (drums) completing the line-up, they were nevertheless a talented outfit. Delivering a varied and classy selection of predominantly high-energy rockers, they infused reggae, rock 'n' roll and pop influences into their songs, making them instantly memorable. Their self-titled debut, released in 1978, is one of the great unheralded classics of this genre. However, a big-seller it was not, and Felice moved over to a career as a Ramones roadie. He also worked as part of the Taxi Boys back in Boston. Borgioli and Ferguson departed to be replaced by Billy Cole and Robby 'Morocco' Morin before the recording of a second album. *Outta Place* was a disappointment, for Felice's new compositions lacked the infectious sparkle that made their debut so special. A shambolic live album, recorded in Paris in 1983, was their final offering before disbanding. Paulino and Borgioli would form the Primitive Souls (one EP), while their former

leader would resurface with John Felice And The Lowdowns. Albums: *The Real Kids* (Red Star 1978), *Outta Place* (Star-Rhythm 1982), *All Kindsa Jerks Live* (New Rose 1983), *Hit You Hard* (New Rose 1983). Compilation: *Girls! Girls! Girls!* (Lolita 1983; comprises Real Kids and Taxi Boys recordings).

Real People

Living down a previous incarnation as Jo Jo And The Real People, which featured a working dalliance with the infamous disco production team of Stock, Aitken And Waterman, the freshly-named Real People were born in 1989 by brothers Tony (b. 7 April 1966, Liverpool, England; bass/vocals) and Chris Griffiths (b. 30 March 1968, Liverpool, England; guitar/vocals). Augmented by Sean Simpson (b. 9 October 1969, Liverpool, England; guitar) and Tony Elson (b. 2 January 1966, Liverpool, England; drums), the foursome started playing local pub gigs in the Bootle area of Merseyside and soon found themselves embroiled in a scene with fellow Scousers, Rain, Top and the La's as all four bands carried the mantle of classic Liverpool pop as instigated three decades earlier by the Beatles. Unfortunately, the Real People's natural instinct for muscular tunes and powerful melodies was undermined by the demands of the music industry. So although the quartet signed to CBS Records (soon to be Sony) at the end of 1989, and had enormous fun spending their advance on a trip to India, it was to be a whole year before any product reached the public. In an environment which thrived on a quick turnover, the Real People suffered a loss of impetus, reaching number 60 in the UK charts with 'Windowpane' when a more hasty work rate could have ensured richer dividends. Album: *The Real People* (1991).

Records

Will Birch (b. c.1950, Essex, England) started out on his drumming career in the 60s with local Southend band the Geezenstacks. He then moved on to the Tradewinds who performed two songs and appeared in a BBC television documentary about young people screened in June 1965. Next up came a stint in the Flowerpots with Wilko Johnson, before he played with Surly Bird, Glory, Cow Pie, the Hot Jets, and even a few gigs with Dr. Feelgood. He later joined the Kursaal Fliers when they formed in October 1973. When the Kursaals split in November 1977 Birch formed a partnership with John Wicks who had been the Kursaals' lead singer for the last few months of their existence (and also played rhythm guitar). In February 1978 they recruited bassist Phil Brown (ex-the Janets) and guitarist Huw Gower, whom Birch spotted playing a one-off gig with Peter Perret's (Only Ones) old band, the Ratbites From Hell. This completed the Records, who made their live debut at Bristol Granary Club in March 1978. The debut single, 'Starry Eyes', was released in November, becoming a minor pop classic in the process. The band then used their connections to join the *Be Stiff* tour ostensibly to back Rachel Sweet, but they also opened the show (the only non Stiff act on board). They signed to Virgin and released further quality pop singles all co-written by Birch, mostly with Wicks as his partner. The best were gathered together on the debut *Shades In Bed* which included an old song dating from Kursaal days,

'Girls That Don't Exist', plus 'Starry Eyes', and 'Teenerama'. Initial copies of the album also included a free 12-inch single featuring Records' cover versions of various well known songs. Ian Gibbons was drafted in to play keyboards on the album. Birch also wrote 'Hearts In Her Eyes' for the Searchers' 1979 comeback album. Gower left just before the second album to be replaced by Judy Cole. He joined David Johannson's band before going solo. By the time of their final album in 1982 the line-up was Birch, Wicks and Brown plus Dave Whelan (guitar) and Chris Gent (vocals). Albums: *Shades In Bed* (1979), *Crashes* (1980), *Music On Both Sides* (1982). Compilation: *Smashes, Crashes & Near Misses* (1988).

Red Guitars

This Hull based guitar pop band featured Jerry Kidd (vocals), Louise Barlow (bass), Hallam Lewis (lead guitar), John Rowley (rhythm guitar), and Matt Higgins (drums). Formed in 1982 by Lewis and Kidd, they released two superb singles, 'Good Technology' and 'Fact', before scoring a number 1 on the independent charts with 'Marimba Jive'. The latter was included on *Slow To Fade* which emerged on Kidd's own Self Drive Records in November 1984. A highly polished and original pop album, with Kidd's analytical lyrics to the fore: 'I said that I love you/God knows I tried/You say you still love me/But you're always saying goodbye'. Fittingly, Kidd himself was to leave barely two months after the album's release. He issued a press statement to the effect that 'Technically we improved a lot during the last year but musically, from my point of view, we were standing still. New ideas and songs I had for the group no longer seemed to fit in. I still favour independence within the record industry and shall continue to look for success, both artistic and commercial, with releases on my own Self Drive Record label.' He was quickly replaced by Robert Holmes, who played his first gig with the band at the University of London Union on 24 May 1985. Lou Howard replaced Barlow on bass as *Tales Of The Expected* saw the band move to One Way Records, through Virgin. Although the lyrical focus of the band had changed, they were still capable of producing highly individual and moving music, notably on singles 'National Avenue' and the yearning 'Be With Me'. Interestingly, both album sleeves featured quotes from poet Sean O'Brien. Hallam and Howard left to form the Planet Wilson in 1987, with drummer Jonah Oxburrow (ex-That Noble Porpoise), and released the album *Not Drowning But Waving*. Hallam now runs his own studio in Hull, while Holmes released his solo album, *Age Of Swing*, for Virgin in 1989. Albums: *Slow To Fade* (Self Drive 1984), *Tales Of The Expected* (Virgin 1985).

Red Letter Day

This Portsmouth, England-based pop punk band formed in 1983, with a line-up consisting of Ade (vocals/guitar), Ian Campbell (lead guitar), Pete White (bass) and Brian Lee (drums). However, nine months and two demos later, Ade was joined by Daryn Price (drums), Keith Metcalfe (bass) and Davie Egan (guitar) in the band's second incarnation. After the single 'Wherever You May Run' they found favour with BBC disc jockey John Peel who secured a session for them on his show. The 12-inch EP *Released Emotions* followed on Quiet Records (they would, confusingly, join a record company with the same name, so called because its boss was a fan of the band). Metcalfe was replaced by a temporary bass player before Steve (ex-Original Mirrors) took over on bass. The highlight of 1987 was one of the support slots at the Polderock Festival in Belgium alongside the Mission, Primitives and Sonic Youth. Now on the Released Emotions label, they recorded a joint album with the Sect, titled *Soft Lights And Loud Guitars*. This picked up a series of good reviews and they also appeared on the Link Records sampler *Underground Rockers*, alongside other bands of a similar persuasion like Mega City Four and the Price. Egan left shortly afterwards, to be replaced by their present guitarist Ray. After a double a-sided single they completed work on their first full long player, *More Songs About Love And War*, in a rockier vein.

Albums: with the Sect *Soft Lights And Loud Guitars* (Released Emotions 1988), *More Songs About Love And War* (Released Emotions 1991).

Red Lorry Yellow Lorry

This post punk gothic band formed in Leeds, England, in 1982, and their first single was 'Take It All Away'. The line-up consisted of Chris Reed (vocals/rhythm guitar), Wolfie (b. Dane Wolfenden; lead guitar, replacing Martin Fagen), Paul Southern (bass; replacing Steve Smith) and Mick Brown (drums). The debut album *Talk About The Weather*, included 'Hollow Eyes', which proved popular in Gothic circles following its regular airing on BBC disc jockey John Peel's BBC Radio 1 show. The album was an intoxicating mix of musical aggression and lyrical minimalism ('It was a strange dream/He stood and stared/Those shining faces/Those darkened eyes/And alone he ran/Alone he ran', comprised the entire scope of the track 'Strange Dream'). After seven singles on Red Rhino Records the band moved on to Situation 2. By this time their material had been revitalized by a broader approach to songwriting: 'People are surprised to find that we have a sense of humour. We do see the irony of things in life', commented Reed. 1988's 'Only Dreaming' attested to this, being their first ballad. In early 1990 the band was forced to cancel four gigs when the current drummer, Chil, was hospitalized for a wrist operation. After eight years' service Wolfie was also absent, leaving Reed as the only surviving original member. His replacement was Gary Weight, alongside bassist Martin Scott.

Albums: *Talk About The Weather* (Red Rhino 1985), *Paint Your Wagon* (Red Rhino 1986), *Nothing's Wrong* (Beggars Banquet 1988), *Blow* (Beggars Banquet 1989), *Drop* (Beggars Banquet 1989), *Blasting Off* (Beggars Banquet 1992). Compilation: *Smashed Hits* (Red Rhino 1988).

Redd Kross

This Los Angeles, California, USA band was formed in 1979. Redd Kross melded elements of 70s glam-rock, 60s psychedelia and 80s heavy metal to become a popular 'alternative' act in the 80s. Originally called the Tourists, the band changed its name to Red Cross. (They were later forced to change the spelling after the International Red Cross

organization threatened to sue.) At the beginning, the band consisted of 15-year-old Jeff McDonald as singer, his 11-year-old brother Steve on bass, Greg Hetson on guitar and Ron Reyes on drums. After gaining local recognition opening for such punk outfits as Black Flag, Red Cross made its first recordings in 1980 for a compilation album on the punk label, Posh Boy Records. Shortly afterwards Hetson left to form the Circle Jerks and Reyes joined Black Flag. Other musicians came and went throughout the band's history, the McDonald brothers being the only mainstay. The group's popularity grew steadily, particularly among those who listened to college radio stations, and by the end of the 80s they had recorded three albums in addition to the debut. Some featured covers of songs by such influences as the Rolling Stones and Kiss, while elsewhere the group's originals seemed to cross 70s punk with the bubblegum hits of the 60s. The group resurfaced in the autumn of 1990 with *Third Eye*, their first album for a major label, Atlantic Records. However, it was 1993's *Phaseshifter* which brought about their commercial breakthrough, with the band signing with Nirvana manager John Silva and continuing to record catchy post-punk homages to 70s kitsch.

Albums: *Born Innocent* (Smoke 7 1982), *Teen Babes From Monsanto* (Gasatanka 1984), *Neurotica* (Big Time 1987), *Third Eye* (Atlantic 1990), *Phaseshifter* (Atlantic 1993).

Redskins

This politically-motivated English trio united the left-wing skinhead movement with a volatile mix of punk and northern soul, aggression and belligerence. Originally formed in York as No Swastikas, they relocated to London where singer/guitarist and *New Musical Express* writer Chris Dean (b. c.1963) assumed the identity of X. Moore. The other original members were Martin Hewes (bass) and Nick King (drums). They were joined in the studio and on stage by a fluid brass section, the most permanent members of which were Lloyd Dwyer and Steve Nicol. After the strident debut, 'Peasant Army', on Leeds based independent CNT Records in 1982, they secured a session for the John Peel BBC Radio 1 programme which would be repeated five times. The follow-up, 'Lean On Me' was voted Single Of The Year by *Sounds* journalist Gary Bushell. Given a high media profile by dint of their exclusively political lyrics (they were all members of the Socialist Workers Party), interest from major record companies soon followed, leading to a deal with London Records. After personal disagreements, King was replaced by Paul Hookham (ex-English Subtitles, Lemons, Woodentops) on the eve of the band's second major tour. By 1984 they had become vigorous supporters of the striking National Union of Miners, playing a host of benefits on their behalf, though 'Keep On Keeping On' and subsequent singles were no match for their earlier promise. The debut album, *Neither Washington Nor Moscow*, was impressive, but critics still cited the band as under-achievers, a fate they condemned themselves to when they broke up in 1986. Hewes returned to life as a motorcycle despatch rider. Album: *Neither Washington Nor Moscow* (London 1986).

Reegs

One of two splinter groups from the ashes of underrated UK

group the Chameleons, the Reegs was formed by guitarists Dave Fielding and Reg Smithies after they split in 1987. They were joined by vocalist Gary Lavery and a drum machine for their 1991 debut under their new title, *The Return Of The Sea Monkeys*. 'We didn't do anything for a while after the Chameleons split, I think we both needed to take some time out. There was never any question of us not working together again.' Fielding had kept busy with production work, the most successful of which was with the Inspiral Carpets. Following the enthusiasm shown by Imaginary Records, they made their first recording with 'See My Friend', for a Kinks' tribute album. The first of their own material came in the shape of two EPs, which formed the basis of the album.
Album: *The Return Of The Sea Monkeys* (Imaginary 1991).

Renees

This UK London-based pop group was loosely formed in 1987, in the aftermath of the break-up of the Gymslips a year earlier. Paula Richards (b. 1 August 1963, Kent, England; guitar/vocals), who had in the meantime been working with the ska/R&B outfits, the Deltones and Potato 5, reunited with Karen Yarnell (b. 2 April 1961; drums) using various friends to perform at gigs, often alongside contemporaries, Coming Up Roses. By 1989 the group had gone full-time with the recruitment of Katrina Slack (b. 14 July 1962; bass), Jacqui Callis (vocals, ex-Delta 5) and the lone male, Paul Seacroft (lead guitar, ex-Potato 5). The single, 'He Called Me A Fat Pig (And Walked Out On Me)', suitably impressed reviewers and the group signed to the French independent label, Squale, releasing their only album, *Have You Got It!*, in 1990. This included an impressive version of 'Mama' Cass Elliot's 'California Earthquake' and the more English-flavoured 'Valerie'. However, with the dissolution of the label the following year, the group broke up, tired of battling against the growing tide of insularity within the capital's live club scene.
Album: *Have You Got It!* (Squale 1990).

Renegade Soundwave

London born and bred esoteric dance trio whose recordings have been variously described as 'Dance-Noise-Terror' and 'Chas 'n' Dave with a beatbox'. The group originally consisted of three multi-faceted instrumentalists, Danny Briotett (ex-Mass), Carl Bonnie and Gary Asquith (ex-Rema Rema, Mass). 'We're a by-product of punk. It forged the way we think, though the sound is nothing to do with it.' Their first single 'Kray Twins' emerged on Rhythm King Records, the sound of a television documentary set to a throbbing bass undertow. After the equally notorious 'Cocaine Sex' they switched to Mute Records because of the greater eclecticism of their catalogue. A series of dancefloor singles like 'Biting My Nails' and 'Probably A Robbery' prefaced a debut album which included an unlikely cover of the Beat's 'Can't Get Used To Losing You'. Their aggressive dancefloor attack was continued the same year with *In Dub*, on which 'Holgertron' made use of the theme music to television's *Doctor Who*. The group re-emerged in 1994 with another fine album, one of the tracks, 'Last Freedom Fighter', announcing that 'We've all been asleep for a very long time'. It was a welcome return,

though Bonnie had long since left for a solo career. Briotett also worked alongside his wife, Linda X, as half of Planet X (who recorded the James Bond tribute, 'I Won't Dance', and 'Once Upon A Dancefloor').
Albums: *Soundclash* (Mute 1990), *In Dub* (Mute 1990), *How Ya Doin?* (Mute 1994), *The Next Chapter Of Dub* (Mute 1995, remix album).

Replacements

This pop-punk group was formed in Minneapolis, Minnesota, USA, in 1979, with Paul Westerburg (b. 31 December 1960, Minneapolis, USA; guitar/vocals), Tommy Stinson (b. 6 October 1966, San Diego, California, USA; bass), Bob Stinson (b. 17 December 1959, Mound, Minnesota, USA; guitar) and Chris Mars (b. 26 April 1961, Minneapolis, USA; drums). Originally the Impediments, their early shambolic, drunken gigs forced a name change to secure further work. Their debut album for the local Twin/Tone label showcased their self-proclaimed power trash style, earning comparisons with hardcore legends Hüsker Dü. Subsequent albums saw the group diversifying to encompass influences from folk, country, and blues without straying far from their winning formula of rock 'n' roll married to the raw passion of punk rock. Beloved by critics on both sides of the Atlantic, the group appeared on the verge of mainstream success in America with the release of *Pleased To Meet Me*. Bob Stinson was replaced by Slim Dunlap (keyboards) and Westerburg was at the height of his songwriting powers on the suicide anthem, 'The Ledge', and the achingly melodic 'Skyway'. Greater success somehow eluded them and *All Shook Down* was a largely subdued affair, hinting at an impending solo career for Westerburg. However, it was Mars who would become the first ex-Replacement to record following the band's dissolution in 1990. Westerburg too would go on to sign under his own name, while Tommy Stinson formed his own band, Bash And Pop. Dunlap would re-appear on former Georgia Satellites mainman Dan Baird's debut solo album. Bob Stinson died on 18 February 1995 of a suspected drug overdose.
Albums: *Sorry Ma, Forgot To Take Out The Trash* (Twin/Tone 1981), *Hootenanny* (Twin/Tone 1983), *Let It Be* (Twin/Tone 1984), *The Shit Hits The Fans* (Twin/Tone 1985, cassette only), *Tim* (Sire 1985), *Pleased To Meet Me* (Sire 1987), *Don't Tell A Soul* (Sire 1989), *All Shook Down* (Sire 1990). Compilation: *Boink!!* (Glass 1986).

Residents

Despite a recording career spanning two decades, the Residents have successfully - and deliberately - achieved an air of wilful obscurity. Mindful of the cult of personality, they studiously retain an anonymity and refuse to name personnel, thus ensuring total artistic freedom. Their origins are shrouded in mystery and mischief, although common currency agrees the group was founded in Shrieveport, Louisiana, USA. They later moved to San Mateo, California, where a series of home-recorded tapes was undertaken. In 1971 the group collated several of these performances and sent the results to Hal Haverstadt of Warner Brothers, who had signed Captain Beefheart. No name had been included and thus the rejected package was returned marked 'for the attention of the residents', which the collective accepted as a sign of distinction. In 1972 the group was resettled in San Francisco where they launched Ralph Records as an outlet for their work. *Meet The Residents* established their unconventional style, matching bizarre reconstructions of 60s pop favourites with ambitious original material. Critics drew comparisons with the Mothers Of Invention, but any resemblance was purely superficial as the Residents drew reference from a wider variety of sources and showed a greater propensity to surprise. *Third Reich Rock 'N' Roll* contained two suites devoted to their twisted vision of contrasting cover versions, whereas *Not Available* comprised material the group did not wish to release. It had been recorded under the Theory Of Obscurity, whereby a record should not be issued until its creators had forgotten its existence, but appeared as a stop-gap release during sessions for the ambitious *Eskimo*. *The Commercial Album* consisted of 40 tracks lasting exactly 1 minute and contrasted the Residents' next project, the *Mole Trilogy*, which comprised *Mark Of The Mole*, *The Tunes Of Two Cities* and *The Big Bubble*. The group undertook extensive live appearances in the US and Europe to promote this expansive work, which in turn spawned several in-concert selections and an EP devoted to music played during the shows' intermission. Their subsequent *American Composers Series* has included *George And James*, a homage to George Gershwin and James Brown, *Stars And Hank Forever*, a celebration of Hank Williams and John Phillip Sousa, and *The King And Eye*, an album of Elvis Presley hits. If this suggests a paucity of original material, it is worth recalling the Residents' strength lies in interpretation and use of cultural icons as templates for their idiosyncratic vision.

Albums: *Meet The Residents* (Ralph 1974), *Ralph Fsette* (Ralph 1975), *Third Reich Rock 'N' Roll* (Ralph 1976), *Fingerprince* (Ralph 1976), *Not Available* (Ralph 1978), *Duck Stab/Buster And Glen* (Ralph 1978), *Eskimo* (Ralph 1979), *The Commercial Album* (Ralph 1980), *Mark Of The Mole* (Ralph 1981), *Intermission* (Ralph 1982), *The Tunes Of Two Cities* (Ralph 1982), *The Big Bubble* (Ralph 1983), *The Mole Show Live In Holland* (Ralph 1983), *George And James* (Ralph 1984), *Vileness Fats* (Ralph 1984), *13th Anniversary Show Live In Holland* (Torso 1986), *13th Anniversary Show Live In Japan* (Ralph 1986), *Stars And Hank Forever* (Ralph 1986), *God In Three Persons* (Rykodisc 1988), *The King And Eye* (Enigma 1989), *Freakshow* (Official Product 1991), *The Residents Present Our Finest Flowers* (Ralph 1993). Compilations: *Nibbles* (Virgin 1979), *Ralph Before '84 Volume 1* (Ralph 1984), *Ralph Before '84 Volume 2* (Ralph 1985), *Buster And Glen/Duck Stab* (Ralph 1995). Further reading: *Meet The Residents*, Ian Shirley.

Revenge

Formed in Manchester in 1987, and now one of three offshoots featuring 'resting' members of New Order. Peter Hook (b. 13 February 1956, Salford, Manchester, England) was initially joined by David Hicks (ex-Southern Death Cult, Lavolta Lakota; guitar) and CJ (Hook's studio engineer, who had previously worked with the Chameleons and the Fall). The band was started because: 'Hooky likes

playing gigs', and they performed their debut at London's Skin 2 Bondage Club in 1990. By this time they featured drummer Ashley Taylor and bassist David Potts, who had worked in Hook's Suite 16 studio. Unlike the more successful Electronic, the first releases by Revenge have garnered mediocre reviews at best. The album was prefaced by disappointing singles '7 Reasons' and 'Pineapple Face'. The third single, 'I'm Not Your Slave', came closest to familiar New Order territory and was the best of the bunch, with Hook's characteristic tugging bass. However, like its predecessors, it failed to make the UK charts. *One True Passion* garnered mixed reviews. Some critics pointed to song titles like 'Surf Nazi' and the recent 'Slave...' single as recalling the flirtation with fascist imagery which had dogged Joy Division and New Order. In spite of this, Hook has repeated his intention that Revenge should be an ongoing project.

Album: *One True Passion* (1990).

Revillos

Formed in March 1979 by Eugene Reynolds and Fay Fife, previously vocalists with the Rezillos. HiFi Harris (guitar), Rocky Rhythm (drums) and three backing singers - Jane White, Jane Brown and Tricia Bryce - completed the group's original line-up, but within months the latter trio had been replaced by Babs and Cherie Revette. The Revillos made their debut with 'Where's The Boy For Me' (1979), but although this exciting performance recalled the best of the previous group, it failed to emulate their success. Internal friction undermined the unit's undoubted potential - guitarists, bassists and singers were replaced with regularity as Reynolds, Fife and Rhythm pursued their uncompromising vision. An album, *Rev-Up*, captured the Revillos' enchanting mixture of girl-group, beat and science-fiction, but they were subsequently dropped by their record company. Undeterred the group inaugurated Superville for ensuing releases and embarked on two gruelling tours of the USA and Canada which they financed themselves. However an anticipated deal failed to materialize and this ebullient act later disintegrated.

Albums: *Rev Up* (1980), *Attack* (1983).

Revolting Cocks

Endearingly titled industrial funk metal band, the name occasionally shortened to RevCo when propriety demands. The Revolting Cocks history stretches back to the mid-80s when Al Jourgenson (also Ministry) met Belgians Richard 23 and Luc Van Acker in a Chicago pool hall. Legend has it that a drunken Van Acker stumbled in to Jourgenson when the latter was attempting to make a winning shot in a $500 game. However, Jourgenson recovered his composure to win, and the three celebrated by wrecking the club. On their exit the manager was heard to remark 'Get out, you revolting cocks!'. The group's first single under their new moniker would be 'No Devotion', housed on Chicago's infamous Wax Trax label. When it made the PMRC's 'Naughty 9' list for its blasphemy something of a noble tradition was born. The lyrical scope of the group's debut offered no respite. Subject matter included rioting soccer fans, sitcom junkies and industrial accidents. Joined in 1987 by multi-instrumentalist

William Rieflin, the next single, 'You Often Forget', featured both 'malignant' and 'benign' versions in tribute to the prevalent media fascination with Betty Ford's breasts. Richard 23 then departed for Front 242, to be replaced by Chris Connelly of Finitribe fame. Paul Barker of Ministry was also on hand to guest and co-produce the half-live *You Goddamned Son Of A Bitch*, recorded at a Chicago show in September 1987. However, *Beers, Steers And Queers* would be the group's second album proper, its title-track a hilarious machismo pile-up of cowboy kitsch and dialogue stolen from the homo-erotic scenes of *Deliverance*. A 'cover' of Olivia Newton John's '(Let's Get) Physical' was also on hand to startle the casual browser - basically consisting of a loop of someone screaming the title. Afterwards the band would move away from Wax Trax (as had Ministry, from whom RevCo would now additionally absorb Roland Barker, Mike Scaccia and Louie Svitek). The madness continued unabated at their new label, with *Linger Ficken' Good* this time seizing Rod Stewart's 'Do You Think I'm Sexy' and righteously deflowering it with additional lyrics from Connelly concerning dentistry. Afterwards RevCo took a break from inflaming moral umbrage while Jourgenson concentrated on Ministry activities.
Albums: *Big Sexy Land* (Wax Trax 1986), *You Goddamned Son Of A Bitch* (Wax Trax 1988), *Beers, Steers + Queers* (Wax Trax 1990), *Linger Ficken' Good And Other Barnyard Oddities* (Devotion 1993).

Revolver

This three piece UK 90s independent label pop group comprised Mat Flint (vocals/guitar), Nick Dewey (drums) and Hamish Brown (bass). Flint and Dewey were both from Winchester, had played in several bands for the previous three years, and met Brown in London in September 1990. Influenced in their efforts by the Beach Boys, Beatles, Byrds, My Bloody Valentine, and the Jesus And Mary Chain, they played their first gig in December 1990. Soon after came the EP, *Heaven Sent An Angel*, after which the media, keen to establish some form of clearly defined trend, picked up on them and numerous others with a similar approach. They were clearly taken unawares by the glare of attention: 'We don't have a desire as individuals to be famous, but we want the band to be a famous name so we can grin down from bedroom walls and get to play in New York.' Possibly due to the fact that all three members of the band were still attempting to pursue a parallel academic career, it would be 1993 before a debut album was released. Its basic rock energy took many journalists, who had written the band off as part of the much reviled 'shoegazing' scene, by surprise.
Album: *Cold Water Flat* (Hut 1993).

Revolving Paint Dream

The Revolving Paint Dream was not only the most mysterious act on Creation Records' original roster back in 1984, but also one of the most inventive. After a memorable psychedelia-tinged single, 'Flowers In The Sky'/'In The Afternoon', in February, the band disappeared for three years before a strange collection of what seemed like out-takes, *Off To Heaven*, reached the shelves in June 1987. 60s-influenced pop sat alongside weird, distorted soundscapes to create an album that lacked any overall identity but was stacked full with ideas. It transpired that the band comprised Primal Scream's second guitarist Andrew Innes, Nico-like vocalist Christine Wanless (also present on several Biff Bang Pow! recordings) and Luke Hayes, with probable involvement from label organizers Alan McGee and Richard Green. January 1989's *Mother Watch Me Burn* was even more experimental and the listener was hard pushed to believe that it was the same band performing the fragrant pop tune, 'Sun, Sea, Sand' (issued as a single) and the ferocious, almost unlistenable instrumentals.
Albums: *Off To Heaven* (Creation 1987), *Mother Watch Me Burn* (Creation 1989).

Rezillos

Formed in Edinburgh, Scotland, in March 1976, the Rezillos were initially an informal aggregation consisting of Eugene Reynolds (b. Alan Forbes; vocals), Fay Fife (b. Sheila Hynde; vocals), Luke Warm aka Jo Callis (lead guitar), Hi Fi Harris (b. Mark Harris; guitar), Dr. D.K. Smythe (bass), Angel Patterson (b. Alan Patterson; drums) and Gale Warning (backing vocals). Their irreverent repertoire consisted of pre-beat favourites by Screaming Lord Sutch and the Piltdown Men, judicious material from the Dave Clark Five and glam-rock staples by the Sweet. Their image, part Marlon Brando, part Shangri-Las, allied them with the punk movement, although their love of pop heritage denied wholesale involvement. The Rezillos' debut single, 'I Can't Stand My Baby', encapsulated their crazed obsessions, but its success introduced a discipline at odds with their initial irreverence. Harris, Smythe and Warning left the line-up, while auxiliary member William Mysterious (b. William Donaldson; bass/saxophone) joined the group on a permanent basis. Now signed to a major label, Sire Records, the quintet undertook several tours and scored a UK Top 20 hit with the satirical 'Top Of The Pops' in August 1978. The group's debut album, *Can't Stand The Rezillos*, also charted, before internal pressures began pulling them apart. Mysterious was replaced by Simon Templar, but in December 1978 the Rezillos folded following a brief farewell tour. Fife and Reynolds formed the Revillos, while the rest of the band became known as Shake. Callis later found fame in the Human League. In the 90s the Revillos/Rezillos reformed for tours in Japan, from which a live album was culled to bookmark their fifteen year career.
Albums: *Can't Stand The Rezillos* (Sire 1978), *Mission Accomplished ... But The Beat Goes On* (Sire 1979). Compilations: *Can't Stand The Rezillos, The (Almost) Complete Rezillos* (Sire 1995), *Live And On Fire In Japan* (Vinyl Japan 1995).

Rhino Records

The Los Angeles-based record company was launched in 1978 by Richard Foos and Harold Bronson as an outgrowth of their Rhino Records retail store. At first the fledgling company specialized in novelty records, including an all-kazoo version of Led Zeppelin's 'Whole Lotta Love' by the Temple City Kazoo Orchestra and an album by one-time Frank Zappa protege Wild Man Fischer. During the 80s the label took to reissuing out-of-print recordings from rock's 'golden era' including the catalogues of the Monkees and the Turtles and hits collections from a diverse list of artists including Jerry Lee Lewis, Nancy Sinatra and the Neville Brothers. Rhino also made an impact with its inventive various artists compilations, including two volumes of nothing but the song 'Louie, Louie' and collections of soul music, novelty records, early 70s AM radio hits, British Invasion, 'Frat Rock' and many others. By the mid-80s Rhino was recognized as the leading repackager in the USA. Compilations: *Rhino Teen Magazine* (1984), *Rhino Brothers Greatest Flops* (1988).

Rich Kids

Formed in London, England, during September 1977, the Rich Kids were the subject of exceptional initial interest. Centred on bassist Glen Matlock (b. 27 August 1956), a former member of the seminal Sex Pistols, his eminent role was emphasized by the inclusion of two 'unknown' musicians, Steve New (guitar/vocals) and Rusty Egan (drums). The group was later completed by Midge Ure, disillusioned frontman of struggling pop group, Slik, and this unusual mixture engendered criticism from unsympathetic quarters. The Rich Kids distanced themselves from punk, and their meagre releases were generally mainstream in execution. Indeed the group's ebullience recalled a 60s bonhomie, but this merely compounded criticism of their 'power pop' approach. The quartet was unable to transform their energy to record, while tension between Matlock and Ure increased to the extent that they were constantly squabbling. The group broke up in November 1978, but denied the fact until free of contractual obligations. Egan and Ure later formed Visage, while their former colleagues pursued several low-key projects. Ure would find the greatest subsequent success as singer with Ultravox, also playing a significant part in the launch of Band Aid.
Album: *Ghosts Of Princes In Towers* (EMI 1978).

Richman, Jonathan

b. 16 May 1951, Boston, Massachusetts, USA. Richman rose to prominence during the early 70s as leader of the Modern Lovers. Drawing inspiration from 50s pop and the Velvet Underground, the group initially offered a garage-band sound, as evinced on their UK hit 'Roadrunner' and the infectious instrumental 'Egyptian Reggae' in 1977. However, Richman increasingly distanced himself from electric music and latterly embraced an acoustic-based direction. He disbanded the group in 1978 to pursue an idiosyncratic solo career in which his naive style was deemed charming or irritating according to taste. His songs, including 'Ice Cream Man', 'My Love Is A Flower (Just Beginning To Bloom)', showed a child-like simplicity which seemed oblivious to changes in trends around him. Richman exhumed the Modern Lovers' name during the 80s without any alteration to his style and the artist continues to enjoy considerable cult popularity.
Albums: *Jonathan Richman And The Modern Lovers* (1977), *Back In Your Life* (1979), *The Jonathan Richman Songbook* (1980), *Jonathan Sings* (1984), *Its Time For Jonathan Richman And The Modern Lovers* (1986), *Jonathan Richman*

& Barence Whitfield (1988), *Modern Lovers 88* (1988), *Jonathan Richman* (1989), *Jonathan Sings Country* (1990), *I, Jonathan* (1993). Compilation: *23 Great Recordings* (1990).

Ride

Formed at Art School in Oxfordshire, England, in 1988 by Mark Gardener (vocals/guitar), Andy Bell (guitar/vocals), Stephan Queralt (bass) and Laurence Colbert (drums), Ride had a rapid impact on the alternative music scene. Initially described as 'The House Of Love with chainsaws', within a year the quartet's serrated guitar melodies were attracting unusual amounts of attention. At the start of 1990 their debut EP reached number 71 in the UK charts - the first time their label, Creation Records, had ever registered such a placing. By the end of the spring, Ride had transcended their independent parameters and entered the Top 40 of the UK chart with the *Play* EP, helped by their youthful good looks and large-scale touring. The success continued with *Nowhere* reaching number 14 in the UK charts before the close of the year. Tours of Japan, Australia and America showed just how impressively swift the band's rise had been, especially when a third EP went straight into the Top 20 of the UK chart. Their success was sealed by a headlining appearance at 1991's Slough Music Festival in front of 8,000 fans. In 1992 Ride consolidated their position as one of the most interesting new bands with the excellent *Going Blank Again* and the hypnotic UK hit single, 'Leave Them All Behind'. *Carnival Of Light* witnessed something of a backlash, however, with the group stalling artistically, seemingly lacking the ideas which had come so quickly at their inception. 1995's *Tarantula* was recorded by the band in London with producer Richard 'Digby' Smith, a veteran of work with Bob Marley and Free.
Albums: *Nowhere* (Creation 1990), *Going Blank Again* (Creation 1992), *Carnival Of Light* (Creation 1994), *Tarantula* (Creation 1995).

Ridgway, Stan

b. Stanard Ridgway, 1954, Los Angeles, California, USA. Ridgway was brought up as a Christian Scientist and his mother's tendency to bring Kirlian photographs home for her son to look at may have contributed to his love of the more perverse elements of life. At school he was nicknamed Mr. Monster and formed the Monster Club. He also admits to being the 'man who cried when Bela Lugosi died!'. A sometime cab driver, Ridgway's first major musical venture was the soundtrack company - Acme - he formed with Marc Morehand. They became Wall Of Voodoo in 1977, the name taken with deference to Phil Spector's 'Wall Of Sound' recording techniques. In 1984 Ridgway collaborated with Stewart Copeland on the soundtrack for Francis Ford Coppolla's movie *Rumblefish*, but Ridgway enjoyed success in 1986 when his wacky 'death disc' 'Camouflage', became a surprise UK hit. The follow-up 'The Big Heat' was equally strong but failed to chart. An album of the same name- recorded with Chapter II, including wife Pietra on keyboards, was highly acclaimed. Ridgway's narrative songs such as 'Drive She Said' were particularly striking. Career problems were compounded when contractual disputes with Miles Copeland at IRS effectively put him out of action for two years. The resultant *Mosquitoes* featured 'Heat Takes A Walk', co-written with Beach Boys collaborator Van Dyke Parks, as well as 'Newspapers', which partially summed up his frustration with his career so far.

Albums: *Camouflage* (1986), *The Big Heat* (1986), *Mosquitoes* (1989).

Riley, Marc, And The Creepers

b. Manchester, England. Riley started playing in a band when he was aged 15, 'then I sort of wormed my way into the Fall when I was 16'. He left to form the Creepers, with Eddie Fenn (drums), Paul Fletcher (guitar) and Pete Keogh (bass). The last two were later replaced by Mark Tilton (guitar) and Phil Roberts (bass). The records that followed were full of hard-hitting humour and remained as opinionated as those of Riley's former boss, Mark E. Smith (who apparently wrote the sarcastic 'Middle Mass' about Riley). Examples included the anti-Paul Weller rallying cry, 'Bard Of Woking'. Riley formed In Tape records with keyboardist Jim Khambatta, who also managed the Creepers. Starved of commercial success, and burdened by his heritage, Riley disbanded the Creepers in 1987 and formed the Lost Soul Crusaders, later undertaking a career in radio.

Albums: *Cull* (In Tape 1984), *Gross Out* (In Tape 1984), *Fancy Meeting God* (In Tape 1985), *Warts 'n' All* (In Tape 1985). The Creepers: *Miserable Sinners* (In Tape 1986), *Rock 'N' Roll Liquorice Flavour* (Red Rhino 1987). Compilation: *Sleeper: A Retrospective* (Bleed 1989).

Rip Rig And Panic

Evolving out of Bristol's the Pop Group, Rip Rig And Panic was formed in 1981 as a conceptual musicians' collective, taking its name from an album by Roland Kirk. The group's prime movers were multi-instrumentalist and songwriter Gareth Sager, jazz trumpeter Don Cherry's stepdaughter Neneh Cherry (b. Stockholm, Sweden; vocals), Cherry's partner and drummer Bruce Smith, Sean Oliver (bass) and Mark Springer (piano). Powerful and disturbing live, their playful, anarchic jazz-funk was well-captured on the irreverent 1981 debut album, *God*, which appeared as two 45rpm discs, but was too radical for daytime airplay or significant sales. They performed at the first WOMAD festival in 1982 shortly before Cherry returned to Sweden to have her first baby. Sean Oliver's sister Andrea temporarily took over vocals, and Louis Moholo joined on drums. The equally experimental second album, *I Am Cold*, appeared in 1982, followed by the more accessible *Attitude* in 1983. Unwilling to compromise further, but feeling the strain of constant innovation, they split in 1985, only to re-align as the smaller outfit, Float Up CP and, briefly, God Mother And Country, before Cherry went on to a successful solo career with Andrea Oliver contributing to some of her songs.

Albums: *God* (1981), *I Am Cold* (1982), *Attitude* (1983).

Robinson, Tom

b. 1 July 1950, Cambridge, England. Robinson's wayward youth included the study of oboe, clarinet and bass guitar, and a spell in Finchden Manor, a readjustment centre in Kent, where he met guitarist Danny Kurstow with whom he formed his first group, Davanq, in 1971. Two years later

Robinson formed Café Society with Hereward Kaye and Ray Doyle and they signed to the Kinks' Konk label. In 1974, *Café Society* was recorded with help from Ray Davies and Mick Avory. During the taping of an intended second album, administrative discord was manifested in what was now the Tom Robinson Band's on-stage mocking of Davies, and, later, the Kinks' reciprocal dig at Robinson in a 1977 b-side, 'Prince Of The Punks' - with whom Robinson's band had been categorized (not entirely accurately) when contracted by EMI Records the previous year. Konk, nevertheless, retained publishing interests in 13 Robinson numbers. Some of these were selected for TRB's *Power In The Darkness* debut and attendant UK Top 40 singles - notably the catchy '2468 Motorway'. Backed by keyboardist Mark Ambler, drummer 'Dolphin' Taylor plus the faithful Kurstow, lead singer Robinson's active support of many radical causes riddled his lyrical output, but the gravity of 'Summer Of 79' and 'Up Against The Wall' was mitigated by grace-saving humour. The quartet's *Rising Free* EP, for example, contained the singalong 'Glad To Be Gay' anthem - which was also a highlight of both TRB's 1978 benefit concert for the Northern Ireland Gay Rights and One Parent Families Association, and Robinson's solo set during a Lesbian and Gay Rights March in Washington in 1979, shortly after parting with his band (Taylor going on to Stiff Little Fingers). This followed a disappointing critical and market reaction to *TRB2* (supervised by Todd Rundgren) - on which the sloganeering was overdone and the musical performance tepid. While Kurstow joined ex-Sex Pistol Glen Matlock in the Spectres, Robinson led the short-lived Section 27 and began songwriting collaborations with Elton John and Peter Gabriel. By 1981 he had relocated to Berlin to record the solo *North By Northwest* and work in alternative cabaret and fringe theatre. Professionally, this period proved fruitful - with 1982's strident 'War Baby' and evocative 'Atmospherics' in the UK Top 40, and a revival of Steely Dan's 'Ricki Don't Lose That Number', from *Hope And Glory*, which fared as well as the original in the same chart. However, when *Still Loving You* produced no equivalent of even this modest triumph Robinson, now a contented father, regrouped his original band. Subsequent engagements were viewed by many as akin to a nostalgia revue - and certainly several old favourites were evident on the Berlin concert set, *Last Tango*. However, Robinson's lyrical eloquence argues that further solid work may lie ahead now he has returned to recording with Cooking Vinyl Records.

Albums: *Power In The Darkness* (Harvest 1978), *TRB2* (Harvest 1979). With Sector 27: *Sector 27* (Fontana 1980). Solo: *North By Northwest* (Fontana 1982), *Hope And Glory* (RCA 1984), *Still Loving You* (RCA 1986), *Last Tango* (Line 1989), with Jakko M. Jakzyk *We Never Had It So Good* (Musidisc 1990), *Living In A Boom Time* (Cooking Vinyl 1992), *Love Over Rage* (Cooking Vinyl 1994). Compilations: *Tom Robinson Band* (EMI 1981), *Cabaret '79* (Panic 1982).

Rockingbirds

Six-piece London band playing country rock in the best traditions of Gram Parsons. The unit were originally based in a Camden squat before eviction notices forced their departure. The initial line-up comprised Alan Tylor

Rockingbirds

Henry Rollins

(vocals/guitar), Andy Hackett (guitar), Dave Golding (bass), Dave Morgan (drums; ex-Loft), Shaun Reid (percussion/backing vocals) and Patrick Harbuthnot (pedal steel guitar). Their second 45, 'Jonathan Jonathan', was a stirring tribute to Jonathan Richman, backed by a cover of the Parsons/Chris Hillman tune, 'Older Guys'. They also covered Tammy Wynette with guest vocals, unlikely as it may seem, by Leslie of Silverfish. Another notable cover was 'Deeply Dippy' as part of their record company's tribute to the genius of Right Said Fred. At the beginning of 1993 they were showcasing material for their second album and taking part in the Cambridge Folk Festival, by which time they had already played a significant part in a new-found, critical accomodation of country music. However, the move from Heavenly Records proved unfortunate, and after line-up changes (losing Bill Prince to a solo career) they only re-emerged in 1995 with a self-deprecating album (produced by Edwyn Collins) for Cooking Vinyl Records, whose title said everything about their commercial malaise.
Album: *The Rockingbirds* (Heavenly 1992), *Whatever Happened To The Rockingbirds* (Cooking Vinyl 1995).

Rollins, Henry

Vocalist Henry Rollins (b. Henry Garfield, 13 February 1961, Washington DC, USA) quickly returned to action following the break-up of Black Flag, releasing *Hot Animal Machine*, followed by the *Drive-By Shooting* EP (under the pseudonym Henrietta Collins and the Wifebeating Childhaters). The Rollins Band was eventually formed in 1987 with Chris Haskett (guitar), Andrew Weiss (bass) and Sim Cain (drums). The group developed their own brand of hard rock, with blues and jazz influences, over several studio and live albums, building a considerable following with their heavy touring schedule. Rollins' lyrics dealt with social and political themes, often unashamedly exorcising personal demons from a troubled childhood. The sight of the heavily-muscled and tattooed frontman on stage, dripping sweat and roaring out his rage, is one of the most astonishing, memorable sights in hard rock music, topping off an enthralling live act. Their commercial rise began with the opening slot on the first Lollapalooza tour, exposing the band to huge audiences for the first time. *The End Of Silence* was a deserved success, and contained some of Rollins' most strikingly introspective lyrics. 'Just Like You' narrated his difficulty in dealing with his similarities to an abusive father: 'You should see the pain I go through, When I see myself I see you'. Rollins' spoken word and publishing activities (his regime is one which allows for little more than a few hours sleep each night) also drew major media interest. An accomplished and experienced spoken word performer with several albums to his credit, Rollins' often hilarious style is in distinct contrast to his musical persona, and has drawn comparisons to Lenny Bruce and Denis Leary (though, in contrast, he implores his audiences not to destroy themselves with 'poisons' like alcohol and tobacco). Despite the humour, there is a serious edge to his words, best animated in the harrowing story of the murder of his best friend, Joe Cole, within feet of him. Rollins' workaholic frame also levers his own publishing company, 2.13.61 (after his birthdate), which has grown from very small beginnings in 1984 to publish a wide range of authors, including Rollins' own prolific output. He also has a music publishing enterprise, Human Pitbull, and co-owns a record label with Rick Rubin, dedicated to classic punk reissues - Rollins himself having graduated from the infamous late 70s Washington DC 'straight edge' scene and bands like SOA. He has additionally broken into film acting, appearing in *The Chase* and *Johnny Mnemonic*. Back with the Rollins Band, *Weight*, produced by long-time soundman Theo Van Rock, saw the first personnel change since the band's inception, with Melvin Gibbs replacing Weiss, and adding a funkier spine to the band's still intense core.
Albums: Henry Rollins: *Hot Animal Machine* (Texas Hotel 1986). Rollins Band: *Life Time* (Texas Hotel 1988), *Do It* (Texas Hotel 1988), *Hard Volume* (Texas Hotel 1989), *Turned On* (Quarterstick 1990), *The End Of Silence* (Imago 1992), *Weight* (Imago 1994). Spoken word: *The Boxed Life* (Imago 1993).
Further reading: all titles by Henry Rollins: *High Adventure In The Great Outdoors* aka *Bodybag*, 1985, *Pissing In The Gene Pool* 1986, *Art To Choke Hearts* 1986, *Bang!* 1987, *One From None* 1987, *See A Grown Man Cry* 1991, *Black Coffee Blues* 1993, *Now Watch 'Em Die* 1993, *Get In The Van: On The Road With Black Flag* 1994.

Room

An adventurous pop band formed in Liverpool, England, the Room quickly attracted strong support from the press with records variously acclaimed for their wit, irony, poise and intelligence. The line-up featured Dave Jackson (vocals), Paul Cavanagh (guitar), Becky Stringer (bass), and Alan Willis (drums). Early singles on Box records ('Bitter Reaction', 'Motion', 'In Sickness And In Health') revealed a talented band , slipstreaming the innovations of Echo And The Bunnymen. More attractive still was their debut for Red Flame, 'Things Have Learnt To Walk That Should Only Crawl'. The band played several dates with Tom Verlaine in 1984, who went on to produce three tracks on *In Evil Hour*. Their first 'complete' album, it also featured John Porter (of Smiths fame) on production. Among the Verlaine slices was 'Jackpot Jack': 'You pulled the lever back/You hit the jackpot jack/And all the radios, are blaring new pop cack'. It was an ambitious statement of intent, and one not missed by critics of the day. However, the single 'New Dreams For Old', also included on the album, saw the band's best, and final, crack at the charts. By this time they had bolstered their line-up with the addition of Peter Baker (organ/synthesizer) and Phil Lucking (trombone/trumpet). However, the band 'just sort of fell out really. . .'. Jackson went on to front Benny Profane taking Stringer and Baker with him.
Albums: *Clear* (1983), *In Evil Hour* (1984), *Nemesis* (1986).

Rose Of Avalanche

This Yorkshire, England-based group came to the fore following heavy airplay from BBC disc jockey John Peel. The debut single, 'LA Rain', finished high in his 1985 'Festive Fifty', although it was released before the band had performed. The follow-up, 'Castles In the Sky', originated from overhearing a man in a pub asking a girl if she wanted to 'See my castle in the sky?'. 'Velveteen', meanwhile, was a

tribute to Nico. The band's principals were Phillip Morris (vocals) and Paul James Berry (guitar), while a host of supporting musicians passed through their ranks. These included: Mark Thompson and Andrew Parker (drums), Alan Davis, Nicol Mackay and Daren Horner (bass) and Glenn Shultz (guitar). Horner and Parker then became encumbants of the rhythm section. After gaining early praise the band were stopped in their tracks for 18 months between 1987 and 1988 following disputes with their label, Fire Records. They responded by setting up their own Avalantic label. Their two most recent collections, *String A Beads* and *I.C.E.* have brought about a transformation in the band's sound. Gone are the heavy rhythms and chiming guitar which saw them pigeon-holed as 'gothic', replaced by material of a comparatively melodic and 'poppy' nature.
Albums: *Always There* (Fire 1986), *First Avalanche* (Fire 1987), *In Rock* (Avalantic 1988), *Never Another Sunset* (Avalantic 1989), *String A Beads* (Avalantic 1990), *I.C.E.* (Avalantic 1991).

Rough Trade Records

Initially based near west London's Portobello Road, the Rough Trade retail shop opened in February 1976, just months prior to the rise of the punk rock phenomenon. Owned by Geoff Travis (b. 2 February 1952, Stoke Newington, London, England), it was an important outlet for punk and independent releases from the UK and USA. Travis's empathy for this musical revolution helped build the shop's reputation as a leading source for import material, British independent releases, complimentary reggae releases and as a selling point for the proliferation of music fanzines. The demand for outlets generated by bands inspired the formation of a distribution network and label, and the Rough Trade record label was launched two years later with the release of 'Paris Maquis' by Metal Urbain, which anticipated the 'Industrial' style flourishing later in the decade. Subsequent releases by reggae artist Augustus Pablo and *avant garde* act Cabaret Voltaire confirmed Rough Trade's reputation as an outlet for diverse talent. Stiff Little Fingers, Young Marble Giants, Aztec Camera, the Raincoats, the Go-Betweens, the Fall, Scritti Politti and the Pop Group maintained the company's reputation as purveyors of challenging music, while a succession of excellent recordings by the Smiths combined perception with popular acclaim, making the group the company's biggest asset for much of its history. The label also became the natural outlet for several US acts, ranging from the guitar-orientated Feelies, Dream Syndicate, the idiosyncratic Jonathan Richman and Camper Van Beethoven, to the experimental styles of Pere Ubu and the offbeat country/folk of Souled American. Many defections to major labels most notably Aztec Camera and Scritti Politti undermined the pitfalls bedevilling independent outlets and in 1984, under the aegis of the giant Warner Brothers corporation, Travis established Blanco Y Negro on which acts who preferred the security of a major company could nonetheless enjoy the intimacy of an independent. Jesus And Mary Chain, Everything But The Girl and Dinosaur Jnr have been among the label's signings, confirming Travis as one of Britain's most astute executives. Rough Trade Records continued to serve as the natural outlet

for independently-minded acts throughout the 80s, but defection to EMI by the aforementioned Smiths was a significant loss. Hopes were then pinned on the Sundays, but the collapse of the Rough Trade distribution network in 1991 put the label's fate in jeopardy. However, a trimming down of staff and operations found the company steadying its position and subsequent recordings by artists such as Robert Wyatt suggest that its long-term future as a haven for adventurism is still assured.
Album: *Wanna Buy A Bridge?* (1980).

Royal Trux

New York duo comprising Neil Hagerty (vocals/guitar), and Jennifer Herrema (vocals, sundry instruments), who specialise in a drug-addled, chemically fuelled dirty rock habit. Royal Trux was formed in 1985 while Hagerty was still playing guitar in Pussy Galore. He was behind the latter's idea to cover the Rolling Stones' *Exile On Main Street* in its entirety. The duo debuted with an untitled 1988 album, and a declared ambition of retracing the US noise scene back to its primal roots (MC5 etc). Descriptions like 'garage psychobilly punk' proliferated in the press. 1990's *Twin Infinitives* double set saw songs based on the works of science fiction writer Philip K Dick, alongside the riffs of Led Zeppelin, Rolling Stones and AC/DC, music which had dominated their youth. Recorded in three months in a deserted warehouse, the touring schedule that ensued saw them physically and aurally confront their audience, *ala* the Swans. In truth Hagerty and Herrema were both heavily strung out on heroin. A third album, also untitled, was released in 1992, and largely essayed their heroin fixation/trials. One result of their ordeals is that they are currently based in Washington DC, having found the ethos of New York a little destructive. Their fourth album, and the first to see them garner serious UK and European press, was recorded in a Virginian country home in 1993. *Thank You* saw them arrange a more permanent band together, and also featured the help of producer David Briggs, a celebrated partner of Neil Young. It included the single 'Map Of The City', as well as confident R&B and rock numbers such as 'Shadow Of The Wasp' and 'Night To Remember'.
Albums: *Untitled* (1988), *Twin Infinitives* (1990, double album), *Untitled* (1992), *Cats And Dogs* (1993), *Thank You* (Virgin 1995).

Rubella Ballet

Formed in the summer of 1979, the first stable line-up of this UK punk band comprised Zillah Minx (b. 31 March 1961, Birkenhead, Merseyside, England; vocals), Sid Attion (b. 18 April 1960, Sutton Coalfield, England; drums), Pete Fender (ex-Honey Bane, Fatal Microbes; guitar), and several bass players. Other early members included Annie Anxiety, Womble, Colin (Flux Of Pink Indians) and the strangely named 'It'. Anxiety was to be the singer, but when she dropped out drummer Sid, who would also work with Flux Of Pink Indians, suggested his girlfriend Zillah fill the position (at extremely short notice). Their first release was the cassette-only 'Ballet Bag', followed by a series of snappy punk pop singles. Gemma (also ex-Fatal Microbes, and brother of Fender) took over the bass position, although still a schoolgirl. The two, incidentally, are the children of the Poison Girls' Vi Subversa. The line-up would continue to be fluid however, with several guitarists passing through the ranks once Fender departed. He would go on to build his own studio, and record the solo single, '4 Formulas'. After spells with Xcentrix and Jungle Records, they formed their own Ubiquitous label with enterprising singles 'Money Talks' and 'Artic Flowers', and eventually three albums. In 1983, they launched a major tour with Death Cult, and were joined by Rachel Minx (b. 12 November 1964, Birkenhead, Merseyside, England; Zillah's sister) on bass. Zillah and Sid later recorded a techno dance track for the compilation *Beyond The Threshold*, under the name Xenophobia, and subsequent singles also appeared under that title.

Albums: *Ballet Bag* (Xentrix 1986), *If* (Ubiquitous 1986), *Cocktail Mix* (Ubiquitous 1987) *Birthday Box* (Ubiquitous 1988), *At The End Of The Rainbow* (Ubiquitous 1990). Video: *Freak Box* (1986).

Runaways

Formed in 1975, the Runaways were initially the product of producer/svengali Kim Fowley and teenage lyricist Kari Krome. Together they pieced together an adolescent female group following several auditions in the Los Angeles area. The original line-up consisted of Joan Jett (b. Joan Larkin, 22 September 1960, Philadelphia, Pennsylvania, USA; guitar/vocals), Micki Steele (bass - later of the Bangles) and Sandy West (drums), but was quickly bolstered by the addition of Lita Ford (b. 23 September 1959, London, England; guitar/vocals) and Cherie Currie (vocals). The departure of Steele prompted several replacements, the last of which was Jackie Fox (b. Jacqueline Fuchs) who had failed her first audition. Although originally viewed as a vehicle for compositions by Fowley and associate Mars Bonfire (b. Dennis Edmonton), material by Jett and Krome helped assert the quintet's independence. *The Runaways* showed a group indebted to the 'glam-rock' of the Sweet and punchy pop of Suzi Quatro, and included the salutary 'Cherry Bomb'. *Queens Of Noise* repeated the pattern, but the strain of touring - the quintet were highly popular in Japan - took its toll on Jackie Fox, who left the line-up and abandoned music altogether becoming an attorney practicing in intellectual property law. Personality clashes resulted in the departure of Cherie Currie, whose solo career stalled following the failure of her debut, *Beauty's Only Skin Deep*. Guitarist/vocalist Vicki Blue and bassist Laurie McAllister completed a revitalized Runaways, but the latter was quickly dropped. Subsequent releases lacked the appeal of the group's early work which, although tarred by novelty and sexual implication, nonetheless showed a sense of purpose. The Runaways split in 1980 but both Jett and Ford later enjoyed solo careers, the former engendering considerable commercial success during the 80s. In 1985 the mischievous Fowley resurrected the old group's name with all-new personnel. This opportunistic concoction split up on completing *Young And Fast*. 1994 brought reports that Fowley was being sued by Jett, Ford, Currie and West over unpaid royalties. Fox was not involved in the action, presumably because she is now herself a practising lawyer.

Albums: *The Runaways* (Mercury 1976), *Queens Of Noise* (Mercury 1977), *Live In Japan* (Mercury 1977), *Waitin' For The Night* (Mercury 1977), *And Now...The Runaways* (Phonogram 1979), *Young And Fast* (Allegiance 1987). Compilations: *Rock Heavies* (Mercury 1979), *Flamin' Schoolgirls* (Phonogram 1982).

Ruts

This punk/reggae-influenced group comprised Malcolm Owen (vocals), Paul Fox (guitar/vocals), Dave Ruffy (drums) and John 'Segs' Jennings (bass). They first came to the fore in 1979 with the UK Top 10 single, 'Babylon's Burning'. Their gigs of that year were the most stunning of punk's second generation, with one in Bradford cited by Justin Sullivan of New Model Army as the biggest influence on his career. Their style resembled that of the Clash, but while Owen was occasionally compared to Joe Strummer, there was something just as original sparking the group's songwriting. The strident 'Something That I Said' gave them another hit and their debut album, *The Crack*, though not representing the band as well as their blistering singles, was well received. The rampaging 'Staring At The Rude Boys' neatly displayed their rock/dub talents, but their progress was arrested by Owen's drug-related death on 14 July 1980. On the run-out groove of their final single together the band scratched the legend 'Can I Use Your Bathroom?' in tribute - Owen having died in the bath. The remaining members were joined by Gary Barnacle and elected to continue as Ruts DC. They recorded two further albums under that name, moving towards funk-influenced reggae. Without Owen, however, the spirit of the group was not the same and they faded from prominence, though their influence lives on in bands such as the Wildhearts and the Almighty. Fox would go on to a successful production career.

Albums: *The Crack* (Virgin 1979), *Grin And Bear It* (Virgin 1980). As Ruts DC: *Animal Now* (Virgin 1981), *Rhythm Collision Vol 1* (Bohemian 1982). Ruts DC And The Mad Professor: *Rhythm Collision Dub Vol. 1* (ROIR 1987, cassette only). Compilations: *The Ruts Live* (Dojo 1987), *The Peel Sessions* (Strange Fruit 1990), *The Best Of The Ruts* (Virgin 1995).

S

Sad Lovers And Giants

This UK post-punk group, based in Watford, Hertfordshire, featured a line-up comprising Grace Allard (vocals), Tristan Garel Funk (guitar), David Wood (keyboards), Cliff Silver (bass) and Nigel Pollard (drums). After the exposure of early singles 'Colourless Dream' and 'Lost In A Moment', it was the release of 'Man Of Straw' and the accompanying *Feeding The Flame* which really established the group as masters of the double-edged lyric and sweeping, emotional textures of guitar and keyboard: 'Like confession whispered slowly, Hate's a word that's spoken softly, Standing lonely trusting no one, In disarray with collar undone'. The band had already fallen apart by the time the *Total Sound* mini-album, recorded live for broadcast on Dutch radio in 1983, was released. Another posthumous release, *In the Breeze*, consisting of demos, live tracks and alternative versions recorded for BBC disc jockey John Peel, pre-dated its release. The group was briefly reactivated in 1987, releasing the disappointing 'White Russians', while only Pollard and Allard were still in place for the subsequent final albums.
Albums: *Epic Garden Music* (Midnight 1982), *Feeding The Flame* (Midnight 1983), *In The Breeze*, (Midnight 1984) *Total Sound* (Midnight 1986, mini-album), *The Mirror Test* (Midnight 1988), *Les Annes Vertes* (Midnight 1988).

Saint Etienne

By far the most dextrous of those bands cursed with the 'indie-dance' label, and one of the few to maintain genuine support in both camps. Pete Wiggs (b. 15 May 1966, Reigate, Surrey, England) and music journalist Bob Stanley (b. 25 December 1964, Horsham, Sussex, England) grew up together in Croydon, Surrey, England. In the early 80s, the pair began to experiment with party tapes, but did not make any serious inroads into the music business until forming Saint Etienne in 1988, taking their name from the renowned French football team. Relocating to Camden in north London, the pair recruited Moira Lambert of Faith Over Reason for a dance/reggae cover of Neil Young's 'Only Love Can Break Your Heart'. Issued in May 1990 on the aspiring Heavenly Records label, the single fared well in the nightclubs and surfaced on a magazine flexidisc remixed by label mates Flowered Up (who appeared on the b-side) in July. Another cover, indie guitar band the Field Mice's 'Kiss And Make Up', was given a similar dance pop overhaul for Saint Etienne's second single, fronted this time by New Zealand vocalist Donna Savage of Dead Famous People. Then came the infectious northern soul-tinged 'Nothing Can Stop Us' in May 1991. Its strong European feel reflected both their name, which helped attract strong support in France, and their logo (based on the European flag). It also benefited from Sarah Cracknell (b. 12 April 1967, Chelmsford, Essex, England)'s dreamy vocals, which would dominate Saint Etienne's debut, *Fox Base Alpha*, released in the autumn. Cracknell had formerly recorded with Prime Time. 'Only Love Can Break Your Heart' was reissued alongside the album, and provided them with a minor chart hit. Throughout the 90s the only critical barb that seemed to stick to Saint Etienne with any justification or regularity was that they were simply 'too clever for their own good'. A criticism which Stanley clearly could not abide: 'The image that the media has built up of us as manipulators really makes us laugh'. *So Tough* revealed a rich appreciation of the vital signs of British pop, paying homage to their forerunners without ever indulging in false flattery. *Tiger Bay*, toted as a folk-album, transcended a variety of musical genres with the sense of ease and propriety that Saint Etienne had essentially patented. The medieval folk/trance ballad, 'Western Wind', and the instrumental, 'Urban Clearway', redolent but not traceable to a dozen prime time television themes, were just two of the bookends surrounding one of the greatest albums of that year. It was followed by a fan club only release, *I Love To Paint*, limited to 500 copies. However, in 1995 Sarah Cracknell was said to be working on a solo album, having already recorded a duet with Tim Burgess of the Charlatans, 'I Was Born On Christmas Day', released at the end of 1993 in a failed attempt to mug the Christmas singles market.
Albums: *Fox Base Alpha* (Heavenly 1991), *So Tough* (Heavenly 1993), *You Need A Mess Of Help To Stand Alone* (Heavenly 1993), *Tiger Bay* (Heavenly 1994).

Saints

Formed in Brisbane, Australia in 1975, the Saints were the first Australian punk band to be recognized as being relevant by the UK media. The band comprised Chris Bailey (vocals/guitar), Kym Bradshaw (bass, replaced by Alisdair Ward in 1977), Ed Kuepper (guitar) and Ivor Hay (drums). They were plucked from obscurity via their single 'I'm Stranded' being reviewed as single of the week by the now defunct UK weekly music paper, *Sounds*. Following this, and encouraging sales for their debut album, the band based itself in the UK. Although labelled a punk band, the Saints did not strictly conform to the English perception of punk, as their roots were more R&B-based. A refusal to imitate the punk fashion was certainly instrumental in their rapid fall from favour, although they have since attained considerable cult status. Co-founder Kuepper left the group in 1978 to form the Laughing Clowns. The band stayed together long enough, with various personnel, to record two more albums, disbanding in 1979. Chris Bailey performed with a variety of musicians during the 80s, using the Saints' name, as well as touring solo, playing acoustic guitar. He reformed the original line-up of the Saints in 1984 (minus Kuepper) and has recorded constantly over the ensuing decade. As a retaliation to Bailey's continued usage of Kuepper's songs in the latter-day Saints line-up, Kuepper formed the Aints in 1990.
Albums: *I'm Stranded* (1977), *Eternally Yours* (1978), *Prehistoric Sounds* (1978), *Monkey Puzzle* (1981), *Casablanca* (1982), *A Little Madness To Be Free* (1984), *Live In A Mud Hut* (1985), *All Fool's Day* (1986), *Prodigal Son* (1989). Compilation: *Songs Of Salvation 1976-1988* (1991).

Salad

Salad

Fronted by ex-MTV presenter Marijne van der Vlugt, UK indie band Salad first took shape when she started writing songs with guitarist Paul Kennedy while working as a photographic fashion model. Signed to Island Records indie offshoot label Red, Salad offer a sparse sound which contrasts with the dense narratives of their lyrics. Both Vlugt and Kennedy, at one time romantically linked, are ex-film students. Kennedy's work includes *The Yoghurt Laugh*, while Vlugt used her own revolving, naked torso as the subject of her film project. Kennedy also worked for a design company before signing up with the band full time, painting betting shop windows. It was through van der Vlugt's original band, Merry Babes, that she was offered the MTV job, being asked for an audition after attempting to press the group's videos onto a member of staff. The song writing on their debut album, *Drink Me*, was split three ways, with Kennedy writing half the songs, Vlugt four and drummer Rob Wakeman (ex-Colenso Parade) three. Bass player Peter Brown is the final, non-writing member of the band. Following 'Your Ma', which explored illicit sexual desires à la *The Graduate*, 'Elixir', penned by Wakeman, gripped the charts in early 1995 portraying the destructiveness of the youth and beauty aesthetic associated with the world of fashion and advertising.

Album: *Drink Me* (Red 1995).

Sammy

Stars of the new 'lo-fi' breed of American artists, a pop format which accentuates the quality of songs above any production expertise and was partly coined in answer to Beck's phenomenal rise, Sammy are a duo of Luke Wood (guitar/bass) and Jesse Hartman (vocals/guitar) who rose to prominence when supporting that artist in the US and UK. The pair met when Hartman noted Wood's Velvet Underground T-shirt in the late 80s, discovering a musical kindred spirit. Together they recorded a debut album, titled simply *Debut Album*, in their occasional drummer Corn's Long Island, New York basement. Though Wood originally worked in the New York press office of Geffen Records, he used the Smells Like Records subsidiary imprint of Geffen artist Steve Shelley (Sonic Youth) to release it. The duo's relationship has become somewhat strained by Woods' job, after he moved to a marketing position with Geffen in Los Angeles. Hartman, still located in New York and employed in his brother's pizza parlour was forced to write with his partner by sending tapes back and forth. However, the approach did not unduly damage the quality of compositions on the album, and both have brought their individual experiences to bear on their songs. 'Rudy', for instance, concerns a 'crack smoking Rastafarian dishwasher' employed at the restaurant, with Hartman's writing primarily influenced by his abiding interest in film. The Long Island lifestyle certainly seemed to offer ample scope:

Sammy

'My piano teacher was a child molester, my high-school teacher was murdered by a gay prostitute and sometimes these characters find their way into my songs'. The album was followed by a 1995 EP, *Kings Of The Inland Empire*.
Album: *Debut Album* (Smells Like 1994).

Sarah Records

This fiercely independent UK Bristol-based label was formed in 1987 by Matt Haynes with Clare Wadd. Hayne's involvement with the UK independent music scene began with the fanzine publication, *Are You Scared To Get Happy?*, which supported the 'back-to-the-roots' idealism of the *New Musical Express*'s C86 compilation. He and Wadd cultivated a label determined to resist the growing fashion for CDs and 12-inch singles by blatantly promoting the 7-inch single and the anti-hi tech flexi-disc. Despite the later deviation from this ideology, the label have continued to promote this format, ignoring industry claims of the death of vinyl and the single format. The musical content, quintessentially English pop, is aptly summed up in the sleeve notes for *Shadow Factory*: the songs are 'full of wrong notes and wrong chords, but crammed with right Everything Elses'. Often derided by their contemporaries for being too soft and twee, the average Sarah group's lyrical content has tended not to stray very far from the timeless subject of boyfriends and girlfriends. Sarah's biggest asset, and the finest exponents of the 'Sarah sound', were, until their break-up in late 1991, the Field Mice. Amongst the other groups who have recorded for the label are the Sea Urchins (who were responsible for the first Sarah release, the *Pristine Christine* EP), the Orchids, the Springfields, Another Sunny Day, St. Christopher, 14 Iced Bears, the Wake, Heavenly and, from Australia, Even As We Speak. Periodically, Sarah issue compilations, containing previously released singles, with the album titles and sleeve artwork reflecting the label's fondness for the Bristol area. While not breaking down any barriers or creating any artistic revolution, Sarah quietly go about their business, ensuring an outlet for their type of music, treating it with love and respect - and continuing to annoy their detractors.
Compilations: *Shadow Factory* (Sarah 1988), *Temple Cloud* (Sarah 1990), *Air Balloon Road* (Sarah 1991, CD only release), *Glass Arcade* (Sarah 1991).

Saw Doctors

Originating in Tuam, County Galway, Eire, the Saw Doctors continue the practice of rock reacquainting itself with traditional Gaelic music. Inspired by the madcap antics of the Pogues et al, the medium is a furious medley of traditional and modern instruments, meshing together in boozy singalongs or sombre ballads. They signed to WEA in 1992 for *All The Way From Tuam*, but they had made their mark with an independent debut featuring 'I Usta Love Her'. The latter would become Eire's biggest selling single of all time. Peviously Leo Moran (vocals) had been playing guitar with the local reggae-folk outfit Too Much For The White Man. Fellow Tuam 'sham'. Singer Davy Corton (guitar) was recruited - or perhaps brought out of retirement might be a more accurate description, the father of three having served time some years previously with local punk force Blase X. The duo next recruited mandolin player and traditional

singer John 'Turps' Burke. Science student Pierce Doherty came in as bass player, the rhythm section filled out by the presence of ex-footballer John Donnelly. The startling sucess of 'I Usta Love Her' brought a re-release of debut single 'N17', and the band, fresh from supports to the Waterboys, were selling out venues on both sides of the Irish sea in their own right. They had been joined at this juncture by Tony Lambert (ex-Racing Cars, Alex Harvey Band; keyboards/piano accordion). Media assertions that these were 'designer bogmen' were enhanced by the choice of producer Phil Tennant (Levellers). However, support slots for bands such as Genesis at Knebworth demonstrated the breadth of their appeal.
Albums: *If This Is Rock 'n' Roll, I Want My Old Job Back* (1991), *All The Way From Tuam* (1992).

Scarlet Party

The short-lived Beatlesque quartet were formed in 1981 by brothers Graham Dye (b. 2 August 1961, Barking, Essex, England; vocals/guitar), Steven Dye (b. 17 September 1963, Barking, Essex, England; bass/vocals/keyboards) and were joined by Sean Heaphy (drums) and Mark Gilmour (guitar), younger brother of Pink Floyd's David Gilmour. Their strong composing ability led them to recording an album at the legendary Abbey Road studios, and performing live at the studio's 50th anniversary party. Much media attention was given to their debut '101 Damn-nations', which was released on the re-activated Parlophone, label 20 years after the Beatles' debut. Graham Dye's John Lennon-influenced vocals was another talking point and the band seemed set for stardom. This immaculate record surprisingly only reached the lower regions of the UK Top 50, and even more disappointing was that their strong follow-up 'Eyes Of Ice' failed to chart. Although they toured, supporting Steve Hackett, Huey Lewis and Sad Cafe, the band disintegrated through lack of commercial success. Graham returned in 1985 singing lead vocal on the Alan Parsons Project track 'Light Of The World', from *Stereotomy*, and again in 1990 with 'Little Hans' from Parsons' *Freudiana*. In 1992, the brothers were working on new material to submit to the record company that failed to capitalize on their remarkably fresh talent a decade earlier.

Scars

The Scars formed in Scotland - Bobby King (vocals), Paul Research (guitar), John Mackie (bass) and Calumn Mackay (drums) - evolved out of Edinburgh's late 70s punk milieu. Early live appearances were enthusiastic rather than accomplished, revealing the group's youthfulness, but they gradually asserted a competence and individuality. 'Adultery', released on the city's Fast Product label, showed an undoubted grasp of melody, and in 1981 the Scars were signed to Charisma Records' short-lived Pre subsidiary. *Author! Author!* was an excellent art/punk selection, but this highly promising set was the group's final recording, and they split up soon after its release.
Album: *Author! Author!* (Pre 1981).

Scratch Acid

Formed in Austin, Texas, USA in 1982, Scratch Acid

Saw Doctors

originally comprised of Steve Anderson (vocals), David Wm. Sims (guitar), Brett Bradford (guitar), David Yow (bass) and Rey Washam (drums), although Anderson was quickly ousted. The reshaped quartet made their live debut as an instrumental act, supporting the Butthole Surfers, following which Yow switched to vocals with Sims taking on bass. Scratch Acid established a reputation as one of the state's leading post-hardcore noise exponents, creating a sound inspired by Killdozer and Big Black. They issued *Scratch Acid* in 1984, but it was two years before the group began recording a full-length album. Although *Just Keep Eating* lacked the arresting power of its predecessor, it confirmed the group's ambition and originality. *Berserker*, completed later the same year, reaffirmed their influential status and is chiefly recalled for its opening track, 'Mary Had A Little Drug Problem'. Scratch Acid then undertook extended tours of the Europe and the USA, but relations within the group had become strained and they split up in May 1987 following a live date at Austin's Cave Club. Sims and Washam then joined Steve Albini (ex-Big Black) in Rapeman, following which Sims was reunited with Yow in the Jesus Lizard.
Albums: *Scratch Acid* (1984), *Just Keep Eating* (1986), *Berserker* (1986). Compilation: *The Greatest Gift* (1991).

Screaming Blue Messiahs

Rising from the ashes of Motor Boys Motor, the Screaming Blue Messiahs were essentially a vehicle for shaven-headed American singer/songwriter and guitarist Bill Carter. Supported by Kenny Harris (drums) and Chris Thompson (bass), Carter churned out a tight, venomous rock formula drawn from R&B and new wave, first heard on the well-received mini-album, *Good And Gone*. Originally issued on Ace's Big Beat label in July 1984, it made sufficient noise to attract WEA Records, who duly re-promoted it a year later. 'Twin Cadillac Valentine' (1985), was a razor-sharp slab of dynamic guitar rock and paved the way for the Screaming Blue Messiahs' most impressive album, *Gun Shy*, the following year. A session previously recorded for BBC disc jockey John Peel in 1984 saw the light of day nearly three years later on the Strange Fruit 'Peel Sessions' series. This preceded the the Screaming Blue Messiahs' relatively low key *Bikini Red* in September 1986. This spawned the closest thing to a hit single the Messiahs ever achieved with the eccentric 'I Wanna Be A Flintstone', which broached the Top 30 in February 1988. It was two years before a new Screaming Blue Messiahs set and when *Totally Religious* (on Atlantic Records) was released in October 1989, it failed to ignite an apathetic public. Although Carter's bite was still evident, the album disappointed in relation to past achievements and they disbanded soon after release. Harris and Thomas would go on to form Lerue.
Albums: *Good And Gone* (Big Beat 1984, mini-album), *Gun Shy* (WEA 1986), *Bikini Red* (WEA 1987), *Totally Religious* (Atlantic 1989). Compilation: *BBC Radio 1 Live In Concert* (Windsong 1992, rec. 1988).

Screaming Trees

Hard-drinking rock band from the rural community of Ellensburg, near Seattle, USA. The Screaming Trees blend 60s music (the Beach Boys being an obvious reference point)

with psychotic, pure punk rage. Not to be confused with the Sheffield, England, synthesizer group of the same name who were also operational in the mid-80s, the Connor brothers (Gary Lee; guitar and Van; bass) are among the largest men in rock, rivalled in their girth only by fellow Seattle heavyweights Poison Idea. The rest of the line-up comprises Mark Lanegan (vocals) and Barrett Martin (drums - replacing original encumbent Mark Pickerell in 1991). *Even If And Especially When*, the best of three strong albums for SST Records, included notable compositions like the live favourite, 'Transfiguration', which typified the group's blend of punk aggression and 60s mysticism. Major label debut *Uncle Anaesthesia* brought production from Terry Date and Soundgarden's Chris Cornell. By the time Screaming Trees moved to Epic Records they had embraced what one *Melody Maker* journalist called 'unashamed 70s Yankee rock', straddled by bursts of punk spite. Lanegan had by now released a solo, largely acoustic album, *The Winding Sheet*, for Sub Pop in 1990. This affecting, intensely personal collection included a cover of Leadbelly's 'Where Did You Sleep Last Night', which Kurt Cobain would later employ as the trump card in Nirvana's *MTV Unplugged* session. Other extra-curricular activities included Gary Lee Conner's Purple Outside project, and his brother Van fronting Solomon Grundy (one album each in 1990).
Albums: *Clairvoyance* (Velvetone 1986), *Even If And Especially When* (SST 1987), *Invisible Lantern* (SST 1988), *Buzz Factory* (SST 1989), *Uncle Anaesthesia* (Epic 1991), *Sweet Oblivion* (Epic 1992), *Change Has Come* (Epic 1993). Compilation: *Anthology* (SST 1991).

Scritti Politti

Scritti Politti was founded by a group of Leeds art students in 1978. By the time of their first single, 'Skank Bloc Bologna', the nucleus of the band was Green Gartside (b. 'Green' Strohmeyer-Gartside, 22 June 1956, Cardiff, Wales; vocals - who prefers not to reveal his actual first name), Matthew Kay (keyboards/manager) and Tom Morley (drums/programming) and Nial Jinks (bass, departed 1980). At this stage, the group was explicitly political (Green had been a Young Communist), encouraging listeners to create their own music in the face of the corporate record industry. Gartside also gained a reputation for convoluted word-play within his lyrics. This early *avant garde* phase gave way to a smooth sound which brought together elements of pop, jazz, soul and reggae on songs like 'The Sweetest Girl' (with Robert Wyatt on piano) and 'Asylums In Jerusalem'/'Jacques Derrida', which appeared on their debut album for Rough Trade Records, produced by Adam Kidron. Morley quit the group in November 1982, by which time Gartside *was* Scritti Politti. *Songs To Remember* became Rough Trade's most successful chart album; number 1 in the UK independent and, in the national chart, peaking at number 12 (beating Stiff Little Fingers' previous effort at number 14). After moving on to Virgin Records, Green linked up with New York musicians David Gamson (guitar) and Fred Maher (drums), who formed the basis of the group that made a series of UK hits in the years 1984-88. Produced by Arif Mardin, these included 'Wood Beez (Pray Like Aretha Franklin)' (number 10), 'Absolute' (number 17) and 'The

Word Girl' (number 6). A three-year silence was broken by 'Oh Patti (Don't Feel Sorry For Loverboy)', lifted from *Provision*, and boasting a trumpet solo by Miles Davis. Gartside again maintained a low-profile for two years after 'First Boy In This Town (Love Sick)', failed to break into the UK Top 60 in late 1988. He returned in 1991 with a revival of the Beatles' 'She's A Woman', featuring leading reggae star Shabba Ranks while another Jamaican star, Sweetie Irie, guested on a version of Gladys Knight And The Pips' 1967 hit, 'Take Me In Your Arms And Love Me'.

Albums: *Songs To Remember* (Rough Trade 1981), *Cupid And Psyche* (Virgin 1985), *Provision* (Virgin 1988).

Sea Urchins

The Sea Urchins were formed in West Bromwich, England, during 1986 by James Roberts (b. 4 March 1970, West Bromwich, West Midlands, England; vocals), Simon Woodcock (b. 2 December 1969, West Bromwich, West Midlands, England; guitar), Mark Bevin (b. 21 January 1970; bass), Bridget Duffy (b. 28 June 1970, Birmingham, England; tambourine, ex-drummer for the Velvet Underwear), Patrick Roberts (drums) and Robert Cooksey (b. 14 November 1969, Solihull, West Midlands, England; guitar). Two flexi-discs in the summer of 1987, 'Clingfilm' and 'Summershine', were available with several fanzines, and revealed the band's love of Byrds harmonies and the more tranquil aspects of the 60s. After Mark was replaced by Darren Martin (b. 25 March 1967) and Bridget had moved onto Vox organ, the Sea Urchins unleashed their first single, and the first for Bristol's Sarah Records in November 1987. The EP, *Pristine Christine*, was a well-received slice of jangly-guitar pop, but the following year's 'Solace' was stronger, the start of their self-confessed mod-rock phase. Both singles had fared well, but Sarah were reluctant to issue a complete album, and Bridget and Darren soon left, Simon switching to bass and James moving to guitar. Eventually, 'A Morning Odyssey' surfaced in the summer of 1990, but when the label refused to issue the rockier 'Low Scene', the band left Sarah for good. In the meantime, Welsh label Fierce issued a Sea Urchins ballad from 1988. The band signed to the Cheree label early in 1991 for 'Please Don't Cry', and were joined on stage by Andy Ellison (ex-John's Children and Radio Stars). In fact, John's Children's John Hewlett was to produce their next single, until Woodcock quit and the Sea Urchins split up after a particularly dismal gig in the summer of 1991. James, Patrick and Robert Cooksey were provisionally working as the Low Scene by the end of the year.

Secret Affair

Led by Ian Page (b. Ian Paine, 1960, England; vocals/trumpet/piano/organ), and Dave Cairns (b. 1959, England; guitar/vocals), Secret Affair, one of the most creative neo-mod groups of the late 70s, emerged out of the lightweight UK new wave band New Hearts who folded in 1978. New Hearts released two lacklustre singles. The Secret Affair line-up was completed by Dennis Smith (bass/vocals, ex-Advertising), and Chris Bennett (drums, ex-Alternative TV). Bennett did not work out and was replaced by Seb Shelton (ex-Young Bucks). They debuted supporting the Jam (as the New Hearts had once done), but made their name at the Bridge House Tavern in Canning Town, London, centre of the mod revival. They appeared on the *Mods Mayday* live compilation but then set up their own I-Spy label through Arista Records. Subsequently they toured with Purple Hearts and Back To Zero under the banner 'March Of The Mods'. Their first single, 'Time For Action', was an immediate success for both band and label, featuring Chris Gent (of the Autographs) on saxophone. They also signed Squire to the I-Spy label. Further singles in differing styles charted and the debut album was well received, particularly the epic title track which referred to their fan following. However, Shelton left late in 1980 to join the Up-Set, then Dexy's Midnight Runners and was replaced by Paul Bultitude. After two singles from the final Secret Affair album failed commercially, they disbanded. Dave Cairns went on to form the duo Flag, with Archie Brown, his former colleague from the Young Bucks. He subsequently formed another band called Walk On Fire with Dennis Smith. Page, who now writes fantasy books, formed Ian Page and Bop whose single 'Unity Street' created some interest. Bultitude joined the Mari Wilson's Wilsations and later founded the Dance Network label. Smith threw in his lot with Nik Kershaw's Krew, and Seb Shelton went on to manage, amongst others, the Woodentops.

Albums: *Glory Boys* (1979), *Behind Closed Doors* (1980), *Business As Usual* (1982).

Section 25

The nucleus of this Blackpool, Lancashire, England group started in November 1979 with brothers Vincent Cassidy (electronics/drum machine) and Larry Cassidy (guitar/vocals). In April 1978, a guitarist called Phil joined and Section 25 performed their first gig on 1 June. November of that year saw Phil replaced by Paul Wiggin. The group then introduced a second drummer, John and, since they were unable to find a suitable keyboard player, the appropriate passages were recorded on a tape machine, having first been constructed at SSRU, the group's rehearsal studio. The sound engineer, John Hurst, played a decisive role in the band's live sound. Their first single, 'Girls Don't Count', came out in early 1980. Over the next two years they toured Europe extensively and frequently supported New Order. After the release of their first album, Wiggin left after a gig in Helsinki. Lee Shallcross (drums) joined in February 1982 and toured with them in the USA. After their second album emerged on the Factory Benelux label, in February 1983, the Cassidys decided to cancel further live shows, drop all their old material and re-think their approach. By August 1983 they returned as a five piece with Angela Flowers (vocals/keyboards) and Jenny Ross (vocals/keyboards), with a first gig in December 1983. Two further albums followed in the mid-80s, but by then Section 25 had become very much the forgotten band at Factory, alongside the similarly unheralded Stockholm Monsters.

Albums: *Always Now* (Factory 1981), *The Key Of Dreams* (Factory 1982), *From The Hip* (Factory 1984), *Love And Hate* (Factory 1986).

Seefeel

An intriguing combination of introspective ambient textures (though they abhor the term) and propulsive guitars have distinguished Seefeel's nascent career. Guitarist and songwriter Mark Clifford answered an advert which Justin Fletcher (drums) had placed on a noticeboard at Goldsmith's College, London. They added Darren 'Delores Throb' Seymour (bass) and set about auditioning over 70 hopefuls for the singer's job. In the end Clifford responded to another ad, 'Wanting to join or form band into My Bloody Vlanetine and Sonic Youth', and called ex-animation student Sarah Peacock, who had placed it. As her tastes reflected Seefeel's personal creed, a distillation of MBV's guitar abuse with ambient's drone, she was immediately taken on board. The made their recording debut with the *More Like Space* EP - which confused BBC Radio 1 disc jockey John Peel as to whether to play it at 33rpm or 45rpm. Two EPs and an album for Too Pure Records quickly followed, 'Pure, Impure' featuring a spectral Aphex Twin remix. They also collaborated and toured with heroes the Cocteau Twins (the question Clifford asked Sarah when he rang her up was whether or not she liked them). Another EP in 1994, *Starethrough*, was their first for Warp Records, and again provoked interest, coinciding with and reflecting a move from indie to dance coverage in the UK music weeklies.
Album: *Quique* (Too Pure 1993).

Selecter

When Coventry's Specials needed a b-side for their own debut, 'Gangsters', they approached fellow local musician Noel Davies. With the assistance of John Bradbury aka Prince Rimshot (drums), and Barry Jones (trombone), Davies concocted the instrumental trac,k 'The Selecter'. Released on the Specials own 2-Tone label, the single took off with both sides receiving airplay. This meant that a band had to be formed to tour. Bradbury was busy drumming for the Specials and Jones had returned to his newsagent business so Davies assembled the Selecter Mk II. This consisted of Pauline Black (vocals), Noel Davis (guitar), Crompton Amanor (drums/vocals), Charles H. Bainbridge (drums), Gappa Hendricks, Desmond Brown (keyboards) and Charlie Anderson (bass). Anderson claims the original ska superstar, Prince Buster, amongst his ancestors. The Debut album featured the renowned ska trombonist Rico Rodriquez. Like many of the bands who first found fame on 2-Tone, the Selecter departed for pastures new - in this case 2-Tone's distributors, Chrysalis. They managed a string of successful singles such as 'On My Radio', 'Three Minute Hero', and 'Missing Words'. Black left in 1981 and recorded the single, 'Pirates Of The Airwaves', with Sunday Best before concentrating on acting. She would reappear to the general public as hostess of the children's pop/games show, *Hold Tight*. However, more impressive performances included a one-woman show, *Let Them Call It Jazz*, plus portrayals of Cleopatra and Billie Holiday, the latter bringing her the *Time Out* award for best actress in 1990. Black rejoined Selector on tour in 1991 as signs of a ska revival in London gained ground, though she also found time to host Radio 5's *Black To The Future* and complete her first novel, *The Goldfinches*. A phone call from Doug Trendle (aka

Buster Blood Vessel from Bad Manners) had prompted the Selecter's reformation, which culminated in the release of their first new material for over a decade in 1994.
Albums: *Too Much Pressure* (1980), *Celebrate The Bullet* (1981), *Out On The Streets* (1992), *The Happy Album* (1994). Compilation: *The Selecter & The Specials: Live In Concert* (1993).

Senseless Things

The Senseless Things formed around the enduring musical partnership of songwriter Mark Keds (vocals/guitar) and Morgan Nicholls (bass, originally guitar), who as 11 year old Twickenham, London, England schoolboys put together Wild Division in the early 80s. With the addition of drummer Cass 'Cade' Browne they became the Psychotics, playing various venues in their local area despite still being at school. Their first gig together as the Senseless Things followed at the subsequently demolished Clarendon in Hammersmith, London, in October 1986. Auxiliary members at this stage included a keyboard player Ben, then a guitarist, Gerry, who deputised for Nicholls while the latter was studying for his 'O' Levels. The definitive Senseless Things line-up finally evolved in summer 1987 when Nicholls returned to take over bass, with new recruit, former BBC clerk Ben Harding acquiring the vacant guitarist's role. Taking their musical cue from the Ramones and the Dickies, and their spiritual lead from fellow guitar outfit Mega City Four, the quartet embarked upon a hectic touring schedule which unveiled their roguish charm and obvious potential. Their youthful zest initially outshone their musical achievements, which were first aired for public consideration on a 7-inch compilation single given away with issue 6 of London fanzine *Sniffin' Rock*. By March 1988 the band had attracted the attention of BBC disc jockey John Peel, who invited them to record the first of two sessions for his programme. Following another fanzine release, three tracks headed by 'I'm Moving', a friend offered to finance a 'proper' release. The impressive 'Up And Coming' 12-inch followed, then 'Girlfriend'/'Standing In The Rain', for Way Cool Records. The musical imbalance which had seen them sacrifice melody for speed had, by the time, been thoroughly redressed. The band's debut mini-album, entitled *Postcard C.V.*, arrived in November 1989. It comprised 22 minutes of scratchy, boisterous punk pop now imbued with more shading and subtlety. Continuing to trawl the independent wasteland, the band joined What Goes On Records just as it collapsed, but the situation was rescued by Vinyl Solution subsidiary Decoy Records, who released the four track EP, *Is It Too Late?*, in May 1990. The group stayed with Decoy for 'Can't Do Anything', which prefaced an appearance at the Reading Festival, but the ground swell of live support eventually saw them snapped up by Epic Records at the start of 1991. The subsequent *The First Of Too Many* introduced acoustic guitars and gentler moods to the punky blitzes of yore, and 'Got It At The Delmar' scuttled into the Top 60 of the UK singles chart. Two further Top 20 singles followed in 1992, 'Easy To Smile' and 'Hold It Down'. The first single from 1993's *Empire Of The Senseless*, 'Homophobic Asshole', was a brave statement but one which ultimately alienated radio programmers. Despite continuing to write quality songs (becoming more reminiscent of the Replacements as time passed by) the momentum had been irretrievably lost. Rumours circulated in March 1995 of the band's impending collapse, having been dropped by their record company. Of the band's new album, *Taking Care Of Business*, guitarist Mark Keds would remark: 'We've achieved a very rounded and accomplished rock record, which is what we always set out to do. We're not going to repeat it. Obviously, we'll be touring the album… after that, I think it's going to be all change. Whatever comes next is going to be completely different.' Keds was falsely rumoured to be joining the Wildhearts, with whom he had formerly appeared, while it was also suggested that drummer Cass might link with friends Urge Overkill.

Albums: *Postcard C.V.* (Way Cool 1989, mini-album), *The First Of Too Many* (Epic 1992), *Empire Of The Senseless* (Epic 1993), *Taking Care Of Business* (Epic 1995).

Senser

This multi-ethnic seven-piece south London band were conceived in 1987. Their *metier* is the synthesis of numerous styles of music into a format which at once stimulates both the feet and grey matter. Fronted by Heitham Al-Sayed (raps/vocals/percussion), Senser proved the only band of their generation to see features in magazines dedicated to heavy metal, hip hop and indie music - and few were in any way grudging. The other members of the band are Nick Michaelson (guitar), Andy 'Awe' (a DJ who once held the national high score on the Asteroids video game), Haggis (engineer), James Barrett (bass), John Morgan (drums) and Kersten Haigh (vocals/flute). This line-up was cemented in 1992, as they began the first of two tours supporting Ozric Tentacles, plus low-key squat and benefit gigs. The first seeds of the band were sewn when Michaelson and Barrett met at a guitarist competition at the Forum, in London. Ex-school friend Haigh fronted the band from 1988 onwards, before the Senser name had been invoked, bringing vocals inspired from her journeys in India. Wimbledon resident Al-Sayed joined in 1991 as a drummer, but soon progressed to rapping duties as the band attempted to tackle their own version of Public Enemy's 'She Watch Channel Zero'. Their 1993 singles, 'Eject' and 'The Key', brought rave reviews across dance and indie periodicals, with their ferocious musical clatter evading categorisation. 'Switch', entering the UK Top 40, in turn announced a Top 5 debut album, *Stacked Up*, and a widely applauded appearance on the 1994 Glastonbury Festival stage. Al-Sayed, meanwhile, was particularly vocal in espousing the cause of the travelling community, under threat in 1994 from a new Criminal Justice bill. Although his throat problems prevented the band from building on their impact for much of 1994, *Stacked Up* would go on to over 80,000 sales.

Album: *Stacked Up* (Ultimate 1994).

Video: *States Of Mind* (1995).

Serious Drinking

Formed after attendance at the University Of East Anglia, Norwich, England in February 1981, this motley assortment of ex-students carved a niche for themselves in the independent charts of the early 80s by injecting their songs with comedic candour. Jem (bass) was an outspoken member of the Socialist Workers Party, although Lance (the only one not to attend UEA, drums), Martin Simon (ex-Higsons) and Eugene (the two singers) and Andy (ex-Farmers Boys; guitar) were more concerned with football and alcoholic beverages. The explanation for the presence of two singers was typically straightforward: 'Eugene is in the band because Martin wanted a lift to a practice and Eugene had a car and he's just stayed ever since'. They took their name from a headline announcing an interview with the Cockney Rejects in *Sounds*. Pigeonholed as leaders of some mythical 'herbert' movement, they did nevertheless have a penchant for traditional British leisure pursuits. The singles 'Love On The Terraces' and 'Hangover' both fared well in the independent charts, the former produced by Mark Bedford of Madness. The latter included the impressive 'Baby I'm Dying A Death' as its b-side, culled from the band's popular John Peel radio session. 1983's *The Revolution Begins At Closing Time* and *They May Be Drinkers Robin, But They're Still Human Beings* fully displayed their eccentricity. The band's philosophy was still crystal clear, 'Basically what we're saying is go out, get drunk and enjoy yourself, and don't be nasty to other people.' Unfortunately, after 'Country Girl Became Drugs And Sex Punk' (another borrowed headline), both Gem and Lance departed. Karen Yarnell (ex-Gymslips) joined on drums and they released *Love On The Terraces*, a collection of favourite tracks and new recordings to coincide with the World Cup in 1990. *Stranger Than Tannadice* followed and was accompanied by sporadic live appearances.

Albums: *The Revolution Begins At Closing Time* (1983), *They May Be Drinkers Robin, But They're Still Human Beings* (1984), *Love On The Terraces* (1990), *Stranger Than Tannadice - The Hits, Misses and Own Goals Of Serious Drinking* (1991).

Servants

David Westlake's carefully crafted guitar pop tunes were the central attraction of west London's Servants. Accompanied by John Mahon (guitar), Philip King (bass - later with Felt, Biff Bang Pow!, the Apple Boutique and See See Rider), and John Wills (drums), the band featured on the *New Musical Express C86* cassette ('Transparent'). Their first single, 'She's Always Hiding', surfaced around the same time on the Head label, followed by a four-track EP, *The Sun, A Small Star*. But Westlake left soon after, joining Creation Records, forming Westlake and releasing a self-titled mini-album in 1987. The Servants second line-up featured Luke Haines (b. 7 October 1967, Walton-On-Thames, Surrey, England; vocals/guitar) and Alice Readman (b. 1967, Harrow, Middlesex, England; bass), alongside former Housemartins' drummer Hugh Whitaker. The results were restricted to a one-off single, 'It's My Turn', and a lone album. Haines and Readman would go on to greater success in the Auteurs.

Album: *Disinterested* (Paperhouse 1990).

Sex Gang Children

This London based post punk/gothic band were briefly in vogue in the early 80s. They were built around vocalist Andi Sex Gang, who talked himself into support slots for which he needed to quickly assemble a new band. He eventually settled on Dave Roberts (bass), Terry McLeay (guitar) and Rob Stroud (drums), who played their first gig under the name Panic Button. The name Sex Gang Children was lifted from a William Burroughs book and was actually on a list of names that fellow King's Road fashion victim Boy George was toying with. It later transpired that Boy George had in turn taken it from Malcolm McLaren's original suggestion for a moniker for the band which would become Bow Wow Wow. By 1982 a number of bands in the same mould began breaking through in the capital. Sex Gang Children's first vinyl release was a 12-inch titled 'Beasts', produced by Nicky Garrett (ex-UK Subs), after which Tony James (Generation X, later Sigue Sigue Sputnik) began to take an interest in the band. Their most fondly remembered release, 'Into The Abyss', closed 1982 with their debut long player arriving early the next year. The single lifted from it, 'Sebastiane', featured Jinni Hewes from Marc And The Mambas on violin. Andi then performed a debut with Marc Almond ('The Hungry Years') for the compilation *The Whip*, which also included a contribution from Roberts' other band, Car Crash International. Stroud left to join Pink And Black (featuring future All About Eve bass player Andy Cousins), and was replaced by Nigel Preston (ex-Theatre Of Hate). He stayed long enough to record the single 'Mauritia Mayer', before he took part in a bizarre 'drummers' swop with Ray Mondo of Death Cult. Events took a further strange turn when the latter was deported back to Sierra Leone for passport irregularities after a USA tour. Roberts also departed, leaving Andi and McLeay to recruit Cam Campbell (bass), and Kevin Matthews (drums). However, only one single, 'Deiche', was released before the band disintegrated and Andi set out on a solo career.

Albums: *Song And Legend* (Illuminated 1983), *Beasts* (Illuminated 1983), *Live* (Arkham 1984), *Re-enter The Abyss* (Dojo 1986), *Blind* (Jungle 1993).

Sex Pistols

This incandescent UK punk group came together under the aegis of entrepreneur Malcolm McLaren during the summer of 1975. Periodically known as the Swankers, with lead vocalist Wally Nightingale, they soon metamorphosed into the Sex Pistols with a line up comprising: Steve Jones (b. 3 May 1955, London, England; guitar), Paul Cook (b. 20 July 1956, London, England; drums), Glen Matlock (b. 27 August 1956, Paddington, London, England; bass) and Johnny Rotten (b. John Lydon, 31 January 1956, Finsbury Park, London, England; vocals). By 1976 the group was playing irregularly around London and boasted a small following of teenagers, whose spiked hair, torn clothes and safety pins echoed the new fashion that McLaren was transforming into commodity. The group's gigs became synonymous with violence, which reached a peak during the 100 Club's Punk Rock Festival when a girl was blinded in a glass-smashing incident involving the group's most fearful follower, Sid Vicious. The adverse publicity did not prevent the group from signing to EMI Records later that year when they also released their first single, 'Anarchy In The UK'. From Rotten's sneering laugh at the opening of the song to the final seconds of feedback, it was a riveting debut. The Pistols promoted the work on London Weekend Television's

Today programme, which ended in a stream of four-letter abuse that brought the group banner headlines in the following morning's tabloid press. More controversy ensued when the group's 'Anarchy' tour was decimated and the single suffered distribution problems and bans from shops. Eventually, it peaked at number 38 in the UK charts. Soon after, the group was dropped from EMI in a blaze of publicity. By February 1977, Matlock was replaced by punk caricature Sid Vicious (b. John Simon Ritchie, 10 May 1957, London, England, d. 2 February 1979). The following month, the group was signed to A&M Records outside the gates of Buckingham Palace. One week later, A&M cancelled the contract, with McLaren picking up another parting cheque of £40,000. After reluctantly signing to the small label Virgin Records, the group issued 'God Save The Queen'. The single tore into the heart of British Nationalism at a time when the populace was celebrating the Queen's Jubilee. Despite a daytime radio ban the single rose to number 1 in the *New Musical Express* chart (number 2 in the 'official' charts, though some commentators detected skullduggery at play to prevent it from reaching the top spot). The Pistols suffered for their art as outraged royalists attacked them whenever they appeared on the streets. A third single, the melodic 'Pretty Vacant' (largely the work of the departed Matlock) proved their most accessible single to date and restored them to the Top 10. By the winter the group hit again with 'Holidays In The Sun' and issued their controversially-titled album, *Never Mind The Bollocks - Here's The Sex Pistols*. The work rocketed to number 1 in the UK album charts amid partisan claims that it was a milestone in rock. In truth, it was a more patchy affair, containing a preponderance of previously released material which merely underlined that the group was running short of ideas. An ill-fated attempt to capture the group's story on film wasted much time and revenue, while a poorly received tour of America fractured the Pistols' already strained relationship. In early 1978, Rotten announced that he was leaving the group after a gig in San Francisco. According to the manager Malcolm McLaren he was fired. McLaren, meanwhile, was intent on taking the group to Brazil in order that they could be filmed playing with the train robber, Ronnie Biggs. Vicious, incapacitated by heroin addiction, could not make the trip, but Jones and Cook were happy to indulge in the publicity stunt. McLaren mischievously promoted Biggs as the group's new lead singer and another controversial single emerged: 'Cosh The Driver'. It was later retitled 'No One Is Innocent (A Punk Prayer)' and issued as a double a-side with Vicious's somehow charming rendition of the Frank Sinatra standard, 'My Way'. McLaren's movie was finally completed by director Julien Temple under the title *The Great Rock 'n' Roll Swindle*. A self-conscious rewriting of history, it callously wrote Matlock out of the script and saw the unavailable Rotten relegated to old footage. While the film was being completed, the Pistols' disintegration was completed. Vicious, now the centre of the group, recorded a lame version of Eddie Cochran's 'C'mon Everybody' before returning to New York. On 12 October 1978, his girlfriend Nancy Spungen was found stabbed in his hotel room and Vicious was charged with murder. While released on bail, he suffered a fatal overdose of heroin and died peacefully in his sleep on the morning of 2 February 1979. Virgin Records continued to issue the desultory fragments of Pistols work that they had on catalogue, including the appropriately titled compilation, *Flogging A Dead Horse*. The group's impact as the grand symbol of UK punk rock has ensured their longevity. The unholy saga appropriately ended in the High Court in 1986 when Rotten and his fellow ex-Pistols won substantial damages against their former manager.

Albums: *Never Mind The Bollocks - Here's The Sex Pistols* (Virgin 1977). Compilations: *The Great Rock 'N' Roll Swindle* (Virgin 1979), *Some Product - Carri On Sex Pistols* (Virgin 1979), *Flogging A Dead Horse* (Virgin 1980), *Kiss This* (Virgin 1992).

Shack

Formed in 1986 by brothers Mick (b. 28 November 1961, Liverpool, England) and John Head (b. 4 October 1965), Shack emerged from the ashes of the Pale Fountains. Having had their fingers burnt by the major records industry - the Pale Fountains reached number 46 in the UK charts with 'Thank You', but were generally misunderstood by their employers - Shack joined up with independent label the Ghetto Recording Company. Experts at the cleverly understated melodic guitar pop song, 1988 saw the release of their acclaimed debut album, *Zilch*. Yet instead of persevering with their commercial instincts, Shack laid low until reappearing with a single in 1991 and a planned second album for the year after, which never materialised.

Album: *Zilch* (Ghetto 1988).

Sham 69

Originally formed in London, England, in 1976, this five-piece skinhead/punk-influenced group comprised Jimmy Pursey (vocals), Albie Slider (bass), Neil Harris (lead guitar), Johnny Goodfornothing (rhythm guitar) and Billy Bostik (drums). Pursey was a fierce, working-class idealist, an avenging angel of the unemployed, who ironically sacked most of the above line-up within a year due to their lack of commitment. A streamlined aggregation featuring Dave Parsons (guitar), Dave Treganna (bass) and Mark Cain (drums) helped Pursey reach the UK charts with a series of anthemic hits including 'Angels With Dirty Faces', 'If The Kids Are United', 'Hurry Up Harry' and 'Hersham Boys'. Although Pursey championed proletarian solidarity, his rabble-rousing all too often brought violence and disruption from a small right-wing faction causing wary promoters to shun the group. After a troubled couple of years attempting to reconcile his ideals and their results, Pursey elected to go solo, but his time had passed. The group reformed in the early 90s and performed at punk nostalgia/revival concerts.

Albums: *Tell Us The Truth* (Polydor 1978), *That's Life* (Polydor 1978), *Adventures Of The Hersham Boys* (Polydor 1979), *The Game* (Polydor 1980), *Volunteer* (Legacy 1988), *Kings & Queens* (CMP 1993). Compilations: *The First, The Best And The Last* (Polydor 1980), *Angels With Dirty Faces - The Best Of* (Receiver 1986), *Live And Loud* (Link 1987), *Live And Loud Vol. 2* (Link 1988), *The Best Of The Rest Of Sham 69* (Receiver 1989), *Complete Live* (Castle 1989), *Live At The Roxy* (Receiver 1990, rec. 1977), *BBC Radio 1 Live In Concert* (Windsong 1993).

Shamen

From the ashes of the moderately successful Alone Again Or (named after the track from Love's *Forever Changes*) in 1986, the Shamen had a profound effect upon contemporary pop music over the next half decade. Formed in Aberdeen by Colin Angus (b. 24 August 1961, Aberdeen, Scotland; bass), Peter Stephenson (b. 1 March 1962, Ayrshire, Scotland), Keith McKenzie (b. 30 August 1961, Aberdeen, Scotland) and Derek McKenzie (b. 27 February 1964, Aberdeen, Scotland; guitar), the Shamen's formative stage relied heavily on crushing, psychedelic rock played by a relatively orthodox line-up. Their debut album, *Drop*, captured a sense of their colourful live shows and sealed the first chapter of the band's career. Soon after, Colin Angus became fascinated by the nascent underground hip hop movement. Derek McKenzie was rather less enamoured with the hardcore dance explosion and departed, allowing William Sinnott (b. 23 December 1960, Glasgow, Scotland, d. 23 May 1991; bass) to join the ranks and further encourage the Shamen's move towards the dancefloor. In 1988, their hard-edged blend of rhythms, guitars, samples, sexually explicit slideshows and furious rhetoric drew anger from feminists, politicians and - after the scathing 'Jesus Loves Amerika' single - religious groups. That same year the band relocated to London, slimmed down to the duo of Angus and Sinnott who concentrated on exploring the areas of altered states with mind-expanding psychedelics. By 1990 the Shamen's influence - albeit unwitting - was vividly realised as the much-touted indie-dance crossover saw bands fuse musical cultures with the likes of Jesus Jones openly confessing to the Shamen's groundbreaking lead. By this time the Shamen themselves had taken to touring with the 'Synergy' show, a unique four hour extravaganza featuring rappers and designed to take the band even further away from their rock roots. After four years of such imaginative adventures into sound, 1991 promised a huge breakthrough for the Shamen and their fluctuating creative entourage. Unfortunately, just as the group inexorably toppled towards commercial riches, Will Sinnott drowned off the coast of Gomera, one of the Canary Islands, on the 23rd of May. With the support of Sinnott's family, the Shamen persevered with a remix of 'Move Any Mountain (Pro Gen '91)' which climbed into the Top 10 of the UK chart, a fitting farewell to the loss of such a creative force. Mr C (b. Richard West), a cockney rapper, DJ and head of the Plink Plonk record label, had joined the band for a section of 'Move Any Mountain (Pro Gen '91)'. Although many found his patois ill-fitting, his rhymes founded the spring board for UK chart success 'LSI', followed by the number 1 'Ebeneezer Goode' - which was accused in many quarters for extolling the virtues of the Ecstasy drug ('E's Are Good, E's Are Good, E's Are Ebeneezer Goode'). The Shamen denied all, and moved on with the release of *Boss Drum*. Its title track provided a deeply affecting dance single, complete with lyrics returning the band to their original, shamanic ethos of universal rhythms. Placed next to the teen-pop of 'LSI' and 'Ebeneezer Goode', such innovative work reinforced the Shamen's position as the wild cards of the UK dance scene.

Albums: *Drop* (Moshka 1987), *In Gorbachev We Trust* (Demon 1989), *Phorward* (Moshka 1989), *En-Tact* (One

Little Indian 1990), *En-Tak* (One Little Indian 1990), *Progeny* (One Little Indian 1991), *Boss Drum* (One Little Indian 1992), *Different Drum* (One Little Indian 1992), *The Shamen On Air* (Band Of Joy 1993).

Shampoo

Adorned in ra ra skirts, pigtails and dayglo T-shirts, Shampoo's arrival on the 1994 British pop scene brought kitsch back to centre stage with a bang. 'The Kylie and Dannii of Baby Tears Punk Rock Pop', as the *New Musical Express* decreed, Jacqui Blake (b. c.1977) and Carrie Askew (b. c.1975) arrived fresh from school in Plumstead, London. The duo's early endeavours included writing a fanzine, *Last Exit*, about the Manic Street Preachers, appearing in one of their videos and earning a reputation for being 'around town'. They then met St. Etienne's Bob Stanley at a party and talked him into giving them a deal on his Icerink label. The resultant single, 'Blisters & Bruises', earned a *Melody Maker* Single Of The Week award for its naive, spunky charm. They wrote the lyrics, while Lawrence of Felt/Denim wrote the music and produced. Shampoo were fully launched with the release of the delinquent 'Trouble' and hopelessly amateur 'Viva La Megababes', the latter a cheap and unruly take on the Voodoo Queens' 'Supermodel': 'Riot girls, diet girls, who really gives a fuck'. 'Trouble', meanwhile, was bizzarely used by BBC television to publicise a Frank Bruno boxing fight, and sold over 150,000 copies. Fabulously popular in Japan, their lyrical concerns for their debut album had expanded to encompass video games, throwing up after dodgy kebabs and sentimental love songs.
Album: *We Are Shampoo* (Food 1994).

Shed Seven

York, England band Shed Seven comprise Rick Witter (b. c.1973; lead vocals), Tom Gladwin (b. c.1973; bass), Paul Banks (b. c.1973; guitar) and Alan Leach (b. c.1970; drums). Together they brought a flash of domesticity and anti-glamour to the independent scene of the mid-90s - their interests including slot machines, bad television (Banks allegedly writes songs while watching *Prisoner Cell Block H*) and cheap alcohol. There was a refreshingly parochial atmosphere to their profile - best symbolised by the fact that Leach is the boyfriend of Witter's sister - despite the fact that their primary influences included Happy Mondays and Stone Roses. The only hint of celebrity, aside from Witter once coming second in a karaoke competition in Cyprus, involved their vocalist's dalliance with Donna Matthews from Elastica. However, as their recorded output demonstrated, and many critics suggested, it remained a thin line between level-headedness and mundanity. To their credit, Shed Seven were unconcerned with the trappings of cool, happily signing to a major, Polydor Records, and making their debut with 'Mark'. After playing the *New Musical Express*' On Into 94 gig, they would make two appearances on *Top Of The Tops*, and score two Top 30 singles and a Top 20 album. The band was clearly at their best live, though, and their 1994 sell-out tours cemented a strong following.
Album: *Change Giver* (Polydor 1994).

Shellac

Rock *enfant-terrible* Steve Albini (ex-Big Black/Rapeman) formed this trio on an informal basis in 1993. Bouyed by the attention garnered in the wake of his producing *In Utero* for Nirvana, Albini (velocity), Bob Weston (mass) and Todd Turner (time) issued 'The Rude Gesture A Pictorial History', the first of two limited-issue singles to appear on the trio's own label. It offered all the trademarks of Albini's previous groups - awkward time changes, thundering bass lines, screaming guitar and frantic vocals. Weston was ex-Volcano Suns, while Trainer had worked with Rifle Sport and Breaking Circus. 'Uranus' followed in similar, exciting fashion. A third single, 'The Admiral', came in a sleeve still showing Albini's caustic remarks referring to how it should be designed. A different version of the 'A' side appeared on *At Action Park*, which developed Albini's distinctive style without subverting its power and direction. His work remains as challenging as ever.
Album: *At Action Park* (Touch And Go 1994).

Shelley, Pete

b. Peter McNeish, 17 April 1955, Leigh, Lancashire, England. When the Buzzcocks disbanded in 1981, Shelley soon embarked on a variety of solo projects. In fact, his solo history extended before, and during, the Buzzcocks career. As one of the Invisible Girls, he helped out on John Cooper Clarke albums while the Buzzcocks were still active. Around the same time he also launched his own independent label, Groovy. On this he released *Free Agents* (subtitled *Three Pounds And Three Pounds Thirty Three R.R.P.*, which was also its original price). This consisted primarily of tape loops and feedback, and general free-for-all improvisation. Meanwhile on New Hormones (the Buzzcocks original label) came *The Tiller Boys* EP, another of Shelley's pet projects. The second release on Groovy was *Sky Yen*, a solo album originally recorded by Shelley in 1974 using electronic instruments. Much akin to work by Kraftwerk, it prefaced the electro dance feel of his later solo work. However, it was 1982's *Homosapien*, a weighty slice of electro-pop concerning bisexuality, which marked the high point in Shelley's solo career. It was produced by Martin Rushent as a launch for his Generic label, and caused much discussion of Shelley's sexuality, and a re-examination of his Buzzcocks lyrics. *XL1* in 1983 was more tame, although it did boast the novelty of including a Sinclair computer programme that reproduced the lyrics. One review compounded matters by mentioning no less than five Buzzcocks titles in comparison, which was perhaps a trifle unfair. Again, it was produced by Rushent, this time with a predominantly disco feel. After 1986's *Heaven And The Sea* Shelley sought the comfort of a band again, and attempted to retain anonymity in Zip.
Albums: *Free Agents* (1980), *Sky Yen* (1980), *Homosapien* (1982), *XL1* (1983), *Heaven And The Sea* (1986).

Shelleyan Orphan

It was in 1980 that Caroline Crawley (vocals/clarinet) and Jemaur Tayle (acoustic guitar/vocals) first got together in their hometown of Bournemouth, England, and discovered they had a mutual appreciation of the poet Shelley. Consequently they took the name of their band from his poem, 'Spirit Of Solitude'. Neither of them could read or write music, or play any of their chosen instruments so, in 1982, Crawley quit her A-Level studies and they moved to London in search of a string section and oboist, with the intention of using these traditionally classical instruments along with the guitar and their two voices in a pop context. Inspired by T-Rex, Nick Drake and Van Morrison, the self-taught duo found their musicians and touted themselves around London, until in June 1984 they won a Kid Jensen BBC radio session. Following a baffling support to the Jesus And Mary Chain at the ICA, where their classical ensemble shocked the assembled crowd, they were swiftly signed up by Rough Trade Records. Two sweet and mellow singles followed, 'Cavalry Of Cloud' and 'Anatomy Of Love', both to ecstatic reviews, and after a memorable appearance on *The Tube* television programme, their controversial debut, *Helleborine*, was released in May 1987. Its swirling romanticism was promptly dubbed 'pretentious' by the music press, gaining Shelleyan Orphan the title of 'Pre-Raphaelite Fruitcakes'. The next two years were spent writing, recording and maturing their sound, and with the addition of more traditional rock instruments to their string orientated line-up, the band produced the more immediate and accessible *Century Flower*. The album was a significant step forward, using unusual time signatures and baroque instrumentation to spectacular effect. The richly harmonic 'Shatter' and superb 'Timeblind' were among the highlights. Supporting the Cure across Europe and America, they showed another side to their gentle image and betrayed a new found energy and exuberance.

Albums: *Helleborine* (Rough Trade 1987), *Century Flower* (Rough Trade 1989), *Humroot* (1993).

Shimmy-Disc

This idiosyncratic label was founded in New York in 1987 by Mark Kramer, formerly of Shockabilly and the Butthole Surfers. Having built his own studio, Noise New York, Kramer set about recording acts of a similar irascible nature. The label's first release, *20th Anniversary Of The Summer Of Love*, was a various artists' compendium which included contributions by Krackhouse, Men & Volts, Allen Ginsberg, Half Japanese and Tuli Kupferberg, many of whom would later record for Shimmy-Disc. The set also featured Bongwater, the group Kramer forged with performance artist Ann Magnuson, whose enthralling double set, *Breaking No New Ground*, was the label's second release. Shimmy-Disc allowed Kramer to indulge his musical fantasies; it provided the vehicle for another of his own bands, B.A.L.L. and several collaborative projects, notably with Jad Fair and John S. Hall. Shimmy Disc reissued albums by Shockabilly and allowed mavericks exposure which might otherwise have been denied them. Zany Brooklyn sextet, When People Were Shorter And Lived Near The Water, unleashed their 15-song 'tribute' to pop crooner Bobby Goldsboro (*Bobby*), before doing the same to *Porgy And Bess* with *Porgy*. Kramer also made international signings, releasing albums by British acts the Walkingseeds and Jellyfish Kiss and Japanese hardcore act, the Boredoms. A highlight of the label's catalogue was *Rutles Highway Revisited*, a various artists' tribute to Beatles' spoof, the Rutles. Das Damen, Galaxie 500 and Peter Stampfel of the Holy Modal Rounders were among the assembled cast; the liner notes were written by Rutles' creator Neil Innes in his guise as 'Ron Nasty'. Late-period Shimmy-Disc signings include the sublime Lydia Husik but, following the release of *The Guilt Trip*, Kramer's solo debut, the label's future was thrown into doubt when Ann Magnuson took out legal action on the acrimonious break-up of Bongwater. Kramer did begin two subsidiary company's, See Eye and Kokopop, in 1993, but at the time of writing all outlets are in limbo.

Shirts

This US pop-rock act were formed from the ashes of the Lackeys and Schemers, who played several low-key gigs in the early 70s. The line-up featured Annie Golden (b. c.1953; vocals), Ronnie Ardito (guitar), Artie La Monica (guitar), Robert Racioppo (bass), John Piccolo (keyboards) and John 'Zeeek' Criscioni (drums). All members provided songs either on their own or in partnership with other personnel. Golden also worked as an actor, having a leading role in the screen adaptation of *Hair* in 1979. Other names which were suggested for the assembly included the Pants and the Sleeves. Shirts was the eventual choice, with the proviso that it should be pronounced Shoits in a thick New York accent. Unsurprisingly this tradition has lapsed with time. They initially earned a crust as a Top 40 covers band playing in bars, before graduating to clubs like CBGB's in 1975. Their first single, 'Tell Me Your Plans', was a surprise hit in Europe. Their big break came with a Peter Gabriel tour, before further singles and albums including the single 'Laugh And Walk Away'. Golden released a solo single in 1984, but the band disappeared from the annals of rock taking their pronunciation with them. They did reunite, however, for one night in 1993 to celebrate the 20th anniversary of their spiritual home, CBGB's.

Albums: *The Shirts* (Capitol 1978), *Street Light Shine* (Capitol 1979), *Inner Sleeve* (Capitol 1980).

Shockabilly

Formed in 1982 by guitarist Eugene Chadbourne, bassist Kramer and drummer Dave Licht, Shockabilly produced music that sounded like an unholy combination of the Electric Prunes and Karlheinz Stockhausen. They specialized in outrageous covers - 'Psychotic Reaction', '19th Nervous Breakdown', 'Day Tripper', 'Purple Haze' - and also more obscure items by John Lee Hooker, John Fogerty and Syd Barrett. When the song appears familiar it gives the listener a thread on which to hang the power trio-chaos they liked to indulge in. Chadbourne's background was in rock, blues, late 60s free jazz and free improvisation - he put it all into Shockabilly with an energy and spleen that gained a response from the more adventurous post-punk audiences. After they folded in 1985 Chadbourne, an inspired songwriter, pursued a solo career while Kramer set up Shimmy Disk, one of the great radical rock labels of the 80s and 90s.

Albums: *The Dawn Of Shockabilly* (1982), *Earth Versus Shockabilly* (1983), *Colosseum* (1984), *Vietnam* (1984), *Heaven* (1985). Compilation: *Greatest Hits* (1983).

Shoes

Formed in Zion, Illinois, USA, this group comprised Jeff Murphy (vocal/guitar), brother John Murphy (bass/vocal), Gary Klebe (guitar/vocal) and Skip Meyer (drums). They preferred composing and recording on a TEAC four-track machine in the Murphy's living room to concert performances. When an architecture scholarship took Klebe to France in 1974, the others taped *One In Versailles* and pressed 300 copies to surprise him. On his return, this privatized policy continued with *Bazooka*, a tape circulated among immediate fans. Containing 15 original compositions, *Black Vinyl Shoes* reached a wider public that included Greg Shaw, who signed them to his Bomp label for a one-shot double a-side, 'Tomorrow Night'/'Okay'. The former was re-made in 1979 in England during sessions for *Present Tense*, the group's debut on Elektra Records. Subsequent product did not, however, include the hits needed to walk the Shoes into the pop mainstream.
Albums: *One In Versailles* (1974), *Black Vinyl Shoes* (1977), *Present Tense* (1979), *Tongue Twister* (1980), *Silhouettes* (1984).

Shonon Knife

Japanese sisters Atsuko Yamano (b. 22 February c.1960, Osaka, Japan) and Naoko Yamano (b. 18 December c.1961, Osaka, Japan) with Michie Nakatani (b. 8 October c.1961, Osaka, Japan) play buzzsaw, distinctly Ramones-derived, pop. Shonen Knife means 'Boy Knife', the brand name of a small Japanese pocket knife. They formed in December 1981, their sporadic recording career starting in Osaka before relocating to the west coast of America. There they came to the attention of US punk pop fans in general, and Nirvana in particular. The latter took them under their wing with support slots, which brought them international recognition. However, they had long been a cult delicacy in American punk circles, made evident when 30 bands each contributed to an album's worth of covers of Shonen Knife songs (*Every Band Has A Shonen Knife Who Loves Them*). Although their charm may be limited in the long-term, a suitable epitaph for their appeal comes from Nirvana's Kurt Cobain: 'They play pop music, pop, pop, pop music'.
Albums: *Burning Farm* (Zero 1983, mini-album), *Yamano Atchan* (Zero 1984, mini-album), *Pretty Little Baka Guy* (Zero 1986, mini-album), *712* (Nippon Crown 1991), *Let's Knife* (MCA Victor 1992), *Rock Animals* (August Records 1993). Compilation: *Shonen Knife* (Giant 1990).

Shop Assistants

Formed in Edinburgh, Scotland, during 1984, this pop band used guitar inflections enthusiastically borrowed from the Buzzcocks. They were originally titled Buba And The Shop Assistants and released a solitary single, 'Something To Do', under that name. With only 500 pressings on the obscure Villa 21 independent, it has gained a reputation amongst record collectors for its monetary value as well as the spirited songwriting. Mainman David Keegan (guitar) was joined by Alex Taylor (vocals), Sarah Kneale (bass) and twin drummers Ann Donald (replaced in 1986 by Joan Bride) and Laura McPhail. 'All Day Long', on the Subway Organisation label, was allegedly Morrissey's favourite single of 1985, but by this time they had garnered adequate plaudits from their exposure in fanzines and magazines. The following year's release on the 53rd & 3rd label (jointly set up by Keegan with Stephen of the Pastels), 'Safety Net', reached number 1 on the UK independent chart. Signing to the major Chrysalis Records label saw the release of their debut album, which made a brief appearance in the Top 100 and then disappeared - as did the band. When Taylor left in 1987 to form the Motorcycle Boy the critical acclaim dried up. Keegan also left, taking up a post as skiing instructor, while Kneale and McPhail went back to college. They reformed in 1990, with McPhail switching to bass and Margarita taking her place on drums. One of the singles produced, 'The Big E', was, typically, a tribute to the guitar chord rather than the fashionable drug of the period. By this time they had signed to Andrew Tulley's Avalanche label, although their status in the independent scene has been somewhat eroded by the passing years. Keegan would eventually make a permanent commitment to the Pastels.
Album: *Shop Assistants* (Chrysalis 1986).

Shriekback

Shriekback originally evolved around a three-man nucleus of ex-Gang Of Four member Dave Allen, Carl Marsh (fresh from his own band, Out On Blue Six), plus Barry Andrews, previously with XTC, League Of Gentlemen and Restaurant For Dogs. The trio fused funk and rock with a unique and complex rhythmic approach, creating a distinctive and influential sound. The first fruits of this project came in 1982 with the EP *Tench* and then 'Sexthinkone' on the Y label, but it was the next two singles, 'My Spine Is the Bassline' (1982) and 'Lined Up' (1983) that established the band. Two further singles, 'Working On The Ground' and 'Afflictions', were enough to secure a deal with Arista Records, releasing *Jam Science* in 1984. The album also spawned two excellent singles, 'Hand On My Heart' and 'Mercy Dash'. The following year saw the release of *Oil And Gold*, which included 'Nemesis' and 'Fish Below The Ice'. Although more commercially based, the band had lost that hard, infectious funk vein that was previously so predominant. A move to Island yielded *Big Night Music*, early in 1987, accompanied by 'Gunning For Buddha' a month earlier. 'Get Down Tonight' followed in 1988, but this presaged the last Shriekback album proper, *Go Bang*. Those looking for an introduction to Shriekback might opt for *The Infinite*, a collection of the Y singles released on the Kaz label. Since then, there have been two further collections, summarising the band's time with Arista and Island respectively.
Albums: *Care* (1983), *Jam Science* (1984), *Oil And Gold* (1985), *Big Night Music* (1987), *Go Bang* (1988), *Sacred City* (Shriek 1994). Compilations: *The Infinite - The Best Of Shriekback* (1985), *The Best Of Shriekback, Volume 2* (1988), *The Best Of Shriekback* (1990).

Sidi Bou Said

Formed in 1990, Sidi Bou Said (pronounced Siddy Boo Sigh) consist of four women from Lewisham, London, England, who were keen to escape the then prevalent 'Riot Grrrl' movement. Indeed, they declined to appear in a

documentary about women in rock music because of their fear of becoming categorised regardless of their music. The group's multi-layered sound was influenced by the folk rock of Soft Machine as well as the all-out guitar assault of the Pixies and was introduced on two fine EPs, *Twilight Eyes* and *Three Sides*, where Claire Lemmon (vocals/guitar) and Lou Howton (vocals/guitar), both classically trained guitarists, shared songwriting credits. After playing dates with Belly they returned to Lincolnshire with the producer Tim Friese-Green to produce *Brooch* which included re-workings of their earlier singles and strong tracks such as 'Big Yellow Taxidermist', which seemingly advocated disembowelling a loved one. However, the rest of their debut disappointed somewhat, and it was left to 1995's *Bodies*, produced by Tim Smith of the Cardiacs, to restore their reputation. This mixture of unusual song constructions, including string sections, harpsichord and flute, embellished highly original lyrics from the pen of Lemmon, backed once again by the rhythm section of Gayl Harrison (bass) and Melanie Woods (drums). Howton had departed in the summer of 1994.
Albums: *Brooch* (Ultimate 1993), *Bodies* (Ultimate 1995).

Sigue Sigue Sputnik

These UK punk/glam revivalists engineered themselves a briefly prosperous niche in the mid-80s. The creation of Tony James (ex-Chelsea, Generation X), Sigue Sigue Sputnik artlessly copied the shock tactics of Sex Pistols manager Malcolm McLaren. Instead of taking on board the Pistols' nihilism, James poached from cyberpunk novels and films (particularly *Blade Runner*) for their image. This consisted of dyed hair piled high, bright colours and an abundance of eye-liner. James had also recruited clothes designer Martin Degville (vocals), Neal X (b. Neil Whitmore; guitar), Ray Mayhew (drums) and Chris Cavanagh (drums), taking pride in their apparent lack of musical experience. Taking their name from a Moscow street gang, they set about a publicity campaign which resulted in EMI Records, understandably keen not to let the next Pistols slip through their hands again, signing them for a reported £4 million pounds. The figure was deliberately exaggerated in order to provoke publicity. Their first single was 'Love Missile F1-11', which soared to number 3 in the UK charts in February 1986. However, though 'Twenty-First Century Boy' also made the Top 20, and a debut album sold advertising space between tracks, James' money-making ruse soon ended. Despite an avalanche of intentionally lurid press, the band dissolved, and Tony James subsequently, albeit briefly, joined the Sisters Of Mercy in 1991. Kavanagh would go on to Big Audio Dynamite, though James would make another attempt at ressurecting Sigue Sigue Sputnik later in the 90s. Degville recorded a dreadful solo album in the interim.
Albums: *Flaunt It* (Parlophone 1986), *Dress For Excess* (EMI 1988). Compilation: *First Generation* (Jungle 1990).

Silkworm

Seattle trio whose literate rock dynamic was initially propelled by Tim Midgett (bass/vocals), Andrew Cohen (guitar/vocals) and Joel Phelps (guitar/vocals). The group were formed in their hometown of Missoula, Montana, in the mid-80s, evolving into Silkworm in 1987. It wasn't until 1990, however, that Silkworm crystallised as a unit, adding drummer Michael Dahlquist and relocating to Seattle. A series of singles followed on a variety of indie labels, before the release of *In The West* in 1993. Their second album, *Libertine*, was the first to grace Seattle indie El Recordo. Both sets were produced by maverick producer Steve Albini (Big Black/Rapeman etc.), while obvious musical reference points included the Minutemen, Mission Of Burma and Gang Of Four. However, Phelps would depart following the release of *Libertine*. Having previously been one of three central songwriters (alongside Cohen and Midgett) in the band, this inevitably shifted the group's creative axis.
Albums: *In The West* (C/Z 1993), *Libertine* (El Recordo 1994).

Silver Jews

Silver Jews is essentially a vehicle for David Berman (b. Virginia, USA) with the backing of friends drawn from Pavement, with whom he had previously co-written songs (he had done the same with Royal Trux). Silver Jew's 1994 set earned admiring glances throughout the underground community, earning comparisons to the Palace Brothers and Violent Femmes despite its billing as a concept album. Fans of Pavement's askew narratives would certainly not be disappointed with the track selection - ranging from improvisational pieces like 'The Moon Is Number 18' to charming, anecdotal dioramas 'Advice To The Graduate' and 'Trains Across The Sea'. Arguably the best composition, 'Secret Knowledge Of Back Roads', would also be played by Pavement on a John Peel session for BBC Radio, ensuring the continued cult growth of Berman's concern.
Album: *Starlite Walker* (Domino 1994).

Silverfish

Silverfish were instigated in 1988 by budding guitarist and regular London gig-goer Andrew 'Fuzz' Duprey (b. 14 June 1963, Kent, England), who thought of the band name and had a desperate urge to play 'noise you could dance to'. Stuart Watson (b. 10 November 1962, Northamptonshire, England; drums) and Chris Mowforth (b. 30 May 1964, Middlesex, England; bass) joined up to start - literally - 'bashing around ideas', until Duprey realised he could not sing and play bass simultaneously. Thus Lesley Rankine (b. 11 April 1965, Edinburgh, Scotland) was discovered b(r)awling at a hardcore gig and subsequently became the vocalist. The title for their first album was derived from an early live review which compared her singing to that of a 'fat Axl Rose' (of Guns N'Roses). Silverfish were confrontational, to say the least: early EP titles included *Total Fucking Asshole* and *Fuckin' Drivin' Or What*, and the expletives were aligned with a suitably ferocious splatterpunk sound which gouged a uniquely noisy niche for itself in the British scheme of things, despite a brief spell spent under the unwanted umbrella of 'Camden Lurch' - a 'scene' half-invented by the ever-imaginative UK music press in an attempt to catagorize the burgeoning state of alternative music in north London. In 1991 Silverfish took a potentially major step up the ladder by switching labels, to Creation Records, prior to causing havoc on their first tour of America. However, the band would grind to a premature halt on their return, with Lesley

Rankine stated to be working on a solo project in 1995.
Albums: *Fat Axl* (Wiiija 1990), *Organ Fan* (Creation 1992).
Compilation: *Cockeye* (Wiiija 1990).

Siouxsie And The Banshees

Siouxsie Sioux (b. Susan Dallion, 27 May 1957, London,
England) was part of the notorious 'Bromley contingent',
including Steve Severin (b. Steven Bailey, 25 September
1955), which followed the Sex Pistols in their early days.
Siouxsie had also taken part in the 100 Club Punk Festival,
singing an elongated version of 'The Lord's Prayer' with a
group that included Sid Vicious on drums. The fledgling
singer also achieved some minor fame after a verbal exchange
with television presenter Bill Grundy which unwittingly
prompted the Sex Pistols' infamous swearing match on the
Today programme. Within months of that incident Siouxsie
put together her backing group the Banshees, featuring Pete
Fenton (guitar), Steve Severin (bass) and Kenny Morris
(drums). Siouxsie flirted with Nazi imagery, highlighted by
black make-up and frequently exposed breasts. By mid-1977
Fenton was replaced by John McGeogh, and the group
supported Johnny Thunders And The Heartbreakers as well
as recording a session for the BBC disc jockey, John Peel. By
1978, the group had signed to Polydor Records (the last of
the important punk bands of the era to be rounded up by a
major) and released their first single, the sublime 'Hong
Kong Garden', which reached the UK Top 10. *The Scream*
soon followed, produced by Steve Lillywhite. Less
commercial offerings ensued with 'The Staircase (Mystery)'
and 'Playground Twist', which were soon succeeded by *Join
Hands*. During a promotional tour, Morris and McKay
abruptly left, to be replaced by former Slits drummer Budgie
(b. Peter Clark, 21 August 1957) and temporary Banshee
Robert Smith, on leave from the Cure. Siouxsie's Germanic
influences were emphasized on the stark 'Mittageisen (Metal
Postcard)', which barely scraped into the Top 50. Both
'Happy House' and 'Christine' were more melodic offerings,
deservedly bringing greater commercial success. After the
success of *Kaleidoscope*, the group embarked on a world tour,
including a concert behind the 'Iron Curtain'. Another Top
10 album, *Juju*, was followed by some extra-curricular
activities. Siouxsie and Budgie formed an occasional offshoot
group, the Creatures, who enjoyed Top 10 success in their
own right, as well as recording an album. Smith and Severin
also recorded successfully together as the Glove. After the
string-accompanied *A Kiss In The Dreamhouse*, the group
reconvened in the autumn of 1983 to play a concert for
Italy's Communist Party. A highly commercial version of the
Beatles' 'Dear Prudence' provided the group with their
biggest UK hit, peaking at number 3. Early in 1984 the
evocative 'Swimming Horses' maintained their hit profile,
while further personnel changes ensued with the enlistment
of John Carruthers from Clock DVA. He, in turn, was
replaced by Jon Klein. Regular albums during the mid-80s
showed that the group had established a loyal cult following
and could experiment freely in the studio without a
significant loss of commercial appeal. Having already
enjoyed success with a cover version, Siouxsie then tackled
Bob Dylan's 'This Wheel's On Fire', which reached the UK
Top 20. An entire album of cover versions followed though

Through The Looking Glass received the most awkward
reviews of the band's career. A change of direction with *Peep
Show* saw the band embrace a more sophisticated sound,
maintaining the eastern nuances of yore but doing so within
an elaborate musical scheme. 1991 returned them to the
charts with the evocative 'Kiss Them For Me' and
Superstition, an album of light touch but contrastingly dense
production. Arguably their greatest achievement of the 90s,
however, was the much-delayed *The Rapture*. Adding
musical adventurism (notably the heavily orchestrated three
movements of the title-track) to familiar but entertaining
refractions from their earlier career ('Not Forgotten'), the
approach of middle age had evidently not weakened their
resolve.

Albums: *The Scream* (Polydor 1978), *Join Hands* (Polydor
1979), *Kaleidoscope* (Polydor 1980), *Juju* (Polydor 1981), *A
Kiss In The Dreamhouse* (Polydor 1982), *Nocturne* (Polydor
1983), *Hyaena* (Polydor 1984), *Tinderbox* (Polydor 1986),
Through The Looking Glass (Polydor 1987), *Peep Show*
(Polydor 1988), *Superstition* (Polydor 1991), *The Rapture*
(Polydor 1995). Compilations: *Once Upon A Time - The
Singles* (Polydor 1981), *Twice Upon A Time* (Polydor 1992).
Video: *Greetings From Zurich* (1994).
Films: *Jubilee* (1978).

Sisters Of Mercy

A post-punk rock outfit whose flirtations with gothic
imagery would dog the public and media perception of them
throughout an eclectic career. They formed in Leeds,
Yorkshire, England in 1980, when Leeds and Oxford
University drop-out Andrew Eldritch (b. Andrew Taylor, 15
May 1959, East Anglia, England; vocals) teamed up with
Gary Marx (guitar) and a drum machine. After releasing
'The Damage Done' (on which Eldritch plays drums and
guitar) on their own Merciful Release label, the band
expanded to include Ben Gunn (guitar) and Craig Adams
(bass) for supports with Clash, Psychedelic Furs and the
Birthday Party. A cult reputation in the North of England
was augmented by excellent press, and further enhanced by
the release of 'Alice'. A magnificent gothic dance saga,
together with the subsequent 'Temple Of Love', it
hallmarked the band's early musical character. Inbetween
these two landmark 45s Gunn left to be replaced by Wayne
Hussey (ex-Pauline Murray, Dead Or Alive). WEA picked
up the distribution for Merciful Release as the band's
reputation continued to grow throughout 1983 and 1984.
However, despite the release of their debut album, the
following year brought a creative watershed. Continuing
rivalries between Marx and Eldritch forced the former to
depart. This was only a stop-gap treaty with the band
announcing a final split in April 1985 after a concert at the
Royal Albert Hall. The rest of the year witnessed
extraordinary legal wrangles between Eldritch on one hand
and Adams and Hussey on the other, each claiming use of
the name Sisters Of Mercy. Eldritch went as far as releasing
a record under the title Sisterhood simply to prevent Adams
and Hussey from adopting this halfway-house title. The duo
eventually settled on the Mission as their new home, while
Eldritch moved to Berlin, West Germany. Still operating
under the Sisters Of Mercy title, Eldritch recruited Patricia

Morrison (b. 14 January 1962, ex-Gun Club) for hit singles 'This Corrosion' and 'Dominion', and the album *Floodland*. A two year spell of inactivity was broken in 1990 with 'More', showcasing another new line-up; Tony James (ex-Generation X, Sigue Sigue Sputnik; bass), Tim Bricheno (b. 6 July 1963, Huddersfield, Yorkshire, England; guitar - ex-All About Eve) and Andreas Bruhn (guitar). The *Vision Thing* indulged Eldritch's penchant for deep rooted, esoteric metaphor, which occasionally makes his lyrics futile and impenetrable. 1991 saw a loss-making, aborted tour with Public Enemy, though this has done little to erase the confidence of the self-confessed 'world's greatest lyricist'.

Albums: *First And Last And Always* (1985), *Floodland* (1988), *Vision Thing* (1990), *Some Girls Wander By Mistake* (1992)

Videos: *The Wake* (1987), *Shot Rev 2.0* (1994).

Skeletal Family

No doubt influenced by the emergence of gothic punk in the early 80s, the Skeletal Family emerged from Bingley in Yorkshire towards the end of 1982. Early demos recorded in September and December featured the input of Anne Marie Hurst (lead vocals), Trotwood (b. Roger Nowell; bass), Stan Greenwood (guitar), Steve Crane (drums) and Karl Heinz (synthesizer). After a debut single, 'Just A Friend', on the Luggage label in March 1983, the band signed to Yorkshire's established indie, Red Rhino Records. By this time Howard Daniels had taken over on drums. 'The Night' shared the same influences championed by the band's 'goth' counterparts - the Cramps, Bauhaus and the Birthday Party. 'Alone She Cries' in January 1984 featured new drummer Martin Henderson, and was followed by 'So Sûre' in June, alongside *Recollect*, a 12-inch EP comprising early demos. By the advent of *Burning Oil* in August, Skeletal Family had attracted a sizeable following, principally through support slots to the Sisters Of Mercy. This ascent continued with 'Promised Land' in February 1985, where they were aided by Graham Pleeth on synthesizer, the a-side backed by a cover of Ben E. King's 'Stand By Me'. *Futile Combat* fared well in the UK independent charts, securing a deal with Chrysalis Records, but singer Anne Marie had left to join Ghost Dance. Recruiting drummer Kevin Phillips and Katrina on vocals, it was a new, more commercial Skeletal Family that issued 'Restless' in March 1986 and 'Just A Minute' in August, but neither made significant headway and the band were soon dropped (a fate that Ghost Dance would soon come to share).

Albums: *Burning Oil* (Red Rhino 1984), *Futile Combat* (Red Rhino 1985), *Ghosts* (Chrysalis 1986).

Skids

A Scottish new wave band founded in Dunfermline in 1977 by Stuart Adamson (guitar/vocals, b. 11 April 1958, Manchester, UK), Richard Jobson (vocals) Tom Kellichan (drums) and Willie Simpson (bass). After issuing 'Reasons' on their own No Bad label, the group were signed by Virgin. David Batchelor produced 'Sweet Suburbia' and 'The Saints Are Coming' before 'Into The Valley' reached the UK Top 10 in 1979. Despite criticism of Jobson's lyrics as pretentious, the Skids enjoyed a further year of chart success

as 'Masquerade' and 'Working For The Yankee Dollar' reached the Top 20. Both came from the second album, which was produced by Bill Nelson of Be-Bop Deluxe. Soon afterwards the band was hit by personnel changes. Russell Webb and Mike Baillie replaced Simpson and Kellichan and more crucially, the Skids' songwriting team was split when Adamson left after the release of the third album, which proved to be the group's most commercial, reaching the Top 10 and containing the minor hit 'Circus Games'. Without Adamson, *Joy*, an exploration of Celtic culture, was more or less a Jobson solo effort. The Skids dissolved in 1982, with *Fanfare* issued by Virgin as a mixture of greatest hits and unreleased tracks. In 1983, Stuart Adamson launched the career of his new band, Big Country. Richard Jobson recorded one album with a new band, the Armoury Show before pursuing a solo career as poet, songwriter and broadcaster. He released albums on Belgian label Les Disques Crepuscules and Parlophone.

Albums: *Scared To Dance* (1979), *Days In Europa* (1979), *Absolute Game* (1980), *Joy* (1981), *Fanfare* (1982). Compilation: *Dumferline* (1993).

Sky Cries Mary

Formed in Seattle, their sound has often been descibed as sponge, as opposed to grunge. The 1995 line-up consists of Anisa Romero, vocals; DJ Fallout, ambient mix and turntables; Bennett James, drums; Gordon Raphael, keyboards; Marc Olsen, guitar and vocals; Joseph E. Howard, bass, sitar and mellotron; Roderick, vocals and lyrics. Two early members now perform with the Posies but this unit prefer a softer mantric approach quite unlike their obvious Hendrixisms. Their creative and original debut *A Return To The Inner Experience* contained mystic lyrics and tribal rhythms together with interestingly different versions of Iggy Pop's 'We Will Fall' and the Rolling Stones' '2000 Light Years'.

Album: *A Return To The Inner Experience* (World Domination 1994).

Slaughter And The Dogs

Formed in Manchester, England, in 1976, this punk quartet comprised Wayne Barrett (vocals); Howard Bates (bass), Mike Rossi (guitar) and Mad Muffet (drums). One of the first groups to sign to Manchester's independent Rabid Records, the group subsequently won a contract with Decca Records for whom they released the glam/punk influenced debut album, *Do It Dog Style*. A dispute with their record company, combined with the departure of Barrett, saw them marooned back in Manchester. Adding Billy Duffy on guitar, they auditioned Morrissey as their new vocalist, before deciding to stay as a four-piece with Rossi singing. An unsuccessful relaunch as Slaughter convinced them to change their name to the Studio Sweethearts, but they fell apart in the summer of 1979. For a time they soldiered on with Barrett briefly returning as vocalist. He was later replaced by Ed Banger (Eddie Garrity) but soon after the unit folded. Duffy went on to form Theatre Of Hate and later joined the Cult. Slaughter And The Dogs did at least leave behind three enduring punk classics; their Rabid debut, 'Cranked Up Really High', and the terrace anthems, 'Where

Sleeper

Have All The Bootboys Gone' and 'You're Ready Now'.
Albums: *Do It Dog Style* (Decca 1978), *Live At The Belle Vue* (Rabid 1979). As Slaughter: *Bite Back* (DJM 1980). Compilations: *The Way We Were* (Thrush 1983), *The Slaughterhouse Tapes* (Link 1989), *Rabid Dogs* (Receiver 1989).

Sleeper

Launched on the UK media primarily by dint of the provocative sexual statements of lead vocalist/guitarist Louise Wener (b. Enfield, Middlesex, England), these have somewhat eclipsed the contribution of fellow members Jon Stewart (b. c.1967; guitar), Andy McClure (b. c.1970, Liverpool, Merseyside, England; drums) and Diid (pronounced Deed) Osman (b. c.1969, Somalia, Africa; bass). The latter pair were recruited by creative axis, Wener and Stewart, after arriving in London from Manchester, where both had studied degrees in politics (and also become romantically linked). Their first gigs were played in October 1992, eventually signing to the newly invoked indie label Indolent the following year. Their debut EP, *Alice In Vain*, was recorded with Boo Radleys/My Bloody Valentine producer Anjeli Dutt at the helm. This set the group's agenda, Wener expressing her disenchantment with the austerity of feminism: 'Really women are as shitty and horrible and vindictive as men are'. Sleeper's musical perspective revealed urgent, stop-go punk pop close in construction to Elastica. February 1994 saw the release of *Swallow*, with a third EP, *Delicious*, following in May. However, it was 'Inbetweener' which brought them to the UK Top 20 the following year. The group's excellent debut album continued the fascination with matters anatomical, 'Swallow' and 'Delicious', which both reappeared, hardly requiring further exposition.
Album: *Smart* (Indolent 1995).

Slits

This UK feminist punk group formed in 1976 with a line-up featuring Ari-Up (b. Arianna Foster; vocals), Kate Korus (guitar), Palmolive (drums; ex-Raincoats) and Suzi Gutsy (bass). Korus soon left to form the Mo-dettes and Gutsy quit to team up with the Flicks. They were replaced by guitarist Viv Albertine and bass player Tessa Pollitt and it was this line-up that supported the Clash during the spring of 1977. The group were known for their uncompromising attitude and professed lack of technique, but their music was as aggressive and confrontational as the best of the punk fraternity. Their failure to secure a record contract during the first wave of the punk explosion was surprising. By the time they made their recording debut, Palmolive had been ousted and replaced by Big In Japan percussionist, Budgie (b. Peter Clark, 21 August 1957). Signed to Island Records, they worked with reggae producer Dennis Bovell on the dub-influenced *Cut*. The album attracted considerable press interest for its sleeve, which featured the group naked, after rolling in the mud. The departure of Budgie to Siouxsie And The Banshees (replaced by the Pop Group's Bruce Smith) coincided with the arrival of reggae musician Prince Hammer and trumpeter Don Cherry (father of Neneh Cherry). A series of singles followed, including a memorable

version of John Holt's 'Man Next Door'. By 1981, the Slits had lost much of their original cutting edge and it came as little surprise when they disbanded at the end of the year.
Albums: *Cut* (Island 1979), *Bootleg Retrospective* (Rough Trade 1980), *Return Of The Giant Slits* (CBS 1981). Compilation: *The Peel Sessions* (Strange Fruit 1988).

Sloan

This Canadian grunge band originated at the Nova Scotia College Of Art in Halifax, where drummer Andrew Scott and bassist Chris Murphy linked with Northern Ireland-born guitarist Patrick Pentland and guitarist/vocalist Jay Ferguson. Sloan developed their own sound from a mixture of hardcore and grunge influences, producing a guitar-fuelled battery of short, sharp songs, releasing the *Peppermint* EP, recorded at a friend's house in Halifax, through their own Murderecords label. A lively performance at Canada's East Coast Music Conference brought the band to the attention of Geffen Records, who liked the EP and promptly signed Sloan. *Smeared* impressed reviewers and public alike, with the pop songwriting and vocal melodies counterpointed by Pentland's raw, aggressive guitar work. In spite of a low-key promotional approach, the record performed well as North American college radio picked up on 'Underwhelmed'.
Album: *Smeared* (Geffen 1992).

Slowdive

Thames Valley indie band formed in 1989 by Rachel Goswell (b. 16 May 1971, Hampshire, England; vocals/guitar), Neil Halstead (b. 7 October 1970, Luton, Bedfordshire, England; vocals/guitar), Brook Christian Savill (b. 6 December 1977, Bury, Lancashire, England; guitar), Nicholas Chaplin (b. 23 December 1970, Slough, Berkshire, England; bass) and Adrian Sell (drums), who departed after six months to go to University. His replacement was Neil Carter, who also played with local Reading band the Colour Mary, until Simon Scott (b. 3 March 1971, Cambridge, England) joined permanently, having drummed for the Charlottes. While this was happening, Slowdive were creating a dreamy sound which frequently escaped analysis, but the main ingredients were floating harmonies and ripples of guitar effects within a traditional three-minute pop framework. Signed by a revitalized Creation Records on the basis of one demo tape, Slowdive made a surprising number of friends with what seemed to be a blatantly esoteric sound; indeed, by the summer of 1991 they had reached number 52 in the UK charts with the *Holding Our Breath* EP. However, something of a press backlash ensued over the following two years, as the 'Thames Valley' scene and 'shoe gazing', a name invoked to describe the motionless, effects-pedal driven dreamy pop of a welter of bands, fell from fashion. Contrary to expectations Slowdive's second album, *Souvlaki*, was named after a Jerky Boys' sketch in which a hotel receptionist is enrolled in an imaginary *ménage-à-trois*. Despite this, and Brian Eno's production of three tracks, Slowdive remained widely perceived to be perennial Cocteau Twins' apprentices. Scott was lost at the end of 1993 because 'he got into acid jazz'. *Pygmalion*, created at Halstead's home studio, saw the group move into ambient soundscapes, including two tracks ('I Believe' and 'Like Up') for an American art house film.

Albums: *Just For A Day* (Creation 1991), *Souvlaki* (Creation 1993), *Pygmalion* (Creation 1995).

Smalltown Parade

London, England indie quartet comprising Robert Moore (b. 1 November 1963, Haverhill, Suffolk, England; bass), Paul Bevoir (b. 29 May 1960, Islington, London, England; vocals/guitar), Simon Smith (b. 3 December 1958, Merton Park, London, England; drums) and Simon Taylor (b. 28 December 1960, Redhill, Surrey, England; keyboards). The band convened first in April 1980 when sleeve designer Bevoir invited Smith (ex-Mood Six) to see his collection of Corgi toy cars. Smalltown Parade were formed thereafter, though the original bass and guitar incumbents, drawn from San Francisco and Berlin, proved temporary. Just two months later the band's 'The Sunday Way Of Life' won Gary Crowley's BBC GLR Demo Clash for five consecutive weeks. In July this was released as a limited edition single on Captain Sensible's Deltic Records, by which time the band had been augmented by the addition of Moore. Following a publishing deal signed in February 1991 with Japanese organization NTVM, 'And We Dance On' was released to strong critical acclaim. By May Taylor (also ex-Mood Six) had introduced himself to the band, and also befriended Rolf Harris at a party. The Australian master of the bilabong duly agreed to appear on the video to third single 'Watching Mary Go Round', painting a 20ft canvas of the group as they performed. A series of gigs ensued as 'token indie pop band' on *Number One* magazine road shows, Moore at one point being mistaken for a member of Take That, before a charity appearance alongside Dannii Minogue at London's Empire Ballroom. However, some of the band's impetus dissipated until in 1993 'Watching Mary Go Round' became a rejuvenated club hit in Japan, prompting Polystar Records to sign the band for a debut album, *Get Beautiful*. Rave reviews in the Orient were commonplace but the band were unable to capitalise due to Bevoir's fear of flying. A second album followed a year later, again to an encouraging response, though by this time the sound was much leaner and more direct. It was followed by a Bevoir solo album, while 1995 saw work begin on a third Smalltown Parade set. Odds and ends were collected on a compilation by Tangerine Records. Albums: *Get Beautiful* (Polystar 1993), *Faces* (Polystar 1994). Compilation: *Best Of* (Tangerine 1995). Paul Bevoir solo: *Paul Bevoir* (Polystar 1994).

S*M*A*S*H

Formed in Welwyn Garden City, Hertfordshire, England, this trio comprising Ed Borrie (vocals/guitar), Rob (drums) and Salvador (bass), actually date back to 1984, when the UK Miners strike was on and irrevocably altered Ed and Sal's political ideals (although both were still schoolboys). Taking on Rob from a nearby squat, Sal moved over from singing to playing bass when the original bass player failed to turn up for rehearsals. To this day Sal still plays the instrument 'wrong side up'. Their first gig did not take place until early 1992, and by the following year the *New Musical Express* had decided they sounded like 'the Stone Roses on PCP', while two singles, 'Real Surreal'/'Drugs Again' and 'Shame'/'Lady Love Your Cunt' were released on their own Le Disques De

Popcor Records. The second single was Single Of The Week in both the *New Musical Express* and *Melody Maker*. Its b-side was a repetition of Germaine Greer's celebrated feminist remark. Showcases like the 100 Club's New Art Riot gig in December 1993 and the NME's On Into 94 event placed them within the New Wave Of The New Wave movement, a description which the band thought of as 'bollocks'. In truth their reputation was built on tireless touring, and their popularity was enhanced by a cheap entry price policy. The 'buzz' was such that admirers included Billy Corgan (Smashing Pumpkins) and Joe Strummer, while the American label, Sub Pop Records, responsible for much of the grunge movement that S*M*A*S*H detested, tried to sign them. Instead they moved to Hi-Rise Records, releasing a mini-album six weeks later (compiling the first two 7-inch singles). A Top 30 hit, it saw them appear on *Top Of The Pops*, and the band later played the London Anti-Nazi Carnival on the back of a float with Billy Bragg. Censorship proved a problem over July's '(I Want To) Kill Somebody', which reached the Top 30 despite being on sale for only one day. Its impact was scuppered by BBC Radio 1 (the song included a hit list of Tory MP's, and was independently edited by the corporation to avoid offence). Their debut album was produced by Chris Allison (Wedding Present) in September 1994.
Albums: *S*M*A*S*H* (Hi-Rise 1994, mini-album), *Self Abused* (Hi-Rise 1994).

Smashing Orange

This initially promising band from Wilmington, Delaware, USA, specialized in loud garage group material flavoured with hardcore. Vocalists Rob Montejo and Sara Montejo were sibling college dropouts, though guitarist Rick Hodgson actually graduated in marketing. They all worked at a record store in Delaware, and established their permanent line-up only five days before their live debut. The other members were Tim Supplee (drums) and Steve Wagner (bass). Their first single was the critically lauded 'My Deranged Heart' on Native Records, while they made a deep impression on domestic audiences supporting Lush at the Marquee Club in New York. Their debut album arrived in the summer of 1991, confirming the band's potential, but when Native Records collapsed in the early 90s it left Smashing Orange in something of a quandry from which they have yet to emerge.
Album: *Smashing Orange* (Native 1991).

Smashing Pumpkins

Once widely viewed as poor relations to Nirvana's major label alternative rock, Chicago, USA's Smashing Pumpkins, led by vocalist/guitarist Billy Corgan (b. 17 March 1967, Chicago, Illinois, USA) have persevered to gradually increasing acceptance and press veneration. Corgan's inspirations, the Beatles, Led Zeppelin, Doors and Black Sabbath, as well as a professional jazz musician father, add up to a powerful musical cocktail over which his lyrics, which frequently cross the threshold of normality and even sanity, float unsettlingly. The rest of the band comprises D'Arcy Wretzky (bass), James Iha (guitar) and Jimmy Chamberlain (drums). Smashing Pumpkins made their official debut with

a drum machine at the Avalon club in Chicago. Chamberlain was then drafted in from a ten-piece showband (JP And The Cats) to fill the percussion vacancy (Corgan had previously played in another local band, the Marked). The group made its debut in early 1990 with the release of 'I Am The One' on local label Limited Potential Records. Previously they had included two tracks on a Chicago compilation, *Light Into Dark*. This led the band to the attention of influential Seattle label Sub Pop, with whom they released 'Tristess'/'La Dolly Vita' in September 1990, before moving to Caroline Records. *Gish*, produced by Butch Vig, announced the group to both indie and metal audiences, and went to number 1 on the influential Rockpool College Radio Chart. Ironically, given the Nirvana comparisons, this came before Vig had produced *Nevermind*. However, it was *Siamese Dream* which launched the band to centre stage with its twisted metaphors and skewed rhythms. A Top 10 success in the US *Billboard* charts, it saw them joined by mellotron, cello and violin accompaniment to give the sound extra depth. However, these remained secondary to the pop hooks and rock atmospherics which have defined the band's sound.
Albums: *Gish* (Caroline 1991), *Siamese Dream* (Virgin 1993).
Video: *Vieuphoria* (1994).
Further reading: *Smashing Pumpkins*, Nick Wise.

Smith, Patti

b. 31 December 1946, Chicago, Illinois, USA. Smith was raised in New Jersey and became infatuated by music, principally the Rolling Stones, the Velvet Underground, Jimi Hendrix and James Brown. Her initial talent focused on poetry and art, while her first major label recording was a version of a Jim Morrison poem on Ray Manzarek's (both Doors) solo album. Her early writing, captured on three anthologies, *Seventh Heaven* (1971), *Kodak* (1972) and *Witt* (1973), was inspired by Arthur Rimbaud and William Burroughs, but as the 70s progressed she was increasingly drawn towards fusing such work with rock. In 1971, Smith was accompanied by guitarist Lenny Kaye for a reading in St Mark's Church, and this informal liaison continued for three years until the duo was joined by Richard Sohl (piano) in the first Patti Smith Group. Their debut recording, 'Hey Joe'/'Piss Factory', was in part financed by photographer Robert Mapplethorpe, later responsible for many of the artist's striking album portraits. By 1974 the unit had become one of the most popular acts at New York's pivotal CBGB's club. Ivan Kral (bass) and J.D. Daugherty (drums) were then added to the line-up featured on *Horses*. This highly-lauded set, produced by John Cale, skilfully invoked Patti's 60s' mentors but in a celebratory manner. By simultaneously capturing the fire of punk, Smith completed a collection welcomed by both old and new audiences. However, *Radio Ethiopia* was perceived as self-indulgent and the artist's career was further undermined when she incurred a broken neck upon falling offstage early in 1977. A lengthy recuperation ensued but Smith re-emerged in July with a series of excellent concerts and the following year scored considerable commercial success with *Easter*. This powerful set included 'Because The Night', co-written with Bruce Springsteen, which deservedly reached the UK Top 5, but

Wave failed to sustain such acclaim. She had previously collaborated on three Blue Öyster Cult albums, with then partner Allen Lanier. Patti then married former MC5 guitarist Fred 'Sonic' Smith, and retired from active performing for much of the 80s to raise a family. She resumed recording in 1988 with *Dream Of Life*, which contained the artist's customary call-to-arms idealism ('People Have The Power') and respect for rock and poetic tradition.
Albums: *Horses* (Arista 1975), *Radio Ethiopia* (Arista 1976), *Easter* (Arista 1978), *Wave* (Arista 1979), *Dream Of Life* (Arista 1988).

Smithereens

Influenced by the 60s pop of the Beatles, Beach Boys and the Byrds, the Smithereens formed in New Jersey in 1980. Members Jim Babjak (guitar) and Dennis Diken (drums) had played together since 1971; Mike Mesaros (bass) was recruited in 1976 and finally Pat DiNizio (vocals). After recording two EPs, they backed songwriter Otis Blackwell ('Great Balls Of Fire') on two obscure albums. In 1986 the group signed to Enigma Records and released their first full album, *Especially For You*, which fared well among both college radio and mainstream rock listeners, as did the single 'Blood And Roses'. After a lengthy tour, the Smithereens recorded their second album, *Green Thoughts*, in 1988, this time distributed by Capitol Records. *Smithereens 11*, was their biggest selling album to date reaching number 41 in the US chart. The group's music has also been featured in several movie soundtracks including the teen-horror film, '*Class Of Nuke 'Em High*'. Their career faltered in 1991 with the poorly received *Blow Up* (US number 120) leaving critics to ponder if the band have run out of ideas.
Albums: *Especially For You* (1986), *Green Thoughts* (1988), *Smithereens 11* (1990), *Blow Up* (1991), *A Date With The Smithereens* (RCA 1994).

Smiths

Acclaimed by many as the most important UK group of the 80s, the Smiths were formed in Manchester during the spring of 1982. Morrissey (b. Steven Patrick Morrissey, 22 May 1959, Davyhulme, Manchester, England) and Johnny Marr (b. John Maher, 31 October 1963, Ardwick, Manchester, England) originally combined as a songwriting partnership, and only their names appeared on any contract bearing the title 'Smiths'. Morrissey had previously played for a couple of months in the Nosebleeds and also rehearsed and auditioned with a late version of Slaughter And The Dogs. After that he wrote reviews for *Record Mirror* and penned a couple of booklets on the New York Dolls and James Dean. Marr, meanwhile, had played in several Wythenshawe groups including the Paris Valentinos, White Dice, Sister Ray and Freaky Party. By the summer of 1982, the duo decided to form a group and recorded demos with drummer Simon Wolstencroft and a recording engineer named Dale. Wolstencroft subsequently declined an offer to join the Smiths and in later years became a member of the Fall. Eventually, Mike Joyce (b. 1 June 1963, Fallowfield, Manchester, England) was recruited as drummer, having previously played with the punk-inspired Hoax and Victim.

During their debut gig at the Ritz in Manchester, the group was augmented by go-go dancer James Maker, who went on to join Raymonde and later RPLA. By the end of 1982, the group appointed a permanent bassist. Andy Rourke (b. 1963, Manchester, England), was an alumnus of various past groups with Marr. After being taken under the wing of local entrepreneur Joe Moss, the group strenuously rehearsed and after a series of gigs, signed to Rough Trade Records in the spring of 1983. By that time, they had issued their first single on the label, 'Hand In Glove', which failed to reach the Top 50. During the summer of 1983, they became entwined in the first of several tabloid press controversies when it was alleged that their lyrics contained references to child molesting. The eloquent Morrissey, who was already emerging as a media spokesperson of considerable power, sternly refuted the rumours. During the same period the group commenced work on their debut album with producer Troy Tate, but the sessions were curtailed, and a new set of recordings undertaken with John Porter. In November 1983 the group issued their second single, 'This Charming Man', a striking pop record that infiltrated the UK Top 30. Following an ill-fated trip to the USA at the end of the year, the quartet began 1984 with a new single, the notably rockier 'What Difference Does It Make?', which took them to number 12. *The Smiths* ably displayed the potential of the group, with Morrissey's oblique genderless lyrics coalescing with Marr's spirited guitar work. The closing track of the album was the haunting 'Suffer Little Children', a requiem to the child victims of the 60s Moors Murderers. The song later provoked a short-lived controversy in the tabloid press, which was resolved when the mother of one of the victims came out on Morrissey's side. A series of college gigs throughout Britain established the group as a cult favourite, with Morrissey displaying a distinctive image, complete with National Health spectacles, a hearing aid and bunches of gladioli. A collaboration with Sandie Shaw saw 'Hand In Glove' transformed into a belated hit, while Morrissey dominated music press interviews. His celibate stance provoked reams of speculation about his sexuality and his ability to provide good copy on subjects as various as animal rights, royalty, Oscar Wilde and 60s films, made him a journalist's dream interviewee. The singer's celebrated miserabilism was reinforced by the release of the autobiographical 'Heaven Knows I'm Miserable Now', which reached number 19 in the UK. Another Top 20 hit followed with 'William, It Was Really Nothing'. While the Smiths commenced work on their next album, Rough Trade issued the interim *Hatful Of Hollow*, a bargain-priced set that included various flip sides and radio sessions. It was a surprisingly effective work, that captured the inchoate charm of the group. By 1984 the Smiths found themselves feted as Britain's best group by various factions in the music press. The release of the sublime 'How Soon Is Now?' justified much of the hyperbole and this was reinforced by the power of their next album, *Meat Is Murder*. This displayed Morrissey's increasingly tendency towards social commentary, which had been indicated in his controversial comments on Band Aid and the IRA bombings. The album chronicled violence at schools ('The Headmaster Ritual'), adolescent thuggery ('Rusholme Ruffians'), child abuse

('Barbarism Begins At Home') and animal slaughter ('Meat Is Murder'). The proseletyzing tone was brilliantly complemented by the musicianship of Marr, Rourke and Joyce. Marr's work on such songs as 'The Headmaster Ritual' and 'That Joke Isn't Funny Anymore' effectively propelled him to the position of one of Britain's most respected rock guitarists. Despite releasing a milestone album, the group's fortunes in the singles charts were relatively disappointing. 'Shakespeare's Sister' received a lukewarm response and stalled at number 26, amid ever growing rumours that the group were dissatisfied with their record label. Another major UK tour in 1985 coincided with various management upheavals, which dissipated the group's energies. A successful trek across the USA was followed by the release of the plaintive summer single, 'The Boy With The Thorn In His Side' which, despite its commerciality, only reached number 23. A dispute with Rough Trade delayed the release of the next Smiths album, which was preceded by the superb 'Big Mouth Strikes Again', another example of Marr at his best. During the same period, Rourke was briefly ousted from the group due to his flirtation with heroin. He was soon reinstated, however, along with a second guitarist Craig Gannon, who had previously played with Aztec Camera, the Bluebells and Colourfield. In June 1986 *The Queen Is Dead* was issued and won immediate critical acclaim for its diversity and unadulterated power. The range of mood and emotion offered on the album was startling to behold, ranging from the epic grandeur of the title track to the overt romanticism of 'There Is A Light That Never Goes Out' and the irreverent comedy of 'Frankly Mr Shankly' and 'Some Girls Are Bigger Than Others'. A superb display of Morrissey/Marr at their apotheosis, the album was rightly placed alongside *Meat Is Murder* as one of the finest achievements of the decade. A debilitating stadium tour of the USA followed and during the group's absence they enjoyed a formidable Top 20 hit with the disco-denouncing 'Panic'. The sentiments of the song, coupled with Morrissey's negative comments on certain aspects of black music, provoked further adverse comments in the press. That controversy was soon replaced by the news that the Smiths were to record only one more album for Rough Trade and intended to transfer their operation to the major label, EMI Records. Meanwhile, the light pop of 'Ask' contrasted with riotous scenes during the group's 1986 UK tour. At the height of the drama, the group almost suffered a fatality when Johnny Marr was involved in a car crash. While he recuperated, guitarist Craig Gannon was fired, a decision that prompted legal action. The group ended the year with a concert at the Brixton Academy supported by fellow Mancunians, the Fall. It was to prove their final UK appearance. After another hit with 'Shoplifters Of The World Unite' the group completed what would prove their final album. The glam rock inspired 'Sheila Take A Bow' returned them to the Top 10 and their profile was maintained with the release of another sampler album, *The World Won't Listen*. Marr was growing increasingly disenchanted with the group's musical direction, however, and privately announced that he required a break. With the group's future still in doubt, press speculation proved so intense that an official announcement of a split occurred in

August 1987. *Strangeways, Here We Come*, an intriguing transitional album, was issued posthumously. The work indicated the different directions that the major protagonists were progressing towards during their final phase. A prestigious television documentary of the group's career followed on *The South Bank Show* and a belated live album, *"Rank"*, was issued the following year. The junior members Rourke and Joyce initially appeared with Brix Smith's Adult Net, then backed Sinead O'Connor, before Joyce joined the Buzzcocks. Morrissey pursued a solo career, while Marr moved from the Pretenders to The The and Electronic, as well as appearing on a variety of sessions for artists as diverse as Bryan Ferry, Talking Heads, Billy Bragg, Kirsty MacColl, the Pet Shop Boys, Stex and Banderas. In 1992 there was renewed interest in the Smiths following the furore surrounding Johnny Rogan's controversial biography of the group, and Warner Brothers acquisition of the group's back-catalogue from Rough Trade.

Albums: *The Smiths* (Rough Trade 1984), *Meat Is Murder* (Rough Trade 1985), *The Queen Is Dead* (Rough Trade 1986), *Strangeways, Here We Come* (Rough Trade 1987), *"Rank"* (Rough Trade 1988). Compilations: *Hatful Of Hollow* (Rough Trade 1984), *The World Won't Listen* (Rough Trade 1987), *Louder Than Bombs* (Rough Trade 1987), *The Peel Sessions* (Strange Fruit 1988), *Best...2* (WEA 1992), *Singles* (WEA 1995).

Videos: *The Complete Picture*.

Further reading: *Morrissey & Marr: The Severed Alliance*, Johnny Rogan.

Snakes Of Shake

This 80s Scottish group comprised Seori Burnette (guitar/lead vocals/harmonica), Tzen Vermillion (guitar), Sandy Brown (piano/accordion/vocals), Robert Renfrew (bass/slide guitar/vocals) and Rhod 'Lefty' Burnett (drums). Their debut album's highlight was the title-track, 'Southern Cross', a slice of cajun-influenced folk pop which was persistently promoted to break the band, without success. Seori Burnette's songwriting talent was often over-shadowed by his excessively dramatic singing style. By the time a second album was released, the line-up comprised Burnette, Brown, Renfrew, Neil Scott (guitar) and Iain Shedden (drums), the last-named previously of pop/punk act, the Jolt. *Gracelands And The Natural Wood* highlighted prefectly the group's blend of folk and rock styles. However, any progress was irretrievably undermined when the group's outlet, Making Waves, went into receivership, and they subsequently split up. Burnett and Shedden quickly resurfaced in a new act, Summerhill.

Albums: *Southern Cross* (Tense But Confident 1985), *Gracelands And The Natural Wood* (Making Waves 1986).

Snapper

This New Zealand band specialising in 60s garage punk rock were formed in Dunedin, a college town at the bottom of South Island, in 1988. Veteran singer/guitarist Peter Gutteridge was a founder member of both the Chills and the Clean, the island's two most inspired outfits of the late 70s and early 80s. Their debut album emerged on the tiny Avalanche label, based in Edinburgh, Scotland, a country which has long harboured a predilection for Antipodean pop. Songs like 'Death And Weirdness In The Surfing Zone' were typical fuzz guitar workouts with Christine Voice's organ augmenting. Gutteridge's love of the Velvet Underground and Stooges shone through much of this work. Album: *Shotgun Blossom* (Avalanche 1991).

SNFU

From Edmonton, Alberta, Canada, SNFU are a hardcore punk band who took obvious influence from both the Subhumans and D.O.A. Their line-ups have always centred around Mr Chi Pig (vocals), and Brent (guitar), with the rhythm section changing with almost every successive album. One of their early drummers, John Card, would later join D.O.A. SNFU have persevered over the years with a formula encompassing largely headlong addrenalin rushes. The most significant interlude was *If You Swear You'll Catch No Fish*, slick titles such as 'Better Homes And Gardens' indicating a growing maturity in the way they conveyed their lyrical gaze. Previously, overtly obvious joke anthems like 'Cannibal Cafe' had been their let-down. By the next album, they were speeding along at a furious rate once more, though some of the early angst had disappeared; 'It's hard to be angry when you live in an environment like this; the physical aspect of Edmonton is so comfortable'. They had definitely not grown in self-importance however; 'We're still the same awful band we were in '81'. Still active, SNFU encapsulate the best traditions of Canadian hardcore; energy, verve and humour. They moved over to Epitaph Records in 1995 for another splintering punk rock album.

Albums: *And No One Else Wanted To Play* (BYO 1984), *If You Swear You'll Catch No Fish* (BYO 1986), *Better Than A Stick In The Eye* (BYO 1988), *Last Of The Big Time Suspenders* (Skullduggery 1992), *The Ones Most Likely To Succeed* (Epitaph 1995).

Snuff

Formed in London in 1988 by Andy (b. 4 July 1963, London England), Duncan (b. 22 August 1964, Louth, England) and Simon (b. 11 December 1966, London, England), Snuff started off as 'a joke' with a hectic mixture of implausibly fast guitars and exquisite melodies. The threesome soon created their own niche in a British music scene sorely lacking the hardcore hardware to rival the host of angry American bands. Next to their own creations such as 'Not Listening' Snuff added a litany of thrashed-up cover versions, ranging from Tiffany to Simon And Garfunkel and numerous British television commercial jingles in between. Such was the band's sense of economy, they once managed to squeeze over 30 tracks onto one 12-inch single! Had the band's ambition matched their liberal taste for cover versions, Snuff's potential would have been huge. However, by consciously adhering to a post-punk manifesto Snuff managed to stay resolutely independent in the face of large financial offers from the corporates. Somewhat fittingly given their stance, when Snuff tired of the demands of the band and the threat of a 'cabaret punk' tag, they immediately called it a day. Their farewell gig was at London's Kilburn National Ballroom in 1991, a great highpoint for any band to depart on. Simon and Duncan started working together on a new project, while bassist Andy joined fellow hardcore band Leatherface.

Album: *SnuffSaidButGorBlimeyGuvIfHeDidn'tThrowA-WobblerChaChaChaChaChaChaChaChaChaChaChaChaYou'reGoingHomeInACosmicAmbience* (1989).

Social Distortion

Formed in Fullerton, Orange County, California, USA, in the summer of 1978, Social Distortion initially featured Mike Ness (guitar), Casey Royer (drums), and the Agnew brothers, Rikk (vocals/guitar) and Frank (bass). That line-up only lasted until the following year, at which point the Agnews departed for fellow Fullerton band, the Adolescents. Dennis Danell then joined on bass, and Ness took over vocals (following experiments with a singer titled Dee Dee), and 'Carrott' replaced Royer. However, this remains a simplification of the band's early line-up shuffles, with other members including Tim Mag (later DI) and Danny Furious (ex-Avengers). After impressing Robbie Fields of Posh Boy Records at a party in Fullerton in 1981, the band booked studio time through him to record their 'Mainliner' 7-inch. This was a one-off affair, however, and afterwards the group moved on to their own 13th Floor Records imprint, also picking up a new and more permanent drummer and backing vocalist, Derek O'Brien (also DI). By this time Danell had switched to rhythm guitar, with Brent Liles becoming the new bass player (making the band a quartet once more). This line-up would last until 1984, spanning the recording of *Mommy's Little Monster*. A superb punk rock debut, this collection revealed more cohesion and tradition than the band's immediate peers, with a sound tracing its heritage back to the Rolling Stones as much as the Sex Pistols. It seemed that Social Distortion had all the ingredients to popularise hardcore ('Another State Of Mind' was achieving plays on MTV long before punk bands were fashionable in that medium), but their breakthrough was delayed by Ness's increasing use of hard drugs. The band practically disintegrated as a result. O'Brien joined DI permanently, while Liles fled for Agent Orange in 1985. Their replacements were John Maurer (bass) and Chris Reece (drums; ex-Lewd). After attending detox clinics Ness finally made a comeback with 1988's *Prison Bound*. A mature, less strident effort, it saw the band flirt with country on tracks such as 'Like An Outlaw', returning to a revved-up Rolling Stones' blueprint for a cover of 'Backstreet Girl' as well as sharp original songs. It also signalled a move towards conventional blues rock which would come to fruition with successive albums for Epic and Sony Records. The best of these was 1992's *Between Heaven And Hell*, by which time the multi-tattooed Ness had moved into prime rockabilly mode, with lyrical inspiration taken from his battles with drink and drugs, ' I live my life for six months as well as I know how, then I sit down with my guitar and it kind of comes out.' In the light of this, songs such as 'Born To Lose' undercut their potential for cliché with the kind of hard-hitting authenticity which had always surrounded the band.

Albums: *Mommy's Little Monster* (13th Floor 1983), *Prison Bound* (Restless 1988), *Social Distortion* (Epic 1990), *Between Heaven And Hell* (Sony 1992).

Soft Boys

When Syd Barrett gave up music for art, another Cambridge musician emerged to take on his mantle. Robyn Hitchcock started out as a solo performer and busker before becoming a member of B.B. Blackberry And The Swelterettes, then the Chosen Few, the Worst Fears, and Maureen And The Meatpackers. It was with the last named that Hitchcock first recorded (in 1976), although the results were not released until much later. His next group, Dennis And The Experts became the Soft Boys in 1976. The Soft Boys first recording session was in March 1977 by which point the line-up was Hitchcock (vocals/guitar/bass), Alan Davies (guitar), Andy Metcalfe (bass), and Morris Windsor aka Otis Fagg (drums). The original sessions remain unreleased but the same line-up also recorded a three track single - known as the *Give It To The Soft Boys* EP - for the notorious local Cambridge label, Raw Records (or rip-off records, to those who knew its owner well). This was released in the autumn of 1977 after which Davies left and Kimberley Rew was installed on guitar, harmonica, and vocals. The Soft Boys, now signed to Radar Records, released the single '(I Wanna Be An) Anglepoise Lamp', but it was not considered representative of their innovative live work. Forming their own Two Crabs label they released *Can Of Bees* in 1979 after which they replaced Metcalfe with Matthew Seligman. Jim Melton, who had been playing harmonica for a while, also left. Their remaining releases came on the Armageddon label and included *Underwater Moonlight*, which is considered amongst Hitchcock's finest moments. They broke up early in 1981 and Hitchcock went on to enjoy an erratic solo career, recruiting along the way Metcalfe and Windsor to form the Egyptians. Rew joined Katrina And The Waves and wrote the classic 'Going Down To Liverpool', while Seligman joined Local Heroes SW9 and continued to contribute to Hitchcock's solo efforts.

Albums: *A Can Of Bees* (Two Crabs 1979), *Underwater Moonlight* (Armageddon 1980), *Two Halves For The Price Of One* (Armageddon 1981), *Invisible Hits* (Midnight 1983), *Live At The Portland Arms* (Midnight 1987, cassette only). Compilations: *Raw Cuts* (Overground 1989, mini-album), *The Soft Boys 1976-81* (Rykodisc 1994).

Some Bizzare Records

Founded by the eccentric teenage entrepreneur, Stevo, the UK-based Some Bizzare Records was one of the most challenging and enterprising labels of the 80s. The pioneering *Some Bizzare Album* brought together an array of fringe groups including Throbbing Gristle, Classix Noveaux, Clock DVA, Cabaret Voltaire, Blancmange, Depeche Mode, Soft Cell and The The. It was the last two acts that were to continue with the label and enable Stevo to continue mining for arcane talent. Cabaret Voltaire also returned for a spell, as did Genesis P. Orridge's Throbbing Gristle offshoot, Psychic TV. Stevo's interest in industrial music saw the signing of the first foreign group to the label, Einsturzende Neubaten. They were soon followed by London's Test Department. Mischievously subversive, sleazy and often controversial, Some Bizzare was a welcome haven for Jim Thirlwell and his various releases under the banner Foetus. By the end of the 80s Stevo had lost a major signing, The The, and, not for the first time, the label's financial future was a matter of conjecture. The power of the label lay in its wilful obscurity aligned with Stevo's remarkable capacity to bring unlikely acts to critical and occasionally acclaim. Whether new signings such as Stex, Tim Hutton and Kandis King will re-invigorate the label's catalogue is part of the test for the 90s.

Sonic Boom

b. Peter Kember, 19 November 1965. UK-based Sonic Boom's solo project was originally planned as an aside for his main love, the Spacemen 3. Signing to the Silvertone label, Sonic issued 'Angel' (a drug-related tale not dissimilar both lyrically and musically to the Velvet Underground's 'Heroin') in 1989. This was followed by *Spectrum* for which Sonic was helped by fellow Spacemen Jason and Will Carruthers, plus the Jazz Butcher and the Perfect Disaster's Phil Parfitt. Spectrum's hypnotic blend of repetitive guitar riffs and keyboard runs betrayed his love of New York duo Suicide, but nevertheless possessed a definite if quiet charm. It even sported a psychedelic, gatefold revolving sleeve. Early buyers could send away for an orange vinyl 10-inch, 'Octaves'/'Tremeloes', which featured two elongated, synthesized notes! Unfortunately, the Spacemen 3 split in his wake to form Spiritualized, although their swan-song appeared later, ironically charting. Sonic re-emerged in the summer of 1991 with a low-key instrumental demo single, '(I Love You) To The Moon And Back', distributed free at gigs.
Album: *Spectrum* (1990).

Sonic Youth

A product of New York's experimental 'No-Wave' scene, Sonic Youth first recorded under the auspices of *avant garde* guitarist Glenn Branca. Thurston Moore (guitar), Lee Ranaldo (guitar) and Kim Gordon (bass) performed together on Branca's *Symphony No. 3*, while the group debuted in its own right on his Neutral label. *Sonic Youth* was recorded live at New York's Radio City Music Hall in December 1981 and featured original drummer Richard Edson. Three further collections, *Confusion Is Sex*, *Sonic Death* and a mini-album, *Kill Yr Idols*, completed the quartet's formative period which was marked by their pulsating blend of discordant guitars, impassioned vocals and ferocious, compulsive drum patterns, courtesy of newcomer Jim Sclavunos, or his replacement, Bob Bert. *Bad Moon Rising* was the first Sonic Youth album to secure a widespread release in both the USA and Britain. This acclaimed set included the compulsive 'I'm Insane' and the eerie 'Death Valley '69', a collaboration with Lydia Lunch, which invoked the horror of the infamous Charles Manson murders. Bob Bert was then replaced by Steve Shelley, who has remained with the line-up ever since. In 1986 the group unleashed *Evol*, which refined their ability to mix melody with menace, particularly on the outstanding 'Shadow Of A Doubt'. The album also introduced the Youth's tongue-in-cheek fascination with Madonna. 'Expressway To Yr Skull' was given two alternative titles, 'Madonna, Sean And Me' and 'The Cruxifiction Of Sean Penn', while later in the year the band were joined by Mike Watt from Firehose in a spin-off project, Ciccone Youth, which resulted in a mutated version of 'Into The Groove(y)'.

(In 1989 this *alter ego* culminated in *Ciccone Youth*, which combined dance tracks with experimental sounds redolent of German groups Faust and Neu.) Sonic Youth's career continued with the highly-impressive *Sister*, followed in 1988 by *Daydream Nation*, a double set which allowed the group to expand themes when required. Once again the result was momentous. The instrumentation was powerful, recalling the intensity of the Velvet Underground or Can while the songs themselves were highly memorable. In 1990 Sonic Youth left the independent circuit by signing with the Geffen Records stable, going on to establish a reputation as godfathers to the alternative US rock scene. Thurston Moore was instrumental in the signing of Nirvana to Geffen Records, while Kim Gordon was similarly pivotal in the formation of Hole. Steve Shelley would also work closely with Geffen on a number of acts. Successive stints on Lollapalooza tours helped to make Sonic Youth the nation's best known underground band, while the group's members continued to collaborate on music and soundtrack projects to a degree which ensured the continuance of an already vast discography.
Albums: *Confusion Is Sex* (Neutral 1983), *Kill Yr Idols* (Zensor 1983), *Sonic Death* (Ecstatic Peace 1984), *Bad Moon Rising* (Homestead 1985), *Evol* (SST 1986), *Sister* (SST 1987), *Daydream Nation* (Blast First 1988), *Goo* (Geffen 1990), *Dirty Boots* (Geffen 1991, mini-album), *Dirty* (Geffen 1992), *Experimental Jet Set, Trash And No Star* (Geffen 1994), *Washing Machine* (Geffen 1995), *Made In USA* (Rhino/WEA 1995; film soundtrack, rec. 1986). Compilation: *Screaming Fields Of Sonic Love* (Blast First 1995). Lee Renaldo solo: *From Here To Infinity* (SST 1987). Thurston Moore solo: *Psychic Hearts* (Geffen 1995).
Further reading: *Confusion Is Next: The Sonic Youth Story*, Alec Foego (1994).

Soul Asylum

Originally a Minneapolis, Minnesota, USA, garage hardcore band, Soul Asylum spent their early years under the yoke of comparisons to the more feted Replacements and Husker Du. Indeed, Bob Mould has been known to fondly describe Soul Asylum as 'our little brothers', and was on hand as producer for their first two long playing sets. Their roots in hardcore are betrayed by the choice of their original name, Loud Fast Rules. Their first formation in 1981 centred around the abiding creative nucleus of Dave Pirner (b. c.1965; vocals/guitar) and Dan Murphy (b. c.1963; guitar), alongside Karl Mueller (b. c.1965; bass) and Pat Morley (drums). Together they specialised in sharp lyrical observations and poppy punk. Morley left in December 1984 to be replaced, eventually, by Grant Young (b. c.1965), who arrived in time for *Made To Be Broken*. As their music progressed it became easier to trace back their heritage to the 60s rather than 70s. *Hang Time*, their third album proper, was their first for a major. It saw them move into the hands of a new production team (Ed Stasium and Lenny Kaye), with a very apparent display of studio polish. The mini-album which was meant to have preceded it (but didn't), *Clam Dip And Other Delights*, included their dismantling of a Foreigner song, 'Jukebox Hero', and a riotous reading of Janis Joplin's 'Move Over'. When playing live they have been

known to inflict their renditions of Barry Manilow's 'Mandy' and Glen Campbell's 'Rhinestone Cowboy' on an audience. Though *The Horse They Rode In On* was another splendid album, the idea of Soul Asylum breaking into the big league was becoming a progressively fantastic one (indeed band members had to pursue alternative employment in 1990, during which time Pirner suffered a nervous breakdown). However, largely thanks to the MTV rotation of 'Somebody To Shove', that was about to change. In its aftermath they gained a prestigious slot on the *David Letterman Show* before support billing to Bob Dylan and Guns N'Roses, plus a joint headlining package with Screaming Trees and the Spin Doctors on a three-month Alternative Nation Tour. Soon they were appearing in front of a worldwide audience of 400 million at the 1993 MTV Awards ceremony, where they were joined by R.E.M.'s Peter Buck and Victoria Williams for a jam of their follow-up hit, 'Runaway Train'. With Pirner dating film starlet Winona Ryder, the profile of a band who seemed destined for critical reverence and public indifference could not have been more unexpectedly high. However, in 1995 the band announced that their next studio sessions would avoid the overt commercial textures of their previous album. They also recruited their fourth drummer, Stirling Campbell, to replace Grant Young.
Albums: *Say What You Will* (Twin Tone 1984), *Made To Be Broken* (Twin Tone 1986), *While You Were Out* (Twin Tone 1986), *Hang Time* (Twin Tone/A&M 1988), *Clam Dip And Other Delights* (What Goes On 1989, mini-album), *Soul Asylum And The Horse They Rode In On* (Twin Tone/A&M 1990), *Grave Dancers Union* (A&M 1993), *Let Your Dim Light Shine* (A&M 1995). Compilations: *Time's Incinerator* (Twin Tone 1984, cassette only), *Say What You Will Clarence, Karl Sold The Truck* (Twin Tone 1989).

Sound

Prior to the Sound's formation Adrian Borland (vocals/guitar) had already released *Calling On Youth* and *Close Up*, and the *One To Infinity* EP as leader of UK's Outsiders from 1977-78. Towards the end of 1978 Graham Green joined the band, replacing the original bass player, Bob Lawrence, and Michael Dudley (drums) was recruited to play alongside Jan (percussion). The new line-up recorded three tracks, which emerged on the Tortch label as the *Physical World* EP in December 1979, credited not as the Outsiders but as the Sound. They had progressed musically from their punk roots and were anxious to leave behind a name that still conjured up the atmosphere of 1977. After the critical acclaim of the debut EP, they signed to Korova Records, releasing a string of singles, 'Heyday', 'Sense Of Purpose', 'Hothouse' and two albums, *Jeopardy* and *From The Lions Mouth*. These stirred a great deal of interest from both critics and public alike, establishing Borland as one of the most creative and mature writers of the post-punk scene. During 1979, Borland and Green created Second Layer, a harder, more experimental project that ran parallel with the Sound, releasing two EPs and an album. Sporadic releases continued throughout the 80s for several different labels with varying degrees of quality and success, but never managing to equal the halcyon days of 1980-81. In addition to the singles 'Counting The Days', 'One Thousand

Reasons', Temperature Drop', 'Hand Of Love' and 'Iron Years', they also collaborated with singer Kevin Hewick on the *This Cover Keeps* EP in 1984. The band finally fragmented in late 1987 but Borland continued to record for Play It Again Sam as Adrian Borland And The Citizens, as well as resurrecting Second Layer.
Albums: *Jeopardy* (Korova 1980), *From The Lions Mouth* (Korova 1981), *All Fall Down* (Korova 1982), *Heads And Hearts* (Statik 1985), *In The Hothouse* (Statik 1985), *Thunder* (Statik 1987).

Soup Dragons

The Soup Dragons emerged from Glasgow, Scotland, as one of a clutch of bands championed by the *New Musical Express* via their *C86* project. The group evolved around Sean Dickson (lead vocals/guitar/songwriter). In early 1985, he met up with Jim McCulloch (guitar), Ross A. Sinclair (drums) and Sushil K. Dade (bass), the collective taking their name from characters in the cult children's television programme, *The Clangers*. A flexi-disc, 'If You Were The Only Girl In The World', emerged at the end of the year, by which time the band were circulating a demonstration tape, *You Have Some Too*. The Subway Organisation label issued the Soup Dragons' first single, 'Whole Wide World' (1986), a tight, exciting slab of Buzzcocks-styled pop, performed at breakneck pace. This attracted ex-Wham! manager Jazz Summers, who set up a new label for them, Raw TV Products, in time for 'Hang-Ten!' (1986). In the meantime, Sean and later Jim had left another group they were serving time with, the BMX Bandits. 'Head Gone Astray' (1987), revealed a marked change away from new wave, towards 60s rock. 'Can't Take No More' and 'Soft As Your Face' fared well commercially but the latter's serene sound was at odds with the band's direction. 'The Majestic Head' (1988) lured Sire Records into a deal, but the next single, 'Kingdom Chains' flopped. A subsequent debut album, *This Is Our Art*, emerged without fanfare. The Stooges'-influenced 'Backwards Dog' and 'Crotch Deep Trash', introduced a rockier feel and this was followed by the dance-orientated 'Mother Universe' (1990). Hinging around a Marc Bolan riff, the single was typical of the tracks on *Lovegod*, the band's second album. By this time, Sinclair had been replaced by new drummer Paul Quinn. After discovering an obscure Rolling Stones track from their 1965 *Out Of Our Heads* collection, the Soup Dragons teamed up with reggae singer Junior Reid and DJ/remixer Terry Farley to create a formidable crossover between white 'indie' rock and dance music. The single was a massive hit, something that had previously eluded the band. *Lovegod* was re-promoted and a remixed 'Mother Universe' was reissued, giving them further chart success. However, accusations of bandwagon-jumping contnued to haunt the band (the press uniting on the fact that Primal Scream had got there first in whichever direction the group pursued). As the 90s progressed diminishing returns became the order of the day, and eventual dissolution with it. Quinn would go on to replace Brendan O'Hare in Teenage Fanclub in 1994, while Sushil joined BMX Bandits and Jim McCulloch moved to Superstar.
Albums: *This Is Our Art* (Sire 1988), *Lovegod* (Raw TV 1990), *Hotwired* (Big Life 1992).

Spacemen 3

Spacemen 3 were instigated in Rugby, Warwickshire, England, in 1982 by Sonic Boom (b. Pete Kember, 19 November 1965) and regional soulmate Jason Pierce (also, strangely enough, b. 19 November 1965). Augmented by the rhythm section of Rosco and Pete Baines, it took Spacemen 3 fully four years to blossom onto record. Initially crying shy of sounding too much like the Cramps, the band carefully evolved into one-chord wonders; masters of the hypnotic, blissed-out groove. Such was their languid approach to working, and so dream-inspiring was their music, Spacemen 3 made a habit of sitting down for the entirety of their gigs. 1989's *Playing With Fire* included the intensely repetitive blast of 'Revolutions'. By this time Baines and Rosco had formed what was tantamount to a Spacemen 3 spin-off in the Darkside, allowing Will Carruthers and John Mattock to step into their places, and although this was the peak of the band's career, fundamental problems were still inherent: Sonic Boom made no secret of his drug dependency, having replaced heroin with methadone, and he and Jason Pierce were gradually growing apart to the point where they were chasing different goals. The relationship became so strained that *Recurring*, although still a Spaceman 3 effort, saw the two forces working separately, Boom being attributed with side one and Pierce with side two. By this stage Boom had embarked upon a solo career and Pierce was working with Mattock and Carruthers in another band, Spiritualized, a situation which further fanned the flames. When *Recurring* finally saw the light of day Spaceman 3's creative forces refused to even be interviewed together. A petty demise to what was, for some time, a creatively intense band.
Albums: *Sound Of Confusion* (Glass 1986), *The Perfect Prescription* (Glass 1987), *Performance* (Glass 1988), *Playing With Fire* (Fire 1989), *Recurring* (Fire 1991).

Spear Of Destiny

Formed from the ashes of Theatre Of Hate in early 1983, Spear Of Destiny took their name from the mythological weapon which pierced the body of Christ, and was supposedly acquired over the years by Attila The Hun, Napoleon and Hitler. This helped the band to attract quite a volume of destructive commentary in the press. The original line-up featured mainstay Kirk Brandon (b. 3 August 1956, Westminster, London, England; vocals/guitar), Chris Bell (drums), Lasettes Ames (saxophone) and Stan Stammers (ex-Theatre Of Hate; bass). They signed to CBS, but maintained their own label design, 'Burning Rome', which had appeared on previous Theatre Of Hate releases. The first single 'Flying Scotsman' arrived in 1983, and was featured on *The Grapes Of Wrath* alongside the relentless single 'The Wheel'. Critical response to the group was divided. By July, Bell and Ames had left, for reasons described by Bell as personal and religious. Brandon and Stammers brought in former Theatre Of Hate saxophonist John Lennard (b. Canada, ex-Diodes) and Nigel Preston (ex Theatre Of Hate, Sex Gang Children). A third line-up added Alan St Clair (guitar) and Neil Pyzor (ex-Case; keyboards, saxophone), Dolphin Taylor (ex-Tom Robinson Band and Stiff Little Fingers; drums) and Nicky Donnelly (ex-Case; saxophone). It was this formation which recorded *One Eyed Jacks*, arguably the band's best album, and

the singles 'Rainmaker', 'Liberator' and 'Prisoner Of Love', the latter signalling a change in direction which would be more fully realized on the follow-up album. When *World Service* arrived, there was considerable disappointment from fans and critics alike. Having built an enviable reputation as a lyricist of considerable vigour, tracks like 'Mickey' seemed grotesque and clumsy. Further personnel changes became commonplace, and by 1987 and *Outlands* the line-up comprised Pete Barnacle (drums), Volker Janssen (keyboards) and Chris Bostock (bass) alongside Brandon. The summer of that year saw Brandon incapacitated for six months with an ankle injury that left him unable to walk, an affliction from which he still carries a limp. However, the band were soon back in the charts with 'Never Take Me Alive', and a support tour with U2. Their 1988 singles 'So In Love With You' and 'Radio Radio' saw them switch from Epic to Virgin. By December 1990, old colleague Stan Stammers returned on bass, alongside new drummer and guitarist Bobby Rae Mayhem and Mark Thwaite. 1991 opened with Brandon touring once more under the joint Theatre Of Hate/Spear Of Destiny banner.
Albums: *The Grapes Of Wrath* (1983), *One Eyed Jacks* (1984), *World Service* (1985) *Outlands* (1987), *The Price You Pay* (1988), *S.O.D.'s Law* (1992), *Live At The Lyceum* (1993).

Specials

This Coventry, England, ska-influenced group was formed in the summer of 1977 as the Special AKA, with a line-up comprising Jerry Dammers (b. Gerald Dankin, 22 May 1954, India; keyboards), Terry Hall (b. 19 March 1959, Coventry, England; vocals), Neville Staples (vocals/percussion), Lynval Golding (b. 24 July 1951, Coventy, England; guitar), Roddy Radiation (b. Rodney Byers; guitar), Sir Horace Gentleman (b. Horace Panter; bass) and John Bradbury (drums). Following touring with the Clash, they set up their own multi-racial 2-Tone label and issued the Prince Buster-inspired 'Gangsters', which reached the UK Top 10. After signing their label to Chrysalis Records, the group abbreviated their name to the Specials. Their Elvis Costello produced debut album was a refreshing, exuberant effort which included the Top 10 single 'A Message To You, Rudi'. The group spearheaded what became the 2-Tone movement and their label enjoyed an array of sparkling hits from Madness, the Beat and the Selecter. In January 1980 the Specials were at their peak following the release of their live EP, *The Special AKA Live*. The pro-contraceptive title track, 'Too Much Too Young', propelled them to number 1 in the UK charts. Further Top 10 hits with 'Rat Race', 'Stereotype' and 'Do Nothing' followed. The Specials ability to 'capture the moment' in pop was most persuasively felt with 'Ghost Town', which topped the charts during the summer of 1981 while Britain was suffering inner-city riots. At this new peak of success, the group fragmented. Staples, Hall and Golding went on to form the intriguing Fun Boy Three, leaving Dammers to continue with a new line-up, which reverted to the old name, the Special AKA. After the minor success of 'Racist Friend' and the anthemic Top 10 hit, 'Nelson Mandela', Dammers became more politically active with Artists Against Apartheid. He was also a major force behind the Nelson

Mandela 70th Birthday Party concert at London's Wembley Stadium on 11 June 1988. The retitled 'Free Nelson Mandela (70th Birthday Remake)' was issued to coincide with the show. However, Dammers was reluctant to record again due to outstanding debts over the *In The Studio* album, which would have to be cleared before he was free of contract. In 1993, with the 2-Tone revival in evidence, Desmond Dekker joined Staples, Golding, Radiation and Gentleman on *King Of Kings*, released on the Trojan Records label. Dammers, meanwhile, had a new band, Jazz Odyssey, but he would soon retire to DJing and studio projects after he developed tinnitus.

Albums. as the Specials *The Specials* (2-Tone/Chrysalis 1979), *More Specials* (2-Tone/Chrysalis 1980), as the Special AKA *In The Studio* (2-Tone/Chrysalis 1984), with Desmond Dekker *King Of Kings* (Trojan 1993). Compilations: *Singles* (Chrysalis 1991), *The Selecter & The Specials: Live In Concert* (Windsong 1993).

Spin

Formed in the UK during the summer of 1989 by Lee Clark (b. 20 January 1963, Cleethorpes, England; vocals), Steve Mason (b. 17 April 1971, Pontypridd, Wales; bass), John Mason (b. 8 August 1967, Bristol, England) and Matt James (b. 20 September 1967, Deptford, London, England). Spin emerged from the ashes of the Go-Hole to claim a place in the legendary Camberwell squat scene in south London. Their first EP, released in the autumn of 1990, was a comfortably contemporary blend of guitars and danceable beats which put Spin in vogue alongside the successes of the Manchester 'Baggy' movement (a phrase culled from the bands' predilection for flared trousers). The quartet's career continued smoothly into 1991 until their first British tour at the end of March, when the tour van - broken down on the hard shoulder of the motorway - was hit by an articulated lorry. Three members of the Spin entourage were hospitalized in intensive care, with bassist John Mason still insufficiently recovered six months later and thus temporarily replaced by Kev Miles. Vocalist Lee Clark meanwhile, ironically the only person not injured in the accident, moved to Paris to become a poet and vowed to never travel by transit again. His post was filled by Martin T. Falls (b. 15 May 1970, Cardiff, Wales) whereupon Spin proved their resoluteness by completing and subsequently releasing their debut album to sympathetic acclaim.
Album: *In Motion* (Foundation 1991).

Spirea X

In 1988, tired of touring incessantly, Jim Beattie (vocals/guitar) left Primal Scream and moved back to Glasgow. Recharged, he formed Spirea X in the summer of 1990, their name taken from a Primal Scream b-side. He had been instrumental in Primal Scream's 'jangly' period, writing the classic 'Velocity Crescent', and he would continue to share Gillespie's nonchalant arrogance: 'We're going to do it. . . by having better songs, better melodies, better arrangements, better everything. By sheer force of ideas'. After a demo in July 1990, which attracted interest almost across the board, they played their first live gig in September at Queen Margaret Student Union. Despite heated competition to get Beattie's signature he eventually settled for the independent label 4AD Records. The band quickly lost their original bass player and guitarist, and by May 1991 featured Andy Kerr (drums), Judith Boyle (Beattie's girlfriend, vocals/guitar), Jamie O'Donnell (bass) and Thomas McGurk (rhythm guitar). Two well received EPs followed, *Chlorine Dream* and *Speed Reaction*, before a debut album titled after a collection of Rimbaud's poetry. Here Beattie's grasp of melody and a fixation with Byrds-styled harmonies was allowed full rein, resulting in a mesmerising selection. The set also included an enthralling rendition of Love's 'Signed D.C.'. Alas *Fireblade Skies* was not a commercial success and the group - now reduced to a duo of Beattie and Boyle was dropped by their label in 1993.
Album: *Fireblade Skies* (4AD 1991).

Spiritualized

This dark, neo-psychedelic band were formed by Jason Pierce (b. 19 November, 1965; vocals, guitar) after his messy split from former writing partner and Spacemen 3 cohort Pete 'Sonic Boom' Kember. Based in Rugby, England, they were inaugurated while Spacemen 3 were still officially active. Pierce took the remnants of that band with him (Will; bass and Jon Mattock; drums) and added his girlfriend Kate Radley (organ) and Mark Retoy (guitar). Their first release was a cover of the Troggs' 'Anyway That You Want Me', then 'Feel So Sad', a sonic opera lasting over 13 minutes. Headliners at ICA's 'Irn Bru' Rock week, their familiar Velvet Underground guitar noise/barrage found favour with old Spacemen 3 bands as well as new converts. Singles like 'Why Don't You Smile' were something of a departure from Pierce's morbid and moribund legacy. Notoriously shy and reticent in interviews, he had a preference for sitting down while playing gigs, which an impressionable audience eagerly imitated. Their efforts thus far, whilst somewhat predictable, have surpassed those of a quiescent Kember.
Albums: *Lazer Guided Melodies* (1992), *Live* (1993).

Spitfire

Formed in 1990, this post-My Bloody Valentine UK guitar pop group made rapid progress. The band consisted of Jeff Pitcher (vocals), younger brother Nick (bass), Simon Walker (guitar), Matt Wise (guitar) and Justin Welch (drums). Original drummer Scott Kenny decided to join his other group Ever, while guitarist Steve White also left because he did not want to tour. They leapt into the fray with two EPs, *Translucent* and *Superbaby*. Their debut included a daring cover of the *Six Million Dollar Man* theme, and 'Superbaby' was produced by That Petrol Emotion's Steve Mack. A tour with Blur helped bring them to national prominence, but more newsworthy were their infamous 'Back Stage' passes. Designed specifically to cater for groupies, their tongues were firmly in cheek, but the press latched on to them as misogynists. It was 1993 before their first full length album emerged, though this still featured all the familiar swager on the title-cut and 'Firebird', which included the intrusion of a flute.
Album: *Sex Bomb* (Fire 1993).

SPK

This industrial noise band has advocated that their name stands for Surgical Penis Klinik, Systems Planning Korporation and other connotations at various points in their career. They began in 1978 when percussionist Derek Thompson was working in a mental hospital looking after brief SPK member Neil, a patient. Together they joined female banshee Sinan, the original conception of SPK being an alias for Sozialistiche Patienten Kollective. This evolved out of homage to the German movement of the same name trying to force improved rights for mental patients. They gained notoriety at early gigs by parading slides and films of medical operations, though later they would embrace flame throwers, oil drums etc. as part of their stage act. In so doing they shared links with the 'metal dance' outfits whose dealings were mainly in metallic percussion; Test Department and Einsturzende Neubaten. However, at a London Venue gig in December 1983, one of their members almost hit members of the audience (including one particularly unimpressed journalist) by swinging a metal chain out in to the auditorium. Such activities would do little to endear them to a largely cynical press, who had already collared them as being too eager to draw any sort of reaction. The situation was exacerbated by the dire mutant industrial creation, 'Metal Dance'. Earlier recordings, notably the inhospitable climate of searing noise and pain which was 1982's *Lichenschrei*, snapped at the heels of what Throbbing Gristle were doing without ever capturing the essence. However, things improved with the arrival of Graham Revell, who brought them to a recorded peak with *Zamia Lehmanni*, which deliberately evoked the sounds of fifth century Byzantium. By the 90s Revell had turned to soundtrack composition and using 'insect' sounds.
Albums: *Leichenschrei* (1982), *From Science To Ritual* (Plasma 1984), *Information Overload* (Normal 1985), *Zamia Lehmanni* (Side Effects 1986), *Auto-Da-Fe* (Walter Ulbright 1984), *Digitalis, Ambigua, Gold & Poison* (Nettwerk 1988), *Oceania* (Side Effects 1988).

Split Enz

Originally formed in Auckland, New Zealand in 1972 as Split Ends, this expansive group evolved around the duo of Tim Finn (b. 25 June 1952, Te Awamuta, New Zealand; vocals/piano) and Jonathan 'Mike' Chunn (b. New Zealand; bass/keyboards) with Geoff Chunn (b. New Zealand; drums - later replaced by Paul Emlyn Crowther), Paul 'Wally' Wilkinson (b. New Zealand; guitar), Miles Golding (b. New Zealand; violin), Rob Gillies (b. New Zealand; saxophone), Michael Howard (b. New Zealand; flute) and Phil Judd (b. New Zealand; vocals/guitar/mandolin). Their reluctance to perform on the traditional bar circuit, left only the college and university venues, as well as the occasional open-air park concert, to enact their brand of theatrical-pop. They featured an eclectic set, wore unusual costumes, facial make-up (which drew comparisons in their homeland to Skyhooks), and even featured a spoons player (percussionist/costume designer Noel Crombie). After three singles released in New Zealand, the band were well established in their homeland, particularly after reaching the final of a national television talent show. After moving to Australia in early 1975, and altering their name, the group recorded their first album for the Mushroom label. At the invitation of Phil Manzanera who had seen the band when they supported Roxy Music on tour in Australia, the band flew to the UK. Signed to the Chrysalis label in Europe, Manzanera recorded the band's second album which included some re-working of their earlier material. Unfortunately, the band's arrival in England coincided with the punk movement and they found acceptance difficult. Returning to Australia in 1977, Split Enz recruited Tim Finn's brother Neil (b. 27 May 1958, Te Awamutu, New Zealand) to replace Judd. The departure of Wilkinson, Crowther and Chunn also made way for Nigel Griggs (b. 18 August 1949, New Zealand; bass) and Malcolm Green (b. 25 January 1953, England; drums). The 1979 album *True Colours*, on A&M Records contained their most successful single, Neil Finn's glorious 'I Got You' with reached number 12 in the UK. Follow-up releases saw the band reach modest positions in the US album charts, but they ran into trouble in the UK when their 'Six Months In A Leaky Boat' was banned by the BBC as its title was considered too provocative at a time when the British were fighting the Falklands war. While Tim Finn recorded a solo album, the group lost their momentum, eventually dissolving in 1985 after the release of *Conflicting Emotions* Tim Finn continued his solo career, while Neil went on to form Crowded House (also with Tim until 1992), with latter years group member Paul Hester (drums). Griggs, Judd and Crombie formed Schnell Fenster. Phil Judd released a solo album in 1983, *Private Lives*, on the Mushroom label.
Albums: *Mental Notes* (1975), *Second Thoughts* (1976), *Dizrhythmia* (1977), *Frenzy* (1979), *True Colours* (1980), *Waiata* (1981), *Time And Tide* (1982), *Conflicting Emotions* (1982), *See Ya Round* (1984), *Livin' Enz* (1985). Compilation: *The Beginning Of The Enz* (1980).

Splodgenessabounds

The origins of this UK group are heavily tinged with apochcrypha. Max (then a drummer) replaced Gerry Healy in Alien Sex Fiend in 1978 and stayed for a few months before forming a duo called the Faber Brothers with guitarist Pat Thetic. They performed at Butlins Holiday Camp in Bognor, Sussex, but were sacked and returned to London to start a band. As Splodgenessabounds, the group started gigging in March 1979 and though various members came and went the line-up briefly comprised Max Splodge (vocals), his girlfriend Baby Greensleeves (vocals), Miles Flat (guitar), Donkey Gut (b. Winston Forbe; keyboards), Whiffy Archer (paper and comb), Desert Island Joe Lurch Slythe and a dog. Robert Rodent joined on bass in early 1980 and Miles Flat left. They came to the public's attention when, to the eternal annoyance of publicans everywhere, they had a freak hit with 'Two Pints Of Lager And A Packet Of Crisps Please' in 1980. Other memorable songs in their repertoire included 'I've Got Lots Of Famous People Living Under The Floorboards Of My Humble Abode', 'Simon Templar', and a savage re-working of Rolf Harris' 'Two Little Boys'. Max was also reputed to be working on a rock opera called *Malcolm*, and appeared in the play *Camberwell Beauty*. His stage performances were somewhat spoiled due to wolf-whistles from his girly fan club (numbering three) throughout the evening. After falling out with Deram in 1982, the band signed to Razor under the shortened title Splodge, where they released *In Search Of The Seven Golden Gussets*, a tribute to mythical items of ladies' underwear. By this time the line-up included the following miscreants; Ronnie Plonker (guitar), Smacked Arse O'Reardon (bass), Poodle (drums) and Tone Tone The Garden Gnome (guitar). Max later recorded solo on Neat releasing the Tony James (Sigue Sigue Sputnik) single 'Phut Phut Splodgenik'.

Albums: *Splodgenessabounds* (1981), *In Search Of The Seven Golden Gussets* (1982).

Squeeze

Formed in the south east London area of Deptford in 1974, Squeeze came to prominence in the late 70s riding on the new wave created by the punk movement. Original members Chris Difford (b. 4 November 1954, London, England; guitar/lead vocals), Glenn Tilbrook (b. 31 August 1957, London, England; guitar/vocals) and Julian 'Jools' Holland (b. 24 January 1958; keyboards) named the group after a disreputable Velvet Underground album. With the addition of Harry Kakoulli (bass), and original drummer Paul Gunn replaced by sessions drummer Gilson Lavis (b. 27 June 1951, Bedford, England), Squeeze released an EP, *Packet Of Three*, in 1977, on the Deptford Fun City label. It was produced by former Velvets member John Cale. The EP's title in itself reflected the preoccupation of the group's main songwriters, Chris Difford and Glenn Tilbrook, with England's social underclass. It led to a major contract with A&M Records and a UK Top 20 hit in 1978 with 'Take Me I'm Yours'. Minor success with 'Bang Bang' and 'Goodbye Girl' that same year was followed in 1979 by two number 2 hits with 'Cool For Cats' and 'Up The Junction'. Difford's lyrics were by now beginning to show an acute talent in capturing the flavour of contemporary south London life with a sense of the tragi-comic. This began to fully flower with the release of 1980's *Argy Bargy* which spawned the singles 'Another Nail In My Heart' (UK Top 20) and the sublime 'Pulling Mussels (From A Shell)'. The set was Squeeze's most cohesive album to date; having finally thrown off any remaining traces of a punk influence they now displayed some of the finest 'kitchen sink' lyrics since Ray Davies' peak. The album also featured the group's new bass player, John Bentley (b. 16 April 1951). In 1980 Holland left for a solo career that included performing and recording with his own band, Jools Holland And The Millionaires (which displayed his talent for the 'boogie-woogie' piano style) and, to a larger extent, hosting the UK television show *The Tube*. His replacement was singer/pianist Paul Carrack, formerly with pub-rock band Ace. He appeared on *East Side Story* which was co-produced by Elvis Costello. Carrack stamped his mark on the album with his performance on 'Tempted' and with the success of 'Labelled With Love' a UK Top 5 hit, the album became the band's most successful to date. Carrack departed soon after to join Carlene Carter's group and was replaced by Don Snow (b. 13 January 1957, Kenya; ex-Sinceros). The follow-up, *Sweets From A Stranger*, was an uneven affair, although it did spawn the superb 'Black Coffee In Bed'. At the height of the group's success, amid intense world tours, including selling out New York's Madison Square Garden,

Difford And Tilbrook dissolved the group. However, the duo continued to compose together releasing an album in 1984. The following year they re-formed the band with Lavis, the returning Holland and a new bass player, Keith Wilkinson. *Cosi Fan Tutti Frutti* was hailed as a return to form, and although not supplying any hit singles, the tracks 'King George Street', 'I Learnt How To Pray' and Difford/Holland's 'Heartbreaking World' stood out. In 1987 Squeeze achieved their highest position in the UK singles chart for almost six years when 'Hourglass' reached number 16 and subsequently gave the group their first US Top 40 hit, reaching number 15. '853-5937' repeated the transatlantic success. The accompanying album, *Babylon And On*, featured contributions from former Soft Boy Andy Metcalfe (horns/keyboards/moog). After the release of 1989's *Frank*, which contained one of the most sensitive lyrics ever written by a man about menstruation ('She Doesn't Have To Shave'), Holland departed once again to concentrate on television work. With Matt Irving joining as a second keyboard player, Squeeze released a live album, *A Round And A Bout*, on their old Deptford Fun City label in 1990, before signing a new record deal with Warner Brothers. The release of *Play* confirmed and continued Chris Difford and Glenn Tilbrook's reputation as one of the UK's finest songwriting teams, with 'Gone To The Dogs' and 'Wicked And Cruel' particularly resonant of earlier charms. *Some Fantastic Place* saw them reunited with A&M Records, although there was some critical carping about their insistence on a group format which did not always augur well for their more adroit and sober compositions.

Albums: *Squeeze* (A&M 1978), *Cool For Cats* (A&M 1979), *Argy Bargy* (A&M 1980), *East Side Story* (A&M 1981), *Sweets From A Stranger* (A&M 1982), *Cosi Fan Tutti Frutti* (A&M 1985), *Babylon And On* (A&M 1987), *Frank* (A&M 1989), *A Round And About* (Deptford Fun City 1990), *Play* (Reprise 1991), *Some Fantastic Place* (A&M 1993). Compilation: *Singles 45 And Under* (A&M 1982).

Stephenson, Martin, And The Daintees

b. c.1965, Durham, England. This singer/songwriter's reputation has been bolstered by virtue of searing live performances throughout the UK. His early love of literature and music led to the formation of the first Daintees line-up in his early teens. With a regular turnover of staff and lack of proper gigs the band nevertheless became something of a busking sensation, on the evidence of which Newcastle record label Kitchenware sent them into the studio. After two singles, notable amongst which was the intoxicating 'Roll On Summertime', a debut album was embarked upon. The Daintees line-up at this time comprised Stephenson (guitar/vocals), Anthony Dunn (bass/acoustic guitar/vocals), John Steel (keyboards/harmonica/bass/vocals) and Paul Smith (drums/percussion). *Boat To Bolivia* was praised by the *New Musical Express* because it 'builds bridges between love and hate, between cradle and grave, between folk and pop, between the past and present'. An example of the candidness and honesty of Stephenson's lyrics is best portrayed on 'Caroline' and 'Crocodile Cryer'. He also revealed his appreciation of the folk/blues rag guitar style with 'Tribute To The Late Rev. Gary Davis' as well as regular live performances of Van Dyke Parks' 'High Coin'. However, a lengthy hiatus delayed the arrival of the follow-up until 1988. *Gladsome, Humour & Blue* contained the superb 'Wholly Humble Heart'. Once again reviews were excellent, and Stephenson already held an impressive reputation for hearty live shows. *Salutation Road* became the songwriter's most politicized work in 1990, prefaced by the single 'Left Us To Burn' which directly attacked Margaret Thatcher. He continues to be a consistent live draw, often appearing solo, or with the Daintees, who comprise any musician who fits the bill. Not yet considered a major songwriter, his elevation to that status may only be a matter of time.

Albums: *Boat To Bolivia* (1985), *Gladsome, Humour & Blue* (1988), *Salutation Road* (1990), *The Boys Heart* (1992), *High Bells Ring Thin* (1993). Compilation: *There Comes A Time: The Very Best Of Martin Stephenson & The Daintees* (1993).

Stereolab

From south London, Stereolab wear their John Cage and John Cale influences on their sleeves, but within a short time span have amassed an impressive body of work. The principal mover is Tim Gane (ex-McCarthy), who was at first joined by his girlfriend Laetitia Sadier (b. 1968, Paris, France), Martin Kean (ex-New Zealand band the Chills), and Th' Faith Healers' drummer Joe Dilworth, also a *Melody Maker* photographer. Tim gave the band their name; after an obscure offshoot of 60s folk label, Vanguard (it has also been stated that the title was taken from a hi-fi testing label). At their early gigs they were joined by Russell Yates (Moose) on guitar and Gina Morris (*New Musical Express* journalist) on vocals. Too Pure signed them, allowing them to keep the Duophonic imprint. By the time of the release of the 'Low-Fi' 10-inch in September 1992, Mary Hansen had arrived to lend keyboard and vocal support, and Andy Ramsay replaced Dilworth on drums. 'John Cage Bubblegum', which some critics have noted as an adequate description of their sound, was released in the US only, on Slumberland, via a limited edition version containing a stick of gum. By the time *The Groop Played Space Age Bachelor Pad Music* was released in March 1993, further line-up changes had occurred, with Duncan Brown joining on bass and ex-Microdisney guitarist Sean O'Hagan also joining. This set was the closest to ambient soundscapes, *ala* Martin Denny or Arthur Lyman, that they had yet come. The group left Too Pure for Elektra Records at the end of 1993, once again retaining the Duophonic Ultra High Frequency Disks imprint for their domestic releases. Duophonic would also issue material by Arcwelder and Herzfeld, the latter featuring another former McCarthy member, Malcolm Eden. The double LP, *Transient Random Noise-Bursts With Announcements*, straddled both indie and dance markets. This was more minimalist than ambient, and maintained their reputation not only as a competent rock outfit, but also a fixture of the experimental dance music axis. 1995's addictive *Music For The Amorphous Body Study Centre* continued to embrace subjects outside of pop music convention, on this occasion acting as a soundtrack to the work of artist Charles Long for an exhibition at New York's Tanya Bonakdar Gallery.

Albums: *Peng!* (Too Pure 1992), *The Groop Played Space Age Bachelor Pad Music* (Too Pure 1993), *Transient Random Noise-Bursts With Announcements* (Duophonic 1993, double album), *Mars Audio Quintet* (Duophonic 1994), *Music For The Amorphous Body Study Centre* (Duophonic 1995, mini-album).

Stiff Little Fingers

This Irish punk band were formed from the ashes of cover group Highway Star. Taking their new name from a track on the Vibrators' *Pure Mania* debut, Stiff Little Fingers soon attracted one of the most fervent fan bases of the era. Present at the Clash's Belfast gig in 1977, Jake Burns (vocals/lead guitar) led Henry Cluney (rhythm guitar), Ali McMordie (bass) and Brian Falloon (drums) as Ireland's first new wave cover band. The original drummer, Gordon Blair, had gone on to play with Rudi. When journalist Gordon Ogilvie saw the band live he urged them to concentrate on their own material, quickly becoming their manager and co-lyricist. They recorded their first two original songs, 'Suspect Device'/'Wasted Life' soon after, on their own Rigid Digits label. The first pressing of 350 copies sold out almost as soon as BBC disc jockey John Peel span it. Rough Trade quickly picked up the distribution, and released the band's second single, 'Alternative Ulster', in conjunction with Rigid Digits. After a major tour supporting the Tom Robinson Band, the group were almost signed to Island, but remained on Rough Trade for their long playing debut, *Inflammable Material*. With songs concentrating on personal experiences in the politically charged climate of Northern Ireland, the album still managed to surprise many with its inclusion of diverse rock patterns and a flawed love song. The release marked the departure of Falloon who was replaced by Jim Reilly. The follow-up, *Nobodys Heroes,* revealed great strides in technique and sophistication with the band branching out into dub, reggae and pop. The dialogue with the audience was still direct, however, urging tolerance, self-respect and unity, and rejecting the trappings of rock stardom. They would still come in for criticism, however, for Ogilvie's patronage. After a disappointing live album, the impressive *Go For It!* saw the band at the peak of their abilities and popularity. Reilly left for the USA, joining Red Rockers shortly afterwards, with Brian 'Dolphin' Taylor (ex-Tom Robinson Band) drafted in as his replacement. 1982's *Now Then* embraced songs of a more pop-rock nature, though in many ways the compromise was an unhappy one. Burns left at the beginning of the following year, forming The Big Wheel. However, live and on record he was unable to shake off comparisons to Stiff Little Fingers, and he soon opted instead for a career as trainee producer at BBC Radio 1. McMordie formed Fiction Groove and contributed to Sinead O'Conner's *The Lion And The Cobra*, while Cluney taught guitar back in Ireland. Taylor returned for a brief stint of drumming with TRB, but the spectre of Stiff Little Fingers remained. One reunion gig gave birth to further events, until 1990 when they re-formed on a permanent basis. McMordie had grown tired of the rock circuit, however, and his replacement was the group's old friend Bruce Foxton (ex-Jam). In the early 90s they embarked on further major tours and recorded two respectable albums, *Flags And Emblems* and *Fly The Flag*, but lost the long-serving Henry Cluney amid much acrimony.

Albums: *Inflammable Material* (Rough Trade 1979), *Nobody's Heroes* (Chrysalis 1980), *Hanx!* (Chrysalis 1980), *Go For It!* (Chrysalis 1981), *Now Then* (Chrysalis 1982), *Flags And Emblems* (Essential! 1991), *Fly The Flag* (Essential! 1993), *Get A Life* (Castle Communications 1994). Compilations: *All The Best* (Chrysalis 1983, double album), *Live And Loud* (Link 1988, double album, reissued as *No Sleep Till Belfast*, Kaz, 1988), *See You Up There* (Virgin 1989, double album), *Live In Sweden* (Limited Edition 1989), *The Peel Sessions* (Strange Fruit 1989), *Greatest Hits Live* (Link 1991), *Alternative Chartbusters* (Link 1991).

Stiff Records

Britain's premier 'new wave' label of the 70s was founded in 1976 by pub-rock producer and promoter, Dave Robinson, and Andrew Jakeman, tour manager of Dr Feelgood. The first release, 'Heart Of The City' by Nick Lowe, was financed by a £400 loan from Dr Feelgood's singer, Lee Brilleaux. From 1976-77, the label released material by a range of London-based pub and punk rock bands such as Roogalator, Lew Lewis, the Adverts and the Damned. Stiff also signed Elvis Costello whose fourth single, 'Watching The Detectives', was the label's first hit. Costello had achieved prominence as a member of Stiff's first package tour of numerous British cities. Like its 1978 successor, the tour served to publicise and popularise the label and its artists. During the early days it was extremely hip to be seen wearing a Stiff T-shirt bearing its uncompromising slogan, 'If it ain't Stiff it ain't worth a fuck'. Towards the end of 1977, Stiff suffered a setback when Jakeman, Costello and Nick Lowe left to join the Radar label. However, Stiff's fortunes were transformed by the success of Ian Dury whose anthem, 'Sex And Drugs And Rock 'n' Roll', had made little impact when first issued in 1977. A year later, however, 'What A Waste' inaugurated a run of four hit singles. Lene Lovich, Jona Lewie and Madness also provided Top 20 records for the label in 1978-80, when Robinson switched distribution from EMI to CBS Records. In the early 80s Stiff flirted with reggae (Desmond Dekker) and soul (various productions by Eddy Grant), but the bulk of its releases still came from artists on the eccentric fringe of the new wave such as Tenpole Tudor and Wreckless Eric. The company also issued one album from Graham Parker before he moved to the larger RCA Records label. There were also hits from the Belle Stars and Dave Stewart with Barbara Gaskin. From the outset, Robinson had been interested in new wave developments in America and over the years Stiff licensed material by such artists as Rachel Sweet, Devo, the Plasmatics and Jane Aire. In 1984 Stiff was merged with Island Records and Robinson became managing director of both companies. This coincided with the departure of Madness to start their own label (Zarjazz), although Stiff's new signing, the Pogues, provided hits throughout the mid-80s. The merger was not a success, however, and in 1986 Robinson resumed control of an independent Stiff, only to see it suffer an immediate cash-crisis. The assets of the company, which had a turnover of £4m at its peak, were sold to ZTT Records for a reputed £300,000. Under the new ownership there were initial releases from the Pogues, hard bop drummer Tommy Chase and female vocal group the

Mint Juleps. But by the 90s the pioneering Stiff had become simply a reissue label.

Stone Roses

A classic case of an overnight success stretched over half a decade, the UK band Stone Roses evolved through a motley collection of Manchester-based non-starters such as the Mill, the Patrol and English Rose before settling down as Stone Roses in 1985. Acclaimed for their early warehouse gigs, at this time the line-up consisted of Ian Brown (b. Ian George Brown, 20 February 1963, Ancoats, Gt. Manchester, England; vocals), John Squire (b. 24 November 1962, Broadheath, Gt. Manchester, England; guitar), Reni (b. Alan John Wren, 10 April 1964, Manchester, England; drums), Andy Couzens (guitar) and Pete Garner (bass). In their hometown, at least, the band had little trouble in working up a following, in spite of their predilection for juxtaposing leather trousers with elegant melodies. In 1987 guitarist Andy Couzens left, later to form the High, and Pete Garner followed soon after, allowing Gary 'Mani' Mounfield (b. 16 November 1962, Crumpsall, Gt. Manchester, England) to take over bass guitar. By this time the band had already made a low-key recording debut, with the ephemeral 45, 'So Young'. By the end of the year the reconstituted foursome were packing out venues in Manchester, but finding it difficult to get noticed in the rest of the country. A deal with the Silvertone Records label in 1988 produced 'Elephant Stone', and showed its makers to be grasping the essence of classic 60s pop. A year later they had carried it over the threshold of the independent scene and into the nation's front rooms. When the follow-up, 'Made Of Stone', attracted media attention, the Stone Roses' ball started rolling at a phenomenal pace. Their debut album was hailed in all quarters as a guitar/pop classic, and as the Manchester 'baggy' scene infiltrated Britain's consciousness, Stone Roses - alongside the funkier, grubbier Happy Mondays - were perceived to be leaders of the flare-wearing pack. By the close of 1989, the Roses had moved from half-filling London's dingiest clubs to playing to 7,500 people at Alexandra Palace. Having achieved such incredible success so quickly, when the band vanished to work on new material, the rumour mongers inevitably came out in force. In 1990 'One Love' reached the UK Top 10, but aside from this singular vinyl artefact, the media was mainly concerned with the Roses' rows with a previous record company, who had reissued old material accompanied by a video made without the band's permission. This resulted in the group vandalising the company's property, which in turn led to a much-publicized court case. As if this was not enough, Stone Roses were back in court when they tried to leave Silvertone, who took an injunction out against their valuable proteges. This prevented any further Stone Roses material from being released, even though the band eventually won their case and signed to Geffen Records for a reported $4 million. At the end of 1991, their eagerly awaited new product was still stuck somewhere in the pipeline while, in true Stone Roses fashion, after their live extravaganzas at Spike Island, Glasgow, London and Blackpool, plans were afoot for a massive open air comeback gig for the following spring. It never happened that year, nor the next. In fact the Stone

Roses absence from the limelight - initially through contractual problems with Silvertone and management squabbles - then seemingly through pure apathy, became something of an industry standing joke. Had their debut album not had such a huge impact on the public consciousness they would surely have been forgotten. Painstaking sessions with a series of producers finally saw the immodestly titled *Second Coming* released in 1995. It was announced in an exclusive interview given to the UK magazine dedicated to helping the homeless, *The Big Issue*, much to the chagrin of a slavering British music press. Almost inevitably, it failed to meet expectations, despite the fact that the US market was now opening up for the band. They also lost drummer Reni, who was replaced within weeks of its release by Robbie Maddix, who had previously played with Manchester rapper Rebel MC. Promotional gigs seemed less natural and relaxed than had previously been the case, while Silvertone milked the last gasp out of the band's legacy with them to compile a second compilation album (from only one original studio set).

Album: *The Stone Roses* (Silvertone 1989), *Second Coming* (Geffen 1995). Compilations: *Turns Into Stone* (Silvertone 1992), *The Complete Stone Roses* (Silvertone 1995).

Stranglers

One of the longest-surviving groups from the British new wave explosion of the late 70s, the Stranglers first rehearsed in Guildford as early as 1974. Two years later, the full line-up emerged comprising: Hugh Cornwell (b. 28 August 1949, London, England; vocals/guitar), Jean Jacques Burnel (b. 21 February 1952, London, England; vocals/bass), Jet Black (b. Brian Duffy, 26 August 1943; drums) and Dave Greenfield (keyboards). Following a tour supporting Patti Smith during 1976 and some favourable press reports (the first to bring comparisons to the Doors), the group were signed by United Artists Records. Courting controversy from the outset, they caused a sensation and saw their date at London's Roundhouse cut short when Cornwell wore an allegedly obscene T-shirt. In February 1977 the Stranglers' debut single, '(Get A) Grip (On Yourself)' reached number 44 in the UK charts and inexplicably dropped out after only one week. According to the chart compilers, the sales were inadvertently assigned to another record, but it was too late to rectify the damage. 'Grip' saw the group at their early best. Bathed in swirling organ and backed by a throbbing beat, the single displayed Cornwell's gruff vocal to strong effect. The b-side, 'London Lady', was taken at a faster pace and revealed the first signs of an overbearing misogynism that would later see them fall foul of critics. Initially bracketed with punk, the Stranglers owed as much to their pub-rock background and it soon emerged that they were older and more knowing than their teenage contemporaries. Nevertheless their first album, *Rattus Norvegicus*, was greeted with enthusiasm by the rock press and sold extremely well. The blasphemous lyrics of 'Hanging Around' and the gruesome imagery of 'Down In The Sewer' seemingly proved less acceptable than the women-baiting subject matter of their next single, 'Peaches'. Banned by BBC radio, the song still charted thanks to airplay offering up the b-side, 'Go Buddy Go'. Rather than bowing to the feminist criticisms levelled against them, the

group subsequently compounded the felony by introducing strippers at a Battersea Park, London concert (though male strippers were also present). Journalists were treated even more cavalierly and the group were renowned for their violent antics against those who opposed them (karate black belt Burnel would attack writer John Savage after one unhelpful review). Having initially alienated the press, their work was almost universally derided thereafter. The public kept faith, however, and ensured that the Stranglers enjoyed a formidable run of hits over the next few years. The lugubrious protest, 'Something Better Change', and faster paced 'No More Heroes' both reached the UK Top 10, while 'Five Minutes' and 'Nice 'N Sleazy' each entered the Top 20. In the background there were the usual slices of bad publicity. Burnel and Black were arrested for being drunk and disorderly before charges were dropped. Cornwell was not so fortunate and found himself sentenced to three months' imprisonment on drugs charges in January 1980. Within two months of his release, the group found themselves under arrest in Nice, France, after allegedly inciting a riot. Later that year they received a heavy fine in a French court. The group's uncompromising outlaw image tended to distract from subtle changes that had been occurring in their musical repertoire. Their brave cover of the Burt Bacharach/Hal David standard, 'Walk On By', reached number 21 in spite of the fact that 100,000 copies of the record had already been issued *gratis* with *Black And White*. Equally effective and contrasting was the melodic 'Duchess', which displayed the Stranglers' plaintive edge to surprising effect. Their albums also revealed a new diversity from *The Raven* (with its elaborate 3-D cover) to the genuinely strange *Themeninblack*. The latter was primarily Cornwell's concept, and introduced the idea of extra-terrestrial hit-men who silence individuals that have witnessed UFO landings - an ever vengeful music press delighted in pulling it to pieces. For their next album, *La Folie*, the group were accompanied on tour by a ballet company. The album spawned the group's biggest hit, the evocative 'Golden Brown', with its startling, classical-influenced harpsichord arrangement. It reached the UK number 2 spot, resting just behind Buck Fizz's 'Land Of Make Believe'. Even at their most melodic the Stranglers ran into a minor furore when it was alleged that the song was concerned with heroin consumption. Fortunately, the theme was so lyrically obscure that the accusations failed to prove convincing enough to provoke a ban. Another single from *La Folie* was the sentimental 'Strange Little Girl', which also climbed into the UK Top 10. The melodic influence continued on 'European Female', but in spite of the hits, the group's subsequent albums failed to attract serious critical attention. As unremittingly ambitious as ever, the Stranglers' 1986 album, *Dreamtime*, was inspired by Aboriginal culture and complemented their outsider image. Just as it seemed that their appeal was becoming merely cultish, they returned to their old style with a cover of the Kinks' 'All Day And All Of The Night'. It was enough to provide them with their first Top 10 hit for five years. Increasingly unpredictable, the group re-recorded their first single, 'Grip', which ironically fared better than the original, reaching the Top 40 in January 1989. Despite their small handful of collaborative ventures, it seemed unlikely that either Cornwell or Burnel would ever consider abandoning the group for solo careers. Perpetual derision by the press finally took its cumulative toll on the lead singer, however, and in the summer of 1990 Cornwell announced that he was quitting the group. The lacklustre *10* was written specifically for the American market, but failed to sell, in light of which Cornwell called time on his involvement. Burnel, Black and Greenfield were left with the unenviable problem of finding an experienced replacement and deciding whether to retain the name Stranglers. The band recruited vocalist Paul Roberts and guitarist John Ellis (formerly of the Vibrators and a veteran of Burnel's Purple Helmets side project). *Stranglers In The Night* was arguably a return to form, but still failed to recapture old glories. A second set with the band's new line-up then emerged in 1995, with strong performances on tracks such as 'Golden Boy', with Cornwell's absence felt most acutely in the unadventurous songwriting.

Albums: *Rattus Norvegicus* (United Artists 1977), *No More Heroes* (United Artists 1977), *Black And White* (United Artists 1978), *Live (X Cert)* (United Artists 1979), *The Raven* (United Artists 1979), *The Meninblack* (Liberty 1981), *La Folie* (Liberty 1981), *Feline* (Epic 1983), *Aural Sculpture* (Epic 1984), *Dreamtime* (Epic 1986), *All Live And All Of The Night* (Epic 1988), *10* (Epic 1990), *Stranglers In The Night* (China 1992), *About Time* (When?/Castle 1995). Compilations: *The Collection* (Liberty 1982), *Off The Beaten Track* (Liberty 1986), *The Singles* (EMI 1989), *Greatest Hits: 1977-1990* (Epic 1990), *The Old Testament (The UA Recordings 1977- 1982)* (EMI 1992), *The Early Years 74/75/76 Rare, Live And Unreleased* (Newspeak 1992), *Saturday Night Sunday Morning* (Castle 1993), *The Stranglers And Friends: Live In Concert* (Receiver 1995, rec. 1980).

Strawberry Switchblade

This colourful duo, comprising Jill Bryson (vocals/guitar) and Rose McDowell (vocals/guitar), emerged as a product of the late 70s Glasgow, Scotland punk scene. Their appearance in polka-dotted frocks with frills, ribbons, flowers and cheap jewellery unfortunately distracted attention from their songwriting. Despite sounding like a happy pop band, their lyrics expressed sadness. The debut single in 1983, 'Trees And Flowers', was written as a result of Bryson's agoraphobia. Signed to the independent Ninety-Two Happy Customers label (under the aegis of producers David Balfe and Bill Drummond), this melancholy song was given a pastoral feel by the oboe playing of Kate St. John (ex-Ravishing Beauties). With added studio assistance from Aztec Camera's Roddy Frame (guitar) and Madness's Mark Bedford (bass), the single reached number 4 in the UK Independent chart. The duo found national success in late 1984 with the chirpy 'Since Yesterday'. An over-produced debut album, far removed from the simplicity of 'Trees And Flowers', entered the UK Top 25 but failed to supply the duo with the expected run of hit singles. Their last hit came in 1985 with a cover of Dolly Parton's classic, 'Jolene'. Following the break-up of the group, McDowell attempted to revive her career without Bryson in the late 80s for a time working under the name Candy Cane, but met with little success.
Album: *Strawberry Switchblade* (Korova 1985).

Stump

Of all the quirky, Captain Beefheart-indebted groups to reside at Manchester's Ron Johnson label, Stump were not only the most distinctive, but also the most endearing. Unlike their manic stablemates, mad-eyed Mick Lynch (vocals), Chris Salmon (guitar), Kev Hopper (bass) and Rob McKahey (drums) avoided an aggressive, staccato-guitar onslaught, opting instead for awkward chord and rhythm changes and a wacky, humorous lyrical content, first heard on the charming EP *Mud On A Colon* in March 1986. BBC disc jockey John Peel was an early admirer and while Stump's Peel session of that year would eventually surface on vinyl the following January, the band were caught up in the *C86* programme organized by the *New Musical Express* and turned up on *The Tube* television show with the offbeat video for their contribution, 'Buffalo'. A debut album, *Quirk Out*, was issued on the Stuff label as Ron Johnson ran into financial problems, and it was not long before Ensign Records lured the band into major territory. 'Chaos' preceded a second album, *A Fierce Pancake*, revealing a Stump that had lost none of their individuality, but it was 'Charlton Heston' (1988), with its 'lights camel action' line and frog-dominated video, that attracted most attention. A full-scale single release for the excellent 'Buffalo' looked set to chart in November, but after it failed, the band all but disappeared.
Albums: *Quirk Out* (Stuff 1987), *A Fierce Pancake* (Ensign 1988).

Style Council

Founded in 1983 by Paul Weller (b. 25 May 1958, England) and Mick Talbot (b. 11 September 1958). Weller had been lead singer of the Jam while Talbot was the former keyboards player with the Merton Parkas and the Bureau. Another constant collaborator was singer D.C. Lee, whom Weller married. Weller's avowed aim with the group was to merge his twin interests of soul music and social comment. In this his most important model was Curtis Mayfield, who appeared on Style Council's 1987 album. The continuing popularity of the Jam ensured that Style Council's first four releases, in 1983, were UK hits. They included the EP, *Paris*. 'Speak Like A Child' and 'Long Hot Summer'. Tracey Thorn from Everything But The Girl was a guest vocalist on the band's first album. Perhaps the most effective Style Council song was the evocative 'My Ever Changing Moods', the first of three Top 10 hits in 1984 and the band's only US hit. During the mid-80s, Weller's political activism was at its height as he recorded 'Soul Deep' as the Council Collective with Jimmy Ruffin and Junior (Giscombe) to raise funds for the families of striking coal miners and became a founder member of Red Wedge, an artists' support group for the Labour Party. Style Council appeared at Live Aid in 1985 and in 1986 made a short film, *JerUSAlem*, a satirical attack on the pop music industry. There were continuing British hits, notably 'The Walls Come Tumbling Down' (1985), 'Have You Ever Had It Blue' (featured in the 1986 film *Absolute Beginners*) and 'Wanted' (1987). With its eclectic mix of soul, classical and pop influences, the 1988 album was less of a commercial success and by 1990, Style Council was defunct. Weller re-emerged the next year with a new band, the Paul Weller Movement, recording for his own Freedom High label.

Albums: *Cafe Bleu* (1984), *Our Favourite Shop* (1985), *Home And Abroad* (1986), *The Cost Of Loving* (1987), *Confessions Of A Pop Group* (1988), *Here's Some That Got Away* (1993).

Sub Pop Records

Based in Seattle, Washington, USA, the Sub Pop label has served as the natural focus for local acts since the late 80s. It has become closely associated with several noise/guitar bands fusing heavy riffs to a sound influenced by the Stooges. Releases by Mudhoney and Tad helped establish a cult following, while the subsequent success of Nirvana focused attention on the group's tenure with the company. Sub Pop was also noted for 'one-off' recordings and Dinosaur Jr, Rapeman and Thin White Rope were among those taking advantage of this practice. The label also established the Sub Pop Singles Club, whereby an annual subscriber would receive an exclusive, limited edition release each month. The idea was later adopted by Rough Trade Records in 1991 as well as several other labels.

Album: *Sub Pop Grunge Years* (Sup Pop 1990).

Subhumans (Canada)

Influential Vancouver punk band who did much of the groundwork for later Canadian left field outfits. However, the Subhumans are possibly more famous for their contribution and inclusion in 'ecological terrorism' activities. Charges included bombing a plant making guidance systems for nuclear missiles, dynamiting a hydro-power station and fire-bombing pornography shops. Gerry 'Useless' Hannah (bass) was the band member implicated and tried, along with four others. He would receive a 10 year custodial sentence. The Subhumans had already marked out their ability to challenge the conventions of the punk movement with *Incorrect Thoughts*' 'Slave To My Dick', an indictment of male stupidity which went against the grain of the macho ethos of 'hardcore' music. The rest of the original band featured; Brian 'Wimpy Boy' Goble (vocals; ex-Skulls), Mike Graham (guitar) and Greg 'Dimwit' James (drums). James was replaced by Jim Iwagama on drums when he joined Pointed Sticks, until he returned on that band's split. Gerry Useless would quit the band after his sentence as he became more interested in environmental issues (he wanted to become a forest warden). Iwagama chose this moment to depart also, for reasons of pure lethargy. The returning James was joined by a new bass player, Ron, again from Vancouver. Goble and James would go on to pursue a lengthy career in D.O.A.. James is the elder brother of original D.O.A. drummer Chuck Biscuits (later Circle Jerks, Black Flag, Danzig etc). Historically, the 'guerilla' activities overshadowed the career of one of the few hardcore bands capable of writing bracing, fully realised songs with a rare lyrical poignancy.

Albums: *Incorrect Thoughts* (Friends 1980), *No Wishes, No Prayers* (SST 1983).

Subhumans (UK)

One of the most popular and entertaining of the 80s anarcho punk bands influenced by the cottage industry approach of Crass. The most significant departure from their bretheren would be in the use of music which traced its heritage more to Led Zeppelin than the Damned. Lyrically, the Subhumans trod familiar territory (vegetarianism, human rights, anti-government sloganeering) though they did so with more humour than many. For instance, 'Are you prepared to die for you beliefs, or just to dye your hair' from 'Work Rest Play Die' questioned the authenticity of the movement they were a part of. The band comprised Dick (b. Richard Lucas; vocals), Bruce (guitar), Grant (bass) and Trotsky (drums), though for *29:29 Split Vision* Phil would replace Grant. On later recordings the Subhumans continued to expand in to other musical areas, largely leaving behind their original thrash based formula (although their debut EP had anticipated such ecelcticism with a reggae number). Members of the band would go on to form Citizen Fish, whose blend of punk and ska would be popularised throughout the UK on the free festival circuit. Dick Lucas stayed true to the band's anarcho roots by continuing to operate his own Bluurg label for releases by both his own bands plus many others.

Albums: *The Day The Country Died* (Spiderleg 1981), *Time Flies But Aeroplanes Crash* (Bluurg 1983), *From The Cradle To The Grave* (Bluurg 1984), *Worlds Apart* (Bluurg 1985), *EP-LP* (Bluurg 1986), *29:29 Split Vision* (Bluurg 1987).

Sudden, Nikki

Following the dissolution of premier UK art punk band Swell Maps, former lead singer and driving force Sudden joined the Abstract label to release *Waiting On Egypt*. He had continued to make music erratically before this. Among these recordings were sessions with Another Pretty Face (later Mike Scott's Waterboys) in Christmas 1980. His first solo single was 'Back To The Start' on Rather Records, before the release of 'Channel Steamer', which would form part of the debut album. He was pleased with the results: 'Nearly everyone I know thinks it's the best thing I've ever done and I must admit when I listen to it I get a pleasant surprise'. Also included were 'Forest Fire' and 'New York', both unreleased Swell Maps songs. The nucleus of musicians that he employed included Scott (guitar), Steve Burgess (bass), Anthony Thistlethwaite (saxophone) and Empire (ex-TV Personalities) on drums. Following *The Bible Belt* in 1983 Sudden would work extensively with Dave Kusworth as the Jacobites, releasing over half a dozen albums for Glass and Creation Records. He also wrote for several music magazines including the later issues of *Zig Zag* during this period, later collaborating on projects with Roland S. Howard. His most recent album, *The Jewel Thief*, saw him work with his long-time fans, R.E.M.

Albums: *Waiting On Egypt* (Abstract 1982), *The Bible Belt* (Flicknife 1983), with Rowland S. Howard *Kiss You Kidnapped Charabanc* (Creation 1987), with the French Revolution *Groove* (Creation 1989), *The Jewel Thief* (Creation 1991).

Suede

This hugely promoted UK band broke through in 1993 by merging the lyrical perspective of Morrissey with the posturings of David Bowie and the glam set. Though Brett

Suede

Anderson (vocals) does have a rare gift for brilliantly evocative mood swings and monochrome diaramas, there is so far little to suggest that the sum of their talents add up to anything approaching those of these celebrated forefathers. Just as much was made of guitarist Bernard Butler's similarities to Johnny Marr (Smiths, Electronic). The rest of the band comprised Matt Osman (bass) and Simon Gilbert (drums), a position which Mike Joyce (ex-Smiths) would try out for. However, it was Anderson's arrogant wit and seedy, sexually ambivalent narratives that fascinated the music press. Their first release, 'The Drowners', arrived in March 1992, and 'My Insatiable One', on the b-side, was a brooding low-life London tale of 'shitting paracetamol on the escalator', which so impressed Morrissey he would later cover it live. Anderson would also get to meet his other spiritual forefather in a two-part joint interview with David Bowie in the *New Musical Express*. By this time, the mainstream music media, starved of an adequate figurehead for the 90s, had latched on to the band in a quite disconcerting manner. *Q* magazine put them on their front cover before the release of their debut album, a previously unthinkable concession. Their appearance at the 1993 televised *Brits* awards gave them massive exposure. On the back of this high profile their debut album went straight to number 1 in the UK charts, going gold on the second day of release. Again, much of the lyrical imagery was deliberately homo-erotic, reflected in the sleeve art work. The picture of two naked women kissing, taken by Tee Corrine, was cut to head and shoulders to hide the identity of those involved. All seemed rosy in the graden until the eve of the group's second album in 1994, when it was announced that Butler had left the band (recent interviews had hinted at rancour between Anderson and the guitarist). He would be replaced by 17-year old 'unknown' Richard Oakes. However, as the writing for *Dog Man Star* (which emerged to mixed reviews) had already been completed, there was little immediate evidence to guage the reshuffled Suede on until 1995. Chart returns, on the other hand, suggested the band's chart thunder may have been stolen by Blur and Oasis. Butler, meanwhile, would go on to write well-regarded new material with McAlmont.
Albums: *Suede* (Nude 1993), *Dog Man Star* (Nude 1994).
Videos: *Love & Poison* (1993), *Bootleg 1* (1993).

Sugar

In the aftermath of Nirvana's commercial breakthrough unhinging a flood of loud, powerful and uncompromising USA-based music, Bob Mould (guitar/vocals) found himself subject to the somewhat unflattering representation 'Godfather of Grunge'. The ex-Hüsker Dü songwriter has earned this accolade on the back of his former group's considerable influence, but with Sugar he seemed set to continue to justify the critical plaudits which have followed his every move. Joined by David Barbe (ex-Mercyland; bass/vocals), and Malcolm Travis (ex-Zulus; drums), he found another powerful triumvirate to augment his own muse. Barbe proved particularly complementary, a talented songwriter in his own right, his presence as a forthright and intelligent counterpoint mirrored the contribution Grant Hart made to Hüsker Dü. Sugar's breakthrough, most visibly

in the UK, came with the arrival of *Copper Blue* in 1992. Populated by energetic, evocative, and determinedly melodic pop noise, the album found critics grasping for superlatives. The Hüsker Dü comparisons were inevitable, but Mould was now viewed as an all-conquering prodigal son. Singles like 'Changes' tied the band's musical muscle to a straightforward commercial skeleton, and daytime radio play became an unlikely but welcome recipient of Sugar's crossover appeal. The historically contrary Mould responded a few months later with *Beaster*, in which the melodies and hooks, though still present, were buried under layers of harsh feedback and noise. Ultimately as rewarding as previous work, its appearance nevertheless reminded long-term Mould watchers of his brilliant but pedantic nature. *F.U.E.L.* offered a hybrid of the approaches on the two previous albums, and again saw Mould venerated in the press, if not with the same fawning abandon that *Copper Blue* had produced. Afterwards, however, Mould ruminated widely about his doubts over the long-term future of Sugar, suggesting inner-band tensions between the trio.
Albums: *Copper Blue* (Creation 1992), *Beaster* (Creation 1993), *F.U.E.L. (File Under Easy Listening)* (Creation 1994).

Sugarcubes

This offbeat pop band was formed in Reykjavik, Iceland on 8 June 1986, the date taken from the birth of Björk's son, Sindri. The settled line-up featured Björk Gundmundsdottir (b. 1966, Reykjavik, Iceland; vocals/keyboards), Bragi Olaffson (bass), Einar Orn Benediktsson (vocals/trumpet), Margret 'Magga' Ornolfsdottir (keyboards, replacing original keyboard player Einar Mellax) Sigtryggur 'Siggi' Balduresson (drums) and Thor Eldon (guitar). Björk's step-father was in a rock showband, and after early stage appearances she completed her first album at the age of 11. She was also the singer for prototype groups Toppie Tikarras then Theyr, alongside Siggi Balduresson. The latter band shot to prominence when Jaz Coleman and Youth (Killing Joke) mysteriously appeared in Iceland in March 1982, paranoid about an impending apocalypse, and collaborated on several projects with Theyr. Björk, Einar and Siggi then went on to form Kukl, who toured Europe and released two records on the Crass label, establishing a link with the UK anarcho-punk scene which would be cemented when the band joined UK independent label One Little Indian Records. Their debut single, 'Birthday', and album, *Life's Too Good*, saw the band championed in the UK press almost immediately. In particular, praise was heaped on Björk's distinctive and emotive vocals. The Sugarcubes ran their own company in Iceland called Bad Taste, an organization which encompassed an art gallery, poetry bookshop, record label, radio station and publishing house. Björk's ex-husband, Thor, a graduate in Media Studies from London Polytechnic and the band's guitarist, sired their son Sindri under a government incentive scheme to boost the island's population, the financial rewards for this action allowing him to buy a pair of contact lenses. He then married Magga Ornolfsdottir (ex-the Giant Lizard), who joined the band in time for their second album. In addition, Siggi Balduresson and Bragi Olaffson, the band's rhythm section, were brother-in-laws, having married twin sisters. Most bizarre of all, however, was the subsequent marriage of Einar and Bragi in Denmark in 1989, the first openly gay marriage in pop history. *Here Today, Tomorrow, Next Week*, its title taken from a line in Kenneth Graeme's book *Wind In The Willows*, was a much more elaborate album, with a full brass section on 'Tidal Wave' and strings on the single, 'Planet'. However, compared with the rapturous reception granted their first album, *Here Today* took a critical pasting. Even label boss Derek Birkett conceded that it was far too deliberate. The press was also quick to seize on the fact that Einar's vocal interjections detracted from the band's performance. After much touring the group returned to Reykjavik, where they followed their own interests for a time. Björk collaborated on the Bad Taste album *Glimg Glo*; 'Just Icelandic pop songs from the 50s with jazz influences'. Balduresson also contributed drums. Members of the band spent time as an alternative jazz orchestra. The band then played a concert for President Mitterand of France, in Reykjavik, and Björk joined 808 State on their *Ex:El* album and single, 'Oops'. The group's third album found them back in favour with the music press and back in the charts with 'Hit', but the inevitable happened shortly afterwards, with Björk heading for a critically and commercially rewarding solo career.

Albums: *Life's Too Good* (One Little Indian 1988), *Here Today, Tomorrow, Next Week* (One Little Indian 1989), *It's It* (One Little Indian 1992, remixes), *Stick Around For Joy* (One Little Indian 1992).

Suicidal Tendencies

Vocalist Mike Muir formed Suicidal Tendencies in the early 80s in the Venice Beach area of Los Angeles, California, USA, enlisting Grant Estes (guitar), Louiche Mayorga (bass) and Amery Smith (drums). Despite an inauspicious start, being voted 'worst band and biggest assholes' in *Flipside* magazine's 1982 polls, the band produced a hardcore classic in *Suicidal Tendencies*, and although they initially fell between hardcore punk and thrash stools, MTV's support of 'Institutionalized' helped the group take off. *Join The Army* was recorded with respected guitarist Rocky George and drummer R.J. Herrera replacing Estes and Smith, and the skateboarding anthem, 'Possessed To Skate', kept the group in the ascendancy. *How Will I Laugh Tomorrow...When I Can't Even Smile Today?* marked the debut of Mike Clark (rhythm guitar) as the group's sound exploded, extending from a balladic title-track to the furious 'Trip At The Brain'. This progression continued on *Controlled By Hatred/Feel Like Shit...Deja Vu*, but as the band's stature increased, so did their problems. Their name and image were easy targets for both the PMRC and the California police, with the former blaming teenage suicides on a band who were unable to play near their home town due to performance permit refusals from the latter, who feared Suicidal Tendencies were an LA gang. Naturally, the outspoken Muir fought vehemently against these bizarre accusations and treatment. Talented bassist Robert Rujillo, with whom Muir formed Infectious Grooves in tandem with Suicidal, made his debut on the excellent *Lights...Cameras...Revolution*, which produced hits in the defiant 'You Can't Bring Me Down' and 'Send Me Your Money', a vitriolic attack on televangelist preachers. The band also re-recorded their debut during these sessions

for release as *Still Cyco After All These Years*. The Peter Collins-produced *The Art Of Rebellion*, with new drummer Josh Freece, was a more ambitious, diverse work, and rather more lightweight than previous albums. Any fears that the band were mellowing were dispelled by furious live shows. *Suicidal For Life*, with Jimmy DeGrasso (ex-White Lion/Y&T) replacing Freece, emphasized the point as the band returned in fast-paced and profanity-peppered style, while continuing to extend individual talents to the full. Shortly after its release news filtered through that the band were no more, and a chapter in hardcore history slammed shut behind them.

Albums: *Suicidal Tendencies* (Frontier 1983), *Join The Army* (Caroline/Virgin 1987), *How Will I Laugh Tomorrow...When I Can't Even Smile Today* (Epic 1988), *Controlled By Hatred/Feel Like Shit...Deja Vu* (Epic 1989), *Lights...Camera...Revolution* (Epic 1990), *The Art Of Rebellion* (Epic 1992), *Still Cyco After All These Years* (Epic 1993), *Suicidal For Life* (Epic 1994). Compilation: *FNG* (Virgin 1992).

Suicide

This US band were an influence on Birthday Party, Soft Cell, Sigue Sigue Sputnik and the Sisters Of Mercy with a potent fusion of rockabilly and electronic music on cheap equipment. Singer Alan Rev (b. 1948) and multi-instrumentalist Martin Rev polarized audiences in Max's Kansas City and other New York clubs in the early 70s, remaining unheard on vinyl until the advent of the new wave when their arrangement of 'Rocket 88' was included on *Max's Kansas City* (1976) compilation. Ramones associates Craig Leon and Martin Thau oversaw the duo's early recording career (on Thau's Red Star label) until a support spot on a Cars tour brought them to the notice of vocalist Ric Ocasek who produced *Alan Vega And Martin Rev* for Ze Records, as well as 'Hey Lord', Suicide's contribution to a 1981 Ze sampler. Ocasek was also involved in the pair's respective solo albums. Of these, Vega's vocal-dominated efforts elicited most public interest - particularly with 1981's *Vega* (containing the European hit 'Juke Box Baby') and *Sunset Strip* with its revival of Hot Chocolate's 'Everyone's A Winner'. Vega also mounted a one-man sculpture exhibition in New York and, with David Bowie and Philip Glass, had a hand in David Van Teighem's collage for the ballet *Fair Accompli* before Suicide resumed corporate activities in 1986.

Albums: *Suicide* (1977), *24 Minutes Over Brussels* (1978), *Live* (1979), *Half Alive* (1981), *Alan Vega And Martin Rev* (1981), *A Way Of Life* (1989). Solo albums: Martin Rev *Martin Rev* (1979), *Clouds Of Glory* (1985), *Cheyanne* (1992); Alan Vega *Vega* (1981), *Sunset Strip* (1983), *Just A Million Dreams* (1985), *Deuce Avenue* (1990), *New Race Is On* (1993).

Sultans Of Ping FC

Formed in 1989 in Cork, Eire, and titled after the Dire Straits' song of similar title, the Sultans Of Ping FC have built up a rabid live following for their cross-dressing antics and tales of the totally unexpected. They chose their name in mock admiration of Mark Knopfler's outfit, being virulently

anti-stadium rock 'n' roll 'baloney'. The band comprise Niall O'Flaherty (vocals), Paddy O'Connell (guitar), Morty McCarthy (drums) and Dat (b. Alan McFeely; bass). Their gigs quickly became legend after a local affair in which the promoter asked the crowd to sit down. The band joined them in solidarity, leading to audience participation of a bizarre nature: a series of floor gymnastics, with kicks to the air from a prone position. The gig that launched them nationally came when taking part in an Irish rock open, where they were the token local Cork entrants. Home support pushed them in to the winner's enclosure. The first single endorsed this lunacy: 'Where's Me Jumper' on Rhythm King Records, revolved around the tale of Niall having his jumper pinched at a dance. In the best traditions of Serious Drinking and Half Man Half Biscuit, the Sultans are a band sharing the esoteric conviction of fellow Cork residents the Frank And Walters. However, their debut album was more than a barrage of jokes; with string and harmonica arrangements backing the strange lyrical observations. These included songs about Jesus' second coming (in a tracksuit), and a pole vaulter unhindered by arms, legs or head. Titles like 'Give Him A Ball And A Yard Of Grass' and 'Riot At The Sheepdog Trials' still gave a fairly strong indication of which planet in the pop universe the Sultans pinged from. *Teenage Drug* emerged to less flattering reviews, but was ultimately no less endearing in its humour, a strain which is often more complex than has been portrayed in some sections of the media.
Albums: *Casual Sex In The Cineplex* (Rhythm King 1992), *Teenage Drug* (Rhythm King 1993).

Summerhill

Arising from the ashes of the Snakes Of Shake, the UK band Summerhill looked to the early Byrds' sound for inspiration, their brand of folk-rock first heard on *I Want You* on the Rocket label in 1988. Their prolific live schedule, often as support act, made the team of Seori Burnette (vocals/guitar), Neil Scott (guitar/vocals), Keith Gilles (bass/vocals) and Ian Shedden (drums) a popular live act and a move to Demon's Diablo label came in time for a mini-album, *Lowdown*, later that year. Signed to Polydor Records, it was a year before the partnership was fruitful, during which time Michael Sturgis had replaced Shedden. 'Here I Am' was an obvious stab at the mainstream and it was March 1990 before *West Of Here*, was released. From it came 'Don't Let It Die' that same month and then a one-off single cover of the Rolling Stones' 'Wild Horses'. Despite some encouraging reviews Summerhill failed to make a sufficient impact on the charts and disbanded later that year. Keith Gilles later joined Sumishta Brahm's group, 13 Frightened Girls, appearing on the Jazz Butcher produced 'Lost At Sea' (1991).
Albums: *I Want You* (1988), *Lowdown* (1988), *West Of Here* (1990).

Sun Dial

The Sun Dial's well-received debut album from 1990, *Other Way Out*, re-created the psychedelic sound of the late 60s with an unnerving accuracy. A myriad of soaring vocals (and trippy lyrics to match), progressive chord changes and some delightful acid rock guitar (plus other strange instruments),

the album's limited run on the Tangerine label soon expired and the trio signed with the UFO label early the following year. Hailing from south London, Sun Dial's roots lay with frontman Gary Ramon (guitar/vocals), previously with Modern Art. He joined up with Anthony Clough (bass/bamboo flutes/organ) and Dave Morgan (drums/percussion). Alongside a reissue/repackage of *Other Way Out*, UFO released its most upfront moment, 'Exploding In My Mind'. By the summer, the band had recruited a second guitarist for live work, while Clough took a smaller role; this was felt on a new single, 'Fireball', treading a mellower, more traditional rock sound. *Acid Yantra* saw better distribution through the auspices of Beggars Banquet Records, and also broadened the band's sound with the addition of a mellotron.
Albums: *Other Way Out* (Tangerine 1990), *Libertine* (UFO 1993), *Acid Yantra* (Beggars Banquet 1995).

Sundays

Indie band formed in London, England, in the summer of 1987, by songwriters David Gavurin (b. 4 April 1963, England; guitar) and Harriet Wheeler (b. June 26 1963, England; vocals), who had already gained prior singing experience in a band called Jim Jiminee. Later joined by the rhythm section of Paul Brindley (b. 6 November 1963, England; bass) and Patrick Hannan (b. 4 March 1966, England; drums), the Sundays' first ever live performance at the seminal Falcon 'Vertigo Club' in Camden Town, London, in August 1988, sparked off abnormally excessive interest from both media and record business circles. Playing what many perceived to be a delicate, flawless mix of the Smiths' guitars and the Cocteau Twins' vocal acrobatics, the band's high profile ensured a Top 50 place in the UK charts for their debut single, 'Can't Be Sure', in January 1989. Despite this dramatic arrival, the Sundays did not capitalize on their success until exactly a year later, when *Reading, Writing, Arithmetic* took everyone by surprise by entering the UK charts at number 4. Despite these rapid advances, the Sundays are notorious for being slow songwriters - legend has it that their label, Rough Trade Records, wanted to release a single from the album but the band did not have any other material for a b-side. This was to be their last release for two years, as touring commitments took the quartet to Europe, Japan and the equally reverential America, where *Rolling Stone* magazine had voted the Sundays' Best Foreign Newcomer. Financial difficulties at their label also held up proceedings while they sought a new record deal during 1991, eventually signing to Parlophone Records in January 1992. A second album was not completed before October of that year, and reactions, though not unkind, lacked the fervour that had greeted their debut.
Albums: *Reading, Writing, Arithmetic* (Rough Trade 1990), *Blind* (Parlophone 1992).

Supergrass

Highly regarded new entrants in the UK's indie guitar band movement of the mid-90s, Oxford's Supergrass comprise Danny Goffey (b. c.1975; drums), Gary Coombes (b. c.1976; vocals/guitar) and Mickey Quinn (b. c.1970; bass). Previously Goffey and Coombes had been part of Ride-

Sundays

Supergrass

wannabe upstarts the Jennifers, who recorded one single for Suede's label, Nude Records. With the addition of Quinn rehearsals took place in various bedrooms in early 1994, with inspiration garnered from the Pixies, Sonic Youth and Buzzcocks. They eventually worked their way up to a ramshackle half hour live set which made up in rakish enthusiasm what it lacked in musical accomplishment. Their debut single, 'Caught By The Fuzz', about being lifted by the constabulary for cannabis possession, would bring them to much wider attention, though not before it had been released on three separate occasions. Bedroom label Backbeat first supplied 250 copies in the summer of 1994. Fierce Panda then included it as part of a six-track EP of various teenage bands on the advent of the group signing to Parlophone Records. Re-released by the major in October, it would climb to number 42 in the UK charts, and by the close of the year it was voted number 5 in disc jockey John Peel's Festive 50 selection. They also toured with Shed Seven and supported Blur at their Alexandra Palace gig, before the release of a second single, 'Man Size Rooster', in early 1995. Their debut album was produced at Sawmills Studios, Golant, with Mystics' singer Sam Williams, while the band also contributed to the Sub Pop Records Singles Club with 'Lose It'.
Album: *I Should Coco* (Parlophone 1995).

Supersuckers
Originally from Austin, Texas, but now relocated to Seattle via Tucson, the Supersuckers are Dan Seigal (drums), Ron Heathman (guitar), Eddie Spaghetti (bass/vocals) and Dan Bolton (guitar). They have recorded for a variety of other outlets since their formation in the late 80s, using eMpTy for their 1991 debut long player, *The Songs All Sound The Same*. This reprised some of their earlier, hard to source 7-inch records for Sympathy For The Record Industry, Lucky and eMpTy themselves. Their debut for new Seattle home Sub Pop Records came with 'Like A Big Fuckin' Train', then 'Hell City Hell'/'Dead Homiez' (the latter a bizarre Ice Cube cover). *The Smoke Of Hell* became their first long player proper in 1992, with a glorious and somewhat attention-grabbing jacket drawn by comic artist Daniel Clowes. It was produced by 'grunge supremo' Jack Endino. Following a first visit to Britain with Reverend Horton Heat in 1993, the Supersuckers entered the studio to work on a follow-up set. *La Mano Cornuda* duly arrived the following year and expanded on previous lyrical and musical themes - hard rocking songs about hard drinking hard men being the overwhelming impression.
Albums: *The Smoke Of Hell* (Sub Pop 1992), *La Mano Cornuda* (Sup Pop 1994). Compilation: *The Songs All Sound The Same* (eMpTy 1991).

Swans
Like many early 80s American bands determined to stretch the boundaries of musical cacophony, the Swans were drawn to the thriving New York underground that has also produced Jim Thirlwell, Lydia Lunch and Sonic Youth over the years. Although the band have endured numerous line-up changes, the Swans always centred on singer Michael Gira and, later, Jarboe. After a raucous debut EP in 1982, *Speak*,

the band released the influential *Filth* on the German Zensor label, which attracted a strong European audience. In 1984 they announced *Cop* on their own Kelvin 422 label, their first record to appear in the UK. Although *Cop* was awash with harsh guitars and awkward, dirge-like sounds, it was easily more accessible than *Filth*, as was the subsequent EP, *Raping A Slave*, in March 1985 (despite the title). 'Time Is Money (Bastard)' kicked off 1986 with a typically uncompromising title, preceding *Greed* in February. Themes of depravity, sex, death and the more sinister aspects of human nature prevailed, also to be heard on *Holy Money* and 'A Screw' later that year. 1987 saw the band move to Product Inc. for a double album, *Children Of The God*, although another less official effort, *Public Castration Is A Good Idea*, also surfaced that year. Most of 1987 was taken up with Jarboe's new project, Skin, although there was a limited German-only Swans release, *Real Love*. Another double album, 1988's *Feel Good Now*, emerged on the Rough Trade Records-distributed Love label. Meanwhile, a sinister cover of Joy Division's 'Love Will Tear Us Apart' climbed the indie charts in June, resulting in a deal with MCA Records. 'Saved', the Swans' first single for the major label in April 1989, revealed a definite shift towards mainstream rock, further evident on *The Burning World*: the sombre, Wagnerian approach was still there, but the ingredients were certainly more palatable. The band also seemed to have worked out of their collective system their monstrous live assaults on an audience, which were generally too painful and horribly loud to be anything other than an exercise in art-house shock tactic indulgence. August's 'Can't Find My Way Home' was far more melodic than earlier singles and it seemed that Swans were on the brink of crossing to a much wider audience. But for the next two years they concentrated on reissues of early material on Gira's own Young God label. In May 1991 the band issued *White Light From The Mouth Of Infinity*, which was both commercial and innovative, illustrating the way in which Gira and companions could always command the attention of those willing to experiment a little in their listening tastes. In 1995 Gira released his first book, *The Consumer And Other Stories*, through Henry Rollins' 21/3/61 publishing house, in tandem with the Swans' latest recording venture; a relatively restrained and accessible collection dubbed *The Great Annihilator*.
Albums: *Filth* (Zensor/Neutral 1983), *Cop* (K.422 1984), *Greed* (PVC 1986), *Holy Money* (PVC 1986), *Children Of The God* (Product Inc/Caroline 1987, double album), *Feel Good Now* (Love 1988, double album), *The Burning World* (Uni-MCA 1989), *White Light From The Mouth Of Infinity* (Young God 1991), *The Great Annihilator* (Young God 1995).
Further reading: *The Consumer And Other Stories*, Michael Gira, 1995.

Sweet Exorcist
(see Cabaret Voltaire)

Sweet, Rachel
b. 1963, Akron, Ohio, USA. Rachel Sweet sang professionally at the age of five, working as a child model for

television commercials in New York and as a support act to Mickey Rooney. At the age of 12 she recorded her first single, the country song 'Faded Rose', on the Derrick label which, along with her follow-up, 'We Live In Two Different Worlds' reached the lower regions of the *Billboard* Country charts. Under the tutelage of manager and songwriter Liam Sternberg, Rachel landed a contract with the pioneering independent UK label Stiff Records. The company had previously distributed a compilation album of Akron acts which included two tracks by the singer. For the Stiff 78 Tour with fellow labelmates Lene Lovich, Wreckless Eric, Jona Lewie and Mickey Jupp, Rachel's backing band were the Records. The single, a version of the Isaac Hayes/David Porter song 'B-A-B-Y', reached the UK Top 40. Sweet possessed a mature voice for someone still in her mid-teens. *Fool Around* saw her tackling Del Shannon's 'I Go To Pieces' and Elvis Costello's 'Stranger In The House' as well as several Sternberg originals. Rachel's obvious talents were dogged by persistent, but tenuous, accusations of her being marketed as 'jail-bait'. After parting with Sternberg in 1979, her second album presented Rachel with a harder image, complete with an advertising campaign bizarrely depicting her as a leather-jacketed, sullen child abductor. Backed by Fingerprintz, the songs on the album contained cover versions of Lou Reed's 'New Age', Graham Parker's 'Fool's Gold' and the Damned's 'New Rose' as well as the usual quota of country rock. As with the first album, *Protect The Innocent* was a commercial failure, although this time it did not enjoy critical approbation. Her departure from Stiff to CBS saw the release of *...And Then He Kissed Me* which included the UK and US Top 40 hit duet with Rex Smith, 'Everlasting Love' in 1981. Despite this encouraging start, the mismanaged talents of Rachel Sweet saw her fade from the scene.
Albums: *Fool Around* (1978), *Protect The Innocent* (1980), *...And Then He Kissed Me* (1981).

Swell Maps

Although associated with the immediate post-punk aftermath, British group Swell Maps was formed in 1972. Five years later Nikki Sudden (guitar/vocals), Epic Soundtracks (drums/vocals), Jowe Head (bass), Richard Earl (vocals) and David Barrington (vocals) founded their own Rather label, which issued material in conjunction with Rough Trade Records. Although their debut single, 'Read About Seymour', became a cult favourite, the group steadfastly refused to become categorized. Despite the pop element of successive singles - 'Dresden Style', 'Real Shocks' and 'Let's Build A Car' - their albums offered a bewildering array of sounds ranging from garage-band simplicity to new-age styled piano instrumentals. Although Swell Maps broke up in 1980, a series of reissues, some of which include archive material, has kept their reputation alive. So too have the fortunes of ex-members Sudden and Epic, who have both begun fruitful solo careers.
Albums: *A Trip To Marineville* (Rather/Rough Trade 1979), *Jane From Occupied Europe* (Rather/Rough Trade 1980). Compilations: *Whatever Happens Next* (Rather/Rough Trade 1981), *Collision Time* (Rather/Rough Trade 1984), *Train Out Of It* (Antar 1987).

Swervedriver

Previously known as Shake Appeal, Swervedriver came into being at the end of 1989 when Adam Franklin (b. 19 July 1968, Essex, England; vocals, formerly of Satan Knew My Father), Jimmy Hartridge (b. 27 November 1967, Oxfordshire, England; guitar) and Adrian Vines (b. 25 January 1968, Yorkshire, England; bass) moved from the Home Counties to London and linked up with Graham Bonnar (b. 28 April 1967, Scotland) who had previously drummed for British hardcore group, Ut. The collective's sound changed accordingly from Stooges-style grunge-rock to a more contemporary American stylisation - a definition which was hardly weakened by the band's apparent lyrical obsession with highways, pick-up trucks and several other things mid-Western. In spite of the unfavourable comparisons, Swervedriver and their effects-driven guitars battled their way from beneath the shadow of their supposedly more credible transatlantic counterparts, reaching number 63 in the UK charts with their third EP, *Sandblasted*. However, Bonnar left in early 1992. By March 1993 his replacement, Jez, had arrived. Vines had also left, in September 1992, but the bass position was still free a year later. A second album, produced by Alan Moulder, who had worked on the band's 'Never Lose That Feeling' single, emerged to little fanfare, with the bass parts shared between Franklin and Hartridge. Vines would go on to work with Skyscraper.
Albums: *Raise* (Creation 1991), *Mezcal Head* (Creation 1993).

Sylvain Sylvain

Although a founder member of the rock band Actress with Johnny Thunders and Billy Murcia, Sylvain only joined his colleagues in their next venture, the pivotal, glam-rock group, the New York Dolls, as a replacement for original guitarist Rick Rivets. He remained with the group until their break-up in 1977, following which the artist formed the Criminals with Bobby Blain (keyboards), Michael Page (bass) and Tony Machine (drums). This highly-respected quartet completed one single, 'The Kids Are Back', for their own Sing Sing label, but progress was hampered by Sylvain's concurrent commitment to former Dolls' vocalist David Johansen. Ties as a composer and backing musician were severed in 1979 when Syl established a new act, Sylvain Sylvain And The Teenage News, with two further refugees from the Johansen band, Johnny Rao (guitar) and Buz Verno (bass). Both *Sylvain Sylvain* and it's follow-up, *And The Teardrops* confirmed the artist's gift for classic pop melody, but were not a commercial success and the artist was subsequently dropped by his label, RCA. He resurrected his independent Sing Sing label for 'Out With The Wrong Woman' (1983), but its creator has since failed to sustain the profile he enjoyed throughout the 70s.
Albums: *Sylvain Sylvain* (1979), *And The Teardrops* (1980). Compilation: *'78 Criminals* (1985).

T

Tad

The monolithic noise engine which is Tad was formed in Seattle, USA, in 1988, by Tad Doyle (b. Idaho; vocals/guitar) and Kurt Danielson (bass), who had previously been working together with the delightfully titled Bundles Of Piss. Fellow miscreants Gary Thorstensen (guitar) and Josh Sinder (drums) joined later. With the rise of the American north west and the Sub Pop imprint in particular, Tad became pre-eminent among that label's bands - though in truth there was always a strong metallic undercurrent which set them aside from the traditional hardcore-rooted sound of grunge. Lyrically too, as *God's Ball* all too clearly demonstrates, they were closer in style to Black Sabbath than Black Flag (song titles included 'Nipple Belt' and 'Satan's Chainsaw'). Whatever, the career of Tad has always proved entertaining. Sharing a touring van with Nirvana in 1989 on their first European jaunt they were ideally placed to see the destruction of the Berlin wall, though on a later European excursion they were offered the perfect contrast when the Belfast hotel in which they were staying was bombed by the IRA (the explosive device malfunctioned). *Salt Lick* saw

production from Steve Albini (Big Black, Rapeman, Shellac) and, understandably, was even noisier as a result. *8-Way Santa* earned much of its notoriety from a sleeve which featured a man fondling a woman's breast - an endearing picture found in a garage-sale photo album. However, this prompted a legal suit in 1991 by the woman concerned (and her second husband) which forced its removal. That was hardly the end of the group's travails, however. On their US tour with Primus in the summer of the same year they narrowly missed being struck by lightning. The following year in Canada further calamity was averted when a mountain boulder descended and crashed through their van, just behind the driver's seat. *Inhaler* would be the group's first album for a major, though bad-tempered songs like 'Grease Box' and 'Lycanthrope' hardly suggested a relaxing of attitudes. Tad Doyle, meanwhile, enjoyed a little celebrity with a small part in Cameron Crowe's *Singles* film, before his band made their debut for a major label with 1995's *Infrared Riding Hood*.

Albums: *God's Balls* (Sub Pop 1989), *Salt Lick* (Sub Pop 1990), *8-Way Santa* (Sub Pop (1991), *Inhaler* (Music For Nations 1993), *Live Alien Broadcast* (Music For Nations 1994), *Infrared Riding Hood* (East West 1995).

Talk Talk

Formed in 1981, this UK pop group comprised Mark Hollis (b. 1955, Tottenham, London, England; vocals), Lee Harris (drums), Paul Webb (bass), Simon Brenner (keyboards).

They were soon signed to EMI who were intent on moulding them into the same league as stablemates Duran Duran. In fact they could not have been more different. They went along with their company's ideas for the first album which produced a number of hit singles including, 'Talk Talk' and 'Today'. Labelled as a 'New Romantic' band, they were very keen to shake off the tag and dismissed their keyboard player to make them a looser, more flexible creative unit. For the next couple of years Hollis spent the time writing new material and assembling a pool of musicians to record a second album. The format was repeated with the highly accessible *The Colour Of Spring*, both records were critically acclaimed and showed the band as a more creative and imaginative act than their debut had suggested. It was their fourth album *Spirit Of Eden* that showed their true musical preferences. A solemn six-track record, it had no commercial appeal, and no obvious single. Its poor showing led to EMI dropping the band who signed with Polydor. It was three years before a new studio album appeared, and to fill in the gap a greatest hits compilation was issued without the band's permission. It nevertheless managed to sell over a million copies and give them three more hit singles. Ironically, their biggest success so far was an EMI reissue of their previous hit 'Its My Life'. *Laughing Stock* picked up where they had left off although to date they have failed to match the catchy commercial appeal of *The Colour Of Spring*.

Albums; *The Party's Over* (1982), *Its My Life* (1984), *Its My Mix* (1984), *The Colour Of Spring* (1986), *Spirit Of Eden* (1988), *Laughing Stock* (1991). Compilations: *Natural History: The Very Best Of Talk Talk* (1990), *History Revisited* (1991, remixes of greatest hits).

Talking Heads

One of the most critically acclaimed groups of the past two decades, Talking Heads pursued an idiosyncratic path of (often) uncompromising brilliance. After graduating from the Rhode Island School of Design, students David Byrne (b. 14 May 1952, Dumbarton, Scotland; vocals/guitar), Chris Frantz (b. Charlton Christopher Frantz, 8 May 1951, Fort Campbell, Kentucky, USA; drums) and Tina Weymouth (b. Martina Weymouth, 22 November 1950, Coronado, California, USA; bass) relocated to New York. In 1975, they lived and rehearsed in Manhattan and named themselves Talking Heads. After appearing at the club CBGBs, they were approached by Seymour Stein of Sire Records, who would eventually sign the group. Early in 1976, the line-up was expanded to include pianist Jerry Harrison (b. Jeremiah Harrison, 21 February 1949, Milwaukee, Wisconsin, USA), a former member of Jonathan Richman's Modern Lovers. The group's art school background, witty invention and musical unorthodoxy was evident on their intriguingly titled debut, 'Love Goes To Building On Fire'. After touring extensively, they issued *Talking Heads '77*, an exhilarating first album, which was widely praised for its verve and intelligence. The highlight of the set was the insistent 'Psycho Killer', a *tour de force*, in which singer Byrne displayed his deranged vocal dramatics to the full. His wide-eyed stare, jerky movements and onstage cool reminded many commentators of Anthony Perkins, star of Hitchcock's movie *Psycho*.

For their second album, the group turned to Brian Eno as producer. *More Songs About Buildings And Food* was a remarkable work, its title echoing Talking Heads' anti-romantic subject matter. Byrne's eccentric vocal phrasing was brilliantly complemented by some startling rhythm work and the songs were uniformly excellent. The climactic 'The Big Country' a satiric commentary on consumerist America, featured the scathing aside: 'I wouldn't live there if you paid me'. The album also featured one cover version, an interesting reading of Al Green's 'Take Me To The River', which was a minor hit. Eno's services were retained for the more opaque *Fear Of Music*, which included the popular 'Life During Wartime'. Byrne next collaborated with Eno on *My Life In The Bush Of Ghosts*, before the group reunited for *Remain In Light*. The latter boasted the superb 'Once In A Lifetime', complete with 'found voices' and African polyrhythms. An edited version of the song provided one of the best hit singles of 1981. During the early 80s, the group's extra-curricular activites increased and while Byrne explored ballet on *The Catherine Wheel*, Franz and Weymouth found success with their spin-off project, Tom Tom Club. The live double *The Name Of This Band Is Talking Heads* served as a stop-gap until *Speaking In Tongues* appeared in the summer of 1983. As ambitious as ever, the album spawned the group's UK Top 10 single, 'Burning Down The House'. While touring with additional guitarist Alex Weir (formerly of the Brothers Four), the group were captured on film in *Stop Making Sense*, the soundtrack of which sold well. The excellent *Little Creatures*, a more accessible offering than their more experimental work, featured three strong singles in the title track, 'And She Was' and 'Road To Nowhere'. The latter brought the group their biggest chart hit and was accompanied by an imaginative and highly entertaining video. In 1986, Byrne moved more forcibly into movies with *True Stories*, for which Talking Heads provided the soundtrack; it was two more years before the group reconvened for *Naked*. Produced by Steve Lillywhite, the work included musical contributions from Level 42 producer Wally Badarou and guitarists Yves N'Djock and Johnny Marr (from the Smiths). Since then Talking Heads have branched out into various offshoot ventures; there was an official announcement of their break-up at the end of 1991. The single- and double-album retrospectives released in October 1992 provided a fairly definitive assessment of their career, including some interesting rarities, but without doing justice to a band rightly regarded as one of the best and most influential of their time.

Albums: *Talking Heads '77* (1977), *More Songs About Buildings And Food* (1978), *Fear Of Music* (1979), *Remain In Light* (1980), *The Name Of This Band Is Talking Heads* (1982), *Speaking In Tongues* (1983), *Stop Making Sense* (1984), *Little Creatures* (1985), *True Stories* (1986, film soundtrack), *Naked* (1988). Compilations: *Once In A Lifetime: The Best Of* (1992), *Popular Favorites 1976 - 1992 (Sand In The Vaseline)* (1992). Videos: *Stop Making Sense* (1986), *Storytelling Giant* (1988).

Talulah Gosh

Formed in Oxford, England, in February 1986, the much-

maligned Talulah Gosh emerged in the aftermath of the *New Musical Express's* influential *C86* promotion. Taking their name from an *NME* Clare Grogan interview headline, the group came to symbolize a movement that would come to be tagged 'shambling'. Its hard-core followers indulged themselves by wearing asexual basin hair-cuts (boys) or straight short fringes (girls), plain anoraks, plus the affectation of a child-like innocence. The music borrowed a great deal from the Ramones, Velvet Underground and US 60s girl-groups while the lyrics dealt with boy/girl relationships but barely mentioned sex in obvious 'rock 'n' roll' terms, and their un-elitist sense of fun endeared them to many. These particular exponents consisted of Peter Momtchiloff (b. 10 March 1962, Weybridge, Surrey, England; guitar), Pebbles (b. Elizabeth Price, 6 November 1966, Bradford, Yorkshire, England; vocals/tambourine), Robert Pursey, replaced early on by Chris Scott (b. 31 October 1961, Hemel Hempstead, Hertfordshire, England; bass), Marigold (b. Amelia Fletcher, 1 January 1966, London, England; vocals/guitar) and her brother Mathew Fletcher (b. 5 November 1970, London, England; drums). One of the group's most popular early songs was 'The Day She Lost Her Pastels Badge', which combined the movement's tweeness with a nod to the band many identified as its figureheads. They scored two UK Independent Top 5 singles with 'Steaming Train'/'Just A Dream' and 'Beatnik Boy'/'My Best Friend', both on the Edinburgh-based 53rd & 3rd label, which were later compiled on the best-selling *Steaming Train* EP in 1987. Elizabeth Price, who left in December 1986, was replaced by Eithne Farry (b. 21 May 1965, Chelsea, London, England) as second vocalist. Price later created the Cosmic English Music label with Gregory Webster (formerly of the Razorcuts) and as a duo also formed the Carousel. One final UK Independent chart hit ensued for Talulah Gosh with 'Bringing Up Baby' the following year and a later album, *They've Scoffed The Lot*, released on Sarah Records, contained tracks from various BBC Radio 1 sessions from both line-ups. The group split in early 1988, due to university commitments and a consensus that the group had run its course. Farry and Scott later appeared in Saturn 5, while Momtchilof, who had briefly played in the final line-up of the Razorcuts, joined the Fletcher siblings in a successful revival of the 'Gosh formula as Heavenly in 1990.
Albums: *They've Scoffed The Lot* (Sarah 1991). Compilation: *Rock Legends Volume 69* (Sarah 1987, collects single releases).

Teardrop Explodes

This Liverpool group was assembled by vocalist Julian Cope (b. 21 October 1957, Bargoed, Wales), a former member of the Crucial Three, which had featured Ian McCulloch (later of Echo And The Bunnymen) and Pete Wylie (later of Wah!). The Teardrop Explodes took their name from a page in a Marvel comic and the original group came together in late 1978 with a line-up featuring Cope, Michael Finkler (guitar), Paul Simpson (keyboards) and Gary Dwyer (drums). After signing to Bill Drummond and Dave Balfe's Liverpool record label Zoo, they issued 'Sleeping Gas' in early 1979. It was soon followed by the eccentric but appealing 'Bouncing Babies'. By then, Simpson had left to be replaced by Balfe, who had previously appeared in the short-lived Lori And The Chameleons. The exuberant 'Treason (It's Just A Story)' was the Teardrop Explodes' most commercial and exciting offering to date, and was unlucky not to chart. The shaky line-up next lost Finkler, who was replaced by Alan Gill, formerly of Dalek I Love You. A distribution deal with Phonogram Records coincided with a higher press profile for Cope, which was rewarded with the minor hit, 'When I Dream'. *Kilimanjaro* followed and displayed the group as one of the most inventive and intriguing of their era. A repromoted/remixed version of 'Treason' belatedly charted, as did the stirring 'Passionate Friend'. By late 1981, Cope was intent on restructuring the group; new members included Alfie Agius and Troy Tate. *Wilder* further displayed the wayward talents of Cope and revealed a group bristling with ideas, unusual melodies and strong arrangements influenced by late 60s psychedelia. When the sessions for a third album broke down, Cope curtailed the group's activities and in 1984 embarked on an erratic yet often inspired solo career. The irreverently-titled *Everybody Wants To Shag The Teardrop Explodes* was posthumously exhumed for release in 1990, using the sessions for that projected third collection.
Albums: *Kilimanjaro* (Mercury 1980), *Wilder* (Mercury 1981), *Everybody Wants To Shag The Teardrop Explodes* (Fontana 1990). Compilations: *Piano* (Document 1990).

Teardrops

The Teardrops were an amalgamation of various stalwarts of the Manchester new wave scene. Buzzcocks bassist Steve Garvey was joined by original Fall bassist Tony Friel, who had played with Contact and the Passage, and drummer Karl Burns, also previously with the Fall and the Passage, plus Public Image Limited. The band's first outing, 'Seeing Double', on local label TJM, was what might have been expected from the members involved: a fairly robust but murky brand of post-punk. After featuring on TJM's *Identity Parade* sampler ('Colours'), the Teardrops released a 12-inch EP, *Leave Me No Choice*, before calling it a day with the appropriately-titled *Final Vinyl* in 1981. Burns rejoined the Fall in time for 'Lie, Dream Of Casino Soul'.
Album: *Final Vinyl* (TJM 1981).

Teenage Fanclub

Formerly the bulk of infamous Glaswegian band the Boy Hairdressers, Teenage Fanclub, a more sober sobriquet than the original suggestion of 'Teenage Fanny', came into being after Norman Blake (b. 20 October 1965, Bellshill, Scotland; guitar/vocals), Raymond McGinley (b. 3 January 1964, Glasgow, Scotland; guitar/vocals) and Francis MacDonald (b. 21 November 1970, Bellshill, Scotland; drums) moved on from that pseudo-punk combo and linked up with Gerard Love (b. 31 August 1967, Motherwell, Scotland; bass/vocals). During 1989 the quartet recorded an entire album - completed three months before the band had even played live - until MacDonald (later to join the Pastels) made way for Brendan O'Hare (b. 16 January 1970, Bellshill, Scotland). As well as the historical connection with the Boy Hairdressers, members of Teenage Fanclub also had dealings with fellow Scots outfit, BMX Bandits. Thus brought up on

Teenage Fan Club

a diet of fun, loud guitars and irreverence, Teenage Fanclub stamped their mark on 1990 with a series of drunken live shows and the erratic but highly promising Americanized rock debut, *A Catholic Education*. In October the band paid tribute to John Lennon by covering his 'Ballad Of John & Yoko', releasing and deleting the record on the same day. A year on and supplemented by the support of a vociferous music press, Teenage Fanclub toned down their sound, allowing the melodies to come through more forcefully in a manner which self-consciously recalled the 70s guitar sound of Big Star and Neil Young (they became fundamental in instigating the former band's revival in the early 90s). Inevitably 'Starsign' - with a cover of Madonna's 'Like A Virgin' on the b-side - threatened the UK charts on the back of the band's new impetus. *Bandwagonesque* arrived at the end of 1991 and became one of the year's most memorable albums. Laced with chiming guitar and irresistible melody, it suggested a band ready to outgrow their humble independent origins. A sense of disappointment accompanied the release of *Thirteen*, completed in eight months after touring the better-received *Bandwagonesque* (which sold 70,000 copies in the UK and 150,000 in the US, where the band are signed to Geffen Records). This resulted in a concerted effort to make the band's fifth studio album, *Grand Prix*, an exceptional return to form. The songs were rehearsed for three months before entering the studio, where everything was fine-tuned over a five week period at the Manor in Oxford with producer Dave Bianco (formerly Black Crowes' producer George Dracoulias' engineer). It also saw the introduction of new drummer Paul Quinn, formerly of the Soup Dragons. Reassuringly, the opening singles from these sessions, 'Mellow Doubt', and 'Sparkey's Dream' showed them still to be writing basic, heroically romantic and happy guitar pop songs.

Albums: *A Catholic Education* (Paperhouse 1990), *The King* (Creation 1991), *Bandwagonesque* (Creation 1991), *Thirteen* (Creation 1993), *Grand Prix* (Creation 1995). Compilation: *Deep Fried Fanclub* (Paperhouse/Fire 1995).

Teenage Jesus And The Jerks

The 17-year-old Lydia Lunch formed Teenage Jesus And The Jerks in the UK during 1976 to channel her feelings of contempt towards a complacent music industry, but almost immediately clashed with founder members James Chance (b. James Siegfried) and Reck, both of whom left before any recordings were completed. Chance later formed the Contortions, Reck going on to front one of Japan's most successful punk acts, Friction. Lunch's distraught singing and atonal guitar cut against drummer Bradley Field and bassist Jim Sclavunos (later replaced by filmmaker Gordon Stevenson) to create an uncompromising, unholy noise labelled 'no wave', which was first heard on their single, 'Orphans', in 1978. 'Baby Doll' reared its ugly head nearly a year later, followed by a mini-album and 12-inch EP. *Pink* boasted seven excellent tracks, while *Pre*, on the Ze label, collected several early recordings. They disbanded in 1980 when Lydia Lunch progressed to the less violent, murkier sound of Beirut Slump. Field moved on to rejoin Chance as one of his Contortions. However, the discordant, tortuous racket they exuded from Teenage Jesus And The Jerks has

influenced a variety of distinguished names since then, from the Birthday Party to Sonic Youth. It is no coincidence that Lunch has worked with them both.
Album: *Pink* (Lust Unlust 1979, mini-album).

Telescopes

Quintessential English indie band formed in 1988 by Stephen Lawrie (b. 28 March 1969, East Hartford, Northumberland, England; vocals), Joanna Doran (b. Wednesbury, West Midlands, England; guitar/vocals), David Fitzgerald (b. 30 August 1966, Wellingborough, Northamptonshire, England; bass), Robert Brooks (b. 11 April 1969, Burton-upon-Trent, Staffordshire, England) and Dominic Dillon (b. 26 September 1964, Bolton, Lancashire, England). The Telescopes started out peddling a fearsome noise which owed much to the path laid earlier in the decade by the Jesus And Mary Chain. Their first release was on a flexidisc shared with Loop and sold with the *Sowing Seeds* fanzine, after which came two temperamental singles on Cheree records followed by a deal with the American What Goes On label. Unfortunately, after a further brace of singles and one album in 1989, What Goes On succumbed to bankruptcy, leaving the Telescopes to battle for the rights to their own songs and sign to Creation Records. The change of label coincided with a change in musical style as the group added lighter shades and harmonies to their intense guitar-based sound, a development which paid dividends when their eighth single, 'Flying', reached number 79 in the UK charts in 1991.
Albums: *Taste* (What Goes On 1989), *Untitled* (Creation 1992).

Television

Lead guitarist/vocalist Tom Verlaine (b. Thomas Miller, 13 December 1949, Mount Morris, New Jersey, USA) first worked with bassist Richard Hell (b. Richard Myers, 2 October 1949, Lexington, Kentucky, USA) and drummer Billy Ficca in the early 70s as the Neon Boys. By the end of 1973, with the addition of rhythm guitarist Richard Lloyd, they reunited as Television. Early the following year they secured a residency at the Bowery club, CBGB's, and found themselves at the forefront of the New York new wave explosion. Conflicts between Verlaine and Hell led to the departure of the latter who would soon re-emerge with the Heartbreakers. Meanwhile, Television found a replacement bassist in Fred Smith from Blondie. The new line-up recorded the raw but arresting 'Little Johnny Jewel', a tribute to Iggy Pop, for their own label, Ork Records. This led to their signing with Elektra Records for whom they recorded their debut album in 1977. *Marquee Moon* was largely ignored in their homeland, but elicited astonished, ecstatic reviews in the UK. where it was applauded as one of rock's most accomplished debut albums. Verlaine's sneering, nasal vocal and searing, jagged twin guitar interplay with Lloyd were the hallmarks of Television's work, particularly on such stand-out tracks as 'Torn Curtain', 'Venus' and 'Prove It'. Although the group looked set for a long and distinguished career, the follow-up, *Adventure*, was a lesser work and the group broke up in 1978. Since then both Verlaine and Lloyd pursued solo careers with mixed results. In November 1991,

Verlaine, Lloyd, Smith and Ficca revived Television and spent the ensuing time rehearsing for a come back album for Capitol Records. They returned to Britain and made an appearance at the 1992 Glastonbury Festival.

Albums: *Marquee Moon* (Elektra 1978), *Adventure* (Elektra 1979), *The Blow Up* (ROIR 1983, rec. live 1978, cassette only), *Television* (Capitol 1993).

Television Personalities

A crass meeting of 60s pastiche and a tongue-in-cheek nod towards punk have characterised Dan Treacy's Television Personalities over their long, erratic career. Treacy teamed up with Edward Ball back in 1977, releasing the privately pressed '14th Floor' the following year. After Ball's solo single as O Level, the pair issued what was to be seen as a pivotal artefact of the time, the EP *Where's Bill Grundy Now?* (1978). BBC disc jockey John Peel latched onto one of the tracks, 'Part Time Punks' (a cruel send-up of a rapidly decaying London scene) and this exposure attracted the interest of Rough Trade Records. Ball spent some time working on his solo projects in the early 80s, the Teenage Filmstars and the Times. The TV Star's debut album, *And Don't The Kids Just Love It*, extended Treacy's exploration of 60s influences. From it came the whimsical 'I Know Where Syd Barrett Lives' as a single, their last for Rough Trade. Treacy then teamed up with Ed Ball to form the Whaam! label, for TVPs and Times products plus other signings, including the Marine Girls. 1982, the group's busiest recording year, saw *Mummy You're Not Watching Me* share the instant appeal of the group's debut. 'Three Wishes' followed, and coincided with a minor psychedelic revival in London. *They Could Have Been Bigger Than The Beatles* was a surprisingly strong collection of demos and out-takes. The band were soon expanded by Mark Flunder (bass), Dave Musker (organ) and Joe Foster (12-string guitar) for a tour of Italy, with Flunder replaced by ex-Swell Maps bass player Jowe Head for a similar tour of Germany. 1983's 'A Sense Of Belonging' saw a one-off return to Rough Trade and caused a minor scandal over its sleeve. But delays meant that *The Painted Word* was not issued until January 1985. Foster and Musker soon left to work at Creation Records. With a new drummer, Jeff Bloom, Treacy set up a new label, after Whaam! was folded due to pressure from pop duo Wham!. In the meantime, the German album, *Chocolat-Art (A Tribute To James Last)*, captured one of their European live gigs. It was not until early 1990 that the next album emerged. *Privilege* included the catchy 'Salvador Dali's Garden Party'. Then the band laid low for a further two years (punctuated by a live album for Overground Records) until the release of *Closer To God*.

Albums: *And Don't The Kids Just Love It* (Rough Trade 1980), *Mummy You're Not Watching Me* (Whaam! 1982), *They Could Have Been Bigger Than The Beatles* (Whaam! 1982), *The Painted Word* (Illuminated 1985), *Chocolat-Art (A Tribute To James Last)* (Pastell 1985), *Privilege* (Fire 1990), *Camping In France* (Overground 1991), *Closer To God* (1992), *I Was A Mod Before You Were A Mod* (Overground 1995).

Temple Of The Dog

This one-off project involved members of Seattle, USA-based bands Mother Love Bone and Soundgarden, and was recorded as a tribute to the late Andrew Wood, former Mother Love Bone vocalist. The 'band' comprised Chris Cornell (vocals), Matt Cameron (drums), Mike McCready (guitar), Stone Gossard (rhythm guitar) and Jeff Ament (bass). Signed to A&M Records, the album received widespread critical acclaim immediately following its release. The music fused the Doors/Joy Division/Stooges fixation of Mother Love Bone with the harder, dirtier and at times funkier rhythms of Soundgarden. It was a moving, powerful and genuine tribute to the first casualty of the 90s Seattle scene. Gossard and Ament later formed Pearl Jam.

Album: *Temple Of The Dog* (A&M 1991).

10,000 Maniacs

This American group was led by enigmatic vocalist Natalie Merchant and backed by Jerome Augustyniak (drums), Robert Buck (guitar), Dennis Drew (keyboards) and Steven Gustafson (bass). The group started playing together in Jamestown, New York, in 1981. They initially specialized in cover versions of songs by such bands as Joy Division, and Gang Of Four, but would later change from a rock-pop format to one which encompassed folk and world traditions. BBC disc jockey John Peel endorsed the group's 'My Mother The War', and it appeared in his Festive 50 selection for 1983. The group were signed to Elektra Records in 1985 and after a UK tour recorded *The Wishing Chair* with Joe Boyd as producer. Original member John Lombardo (guitar) left the group in 1986 following strenuous touring. 1987 saw a change of producer for *In My Tribe*, with Peter Asher stepping in, as he did with the subsequent release, *Blind Man's Zoo*. The production change obviously worked as the latter album went into the US Top 40 in 1987, going gold in 1988 and platinum the following year. 'Peace Train', taken from the former album, received a great deal of airplay, but following alleged death threat declarations to American servicemen by Yusuf Islam, formerly Cat Stevens, the writer of the song, the group insisted that any re-pressing of the album should exclude the aforementioned track. *Blind Man's Zoo* went into the US Top 20 in 1989, achieving gold status the same year. Following the release of *Blind Man's Zoo*, the group were on the road from June to December of 1989. This consolidated their standing as a highly original group, albeit one utilising several musical influences. This was superbly demonstrated with *Our Time In Eden* including the lilting 'Noah's Dove' and the punchy brass of 'Few And Far Between'. Merchant's 'Jezabel' had the strings arranged by Paul Buckmaster. *Hope Chest* was a remixed compilation of the group's first two independently released albums. In September 1993 Merchant departed to develop her solo career, commenting 'There is no ill will between the members of the group, this is a natural passage.' The 10,000 Maniacs persevered by recruiting former member John Lombardo and new lead singer Mary Ramsey, with whom Lombardo had spent the intervening years recording with as John And Mary.

Albums: *Human Conflict Number 5* (Christian Burial 1982), *Secrets Of The I Ching* (Christian Burial 1983), *The Wishing Chair* (Elektra 1985), *In My Tribe* (Elektra 1987), *Blind Man's Zoo* (Elektra 1989), *Our Time In Eden* (Elektra 1992),

10,000 Maniacs

10,000 Maniacs MTV Unplugged (Elektra 1993). Compilation: *Hope Chest (The Fredonia Recordings 1982-1983)* (Elektra 1990).
Video: *MTV Unplugged* (1994).

Tenpole Tudor

This theatrical UK punk-pop group was led by the inimitable Edward Tudor-Pole (b. 6 December 1955, London, England) who first took to the stage at the age of nine when he appeared in *A Christmas Carol*. After a course at Chiswick Polytechnic he went to train at the Royal Academy of Dramatic Arts. In 1977 he joined a band called the Visitors which also included future *Riverside* BBC televsion host Mike Andrews. Edward formed the band Tenpole Tudor with Visitors Gary Long (drums), Dick Crippen (bass) and Bob Kingston (guitar). Kingston came from a musical family and had previously been a member of Sta-Prest with his brother Ray, himself later in the Temper. His sister June would soon become a member of the Mo-Dettes. Tudor appeared in the film *The Great Rock 'N' Roll Swindle* (Malcolm McLaren had been an early mentor) and performed 'Who Killed Bambi', which appeared on the b-side of the Sex Pistols' 'Silly Thing'. Eddie also helped Paul Cook and Steve Jones write the title song to the film. His first single under their own name was 'Real Fun', which came out on Korova Records. After signing to Stiff Records the group released 'Three Bells In A Row'. Over the next few months they took part on the *Sons Of Stiff* tour, hit the charts three times starting with the raucous 'Swords Of A Thousand Men', recruited a second guitarist in the form of Munch Universe, and released two albums, before they suddenly went out of fashion again. In 1982 Eddie decided to split the band up. Crippen, Long, and Kingston became the Tudors and released 'Tied Up With Lou Cool' whilst Eddie formed a new cajun-style Tenpole Tudor and put out the 'Hayrick Song'. He then left Stiff and moved in to jazz and swing style bands whilst also reviving his acting career. In 1985 he formed an old style Tenpole Tudor and toured the country dressed in armour but left the following year to concentrate on acting. He subsequently appeared on stage (*The Sinking Of The Belgrano*), film (*Straight To Hell*, *Absolute Beginners* and *Walker*) and television (in the comedy *Roy's Raiders*). He also reformed Tenpole Tudor again in 1989 and it seemed likely that he would continue to do so at regular intervals until his acting career took off. Memorably playing the narrator in stage play *The Road*, Tudor then took over the host's role in Channel 4 television's *The Crystal Maze*.
Albums: *Eddie, Old Bob, Dick And Gary* (Stiff 1981), *Let The Four Winds Blow* (Stiff 1981). Compilation: *Wunderbar* (Dojo 1992).

Test Department

This UK experimental/industrial band comprised Paul Jamrozy (b. 3 March 1959), Graham Cunnington (b. 23 August 1960), Alistair Adams (b. 5 October 1959), Tony Cudlip (b. 9 September 1959) and Gus Ferguson. Originally forming in 1982 as a loose collective in New Cross, London, England, they were all co-directors of Test Department's stable, Ministry of Power Records. However, they liaised with a variety of other artists and musicians in order to empower their large-scale projects. The most recent and impressive of these was the huge *The Second Coming* show for Glasgow's 1990 Year Of Culture, set in the abandoned St. Rollox Railway Works. This served as the culmination of several years inaugurating spectacular musical events in unlikely settings. Others have included Cannon Street Station, Bishopsbridge Maintenance Depot, a sand quarry, a car factory in Wales and an ice rink in Friesland. 'From the beginning there was a realization that we wanted to make things pretty monumental', they concede. Allied to their innovative use of spectacle was the employment of instruments from the natural and unnatural environment; scrap metal and industrial cast-offs beating a rhythm to film and slide shows. Powered by a four-piece anvil chorus, the music splendidly complemented visuals drawn from 20s and 30s industrial monochromes. Originally signed up to Stevo's Some Bizzare label, they came in the same wave as fellow travellers SPK and Einsturzende Neubaten. In early 1984 they published an open manifesto in a letter to the *New Musical Express*: '...we will continue a disciplined attack on the official wall of ignorance both in music and in politics'. This remains a constant objective, as witnessed by their *Pax Britiannica* album, recorded with the help of the Scottish Chamber Orchestra and Choir as a critique of Thatcherism.
Albums: *Beating The Retreat* (Some Bizzare 1984), *Shoulder To Shoulder With South Wales Striking Miners* (Some Bizzare 1985), *The Unacceptable Face Of Freedom* (Ministry Of Power/Some Bizzare 1986), *A Good Night Out* (Ministry Of Power/Some Bizzare 1988), *Terra Firma* (Sub Rosa/Ministry Of Power 1988), with Brith Gof *The Gododdin* (Ministry Of Power 1989), *Pax Britannica* (Ministry Of Power 1991), *Proven In Action* (Ministry Of Power 1991, live album). Compilation: *Legacy (1990-1993)* (Ministry Of Power 1994).

That Petrol Emotion

This critically lauded and highly skilled pop group's efforts to break in to the mainstream were been consistently thwarted despite a splendid arsenal of songs. The band was originally formed when the O'Neill brothers (Sean; guitar, Damian; bass) parted from the fragmenting Undertones. A new approach was immediate with Sean reverting to his Irish name (having always appeared as John in his former band), and Damian switching to bass instead of guitar. They added Ciaran McLaughlin (drums), Reamann O'Gormain (guitar; ex-Bam Bam And The Calling), and, most importantly, dynamic Seattle-born front man Steve Mack (vocals). They debuted with a single, 'Keen', on the small independent label, Pink. Both that and the subsequent 'V2' proved radical departures for those clamouring for a re-run of the Undertones, with frothing guitar and a fuller sound. There was now a political agenda too, ironic in view of the press bombardment of the Undertones as to why they did not write songs about the troubles in Northern Ireland. The questioning of British imperialism, explored through factors like 'racist' jokes and the fate of political prisoners, would became a tenet of their music (and more particularly record sleeves). Both their pop-based debut and *Babble* were dominated by frantic guitar and Mack's wholehearted

The The

delivery. However, their one album deal with Polydor Records finished with *Babble* and they moved on to Virgin Records for the more diverse *End Of The Millenium Psychosis Blues*. This included the controversial but poignant ballad 'Cellophane', bone-shattering disco of 'Groove Check', and Sonic Youth-tainted 'Under The Sky'. Big Jimmy (trombone) and Geoff Barrett (saxophone), ex-Dexy's Midnight Runners, had been added to bolster the sound but finances could not stretch to take them on tour. McLaughlin was beginning to step out as a major songwriting force, as Sean O'Neill elected to give family matters more prominence and returned to Derry. His brother switched to guitar with John Marchini taking over on bass. *Chemicrazy* which followed was exceptionally strong, especially on singles 'Hey Venus' and 'Sensitize'. In the light of its commercial failure the group were dropped by Virgin, going on to release a final album on their own label, Koogat. However, its lack of sales again contrasted with its critical reception, and in March 1994 press announcements of the band's split reached the music press (though the group had already been inactive for some time). Despite constant campaigning on their behalf by the press, 'Big Decision', a direct call to political activism which reached a paltry UK number 42, remained their biggest chart success.

Albums: *Manic Pop Thrill* (1986), *Babble* (1987), *End Of The Millenium Psychosis Blues* (1988), *Chemicrazy* (Virgin 1990), *Fireproof* (Koogat 1993).

The The

Formed in 1979, this UK group was centred on the activities of singer/songwriter Matt Johnson. Initially, the unit included Keith Laws and cartoonist Tom Johnston, but the line-up was continually changing and often featured Johnson alone. Following their debut at London's Africa Centre on 11 May 1979, The The's first single, 'Controversial Subject', was issued by 4AD Records. Two years later, they signed with Stevo's Some Bizzare Records and released the excellent 'Cold Spell Ahead'. Since 4AD still had a one-record option, Johnson issued *Burning Blue Soul* for them under his own name. Manager Stevo found it difficult to license The The's material to a major label but eventually Phonogram Records invested £8,000 in 'Uncertain Smile' (a retitled version of 'Cold Spell Ahead'), produced in New York by Mike Thorne. It was an exceptionally impressive recording, but its impact was overshadowed by contractual machinations which saw Johnson move to another label, CBS Records. A projected album, *The Pornography Of Despair*, took longer to complete than expected and was vetoed by Johnson. It was eventually replaced by the superb *Soul Mining*, one of the most critically acclaimed albums of 1983. By now, Johnson was already known for his uncompromising attitude and lust for perfection. Three years passed before the release of *Infected*, but it was well worth the wait. The album served as a harrowing commentary on the sexual, spiritual, political and economic malaise of 80s Britain. The production was exemplary and emphasized Johnson's standing as one of the most important cult artists to emerge during the decade. In 1988, Johnson established a new version of The The featuring former Smiths guitarist Johnny Marr, bassist James Eller and drummer Dave Palmer. A worldwide tour

coincided with the release of *Mind Bomb*, which garnered the least promising reviews of Johnson's career. The work was bombastic in tone and filled with lyrical diatribes and anti-religious rants allied to distinctly unmelodic songs. Johnson retained the new group for another album released in 1993, which recovered some of the lost ground. 1995's *Hanky Panky* saw Johnson deliver 11 cover versions of Hank Williams' songs to coincide with the publication of a new biography on the subject.

Albums: *Soul Mining* (Some Bizzare 1983), *Infected* (Epic 1986), *Mind Bomb* (Epic 1989), *Dusk* (Epic 1993), *Hanky Panky* (Epic 1995).

Videos: *Infected* (1989), *From Dawn 'Til Dusk* (1993).

Theatre Of Hate

Formed in September 1981, this UK post-punk group comprised Kirk Brandon (vocals; ex-Pack), John Lennard (saxophone), Stan Stammers (bass), Billy Duffy (guitar) and Nigel Preston (drums). This was in fact the band's second line-up, Brandon having ditched all his former Pack; Jonathan Werner (bass), Jim Walker (drums) and Simon Werner (guitar), following the release of the first of a series of live albums and three singles. After establishing a strong live reputation for their hard, uncompromising lyrics, and harrowing, martial rhythms, the group recorded their 1982 debut album, *Westworld*. Produced by Mick Jones of the Clash, the work proved commercial enough to infiltrate the UK Top 20. The attendant single, 'Do You Believe In The Westworld?' also gave the group their only Top 40 singles entry. Drummer Preston was replaced by Luke Rendle, while Duffy went on to form the Cult. Despite their promise and strong following, the group fell apart a year after their inception with Stammers and Brandon going on to form Spear Of Destiny.

Albums: *He Who Dares Wins Live At The Warehouse Leeds* (SS 1981), *Live At The Lyceum* (Straight 1982), *Westworld* (Burning Rome 1982), *He Who Dares Wins Live in Berlin* (SS 1982). Compilations: *Revolution* (Burning Rome 1993), *Ten Years After* (Burning Rome 1993).

Therapy?

Northern Irish hard rock/indie metal trio comprising Andy Cairns (guitar/vocals), Michael McKeegan (bass) and Fyfe Ewing (drums). Cairns and Ewing first met by chance at a charity concert in the late 80s. At that time both were playing in covers bands, but decided to begin writing together. McKeegan was drafted in for live support (having originally lent his bass to the duo's bedroom sessions) and the enduring Therapy? line-up was in place. They played their first gig supporting Decadence Within at Connor Art College in the summer of 1989, by which time they had already composed some 30 songs. After two demos failed to ignite attention from suitable labels, the band released their debut single, 'Meat Abstract'/'Punishment Kiss', on their own Multifuckingnational imprint. Following approving plays from John Peel the group found their way on to Wiiija Records, via the intervention of Silverfish's Leslie. Their debut single was then added to new material for a mini-album, *Baby Teeth*. This was followed in short order by a second abbreviated set, *Pleasure Death*. Both these collections

went to number 1 in the UK indie charts, but the band remained hamstrung by lack of finance from their record company. Therapy? signed to A&M in 1992, and collected a much bigger budget for a new album, *Nurse*, and touring. However, at best the press were neutral about the record, which featured more complex arrangements and themes than the punk-descended speed burnouts of earlier releases. The band's career was revitalized in March 1993 when 'Screamager' made the UK Top 10. Almost a year later *Troublegum* was unveiled, which returned to more familiar Therapy? elements - buzzsaw guitar, harsh but persistent melodies and musical adrenalin - aided by a cleaner, leaner production than had previously been the case. Nominated for the Mercury Prize - alongside the Prodigy easily the most extreme record to be offered as a candidate - it enshrined Therapy?'s progress as the most commercially successful British band working in their territory. 1995's *Infernal Love* offered a significant departure. Alongside the trademark grinding hardcore sound came ballads, string quartets and upbeat lyrics, indicating a band able to shed their old skins musically and lyrically, where it might have been easier to retread former glories. How this transformation will sit with their existing audience, however, is another matter.
Albums: *Baby Teeth* (Wiiija 1991, mini-album), *Pleasure Death* (Wiiija 1992, mini-album), *Nurse* (A&M 1992), *Troublegum* (A&M 1994), *Infernal Love* (A&M 1995).

These Animal Men

Essential but nevertheless relatively aged participants in the media-led New Wave Of The New Wave movement, These Animal Men's debut single was 'Speeed King', a tribute to the power of amphetamines. It arrived in a cover with a bowl of white powder and four straws, prompting Brighton MP Andrew Bowden to criticise their attitude to drugs as 'appalling'. The local council of Plymouth banned them full stop. Like an even more ill-mannered Manic Street Preachers, elsewhere their ten commandments included such errant nonsense as 'Get A Catholic Education' and 'Love's Good, But Not As Good As Wanking'. The latter statement got them into trouble when they offered to demonstrate its advantages live on a youth television show. The band was formed in Brighton by Hooligan (b. Julian; guitar) and bass player Patrick (b. Liverpool, Merseyside, England), who knew each other from nursery school. They added additional members Boag (vocals) and Stevie (drums), following 'Speeed King' with 'You're Not My Babylon'. A stop-gap release compiled both with a live version of the title-track, 'Too Sussed', recorded live for the last ever edition of BBC Radio 5's *Vibe* programme. Breaking the UK Top 40, it also brought the band to the *Top Of The Pops* stage. A full album, produced by Dave Eringa, was available before the end of the year, and replicated the punk-pop approach of the debut with some particularly virulent lyrics ('Flawed Is Beautiful' and 'Sitting Tenant' in particular).
Albums: *Too Sussed* (Hi-Rise 1994, mini-album), *(Come On, Join) The High Society* (Hi-Rise 1994), *Taxi For These Animal Men* (Hi-Rise 1995, mini-album).

They Might Be Giants

John Flansburgh and John Linnell formed this New York based duo in 1984 after an initial meeting in Massachusetts, USA. The group took their name from a 1972 George C. Scott movie. Their original intention to recruit a full band was abandoned, but Linnell learned the accordion and Flansburgh mastered the guitar. Following Linnell's broken wrist which decimated their early tour dates, they devised the 'Dial-A-Song Service', which still operates today, premiering their intelligent pop skills. A self-titled debut album collated many of these early songwriting ventures, gaining the band a considerable cult reputation. MTV picked up on their quirky visual appeal, and *Lincoln* became the biggest selling independent album of 1989 in the USA. With wry and perverse lyrics like 'I can't help but feel jealous each time she climbs on his knee' ('Santa's Beard') they struck an immediate chord with college radio. The UK independent label One Little Indian Records released the album before the group tied up a major deal with Elektra Records. *Flood* showcased their obtuse lyrical approach, contrasting influences as diverse as the Ramones and Love. The UK hit single, 'Birdhouse In Your Soul', was a beautifully crafted pop song highlighting the band's affection for the naive charm of the 60s ballad. While *Apollo 18* brought minor hits in 'The Statue Got Me High' and 'The Guitar (The Lion Sleeps Tonight)', *John Henry* saw them introduce a full band for the first time, including Brian Doherty (ex-Silos; drums), Tony Maimone (ex-Pere Ubu, Bob Mould; bass), Kurt Hoffman (ex-Ordinaires, Band Of Weeds; saxophone/keyboards) and Steven Bernstein (ex-Spanish Fly; trumpet). 1995 brought the band an unlikely appearance, with 'Sensurround', on the soundtrack to global kids film smash, *Mighty Morphin Power Rangers*.
Albums: *They Might Be Giants* (Elektra 1987), *Lincoln* (Elektra 1989), *Don't Let's Start* (Elektra 1989), *Flood* (Elektra 1990), *Apollo 18* (Elektra 1992), *John Henry* (Warners 1994).

Thin White Rope

Formed in Sacramento, California, USA, in 1984, Thin White Rope initially comprised; Guy Kyser (vocals/guitar), Roger Kunkel (guitar), Kevin Stayhodor (bass/vocals) and Frank French (drums, ex-True West). However, by 1985 Stayhodor had been replaced by Steve Tesluk while the group's notoriously unsettled drumming position had been filled by Joe Becker. Taking their name from William Burroughs' slang description of male ejaculation, *Exploring The Axis* was an exceptionally powerful debut, marked by Kyser's distinctive voice and ragged guitar style. The balance between power and heavy-handedness was perfectly struck although subsequent releases, in particular *Moonhead* and *In The Spanish Cave*, have veered towards the latter. Two mini-albums, *Bottom Feeders* and *Red Sun*, show the group's quirkiness in a better light. The former was marked by a suitably idiosyncratic reading of blues singer Jimmy Reed's 'Ain't That Lovin' You Baby', while the latter offers other cover versions, including 'Town Without Pity' (Gene Pitney) and 'Some Velvet Morning' (Nancy Sinatra and Lee Hazelwood). Despite limited commercial acceptance, Thin White Rope continued to record interesting, if erratic, music, which in 1991 included 'Ants Are Cavemen' on the Sub Pop Records label. However, the split came in the summer of the following year, ostensibly because they felt it was time to try their hands at something different. Kyser would go on to study for a degree, though he continued to write songs with his girlfriend.

Albums: *Exploring The Axis* (Frontier 1985), *Moonhead* (Frontier 1987), *In The Spanish Cave* (Frontier 1988), *Sack Full Of Silver* (Frontier 1990), *Squatter's Rights* (Frontier 1991, mini-album), *The Ruby Sea* (Frontier 1991), *The One That Got Away (Live)* (Frontier 1992). Compilation: *Spoor* (Frontier 1995).

Thirwell, Jim

(see Foetus)

This Heat

This English group comprised Charles Bullen (guitar, clarinet, viola, vocals) Charles Heyward (drums, vocals, keyboards) and Gareth Williams (guitar, bass, vocals, keyboards). Bullen and Heyward had first met in 1972 when Heyward answered a *Melody Maker* ad from Liverpudlian guitarist Bullen and travelled down to London, where the duo briefly formed Radar Favourites. Heyward had previously been in Quiet Sun with Phil Manzanera (1968-70), the Amazing Band (1970-72) and Gong (1972). In February 1974 they formed the short-lived Dolphic Logic. Phil Manzanera's reformed Quiet Sun led to Heyward appearing on both Manzanera's solo stab, *Diamond Heat*, and Quiet Sun's *Mainstream* in 1975. In January 1976 Gareth Williams joined the duo and they became This Heat. Williams had never played keyboards, which altered both the musical attitude and instrumental approach, allowing the unit space to improvise and compose more freely. Three weeks later, they played their first London gig. Between 1976 and 1977 they continued to rehearse, made home recordings and performed live, building up a solid reputation for their uncompromising sound. At times schizophrenic, it swung from moments of quiet beauty to an all-out wall-of-noise assault. This was no better exemplified than in two sessions they did for John Peel's BBC Radio 1 show which still defy description. Towards the end of 1977 they met and performed with Ghanaian percussionist Mario Boyar Diekvuroh, who in turn had an immense influence on them. Private recordings made at the time were eventually released on a limited edition cassette, through the y French Tago Mago label in 1981. At the same time, the group moved into rehearsal rooms and were able to record at their own convenience. Throughout 1977 and 1978 the pressure to release a record came from various labels but the group maintained an independent stance. *This Heat* was finally released in 1979, produced by David Cunninhams and Slapp Happy guitarist Antony More. It received unanimous acclaim, despite criticism being levelled at Heyward's Robert Wyatt-esque vocals. In July 1981 Williams played his last concert as a member of the group before travelling to India, but not before the excellent 12-inch EP, *Health & Efficiency*, was released. Later the same year *Deceit* was unveiled on Rough Trade Records. During 1981 Heyward also found time to play drums on both Laura Logic's *Pedigree Charm* and the Raincoats' *Odyshape*, touring the UK with the latter as their drummer. In April 1982 Heyward and Bullen were joined by Trefor Goronwy (bass/vocals) and Ian Hill (keyboards/vocals). This formation was short-lived and played only a handful of European dates before returning to the UK to play their final gig on May 18 to enthusiastic reviews. Despite only two studio albums, a 12-inch single and two cassette-only releases, This Heat's influence remains, and the fact that their work still sounds as adventurous and daring today as it did when released is a testament to their originality. Following their demise, Bullen concentrated on working as a recording engineer, Heyward and Goronwy were joined by Stephen Rickard (tapes/autoharp) to form the sadly-ignored Camberwell Now, who utilized an early version of sampling called the tape switchboard, devised by Rickard. While the group never quite captured the intensity of their predecessors, they did stretch the melodic elements further. Their limited discography amounts to *The Ghost Trade*, and a 12-inch single, 'Green Fingers' (an old This Heat song). During a hiatus in Camberwell Now activity Heyward aligned himself with two other drummers, Rick Brown and Guigou Chenebier to record *Noisy Champs* under the cheeky moniker, Les Batteries. After Camberwell Now's demise in 1986 Heyward went on to record a simple melodic album, *Survive The Gesture*. Two further collections followed, both equally diverse in their sound and subject matter: *Skew Whiff*, a tribute to American painter Mark Rothko, and *Switch On War*, prompted by the 1991 Gulf War. Heyward has also been active playing live with ex-Henry Cow and Art Bears guitarist Fred Frith in group titled Keep The Dog, and also worked with Nick Doyne-Ditmus (ex-Pinski Zoo) on a project entitled Carol, Singing.

Albums: *This Heat, This Heat* (Piano 1979), *Deceit* (Rough Trade 1981).

This Mortal Coil

This group was essentially the creation of Ivo Watts-Russell (b. c.1955, England), the co-owner of 4AD Records, a highly successful Wandsworth, London-based independent label. This Mortal Coil was actually a collaboration of musicians recording in various permutations, overseen and directed by Ivo. The first single, an epic cover of Tim Buckley's 'Song To The Siren', was originally intended as a b-side. However, bolstered by the considerable talents of Robin Guthrie and Elizabeth Fraser (Cocteau Twins), it saw its own release and became a near permanent fixture in the independent charts as a result. The album which followed set the pattern for the occasional outings to come. Featuring a selection of artists from the 4AD roster plus various outsiders, the albums included several covers of Ivo's favourite songwriters (Buckley, Alex Chilton, Roy Harper, Gene Clark and Syd Barrett). At times shamefully indulgent, the series has nevertheless highlighted the occasional stunning performance and breathtaking arrangement. The most recent outing, which Ivo promises to be final, continues this tradition. In addition to label favourites Kim Deal (Pixies), Tanya Donelly (Throwing Muses/Breeders/Belly) and Heidi Berry, also recruited was Caroline Crawley (Shelleyan Orphan). Previous encumbents have included Howard Devoto and Gordon Sharp (Cindytalk).

Albums: *It'll End In Tears* (4AD 1984), *Filigree And Shadow* (4AD 1986), *Blood* (4AD 1991).

Thomas, David, And The Pedestrians

After the original Pere Ubu broke up, the group's central figure, David Thomas, embarked on a fascinating body of work with the Pedestrians that was both musical and experimental. Alongside veteran female jazz pianist Lindsay Cooper, Thomas stayed at Rough Trade for a 45rpm album, *The Sound Of The Sand And Other Songs Of The Pedestrians*. A subsequent lull was broken by *Variations On A Theme* in 1984, continuing Thomas's avenue of *avant garde* rock. The release of *More Places Forever* and *The Monster Walks On Winter Lake* (with the Wooden Buds) allowed Thomas to interact with a plethora of diverse talent; he has worked with Chris Cutler, Mayo Thompson, Ralph Harney, Scott Kraus, Ian Green, Richard Thompson, Anton Fier, Philip Moxham (Young Marble Giants), Eddie Thornton and Allen Ravinstein. After the issuing *Winter Comes Home* on the experimental label Recommended, followed by *Blame The Messenger* on Rough Trade, the idiosyncratic Thomas later reformed Pere Ubu.
Albums: *The Sound Of Sand And Other Songs Of The Pedestrians* (1981), *Variations On A Theme* (1984), *More Places Forever* (1985), *The Monster Walks On Winter Lake* (1986), *Winter Comes Home* (1986), *Blame The Messenger* (1987).

Thompson Twins

The origins of this UK synthesizer pop act were much less conventional than their chart material might suggest. Their name derived from the *Tin Tin* cartoon books of Herge. Formed in 1977, the line-up featured Tom Bailey (b. 18 June 1957, Halifax, Yorkshire, England; vocals, keyboards, percussion), Peter Dodd (b. 27 October 1953; guitar) and John Roog (guitar, vocals, percussion), who were friends living in Chesterfield when they decided to experiment with music. Several gigs later they relocated to London where they picked up drummer Chris Bell (later Spear Of Destiny and Gene Loves Jezebel). After sporadic gigs 1981 saw their line-up extended to include Joe Leeway (b. 15 November 1957, Islington, London, England; percussion, vocals), Alannah Currie (b. 20 September, 1959, Auckland, New Zealand; percussion/saxophone), and Matthew Seligman (ex-Soft Boys; bass). This seven-piece became a cult attraction in the capital, where their favourite gimmick involved inviting their audience on stage to beat out a rhythmic backdrop to the songs. Their motivation was similar to that of the punk ethos: 'We were angry with the world in general - the deceit and the lies'. However, when *A Product Of...* was released it showed a band struggling to make the transition from stage to studio. Producer Steve Lillywhite took them in hand for *Set*, and the Bailey-penned 'In The Name Of Love' saw them gain their first minor hit in the UK. It did much better in the US, staying at the top of the *Billboard* Disco charts for five weeks. Before this news filtered back, four of the band had been jettisoned, leaving just Bailey, Currie and Leeway. The cumbersome bohemian enterprise had evolved into a slick business machine, each member taking responsibility for either the music, visuals or production, in a manner not dissimilar to the original Public Image Limited concept. Reinventing their image as those of the Snap, Crackle and Pop characters of the Kelloggs' breakfast cereal, they set about a sustained assault on the upper regions of the UK charts. 1983's 'Love On Your Side' was their first major domestic hit, preceding *Quick Step And Side Kick*, their first album as a trio which rose to number 2 in 1983. Highly commercial singles 'Hold Me Now', 'Doctor Doctor' and 'You Take Me Up' put them firmly in the first division of UK pop acts. Further minor hits followed, most notably the anti-heroin 'Don't Mess With Doctor Dream'. However, when Leeway left at the end of 1986 the Thompson Twins became the duo their name had always implied. Bailey and Currie had been romantically involved since 1980, and had their first child eight years later. Unfortunately, success on the scale of their previous incarnation deserted them for the rest of the 80s although their songwriting talents earned Deborah Harry a UK Top 20 hit in 1989 with 'I Want That Man'.
Albums: *A Product Of...* (1981), *Set* (1982), *Quick Step And Side Kick* (1983), *Into The Gap* (1984), *Here's To The Future* (1986), *Close To The Bone* (1987), *Big Trash* (1989), *Queer* (1991). Compilations: *Greatest Mixes* (1988), *The Greatest Hits* (1990).

Three Johns

This Leeds, Yorkshire pop punk band, formed on Royal Wedding Day in 1981, set themselves a characteristic precedent by being refused permission to play a 'Funk The Wedding' gig because they were drunk. The line-up featured John Brennan (ex-25 Rifles; bass), John Langford (ex-Mekons; guitar) and John Hyatt (ex-Sheeny And The Goys, Another Colour; vocals). They met in Leeds while they were at college, although individually they are from Wales, Belfast and Wolverhampton. A drum machine was used in preference to an extra member, although, ironically, all three musicians were competent percussionists. They signed to CNT Records in 1982 and released two singles, one of which, 'English White Boy Engineer', was a re-working of an old Mekons number. The lyrical focus of the song attacked hypocritical attitudes towards South Africa and apartheid, and the group were quickly designated as left wing rockers, albeit heavy drinking ones: 'We all have socialist convictions and obviously that comes through ... but we're not a socialist band. We're a group of socialists who are in a band. It's a fine distinction but an important one'. They quickly made their reputation via frenetic and comic live shows, even performing a version of Madonna's 'Like A Virgin'. A legacy of fine singles populated the independents charts, including 'Pink Headed Bug', 'Men Like Monkeys' and 'Do The Square Thing'. 1985's 'Death Of A European' was a *New Musical Express* Single Of The Week, although by misfortune it emerged in the aftermath of the Heysel football tragedy and hence achieved no airplay. Unfortunately, there was insufficient success to allow the band to give up their day jobs. Langford earned his living as a part-time graphic designer for the Health Education Service, and Hyatt (who designed the band's covers) was a teacher of Fine Art at Leeds Polytechnic. Their debut album, *Atom Drum Bop*, bore the legend 'Rock 'n' Roll versus Thaatchiism', and included contributions from schoolgirl Kate Morath on oboe. They worked with Adrian Sherwood on 1987's *Never And Always*, while 1988's *The Death Of Everything And More* was summed up by one critic as 'messy, snappy, guttural'. After that came a long break in their musical endeavours: 'We basically stopped working after our last gig in December 1988. We'd done a US tour which was a total disaster and we didn't speak to each other after that, we were all too busy having babies and things'. Hyatt produced an art exhibition at Liverpool's Tate Gallery, and Langford continued to work with the Mekons. They returned with *Eat Your Sons* in 1990, a concept album dealing with, of all things, cannibalism.

Albums: *Atom Drum Bop* (Abstract 1984), *The World By Storm* (Abstract 1986), *Live In Chicago* (Last Time Round 1986), *Deathrocker Scrapbook* (ROIR 1988, cassette only), *Death Of Everything* (Caroline 1988), *Eat Your Sons* (Tupelo 1990). Compilation: *Crime Pays...Rock 'n' Roll In The Democracy* (Abstract 1986).

3 Mustaphas 3

This pseudo-Balkan group have often been included under the 'World Music' banner. Each group member has adopted 6 August as an official birthday in order to avoid confusion. Niaveti Mustapha III (flutes/German bagpipes), Hijaz Mustapha (violin/bouzouki), Houzam Mustapha (drums), Sabah Habas Mustapha (bass/percussion), Kemo "Kem Kem" Mustapha (accordion/piano), and Daoudi Mustapha (clarinet) made their UK debut in August 1982. They hail from Szegerley, and their major breakthrough was going from Balkan Beat Bastard Bad Boys to Godfathers Of World Music, without changing their direction. The Mustaphas are occasionally joined by Expensive Mustapha (trumpet). The humorous ensemble was first brought to public attention by John Peel. The group have attracted a degree of criticism for not taking their music seriously, but the end product is still extremely popular with audiences both in Europe and the USA. As an indication of this, *Soup Of The Century* was number 1 in the *Billboard* World Music charts, and was voted the 'Best World Music/International' album for 1990 by NAIRD (National Association of Independent Record Distributors), in the USA. For *Heart Of Uncle*, on Globestyle Records, the group were joined by their sister Laura Tima Daviz Mustapha (vocals). They have backed a number of other artists, such as Ofra Haza where they sang 'Linda Linda' and managed to offend some people by singing half the lyrics in Hebrew and half in Arabic.

Albums: *Bam! Mustaphas Play Stereo* (1985), *From The Balkans To Your Heart-The Radio Years* (1985), *L'Orchestre Bam de Grand Mustapha International & Party Play "Local Music"* (1986), *Shopping* (1987), *Heart Of Uncle* (1989), *Soup Of The Century* (1990). Compilation: *Friends, Fiends & Fronds* (1991).

Three O'Clock

Of all the early 80s west coast outfits to profess a liking for psychedelia, the Three O'Clock were the most overtly pop-influenced. From Sun Valley, California, USA, Michael Quercio (lead vocals/bass), Louis Guttierez (guitar), Mike Mariano (keyboards) and Danny Benair (drums) had their debut, *Sixteen Tambourines*, released in Europe in 1984 by the French label Lolita. Riding on the crest of the so-called 'paisley underground' wave of publicity, the album created enough of a stir to clinch a deal with IRS, releasing *Arriving Without Travelling* (from which was drawn 'Hand In Hand').

But like their debut, this only hinted at psychedelia and owed more if anything to that other late 60s musical form, bubblegum. The release of *Ever After* in 1987 saw Guttierez replaced Steven Altenberg, and though melodically strong, suffered from its stylized production. There was even a hint of Prince in there somewhere, not least on the single 'Warm Aspirations', so it was no surprise when the band teamed up with his Paisley Park operation in 1988. But since *Vermillion*, issued soon after, the Three O'Clock have kept a low profile.

Albums: *Sixteen Tambourines* (1984), *Arriving Without Travelling* (1985), *Ever After* (1987), *Vermillion* (1988).

Throbbing Gristle

Formed in London in September 1975, the group comprised Genesis P-Orridge (vocals), Cosey Fanni Tutti (guitar), Peter Christopherson (electronics) and Chris Carter (synthesizers). Essentially a performance art ensemble whose work often bordered on the obscene, they achieved a vague cult status in the wake of punk. Although boasting their own record company, early releases were limited to a few hundred copies. Some of their best known compositions were characteristically tasteless with such titles as 'Hamburger Lady' and 'Five Knuckle Shuffle'. Their generally formless approach was sprinkled with arty in-jokes, such as speeding up a single to last a mere 16 seconds for inclusion on their second album. Other tricks involving misplaced grooves and misleading album titles were commonplace. Although derided or ignored by the music press they influenced a number of post-punk acts, not least Cabaret Voltaire. In May 1981 they split with the announcement: 'T.G. was a project not a life. . . we've exploited it completely - there's nothing else to say'. Except perhaps that their debut album *Second Annual Report* was reissued with the recording played backwards. Orridge and Christopherson soon resurfaced as Psychic TV while their erstwhile partners continued as Chris And Cosey.

Albums: *Second Annual Report* (1977), *D.O.A. The Third And Final Report* (1978), *20 Jazz Funk Greats* (1979), *Heathen Earth* (1980), *Second Annual Report* (1981), *Funeral In Berlin* (1981), *Music From The Death Factory* (1982), *Journey Through A Body* (1982), *Assume Power Focus* (1982), *Live At The Death Factory, May '79* (1982), *Live Box Set* (1993). Compilation: *Greatest Hits* (1984).

Throwing Muses

Formed in Newport, Long Island, USA, by Kristin Hersh (b. c.1966, Atlanta, Georgia, USA; vocals/guitar), Tanya Donelly (b. 14 August 1966, Newport, Rhode Island, USA; vocals/guitar), Elaine Adamedes (bass) and David Narcizo (drums), Throwing Muses added an entirely new perspective to the pop model of the late 80s. The band was formed by step-sisters (who had previously been best friends) Hersh and Donelly, though Hersh was the primary influence: 'The band was totally my idea. We were 14, and I was a pain in the ass about it, Tanya didn't even want to play anything for a year'. The duo picked up the services of Narcizo in their junior year in high school after he invited them to play a set at his parents' house. Previously he had only played marching drums, while the cymbal-less set-up of his kit was the result of borrowing from a friend who had mislaid them, rather than any great conceptual plan. The band's first bass player, Adamedes, departed while Donelly was still playing a Casio placed on an ironing board. Dreadlocked vegetarian Leslie Langston arrived in Adamedes' stead and the band relocated to Boston, Massachusetts. Seemingly unaware of conventional constraints, the quartet went on to peddle an off-kilter brand of guitar noise which accentuated the female self-expression implicit rather than explicit in their songs. Yet contrary to becoming too awkward for their own commercial good, the band were picked up by Britain's 4AD Records and thrust into the European limelight alongside local contemporaries the Pixies. Over the next five years and five albums, the media made much of singer Hersh's psychological disorders, drawing parallels between her state of mind and the music's unsettling idiosyncrasies. Langston departed to be replaced by bassist Fred Abong for *The Real Ramona*, and more problems were to manifest themselves by the end of the decade as Throwing Muses became embroiled in a series of legal disputes with their manager (Ken Goes), the Musician's Union and over personal aspects of individual band members' lives. During the recording of *The Real Ramona*, guitarist Tanya Donelly - who had also moonlighted in the Breeders - announced her permanent departure from the Muses, although she stayed on for the subsequent tour before forming Belly. The amicable split had come about because, instead of wishing to contribute her usual one or two songs to the new album, Donelly had written seven, and there was no room to accommodate these in the final selection. This left the Throwing Muses' picture in a decidedly muddled state by the close of 1991. By the following year the core of the group comprised the trio of Hersh, Narcizo and Bernard Georges (bass). This line-up recorded the critically acclaimed *Red Heaven*, but the group all but broke up the following year. Hersh attempted to retreat to Newport to concentrate on her family, but the 'muse' would not leave her, and the band regrouped in 1994 following her well-received solo album, *Hips And Makers*. 1995's *University* served to remind doubters of what had made Throwing Muses so unique in the first place - a wilfully adventurous approach to song writing, though this time there were also more songs of potential commercial import.

Albums: *Throwing Muses* (4AD 1986), *The Fat Skier* (Sire/4AD 1987, mini-album), *House Tornado* (Sire/4AD 1988), *Hunkpapa* (Sire/4AD 1989), *The Real Ramona* (Sire/4AD 1991), *Red Heaven* (Sire/4AD 1992), *University* (Warners/4AD 1995).

Thrum

Glasgow, Scotland band whose debut self-titled EP in May 1993 brought comparisons to the Flying Burrito Brothers, or closer to the fact, 'Sonic Youth meets k.d. lang'. Comprising Johnny Smillie (guitar), Gary Johnston (drums), Monica Queen (vocals/guitar) and Dave McGowan (bass), the group's regional location of Bellshill, famed for its production of indie bands the Pastels, Eugenius, Teenage Fanclub etc., proved no handicap when it came to interpreting the country blues of their favoured American artists. Smillie, heavily influenced by Neil Young, met his future song writing partner Queen after catching her singing

in a youth theatre production of *Godspell*. She had been influenced by the great country singers Patsy Cline, Johnny Cash and Tammy Wynette. A Pentecostal upbringing at first led to her joining a Christian rock band, before her meeting with Smillie 'corrupted' her. They were initially going to call themselves Thrush until they heard about Come having to explain their name to their parents. Hailing from strict working class Catholic roots they decided on something a little less sensational, signing to Fire Records on 1 January 1993. The dictionary definition of thrum is to 'strum a stringed instrument monotonously', though they did not learn this until after airing the name on an early gigging schedule which included an acoustic support to the Jayhawks at Glasgow's King Tut's venue. Following two further acclaimed singles, 'So Glad' in September 1993 and 'Here I Am' in June 1994, the band recorded their debut album in San Francisco at the behest of big fan Grant Phillips of Grant Lee Buffalo. This proved a heady, stirring collection of guitar-driven country bar rock tunes (the title, *Rifferama*, proved astutely onomatopoeic), given a legitimacy they might otherwise have lacked via Queen's confident delivery. Album: *Rifferama* (Fire 1994).

Thunders, Johnny

b. John Anthony Genzale Jnr., 15 July 1952, New York City, New York, USA, d. 23 April 1991, New Orleans, Louisiana, USA. Johnny Thunders first gained recognition as a member of the New York Dolls, an aggregation that built a reputation for its hard R&B-influenced rock sound and glam/punk appearance in the early 70s. First calling himself Johnny Volume, the guitarist joined the high school band Johnny And The Jaywalkers, then a local band called Actress, which included in their line-up two other future Dolls members, Arthur Kane and Billy Murcia. Actress evolved into the New York Dolls in late 1971. Genzale, now renamed Johnny Thunders, recorded two albums for Mercury Records with the Dolls. After leaving the band in 1975 along with drummer Jerry Nolan, the pair formed a new band alongside ex-Television guitarist Richard Hell called the Heartbreakers. This line-up was completed with the addition of guitarist Walter Lure. Hell left the group soon after to form the Voidoids with Billy Rath replacing him. Thunders and the Heartbreakers recorded prolifically for USA and UK labels such as Track and Jungle Records. The group achieved greater popularity in the UK, where they were accepted as peers by early punk-rock bands that had idolized the Dolls. Thunders earned a reputation for his shambling stage performances owing to an excess of drugs and alcohol, and he often made unscheduled guest appearances with other artists. His first solo collection, *So Alone*, found him supported by many UK musicians, including Phil Lynott, Peter Perrett (Only Ones), Steve Jones and Paul Cook (Sex Pistols), Steve Marriott (Humble Pie/Small Faces) and Paul Gray (Eddie And The Hot Rods/Damned). Thunders later gigged with fellow junkie, Sid Vicious, in the Living Dead. The Heartbreakers broke up and reformed numerous times, recording their last album together in 1984. Thunders then produced an album of 50s and 60s R&B/pop covers with singer Patti Palladin and an album with ex-MC5 guitarist Wayne Kramer. The latter featured a group called Gang War

Tindersticks

formed by Thunders and Kramer in the late 80s and early 90s. Despite the promise of all this activity, Thunders was found dead in a hotel room in New Orleans, Louisiana in mysterious circumstances in 1991. He was 38. Despite Thunders' notorious drug dependency, the autopsy failed to reveal the cause of death although later reports cited a heroin overdose.

Albums: *So Alone* (Real 1978), *In Cold Blood* (New Rose 1983), *Too Much Junkie Business* (ROIR 1983, cassette only), *Hurt Me* (New Rose 1984), *Que Sera Sera* (Jungle 1985), *Stations Of The Cross* (ROIR 1987, cassette only), with Patti Palladin *Copy Cats* (Restless 1988), *Gang War Featuring Johnny Thunders And Wayne Kramer* (Zodiac 1990), *Bootlegging The Bootleggers* (Jungle 1990).

Timbuk 3

Formed in Madison, Wisconsin, USA in 1978, Timbuk 3 was a duo consisting of husband and wife, Pat MacDonald and Barbara Kooyman MacDonald. The pair met while attending the University of Madison and began writing and performing their songs. They went to New York City where they played on the street for tips before settling in Austin, Texas. While in Austin they became regulars at clubs such as the Hole in the Wall and the Austin Outhouse. They recorded a demo and made an appearance on MTV's *I.R.S. The Cutting Edge*, which led to a record deal with I.R.S. Records. Using a boombox for their rhythm section, the duo (playing acoustic and electric guitars) began making

appearances on other television programmes and recorded their debut, *Greetings From Timbuk 3*, in 1986. It reached number 50 in the US, largely on the strength of the sparkling first single, 'The Future's So Bright, I Gotta Wear Shades', a danceable novelty song which climbed to number 19 (21 in the UK). The album was a mixture of similarly light fare and darker, more serious themes, as was the 1988 follow-up, *Eden Alley*. Following the release of *Edge Of Allegiance*, the couple was joined by drummer Wally Ingram, and by *Big Shot In The Dark* they had evolved into a full band with the addition of bassist Courtney Audain.

Albums: *Greetings From Timbuk 3* (1986), *Eden Alley* (1988), *Edge Of Allegiance* (1989), *Big Shot In The Dark* (1991).

Timelords

Conceived by the mischievous Bill Drummond and Jim Cautry, this fictitious group registered a surprise UK number 1 with the novelty 'Doctorin' The Tardis' in the summer of 1988. Inspired by the television series *Dr Who*, the insistent tune incorporated the glam rock thud of Gary Glitter, who even joined the duo when they performed the song. The spoof was continued in *The Manual*, a book credited to the Timelords, in which Drummond espoused his theories of how to create a number 1 hit. The front cover of the tome enthused 'The Justified Ancients Of Mu Mu Reveal Their Zenarchistic Method Used In Making The Unthinkable Happen'. The Drummond/Cautry partnership soon enjoyed even greater success with the dance-orientated KLF, whose

title also served as the Timelords' record label.
Further reading: *The Manual*, The Timelords.

Tindersticks

Formed in the UK from the ashes of Nottingham group, Asphalt Ribbons, Tindersticks revolve around the melancholic tones of singer Stuart Staples. Dickon Hinchcliffe (violin) and Dave Boulter (keyboards) joined him in the new act, which was completed by Neil Fraser (guitar), Mark Cornwill (bass) and Al McCauley (drums). The sextet made its debut in November 1992 with 'Patchwork', released on their own Tippy Toe label. A second single, 'Marbles', presaged 'A Marriage Made In Heaven', a collaboration with Niki Sin of Huggy Bear, issued on the Rough Trade Records Singles' club. Having then completed the *Unwired EP*, the Tindersticks were signed by Andrew Lauder for his newly-formed This Way Up company. The ensuing *Tindersticks* was rightly lauded as a masterpiece, centring on Staples' lugubrious vocals, which are part Scott Walker, part Ian Curtis (Joy Division) and part Lee Hazelwood. Its atmosphere of late-night disenchantment was matched by haunting melodies and beautiful instrumentation. Ensuing releases included a version of 'We Have All The Time In The World', written by John Barry for the Bond film, *On Her Majesty's Secret Service* and a live collection. The group's second, unimaginatively titled studio album arrived in 1995, recorded at Conny Plank's studio in Cologne, Germany, and London's Abbey Road. Again the preoccupations were doomed romance and life on the edge, with a guest appearance from the like-minded Terry Edwards of Gallon Drunk on saxophone and trumpet, and the Walkabouts' Carla Torgerson on the duet, 'Travelling Light'. Once more the reaction was overwhelmingly positive.
Albums: *Tindersticks* (This Way Up 1993), *Amsterdam 1994* (This Way Up 1994), *The Second Tindersticks Album* (This Way Up 1995).

Toad The Wet Sprocket

This US rock band were formed in the mid-80s at high school in Santa Barbara, California, by friends Dean Dinning (bass/backing vocals/keyboards), Randy Guss (drums), Todd Nichols (guitar/vocals) and Glen Phillips (vocals/guitar/keyboards). The unconventional name came from British television's cult comedy series, *Monty Python*. By the time they had established their reputation on the local Santa Barbara club circuit, none of the band had even reached the legal drinking age required for entrance. Despite the irreverence of their name, the group's lyrics were delivered with intelligence and poise, and addressed social issues and personal relationships. With a budget of just $650, their debut album was recorded in a cramped living room, but still caught the immediacy of their live show. Sold at local stores and gigs, it allowed them to finance the release of a second set, before the major record labels began to notice their local popularity. The group signed to Columbia Records in 1988, who agreed to re-release both albums in their original form. As Phillips recalls, 'We got signed in the summer after what was going to be our last year together. When the summer ended I was supposed to go off to college.' What they did instead was to depart on support tours with the B-52's, Debbie Harry and Michael Penn. The group's major label debut, *Fear*, followed in August 1991. With 'Hold Her Down' receiving widespread airplay the 100,000 sales return of the album satisfied both artist and record company. Then, quite unexpectedly, Toad The Wet Sprocket took a giant commercial leap forward. 'All I Want' entered the US Top 40, as did its follow-up, 'Walk On The Ocean'. With nearly 300 shows played in 18 months across North America and Europe, *Fear* acquired platinum status. When they finally came off the road the band returned to the studio, this time the Site in Marin County, California, with the express intention of rediscovering the organic writing process which had produced their earliest songs (in interviews they expressed the collective view that *Fear* was too 'manicured'). Produced with Gavin MacKillop, *Dulcinea* took its title from the story of Don Quixote, specifically the love of his life. The idea of unattainable perfection was central to the album's concept, further explored in opening single 'Fall Down', 'She hates her life, she hates her skin / She even hates her friends / Tries to hold on to all the reputations / She can't mend'. Alternating lead vocals from Nichols and Phillips added further musical contrast to a selection of songs which drew heavily on folk and country as well as rock traditions, paying homage to Nanci Griffith and Loretta Lynn on 'Nanci'.
Albums: *Bread And Circus* (Abe's 1989), *Pale* (Abe's 1988), *Fear* (Columbia 1991), *Dulcinea* (Columbia 1994).

Tom Tom Club

This US group was a spin-off of the Talking Heads featuring bassist Tina Weymouth (b. Martina Weymouth, 22 November 1950, Coronade, California, USA) and her husband, drummer Chris Frantz (b. Charlton Christopher Frantz, 8 May 1951, Fort Campbell, Kentucky, USA). The pair were on holiday in Nassau in the Bahamas (later buying a house there) when they met Stephen Stanley, the engineer at the studios and a keyboard player. They also met Monty Brown, the guitarist with T-Connection who were recording there. The four set about rehearsing and recording together and came up with 'Wordy Rappinghood' which was a UK hit in 1981 under the group name the Tom Tom Club, taken from the name of a hall where they practised. The quartet stayed together on and off as a studio project utilizing various other people when necessary. These included Tina's two sisters on vocals, plus Steve Scales (percussion), Alex Weir (guitar) and Tyron Downie (keyboards). 'Genius Of Love' topped the US disco charts, and was followed by a cover of 'Under The Boardwalk'. It seemed as though they were in danger of overstating their separateness from Talking Heads: 'We've deliberately embraced all the types of music that Talking Heads hasn't. We like the accessibility and fun of dance music, but that's not all we do'. Frantz and Weymouth had produced Ziggy Marley early in 1988, and September saw the band playing a three-week stint at CBGB's with Lou Reed and Debbie Harry as guests. They began a UK tour with guitarist Mark Roule and keyboard player Gary Posner as the latest semi-permanent personnel. After the release of their third album, which this time included a cover of the Velvet Underground's 'Femme Fatale', they rejoined Byrne for Talking Heads' first live

appearance since 1984 at the Ritz, New York.
Albums: *Tom Tom Club* (1981), *Close To The Bone* (1983), *Boom Boom Chi Boom Boom* (1989).

Tones On Tail

This three-piece *avant garde* rock band's brief tenure stretched from the summer of 1983 to late 1985. The band was built around the remnants of the higher profile Northampton group, Bauhaus. Both Kevin Haskins (drums) and Daniel Ash (vocals/guitar) had been an essential part of that band, and Glenn Campling (bass/keyboards) had previously been their roadie. 'We're doing things the other way round to what Bauhaus did. They started off as a live band, then went into the studio. We started off as a studio band and have to branch off into live to show ourselves', Ash ruminated to the press. However, when David J finished recording with the Jazz Butcher, he linked once more with his old Bauhaus colleagues and the more successful (and rock orientated) Love And Rockets signalled the death knell for Tones On Tail.
Album: *Pop* (Beggars Banquet 1984). Compilations: *Tones On Tail* (Situation 2 1985), *Night Music* (Beggars Banquet 1987), *Tones On Tail* (Beggars Banquet 1990, different track-listing to Situation 2 album).

Tourists

A UK power-pop group of the late 70s, the Tourists were notable as the first setting in which the David A. Stewart-Annie Lennox partnership came into the spotlight. The band grew out of an earlier duo formed by ex-Longdancer guitarist Stewart (b. 9 September 1952, Sunderland, Tyne & Wear, England) with fellow Sunderland singer-songwriter Pete Coombes who had been a member of Peculiar Star. The pair played folk clubs and cabaret around Europe in 1974-76. Returning to London, they met Lennox (b 25 December 1954, Aberdeen, Scotland) a former Royal Academy of Music student who had toured with jazz-rock big band Red Brass. As Catch they made one single, 'Black Blood' (Logo 1977), before re-forming as the five-strong Tourists with Jim Toomey (drums) and Eddie Chin (bass). The first album appeared on Logo Records in 1979, recorded with German producer Conny Plank. All the songs, including two minor hit singles, were by Coombes, but the band's first real success came with a revival of the 1963 Dusty Springfield hit 'I Only Want To Be With You' and 'So Good To Be Back Home Again', which both reached the Top 10. After a contractual dispute with Logo, the Tourists made *Luminous Basement* for RCA, produced by Tom Allom at George Martin's studio in Montserrat. It sold poorly and after a final UK tour The band split in 1980. Coombes and Chin formed Acid Drops while Lennox and Stewart re-emerged the next year as the Eurythmics.
Albums: *The Tourists* (1979), *Reality Effect* (1979), *Luminous Basement* (1980).

Tovey, Frank

Leaving behind his somewhat self-destructive *alter ego* Fad Gadget, Tovey continued to release an eclectic selection of recordings on the Mute Records label. After attending London's St. Martins School Of Art in 1974 he moved to Leeds Polytechnic, graduating in Fine Arts. Using the rising tide of techno pop as a flag of convenience, Gadget released five albums and 15 singles before he shed his skin and introduced himself as Tovey. Although the performance art was toned down, the melodrama of Tovey's soundscapes and lyrics was more familiar: 'So meet me by the old bridge when the sun is setting low/There's a new gambling game they call the Lemming Show/I've got two tickets front row seats for the river side/We can take a picnic and watch suicides' (from early single 'Bridge St. Shuffle', a testament to the madness of daily life in the UK's capital). By now Tovey had introduced many traditional rock elements to aid the electronic rhythms. This was much in evidence on Tovey's debut, *Snakes And Ladders* under his real name. Produced by Tovey and E.C. Radclife (ex-Assembly), who also featured as lead guitarist, its theme shifted to that of Spanish colonialism (British Imperialism had already been the subject of Gadget's 1982 effort, *Under Two Flags*). A further shift came with 1989's *Tyranny And The Hired Hand*, whose songs were firmly rooted in the traditions of acoustic folk. Soon afterwards Tovey was joined by the Pyros, consisting of Irish musicians Paul Rodden (banjos), John Cutliffe (bass) and Charlie Llewelyn (drums).
Albums: *Snakes And Ladders* (Mute 1986), *The Fad Gadget Singles* (Mute 1986), *Civilian* (Mute 1988), *Tyranny And The Hired Hand* (Mute 1989). With the Pyros: *Grand Union* (Mute 1991), *Worried Men In Secondhand Suits* (Mute 1992).

Towering Inferno

Based in south London, England, Towering Inferno are a performance art duo consisting of the musicians and film-makers Richard Woolfson and Andy Saunders, whose pioneering soundscapes combine freeform jazz, classical elements and samples. The subject of *Kaddish*, the 1993 debut release which provoked all the interest, was their mutual Jewish background, exploring the Holocaust through improvised music and sampled dialogue from Adolf Hitler's speeches of the 30s and 40s. They met six years before the album's release and established a spiritual link which they could only put down to their ethnic origins. 'We became bored of the labels which are attached to rock, classical or jazz. We're interested in each of those areas and wanted to put everything together and incorporate all the music we love most.' *Kaddish*, Hebrew for 'Lament', soon attracted significant support, including the patronage of Brian Eno, who commented in an internet conversation with David Bowie for *Q* magazine's 100th issue, 'Have you heard about Towering Inferno? They are doing something amazing.' After initial interest from U2's Mother Records label, the duo signed to Island Records, making their live debut on 4 February 1995 with a multi-media show at the Queen Elizabeth Hall in London. The show was then performed again in Berlin to mark the 50th anniversary of the end of World War II.
Album: *Kaddish* (Recommended 1993).

Toy Dolls

From Sunderland, England, the Toy Dolls are a punk trio centred around supremo Olga. Other personnel, at various

Tragically Hip

times, comprised some five bass players, 14 drummers and 39 drivers and roadies. And that was only by the end of the decade. The Toy Dolls have long been a cult attraction, their scampering, hyperactive anthems to the absurd earning them a dedicated following. However, they would go on to national notoriety and a number 2 chart hit with a breakneck revision of 'Nellie The Elephant' in Christmas 1984. Its ludicrous nature was not out of place with their standard fare: 'Yul Brynner Was A Skinhead', 'Nowt Can Compare To Sunderland Fine-Fare', 'Geordies Gone To Jail' . They also launched attacks on television personalities Deirdre Barlow from *Coronation Street* ('Deirdre's A Slag') and Anne Diamond. They did little, however, to reinforce their punk street cred by composing a new theme tune to the children's television pop show *Razamatazz*.

Albums: *A Far Out Disc* (Volume 985), *Bare Faced Cheek* (Neat 1987), *Dig That Groove Baby* (Volume 1988), *Idle Gossip* (Volume 1988), *Wakey Wakey* (Volume 1989). Compilation: *Singles 1983-84* (Volume 1986). Video: *We're Mad* (1988).

Toyah

One of the more talented individuals to have risen under the banner of punk, Toyah (b. Toyah Ann Wilcox, 18 May 1958, Kings Heath, Birmingham, England) roamed with the gangs of Birmingham before channelling her energy into Birmingham Old Rep Drama School. She later worked as a mime artist at the Ballet Rambert before getting her first professional acting role in the BBC television play *Glitter* with Noel Edmonds and Phil Daniels, in which she sang with the band Bilbo Baggins. Her next major role was as Emma in *Tales From The Vienna Wood*. Actor Ian Charleston then took her to tea with film maker Derek Jarman who offered her the part of Mad in *Jubilee*. It was here she met Adam Ant and for a time the pair, plus Eve Goddard, formed a band called the Man Eaters. However, the clash of egos ensured that the band was shortlived. While acting in Vienna they formed their first group with Peter Bush (keyboards), Steve Bray (drums, ex-Boyfriends) and Mark Henry (bass). Toyah then appeared in the film *The Corn Is Green* with Katharine Kepburn, and played Monkey in *Quadrophenia*. The band was signed to Safari in 1979 and released 'Victims Of The Riddle'. In August, Charlie Francis (ex-Patrick Fitzgerald group) replaced Henry. Toyah's extravagant vocal style and arresting lyrical subject matter were particularly evident on the powerful 'Bird In Flight'. While she was appearing in *Quatermass* the band started recording the *Sheep Farming In Barnet* mini-album. 1979 was one of Toyah's busiest years as she also hosted the *Look! Hear!* television series for BBC Midland, had a bit part in *Shoestring*, and made several other acting appearances. She was considered for the leading role in *Breaking Glass*, but it was eventually offered to Hazel O'Connor. Further singles followed the release of *Blue Meaning*, before Toyah was rewarded with the success of the *Four From Toyah* EP in 1981. Of the offerings, the repetitive lisp of 'Its A Mystery' carved out her identity with both public and press. Her first UK Top 10 hit, 'I Want To Be Free' came across as a petulant nursery anthem, but was attractive enough to appeal to a nation's teenagers. 1981 ended with Toyah's biggest hit, the exuberant 'Thunder In

The Mountains', which peaked at number 4. The following year, she also charted with the startling, hypnotic 'Ieya' and the raucous 'Be Loud Be Proud (Be Heard)'. Bogan remained by her side musically but subsequent albums were recorded using session musicians instead of the band. Further acting roles came with the movie *The Tempest* and the stage play *Trafford Tanzi*. She became a Buddhist, married guitarist Robert Fripp and later recorded with him. She stayed with Safari until *Minx*, after which she went to Epic and then EG. Her last major hit was with a cover of 'Echo Beach' in 1987. In Autumn 1991 she was appearing with Tim Piggott-Smith in Peter Shaffer's *Amadeus Of Bradford*.

Albums: *Sheep Farming In Barnet* (1980), *The Blue Meaning* (1980), *Toyah Toyah Toyah* (1981), *Anthem* (1981), *The Changeling* (1982), *Warrior Rock (Toyah On Tour)* (1982), *Love Is The Law* (1983), *Minx* (1985), *Mayhem* (1985), *Desire* (1987), *Prostitute* (1988), *Ophelia's Shadow* (1991), *Dreamchild* (Cryptic 1994).

Tragically Hip

Politically correct Canadian guitar rock band who have proved massively popular in their native country, and earned comparisons to Green On Red and early R.E.M. further abroad. The line-up comprises: Bobby Baker (guitar), Gordon Downie (vocals), Johnny Fay (drums), Paul Langlois (guitar/vocals), and Gordon Sinclair (bass/vocals). Downie is an accomplished songwriter, his keen eye recognisable on early songs such as 'Small Town Bringdown' (1987). Now signed to MCA, the Ontario based band earned further recognition from their native country in the shape of a Juno Award for *Fully Completely*.

Albums: *Road Apples* (1991), *Fully Completely* (1993).

Transvision Vamp

Transvision Vamp was founded by the media-conscious Wendy James (b. 21 January 1966, London, England) and songwriter/guitarist Nick Christian Sayer (b. 1 August 1964). The group was completed by the arrival of Tex Axile (b. 30 July 1963; keyboards), Dave Parsons (b. 2 July 1962; bass) and Pol Burton (1 July 1964; drums). The band borrowed heavily, in terms of image and content, from a variety of sources such as T. Rex, the Clash and most notably, Blondie. James was frequently compared, unusually favourably, to Blondie's former lead singer, the peroxide blonde Debbie Harry. Despite being an easy target for her detractors, James filled the space that had been long open for a British female teenage-rebel figure. On signing to MCA Records, Transvision Vamp made their initial foray on to the UK pop scene in 1987 with the single, 'Revolution Baby', but it was not until the cover of Holly And The Italians' 'Tell That Girl To Shut Up' that they made any impact on the UK chart, while the follow-up, 'I Want Your Love' reached the UK Top 5. Their first album, *Pop Art* reached the UK Top 5. In 1989 further single chart hits with 'Baby Don't Care' (number 3), 'The Only One' and 'Landslide Of Love' (both Top 20) paved the way for the number 1 album, *Velveteen*. This run of success halted in 1991, with the result that MCA refused to release *The Little Magnets Versus The Bubble Of Babble* in the UK. Transvision Vamp's low profile since has resulted in persistent rumours of a break-up. James's sense of self-publicity and cheap outrage has given the group's name a consistent high profile, making it increasingly likely that it will be her image and not the group's music that will have any lasting impression.

Albums: *Pop Art* (1988), *Velveteen* (1989), *The Little Magnets Versus The Bubble Of Babble* (1991).

Trettine, Caroline

b. Caroline Halcrow. Former Blue Aeroplanes member Trettine left the group in 1987 (where she appeared under her real name) and forged a solo career as an acoustic guitar playing singer/songwriter in the mould of Joni Mitchell and contemporary Tanita Tikaram. Her strength lay in the haunting and melancholic style of such songs as 'Sleep With Me' and 'Guilty, Imagination And Turning'. She signed to Billy Bragg's re-activated Utility label, recording one mini-album with assistance from Nick Jacobs (electric guitar), Ian Kearey (electric and acoustic guitar) and Tone Bank (drums). Her later live performances in London drew much critical praise upon which she has yet to capitalize.

Album: *Be A Devil* (1990).

Triffids

Hailing from the isolated Western Australian city of Perth, David McComb's group has, along with the Go-Betweens and Nick Cave, contributed greatly to increasing the northern hemisphere's respect for Antipodean rock, which for a long time was seldom taken seriously. The line-up was completed by McComb (b. 1962; lead vocals/guitar/keyboards), 'Evil' Graham Lee (pedal and lap steel guitar), Jill Birt (keyboards/vocals), Robert McComb (violin/guitar/vocals), Martyn Casey (bass) and Alsy MacDonald (drums/vocals). The group's biggest success, providing the great break-through into the European market was 1986's *Born Sandy Devotional* on the Australian independent Hot label. This atmospheric set boasted a brooding, almost Bruce Springsteen-like 'Wide Open Road' and the desolate 'Sea Birds'. The follow-up found the Triffids returning to a simpler recording technique - an outback sheep-shearing shed and an eight-track recorder, producing a collection of Australian C&W/folk-blues songs. Departing from Hot, the Triffids landed a major deal with Island Records. McComb's lyrics, which are starkly evocative of the rural Australian townships and psyche, reached new peaks on *The Black Swan*, their most mature set to date. *Stockholm* was a live set released on the MNW label

Albums: *Treeless Plain* (1983), *Raining Pleasure* (1984), *Born Sandy Devotional* (1986), *In The Pines* (1986), *Calenture* (1987), *The Black Swan* (1989), *Stockholm* (1990, a live set).

Truman's Water

This San Diego quartet - Kevin (bass), Ely (drums), Glen (guitar) and Kirk (guitar) - made its debut in 1992 with an EP, *Our Scars Like Badges*. 'Hey Fish'/'Mr E'/'Empty Queen', a single issued on the cult Drunken Fish label, ensued, but the quartet's métier was more fully exposed on *Of Thick Tum*. Braying vocals, oblique rhythms and gunshot guitar merged to create a sound invoking Captain Beefheart, Sonic Youth and Wire without ever seeming copyist. Their sense of

adventure (and humour) was caught to perfection on *Spasm Smash XXXOXOX Ox And Ass*, a wondrous double-set crammed with inventiveness which was rightly lauded as one of 1993's finest releases. Radio 1 disc jockey John Peel played the set in its entirety during one show. A six-song EP, *10 X My Age*, maintained Truman's Water's grasp of avant-pop, prior to issuing the forthright *God Speed The Punchline*. They remain one of the most rewarding bands to emerge from the US during the 90s.

Albums: *Of Thick Tum* (Justice My Eye/Elevated Loin 1992), *Spasm Smash XXXOXOX Ox And Ass* (Justice My Eye/Elevated Loin 1993, double album), *God Speed The Punchline* (Justice My Eye/Elevated Loin 1994).

TSOL

Los Angeles based punk band, whose name, after much speculation, was identified as representing True Sounds Of Liberty. They formed officially in 1980 in Long Beach, California, quickly becoming one of the biggest draws in the area. Emery was joined by Jack Grisham (aka Lloyd, Gregger; vocals), Mike Roche (bass) and Francis Gerald 'Todd' Barnes (drums). Their high energy, chaotic shows would become the stuff of local legend, and led to a contract with the Posh Boy label. Subsequent releases combined rock muscle with irreverent punk asides, the arrangements some way ahead of their peers. Greg Kuehn joined on keyboards for *Beneath The Shadows*, a more experimental album which echoed mid-period Damned leanings. They also toured with Frank Agnew (Adolescents) on loan as second guitarist. Huge shows snowballed into a set on Sunset Boulevard in Hollywood in 1983, when riot police broke up the show. From then on assumed names were necessary to secure gigs, and they split shortly after. Kuehn went on to play with, of all people, Bob Dylan. Grisham formed Tender Fury. TSOL re-emerged in 1984 with Joe Wood (vocals/guitar; ex-Hated) and Mitch Dean (drums; ex-Joneses). However, when they turned in to a heavy metal act both Roche and Barnes, the remaining original members, fled. The original line-up reformed in 1990, largely for beer money, though the second TSOL were still active and playing that same night in Los Angeles. It was a sad epitaph to the career of a once vital band.

Albums: *Dance With Me* (Frontier 1981), *Beneath The Shadows* (Alternative Tentacles 1982), *Change Today* (Enigma 1984), *Hit And Run* (Enigma 1987), *TSOL Live* (Restless 1988), *Strange Love* (Enigma 1990). Compilation: *Thoughts Of Yesterday* (Posh Boy 1987).

Tubes

Never short of personnel, the Tubes comprised Rick Anderson (b. 1 August 1947, Saint Paul, Minnesota, USA; bass), Michael Cotten (b. 25 January 1950, Kansas City, Missouri, USA; keyboards), Prairie Prince (b. 7 May 1950, Charlotte, North Carolina, USA; drums), Bill Spooner (b. 16 April 1949, Phoenix, Arizona, USA; guitar), Roger Steen (b. 13 November 1949, Pipestone, Minnesota, USA; guitar), Re Styles b. 3 March 1950, USA; vocals), Fee Waybill (b. John Waldo, 17 September 1950, Omaha, Nebraska, USA; vocals) and Vince Welnick (b. 21 February 1951, Phoenix, Arizona, USA; keyboards). Founder members Anderson,

Spooner and Welmick got together in Phoenix in the late 60s, but it was in San Francisco in 1972 that the Tubes were born. Fronted by Waybill, the band's stage act became wilder and crazier, a manic mixture of loud rock music, outrageous theatrics and burlesque. The videos were risque with scantily-clad women, a 'drugged-out superstar' Quay Lude and 'a crippled Nazi' Dr. Strangekiss. The group were signed to A&M Records in 1975 and their debut album, produced by Al Kooper, included the bombastic UK Top 30 hit 'White Punks On Dope'. Their alleged sexism was tempered somewhat during the late 70s. Their fourth album, *Remote Control*, was produced by Todd Rundgren, after which they left A&M for Capitol Records. *The Completion Backward Principle* was regarded as a compromise, despite its AOR potency with flashes of humour. The group's satirical thrust declined due to over-familiarity but prior to their demise, they enjoyed their greatest commercial success with the US Top 10 hit 'She's A Beauty' in 1983.

Albums: *The Tubes* (1975), *Young And Rich* (1976), *Now* (1977), *What Do You Want From Your Life* (1978), *Remote Control* (1979), *The Completion Backward Principle* (1981), *Outside Inside* (1983). Compilations: *T.R.A.S.H./Best Of The Tubes* (1981), *The Best Of* (1993).

Turbines

Powerful blues-based rock quartet from Roxbury, Massachusetts, USA, who sparked to life briefly in the mid-80s but disappeared just as quickly. With a line-up of Jack Hickey (guitar), John Hovorka (guitar/vocals), Fred Nazzaro (drums) and David Shibler (drums), the Turbines occupied a space somewhere between the frenzied rockabilly of the Cramps and the mannered dark élan of early Nick Cave. It later transpired that the band were close allies of the Blasters, whose country punk experiments was another comparison invoked over the course of their two albums.

Albums: *Magic Fingers And Hourly Rates* (New Rose 1985), *Last Dance Before The Highway* (Big Time 1986).

TV Smith

An under-rated singer-songwriter, Smith (b. Timothy Smith) was previously better known as a the principal behind 70s punk band, the Adverts. After which he would experiment with a variety of musical ensembles, including TV Smith's Explorers (notably one glorious single, 'Tomahawk Cruise') and Cheap. Before this he had released a debut solo album, the gritty *Channel 5*. In 1992 he released his second solo collection, *March Of The Giants*, on Cooking Vinyl Records. It marked a return to form for his poignant writing and arrangements, and fused punk sensibility with gentle guitar, vocal and strings.

Albums: *Channel 5* (Expulsion 1983), *March Of The Giants* (Cooking Vinyl 1992).

TV Smith's Explorers

Formed from the punk debris of the Adverts, the Explorers saw TV Smith (b. Timothy Smith; vocals) and Tim Cross (guitar) combine with Erik Russell (guitar), Colin Stoner (bass) and John Towe (drums). After only one gig at the London Marquee in March 1980, Cross quit and, three performances later, Towe followed suit. With Mel Wesson and Dave Sinclair, respectively, stopping the musical gap, the new line-up signed to Chiswick Records. The aggressive 'Tomahawk Cruise' was voted Single Of The Week in *Sounds* music paper, but failed to chart. Over the next two years the group recorded several singles and an album for the Epic Records subsidiary Kaleidoscope, until Smith moved on to a solo career. After recording 'War Fever' and *Channel Five* (1983), he formed a new group, Cheap, though he remains best known for his work with the Adverts.

Album: *Last Words Of The Great Explorer* (Kaleidoscope 1981).

Twinkeyz

The Twinkeyz were one of the originators of a small, but thriving new wave scene in Sacramento, California, USA. Donnie Jupiter (guitar/bass/vocals), Honey (guitar/bass/vocals), Tom Darling (guitar/bass) and Keith McKee (drums) began performing together in 1976 and secured their early reputation with a series of excellent singles, notably 'Aliens In Our Midst'. This quirky composition inspired a cult following for the group when copies were imported to Europe and the Twinkeyz' lone album, *Alpha Jerk*, was released on the Dutch-based Plurex label. The quartet split up soon afterwards, following which Darling joined another Sacramento attraction, the Veil, before switching to Game Theory, the city's prime pop/rock attraction.

Album: *Alpha Jerk* (1979).

Two Nice Girls

Two Nice Girls from Austin, Texas, USA, emerged as a trio in 1989 and by the following year had expanded to a quartet. Gretchen Phillips, Kathy Korniloff and Laurie Freelove were the nucleus that sang and played guitars on the group's debut *2 Nice Girls*. An enticing work, filled with entwining vocal arrangements, the album showed the girls capable of writing songs of great sensitivity and humour. Phillips' songs, ranging from the sensuous 'The Sweet Postcard' (co-composed by Barbara Hofrenning) to the feminist Nashville pastiche 'I Spent My Last $10.00 (On Birth Control And Beer)' and the tenderly penetrating narrative of jealousy 'My Heart Crawls Off' announced the arrival of a considerable talent. Both Freelove and Korniloff also offered strong arrangements and well-scripted lyrics on such songs as 'Money' and 'The Holland Song'. A mini-album of covers, including a second airing of their fusion of the Velvet Underground's 'Sweet Jane' and Joan Armatrading's 'Love And Affection', followed. Line-up fluctuations in 1990 saw the apparent departure of Freelove and the arrival of Pam Barger and Meg Hentges.

Albums: *2 Nice Girls* (1989), *Like A Version* (1990). Solo album: Laurie Freelove *Smells Like Truth* (1991).

U

U2

Indisputably, the most popular group of the 80s in Britain, Irish unit U2 began their musical career at school in Dublin back in 1977. Bono (b. Paul Hewson, 10 May 1960, Dublin, Eire; vocals), The Edge (b. David Evans, 8 August 1961, Barking, Essex; guitar), Adam Clayton (b. 13 March 1960, Chinnor, Oxfordshire, England; bass) and Larry Mullen (b. Laurence Mullen, 1 October 1960, Dublin, Eire; drums) initially played Rolling Stones and Beach Boys cover versions in a group named Feedback. They then changed their name to the Hype before finally settling on U2 in 1978. After winning a talent contest in Limerick that year, they came under the wing of manager Paul McGuinness and were subsequently signed to CBS Ireland. Their debut EP *U2:3* featured 'Out Of Control' (1979), which propelled them to number 1 in the Irish charts. They repeated that feat with 'Another Day' (1980), but having been passed by CBS UK, they were free to sign a deal outside of Ireland with Island Records. Their UK debut '11 O'Clock Tick Tock', produced by Martin Hannett, was well received but failed to chart. Two further singles, 'A Day Without Me' and 'I Will Follow', passed with little sales while the group prepared their first album, produced by Steve Lillywhite.

Boy, a moving and inspired document of adolescence, received critical approbation, which was reinforced by the live shows that U2 were undertaking throughout the country. Bono's impassioned vocals and the group's rhythmic tightness revealed them as the most promising live unit of 1981. After touring America, the group returned to Britain where 'Fire' was bubbling under the Top 30. Another minor hit with the impassioned 'Gloria' was followed by the strident *October*. The album had an anthemic thrust reinforced by a religious verve that was almost evangelical in its force. In February 1983 the group reached the UK Top 10 with 'New Year's Day', a song of hope inspired by the Polish Solidarity Movement. *War* followed soon after to critical plaudits. The album's theme covered both religious and political conflicts, especially in the key track 'Sunday Bloody Sunday', which had already emerged as one of the group's most startling and moving live songs. Given their power in concert, it was inevitable that U2 would attempt to capture their essence on a live album. *Under A Blood Red Sky* did not disappoint and as well as climbing to number 2 in the UK brought them their first significant chart placing in the US at number 28.

By the summer of 1984, U2 were about to enter the vanguard of the rock elite. Bono duetted with Bob Dylan at the latter's concert at Slane Castle and U2 established their own company Mother Records, with the intention of unearthing fresh musical talent in Eire. *The Unforgettable Fire*, produced by Brian Eno and Daniel Lanois, revealed a new maturity and improved their commercial and critical standing in the US charts. The attendant single, 'Pride (In

The Name Of Love)', displayed the passion and humanity that were by now familiar ingredients in U2's music and lyrics. The group's commitment to their ideals was further underlined by their appearances at Live Aid, Ireland's Self Aid, and their involvement with Amnesty International and guest spot on Little Steven's anti-Apartheid single, 'Sun City'. During this same period, U2 embarked on a world tour and completed work on their next album. *The Joshua Tree* emerged in March 1987 and confirmed U2's standing, now as one of the most popular groups in the world. The album topped both the US and UK charts and revealed a new, more expansive sound, which complemented their soul-searching lyrics. The familiar themes of spiritual salvation permeated the work and the quest motif was particularly evident on both 'With Or Without You' and 'I Still Haven't Found What I'm Looking For', which both reached number 1 in the US charts. After such a milestone album, 1988 proved a relatively quiet year for the group. Bono and the Edge appeared on Roy Orbison's *Mystery Girl* and the year ended with the double-live album and film, *Rattle And Hum*. The group also belatedly scored their first UK number 1 single with the R&B-influenced 'Desire'. The challenge to complete a suitable follow-up to *The Joshua Tree* took considerable time, with sessions completed in Germany with Lanois and Eno. Meanwhile, the group appeared on the Cole Porter tribute album *Red Hot + Blue*, performing a radical reading of 'Night And Day'. In late 1991, 'The Fly' entered the UK charts at number 1, emulating the success of 'Desire'. *Achtung Baby* was an impressive work, which captured the majesty of its predecessor yet also stripped down the sound to provide a greater sense of spontaneity. The work emphasized U2's standing as an international group, whose achievements since the late 70s have been extraordinarily cohesive and consistent and although the critics were less than generous with Zooropa the band remain one of ther most popular 'stadium' attractions of the 90s.

Albums: *Boy* (1980), *October* (1981), *War* (1983), *Under A Blood Red Sky* (1983), *The Unforgettable Fire* (1984), *Wide Awake In America* (1985), *The Joshua Tree* (1987), *Rattle And Hum* (1988), *Achtung Baby* (1991), *Zooropa* (1993).

Videos: *Unforgettable Fire* (1985), *Under A Blood Red Sky (Live At Red Rocks)* (1988), *Under A Blood Red Sky* (1988), *Rattle And Hum* (1989), *Actung Baby* (1993), *Numb* (1993), *U2: Zoo TV Live From Sydney* (1994).

Further reading: *Unforgettable Fire: The Story Of U2*, Eamon Dunphy. *The U2 File: A Hot Press U2 History*, Niall Stokes (ed.). *U2: Three Chords And The Truth*, Niall Stokes (ed.). *Rattle And Hum*, Peter Williams and Steve Turner. *U2: Stories For Boys*, Dave Thomas. *U2: Touch The Flame. An Illustrated Documentary*, Geoff Parkyn. *U2 The Early Days: Another Time, Another Place*, Bill Graham. *U2: A Conspiracy Of Hope*, Dave Bowler and Brian Dray. *U2: The Story So Far*, Richard Seal. *U2: Burning Desire - The Complete Story*, Sam Goodman. *U2 Live*, Pimm Jal De La Perra. *Race Of Angels: The Genesis Of U2*, John Waters. *U2, The Rolling Stones File*, editors of *Rolling Stone*. *U2 At The End Of The World*, Bill Flanagan.

UK Decay

Starting life as the Resistors, this somewhat under-rated post-

punk band formed in Luton, Bedfordshire, England, in the summer of 1978, a period when many of the original punk bands were already splitting up. After a few line-up changes, the band stabilized with Abbo (b. John Abbott; vocals/guitar), Segovia (b. Martyn Smith; bass) and Steve Harle (drums). During 1979, Adam And The Ants appeared to be their principal influence, both musically and visually. The Resistors' atmospheric live shows included 'Necrophilia', 'Middle Of The Road Man', 'Rising From The Dread', 'Disco Romance' and 'Christian Disguise'. In May they left behind the name and image of just another anonymous punk band and transformed into UK Decay, the title of one of their songs. 'UK Decay' and 'Carcrash' emerged on the Plastic label in August as part of a joint EP release with Pneu-Mania, another Luton punk band. It was pressed in a very limited edition which quickly sold out and demonstrated an early example of gothic punk. The band became a four-piece with the addition of Steve Spon, the guitarist from Pneu-Mania, and in early 1980 they released *The Black Cat* EP, which continued in the same vein as their debut, but with wider distribution. The early 80s saw a huge increase in the popularity of gothic punk and, riding on this crest, UK Decay achieved a great deal of independent chart success with their subsequent releases: 'For My Country', 'Unexpected Guest', 'Sexual', the re-release of *The Black Cat* EP and 'Rising From The Dread'. After Segovia's departure and a brief experimentation with Lol from the disbanded Twiggy, the bass position was finally filled by Eddie Branch. It was almost a year before the *Rising From The Dread* EP was released. A few months later the band recorded their farewell concert at 'The Klub Foot', Clarendon Ballroom, Hammersmith, London, on 30 December, for the tape-only release, *A Night For Celebration*.
Albums: *For Madmen Only* (Fresh 1981), *A Night For Celebration* (Decay 1983, cassette only).

UK Subs

This London band was formed in 1976 by veteran R&B singer Charlie Harper. Recruiting Nicky Garratt (guitar), Paul Slack (bass) and Pete Davies (drums), they specialized in shambolic sub-three minute bursts of alcohol-driven rock 'n' roll, but lacked the image and songs of peers such as the Damned, Clash and Sex Pistols. They did, however, attain a string of minor classic singles during the late 70s, including 'I Live In A Car', 'Stranglehold' and 'Tomorrow's Girls'. The latter two dented the lower reaches of the UK Top 40 singles chart. Both *Another Kind Of Blues* and *Brand New Age* were vintage Subs collections, but arguably the definitive statement came with *Crash Course*, which captured the band in all its chaotic glory in front of a live audience. It became their most successful chart album and biggest seller. The band's line-up has rarely been stable, with only Harper surviving each new incarnation. The arrival of Alvin Gibbs (bass) and Steve Roberts (drums) marked a change in emphasis, with the band including metal elements in their songs for the first time. Harper also had a side-line project between 1983 and 1985, Urban Dogs, who were a Stooges/MC5 influenced garage outfit. He had earlier released a solo album. The UK Subs are still active today, but their audience continues to diminish. *Mad Cow Fever*, released in 1991 was a sad testimony to the band's longevity, featuring an even mixture of rock 'n' roll standards and originals, without the drive and spontaneity of old. At least Harper had the compensation of a fat royalty cheque to retire on following Guns N'Roses' version of his 'Down On The Farm'.
Albums: *Another Kind Of Blues* (Gem 1979), *Brand New Age* (Gem 1980), *Crash Course* (Gem 1980), *Diminished Responsibility* (Gem 1981), *Endangered Species* (NEMS 1982), *Flood Of Lies* (Scarlet/Fall Out 1983), *Gross Out USA* (Fall Out 1984), *Huntington Beach* (Revolver 1986), *Killing Time* (Fall Out 1987), *Japan Today* (Fall Out 1990), *In Action* (Red Flame 1990), *Mad Cow Fever* (Jungle 1991), *Normal Service Resumed* (Jungle 1993). Compilations: *Live At Gossips* (Chaos 1982, cassette only), *Demonstration Tapes* (Konexion 1984), *Subs Standards* (Dojo 1986), *Raw Material* (Killerwatt 1986), *Left For Dead* (ROIR 1986, cassette only), *Recorded 1979-81* (Abstract 1989), *Greatest Hits (Live In Paris)* (Released Emotions 1990), *Down On The Farm (A Collection Of The Less Obvious)* (Streetlink 1991), *The Singles 1979-81* (Abstract 1991), *Europe Calling* (Released Emotions 1992), *Scum Of The Earth - The Best Of* (Music Club 1993).

Ultra Vivid Scene

Indie pop band built around the pivotal figure of Kurt Ralske (b. 1967, New York, USA). After spending much of his youth playing in various New York bands (tackling everything from hardcore to jazz; he followed a jazz improvisation course at the Berklee College Of Music in Boston), Ralske moved to London in 1986. Inspired by the innovative work of the Jesus And Mary Chain and My Bloody Valentine, he returned to New York to form Ultra Vivid Scene. By 1988 he had signed to 4AD Records, his first EP, *She Screamed*, following in August of that year. It included the cult favourite 'Not In Love (Hit By A Truck)', dedicated to both Hank Williams and the Maquis De Sade. When the debut album arrived, it was written, performed and produced in its entirety by Ralske. The follow-up would be produced by Hugh Jones, though it continued to tread a thin line between pure pop abandon and disconcerting subject matter. It topped the UK independent charts and was voted College Radio album of the year in the US. *Rev* would prove to be a much more raw, rocky affair. For the first time a band had been assembled; roughly comprising Jack Daley (bass) and Julian Klepacz (drums), alongside Ralske (vocals/guitar). Other musicians arrived and departed according to individual tracks' demands. Lyrics tackled familiar issues; suicide, salvation, sex, schizophrenia, and other extremes of the emotional range. Afterwards Ralske would concentrate on production duties, including work with American singer Lida Husik.
Albums: *Ultra Vivid Scene* (4AD 1988), *Joy 1967-1990* (4AD 1989), *Rev* (4AD 1992).

Uncle Sam

Formed in 1987, Uncle Sam were the brainchild of guitarist Larry Millar. With the recruitment of fellow New Yorkers David Gentner (vocals), Bill Purol (bass) and Jeff Mann (drums), they signed with the independent Razor Records.

Influenced by both the punk and thrash movements, their songs were short, frantic and sometimes devoid of melody. Gentner's vocals were monotonous while the back beat lacked depth or colour. At best they came across as an updated, but pale version of the Stooges or MC5, and their were few mourners when the band collapsed in the 90s.
Albums: *Heaven Or Hollywood* (Razor 1988), *Letters From London* (Razor 1990).

Undertones

Formed in Londonderry, Northern Ireland, this much-loved punk/pop quintet comprised Feargal Sharkey (b. 13 August 1958, Londonderry, Northern Ireland; vocals), John O'Neill (guitar), Damian O'Neill (guitar), Michael Bradley (bass) and Billy Doherty (drums). By 1978 the group were offered a one-off deal with the Belfast label, Good Vibrations. Their debut EP, *Teenage Kicks*, was heavily promoted by the influential BBC disc jockey John Peel, who later nominated the lead track as his all-time favourite recording, saying that he cried when he first heard it. By the spring of 1979, the group had entered the Top 20 with the infectious 'Jimmy Jimmy' and gained considerable acclaim for their debut album, which was one of the most refreshing pop records of its time. The group's genuinely felt songs of teenage angst and small romance struck a chord with young listeners and ingratiated them to an older public weaned on the great tradition of early/mid-60s pop. *Hypnotised* was a more accomplished work, which featured strongly melodic hit singles in 'My Perfect Cousin' and 'Wednesday Week'. The former was particularly notable for its acerbic humour, including the sardonic lines: 'His mother bought him a synthesizer/Got the Human League in to advise her'. Following a major tour of the USA, the group completed *Positive Touch* in 1981. The insistent 'It's Going To Happen' was a deserved success, but the romantic 'Julie Ocean' was not rewarded in chart terms. The Undertones' new-found maturity did not always work in their favour, with some critics longing for the innocence and naïvety of their initial recordings. With *The Sin Of Pride* and attendant 'The Love Parade', the group displayed a willingness to extend their appeal, both musically with the introduction of brass, and thematically with less obvious lyrics. With a growing need to explore new areas outside the restrictive Undertones banner, the group ended their association in June 1983. Sharkey went on to team up with Vince Clarke in the short-lived Assembly, before finding considerable success as a soloist. The O'Neill brothers subsequently formed the critically-acclaimed That Petrol Emotion.
Albums: *The Undertones* (Sire 1979), *Hypnotised* (Sire 1980), *Positive Touch* (Ardeck/EMI 1981), *The Sin Of Pride* (Ardeck/EMI 1983), *The Peel Sessions Album* (Strange Fruit 1991). Compilations: *All Wrapped Up* (Ardeck/EMI 1983), *Cher O'Bowlies: Pick Of Undertones* (Ardeck/EMI 1986), *The Best Of: Teenage Kicks* (Castle 1993).

Underworld

Based in Romford, Essex, England, Underworld were formed from the ashes of Freur in the late 80s, featuring former members of that band Karl Hayde (vocals), Alfie Thomas and Rick Smith, alongside Baz Allen (bass) and video-maker John Warwicker. Smith had also performed on sessions for Bob Geldof, while Hyde worked with Debbie Harry. After their debut album as Underworld, a funk-rock affair produced by Tom Bailey of the Thompson Twins, Burrows was replaced by Pascal Consolli (ex-Boys Wonder). By 1990 Thomas too had departed. Hyde (who had by now taken part in sessions for Prince at his Paisley Park studio complex) and Smith continued with the addition of DJ Darren Emerson - a journeyman of clubs like the Limelight and Milky Bar. Allen and Consolli went on to become the rhythm section of D-Influence, Burrows eventually joining Worldwide Electric. Mark II of the band debuted as Lemon Interrupt with the harmonica-drenched 'Big Mouth'. Underworld's breakthrough single, though, was the wonderful 'MMM...Skyscraper I Love You', released on Junior Boy's Own, encapsulating the chilled-out house movement perfectly. It was hailed as influential to the likes of Fluke, One Dove and Orbital, but many others have took it as a signpost in the emergence of dance music in the 90s. Underworld mix live instruments with their studio wizardry, expanded by an eclectic, often plain odd collection of samples. They confounded expectations by playing live on the MIDI Circus roadshow and are one of the few techno outfits to actually relish such activity, mixing live on the decks for a unique experience at each date. Accordingly they were applauded for a stunning, improvised set at Glastonbury in 1992. They are also part of the Tomato collective, a multi-media enclave which produces art, film and graphics for the band's record sleeves, as well as advertising campaigns for prestigious accounts like Red Mountain, Nike and Adidas - all of which feature Underworld's soundtracks. The follow-up single to 'Skyscraper' was 'Rez', but it was the attendant album, *Dub No Bass With My Head Man*, that engendered further excitement. Among the more modest critical responses, the album was described as a 'fantastic synthesis of dance, techno, ambient, dub, rave, trance and rock...the most important album since the Stone Roses and the best since *Screamadelica*'. More than any other artefact, it was the one single record that saw audiences and critics switch allegiances from guitar bands to more 'progressive' outfits. Some even suggested it was the soundtrack to the death of rock 'n' roll, which was, perhaps, overstating the case.
Albums: *Underneath The Radar* (Sire 1988), *Change The Weather* (Sire 1989), *Dub No Bass With My Head Man* (Junior Boy's Own 1994).

Urge Overkill

Formed in 1986 in Chicago, Illinois, USA, Urge Overkill are led by National 'Nash' Kato (vocals) and his co-vocalist and drumming partner Blackie 'Black Caesar' Onassis (b. Johnny Rowan, Chicago, Illinois, USA). The line-up is completed by bass player Eddie 'King' Roeser. They took their name from an old Funkadelic song, and combined the upfront rock riffs of AC/DC with the pop of the Raspberries and Cheap Trick. After releasing a lacklustre debut 12-inch, the *Strange, I...* EP, Urge Overkill went on to record four albums for seminal Chicago punk label Touch & Go Records, and supported Nirvana. With producers that included Steve Albini and Butch Vig, no one could contest their punk rock credentials. However, such product placement proved misleading They covered Neil Diamond 'Girl', stating that he was more important to their development than any late 70s band. As they revealed, 'We come from the fine tradition of James Brown and the soul bands, for whom looking good was paramount.' As if to confirm their lack of sympathy for the growing punk movement Urge Overkill took delight in wearing outlandish ethnic clothes, touring Chicago in an open-top car, with chilled champagne nestling in the boot. They also flew in the face of grunge fashion by filming videos about picnics, yachting and their second most-favoured form of transport - the horse drawn carriage. Such behaviour won them few friends within the tightly knit Chicago scene, the most public demonstration of their rejection coming from Albini (he cited them as 'freakish attention-starved megalomaniacs'). *The Supersonic Storybook* saw the band trade in overblown images of Americana, resenting the new austerity which had swept the nation and deprived its teenagers of opportunities for excess - in particular the band's favoured drug, the hallucinogenic artane. *Stull* was inspired by a visit to the ghost town of the same name, situated exactly at the mid-point of the US, 40 miles away from Kansas. *Saturation*, their debut record for major label Geffen Records, was produced by hip hop duo the Butcher Brothers, once again revealing a much more gaudy, vaudeville and escapist outlook than other Chicago bands.

Album: *Jesus Urge Superstar* (Touch & Go 1989), *Americruiser* (Touch & Go 1990), *The Supersonic Storybook* (Touch & Go 1991), *Stull* (Touch & Go 1992, mini-album), *Saturation* (Geffen 1993).

Ut

Formed in New York, USA, in 1978, Ut comprised Nina Canal, Jacquie Ham and Sally Young. Renowned for trading instruments after each song, the trio shared kinship with the city's 'no-wave' practitioners Teenage Jesus And The Jerks. They decamped to London in 1980 when the label to which they signed, Lust/unlust, folded. *Ut Live*, a cassette-only release, and *UT EP*, capture the trio in its primitive, raw state, while, *Conviction*, the first of four albums for the Blast First label, shows their noise ameliorated by a sense of structure. *In Gut's House* invoked parallels with Sonic Youth, blending discordant melody with rage. This excellent set was succeeded by the equally powerful *Griller*, which was produced by Steve Albini (Big Black/Rapeman), but Ut frustratingly split up following its release.

Albums: *Ut Live* (Out 1981, cassette only), *Conviction* (Out/Blast First 1986), *Early Live Life* (Out/Blast First 1987), *In Gut's House* (Blast First 1988), *Griller* (Blast First 1989).

V

Valley Of The Dolls

This UK group was formed in 1987 by ex-Geisha Girl Jill Myhill (vocals/keyboards) and ex-Fischer Z member Mandy Monkham (vocals), with a flux of transient personnel. Breaking away from the confines of their native Berkshire, they were to prove popular on the London club circuit as well as in northern Europe, with Myhill's street-urchin charm a potent ingredient in this success. Monkham and Myhill also became much in demand as session musicians for Dave Berry, Red Lorry Yellow Lorry and Alan Clayson. However, with no product in their own right issued, Monkham elected to front a new group while Myhill moved centre stage in a Valley Of The Dolls with Leila Liran (guitar), Beverley de Schoolmeester (bass) and Vas Antoniadou (drums) as permanent members. A self-composed repertoire was flavoured with a quirkiness that made songs like 'Where Were You', 'Driver' and 'Hello (Your World Is Next To Me)' distinctive. Produced by That Petrol Emotion's Steve Mac, the latter was the single attending *Cloud Cuckoo*.

Album: *Cloud Cuckoo* (1992).

Vapors

This power pop quartet, based in Guildford, Surrey, England, came together officially in April 1979, although an earlier incarnation had existed a year earlier. The common thread was Dave Fenton, a graduate who dabbled in the legal profession before turning to music. His first band, the Little Jimmies, was formed while he studied at Nottingham University. To his rhythm guitar and vocals were added the lead guitar of Ed Bazalgette and the drums of Howard Smith, both former members of Ellery Bop. The line-up was completed by former Absolute drummer Steve Smith, who switched over to bass guitar. An early Vapors gig was watched by the Jam's Bruce Foxton who was impressed by their gutsy pop, not unlike the Jam's own style, and invited them to appear on the *Setting Sons* tour. Foxton also became the band's manager in partnership with John Weller. After a promising but unsuccessful debut single, 'Prisoners' for United Artists, the follow-up 'Turning Japanese' catapulted them to number 3 in the UK charts. By May 1980 *New Clear Days* was released. The most notable track was the single, 'News At Ten', which underlined teenage insecurity with a power pop beat that recalled the Kinks. *Magnets* was more adventurous, with the lyrical focus moving from the Oriental to Americana. Unfortunately the band were receiving few plaudits for their ambitious efforts, with most critics unable to move away from the earlier Jam comparisons, which were no longer valid. The band disappeared from the scene quickly; the most recent sighting of Fenton was as the landlord of a public house in Woking, Surrey, and Steve Smith joined with ex-World Domination Enterprises bass player Steve Jameson to form Cut.

Albums: *New Clear Days* (United Artists 1980), *Magnets* (United Artists 1981).

Vaselines

Formed in Bellshill, Lanarkshire, Scotland, in 1986, the Vaselines initially comprised Eugene Kelly and Frances McKee. The duo completed two singles, 'Son Of A Gun' and 'Dying For It', which balanced Kelly's abrasive guitarwork with his partner's more melancholic style. McKee's quirky intonation was particularly evident on the b-side of the latter, 'Molly's Lips', a song later adopted by US group Nirvana, who maintained an affection for the Vaselines' work. James Seenan (bass) and Charles Kelly (drums) joined the pair for *Dum Dum*, which emphasised the group's irrascable fascination with matters carnal, evident on titles such as 'Sex Sux (Amen)' and 'Monster Pussy'. Shop Assistants' guitarist David Keegan augmented the Vaselines prior to their demise in 1987, after which Kelly briefly joined the Pastels before founding Captain America (later Eugenius) with Seenan.

Album: *Dum Dum* (53rd & Third 1987). Compilation: *All The Stuff And More...* (Avalanche 1992).

Velocity Girl

An alternative rock pop quintet from Washington DC, USA, Sub Pop Records stalwarts Velocity Girl comprise Archie Moore (guitar/bass/vocals), Brian Nelson (guitar), Kelly Riles (guitar/bass), Sarah Shannon (vocals) and Jim Spellman (drums). Formed from the remains of a University band put together by Riles and Moore in 1988, the group took on a permanent footing a year later. However, despite their emergence on *the* 'grunge' label, Velocity Girl took their name from a (much lauded) Primal Scream b-side, and play songs in a manner not dissimilar to mid-80s shambling bands like the June Brides or Loft. Indeed, the group are all self-confessed Anglophiles. Several compilation and 7-inch appearances preceded the arrival of 'My Forgotten Favorite' on Slumberland Records, which earned a degree of press attention. Shortly after its release, the group recorded a split-single for Sub Pop's celebrated singles club. Signing to the label shortly thereafter, they completed their first full length album with the assistance of Sebadoh producer Bob Weston. It was their label's biggest seller since Nirvana's *Bleach*. For its follow-up, Englishman John Porter (Roxy Music, Smiths) stepped in, to produce a more polished sound, and one even closer aligned to English pop semantics. The lead-off single, 'I Can't Stop Smiling', with its carefree, jangling guitar, even recalled the restrained dynamic of the Sarah Records roster.

Albums: *Copacetic* (Sub Pop 1993), *!Simpatico!* (Sub Pop 1994).

Verlaine, Tom

b. Thomas Miller, 13 December 1949, Mount Morris, New Jersey, USA. Trained as a classical pianist, guitarist/vocalist Verlaine became interested in rock music upon hearing the Rolling Stones' '19th Nervous Breakdown'. In 1968 he gravitated to New York's lower east side, and formed the Neon Boys with bassist Richard Hell and drummer Billy Ficca. Although collapsing within weeks, the band inspired the founding of Television, which made its debut in March 1974. Verlaine's desire for a regular venue transformed CBGB's from a struggling bar into New York's premier punk haven. Although his own group did not secure a major deal until 1976, his flourishing guitar work appeared on early releases by the Patti Smith Group. Television's debut, *Marquee Moon*, was acclaimed a classic, although a lukewarm reception for the ensuing *Adventure* exacerbated inner tensions. The group was disbanded in 1978, and Verlaine began a solo career. *Tom Verlaine* and *Dreamtime* continued the themes of the artist's former outlet, but failed to reap due commercial reward. *Words From The Front*, which featured the lengthy 'Days On The Mountain', attracted considerable UK interest and when *Cover* was issued to fulsome reviews, Verlaine took up temporary residence in London. *Flash Light* and *The Wonder* revealed an undiminished talent with the latter his most consistent release to date. Verlaine's gifted lyricism and brittle, shimmering guitar work has ensured a reputation as one of rock's most innovative and respected talents. In 1991 a decision was made to reform the original Television line-up and the following year was spent in rehearsals and recording. Meanwhile, Verlaine continued with his solo career, releasing the instrumental set, *Warm And Cool* early in 1992.

Albums: *Tom Verlaine* (Elektra 1979), *Dreamtime* (Warners 1981), *Words From The Front* (Warners 1983), *Cover* (Warners 1984), *Flash Light* (Fontana 1987), *The Wonder* (Fontana 1990), *Warm And Cool* (Rough Trade 1992).

Verlaines

This New Zealand pop legend was formed in 1981. The line-up consisted of Graeme Downes (vocals/guitar), John Dodds (bass) and Robbie Yeats (drums). The complex arrangements which hallmarked the Verlaines sound was at least partially down to Downes' classical training. Inspired in equal part by Brahms, Mahler, Bob Dylan and Van Morrison, songs such as 'Ten O'Clock In The Afternoon' (from their venerated 1984 EP of the same title) or 'Death And The Maiden' revealed an outstanding talent for bending the rules of song composition. While albums often contained horns, keyboards, cello and even clarinet, the savagery of Downes voice was never too far afield.

Albums: *Hallelujah All The Way Home* (Flying Nun 1985), *Juvenilia* (Homestead 1987), *Birddog* (Flying Nun 1988), *Some Disenchanted Evening* (Flying Nun 1990), *Way Out Where* (Flying Nun 1994).

Veruca Salt

Chicago quartet formed in 1992 around singer/guitarists Nina Gordon and Louise Post, eventually joined by bass player Steve Lack and drummer Jim Shapiro (Gordon's brother). 'We started off playing acoustic together and our songs tended to be slower. When we switched to electric and playing distorted guitar they were still kind of slow and we thought of ourselves as dreamy and ethereal with a heavy bottom. Then Steve added a lot of depth to the songs and Jim turned us into a rock band'. Playing their first tentative gigs in September 1993, they went on to release a single, 'Seether', on Jim Powers' Minty Fresh Records. This impressed the flock of A&R personnel descending on the mid west following the success of the Smashing Pumpkins,

Liz Phair and Urge Overkill, with *Billboard* proclaiming Chicago 'the capital of the cutting edge'. After a bidding war between Virgin and Geffen Records the band opted to stay on the Minty Fresh imprint for their first album. The ensuing debut, released in September 1994, was named after a line in AC/DC's 'You Shook Me All Night Long', and became an instant favourite among MTV viewers and followers of literate US rock. The following month Veruca Salt would ink a deal with Geffen, which had by now also signed up Powers for A&R, along with his label. Joining new label mates Hole on their 1994 tour helped generate further interest, the group's appeal spreading quickly to the UK also. Central to that Veruca Salt attraction is the space with which they allow ideas to develop - despite a full sound, there is a sparsity to their instrumentation which distinguishes them musically. Indeed, some commentators noted how Veruca Salt represented the first post-grunge pop group, in a similar manner in which Blondie represented post-punk pop in the late 70s.
Album: *American Thighs* (Minty Fresh 1994).

Verve

UK indie band Verve released their first record in March 1992 with 'All In The Mind'. However, they had already been in existence for several years, having made their live debut at Winstanley College, Wigan, in the Autumn of 1989 (three of the band members studied there). Verve comprise Peter Salisbury (b. Peter Anthony Salisbury, 24 September 1971, Bath, Avon, England; drums), Richard Ashcroft (b. Richard Paul Ashcroft, 11 September 1971, Billinge, Wigan, Lancashire; vocals), Simon Jones (b. 29 July 1972, Liverpool, Merseyside, England; bass) and Nick McCabe (b. 14 July 1971, St Helens, Lancashire, England; guitar). After a run of singles which covered '(She's A) Superstar', 'Gravity Grave' and 'Blue' (all released on Virgin Records 'indie' subsidiary Hut), their debut album arrived in June 1993. Surprisingly the hits were omitted in favour of new material which saw further comparisons to artists as diverse as T Rex and the Stone Roses. On the back of this rise to prominence the group had come to the attention of the Verve Records jazz label, who insisted on copyright of the name. Failing to accept a compromise 'Verv' spelling, after a two year battle the group were re-christened The Verve. The group then embarked on 1994's Lollapalooza tour, before joining with Oasis for a double-headed package later that year. Progress in 1995 was interrupted when McCabe broke his finger during an attack by a bouncer at the Paris Bataclan venue on April 20, from which litigation ensued. However, they had the consolation of an overwhelming press response to 1995's *A Northern Soul*, which included Oasis' Noel Gallagher, who added handclaps to one track, 'History', citing it as the 'third best album of the year'.
Album: *Storm In Heaven* (Hut 1993), *A Northern Soul* (Hut 1995). Compilation: *No Come Down* (Virgin 1994).

Very Things

The Very Things were one of various outfits launched under the umbrella organization of the Dada Cravats Laboratory (DcL), based in Redditch, Worcestershire, England. This group operated a number of musical projects under Dada

principals: 'Using that banner was a lot simpler than delivering lengthy manifestos'. The key personnel involved were The Shend (b. Chris Harz; vocals) and Robin R. Dallaway (aka Robin Raymond; guitar), plus Gordon 'DisneyTime' (drums), and Fudger O'Mad aka Budge (ex-And Also The Trees; bass). Other groups operating out of the same stable included the Cravats, Babymen, and DcL Locomotive. Their first single, 'The Gong Man', explored responsibility and the work ethic. Although they were coming from a less strident political standpoint, they found allies in anarcho-punk band Crass, with this being the second of two singles coming out on their label (the previous one under the Cravats logo being 'Rub Me Out'). On the back of this, and a very successful radio session for BBC disc jockey John Peel, they were signed to Reflex Records for the release of *The Bushes Scream While My Daddy Prunes*. An early appearance on television music programme *The Tube* helped bolster their fortunes, while the follow-up single, 'Mummy You're A Wreck', was an equally entertaining offbeat production. After a series of personnel changes, they folded in 1988, leaving behind the Motown-influenced *Motortown* (produced by Ray Shulman ex-Gentle Giant and Derek Birkett ex-Flux Of Pink Indians). The Shend turned to an acting career appearing in television series such as *The Bill* and *Eastenders* playing, somewhat predictably, intimidating characters. The two 'Robs' departed to form their own band under the title Hit The Roof.
Albums: *The Bushes Scream While My Daddy Prunes* (Reflex 1984), *Motortown* (DCL 1988).

Vibrators

This first wave UK punk band were formed in February 1976 by Knox Ian Carnochan (b. 4 April 1945; vocals/guitar), John Ellis (b. 1 June 1952; guitar), Pat Collier (b. October 1951; bass), and Eddie (b. 1 April 1951; drums). Their first gig came as support to the Stranglers at Hornsey College of Art, before joining the Sex Pistols at the 100 Club during the summer of 1976. By September they were at the same venue supporting guitarist Chris Spedding (ex-Grease Band, and solo hitmaker for Rak). He helped get the band signed to Rak and in November 1976 they released their debut 45, 'We Vibrate', which earned a *New Musical Express* Single Of The Week plaudit. At the same time they also released a single with Spedding called 'Pogo Dancing', a cash-in on the new dance craze. They left Rak for Epic Records in 1977 to release their debut album, *Pure Mania*. Contained therein were the seminal Vibrator tracks 'Whips And Furs', and 'Stiff Little Fingers' (from whence a Northern Irish band took their name). Collier left after a tour with Ian Hunter and formed the Boyfriends, later enjoying a significant production career. His replacement was Gary Tibbs, whose CV would later include Adam And The Ants, Roxy Music, Mick Farren's Good Guys and many more. In 1978 they scored their first UK hit with 'Automatic Lover'. It was followed by *V2*, produced by Vic Maille. Ellis left soon afterwards to play for Peter Grabriel, the Purple Helmets and the Stranglers. He was replaced by Dave Birch on guitar and the band's sound was augmented with Don Snow on keyboards. Snow had formerly appeared with the Rezillos and Squeeze. The new single, 'Judy Says (Knock You In The

Violent Femmes

Head)', became their second hit. Birch, Snow and Tibbs were the next departures and were replaced by Ben Brierly on bass and American Greg Van Cook on guitar. This line-up was short lived though as Know embarked on a solo career (it produced two good singles in a cover of Syd Barrett's 'Gigolo Aunt' and the poppy 'She's So Good Looking'). This signalled the end of the first phase of the VIbrators' career, with Eddie going on to drum for PiL and the Inmates. In 1980 a new Vibrators were formed with Kip (vocals), Jimmy V and the Birdman (guitars), Ian Woodcock (bass), and the only constant - Eddie (drums). They released two singles before, once again, splitting up. In 1982 the original line-up reformed. Since then the band have continued to tour (particularly on the continent) and record. There have been a few further line-up changes. Most significant was the departure of Pat Collier. His replacements were Noel Thompson, then Marc Duncan (b. 9 May 1960) from Doll By Doll. Ellis also departed to become a temporary then permanent Strangler. Mickie Owen (b. 3 March 1956) took over initially but was then replaced by ex-Members guitarist Nigel Bennett.
Albums: *Pure Mania* (Columbia 1977), *V2* (Epic 1978), *Batteries Not Included* (CBS 1980), *Guilty* (Anagram 1982), *Alaska 127* (Ram 1984), *Fifth Amendment* (Ram 1985), *Vibrators Live* (FM-Revolver 1986), *Recharged* (FM-Revolver 1988), *Meltdown* (FM-Revolver 1988), *Vicious Circle* (FM-Revolver 1989), *Volume 10* (FM-Revolver 1990), *Power Of Money* (Anagram 1992), *Live Marquee '77* (Released Emotions 1992), *Hunting For You* (FM-Revolver 1994). Compilations: *Yeah Yeah Yeah* (Repetoire 1988), *The Best Of The Vibrators* (1992).

Vice Squad

Formed in Bristol, Avon, England, in 1978, Vice Squad emerged from two local bands, Contingent and TV Brakes. The line-up comprised Beki Bondage (b. Rebecca Louise Bond, 3 June 1963, Bristol, England; vocals) Dave Bateman (guitar) Mark Hambly (bass) and Shane Baldwin (drums). Their first single, 'Last Rockers', was released on their own Riot City Records in 1980, and brought them some press in the weekly music press paper, *Sounds*. Their EPs *Resurrection* and *Out Of Reach* were distinctively melodic. However, the debut album was disappointing. After signing a deal licensing the Riot City label to EMI, for which they would come in for a fair amount of criticism from politically-minded punk artists, they were rushed into the studio. Taking only three days, the finished product was barely listenable. Much more polish went in to the superior *Stand Strong Stand Proud*, only six months later. Despite Beki's increasingly high profile and naïve exploitation of her sex (she was voted 'Punk's Prime Minister' in an absurd contest in *Punk Lives!* magazine), EMI wanted their success to transfer from the independent to national chart. Bondage left amid some degree of acrimony, commenting: 'It was very hard. I'd wanted to go for about a year. I realised that I wasn't doing anything. Looking back, it seems a funny situation. I joined when I was 15, the others were 17 and 18, and everyone was really nasty from the start. I never liked them and they never liked me.' The singer formed the short-lived Ligotage and then Beki And The Bombshells, while the band continued for a short time, recruiting a new female singer called Lia and guitarist Sooty. They released three excellent singles and an album, *Shot Away*, as such.
Albums: *No Cause For Concern* (Zonophone 1981), *Stand Strong Stand Proud* (Zonophone 1982), *Shot Away* (Anagram 1985).

Violent Femmes

From Milwaukee, Wisconsin, USA, the Violent Femmes comprise Gordon Gano (b. 7 June 1963, New York, USA; vocals/guitar), Brian Ritchie (b. 21 November 1960, Milwaukee, Wisconsin, USA; bass) and Victor De Lorenzo (b. 25 October 1954, Racine, Wisconsin, USA; drums). Gano and Ritchie first teamed up for an acoustic set at the Rufus King High School, Ritchie having formerly played with Plasticland (one single, 'Mushroom Hill'/'Color Appreciation'). Joined by De Lorenzo, they recorded a debut album (through Rough Trade Records in the UK). Its rough, acoustic style failed to hide the Femmes' intriguing variety of songs and lyrics; and although they have since mellowed, this formed the basis of what was to follow. Two acclaimed singles, 'Gone Daddy Gone' and 'It's Gonna Rain' (both 1984) were drawn from *Violent Femmes* before *Hallowed Ground* followed a year later, a more full-bodied work that lacked the shambolic nature of their debut. *Hallowed Ground* contained, what is for many, the classic Violent Femmes composition, the macabre 'Country Death Song'. *The Blind Leading The Naked* nearly gave the group a hit single in their cover of T.Rex's 'Children Of The Revolution' early in 1986. There was then a long pause in the Femmes' activities while Gordon Gano appeared with his side-project, the gospel-influenced Mercy Seat, and Ritchie recorded two solo sets for the SST Records label, and one for Dali-Chameleon. De Lorenzo released 'Peter Corey Sent Me' in 1991 and played on Sigmund Snpek III's album, which also featured Ritchie. The release of the succinctly-titled *3* re-introduced a more sophisticated Violent Femmes, although the grisly subject matter continued, while 1991's *Why Do Birds Sing?* included a savage version of the Culture Club hit, 'Do You Really Want To Hurt Me?'
Albums: *Violent Femmes* (Rough Trade 1983), *Hallowed Ground* (Slash 1985), *The Blind Leading The Naked* (Slash 1986), *3* (Slash 1989), *Why Do Birds Sing?* (Slash 1991), *New Times* (Elektra 1994). Solo albums: Gordon Gano in Mercy Seat: *The Mercy Seat* (1988); Brian Ritchie: *The Blend* (SST 1987), *Sonic Temple And The Court Of Babylon* (SST 1989).

Virgin Prunes

This Irish performance-art/*avant garde* musical ensemble was originally formed in 1976. Fionan Hanvey, better known under his pseudonym Gavin Friday, was invited by Paul Hewson (later Bono of U2) to join a group of Dublin youths with artistic leanings who were inspired by the new wave explosion in the UK. A rough community had been formed under the title of the Village, a social club bound in secrecy. The Virgin Prunes became an official band, and an extension of the Village, by the end of 1977. Friday was joined by Guggi (Derek Rowen) and Dave-id (b. David Watson; vocals), Strongman (b. Trevor Rowen; bass), Dik Evans

Voice Of The Beehive

(brother of U2's The Edge; guitar) and Pod (b. Anthony Murphy; drums). Early gigs were very much performance events, with audiences bemused by the expectations placed on them. However, by the turn of the decade they had attracted strong cult support, and on the strength of the self-financed 'Twenty Tens', were signed to Rough Trade Records. Pod was the band's first casualty, opting out of their new disaffected religious stance. As a manifestation of their unconventional approach their first album was initially released as a set of 7, 10 and 12-inch singles, with component parts making up *New Forms Of Beauty*. After the brief tenure of Haa Lacka Binttii, Mary O'Nellon took over on drums. His instalment was in time for the band's second, and first complete album, *If I Die...I Die*. Less experimental and perverse than its predecessor, it continued nevertheless to explore the tenets of purity and beauty. At the same time a mixed studio/live album, *Heresie*, was released, which emphasized that the performance-art aspect of the group had not been totally neglected. By 1984 Guggi had become disenchanted with the music industry and departed. When Dik Evans defected for similar reasons, O'Nellon switched to guitar and Pod re-joined as drummer. 1986's *The Moon Looked Down And Laughed* witnessed another change in direction. Produced by Soft Cell's Dave Ball, it consisted largely of ballads and melodic pop, with little hint of the band's usual confrontational approach. However, following the continued lack of response from the record-buying public, Friday called a halt to his involvement with the band. Subsequent solo endeavours from former members failed to sustain the Virgin Prunes original spirit of adventure, although Gavin Friday's *Adam And Eve* set attracted music press acclaim.

Albums: *New Forms Of Beauty* (Rough Trade 1981), *If I Die...I Die* (Rough Trade 1982), *Heresie* (L'invitation Au Suicide 1982), *The Moon Looked Down And Laughed* (Baby 1986), *Hidden Lie* (Baby 1976).

Visage

A synthesizer 'jamming' band fronted by Steve Strange (b. Steve Harrington, 28 May 1959, Wales). Other members of the band included Midge Ure (b. James Ure, 10 October 1953, Cambuslang, Scotland; guitar), Rusty Egan (b. 19 September 1957), Billy Currie (b. 1 April 1952; violin), Dave Formula (keyboards), John McGeogh (guitar) and Barry Adamson (bass). The last three named were all members of Magazine. Ure rose to fame with teenybopper stars Slik before joining the Rich Kids with whom Egan played drums. Both Egan and Ure also played in the short lived Misfits during 1979 before Egan briefly joined the Skids and Ure linked with Thin Lizzy, then replaced John Foxx in Ultravox. Billy Currie was also in both Ultravox and Visage, not to mention Gary Numan's band at more or less the same time. The roots of Visage came about in late 1978 when Ure and Strange recorded a version of the old Zager And Evans' hit 'In The Year 2525' as a demo for EMI Records but had it turned down. The duo started recruiting instead, picking up the above-named musicians for rehearsals. The demo was hawked to Radar Records who signed them and released their first single, 'Tar', which concerned the joys of smoking. It was produced by Martin Rushent. Any hopes of releasing a follow-up on the label were dashed when Radar's parent company pulled the purse-strings tight and wound the label up. Polydor picked up on the band and were rewarded with a massive hit in 'Fade To Grey', which fitted in with the burgeoning synthesizer pop scene of the early 80s (New Romanticism). Although all of the band had other commitments, Visage made a brief effort to continue their existence. The third single, 'Mind Of A Toy', with its memorable Godley And Creme-produced video (their first), was a Top 20 hit but subsequent singles were released at greater and greater intervals and did increasingly less well. The band fizzled out in the mid-80s, with Strange forming Strange Cruise with Wendy Wu (ex-Photos), and his collaborators returning to their main bands. Albums: *Visage* (1980), *The Anvil* (1982). Compilation: *The Singles Collection* (1983).

Voice Of The Beehive

Formed by sisters Tracey Bryn (b. 17 May 1962, Encino, California, USA) and Melissa Brooke Belland (b. 6 February 1966, Los Angeles, California, USA), this pop group had a strong pedigree. The girls' father was Brian Belland, a former member of the hit group, the Four Preps. Following a showbusiness childhood, in which they acted in various television commercials, the female duo decided to move to England and start a group. They soon infiltrated rock circles and were frequently seen in the company of Zodiac Mindwarp. After appearing on Bill Drummond's solo album, they formed Voice Of The Beehive, the title borrowed from a Bette Davis movie. With guitarist Mick Jones, the group began recording various demos. Their line-up was soon expanded following the recruitment of Dan Woodgate (b. 19 October 1960, London, England; drums) and Mark Bedford (b. 24 August 1961, London, England; bass), who had previously played in Madness. After signing with David Balfe's Food label, they appeared on an EMI compilation album and subsequently recorded for London Records. Their early singles 'Just A City', 'I Say Nothing' and 'I Walk The Earth' encouraged comparisons with the Bangles and Blondie. Bedford, meanwhile, had left to form Butterfield 8 and was replaced by Martin Brett, who arrived in time to assist with the group's debut album. *Let It Bee* was a pleasant, witty pop confectionery, which included the UK Top 20 single, 'Don't Call Me Baby'. Further success followed with the Top 10, 'The Man In The Moon'. The appealing pop of Voice Of The Beehive continued on the punningly-titled *Honey Lingers* which climaxed in the heat of the summer of 91 with a series of live appearances in London which, tongue in cheek, were entitled Orgy Under The Underworld.

Albums: *Let It Bee* (1988), *Honey Lingers* (1991).

W

Waitresses

Formed in 1978 in Akron, Ohio, USA, the Waitresses were a new wave/pop band which achieved moderate popularity after relocating to the New York area in the early 80s. The group was led by Chris Butler (guitar, formerly of Tin Huey, an Akron, Ohio-based *avant garde* rock band), Patty Donahue (vocals), Dan Klayman (keyboards), Mars Williams (saxophone), Tracy Warmworth (bass), and Billy Ficca (drums, formerly of Television). After releasing an independent single on the Clone label in 1978, the Waitresses signed to the PolyGram subsidiary Ze Records in 1982. Their single 'I Know What Boys Like', which cast Donahue as a tease who delighted in *not* giving boys what they liked, was a popular dance hit in clubs and received substantial college radio airplay, reaching number 62 in the USA. The debut, *Wasn't Tomorrow Wonderful?*, on Polydor, received critical acclaim and was their highest-charting record at number 41. The group's 1982 mini-album was issued in the USA under the title *I Could Rule The World If I Could Only Get The Parts*, and in the UK as *Make The Weather*; the USA version featured 'Christmas Wrapping', which became a popular rap hit in clubs.
Albums: *Wasn't Tomorrow Wonderful?* (1982), *I Could Rule The World If I Could Only Get The Parts* (1982), *Bruiseology* (1983).

Walkabouts

Seattle, USA band the Walkabouts are built around a nucleus of Chris Eckman (vocals/guitar), Carla Torgerson (vocals/guitar), Michael Wells (bass), Glenn Slater (keyboards) and Terri Moeller (drums), with guests like touring member and Glitterhouse recording artist Larry Barrett providing banjo, mandolin and additional guitar. They were formed by Eckman and Torgerson on the understanding that 'twisting a take on punk didn't rule out a love for Appalachian mountain music'. Their early career saw their distinctive brand of energised folk-rock weakened by limited budget recordings, beginning with a self-titled EP in 1984. A second outing for Necessity Records, the *22 Disasters* EP, followed a year later. Afterwards they would sign permanently to the geographically but not necessarily musically local Sub Pop Records. It was *Contract* in 1989 that truly marked their arrival, a clutch of fine songs spearheaded by the stinging lament of 'Hell's Soup Kitchen'. *New West Motel* brought further acclaim, and was swiftly followed by *Satisfied Mind*, a covers project, lifting material from blues, country and rock traditions. Guests included Peter Buck (REM), Mark Lanegan (Screaming Trees) and Ivan Kral (Patti Smith Group), while the chosen selections included songs drawn from Nick Cave, Neil Young and Charlie Rich. 1994's *Setting The Woods On Fire* lifted its title from an old Hank Williams' song. This strong collection, comprising over 60 minutes of original material embossed by fiddle, pedal steel guitar, mandolin and the mysterious Tiny Hat Orchestra, saw the band court comparisons to a 90s version of Neil Young & Crazy Horse. Certainly they were no 'typical Sub Pop band'.
Albums: *See Beautiful Rattlesnake Gardens* (PopLlama Products 1987), *Contract* (Sub Pop 1989), *New West Motel* (Sup Pop 1992), *Satisfied Mind* (Sub Pop 1993), *Setting The Woods On Fire* (Sub Pop 1994).

Walking Seeds

Liverpool's premier psychedelic 'grunge' specialists arose early in 1986 out of the ashes of the Mel-O-Tones. In between, John Neesam (drums), Frank Martin (vocals) and Bob Parker (bass/guitar) formed the Corinthians for three months, recording a seven-track demo that formed the basis of the Walking Seeds set. The group's first EP, *Know Too Much* (1986), set the pace, fronted by the strong 'Tantric Wipeout'. By the time of the follow-up, 'Mark Chapman' (1987), Neesam had been replaced by two former members of Marshmallow Overcoat, Tony Mogan (drums) and Baz Sutton (guitar). This was followed by the extreme but patchy *Skullfuck* (the title influenced by a Grateful Dead album cover) later that year. After lying low, the band signed to Glass Records, issuing *Upwind Of Disaster, Downwind Of Atonement* in 1989. Recorded in New York, the presence of Bongwater's Mark Kramer as producer helped create a more defined, but nevertheless uncompromising aura to the proceedings. Sutton left to join the La's and was briefly replaced by Andy Rowan for 1989's *Shaved Beatnik* EP (wherein the band admirably slaughtered Cream's 'Sunshine Of Your Love'). The mini-album, *Sensory Deprivation Chamber Quartet Dwarf*, was assisted by psychedelic wizard Nick 'Bevis Frond' Saloman and new bassist Lee Webster. When Glass folded, the Walking Seeds recorded 'Gates Of Freedom' (1990) which included a b-side cover of Pink Floyd's 'Astronomy Dominé'. This coincided with *Bad Orb...Whirling Ball*, a more considered but still aggressively garage-like effort. The Seeds tore through Bevis Frond's 'Reflections In A Tall Mirror' (1990), backed by Bevis's interpretation of the band's 'Sexorcist'. But at this point, the band 'self-destructed', despondent about their lack of success, despite recruiting ex-Dinosaur Jr. guitarist Don Fleming. A swan-song was offered in *Earth Is Hell* on the Snakeskin label, housing live material recorded in Germany earlier that year. Tony and Bob then set up the Del-Bloods, issuing 'Black Rabbit' (1991). The pair also surfaced in White Bitch for 'Animal Woman' and teamed up with Frank for Batloaf's 'Meat Out Of Hell' soon afterwards. Webster, meanwhile, had joined Baz Sutton in Froth that same year.
Albums: *Skullfuck* (Probe 1987), *Upwind Of Disaster, Downwind Of Atonement* (Communion 1989), *Sensory Deprivation Chamber Quartet Dwarf* (Glass 1989), *Bad Orb...Whirling Ball* (Shimmy Disc 1990), *Earth Is Hell* (Snakeskin 1990).

Wall

Formed in Sunderland, England, in early 1978, they settled on their first permanent line-up: Andzy, (bass/vocals), Lowery (vocals), Rab Fae Beith (drums) and Nick Ward (guitar, ex-Urban Gorillas). The band released their debut

'Exchange' for the Small Wonder label, shortly after which Lowery quit to be replaced by Keely, ex-Ruefrex. This line-up lasted from September 1979 to June 1980, and during this time they took on a fifth member, Heed, who had been with the Straps. The band had just released their *Ghetto* EP and *Personal Troubles And Public Issues* for Fresh Records. As 1980 closed Ward and Kelly both left, and the band continued as a three-piece. 'Ghetto' was reissued on Polydor, along with the single 'Remembrance', and the Wall set about a national tour in support of Stiff Little Fingers. An album followed but by now they were in dispute with their label over career direction. The next release was back on an independent, and featured a frenetic cover of the Beatles' 'Day Tripper'. Lowery later joined Ski Patrol and the Folk Devils.
Albums: *Personal Troubles And Public Issues* (1981), *Dirges And Anthems* (1982).

Wall Of Voodoo

Formed in Los Angeles, California, USA, in the immediate punk aftermath, Wall Of Voodoo was initially comprised of Stan Ridgway (vocals/keyboards), Bill Noland (guitar/vocals), Charles Gray (bass/keyboards/synthesizer) and Joe Nanini (drums). However, by the release of *Dark Continent*, Noland had been replaced by Marc Moreland while Bruce Moreland had been added on bass. The latter was then dropped for *Call Of The West*, arguably the unit's finest album, on which their sense of rhythm and wash of synthesizer lines underscored Ridgway droning, offhand vocals. Any potential this offered was sadly sundered with the singer's departure in 1985. While Ridgway enjoyed a UK Top 5 single with 'Camouflage', Wall Of Voodoo pursued a less successful career led by new vocalist Andy Prieboy. Further personnel changes undermined the group's progress and subsequent albums, although of intermittent interest, lacked the adventure of their second set.
Albums: *Dark Continent* (1981), *Call Of The West* (1982), *Seven Days In Sammy's Town* (1985), *Happy Planet* (1987), *The Ugly Americans In Australia* (1988). Compilation: *Grandma's House* (1984).

Warrior Soul

This psychotic art-rock quartet from New York is the brainchild of poetry-reading, one-time video DJ and L7 (the Detroit, rather than all-female Los Angeles version) drummer Kory Clarke. With the help of Pete McClanahan (bass), John Ricco (guitar) and Paul Ferguson (drums), *Last Decade, Dead Century* was released in 1990, with Clarke leading from the front with vocals and lyrics which took few prisoners: 'At that time everybody was hooked on Hollywood and the whole vibe of 80s Republican morality. But all that lame ass shit had no content'. Influences as diverse as the Doors, Metallica, the Stooges and Joy Division were combined to produce a dark, intense, angst-ridden debut album. Lyrically it criticised the establishment's inability to solve contemporary social problems, with references to political and police corruption, the homeless and narcotics. Mark Evans took over as drummer on *Drugs, God And The New Republic*, which built on previous themes, but increased the musical intensity of their delivery, honed

on US supports to Queensrÿche, whose philosophical angle, if not musical, they echoed. The message for *Salutations From The Ghetto Nation* was succinct if not polite: 'I don't think you have to be particularly intelligent to understand Fuck The Government!' These works received considerable critical acclaim, but it would be *Chill Pill* and *Space Age Playboys* which converted this into album sales. If anything *Chill Pill* was more resentful and hate-filled than previous offerings, but by *Space Age Playboys* the band looked to have exhausted this avenue. What listeners received instead was an 'up' record, which maintained Clarke's political allegiances, but allied them to a collage of images and events which eschewed earlier didacticism.
Albums: *Last Decade, Dead Century* (Geffen 1990), *Drugs, God And The New Republic* (Geffen 1991), *Salutations From The Ghetto Nation* (Geffen 1992), *Chill Pill* (Geffen 1993), *Space Age Playboys* (Music For Nations 1994).

Waterboys

Formed by vocalist Mike Scott (b. 14 December 1958, Edinburgh, Scotland), a former fanzine writer, the Waterboys evolved from Another Pretty Face, which included John Caldwell (guitar) and a frequently changing line-up from 1979-81. A series of failed singles followed until Scott elected to form a new group. Borrowing the name Waterboys from a line in 'The Kids' from Lou Reed's *Berlin*, Scott began advertising in the music press for suitable personnel. Anthony Thistlethwaite (b. 31 August 1955, Leicester, England; saxophone) and Karl Wallinger (b. 19 October 1957, Prestatyn, Clwyd, Wales; keyboards/percussion/vocals) were recruited and work was completed on 'A Girl Called Johnny', a sterling tribute to Patti Smith that narrowly failed to become a big hit. The group's self-titled debut was also a solid work, emphasizing Scott's ability as a singer/songwriter. 'December', with its religious connotations, was an excellent Christmas single that again narrowly failed to chart. Augmented by musicians Kevin Wilkinson (drums), Roddy Lorimar (trumpet) and Tim Blanthorn (violin), the Waterboys completed *A Pagan Place*, which confirmed their early promise. The key track for many was 'The Big Music', which became a handy simile for Scott's soul-searching mini-epics. For the following year's *This Is The Sea*, Scott brought in a new drummer Chris Whitten and added a folk flavour to the proceedings, courtesy of fiddler Steve Wickham. The attendant 'The Whole Of The Moon' only reached number 28 in the UK but later proved a spectacular Top 10 hit when reissued in 1990. It was a masterwork from a group seemingly at the height of its powers. Despite their promise, the Waterboys remained a vehicle for Scott's ideas and writing, a view reinforced when Karl Wallinger quit to form World Party. At this point Wickham, who had previously played with In Tua Nua, U2 and Sinead O'Connor, took on a more prominent role. He took Scott to Eire and a long sojourn in Galway followed. Three years passed before the Waterboys released their next album, the distinctively folk-flavoured *Fisherman's Blues*. Scott's assimilation of traditional Irish music, mingled with his own spiritual questing and rock background coalesced to produce a work of considerable charm and power.

Waterboys

Back in the ascendant, the group completed work on *Room To Roam*, which retained the folk sound, though to a lesser extent than its predecessor. Within days of the album's release, Wickham left the group, forcing Scott to reconstruct the Waterboys' sound once more. A revised line-up featuring Thistlethwaite, Hutchinson and new drummer Ken Blevins toured the UK playing a rocking set, minus the folk music that had permeated their recent work. After signing a US/Canadian deal with Geffen Records, the Waterboys line-up underwent further changes when, in February 1992, long-serving member Anthony Thistlethwaite left the group. During the rebuilding of the group, former Wendy And Lisa drummer Carla Azar took over the spot vacated by Ken Blevins, and Scott Thunes was recruited as the new bassist. Mercurial and uncompromising, Scott has continually steered the Waterboys through radically different musical phases, which have proven consistently fascinating.

Albums: *The Waterboys* (1983), *A Pagan Place* (1984), *This Is The Sea* (1985), *Fisherman's Blues* (1988), *Road To Roam* (1990), *This Is The Sea* (1992), *Dream Harder* (1993). Compilation: *The Best Of 1981-90* (1991).

Wax Trax Records

Along with Touch & Go Records, Wax Trax is Chicago's most important post-punk label. Headed by proprietors Jim Nash and Dannie Flesher, the keynote to the company's performance since 1979 has been a dogged sense of independence, and an unwillingness (perhaps even an inability) to compromise its artistic vision. While this could be argued to have been the central cause of the label's temporary bankruptcy, it did provide outsiders with a decade and a half of incredible sounds. The music on offer, generally rock distilled through electronics, samplers and synthesizers, could have been purpose built to defy fashion or fandom. Yet over the years the label was home to a number of groups whose influence was probably not truly felt at the time - Front 242, Meat Beat Manifesto, KMFDM, My Life With The Thrill Kill Kult, the Revolting Cocks, Finitribe and Ministry, to name but a few. Thematically inspired by the slow death of the industrial age, these groups proselytised the wake with martial rhythms and dense imagery - though genre classics such as the Cocks' 'Beers, Steers And Queers' pointed out that this was no exercise in austerity. The mid-90s saw a now fully-recovered and financially stable Wax Trax working with artists which fitted with their musical tradition - Die Warzau, Chris Connelly, etc., also licensing UK dance experimentalists Underworld.

Selected album: various artists *Black Box: A 13 Year History Of Wax Trax Records* (Wax Trax 1994).

We Are Going To Eat You

This UK band were formed in 1986 by Julie Sorrell (b. London, England; vocals), Paul Harding (b. London, England; guitar), Paul 'Veg' Venables (b. London, England; bass) and Chris Knowles (b. London, England; drums). The cumbersomely-named group peddled a hybrid of pop and rock infused with a punk spirit. After several years of intense gigging and low-key releases, an appearance on BBC television's alternative *Snub TV* show, at the start of 1989, attracted copious amounts of interest from music business circles, resulting in a burst of media activity and much talk of a major record label deal. Unfortunately, the band's independent backers refused to allow the band to sign unless the price was right. In the ensuing legal mess the band lost the all-important momentum and therefore by the time they were free of their old constraints, the quartet struggled to rekindle outside interest, in spite of a prestigious American deal. Eventually these frustrations came to a head in 1990 when the band vanished into the studio and reappeared with a new, more fashionable sound and the infinitely more sociable name of Melt.

Album: *Everywhen* (TVT 1990).

We've Got A Fuzzbox And We're Gonna Use It

Formed in Birmingham, England, in 1985, this all-female quartet comprised Maggie Dunne (b. 5 June 1964, Solihull, West Midlands, England; vocals/keyboards/guitar), Jo Dunne (b. 12 November 1968, Birmingham, England; bass/piano), Vickie Perks (b. 9 October 1968, Birmingham, England; vocals) and Tina O'Neill (b. 20 January 1969, Solihull, West Midlands, England; drums/percussion/saxophone). Their unusual name was coined after they had purchased a fuzzbox for their guitars and Maggie casually announced: 'We've Got A Fuzzbox And We're Gonna Use It!' The fuzzbox drone dominated their early work, particularly on such songs as 'XX Sex' and 'Rules And Regulations', which displayed a raw, intense sound overladen with strong harmonies and barbed sloganeering lyrics. The delightfully unselfconscious amateurish style of their work was reflected in their bizarre technicolour cartoon image, with multicoloured, geometric hairstyles and garish clothes. Their schoolgirl playfulness and frequently-voiced disregard for musical precision extracted a condescending chauvinism from the music press of the period. This patronizing attitude was undeserved for Fuzzbox were considerably more interesting, technically and otherwise, than many of their male contemporaries. They played a variety of instruments, showed no reluctance to undertake major tours and wrote and arranged their own material. An appearance on their record label's *Vindaloo Summer Special* spawned a minor hit EP, *Rockin' With Rita*, produced by Stuart Colman. A contract with WEA Records followed and in 1986 they scored another small UK hit with the glorious 'Love Is The Slug', with its distinctive wall of sound guitars, embellished by piercing yet barely coherent vocals. Their debut album, *Bostin' Steve Austin*, included several old singles, plus the stage favourite 'What's The Point?'. After further touring, the group re-emerged without their bizarre hairstyles for the 1989 UK Top 20 hit 'International Rescue'. Another high-powered production, the single saw Fuzzbox dressed as *Thunderbirds* puppets with Vickie playing the role of Jane Fonda's *Barbarella*, complete with bacon-foil space garb, in the accompanying video. Having virtually abandoned their 'fuzzbox sound', they also reluctantly accepted the advice of their record company and abbreviated their name to 'Fuzzbox'. Thereafter, they moved increasingly towards the mainstream. The next hit 'Pink Sunshine' was catchy enough, but lacked the distinction and originality of their earlier work. The accompanying *Big Bang!* was another largely self-penned effort, but included a surprise hit reading

of Yoko Ono's 'Walking On Thin Ice'. A highly accomplished closing track, 'Beauty', displayed their oft-neglected vocal and arranging talents to the full. In July 1990 after some months of speculation, Vickie Perks announced her intention to pursue a solo career. The remaining members agreed to end the the Fuzzbox saga at that point and start afresh.
Albums: *Bostin' Steve Austin* (WEA 1987), *Big Bang!* (WEA 1989).

Wedding Present

Forthright and briefly fashionable indie band formed in Leeds, Yorkshire, England, in 1985 from the ashes of the Lost Pandas by David Gedge (b. 23 April 1960, Leeds, Yorkshire, England; guitar/vocals) with Keith Gregory (b. 2 January 1963, Co. Durham, England; bass), Peter Salowka (b. Middleton, Gt. Manchester, England; guitar) and Shaun Charman (b. Brighton, East Sussex, England; drums). The Wedding Present embodied the independent spirit of the mid-80s with a passion that few contemporaries could match. Furthermore, they staked their musical claim with a ferocious blend of implausibly fast guitars and lovelorn lyrics over a series of much-lauded singles on their own Reception Records label. As some cynics criticized the band's lack of imagination, *George Best* shared the merits of the flamboyant but flawed football star and reached number 47 in the UK chart. Similarly, as those same critics suggested the band were 'one-trick phonies', Pete Salowka's East European upbringing was brought to bear on the Wedding Present sound, resulting in the frenzied Ukrainian folk songs on *Ukrainski Vistupi V Johna Peel*, so called because it was a compilation of tracks from sessions they had made for John Peel's influential BBC Radio 1 show. Shaun Charman left the band as their debut was released, to join the Pop Guns, and was replaced by Simon Smith (b. 3 May 1965, Lincolnshire, England). Capitalizing on a still-burgeoning following, 'Kennedy' saw the band break into the Top 40 of the UK singles chart for the first time and revealed that, far from compromising on a major label, the Wedding Present were actually becoming more extreme. By their third album, *Seamonsters*, the band had forged a bizarre relationship with hardcore exponent Steve Albini (former member of the influential US outfit Big Black), whose harsh economic production technique encouraged the Wedding Present to juggle with broody lyrical mumblings and extraordinary slabs of guitar, killing the ghost of their 'jangly' beginnings. Before *Seamonsters* was released in 1991, Salowka made way for Paul Dorrington, although he remained in the business side of the band and formed the Ukrainians. In 1992 the Wedding Present undertook the ambitious project of releasing one single, every month, throughout the year. Each single charted in the UK Top 40 (admittedly in a depressed market), making the tactic a success, though the ever candid Gedge revealed that it had been done against a backdrop of record company opposition. Their relationship with RCA ended following the accompanying *Hit Parade* compilations, though Island Records were quick to pick up the out of contract band. Gregory also left the fold before *Watusi* restored the band to their previous status (reviled by certain sections of the UK media, venerated by hardcore supporters).

Albums: *George Best* (Reception 1987), *Bizarro* (RCA 1989), *Seamonsters* (RCA 1991), *Watusi* (Island 1994). Compilations: *Tommy* (Reception 1988), *The Hit Parade Part One* (RCA 1992), *Ukrainski Vistupi V Johna Peel* (RCA 1989), *The Hit Parade Part Two* (RCA 1993).

Weddings, Parties, Anything

Formed in Melbourne, Australia, in 1984, and based around Mike Thomas (guitar/bass/vocals) and David Steel (guitar/vocals), the closest comparison to WPA's sound is that of the Pogues, and the Sydney-based, Roaring Jack - both punk-influenced bands who also derived their inspiration from traditional Irish folk music. The line-up also comprised Mark Wallace (piano accordion), David Adams (drums, replaced in 1986 by Marcus Schintler) and Paul Clark (guitar). Their songs are concerned with Australian social issues, whilst the music, featuring Wallace's accordion complements the biting lyrics that depict the life of the down-and-out. The departure of song writer Steel (who later recorded his own well received solo album), in 1988, did no harm to the band. After their mini-album *No Show Without Punch*, was released on Billy Bragg's Utility label, and the band attracted some favourable reviews in the UK. Though they failed to capitalize commercially, they retain numerous high-profile supporters, including Shane MacGowan and Bono of U2, who once remarked: 'I really admire Michael Thomas. He writes songs that old men can sing in pubs and kids can dance to. We've been trying to do that for ages'.
Albums: *Scorn Of The Women* (1987), *Roaring Days* (1988), *The Big Don't Argue* (1989), *Difficult Loves* (Cooking Vinyl 1993), *Kingtide* (East West 1994).

Weekend

After the demise of the Young Marble Giants in 1980, Alison Statton (b. March 1958, Cardiff, Wales; vocals/bass) and fellow Cardiffian, Spike (guitarist/viola), moved to London. After teaming up the following year with Simon Booth (b. 12 March 1956), who worked at Mole Jazz record shop, they formed Weekend. Their debut single on Rough Trade Records, 'The View From Her Room', produced by Simon Jeffes of the Penguin Cafe Orchestra, presented a breezy jazz-shuffle driven by Statton's excellent bass-line. Amongst the studio support were two veterans of the British jazz scene, Harry Beckett (trumpet/flugelhorn) and former Centipede member Larry Stabbins (b. 9 September 1949; tenor sax). Mixed with Statton's introspective lyrics, the band's image of an 'anti-rock' outfit drawing on multi-cultural jazz influences, from the bossa nova of Gilberto Gill and Astrud Gilberto to the light African guitar style of King Sunny Ade, was quickly picked up by the then fashionable youthful London 'jazz-club' scene. Later singles 'Past Meets Present' and 'Drumbeat For Baby' gave Weekend further independent chart hits. Their debut *La Variété* perfectly captured the group's light summery feel. While live performances were few and far between, London was blessed one memorable weekend in 1983 with two concerts, one at the Africa Centre, Covent Garden and another at the legendary Ronnie Scott's Club in Soho, where they were joined onstage by Keith Tippett. This set was recorded and later released on a posthumous mini-album. Statton's unease with live performances and Booth's desire to lead the group down a harder jazz-dance direction led to the group splitting, with Stabbins and Booth carrying on the bloodline with the formation of Working Week. Statton returned to Cardiff and her college studies, re-emerging in the late 80s with the duo Devine And Statton.

Albums: *La Verité* (1982), *Live At Ronnie Scott's* (1983). Compilation: with the Young Marble Giants and the Gist *Nipped In The Bud* (1984).

Weezer

'Post-slacker' US guitar pop artisans from Los Angeles, California, comprising Rivers Cuomo (b. c.1971, Connecticut, USA; vocals/guitar), Brian Bell (b. Tennessee, USA; guitar), Matt Sharp (bass) and Patrick Wilson (b. Buffalo, New York State, USA; drums). Cuomo grew up in rural Connecticut until deciding to move to Los Angeles at age 18 to form a band. It was to little immediate success, but, tortured by the sundering of his relationship, he began to write his own songs. Sharp brought the unlikely influences of Talk Talk and Gary Numan to the bass player's role. Bell first learnt guitar in Tennessee by playing along to television shows like *Hee Haw*, picking on a ukulele his grandmother won at a bingo game. Wilson was introduced to the other members via fellow Buffalo citizen Pat Fin (of Winkler). The four protagonists had met as strangers who found themselves abroad in Los Angeles, and decided to form a band together. The official date of formation would be 14 February 1992, signing to DGC Records in June of the following year. On the back of offbeat singles, 'Undone - The Sweater Song' and 'Buddy Holly' (a tale of high school prom rejection), and seven months touring their native country, their self-titled debut album, produced by Ric Ocasek of the Cars and Chris Shaw in New York, would sell nearly a million copies. Their preference for goofy garage aesthetics soon distinguished them, and, with fuzz boxes and falsetto harmonies (from Sharp) to the fore, comparisons to They Might Be Giants hardly delineated their musical compass, despite helping to pinpoint their humour. The participants, meanwhile, remained awe-struck at the depth of their appeal: 'We've sold all these albums when, honestly speaking, we're a super straight-ahead American guitar garage rock band'.

Album: *Weezer* (Geffen 1994).

Weirdos

One of the strongest bands to emerge from the Los Angeles, California, USA punk explosion, the Weirdos were formed in 1976 following a short spell known as the Barbies and Luxurious Adults. Comprising John Denny (vocals), Dix Denny (guitar), Cliff Roman (guitar), David Trout (bass) and Nickey Beat (drums), the Weirdos recorded several excellent singles, notably 'Destroy All Music' (1977) and 'We Got The Neutron Bomb' (1978) for cult label Dangerhouse Records, but the group were plagued by internal problems. The EP, *Who, What, When, Where, Why?*, showed some of the Weirdos' early fire but further changes in the rhythm section undermined their progress. They broke up in 1981, but reformed in 1990 for *Condor*.

Album: *Condor* (Frontier 1980). Compilation: *Weird World 1977-1981 Time Capsule Volume One* (Frontier 1991).

Weller, Paul

b. 25 May 1958, Woking, Surrey, England; vocals/guitar. The rise and fall from critical grace, and subsequent rise of Paul Weller could occupy a small chapter in any book on UK rock music of the 70s, 80s and 90s. The recipient of almost universal acclaim and 'spokesman for a generation' type accolades with the Jam, after the release of the Style Council's second album his relationship with the press became one of almost total antipathy. Some might argue with good reason, the thread of soul-stirring passion which had always seen Weller at his most affecting had been squandered in a less earnest quest for dry musical sophistication. The fact that he was now married (to Style Council backing vocalist D.C. Lee) and a father contributed to what he later admitted was a lack of thirst for music. By 1990 he found himself without either a band or a recording contract for the first time in 13 years. This period saw him reacquaint himself with some of his old influences, the omnipresent Small Faces/Steve Marriott fixation, as well as discover new ones like house and acid jazz, as well as Traffic, Spooky Tooth, Tim Hardin and Tim Buckley. Inspired enough to write new material, despite his recent travails with the Style Council having drained him of confidence, he began to set up a new band in the autumn. Comprising Paul Francis (bass), Max Beesley (keyboards/vibraphone), Jacko Peake (saxophone/flute), Joe Becket (percussion), Damon Brown (trumpet/flugelhorn), Chris Lawrence (trombone) as well as Jam biographer and 'best friend' Paulo Hewitt (DJ) and Style Council drummer Steve White, the band was christened the Paul Weller Movement. They made their live debut on UK tours in November and December, with a second spree in April 1991. These served to renew Weller's previous unimpeachable self-belief and test new songs like 'Round And Round' and 'Kosmos'. The line-up now saw Henry Thomas (formerly of music education television programme *Rock School*) on bass, with the brass section reduced to Gerard Prescencer (trumpet/flugelhorn), with Zeta Massiah and Lina Duggan on backing vocals. Weller released his first solo single, 'Into Tomorrow', on his own Freedom High label in May, before contributing seven compositions to wife D.C. Lee's Slam Slam project. However, he was still refining his muse and the vast majority of the Movement and the name itself were dispensed with, leaving a kernel of White and Peake with guests including Robert Howard (aka Dr. Robert of the Blow Monkeys), Marco Nelson of the Young Disciples, Style Council bass player Camille Hinds and singer Carleen Anderson. However the debut album was delayed for almost a year while he searched for a suitable label. It was initially released on Pony Canyon in Japan, where Weller maintained a formidable personal popularity, six months before a UK issue on Go! Discs. *Paul Weller* was strangely overlooked by the UK press who at this stage seemed resistant to the artist's revival, despite the presence of fine songs in 'Clues' and 'Strange Museum'. Further line-up changes accrued during the quiet early months of 1992, with Orange Juice drummer Zeke Manyika joining, as did former Style Council compatriot Helen Turner (organ). The subject of second single 'Uh Huh, Oh Yeh' was Weller's Woking youth, and its

Paul Weller

Top 20 UK status kindled a prodigal son welcome from the UK press. This was confirmed in 1993 with the release of 'Sunflower', a breezy, Traffic-inspired folk rock enterprise, and *Wild Wood*, arguably the finest collection of songs Weller had written since the Jam's *All Mod Cons*. With a fresh, natural production from Brendan Lynch, and multitudinous musical accompaniment from White, Turner, Beesley and Howard plus Mick Talbot (Weller's former Style Council song writing collaborator), D.C. Lee, Simon Fowler and Steve Craddock (Ocean Colour Scene) and new bass player Marco Nelson, the set was nevertheless firmly located in the classic English singer/songwriter pantheon. Live favourite 'The Weaver' and 'Hung Up' again breached the charts as Weller was at last able to shake off the albatross of his previous musical ventures. He was joined on tour in Japan by new bass player Yolanda Charles in October, while early 1994 saw him jamming on stage with Kenney Jones (Faces), James Taylor and Mother Earth for the filming of *The History Of Acid Jazz*. The summer of that year saw euphoric performances at the Glastonbury and Phoenix Festival stages, before a 1994 double live album drawn from four different sets between late 1993 and mid-1994. For the first time in a decade Weller had cultivated a new set of fans, rather than dragging existing followers with him, and this fact drew evident satisfaction. 1995's *Stanley Road* was titled after the street in which Weller grew up, and featured Oasis' Noel Gallagher on a cover of Dr. John's 'Walk On Gilded Splinters'. Of more enduring interest were the Weller originals, however, which spanned a wide range of musical styles unified by the 'live' approach to recording.
Albums: *Paul Weller* (Go! Discs 1992), *Wild Wood* (Go! Discs 1994), *Live Wood* (Go! Discs 1994, double album), *Stanley Road* (Go! Discs 1995).
Videos: *The Paul Weller Movement Live* (1991), *Live Wood* (1994).

Wiedlin, Jane

b. 20 May 1958, Oconomowoc, Wisconsin, USA. Wiedlin was originally the guitarist of the top US female band, the Go-Go's. When the split came in 1984, all five members embarked on solo careers. Wiedlin released a self-titled album which contained a minor hit 'Blue Kiss'. However, her heart was also set on pursing an acting career and she made cameo appearances in *Clue* and *Star Trek 4: The Voyage Home*. A successful return to recording came in 1988 with the superb transatlantic hit, 'Rush Hour'. Much of Wiedlin's chart success however has largely been confined to the US charts. Her energies in the early 90s have been directed towards her involvement in the anti-fur trade movement. This resulted in the Go-Go's reforming briefly in 1990 at a benefit for PETA (People for the Ethical Treatment of Animals).
Albums: *Jane Wiedlin* (1986), *Fur* (1988), *Tangled* (1990).

Wild Flowers

Like Del Amitri, Wolverhampton's Wild Flowers became tired of a disinterested UK pop scene and looked to America for inspiration and appreciation. After two singles, 'Melt Like Ice' and 'Things Have Changed' and an album, *The Joy Of It All*, on Reflex in 1984, the fledgling outfit were dealt a blow when original guitarist Dave Newton left to form the Mighty Lemon Drops. The remaining members, Neal Cook (guitar/vocals), Mark Alexander (bass) and Dave Fisher (drums) eventually found a replacement in Dave Atherton, and the band duly signed to aspiring local label Chapter 22. They broke their two-year silence in 1986 with 'It Ain't So Easy' and was followed later that year by 'A Kind Of Kingdom'. Both singles were then coupled on a mini-album, *Dust*, primarily aimed at introducing the Wild Flowers to the US market which was more sympathetic to their New York-influenced rock sound. The band became the first British act to sign with Slash in the USA, releasing *Sometime Soon* in 1988, preceded by 'Broken Chains' and 'Take Me For A Ride' in the UK. The band's *Tales Like These* was recorded in the inspirational surroundings of California, by which time a new drummer, Simon Atkins, had been found. The album made little headway in the UK (where Slash is handled by London Records) and since then, the group have concentrated more on performing in the USA.
Albums: *The Joy Of It All* (1984), *Dust* (1987), *Sometime Soon* (1988), *Tales Like These* (1990).

Wild Swans

'Revolutionary Spirit', the last single for Liverpool's influential Zoo label, created quite a stir for the Wild Swans back in early 1982. A moving slice of uplifting pop set against guitar and synthesizer, the song looked set to elevate the band alongside those other Zoo graduates, Echo And The Bunnymen and the Teardrop Explodes. However, the song's over-loud production did result in a loss of sound quality, and it could be argued that this prevented healthier sales. But instead, Paul Simpson (vocals, ex-Teardrop Explodes), Jerry Kelly (guitar, ex-Systems), Ged Quinn (keyboards), Alan Mills (drums) and Modernaires bassist Alan disbanded soon after, forming the Lotus Eaters. But 'Revolutionary Spirit' became a cult favourite and after the recording of a John Peel BBC radio session was warmly received in September 1986, the band decided to re-form. *Bringing Home The Ashes* was issued in 1988. Like its single offspring, 'Young Manhood' and 'Bible Dreams', the album hinted at the Wild Swans' originality without really leaving a lasting impression. The more psychedelic-tinged *Space Flower* also failed to revive fortunes.
Albums: *Bringing Home The Ashes* (Sire 1988), *Space Flower* (Sire 1990).

Wilson, Mari

b. Mari MacMillan Ramsey Wilson, 29 September 1957, London, England. In the mid-80s, Mari Wilson single-handedly led a revival of the world of 50s/early 60s English kitsch. Sporting a bee-hive hairdo, wearing a pencil skirt and fake mink stole, her publicity photos depicted a world of long-lost suburban curtain and furniture styles, tupperware, garish colours (often pink) and graphic designs from the period. The songs were treated in the same way, only affectionately and with genuine feeling. The whole image was the idea of Tot Taylor who, composing under the name of Teddy Johns and gifted with the ability to write pastiche songs from almost any era of popular music, also ran the Compact Organisation label. The label's sense of hype excelled itself as they immediately released a box-set of Compact Organisation artists, all of which, with the exception of Mari, failed to attract the public's attention, (Although 'model agent' Virna Lindt was a music press favourite.) Mari was quickly adopted by press, television and radio as a curiosity, all aiding her early 1982 singles 'Beat The Beat' and 'Baby It's True' to have a minor effect on the chart. 'Just What I Always Wanted' a Top 10 hit, fully encapsulated the Wilson style. However, it was the following year's cover of the Julie London torch-song number, 'Cry Me A River' which, despite only reaching number 27, most people have come to associate with Mari. The song also generated a revival of interest in London's recordings, resulting in many long-lost (and forgotten) albums to be re-released. After touring the world with her backing vocal group, the Wilsations - which included within the line-up Julia Fordham - the return home saw a slowing-down in activity. Although for the most part Mari was out of the lime-light, she provided the vocals to the soundtrack to the Ruth Ellis bio-pic Dance With A Stranger. In 1985, she started playing small clubs with her jazz quartet performing standards, as well as writing her own material which led to her appearance with Stan Getz at a London's Royal Festival Hall. Although still affectionately remembered for her beehive, she has been able to put that period behind her and is now taken more seriously as a jazz/pop singer and is able to fill Ronnie Scott's club for a season.

Albums: Show People (1983), Dance With A Stranger (1987, film soundtrack), The Rhythm Romance (1992).

Win

After the Fire Engines folded on New Year's Eve 1981, Davey Henderson formed Heartbeat with former Flower singer Hilary Morrison, releasing just one track, on a New Musical Express cassette. By mid-1984 he was working with former Dirty Reds and Fire Engines member Russel Burns (drums) once more, linking with Ian Stoddart from Everest The Hard Way to form Win in his native Edinburgh. Straight away they won Single Of The Week awards with their debut for London Records, 'You've Got The Power'. Live, they played advertising jingles between songs, and appropriately 'You've Got The Power' was used in a television advertising campaign by McEwans lager. With obvious irony the band's lyrics discussed mass media communication, paranoia and conspiracy. After its release Win were augmented by keyboard player Will Perry (cousin of Andy Stewart), bass player Manny and guitarist/backing vocalist Simon Smeeton. As Postcard Records boss Alan Horne noted: 'Win are the most exciting thing I've come across since Orange Juice were starting out'. However, just like the Fire Engines before them, Win proved too subtle to procure a mainstream audience, splitting in 1990. The New Musical Express was one of many papers that mourned their passing: '(they) ... must be both proud and guilty in the knowledge that they made some of the greatest pop never heard'. Henderson took the name Nectarine No. 9 for an album for Postcard, See With Three Stars, that included Smeeton in the line-up. Stoddart joined the ill-fated Apples before becoming a member of Captain Shifty. Manny joined Jive Records-recording artists Yo Yo Honey, while Russell Burns recorded

for Creation Records under the Pie Finger mantle. Willie Perry is believed to have moved to India via Ibiza.

Albums: Uh! Tears Baby (London 1987), Freaky Trigger (Virgin 1989).

Wipers

From Portland, Oregon, USA, the Wipers formed in 1977, and have been active almost continuously since. Greg Sage, formerly of 60s obscurists Beauregarde, is the only original member remaining, and the engine of all Wipers material. He had made his recording debut in the early 70s providing backing for an album by a celebrity (villain) pro-wrestler. His original partners were Dave Koupal (bass) and Sam Henry (drums). Brad Naish and Brad Visdson arrived in time for the band's best albums, Youth Of America and Over The Edge. By 1986's Land Of The Lost Steve Plouf had taken over drums. Their legacy of scouring, audacious rock has recently become a subject of joy not only to hardcore archivists; a whole new generation has tuned in thanks to the public veneration of the band's achievements by Nirvana. This despite an inconsistent line-up and no secure record label or pigeonhole. Sage, who has also recorded two solo albums, is the mainstay of the band with his distinctive guitar style, a rhythmic assault with understated vocals whose dynamics were revisited by most of the late 80s/early 90s 'Seattle scene'. Sage continued to fend off offers from Nirvana for the Wipers to support them on tour, keeping a dignified distance from the vagueries of fashion.

Albums: Is This Real? (Park Avenue 1980), Youth Of America (Park Avenue 1981), Over The Edge (Brain Eater 1983), Wipers/Live 84 (Enigma 1985), Land Of The Lost (Enigma 1986), Follow Blind (Restless 1987), The Circle (Restless 1988), Silver Sail (T/K 1994). Compilation: Best Of Wipers & Greg Sage (Restless 1990).

Wire

This inventive UK group were formed in October 1976 by Colin Newman (b. 16 September 1954, Salisbury, Wilshire, England; vocals/guitar), Bruce Gilbert (b. 18 May 1946, Watford, Hertfordshire, England; guitar), Graham Lewis (b. 22 February 1953, Grantham, Lincolnshire, England; bass/vocals) and Robert Gotobed (b. Mark Field, 1951, Leicester, England; drums) along with lead guitarist George Gill - the latter member had previously been a member of the Snakes, releasing a single on the Skydog label, while the rest of Wire all had art school backgrounds. Their early work was clearly influenced by punk and this incipient era was captured on a various artists' live selection, The Roxy, London, WC2, their first recording as a four-piece following Gill's dismissal. Although not out of place among equally virulent company, the group was clearly more ambitious than many contemporaries. Wire was signed to the Harvest Records label in September 1977. Their impressive debut, Pink Flag, comprised 21 tracks, and ranged from the furious assault of 'Field Day For The Sundays' and 'Mr Suit' to the more brittle, almost melodic, interlude provided by 'Mannequin', which became the group's first single. Producer Mike Thorne, who acted as an unofficial fifth member, enhanced the set's sense of tension with a raw, stripped-to-basics sound. Chairs Missing offered elements found in its predecessor, but couched them in a newfound maturity. Gilbert's buzzsaw guitar became more measured, allowing space for Thorne's keyboards and synthesizers to provide an implicit anger. A spirit of adventure also marked *154* which contained several exceptional individual moments, including 'A Touching Display', a lengthy excursion into wall-of-sound feedback, and the haunting 'A Mutual Friend', scored for a delicate *cor anglais* passage and a striking contrast to the former's unfettered power. However, the album marked the end of Wire's Harvest contract and the divergent aims of the musicians became impossible to hold under one banner. The quartet was disbanded in the summer of 1980, leaving Newman free to pursue a solo career, while Gilbert and Lewis completed a myriad of projects under various identities including Dome, Duet Emmo and P'o, plus a number of solo works. Gotobed meanwhile concentrated on session work for Colin Newman, Fad Gadget and later organic farming. A posthumous release, *Document And Eyewitness*, chronicled Wire's final concert at London's Electric Ballroom in February 1980, but it was viewed as a disappointment in the wake of the preceding studio collections. It was not until 1985 that the group was resurrected and it was a further two years before they began recording again. *The Ideal Copy* revealed a continued desire to challenge, albeit in a less impulsive manner, and the set quickly topped the independent chart. *A Bell Is A Cup (Until It Is Struck)* maintained the newfound balance between art and commercial pop, including the impressive 'Kidney Bingos'. In 1990 the group abandoned the 'beat combo' concept adopted in 1985 and took on board the advantages and uses of computer and sequencer technology. The resulting *Manscape* showed that the group's sound had changed dramatically, but not altogether with satisfactory results. Following the album's release Gotobed announced his departure. The remaining trio ironically changed their name to Wir, but not until *The Drill* had been released. It contained a collection of variations on 'Drill', a track that had appeared on the EP *Snakedrill* in 1987. The new group's first release 'The First Letter', showed a harder edge than their more recent work, amusingly containing some reworked samples of *Pink Flag*. Wire subsequently became the subject of renewed interest in the mid-90s when indie darlings Elastica not only name-checked but also borrowed liberally from their back-catalogue.

Albums: *Pink Flag* (Harvest 1977), *Chairs Missing* (Harvest 1978), *154* (Harvest 1979), *Document And Eyewitness* (Rough Trade 1981), *The Ideal Copy* (Mute 1987), *A Bell Is A Cup Until It Is Struck* (Mute 1988), *It's Beginning To And Back Again* (Mute 1989), *Manscape* (Mute 1990), *The Peel Sessions* (Strange Fruit 1990), *The Drill* (Mute 1991). As Wir *The First Letter* (Mute 1991). Compilations: *Wire Play Pop* (Pink 1986), *On Returning* (Harvest 1989).

Further reading: *Wire ... Everybody Loves A History*, Kevin S. Eden.

Wishplants

Indie band the Wishplants had been playing together for some time in their native Northamptonshire, England, as a trio of Ed Gilmour (guitar), James Fitzgerald (drums) and Paul Simpson (bass), before cementing the line-up with the addition of vocalist Saul in March 1992. Taking their name from an episode of science fiction television programme *Star Wars*, they played a few shows before entering a local studio to record demos with Wonder Stuff/Neds Atomic Dustbin producer Simon Efemey. It was he that introduced the band to their manager and set their career in motion by inviting the Wonder Stuff along to see them. The result was the support slot on that band's Scottish tour, before they had played 20 shows under their own auspices. Saul's charismatic performances soon attracted the attention of the UK indie press prompting the *New Musical Express* to describe him as 'clearly one leg short of a full pair of trousers'. Despite record company interest the group elected to record an EP, *Circus Rain*, with Efemey, released in February 1993 on China Records. Afterwards they embarked on a first UK tour proper with Power Of Dreams, taking in both the Phoenix and Glastonbury Festivals. The *Tortoiseshell* EP followed in July to further strong reaction, prefacing a well-received debut album in October.

Album: *Coma* (China 1993).

Wobble, Jah

(see Jah Wobble)

Wolfgang Press

'None of us are very good musicians and I think that helps a lot'. Despite a reputation as 4AD Records' longest-serving glacial post-punk outfit, such generic descriptions hardly embrace the width of the Wolfgang Press' songwriting arsenal. Comprising Andrew Gray (guitar), Mark Cox (keyboards) and Mick Allen (vocals), they took more responsibility for their packaging and image than many of their label's fellow travellers, producing an intriguing range of records, covers and videos. Their recorded fare, however, continued to be imaginative but insubstantial. Support slots on tours with the Pixies and Nick Cave had given the band a higher profile in Europe and the USA than they enjoyed domestically by the close of the 80s, where their sound collages were viewed as too eclectic to fit any particular strain of modern 'indie' music. Following several albums of edgy, fragmented pop sounds, they began the next decade with a plunge into the dance market, primarily inspired by De La Soul's *Three Feet High And Rising*. *Queer* won many favourable reviews, and was a successful accomodation of new musical innovations. So too 1995's *Funky Little Demons*, though this wide-ranging collection of songs was not the result of inflated art school egos, Allen commenting: 'You could see music as being magical but it's more like a lot of hard work, not far removed from building a house.' Whatever they have served as architects of, the Wolfgang Press have grown significantly in ability as the years have passed.

Albums: *The Burden Of Mules* (4AD 1983), *The Legendary Wolfgang Press And Other Tall Stories* (4AD 1985), *Standing Up Straight* (4AD 1986), *Bird Wood Cage* (4AD 1989), *Queer* (4AD 1991), *Funky Little Demons* (4AD 1995).

Wolfhounds

Formed in Essex, England, in 1985, the Wolfhounds' first recording line-up was Dave Callahan (vocals), Andrew

Jah Wobble

Bolton (bass), Paul Clark (guitar), Andrew Golding (guitar) and Frank Stebbing (drums). Having spent their formative months supporting dubious pub/punk rock bands around London, the Wolfhounds became fortuitously involved in the *New Musical Express*'s C86 venture. Toying with a gritty, angular guitar framework over which Callahan's vocals wandered, the Wolfhounds were famed for having as many labels as album releases; they bounced from Pink Records to Idea and on through September and Midnight Music Records, fittingly experiencing an alarming number of personnel changes. In spite of - or perhaps because of - their stubborn outlook, the band never achieved the respect they truly warranted, and finally ground to a halt at the end of the 80s. After their demise, Dave Callahan initiated a new band called Moonshake.

Albums: *Unseen Ripples From A Pebble* (Pink 1987), *Blown Away* (Idea 1989). Compilation: *Essential Wolfhounds* (Midnight 1988).

Wonder Stuff

Formed in Stourbridge, West Midlands, England, in April 1986, the Wonder Stuff featured Miles Hunt (vocals/guitar), Malcolm Treece (guitar), Rob Jones (b. 1964, d. 30 July 1993, New York, USA; bass, replacing original member Chris Fradgley) and former Mighty Lemon Drops drummer, Martin Gilks. The roots of the band lay in From Eden, a short-lived local group which featured Hunt on drums, Treece on guitar and Clint Mansell and Adam Mole, later of peers Pop Will Eat Itself, occupying the remaining roles. After amassing a sizeable local following the Wonder Stuff released their debut EP, *It's A Wonderful Day*, to favourable small press coverage in 1987. Along with the aforementioned PWEI and other Midlands hopefuls Crazyhead and Gaye Bykers On Acid, they were soon pigeonholed under the banner of 'grebo rock' by the national music press. Despite this ill-fitting description, the Wonder Stuff's strengths always laid in melodic pop songs braced against an urgent, power pop backdrop. After an ill-fated dalliance with EMI Records' *ICA Rock Week*, a second single, 'Unbearable', proved strong enough to secure a deal with Polydor Records at the end of 1987. 'Give Give Give Me More More More' offered a minor hit the following year, and was succeeded by arguably the band's best early song. Built on soaring harmonies, 'A Wish Away' was the perfect precursor to the Wonder Stuff's vital debut, *The Eight Legged Groove Machine*, which followed later that year and established them in the UK charts. 'It's Yer Money I'm After Baby', also from the album, continued to mine Hunt's cynical furrow (further evident on the confrontational b-side, 'Astley In The Noose' - referring to contemporary chart star, Rick Astley) and began a string of UK Top 40 hits. 'Who Wants To Be The Disco King?' and the more relaxed 'Don't Let Me Down Gently', both from 1989, hinted at the diversity of the group's second album, *Hup*. Aided by fiddle, banjo and keyboard player Martin Bell (ex-Hackney Five-O), the album contrasted a harder, hi-tech sound with a rootsy, folk feel on tracks such as 'Golden Green', a double a-side hit when combined with a cover of the Youngbloods' 'Get Together'. The band's well-documented internal wrangles came to a head with the departure of Rob Jones at the end of

the decade. He moved to New York to form his own band, The Bridge And Tunnel Crew, with his wife Jessie Ronson, but died of heart failure in 1993. 'Circlesquare' introduced new bass player Paul Clifford. A subsequent low profile was broken in April 1991 with 'Size Of A Cow'. A UK Top 10 hit, this was quickly followed by 'Caught In My Shadow' and *Never Loved Elvis*. Once again, this third album revealed the Wonder Stuff's remorseless progression. Gone were the brash, punk-inspired three-minute classics, replaced by a richer musical content, both in Hunt's song writing and musical performances. The extent of their popularity was emphasized in late 1991 when, in conjunction with comedian Vic Reeves, they topped the UK charts with a revival of Tommy Roe's 'Dizzy'. The group made a swift return to the Top 10 in 1992 with the *Welcome To The Cheap Seats* EP, the title-track's post-punk jig (with Kirsty MacColl on backing vocals) typifying the direction of the following year's *Construction For The Modern Idiot*. With songs now imbued with far more optimism due to Hunt's improved romantic prospects, singles such as 'Full Of Life' and 'Hot Love Now!' replaced previous uncertainties with unforced bonhomie. Thus it came as something as a surprise when Hunt announced the band's dissolution to the press in July 1994 long before any grape's could sour - a decision allegedly given impetus by Polydor's insistence that the band should crack the US (a factor in striking down the label's previous great singles' band, the Jam). They bowed out at a final gig in Stratford Upon Avon, Hunt leaving the stage with a pastiche of the Sex Pistols' epigram, 'Every Feel You've Been Treated?', ringing in fan's ears. Writer James Brown offered another tribute in his sleevenotes to the compulsory posthumous singles' compilation: 'It was pointed out that if the writer Hunter S. Thompson had been the presiding influence over the Beatles, they they might have looked and sounded like the Wonder Stuff'. Suitably abbreviated, it provided less accurate testimony than 'greatest hits', perhaps, but it was certainly more in keeping with the band's legacy. Former members of the band (Treece, Clifford and Gilks) regrouped in 1995 as Weknowwhereyoulive, with the addition of former Eat singer Ange Doolittle on vocals. Hunt also gave up his job as host of MTV's *120 Minutes* to put together a new band.

Albums: *The Eight Legged Groove Machine* (Polydor 1988), *Hup* (Polydor 1989), *Never Loved Elvis* (Polydor 1991), *Construction For The Modern Idiot* (Polydor 1993). Compilation: *If The Beatles Had Read Hunter...The Singles* (Polydor 1994).

Woodentops

At one point, it seemed likely that the Woodentops from Northhampton, England, would be commercially successful. After the offbeat 'Plenty', a one-off single for the Food Records label in 1984, songwriter Rolo McGinty (guitar/vocals), Simon Mawby (guitar), Alice Thompson (keyboards), Frank de Freitas (bass) and Benny Staples (drums) joined Geoff Travis's Rough Trade Records and issued a string of catchy singles that fared increasingly well commercially. 1985's jolly 'Move Me' was followed by the menacing pace of 'Well Well Well' while 'It Will Come' seemed a likely hit. The band's critically acclaimed debut album, *Giant*, was an enticing mixture of frantic acoustic guitars and a warm yet offbeat clutch of songs. After 'Love Affair With Everyday Living' (1986), McGinty decided upon a change in direction, hardening up the Woodentops' sound and incorporating new technology within their live repertoire. The results were heard the following year on *Live Hypnobeat Live*, which relied on material from *Giant*, albeit performed live in a drastically revitalized way. *Wooden Foot Cops On The Highway* and the accompanying single, 'You Make Me Feel'/'Stop This Car', showed how far the Woodentops had progressed by early 1988. Although less uncompromising than their live project, the sound was more mature with an emphasis on detail previously lacking. What the band failed to achieve in commercial terms was more than compensated for by the level of critical and public respect they earned.

Albums: *Giant* (Rough Trade 1986), *Live Hypnobeat Live* (Upside 1987), *Wooden Foot Cops On the Highway* (Rough Trade 1988).

World Domination Enterprises

Rock-dance fusion trio who, though passing largely unacknowledged in their own lifetime, have achieved something akin to cult status in their retirement. The band comprised Keith Dobson (guitar, vocals), Steve Jameson (bass) and Digger (drums). Dobson had formerly drummed with hippie monoliths Here And Now, and set up his own cassette label, invitingly titled Fuck Off Records. World Domination Enterprises first arrived in 1985, when they played a flurry of gigs around the UK to coincide with the Live Aid phenomenon. This was followed by the release of their debut single, and their signature song, Asbestos Lead Asbestos'. Its gravelly, savage delivery neatly counterpointed Dobson's environmental concerns with a rumbling, bass-dominated resonance. Contrastingly, other material included 'Hotsy Girl', a tribute to their Morris Minor and the art of stock car racing. As the 80s developed the group played at many of the warehouse parties during the early acid house epoch, notably those organised by the Mutoid Waste Company. In the meantime they had released two LPs, but split after returning from a tour of Russia when Digger elected to pledge his faith to the Jehovah's Witness movement. There was no way back from that, and Dobson split the group and set up home in Spain, though he did return to London in 1993. Jameson joined with Steve Smith (ex-Vapors) in a new outfit, Cut, while Digger continues merrily on his way to this day, imparting the good news via the latest issue of Watchtower.

Albums: *Let's Play Domination* (Product Inc 1988), *Hot From Hit City* (Product Inc 1988).

World Party

Founded on the talents of ex-Waterboy Karl Wallinger, World Party have worked hard to shrug off comparisons to

World Party

the former group. Which is a little unjust, bearing in mind Wallinger's quite separate, but in many ways equal, song writing abilities. Wallinger was born in Prestatyn, North Wales, the son of an architect father and housewife mother. There he was brought up on a diet of 60s ephemera, from the Supremes, Spencer Davis Group and Merseybeat. His first musical experience arrived in 1976 with Quasimodo; who would eventually lose their hump to become the Alarm. Later he moved to London to become a clerk for ATV/Northern Songs, who counted the Beatles catalogue amongst their clients. He delved back in to performance in his own time, eventually going on to become musical director of *The Rocky Horror Show* in the West End of London. A short residency with funk band the Out overlapped his liaison with the Waterboys. After he split amicably from Mike Scott, Wallinger set out on a solo career that would see him sign to Prince's management. He also helped Sinead O'Connor on her *Lion And The Cobra* set. Wallinger recorded the first two World Party albums practically single-handed, though 1993's *Bang!* saw him joined by Chris Sharrock (drums) and Dave Catlin-Birch (guitars, keyboards). The early hit single 'Ship Of Fools' (1987) showcased Wallinger's muse, a relaxed and melancholic performance reminiscent of mid-period Beatles. This has not so much been updated as revitalised on his subsequent, sterling work. A minor breakthrough was made with *Bang!*

Albums: *Private Revolution* (1987), *Goodbye Jumbo* (1990), *Bang!* (1993).

Wreckless Eric

b. Eric Goulden, Newhaven, Sussex, England. Launched by Stiff Records in the heyday of punk, Wreckless Eric, as his name suggested, specialized in chaotic, pub rock and roots-influenced rock. His often tuneless vocals belied some excellent musical backing, most notably by producer Nick Lowe. Wreckless' eccentric single, 'Whole Wide World'/'Semaphore Signals' has often been acclaimed as one of the minor classics of the punk era. During 1977-78, he was promoted via the famous Stiff live revues where he gained notoriety off-stage for his drinking. For his second album, *The Wonderful World Of Wreckless Eric*, the artist provided a more engaging work, but increasingly suffered from comparison with the other stars on his fashionable record label. Wreckless' commercial standing saw little improvement despite an attempt to produce a more commercial work, the ironically-titled *Big Smash*. Effectively retiring from recording for the first half of the 80s, Wreckless returned with *A Roomful Of Monkeys*, credited to Eric Goulden, and featuring members of Ian Dury's Blockheads. He then formed the Len Bright Combo with ex-Milkshakes members Russ Wilkins (bass) and Bruce Brand (drums), who released two albums and found nothing more than a small cult-following on the pub/club circuit. The eventual dissolution of that group led to the formation of Le Beat Group Electrique with Catfish Truton (drums) and André Barreau (bass). Now a resident in France, and a more sober personality, Eric has found an appreciative audience.

Albums: *Wreckless Eric* (1978),*The Wonderful World Of Wreckless Eric* (1979), *The Whole Wide World* (1979), *Big Smash* (1980), as Eric Goulden *A Roomful Of Monkeys* (1985), *The Len Bright Combo Present The Len Bright Combo* (1986), *Le Beat Group Electrique* (1989), *At The Shop* (1990), *The Donovan Of Trash* (1991).

Wyatt, Robert

b. 28 January 1945, Bristol, Avon, England. As the drummer, vocalist and guiding spirit of the original Soft Machine, Robert Wyatt established a style which merged the *avant garde* with English eccentricity. His first solo album, *The End Of An Ear*, presaged his departure from the above group, although its radical content resulted in a muted reception. Wyatt's next venture, the excellent Matching Mole, was bedevilled by internal dissent but a planned relaunch was forcibly abandoned following a tragic fall from a window, which left him paralyzed and confined to a wheelchair. *Rock Bottom*, the artist's next release, was composed while Wyatt lay in hospital. This heartfelt, deeply personal collection was marked by an aching vulnerability which successfully avoided any hint of self-pity. This exceptional album was succeeded by an unlikely hit single in the shape of an idiosyncratic reading of the Monkees hit, 'I'm A Believer'. *Ruth Is Stranger Than Richard*, released in 1975, was a more open collection, and balanced original pieces with outside material, including a spirited reading of jazz bassist Charlie Haden's 'Song For Che'. Although Wyatt, a committed Marxist, would make frequent guest appearances, his own career was shelved until 1980 when a single comprising of two South American songs of liberation became the first in a series of politically motivated releases undertaken for the Rough Trade label. These performances were subsequently compiled on *Nothing Can Stop Us*, which was then enhanced by the addition of 'Shipbuilding', a haunting anti-Falkland War composition, specifically written for Wyatt by Elvis Costello which was a minor chart entry in 1983. Wyatt's fluctuating health has undermined his recording ambitions, but his commitment remains undiminished. He issued singles in aid of Namibia and the British Miners' Hardship Fund, and contributed a compassionate soundtrack to the harrowing 1982 *Animals* film.

Albums: *The End Of An Ear* (1970), *Rock Bottom* (1974), *Ruth Is Stranger Than Richard* (1975), *Nothing Can Stop Us* (1982), *Animals* (1984), *Old Rotten Hat* (1985), *Dondestan* (1991), *A Short Break* (1992).

Wynn, Steve

Guitarist/vocalist Wynn is one of the pivotal figures in the Los Angeles 'paisley underground' rock scene of the early 80s. A former member of the Suspects, which included Gavin Blair and Russ Tolman, later of True West, he briefly joined the Long Ryders, before founding the Dream Syndicate in 1981. Starved of a suitable record label, Wynn established Down There Records, which issued important early sets by Green On Red and Naked Prey in addition to his own group's debut. Dream Syndicate have since pursued an erratic career, blighted by commercial indifference. During a hiatus in its progress Wynn joined Dan Stuart from Green On Red in a ragged, bar-room influenced collection, *The Lost Weekend* (1985). Billed as by Danny And Dusty, the album featured support from friends and contemporaries and paradoxically outsold the musicians' more serious endeavours.

Albums: *The Lost Weekend* (1985), *Kerosene Man* (1990), *Fluorescent* (Mute 1994).

X

Formed in Los Angeles, California, USA in 1977, X originally comprised Exene Cervenka (b. Christine Cervenka, 1 February 1956, Chicago, Illinois, USA; vocals), Billy Zoom (b. Tyson Kindale, Savannah, Illinois, USA; guitar), John Doe (b. John Nommensen, Decatur, Illinois, USA; bass) and Mick Basher (drums), although the last-named was quickly replaced by D.J. (Don) Bonebrake (b. North Hollywood, California, USA). The quartet made its debut with 'Adult Books'/'We're Desperate' (1978), and achieved a considerable live reputation for their imaginative blend of punk, rockabilly and blues. Major labels were initially wary of the group, but Slash, a leading independent, signed them in 1979. Former Doors' organist, Ray Manzarek, produced *Los Angeles* and *Wild Gift*, the latter of which established X as a major talent. Both the *New York Times* and the *Los Angeles Times* voted it Album Of The Year and such acclaim inspired a recording deal with Elektra Records. *Under The Big Black Sun* was another fine selection, although reception for *More Fun In The New World* was more muted, with several commentators deeming it 'over-commercial'. In the meantime X members were pursuing outside projects. *Adulterers Anonymous*, a poetry collection by Cervenka and Lydia Lunch, was published in 1982, while the singer joined Doe, Henry Rollins (Black Flag), Dave Alvin (the Blasters) and Jonny Ray Bartel in a part-time country outfit, the Knitters, releasing *Poor Little Critter On The Road* on the Slash label in 1985. Alvin replaced Billy Zoom following the release of *Ain't Love Grand* and X was subsequently augmented by ex-Lone Justice guitarist Tony Gilkyson. However, Alvin left for a solo career on the completion of *See How We Are*. Despite the release of *Live At The Whiskey A Go-Go*, X were clearly losing momentum and the group was dissolved. Doe and Cervenka have both since recorded as solo acts. They reunited in 1993 with a new recording contract for *Hey Zeus!*

Albums: *Los Angeles* (Slash 1980), *Wild Gift* (Slash 1981), *The Decline...Of Western Civilization* (Slash 1981, soundtrack), *Under The Big Black Sun* (Elektra 1982), *More Fun In The New World* (Elektra 1983), *Ain't Love Grand* (Elektra 1985), *See How We Are* (Elektra 1987), *Live At The Whiskey A Go-Go On The Fabulous Sunset Strip* (Elektra 1988), *Major League* (Curb 1989, soundtrack), *Hey Zeus!* (Big Life/Mercury 1993). John Doe: *Meet John Doe* (DGC/Geffen 1990). Exene Cervenka: with Wanda Coleman *Twin Sisters: Live At McCabe's* (Freeway 1985), *Old Wives' Tales* (Rhino 1989), *Running Scared* (RNA 1990).

X-Ray Spex

One of the most inventive, original and genuinely exciting groups to appear during the punk era, X-Ray Spex were the brainchild of the colourful Poly Styrene (Marion Elliot), whose exotic clothes and tooth brace established her as an instant punk icon. With a line-up completed by Lora Logic, later replaced by Glyn Johns (saxophone), Jak Stafford (guitar), Paul Dean (bass) and B.P. Hurding (drums), the group began performing in 1977 and part of their second gig was captured for posterity on the seminal *Live At The Roxy WC2*. A series of extraordinary singles including 'Germ Free Adolescents', 'Oh Bondage Up Yours', 'The Day The World Turned Dayglo' and 'Identity' were not only rivetting examples of high energy punk, but contained provocative, thoughtful lyrics berating the urban synthetic fashions of the 70s and urging individual expression. Always ambivalent about her pop-star status, Poly dismantled the group in 1979 and joined the Krishna Consciousness Movement. X-Ray Spex's final single, 'Highly Inflammable' was coupled with the pulsating 'Warrior In Woolworths', a parting reminder of Poly's early days as a shop assistant. Although she reactivated her recording career with the album *Translucence* (1980) and a 1986 EP *Gods And Goddesses*, no further commercial success was forthcoming.

Album: *Germ Free Adolescents* (EMI 1978).

XL Capris

Formed in Sydney, Australia at the end of 1978, the XL Capris soon acquired a healthy following on the punk/alternative circuit when they formed their own Axle Records and released two singles and an album in 1980. The songs on the album were mainly written by guitarist Tim Gooding, featuring simple instrumentation, sparse production and the plaintive vocals of Johanna Pigott (bass), singing lyrics that were very Sydney-orientated. Joining Julie Anderson aka Nancy Serapax (drums), former Dragon guitarist Todd Hunter boosted the line-up and a second album was recorded. *Weeds* featured many Pigott-Hunter compositions, obtaining a fuller, more polished sound. The band employed a second drummer, Michael Farmer - an unusual move which did not enhance the material and the band broke up shortly afterwards at the end of 1981. XL Capris were certainly one of the most original and interesting bands to emerge out of the punk era, but they did not achieve mainstream success. Hunter returned to the reformed Dragon and Piggott recorded three albums under the name Scribble before finding acclaim as a songwriter for Dragon. Original drummer Julie Anderson married the vocalist from UK band the Vapours and guitarist Kimble Rendall was a founder member of the Hoodoo Gurus.

Albums: *Where Is Hank* (1980), *Weeds* (1981).

Xmal Deutschland

This experimental and atmospheric band formed in the

autumn of 1980 and were based in Hamburg, Germany. With no previous musical experience, the essential components were Anja Huwe (vocals), Manuela Rickers (guitar), and Fiona Sangster (keyboards). Original members Rita Simon and Caro May were replaced by Wolfgang Ellerbrock (bass) and Manuela Zwingmann (drums). Insisting on singing in their mother tongue and refusing to be visually promoted as a 'female' band (Ellerbrock is the 'token' male), they have continued to plough a singular, and largely lonely, furrow since their inception. They first came to England in 1982 to support the Cocteau Twins, joining 4AD Records soon afterwards. The debut *Fetisch* highlighted a sound which tied them firmly to both their Germanic ancestry and the hallmark spectral musicianship of their new label. Huwe's voice in particular, was used as a fifth instrument which made the cultural barrier redundant. After the release of two well-received singles, 'Qual' and 'Incubus Succubus II', they lost drummer Zwingmann who wished to remain in England. Her replacement was Peter Bellendir who joined in time for rehearsals for the second album.
Albums: *Festisch* (1982), *Tocsin* (1984).

XTC

Formed in Wiltshire, England, in 1972 as Star Park (an anagram of Rats Krap) this widely-beloved UK pop unit became the Helium Kidz in 1973 with the addition of Colin Moulding (b. 17 August 1955, Swindon, Wiltshire, England), Terry Chambers (b. 18 July 1955, Swindon, Wiltshire) and a second guitarist Dave Cartner, to the nucleus of. Andy Partridge (b. 11 December 1953, Swindon, Wiltshire, England; guitar/vocals). The Kidz were then heavily influenced by the MC5 and Alice Cooper. In 1975 Partridge toyed with two new names for the band, the Dukes Of Stratosphear and XTC. At this time Steve Hutchins passed through the ranks and in 1976 Johnny Perkins (keyboards) joined Moulding, Partridge and Chambers. Following auditions with Pye, Decca and CBS Records they signed with Virgin Records - at which time they were joined by Barry Andrews (b. 12 September 1956, West Norwood, London, England). The band's sparkling debut, *White Music*, revealed a keener hearing for pop than the energetic new wave sound they were often aligned to. The album reached number 38 in the UK charts and critics marked their name for further attention. Shortly after the release of *Go2*, Barry Andrews departed, eventually to resurface in Shriekback. With Andrews replaced by Dave Gregory, both *Go2* and the following *Drums And Wires* were commercial successes. The refreshing hit single 'Making Plans For Nigel' exposed them to a new and eager audience. Singles were regularly taken from their subsequent albums and they continued making the charts with quality pop songs, including 'Sgt Rock (Is Going To Help Me)' and the magnificently constructed 'Senses Working Overtime', which reached the UK Top 10. The main songwriter, Partridge, was able to put his sharp observations and nursery rhyme inflences to paper in a way that made his compositions vital while eschewing any note of pretension. The double set, *English Settlement*, reached number 5 on the UK album charts in 1982. Partridge subsequently fell ill through exhaustion and nervous breakdowns, and

announced that XTC would continue only as recording artists, including promotional videos but avoiding the main source of his woes, the stage. Subsequent albums have found only limited success, though those of the Dukes Of Stratosphere, their *alter ego*, have reputedly sold more copies. *Mummer, The Big Express* and the highly underrrated Todd Rundgren-produced *Skylarking* were all mature, enchanting works, but failed to set any charts alight. *Oranges And Lemons* captured the atmosphere of the late 60s perfectly, but this superb album also offered a further, perplexing commercial mystery. While it sold 500,000 copies in the USA, it barely made the UK Top 30. The highly commercial 'Mayor Of Simpleton' found similar fortunes, at a desultory number 46. Partridge remains a home-bird and is at his happiest when in Wiltshire. The lyric from follow-up single 'Chalkhills And Children' states; 'Chalkhills and children anchor my feet/Chalkhills and children, bringing me back to earth eternally and ever Ermine Street.' In 1992 *Nonsuch* entered the UK album charts and two weeks later promptly disappeared. 'The Dissappointed', taken from that album, was nominated for an Ivor Novello songwriters award in 1993, but could just as easily have acted as a personal epitaph. In 1995 the Crash Test Dummies recorded 'Ballad Of Peter Pumpkinhead' for the movie *Dumb And Dumber* and in turn reminded the world of Partridge's talent. Quite what he and his colleagues in the band and Virgin Records feel they have to do remains uncertain. Partridge once joked that Virgin retain them only as a tax loss. XTC remain one of the most original pop bands of the era and Partridge's lyrics place him alongside Ray Davies as one of the UK's most imaginative songwriters.
Albums: *White Music* (Virgin 1978), *Go2* (Virgin 1978), *Drums And Wires* (Virgin 1979), *Black Sea* (Virgin 1980), *English Settlement* (Virgin 1982), *Mummer* (Virgin 1983), *The Big Express* (Virgin 1984), *Skylarking* (Virgin 1986), *Oranges And Lemons* (Virgin 1989), *Nonsuch* (Virgin 1992). Compilations: *Waxworks: Some Singles 1977-1982* (Virgin 1982, originally released with free compilation, *Beeswax*, a collection of b-sides), *The Compact XTC* (Virgin 1986), *Live In Concert 1980* (Windsong 1992).
Further reading: *Chalkhills And Children*, Chris Twomey.

Y

Yachts

Another UK new wave act to emerge from the Liverpool art school student pool of the late 70s, the Yachts started life as the seven-piece Albert And The Cod Fish Warriors. Reduced to a five-piece of Henry Priestman (vocals/keyboards), J J Campbell (vocals), Martin Watson (guitar), Martin Dempsey (bass), and Bob Ellis (drums), they played their debut gig at Eric's in Liverpool supporting Elvis Costello. This led Stiff Records to sign them in October 1977 and they released one Will Birch-produced single before they departed (with Costello and Nick Lowe) for the newly formed Radar. Campbell left at this point but with Priestman in control they released several singles including the minor new wave classic 'Love To Love You'. They recorded their debut album in New York with Richard Gottehrer at the helm. Dempsey left in January 1980 to join Pink Military and when Radar was liquidated they switched to Demon for a further single. Inevitably they disintegrated and Priestman spent some time with It's Immaterial before forming the Christians. The Yachts' popularity was fleeting but they left behind several great three-minute slices of pop, including a cover of R. Dean Taylor's 'There's A Ghost In My House'.
Albums: *The Yachts* (1979), *Yachts Without Radar* (1980).

Yargo

Formed in the mid-80s, Yargo fused jazz, soul, blues and reggae forms in so uniquely that it proved too distinctive to break them commercially. But within the annals of rock history, this Manchester quartet will reside as major innovators in black music. While vocalist Basil Clarke injected a penetrating, yearning quality into his voice, occasionally reminiscent of an urgent Marvin Gaye, the rhythm section of drummer Phil Kirby and enigmatic bassist Paddy Steer created a minimal but infectious backing akin to Sly And Robbie, alongside guitarist Tony Burnside. Primarily a live outfit at first, Yargo issued three promising singles - 'Get High' (Skysaw 1986), 'Carrying Mine' (Racket Manufacture 1987), and 'Help' on their own Bodybeat label, and attracted sizeable interest when they appeared on the UK television programme *The Tube*. But it was *Bodybeat*, that garnered the most praise, combining the singles with a hypnotic title cut to create a sparse but mesmerising soundtrack, set against tales of urban Manchester. August 1989 saw the band's theme for ITV television's *The Other Side Of Midnight* released, drawn from the long-awaited *Communicate*, issued in October. Smoother and fuller than *Bodybeat*, this should have established Yargo as a major commercial act, but it was sadly ignored by a nation taken with house music and it was not long before the band fragmented.
Albums: *Bodybeat* (Bodybeat 1987), *Communicate* (Bodybeat 1989).

Yeah Jazz

Hailing from Uttoxeter, Staffordshire, England, and formed in 1986 by Kevin Head (b. 11 April 1964, Staffordshire, England; vocals) and Chute (b. Mark Charfield, 1 April 1962, Staffordshire, England; guitar), Yeah Jazz were completed by Stu Ballantyne (bass) and Ian Hitchens (drums). Their attempt to fuse pop and folk while chronicling the sagas of everyday life in a west Midlands rural town gained an Independent Top 30 hit in 1986 with 'This Is Not Love'. The addition of former Higsons' saxophonist and guitarist Terry Edwards to the line-up and the transferring to the Cherry Red label strengthened the group's sound. Edwards also lent his production talents to Yeah Jazz's only album. Despite encouraging reviews and positive audience reaction their fortunes took a downward turn. Freeing themselves from their Cherry Red contract, the band re-surfaced in 1991, working on the west Midlands circuit with the promise of recording again in the near future. That promise materialised in June 1993 when they signed to Native Records and released *April*.
Albums: *Six Lane Ends* (Cherry Red 1988), *April* (Native 1993).

Young Fresh Fellows

Operating out of Seattle, USA since the early 80s, the Young Fresh Fellows have released a body of rough hewn, understated pop gems. Their debut album was recorded in 1983 and released a year later. The band comprises Scott McCaughey (vocals), Chuck Carroll (guitar) and Tad Hutchinson (drums). *The Fabulous Sounds Of The North Pacific* picked up immediate plaudits, *Rolling Stone Record* going so far as to describe it as 'perfect'. Joined by Jim Sangster (Jimbo) (bass), they become a fully fledged off-beat new wave act, the dry humour and acute observations of their lyrics attracting a large college following. Their stylistic fraternity with the higher profile Replacements was confirmed by their joint tours, both bands sharing what *Billboard* magazine described as 'a certain deliberate crudity of execution'. After the mini-album *Refreshments* they moved to Frontier Records for 1988's *Totally Lost*. Despite being dogged by a 'joke band' reputation, brought about by an aptitude for satirizing high school traumas, the band's critical reaction was once more highly favourable. However, Carroll played his last gig for the band in winter 1989 in Washington. He was replaced by the Fastbacks guitarist Kurt Bloch (who continues with both bands). Their most polished album yet, *This One's For The Ladies*, highlighted McCaughey's successful adaptation of the spirit of the Kinks while Bloch's guitar melodies fitted in seamlessly. Elsewhere, McCaughey released his first solo album and toured as second guitarist with R.E.M. in 1995.
Albums: *The Fabulous Sounds Of The Pacific Northwest* (1984), *Topsy Turvy* (1986), *The Men Who Loved Music* (1987), *Refreshments* (1987), *Totally Lost* (1988), *Beans And Intolerance* (1989), *This One's For The Ladies* (1989), *Electric Bird Digest* (1991), *It's Low Beat Time* (1993).

Young Gods

This heavily experimental trio originated from Geneva, Switzerland and specialized in hard electronic rock and rhythm. The main artistic engine was Franz Treichler (vocals), alongside original collaborators Cesare Pizzi (samples) and Frank Bagnoud (drums). Although singing mainly in French, they found an audience throughout Europe via the premier outlet for 'difficult' music, Play It Again Sam Records. Notable among their releases were 'L' Armourir', a version of Gary Glitter's 'Hello Hello I'm Back Again', and *Young Gods Play Kurt Weill*, which stemmed from a commission to provide a tribute performance of the composer's works. They had already been awarded a French Government Arts grant to tour the USA in 1987, where they maintain cult popularity.

Albums: *The Young Gods* (1987), *L' Eau Rouge* (1989), *Play Kurt Weill* (1991), *TV Sky* (1991), *Live Sky Tour* (1993).

Young Marble Giants

Formed in 1978 as 'a desperate last-ditch attempt at doing something with my life' by Stuart Moxham (guitar/organ), this seminal, yet short-lived trio, from Cardiff, Wales, comprised the latter as the group's main songwriter, his brother Philip Moxham (bass) and Alison Statton (b. March 1958, Cardiff, Wales; vocals). Together they made their debut on *Is The War Over?*, a compilation of Cardiff groups, released in 1979. Their contribution reached the ears of Geoff Travis at Rough Trade who promptly invited them to record an album. Playing within minimalist musical landscapes the group utilized the superb, lyrical bass playing of Philip Moxham. The combination of Stuart's twangy/scratchy guitar and reedy organ with Alison's clear diction was evident on tracks such as 'Searching For Mr Right', 'Credit In The Straight World' and 'Wurlitzer Jukebox' from *Colossal Youth*. This highly acclaimed album was followed the next year by the impressive *Testcard* EP, which reached number 3 in the UK independent charts, by which time the group had amicably split. The brothers noted that recording separately would be the only way to maintain a healthy sibling relationship. Statton formed Weekend for two jazz-inspired albums, before joining Ian Devine (ex-Ludus) in Devine And Statton, releasing two albums, *The Prince Of Wales* and *Cardffians*. Stuart Moxham established the Gist, recording *Embrace The Herd* (1983). This included the gorgeous 'Love At First Sight' which reached the UK independent Top 20,. Stuart's producing talents where called upon to oversee the recording of the Marine Girls second album, *Lazy Ways*. Other projects in the 90s included work with Beat Happening and a solo album, *Signal Path*, on Feel Good All Over Records, with Statton guesting on one track. In later years his other profession, that of animation painter, gave him a credit on the film *Who Killed Roger Rabbit?* Phil Moxham found work sessioning for both Weekend and the Gist. In 1987, the Young Marble Giants reformed briefly to record a French release, 'It Took You'.

Album: *Colossal Youth* (Rough Trade 1980). Compilation: with Weekend and the Gist *Nipped In The Bud* (1984). Videos: *Live At The Hurrah!* (1994).

Z

ZTT Records

Formed in 1983 by producer Trevor Horn, a former member of the Buggles and Yes, and his wife Jill Sinclair, ZTT was one of the most innovative UK labels of the early 80s. Horn employed the sharp marketing skills of former *New Musical Express* journalist Paul Morley, whose obtuse style and interest in unearthing obscure talent was allied to a love of ephemeral pop. ZTT was an abbreviation of Zang Tumb Tuum, a phrase used by the Italian futurist Russulo to describe the sound of machine-gun fire. The artistic notions of the label were emphasized through elaborate artwork and a release policy that encouraged the use of multi-format pressings. The label was distributed by Island Records until 1986, after which it pursued the independent route. Among the early signings to the label were the Art Of Noise and Propaganda, both of whom enjoyed chart success and enhanced the label's *avant garde* reputation. The key act, however, was undoubtedly Frankie Goes To Hollywood, which conjured a trilogy of spectacular UK number 1 hits in 1984 with 'Relax', 'Two Tribes' and 'The Power Of Love'. Their double album, *Welcome To The Pleasure Dome* was quintessentially ZTT with arresting artwork, political slogans, and mock merchandising ideas included on the sleeve. The Frankie flame burned brightly until the second album, *Liverpool*, which proved expensive and time consuming and sold far fewer copies than expected. The label continued its search for original talent, but all too often signed notably obscure acts who failed to find success in the mainstream. Among the artists who joined ZTT were Act, Anne Pigalle, Insignificance, Nasty Rox Inc. and Das Psych-Oh Rangers. Roy Orbison was also signed for a brief period and Grace Jones provided a formidable hit with 'Slave To The Rhythm'. ZTT suffered its most serious setback at the hands of former Frankie Goes To Hollywood singer Holly Johnson, who successfully took the label to the High Court in 1988 and won substantial damages after the group's contract was declared void, unenforceable and an unreasonable restraint of trade.

INDEX

A

A Cappella, 17, 59, 180, 185
A Certain Ratio, 5, 138
A.D., 27, 43, 89, 96, 110-111, 133, 225, 235, 244, 252, 324, 336, 358
A Flock Of Seagulls, 247
A House, 5-6, 72, 88, 94, 112, 120, 190, 250, 257, 361, 370, 386
A&M Records, 5-9, 11-17, 19-22, 24, 26-27, 29-31, 33-35, 37, 39, 41, 43, 45-46, 48-49, 51-53, 55, 57-65, 67-74, 76-80, 82-94, 96, 98, 100-107, 109-120, 122-123, 125-139, 141, 143-158, 161-162, 164-180, 182-187, 189-204, 206-208, 210-212, 214-218, 220-223, 225-231, 233-253, 255-259, 261, 263, 265-269, 271-276, 278-280, 282-284, 286, 288-296, 299-302, 304-305, 307-318, 320-336, 338-340, 343-347, 349-350, 352, 354-362, 364-372, 374, 376-378, 380-382, 384-386, 388-394
A's, 7
A Tribe Called Quest, 35
A Witness, 5, 7-8
A-Ha, 248
Abba, 129, 197, 201, 204
Abbot, Jacqui, 37
Abbott, John, #68
ABC, 157, 172, 177, 251
ABC Records, 172
Abong, Fred, 39, 359
Absolute Beginners, 335, 352
Absolute Gray, 7
Accelerators, 7
Accept, 180, 372
Ace, 162, 236, 242, 278, 307, 331
Ace, Martin, 242
Ace Records, 278
Acid House, 43, 69, 86, 112, 129, 153, 382, 389
Acid Jazz, 112, 320, 382, 384
Acland, Chris, 239
Across The Room, 22
Actifed, 7
Action Pact, 7-8
Adam And The Ants, 8-9, 61, 133, 238, 368, 372
Adam Ant, 8-9, 147, 226, 238, 364
Adams, Alistair, 352
Adams, Allen, 115
Adams, Bronwyn, 101
Adams, Craig, 235-236, 317
Adams, David, 381
Adams, Justin, 190
Adams, Richard, 105
Adamson, Barry, 46, 74, 113, 220, 235, 376
Adamson, Stuart, 318
Adderley, Cannonball, 253
Addiction, 191, 203, 210, 218, 256, 278, 311
Addie, 256
Ade, King Sunny, 381
Adge, Mark, 261
Adicts, 9
Adolescents, 9, 12, 325, 365, 391
Adrenalin, 109, 355

Adult Net, 11, 37, 55, 141, 324
Adulterers Anonymous, 216, 391
Adventures, 8, 10-11, 91, 123, 176, 184, 257, 312
Adverts, 11, 133, 164, 194, 265, 333, 366
Aeroplanes, 41, 53-54, 78, 215, 242, 336, 365
Aerosmith, 39
Affinity, 170, 182, 207
Afraid Of Mice, 12
Afrika Bambaataa, 282
Afros, 35
After The Fire, 152, 212, 275, 385
Aftermath, 86, 288, 292, 327, 338, 344, 347, 357, 378
Agar, David, 261
Age Of Chance, 12
Agent, 9, 12-13, 325, 385
Agent Orange, 9, 12-13, 325
Agnew, Alfie, 9
Agnew, Frank, 9, 365
Agnew, John, 234
Agnew, Rikk, 9, 11, 79, 325
Ainge, Gary, 146
Aire, Jane, 13, 112, 131, 138, 161, 263, 333
Airforce, 197
Airhead, 13
Al-Sayed, Heitham, 310
Alabama, 9, 20
Aladdin, 171
Alarm, 11, 13, 390
Alaska, 233, 374
Albarn, Damon, 57, 133
Albatross, 65, 227, 384
Albertine, Viv, 236, 320
Alberto Y Lost Trios Paranoias, 13-14
Albin, Rich, 126
Albini, Steve, 43, 63, 73, 194, 228, 252, 268-269, 289, 307, 313, 316, 345, 369-370, 381
Albion Records, 228
Albrow, Mark, 185
Alder, John, 241
Alex, Duncan Robert, 257
Alexander, Dave, 187
Alexander, James, 187
Alexander, Mark, 384
Alexander, Van, 132
Alice Cooper, 14, 129, 228, 392
Alien, 14, 72, 80, 90, 330, 345
Alien Sex Fiend, 14, 330
Alizojvodic, Alan, 94
All About Eve, 14, 82, 164, 311
All Night Long, 372
Allard, Grace, 302
Allardyce, Michéle, 155
Allen, Baz, 155, 369
Allen, Carl, 315
Allen, Dave, 161, 315
Allen, Lee, 49
Allen, Mick, 386
Allen, Phil, 45
Allen, Rodney, 53, 78
Allen, Ros, 113
Allen, Sarah, 33

Allen, Steve, 111-112
Allen, Thomas R., 234
Allen, Woody, 257
Alliance, 53, 115, 186, 225, 235, 241, 247, 324
Alliance Records, 186
Allies, 366, 372
Alligator, 231
Alligator Records, 231
Allin, G.G., 15
Allison, Chris, 321
Allison, Peter, 79
Allman Brothers, 57
Allom, Tom, 362
Almaas, Steve, 35
Almighty, 301
Almond, Marc, 86, 152, 311
Almqvist, Jonas, 204
Alquover, Endre, 118
Altenberg, Steven, 358
Alter Ego, 127, 165, 201, 272, 326, 362, 392
Altered Images, 15, 168, 180
Alternative Tentacles, 67, 110-111, 122, 143, 365
Alternative TV, 15-16, 30, 266, 380
Alvin, Dave, 49, 150, 391
Alvin, Phil, 49
Always Billy, 62
Aly, Brando, 64
Amanor, Crompton, 309
Ambel, Eric 'Roscoe', 113
Ambrose, 267
Ament, Jeff, 171, 241, 263, 350
American Breed, 304
American Music Club, 16, 114
Amorphous, 332
Amos, Tori, 179
Amphlett, Chrissie, 120
An Emotional Fish, 17
Anastasia Screamed, 17
And All Because The Lady Loves, 17
Anderson, Brett, 133, 336
Anderson, Bruce, 244
Anderson, Carleen, 382
Anderson, Charlie, 309
Anderson, Emma, 217
Anderson, Gary, 170
Anderson, Ian, 98
Anderson, Jimmy, 169
Anderson, Julie, 391
Anderson, Rick, 365
Anderson, Steve, 307
Andrew, John, 200
Andrews, Barry, 315, 392
Andrews, Bob, 164
Andrews, Julie, 9
Andrews, Mike, 352
Andy 'Awe', 310
Angel, 19, 30, 45, 76, 141, 194, 233, 245, 294, 312, 326
Angel Dust, 19, 141
Angelic Upstarts, 17, 153
Angels, 35, 64, 83, 86, 89, 132, 164, 175, 179, 191-192, 234, 261, 312, 367
Angry Samoans, 19
Angus, Colin, 312

Animal Nightlife, 194
Animal Records, 172
Animals, 18-19, 72, 92, 167, 267, 272, 315, 384, 390
Animals That Swim, 18-19
Annihilator, 343
Anthony, John, 249, 359
Anthony, Richard, 162
Anti-Nowhere League, 19
Anti-Pasti, 19, 119
Antietam, 19-20
Anton, Alan, 94
Antoniadou, Vas, 370
Anvil, 352, 376
Aphex Twin, 61, 309
Apocalypse, 59, 119, 137, 199, 204, 338
Apollo, 355
Appelby, Paul, 210
Apperley, Paul, 250
Applause, 17, 289
Apple Mosaic, 134
Apple Records, 155
Apples, 13, 20, 128, 364, 385
AR Kane, 20, 152, 222
Arby, 139
Ardito, Ronnie, 314
Arery, John, 185
Arigato, Domo, 128
Arista Records, 7, 107, 157, 167, 186, 189, 308, 315
Arm, Mark, 171, 242, 263
Armageddon, 173, 180, 325
Armatrading, Joan, 366
Armour, Jeff, 244
Armour, Paul, 102
Armoury Show, 20, 104, 194, 282, 318
Armstrong, Billy Joe, 171
Armstrong, Kevin, 261, 279
Armstrong, Simon, 58
Arrow, 195
Art Bears, 51, 356
Art Of Noise, 91, 394
Artery, 20
Arthurs, Paul 'Bonehead', 255
Ash, 20-21, 34, 152, 214, 243, 362
Ash, Daniel, 21, 34, 152, 214, 243, 362
Asher, Peter, 350
Asheton, Ron, 115, 187, 284
Ashley, Dave, 13
Ashley, Tyrone, 282
Ashman, Matthew, 61
Ashton, John, 279
Ashworth, Peter, 195
Askew, Carrie, 313
Asphalt Ribbons, 21, 361
Aspinall, Vicky, 288
Asquith, Gary, 292
Ass Ponys, 21
Associates, 21, 180, 223, 339
Astbury, Ian, 30, 103
Astley, Rick, 388
Astley, Virginia, 21
Aston, Jay, 164
Aston, Mike, 162, 164
Astor, Peter, 196, 211
Asylum Records, 117

Atchan, Yamano, 315
Atherton, Dave, 233, 384
Atkin, James, 134
Atkins, Martin, 199, 280
Atkins, Simon, 384
Atkinson, Steve, 167
Atlantic Records, 51, 87, 153, 178, 199, 218, 234, 278, 291, 307
Atom Heart, 87
Atomic Dustbin, 125, 246, 386
Attaway, Murray, 172
Atterson, Phil, 115
Attic Records, 241
Attila The Stockbroker, 22, 83, 250
Attion, Sid, 300
Attractions, 22, 24, 68, 76, 78, 92, 101, 210, 253, 367
Atwell, Billy, III, 143
Au Pairs, 22, 113
Auckerman, Milo, 115
Audain, Courtney, 360
Auer, Jonathon, 274
Auge, Jymn, 180
August Records, 20, 135, 315
Aural Assault, 45, 101
Aurora, Sonya, 130
Ausgang, 22, 24
Austin, Steve, 380-381
Austin, Vernon, 208
Autechre, 87
Autograph, 77
Autoharp, 356
Autopsy, 360
Avalanche, 58, 155, 162, 222, 299-300, 315-316, 324, 371
Avalon, 322
Avant Gardeners, 24
Avengers, 24, 26
Averre, Berton, 202
Avison, Richard, 33
Avory, Mick, 296
Axile, Tex, 364
Axiom, 227
Axis, 76, 152, 180, 255, 316, 320, 332, 355-356
Axle Records, 391
Ayers, Ben, 90
Ayers, David Wesley, Jnr., 71
Ayers, Kevin, 30, 272
Ayre, Tony, 11
Azar, Carla, 380
Azoff, Irving, 45
Aztec Camera, 26, 43, 55, 88, 210, 256, 275, 300, 323, 335

B

B., Derek, 151, 194, 255, 312
B.A.L.L., 27, 118, 173, 182, 314
B-52's, 26, 189, 361
B-Movie, 27, 111
Babes In Toyland, 27, 182, 190
Bacharach, Burt, 334
Back To The Planet, 28-29
Backs Records, 179
Bacon, Kevin, 89
Bad Boy, 9
Bad Brains, 29, 102, 141, 148
Bad Manners, 309
Bad News, 157
Bad Religion, 29, 117, 202
Bad Samaritans, 8
Badarou, Wally, 346
Badenious, Richard, 245
Badfinger, 193
Badowski, Henry, 29, 71
Baggett, Tony, 103
Bagnall, Nick, 269
Bagnoud, Frank, 394
Bailey, Chris, 302
Bailey, Steven, 317
Bailey, Tom, 357, 369
Baillie, Mike, 318
Bainbridge, Charles H., 309
Baine, John, 22
Baines, Pete, 328
Baines, Una, 55, 141
Baird, Dan, 292

Baker, Arthur, 248
Baker, Bobby, 364
Baker, Danny, 266
Baker, David, 229
Baker, Gary, 223, 225, 228
Baker, Ginger, 282
Baker, Jim, 183
Baker, Jon, 77
Baker, Peter, 39, 299
Baker, Robert, 84
Balaam And The Angel, 30
Balalaika, 70
Balam, Pam, 94
Balance, John, 86
Balbi, Paul, 93
Baldinger, Dana, 274
Balduresson, Siggi, 338
Baldwin, Dave, 187
Baldwin, Neil, 169
Baldwin, Shane, 374
Balearic, 86, 147, 248
Balfe, David, 45, 57, 106, 129, 152, 214, 335, 347, 376
Ball, Dave, 69, 376
Ball, Ed, 350
Balmer, Peter, 138
Bambi Slam, 30
Bamonte, Perry, 104
Bananarama, 55, 114
Band Aid, 61, 80, 295, 323
Band Of Blacky Ranchette, 165
Band Of Susans, 30, 178
Bandit Queen, 31
Bandulu, 169
Bangles, 31, 53, 126, 183, 197, 212, 223, 301, 376
Banks, Paul, 313
Bar B Q Killers, 88
Barbara, Santa, 361
Barbarian, Lydia, 105
Barbarossa, David, 61
Barbe, David, 61, 338
Barber, Simon, 78
Barbieri, Richard, 192
Barclay, Alan, 176
Barely Works, 33, 61
Barenaked Ladies, 31-33
Bargeld, Blixa, 74, 76, 132
Barger, Pam, 366
Barham, Meriel, 259
Barker, Al, 19
Barker, Clive, 86-87, 261
Barker, Hugh, 19
Barker, Rocco, 149
Barker, Roland, 294
Barker, Simon, 194
Barlow, Lou, 119
Barlow, Louise, 290
Barnacle, Gary, 301
Barnacle, Pete, 328
Barnes, Adam, 185
Barnes, Kathy, 172
Barnes, Lloyd, 114
Barone, Richard, 35
Barracudas, 33
Barreau, André, 390
Barrett, Geoff, 354
Barrett, Howard, 318
Barrett, James, 310
Barrett, Jeff, 177
Barrett, Larry, 377
Barrett, Russell, 77
Barrett, Syd, 30, 90, 112, 180, 193, 236, 314, 325, 350, 356, 374
Barrington, David, 344
Barron, Chris, 55
Barry, John, 361
Barson, Mike, 218
Bartel, Jonny Ray, 391
Bartram, Hazel, 111
Basher, Mick, 391
Bashford, Chris, 78
Basil, Toni, 239
Basinger, Kim, 80
Bass, Paul, 8, 11, 64, 93, 102, 120, 126, 131, 148, 167, 170, 176, 192, 199, 202, 243, 259, 267, 279, 291, 313,

321, 345, 368, 382, 386, 388, 391
Bassheads, 48
Batchelor, David, 318
Bateman, Bill, 49, 150
Bateman, Brian, 286
Bates, Ashley, 77
Bates, Howard, 318
Bates, Martyn, 33, 137
Bators, Stiv, 34, 110, 168, 212
Batt, David, 192
Batt, Steven, 192
Battered Ornaments, 197
Batts, Fraser, 79
Batz, Guana, 172, 231
Bauhaus, 21, 34, 37, 46, 103, 106, 152, 214, 243, 252, 318, 362
Bay City Rollers, 215
Bazalgette, Ed, 370
Bazz, John, 49, 150
Be-Bop Deluxe, 83, 246-247, 318
Beach, Howard, 46
Beach Boys, 11, 33, 49, 294, 296, 307, 322, 367
Beach Party, 111, 222
Beales, Nick, 250
Beastie Boys, 34
Beat, 35
Beat Happening, 37, 394
Beat Rodeo, 35
Beatles, 12, 27, 31, 48, 57, 60, 62-63, 82, 106, 109, 120, 155, 164, 166, 193, 195, 201-203, 248, 255, 259, 266, 286, 290, 294, 305, 308, 314, 317, 321-322, 350, 378, 388, 390
Beats International, 166, 185, 222
Beattie, Jim, 329
Beaujolais, Roger, 139
Beautiful South, 35, 37, 166, 185, 200
Beauvoir, Jean, 269
Bechdel, John, 279
Beck, 36-37, 89, 227, 304
Beck, Lori, 227
Beck, Pauline, 89
Becker, Joe, 161, 355
Becker, Nancy, 161
Becker, Peter, 33, 137
Becker, Walter, 79
Becket, Joe, 382
Beckett, Harry, 381
Bedford, Dave, 87
Bedford, David, 155
Bedford, Mark, 67, 179, 218, 220, 310, 335, 376
Bedlam, 190-191
Beech, Wes, 269
Beecham, John, 144
Been, Michael, 69
Beers, Garry, 237
Beesley, Max, 382
Beesley, Simon, 196
Beeston, Julian, 118, 253
Beetlestone, Jan, 143
Beggars Banquet Records, 11, 21, 37, 46, 53, 77, 126, 150, 152, 166, 186-187, 340
Beith, Rab Fae, 377
Beki Bondage, 120, 374
Bel Canto, 37
Belanger, George, 79
Belben, Richard, 112
Belew, Adrian, 175
Bell, Andy, 295
Bell, Brian, 382
Bell, Chris, 164, 328, 357
Bell, Marc, 177, 288
Bell, Martin, 388
Bell, Robert, 53
Belland, Brian, 376
Belland, Melissa Brooke, 376
Belle Stars, 37, 223, 236, 333
Belly, 17, 29, 39, 41, 59, 63-64, 74, 96, 153, 178, 316, 356, 359
Beloved, 38-39, 51, 70, 292
Belsham, Lee, 125
Belushi, John, 55
Benair, Danny, 358
Benatar, Pat, 113

Bendelow, Ian, 203
Beninato, Jeff, 110
Benji, 127
Bennett, Chris, 308
Bennett, Dave, 98
Bennett, James, 318
Bennett, Justin, 185
Bennett, Nigel, 228, 374
Bentham, Jeremy, 158
Bentley, Billy, 198
Bentley, Jay, 29
Bentley, John, 331
Benzini Brothers, 184
Berenyi, Miki, 217, 239
Berk, Dave, 30, 106, 195
Berk Brothers, 195, 276
Berklee College Of Music, 368
Berlin, Steve, 49, 150
Berman, David, 316
Bernhardt, Sandra, 94
Berry, Bill, 180, 283-284
Berry, Christopher, 39
Berry, Dave, 370
Berry, Heidi, 39, 41, 356
Berry, John, 34
Berry, Mark, 174
Bert, Bob, 326
Bertzger, Brian, 161
Beserkley Records, 41, 237
Best, Eddy, 34
Best, George, 381
Betrock, Alan, 109
Bettie Serveert, 40-41
Betty, 64, 178, 294
Bevin, Mark, 308
Bevis Frond, 41, 377
Bevoir, Paul, 321
Biafra, Jello, 110, 122, 143, 156, 173, 234
Bible, 12, 41-43, 179, 197, 221, 336, 384
Bickers, Terry, 39, 87, 184, 207
Bidwell, Claire, 261
Biff Bang Pow, 43, 100, 217, 225, 294, 310
Big Audio Dynamite, 43-44, 84, 316
Big Beat, The, 278-279
Big Black, 43, 63, 73, 178, 228, 252, 268-269, 307, 316, 345, 370, 381, 391
Big Country, 103, 318, 346
Big Flame, 45
Big Fun, 150
Big Head Todd And The Monsters, 45, 57
Big In Japan, 45, 106, 111, 127, 208, 214, 267, 320
Big John, 136, 148, 169
Big Life, 112, 199, 227, 257, 327, 391
Big Star, 65, 112, 161, 274, 349
Big Youth, 12
Biggs, Ronnie, 226, 311
Bigham, John, 148
Bikini Kill, 45, 185
Bikinis, 77
Billboard, 45, 87, 98, 193, 223, 244, 322, 344, 357-358, 372, 393
Billingsley, Wendy May, 61
Billy Boredom, 45
Bilt, Peter, 263
Bingenheimer, Rodney, 12, 135, 226
Biohazard, 45-46
Birch, Dave, 372
Birch, Gina, 288
Birch, Will, 290
Birkett, Derek, 151, 255, 339, 372
Birthday Party, 34, 46, 74, 101, 107, 118, 132, 152, 161, 216, 244, 252, 317-318, 329, 339, 349
Biscuits, Chuck, 82, 122, 336
Bishop, Glen, 150
Bison, Fred, 41
Bitch, 48, 189, 269, 294, 377
Bitter Sweet, 199
Bivouac, 46
Bizarro, Mondo, 288-289
Bjelland, Kat, 27, 182
Björk, 47-48, 131, 256, 269, 338-339

Black, 48
Black, Burundi, 9
Black, Daniel, 280
Black, Frank, 49, 112, 153, 220, 268
Black, Jack, 62
Black, Pauline, 309
Black, Ray, 79
Black, Roy, 187
Black Box, 380
Black Crowes, 186, 192, 225, 278, 349
Black Flag, 19, 29, 48-49, 70, 115, 122, 143, 164, 291, 299, 336, 345, 391
Black Francis, 49, 267
Black Rose, 48
Black Sabbath, 67, 91, 117, 228, 321, 345
Black Witch Climax Blues Band, 195
Blackborow, Richard, 58
Blackmore, Ritchie, 180
Blackout, 136, 272
Blackwell, Chris, 26
Blackwell, Otis, 322
Blade, 91, 120, 126, 129, 316
Blain, Bobby, 344
Blair, Gavin, 390
Blair, Gordon, 258, 332
Blake, David, 261
Blake, Jacqui, 313
Blake, Norman, 58, 261, 347
Blake, Sam, 245
Blake, William, 197
Blake Babies, 49, 63, 176, 204
Blameless, 49
Blamey, Chris, 51
Blamire, Robert, 244, 265
Blancmange, 146, 325
Blanco Y Negro, 5, 30, 100, 119, 136, 193, 238, 300
Blanthorn, Tim, 378
Blast First Records, 129, 216
Blasters, 49, 366, 391
Blazyca, Rita, 117
Bleach, 50-52, 251-252, 371
Bleasdale, Alan, 92
Blegvad, Peter, 51, 169
Blessing, 131, 199
Blevins, Ken, 380
Blind Illusion, 278
Blind Melon, 51-52
Blitz, 110
Blitz, Johnny, 110
Bloch, Alan, 89
Bloch, Kurt, 393
Blockheads, 128, 198, 263, 390
Blondie, 31, 35, 51-52, 76, 109-110, 133, 135, 149, 167, 182, 202, 222, 247, 278, 349, 364, 372, 376
Blood, Dave, 111
Blood Brothers, 286
Blood On The Saddle, 31, 52-53, 212
Blood Sausage, 53
Bloom, Jeff, 350
Blow Monkeys, 382
Blow Up, 74, 154, 322, 350
Blue, Billy, 141
Blue, Vicki, 301
Blue Aeroplanes, 41, 53-54, 78, 365
Blue Moon, 94
Blue Nile, 53
Blue Orchids, 55
Blue Sky Records, 194
Blue Zoo, 283
Bluebell, Bobby, 55
Bluebells, 55, 92, 275, 323
Blues Band, 57, 78, 187, 195
Blues Brothers, 55
Blues Traveler, 55, 57
Blum, Richard, 117
Blunt, Martin, 77
Blur, 19, 56-57, 60, 72, 74, 100, 107, 133, 136, 149, 152, 329, 338, 343
Blurt, 57-58, 267
Blyth Power, 22, 58, 98
BMG Records, 114
BMX Bandits, 58, 71, 135, 327, 347
Boast, Tony, 241
Bob, 58-59

Bobs, 59
Bock, Charlie, 17
BoDeans, 45
Bodines, 59, 225
Bodysnatchers, 37
Bogdan, Henry, 178
Bogle, Eric, 229
Bolan, Marc, 27, 103, 170, 265, 327
Bollen, Andy, 71
Bollock Brothers, 59
Bolt Thrower, 245
Bolton, Dan, 343
Bomb The Bass, 48
Bonas, Peter, 243
Bond, James, 214, 292
Bond, Rebecca Louise, 374
Bonebrake, 150, 164, 391
Bonebrake, Don, 150, 164, 391
Boneyard, 39
Bonfire, 301
Bong Load Custom Records, 37
Bongwater, 27, 59, 67, 173, 199, 314, 377
Bonnar, Graham, 344
Bonney, Simon, 101
Bonnie, Carl, 292
Bono, 211, 367, 374, 381
Bonzo Dog Doo-Dah Band, 13
Bonzo Goes To Washington, 175
Boo Radleys, 43, 59-60, 100, 320
Boogie, 14, 208, 217, 284
Boogie Down Productions, 284
Booker T. And The MGs, 77
Boomtown Rats, 13, 61
Boon, Clint, 189, 255
Boon, Richard, 216
Booth, Andy, 74
Booth, Blair, 88
Booth, Carrie, 238
Booth, Simon, 381
Boothill Foot-Tappers, 33, 61
Bor, Rachel, 71, 123
Bordin, Mike, 139
Boredoms, 314
Borgioli, Billy, 289
Borland, Adrian, 327
Borrie, Ed, 321
Bortman, Terry, 7
Boss, 59
Bostik, Billy, 312
Bostock, Chris, 167, 328
Bostrom, Derrick, 226
Botany, 61
Botany 5, 61
Botelho, Ron, 52
Boulevard, 365
Boulter, Dave, 21, 361
Boulter, Roy, 144
Bourton, A.J.W., 53
Bovell, Dennis, 88, 230, 320
Bow Wow, 9, 61-62, 133, 194, 226, 311
Bow Wow Wow, 9, 61-62, 133, 194, 226, 311
Bowers, Tony, 13, 127
Bowie, David, 12, 21, 34, 103, 169, 187, 229, 237, 241, 261, 336, 338-339, 362
Bowler, Johnny, 172
Box Of Laughs, 94
Box Tops, 7
Boy, Andy, 331
Boy's Own, 107, 190, 369
Boyce, Mark, 259
Boyd, Craig, 114
Boyd, Joe, 350
Boyfriend, 11, 64, 114, 200, 238, 241, 273, 276, 313
Boyle, Judith, 329
Boyle, Ray, 135
Boys, 62
Brad, 7, 51, 64, 96, 122, 162, 183, 226, 252, 265, 385
Bradbury, Brad, 162
Bradbury, John, 309, 328
Bradford, Brett, 307
Bradley, Michael, 369

Bradshaw, Kim, 30, 216, 302
Brady, Eunan, 182
Bragg, Billy, 49, 62-63, 89, 110, 166, 168, 217, 225, 321, 324, 365, 381
Brahm, Sumishta, 340
Brain, Brian, 280
Bramham, 43
Bramah, Martin, 55, 141
Braman, Winston, 157
Bramley, Clyde, 183
Brammer, Keith, 117
Branca, Glenn, 63, 326
Branch, Eddie, 243, 368
Brand, Bruce, 64, 233, 390
Brand New Heavies, 127
Brandenburg, Tony 'Montana', 9
Brando, Marlon, 294
Brandon, Kirk, 328, 354
Brandt, Bill, 247
Brass Construction, 153
Brats, 9, 62, 182, 211
Bray, Steve, 364
Bread, 128, 250, 361
Breaking Glass, 107, 215, 253, 255, 364
Breathless, 176
Brecht, Eric, 126
Brecht, Kurt, 126
Breeders, 31, 39, 43, 63-64, 119, 153, 218, 266, 268, 356, 359
Brel, Jacques, 238
Bremner, Rick, 34
Brenner, Simon, 345
Bret, David, 241
Brett, Martin, 376
Brewer, Des, 212
Bricheno, Tim, 14, 318
Brickell, Edie, And The New Bohemians, 64
Brierly, Ben, 374
Brigandage, 64
Briggs, David, 300
Bright, Ann, 111
Bright, Bette, 64, 111, 218
Bright, Len, Combo, 64, 390
Bright, Sandy, 111
Brilleaux, Lee, 208, 333
Brilliant, 64-65, 127-128, 152, 157, 196, 199, 201, 225, 238, 257, 338
Brilliant Corners, 65
Brindley, Paul, 340
Brinsley Schwarz, 78, 215
Briquette, Pete, 13, 61
Bristow, John, 7
Britain, John, 167
Broad, William, 164
Broadrick, Justin, 168, 245
Brockman, Jake, 130
Brodie, Nicky, 88
Brodsky Quartet, 92
Brody, Bruce, 211, 225
Brokaw, Chris, 86, 88
Bromberg, Craig, 226
Bromley, Gary, 118
Bronson, Harold, 294
Brooke, Jaquie, 147
Brookes, Jon, 77
Brookes, Tom, 259
Brooks, Elkie, 65
Brooks, Ernie, 175, 237
Brooks, Meredith, 167
Brooks, Robert, 349
Brotherhood, 248-249
Brothers Four, 346
Brothers Records, 55, 100, 186, 225, 243
Brotherton, Paul, 59
Broudie, Ian, 45, 59, 64, 155, 187, 194, 208
Brown, Alan, 5, 45
Brown, Amanda, 167
Brown, Archie, 308
Brown, Beth, 7
Brown, Colleen, 176
Brown, Damon, 382
Brown, Daniel, 227
Brown, Darren, 227

Brown, Dave, 39, 290
Brown, David, 45
Brown, Desmond, 309
Brown, George, 333
Brown, Hamish, 294
Brown, Ian, 333
Brown, James, 65, 69, 137, 222, 267, 273, 293, 322, 370, 388
Brown, Jane, 293
Brown, Jerry, 110
Brown, Lee, 231
Brown, Mick, 235, 237, 291
Brown, Monty, 361
Brown, Nick, 228
Brown, Paula, 165
Brown, Peter, 304
Brown, Phil, 290
Brown, Rick, 356
Brown, Sam, 48
Brown, Sandy, 324
Brown, Timothy, 59
Browne, Cass 'Cade', 309
Browne, Colleen, 259
Brownson, Derry, 134
Browse, Paul, 84
Bruce, Dunstan, 80
Bruce, Jack, 145, 169
Bruce, Lenny, 299
Bruhn, Andreas, 318
Brutal Truth, 92
Brücken, Claudia, 279
Bryant, Gerald, 227
Bryant, Terl, 243
Bryce, Tricia, 293
Brydon, Mark, 69, 73, 183
Bryn, Tracey, 376
Brynner, Yul, 364
Bryson, Jill, 335
Brzezicki, Mark, 103
Buchanan, Paul, 53
Buck, Mike, 283
Buck, Peter, 145, 283, 327, 377
Buckler, Paul Richard, 191
Buckler, Rick, 154, 191
Buckley, David, 33
Buckley, Jeff, 41, 65-66
Buckley, Tim, 65, 85, 356, 382
Buckmaster, Paul, 350
Budd, Harold, 85-86
Buddy, 100-101, 170, 179, 231, 334, 382
Budgie, 45, 100, 208, 317, 320
Buffalo, 30, 65, 114, 170, 172, 212, 226, 229, 265, 335, 359, 382
Buffalo Springfield, 212, 265
Buffalo Tom, 65
Buggles, 394
Bulldozer, 43
Bullen, Charles, 143, 356
Bullen, Nick, 245
Bultitude, Paul, 308
Bunbury, Fergal, 5
Bundles Of Piss, 345
Bunnage, Michael, 112
Burden, Martin, 114
Burdett, Christopher, 17
Burdon, Eric, 272
Bureau, 144, 230, 335
Burgess, Mark, 76
Burgess, Paul, 187
Burgess, Steve, 336
Burgess, Tim, 77, 302
Burke, Clem, 11
Burke, Clement, 51
Burke, Noel, 130
Burn, 46, 123, 147, 271-272, 279, 294, 332
Burn, Russell, 147
Burnel, Jean Jacques, 65, 334
Burnett, Andrew, 84
Burnett, T-Bone, 92-93, 169
Burnette, Seori, 324, 340
Burnham, Hugo, 161
Burns, Jake, 332
Burns, Karl, 55, 141, 244, 280, 347
Burns, Ray, 195
Burns, Raymond, 71

Burns, Russell, 385
Burroughs, William, 87, 242, 280, 311, 322, 355
Burrows, Bryn, 155
Burrows, Chris, 168
Burton, Cliff, 141
Burton, Don, 96
Burton, James, 92
Burton, Mike, 77
Burtonwood, Tim, 59
Bush, John, 64
Bush, Kate, 253
Bush, Peter, 364
Bush, Richard, 7
Bushell, Gary, 119, 291
Bushwackers, 67
Butcher Brothers, 370
Butler, Alan, 169
Butler, Andy, 115
Butler, Bernard, 223, 338
Butler, Chris, 377
Butler, Richard, 279-280
Butler, Tim, 279
Butterfield, Paul, 187
Butterfield 8, 67, 179, 220, 376
Butterfield Blues Band, 187
Butterworth, William, 201
Butthole Surfers, 59, 67, 111, 149, 307, 314
Butty, Jean-Marc, 269
Buzzcocks, 67-68, 83, 115-116, 119-120, 151, 168, 174, 210, 216, 220, 227, 265, 282, 289, 313, 315, 324, 343, 347
Byers, Rodney, 328
Byfield, Joe, 161
Byrds, 77, 82, 186, 197, 221, 236, 283, 286, 289, 294, 308, 322, 340
Byrne, David, 20, 68, 76, 88, 134, 346
Bywaters, Peter, 266

C

Cabaret Voltaire, 68-69, 79, 153, 216, 244, 300, 325, 343, 358
Cacavas, Chris, 171
Cacophony, 151, 343
Cactus, 268
Cadenza, Dez, 48
Cadmon, Arthur, 215
Café Society, 296
Caffey, Charlotte, 167
Cafritz, Julie, 155
Cage, John, 82, 332
Caiati, Manny, 113
Cain, Mark, 312
Cain, Sim, 299
Caine, Michael, 218
Caine, Ron, 73
Cairns, Dave, 308
Caldwell, John, 378
Cale, John, 62, 164, 174, 187, 211, 237, 322, 331-332
California, Randy, 103
Call, 69
Callahan, Dave, 386, 388
Callahan, Ken, 192
Callender, Gus, 126
Callis, Jacqui, 292
Callis, Jo, 294
Calvert, Phil, 46
Cambridge Folk Festival, 299
Camel, 11, 202, 335
Camel Lips, 202
Cameo, 21, 34-35, 265, 384
Cameron, Matt, 263, 350
Cameron, Mike, 350
Campbell, Cam, 311
Campbell, Gia, 167
Campbell, Glen, 245, 327
Campbell, Ian, 290
Campbell, J., 190, 393
Campbell, J.J., 190, 393
Campbell, Martin, 208, 286, 393
Campbell, Tony, 96
Camper Van Beethoven, 69-70, 94, 300
Campsie, Col, 283
Canal, Nina, 370

Cancer, 26, 162
Candlebox, 70-71
Candyland, 71
Cantwell, Dennis, 166
Canty, Brendan, 157
Capitol Records, 169, 202, 223, 241, 269, 322, 350, 366
Capris, 391
Captain America, 58, 71, 135, 261, 371
Captain Beefheart, 5, 33, 49, 76, 90-91, 112, 190, 218, 236, 244, 246, 265, 268, 292, 365
Captain Sensible, 30, 71, 98, 106, 125, 180, 195, 241, 248, 321
Captain Shifty, 20, 385
Caravan, 166, 185
Carcass, 201, 245
Card, Jon, 122
Card, The, 307
Cardiac Arrest, 72
Cardiacs, 72, 316
Cardinal, 72
Carefree, 371
Caretaker Race, 58, 72, 78, 149, 211
Carey, Scott, 261
Carlier, Ramona, 236
Carlisle, Belinda, 164, 167, 206
Carlotti, Rachael, 176
Carlotti, Rose, 176
Carlson, Angie, 206
Carmel, 61
Carmen, Eric, 27
Carnival, 272, 295, 321
Carnivore, 45
Carnochan, Ian, 372
Carousel, 107, 347
Carozzo, Angela, 180
Carpenter, Chip, 267
Carr, Martin, 59
Carr, Tim, 27
Carrack, Paul, 215, 331
Carrera, Jackie, 72, 149
Carrie, 238, 313
Carrigan, Andy, 227
Carrion, Doug, 115
Carroll, Cath, 72
Carroll, Chuck, 393
Carroll, Jean-Marie, 228
Carruthers, John, 84, 317, 328
Carruthers, Will, 326, 328
Cars, 69, 73, 111, 117, 218, 237, 305, 321, 339, 382
Carson, Salli, 51
Carter, Bill, 307
Carter, Carlene, 215, 331
Carter, Chris, 79, 358
Carter, John, 241
Carter, Judy, 143
Carter, Leslie, 73
Carter, Neil, 320
Carter USM, 58, 73, 190, 227, 273
Casale, Bob, 116
Casale, Gerald, 116
Case, Peter, 35
Casebolt, Arika, 83
Casey, Jayne, 45, 267
Casey, Martyn, 365
Cash, Al, 27
Cash, Johnny, 359
Cash, Nick, 138, 198, 251
Cashan, James, 200
Casino Steel, 62, 182, 211
Cassandra Complex, 74
Cassidy, Larry, 308
Cassidy, Spike, 126
Cast, 74
Castle Communications, 333
Casual, 175, 294, 340
Casual Gods, 175
Cathedral, 245
Catherine Wheel, 68, 74, 346
Catlin-Birch, Dave, 390
Cats, 104, 229, 300, 322, 331, 360
Catto, Malcolm, 266
Cautry, Jim, 360
Cauty, Jimmy, 65, 196, 201, 257
Cavalera, Max, 156

Cavanagh, Chris, 316
Cavanagh, Paul, 299
Cave, Nick, 29, 46, 74-76, 96, 101, 132, 152, 161, 244, 263, 269, 365-366, 377, 386
Cave, Nick, And The Bad Seeds, 29, 74, 101, 269
Cawthra, Mark, 72
CBGB's, 27, 76, 102, 110, 117, 234-235, 288, 314, 322, 349, 361, 371
CBS Records, 83, 89, 256, 290, 333, 354, 392
Celebration, 73, 107, 114, 214, 293, 368
Centipede, 381
Cervenka, Christine, 391
Cervenka, Exene, 391
Chadbourne, Eugene, 314
Chadwick, Guy, 184, 207
Chadwick, Mark, 206
Chamberlain, Matt, 64
Chambers, David, 90
Chambers, Jimmy, 229
Chambers, Martin, 276
Chambers, Terry, 392
Chameleons, 45, 76, 127-128, 214, 292-293, 347
Champagne, 370
Champion, 15, 153, 222, 241, 271
Champs, 356
Chance, James, 90, 349
Chandler, Jon, 200
Change, Willie, 241
Channel 3, 12, 76-77
Channels, 151
Channing, Chad, 251
Chaplin, Gary, 265
Chaplin, Nicholas, 320
Chapman, Dave, 53
Chapman, Mark, 134, 377
Chapman, Mike, 15, 52, 202
Chapman, Tracy, 128
Chapterhouse, 77, 245
Charisma Records, 12, 305
Charlatans, 46, 74, 77, 129, 250, 279, 302
Charles, Bryan, 263
Charles, Kelly, 371
Charles, Ray, 92
Charles, Yolanda, 384
Charleston, Ian, 364
Charlottes, 320
Charman, Shaun, 273, 381
Charms, 193, 331
Charterton, Simon, 179
Chas And Dave, 292
Chase, Tommy, 333
Chatfield, Mark, 393
Chatham, Rhys, 30
Chau, Ted, 282
Cheap Trick, 369
Cheatham, Bill, 187
Cheek, Randy, 21
Cheex, George, 8
Chefs, 77, 177
Chelsea, 11, 29-30, 78, 164, 211, 225, 228, 347
Chenebier, Guigou, 356
Cher, 117, 276, 369
Cherry, Don, 128, 296, 320
Cherry, Neneh, 134, 296, 320
Cherry, Sophie, 88
Cherry Red Records, 14, 22, 110, 123, 136, 146, 182, 200, 222
Cherry Vanilla, 78
Cheslin, Matt, 246
Chesterfields, 78
Chevette, Brian, 129
Chevron, Philip, 269
Chic, 26, 110, 255
Childish, Billy, 53, 233, 243
Childress, Ross, 87
Chilli Willi And The Red Hot Peppers, 22, 78
Chills, 78-79, 324, 332
Chilton, Alex, 94, 356
Chimes, 27, 83, 164, 211

Chimes, Terry, 83, 164, 211
Chin, Eddie, 362
China Crisis, 79
China Records, 49, 206, 386
Chippington, Ted, 250
Chiswick Records, 93, 256, 366
Choir, 34, 274, 352
Chorley, Dennis Leigh, 154
Chosen Few, 101, 149, 187, 325
Chris And Cosey, 79, 358
Christian Death, 9, 79-80
Christians, 393
Christie, 61
Christie, Stevie, 61
Christopherson, Peter, 86, 280, 358
Chrome, 74, 80, 92, 110, 263
Chrysalis Records, 11, 43, 52, 73, 112, 125, 164, 166, 179, 200, 233, 242, 315, 318, 328
Chumbawamba, 80-82, 256
Chung, Marc, 132
Chunn, Geoff, 330
Church, 14, 24, 33-34, 80, 82, 94, 110, 145, 167, 179, 197, 212, 322
Chylinski, Mike, 126
Ciccone Youth, 82, 326
Cieka, Robert, 60
Circle Jerks, 19, 29, 48, 82-83, 122, 291, 336
Circus Lupus, 83
City Records, 120, 374
Claesson, Gert, 204
Clandinning, Linda, 87
Clark, Anne, 137
Clark, Dave, 294
Clark, Dave, Five, 294
Clark, Gene, 356
Clark, Lee, 329
Clark, Michael, 143
Clark, Mike, 339
Clark, Ned, 286
Clark, Paul, 381, 388
Clark, Petula, 102
Clarke, Anne, 128
Clarke, Basil, 46, 393
Clarke, Gilby, 111
Clarke, John, 83, 244, 313
Clarke, John Cooper, 83, 244, 313
Clarke, Johnny, 266
Clarke, Kory, 378
Clarke, Margi, 173
Clarke, Mervin, 8
Clarke, Nick, 102
Clarke, Nigel, 123
Clarke, Ronan, 189
Clarke, Ross, 105
Clarke, Simon, 155
Clarke, Stanley, 29
Clarke, Vince, 114, 369
Clash, 13-14, 17, 27, 39, 43, 62, 64, 69, 80, 83-84, 98, 107, 123, 149, 151, 164, 167-168, 176, 184, 210-211, 218, 250, 256, 269, 271, 280, 284, 301, 317, 320-321, 328, 332, 354, 364, 368
Classix Nouveaux, 84
Clay, Roger, 126
Clay Records, 119
Claypool, Les, 278
Clayson, Alan, 370
Clayton, Adam, 367
Clayton, Keith, 145
Clayton, William, 145
Clea And McLeod, 63
Clean, Dean, 111
Cleaver, Chuck, 21
Clifford, John, 89
Clifford, Mark, 309
Clifford, Paul, 388
Clift, Anne, 138
Climax, 195
Climax Blues Band, 195
Cline, Patsy, 92, 359
Clinton, George, 278
Clock DVA, 84, 317, 325
Clockwork Orange, 9, 35
Close Lobsters, 84-85
Clouds, 109, 257, 339

Clough, Anthony, 340
Clover, 92, 215
Clowes, Daniel, 343
Club, Billy, 117
Coasters, 203
Cobain, Kurt, 104, 135, 176, 182, 227, 268, 251, 262, 265, 288, 307, 315
Cobra, 332, 390
Cochran, Eddie, 100, 170, 311
Cockney Rejects, 85, 153, 310
Cocksman, Kid, 271
Cocteau Twins, 20, 37, 85-86, 88, 96, 118, 146, 152-153, 180, 217, 226, 239, 309, 320, 340, 356, 392
Codeine, 20, 86, 88
Codemo, Luciano, 27
Coffee, 178, 274, 299, 331
Cohen, Andrew, 316
Cohen, Leonard, 65
Coil, 20, 39, 85-87, 152, 155, 180, 280, 356
Colbert, Laurence, 295
Colbourn, Chris, 65
Cold Blood, 360
Cold Sweat, 76
Cole, B.J., 61
Cole, Bob, 61
Cole, Gardner, 283
Cole, Joe, 299
Cole, Judy, 290
Cole, Lloyd, 87, 167, 180
Coleman, Jaz, 199, 338
Coleman, Ornette, 90
Colenso Parade, 87
Collard, Dave, 167
Collective Soul, 87
Collectors, 41, 204, 271, 315
Colley, Dana, 239
Collier, Pat, 98, 372, 374
Collimore, Stan, 185
Collins, Bootsy, 169, 175
Collins, Charlie, 84
Collins, Edwyn, 5, 88, 154, 256, 275, 299
Collins, Henrietta, 299
Collins, Paul, 35
Collins, Phil, 5
Collins, Rachel, 17
Collins, Rob, 77
Collins, Robert, 113
Colman, Stuart, 380
Colorado, 45, 110
Colorblind James Experience, 88
Colosseum, 314
Colour Field, 88
Colour Mary, 320
Coltrane, Ruth, 53
Columbia Records, 35, 148, 177, 361
Colvin, Douglas, 288
Colvin, Monty, 158
Combe, Nick, 161
Come, 88
Coming Up Roses, 63, 88, 125, 292
Commodores, 141
Communards, 236
Company Of Wolves, 109
Comsat Angels, 89
Concert For Bangla Desh, The, 27
Concrete Blonde, 89
Conflict, 31, 73, 89-90, 98, 118, 138, 162, 226, 247, 350
Conspiracy, 179, 192, 201, 367, 385
Conti, Neil, 275
Contortions, 90, 349
Conway, Billy, 239
Conway, Dave, 244

Conway, Deborah, 122
Cooder, Ry, 215
Coogan, Martin, 236
Cook, Greg, 374
Cook, Norman, 166, 185, 222
Cook, Paul, 88, 171, 279, 311, 352, 359
Cooksey, Robert, 308
Cool, Tre, 171
Coombes, Gary, 340
Coombes, Pete, 362
Cooper, Alex, 197
Cooper, Chris, 259
Cooper, Lindsay, 357
Cooper, Ray, 115
Cope, Julian, 90, 127, 129, 175, 347
Cope, Matt, 96
Copeland, Miles, 31, 82, 110, 150, 167, 212, 266, 272, 295
Copeland, Stewart, 201, 272, 295
Cora, Tom, 136
Corbijn, Anton, 114
Cordelia, Josephine Miranda, 63, 266
Cordelia Records, 125
Corea, Chick, 29
Corkhill, Roy, 187
Cornell, Chris, 263, 307, 350
Cornershop, 53, 90-91
Cornetto, Chris, 246
Cornwill, Mark, 361
Corrigan, Briana, 35
Corris, Katherine, 236
Cortinas, 91
Costello, Elvis, 22, 53, 91-92, 215, 221, 229, 269, 274-275, 328, 331, 333, 344, 390, 393
Costello, Nick, 92, 333, 393
Coté, Billy, 218
Coté Coté, 218
Cotillard, Vaughan, 114
Cotten, Michael, 365
Coudanne, Vincent, 67
Cougar, John, 49, 184
Coughlan, Cathal, 145, 231, 274
Count Bishops, 92-93
Count Duckula, 14
Country Folk, 131, 239, 283, 292, 300, 361
Country Joe And The Fish, 265
Countrymen, 129, 147
Court, Paul, 278
Couse, Dave, 5
Cousin, Andy, 14, 385
Cousins, Andy, 311
Couzens, Andy, 179, 333
Cow Cow, 7, 51, 164, 173, 189, 243, 269, 290, 356, 368, 388
Cow Records, 189
Cowan, Blair, 87
Cowboy Junkies, 93-94
Cowboys, Galactic, 158-159
Cowen, Steve, 236
Cox, Alex, 182
Cox, Mark, 386
Coxhill, Lol, 41
Coxon, Graham, 57
Coyle, Peter, 214
Coyne, Chris, 168
Coyne, Kevin, 265
Coyne, Mark, 149
Coyne, Wayne, 149
Coyote Records, 35
Crabb, Graham, 273
Cracker, 70, 94
Craddock, Steve, 384
Cramer, Philo, 145
Cramps, 76, 94, 96, 150, 157, 172, 183, 230, 244, 318, 328, 366
Cranberries, 95-96
Crane, Lex, 238
Crane, Steve, 318
Cranes, 96
Crash, Johnny, 237
Crash Test Dummies, 96-98, 175, 392
Crass, 48, 71, 80, 89, 98, 119, 151, 182, 271, 273, 336, 338, 350, 372
Crass Records, 98, 151

Cravats, 98, 372
Crawford, Ed, 148, 235
Crawford, Justin, 247
Crawley, Caroline, 313, 356
Crazy Horse, 134, 288, 377
Crazyhead, 98-99, 152, 388
Creamin' Jn, 151, 153, 311
Creaming Jesus, 98, 100
Creation Records, 5, 39, 43, 58-60, 79, 94, 100, 135, 146, 177, 184, 192-193, 196, 211, 226, 228, 238, 245, 255, 273, 289, 294-295, 310, 316, 320, 336, 349-350, 385
Creatures, 34, 85, 100, 157, 229, 317, 346
Credit To The Nation, 256
Creed, 80, 131, 309
Creedence Clearwater Revival, 231
Creek, 16
Creese, Pete, 57
Crego, Michael, 175
Crenshaw, Marshall, 100-101
Crews, Harry, 175, 216
Crickmore, David P., 146
Crime, 19, 24, 34, 46, 101, 110, 132, 135, 162, 244, 358
Crime And The City Solution, 46, 101, 132, 135, 244
Criminal Records, 24
Crippen, Dick, 352
Crispy Ambulance, 101
Critchley, Martin, 228
Cro-Mags, 45, 101-102
Crockford, Allan, 278
Crockford, Jane, 236
Crombie, Noel, 330
Cromby, Bur, 127
Crosby, David, 184
Cross, Dan, 266
Cross, Tim, 366
Crossfire, 118
Crossley, Nigel, 173
Crover, Dale, 227
Crow, 178, 210, 250
Crow, Joe, 210, 250
Crowded House, 330
Crowder, Paul, 11
Crowe, Cameron, 265, 345
Crowe, Dave, 282
Crowe, Simon, 61
Crowell, Rodney, 39
Crowley, Gary, 123, 149, 321
Crows, 93-94, 192
Cruise, Julie, 26
Cruise, Tom, 225
Crump, Simon, 185
Crusaders, 296
Crying, 103, 328
Cuban Heels, 102
Cubitt, Robert, 246
Cud, 102-103, 233
Cuddly Toys, 103
Cuffe, Laurie, 102
Cugini, Christopher, 17
Cullen, Keith, 5
Cult, 103
Culture Club, 13, 62, 112, 131, 199, 211, 226, 374
Cummings, Dave, 179
Cummings, David, 112
Cummings, John, 288
Cunningham, 156, 206, 222
Cunningham, Jeremy, 206
Cunningham, Neil, 156
Cunningham, Phil, 222
Cunnington, Graham, 352
Cuomo, Rivers, 382
Cupid, 308
Curb, 391
Curd, John, 7
Cure, 96, 104-105, 119, 166, 239, 273, 314, 317
Curley, John, 11-12, 21
Curnon, Ian, 13
Currie, Billy, 376
Currie, Nicholas, 238

Curry, Mickey, 103-104
Curtis, Alan, 118
Curtis, Dave, 118
Curtis, Ian, 101, 196, 248, 361
Curtis, Jon, 77
Curtis, Keith, 5, 228
Curve, 105, 110
Cutler, Chris, 357
Cutler, Ian, 13
Cutliffe, John, 362
Cyborg, John L., 80
Cyclone, 229
Czukay, Holger, 155, 190-191

D
D.A.D., 27, 43, 89, 96, 110-111, 133, 225, 235, 244, 252, 324, 336, 358
D'Arby, Terence Trent, 139
D Records, 107
Da Silva, Ana, 288
Dada, 98, 372
Dade, Sushil K., 327
DAF, 105
Dahlheimer, Patrick, 210
Dahlquist, Michael, 316
Daisy Chainsaw, 105, 256
Dalek I Love You, 106, 347
Daley, 49, 368
Daley, Jack, 368
Daley, Jared, 49
Dali, 34, 106, 243, 350
Dali's Car, 34, 106, 243
Dallaway, Robin, 98, 372
Dallion, Susan, 317
Dalton, Nic, 206
Dalwood, Dexter, 91
Dulji Guiji, 79
Daly, Steven, 195, 256
Dames, 39
Damian, 180, 352, 369
Dammers, Jerry, 328
Damned, 11, 13-14, 17, 29-30, 34, 71, 76, 106-107, 110, 125, 131, 195, 211, 215, 235, 241, 253, 333, 336, 344, 359, 365, 368
Dana, 239, 274
Dance Band, 19, 45, 71, 253, 365
Dance Craze, 372
Dancing Did, 107
Dando, Evan, 49, 135, 176, 204
Danell, Dennis, 325
Danger, 69, 167, 210, 255, 361
Danger, Danger, 69, 167, 210, 255, 361
Dangerfield, Matt, 62, 211
Dangerhouse Records, 135, 382
Dangerous Birds, 88
Daniels, Howard, 318
Daniels, Phil, 107, 364
Daniels, Phil, And The Cross, 107
Danielson, Kurt, 345
Dankin, Gerald, 328
Danse Society, 107
Dantalians, 272
Danzig, 46, 82, 91, 122, 235, 336
Danzig, Glenn, 235
Darbyshire, Keith, 101
Dark Star, 276
Darling, Tom, 366
Darling Buds, 108-109, 134, 217
Darts, 76
Darvill, Benjamin, 96
Date, Terry, 307
Daugherty, Dee, 82
Daugherty, J.D., 322
Davenport, Robert, 101
David, Charles, 174
David, Hal, 334
David, Jay, 34, 152, 214
David Z, 45
Davidson, Aaron, 237
Davidson, Eric, 247
Davidson, Jim, 247
Davidson, Pete, 9
Davies, Alan, 325
Davies, Annemari, 146
Davies, Dickie, 173
Davies, Gary, 286

Davies, Geoff, 173
Davies, Noel, 309
Davies, Pete, 368
Davies, Ray, 91-92, 191, 276, 296, 331, 392
Davies, Richard, 72
Davies, Simon, 179
Davis, Alan, 300
Davis, Bette, 376
Davis, Gary, 331
Davis, Gary, Rev., 331
Davis, Greg, 52
Davis, Jeff, 241
Davis, Martha, 241
Davis, Michael, 115
Davis, Miles, 20, 308
Davis, Noel, 309
Davis, Paul, 174
Davis, Spencer, 390
Davis, Spencer, Group, 390
Davis, Thomas, 111
Davison, Michael, 9
Davison, Simon, 246
Dawn, 7, 20, 117, 147, 153, 198, 236, 314, 354
Dawn, Golden, 20
Dawn Records, 20
Dax, Danielle, 109, 147
Day, Doris, 78
Day, Graham, 278-279
Day, Mark, 174
Day, Terry, 197
De Arsten, 41
De Borg, Jerry, 193
De Freitas, Pete, 129
De La Soul, 386
De Lorenzo, Victor, 374
De Monierre, Françoise, 187
De Salvo, Debra, 143
Deacon, 169
Deacon Blue, 169
Dead Boys, 34, 76, 110
Dead Can Dance, 33, 152
Dead Dead Good, 27, 77, 125
Dead Famous People, 63, 110, 302
Dead Kennedys, 29, 102, 110-111, 122, 148, 164, 245, 253
Dead Milkmen, 111
Dead Or Alive, 235, 317
Deaf School, 13, 64, 111-112
Deakin, Graham, 151
Deal, Kim, 39, 63-64, 266-268, 356
Dean, Chris, 291
Dean, James, 220, 240, 322
Dean, Mitch, 365
Dean, Paul, 391
Dean, Rob, 192
Death Of Vinyl, 305
Death Records, 122
Debaun, Jack, 77
Decca Records, 318
Decharne, Max, 161
Decloedt, Mark, 134
DeConstruction, 78
Decouffle, Phillipe, 248
Decoy Records, 227, 309
Dedona, Paul, 29
Dee, Jay, 82
Dee, Johnny, 78
Dee, Kid, 9
Deebank, Maurice, 146
Deep Freeze Mice, 112
Deep Freeze Productions, 112
Deevey, Andrew, 72
Defever, Warren, 180
DeFreitas, Rosemarie, 176
DeGrasso, Jimmy, 339
Degville, Martin, 316
Deily, Ben, 204
Dekker, Desmond, 329, 333
Del Amitri, 112-113, 169, 180, 384
Del Lords, 113
Delaney, Alan, 147
Delanian, Mike, 161
Delgado-Lopez, Gabi, 105
Delisle, Wayne, 229
Delta 5, 113

Deltic Records, 321
Deltones, 173, 292
Demon, 14, 17, 88, 92, 112, 114, 215, 229, 256, 312, 340, 393
Demon Records, 114
DeMores, Anthony, 8
Dempsey, Martin, 393
Dempsey, Michael, 104, 214
Den, 132
Dench, Ian, 134
Denison, Duana, 113
Dennis, Dean, 84
Dennis And The Experts, 325
Denny, Dix, 382
Denny, John, 382
Denny, Martin, 332
Dentists, 113, 233
DeNuzio, Vinny, 145
Denzil, 113-114
DePace, Steve, 150
Department S, 114, 325, 352
Depeche Mode, 114, 156, 235, 244, 253, 325
Deram Records, 27
Derf Scratch, 145
Derrida, Jacques, 307
Descendents, 114-115
Desires, 304
Desperate Bicycles, 115
Destiny, 117, 164, 178, 238, 253, 328, 354, 357
Destri, James, 51
Destroy All Monsters, 115, 187
Destructors, 115
Detectives, 24, 92, 333
Detours, 9
Detrick, Ritchie, 253
Detroit, 100, 116, 136, 180, 187, 212, 284, 378
Deupree, Jerome, 239
Deutsch, Stu, 269
DeVille, Willy, 234
Devine, Ian, 115, 216, 394
Devine And Statton, 115, 216, 382, 394
Devo, 91, 116, 333
Devoto, Howard, 68, 116, 216, 220, 356
Dewey, Nick, 294
Dewing, Thomas, 86
Dexys Midnight Runners, 230
DFC, 266
Dharma Bums, 116
Diagram, Andy, 120, 259
Diagram Brothers, 120, 259
Diamond, Anne, 364
Diamond, Neil, 370
Diamond D, 34
Diamonds, 20
Dicken, Bernard, 196, 248
Dickie, Dave, 48
Dickies, 19, 117, 309
Dickinson, Bob, 220
Dickinson, Rob, 74
Dickson, Jim, 33, 58
Dickson, Sean, 58, 327
Dictators, 76, 117
Diddley, Bo, 107, 136
Die Cheerleader, 117
Die Kreuzen, 117-118
Diesel Park West, 152
Dif Juz, 85, 118, 152
Difford, Chris, 331
Difford And Tilbrook, 331
DiFonzo, Rick, 7
Diggle, Steve, 68
Digital, 67, 84, 258
Diken, Dennis, 322
Dillon, Dominic, 349
Dillon, Mavis, 80
Dillon, Paul, 74
Dils, 24, 118, 289
Dilworth, Joe, 332
Dim Stars, 118-119, 178
Dimension, 167, 204, 241
DiNizio, Pat, 322
Dinning, Dean, 361

Dinosaur Jr, 15, 48-49, 60, 65, 76, 119, 135, 229, 233, 251, 263, 336
Dinsdale, Steve, 183
Dire Straits, 242, 251, 273, 339
Dirnt, Mike, 171
Discharge, 115, 119, 151, 158
Dislocation Dance, 119-120, 259
Disorder, 120, 127, 196
Disorder Records, 120
Distractions, 120
Divine Comedy, 120-121
Divinyls, 120, 122, 127
Dixie Cups, 37
Dixon, Don, 7, 35, 122, 169, 172
Dixon, Greg, 273
Dixon, Nigel, 176
Dixon, Pat, 273
Dixon, Willie, 92
DJ Curtis W. Casella, 204
DJ Fallout, 318
DJ Hurricane, 35
DJ Milf, 134
DJ Zonka, 43
DJM Records, 266
Dmochowski, Wojtek, 53
Do Ré Mi, 122, 127
DOA, 122
Dobson, Mark, 146
Doctor, 116, 122, 292, 357
Doctor And The Medics, 122
Doctor Detroit, 116
Doctors Of Madness, 11, 106, 123
Dodds, John, 371
Dodds, Roy, 138
Dodgy, 123-124, 313
Doe, John, 150, 391
Doffman, Mark, 143
Doherty, Billy, 369
Doherty, Chris, 161, 229
Doherty, Mike, 155
Doherty, Pierce, 305
Doiron, Julie, 135
Dolby, Thomas, 275
Dolittle, Ange, 129
Doll, 27, 37, 123, 171-172, 182, 204, 349, 374
Doll By Doll, 123, 374
Dollar, 134, 243, 318, 329
Dollar, Johnny, 134
Dollimore, Kris, 34, 168
Dolly Mixture, 71, 123, 125
Don, Ricki, 296
Donahue, John 'Dingus', 149
Donahue, Jonathan, 229
Donahue, Patty, 182, 377
Donaldson, William, 294
Donato, Chris, 100
Donegan, Lawrence, 55, 87
Donelly, Tanya, 17, 39, 64, 74, 178, 266, 356, 358-359
Donnelly, John, 305
Donnelly, Nicky, 328
Donnelly, Thomas, 84
Donovan, 11, 43, 67, 174, 390
Donovan, Dan, 43
Donovan, Terence, 43
Dooge, Michel, 98
Doors, 7, 30, 111, 129-130, 169, 187, 191, 211, 263, 265, 308, 321-322, 334, 350, 378, 391
Doran, Joanna, 349
Dormer, Martyn, 107
Dornacker, Jane, 263
Dorney, Tim, 151
Doroschuk, Colin, 229
Dorrell, Dave, 222
Dorrian, Lee, 245
Dorrington, Paul, 381
Doss, Alan, 158
Doughton, Shannon, 63
Douglas, Graeme, 131
Douglas, Steve, 234
Dover, Eric, 193
Dowd, Gordon, 148
Dowd, Tom, 278
Downes, Graeme, 371
Downie, Gordon, 364

Downie, Tyron, 361
Doyle, John, 20, 220
Doyle, Maria, 184
Doyle, Peter, 203
Doyle, Ray, 296
Doyle, Tad, 345
Doyne-Ditmus, Nick, 356
Dr. Feelgood, 92-93, 131, 161, 208, 215, 290, 333
Dr. John, 384
Dr. Robert, 382
Dragon, 16, 391
Drake, Nick, 141, 314
Drake, William D., 72
Drakoulias, George, 192, 225, 278
Dramatics, 346
Dransfield, Andy, 27
Drayton, Charley, 104
Dream 6, 89
Dream Academy, 272
Dream Syndicate, 7, 31, 125, 134, 171, 212, 300, 390
Dream Theater, 76
Dreams, 27, 84, 92, 96, 186, 212, 247, 280, 288-289, 299, 308, 339, 384, 386
Drecker, Anneli Marian, 37
Dredd, Colin, 250
Drewitt, Steve, 60
DRI, 91, 125-126
Drifters, 234
Drive, She Said, 295
Driver, 8, 11, 65, 114, 128, 295, 311, 345, 370
Drojensky, Steve, 19
Drone, M.J., 126
Drones, 126
Droogs, 126
Drozd, Steven, 149
Drugstore, 126, 166
Drum Theatre, 126
Drummond, Bill, 45, 127, 129, 137, 196, 201, 214, 335, 347, 360, 376
Drums And Wires, 392
Dub, 29, 127, 131, 166, 190, 292, 301, 332, 369
Dub War, 127
Duck, Dennis, 125
Ducks Deluxe, 242
Dudanski, Richard, 236, 256, 280
Dudfield, Simon, 137
Dudley, Anne, 199
Dudley, Michael, 327
Duff, Jeff, 37
Duffield, Andrew, 237
Duffy, Billy, 103, 155, 318, 354
Duffy, Brian, 334
Duffy, Bridget, 308
Duffy, Eamonn, 250
Duffy, Martin, 39, 146, 276
Duffy, Stephen 'Tin Tin', 208
Duggan, Lina, 382
Dugites, 127
Dukes, 127, 280, 392
Dukes Of Stratosphear, 127, 392
Dukowski, Chuck, 48
Dullaghan, Steve, 33, 278
Dunbar, Derek, 194
Dunbar, Robbie, 128
Dunbar, Sly, 128
Duncan, Big John, 136, 169
Duncan, Davie, 102
Duncan, Gerald, 7
Duncan, John, 79, 136, 169
Duncan, Marc, 374
Dunlap, Slim, 292
Dunn, Anthony, 331
Dunne, Jo, 380
Dunne, Maggie, 380
Dunphy, Eamon, 367
Dunphy, Mike, 102
Duplantier, Carla, 194
Duran Duran, 210, 346
Durand, Marc, 229
Durutti Column, 14, 127-128, 138, 244
Dury, Ian, 128, 197-198, 251, 263, 333, 390

Dust Brothers, 35
Dwyer, Gary, 347
Dwyer, Lloyd, 291
Dye, Graham, 305
Dye, Steven, 305
Dylan, Bob, 64, 83, 92, 148, 164, 166, 211, 229, 268, 271, 275, 317, 327, 365, 367, 371

E
Eadie, James, 189
Eagles, 267
Eagles, Steve, 267
Earache Records, 119, 127, 156, 169
Earl, Richard, 344
Earle, Steve, 11
Earls, 161
Earls Of Suave, 161
Earth Opera, 193
East 17, 149
East End, 20, 53
East West Records, 148, 178
Easter, Mitch, 7, 35, 109, 122, 161, 206
Easterhouse, 128
Eastern Bloc, 131, 151
Easther, Caroline, 79
Easton, Elliot, 73
Easy, 13, 24, 27, 31, 80, 85, 87, 103-104, 114, 129, 138, 141, 201, 221, 286, 309, 338-339, 364, 384
Easy Action, 114
Easybeats, 41
Eat, 15, 52, 74, 82, 98, 111, 127, 129, 154, 179, 200, 273, 350, 300, 300
Eater, 129, 385
Eaves, David, 64
Ebert, John, 88
Echeverria, Rob, 178
Echo And The Bunnymen, 7, 12, 21, 87, 90, 127, 129-130, 201, 208, 233, 299, 347, 384
Echobelly, 105, 126, 130, 149
Echoes, 30, 85, 158, 278
Eckman, Chris, 377
Ed Banger And The Nosebleeds, 127, 216
Eddie And The Hot Rods, 92, 106, 131, 208, 359
Eden, Kevin S, 386
Eden, Malcolm, 223, 225, 332
Edge, 12-13, 21, 57, 80, 106, 131, 143, 148, 155, 185, 190-191, 193, 208, 211, 227, 231, 234, 263, 299, 320, 334, 360-361, 367, 372, 376, 385-386
Edge, Brian, 143
Edge, Damon, 80
Edmonds, Noel, 364
Edmonton, Dennis, 301
Edmunds, Dave, 92, 208, 215
Edmunds, Lu, 13, 106, 131, 282
Edson, Richard, 326
Edwards, Mike, 193
Edwards, Richey, 220
Edwards, Simon, 61, 138
Edwards, Terry, 67, 161, 179, 220, 361, 393
Efemey, Simon, 386
EG Records, 257
Egan, Davie, 290
Egan, John, 259
Egan, Rusty, 111, 295, 376
Egeness, Brian, 117
Egg, 109, 129
Eider, Max, 192
808 State, 5, 46, 48, 131, 189, 339
18 Wheeler, 100, 131-132, 255
Eighth Wonder, 43
Einsturzende Neubaten, 46, 101, 132, 325, 330, 352
Eitzel, Mark, 16
Elastica, 19, 132-133, 162, 313, 320, 386
Eldon, Thor, 338
Eldritch, Andrew, 118, 235, 317
Electric Prunes, 231, 314
Electro Hippies, 133-134

Electronic, 5, 64, 74, 106, 116, 127, 134, 138, 176, 195, 204, 222, 238, 248-249, 252, 255, 258, 293, 313, 324, 338-339, 362, 393
Elektra Records, 11-12, 117, 176, 187, 206, 315, 332, 349-350, 355, 391
Elemental Records, 19
Eleventh Dream Day, 134
Elias, Manny, 67, 91
Elixir, 304
Eller, James, 11, 354
Elliot, 'Mama' Cass, 292
Elliot, Cass, 292
Elliot, Mari, 272
Elliot, Marion, 272, 391
Elliot, Niki, 53
Elliot, Sean, 258
Elliot, Stuart, 78
Elliot-Kemp, Simon, 84
Elliott, Melissa, 100
Ellis, John, 65, 335, 372
Ellis, Mark, 203
Ellis, Mel, 9
Ellis, Rob, 268
Ellis, Ruth, 385
Ellis, Shirley, 37
Ellison, Andy, 284, 308
Elson, Tony, 290
Elvidge, Steve, 12
Ely, Vince, 279
Embury, Shane, 245
Emerson, 369
Emerson, Darren, 369
Emery, Jill, 182
EMF, 20, 43, 134, 193
EMI Records, 62, 151-152, 240, 247, 296, 311, 316, 323, 376, 388
Emmanuel, Tommy, 67
Emotionals, 134-135
Emotions, 199, 217, 276, 291, 330, 368, 374
End Of Chat, 22
Endicott, James, 212
Endino, Jack, 27, 243, 343
Enfield, Harry, 179
England, John, 223, 312, 333
England, Paul, 64, 311, 321, 380
Engle, John, 86
Englishman, 371
Enigma, 12-13, 77, 92, 96, 111, 115, 116, 121, 125-126, 161, 179, 197, 288, 293, 322, 365, 385
Enigma Records, 12, 77, 125, 179, 322
Eno, Brian, 68, 116, 320, 346, 362, 367
Ensign Records, 61, 190, 335
Eon, 12
Epic Records, 15, 20, 83, 109, 117, 168, 187, 208, 247, 263, 279, 307, 309, 366, 372
Epic Soundtracks, 101, 135, 344
Epitaph, 29, 91, 202, 256, 288-289, 315, 324, 365, 392
Equals, 122
Erasmus, Alan, 138
Erasure, 73, 244
Erdelyi, Tommy, 288
Eric B, 110-111, 269, 390
Eric's Trip, 135
Erickson, Roky, 90
Ericson, Tommy, 129
Eringa, Dave, 355
Escovado, Alejandro, 118, 253
Espiritu, 155, 177
Esquibel, Zecca, 78
Essential Logic, 135, 212
Estes, Grant, 339
Estonian Gauchos, 94
Etchells, Paul, 236
Eternal, 31, 48, 111, 137, 201, 212, 228, 250, 330
Etzioni, Marvin, 211, 225
Eugene, 58, 71, 135, 258, 261, 293-294, 310, 314, 371
Eugenius, 58, 71, 135, 261, 359, 371
Eurogliders, 127
Eurovision, 274

Eurythmics, 52, 79, 105, 138, 362
Evans, Anthony, 144
Evans, Carl, 77
Evans, David, 367
Evans, Dik, 374, 376
Evans, Kevin, 223
Evans Mark, 378
Evans, Mike, 111
Evans, Nick, 19
Evans, Pete, 184
Evans, Seamus, 274
Evans, Shane, 87
Evans, Slim, 289
Evans, Terry, 184
Everett, Kenny, 200
Everett, Steve, 259
Evergreen, 15
Everly Brothers, 289
Everman, Jason, 251
Everything But The Girl, 135, 194, 222, 300, 335
Ex, 48, 131, 136, 215, 328, 339
Executives, 96, 300
Exile, 118, 189, 221, 300
Exploding White Mice, 136
Exploited, 19, 119, 136-137, 158, 169, 195, 358
Explorers, 11, 366
Expresso Bongo, 229
Extreme, 85, 133, 137, 156, 158, 201, 223, 245-246, 273, 355, 377, 381
Eyeless In Gaza, 33, 137

F
F.M., 132, 177
Faber Brothers, 330
Fabulous, 33, 126, 137, 215, 241-242, 391, 393
Face The Music, 307
Faces, 57, 64, 67, 162, 204, 241, 265, 291, 312, 321, 359, 382, 384
Factory Records, 5, 46, 68, 73, 101, 127, 134, 138, 174, 196, 248, 253, 286
Fad Gadget, 132, 138, 244, 362, 386
Fagg, Otis, 325
Fahey, Siobhan, 55
Fairground Attraction, 138-139
Fairport Convention, 107
Fairweather, 171, 241
Fairweather, Bruce, 171, 241
Faith No More, 27, 139, 141, 178, 182, 191, 278
Faith Over Reason, 141, 302
Falconi, Ted, 150
Fall, 8-9, 11, 24, 31, 37, 55, 58, 67, 112, 141-143, 168-169, 174, 183, 190, 208, 218, 220, 223, 244, 246-247, 263, 265, 271-272, 280, 293, 296, 300, 302, 318, 322-323, 327, 334, 347, 361, 368, 382, 390
Falloon, Brian, 332
Falls, Martin T., 329
False Prophets, 80, 143
Family Cat, 143, 268
Family Fodder, 143
Famous, Richard, 271
Fancher, Lisa, 117
Fanny, 347
Farewell Performance, 157
Farley & Heller, 144, 257, 327
Farley, Terry, 144, 327
Farm, 22, 93, 144, 147, 152, 182, 231, 268-269, 315, 368
Farmer, Michael, 391
Farmers Boys, 144
Farmery, Steve, 228
Farndon, Pete, 276
Farrell, Perry, 191
Farren, Mick, 372
Farry, Eithne, 347
Fashion, 21, 43, 65, 80, 116-117, 126, 144, 154, 161, 174, 194, 197, 218, 225, 302, 304-305, 311, 313, 320, 333, 352, 370, 380, 386
Fatima Mansions, 144-145, 231, 274
Fats, 49, 293
Faulkner, Dave, 183

Faust, 156, 212, 326
Fawcett, Tom, 246
Fay, Johnny, 364
Fear, 19, 77, 103, 145-146, 151, 192, 227-228, 234, 245-246, 271, 316, 321, 346, 361
Fearnley, James, 269
Featherby, Marcus, 107
Feelies, 145, 300
Feeney, Seamus, 274
Feldman, Eric, 49, 269
Feldman, Eric Drew, 49
Feldon, Roy, 30
Felice, John, 289-290
Felix, 71, 110, 126, 143, 192
Fellows, Stephen, 89
Felt, 33, 39, 55, 120, 141, 146, 170, 178, 190, 193, 217, 225, 248, 250, 310, 313, 328, 335, 340, 356, 369, 380
Femme Fatale, 77, 175, 361
Fenn, Eddie, 296
Fenner, Chris, 73
Fenster, Schnell, 330
Fenton, Dave, 370
Ferda, Mark, 190
Ferguson, Alex, 266, 280
Ferguson, Gus, 352
Ferguson, Howard, 289
Ferguson, Jay, 320
Ferguson, Paul, 64, 199, 378
Ferry, Bryan, 324
Fetchin Bones, 19
Fewins, Mike, 91
Fiat Lux, 146
Ficca, Billy, 349, 371, 377
Fidler, Michael, 20
Fieger, Doug, 202
Field, Bradley, 349
Field, Mark, 385
Field Mice, 110, 146, 177, 302, 305
Fielding, Dave, 76, 292
Fields, Danny, 187
Fields, Dougie, 241
Fields, Robbie, 12, 77, 325
Fields Of The Nephilim, 37, 146-147, 266
Fier, Anton, 51, 145, 169, 242, 357
53rd & 3rd, 20, 58, 261, 273-274, 315, 347, 371
Fin, Pat, 382
Finch, Jennifer, 27, 202
Fine Young Cannibals, 45
Finer, Jem, 269
Finestone, Pete, 29
Fingers, Johnny, 61
Finitribe, 147, 255, 294, 380
Finkel, Howie, 78
Finkler, Michael, 347
Finlay, John, 58
Finn, Tim, 330
Finney, Mike, 120
Fiona, 259, 392
Fire Engines, 147-148, 218, 246, 275, 385
Fire Records, 17, 53, 87, 233, 259, 266, 300, 359
Firefly, The, 39
Firehose, 82, 148, 235, 326
Firm, 62, 85, 231
Fisch, Alan, 185
Fischer Z, 148
Fish, Alan, 185
Fish, Pat, 192
Fishbone, 148
Fisher, Bob, 225
Fisher, Dave, 233, 384
Fisher, Dean, 176
Fisher, John, 148
Fisher, Norwood, 148
Fist, 153, 279
Fitzgerald, David, 349
Fitzgerald, James, 386
Fitzgerald, Patrick, 200
Five Star, 189
Five Thirty, 148
Fix, Frankie, 101
Fizman, Nicolas, 116

Flakner, Jason, 193
Flamin' Groovies, 33, 101, 113, 182, 242
Flaming Lips, 149
Flamingoes, 149
Flanagan, Paul, 8
Flanegan, Harley, 101
Flansburgh, John, 355
Flash, 151, 313, 371
Flatmates, 149, 261
Fleetwood Mac, 265
Fleming, Don, 12, 27, 118-119, 173, 178, 182, 274, 377
Flesh For Lulu, 149-150
Flesheaters, 150
Flesher, Dannie, 380
Fleshtones, 150, 183
Fletcher, Amelia, 177, 347
Fletcher, David, 29
Fletcher, Mathew, 177, 347
Fletcher, Mervyn, 127
Fletcher, Paul, 296
Fletcher, Sarah, 149
Fletcher, Tony, 76, 284
Flickernoise, 286
Flickknife Records, 174
Flipper, 101, 150-151, 228
Flippermen, 253
Flirtations, 167, 266, 317
Flock, 148, 247, 371
Flowered Up, 151, 177, 302
Flowers, Angela, 308
Floyd, Neale, 265
Fluke, 48, 369
Flunder, Mark, 350
Flux Of Pink Indians, 98, 151, 255, 300
Flying Burrito Brothers, 192, 226, 359
Flying Records, 79, 110, 289
Flys, 151-152
FM, 24, 217
FM Records, 24
FM Revolver Records, 24
Foad, Paul, 22
Foetus, 63, 86, 132, 134, 152, 216, 325, 356
Foetus, Jim, 132, 134, 152, 356
Fogerty, John, 177, 314
Foley, Zak, 134
Fonda, Jane, 380
Fong, Lincoln, 239
Fontana Records, 11, 74, 86, 184
Fontayne, Brit Shayne, 211
Food Records, 45, 57, 152, 193, 388
Foos, Richard, 294
Foote, Mickey, 83
Forbe, Winston, 330
Forbes, Alan, 294
Forbes, Derek, 279
Forbidden, 226, 286
Ford, Betty, 294
Ford, Lita, 301
Ford, Martin, 127
Fordham, Julia, 385
Foreigner, 326
Foreman, Chris, 218, 220
Forest, 68, 87, 104, 134, 336
Forgie, Jackie, 87
Formations, 106, 116, 231
Formula, Dave, 220, 376
Forster, Robert, 166-167
Forsyth, Bill, 15
Fortune, Carey, 65
Foster, 244, 276, 320, 350
Foster, Joe, 244, 350
Foster, Malcolm, 276
Foundation, 72, 111, 115, 201, 234, 268, 329
Foundations, 128
4AD Records, 20, 39, 46, 49, 85-86, 118, 152, 180, 195, 216-217, 237, 259, 267, 329, 354, 356, 359, 368, 386, 392
Four Horsemen, 59
400 Blows, 153
4 Non Blondes, 153
Four Preps, 376
Four Seasons, 210

4 Skins, 153-154
14 Iced Bears, 154, 305
Fowler, Simon, 384
Fowley, Kim, 301
Fox, Dave, 274
Fox, Jackie, 301
Fox, Jane, 222
Fox, Mark, 130
Fox, Mat, 33
Fox, Paul, 276, 301
Foxton, Bruce, 154, 191, 332, 370
Foxx, John, 154, 376
Frame, Roddy, 26, 88, 256, 275, 335
Frampton, Peter, 256
Francis, Charlie, 364
Francis, Paul, 382
Francollini, Dave, 207
Francombe, Mark, 96
Frank, Ken, 88
Frank And Walters, 88, 154, 166, 190, 208, 340
Frank Chickens, 154-155
Frankie Goes To Hollywood, 45, 208, 267, 279, 394
Franklin, Adam, 344
Franklin, Aretha, 307
Franks, Billy, 139
Frantz, Chris, 174, 346, 361
Fraser, Elizabeth, 85-86, 146, 356
Fraser, Liz, 118
Fraser, Neil, 361
Frazer, Liz, 86
Frazier Chorus, 155, 208
Frederick, Martin, 143
Free Kitten, 27, 155, 175
Freece, Josh, 339
Freeez, 37
Freegard, Mark, 218
Freelove, Laurie, 179, 366
Freeman, David, 151
Freeman, Roger, 267
Freeman, Tim, 155
French, Frank, 355
Fresh Records, 8, 103, 371, 378
Freshies, 155
Freud, James, 237
Freur, 155, 369
Frew, Dave, 17
Freytag, Susanne, 279
Frez, Milan, 203
Friday, Gavin, 225, 374, 376
Fridmann, David, 229
Friedorowicz, Felix, 143
Friel, Tony, 55, 141, 347
Friend, Simon, 206
Friends Again, 57, 156, 214
Friese-Green, Tim, 316
Fripp, Robert, 109, 272, 364
Frischmann, Justine, 132
Frith, Fred, 59, 173, 356
Front 242, 118, 156, 257, 294, 380
Frontier Records, 9, 117, 190, 393
Frost, B.J., 138
Frost, Jack, 82, 167, 197
Fryday, Paul, 89
Fryer, John, 138
Fuchs, Jacqueline, 301
Fudge Tunnel, 156
Fugazi, 46, 136, 156-157
Fun Boy Three, 88, 167, 236, 328
Fun-Da-Mental, 103
Fundamental Records, 7
Fungus, 8
Fungus, Joe, 8
Funicello, 117
Funkadelic, 369
Furious, Danny, 24, 325
Furniture, 136, 157, 191, 384
Fury, Billy, 176
Futter, Brian, 74
Fuzztones, 157
Fuzzy, 157, 170-171

G.B.H., 158
Gabriel, Peter, 207, 296, 314
Gabrielle, 166

Gaitsch, Bruce, 283
Galas, Diamanda, 158, 244
Galaxie, 158, 314
Galaxie 500, 158, 314
Gallagher, Mickey, 128
Gallagher, Nicky, 263
Gallagher, Noel, 255, 372, 384
Galley, David, 31
Gallon Drunk, 160-161, 361
Gallup, Simon, 104
Game Theory, 161, 366
Gamson, David, 307
Gane, Mark, 222-223
Gane, Tim, 223, 225, 239, 332
Gang Green, 161
Gang Of Four, 12, 138, 161-162, 236, 316, 350
Ganley, Len, 173
Gannon, Craig, 11, 55, 203, 210, 240, 323
Gano, Gordon, 374
Gant, Frances, 110
Garcia, Dean, 105
Gardner, Suzi, 202
Garfield, Henry, 299
Garner, Pete, 333
Garon, Jesse, And The Desperadoes, 162
Garrett, Nicky, 311
Garrett, Pat, 118, 150
Garrett, Peter, 231
Garrity, Eddie, 318
Garside, Katie Jane, 105
Gartside, Green, 307
Garvey, Nick, 7, 147, 242
Garvey, Steve, 68, 347
Gary, Bruce, 202
Gaskin, Barbara, 333
Gates, Clive, 248
Gaudet, Mark, 135
Gaumont, Mark, 8
Gavurin, David, 340
Gaye, Marvin, 393
Gaye Advert, 11
Gaye Bykers On Acid, 16, 162, 186, 388
Gayle, Crystal, 116
Gedge, David, 381
Geffen, David, 37
Geffen Records, 11, 37, 63-64, 76, 210, 251, 253, 274, 304, 320, 326, 333, 349, 370, 372, 380
Geggus, Micky, 85
Gehman, Don, 184
Geldof, Bob, 61, 369
Gems, 26, 71, 208, 276, 393
Gen, 119, 164, 193, 312
Gene, 14, 24, 37, 49, 78, 109-110, 126, 128, 150, 162-164, 176, 299, 355-357
Gene Loves Jezebel, 14, 24, 37, 162, 164, 357
General Public, 248, 273, 309
Generation X, 7, 11, 164, 167, 211, 265, 311, 316
Genesis, 72, 86, 101, 132, 204, 274, 280, 305, 325, 358, 367
Gent, Chris, 290, 308
Gentleman, Horace, 328
Geoghegan, Mick, 233
Geordie, 199
George, Boy, 62, 226, 231, 311
George, Jon, 258
George, Rocky, 339
George Records, 192
Georges, Bernard, 359
Georgia Satellites, 292
Gerald, Francis, 365
Gerald, Michael, 198
Geraldo, 113
Geraldo, Neil, 113
Gerber, Scott, 165
Germs, 14, 164
Gersch, Gary, 63
Gershwin, George, 293
Getz, Stan, 136, 385
Ghost Dance, 164-165, 318
Giammalvo, Chris, 218

Giant Records, 45, 113
Giant Sand, 165
Giant Sandworms, 165
Gibbons, Ian, 290
Gibbs, Alvin, 368
Gibbs, Melvin, 299
Gibson, 67, 150, 168
Gibson, Alex, 150
Gifford, Alex, 67, 91
Gilbert, Bruce, 30, 152, 165, 385
Gilbert, Gillian, 248, 257
Gilbert, Nick, 146
Gilbert, Simon, 338
Gilberto, Astrud, 381
Gilbey, Alan, 220
Gilchrist, Paul, 136
Gilder, Maya, 157
Gilks, Martin, 233, 388
Gilkyson, Tony, 391
Gill, Alan, 106, 347
Gill, Andy, 161
Gill, Craig, 189
Gill, George, 385
Gill, Jayne, 261
Gilles, Keith, 340
Gillespie, Bobby, 193, 276
Gillett, Charlie, 182, 197
Gilliam, Terry, 208
Gillies, Rob, 330
Gilmartin, Paul, 107
Gilmore, Gary, 11
Gilmour, David, 279, 305
Gilmour, Mark, 305
Ginn, Greg, 48
Ginsberg, Allen, 246, 314
Giornio, John, 63
Gira, Michael, 216, 343
Girl Crazy, 117
Girl Friend, The, 73
Giscombe, Junior, 62, 335
Gladwin, Tom, 313
Glaisher, Mik, 89
Glascock, Brian, 187, 241
Glass, David, 80
Glass, Philip, 63, 339
Glass Records, 98, 261, 377
Glenn, Will, 288
Glenn And Chris, 331
Glitter, Gary, 59, 197, 201, 360, 394
Glossop, Mick, 265
Glove, 104, 166, 197, 317, 323
Glover, Martin, 64, 127, 199
Glover, Richie, 127
Gloworm, 166
Gluck, Jeremy, 33
Go-Betweens, 16, 37, 46, 72, 82, 166-167, 197, 275, 300, 365
Go-Go's, 31, 167, 384
Goddard, Eve, 364
Goddard, Leslie, 8
Goddard, Paul, 167
Goddard, Vic, 88, 167-168
Godfathers, 168, 242, 326, 358
Godfrey, Andy, 238
Godspell, 359
Godwin, Peter, 182
Goffey, Danny, 340
Gogan, Barbara, 261
Going Steady, 68
Golden, Annie, 314
Golden Boy, 335
Golden Palominos, 169, 242
Golden Records, 20
Golding, Andrew, 388
Golding, Dave, 299
Golding, Lynval, 328
Golding,Tracy, 31
Goldsboro, Bobby, 314
Goldsmith, Glen, 112
Goldstar, Rick, 55
Goldsworthy, David, 78
Gong, 356, 372
Good News, 227, 389
Good Times, 203
Goodacre, Martin, 137
Gooday, David, 253
Goodbye Mr. Mackenzie, 137, 169

Goodier, Mark, 17, 190
Gooding, Tim, 391
Goodroe, Michael, 241
Goodwin, Chris, 179
Googe, Debbie, 244
Gordon, Chris, 261
Gordon, Jim, 371
Gordon, Kim, 82, 135, 155, 175, 193, 216, 326
Gordon, Martin, 284
Gordon, Nina, 371
Gore, Joe, 269
Gore, Martin, 114
Gorillas, 169-170, 377
Gorl, Robert, 105
Gorman, Chris, 39
Gorman, Leigh, 13, 61
Gorman, Thomas, 39
Goronwy, Trefor, 356
Gosh, Talulah, 177, 261, 346-347
Gossard, Stone, 171, 241, 263, 350
Goswell, Rachel, 320
Gotobed, Robert, 138, 249, 385
Gottehrer, Richard, 52, 167, 182, 393
Gould, Bill, 139
Goulden, Eric, 64, 390
Goulding, Steve, 104, 164, 227
Gouldman, Graham, 288
Gousden, Guy, 39
Gower, Huw, 290
Grab Grab The Haddock, 222
Grabriel, Peter, 372
Grace, Clinton, 7
Gracey, Chad, 210
Graduate, The, 68, 77, 304, 316
Graeme, Kenneth, 339
Graffin, Greg, 29
Graham, Bill, 35, 57, 367
Graham, Lee, 365
Graham, Mike, 336
Graning, Chick, 17
Grant, Eddy, 333
Grant, James, 156, 214
Grant, John, 164
Grant Brothers, 263
Grant Lee Buffalo, 114, 170, 172, 359
Grantham, Anthony, 222
Grass Roots, 11, 265
Grateful Dead, 94, 182, 265, 377
Graves, Leonard, 117
Gray, Andrew, 305
Gray, Charles, 378
Gray, Eddie, 106, 359
Gray, Kelly, 71
Gray, Marcus, 284
Gray, Mark, 386
Gray, Paul, 71, 106, 125, 131, 359
Gray, Robbie, 237
Graziedi, Billy, 45
Grease, 345
Greasy Bear, 13
Great Divide, 43, 179
Great Rock'n'Roll Swindle, The, 111, 226, 236, 311-312, 352
Great White, 273
Greaves, John, 51
Greco, Paul, 80
Greco, Ron, 101
Greedies, 171
Green, Alex, 192
Green, Dave, 187
Green, David, 168
Green, Dick, 43
Green, Graham, 327
Green, Ian, 357
Green, Malcolm, 330
Green, Richard, 294, 357
Green, Steve, 236
Green Day, 21, 157, 171
Green On Red, 126, 165, 171, 212, 245, 286, 364, 390
Greenaway, Peter, 63
Greenbaum, Norman, 122
Greenblatt, Nanette, 246
Greene, Richard, 289
Greenfield, Dave, 67, 334
Greenhalgh, Tom, 227

Greening, Derek, 150, 266
Greensleeves, 330
Greenwood, Colin, 286
Greenwood, Gail, 39
Greenwood, Russell, 77
Greenwood, Stan, 318
Gregg, Dave, 122
Gregg, Fiona, 259
Gregg, Stephen H., 259
Gregory, Bryan, 94
Gregory, Keith, 381
Gregory, Peter, 112
Gregson, Clive, 179
Gremp, Ron, 239
Gretsch, 62
Gretton, Rob, 5, 101, 138
Grey, Crispin, 105
Grey, Hemmingford, 286
Greyhound, 139
Gribben, Pat, 11
Grid, 69
Griffin, Alex, 246
Griffin, Felix, 126
Griffin, Sid, 211
Griffith, Nanci, 361
Griffiths, Gavin, 259
Grigg, Robert, 113
Griggs, Nigel, 330
Grimes, Steve, 144
Grisham, Jack, 19
Grogan, Clare, 15, 347
Groothuizen, Chris, 184
Groovies, 33, 101, 113, 182, 242
Grossman, Rick, 184
Grundy, Bill, 317, 350
Grundy, Solomon, 307
GTO Records, 272
Guadalcanal Diary, 172
Guerilla, 136, 336
Guess Who's, 5
Guild, 14
Gullaghan, Steve, 137
Gumball, 12, 27, 119, 173, 178, 182
Gun Club, 94, 172
Gunn, Ben, 317
Gunn, Paul, 331
Guns N'Roses, 51, 76, 104, 119, 189, 204, 221, 316, 327, 368
Gunshot, 118, 365
Guru Guru, 45, 146, 155, 226
Guss, Randy, 361
Guthrie, Robin, 20, 85-86, 88, 118, 146, 217, 226, 356
Guthrie, Woody, 37
Gutsy, Suzi, 320
Gutteridge, Peter, 324
Guttierez, Louis, 358
Guy Called Gerald, A, 131
Gymslips, 172, 292
Gypsies, 107
Gypsy, 123

H

Haas, Andy, 223
Hackett, Andy, 299
Hackett, Steve, 305
Haddow, Steven, 131
Haden, Charlie, 390
Hag Records, 206
Hagen, Nina, 145
Haglof, Karen, 30
Hague, Stephen, 248
Haig, Alan, 79
Haig, Paul, 173, 195
Haigh, Kersten, 310
Hair, 13-14, 74, 104, 202, 206, 222, 229, 246, 258, 272, 275, 311, 314, 316, 336
Haircut 100, 130
Haitt, John, 101
Hake, Alan, 131
Halcrow, Caroline, 53, 365
Half Japanese, 314
Half Man Half Biscuit, 173, 340
Halford, Paul, 195
Hall, John S., 199, 314

Hall, T., 49
Hall, Terry, 88, 130, 167, 328
Hall, Tom T., 49
Hall And Oates, 49
Halliday, Neil, 131
Halliday, Toni, 105
Halstead, Neil, 320
Ham, Jacquie, 370
Hambel, Bobby, 45
Hambly, Mark, 374
Hamely, Chris, 83
Hamer, Harry, 80
Hamilton, Andrew, 144
Hamilton, Ferdy, 166
Hamilton, Graham, 22
Hamilton, Mark, 20
Hamilton, Page, 30, 178
Hammer, 33, 45, 109, 125, 169, 246, 320
Hammerdoll, 210
Hammerstein, Oscar, II, 71
Hammond, Dave, 84
Hammond, Pete, 22
Hampshire, Mickey, 233
Hampshire, Paul, 107
Hampson, Robert, 169, 212
Hancock, Herbie, 67
Hancock, Polly, 274
Hancox, Pip, 172
Hand, David, 339
Handyside, Paul, 185-186
Hankin, Paul, 259
Hanna, Kathleen, 45
Hannan, Patrick, 340
Hannett, Martin, 83, 101, 127, 138, 174, 196, 244, 247, 367
Hannon, Neil, 120
Hanoi Rocks, 175
Hansen, Al, 37
Hansen, Mary, 332
Hanson, Ray, 186
Hanvey, Fionan, 374
Happy Mondays, 77, 134, 138, 144, 151, 174, 177, 189, 200, 247, 253, 255, 313, 333
Harbuthnot, Patrick, 299
Harder They Come, The, 220
Hardin, Tim, 382
Harding, 13, 222, 309, 380
Harding, Jim, 309
Harding, Bob, 13
Harding, Jamie, 222
Harding, Paul, 380
Hardy, Lawrence Paul, 200
Hardy, Loz, 200
Hardy, Russell, 197
Harle, Steve, 368
Harney, Ralph, 357
Harper, Charlie, 174, 368
Harper, Roy, 356
Harpsichord, 72, 316, 334
Harrington, Steve, 376
Harris, HiFi, 293-294
Harris, Kenny, 307
Harris, Lee, 345
Harris, M.J., 33
Harris, Mark, 294
Harris, Mick, 137, 245
Harris, Micky, 208
Harris, Neil, 312
Harris, Noel, 144
Harris, Paul, 345
Harris, Rolf, 321, 330
Harris, Tim, 19
Harrison, Dick, 55, 119
Harrison, Gayl, 316
Harrison, George, 27, 272
Harrison, Jeremiah, 175, 346
Harrison, Jerry, 98, 175, 237, 346
Harrison, Nigel, 52, 135
Harrison, Ollie, 267
Harrison, Tim, 107
Harry, Debbie (Deborah), 51-52, 143, 189, 288, 357, 361, 364, 369
Harry, Neil, 165
Harry Crews, 175, 216
Hart, Charlie, 197

Hart, Douglas, 162, 193
Hart, Grant, 175, 186, 253, 338
Hartley, Mathieu, 104
Hartley, Sam, 13
Hartman, Dan, 175
Hartman, Jesse, 304
Harvey, Alex, 59, 305
Harvey, Laurence, 67
Harvey, Mick, 46, 74, 76, 101, 167, 269
Harvey, Polly, 176, 268
Harvie, Iain, 112
Harz, Chris, 98, 372
Haskett, Chris, 299
Haskins, Kevin, 34, 214, 362
Hasler, Mike, 114
Hassell, Dave, 244
Hassell, Jon, 253
Hatfield, Juliana, 176, 206, 220
Haunted, 14, 162, 275
Havana 3 A.M., 176
Havard, Glyn, 13, 131
Havard, Tim, 39
Hawes, David, 74
Hawkes, Greg, 73
Hawkins, Dick, 164
Hawkins, Jay, 92
Hawkins, Nick, 43
Hawks, 226
Hawkwind, 101, 212
Hay, Ivor, 284, 302
Hayde, Karl, 369
Hayes, Christian 'Bic', 207
Hayes, Dennis, 123
Hayes, James, 311
Hayes, Luke, 294
Haynes, Deb, 149
Hayward, Martin, 261
Haywoode, 283
Haza, Ofra, 358
Head, John, 312
Head, Michael, 259
Head, Sean, 174
Head Records, 273
Headon, Nicky, 83, 211
Headon, Topper, 43, 83, 211
Healy, Gerry, 330
Healy, Martin, 5
Heaphy, Sean, 305
Heart Throbs, 176, 255-256
Heartbreakers, 78, 94, 118, 176-177, 211, 249, 289, 317, 349, 359
Heather, Charlie, 206
Heathfield, Simon, 53
Heathman, Ron, 343
Heatley, Merrill, 61
Heaton, Paul, 35, 185, 200
Heaton, Robb, 247
Heavenly, 151, 164, 177, 211, 299, 302, 305, 347
Heavenly Records, 177, 211, 299, 302
Heavy Metal Kids, 242
Hector, Jesse, 169
Hedges, Mike, 150
Heffington, Don, 192, 211, 225
Heffner, Des, 46
Hegley, John, 33
Heinz, 318
Heinz, Karl, 318
Helen And The Horns, 61, 77, 177
Hell, Richard, 76, 118-119, 135, 176-177, 210, 288, 349, 359, 371
Heller, 257
Hello, 64, 370, 394
Hellyer, Mark, 55
Helmet, 30, 178
Help!, 7, 17, 59, 63, 90, 94, 104, 106, 118, 144, 162, 171-172, 179, 182, 185, 194, 196, 206-207, 217, 225, 235, 241, 247, 249-250, 255, 261, 296, 300, 302, 352, 355, 378, 392-393
Hemmings, Paul, 202, 208
Hemmingway, Dave, 185
Hemmingway, David, 35
Hemphill, Stuart, 7
Hempsall, Alan, 101

Henderson, Andy, 130
Henderson, Davey, 246, 385
Henderson, David, 147
Henderson, Graham, 139
Hendrickse, Carl, 29
Hendrix, Jimi, 41, 71, 74, 82, 123, 170, 210, 218, 322
Hendry, Rob, 242
Hendryx, Nona, 175
Hennin, Martin, 55
Henry, John, 355
Henry, Julian, 73
Henry, Mark, 139, 182, 364
Henry, Richard, 127
Henry, Robert, 276
Henry, Sam, 385
Herbage, Mike, 114
Herd, 394
Herman, 27, 41
Herman, Maureen, 27
Herrera, R.J., 339
Hersh, Kristin, 39, 178, 358
Hersom, Henry, 72
Hersom, Stephen, 58
Hertz, Paul, 107
Hesler, Chris, 175
Hester, Paul, 330
Heston, Charlton, 335
Hetson, Greg, 29, 82, 291
Heukamp, Andrea, 184
Heveron, Bernie, 88
Hewerdine, Boo, 43, 178
Hewes, Jinni, 311
Hewes, Martin, 291
Hewick, Kevin, 327
Hewison, Dolan, 247
Hewitt, Paulo, 382
Hewlett, John, 308
Hewson, Paul, 367, 374
Heyward, Charles, 356
Hiatt, John, 126, 184, 215
Hibbert, Jimmy, 13
Hibtone Records, 283
Hickey, Jack, 366
Hickman, Johnny, 94
Hicks, David, 293
Higgs, Dave, 131, 208
High, 179
High Note, 77
High Society, 355
High Tide, 52
Higher And Higher, 146, 247
Highlights, 226, 243, 314
Highway, John, 267
Higson, Charlie, 179
Higsons, 67, 144, 164, 179-180, 393
Hill, Brendan, 57
Hill, Ian, 143, 356
Hill, Rob, 24
Hillhouse, Christa, 153
Hillman, Chris, 299
Hinchcliffe, Dickon, 21, 361
Hinds, Camille, 382
Hindu Love Gods, 180
Hines, David, 12
Hingley, Tom, 189
Hinkler, Simon, 20, 235
Hinton, Joie, 259
Hipgnosis, 74
Hipsway, 15, 156, 180
Hirons, Lee, 139
Hirsch, Larry, 53
Hirst, Rob, 231
His Name Is Alive, 180
Hiscock, Michael, 146
Hit The Deck, 267
Hitchcock, Robyn, 71, 113, 180, 325
Hoagland, Byron, 206
Hobbs, Mick, 143
Hobson, Andy, 236, 276, 278
Hobson, Bill, 198
Hodgson, Rick, 321
Hodkinson, Anthony, 46
Hoffs, Susanna, 31, 223
Hofrenning, Barbara, 366
Hogan, Anne, 152
Hogan, Noel, 96

Hohki, Kazuko, 154
Hold My Hand, 184
Hold On!, 62, 91, 157, 175, 286, 361
Holden, Brendan, 78
Holder, Gene, 109
Holder, Noddy, 236
Holder, Roy, 111
Hole, 11, 27, 49, 67, 141, 152, 162, 181-182, 247, 250-251, 282, 326, 360, 372
Holiday, Billie, 309
Holland, Annie, 133
Holland, Doug, 101
Holland, Jools, 91, 331
Holland, Julian, 331
Holland, Nicola, 21
Holliday, Rick, 27
Hollies, 274
Hollis, Mark, 345
Holly, Buddy, 100-101, 170, 382
Holly And The Italians, 182, 364
Hollywood Brats, 62, 182, 211
Holmes, Kate, 155
Holmes, Robert, 290
Holmlund, Johan, 129
Holocaust, 137, 221, 362
Holsapple, Peter, 109-110, 126
Holt, John, 320
Holt, Stephen, 189
Holy Men, 15
Holy Modal Rounders, 314
Homegrown Records, 21
Homer, Todd, 19
Homestead Records, 15
Honey Bane, 182
Honeyman-Scott, James, 276
Honeysmugglers, 183
Honky, 227
Hoodoo Gurus, 183-184, 391
Hook, Peter, 116, 196, 248, 293
Hooker, John Lee, 314
Hooker, Lee, 314
Hookham, Paul, 33, 291
Hooper, Phil, 148
Hootie, 184
Hootie And The Blowfish, 184
Hooton, Peter, 144
Hoover, Jamie, 122
Hope, Dave, 367
Hope, Peter, 69
Hopkins, Steve, 244
Hopper, Kev, 335
Horn, Trevor, 279, 394
Hornby, Paul, 267
Horne, Alan, 148, 166, 246, 275, 385
Horner, Ashley, 259
Horner, Daren, 300
Horwitz, Adam, 35
Horwitz, Israel, 34
Hoskins, Bob, 91
Host, 9, 58, 62, 111, 128, 174, 184, 189, 228, 242, 291, 300, 309, 324, 352, 388
Hostnik, Tomaz, 203
Hot, Roland, 211
Hot And Blue, 189
Hot Chocolate, 103, 339
Hot Tuna, 21
Hothouse Flowers, 96, 183-184, 190
Houghton, Chris, 107
Hound Dog, 131
House Of Love, 87, 100, 129, 184, 207, 220, 225, 295
House Of Pain, 46, 178
Housemartins, 33, 35, 166, 185, 283, 310
Houser, Brad, 64
Hovington, Steve, 27
Hovorka, John, 366
Howard, Harry, 101
Howard, Joseph E., 318
Howard, Lou, 290
Howard, Michael, 330
Howard, Pete, 83, 291
Howard, Robert, 382
Howard, Rowland S., 101, 132, 152, 216, 336

Howard And David, 279
Howard Pickup, 11
Howbs, Neil, 12
Howe, Mark, 231
Howell, Myles, 200
Howell, Owen, 87
Howells, Pete, 65
Howes, Andrew, 259
Howlett, Mike, 265
Howlett, Steve, 139
Howlin' Wolf, 119, 187
Howton, Lou, 316
Hubley, Georgia, 19
Hudson, Earl, 29
Hudson, Ian, 162
Hudson, Paul, 29
Huggins, Ben, 158
Huggy Bear, 45, 53, 185, 361
Hughes, Bruce, 94
Hughes, Chris, 9, 106
Hughes, Dave, 106
Hughes, David, 185-186
Hughes, Howard, 243
Hughes, Jimmy, 109
Hughes, Joe, 151
Hughes, Sean, 120
Hula, 185
Hull, Stephen, 286
Human League, 126, 294, 369
Humble Pie, 359
Hunt, Darryl, 269
Hunt, Mike, 64
Hunt, Miles, 388
Hunt, Neville, 231
Hunter, Carl, 144
Hunter, Faye, 206
Hunter, Ian, 372
Hunter, Jon, 196
Hunter, Kevin, 151
Huntrods, Patrick, 192
Hurley, George, 148, 234
Hurley, Pete, 137
Hurrah, 185-186, 394
Hurricane, 13-14, 35, 278
Hurst, John, 308
Hurt, John, 37
Hurt, Mississippi John, 37
Husick, Anne, 30
Hussey, Wayne, 235, 244, 317
Hutchins, Steve, 392
Hutchinson, 12, 380, 393
Hutchinson, Charles, 12
Hutchinson, Tad, 393
Huth, Todd, 278
Hutton, Tim, 326
Huwe, Anja, 392
Hüsker Dü, 48, 65, 110, 143, 175, 186, 242, 263, 267, 274, 292, 338
Hyatt, John, 357
Hyde, Karl, 155
Hyman, Jeffrey, 288
Hynde, Chrissie, 195, 275
Hynde, Sheila, 294
Hypnotics, 135, 186
Hypnotics, Thee, 135, 186

Ian, Scott, 357
Ibald, Mark, 155, 261
Ice Cube, 343
Icicle Works, 37, 187, 208
Icon, 15, 51, 107, 391
Ideals, 91, 98, 119, 278, 312, 321, 367
Idol, Billy, 164, 211
Ielpi, Stephan, 143
Iggy Pop, 16, 30, 110, 117, 137, 187, 189, 204, 243, 318, 349
Ignorance, 136, 156, 179, 210, 247, 352
Ignorant, Steve, 89, 98
Igoe, Kim, 8
Ill, 34-35, 90, 127, 236, 350, 392
Illegal, 78, 96, 212, 272
Illusion, 31, 51, 278
Imaginary Records, 292
Imagination, 116, 127, 246, 365, 381
Imagine, 80, 130

Immaculate Fools, 188-189
Immerwahr, Steve, 86
In Crowd, 230
In The Air, 41, 223
In Tua Nua, 378
Incubus Succubus, 392
Independents, 48, 100, 276, 357
Indigo Girls, 184
Infante, Frank, 52
Ingram, Wally, 360
Inmates, 261, 374
Inner City, 78, 137
Innes, Andrew, 276, 278, 294
Innes, Neil, 314
Innocence, 22, 30, 172, 261, 347, 369
Innocents, 259
Inspiral Carpets, 55, 189, 244, 255, 279, 292
Into Paradise, 5, 154, 189-190
Into The Woods, 69
Intro, 282
INXS, 17, 237
Iona, 214
Iovine, Jimmy, 211
Ireland, Sam, 117
Iron Curtain, 317
Iron Maiden, 74
Irons, Jack, 263
Irvin, James, 157
Irvine, Stephen, 87
Irving, Matt, 331
Irwin, Michael, 161
Island Records, 26, 89-90, 96, 120, 154, 191, 199, 228, 244-245, 269, 288, 304, 320, 333, 362, 365, 367, 381, 394
Its Immaterial, 190
Ives, Burl, 242
Ivins, Michael, 149
Iwagama, Jim, 336

J
Jabbers, 15
Jack Plug And The Sockets, 282
Jackel, James, 199
Jacket Hangs, 53
Jacks, 328
Jackson, Andy, 115, 151
Jackson, Dave, 39, 299
Jackson, Janet, 48
Jackson, Joe, 228
Jackson, Luscious, 35
Jackson, Mahalia, 43
Jackson, Martin, 155, 220
Jackson, Michael, 31, 33, 251
Jackson, Paul, 299
Jackson, Roger, 180
Jackson, Sean, 131
Jacob's Mouse, 46, 190
Jacobs, Nick, 53, 365
Jacques, Jean, 65, 334
Jagolinzer, Andy, 17
Jah Wobble, 48, 118, 147, 190-191, 280, 386-387
Jakeman, Andrew, 333
Jam, 34-35, 49, 57, 76, 131, 148-149, 154, 171, 191, 202, 230, 241-243, 252, 263-265, 308, 315, 327, 335, 350, 370, 382, 384, 388
Jam & Spoon, 34-35, 49, 57, 76, 131, 148-149, 154, 171, 191, 202, 229-230, 241-243, 252, 263-265, 308, 315, 327, 335, 350, 370, 382, 384, 388
James, 129, 138, 189, 286
James, Alex, 57
James, Bennett, 318
James, Brian, 11, 34, 65, 71, 78, 106, 110, 212, 241
James, David, 14
James, Kieron, 134
James, Matt, 162, 329
James, Paul, 300
James, Peter, 202
James, Philip, 286
James, Tony, 7, 164, 211, 311, 316, 318, 331
James, Valerie A., 73
James, Wendy, 207, 364

Jameson, Robyn, 150
Jamiroquai, 127
JAMMS, 127, 197
Jamrozy, Paul, 352
Jan And Dean, 231
Jane Aire And The Belvederes, 13, 131, 138, 161, 263
Jane's Addiction, 191, 210, 278
Janikel, Chas, 14
Janney, Eli, 63
Janowitz, Bill, 65
Jansen, Steve, 192, 279
Janssen, Volker, 328
Japan, 192
Jaworski, Al, 193
Jay, David, 34, 152, 214
Jay, Michael, 157
Jayhawks, 192, 225, 359
Jaymes, David, 208
Jazz Butcher, 53, 113, 192, 214, 326, 340, 362
Jazzie B, 35
Jefferson, 12-13, 85, 106, 265
Jefferson Airhead, 13
Jefferson Airplane, 12-13, 106, 265
Jeffes, Simon, 381
Jelbert, Stephen, 143
Jelly Beans, 82
Jellybean, 27
Jellyfish, 192-193, 314
Jellyfish Kiss, 314
Jenkins, Alan, 112
Jenner, Peter, 62
Jennifer, Darryl, 29
Jennings, Craig, 30
Jennings, John, 301
Jerwood, Colin, 89
Jesus And Mary Chain, 67, 100, 118, 129, 176, 193, 223, 225, 244, 266, 276, 294, 300, 314, 349, 368
Jesus Jones, 20, 43, 134, 152, 193, 246, 312
Jesus Lizard, 46, 63, 76, 113, 194, 289, 307
Jet, 71, 203, 238, 241, 284, 326, 334
Jethro Tull, 103, 265
Jets, 290
Jett, Joan, 45, 76, 301
Jewel, Little Johnny, 189, 349
Jewels, 149, 204
Jigsaw, 282
Jilted John, 194
Jimmy The Hoover, 194
Jive Records, 89
Jo Jo And The Real People, 290
JoBoxers, 168
Jobson, Richard, 20, 128, 194, 318
Jody And The Creams, 112
Johannson, David, 290
Johansen, David, 194-195, 249, 344
Johansson, Glenn, 130
John, Elton, 203, 296
John, Graham, 83
John, Lee, 314
John, Robert, 265
John's Children, 284, 308
Johnasen, Nils, 19
Johnny And The Self Abusers, 102
Johnny Backbeat, 145
Johnny Moped, 30, 71, 106, 195
Johnny Moped And The 5 Arrogant Superstars, 195
Johnny Moped's Assault And Buggery, 195
Johns, Glyn, 39, 83, 391
Johns, Teddy, 384
Johnson, Andy, 27
Johnson, Arthur, 88
Johnson, Billy, 53
Johnson, Bruce, 127
Johnson, Calvin, 37
Johnson, Dean, 271
Johnson, Denise, 276
Johnson, Dennis, 126
Johnson, Donald, 5, 127
Johnson, Gazza, 79
Johnson, Holly, 45, 111, 208, 394

Johnson, Jo, 53
Johnson, Mark, 90, 161, 196, 223
Johnson, Martha, 222
Johnson, Matt, 134, 152, 195, 354
Johnson, Michael, 195
Johnson, Mike, 119
Johnson, Robert, 172
Johnson, Roy, 5, 7, 13, 210, 333
Johnson, Terry, 161
Johnson, Tom, 195
Johnson, Tommy, 172
Johnson, Vince, 105
Johnson, Wilko, 128, 161, 208, 290
Johnston, Gary, 359
Johnston, Ian, 96
Johnston, James, 161
Johnston, Tom, 195, 354
Johnstone, James, 267
Jones, Alison, 33
Jones, Barry, 309
Jones, Brian, 170, 280
Jones, Chris, 112, 227
Jones, David, 279
Jones, Dean, 137
Jones, George, 92
Jones, Grace, 276, 394
Jones, Howard, 146, 279
Jones, James, 186, 211, 384
Jones, Jeff, 34
Jones, John, 158, 236
Jones, John Paul, 158, 236
Jones, Kendall, 148
Jones, Lee, 149, 257
Jones, Marc, 170
Jones, Marti, 122
Jones, Mick, 43, 66, 83, 84, 211, 334, 376
Jones, O.P., 192
Jones, Paul, 112, 158, 236, 359
Jones, Phil, 12, 106, 137
Jones, Pim, 180
Jones, Quincy, 248
Jones, Ray, 186
Jones, Rickie Lee, 257
Jones, Rob, 388
Jones, Ron, 149
Jones, Russell, 231
Jones, Shay, 112
Jones, Simon, 372
Jones, Steve, 26, 171, 189, 279, 311, 352, 359
Jones, Tom, 122, 257
Jonsson, Tommy, 129
Joplin, Janis, 225, 326
Jordanaires, 19
Jormin, Rikard, 129
Josef K, 147-148, 173, 195-196, 275
Joseph, John, 101
Joshua, 367
Jourard, Jeff, 241
Jourgensen, Alain, 234
Jourgenson, Al, 293
Joy Division, 101, 138, 174, 196, 199, 237, 247-248, 265, 286, 293, 343, 350, 361, 378
Joyce, Chris, 127, 267
Joyce, Mike, 11, 68, 240, 282, 322, 338
Joyce, Miranda, 37
Jubilee, 9, 78, 176, 311, 317, 364
Judd, Phil, 330
Juhos, Fred, 161
Julian, Ivan, 177
Jumbo, 390
June Brides, 196, 371
Jungle Book, The, 39
Jungle Brothers, 148
Jungr And Parker, 63
Junkyard, 46, 171
Jupiter, Donnie, 366
Jupp, Mickey, 214, 344
Jury, 119
Justified Ancients Of Mu Mu, 127, 196, 201, 214, 360

K

Kaballero, Karlos, 117

Kabaret Noir Records, 24
Kabuki, 22
Kahne, David, 148
Kaiser, Henry, 169, 244
Kakoulli, Harry, 331
Kaleidoscope, 79, 204, 244, 317, 366
Kaliphz, 131
Kalwa, Eddie, 288
Kamera Records, 22, 107
Kamura, Atsuko, 154
Kane, Arthur, 249, 359
Kane, Arthur Harold, 249
Kane, Eden, 120
Kapelle, Schwarze, 261
Kaplan, Ira, 19
Karn, Mick, 34, 106, 192, 243
Kat, 27, 182
Kato, National 'Nash', 369
Katrina And The Waves, 31, 197-198, 375
Katsis, Dan, 223
Kaufman, Matthew, 41
Kaukonen, Jorma, 263
Kavanagh, Chris, 43
Kay, Matthew, 307
Kaye, Hereward, 296
Kaye, Joey, 30
Kaye, Lenny, 178, 322, 326
Kean, Martin, 79, 332
Kearey, Ian, 41, 53, 365
Keating, Ashley, 154
Keay, Jane, 89
Keds, Mark, 309-310
Keegan, David, 261, 315, 371
Keegan, Guy, 286
Keeler, Christine, 176
Keen, Gordon, 58, 71, 135
Keen, Speedy, 177
Keen Records, 316
Keigher, Charley, 200
Kelley, Larry, 76
Kellie, Mike, 256
Kelly, Charles, 371
Kelly, Derek, 169
Kelly, Eugene, 58, 71, 135, 261, 371
Kelly, Jerry, 384
Kelly, Malcolm, 166
Kelly, Martin, 228
Kelly, Mike, 24
Kelly, Sean, 237
Keltner, Jim, 94, 215
Kember, Peter, 326
Kempner, Scott, 113
Kendrick, David, 116
Kennedy, J.F., 235
Kennedy, John, 73
Kennedy, Nigel, 11
Kennedy, Paul, 304
Kenny, Claire, 88
Kenny, Scott, 329
Kensit, Patsy, 43
Kent, Nick, 106, 276
Keogh, Pete, 296
Kepburn, Katharine, 364
Kerouac, Jack, 246
Kerr, Andy, 329
Kerr, Gordon, 61
Kerr, Jeremy, 5
Kerr, Jim, 276
Kerr, Stuart, 156, 214
Kershaw, Andy, 257
Kershaw, Nik, 308
Kesteven, Ben, 13
Kesteven, Sam, 13
Key, Tara, 19
Key, Ted, 185
Keyser, Alex, 130
Khambatta, Jim, 296
Khan, Chaka, 283
Khan, George, 197
Kibby, Walter, 148
Kick, Johnny, 218
Kick, Richard, 64
Kidd, Jerry, 290
Kidron, Adam, 307
Kihn, Greg, 41

Kilbey, Steve, 82, 167, 197
Kilburn, Duncan, 279
Kilburn And The High Roads, 128, 197-198, 251
Killdozer, 117, 198, 307
Killers, 88, 249, 251
Killing Joke, 64, 162, 178, 198-199, 225, 257, 279, 338
Kimball, James, 113
Kimble, Paul, 170
Kin, Joe, 55
Kinchla, Chan, 57
Kindale, Tyson, 391
King, 199
King, B.B., 217
King, Ben E., 318
King, Bobby, 305
King, Eddie, 131, 369
King, Howard, Jnr, 175
King, Jon, 161
King, Jonathan, 41, 71
King, Louis, 35
King, Nick, 76, 291
King, Paul, 199, 305
King, Pete, 151-152
King, Phil, 217
King, Philip, 310
King, Stu Boy, 117
King, Tony, 199
King Kurt, 172
King Of The Slums, 200
King Records, 292, 340
Kingmaker, 200, 286
Kings X, 158
Kingsmill, Mark, 183
Kingston, Bob, 236, 352
Kinks, 57, 126, 141, 169, 191, 218, 236, 276, 292, 296, 334, 370, 393
Kinman, Chip, 118, 289
Kinman, Tony, 118, 289
Kippington Lodge, 214
Kirby, Phil, 46, 393
Kirk, Don, 150
Kirk, James, 256
Kirk, Richard H., 68-69
Kirkland, Mike, 279
Kirkwood, Cris, 226
Kirkwood, Curt, 226
Kiss, 12, 27, 30, 65, 104-105, 110, 112-113, 128, 139, 146, 164, 194, 220, 228, 245, 248, 257, 269, 291, 302, 312, 314, 317, 336, 354, 384
Kiss Of Life, 164
Kitchens Of Distinction, 200, 255
Kitson, Dave, 250
Kizys, Algis, 63
Klark Kent, 201, 272
Klebe, Gary, 315
Klein, Jon, 317
Kleingers, Dan, 21
Klepacz, Julian, 368
Klett, Peter, 70
KLF, 45, 73, 127, 137, 153, 197, 201-202, 214, 257, 360
Knack, 202, 273
Knight, Dave, 109
Knight, Gladys, And The Pips, 308
Knight, Kelvin, 113
Knight, Phillip, 204
Knight, Steve, 109
Knopfler, Mark, 339
Knowles, Chris, 380
Knox, Nick, 94
Koch, Lydia, 216
Kolderie, Paul Q., 49
Kolkowski, Alex, 30
Kongos, John, 136, 174
Kooper, Al, 171, 366
Kopelle, Rote, 162
Koppes, Peter, 82
Korab, Krzysztof, 236
Korniloff, Kathy, 366
Korus, Kate, 236, 320
Kottke, Leo, 45
Kowalcyzk, Ed, 210
Krackhouse, 314
Kraftwerk, 313

Kral, Ivan, 189, 322, 377
Kramer, Amanda, 169
Kramer, Mark, 27, 59, 314, 377
Kramer, Wayne, 359-360
Kraus, Scott, 357
Krause, Dagmar, 51
Kravitz, Lenny, 258
Kreator, 46
Krome, Kari, 301
KRS-1, 284
Krukowski, Damon, 158
Krummenacher, Victor, 70
Krusen, Dave, 263
Kubinski, Dan, 117
Kubrick, Stanley, 9
Kuehn, Greg, 365
Kuepper, Ed, 203, 302
Kupferberg, Tuli, 314
Kurious, 143
Kursaal Flyers, 131, 215, 242
Kurstow, Danny, 296
Kusworth, Dave, 336
Kyle, Kyle, 126
Kyser, Guy, 355

L

L7, 27, 182, 202, 228, 378
La's, 19, 37, 39, 74, 166, 187, 202-203, 208, 290, 377, 386
Lacey, John, 79
Lack, Steve, 371
Ladd, Rob, 206
Ladly, Martha, 223
Laff, Mark, 164, 167
Laibach, 203, 244
Lally, Joe, 157
Lalonde, Larry, 278
Lamacq, Steve, 220, 227
Lambdin, John, 80
Lambert, Graham, 189
Lambert, Moira, 141, 302
Lambert, Tony, 305
Lambrettas, 203
Lambyekski, Graham, 59
Land, Erp, 259
Land Speed Record, 186
Landray, Jeanette, 104, 166
Landscape, 111, 138, 246
Lanegan, Mark, 307, 377
Laney, Roz, 134
Lang, Damian, 180
lang, k.d., 359
Langan, Gary, 91
Lange, Mutt, 242
Langer, Clive, 64, 79, 100, 111, 151, 225, 240
Langford, John, 357
Langford, Jon, 21, 136, 227
Langham, Phil, 8
Langley, Gerard, 53
Langlois, Paul, 364
Langston, Leslie, 39, 359
Lanier, Allen, 322
Lanois, Daniel, 367
Lansford, Jay, 12
Larcombe, Dave, 43
Larkin, Joan, 301
Larkins, Tom, 165, 245
Last, James, 350
Last Exit, 313
Laswell, Bill, 87, 90, 169
Lauder, Andrew, 229, 361
Laugh, 199, 203-204, 302, 304, 311, 314, 339
Laughing Clowns, 203-204, 302
Laurie Driver, 11
Lavelle, Caroline, 128
Lavery, Gary, 292
Lavilla, Maz, 129
Lavis, Gilson, 331
Lawler, Fergal, 96
Lawrence, Bob, 327
Lawrence, Chris, 382
Lawrence, June, 65
Lawrence, Roy, 135
Lawrence, Sherree, 112
Lawrie, Stephen, 349

Laws, Keith, 195, 354
Lawson, Neil, 87
Lay, Sam, 187
Layhe, Chris, 187
Lazy Records, 278
Le Noble, Martyn, 191
Lea, Jim, 236
Lea, Tim, 7
Leach, Alan, 313
Leach, Ben, 144
Leadbelly, 37, 307
Leary, Denis, 299
Leary, Paul, 67
Leather Nun, 204
Leavell, Chuck, 57
Leckie, John, 74, 208, 274, 286
Led Zeppelin, 34, 59, 103, 117, 201, 210, 222, 236, 294, 300, 321, 336
Lee, Brian, 290
Lee, C.P., 13-14
Lee, D.C., 335, 382, 384
Lee, Erick Erick, 94
Lee, Graham, 365
Lee, Hamilton, 157
Lee, Jack, 35
Lee, Jeanette, 96, 282
Lee, Jerry, 295
Lee, John, 314
Lee, Michael, 149
Lee, Stan, 117
Leer, Thomas, 279
Leeway, Joe, 357
Leftfield, 105, 282
Legendary Pink Dots, 204
Legends, 19, 68-69, 148, 150, 183, 206, 223, 292, 347
Leggett, Dean, 58
Lehmann, Edie, 283
Lehrer, Lucky, 82
Leigh, Dennis, 154
Leigh, Mike, 141, 282
Leila And The Snakes, 263
Lemmon, Claire, 316
Lemon Kittens, 109
Lemonheads, 49, 135, 153, 157, 176, 204-206
Lendor, Leroy, 43
Lennard, John, 328, 354
Lennon, John, 12, 26, 80, 92, 100, 134, 194, 206, 255, 272, 349
Lennon, Julian, 55, 103
Lennox, Annie, 128
Leon, 27, 247, 339
Leon, Craig, 247, 339
Leon, Michelle, 27
Lepere, Louis, 78
Lerner, Scott, 17
Let Loose, 216
Let's Active, 7, 109, 122, 206
Letts, David, 106
Letts, Don, 43, 84
Level 42, 346
Levellers, 206-207, 259, 284, 305
Leven, Jackie, 123
Levene, Keith, 30, 83, 280
Levesque, James, 12
Leviathan, 51
Levitation, 39, 72, 87, 184, 207
Levy, Steve, 144
Lewie, Jona, 214, 333, 344
Lewis, Andrea, 109
Lewis, Graham, 152, 165, 385
Lewis, Hallam, 290
Lewis, Huey, 92, 305
Lewis, Jerry, 295
Lewis, Jerry Lee, 295
Lewis, Lee, 295
Lewis, Lew, 65, 131, 207-208, 333
Lewis, Nigel, 230
Lewis, Simon, 67
Leyland, Biddy, 110
Leyton, John, 231
Leyton Buzzards, 208
Libertine, Eve, 98
Libertines, 21
Liberty Horses, 179
Liberty Records, 84

Licht, David, 27, 59
Life And Times, 15
Lifetime, 114, 126, 141, 346, 389
Lightning Seeds, 45, 59, 64, 74, 155, 187, 194, 208-209
Lilac Time, 208, 210
Liles, Brent, 13, 325
Lillywhite, Adrian, 199, 228
Lillywhite, Steve, 217, 223, 228, 241, 265, 271, 279, 317, 346, 357, 367
Lincoln, Abraham, 180
Lindsay, Ian, 103
Lindsay, Steve, 111-112
Lindt, Virna, 385
Linehan, Niall, 154
Linehan, Tony, 233
Link Records, 291
Linna, Miriam, 94
Linnell, John, 355
Lion, 332, 339, 355, 390
Liquid Jesus, 210
Lisa Lisa, 117, 380
Lisher, Greg, 70
Lishrout, Jay, 29
Lister, Sim, 73
Lithman, Phil, 78
Litt, Scott, 35
Little Angels, 191
Little Buddy, 100
Little Me, 112
Little Richard, 148
Little Village, 94, 215
Littlewhite, Steve, 154
Littlewood, Joan, 57
Live, 210
Live Aid, 61, 73, 92, 276, 335, 367, 389
Liverpool Scene, 12, 127, 196
Living Colour, 29, 148, 278
Lizard, John-Bill, 24
Lizards, 169
Llewellyn, Charles, 223
Llewelyn, Charlie, 362
Lloyd, Andy, 250
Lloyd, Mick, 146
Lloyd, Richard, 210, 349
Lloyd, Robert, 210, 250
Lloyd, William, 141
Locomotive, 372
Locust, 67
Loft, 72, 78, 100, 210-211, 225, 371
Loizides, Nicholas, 266
Lolita, 20, 34, 161, 172, 290, 358
Lombardo, Dave, 126
Lombardo, Tony, 114
Lomond, Simon, 250
London, John, 190
London, Julie, 385
London, Richard, 98
London, Tim, 111
London Calling!, 83-84
London Records, 29, 55, 117, 166, 179, 222, 226, 291, 376, 384-385
London SS, 62, 83, 106, 182, 211
London Town, 61, 193, 230, 274, 308, 340
Lone Justice, 211, 225
Lonely, Johnny, 210
Long, Bonnie, 292
Long, Dave, 189
Long, Gary, 352
Long, Janice, 53, 78, 107, 149, 211, 256
Long Ryders, 126, 147, 171, 211-212, 390
Looking Glass, 7, 41, 317
Loop, 169, 212, 217, 294, 349
Lora Logic, 58, 135, 212, 391
Lord Buckley, 11
Lordan, Tony, 114
Lords Lords Of The New Church, 33-34, 110, 212
Lori And The Chameleons, 45, 127, 213-214, 347
Lorimar, Roddy, 378
Lorinczi, Seth, 83
Lorson, Mary, 218

Los Lobos, 49, 170
Lotus Eaters, 214, 384
Louie, Louie, 174, 234, 294-295
Louis & Clark, 35, 67, 78, 83, 87, 102, 137, 143, 182, 226, 244, 286, 294, 296, 317, 320, 329, 339, 356, 358, 381, 388
Louris, Gary, 192, 225
Louvin, Ira, 192
Love, Courtney, 27, 141, 182, 251-252
Love, Gerard, 347
Love Affair, 21, 389
Love Again, 182
Love And Money, 156, 213-214
Love And Rockets, 21, 34, 214, 362
Love Life, 53
Love Parade, The, 369
Loveday, Bob, 61
Lovell, Steve, 128
Lover Speaks, The, 152
Loverboy, 308
Lovering, Dave, 43
Lovich, Lene, 147, 214, 333, 344
Lovin' Spoonful, 249
Lovre, Eric, 116
Low, Mike, 80
Lowe, Nick, 92, 106, 122, 214-215, 229, 276, 286, 333, 390, 393
Lowery, David, 69-70, 94
Lu Win, Annabella, 62, 226
Lucas, 168, 197-198, 215, 251, 336
Lucas, Dick, 215, 336
Lucas, Keith, 197-198, 251
Lucas, Richard, 336
Luciano, 27
Lucking, Phil, 299
Luckman, Dominic, 72
Ludus, 115, 215-216
Lugosi, Bela, 34, 295
Lukin, Matt, 171, 227, 242
Lulu, 149-150
Lunachicks, 216
Lunch, Lydia, 46, 132, 152, 175, 216, 326, 343, 349, 391
Lunchbuddies, 21
Lundon, Eddie, 79
Lure, Walter, 176, 359
Lurkers, 37, 62, 216, 230
Luscious Jackson, 35
Lush, 62, 77, 86, 118, 129, 153, 217, 223, 239, 245, 255, 321
Lux, 94, 146
Lycett, Kevin, 227
Lydon, John, 64, 169, 280, 311
Lyman, Arthur, 332
Lymon, Frankie, 62
Lynch, Brendan, 384
Lynch, Mick, 335
Lynch, Stan, 289
Lynn, Loretta, 361
Lynott, Phil. 171, 359
Lynyrd Skynyrd, 94
Lyons, Toby, 88

M

M.A.R.S., 20, 153, 283
M Records, 5, 30, 48, 57, 103, 106, 110, 112, 117, 123, 125, 167, 176, 180, 226-227, 263, 311, 330-331, 350, 366
Mac, Steve, 370
Macabre, 11, 240, 374
Macc Lads, 217
MacColl, Ewan, 217
MacColl, Kirsty, 13, 62, 131, 195, 208, 217, 271, 324, 388
MacDonald, Alsy, 365
MacDonald, Eddie, 13
MacDonald, Francis, 58, 347
MacDonald, Pat, 360
MacGowan, Shane, 218, 228, 269, 381
MacGuire, Steve, 73
Machine, Tony, 344
Mack, Steve, 117, 329, 352
Mackay, Calumn, 305
Mackay, Nicol, 300
MacKay, Steve, 187

MacKay, Steven, 187
MacKaye, Ian, 156
MacKenzie, Billy, 21
Mackenzie, Neil, 20
Mackenzies, 218
Mackie, John, 305
MacKillop, Gavin, 361
Mackintosh, C.J., 222
Mackowiak, Sean 'Grasshopper', 229
Maclean, Bryan, 211
MacNicol, Alex, 171
MacPherson, Jim, 64
Mad Dog, 168
Mad Professor, 127, 301
Madder Rose, 218
Madeley, Gary, 101
Madell, Josh, 20
Madness, 11, 57, 64, 90, 106, 111, 114,
123, 151, 158, 179, 203, 212, 218-220,
231, 241, 251, 259, 269, 294, 302,
310, 328, 333, 335, 362, 376
Madonna, 29, 48, 51, 71, 82, 109, 326,
349, 357
Mae, Sadie, 175
Mag, Tim, 325
Magazine, 220
Magicians, 173
Maginnis, Tom, 65
Magnet Records, 123, 229
Magnum, 110, 184, 212, 258
Magnum, Jeff, 110
Magnuson, Ann, 59, 314
Maher, Fred, 87, 178, 307
Maher, George, 144
Maher, John, 68, 134, 244, 322
Maher, Johnny, 240
Maher, Liam, 151
Mahon, John, 310
Mahoney, Damien, 186
Mahoney, Dave, 244
Maimone, Tony, 242, 355
Main, Graham, 147
Main Source, 37, 392
Mair, Alan, 256
Majors, 29, 106, 223
Maker, James, 323
Malarky, John, 102
Malkmus, Steve, 261
Mallinder, Stephen, 68-69
Mamas And The Papas, 31, 259
Mancini, Hilken, 157
Mandelson, Ben, 220
Manic Street Preachers, 127, 137, 177,
215, 220, 313, 355
Manilow, Barry, 327
Manitoba, Dick, 117
Mankey, Earle, 274
Mankey, Jim, 89
Mann, Aimee, 221
Mann, Carl, 100
Mann, Herbie, 100
Mann, Jeff, 368
Manning, Chris, 193
Manning, Mark, 103
Manning, Roger, 193
Manns, Dominic, 78
Manor, Wayne, 182
Mansell, Clint, 273, 388
Mansfield, Tony, 248
Manson, Charles, 204, 280, 326
Manson, Shirley, 169
Manton, Robert, 282
Manyika, Zeke, 61, 88, 256, 382
Manzanera, Phil, 330, 356
Manzarek, Ray, 130, 322, 391
Marauders, 174
Marbles, 361
Marc And The Mambas, 311
Marc Riley And The Creepers, 296
March, Rob, 167
March Violets, 222
Marchini, John, 354
Marcum, Mark, 288
Marcus, Greil, 201
Mardi Gras, 280
Mardin, Arif, 307
Margo, 94

Margolis, Kenny, 234
Mariano, Mike, 358
Marietta, 172
Marine Girls, 136, 222, 350, 394
Marion, 123, 222, 272, 391
Marionette, 196
Markie, Biz, 35
Markosek, Ervin, 203
Marley, Bob, 093
Marley, Ziggy, 361
Marr, Johnny, 134, 218, 249, 255, 322-
323, 338, 346, 354
Marriott, Steve, 359, 382
MARRS, 222
Mars, 45, 82, 183-184, 247, 292, 301,
332, 377
Mars, Chris, 45, 292
Mars Bonfire, 301
Marsalis, Wynton, 184
Marsden, Gerry, 144
Marsden, Granville, 46
Marsh, Carl, 315
Marsh, Jon, 39
Marsh, Nick, 149
Marsh, Paul, 233
Marsh, Richard, 273
Marsh, Sam, 190
Marshall, Nick, 55
Marshall, Phillip, 88
Marshall, Steve, 13
Martha And The Muffins, 222-223
Martin, Ann, 111
Martin, Anne, 64
Martin, Bardi, 70
Martin, Barrett, 307
Martin, Darren, 308
Martin, Dave, 280
Martin, Frank, 377
Martin, George, 362
Martin, Jim, 118, 139, 141
Martin, Kevin, 70
Martin, Mike, 141
Martin, Moon, 234
Martin, Paul, 291
Martin, Wes, 64
Marx, Gary, 164-165, 317
Mascis, J., 15, 65, 76, 119, 135, 251
Mason, John, 329
Mason, Nick, 106
Mason, Pete, 200
Mason, Richard, 289
Mason, Steve, 162, 329
Massacre, 137
Masters, Barrie, 131
Masters, Ian, 259
Masuak, Chris, 284
Matador, 132
Matching Mole, 265, 390
Material Issue, 332
Matheson, Andrew, 182
Matlock, Glen, 111, 189, 295-296, 311
Mattacks, Dave, 136
Matthew, Mark, 113
Matthews, Dave, Band, 223
Matthews, Donna, 133, 313
Matthews, Eric, 72
Matthews, John, 179
Matthews, Kevin, 311
Matthews, Simon, 193
Mattock, Jon, 64, 329
Matumbi, 230
Maureen And The Meat Packers, 180
Maurer, John, 325
Mavericks, 314
Maximum Joy, 223
May, Caro, 392
May, Phil, 186
Mayer, Mauritia, 311
Mayfield, Curtis, 148, 335
Mayhem, 15, 328, 364
Mayhem, Bobby Rae, 328
Mayhew, Parris Mitchell, 102
Mayo, John, 93
Mayorga, Louiche, 339
Maze, 46, 352
Mazur, George, 168
MC Tunes, 131

MC5, 15, 65, 115-116, 131, 186, 212,
241, 249, 263, 284, 300, 322, 368-369,
392
MCA Records, 14, 48, 169, 343, 364
McAffer, Guy, 29
McAllister, Laurie, 301
McAlmont, 223, 338
McAlmone, David, 223
McAloon, Martin, 275
McAloon, Paddy, 275
McAvaney, Jim, 88
McCaffrey, Chris, 259
McCallum, Helen, 77
McCallum, James, 77
McCarrick, Martin, 39
McCarroll, Tony, 255
McCarthy, 212, 223, 225, 229, 252-
253, 332, 360
McCarthy, Allan, 229
McCarthy, Douglas, 252
McCarthy, Stephen, 212
McCartney, Paul, 92, 203, 206
McCaughey, Scott, 117, 393
McCauley, Al, 361
McClanahan, Pete, 378
McClure, Andy, 320
McCluskey, David, 55
McCluskey, Ken, 55
McCluskey Brothers, 55
McClymont, David, 256
McComb, David, 365
McComb, Robert, 365
McCombs, Douglas, 134
McCookerybook, Helen, 77
McCormack, Gary, 195
McCormick, Gary, 136
McCowall, Dean, 86
McCready, Mike, 263, 350
McCreeth, Andy, 53
McCulloch, Ian, 7, 87, 90, 129-131,
144, 347
McCulloch, Jim, 58, 327
McDaid, Tony, 15
McDonagh, Chris, 109
McDonald, Andy, 115, 166
McDonald, Dave, 115
McDonald, Jeff, 291
McDowell, Gary, 237
McDowell, Rose, 335
McElhone, Johnny, 15
McElhone, Jon, 180
McEntee, Mark, 120
McFadyen, Stewart, 84
McGeachin, Stuart, 179
McGee, Alan, 43, 59, 79, 100, 184,
193, 211, 224-225, 255, 273, 294
McGee, Brian, 279
McGeechan, 156, 214
McGeechan, Paul, 156, 214
McGeoch, John, 20, 207
McGeogh, John, 104, 220, 243, 282,
317, 376
McGinley, Raymond, 347
McGinty, Rolo, 192, 388
McGough, Roger, 83
McGovern, Tim, 241
McGowan, Dave, 359
McGrann, Mike, 76
McGuigan, Matthews, 86
McGuigan, Paul 'Guigs', 255
McGuigan, Tony, 286
McGuinn, Roger, 92, 221
McGuinness, Paul, 367
McGurk, Thomas, 329
McIntire, Dave, 88
McIntosh, David, 123
McIntosh, Robbie, 276
McIntyre, Douglas, 214
McKahey, Rob, 335
McKay, John, 212
McKean, Ian, 30
McKechnie, Alex, 12
McKechnie, Joseph, 39
McKee, Frances, 371
McKee, Keith, 366
McKee, Maria, 184, 192, 211, 225
McKenzie, Ali, 102

McKenzie, Derek, 312
McKenzie, Derrick, 71
McKenzie, Keith, 312
McKeown, Jennie, 37
McKillop, Kevin, 239
McLad, Muttley, 217
McLaren, Malcolm, 9, 51, 177, 190,
194, 225-226, 249, 276, 311, 316, 352
McLaughlin, Ciaran, 352
McLean, Don, 49
McLeay, Terry, 311
McLennan, G.W., 167
McLennan, Grant, 82, 166-167, 197
McLeod, Ian, 284
McLusky, Sean, 167
McManus, Declan, 91
McManus, Louis, 67
McManus, Ross, 91
McMaster, Andy, 242
McMillan, Andrew, 233
McMordie, Ali, 332
McMullan, Pat, 93
McMurray, Rick, 20
McNabb, Ian, 187
McNair, Callum, 20
McNally, John, 118
McNally, Rand, 118
McNeilly, Mac, 194
McNeish, Peter, 68, 313
McPake, Angus, 162
McPherson, Graham, 64, 218
McPherson, Suggs, 64, 218
McQueen, Steve, 275
McRobbie, Stephen, 261
McTell, Ralph, 19, 123
McVann, Andy, 144
McVeigh, Ray, 279
McVey, Tim, 143
Meany, Dick, 149
Meat Puppets, 48, 226
Medicine Head, 265
Mega City Four, 115, 226-227, 233,
291, 309
Mekons, 13, 21, 131, 136, 227, 282,
357-358
Melanie, 278, 316
Mellencamp, John, 49, 184
Mellencamp, John Cougar, 49, 184
Mellor, Linda, 30
Mellotron, 318, 322, 340
Melody Dog, 261
Melody Maker, 17, 30, 111, 157, 174,
182, 206, 218, 228-229, 307, 313, 321,
332, 356
Melton, Jim, 325
Melvin, Rod, 198
Melvins, 171, 227-228
Members, 228
Members, Dave, 220, 282
Membranes, 7, 125, 228
Men They Couldn't Hang, 207, 228
Men Without Hats, 229
Menor, John, 126
Mental As Anything, 229
Mercado, Scott, 70
Mercury Records, 14, 69, 156, 180,
194, 246, 359
Mercury Rev, 149, 229-230
Merkl, Tom, 175
Merry Babes, 304
Mertens, Michael, 279
Merton Parkas, 203, 230, 335
Mesaros, Mike, 322
Metallica, 102, 118-119, 141, 158, 199,
378
Metcalfe, Andy, 180, 325, 331
Metcalfe, Keith, 290
Metcalfe, Martin, 169
Meteors, 172, 230-231
Mew, Dave, 72
Meyer, Skip, 91
Miall, Terry Lee, 9
Miaow, 37, 73
Michaelson, Nick, 310
Michel, 98, 257
Michel, Jean, 257
Mickey And The Milkshakes, 233

Microdisney, 17, 145, 231-232
Middle Of The Road, 276, 368
Midgett, Tim, 316
Midnight Oil, 231, 233
Midnight Runners, 179, 230, 308, 354
Migdol, Brian, 48
Mighty, Ray, 13
Mighty Baby, 78
Mighty Lemon Drops, 233, 384, 388
Mighty Mighty, 13, 78, 92, 171, 199, 233-234, 279, 355, 384, 388
Mike And The Mechanics, 174
Miles, Buddy, 179
Miles, Kev, 329
Miles, Kevin, 162
Miles-Kingston, June, 236
Milestone Records, 100
Milkshakes, 113, 233-234, 279
Millar, Larry, 368
Millar, Robin, 48
Millenium, 354
Miller, Andy, 123
Miller, Ben, 115
Miller, Besti, 279
Miller, Brian, 71
Miller, Chris, 71, 106, 211
Miller, Daniel, 114, 138, 185, 244
Miller, David, 147
Miller, Frankie, 242
Miller, John, 151
Miller, Larry, 115
Miller, Robert, 167
Miller, Roger, 236
Miller, Scott, 12, 161
Miller, Thomas, 349, 371
Milligan, Spike, 228
Millington, Mary, 162
Million, Bill, 145
Mills, Alan, 384
Mills, Kevin, 150
Mills, Mike, 12, 180, 283
Mills, Rodney, 172
Milton, Doc, 14
Milton, Tara, 148
Milton, Ted, 57
Mimms, Howie, 187
Mindfunk, 251
Ministry, 87, 147, 162, 178, 199, 234, 293-294, 352, 380
Mink Deville, 234
Minkoff, Myrna, 72
Minks, Jasmine, 100, 225
Minnery, John, 156
Minogue, Dannii, 321
Minor Threat, 156-157, 251
Mint Juleps, 333
Minty Fresh Records, 371
Minutemen, 21, 48, 148, 234-235, 316
Minx, Rachel, 301
Miracles, 53, 192
Miro, 253
Miro, Jennifer, 253
Misfits, 167, 206, 235, 376
Mission, 14, 17, 20, 87, 147, 162, 165, 235-236, 244, 291, 294, 316-317
Mission Of Burma, 316
Misunderstood, 92, 116, 312
Mitchell, Alex, 105
Mitchell, Bruce, 13, 127
Mitchell, James, 149
Mitchell, Joni, 253, 365
Mittler, Martin, 203
Mizan, Stuart, 114
Mnemonic, Johnny, 299
Mo-Dettes, 236, 320, 352
Moby, 244, 257, 265
Moby Grape, 265
Mock Turtles, 57, 236-237
Models, 35, 154, 237
Modern English, 152, 237
Modern Lovers, 41, 175, 237-238, 295, 346
Modern Romance, 208
Modernaires, 384
Moeller, Terri, 377
Moen, John, 116
Mogan, Tony, 377

Moginie, Jim, 231
Mohan, John, 146
Moholo, Louis, 296
Mohr, Todd Park, 45
Mole, Adam, 273, 388
Moles, 72
Molo, John, 210
Mombasa, Reg, 229
Momtchiloff, Peter, 177, 347
Momus, 225, 238
Monasterio, Juan, 63
Monk, Dave, 208
Monk, Thelonious, 65
Monkees, 59, 117, 144, 166, 261, 295, 390
Monkham, Mandy, 370
Monks, 46, 70
Monochrome Set, 8, 238, 246
Monster Magnet, 263
Montana, Tony, 9
Montejo, Rob, 321
Montejo, Sara, 321
Monterio, Isabel, 126
Monty Python, 22, 208, 361
Mood Six, 230, 238-239
Moody, Bill, 220
Moody Blues, 59, 117
Moody Boyz, 153
Moon, Gill, 110
Moon, Keith, 149, 233
Moon Records, 69, 156
Mooney, Kevin, 9
Mooney, Tim, 16
Moore, Angelo, 148
Moore, Anthony, 51
Moore, Archie, 371
Moore, Jem, 179
Moore, John, 193
Moore, Keith, 33
Moore, Ollie, 267
Moore, Paul Joseph, 53
Moore, Robert, 321
Moore, Sean, 220
Moore, Terry, 79, 179
Moore, Thurston, 12, 63, 82, 118, 136, 178, 326
Moors Murderers, 195, 201, 276, 323
Moorshead, Jem, 129
Moose, 77, 227, 239, 247, 332
Morales, David, 48
Morath, Kate, 357
Morbid Angel, 245
More, Antony, 356
Morehand, Marc, 295
Moreland, Bruce, 378
Morells, 259
Morgan, Charles, 93
Morgan, Dave, 211, 299, 340
Morgan, John, 310
Morgan, Tom, 206
Morgan, Wendy, 273
Morley, Paul, 228, 279, 394
Morley, Tom, 307
Moroder, Giorgio, 52
Morphine, 239-240
Morrell, Brad, 252, 265
Morricone, Ennio, 176
Morris, Adam, 257
Morris, Gina, 332
Morris, Jem, 58
Morris, Keith, 48, 82
Morris, Phillip, 300
Morris, Roger, 279
Morris, Stephen, 248, 257
Morris, Steven, 196
Morris Brothers, 30
Morrison, Dave, 21
Morrison, Hilary, 385
Morrison, Jim, 129, 169
Morrison, Lindy, 166-167
Morrison, Patricia, 317
Morrison, Van, 65, 93, 218, 314, 371
Morrissey, 90, 128, 215-216, 218, 222, 239-241, 267, 315, 318, 322-324, 336, 338
Moscrop, Martin, 5
Moss, Joe, 222, 323

Moss, Jon, 13, 106, 131, 211
Most Wanted, 274
Motello, Elton, 241
Motels, 187, 241
Mother Earth, 384
Mother Goose, 34
Mother Love Bone, 171, 241, 263, 350
Mother Records, 362, 367
Mothers Of Invention, 112, 293
Mothersbaugh, Bob, 116
Mothersbaugh, Mark, 116
Motorcycle Boy, 242, 315
Motors, 7, 147, 242
Mott, 114
Mott The Hoople, 114
Motter, Paul, 126
Mould, Bob, 41, 169-170, 175, 186, 220, 242, 326, 338, 355
Moulding, Colin, 392
Mountain, 55, 180, 217, 242, 312, 345, 369, 371, 377
Mousa, Murad, 222
Mowforth, Chris, 316
Moxham, Philip, 357, 394
Moxham, Stuart, 394
Moyet, Alison, 114, 138, 151, 208
Mr. Big, 257
MTV, 37, 51, 87, 93, 149, 199, 212, 234, 251-252, 265, 304, 307, 325, 327, 339, 352, 355, 360, 372, 388
Mu, 127, 196, 201, 214, 360
Mud, 278, 302, 320, 335
Mudhoney, 171, 182, 228, 242-243, 251, 263, 274, 336
Mueller, Andrew, 17
Muir, Mike, 339
Muir, Nick, 229
Mullen, Keith, 144
Mullen, Larry, 367
Mullen, Laurence, 367
Mulligan, John, 144
Mulreany, Paul, 53, 192
Mulvey, Linda, 215
Munro, Jane, 22
Murch, Russell, 24
Murcia, Billy, 249, 344, 359
Murder Inc, 279
Murder Junkies, 15
Murphy, Jeff, 315
Murphy, John, 164, 315
Murphy, Kevin, 168
Murphy, Martin, 17, 229
Murphy, Michael, 113
Murphy, Pete, 27
Murphy, Peter, 34, 106, 243
Murphy, Spud, 11
Murray, Martin, 237
Murray, Mike, 128
Murray, Pauline, 127, 244, 256, 265
Mushroom, 19, 330, 374
Musker, Dave, 350
Mustafa, Tim, 166
Mute Records, 30, 69, 138, 158, 189, 244, 253, 292, 362
Mutler, Stuart, 230
MX-80 Sound, 244
My Bloody Valentine, 96, 100, 161, 184, 225, 229, 239, 244-245, 294, 320, 368
Myers, Alan, 116
Myers, Colvin, 72
Myers, Paul, 167, 279
Myers, Richard, 177, 349
Myhill, Jill, 370
Myles, Geoff, 78
Myrick, Gary, 176
Mystics, 343

N

N'Dour, Youssou, 134
Naish, Brad, 385
Nakatani, Michie, 315
Naked Prey, 165, 245, 390
Naked Skinnies, 16
Nanette, 146
Nanini, Joe, 150, 378
Napalm Death, 33, 137, 169, 245

Napier-Bell, Simon, 192
Napolitano, Johnette, 89
Narcizo, David, 63, 358
Nash, Jim, 380
Nash, Johnny, 184
Nason, Steven, 22, 92
Nation Records, 76
National Health, 323
Native Hipsters, 246
Native Records, 109, 135, 321, 393
Navarro, David, 191
Navetta, Frank, 114
Naylor, Liz, 72
Naysmith, Graeme, 259
Nazzaro, Fred, 366
Necessity Records, 377
Nectarine No.9, 148, 246, 385
Ned's Atomic Dustbin, 125, 246
Neesam, John, 377
Neil, Barry, 107
Neil, Peter, 256
Nelson, Bill, 83, 146, 237, 244, 246-247, 318
Nelson, Brian, 371
Nelson, Ian, 146
Nelson, Marco, 382, 384
Nelson, Phil, 206
Nelson, Red, 246
Nelson, William, 246
Nemesis, 299, 315
Neon Boys, 177-178, 349, 371
Nervous, 22, 48, 77, 221, 265, 284, 314, 327, 371, 392
Nesmith, Michael, 206
Ness, Mike, 325
Netherlands, 190, 204
Network, 112, 154, 187, 197, 231, 300, 308
Neville Brothers, 295
Nevin, Brian, 45
Nevin, Mark, 138
New, Steve, 295
New Bomb Turks, 247
New England, 62, 120, 182, 217, 239
New Fast Automatic Daffodils, 57, 247
New Kids On The Block, 206
New Model Army, 207, 247, 301
New Musical Express, 7, 29, 31, 45, 53, 64-65, 72, 84, 127, 145, 147, 156, 158, 161-162, 174, 200, 203, 217-218, 220, 223, 227, 233, 238, 261, 266, 269, 273, 276, 291, 305, 310-311, 313, 321, 327, 331-332, 335, 338, 347, 352, 357, 372, 385-386, 388, 394
New Musik, 248
New Order, 5, 39, 96, 101, 116, 131, 134, 138, 156, 174, 187, 196, 248-249, 257, 293, 308
New Orleans, 249, 359-360
New Seekers, 255
New York City, 20, 51, 73, 109, 117, 150, 234, 249, 269, 359-360
New York Dolls, 176-177, 182, 194, 225, 235, 240, 249, 322, 344, 359
Newby, Christine, 79
Newby, Gary, 286
Newman, 152, 249, 385-386
Newman, Colin, 152, 249, 385-386
Newport, Alex, 156
Newton, Adi, 84
Newton, Dave, 384
Newton, Dobe, 67
Newton, Tony, 233
Newtown Neurotics, 228, 249-250
Niagara, 115
Nice, 39, 155, 176, 182, 334, 366
Nicholls, Morgan, 309
Nicholls, Pip, 120
Nichols, Todd, 361
Nico, 83, 187, 300
Nicol, Steve, 131, 291
Nieve, Steve, 22, 92, 112, 210
Night And Day, 30, 136, 222, 367
Nightingale, Wally, 311
Nightingales, 210, 225, 250, 275
Nightmare, 22, 87, 119, 179, 229
999, 119, 198, 251

Nitzer Ebb, 118, 244, 252
Nitzsche, Jack, 234
Nix, Bern, 90
No Means No, 110-111
No Strings, 112, 226
Noakes, Terry, 103
Nobacon, Danbert, 80
Nobel, Max, 129
Nobel, Paul, 129
Noel, Lester, 222
Nolan, Jerry, 176-177, 249, 359
Nommensen, John, 391
North, Richard, 64
Northside, 174, 179, 208, 253
Norton, Gil, 71, 74
Norton, Greg, 186
Nova Mob, 175, 253
Novak, Ivan, 203
Novamute, 244
Novello, Ivor, 392
Nude Records, 343
Numan, Gary, 37, 154, 376, 382
Nuns, 110, 150, 253, 289
Nuttal, Tim, 64
Nutter, Alice, 80
NWA, 34
Nye, Steve, 172
Nyman, Michael, 120
Nymphs, 72

O

O'Brien, Derek, 325
O'Brien, Ed, 286
O'Brien, Sean, 88, 290
O'Connell, Billy, 178
O'Connor, Hazel, 107, 151, 253, 364
O'Connor, Sinead, 190, 324, 378, 390
O'Dean, Michelle, 63
O'Gorman, Andrew, 145
O'Hare, Brendan, 71, 135, 327, 347
O'Keefe, Johnny, 189
O'Keefe, Laurence, 39, 192, 207
O'Neill, Keith, 74
O'Riordan, Delores, 96
Oakenfold, Paul, 112, 155
Oasis, 21, 43, 60, 100, 123, 131, 162, 225, 254-255, 338, 372, 384
Obscure Records, 235
Obsession, 79, 161, 203, 240, 344
Ocasek, Ric, 29, 73, 339, 382
Ocean, 130, 197, 361, 369, 384
Ocean, Julie, 369
October, Gene, 78
Ogden, Richard, 242
Ogg, Alex, 154
Ogier, Cliff, 253
Ogilvie, Gordon, 332
Oklahoma!, 149, 153, 265
Okra Records, 21
Olaffson, Bragi, 338
Olaverra, Margot, 167
Olener, Jeff, 253
Oliver!, 58, 92, 152, 180, 247, 251, 296
Oliver, Karin, 180
Oliver, Sean, 296
Olsen, Anders, 204
Olsen, Henry, 276
Olsen, Mark, 225
Olson, Marc, 192
OMD, 138, 174
On A Friday, 286
On The Town, 71, 216, 284
Onassis, Blackie 'Black Caesar', 369
One Dove, 369
One Little Indian Records, 20, 106, 151, 176, 200, 255, 274, 338, 355
101ers, 83, 211, 256
One Records, 43, 106, 290, 325
1,000 Violins, 256
One Way Records, 290
Only Ones, 170, 174, 182, 256, 290, 359
Ono, Yoko, 33, 134, 158, 381
Onslaught, 119, 148, 212, 266, 274, 335
Onyx, 46

Open Road, 365
Opitz, Mark, 150
Oracle, 112, 249
Orange Juice, 55, 61, 88, 147, 180, 195-196, 233, 256, 275, 382, 385
Orange Records, 15
Orb, 61, 201, 257, 377
Orbison, Roy, 367, 394
Orbital, 147, 369
Orchestral Manoeuvres In The Dark, 12
Oregon, 27, 116, 178, 182, 271, 385
Organization, 149, 167-168, 291, 321, 338, 372
Original Concept, 35
Originals, 13, 91, 102, 126, 136, 256, 269, 291, 344, 368, 384
Ork Records, 349
Orleans, 249, 359-360
Orpheus, 74
Orpheus, Rodney, 74
Orr, Benjamin, 73
Orridge, Genesis P., 86, 101, 132, 204, 274, 280, 325
Osbourne, Stuart, 172
Oscar, 71, 87, 323
Osman, Kenediid, 71
Osman, Matt, 338
Osmond, Donny, 31
Otcasek, Richard, 73
Other Two, 87, 127, 155, 170, 204, 240, 249, 257, 356, 359
Otway, John, 22, 151, 257
Our Daughters Wedding, 258
Out Of My Hair, 258
Outcasts, 55, 258
Outsiders, 327, 356, 380
Overkill, 172, 310, 369-370, 372
Overtones, 24, 51, 116, 147, 154, 193, 210, 241
Owen, Malcolm, 301
Owen, Mickie, 374
Owen, Sarah-Jane, 37
Owen, Stuart, 200
Owens, Campbell, 26
Oxburrow, Jonah, 290
Ozric Tentacles, 258-259, 310

P

Pablo, 237, 251, 286, 300
Pablo, Augustus, 300
Pachelbel, Johann, 144
Padgham, Hugh, 272
Padovani, Henry, 272
Pagan Tango, 79
Page, Ian, 308
Page, Michael, 344
Page, Steven, 31
Pain, Clive, 61
Paine, Ian, 308
Paint Your Wagon, 291
Palaminos, 51, 145
Pale Fountains, 120, 259, 312
Pale Saints, 153, 259-260
Palladin, Patti, 359-360
Palm, Mike, 12
Palmer, Dave, 354
Palmer, N.A., 98
Palmer, Robert, 48, 82
Pandela, Nelson, 59
Pandemonium, 149, 199
Pandora, 164
Panter, Horace, 328
Pantera, 46, 169
Panunzio, Thom, 113
Papp, Josh, 161
Pappalardi, Felix, 110
Papworth, Dave, 115
Parachute Men, 259
Paradis, Vanessa, 24
Paradox, 69
Paragons, 52
Parashar, Rick, 51, 263
Parfitt, Phil, 207, 266, 326
Paris Angels, 261
Parker, Alan, 300
Parker, Andrew, 300
Parker, Bob, 377

Parker, Chuck, 169
Parker, Graham, 78, 333, 344
Parker, John, 125, 265
Parker, Maceo, 90
Parker, Matthew, 259
Parker, Robert, 103, 265
Parkin, Adrian, 156
Parkin, Matthew, 259
Parks, Van Dyke, 110, 296, 332
Parliament, 233, 253
Parlophone Records, 134, 151, 194, 256, 340, 343
Parrish, John, 269
Parry, Chris, 104, 282
Parry, Steve, 284
Parsons, Alan, 305
Parsons, Dave, 312, 364
Parsons, Gram, 135, 206, 212, 296
Parsons, Judy, 37
Parsons, Ted, 279
Parton, Dolly, 335
Partridge, Andy, 51, 96, 127, 208, 392
Passion, 13, 33, 62, 64, 69, 76, 78, 80, 83, 103, 113, 123, 169, 172, 186, 235, 261, 278, 292-293, 367, 381-382
Passions, 253, 256, 261
Passport Records, 35, 195
Pastel, Stephen, 261
Pastels, 100, 225, 261-262, 315, 347, 359, 371
Paterson, Alex, 257
Pates, Allison, 266
Patman, Stephen, 77
Patrick, James, 308
Patrick, Steven, 239, 322
Patterson, Alan, 294
Patterson, Angel, 294
Patterson, Bobby, 214
Patterson, Les, 129
Patton, Brian, 22
Patton, Mike, 141
Paul, Alan, 210, 250
Paul, Dean, 391
Paul, John, 158, 215, 236
Paul, Owen, 101, 301
Paul, Peter, 267
Paul, Tim, 271
Pavement, 21, 261, 316
Pavlov's Dog, 24
Payne, Chris, 13, 228
Payne, Colin, 71
Payne, Davey, 197
Peacock, Sarah, 309
Peake, Andy, 89
Peake, Jacko, 382
Pearce, Kevin, 177
Pearl Harbor And The Explosions, 80, 263
Pearl Jam, 49, 76, 171, 202, 241-243, 252, 263-265, 350
Pearlman, Sandy, 83
Pearson, Danny, 16
Pedham, Mike, 27
Pedro, 234-235
Peel, John, 5, 7-8, 12, 15, 22, 39, 46, 58, 60, 77, 80, 85, 88, 96, 107, 112-113, 125, 129, 134, 137, 141, 145, 154, 164, 168, 173, 179, 185, 187, 189-190, 195, 199, 203, 210, 212, 217, 222, 227-229, 245-246, 250, 257-258, 265, 279, 282, 291, 299, 302, 307, 309-310, 316-317, 332, 335, 343, 350, 354, 356, 358, 365, 369, 372, 381, 384
Peel, Tina, 157
Penetration, 244, 265-266
Penguin Cafe Orchestra, 381
Penn, Dan, 58
Penn, Sean, 326
Penney, Jonn, 246
Pennington, Mark, 172
Penny, Jan, 12
Pentes, Danna, 19
Peopler, Merv, 259
Pepper, Will, 135, 186
Peretz, Jesse, 204
Perez, David Charles, 174
Perfect, Pete, 126

Perfect Disaster, 39, 63-64, 266, 326
Perkins, Anthony, 346
Perkins, Johnny, 392
Perkins, Stephen, 191
Perks, Vickie, 380-381
Perlman, Marc, 192
Perrett, Daniel, 258
Perrett, Peter, 182, 256, 359
Perrin-Brown, Steve, 120
Perrson, Hans, 150
Perry, Ivor, 128
Perry, John, 256
Perry, Linda, 153
Perry, Mark, 15, 30, 266
Perry, Neil, 236
Perry, Willie, 385
Persuasions, 201
Pestilence, 112
Pet Shop Boys, 73, 134, 147, 190, 248, 324
Peter, Paul And Mary, 267
Peter And The Test Tube Babies, 266
Peter Pan, 73
Peters, Bethan, 113
Peters, Dan, 171, 242, 251
Peters, Joey, 170
Peters, Mike, 13
Peters, Rob, 179
Peterson, Alex, 201
Peterson, Anders, 129
Peterson, Debbi, 31
Peterson, Vicki, 31
Pettitt, Tony, 147
Petty, Tom, 94, 211, 252, 289
Petty, Tom, And The Heartbreakers, 94, 289
Pew, Tracy, 66
Phair, Liz, 372
Phelps, Joel, 316
Phield, Paddy, 103
Phillipps, Martin, 79
Phillips, Glen, 361
Phillips, Grant Lee, 170, 359
Phillips, Gretchen, 366
Phillips, Julian, 222
Phillips, Kevin, 318
Philo, 145
Phoenix, 35, 43, 46, 126, 365-366, 384, 386
Phoenix, River, 35
Phonogram Records, 347, 354
Photos, 85, 231, 266-267, 384
Phranc, 267
Piaf, 65
Piaf, Edith, 65
Picciotto, Guy, 157
Piccolo, John, 314
Pickerell, Mark, 307
Pierce, Jason, 266, 328-329
Pierce, Jeffrey Lee, 172
Pierson, Kate, 26, 189, 284
Pigalle, Anne, 394
Pigbag, 223, 267, 273
Piggott-Smith, Tim, 364
Pigott, Johanna, 391
PiL, 13, 30, 162, 169, 190-191, 207, 218, 256, 267, 280, 282, 374
Pilf, Philip, 72
Pilnick, Paul, 111
Pilot, 183-184
Piltdown Men, 294
Pincombe, Ian, 115, 216
Pink Fairies, 78, 241
Pink Floyd, 74, 106, 229, 257, 265, 305, 377
Pink Industry, 45, 267
Pink Military, 45, 111, 267, 393
Pink Records, 73, 267, 388
Pinker, Jeff, 67
Pins And Needles, 261
Pinsky, David, 147
Pinsky, Philip, 147
Pintado, Jesse, 245
Pioneers, 45, 79, 211, 245
Pirate, The, 265
Pirate Radio, 265
Pirates, 309

Pirroni, Marco, 9
Pisteer, Bob, 204
Pitcher, Jeff, 329
Pitney, Gene, 355
Pittsburgh, 149
Pixies, 39, 43, 49, 63-64, 71, 119, 134, 143, 152-153, 229, 266-268, 316, 343, 356, 359, 386
PJ Harvey, 43, 48, 143, 176, 268-270
Placebo Thing, 179
Plain, John, 62, 216
Plakas, Dee, 202
Plank, Conny, 155, 361-362
Plant, Robert, 45, 218
Plasmatics, 269, 333
Plastic Bertrand, 71, 241
Plath, Sylvia, 194
Platters, 125
Playboy Records, 41
Player, John, 55, 126, 236, 331
Playtime Records, 31
Plaza, Martin, 229
Pleeth, Graham, 318
Plimsouls, 35
Plonker, Ronnie, 331
Ploog, Richard, 82
Poe, John, 172
Poets, 22
Pogues, 84, 92, 218, 228, 269, 271, 305, 333, 381
Poindexter, Buster, 195
Poison Girls, 98, 182, 271, 301
Poison Idea, 271, 307
Police, 12, 17, 19, 49, 69, 82, 89, 115, 136, 144, 151, 153, 156, 176, 186, 201, 242, 272, 280, 339, 365, 378
Pollard, Nigel, 302
Pollitt, Tessa, 320
Poly Styrene, 135, 272, 391
Polydor Records, 74, 84, 89, 123, 150, 162, 191, 251, 256, 261, 275, 313, 317, 340, 354, 388
Pomus, Doc, 234
Ponce, Daniel, 169
Pond, 109
Pooh Sticks, 273
Poole, Brian, 62
Poole, Brian, And The Tremeloes, 62
Pop Art, 241, 364-365
Pop Group, 13, 35, 55, 104, 112, 131, 134, 155, 185, 197, 212, 218, 231, 242, 248, 256, 267, 273, 292, 294-296, 300, 320, 329, 336, 345, 352, 372, 376
Pop Will Eat Itself, 98, 127, 273, 388
Pope, Tim, 104
Popguns, 16, 273-274
Popinjays, 200, 255, 274
Popper, John, 55
Porgy And Bess, 314
Porno For Pyros, 149, 191
Porta, Josef, 58, 98
Porter, Cole, 136, 222, 367
Porter, David, 344
Porter, John, 299, 323, 371
Porterhouse, David, 185
Portnoy, Elan, 157
Posh Boy Records, 9, 12, 291, 325
Posies, 114, 274, 318
Posner, Gary, 361
Poss, Robert, 30
Possessed, 196, 269, 289, 326, 339, 344
Possum Dixon, 274
Post, Louise, 371
Postcard Records, 112, 131, 147, 166, 195, 233, 246, 256, 274-275, 385
Potter, Dennis, 272
Potts, David, 293
Povey, Gavin, 13, 131, 208
Power, John, 74, 202
Powers, Jim, 371
Prater, Dan, 35
Pre Records, 113, 305
Precoda, Karl, 125
Prefab Sprout, 275
Prelude, 68, 178
Prescencer, Gerard, 382

Prescott, Peter, 236
Presence, Orson, 238
Presley, Elvis, 76, 170, 271, 275, 284, 293
Preston, Nigel, 103, 311, 328, 354
Pretenders, 67, 134, 195, 200, 215, 222, 275-276, 324
Pretty Things, 186, 241, 352
Price, 14, 62, 79, 112, 131, 186-187, 237, 247, 271, 276, 290-291, 313, 321, 325, 328, 347, 380
Price, Daryn, 290
Price, Elizabeth, 347
Price, Mark, 14, 237
Price, Martin, 131
Price, Steve, 186
Prieboy, Andy, 378
Priest, Matthew, 123
Priestman, Henry, 111, 393
Primal Scream, 100, 177, 190, 193, 225, 257, 276, 278, 294, 327, 329, 371
Prime Minister, 78, 98, 269, 374
Prime Time, 30, 90, 302
Primitives, 33, 109, 134, 137, 208, 244, 277-278, 291
Primus, 153, 278, 345
Prince, Bill, 210, 299
Prince Buster, 218, 309
Prince Hammer, 320
Prior, Les, 13-14
Prisoners, 113, 233-234, 278-279, 352, 370, 378
Private Lives, 85, 330
Proclaimers, 33
Prodigy, 48, 355
Profane, Benny, 39, 299
Professionals, 171, 279
Prohourn, Chris, 122
Promises, 68, 158, 356
Prong, 279
Propaganda, 118, 279, 394
Prophet, Chuck, 171
Protrudi, Rudi, 157
Psychedelic Furs, 46, 174, 279-280, 317
Psychic TV, 16, 86, 132, 274, 280, 325, 358
Psychick Warriors, 169
Psychotics, 309
Ptacek, Rainer, 165
Public Enemy, 12, 34, 310, 318
Public Image Limited, 30, 96, 190, 267, 280, 347, 357
Pugh, Mick, 72
Pukulski, Jan Marek, 150
Pulsallama, 59
Punk In London, 71, 118
Purcell, Sean, 103
Purol, Bill, 368
Purple Gang, 120
Purple Hearts, 282, 308
Purser, Fred, 265
Pursey, Jimmy, 85, 174, 182, 212, 312
Pursey, Robert, 177, 347
Pussy Galore, 155, 300
Pussycat, 275
Puttnam, Carl, 102
Pynchon, Thomas, 39
Pyzor, Neil, 328

Q
Quail, Roger, 84
Quargnolo, Debbie, 117
Quatermass, 364
Quatro, Suzi, 173, 301
Queen, 31, 59, 135, 141, 180, 193, 210, 216, 221, 235, 311, 323-324, 329, 359, 362, 365
Queen, Monica, 359
Quercio, Michael, 161, 358
Quest, 35, 143, 367, 382
? And The Mysterians, 131
Questions, 60, 111, 150, 192, 250
Quick, 283
Quine, Bob, 177
Quine, Robert, 87, 119
Quinn, Ged, 384
Quinn, Mickey, 340

Quinn, Paul, 55, 256, 327, 349
Quinnones, Vanessa, 155
Quinton, David, 34
Quiver, 22
Quixote, Don, 361
Quy, Tim, 72

R
R.E.M., 12, 53, 63, 110, 116, 122, 145, 161, 169, 178, 180, 184, 195, 206, 220, 236, 242, 283-284, 327, 336, 364, 393
Rabbit, Jack, 276
Rabid, Jack, 29
Rabid Records, 83, 194, 318
Race, Tony, 146
Racioppo, Robert, 314
Radalj, Rod, 183
Radar Records, 325, 376
Radclife, E.C., 362
Radcliffe, Eric, 138
Radcliffe, Leroy, 237
Radiation, Roddy, 152, 328
Radiators, 290
Radiators From Space, 269
Radical Dance Faction, 284
Radio Birdman, 284
Radio On, 14, 35, 48, 55, 60, 247, 265, 286, 302, 309
Radio Stars, 237, 284, 308
Radiohead, 49, 284-286
Radley, Kate, 329
Rage, 8, 11, 172, 199, 235, 241, 296, 299, 307, 370
Rage Records, 8
Ragga, 127
Raggamuffin, 261
Railway Children, 286-287
Rain, 26, 31, 51, 57, 100, 103, 112, 116, 118, 120, 130, 135, 154, 162, 165, 171, 184, 196, 211-212, 218, 223, 229, 242, 255, 263, 283, 286, 288, 290, 299, 309, 374, 386
Rain Parade, 31, 116, 171, 212, 223, 288
Rainbow, 184, 301
Raincoats, 212, 256, 280, 288, 300, 356
Rainer, 165
Rainford, Phil, 127
Ralph Records, 293
Ralske, Kurt, 368
Ramirez, Joe, 150
Ramon, Gary, 340
Ramone, Dee Dee, 34, 177, 288
Ramone, Joey, 76, 182, 288
Ramone, Johnny, 288
Ramone, Marky, 288
Ramone, Tommy, 288
Ramones, 19, 21, 34, 37, 68, 76, 110, 117, 136, 149, 158, 165, 177-178, 187, 195, 199, 204, 216, 231, 247, 250, 261, 265-266, 278, 288-289, 309, 339, 347, 355
Rampage, Randy, 122
Rampling, Danny, 225
Ramsay, Andy, 332
Ranaldo, Lee, 63, 326
Random, Eric, 69
Rank And File, 118, 245, 253, 289
Ranken, Andrew, 269
Rankine, Alan, 21
Rankine, Lesley, 316
Ranking Roger, 273
Ranks, Shabba, 308
Rao, Johnny, 344
Rapeman, 43, 63, 194, 252, 269, 289, 307, 313, 316, 336, 345, 370
Raphael, Gordon, 318
Raphael, Jeff, 253
Rasa, Tabula, 132
Rasor, Mitch, 7
Raspberries, 34, 369
Rat Fink Junior, 14
Rat Scabies, 71, 106, 195, 211
Rath, Billy, 176, 359
Raven, 64, 126, 199, 279, 334-335

Raven, Kyle, 126
Raven, Paul, 64, 199
Raw Records, 325
Ray, Felix, 192
Ray, Willie, 92
Raymond, Robin, 372
Raymonde, Simon, 85-86, 239
Rays, 220
Razor Records, 9, 203, 250, 368
Razorcuts, 289, 347
RCA Records, 114, 223, 258, 273, 278, 333
Reader, Eddi, 138, 179
Reagan, Ronald, 288
Real Kids, 289-290
Real Life, 178, 220
Real People, 290
Real Thing, 141
Rebel MC, 334
Reber, Matt, 247
Reception Records, 381
Reckless, 41, 229, 283
Reckless Records, 41
Records, 290
Red Bird, 128-129
Red Crayola, 14, 135, 212
Red Flame Records, 20, 118
Red Guitars, 290
Red Hot Chili Peppers, 145, 148, 191, 210, 228, 263
Red Letter Day, 65, 290
Red Lorry Yellow Lorry, 164, 291, 370
Red Records, 14, 20, 22, 110, 118, 123, 136, 146, 182, 200, 222, 291, 318
Red Rhino Records, 291, 318
Redd Kross, 291
Redding, Otis, 128
Redskins, 33, 291
Reece, Chris, 325
Reed, Chris, 291
Reed, Jimmy, 355
Reed, Lou, 13, 87, 94, 125, 178, 191-192, 218, 256, 344, 361, 378
Reegs, 76, 291-292
Reeves, Jim, 173
Reeves, Steve, 109
Reeves, Vic, 388
Reflections, 16, 377
Reflex, 98, 186, 372, 384
Refugee, 51, 133
Regan, Julianne, 14, 164
Regan, Riff, 211
Reid, Ellen, 96
Reid, Jim, 193
Reid, Junior, 327
Reid, Shaun, 299
Reid, William, 193
Reilly, Jim, 332
Reilly, Vini, 127-128, 240, 244
Reininger, Blaine, 116, 127
Relativity, 83, 87, 91, 180
Remick, Lee, 166
Renaldo, Lee, 82, 119, 136, 326
Rendall, Kimble, 391
Rendle, Luke, 354
Renees, 173, 292
Renegade Soundwave, 292
Renfrew, Robert, 324
Reparata And The Delrons, 64
Replacements, 45-46, 55, 84, 94, 182, 245, 250, 263, 292, 301, 310, 325-326, 374, 393
Requiem, 323
Research, Paul, 305
Residents, 78, 244, 292-293, 340
Restless Records, 31
Retoy, Mark, 329
Return To The Forbidden Planet, 286
Rev, Martin, 339
RevCo, 293-294
Revell, Graham, 330
Revell, Mark, 187
Revenge, 67, 158, 189, 195, 234, 249, 269, 279, 293
Revette, Cherie, 293
Revillos, 206, 293-294
Revolting Cocks, 147, 234, 293, 380

Revolver, 24, 217, 294, 368
Revolving Paint Dream, 100, 294
Rew, Kimberley, 31, 197, 325
Rey, Daniel, 199
Reyes, Ron, 291
Reynolds, Eugene, 293-294
Rezillos, 293-294, 372
Rhino Records, 19, 291, 294, 318
Rhythm King, 131, 292, 340
Ribot, Marc, 116
Ricardo, 200
Ricco, John, 378
Rice, Boyd, 138
Rich, Charlie, 377
Rich, S., 45, 283-284, 377
Rich Kids, 295, 376
Richard, Cliff, 102, 144
Richard, Paul, 191, 372
Richard 23, 73, 156, 293-294
Richards, Paula, 172, 292
Richardson, Dawn, 153
Richardson, Rudy, 211
Richman, Jonathan, 41, 58, 158, 173, 192, 237-238, 295, 299-300, 346
Rickard, Stephen, 356
Rickenbacker, 191, 286
Rickers, Manuela, 392
Rico, 258, 309
Rico, Layne, 258
Ride, 59, 100, 110, 115, 225, 295, 340, 384
Ridgway, Stan, 150, 295, 378
Rieflin, William, 294
Riff Raff, 62
Rigby, Will, 109
Riggs, 113
Riggs, Alan, 113
Right Said Fred, 177, 299
Rigione, Todd, 210
Riley, Kelly, 371
Riley, Dave, 43
Riley, Marc, 141, 196, 296
Riley, Mike, 141
Riley, Paul, 78
Rimbaud, Arthur, 322
Rimbaud, Penny, 98
Riordan, Vince, 85
Riot City Records, 120, 374
Riot Squad, 22
Rip Rig And Panic, 273, 296
Riperton, Minnie, 257
Rippington, Tim, 149
Ripple, Max, 111
Rippon, Steve, 217
Ritchie, Brian, 374
Ritchie, Ian, 13, 111
Ritter, Melissa, 236
Ritter, Rob, 172
Rivers, John, 289
Rivets, Rick, 249, 344
Rizzo, Peter, 164
Rizzo, Rick, 134
Roach, Martin, 236
Roadhouse, 265
Roadrunner Records, 126, 282
Roback, David, 125, 223, 288
Robb, John, 125, 228
Roberts, Brad, 96
Roberts, Dave, 311
Roberts, Gerry, 61
Roberts, Greg, 43
Roberts, James, 199, 308
Roberts, Matt, 212
Roberts, Mick, 199
Roberts, Mike, 24
Roberts, Patrick, 308
Roberts, Paul, 149, 335
Roberts, Steve, 212, 368
Robertson, Brian, 106
Robertson, Jason, 61
Robertson, Justin, 48
Robertson, Mark, 231
Robertson, Robbie, 55
Robie, John, 248
Robinson, Chris, 186
Robinson, Daron, 126
Robinson, Dave, 92, 215, 333

Robinson, David, 73, 237
Robinson, Harry, 136
Robinson, Smokey, 91, 192
Robinson, Steve, 120
Robinson, Tom, 296, 332
Robinson, Wendy, 274
Rocha, Roger, 153
Roche, Mike, 365
Rock, Bob, 104
Rock 'n' Roll High School, 136, 288
Rock, Pete, 83
Rock Steady, 5
Rocket 88, 339
Rocket Records, 203
Rockets, 21, 29, 34, 155, 214, 362
Rockingbirds, 177, 211, 296-297, 299
Rocky Horror Show, The, 390
Roddy Radiation And His Tearjerkers, 152
Rodent, Robert, 330
Roderick, 318
Rodgers, Nile, 26
Rodgers, Richard, 71
Rodgers, Steve 'Soto', 9, 12
Rods, 65, 92, 106, 131, 208, 359
Roe, Tommy, 388
Roeser, Eddie 'King', 369
Rogan, Johnny, 226, 241, 324
Roger, Scott, 118
Rogers, Anne, 274
Rogers, Cathy, 177
Rogers, David, 7
Rogers, Ian, 55
Rogers, Kenny, 58
Roland, Dean, 87
Roland, Ed, 87
Rolling Stone, 7, 16, 41, 51, 83, 184, 233, 252, 283, 340, 367, 393
Rolling Stones, 75, 88, 116, 118, 131, 164, 194, 218, 236, 245, 249, 258, 269, 278, 280, 291, 300, 318, 322, 325, 327, 340, 367, 371
Rollins, Henry, 48-49, 117, 156, 176, 298-299, 343, 391
Rollins Band, 299
Roman, Cliff, 382
Romero, Anisa, 318
Romero, George A., 235
Romweber, Sam, 206
Rondolet Records, 228
Ronettes, 288
Ronson, Mick, 241
Ronstadt, Linda, 92, 211
Roog, John, 357
Roogalator, 333
Room, 9, 22, 31, 39, 41, 100-101, 129, 138, 143, 147-148, 180, 190, 202, 207, 210-211, 225, 229, 299, 311, 315, 359-361, 380-381
Rooney, Mickey, 344
Roots, Simon, 141
Roper, Martin, 19
Rorschach, Ivy, 94
Rose, Axl, 51, 316
Rose, Billy, 218
Rose, Jeff, 127
Rose, The, 174, 191, 311, 344
Rose Of Avalanche, 299
Ross, Andy, 57, 152, 189
Ross, Jenny, 308
Ross, Jonathan, 22
Ross, Malcolm, 195-196, 256
Ross, Peter, 189
Ross, Rick, 231
Rossi, Mike, 318
Rossiter, Martin, 162
Rotheray, David, 35
Rothko, Mark, 356
Rotsey, Martin, 231
Rotten, Johnny, 226, 280, 311
Rough Trade Records, 20-21, 49, 58, 60, 68, 73, 79, 96, 100, 113, 125, 128, 135, 141, 158, 166, 175, 201, 210, 238, 242, 244, 250, 288, 300, 307, 314, 323, 336, 340, 344, 350, 356, 361, 374, 376, 381, 388
Roule, Mark, 361

Rourke, Andy, 11, 55, 240, 323
Rourke, Carl, 284
Roustabout, 72
Roustabout Records, 72
Rowan, Andy, 377
Rowbotham, Dave, 127-128, 244
Rowe, Simon, 77
Rowe, Buck, 374
Rowland, John, 59
Rowley, John, 290
Rowley, Keith, 233
Rowntree, Dave, 57
Roxy, Eddie, 114
Roxy Music, 149, 214, 330, 371-372
Royal Wedding, 357
Royer, Casey, 9, 325
RPM Records, 89
RSO Records, 53
Rubella Ballet, 151, 300
Rubin, Rick, 34, 103, 192, 299
Rubinoos, 41
Rucker, Darious, 184
Rude Boy, 84
Ruffin, Jimmy, 335
Ruffy, Dave, 301
Rufus, 374
Ruin, Clint, 86, 152, 216
Rujillo, Robert, 339
Rumbles, Kenny, 258
Rumour, 92, 192, 227, 333
Run DMC, 82
Runacres, Ian, 119
Runaways, 31, 35, 301
Rundgren, Todd, 279, 296, 366
Rupe, Bob, 59
Rush, 68, 94, 109, 200, 229, 231, 247, 278, 384
Rushakoff, Harry, 85
Rushent, Martin, 15, 313, 376
Rushton, Geoff, 280
Rushton, Nicky, 17
Russell, Erik, 366
Rust Never Sleeps, 116
Ruth, Amanda, 289
Rutles, 314
Ruts, 151, 266, 284, 301
Ryan, Barry, 107
Ryan, David, 157, 206
Ryan, Mick, 59
Ryan, Paul, 59
Ryder, Paul, 174
Ryder, Sean, 174
Ryley, Dave, 156

S
S'Express, 29, 276, 305, 347, 388
Sabin, Lance, 128
Sad Cafe, 305
Sad Lovers And Giants, 302
Sade, 280, 368
Sadier, Laetitia, 332
Safety Net Records, 59
Saga, 180, 226, 312, 317, 381
Sage, Greg, 385
Sager, Gareth, 296
Saint Etienne, 110, 141, 146, 177, 302
Saints, 153, 203, 259-260, 284, 302, 318
Sakamoto, Ryûichi, 282
Salad, 87, 148, 211, 303-304
Sale, Julz, 113
Salem, Kevin, 218
Sales, Tony, 187, 189
Salewicz, Chris, 63
Sally, 72, 157, 227, 370
Saloman, Nick, 41
Salowka, Pete, 381
Saltwell, John, 266
Salvation, 200, 302, 367-368
Samhain, 235
Sammy, 304, 378
Sampling, 127, 144, 175, 196, 273, 279, 356
Sanctuary, 103, 248, 261
Sanders, Tim, 155
Sanderson, Nick, 84, 172
Sandman, Mark, 239

Sangster, Jim, 393
Santana, Carlos, 57
Santiago, Joey, 49, 267
Sarah Records, 146, 177, 305, 308, 347, 371
Sardi, Sam, 172
Sparks, Nicki, 133
Satan, 74, 158, 177, 344-345
Satie, Erik, 253
Satriani, Joe, 278
Saturday Night Fever, 193
Saunders, Andy, 362
Saunders, Martin, 24
Saunders, Mike, 19
Saunders, Pete, 179
Sauter, Brenda, 145
Savage, 8, 110, 116, 141, 164, 199, 226, 246, 253, 268, 302, 330, 334, 374, 389
Savage, Donna, 110, 302
Savill, Brook Christian, 320
Saville, Peter, 138
Savoy, Dave, 175
Savoy Brown, 78
Saw Doctors, 305-306
Scaccia, Mike, 234, 294
Scales, Steve, 361
Scandal, 176, 192, 214, 350
Scanlon, Craig, 141
Scarface, 204
Scarlet, 14, 242, 305, 368
Scarlet Party, 305
Scarpantoni, Jane, 242
Scars, 305, 365
Scharin, Douglas, 86
Scheff, Jerry, 234
Schinzler, Matthew, 301
Schneider, Fred, 26
Schock, Gina, 167
Schofield, Brian, 76
Schofield, Marcia, 55, 143
Schoolboys, 309, 321
Schoppler, Fran, 162
Schuler, Danny, 45
Schultz, Charles, 19
Schunk, Bill, 35
Scientist, 111, 295
Sclavunos, Jim, 94, 326, 349
Scobie, Rona, 169
Scorn, 137, 169, 381
Scott, Andy, 210
Scott, Chris, 347
Scott, Colin, 167
Scott, David, 242
Scott, George, 355
Scott, Mike, 170, 179, 336, 378, 390
Scott, Neil, 146, 324, 340
Scott, Ronnie, 381-382, 385
Scott, Simon, 320
Scott, Steve, 51, 336
Scott, Suzanne, 17
Scratch Acid, 194, 289, 305, 307
Screaming Blue Messiahs, 307
Screaming Trees, 119, 307, 327, 377
Scritti Politti, 220, 300, 307
Scumfucs, 15
Sea Urchins, 305, 308
Seacroft, Paul, 292
Seal, 26, 89, 367
Seaman, David, 239
Searchers, 290
Seaweed, 48
Secret Affair, 203, 282, 308
Secret Knowledge, 316
Secrets, 11, 17, 111, 146, 350
Section 25, 138, 308
Sed, Billy, 165
Seefeel, 309
Seeger, Pete, 13
Seekers, 255
Seenan, James, 71, 371
Segal, Jonathan, 70
Seger, Dave, 165
Seger, David, 245
Seidelman, Susan, 178
Seigal, Dan, 343
Seinfeld, Evan, 45

412

Selecter, 309, 328-329
Self Drive Records, 290
Seligman, Matthew, 325, 357
Sell, Adrian, 320
Sellers, Peter, 228
Selway, Phil, 286
Semple, Andy, 117
Senac, Hermann, 52
Sensations, 255
Senseless Things, 115, 190, 227, 309
Senser, 127, 310
September Records, 225
Sepultura, 46, 156
Sequel Records, 180
Serapax, Nancy, 391
Sergeant, 129-130
Serious Drinking, 173, 310, 340
Servants, 24, 217, 310
Severin, Steve, 15, 104, 166, 317
Sewell, Tim, 129
Sex Gang Children, 46, 103, 310-311,
328
Sex Pistols, 8, 14, 17, 26, 59, 61, 68,
83-84, 106, 117, 119, 137, 155, 167,
169, 171, 177, 193-194, 210, 225-226,
249, 256, 265, 279-280, 295, 311-312,
316-317, 325, 352, 359, 368, 372, 388
Seymour, 57, 109, 144, 276, 309, 344,
346
Seymour, Adam, 276
Shack, 5, 26, 312
Shadbolt, Jeff, 282
Shadows, 89, 365
Shaffer, Paul, 55, 57
Shaffer, Peter, 364
Shah, 67
Shakespeare, Robbie, 128
Shakin' Street, 19, 33, 117
Shallcross, Lee, 308
Sham 69, 85, 110, 119, 153, 182, 212,
312
Shame, 103, 107, 109, 156, 164, 206,
208, 222, 321
Shamen, 147, 255-256, 312-313
Shampoo, 145, 152, 313
Shangri-Las, 125, 294
Shank, Barry, 211
Shannon, 51, 63, 220, 344, 371
Shannon, Del, 344
Shannon, Sarah, 371
Shapiro, Elliot, 73
Shapiro, Jim, 371
Shark, Eric, 111
Sharkey, Feargal, 211, 218, 369
Sharle, Karl, 88
Sharp, David, 13
Sharp, Gordon, 356
Sharp, Matt, 382
Sharpe, Terry, 11
Sharrock, Chris, 187, 208, 390
Shaw, Chris, 106, 382
Shaw, Dale, 53
Shaw, David, 123
Shaw, Greg, 34, 315
Shaw, Jim, 96
Shaw, Joe, 123
Shaw, Sandie, 138, 323
Shea, Robert, 201
Shear, Jules, 31, 221
Shed Seven, 123, 313, 343
Shedden, Iain, 310
Sheehan, Bobby, 57
Sheila, 294, 323
Shellac, 43, 313, 345
Shellenbach, Kate, 34
Shelley, Pete, 68, 244, 313
Shelley, Steve, 178, 288, 304, 326
Shelleyan Orphan, 313-314, 356
Shells, 167
Shelly, Steve, 118
Shelton, Seb, 308
Shenkman, Eric, 55
Sheperd, Brad, 183
Shepherd, Tony, 43, 179
Sheppard, Nick, 91
Sheriff Fatman, 73
Sherriff, 77

Sherriff, Andrew, 77
Sherrill, Billy, 92
Sherwood, Adrian, 223, 273, 357
Sherwood, Eddie, 46
Shibler, David, 366
Shields, 17, 244
Shields, Kevin, 244
Shimmy Disc, 27, 199-200, 314, 377
Shirelles, 125
Shirley, Ian, 293
Shirts, 76, 199, 233, 273, 314
Shiva, 170
Shockabilly, 27, 59, 67, 173, 314
Shocked, Michelle, 17, 184
Shocking Blue, 251
Shoes, 61, 161-162, 178, 315
Shonen Knife, 315
Shop Assistants, 78, 113, 162, 242,
261, 315, 371
Shout, 116
Shriekback, 161, 223, 315, 392
Shulman, Ray, 372
Shultz, Glenn, 300
Shy, 51, 307, 328-329
Side, Mark, 176
Sidebottom, Alec, 120
Sidebottom, Frank, 155
Sidi Bou Said, 72, 315
Siegfried, James, 90, 349
Sievey, Chris, 155
Siffre, Labi, 218
Sigman, Carl, 100
Signal, 30, 214, 234, 394
Sigue Sigue Sputnik, 34, 43, 164, 311,
316, 318, 331, 339
Siguenza, Ruben, 234
Silhouettes, 315
Silk, 136
Silkworm, 316
Silva, John, 291
Silva, Keith, 258
Silva, Paula, 73
Silver, Cliff, 302
Silver Jews, 316
Silver Mountain, 180
Silverfish, 156, 299, 316, 354
Silvers, John, 118
Sim, Mark, 185
Simenon, Paul, 211
Simenon, Tim, 48
Simmonds, Paul, 228
Simmons, David, 138
Simmons, Desmond, 249
Simon, Carly, 109
Simon, John, 311
Simon, Paul, 64, 226
Simon, Rita, 392
Simon, Robin, 220
Simon, Scott, 320
Simon And Garfunkel, 31, 206, 324
Simonon, Paul, 83, 176
Simple Minds, 20, 89, 102, 180, 218,
233, 276
Simply Red, 14, 46
Simpson, Gerald, 131
Simpson, Paul, 208, 347, 384, 386
Simpson, Sean, 290
Simpson, Willie, 318
Sims, David Wm., 289, 307
Sims, Neil, 74
Sims, Paul, 112
Sinatra, Frank, 311
Sinatra, Nancy, 259, 295, 355
Sinclair, Charlie, 197
Sinclair, Dave, 11, 366
Sinclair, Gordon, 364
Sinclair, Jill, 394
Sinclair, Ross A., 327
Sinder, Josh, 345
Sinek, Roger, 39
Singer, Kurt, 182
Singh, Tjindar, 90
Singleton, Nick, 51
Sinnott, Will, 312
Siouxsie And The Banshees, 15, 20, 39,
45, 85, 100, 104, 138, 166, 208, 220,
265, 282, 317, 320

Sire Records, 109-110, 144, 166, 237,
294, 327, 346
Siren Records, 80, 190, 237
Sister Sledge, 27
Sisters Of Mercy, 14, 118, 147, 164,
235, 244, 316-318, 339
Ska, 29, 70, 88, 114, 153, 215, 218,
284, 292, 309, 336
Skeletal Family, 164, 318
Skeleton Records, 173
Skid Row, 235
Skids, 20, 194, 247, 318, 376
Skinner, Graham, 180
Skopelitis, Nicky, 169
Skull, 58, 88, 150, 326
Sky Cries Mary, 318
Skyclad, 256
Skyhooks, 67, 330
Skyscraper, 344, 369
Slack, Katrina, 292
Slack, Paul, 368
Slack, Sue, 236
Slade, 147, 236, 247
Slam, 30, 145, 382
Slapp Happy, 51, 59, 356
Slater, Glenn, 377
Slaughter, 240, 242, 318, 320, 322-323
Slaughter And The Dogs, 240, 318, 322
Slaughterhouse, 27, 320
Slayer, 126, 271
Sleak, Norman, 13
Sleeper, 208, 257, 296, 319-320
Sleeping Bag Records, 175
Sleeping Beauty, 225
Slick, 29, 168, 195, 233, 279, 324, 357
Slider, Albie, 312
Slik, 295, 376
Slim Chance, 94
Slits, 5, 45, 113, 210, 236, 288, 317,
320
Slowdive, 77, 245, 320
SLR Records, 200
Slumberland Records, 371
Sly And Robbie, 128, 393
Sly And The Family Stone, 88
Small Wonder Records, 98, 104, 208,
271
Smalley, Dave, 115
Smallman, Gary, 265
Smalltown Parade, 321
S*M*A*S*H, 321
Smash, Chas, 218
Smashing Orange, 321
Smear, Pat, 164, 252
Smedley, Martin, 27
Smeeton, Simon, 385
Smells Like Records, 304
Smillie, Johnny, 359
Smith, Alex, 105
Smith, Amery, 339
Smith, Andrew, 229
Smith, Andy, 130
Smith, Brix, 11, 324
Smith, Bruce, 282, 296, 320
Smith, Darden, 179
Smith, Dave, 11
Smith, David, 289
Smith, Debbie, 105, 130
Smith, Dennis, 308
Smith, Fred, 51, 322, 349
Smith, Garth, 68
Smith, Hester, 88, 125
Smith, Ian, 113, 216
Smith, Kendra, 105, 223, 288
Smith, Laura Elise, 141
Smith, Mark, 11, 141, 143, 296
Smith, Mark E., 11, 141, 296
Smith, Martyn, 368
Smith, Micky, 15
Smith, Oliver, 296
Smith, Patti, 76, 82, 88, 166, 178, 265,
322, 334, 371, 377-378
Smith, Paul, 164, 167, 331
Smith, Rex, 344
Smith, Richard, 76, 295
Smith, Rick, 155, 369
Smith, Robert, 104-105, 119, 166, 317

Smith, Robert B., 104
Smith, Roger, 107
Smith, Sara, 72
Smith, Simon, 175, 230, 238-239, 321,
381
Smith, Steve, 164, 291, 370, 389
Smith, Stevie, 216
Smith, Terry, 33
Smith, Tim, 11, 72, 193, 316
Smith, Wendy, 275
Smithereens, 122, 178, 322
Smithies, Reg, 76, 292
Smiths, 11, 19, 55, 68, 112-113, 128,
134, 141, 162, 194, 203, 210, 218,
222, 240-241, 249, 255, 286, 299-300,
322-324, 338, 340, 346, 354, 371
Smoke, 37, 58, 82, 244, 291, 343
Smokey, 91, 192
Smooth, 73, 116, 171, 229, 283, 307
Smythe, Cathal, 218
Snakefinger, 78
Snakes Of Shake, 324, 340
Snap!, 51, 83, 112, 191, 357
Snapper, 324
Sneef, Paul, 67
SNFU, 122, 324
Snook, Paul, 126
Snow, 67, 137, 158, 237, 331, 372, 374
Snow, Don, 331, 372
Snowblind, 85
Snpek, Sigmund, 374
Snuff, 13-14, 324
Snyder, Mike, 7
Social Distortion, 9, 325
Society Records, 107
Soft Boys, 31, 180, 197, 325
Soft Cell, 69, 325, 339, 376
Soft Machine, 57, 59, 71, 112, 265,
272, 316, 390
Sohl, Richard, 322
Soho, 13, 43, 261, 381
Sojourn, 145, 199, 226, 378
Sok, G.W., 136
Solicitors, 22
Solitude, 314
Solo, Robert, 105, 167
Some Bizzare Records, 84, 132, 195,
325, 354
Some People, 74, 122, 358
Somers, Andrew, 272
Somerville, Jimmy, 62
Sonic Boom, 326, 328-329
Sonic Youth, 12, 27, 48, 63, 76, 82,
101, 118-119, 135-136, 143, 155, 175,
178, 182, 216, 228-229, 242, 288, 291,
304, 309, 326, 343, 349, 359, 365, 370
Sonnier, Dane, 158
Sonny And Cher, 117, 276
Sorrell, Julie, 380
Sorum, Matt, 104
Soul Asylum, 65, 157, 192, 326-327
Soul II Soul, 35
Souled American, 300
Sound, 327
Sound Of Music, The, 9, 87, 110
Sound Systemme, 166
Soundgarden, 51, 76, 91, 116, 171,
199, 251, 263, 307, 350
Soup Dragons, 58, 327, 349
Southern, Paul, 164, 291
Southernaires, 166
Spacemen 3, 77, 186, 212, 242, 326,
328-329
Spaghetti, Eddie, 343
Spain, Gary, 80
Spandau Ballet, 261
Sparkes, Gary, 200
Sparks, 39, 89, 116, 147, 182, 189,
202, 282, 284
Sparks, Donita, 202
Sparks, Frank, 39
Sparks, Gary, 282
Sparks, Louis, 182
Sparrow, 267
Sparrow, Dave, 267
Spear, 14, 328, 354, 357
Spear, Roger Ruskin, 14

Spear Of Destiny, 328, 354, 357
Specials, 88, 92, 309, 328-329
Spector, Phil, 119, 288, 295
Spectrum, 326
Spedding, Chris, 276, 372
Speedball, 93, 218
Speedball Baby, 218
Speight, Jay, 97
Speight, Ted, 197-198
Spellman, Jim, 371
Spence, Chris, 183
Spencer, Barry, 155
Spencer, Paul, 220
Spheeris, Penelope, 145
Spider, 200, 231, 269, 271
Spigel, Malka, 249
Spin, 11, 55, 76, 131, 153, 265, 327, 329
Spin Doctors, 55, 76, 153, 327
Spirea X, 329
Spires, 116
Spirits, 58, 191, 255, 272
Spiritualized, 64, 266, 326, 328-329
Spit Stix, 145
Spitfire, 329
Spitzer, Ron, 30
SPK, 164, 330, 352
Splinter, 37, 291
Split Enz, 330
Splodge, Max, 330
Splodgenessabounds, 330-331
Spon, Steve, 368
Spooky, 217, 253, 256, 382
Spooky Tooth, 256, 382
Spooner, Bill, 365
Sports, 173
Spreafico, Robin, 123
Spring Records, 346
Springer, Mark, 296
Springfield, Dusty, 13, 362
Springfields, 305
Springsteen, Bruce, 49, 169, 172, 322
Spud, 11
Spungen, Nancy, 84, 311
Spy, 62-63, 184, 214, 216
Squad, Vice, 120, 269, 374
Square, Lester, 8, 238, 246
Squeeze, 92, 113, 274, 324, 331, 372
Squire, John, 333
Squirell, Johnny, 208
Squires, Rob, 45
SST Records, 48, 65, 119, 175, 186, 226, 235, 307, 374
St. John, Kate, 21, 335
St Clair, Alan, 328
Stabbins, Larry, 381
Stacy, Jeremy, 114
Stafford, Jak, 391
Stagger, Matt, 199
Stalin, Joe, 70
Stamey, Chris, 109
Stammers, Stan, 328, 354
Stampede, 231
Stampfel, Peter, 314
Stanier, John, 178
Stanley, Bob, 177, 302, 313
Stanley, Stephen, 361
Staples, 21, 294, 328-329, 361, 388
Staples, Neville, 328
Staples, Stuart, 21, 361
Stapleton, John, 53
Stapleton, Steve, 204
Stardust, 34
Starjets, 11
Starkey, Zak, 187
Starr, Ringo, 27, 187, 193
Starrs, Hank, 19
Stasium, Ed, 46, 326
Statham, Paul, 27, 243
Statton, Alison, 115, 216, 381, 394
Status Quo, 14, 70, 190, 208
Stayhodor, Kevin, 355
Stead, David, 35
Steadman, Ralph, 148
Stealers Wheel, 111
Steam, 58, 229-230
Stebbing, Frank, 388

Stebbing, Simon, 282
Steed, Mike, 150
Steel, John, 165, 331
Steel, Richard, 164
Steele, Michael, 31
Steele, Micki, 301
Steeleye Span, 107, 269
Steely Dan, 296
Steen, Roger, 365
Steer, Bill, 245
Stein, Chris, 51, 172
Stein, Seymour, 109, 144, 346
Stench, Hilary, 80, 263
Stench, John, 263
Stenger, Susan, 30
Stephanoff, Nick, 94
Stephens, Jeff, 136
Stephens, Nick, 115
Stephens, Roger, 115
Stephenson, Karl, 87
Stephenson, Marnie, 61
Stephenson, Martin, And The Daintees, 331
Stephenson, Peter, 312
Steppin' Out, 203
Steptoe, Kevin, 208
Stereolab, 225, 239, 268, 332
Stern, Thomas, 101
Sternberg, Liam, 13, 31, 344
Stevens, Cat, 57, 102, 350
Stevens, Guy, 83
Stevens, Tom, 212
Stevenson, Bill, 114
Stevenson, Gordon, 349
Stevenson, James, 30, 164
Stevenson, Robert, 164
Stevo, 27, 84, 114, 132, 152, 325-326, 352, 354
Stewart, Andy, 385
Stewart, Dave, 333
Stewart, Dave, And Barbara Gaskin, 333
Stewart, David, 105
Stewart, David A., 105
Stewart, Jamie, 30, 103
Stewart, John, 22
Stewart, Jon, 320
Stewart, Mark, 273
Stewart, Rod, 265, 294
Stewart, Tyler, 44
Stiff Little Fingers, 191, 226, 296, 300, 307, 328, 332, 372, 378
Stiff Records, 11, 13-14, 30, 37, 87, 92, 106-107, 114, 128, 157, 167, 177, 208, 215, 217-218, 228, 269, 279, 333, 344, 352, 390, 393
Sting, 272
Stinson, Bob, 292
Stipe, Michael, 63, 169-170, 178, 220, 283-284
Stock, Aitken And Waterman, 109, 290
Stockhausen, Karlheinz, 314
Stoddart, Ian, 20, 385
Stoker, Martin, 144
Stokes, Niall, 367
Stone, Martin, 78
Stone, Oliver, 251
Stone, Sly, 148, 288
Stone Roses, 77, 134, 174, 179, 184, 189, 247, 255, 274, 313, 321, 333-334, 369, 372
Stone Temple Pilots, 149
Stoner, Colin, 11, 366
Stooges, 88, 110, 136, 149, 187, 189, 212, 223, 241, 249, 263, 324, 327, 336, 350, 368-369, 378
Stop The World, 112, 165
Storch, Larry, 183
Storm, 13, 74, 111, 165, 244, 358, 372
Storyteller, 289
Stotts, Richie, 269
Strange, Richard, 123
Strange, Steve, 220, 267, 376
Strange Fruit Records, 7
Strangeloves, 62
Stranger, 17, 59, 98, 139, 310, 331, 344, 385, 390

Strangeways, 324
Stranglers, 65, 67, 91, 133, 212, 231, 334-335, 372
Strauks, Freddie, 67
Straw, Syd, 51, 110, 113, 145, 169
Strawberry Alarm Clock, 11
Strawberry Switchblade, 335
Street, Stephen, 96, 109, 222
Strickland, Andy, 72, 78, 210
Strickland, Keith, 26
Stride, Pete, 62, 216
Strife, 29, 161
Strike, Johnny, 101
Striker, 194
Striknine, Aldine, 271
Stringer, Becky, 39, 299
Stringfellow, Ken, 274
Strip, The, 51
Strohm, John, 49, 204
Strong, Keith, 150
Strongman, Phillip, 144
Structure, 85, 155, 198, 288, 370
Strummer, Joe, 43, 83, 211, 256, 261, 271, 301, 321
Stuart, Dan, 171, 245, 390
Stuart, Leslie, 8
Stubbs, Levi, 62
Studio One, 27, 334
Stump, 335
Sturgess, Ian, 109
Sturgis, Michael, 340
Sturmer, Andy, 193
Style Council, 114, 191, 230, 335, 382, 384
Styx, 177
Sub Pop Records, 11, 27, 86, 88, 119, 135, 242, 251, 274, 321, 336, 343, 355, 371, 377
Sub Sub, 11-12, 27, 86, 88, 119, 135, 147, 169, 171-172, 186, 203, 242-243, 251-252, 274, 289, 307, 321-322, 336, 343, 345, 352, 355, 371, 377
Subhumans, 215, 255, 324, 336
Subterraneans, The, 106, 211
Subway Organisation Records, 78
Sudden, Nikki, 100, 135, 225, 336, 344
Suede, 133, 162, 286, 336-338, 343
Sugar, 17, 27, 46, 55, 175, 182, 186, 242, 338
Sugarcubes, 48, 233-236, 338
Sugarhill Records, 273
Suicidal Tendencies, 339
Suicide, 8, 13, 15, 35, 59, 80, 90, 117, 175-176, 196, 212, 215, 221, 226, 230, 248-249, 251-253, 292, 326, 339, 368, 376
Sultans Of Ping FC, 339
Summerhill, 324, 340
Summers, Andy, 272
Summers, Graham, 112
Sumner, Bernard, 131, 134, 248
Sumner, Gordon, 272
Sun Dial, 340
Sun Ra, 282
Sun Records, 94
Sundays, 141, 300, 340-341, 385
Sunny, 146, 244, 267, 305, 381
Sunset Boulevard, 365
Supergrass, 340, 342
Superman, 96, 174
Superstar, Brian, 261
Supersuckers, 343
Supplee, Tim, 201
Supremes, 92, 151, 183, 390
Surgeoner, Billy, 103
Surrender, 191
Surtees, Robin, 39
Survivor, 245, 265
Sutch, Screaming Lord, 294
Sutcliffe, Stuart, 12
Sutherland, Steve, 105, 175, 239
Sutherland Brothers, 22
Sutton, Baz, 377
Sutton, Greg, 211
Svitek, Louie, 294
Swales, Julian, 200
Swan, Daniel, 91

Swans, 63, 76, 152, 208, 214, 300, 343, 384
Swanson, Bernice, 261
Sweet, Rachel, 13, 31, 214, 290, 333, 343-344
Sweet Charity, 102
Sweet Childish, 171
Sweet Dreams, 92, 280
Sweet Love, 221
Sweethearts, 318
Sweetie Irie, 308
Swell Maps, 135, 212, 263, 336, 344
Swenson, Rod, 269
Swervedriver, 344
Swift, David, 189
Swing Out Sister, 155
Swirl, 31
Sword, 69, 206
Swordfish, 169, 208
Sylvain Sylvain, 249, 344
Sylvia, 194
Sylvian, David, 192, 279
Symons, Johnny, 278
System, 22, 58, 63, 82, 91, 134, 158, 173, 221, 255, 343

T

T. Rex, 34, 129, 210, 246, 364, 372, 374
Taang Records, 161
Tackhead, 147
Tad, 43, 117, 336, 345, 393
Tagg, Peter, 72
Taguchi, Kazumi, 154
Tajti, Steven, 261
Takarrass, Tappi, 48
Take That, 45, 321
Talbot, Danny, 230
Talbot, Mick, 230, 335, 384
Talcum, Joe Jack, 111
Talk Talk, 15, 62, 69, 71, 106, 120, 122, 125, 136, 144, 167, 184, 272, 276, 279-280, 291, 345-346, 380, 382
Talking Heads, 5, 59, 68, 76, 98, 110, 145, 166, 174-175, 195, 218, 237, 274, 286, 288, 324, 346, 361
Tall Stories, 386
Talstra, Jim, 116
Tanks, 62, 106, 210
Taplin, Chris, 155
Tappin, Chris, 157
Tarcia, David, 8
Tate, Troy, 214, 323, 347
Tayle, Jemaur, 313
Taylor, Alex, 242, 315
Taylor, Andrew, 317
Taylor, Ashley, 293
Taylor, Brian, 261, 332
Taylor, Chad, 210
Taylor, Dick, 186
Taylor, Dolphin, 296, 328, 332
Taylor, Elizabeth, 67
Taylor, Gene, 49, 150
Taylor, Geoff, 12
Taylor, James, 84, 112, 278-279, 384
Taylor, James, Quartet, 112, 279
Taylor, John, 150
Taylor, Johnny, 208
Taylor, Mark, 104, 114
Taylor, Neil, 128
Taylor, Phil, 186
Taylor, R. Dean, 141, 393
Taylor, Rick, 208
Taylor, Simon, 239, 321
Taylor, Steven, 84, 143
Taylor, Steven James, 84
Taylor, Tim, 63
Taylor, Tot, 384
Teardrop Explodes, 12, 21, 45, 90, 127, 129, 152, 155, 201, 208, 214, 347, 384
Teardrops, 344, 347
Tearle, Robin, 110
Tears For Fears, 67, 91
Techno, 79, 105, 131, 169, 201, 244, 286, 301, 362, 369
Teenage Fanclub, 27, 58, 71, 100, 135, 225, 233, 261, 274, 327, 347, 349, 359

Teenage Head, 112
Teenage Jesus And The Jerks, 216, 349, 370
Teeter, Richie, 117
Tek, Deniz, 284
Telescopes, 349
Television,
Television Personalities, 222, 225, 261, 350, 364
Temple, Julien, 311
Temple, Shirley, 15
Temple, Steve, 112
Temple Of The Dog, 241, 263, 350
Temptations, 126, 214, 272
10cc, 193
10,000 Maniacs, 350-352
Ten Years After, 354
Tench, Benmont, 94, 211
Tennant, Neil, 134
Tennant, Phil, 206, 305
Tenpole Tudor, 236, 333, 352
Tepper, Jeff Morris, 49
Terel, Peter, 5
Terrorvision, 117
Tesco, Nicky, 228
Tesluk, Steve, 355
Test Department, 325, 330, 352
Texas, Austin, 67, 194, 289, 305, 343, 360, 366
Tharp, Twyla, 63, 68
That Petrol Emotion, 196, 329, 352, 369-370
That Summer, 30, 106, 135, 207, 222, 328, 384
Thayer, Donnette, 161, 197
The The,
Theatre Of Hate, 103, 318, 328, 354
Then Jerico, 27
Therapy, 46, 231, 263, 354-355
Therapy?, 46, 231, 263, 354-355
These Animal Men, 149, 355
They Might Be Giants, 255, 355, 382
Thin Lizzy, 376
Thin White Rope, 161, 336, 355
Third Rail, 288
Thirlwell, Jim, 132, 152, 216, 325, 343
Thirteenth Floor Elevators, 59, 235
This Heat, 356
This Mortal Coil, 20, 39, 85, 152, 155, 180, 356
Thistlethwaite, Anthony, 182, 336, 378, 380
Thoman, John, 288
Thomas, Alfie, 155, 369
Thomas, Bruce, 22, 92
Thomas, Dave, 367
Thomas, David, 357
Thomas, David, And The Pedestrians, 357
Thomas, Denzil, 114
Thomas, Henry, 382
Thomas, Joseph, 263
Thomas, Ken, 106
Thomas, Marco, 146
Thomas, Mike, 381
Thomas, Owen, 53
Thomas, Pat, 7
Thomas, Pete, 22, 78, 92, 210
Thomas, Richard, 85, 118
Thomas, Rick, 369
Thomas, Steve, 22
Thomas, Timmy, 223
Thomas, Tony, 146
Thomas, Tyrone, 266
Thompson, Alice, 192, 388
Thompson, Chris, 33, 61, 135, 220, 307
Thompson, D. Clinton, 239
Thompson, Danny, 51, 136
Thompson, Dave, 105, 114, 136, 252
Thompson, Dennis, 115, 284
Thompson, Derek, 330
Thompson, Jim, 239
Thompson, Lee, 218, 220
Thompson, Mark, 186, 300
Thompson, Mayo, 357
Thompson, Michael, 267

Thompson, Noel, 374
Thompson, Paul, 89
Thompson, Porl, 104
Thompson, Richard, 101, 136, 169, 357
Thompson Twins, 175, 357, 369
Thomson, Chris, 83, 156
Thor, 338
Thorn, Tracey, 135-136, 222, 335
Thornalley, Phil, 5
Thorne, Mike, 249, 354, 385
Thornton, 357
Thorpe, Suzanne, 229
Thorstensen, Gary, 345
Three Cheers For Tokyo, 123
Three Johns, 357
Three O'Clock, 161, 358
3 Mustaphas 3, 282, 358
Throb, Delores, 309
Throbbing Gristle, 74, 79-80, 84, 86, 153, 204, 226, 244, 280, 325, 330, 358
Throbs, 176, 255-256
Thrower, Stephen, 86
Throwing Muses, 17, 39, 63, 88, 135, 152-153, 178, 266, 356, 358-359
Thrown Ups, 242
Thrum, 359
Thunder, 64, 134, 225, 248, 258, 327, 338, 364
Thunders, Johnny, 34, 78, 103, 176-177, 249, 317, 344, 359-360
Thunders, Johnny, And The Heartbreakers, 78, 317
Thunes, Scott, 380
Thurston, Colin, 256
Thurston, Scott, 187
Tibbs, Gary, 9, 372
Tice, Dave, 93
Tickle, David, 153
Tickner, Myrtle, 271
Tiffany, 324
Tiger, 302
Tighe, Michael, 65
Tighe, Rachael, 189
Tikaram, Tanita, 365
Tilbrook, Glenn, 331
Tilson, Martha, 5
Tilton, Mark, 228, 296
Timbuk 3, 360
Time Records, 43, 78
Timelords, 127, 197, 201, 214, 360-361
Timmins, Michael, 93
Timms, Sally, 227
Timperley, Clive, 256, 261
Timson, John, 202
Tin Pan Alley, 197
Tin Soldier, 198
Tin Tin, 33, 64, 112, 192, 197-198, 208, 269, 280, 357, 377
Tina, 157, 174, 244, 346, 361, 380
Tinderbox, 317
Tindersticks, 21, 126, 360-361
Tiny, 45, 85, 150, 208, 261, 324, 377
Tiny Hat Orchestra, 377
Tippett, Keith, 381
Titley, Jeff, 115
TNT, 286
Toad The Wet Sprocket, 361
Tobin, Penny, 67
Tod, Felix, 71
Todd, Andrew, 79
Todd, Jane, 79
Together Records, 87
Tolhurst, Lol, 104
Tolman, Russ, 390
Tom The Monk, 157
Tom Tom Club, 288, 346, 361-362
Tonche, Frank, 234
Tones On Tail, 21, 152, 214, 362
Too Short, 101
Tool, 86, 263
Toole, John Kennedy, 73
Toomey, Jim, 362
Top Records, 55, 333
Topping, Simon, 5, 127
Torgerson, Carla, 361, 377

Toronto, 30-31, 34, 94, 167, 222, 236, 280
Torrance, Ron, 195
Toulouse, Vaughan, 114
Tourists, 291, 362
Tovey, Frank, 132, 138, 362
Towe, John, 11, 15, 164, 366
Towering Inferno, 362
Towner, Phil, 248
Townshend, Pete, 122, 257, 275
Townshend, Robert, 273
Toy Dolls, 362, 364
Toyah, 9, 62, 364
Toyne, Steve, 55
Toys, 103, 222
Tracey, Scott, 210
Trachten, Doug, 204
Tracy, Donna, 182
Tradewinds, 290
Traffic, 214, 382
Trafford, Howard, 68
Tragically Hip, 363-364
Trammps, 12
Transvision Vamp, 182, 207, 364
Trap, Tony, 120
Travis, Geoff, 5, 30, 96, 166, 300, 388, 394
Travis, Malcolm, 338
Trax Records, 147, 380
Treacy, Dan, 350
Treat Her Right, 239
Tree, Penelope, 146
Treece, Chuck, 172
Treece, Malcolm, 388
Trees, 118-119, 208, 307, 327, 335, 372, 377
Treganna, Dave, 34, 212, 312
Treichler, Franz, 394
Tremeloes, 62, 326
Trent, Tyler, 63
Trent D'Arby, Terence, 139
Trettine, Caroline, 53, 63, 365
Trezise, Henry, 139
Tricky, 131
Triffids, 365
Trinity, 94, 168
Trip, The, 12, 14, 164, 284, 311, 314, 323, 339
Tristan, Brian, 94, 172
Triumph, 296
Troggs, 329
Trojan, 329
Trojan Records, 329
Trotter, Howard, 116
Trout, David, 382
Truman's Water, 365
Trumpet Records, 267
Trust, 39, 79, 92, 111, 246, 312
TSOL, 365
Tubes, 263, 365-366
Tubeway Army, 37, 106
Tudor-Pole, Edward, 352
Tuff, 69, 76
Tully, Andrew, 162
Tunison, Eric, 117
Turbines, 366
Turner, Dave, 172
Turner, Helen, 123, 382
Turner, Jefferson, 85
Turner, Joe, 234
Turner, Nicky, 33-34, 212
Turner, Paul, 123
Turner, Pete, 235
Turner, Simon, 137
Turner, Steve, 171, 242, 263, 367
Turner, Todd, 313
Turpin, Will, 87
Turtles, 29, 57, 236-237, 295
Tutt, Ron, 234
TV Smith, 11, 22, 366
TV Smith's Explorers, 11, 366
Tweedie, Pete, 278
Twiggy, 368
Twinkeyz, 366
Twist, 13, 17, 148, 176, 234, 253, 317
Twist, Nigel, 13
Twisted Sister, 117

Two Nice Girls, 366
2-Tone, 37, 179, 218, 309, 328-329
Tyla, Sean, 41
Tyler, Watt, 58
Tylor, Alan, 296
Tyner, Robin, 131
Tyrannosaurus Rex, 265

U
U2, 13, 17, 33, 69, 89, 145, 174, 184, 186, 190, 211, 255, 269, 278, 284, 328, 362, 367, 374, 376, 378, 381
UB40, 31, 131, 276
Ubu, Pere, 5, 112, 169, 230, 242, 300, 357
UFO, 85, 91, 216, 334, 340
Ugly Kid Joe, 157
UK Decay, 367-368
UK Reggae, 284
UK Subs, 174-175, 368
Ukrainians, 381
Ullman, Tracey, 217
Ulmer, James 'Blood', 90
Ultra Vivid Scene, 368
Ultravox, 154, 220, 295, 376
Uncle Sam, 220, 368
Undertones, 125, 211, 265, 352, 369
Underwood, Russel, 137
Underwood, Simon, 267, 273
Underworld, 48, 155, 256, 280, 369, 376, 380
Unforgiven, 94
Union City, 52
United Artists Records, 251, 334
Units, Vincent, 236
Unruh, N.U., 132
Unusuals, 195
Up The Junction, 331
Urban Folk, 174
Ure, James, 376
Ure, Midge, 154, 295, 376
Urge Overkill, 172, 310, 369-370, 372
Ut, 344, 370
Utility Records, 89, 110
Uzi, 88

V
Vai, Steve, 282
Valdez, 233
Valentine, Gary, 51-52
Valentine, James, 237
Valentine, Jeremy, 91
Valentine, Kathy, 167
Valentinos, 322
Valley Of The Dolls, 164, 370
Van Acker, Luc, 293
Van Borsig, Alexander, 132
Van Der Sman, Liduina, 246
van der Vlugt, Marijne, 304
Van Dijk, Carol, 41
Van Halen, 87, 161
Van Hoorne, Nils, 204
Van Rock, Theo, 299
Van Teighem, David, 339
Vanden, Peter, 128
Vangelis, 59
Vanian, Dave, 71, 106
Vanity, 252
Vapors, 370
Varney, Mike, 253
Vaselines, 71, 135, 273, 371
Vass, Tim, 289
Vearncombe, Colin, 48
Vedder, Eddie, 263
Vega, Alan, 339
Vega, Suzanne, 206
Velocity Girl, 100, 276, 371
Velvet Underground, 7, 49, 68, 77, 112, 145, 149, 158, 166, 173-174, 191, 195, 218, 236-237, 241, 246, 263, 265, 279, 295, 304, 322, 324, 326, 329, 331, 347, 361, 366
Velvets, 331
Venner, Cliff, 248
Venom, 158, 194
Verlaine, Tom, 143, 177, 210, 299, 349, 371

Verlaines, 79, 371
Vermillion, Tzen, 324
Verner, David, 128
Verno, Buz, 344
Vernon, 208
Verta-Ray, Matt, 218
Veruca Salt, 371-372
Verve Records, 372
Very Things, 98, 255, 372
Vibrations, 280, 369
Vibrators, 242, 274, 332, 335, 372, 374
Vicious, Sid, 84, 136, 226, 311, 317, 359
Vick, William, 147
Vickers, Robert, 166-167
Victor, Tommy, 279
Vig, Butch, 117, 134, 178, 263, 322, 369
Vinall, Phil, 162
Vincent, Gene, 128, 176
Vincent, Nick, 49
Vine, Emma, 134
Vines, Adrian, 344
Ving, Lee, 145
Vinyl Records, 11, 296, 299, 366
Violent Femmes, 170, 178, 274, 316, 373-374
Virgin Mary, 145, 228
Virgin Prunes, 374, 376
Virgin Records, 12-13, 20, 24, 30, 51, 53, 69-70, 79, 94, 102, 105-106, 123, 125, 139, 155, 162, 192, 210, 220, 227-228, 231, 239, 261, 265, 267, 282, 286, 290, 307, 311-312, 354, 372, 392
Virtues, 39, 161, 192, 217, 312
Visage, 220, 229, 295, 376
Visconti, Tony, 12-13, 15, 246, 253, 267
Viscounts, 67
Visdson, Brad, 385
Visser, Peter, 41
Vockeroth, Bill, 19
Voice Of The Beehive, 152, 375-376
Voidoids, 119, 135, 176-177, 359
Volumes, 100, 116, 295
Von, Eerie, 235

W

Wadd, Clare, 305
Wadden, Wayne, 267
Waddington, John, 223
Waddington, Steve, 39
Wade, Christine, 14
Wade, Nick, 14
Wagner, Steve, 321
Wagon, Chuck, 117
Wagstaff, Paul, 261
Wah-Wah, 186, 212
Wahl, Chris, 150
Waite, Tony, 123
Waitresses, 109, 182, 377
Waits, Tom, 96, 116, 278
Wakeman, Rob, 304
Wakeman, Robert, 87
Waldo, John, 365
Waldron, Pete, 233
Walkabouts, 361, 377
Walker, Gary, 190
Walker, Ian, 361
Walker, Joe, 286
Walker, Joe Louis, 286
Walker, Margin, 157
Walker, Paul, 259
Walker, Scott, 90, 96, 120, 361
Walker, Simon, 184, 329
Walker, Stephen, 237
Walking Seeds, 377
Walkington, Pat, 273
Wall, 5, 46, 119, 131, 144, 150, 185, 199, 216, 221, 250, 261, 295-296, 345, 352, 360, 377-378, 380
Wall, Howard, 216
Wall, Mick, 199
Wall, Tony, 199
Wall Of Voodoo, 150, 295, 378
Wallace, Kirsty Marlana, 94
Wallace, Mark, 381

Wallinger, Karl, 378, 389
Wallis, Glenn, 79
Wallis, Larry, 228
Wallis, Michael, 13
Walmsley, Tim, 33
Walsh, Kevin, 61
Walsh, Martin, 189
Walsh, Paul, 253
Walsh, Peter, 204
Walsh, Steve, 266
Walsh, Timmy, 253
Walter, John, 34
Walters, John, 154, 265
Walton, Mark, 165
Wanless, Christine, 294
Warburton, Damien, 239
Ward, Alan, 241
Ward, Algy, 106
Ward, Alisdair, 302
Ward, Ken, 45
Ward, Nick, 82, 377
Ward, Richard, 82
Ward, Sally, 72
Ward, Stephen, 176
Wardle, John, 190
Wareham, Dean, 158
Warhol, Andy, 11, 218
Warleigh, Ray, 13
Warmworth, Tracy, 377
Warner Brothers Records, 55, 100, 186, 225, 243
Warnick, Kim, 274
Warp, 69, 248, 309
Warrant, 77, 144, 166
Warren, Andy, 8, 238
Warrington, Keith, 85
Warrior, 153, 364, 378, 391
Warrior Records, 153
Warrior Soul, 378
Warwick, Gilbert, 284
Warwicker, John, 155, 369
Was, Don, 26, 193
Washam, Rey, 289, 307
Watchtower, 389
Waterboys, 5, 170, 179, 183, 206, 305, 336, 378-380, 390
Waterman, Mark, 139
Waters, John, 202, 367
Waterson, Jack, 171
Watson, Chris, 68
Watson, David, 374
Watson, Martin, 393
Watson, Stuart, 316
Watt, Ben, 135-136, 222
Watt, John, 87
Watt, Mike, 82, 148, 234, 326
Watts, David, 191
Watts, John, 148
Watts, Louise Mary, 80
Watts, Mario, 123
Watts, Martin, 109
Watts, Skidillion, 173
Watts, Tony, 89
Watts-Russell, Ivo, 85, 152, 356
Wax Trax Records, 147, 380
Way, Mickey, 5
Way, Pete, 85
Waybill, Fee, 365
Wayne, John, 199
We Are Going To Eat You, 380
We've Got A Fuzzbox And We're Gonna Use It, 250, 380
WEA Records, 26, 48, 111, 307, 380
Weapon, 136, 207, 328
Weatherall, Andy, 189-190, 245, 278
Weatherall, Kevin, 189
Weatherall, Paul, 189
Webb, Paul, 345
Webb, Russell, 20, 318
Weber, Jim, 247
Webster, Gregory, 289, 347
Weckerman, Dave, 145
Wedding Present, 65, 85, 103, 166, 321, 381
Weddings, Parties, Anything, 63, 381
Wednesday, Jamie, 58, 73, 273

Weekend, 57, 71, 87, 89, 107, 115, 120, 171, 208, 238, 265, 311, 381, 390-391, 394
Weezer, 73, 382
Weighall, Paul, 49
Weight, Gary, 291
Weill, Kurt, 394
Weinert, Michael, 19
Weir, Alex, 346, 361
Weirdos, 83, 200, 382
Weiss, Andrew, 299
Welch, Chris, 9
Welch, Justin, 133, 329
Welch, Sean, 35
Welchel, Doug, 7
Weller, John, 370
Weller, Paul, 61-62, 114, 125, 162, 166, 191, 203, 335-336, 382-384
Welles, Orson, 116
Wells, Michael, 377
Welnick, Vince, 365
Wenders, Wim, 76, 101, 132
Wendy And Lisa, 380
Wener, Louise, 320
Wernham, Ricky, 242
Wesolowski, Nick, 238
Wesson, Dave, 366
Wesson, Mel, 366
West, Andy, 91
West, Mike, 9
West, Richard, 312
West, Sandy, 301
West, Steve, 263
West-Oram, Jamie, 123
Westerburg, Paul, 292
Westermark, Greg, 24
Westlake, David, 310
Weston, Bob, 313, 371
Weston, Kristian, 257
Weston, Mel, 11
Westwood, Vivienne, 225
Wet Wet Wet, 59, 62, 169, 229, 361
Weymouth, Martina, 346, 361
Weymouth, Tina, 174, 346, 361
Wham!, 155, 194, 350
Wheeler, Harriet, 340
Wheeler, Tim, 20
Whelan, Dave, 290
Whelan, Gary, 174
Whelan, Thomas, 259
Whelan, Timothy, 157
Wheland, Gerard, 17
When People Were Shorter And Lived Near The Water, 314
Whirlwind, 276
Whispers, 70
Whitaker, David, 107
Whitaker, Hugh, 185, 310
Whitby, Susan, 212
White, Alan, 154
White, Barry, 248
White, James, 90
White, James, And The Blacks, 90
White, Jane, 293
White, Mark, 172, 227
White, Mick, 231
White, Paul, 255
White, Pete, 290
White, Rick, 135
White, Robert, 207
White, Simon, 13
White, Steve, 329, 382
White, Trevor, 284
White Zombie, 199
Whitehead, Annie, 246
Whitehead, J., 190
Whitehead, Martin, 149
Whiteread, Rachel, 201
Whites, 339
Whitney, Lou, 239
Whittaker, Tim, 111
Whitten, Chris, 378
Whitten, Danny, 136
Wickens, Barry, 189
Wickham, Steve, 378
Wicks, John, 290
Wiczling, Dogdan, 147

Widger, Paul, 84
Wiedlin, Jane, 167, 384
Wiggs Jn, 39
Wiggs, Josephine, 63, 266
Wiggs, Pete, 302
Wiggs, Susan, 63, 266
Wigley, Danny, 115
Wiiija Records, 53, 90, 190, 354
Wilcox, Toyah, 364
Wild Child, 189
Wild Division, 309
Wild Flowers, 233, 384
Wild Horses, 340
Wild In The Country, 62
Wild Man, 294
Wild Planet, 8, 26
Wild Swans, 208, 214, 384
Wilde, Oscar, 323
Wilder, Alan, 114
Wildhearts, 301, 310
Wilding, William, 246
Wilkins, Russ, 64, 233, 390
Wilkinson, Keith, 74, 331
Wilkinson, Kevin, 79, 378
Wilkinson, Paul, 330
Wilkinson, Peter, 74
Willé, Tony, 146
Williams, Andy, 179
Williams, Boris, 104
Williams, Colin, 179
Williams, Gareth, 356
Williams, Hank, 293, 354, 368, 377
Williams, Harvey, 146
Williams, Hue, 273
Williams, John, 293
Williams, Mars, 377
Williams, Peter, 367
Williams, Richard, 261
Williams, Rozz, 79
Williams, Sam, 343
Williams, Steve, 367
Williams, Terry, 242, 273
Williams, Tig, 278
Williams, Tony, 282
Williams, Travis, 176
Williams, Victoria, 192, 327
Williams, Wendy O., 269
Williamson, 187, 189, 223
Williamson, James, 187, 189
Williamson, John, 223
Willis, Alan, 299
Willner, Hal, 65
Willows, 339
Wills, John, 212, 310
Wills, Robin, 33
Willson-Piper, Marty, 14, 82
Willsteed, John, 167
Wilsher, Mark, 141
Wilson, Anthony, 127
Wilson, Brian, 49, 193, 280
Wilson, Cassandra, 90
Wilson, Chris, 33
Wilson, Cindy, 26
Wilson, Dennis, 217
Wilson, Gary, 20
Wilson, Gordon, 214
Wilson, Jeremy, 116
Wilson, Mari, 248, 308, 384
Wilson, Martin, 151
Wilson, Patrick, 382
Wilson, Phil, 196
Wilson, Rick, 143
Wilson, Ricky, 26
Wilson, Robert, 68, 201
Wilson, Roger, 179
Wilson, S., 49, 90, 120, 138, 201, 217, 308
Wilson, Tony, 120, 138
Wilson-Wright, Icarus, 247
Win, 62, 70, 111, 134, 148, 153, 208, 226, 246, 275, 293, 385
Wincer, Paul, 203
Windbreakers, 7
Windsor, Morris, 180, 238, 325
Wings, 57, 76, 96, 101, 110, 123, 218
Winstanley, Alan, 79, 240
Winston, 65, 157, 330

Winter, Hazel, 53
Winter, Martin, 27
Wipers, 385
Wire, 30, 101, 105, 133, 138, 165-166, 193, 220, 230, 236, 242, 249, 275, 365, 385-386
Wire, Nicky, 220
Wired Records, 112
Wise, Matt, 329
Wishplants, 386
Withrow, Kenny, 64
Witter, Rick, 313
Wohlrabe, Nils, 204
Wolfenden, Dave, 236
Wolfgang Press, 118, 152, 386
Wolfhounds, 386, 388
Wolstenholme, Janet, 31
Wolverines, 110
Womb, 112, 158
Wonder, Stevie, 275
Wonder Stuff, 24, 49, 129, 233, 236, 386, 388
Wonderland, 166
Wood, Andrew, 171, 241, 263, 350
Wood, Anne, 288
Wood, David, 302
Wood, Joe, 365
Wood, John, 111
Wood, Luke, 304
Woodcock, Ian, 129, 374
Woodcock, Simon, 308
Woodentops, 192, 291, 308, 388-389
Woodgate, Dan, 218, 376
Woods, Lesley, 22
Woods, Melanie, 316
Woods, Terry, 269
Woodstock, 57, 171, 182, 251, 258
Woodward, Davey, 65
Woolfson, Richard, 362

Wordle, John, 280
Words And Music, 143
Working Week, 139, 382
World Famous Supreme Team Show, 226
World Party, 114, 187, 378, 389-390
Woronzow Records, 41
Worrall, Simon, 261
Worrell, Bernie, 175
Wozitsky, Jan, 67
Wrafter, Tony, 223
Wratten, Robert, 146
Wreckless Eric, 30, 64, 182, 233, 333, 344, 390
Wren, John, 333
Wright, Adrian, 120
Wright, Aggi, 261
Wright, Betty, 64
Wright, Martin, 203, 261
Wright, Pete, 98
Wright, Ron, 185
Wright, Steve, 146, 261
Wright, Tim, 107
Writing On The Wall, 131, 144
Wu, Wendy, 267, 376
Wurrell, Neil, 230
Wurzels, 107
Wyatt, Enda, 17
Wyatt, Robert, 20, 92, 300, 307, 390
Wykes, Debsey, 88, 123
Wylder, Thomas, 76
Wylie, Pete, 48, 90, 129, 144, 175, 347
Wynette, Tammy, 197, 201, 299, 359
Wynn, Steve, 125, 171, 212, 390
Wynne, Ed, 258

X
X, 391
X-Ray Spex, 135, 155, 212, 272, 391

Xentrix, 301
Xerxes, 195
XL Capris, 391
Xmal Deutschland, 391
XTC, 51, 59, 96, 113, 127, 208, 274, 315, 392
Xymox, 152

Y
Y Records, 158
Yachts, 45, 393
Yamano, Atsuko, 315
Yang, Naomi, 158
Yard, 9, 11, 111, 204, 340
Yargo, 46, 393
Yarnell, Karen, 172, 292, 310
Yates, Peter, 147
Yates, Russell, 239, 332
Yazoo, 114, 244
Yeadon, Paul, 46
Yeah Jazz, 67, 179, 393
Yeats, Robbie, 371
Yellow Magic Orchestra, 257
Yellow Submarine, 166
Yes, 16, 98, 172, 174, 223, 261, 394
Yesno, Johnny, 69
Yetties, 107
Yianni, Adonis, 123
Yianni, Christos, 123
Yo Yo, 19, 112, 385
York, Keith, 48, 125
York, Steve, 182
Yorke, Thom, 284
Yoshimi, 155
Youé, Curtis, 58
Young, Faron, 275
Young, Gary, 261, 263
Young, Neil, 43, 65, 116, 119, 125, 134, 153, 158, 170-171, 192, 288, 300,

.., ,/7
.aul, 174
.. Robert, 276
Young, Sally, 370
Young, Steve, 182
Young At Heart, 55
Young Disciples, 382
Young Fresh Fellows, 117, 393
Young Gods, 96, 393-394
Young Marble Giants, 182, 300, 357, 381-382, 394
Young Snakes, 221
Youngbloods, 388
Younger, Rob, 284
Yow, David, 113, 194, 307

Z
Z, David, 45
Zabrecky, Robert, 274
Zager And Evans, 376
Zappa, Frank, 211, 244, 278, 294
Zaremba, Peter, 150
Ze Records, 339, 377
Zedek, Thalia, 88
Zero, Jimmy, 110
Zettner, Zeke, 187
Zevon, Warren, 180
Zientara, Don, 83
Ziffel, Arnold, 183
Zilinkas, Annette, 31, 53
Zombies, 238
Zoo Records, 45, 196
Zoom, Billy, 391
Zorn, John, 51, 173
ZTT Records, 131, 157, 279, 333, 394
Zwingmann, Manuela, 392